WORLD HISTORY
A STORY OF PROGRESS

Terry L. Smart
Professor of History • Trinity University

Allan O. Kownslar
Professor of History • Trinity University

Holt, Rinehart and Winston, Publishers
New York • Toronto • Mexico City • London • Sydney • Tokyo

·A U T H O R S·

TERRY L. SMART is Professor of History and Chairman of the Department of History at Trinity University in San Antonio, Texas. He was formerly a world history teacher and social studies curriculum writer in the Houston, Texas schools. Dr. Smart, who is a specialist in both Asian and European history, received his doctorate in history from the University of Kansas. He is coauthor of Essentials of Economics and Free Enterprise, Fundamentals of the American Free Enterprise System, American Government, *and* Civics: Citizens and Society. *He has conducted advanced placement institutes in both European and American history for the College Board examinations as well as workshops focusing on the use of critical thinking in high school social studies courses. He has also served as a consultant in social studies curriculum development to numerous private schools and public school systems.*

ALLAN O. KOWNSLAR is Professor of History at Trinity University in San Antonio, Texas. He was formerly Research Historian at Carnegie-Mellon University, where he received his doctorate in history. Dr. Kownslar has taught social studies on the junior and senior high school levels in San Antonio, Texas, Amherst, Massachusetts, and Pittsburgh, Pennsylvania. He is coauthor of American Government *and* Civics: Citizens and Society. *In 1974 Dr. Kownslar served as editor of* Teaching American History: The Quest for Relevancy, *the forty-fourth Yearbook of the National Council for the Social Studies, and in 1979 wrote* Teaching about Social Issues in American History *for the Social Science Education Consortium. He has also conducted advanced placement institutes in both European and American history for the College Board Examinations, as well as workshops focusing on the use of critical thinking in secondary level social studies courses.*

Cover photo by Roland and Sabrina Michaud/Woodfin Camp

Cover illustration

In the first century B.C., Antiochus I of Commagene had these sculptures constructed. The sculptures were among a series that honored the mixed pantheon of Greco-Persian deities, and are thus symbolic of the blending of eastern and western cultures. The statues, though damaged by earthquakes, still endure, overlooking the mountains of Anatolia and the headwaters of the Euphrates River. Now located in modern-day Turkey, Commagene once belonged to the Assyrian Empire and later became a part of the Persian and Roman empires.

Art and photo credits begin on page 737.
Acknowledgments for previously copyrighted matter appear with the materials used.

ISBN 0-03-005228-9

1 0 3 9 9 8 7 6 5

·CONSULTANTS·

CONTENT SPECIALISTS

WINTHROP LINDSAY ADAMS
Department of History
The University of Utah
Salt Lake City, Utah

PAUL BUSHKOVITCH
Department of History
Yale University
New Haven, Connecticut

LAWRENCE A. CLAYTON
Latin American Studies Program
University of Alabama
University, Alabama

DALE LOTHROP CLIFFORD
Department of History
University of North Florida
Jacksonville, Florida

HELEN DELPAR
History Department
University of Alabama
University, Alabama

DAVID HICKS
Department of History
New York University
New York, New York

MARTIN J. HILLENBRAND
The Center for Global Policy Studies
The University of Georgia
Athens, Georgia

DAMODAR R. SARDESAI
Department of History
University of California
Los Angeles, California

STUART SCHAAR
Department of History
Brooklyn College
The City University of New York
Brooklyn, New York

ALEXANDER SEDGWICK
Department of History
University of Virginia
Charlottesville, Virginia

ROBERT L. TIGNOR
Department of History
Princeton University
Princeton, New Jersey

Y. S. YÜ
Department of History
Yale University
New Haven, Connecticut

WOMEN'S STUDIES SPECIALIST

MARYJO WAGNER
Department of History
University of Oregon
Eugene, Oregon

PHONETIC CONSULTANT

MARK CALDWELL
Department of English
Fordham University
New York, New York

TEACHER REVIEWERS

SUSAN EDGERTON COORE
Union Pines High School
Carthage, North Carolina

SHIRLEY HOOVER
Upper Arlington City Schools
Columbus, Ohio

RAYMOND C. KARTCHNER
Granite School District
Salt Lake City, Utah

JANE C. McCUE
Shawnee Mission East High School
Shawnee Mission, Kansas

· C O N T E N T S ·

UNIT ·2·

CLASSICAL CIVILIZATIONS
(3000 B.C.–650 A.D.)

THE WORLD OUTSIDE MEDIEVAL WESTERN EUROPE
(5500 B.C.–1800 A.D.)

FROM MEDIEVAL TO EARLY MODERN EUROPE
(1350–1763)

A WORLD OF SOCIAL AND POLITICAL CHANGE
(1600–1900)

THE ERA OF NATIONALISM AND REFORM
(1815–1914)

THE TWENTIETH CENTURY TO 1945

·*SPECIAL FEATURES*·

PRIMARY SOURCES

PEOPLE IN HISTORY

SOCIAL SCIENCE SKILLS

·MAP LIST·

From Medieval to Early Modern Europe

A World of Social and Political Change

The Era of Nationalism and Reform

The Twentieth Century to 1945

The World Since 1945

·TO THE STUDENT·

As you begin your study of world history in World History: A Story of Progress, *we would like you to keep several things in mind about the study of history in general and the study of this book in particular.*
The first thing to remember is that much of what happened in the past was never recorded. Only a fragment of what took place was written down. One reason for this is that people of the past did not recall everything that happened around them, any more than you can recall everything that has happened in your life. Also, people of the past, like people of today, noticed and recorded only what they thought was important.

Sometimes, however, people in the same society had different ideas about what was important. This influenced the way they recorded events. For instance, two observers of the same event might emphasize different aspects of it; or, the event might seem important to them for different reasons. As a result, historians often find differing, and even conflicting, records of what happened in the past. When writing about the past, historians assess available records and then draw their own conclusions.

Historians use primary source materials, or documents, written in the period they are researching when writing about the past. When using source materials, historians usually have one or more questions in mind to help them focus on a specific topic. For example, a historian examining a collection of letters written by ancient Chinese men and women might focus his or her attention on a question such as: What do these letters reveal about ancient Chinese family life? When you are using primary sources, whether from this book or from elsewhere, you too will benefit by keeping some questions in mind to help you focus your study.

As you read the book, you will notice that some questions are set off by this symbol: ▪. This symbol indicates that these questions have a special purpose: to encourage you to consider how a study of world history could relate to your own life. Such critical thinking questions will aid you in making relationships between the past and present.

The information and questions contained in World History: A Story of Progress *will help you to gain the knowledge and skills that will enable you to assume the responsibilities of citizenship. How you and your contemporaries exercise your responsibilities as citizens will be one of the most important things future historians will study about your generation.*

Terry L. Smart
Allan O. Kownslar

BUILDING YOUR GEOGRAPHY SKILLS

Objectives

- *To summarize ways in which geography relates to a study of world history*
- *To identify map projections and explain how information is presented on a globe and on a map*

*G*eography is mainly the study of particular places on the surface of the earth. In their studies, geographers attempt to find out all the characteristics that make one place different from other places. Most important, geographers try to learn how these characteristics are related.

RELATING GEOGRAPHY TO A STUDY OF WORLD HISTORY

When you study geography in relation to world history, you will be concerned mainly with studying how people in history have used, shaped, and lived in their physical environment. You may consider questions like these: How did they use the available resources to improve their lives? How did these peoples learn to live in their surroundings? How did they change their environment so that they could live in it without constant concern for survival?

You will find it helpful to form your questions about geography around the following topics.

1. The earth is divided into many different regions. A region is an area of any size that has common physical and cultural characteristics.
2. Physical characteristics of a region include the climate, land forms, and resources.
3. Cultural characteristics of a region include the number of people living there, their religious beliefs, technical skills, types of food, and quality of life.
4. A region's physical and cultural characteristics are related to one another.

5. People in regions interact with each other and are interdependent. Interdependence means the exchange of ideas, goods, or services by two or more groups of people so that the needs of everyone are satisfied.

6. Political and economic relations between areas are always undergoing change. Your study of world history will view relations among countries and people in given regions and how these relations have strengthened or weakened over the years. For example, the building of the Suez Canal and increased demand for oil affected the importance of the Middle East.

GATHERING INFORMATION

Imagine that you are a geographer studying modern Iraq. Where would you begin your study? First, you would look at the area's physical environment. Physical environment includes the formation of the land—the mountains, valleys, plateaus, and so on. You also would look at the climate. Is the area under study a desert area? Second, you would want to know something about the cultural characteristics of the area. Some of the questions to investigate here might include: Where do the people live? What jobs do they have? What do they eat? What are their beliefs? What is important to them? Finally, you would find out how all the physical and cultural characteristics of the area are related to each other. How do they influence one another? How do they make this area different from other areas in the world?

Geographers use many methods used by other social scientists in studying and identifying regions on the earth. Geographers gather information, classify it, measure it, and then form a hypothesis, or educated guess, about the meaning of the information.

Field Observation

The process of gathering information is carried out in a variety of ways. One way, called field observation, is to travel to a place and observe its physical and cultural characteristics. For example, a geographer would study the rise and fall of a river's water level and compare it to some observation made by another geographer years, and maybe centuries, before. A geographer would compare the location and appearance of a present-day city to those of the same city as it existed in the past. To make these comparisons a geographer, like a historian, would use written records, descriptions, drawings, paintings, photographs, and maps from the past.

Statistical Analysis

Once information is gathered, the data are fed into a computer to be analyzed. By doing this statistical analysis, a geographer can get results or answers that are mathematically exact. Some of the information gathered in this way then can be used by mapmakers, or cartographers, to produce new maps.

GLOBES AND MAPS

Maps and globes are the tools used most often by geographers. Over the course of history the process of making maps and globes has changed. The earliest known maps were scratched on clay tablets in ancient Babylonia. Later, maps were drawn by

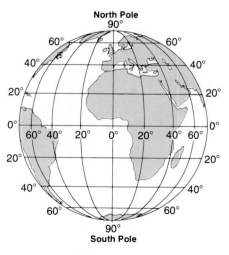

Globe with Full Grid

sailors on sheepskin. The first globes were probably made in the late fifteenth century. We now have maps that are based on information provided by cameras in spacecraft. Some maps are drawn with computer assistance. New technological developments will continue to improve the ways we have of representing the earth.

Globes

A globe is a miniature model of the earth. It is the most reliable representation of the earth available to us. A globe accurately shows distance, direction, shape, and area.

If you look at a globe, you will notice the variety of information shown: oceans, rivers continents, islands, mountains, deserts, cities, and so on. You will also notice the network of lines covering the globe. These lines were devised by geographers and mapmakers to help you locate places on the earth's surface and to help in the construction of maps.

Latitude and Longitude

Lines drawn on the globe from the North Pole to the South Pole are called meridians. All meridians are of equal length and converge at the poles. The prime meridian is marked 0° and runs through Greenwich (GREN-ich), England, a suburb of the city of London. (Refer to the maps on the right.) The prime meridian is used as a starting line for measuring meridians of longitude—distances east and west of it.

Longitude is measured in degrees (°), minutes ('), and seconds ("). There are 180° of east longitude and 180° of west longitude. Any place in the world 10 degrees east of the prime meridian is said to be 10 degrees east longitude (10°E). Any place that is 20 degrees west of the prime meridian is said to be 20 degrees west longitude (20°W).

The lines drawn east to west parallel to the equator are called parallels of latitude. All parallels of latitude circle the earth, although their circumferences (distances around the earth) become smaller toward the poles. The equator is the largest parallel. It is used as a starting line for measuring other parallels of latitude—distances north and south of the equator. The equator is marked 0°. Latitude also is measured in degrees (°), minutes

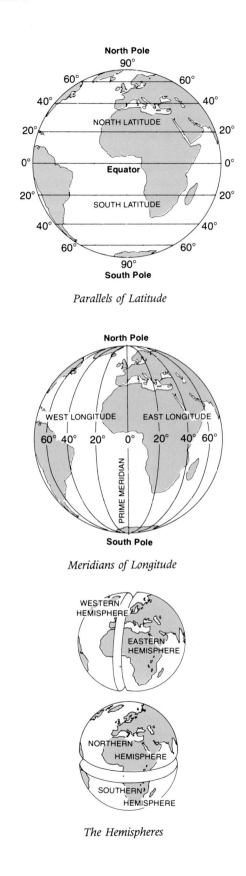

Parallels of Latitude

Meridians of Longitude

The Hemispheres

('), and seconds ("). From the equator to either the North or South Pole is 90 degrees. The North Pole is 90 degrees north latitude. Any place in the world 10 degrees north of the equator is 10 degrees north latitude (10°N). Any place that is 30 degrees south of the equator is 30 degrees south latitude (30°S).

All parallels of latitude and meridians of longitude intersect at right angles except at the poles. You can locate any place on earth by using the intersections of latitude and longitude. New York City, for example, is 41°N latitude and 74°W longitude.

The earth may be divided into hemispheres, or halves, along any meridian of longitude. The only parallel of latitude that cuts the earth in half is the equator.

Maps

Maps were developed as a convenient way to show information about the earth. Unlike globes, they are easy to carry and store. They also are capable of showing the entire surface of the earth at one time. You probably have more maps than you realize. You may find four or five in the glove compartment of your family car. You also may have a map showing bus and train routes in your city or town. Road maps and route maps are special-purpose maps. There are many other useful, common special-purpose maps. An economic map shows the location and distribution of economic activities in a region. Climate maps show the types and location of climates in an area. Population density maps show the number of people per square mile or square kilometer.

For all their convenience, maps can have some serious drawbacks. Geographers and mapmakers tried to transfer the information on a globe to a flat surface, but there were real problems in doing this. The curved surface of the earth cannot be transferred to a flat piece of paper. Imagine cutting an orange in half and removing the inside. You cannot make the skin of the orange lie down flat without cutting it again. In order to show one type of information accurately on a flat surface, other types of information have to be distorted. For example, in showing direction correctly on a map, mapmakers could not show distance correctly. The solution at which they arrived was to draw different maps for different uses.

Map Projections

Imagine a glass globe with a light bulb inside of it. Mapmakers can project the outlines of land areas, parallels, and meridians from the globe onto a cylinder-shaped piece of paper. Then they cut the cylinder and roll it out flat. The lines of longitude and of latitude are now on paper. Mapmakers are ready to plot locations and make a map of the earth. This method of flattening a globe onto a piece of paper is called projection.

Using a glass globe is only one way of making a map projection, and there are many different kinds of projections. Some of these different projections are described and illustrated in the following pages. How may of these projections do you recognize? How many are new to you?

Mercator Projection

The Mercator projection is a modification of a cylindrical projection. The lines of latitude and of longitude form a rectangular grid. The shapes of the land areas are accurate closest to the equator. The farther the distance from the equator, however, the more the land areas become distorted. For example, although South America is, in reality, ten times larger than Greenland, Greenland seems larger on a Mercator map. Despite distortions in land size, this projection shows all directions correctly. The Mercator projection was often used by ship's navigators in the sixteenth century because no other projection showed directions as accurately.

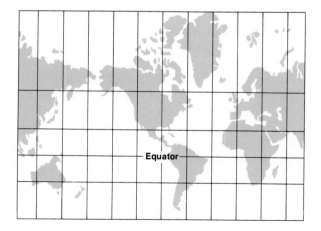

Mercator Projection

Azimuthal Equidistant Projections

On the azimuthal equidistant projection, or polar projection, the meridians of longitude are straight lines projected outward from the poles. Parallels of latitude are equally spaced concentric circles. The relationships of the land areas around the North Pole are shown accurately. Land areas away from the poles are increasingly distorted. The advantages of this projection are that the distance along the meridians and the direction from the central point, or pole, are correct. Polar projections are used extensively by airplane pilots. The straight lines that radiate from the center of the map are called great circle routes. Distances for air travel can be easily measured because all the great circles are straight lines on the projection.

Conic Projections

A conic projection is made by placing a paper cone over the globe. Longitude lines are lines that radiate down the peak of the cone. Latitude lines are arcs, or portions, of concentric circles. The projection shown here is a modified conic projection with one standard parallel, the one where the cone touches the globe. This is the area of least distortion. Distortion increases slowly as the distance from the standard parallel increases. Conic projections are particularly good for showing large areas that extend primarily in an east-west direction. They are useful for representing the United States, the Soviet Union, or Europe.

Interrupted Projections

Interrupted projections are used when the purpose of a map is to show landmasses and the oceans are not a major interest. In an interrupted projection, there is a central meridian for each continent so that no land area is far from a meridian. The concept used is that of taking the skin of an orange and cutting away sections so it can be flattened out. The interruptions, or cuts, in this map have been made in the oceans in order to keep the shape and size of the land areas as accurate as possible.

No matter what map projection is used, there will always be distortion. By comparing a map to a globe, it is possible to identify the type of distortion and to compensate for it.

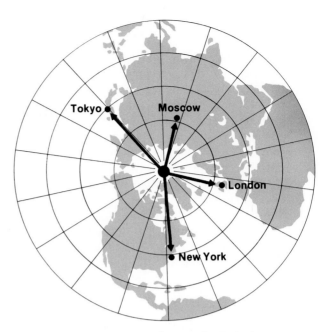

Polar airline routes imposed on a Polar Projection

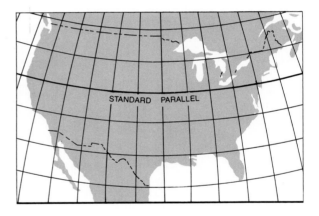

Conic Projection

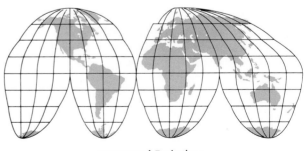

Interrupted Projections

Scales on Maps and Globes

The scale on a map or globe tells us what distance on the earth is represented by a certain distance on the map or globe. The scale, in miles or kilometers, may be a graph or it may state that one centimeter or one inch equals a certain number of miles of kilometers. In an atlas, a world map may show a scale of 1:140,000,000 inches (1:350,000,000 centimeters). This means that one inch represents 140 million inches or that one centimeter represents 350 million centimeters on the actual surface of the earth. On a 12–inch (30–centimeter) globe, the scale is usually 1:41,817,600 inches or about 660 miles to an inch (1:104,544,000 centimeters or 1,056 kilometers to a centimeter).

Symbols on Maps

Symbols or pictures represent certain information on a map. While there are no standard symbols for all maps, there are some that are used very often.

In order to be sure that people understand what they are reading on a map, mapmakers include a legend. A legend is a small section of the map that displays the symbols and shows how they are used. Examples of some symbols are included on page 7. How many can you recognize? Can you identify any of the symbols used on the map of Allentown and what they represent? What conclusions can be drawn about Allentown from the map? Look through the book at other maps. What symbols are used for battle sites, invasions, trade routes, and other historical information?

Another symbol commonly found on maps is the directional indicator. This is often an arrow that points north. Most of the maps in this book show only a small portion of the earth's surface. Without lines of longitude and latitude drawn on the maps, it is difficult to determine the direction accurately. By consulting the directional indicator, or arrow, you can tell the orientation of the map. On some maps, direction is indicated by a compass rose that displays the four directions.

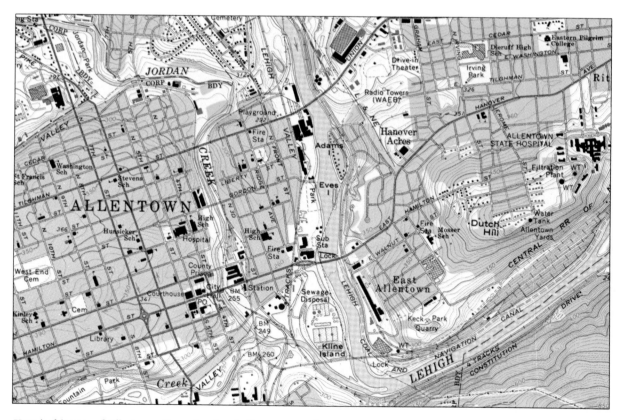

How is this map of Allentown, Pennsylvania, similar to maps of your community?

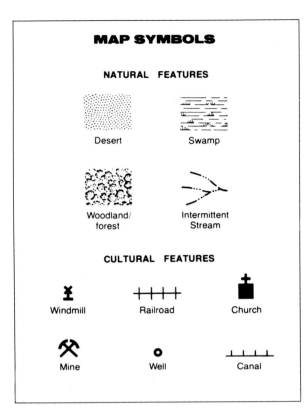

MAP SYMBOLS

NATURAL FEATURES

Desert

Swamp

Woodland/forest

Intermittent Stream

CULTURAL FEATURES

Windmill

Railroad

Church

Mine

Well

Canal

Using Maps

When you are studying history, you will encounter many maps that provide useful information. The political maps show the boundaries of political units, that is, boundaries established by people and not nature. In a book of this type, there are many historical maps that show the political boundaries of a region at different points in time. By comparing these maps, it is possible to detect changes that have occurred over the course of history. Political maps can be compared to the physical maps in the Atlas. In this way, certain conclusions can be drawn about the influence of physical features on the cultural and political development of an area.

The first step to take when using a map is to read the title. The title will tell you what information you will find on the map. Then look over the map to see how the information is presented. Look at the symbols on the map legend and locate them on the map itself. If distance is an important factor, consult the scale to get an accurate estimate. Read the map caption. The question will focus your attention on some major aspect of the map.

Color in Maps

The maps in the Atlas, located in the back of the book, use color to indicate the various elevations on the earth. Areas near sea level may be green, plains areas may be orange, and mountains may be reddish brown. Color is also used to show different kinds of vegetation.

On a political map, the mapmaker explains in the legend what information is represented by certain colors on the map. In this book, colors are used sometimes to show the extent of empires, kingdoms, colonies, and other political units.

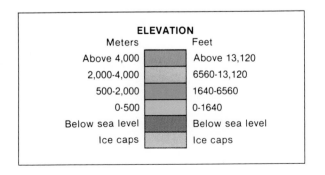

ELEVATION

Meters		Feet
Above 4,000		Above 13,120
2,000-4,000		6560-13,120
500-2,000		1640-6560
0-500		0-1640
Below sea level		Below sea level
Ice caps		Ice caps

REVIEWING THE LESSON

1. In your own words, briefly define or identify: geographer, meridian, prime meridian, parallels of latitude, equator.
2. Why is it important to study the geography of an area along with its history?
3. Using the Atlas maps in the back of the book, locate by means of latitude and longitude coordinates each of the following: Dallas, Texas; Adelaide, Australia; Bogotá, Colombia; Calcutta, India; Munich, West Germany; Astrakhan, U.S.S.R.; Nairobi, Kenya; Tokyo, Japan.
4. Using the Atlas, find the distance in miles and kilometers between each of the following cities: Atlanta, Georgia and Toronto, Canada; Recife, Brazil and Lima, Peru; Oslo, Norway and Copenhagen, Denmark.
5. Using the elevation guide, list the highest and lowest elevations shown. Then turn to the Atlas map that shows the area in which you live and give its elevation.

UNIT · 1 ·

The EARLY ANCIENT WORLD

4500 B.C.–250 B.C.

CHAPTER ·1·

EARLY PEOPLES

4500 B.C.–300 B.C.

Objectives

- To describe what archaeologists have learned about prehistoric people

- To discuss the civilization that developed in ancient Sumer

- To explain the contributions made by the Amorites to civilization in the ancient Middle East

- To describe how the use of iron affected the Hittites and the Assyrians

- To discuss how the Persians extended and controlled their empire

- To describe the lasting contributions of the Phoenicians and the Hebrews

*I*n this chapter, you will learn about the early people who inhabited the Earth and how scholars reached their conclusions about the way they lived. Your study will take you from these first human beings through the series of developments that affected their future and our past. You will see how the development of agriculture changed people's relationship to their environment as well as to each other. As people began to settle in one place and gradually were freed from the daily search for food, they were able to devote a portion of their time to other pursuits, such as political organization, religion, and art.

About 4500 B.C. the Sumerians developed the first civilization, or advanced society, in which members depended on others in the group rather than worked and lived independently. Their economic and political systems centered on shared efforts to deal with their environment and please their gods. Their civilization emerged in a fertile river valley between the Tigris (TIE-gris) and the Euphrates (yoo-FRAY-teez) rivers in present-day Iraq. As groups of nomads invaded Sumer, they were influenced by the accomplishments of the Sumerians. The nomads took what they learned and built on it. The achievements made here and in other river valleys at approximately the same time would have a lasting impact on later civilizations.

PREHISTORIC PEOPLE

People have always wondered about the first inhabitants on Earth. It is difficult to know much about these early people because they had no system of writing. As no written records were left for historians to study, this period is called **prehistory**—a time before written history.

Archaeology

In order to understand this period, we depend on archaeologists, scientists who study the remains of the cultures of ancient people. They examine artifacts such as tools, weapons, and ornaments that have been found at the sites where prehistoric people lived.

The task of interpreting archaeological remains is not an easy one. Archaeologists like Mary and Louis Leakey have devoted their lives to searching for clues to the life of prehistoric people. In the Olduvai Gorge (OLE-duh-vie GAWRJ) in northern Tanzania (Tan-zuh-NEE-uh) in 1959, Mary Leakey discovered teeth and pieces of a skull. Study of these fossils led the Leakeys to believe they belonged to a hominid, or human-like individual, who lived about 1.75 million years ago. Years later in 1978, in a region south of the Olduvai Gorge, Mary Leakey found hominid footprints that were very much like those of modern people. She and her colleagues believe that these footprints are nearly 3.5 million years old.

Archaeologists use a method called **carbon 14 dating** to determine the age of various archaeological finds. This process measures the amount of radioactive carbon (radiocarbon) left in an object. All living things absorb radiocarbon from the air, and when a living thing dies, this radiocarbon loses radioactivity at a specific rate over a certain period of time. For example, the radiocarbon content in a bone fossil is half gone in about 5,700 years and it continues to lose half of its remaining radioactivity every 5,700 years. Scientists can measure the amount of radioactivity from radiocarbon left in a fossil to determine just how old it is.

Another method used by scientists to find the age of certain remains is **dendrochronology** (den-droe-kruh-NAHL-uh-jee), the name given to tree-ring dating. Using this method, archaeologists determine the age of wood remains by comparing their growth rings with those of a tree trunk whose age is known. The most important factor in dendrochronology is to match the ring patterns that are present in different wood remains.

As archaeologists unearth new findings and scientists develop new ways of interpreting these artifacts, our present ideas about how early people lived may be reinforced or contradicted. Our history began millions of years ago and much remains to be learned about it.

The Old Stone Age

Prehistory is divided into periods according to the kinds of tools that people used. The earliest phase is called the Old Stone Age, or **Paleolithic** (pay-lee-uh-LITH-ik) **Age.** The word Paleolithic comes from the Greek words *palaios* (pah-lie-OSE), meaning old, and *lithos*, meaning stone. The era is so named because people living during this period made tools from stone, as well as from wood and bone. Most scholars think that the Old Stone Age began millions of years ago and lasted until about 8000 B.C. Ninety-nine percent of our history on earth has been spent in the Old Stone Age.

Scientists do not know much about the people of the Old Stone Age, but they believe that these people were nomads or wanderers who lived by hunting animals and gathering wild plants. The study of ancient campsites shows that Stone Age hunters usually lived in small groups of perhaps twenty to sixty people. They remained in one area for as long as a supply of plants and animals was available. Then they had to move on in their constant search for food.

In order to hunt successfully, early people had to reach a certain level of development and there had to be some sort of social organization. Someone, perhaps an older member of the group or a hunter respected for skill and prowess, had to assume the role of leader. There also had to be a means through which the leader could communicate instructions to his followers, perhaps through sounds or sign language.

Archaeologists believe there were several kinds of Stone Age people. It is believed that one type of early people lived between 1,200,000 and 300,000 years ago. Their remains have been found in Java, an island of Indonesia, and in China near Beijing (Peking).

Scientists think the early people who lived in Java used spoken language, kindled fires, and made some of the first hand axes. Although their brains were larger than those of some other prehistoric people, they were smaller than ours today. The prehistoric people in China apparently also created fire and developed advanced stone tools. For some unknown reason these people ceased to exist probably about 300,000 years ago.

Remains from another group of early people— the so-called **Neanderthal** (nee-AN-dur-thal) people—believed to have emerged about 120,000 years ago, were discovered in the Neander Valley in Germany. During the years 80,000 B.C. to 40,000 B.C. Neanderthal people were the main inhabitants of Europe and neighboring areas of Africa and Asia.

Neanderthal men and women stood about five feet (150 centimeters) tall, had relatively short arms and legs, and were probably heavy for their height. Makers of advanced tools and weapons, their use of fire helped them survive the cold glacial periods. Scientists think that Neanderthal people believed in an afterlife, because they buried their dead with tools and other materials that would have been useful to them in a successive life. This indicates that Neanderthal people may have practiced some form of religion, since belief in an afterlife is a common denominator in many religions.

Why Neanderthal people disappeared has never been determined. One possible explanation is that they were victims of an epidemic. Another theory is that they were destroyed by a more advanced prehistoric people called **Cro-Magnons.**

Cro-Magnon people may have emerged as far back in time as 70,000 years ago. Remains of these people have been discovered in southern France and in Spain. They were probably taller than the Neanderthals, and made more complex weapons than did their predecessors. They may have been the first to use the fishhook, the harpoon, and, eventually, the bow and arrow. Scientists believe that Cro-Magnon people also developed several forms of art as early as 30,000 years ago. Pictures of their daily lives, drawn on cave walls in France

The people who created this example of cave art left no written records. What conclusions could an archaeologist draw about the people depicted here?

and Spain between 15,000 B.C. and 10,000 B.C., are the most outstanding contribution of the Cro-Magnons. By about 20,000 years ago, these new homo sapiens had already migrated not only throughout Europe but also to Asia, Africa, the Americas, and even as far away as Australia.

The New Stone Age

During long periods of the Earth's history, its climate was much colder than it is today. Glaciers, or ice sheets, covered large areas of the world. The most recent ice age, as these periods are called, began more than 1.5 million years ago. During this era prehistoric peoples hunted the hardy animals that thrived in the rugged climate. The life of prehistoric hunters was difficult because they depended entirely upon the availability of game for their survival.

About 10,000 years ago the Earth's climate began to grow warmer. The large animals that people hunted previously, such as the wooly rhinoceros and the mammoth, began to perish as vegetation changed. However, there was a great increase in the number of smaller animals, which were easier to hunt. Instead of hunting big game, people gradually began to rely on these smaller animals, as well as fish and shellfish. Their diets began to include more vegetation such as wild grains, nuts, and fruits, which grew in warmer weather. At first, people gathered only what they needed each year. Once the wild plants in an area became exhausted, people migrated in search of other sources of food. They had to search farther and farther to find enough to eat, until they discovered how to grow their own plants. Some people became less nomadic and experimented with farming, but the development of agriculture was a slow process. Scientists think that farming could have begun 11,000 years ago in Israel and Jordan, and that by 5000 B.C. farming had spread to eastern Europe, and by 3000 B.C. to Great Britain. Farming may have developed independently in the Americas.

Farmers had different needs than the nomadic hunters and gatherers had, and these needs spurred a series of developments. Farmers began to improve their stone tools and those that they developed are called **neoliths** (NEE-uh-liths). The age in which they were developed is called the New Stone Age, or the **Neolithic Age.** Toward the end of this era, the art of making stone tools was perfected. Farmers learned that axes made by polishing, rather than by chipping, the cutting edges were stronger and could cut more deeply into the wood surface than could the chipped tools they had made previously. The same techniques may have been used to develop the wheel during this period.

People also began to domesticate, or tame, sheep, goats, cows, horses, and pigs during the New Stone Age. These animals became more useful to people as agriculture developed.

No one knows exactly how people learned to tame animals. One theory is that a few wild dogs strayed near human camping areas in search of food. The hunters may have noticed that the dogs could help them spot game and hunt more efficiently. In return for their services, the dogs were fed. Because of their success with dogs, people may have decided to domesticate other animals as well.

The farmers' need for containers to hold grain and seed may have encouraged yet another development. Remains found at Neolithic sites reveal that the art of pottery making was known during much of the New Stone Age. Pottery is not easy to make, and the development of this skill shows that technology was advancing well before people knew how to write.

Early people had to make several discoveries prior to becoming good potters. First, they learned to use special clay that could be softened with water in order for it to be molded. Secondly, they found that adding other material, such as sand, would give body to the clay so that it would hold its shape. Neolithic people invented the process of firing, or baking, to make the pottery hard and durable. Several of the processes they invented are still in use today.

Neolithic people also were talented weavers who made baskets, mats, and nets. As agriculture and domesticated animals began to provide more fibers, clothmaking became possible. Scientists have found remains of heavy tools and primitive looms at Neolithic campsites. Scholars believe that people began to form more settled communities out of necessity during the New Stone Age, since tools for making pottery and looms for weaving

As people settled down, each village had its own kiln for firing pottery. In what ways does this pot reflect a higher level of civilization than cave art?

could not be carried easily. The heavy implements would have hindered the mobility of people who hunted as a means of survival. The development of agriculture and the establishment of permanent communities were two of the most important advances toward society as we know it today.

Culture and History

Culture means all the behavior patterns, arts, beliefs, and institutions possessed by a community or population. The culture of a society includes such things as science, art, economic activity, religious beliefs, and government. Societies develop their cultures over a period of many years by passing on, and thus preserving from one generation to the next, certain aspects of their way of life.

The development of agriculture and the changes it brought about laid the basis for the emergence of more complex cultures, called civilizations. A **civilization** is a state of human society marked by relatively advanced levels of economy, government, arts, and technology. Progress was slow at first. Small village communities replaced wandering bands of hunters. A steady supply of food enabled people to settle permanently in primitive farming communities, where the first forms of government probably began to develop.

As farmers in these villages developed better farming methods, they improved the variety and quality of their crops. They began to use plows, then plows pulled by animals. As people had more to eat and began to live longer, the population increased.

Gradually, the farmers were able to produce surplus crops. Since there was extra food, people no longer had to spend most of their time working only at agriculture. They had more free time to try new things, to create and develop crafts and trades, and to make many new and important inventions.

As technology advanced, some people became specialists in one particular craft. For example, one family may have made the tools used by several farmers. Clothmaking began with the basic weaving techniques of Neolithic peoples. Skilled workers employed in these crafts were called **artisans.** As towns grew, the artisans became an important element in society.

The division of labor among several artisans gave rise to the need for trade. The services of traders and merchants were necessary to ensure a smooth flow of goods between the artisans and their customers. The growth of a merchant group within a community gave rise to the need for accountants to help tradespeople keep records of their transactions. Many scholars think that writing may have been invented so that people could keep permanent records of what was bought and sold. This invention marks the beginning of the **historic** period. Once people began to write they kept a record, or history, of their ideas, beliefs, attitudes, and events from their daily lives, as well as statistical records.

Most of these changes took place first in four major river valleys: the Tigris-Euphrates in Mesopotamia, the Nile in Egypt, the Indus in India, and the Huang He (Yellow River) in China. While some people were still hunting and gathering, other groups began to migrate into the river valleys. These regions contained the fertile soil, water, and growing season that would support agriculture. From this combination of circumstances and opportunity sprang the first civilizations.

SECTION REVIEW

1. Mapping: Use the Atlas maps on pages 755, 756, and 758 to describe the location of Tanzania, Java, Germany, Spain, and France.
2. What is an artifact?
3. What is the main function of an archaeologist?
4. What is meant by prehistory?
5. What are two methods used to date archaeological finds?
6. About when did the Old Stone Age end and the New Stone Age begin?
7. What one thing seems to distinguish the culture of Neanderthal people from that of the Cro-Magnons?
8. What is one main difference between the meanings of the terms culture and civilization?
- How were the aspects of your culture passed on to you?

THE SUMERIANS

In the region that is now Iraq (ih-RAHK), eastern Syria, and southern Turkey, the Tigris and Euphrates rivers flow side by side for more than 1,000 miles (1,600 kilometers). Between these two great rivers lies a fertile valley that the ancient Greeks called **Mesopotamia** (mes-uh-puh-TAY-mee-uh), which means "land between the rivers." This rich valley forms the eastern part of the **Fertile Crescent.** The Fertile Crescent is a strip of rich, well-watered land that extends in a great arch from the coast of the Mediterranean Sea to the Persian (PUR-zhun) Gulf. (See the map below.) Many of the ideas of Western civilization developed in this region, and much of the flora and fauna we have today were first domesticated here.

People began to move into Mesopotamia at a very early time. They settled at the lower end of the valley where the rivers empty into the Persian Gulf and called their land Sumer. Probably the most important achievement of the **Sumerians** (soo-MER-ee-unz), the people of Sumer, was that they were among the first people to leave written records. Most scholars agree that the development of a system of writing is one of the main prerequisites for the development of a civilization.

By about 4000 B.C. the Sumerians were living in large villages with buildings made of sun-dried mud brick. By about 3300 B.C. writing began. By

MIDDLE EAST

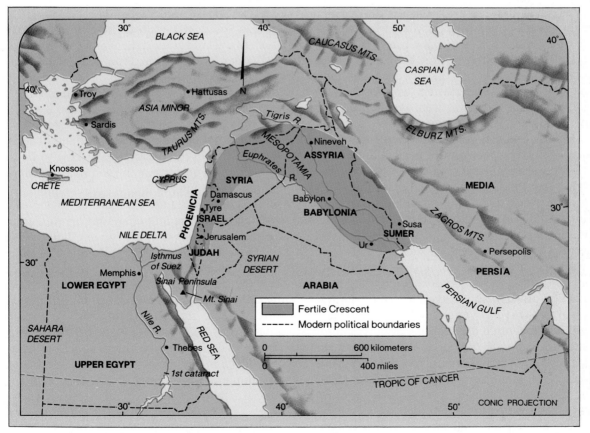

The Fertile Crescent provided a number of natural advantages including a warm climate and fresh water. What civilizations developed in this region?

that time the Sumerians had animal-drawn plows and the wheel. By about 3000 B.C. they had become prosperous enough to develop the cities of Uruk (OO-rook), Nippur (nih-POOHR), Ur (UHR), and Lagash (LAY-gash). (See the map on the previous page.)

Taming the Rivers

The Tigris is the deeper of the two rivers of the Fertile Crescent and carries a larger amount of water. The Euphrates, however, is faster and carries large amounts of soil along with its waters. This soil gradually sinks to the bottom of the river and makes the river more shallow. For this reason, the Euphrates often overflows its banks and floods the valley. This can be dangerous because it is not always possible to predict when the floods will occur or to know how much water will cover the land.

Historians believe that the Tigris and Euphrates rivers played important roles in the development of the great Sumerian cities. The early settlers in the valley realized how crucial it was to control the floodwaters of the rivers. They built a large irrigation system with a network of canals and dikes. The canals led water from the rivers to the fields. The dikes kept the rivers from flooding the land and washing away crops and homes.

This irrigation system finally grew so large that each year many people were needed to clean the irrigation channels and repair the dikes. Work on such a large scale had to be organized in order to be done efficiently. Some historians believe that the need to plan and supervise large work projects helped the Sumerians develop the additional skills necessary to form a complex society.

For example, it was not possible for individual farmers to finance the construction of large-scale irrigation projects, and this resulted in the foundation of a system of government that made the decisions and organized the available resources. In the early years priests served as the managers and planners. They designated the use of land, kept the boundaries, made sure surplus grain was stored, and organized groups of workers. Later, this role was taken over by kings and their officials.

The Sumerians could support their population on the same land year after year, even though the number of people continued to increase. Not only did the irrigated fields produce more crops than those that used only rainfall, but the rich soil carried by the rivers helped keep the land fertile.

Sumerian City-States Develop

In early Sumer many people lived in farming villages. As the food supply became more plentiful and a share of the surplus grain was stored in the temples, not everyone was needed to work in the fields. This surplus freed some people to develop their skills and work at other jobs. At first they worked as carpenters, potters, metalworkers, and stone carvers. Gradually they developed more specialized skills. During the height of the Sumerian civilization, there were boat builders, scribes who kept written records, jewelers, and people who made tools and weapons of bronze.

By 3000 B.C. the farming villages had developed into large cities. In fact, Sumerian cities were like large states. Historians often call cities such as those in Sumer **city-states.** These cities controlled much of the land around them and competed with each other for leadership. From a study of Sumerian writings, historians believe that the cities were ruled first by groups of adult free men. Only in time of danger did the citizens choose a king to lead them. Later, when cities had grown to great size, the kings became permanent rulers. The Sumerians, however, considered the king to be the representative on earth of the god who owned the city and everything in it.

The most outstanding feature of the city-state was its temple. The Sumerian temples were called **ziggurats** (ZIG-uh-rats). They were built of sun-dried mud brick and had several stories. Ziggurats, possibly representing mountains, were often more than 150 feet (45 meters) high. They towered over the countryside and could be seen for miles. Some were so large that their bases covered 500,000 square feet (45,000 square meters). The top story was set aside for the worship of an important god or goddess. In addition to its religious importance, the temple was the center of economic and commercial activity. Located around the ziggurats were storehouses that held sacks of grain, precious gems, metals, and fine textiles. The priests, who interpreted the wishes of the gods, used the grain to serve the gods' needs.

Ziggurats had names such as "House of the Mountain" and "Bond Between Heaven and Earth." What buildings today have names with strong symbolic meanings?

Sumerian Religion

Many aspects of life in Sumer were affected by religious beliefs. The Sumerians believed that a god founded and owned each city-state. Everyone was a slave of the gods and had to try to please them or risk being greatly harmed. It was the responsibility of the priest or the king to interpret what the gods wanted and relay the information to the people. Kings usually communicated with the gods through dreams. The king, for example, would visit the temple area of the ziggurat, which contained an altar and a couch. Once there, the king could sleep and, according to tradition, receive the gods' orders through dreams. Orders were passed down by the king to the lowest order of citizens, telling them what the gods wanted them to do. Many people were directed to build temples, roads, and irrigation projects. The people would obey the king in order to please the gods and forestall their anger. In this way the king maintained control over the people. The belief in the Sumerian gods, therefore, played an important role in the development of Sumerian civilization. It was the basis of authority for the priests and kings.

Sumerian Society

Free citizens and slaves made up the two major classes of people at the height of Sumerian civilization. The most influential free citizens were princes, who often were in charge of large estates worked by others, and soldiers of high rank. The second most important group included farmers, manufacturers, merchants, and artisans. They, like the princes and soldiers, had a say in the political process.

Slaves also had a place in Sumerian society. Though a slave might be a war captive, criminal, or a person sold temporarily into bondage because of debts, a slave was not without some rights. A master could beat, but not murder, a slave. Slaves could borrow money, start a business, and even purchase their own freedom. The children of a free parent were born free even if the other parent happened to be a slave.

Sumerian women also had rights. They could own private property, enter into businesses, and serve as witnesses in civil and criminal trials. However, parents or guardians continued to arrange marriages for women and, if a marriage failed to produce children, a husband was allowed to obtain a divorce and remarry, if he so wished. Divorce was very difficult for women to obtain, but not for men.

At birth, Sumerian children became the property of their father. By law, he could disinherit them or sell them into slavery, although there is no evidence that either was a common practice. Scholars studying Sumerian writing have ascertained that children, in fact, were regarded with great affection by their parents and that parents wished their offspring to receive as good an education and training as possible.

SOURCES

The Epic of Gilgamesh

Among the best-known tales in Mesopotamian literature is the ancient Epic of Gilgamesh (GIL-guh-mesh). This myth poses two universal questions. First, why must a good person suffer and die? Second, can a person ever obtain immortality, or everlasting life?

In this passage Gilgamesh laments the death of his best friend Enkidu (en-KID-yoo). Later, Gilgamesh sets out to find a life-giving plant to revive his friend. Though he succeeds in getting the plant, he loses it to a snake and concludes the dead cannot be brought back to life.

"Enkidu, my friend, my younger brother—who with me . . . hunted . . . panther in the plains; who with me could do all, who climbed the crags. . . . Now—what sleep is this that seized you?. . ."
He did not raise his eyes.
Gilgamesh touched his heart, it was not beating . . . .
Again and again he turned toward his friend, tearing his hair and scattering the tufts, stripping and flinging down the finery off his body.

Refusing to accept his friend's death, Gilgamesh sets out to discover the secret of immortality. In the end, *however, he is defeated. The advice Gilgamesh receives on his difficult quest is described below.*

Life, which you look for, you will never find.
For when the gods created man, they let death be his share, and life withheld in their own hands.
Gilgamesh, fill your belly . . . dance and make music day and night.
And wear fresh clothes, and wash your head and bathe.
Look at the child that is holding your hand. . . .
These things alone are the concern of men.

Source: Adapted from H. and H.A. Frankfort, John A. Wilson, Thorkild Jacobsen, *The Intellectual Adventure of Ancient Man.* Copyright © 1946 by University of Chicago Press.

1. How does Gilgamesh feel about his friend's death?
2. What does the advice that Gilgamesh received tell us about Mesopotamian people and their view of life and death?
3. What tales do we have that might reveal our view of life to historians? List and discuss them.

A Writing System

The writing system invented by the Sumerians is called **cuneiform** (kyoo-NEE-uh-fawrm) writing. The word cuneiform is derived from the Latin word *cuneus,* meaning wedge, because of the wedge-shaped marks made by a reed stylus on wet clay. Nearly one-half million clay tablets have survived the ages, providing us with an invaluable record of ancient Sumerian civilization. Cuneiform writing, probably the greatest creation of the Sumerians, was developed so that temple priests could keep track of goods entering and leaving the storehouses. For each item, a different wedge-shaped mark was made on a wet clay tablet that was kept as a permanent record. At first, cuneiform began as a kind of picture writing. This system worked well while the storehouses were small, but as the cities grew, the types of things recorded became more varied and numerous. New marks had to be invented to record them all, and soon it became impossible to continue using this system.

Instead, the Sumerians began to use existing or new symbols to represent separate sounds. In this way, the name of a person or thing was represented by a combination of symbols. The picture

DEVELOPMENT OF CUNEIFORM

MEANING	Earth	Man	Woman	Water In	To Drink	Fish
EARLY CUNEIFORM						
PICTOGRAPH IN POSITION OF LATER CUNEIFORM						
ORIGINAL PICTOGRAPH						
CLASSIC ASSYRIAN						

writing was gradually simplified so it would be easier to draw. From this simpler style, cuneiform developed. There were about 600 cuneiform signs representing ideas, objects, syllables, or single sounds, and the Sumerians were able to write entire sentences with these signs.

The Contributions of the Sumerians

The Sumerians wrote down more than lists of goods. They left a rich literature, which included poetry about the deeds of their gods and myths about their own creation. The Sumerians also wrote down prayers to the gods, fables that were designed to teach proper behavior, scientific writings, legal documents, and a great deal of history.

Education was highly valued by the Sumerians but was available only to boys of the upper classes. Priests conducted the lessons in the temples, where students learned reading, writing, history, mathematics, foreign languages, and mapmaking. Some also studied law and medicine.

The Sumerians developed many new ideas that are now part of our daily lives. They created some of the rules of algebra, and they invented a calendar based on the movements of the moon that enabled farmers to time their planting. The calendar divided the year into two seasons: winter and summer. It had twelve months, some with twenty-nine days and some with thirty. When necessary, the Sumerians added an extra month to the calendar so it would conform to the proper season. Rather than use a formal numbering system, the Sumerians recorded years by means of some significant event. The Sumerians also devised a method for measuring time. They divided a circle into 360 degrees, each degree composed of 60 minutes, and each minute divided into 60 seconds. This is the same system we use today.

Sumerians and the Bronze Age

The Sumerians were among the first people known to use bronze. They learned to make bronze about 3500 B.C., at which time it began to replace stone and soft copper as the main material for making implements. For this reason, historians call this new period the **Bronze Age.**

Statues of Gudea, a ruler of Lagash in Mesopotamia, also included lists of his accomplishments. What methods do we use today to record the lives and deeds of our leaders?

Bronze, a very strong metal, is a mixture of copper and tin. Other materials can also be combined with bronze to make it more useful. Phosphorus, for example, helps strengthen bronze, especially in the making of tools and weapons. Lead lowers the melting point of bronze so that it can be poured into molds.

The Sumerians used bronze to make cups, vases, battle axes, helmets, knives, shields, spear points, swords, various ornaments, and even cooking stoves. Bronze continued to be used on a wide scale by many ancient peoples until it was replaced about 1200-1000 B.C. At that time a much stronger substance, iron, replaced bronze in the making of weapons and tools. The **Iron Age** will

be discussed in greater detail when you study about the Hittites and the Assyrians.

In spite of their great civilization, the Sumerians never developed lasting political unity. Repeated warfare between city-states over territory and water weakened the Sumerians. The shift of the riverbed of the Euphrates River left the cities of Ur and Eridu without water for irrigation or access to harbors for shipping. By 2500 B.C. the government of Sumerian city-states had begun to decline in strength. Other regions to the north of Sumer became more powerful and began to take over Sumer. Within 400 years the Sumerian language was no longer spoken.

SECTION REVIEW

1. Mapping: Use the map on page 15 to describe the relationship and location of: Mesopotamia, the Tigris and Euphrates rivers, the Persian Gulf, Sumer.
2. In your own words, briefly identify: Mesopotamia, Fertile Crescent, cuneiform writing, city-state, ziggurat.
3. Briefly describe the physical geography of Mesopotamia. How might it have affected life in Sumer?
4. What was the role of the king in the Sumerian religion? How did this role affect Sumerian society?
■ How was the history of ancient Sumer recorded? How are historical events recorded today? List the different methods. Which method do you think would be the most useful to future historians in describing life today? Explain.

THE AKKADIANS AND THE AMORITES

Throughout the history of the ancient Middle East, cities and high civilizations were conquered by desert nomads. As the population of the nomads increased and their needs became greater, they began to press closer and closer to the borders of the city-states, threatening invasion. The river valley in which the Sumerians developed their civilization provided no natural barriers against invasion. Where civilization was deeply rooted, the invaders sought to enjoy rather than destroy what they had conquered. Cultures developed that were a blend of both the Sumerian culture and that of the intruders.

Akkadians

One important group of nomads was the **Semites,** the people who in ancient times were located in Mesopotamia and on the grasslands west of the Euphrates River (in present-day Syria and Saudi Arabia). The first nomadic Semites wandered with their herds in search of available grasslands. When overpopulation, poor grazing seasons, or restlessness drove them into settled communities, they quickly adapted to new ways of living. Many became successful farmers or merchants.

When groups of Semites moved south along the Euphrates River, more and more of them began to live in the Sumerian city-states. The Semites became an especially strong force in Akkad, a city-state just north of Sumer, and were known as **Akkadians.** A Semite leader named Sargon emerged and eventually led his forces to control not only Akkad but Sumer itself. Around 2200 B.C. the Akkadians weakened and the Sumerian city-states reasserted their power.

AMORITE EMPIRE ABOUT 1700 B.C.

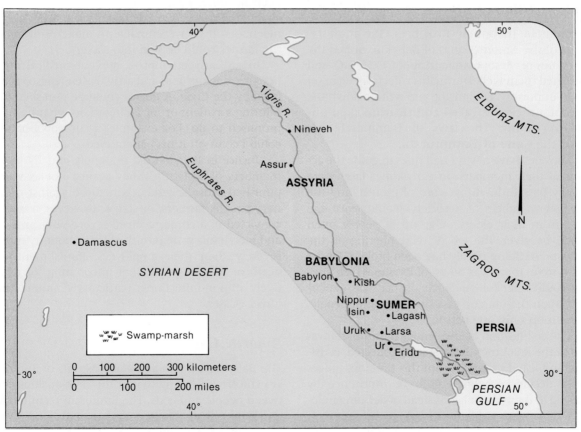

Describe the extent of the Amorite Empire. How would you account for the distribution of cities along the banks of the Tigris and Euphrates rivers?

Amorites

In a pattern that recurred in the Fertile Crescent, another band of invaders rose to power on the fringe of the river valley. This time it was the **Amorites** who gained political control of Mesopotamia. By about 2000 B.C. they had migrated into the Euphrates River valley area and settled in Babylon (BAB-uh-lun) north of Akkad. The Semitic Amorites were nomads who lived in the Syrian (SIR-ee-un) Desert. The Amorites swept in from the deserts, and the stability of Sumer was again threatened. Around 1900 B.C. they managed to overcome the Sumerians and take over the village of Babylon, which became the capital of the whole region. (See the map on page 21.) Later, Amorite rulers used the city of Babylon as a base for building a large empire called Babylonia (bab-uh-LOE-nyuh).

Code of Hammurabi

Hammurabi (ham-moo-RAH-bee), the most famous of the Amorite kings of Babylon, united the city-states of Mesopotamia in about 1750 B.C. and governed them well. During his rule, laws were set down uniformly. Organizing and writing down the laws of a society is called **codification** (kod-uh-fuh-KAY-shun). The laws of Hammurabi are called the **Code of Hammurabi.**

Societies have always had rules to guide the actions of their members. In early times laws were usually passed down by word of mouth, and the younger members of a society would learn the rules from their elders. A group of people often would be given the job of remembering all the laws and deciding if they had been broken. Under this system, there was no list of laws to which anyone could refer for guidance. Justice was dependent upon the opinion of a small group of people, or even on only one person.

The codification of laws under Hammurabi was one of the first times that a society collected, classified, and listed its laws. From this time on, judges could decide someone's guilt or innocence by looking at the written law instead of deciding independently what judgment should be passed.

The Code of Hammurabi tells historians much about life in ancient Mesopotamia. Women held a high position in society, and foreigners were treated well. There were many laws that regulated industry and trade; therefore, historians conclude that these must have been important activities. The Code also indicates that land was privately owned, but peasants who rented land could not be evicted from it until their leases had run out.

Marriage was a legal contract, and both husband and wife had definite rights. Even though a wife was considered to be chattel, or the property of her husband, she could return to her family if he mistreated her. If divorced, she was allowed to keep her children. Women were allowed to conduct business and had the same rights in business as did men.

People who falsely accused others of crimes received the punishment that the accused would have received. If a city was not able to catch a thief, that city had to repay the victim of the robbery. Members of society had special duties toward their neighbors. For example, a farmer who did not keep his dikes in good repair was financially responsible for any flood damage to the fields of his neighbors. If he were unable to make restitution, the farmer could be sold into slavery.

In an early attempt to prevent medical malpractice, doctors' fees and activities were also regulated by the Code. A doctor could be punished for injuring a patient or for failing to do what he had promised to do. For example, a surgeon's hands could be cut off if his patient died.

Justice in Babylon did not apply equally to all members of society. Crimes against nobles were punished more severely than those against ordinary people, farmers, or slaves. However, a noble convicted of a crime received severe punishment, and merchants were punished for dishonesty more severely than their employees. Punishment by death or mutilation was not uncommon for relatively minor infractions, particularly among the lower classes.

Amorite Culture

The Babylonians adopted many aspects of Sumerian culture, including that of the relationships between people and gods. The Sumerian technology for dealing with the river and annual floods was also adopted with little change. Whenever possible, the Babylonians built on foundations laid by the Sumerians. In mathematics, the Babylonians took advantage of the achievements of the Sumerians and went on to develop multiplication tables, exponents, and even mathematics textbooks.

Fall of the Amorite Kingdom

By 1600 B.C. other groups had invaded the Amorite kingdom. At first, the Hittites conquered Babylon but then withdrew because they could not maintain their position. Then came the **Kassites** (KASS-ites), who had established secure positions in the northern part of Mesopotamia from the time of the rule of Hammurabi's son. The Hittite and Kassite invasions were part of a larger movement of nomads who, with their horse-drawn chariots, disrupted the relative stability of the major river valley civilizations. The Kassites ruled for about four hundred years until they were swept away by invading Assyrians.

SECTION REVIEW

1. Mapping: Use the map on page 21 to locate the latitude and longitude coordinates for the city of Babylon.
2. In your own words, briefly identify: Hammurabi and the Code of Hammurabi.
3. Explain how and why the Semites changed their life-style.
4. What does the Code of Hammurabi tell us about life in ancient Babylon?
■ Do you live by any code or set of laws? What are they? Choose one and tell how you think future historians would use it to describe our society.

THE HITTITES AND THE ASSYRIANS

The Hittites were one of several civilizations that developed along the borders of the irrigated river valleys about 2000 B.C. They were probably nomadic herders in the grasslands north of the Black and Caspian (KAS-pee-un) seas. About 1650 B.C.

they moved south through the Caucasus (KAW-kuh-sus) Mountains and into the area that is now modern Turkey. By 1600 B.C. the Hittites had formed a confederation of states with a capital at Hattusus (HAT-too-shus). As you just read, the Hittites invaded Babylon about 1600 B.C. but withdrew to the west of Mesopotamia.

The Hittite Empire

At the height of their power, the Hittites had a strong army, and their confederation was ruled by a king. One Hittite king, Suppiluliumas (soo-pee-loo-lee-OO-mus) I, who ruled from 1375 B.C. to 1335 B.C., extended his rule almost to the borders of Egypt. While problems within Egypt diverted the attention of its rulers, the Hittites tore away the region of northern Syria from Egypt.

For many years thereafter, the Hittites and Egyptians often clashed. A peace treaty was finally arranged after a battle in 1296 B.C. between the Hittite king, Muwatallis (moo-wah-TAHL-iss), and Ramses (RAM-seez) II of Egypt. Peace then reigned for about seventy years, but the Hittites never fully recovered from the effects of the wars. By the end of that time, the Hittite Empire had lost much of its power. About 1200 B.C. the Hittites were overcome by warlike people from southeast Europe and from the Aegean (ih-JEE-un) Sea region. However, during their reign, the Hittites made important contributions to the civilization of the ancient Middle East.

Hittite Art and Architecture

The Hittite art that has survived includes primarily sculpture and architecture. It can be seen in the remains of huge, squat public buildings, ornamental gateways, and reliefs. The sculptured reliefs depict gods in the form of human beings. All Hittite gods are pictured with sacred animals: for example, the characteristic animal for the weather god was the bull; that for the sun-goddess was a lion.

The architecture of Hittite defense fortifications was outstanding for its time. The Hittites built their towns in places where nature provided protection. Their capital, Hattusas, was located on a peninsula at the intersection of two deep gorges with sheer cliff faces. Strong fortifications appeared on the side that allowed easy access. The Hittites built two

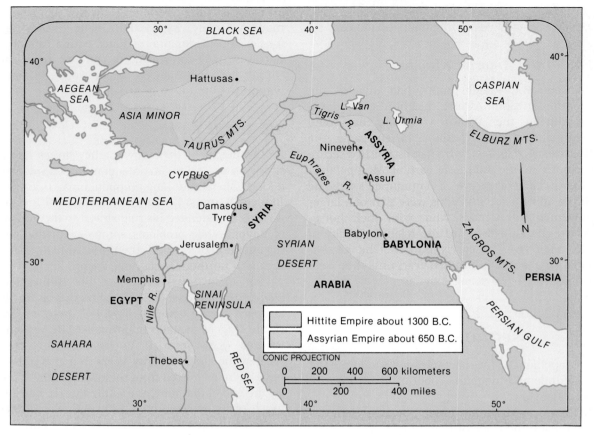

Even with a centralized administration, the Assyrians had difficulty controlling their empire. Why do you think this was so?

parallel stone walls with linking cross walls between them and filled the extra space with rubble. Above this were brick superstructures.

The Hittites planned all gateways, walls, and towers so that any visitors or invaders would be exposed to the Hittite defenders. A tunnel to permit surprise expeditions against the enemy existed under the wall of one of the gates.

Hittite Law

The legal system of the Hittites was one of their most significant achievements. Their code was less severe than the Code of Hammurabi. Punishment by death was limited to serious crimes, such as treason, and the payment of fines was a more common punishment for lesser offenses. Elders served as judges in local courts and attempted to make unbiased judgments. Persons accused of crimes were allowed to question their accusers and to defend themselves during their trials.

Commerce and trade were vital to the Hittites, and their laws strictly controlled economic life. Set prices were established for luxuries and necessities. Wages and fees were also set, and a woman was paid less than half of a man's salary.

The Hittites' Ironworking

Although bronze was in wide use in the ancient Middle East by 2000 B.C., the Hittites were the first people to successfully use iron for making tools and weapons. Earlier peoples, like the Sumerians you have studied, had known of iron but did not

This detail from a silver cup of the Hittite period shows a male god standing on a deer. What does the existence of such a vessel reveal about the Hittites?

burn hotter, could produce enough heat to purify the iron ore by separating it from other elements. The new process produced strong, rust-resistant iron tools and weapons. These tools and weapons gave the Hittites a great advantage over their neighbors.

For a long time the Hittites kept their method of making iron a secret, and they would not trade iron goods with other people out of fear that their methods of iron production would be discovered. However, about 1200 B.C. when the Hittite Empire fell, the metalworkers moved to other parts of the Middle East, taking their knowledge of ironworking with them. As a result, the use of iron tools and weapons spread throughout the region. Historians mark this time as the end of the Bronze Age and the beginning of the Iron Age in the ancient Middle East.

The eventual spread of iron production throughout the ancient Middle East after 1000 B.C. brought important changes to farming as well as to warfare. Iron plows and sickles helped farmers clear more fields and increase food production. Farmers now had to have specialists to make their iron tools, so they had to depend on people in the towns. Thus, ironworking brought about a closer relationship between the people of the countryside and the towns.

The Assyrian Empire

The fall of the Hittite Empire was, in part, due to a general wave of invaders throughout much of the Middle East. One of those groups was the Assyrians, who for years had waged wars against the Babylonians and aggressive mountain people to the north and east of Babylonia. Years of warfare turned these fiercely independent Assyrian farmers into an efficient military organization. By about 900 B.C. the Assyrians moved into the northern part of Mesopotamia and built city-states. The first people to use iron widely, they expanded their vast empire by warfare, using iron weapons, chariots, and cavalry. An especially useful device was an iron battering ram that could be used to break through city walls.

The Assyrians, who killed or deported conquered people who resisted their rule, could be brutal, but they were generally efficient soldiers

make as much use of it. Some peoples in the Middle East had made a few tools by hammering iron from fallen meteors. However, such supplies of iron ore were very limited, and the use of them was very expensive.

Around 1400 B.C. the Hittites developed a new method of ironworking. They invented a furnace which, by forcing air through it to make the fire

This Assyrian relief carving shows a detail of a royal lion hunt. What clues does it provide as to why the Assyrians were successful fighters?

and governors. They united a large area by building roads to link all parts of the empire. They also created a messenger service to carry news of important events to the capital.

Nineveh (NIN-uh-vuh), the Assyrian capital, was a large and prosperous city. It had a continual supply of fresh water that was brought in from mountain streams. It also had the world's largest cuneiform library, built on the orders of Assurbanipal (ah-shoor-BAHN-ih-pahl), an Assyrian king. The library contained thousands of clay tablets from all over Mesopotamia and, from these preserved records, scholars have been able to trace how this once peaceful people became a warrior society. The tablets have also provided information about the Assyrian religion and indicate that many of the Assyrian religious beliefs were borrowed from the Sumerians. Indeed, Assyrian scribes copied, studied, and accepted the ideas in many Sumerian and Babylonian texts.

The Assyrians made great contributions to the science of warfare and the organization of government. They divided their army into corps of infantry, chariotry, engineers, and supply, even using camels for desert warfare. They organized their empire into provinces or states, each ruled by a governor and protected by a military garrison. In order to control rebellious peoples they even moved entire populations in some areas, but this was not enough to preserve their empire. There

were often revolts by the people they had conquered and the continual warfare depleted the supply of soldiers. In order to keep the army at its full strength, soldiers had to be drafted from among the defeated enemies. These foreign soldiers did not fight as willingly as did the Assyrian troops; the capital of the weakened Assyrian Empire finally fell about 612 B.C.

SECTION REVIEW

1. Mapping: Use the map on page 24 to describe the relative location of: the Hittite Empire, the Black Sea, the Syrian Desert, Egypt, Hattusas.
2. In your own words, briefly identify: the Hittites, the Assyrians.
3. Why did the Hittites and Egyptians clash with each other?
4. What contribution did the Hittites make to ironworking?
5. List two contributions made by the Assyrians to life in the ancient Middle East.
6. What did the remains of iron goods tell archaeologists about life in the ancient Middle East?
■ Do you own any things made of metal? Pick three of these things and describe what archaeologists would be able to tell about your life by examining these items.

THE CHALDEANS AND THE PERSIANS

The Assyrian Empire was defeated by an alliance of **Chaldeans** (kal-DEE-unz) who came from Babylon, Medes (MEEDZ) who came from a plateau area in the east called Media, and the **Scythians** (SITH-ee-unz) who came from the area north of the Caspian and Aral (AR-ul) seas. Ironically, it was these people who had adopted the military innovations of the Assyrians and improved upon them. They were part of a military revolution that occurred between 850 B.C. and 700 B.C. in the Middle East. People learned how to handle weapons effectively while mounted on horseback or camelback. The ability to maneuver quickly gave them a significant advantage over foot soldiers.

Soon after the Assyrians were defeated by this group led by the Chaldeans, the alliance crumbled. The Scythians returned home with their booty, and the Chaldeans and Medes divided up the conquered territory with the Egyptians, who had been overrun by the Assyrians about 900 B.C.

The Chaldean Empire

The Chaldeans combined the remains of the Assyrian Empire with their own kingdom to form a new empire ruled by the strong leader Nebuchadnezzar (neb-uh-kud-NEZ-ur). At its height, the empire covered most of the Fertile Crescent. (See the map on page 28.)

About 600 B.C., during the rule of Nebuchadnezzar, Babylon was rebuilt. It was surrounded by a wall more than 13 miles (20 kilometers) long and beautiful buildings were built within. Among the greatest of these were the ziggurat and the palace of the king, the latter containing gardens of hanging tropical plants. These hanging gardens of Babylon were considered one of the seven wonders of the ancient world, and the ziggurat is believed to be the largest ever built.

Babylon was a rich and important city in which the arts and commerce were highly developed. In its schools, scientists made maps of the heavens and also worked out a system for recording the length of the year, similar to the one we use today.

The Medes

At the height of the Chaldean Empire the Medes were also growing in power. The Medes gradually extended their empire across upper Mesopotamia and Syria, and westward toward Babylon. As the Medes added to their territory, they conquered the Persians who, in time, rebelled against the Medes. A Persian prince named Cyrus (SIE-rus) united both of these groups under one rule. Together, the Medes and the Persians were a powerful force and, as they continued their expansion westward into the Fertile Crescent, they became a threat to the Chaldean Empire.

The snarling lion adorned the foundation of a temple in northern Mesopotamia. Why do you think the lion was a popular subject for art throughout early civilizations?

Cyrus the Great

Cyrus was one of the greatest conquerers in the history of the ancient Middle East. In only eleven years, between 550 B.C. and 539 B.C., he invaded lands from the heart of India in the east to Babylonia in the west. Cyrus' armies entered Babylon in 539 B.C. and, according to his own records, the city surrendered to his army without a battle. This event marked the end of the independent political organization of the older civilizations of Mesopotamia. From this time onward, the cities of the river valleys were united under one administration with the plateau region of present-day Iran. Thus, the Chaldean Empire was added to Cyrus' other lands and became part of the Persian Empire.

The Persian Empire

The Persian Empire was larger than either the Assyrian or the Chaldean. It stretched east to India and west to the Aegean Sea. The well-organized and well-governed empire was divided into provinces with capitals that included Babylon, Persepolis (pur-SEP-uh-lus), and Susa (SOO-zuh). Each province was under the control of a government official called a **satrap** (SAY-trap) who was responsible for governing the provinces and for supplying soldiers in time of war. The officials, in turn, were evaluated by representatives of the king and faced dismissal if they were ruling improperly. The satraps could also be dismissed for disloyalty to the emperor or for crimes such as taking bribes.

CHALDEAN AND PERSIAN EMPIRES

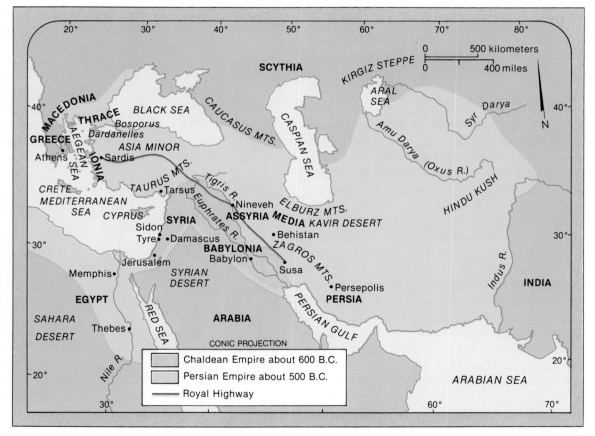

Cyrus extended the boundaries of Persian Empire. What natural barriers limited the extent of his conquests?

Messengers went to and from Susa, the capital city, and the major cities of the empire by a network of highways built by slaves. The excellent system of roads also aided trade.

The Persians did not try to change the customs of the people they conquered. Those who did not try to rebel against Persian rule were allowed religious freedom and some say in local government. Many people were even allowed to join the Persian army or become traders on Persian ships. Native Persians, however, were taxed less than others and received the best government posts.

Persian Religion

At the height of Persian power, a new religion became popular among many people in Persia and Mesopotamia. Its founder was a prophet named Zoroaster (ZORE-oe-as-tur) or Zarathustra (zar-uh-THOO-struh), who probably lived during the seventh century B.C., but undoubtedly borrowed many of his ideas from earlier times. According to him, the god of light and goodness had created the world. This god, known as Ahura-Mazda (AH-hoo-ruh-MAZ-duh), was in a never-ending battle with Ahriman (AH-rih-mun), the god of darkness or wickedness. People had an obligation to help Ahura-Mazda in his struggle against Ahriman. Zoroaster also preached a definite belief in a future life after physical death.

The Persian Empire lasted for more than 200 years, eventually being defeated about 330 B.C. by the armies of Alexander the Great.

SECTION REVIEW

1. Mapping: Use the map on page 28 to describe the location of the homelands of the Medes, the Scythians, the Chaldeans, and the Persians.
2. In your own words, briefly identify: the Medes, the Persians, the Chaldeans, the Scythians, Nebuchadnezzar, Cyrus, Alexander the Great.
3. How did the Persian highway system contribute to life in ancient Mesopotamia?
4. Who was Zoroaster?
■ What do you regard as one important contribution made by your society? Describe how that contribution might affect future generations.

THE PHOENICIANS AND THE HEBREWS

For about four hundred years, beginning around 1200 B.C., portions of the Fertile Crescent were free from disruptive invaders. During this time, the Phoenicians and the Hebrews had the opportunity to develop their own cultures. An outstanding, lasting achievement of the Phoenicians was their alphabet. That of the Hebrews was their religion.

Phoenicia

Phoenicia (fuh-NISH-ee-uh) is the ancient Greek name for a narrow strip of land about 12 miles (19 kilometers) wide and 200 miles (320 kilometers) long, located on the eastern coast of the Mediterranean Sea. This land, in the region of present-day Syria and Lebanon (LEB-uh-nun), was made up of a group of loosely united city-states. These states usually paid tribute to other more powerful states in the area, such as Assyria, to ensure their own survival.

Phoenicia was a hilly land with poor soil that made large-scale agriculture impossible, and so the Phoenicians turned to the sea for their livelihood. They were highly skilled sailors and successful traders. They founded colonies throughout the Mediterranean region and in northwest Africa. Phoenicia reached the height of its power about 1000 B.C. to 774 B.C.

Phoenician Traders

The Phoenicians carried on active trade with the people of the region that is present-day Spain. They sailed as far as the British Isles for tin. It is quite likely that, at the beginning of the seventh century, a Phoenician fleet sailed completely around the African continent.

About 800 B.C. the Phoenicians began to develop their trading posts into colonies. One of the most important of these colonies was Carthage (KAHR-thij), in North Africa. In time, Carthage gained its independence and spread its influence throughout the Mediterranean. Carthage was especially important because of its strategic location on the northern coastline of Africa and because it was a stopover point for Phoenician merchants and sailors on their longer voyages westward.

The Phoenicians were also skilled at crafts. They brought raw materials from other lands and used them to make objects of gold, silver, copper, and bronze, as well as beautiful glass and textiles. One of their most valuable products was cloth tinted a rich purple by a dye made from a shellfish found along the Mediterranean coast.

The Phoenician Alphabet

The most important invention of the Phoenicians was their alphabet. It was not actually their own creation, but something they took over from the Aramaeans (ar-uh-MEE-uns) and improved upon. As you know, the Sumerians developed a form of writing called cuneiform, which did not use an alphabet but instead was made up of symbols that represented specific things or syllables.

The first alphabet, or set of signs, each standing for a single sound, was invented some time between 1700 B.C. and 1500 B.C. by the Aramaeans who lived in the area of the Sinai (SIE-nie) Peninsula and northern Syria. These people used fewer than thirty signs to represent all the sounds of their speech. They used only consonants, no vowels. The Phoenicians adopted this system and developed their own alphabet consisting of twenty-two consonants, which was easily learned and simple to use.

The alphabet we use today is based on the Phoenician alphabet, which in turn was adopted by the Greeks. The Greeks improved upon it by adding signs to represent vowel sounds,making it more versatile as well as easier to use. The alphabet used today is a further reinforcement of the one adapted by the Greeks and passed via the Etruscans to the Romans.

The Hebrews

The Hebrews were a nomadic people who lived by herding sheep. About 1800 B.C. they moved with their flocks from the Sumerian city of Ur to the region that we know today as Israel. This area, called Canaan (KAY-nun), home of the Canaanites, was located in the eastern part of the Fertile Crescent between the Jordan River and the Mediterranean Sea.

The Hebrews were led into Canaan first by Abraham and then by his son Isaac and his grandson Jacob. Years later, when Jacob was an old man, famine struck and the Hebrews were forced to move south into Egypt where grain was available. There they remained for many years and were made slaves by the pharaoh Ramses II. Then about 1275 B.C. Moses, the leader of the Hebrews, led them back toward Canaan. But before he reached his goal he died on the journey, which is said to have taken the Hebrews forty years.

The Hebrew Kingdoms

When they first moved back into Canaan, the Hebrews were organized into twelve tribes that cooperated with each other during emergencies. Common problems were settled by judges who were chosen for their holiness.

The Hebrews' struggle to establish a homeland finally led to war with their neighbors, the Canaanites. When war broke out, the Hebrews realized that they needed to be unified. Samuel, the last of the judges, gathered all the tribes together and then chose from among them a strong and able young man named Saul (SAWL) to be their king.

Saul, who led the Hebrews from about 1020 B.C. to 1004 B.C., was killed in a battle with the Canaanites and was succeeded by his son-in-law, David. David defeated the Canaanites, captured the city of Jerusalem (juh-ROO-suh-lum) and made it the capital of the Hebrew kingdom.

By the time David became king, the Hebrews were no longer simple nomads. From their neighbors they had learned horse breeding, engineering techniques, chariot warfare, ironworking, and other crafts and skills. David's reign, from 1004 B.C. to 965 B.C., was relatively peaceful. The Hebrews had good relations with neighboring kingdoms, and trade developed. Under the rule of David's son, Solomon (SOL-uh-mun), the well-organized Hebrew kingdom reached a new level of peace, wealth, and cultural development during the years 965 B.C. to 925 B.C. Beautiful buildings were constructed in Jerusalem, including the great temple, which was later destroyed by the Chaldeans. Commerce and trade increased, and learning and the arts were encouraged.

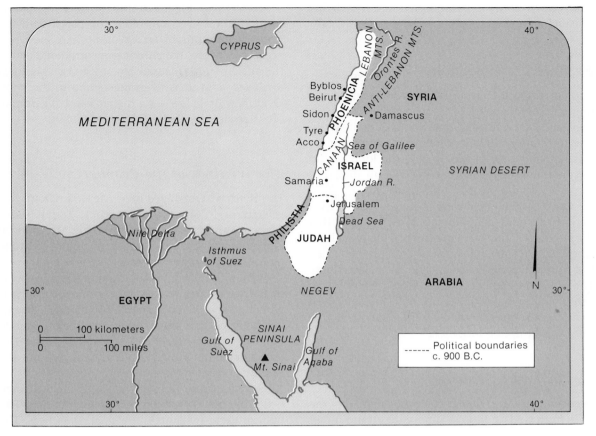

30° · CYPRUS

MEDITERRANEAN SEA

Byblos
Beirut
Sidon
Tyre
Acco

PHOENICIA · LEBANON MTS. · Orontes R. · ANTI-LEBANON MTS.

SYRIA

• Damascus

Sea of Galilee

CANAAN

ISRAEL
Samaria •
Jordan R.

SYRIAN DESERT

PHILISTIA

• Jerusalem

Dead Sea

JUDAH

Nile Delta

Isthmus
of Suez

NEGEV

ARABIA

N

30°

EGYPT

0   100 kilometers
0   100 miles

Gulf of
Suez

SINAI
PENINSULA

▲
Mt. Sinai

Gulf of
Aqaba

30°

----- Political boundaries
c. 900 B.C.

30° · 40°

What advantages resulted from the location of Phoenician cities on the coast of the Mediterranean Sea?

Solomon was known for his great wisdom and skillful administration. Like other great kings of his time, he spent large amounts of money to encourage the arts and construct huge buildings. People were heavily taxed, and some had to work without pay for projects they considered extravagant. Despite Solomon's accomplishments, unrest and bad feelings began to endanger the kingdom.

The Fall of Israel and Judah

After Solomon's death in 925 B.C., the kingdom was split in two by a civil war. The northern kingdom was called Israel and was ruled from the city of Samaria (suh-MER-ee-uh), while the southern kingdom was called Judah and was ruled from Jerusalem. (See the map above.) For nearly 200

years the kingdoms fought with each other periodically, and the conflict so weakened the two kingdoms internally that they were incapable of resisting outside attacks.

In 721 B.C. the kingdom of Israel fell to the Assyrians. In 586 B.C. Judah was conquered by the Chaldeans from the east. Nebuchadnezzar, the king of the Chaldeans, destroyed the temple at Jerusalem and exiled to Babylon many of those living in Judah. After the Persians conquered the Chaldeans, many Hebrews were allowed to return to their homeland, but they remained subjects of the Persians until about 165 B.C.

After the Hebrews returned to Jerusalem, the first five books of the Old Testament, called the *Torah*, were written. Hebrews who accepted the teachings of the Old Testament and worshiped at

Jerusalem were first called Israelites and later came to be known as Jews. In modern times, Jews living in Israel are called Israelis.

Early Hebrew Religion

Prior to going to Egypt, the Hebrews had been a nomadic desert people. As one grazing area was used up, they moved to another with their flocks. The rules of conduct they followed were based on this nomadic way of life. During the long stay in Egypt, however, the Hebrews gave up their nomadic ways and settled in one place.

Once the Hebrews were to return to their lives as nomadic herders in Canaan, Moses realized that they required rules to govern their daily actions. Knowledge of the old rules of conduct had been lost and new ones were created to replace them. The old rules had been passed from generation to generation by word of mouth, but Moses believed that the new ones should be written down, so that they would not be forgotten.

Mosaic Law

According to the Hebrews, Moses received the rules from God on Mount Sinai, a desert mountain between Egypt and Canaan. These rules, called the Ten Commandments, governed the actions of the Hebrews in their religious, family, and community life. These commandments today are observed by Christians as well as by Jews, the descendants of the ancient Hebrews.

For the ancient Hebrews the Ten Commandments also form part of the *Sinai Covenant,* or pact with the Hebrew God. This covenant unified the Hebrews in worshiping God and obeying the laws set forth in the *Torah.* According to Hebrew belief, the Hebrews were chosen to proclaim the existence and glory of God, who promised to protect them and grant them the Land of Canaan, much of present-day Israel. In exchange, the Hebrews were to continue to fulfill the promises, obligations, and details of the Covenant.

The Ten Commandments were the foundation of Hebrew law, but gradually other rules developed around them. Because Moses was the first lawgiver of the ancient Hebrews, these laws are known as **Mosaic** (moe-ZAY-ik) **law.** At least some of the rules that make up Mosaic law are believed to have originated much earlier in Hebrew history. These laws are often compared with the Code of Hammurabi. In a world where everyone accepted slavery, which was not considered evil in the ancient world, Mosaic law insisted on kindness to slaves, as well as to strangers and to the poor. Overall, Mosaic law set a higher value on human life than did the Code Of Hammurabi.

The Writings of the Prophets

The Hebrews worshiped only one God whom they referred as **Yahweh** (YAH-way). Today many Jews use the word *Adonai,* meaning My Lord, in place of Yahweh, which is considered by some to be too sacred to pronounce.

When the Hebrews returned to Canaan, however, they came into contact with the fertility gods worshiped by the Canaanite farmers. The Canaanites believed that their fertility gods ensured rich harvests and prosperity. Soon many of the Hebrews began to worship not only Yahweh but the fertility gods as well.

Among those Hebrews who still held to their belief in one God were the **prophets** (PRAHF-uts), or great religious thinkers and teachers. The prophets said that it was wrong to worship any god other than Yahweh. They also said that Yahweh would punish the Hebrews for worshiping the fertility gods. The written words of the prophets became part of the Hebrew holy writings because the prophets were believed to speak for Yahweh. The Hebrew people studied the holy writings to find out how God wished them to behave. Besides being a source of religious wisdom and a guide to proper conduct, the writings of the prophets contain some of the world's most beautiful poetry.

Many of the sacred writings of the ancient Hebrews are included in the books of the Bible. They contain the rules of conduct that form Hebrew law, the writings of the prophets, and books of poetry. They also contain a detailed record of Hebrew history. The Hebrews recorded major events of their history because they believed that Yahweh's will was involved in those events. As a result, we have a more extensive written record of history of the Hebrews than of any other peoples in the ancient Middle East.

This is a fragment from the Dead Sea Scrolls found in 1947. Why is such a find so valuable to scholars?

Ethical Monotheism

Most of the peoples in the ancient Middle East worshiped a number of gods. According to their religions, these gods carried on their own activities with little concern for the people who worshiped them. The Hebrew religion was different. First, the Hebrews taught the worship of only one God, Yahweh. The worship of one God is called **monotheism** (MON-uh-thee-iz-um). In addition, the religion of the Hebrews focused on the daily lives and values of the people, and it encouraged the good behavior of individuals—both in their own personal lives and toward others. This study of moral values is called **ethics** (ETH-iks). The Hebrew religion is the first example in recorded history of **ethical monotheism,** which encourages worship of one God and teaches that God requires proper conduct on the part of the people.

The Synagogue

While they were in exile in Babylon, the Hebrews developed a new form of worship. It centered on the **synagogue** (SIN-uh-gahg), a meeting place where the Hebrews would come together each week to read and learn about the **scriptures,** or holy writings. Every person could not be an expert in these writings, so in time each synagogue had one person who was specially trained in explaining them. It was the duty of this teacher, called a rabbi (RAB-ie), to interpret the holy writings for others.

The creation of the synagogue was an important step in the development of religion. Before this, people believed that gods or goddesses could be worshiped only in specific sacred places, and that a special ritual had to be performed by a priest or priestess. After the synagogue was created, people could worship wherever they could gather together. Their religion was no longer tied to a certain location—synagogues could be found in many places.

A synagogue was also important because it helped the Hebrews to keep their identity as a separate people. This was an important development because in most other religions only the priest or priestess was permitted to read the holy writings and to interpret the gods' or goddesses' wishes for the people. Hebrews were allowed to read the holy writings of their religion together, and thus they strengthened one another's faith, even though they were living in a foreign land.

SECTION REVIEW

1. Mapping: Use the map on page 31 to describe the location of: Phoenicia, Canaan, Egypt, Israel, Judah, Jerusalem.
2. In your own words, briefly identify: alphabet, ethical monotheism, the prophets, synagogue, rabbi.
3. Why do you think the Phoenician alphabet is considered such an important contribution to the ancient world?
4. List the major events in Hebrew history from the time of Abraham to the return of the Hebrews from their exile in Babylon.
5. What was different about the religious ideas of the Hebrews? Explain briefly.
■ Both the Phoenicians and the Hebrews made lasting cultural contributions. How have their achievements affected your own life? Give a specific example.

Reviewing the Chapter

Chapter Summary

We owe a great debt to many of the early peoples of the ancient Middle East. The Sumerians were among the first to leave a written record, in cuneiform, of their lives. The Amorites developed one of the earliest known written codes of law, the Code of Hammurabi, about 1750 B.C. A new method of ironworking was introduced by the Hittites about 1400 B.C. The Assyrians, however, were the first people to use iron widely. They also maintained a large library of cuneiform tablets. Their civilization reached its peak about 800 B.C.

While the Assyrians gained power, the Phoenicians built a great sea-trading civilization that reached its height from about 1000 B.C. to 774 B.C. Their most important contribution was the development of an alphabet. It provided the basis for the one we use today.

The Hebrews organized themselves under the leadership of prophets, judges, and kings. The Hebrews contributed ideas such as those expressed in the Ten Commandments. They were conquered by the Chaldeans in 586 B.C.

Culture continued to develop in the ancient Middle East even after the decline of these civilizations. For example, by 600 B.C. the Chaldeans had rebuilt Babylon into a beautiful capital city. The Persians created a well-organized empire that lasted from about 500 B.C. to 330 B.C.

1. What people left the first written records of their lives? What is this writing called?

2. What is the Code of Hammurabi? When and by whom was it developed?

3. For what will the Hittites be remembered? The Assyrians? The Phoenicians?

Using Your Vocabulary

1. What is the difference between history and prehistory?
2. What is the origin of the word Paleolithic? Why do scientists use it to describe the earliest phase of prehistory?
3. What is an ice age? How did prehistoric people survive during these times?
4. What is the origin of the word Neolithic? What is another name for this age? What important invention was created in this era?
5. What does the word domesticate mean? How did the domestication of animals help to develop civilization?
6. What is culture? How is it developed?
7. What is an artisan? Explain the artisan's role in developing society.
8. What is the origin of the word cuneiform? Explain the uses of cuneiform writing in Sumerian society as well as its importance in history.
9. What is codification? Why is it considered an important development in human history?
10. Who were the satraps? What were their principal responsibilities?
11. Define Mosaic Law. On what was it based?
12. What synonym is often substitued by the Hebrews for Yahweh? Why?
13. What are monotheism and ethical monotheism? Who were the first people to develop a civilization based on these terms?

Developing Your Geography Skills

1. Look at the map of the Fertile Crescent on page 15 and the map of the Middle East and Southwestern Asia on page 754. What modern countries are located in what was then the Fertile Crescent? What modern countries are now located in the valley between the Tigris and Euphrates rivers?
2. Look at the map of the Persian Empire on page 28 and the map of the Middle East and Southwestern Asia on page 754. What modern countries are located in what was then the Persian Empire?

3. Look at the map on page 28. What are the co-ordinates of latitude and longitude for Jerusalem, Persepolis, Susa, and Nineveh?

Recalling the Facts
---

1. Who were the Java and Peking people? Where and when did they live? What kinds of tools did they use and how did they get food?
2. When and where did the Neanderthals live?
3. What is the main contribution to human civilization of the Cro-Magnon people?
4. What distinguishes the Neolithic from the Paleolithic Age? What were the major innovations of the Neolithic Age?
5. Where did the Sumerians live? What were their major contributions? Describe how their city-states were organized.
6. When, how, and by whom was ironworking developed? How did the use of iron affect the peoples of the ancient Middle East?
7. What event marked the end of the independent political organization of the older civilizations of Mesopotamia? What religion did the conquering people have?
8. What were the important contributions of the Phoenicians? What was the name of their most important trading post?
9. Who invented the first alphabet? When was it developed? Which people adopted this system and developed it further?
10. Where were the Hebrews from originally? Why did they migrate to Egypt and why did they later leave Egypt? Who were Saul, David, and Solomon? What were their contributions to Hebrew civilization?

Essay Questions
---

1. Describe the development of prehistoric people from the nomadic to the settled stage. Explain how and why the development of agriculture and the establishment of permanent communities were so important to the advancement of culture and society.
2. Describe the achievements of Sumerian society and explain how the necessity to control the Tigris and the Euphrates rivers was a very important factor in the development of Sumerian society.
3. Compare Sumerian and Hebrew religion. How did their conception of God or the gods influence their social, cultural, and political development?
4. Describe the specific elements of Hammurabi's Code, Hittite Law, and Mosaic Law. How were they similar? How did they differ?
5. Describe characteristic elements of modern civilization. Make sure to include significant social and cultural institutions, as well as common implements of modern technology.

Critical Thinking

Determining Verifiable Facts

Critical thinking involves a variety of skills, each of which to some degree combines analysis and evaluation. One of the most important critical thinking skills is that of **determining verifiable facts.** A verifiable fact is something that can be proven by the presentation of objective evidence. For example, a verifiable fact would be: "In January of 1985 Ronald Reagan began serving his second term as President of the United States." Documentary evidence for such a claim can be found in public records and the electoral votes cast for United States President in 1985. Few, if any, people would dispute such a claim. Keep in mind the definition of a verifiable fact as you answer the following questions.

1. What are two techniques used for verifying the dates and authenticity of archaeological finds?
2. How can we verify that the peoples of the ancient Middle East had knowledge of ironworking?
3. How do we know about the government of Sumerian cities?
4. Why do you believe that it is difficult to verify facts about ancient civilizations?
5. What souces will historians one hundred years from now have to discover facts about our society?

CHAPTER ·2·

THE EGYPTIANS

2850 B.C.–670 B.C.

Objectives

- To describe the importance of the Nile River to ancient Egypt

- To explain the role of the pharaohs in the Old Kingdom

- To discuss the struggles for control of Egypt during the Middle Kingdom and New Kingdom

- To explain the reasons for the decline of Egypt during the New Kingdom

- To describe the achievements of the ancient Egyptians

As you know, the first true civilization developed in Sumer where, over the centuries, Neolithic farming communities gave way to city-states. However, no one city-state gained enough power to control the others and unite Sumer under one rule.

This political disunity, coupled with several natural disasters such as the change in the flow of the Euphrates River, weakened Sumer. At the same time, the nomads who inhabited the regions beyond this irrigated river valley gathered strength. Tempted by the wealth of the city-states and their lack of natural defenses, invaders repeatedly overran Sumer. However, instead of destroying the civilization they encountered, the nomads adopted many traits of Sumerian society and, in turn, left their own mark on the region they invaded. Some of the invaders were able to impose unity on Sumer, but it was not lasting.

While Sumerian civilization was emerging in the Tigris-Euphrates River valley, similar developments occurred elsewhere-in the Nile River valley of Egypt.

In this chapter you will learn how Egyptian civilization, its people united by the Nile River and protected by a barren desert, remained practically undisturbed by outsiders for hundreds of years. The geography of the Nile River valley differed from that of Sumer and, as you will see, helped give Egyptian civilization its own, unique character.

EARLY EGYPT

The Egyptians developed a great civilization along the Nile River in the northeastern part of Africa. (See the map on page 15.) Although historians now believe that this civilization emerged after the Sumerians, both arose from a similar Neolithic background.

The Nile River

The Nile River has two main sources: the highlands of Ethiopia, and Lake Victoria, in present-day Uganda. It flows northward for about 4,200 miles (6,700 kilometers) until it reaches the Mediterranean Sea. In its course, the river cuts through the Nile Valley which is about 12 miles wide (19 kilometers) and 880 miles (1,400 kilometers) long.

The valley is bordered on both sides by high rock walls, beyond which is desert. Both the rock walls and the desert form a natural barrier that helped protect the people of the Nile Valley from raids by desert nomads.

As it nears the Mediterranean, the Nile River branches into many smaller rivers and flows through the Nile Delta. This is a broad, fan-shaped plain of fertile soil deposited by the river as it empties into the sea. Owing to the richness of the soil, the Nile Delta has been heavily populated throughout Egypt's history.

To the east of the delta lies the Isthmus of Suez, bordered on the north by the Mediterranean Sea and on the south by the Red Sea. This narrow neck of land connects the northeastern part of Africa with Asia. (See the map on page 15.) The Isthmus of Suez is the only break in the natural barriers formed by the rock walls of the Nile Valley. It

The Nile River is a valuable natural resource. In ancient Egypt sailboats similar to these carried goods up and down the river. Fish were caught, water was drawn for irrigation, and the annual floods replenished the soil with mineral-rich silt.

Barges such as this one carried Egyptian nobles over the Nile. The seated noble was attended to by a crew of rowers, servants, and hunters and fishers to provide meals.

linked Egypt with the rest of the ancient Middle East and provided a route to and from Egypt for both travelers and invaders. This route was used by the Hebrews to travel to Egypt.

The Greek historian Herodotus called Egypt the "gift of the Nile" because when the river floods each summer, it deposits a layer of rich soil on the land. From very early times, Egyptian farmers relied heavily on the yearly floods. After harvesting their crops in March and April, the farmers waited for the great river to overflow its banks and deposit the rich black soil carried by its waters. After that, they planted their next crop. Farmers were able to plant as many as three crops a year in this very fertile soil. Each new generation was able to reuse the same land because the Nile renewed the soil year after year.

The Egyptian farmers used a network of dikes and canals to water their land, much as was done in ancient Mesopotamia. Dikes were built all around a field, and canals were used to lead the water from the Nile. Then the dikes were opened in such a way that the water irrigated one field at a time. The cooperation necessary for such endeavors created a need for organization and leadership. This provided a stimulus for the emergence of civilization in Egypt.

The Nile River gave the Egyptians another advantage as well. The northward flow of the river carried boats toward the Mediterranean. On the return trip a ship's sails could catch the prevailing winds that blow in a southerly direction across Egypt most of the time. River travel took precedence over all other means of transportation in Egypt. It encouraged a lively river trade that helped unify the country's economy and also fostered political unity: a ruler who could control river transportation could control the country.

Natural Resources of Ancient Egypt

Because of its rich natural resources, ancient Egypt was a prosperous land. A wide variety of crops were grown in the fertile soil of the delta and on the farmlands bordering the Nile River. There were pastures for cattle, goats, and sheep. Fish were plentiful, and birds were hunted in the tall reeds that grew along the river banks. The reeds themselves provided material for baskets, mats, sandals, and boats. Most important of all, the Egyptians invented a method of splitting and pressing the river reeds together to make a substance similar to present-day writing paper. The plant used to make this paperlike material was called **papyrus** (puh-PIE-rus). Papyrus also had many other uses. Its roots could be used as a source for fuel. The fleshy tissue in the stem of the papyrus could be used as food.

The fine river mud was used for making bricks and clay pots, jars, and other containers. Blocks of limestone and sandstone, cut from the rock walls bordering the Nile, were used in building the great pyramids and temples of ancient Egypt. Copper was mined in the eastern desert and the Sinai Peninsula, and gold came from the nearby desert and from Nubia, a region to the south. In addition there was the Nile itself, which could be called the Egyptians' greatest natural resource.

Prehistoric Egypt

Egyptians capitalized on the resources that nature provided and developed a civilization that paralleled and even surpassed, in some ways, that of ancient Sumer. From the work of archaeologists and from myths and customs passed down through the ages, historians have been able to piece together a picture of life in Egypt. Archaeologists found the oldest Egyptian remains in the cliffs that border the Nile Valley and in the desert beyond. There, scientists found the bones of ancient animals, in addition to stone tools used by the hunters who lived there nearly 12,000 years ago. During the Paleolithic Period when hunters roamed the northern part of Africa, it was covered with broad, rolling grasslands and many rivers. Wild animals were abundant and were a source of food for the hunters and their families.

Gradually the climate became drier as the earth warmed after the most recent Ice Age, and the region became a desert. People were forced to move to places with a greater water supply. Some of them moved to the banks of the Nile and settled in the low desert that bordered the swamps of the Nile Valley. Ancient houses and cemeteries found in that area indicate that over a period of 4,000

years the swamps, once inhabited by crocodiles and hippopotamuses, were cleared and settled.

As the swamps were cleared, Neolithic people began to farm the fertile land. Historians think that the first crops in Egypt were planted about 7,000 years ago. The prehistoric Egyptians learned to domesticate wild animals. They made tools from wood and stone, fashioned pottery on a rotating wheel, and worked with copper. They even learned to grow flax and weave the fibers into linen for clothing. Some prehistoric Egyptians engaged in limited trade. Popular trade items included materials used in the making of perfumes and goods made from copper and ivory.

These early farmers formed villages along the Nile and built their homes of reeds and mud from the river banks. Remains of their cemeteries show that the Nile farmers buried their dead in shallow graves. The bodies were placed on their sides and the hot, dry sands of the desert often preserved the bodies for thousands of years. Pots, weapons, and food were usually found placed beside the deceased, suggesting that the prehistoric Egyptians believed in an afterlife.

SECTION REVIEW

1. Mapping: Use the map on page 44 to describe the relative location of the Mediterranean Sea to Egypt, the Nile Delta, the Nile River, the Gulf of Suez.
2. In your own words, briefly identify: flax, Isthmus of Suez, delta, papyrus, Nile Valley.
3. List the chief natural resources of ancient Egypt. Why do you think these natural resources were so important to the development of civilization in this area?
4. Where have the oldest prehistoric Egyptian remains been found? What do these remains tell archaeologists about prehistoric Egyptian life?
5. What technological aspect did the Egyptian and Sumerian civilizations have in common?
■ Where would future archaeologists find the remains of the earliest days of your community? What might these remains be? What would they indicate about the earliest life of your community?

THE OLD KINGDOM

Historians divide Egyptian history into three main periods: the Old Kingdom (2850 B.C. to 2200 B.C.), the Middle Kingdom (2050 B.C. to 1792 B.C.), and the New Kingdom (1570 B.C. to 1090 B.C.). As you will see, these dates are only approximations because of the kinds of records the Egyptians kept. Historians do not have enough information to say exactly when each period began or to know precisely how long it lasted.

The Uniting of Egypt

Before the beginning of the Old Kingdom, Egypt was divided into two separate kingdoms called Upper Egypt and Lower Egypt. (The map on page 44 shows the location of Upper and Lower Egypt.) Upper Egypt, the southern kingdom, was located along the banks of the upper Nile, or the part of the river closest to its source. Lower Egypt, the northern kingdom, was located along the lower Nile, or the part of the river closest to the Nile Delta. In other words, Upper Egypt was upriver and Lower Egypt was downriver.

A king of Upper Egypt named Menes (MEE-neez) conquered Lower Egypt and united the two into one kingdom. He founded his capital city at Memphis, located near modern Cairo (KIE-roe). This unification marked the beginning of the Old Kingdom, a time in which Egypt remained united politically and Egyptian civilization reached its height. Power passed smoothly from one member of the Menes family to another. One explanation for this period of political stability is that Egypt's hostile neighbors lacked sufficient numbers to present a serious threat.

Menes and his successors were what is called a **dynasty** (DIE-nuh-stee), or a family of rulers. In a dynasty the power to rule passes from one generation to the next within a family, ending only when that family dies out or is overthrown. The Egyptians dated their histories by reigns of various rulers and used a reign, rather than a year, to refer to when an event occurred. This is why historians are not always sure exactly when many events took place. For example, tradition puts the start of the Old Kingdom at about 3100 B.C., but modern scholars feel 2850 is a more likely date.

Egyptian Religion

In ancient Egypt, religion was very complex. It played a vital role in Egyptian life, often following political developments. Each local area had its own gods and goddesses. As areas united, their gods and goddesses were accepted by the whole region. The leading god or goddess of Egypt was often the predominant god worshiped in the place where the ruler came from. Early rulers claimed to be the descendants of Horus, the falcon god of the sky. By the Fifth Dynasty, rulers claimed also to be descended from Re (RAY), the sun god. Archaeologists have found boats in the rulers' tombs that they think were intended to be used to accompany Re on journeys through the sky and the underworld. Egyptians also identified deceased rulers with Osiris (oe-SIE-rus), who ruled the world of the dead. By virtue of their union with Osiris, rulers claimed immortality. By obeying the rulers, Egyptians felt that they too could participate in life after death. Thus, as in Sumerian society, religious beliefs formed the basis of authority for the rulers. By claiming to be gods, Egypt's rulers held even greater power over their subjects than Sumerian

Egyptian artists portrayed pharaohs larger than other people to emphasize the pharaohs' greatness. Rate the importance of the two remaining human figures.

rulers. This belief, combined with the unifying influence of the Nile, allowed Egyptian rulers to control all of Egypt.

The Pharaohs

In Egypt there was no separation of church and state. Egyptian rulers were religious leaders as well as political leaders. During the Old Kingdom, the ruler was called a **pharaoh** (FAIR-oe). This is from the Egyptian word meaning "great house." As a god, the pharaoh was thought to have special powers that made it possible for him or her to rule Egypt with perfect judgment and complete power. The pharaoh was believed to control not only people, but also the natural world. Therefore, in Egyptian art the pharaoh is always shown larger than other humans or animals. The Egyptians also believed the pharaohs' powers were responsible for the flooding of the Nile. If the river rose too much or too little, it was believed to be the pharaoh's fault. Fortunately for the pharaohs, the flooding of the Nile followed a much more regular pattern than that of the Tigris-Euphrates rivers. The Nile was therefore a source of more praise than blame for the pharaohs.

As the descendant of the gods, a pharaoh was the supreme ruler of all Egypt and the judge of all the people. Egyptians believed that the law, which was based on custom, encompassed the will of the gods. Despite their position as gods, even pharaohs were considered to be subject to the law. They were also expected to prepare themselves to be rulers and to provide for the public welfare. A pharaoh's heir had to study about the needs of Egypt and the management of irrigation, mining, and construction. A new pharaoh was expected to ascend the throne ready to rule and to direct the economy.

The power and prestige of the pharaoh was so great that government officials never spoke on their own authority. They always said they were speaking for the pharaoh. The pharaoh also owned all the land in Egypt and received taxes on goods and services from the farmers. Pharaohs allowed the people to use the land, but they always maintained the right to take away any part of the land they wished. Pharaohs also ordered mining and trading expeditions that brought more wealth to the kingdom.

Egyptian Government

During the Old Kingdom, the relative wealth of Egypt and its natural barriers to invasion promoted a government based on peace. Egypt had no standing army or professional military corps. Government was based on cooperation rather than force. The pharaoh administered control over Egypt through civil officials. The most important official was the **vizier** (vuh-ZIR), or prime minister. Viziers emerged in Egyptian society by the beginning of the Old Kingdom and gradually came to run almost every part of Egyptian government when the pharaoh's power declined in later dynasties.

Among his many duties, the vizier acted as judge, trying cases and hearing appeals. He also appointed judges in the local courts, and controlled irrigation and agriculture. He was responsible for collecting taxes, and entertained important visitors from other lands. It was the vizier's duty to keep the roads and buildings in good repair.

Other important government officials included the high priest, the chief architect, the royal treasurer, the royal official who looked after the pharaoh's household, and the teachers of the royal children.

The Pyramids

Egyptians built pyramids to provide a fitting burial place for their pharaoh god-kings because they believed the pharaohs held the key to the afterlife for all. Pyramids reflected the Egyptians' strong conviction in life after death. They also reflected the ability of the pharaohs of the Old Kingdom to marshal the resources of Egypt to provide the labor and materials for these huge monuments.

The first pyramid, which was built for the pharaoh Zoser (ZOE-sur), was begun about 2600 B.C. The pyramid was made in steps of small, square stones and was surrounded by beautiful white limestone temples and other buildings used for worshiping the dead pharaoh.

The building of a pyramid was a huge public-works project taking many years to complete. Thousands of Egyptians worked under the direction of architects and overseers during the seasons when fewer workers were needed on the farms. Herodotus recorded that the building of Cheops (KEE-ops), known to us as Khufu, required the labor of 100,000 people over a twenty-year period. The structure, which contains over two million limestone blocks fitted together with almost perfect precision without using mortar or cement, rose to a height of 480 feet (146 meters).

SECTION REVIEW

1. Mapping: Use the map on page 44 to describe in which region of Egypt the city of Memphis was located.
2. In your own words, briefly identify: dynasty, pharaoh, vizier, pyramid.
3. Why is it difficult to find exact dates for events in ancient Egyptian history?
4. What part did religion play in the political development of Egypt? What other factor was important in the unification of Egypt?
■ Name the important officials of the Egyptian government. How do their positions compare with officials of our own government?

THE MIDDLE KINGDOM AND THE NEW KINGDOM

In time the pharaohs were no longer able to control all of Egypt. At the height of the Old Kingdom, a few officials ruled Egypt. Many were related to the pharaoh and owed their well-being to the pharaoh's generosity. As the number of officials increased, some left the pharaoh's household. Many official positions became hereditary, and people of ambition and talent were cut off from the opportunity to serve the kingdom. Less able administrators inherited positions of power and influence. At the same time, the Egyptian economy was being drained by taxation to support the ceremonies held at the pharaohs' temples.

Between 2200 B.C. and 2050 B.C., a great struggle for power took place in Egypt as the influence of the pharaoh waned. Priests and local nobles fought among themselves for leadership, and Egypt became a divided country. As the central government collapsed, local nobles usually became the real rulers.

Artists hoped to render the dangerous hippopotamus harmless by portraying it as a delicate art object.

The decentralization of power had an impact on other phases of Egyptian life as well. The quality of art produced by artisans of the pharaoh's household declined, and the building of great monuments was sharply curtailed.

The Middle Kingdom

Around 2130 B.C., a prince from the city of Thebes (THEEBZ) began to restore the power of the pharaoh and the local rulers and to reunite the country. Thus began the period known as the Middle Kingdom, which lasted from 2050 B.C. to 1792 B.C.

The work of reuniting Egypt was completed by a new pharaoh, Amenemhet I (ah-meh-NEM-het). During his rule, and during the next two dynasties, the role of the pharaoh changed. As before, pharaohs were considered to be gods, but they no longer had absolute power. Now they had to share their power and wealth with the nobles and priests. The people no longer believed that a person could achieve a place in the afterlife only through association with the pharaoh. In addition, the people no longer feared the pharaohs, but instead considered them to be their protectors. The pharaohs themselves seemed more concerned with the welfare of the people than they had previously. Tales of pharaohs trying to ensure justice and good government for the people appeared in Egyptian literature of the time.

The Middle Kingdom brought about other

changes. One was a decline in the building of stone pyramids and an increase in construction of rock-cut chamber tombs, which were less expensive and less time-consuming to build. Glassmaking also appeared at this time, but scholars are not certain just how that invention emerged. It may have occurred accidentally due to the overfiring of faience (fay-AHNS) ware, a fine, glazed pottery with partially fused minerals in it. During the Middle Kingdom Egyptians made glass objects such as statuettes and jewelry.

The Middle Kingdom was a time of peace and prosperity. Trade with other nations expanded under the protection of the pharaoh. Since all classes of people were thought of as equals in the next world, even the poor received fine funerals. One of the most important changes of this period was in the role of priests. They were given more religious duties and acted as intermediaries between the people and the officials of the royal household. Gradually the position of priest was passed down from father to son, and they formed a large, wealthy class whose power rivaled that of the pharaohs.

The strengthening of the priests' influence and the weakening of the pharaoh's power changed the character of Egyptian government. Authority became decentralized. The kingdom became divided when local nobles refused to submit to the pharaoh's authority. Thus political unrest disrupted Egypt's unity once again.

The Hyksos Invade Egypt

Although little is known about the last pharaohs of the Middle Kingdom, the existence of natural barriers may have lulled them into a false sense of security. Frontier defenses to the north became lax, due in part to the Egyptians' belief in their own superiority. Egyptians thought that their country was the only one protected by the gods and, according to this way of thinking, all other peoples were subject to them. However, not all other peoples accepted such a notion, and some made plans to conquer Egypt.

Among the invaders poised beyond Egypt's borders and ready to take advantage of any sign of weakness were the Hyksos (HIK-soes), which is what the ancient Egyptians called the Asians. The Hyksos invasion was part of a wave of invasions,

including those of the Hittites and Kassites in Mesopotamia, that disrupted civilization in the Middle East. The Hyksos were a conquering people who had entered Canaan about twenty years prior to entering Egypt. By 1730 B.C. they had traveled over the Isthmus of Suez and through the Nile Delta. Some scholars believe that the Hebrews entered Egypt with the Hyksos and that Joseph, son of Jacob, served under one of their last kings.

The Hyksos quickly defeated the Egyptians and established their capital at Avaris, in the northern delta of Egypt. The success of the Hyksos, like that

The Egyptian pharaoh Ramses is seen here fighting a Hyksos soldier. Again the pharaoh is shown as larger than life to make clear his superiority. What qualities of Ramses does the artist attempt to emphasize in this relief?

of the Kassites in Sumer, was linked to their use of lightweight chariots pulled by fast horses. This gave the Hyksos the ability to maneuver easily and strike swiftly. They ruled Egypt for over 100 years, and even established their own dynasties. While the Egyptians hated these foreigners and resisted many of their ways, the Hyksos did bring some prosperity to the country. They repaired the old roads or built new ones to connect northern Egypt with routes to Asia. Hyksos forts and well-armed garrisons provided protection for travelers and traders who used those roads.

Gradually, however, the Hyksos allowed some Egyptian princes, such as those at Thebes, to gain local independence. Once those princes had effectively learned to use the Hyksos' weapons and basic military techniques, they waged a patriotic war against the Hyksos and by 1570 B.C. drove them from Egypt. According to ancient Egyptian legend, this rebellion began when a Hyksos pharaoh ordered a Theban prince to "silence the bellowing of the hippopotamuses who were disturbing his sleep." The Egyptian prince, who had attached great significance to the animals and greatly admired them, refused to obey the Hyksos king's order. Unfortunately for later scholars, the Egyptians, in the course of winning the war, destroyed most of the records of Hyksos rule.

The New Kingdom

After the Hyksos were driven out, Egypt entered another period of unity called the New Kingdom, which lasted from about 1570 B.C. to 1090 B.C.

EGYPTIAN EMPIRE ABOUT 1450 B.C.

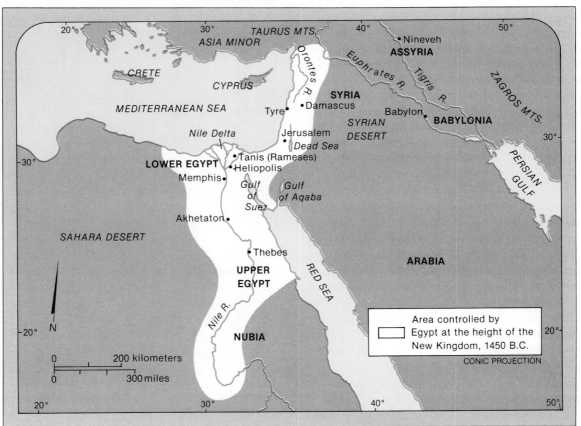

Compare this map with the one on page 15. Which states did Egypt take over?

During this time a series of strong pharaohs ruled Egypt from the capital city of Thebes. As were those of the Old Kingdom, the pharoahs of the New Kingdom were absolute rulers. They stripped the priests and the nobles of some of their power and kept tight control over the government.

After the Hyksos invasion, the Egyptians realized that it was possible for invaders to enter and occupy their land. They could no longer maintain the isolated position from events in the Middle East that had marked their previous history. They realized that they had to protect themselves and, as the first step in that direction, they formed an army. The Egyptians felt that safety would come only from controlling the surrounding areas, and thereby keeping this territory out of the hands of rival powers. The Egyptian army of the New Kingdom was a professional army and much larger than that of the Middle Kingdom. Modeled on the Hyksos army, it used horses, chariots, and bronze weapons.

The Egyptian Empire

Just as the Hittites had used the chariot in the creation of their huge empire, the Egyptians used it to expand their territory. The pharaoh had a full-time army, ready to fight at a moment's notice. Many of the soldiers were former prisoners of war who could gain their freedom by serving in the Egyptian army. With this new and stronger army, the Egyptians conquered the whole area along the eastern coast of the Mediterranean area as far north as the Taurus (TAW-rus) Mountains. They then moved south into the region that is now the Sudan (soo-DAN).

As the Egyptians took more and more land, the empire grew rapidly. The pharaohs, however, soon found that it was sometimes easier to conquer a land than to rule it. During the reigns of weak pharaohs, parts of the empire revolted and tried to break away. Only the strongest pharaohs were capable of holding the empire together. By the twelfth century B.C., most of the conquered land had been lost.

Two Pharaohs of the New Kingdom

Among the ablest and most powerful pharaohs of the Egyptian Empire were Hatshepsut (hat-SHEP-soot) and her husband, nephew, and stepson, Thutmose III (thoot-MOE-suh). Hatshepsut was a wise and strong pharaoh who ruled jointly with Thutmose III from about 1500 B.C. to 1480 B.C. Hatshepsut was more interested in building a secure and prosperous Egyptian society than in expanding the empire. During Hatshepsut's rule, Egyptian women enjoyed a better position than had women in most other parts of the ancient world. They had full legal rights and could inherit and sell property without first receiving the consent of their husbands.

In addition to completing huge building projects, Hatshepsut restored the temples that had been ruined during the Hyksos occupation. The new paintings and carvings that decorated the walls of these temples highlighted important events that took place during her rule.

After Hatshepsut's death, Thutmose III ruled alone from 1468 B.C. to 1436 B.C. Possibly driven by jealousy, Thutmose destroyed many of the paintings, sculptures, and buildings that Hatshepsut had created during her rule. Thutmose and his followers even destroyed the tombs of her most faithful servants.

Thutmose III set out to establish himself quickly as one of Egypt's most forceful rulers. He extended the borders of the empire as far as the Euphrates River and gained control over Palestine and Syria that lasted into the next century. (See map on opposite page.) He also improved the Egyptian army and set up military posts primarily designed to put down revolts throughout the empire. These posts served as a constant reminder of Egyptian power and ensured that the conquered people would pay tribute to the pharaoh.

Thutmose held the children of conquered princes as hostages and educated them in Egypt. The children were taught that the pharaohs were powerful enough both to protect conquered peoples and to punish those who tried to revolt. It was hoped that this indoctrination would persuade the children, once they grew up and became rulers of their own lands, not to dare oppose the regime of the pharaoh.

Thutmose was a very able ruler. He devoted much time to the ruling of his empire, and personally judged legal cases. He also rebuilt temples with the labor of prisoners of war and decorated the temples with chalices and urns of his own design.

The funerary temple of Hatshepsut, the only temple to be built by a woman pharaoh, was carved in the Valley of the Kings and completed around 1485 B.C.

Wall paintings from about 1500 B.C. show foreign sailors bringing the products of their lands to exchange for Egyptian goods, indicating that trade with other countries also increased during the rule of Thutmose.

The Common People Lose Their Rights

The military victories of Thutmose and other pharaohs of the New Kingdom made Egypt rich and powerful. The tribute collected from conquered peoples helped make the pharaohs and the nobles wealthy, but the benefits reaped did not filter down to the common people.

Most of the Egyptian people lived in poverty, while the rulers grew rich and corrupt. The free-

dom of the common people decreased as the pharaohs' power increased. They had no political rights and depended entirely on the whims of the pharaohs for justice. The whole concept of the rule of the pharaohs had changed from one based on national unity to one based on military strength.

As you know, during the Old Kingdom the pharaohs owned all property in Egypt. Until the New Kingdom, the pharaohs had allowed the people to use the land as if it were their own. The pharaohs of the New Kingdom, however, treated large parcels of land as their private property and forced the peasants to work the land for them. Periodically the peasants were forced to work on huge building projects, which caused great discontent among the Egyptian people.

1. Mapping: Use the map on page 44 to describe the locations of: Thebes, Taurus Mountains.
2. In your own words, briefly identify: Amenemhet I, the Hyksos, Hatshepsut, Thutmose III.
3. How did the pharaoh's role in Egyptian society change during the Middle Kingdom?
4. What other changes occurred during the Middle Kingdom?
5. Why were the Hyksos able to conquer the Egyptians so easily?
6. What changes were made in Egyptian society during the New Kingdom?
7. What rights did Egyptian women have during Hatshepsut's reign?
■ What are some of the rights you have? Make a list of five or more. Pick one right from your list and tell how your life would be different if you did not have that right.

THE DECLINE OF THE NEW KINGDOM

The New Kingdom reached its greatest heights during the long rule of Amenhotep III (ahm-un-HOE-tep). During his reign (1417 B.C.–1379 B.C.), the priests and nobles enjoyed many years of prosperity as wealth poured into Egypt from the army's conquests. Amenhotep, the last of the great builders, constructed a temple at Luxor that was connected by a mile-long road to the temple at Karnak. Flanking the road were statues of rams, and two seventy-foot-high statues adorned Amenhotep's funeral temple. His tomb was so large that it was never completed. In order to display his wealth, Amenhotep personally gave valuable gifts to important visitors to Egypt.

A New Egyptian Religion

Amenhotep III's son and successor, Amenhotep IV, was not a strong ruler. He had little interest in saving the empire, some of whose subjects were transferring their loyalty to the Hittites. He was interested, however, in reestablishing the Old Kingdom idea that the pharaoh was the only key to an afterlife. In order to do this, Amenhotep IV undertook a reformation of Egyptian religion.

During the New Kingdom one of the most important gods was **Aton** (AH-ton), the sun god. Around 1375 B.C. Amenhotep IV elevated the ancient cult of the sun god to a position approaching monotheism. His premise was that Aton was the only true god—not just the most important. To demonstrate his conviction, Amenhotep changed his own name to Akhenaton (ak-keh-NAH-ton), which means "he who serves the Aton."

In honor of Aton, the pharaoh built a new capital city named Akhetaton, which was located on the site of the present-day town of Tell el-Amarna (TELL el-uh-MAHR-nuh). There scholars have discovered pictures of the pharaoh, his wife, Queen Nefertiti (neh-fer-TEE-tee), and their children. In contrast to the traditional, static representation of pharaohs in earlier art, the royal family here is depicted in various aspects of everyday life, and their facial expressions reveal feelings and emotions. This art style is called the **Amarna** (uh-MAHR-nuh) **style** or period, named after the town where the pictures were found.

The priests of the older religion, whose main god was **Amon** (AH-mun), the ram-headed god of Thebes, had grown very powerful, particularly during the Middle Kingdom era. Now that Thebes was no longer the religious center and the pharaoh sought to suppress worship of Amon, the priests lost much of their power. Akhenaton believed he was the son of Aton and, as such, allowed the god to be worshiped only through himself—not through the priests. Therefore, the priests' importance in society diminished, and the wealth they received in the form of gifts from the worshipers of Amon declined.

The priests of the older religion were angered by Akhenaton's power over the Egyptian people. To make matters worse, Akhenaton placed his followers in high positions that previously had been held by priests. Also, the wealth that formerly went both to the priests of Amon and for building temples to the former gods went instead to the pharaoh's new temples for Aton.

Thus, while Akhenaton and Queen Nefertiti

were focusing their attention on founding a new religion, the Egyptian Empire continued to decline. The Egyptian common people were unhappy about the pharaoh's new religion because it offered them little hope of a life in the next world. Foreign princes were challenging the pharaoh's strength and trying to gain control. Rebellions against Egyptian rule had already succeeded in Canaan, and it seemed as if the empire was on the brink of collapse.

Tutankhamun Succeeds Akhenaton

The priests of Amon and the other gods maintained some control over the people by continually stirring up discontent over the new religion. In 1361 B.C. the young prince Tutankhaton (too-tahng-KAHT-un), whose name was changed to Tutankhamun (too-tahng-KAHM-un) in honor of the god Amon, succeeded Akhenaton as pharaoh.

Pressured by the priests, he restored the old Egyptian religion and returned the capital to Thebes.

However, Tutankhamun was unable to stop Egypt's decline and the empire continued to fall into disorder. The situation improved somewhat under the direction of the army general who succeeded Tutankhamun. What followed, however, was the final stages of the Egyptian Empire.

Ramses II

The most famous pharaoh of this dynasty was Ramses II (RAM-seez), who ruled from 1279 B.C. to 1212 B.C. He managed to collect enough taxes to construct huge buildings and also built a new capital at Tanis (TAY-nus), in the Nile Delta. (See the map on page 44.) This city was called Ramses. One of Ramses II's battles against the Hittites concluded with the first recorded peace treaty in history. This battle was followed by years of peace,

Compare this stone relief done in the Amarna Style with works on pages 40 and 43.

People in History

Tutankhamun

The reign of Tutankhamun hardly would have received any mention in most history books had it not been for the discovery of his tomb. Tutankhamun ruled as pharaoh in ancient Egypt from about 1361 B.C. to 1352 B.C. He was eight or nine years of age when he became pharaoh by his childhood marriage to a daughter of the pharaoh Akhenaton. Tutankhamun died when he was only nineteen years old and was buried in a small four-room tomb in the Valley of the Kings.

Tutankhamun's tomb was the first ancient royal Egyptian tomb to be examined that was somewhat intact from the day of his burial. Previously, all known royal tombs in the Valley of the Kings had been thoroughly plundered by robbers. While Tutankhamun's tomb had been entered on several occasions after his death, much of the tomb's contents remained untouched.

The search for his tomb began with two Englishmen, Lord Carnarvon and Howard Carter. In 1907 they began an archaeological dig that continued for many years.

The debris left from other excavations in the valley complicated the search for the tomb. Previous archaeologists, digging into other tombs, had piled rubble outside the entrance to Tutankhamun's tomb. By some good fortune, it was some of that very rubble that actually saved this tomb from later plunderers. Debris from a nearby tomb had covered the entrance, hiding the tomb from view. Carter was removing some of the waste material when, on November 4, 1922, he discovered a stone step leading down. He uncovered fifteen other steps, then a blocked doorway.

Carter sent for Carnarvon, who was then in England. Upon his arrival on November 24, the two began to make one of the most important archaeological discoveries of the twentieth century. As Carter slowly worked his way into the tomb, he recalled: "My eyes grew accustomed to the light, details of the room within emerged slowly, and gold—everywhere the glint of gold. For the moment—an eternity it must have seemed to the others standing by—I was struck dumb with amazement, and when Lord Carnarvon, unable to stand the suspense any longer, enquired anxiously, 'Can you see anything?' It was all I could do to get out the words, 'Yes, wonderful things!'."

Included among the treasures were the three coffins of the king and an effigy of the young ruler made of gold, colored stones, and glass—all undisturbed for more than 3,000 years! Many of the items from the tomb were sent by Egypt on a tour of the United States in the late 1970's so that Americans could share the experience of discovering these "wonderful things."

1. What did Howard Carter find in 1922?
2. Why was his discovery important?
3. Do you think important evidence about our culture could ever get "buried"? Explain.

even though nomadic tribes called Sea Peoples continued to challenge Egypt's rule in Canaan.

Ramses II was the last pharaoh to win a major victory over Egypt's rivals. After his reign, Egypt was no longer able to fight off invaders. Disorder spread rapidly, and Egypt was conquered repeatedly. Invaders, from Libya to the west, controlled the government for a while. These were followed by Ethiopians who invaded Egypt from the south, and the Assyrians who approached from the northeast in 670 B.C. Although the latter conquered the entire country, they were defeated by the Persians around 525 B.C. At this point Egypt's history as an independent state in the ancient world ended. The Persians ruled Egypt until they, in turn, were defeated by Alexander the Great in 332 B.C. It was not until the twentieth century, after falling under the domination of the Romans, Turks, French, and British, that Egypt again became independent.

SECTION REVIEW

1. Mapping: Use the map on page 44 to locate by means of latitude and longitude coordinates: Akhetaton, Thebes, Tanis.
2. In your own words, briefly identify: Amenhotep III, Akhenaton, Nefertiti, Aton, Tutankhamun, Ramses II.
3. Describe the new religion started by Akhenaton. Why was it disliked by the priests and common people?
■ What were some of the causes of the collapse of the Egyptian Empire? What could your religious beliefs tell a future historian about your life? Give two examples.

SOCIAL AND CULTURAL PATTERNS

From simple beginnings as a group of agricultural villages, Egyptian society reached a high level of political, religious, and artistic achievement.

Egyptian Writing

Many visitors to Egypt are struck with the beauty of ancient inscriptions found on walls and tombs. This form of writing is called **hieroglyphics** (hie-ur-uh-GLIF-iks), a name that comes from the Greek word meaning "sacred carving," and dates back to about 3000 B.C. Hieroglyphics were composed of more than 600 signs, which were carved into stone monuments. They were used mainly by priests for religious purposes. The Egyptians did not develop a true alphabet as the Phoenicians later did, but they gradually made hieroglyphic writing more simple. One of these simpler writing systems was a type of handwriting called hieratic (hie-uh-RAT-ik). While hieroglyphics were carved in stone, hieratic writing was written on papyrus with a brush dipped in ink.

Much of our present knowledge about Egypt is based on the deciphering of hieroglyphics. In the late eighteenth century a stone was discovered near the mouth of the Nile River. Named for the city near where it was found, the Rosetta stone contained three different types of writing: Greek, which was known, hieroglyphics and a later form of Egyptian writing, which were not known. The stone is inscribed with a decree honoring a king's restoration of a temple. A French scholar, Jean François Champollion, used the Greek to interpret the other two writings, and published his findings in 1822.

Scribes

The tremendous amount of Egyptian writing that even today remains intact was the work of **scribes,** or official writers. Scribes, who were among the most important members of Egyptian society, attended a special school for twelve years. Anyone who studied at this school learned to read and write and was taught the literature and history of Egypt. Scribes also had to know mathematics, bookkeeping, mechanics, surveying, and law. Some scribes rose to the rank of nobility because Egypt had a great need for educated men during the time of the Old Kingdom. If a man managed to learn to read and write and succeeded in impressing a pharaoh, noble, or priest, his promotion was swift. Pharaohs often rewarded scribes with land, jewels, or a precious metal such as gold. Scribes were needed to serve in the temples, on nobles' estates, and in the pharaohs' households. They wrote their records on a roll of papyrus which had fifty times the writing surface of a cuneiform clay tablet. The convenience of writing on papyrus, which could be carried easily, helped spread Egyptian writing to Phoenicia. It later led to the development of the Phoenician alphabet.

Egyptian Society

The most important figure in Egyptian society was, of course, the pharaoh. Sharing in the pharaoh's wealth and prestige were the officials who helped administer Egypt, and the priests who advised the pharaohs and carried out ceremonies in the temples. In later Egyptian society, local princes and administrators arose who were not closely related to the pharaoh's household. As Egyptian civilization progressed, merchants and artisans became important members of Egyptian society. During the Middle Kingdom they even revolted against the priests and nobles in order to get more rights. During the New Kingdom, when the role of the army became important, professional soldiers occupied a place in society just below the nobles.

The bulk of the Egyptian population, however were peasant farmers who lived in rural areas along the banks of the Nile. The cost of supporting the royal household and building the pyramids fell mainly on their shoulders. It is probable that farmers were assessed one-fifth or more of their crop production each year. There was a vast gulf between the standard of living of the nobles and that of the poor. The life of the peasant was hard and changed little from century to century.

Slaves were at the bottom rung of Egyptian society. Slavery, which was uncommon in the Old Kingdom, became widespread when Egypt embarked on wars of conquest during the New Kingdom. Most slaves lived short, brutal lives, rowing the pharaohs' boats or laboring in the pharaohs' mines or quarries.

Women in the upper classes were generally well respected. They oversaw their homes and a large staff of servants. Women could carry on a business and own and inherit property. It is unlikely, however, that women took official part in the government, with the exception of three women pharaohs.

Egyptian Architecture

Surrounded as they were by cliffs, Egyptians of the Old Kingdom made important advances in building with stone. To build temples, palaces, and pyramids, they learned to move huge blocks of stone

In 1880, over 3000 years after it was built by Pharaoh Thutmose III, this obelisk was given to the United States by the Persian Shah Ismail Pasha.

weighing several tons from one place to another. They cut the stones into the proper shapes with copper saws and then fitted them tightly into place.

The Egyptians used a special unit of measure called the royal cubit (KYOO-but), which measured about 21 inches (53 centimeters), or about the length of an Egyptian's arm from fingertips to elbow. They also used the width of a hand (without the thumb) and the width of a single finger as units of measure. With this simple measuring system, the Egyptians were able to build pyramids having bases the size of eleven football fields!

As the Egyptians became more skilled, they built other kinds of monuments. **Obelisks** (AHB-uh-lisks), or tall, pointed stone columns shaped like huge needles, were erected for Thutmose III, who began his rule in 1480 B.C., during the New Kingdom. Originally built at Heliopolis (hee-lee-AHP-uh-lus), they were later removed and now stand in Istanbul, London, New York, and Rome.

Egyptian Art

Like the pyramids, Egyptian art was also a reflection of Egyptian culture. Much of it appeared in tombs. During the Old Kingdom, skilled artisans and artists worked with fine materials and deliberate care. Pictures on the walls of tombs displayed a colorful view of life in Egypt. They were painted to provide the dead with reminders of their life on earth. Inscriptions and drawings on the walls of officials' tombs depicted their service to the ruler. A king might be shown defeating his enemies. Farmers were shown working in their fields.

Sculpture was a highly developed art form. The face on the statue was realistic since food and drink were provided for the dead. Statues of the dead were thought to contain some part of the spirit of the deceased. Therefore, the body appeared imposing and static to show timelessness.

Temples, such as the one at Karnak (KAHR-nak), were decorated with sculptured stone **sphinxes** (SFINGKS-us). A sphinx is a figure having the head of a human being, ram, or hawk, and the body of a lion. One of the best known Egyptian sphinxes is the one found at Giza (GEE-zuh), which has the head of a man and the body of a lion.

The Great Sphinx of Giza, carved from a leftover mound of quarry stone, symbolized the pharaoh. What qualities were emphasized in choosing the combination of lion and man to symbolize the pharaoh?

Other artwork included beautifully worked small figures of people and animals in copper, bronze, stone, or coal.

Egyptian Science

The Egyptians were experts in astronomy and geometry. They developed an accurate calendar so that they could predict the flooding of the Nile River. They also measured the angle of the sun's rays at various times in order to arrange the construction of the temples so that the rays of the sun would fall on specific important places during special rituals.

The Egyptians based the length of their year, 365 days, on the time that passed between the appearances of the star Sirius (SIR-ee-us), or the Dog Star. The 365 days were then divided into twelve months of thirty days each. At the end of each

SOCIAL SCIENCE SKILLS

READING FOR THE MAIN IDEA

In order to understand what you read, it is important to be able to determine the main idea of a passage. To do this, ask yourself: What is the topic or subject of the reading? What is the most important point the writer makes? Do the other ideas support the main idea? Consider these questions as you read the following passages and determine the main ideas of each.

The Egyptians carried out elaborate procedures when burying a pharaoh, with the purpose of preserving the body and guaranteeing immortality. One requirement was that the vital organs, removed to prevent decay, be stored in jars near the body. The body and the organs were treated with a chemical that dried up body fat and left the skin leathery. The body was then made to appear as lifelike as possible. False eyes were put in the eye sockets and the body was wrapped in cloth, preserving its natural shape. If the heart was removed it was replaced by a carved replica of a beetle, called a scarab.

1. The most important idea of this passage is:
   a. Organs had to be kept near the body to guarantee immortality.
   b. The body was made to appear lifelike.
   c. The body was treated with preservatives.
   d. The Egyptians carefully prepared the pharaoh for burial.

The correct answer is *d*. Note, however, that the main idea does not necessarily have to be in the first sentence of a paragraph.

In recognition of their special talents, scribes were not required to labor on the pharaoh's projects, were exempt from military service, and did not pay land taxes. An orphan or the son of a poor man could rise from a low rank in society by becoming a scribe. Scribes worked for the army, navy, treasury, traders and merchants, and in temples. They accompanied missions to foreign lands and served in embassies.

2. The most important idea of this passage is:
   a. Scribes were exempt from military service.
   b. A scribe could rise in society.
   c. Scribes served as ambassadors.
   d. Scribes held a special place in society.

Sometimes the main idea of a passage is expressed in not only one, but several sentences. Keep in mind the questions to ask yourself, and you will find it easier to identify the main idea.

Some early Egyptian medical documents contain accurate descriptions of the heart and the pulse. Less accurate were Egyptian beliefs about circulation: they thought the veins carried air and water. Based on fairly accurate scientific observation the Egyptians did, however, describe the treatment for forty-eight different disorders. Egyptian doctors treated wounds with ointments, stitched cuts, and set broken bones. They wrote some effective prescriptions, but also called on disease-causing spirits to leave the body.

3. The most important idea of this passage is:
   a. Egyptian medicine is based on early documents.
   b. Egyptian medicine was based on a combination of science and misconception.
   c. Egyptian doctors could treat forty-eight diseases.
   d. Egyptian medicine was the most advanced in the ancient world.

4. After you have read the following paragraph, write a first sentence to express the main idea.

Egyptian women pursued a variety of occupations. According to various sources, women held positions such as priestess, workshop superintendent, director of a wig shop, and choir leader. Egyptian women could inherit property, own a house and slaves, and adopt children. In many instances Western women did not acquire these rights until the nineteenth century.

year, the five days remaining were observed as holidays.

As you know, the ancient Egyptians numbered the years by the rule of the pharaohs. For example, they spoke of an event as occurring in the tenth year of the rule of Hatshepsut. Using this system of dating, historians have been able to trace Egyptian history back to about 2700 B.C.

Egyptian geometry developed for very practical reasons. In a land where the borders of fields might be wiped out by the yearly floods, it was necessary to have exact measurements in order to restore these borders. Geometry was also used to lay out the system of dikes and canals that watered the fields. The pyramids and other great monuments of the Old Kingdom were planned and built according to complex geometrical formulas.

In contrast to their extensive knowledge of geometry, the Egyptians had a simple numbering system. Numbers were written using signs for ones, tens, hundreds, thousands, and so forth, up to one million. For example, the number 22 would be written 10 + 10 + 1 + 1. At least twenty-seven separate signs were needed to write 999. The Egyptians multiplied by doubling numbers until they reached the multiple they were looking for. They used the same process in reverse when dividing numbers. Fractions were used, but no fraction could be written unless it contained the number one as the numerator. Thus the fraction 3/4 would be written 1/2 + 1/4. Although this system had limited use, the Egyptians were able to use it to solve most of their practical problems.

Egyptian Medicine

Medical writings on papyrus provide much information about Egyptian medicine. The writings cite important cases that were treated and also tell how a patient was examined, what treatment was prescribed, and how the doctor thought the case would develop. Sometimes possible causes of a disease were listed. Drawings indicate that doctors

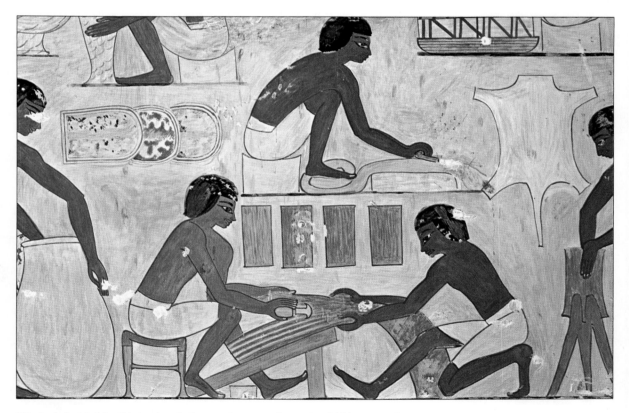

Workers depicted in this tomb painting are busy tanning animal hides to produce leather. Why are paintings such as this valuable resources to historians?

In the top part of this picture, Egyptians are measuring a field of grain. In the bottom part, the grain is being delivered to the storehouse where scribes record the amount of the harvest. How would a similar pictorial record of farm activities today differ from the activities recorded here?

knew a great deal about human anatomy, and it is believed that they gained this knowledge while preparing bodies for burial.

Egyptian medicine was valued throughout the ancient world. Egyptian doctors were sent to distant lands to treat rulers and nobles, and most of the large temples had medical libraries and medical schools for training doctors. Foreign doctors often described the drugs and methods of treating disease they learned while studying in the Egyptian temple schools.

Trade in Ancient Egypt

The Egyptians traded with many parts of the ancient world. By the time of the New Kingdom, their ships brought timber from Phoenicia, finely worked objects from Sumer, and carved ivories and weapons from Syria. They also brought olive oil, honey, copper, wine, tin, lead, and iron from other countries of the ancient Middle East. Caravans brought back ebony, ivory, animal skins, and gold, as well as slaves, from the lands south of Egypt. There is some evidence that Egyptian ships sailed as far as the Aegean Sea, the Persian Gulf, and the coast of India to trade.

Most trade was conducted by barter, or the exchange of one type of thing, such as timber, for another of equal value, such as ivory. This is particularly true of trade done by peasants and poor farmers. In some cases, rings of copper and gold were used as currency in larger dealings by merchants and traders. Historians believe that Egyptian trade was well organized. From early times Egyptians developed elementary methods of accounting and bookkeeping. Egyptians also originated deeds, wills, and written contracts. A few commercial records on papyrus have been found. The Egyptian records, however, are not as complete as the cuneiform tablets historians have analyzed from other ancient Middle Eastern peoples.

Egyptian Agriculture and Industry

The first people who lived in the Nile Valley caught fish and game and gathered wild fruits and vegetables. Later, barley and wheat brought into Egypt from lands to the east were grown in the fertile Nile Delta and the Nile Valley. These were the two most important **staple crops** of ancient Egypt. A staple crop is one that is used widely and continually and, for this reason, is usually grown in large amounts. Staple crops were grown on large estates, and production was increased by using wooden plows and hoes. Once the use of iron was known, farm implements were made of that metal because it was more durable.

Why did Egyptian tombs contain statues of servants carrying food and other articles for the deceased?

Another important aspect of Egyptian economic life was manufacturing. As early as 3000 B.C. large numbers of people, generally working alone, were able to specialize in crafts. In later years people began to work in groups in factories. Some of the leading industries were quarrying, textiles, glassmaking, pottery, and shipbuilding. Egyptian industries provided the goods for Egyptian trade.

Egyptian Beliefs About Death

Egyptian beliefs about death changed over the centuries. Egyptians believed that they could participate in an afterlife through their associations with the pharaoh. By the time of the Middle Kingdom, elaborate preparations were made to preserve the body of the pharaoh. The Egyptians believed that the soul of the dead pharaoh would return to the body it had occupied during life. For this reason, it was important to preserve the body as carefully as possible. The body of the pharaoh was prepared for burial by a process called mummification (mum-ih-fuh-KAY-shun). The whole process took about seventy days. The brain was drawn out of the skull through the nose. The heart was left in the body because it was thought to be the center of a person's will and intelligence. Other organs were removed and preserved in jars that were placed in the tomb near the mummy. Dehydrating agents were put inside the stomach area to keep the body from decaying. Finally, the body was very carefully wrapped in hundreds of strips of linen. The mummy of the pharaoh was then placed in a pyramid along with food and drink to nourish him or her in the afterlife. To discourage thieves from trying to enter the tomb, workers let huge stone blocks crash down to seal the entrance. The only openings left were two secret air holes to allow the pharaoh's spirit to enter and leave the tomb.

Despite these careful preparations, most mummified bodies were damaged or destroyed by vandals or thieves. The bodies of poor people, conversely, were buried in the hot, dry desert sand, and often were better preserved.

By the time of the New Kingdom, the Egyptians believed that after they were buried their spirits would be sent to a great hall where their sins were judged. There they pleaded before forty-two gods for eternal life. The dead had to declare virtue, know the secret names of the gods, and be able to cast magic spells that would drive off dangerous snakes and crocodiles. Spells were necessary to survive the dangers of a journey across a lake of fire, and to keep the dead from forgetting their own names. The Egyptians believed that if a dead person were to forget his or her name, that individual would die again. If the dead surmounted all these trials, they would arrive at a place called the "Field of Rushes," where their lives would remain pleasant forever. These Egyptian beliefs about death and eternal life, developed over thousands of years, were finally recorded about 1500 B.C. in the *Book of the Dead.* Just as the *Epic of Gilgamesh* reveals some of the basic views of the Sumerians about life and death, the *Book of the Dead* reveals a great deal about the Egyptians' views. This large collection of spells and information about Egyptian beliefs has been a valuable resource for historians.

SECTION REVIEW

1. Mapping: Use the maps on pages 15 and 44 to describe the location, in relation to Egypt, of: Phoenicia, Sumer, Nubia, the Persian Gulf.
2. In your own words, briefly identify: staple crop, scribes, hieroglyphic writing, royal cubit, obelisk, sphinx.
3. Explain the importance of the discovery of the Rosetta Stone.
4. What were some Egyptian advances in stone building?
5. What scientific advances did the ancient Egyptians make?
6. What were Egypt's leading industries?
■ What changes or developments do you think trade and commerce encouraged in Egyptian society? How do commerce and trade affect our society and economy?

To assist the dead in the afterlife, magic spells from a body of work called the Coffin Texts were included in the mummy's coffin. One such spell is visible along the top of the background wall. What kind of life did ancient Egyptians expect after death?

Reviewing the Chapter

Chapter Summary

In Chapter 1 you learned that the peoples of the Tigris-Euphrates River valley, and areas immediately adjacent, or next to it, developed advanced civilizations early in world history. Farther to the west, the ancient Egyptians were using the waters of the Nile River to develop their land. Egyptian rulers, called pharaohs, were religious as well as political leaders. Historians know a great deal about the early Egyptians because of the hieroglyphic and hieratic writings that have been deciphered. Their mathematical and stonebuilding skills are also evident from the many monuments they constructed.

The highlights of ancient Egyptian history focus on three major time periods. The Old Kingdom began about 2850 B.C. and was the time when the Egyptian dynasties emerged. It was also the period when Egyptians built their great pyramids.

The Middle Kingdom, which lasted from about 2050 B.C. to 1792 B.C., was a period in which the power of the pharaoh, which had declined by 2200 B.C., again was revived, especially through the efforts of Amenemhet I. The Middle Kingdom was a time of great peace, trade, and prosperity, too. It ended with the invasion of the Hyksos who ruled Egypt from 1730 B.C. to 1570 B.C. After the Hyksos were driven out, Egypt entered another period of unity, called the New Kingdom, lasting from about 1570 B.C. to 1090 B.C. During that time, the Egyptians created an empire founded, in part, on the techniques and inventions they had acquired from the Hyksos and the Hittites. This empire endured until invaders, which included the Libyans, the Ethiopians, the Assyrians, the Persians, and the Greeks, conquered Egypt during a time span that covered the years 670 B.C. to 332 B.C.

1. Why do historians know a great deal about ancient Egyptian civilization?
2. What are three main time periods of ancient Egyptian history? Name one characteristic of each.
3. When and why did the ancient Egyptian Empire collapse?

Using Your Vocabulary

1. What is the difference between cuneiform, hieroglyphic, and hieratic writing? Which type was the most practical? Why?
2. How are the terms pharaoh and dynasty related to one another?
3. Name and describe three types of monuments constructed by the Egyptians.
4. What is a scribe? Describe the scribe's role in Egyptian society.
5. What does the process of mummification tell us about ancient Egyptian beliefs and medical knowledge?
6. What is barter? Would you prefer to see trade conducted by barter or through a monetary system? Why?
7. What pharaoh introduced a religion approaching monotheism to the Egyptians? What did his name mean? Who was Aton? What other people of the ancient world practiced a monotheistic religion? What do you think the word polytheism means?
8. In your own words, define the terms religion and government. Why do you think these terms can have different meanings for different peoples? Explain.

Developing Your Geography Skills

1. Using the map on page 44 and the descriptions on pages 37 and 38, describe how the Nile River and Delta areas helped the ancient Egyptians to develop a civilization based on agriculture.
2. Compare the map on page 44 to the atlas maps on pages 754 and 758. What modern countries are now located in what was the ancient Egyptian Empire?

Recalling the Facts

1. Describe the role that the Nile River played in the economic development of early Egyptian civilization.
2. What importance did the Isthmus of Suez have in the development of Egyptian civilization?
3. Name and describe two significant developments that occurred in Egypt during the period of the Old Kingdom.
4. Name and describe two significant developments that occurred in Egypt during the Middle Kingdom.
5. Name and describe two significant developments that occurred in Egypt during the New Kingdom.
6. What role did the vizier play in ancient Egyptian government?
7. What means of transportation did the ancient Egyptians use? Why?
8. What were two characteristics of ancient Egyptian trade?
9. What were two characteristics of ancient Egyptian science? Medicine?
10. What were two characteristics of ancient Egyptian agriculture? What crops did they cultivate?
11. What types of art were developed by the Egyptians?
12. Describe the role played by Egyptian priests during the period of the Middle Kingdom. How did this role affect the power of the pharaoh? How did this role change during the period of the New Kingdom?
13. How did the success of the Hyksos invasion affect the way the Egyptians viewed themselves and their relationship to other states in the Middle East?
14. What changes in the Egyptian army were made as a result of the success of the Hyksos army?
15. Describe how the style of art known as the Amarna Style differed from traditional Egyptian art.
16. Who were Jean François Chapollion and Howard Carter? What discovery did each of these two men make and how did their discoveries help modern historians to learn more about life in ancient Egypt?

Essay Questions

1. Describe the changing role of the pharaoh in the Old, Middle, and New Kingdoms. Explain how and why this happened.
2. What were two main differences between the history of the Old Kingdom period and the Middle Kingdom period in Egyptian history? How can you account for that?
3. What were two main differences between the Middle Kingdom period and the New Kingdom period in Egyptian history?
4. Explain the role of the Hyksos and Hittites in ancient Egyptian history. How did they affect or influence Egyptian civilization?
5. What were the major developments in Egyptian religion from 2850 B.C. to 1090 B.C.?
6. What do you regard as the two most important contributions by the ancient Egyptians to world civilization? Why?

Critical Thinking

Determining Value Claims

Critical thinking involves **determining value claims.** A "value" is a quality considered worthwhile or desirable. No two civilizations value the same things equally. What is important to one person or group may not be of equal value to others even within the same culture.

1. How did the ancient Egyptians view their pharaoh? What value claim did they make concerning the pharaoh?
2. What value did the ancient Egyptians place on religion?
3. What series of events led to a change in the value the Egyptians placed on the military? How did this value change help Egypt?
4. What important value did the common people of Egypt believe to be missing from the worship of the sun god Aton? Why do you think the common people felt this was such an important value?
5. Choose five values that you consider important and describe the significance of each. There are many values to choose from; choose only those you feel comfortable discussing.

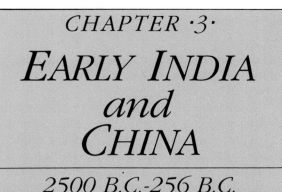

CHAPTER ·3·
EARLY INDIA and CHINA
2500 B.C.-256 B.C.

Objectives

- To describe how India's geography helped shape its early civilization

- To compare and contrast the main beliefs of Hinduism and Buddhism

- To describe the origins of Chinese civilization

- To discuss the system of government that evolved in ancient China

- To explain the main ideas of Confucianism and Taoism

You have learned that the advanced civilizations that emerged in the ancient Middle East developed in the great river valleys of the Tigris, Euphrates, and Nile rivers. These are the cultures of the Sumerians, the Hittites, the Assyrians, and the Egyptians. Far to the east, other river valley civilizations emerged at about the same time. One of these civilizations included the early cultures of the Indians, which developed along the valleys of the Indus and the Ganges (GAN-jez) rivers. Another is the culture of the Chinese, which developed near the Yellow and the Yangtze (YANG-SEE) rivers in the Far East.

The people of the ancient Middle Eastern and Mediterranean lands were isolated from the people of the Far East not only by great distances, but by formidable geographic barriers as well. Vast deserts and high mountain ranges limited contact between these parts of the ancient world. The huge subcontinent of India, for example, was cut off from its neighbors by the towering Himalaya (him-uh-LAY-uh) range, the surrounding seas, and Indochina, a large land mass that juts southward into the sea.

Yet despite geographical barriers, these lands of the ancient Far East maintained some contact with one another. Asian traders and scholars traveled to other parts of the world. Occasionally non-Asians visited these ancient empires and kingdoms. Due, in part, to such interchange, the cultures of China and India influenced much of the world.

EARLY CIVILIZATION IN INDIA

Today much is known about the early civilizations of the Middle East. Scholars, however, know far less about the history of ancient India. What little we do know is based on the work of archaeologists. For example, we know that the culture of ancient India was highly developed as early as 2500 B.C. This is about the same time that the first pyramids were being built in Egypt and about the same time that the government of ancient Sumer was beginning to collapse. We do not know, however, who these early people of ancient India were, where they originally came from, or what it was that finally destroyed their civilization.

The Geography of Ancient India

Ancient India was a land about half the size of the present-day continental United States. Its physical boundaries served to isolate the subcontinent. In the north, high mountains made travel difficult. Water surrounded the Indian peninsula on three sides: the Indian Ocean to the south, the Arabian Sea to the west, and the Bay of Bengal to the east. Despite these barriers, invaders filtered through mountain passes into India. Their path of conquest was shaped by India's geography and climate.

India can be divided into three geographical areas. These are the Himalayas, India's northernmost mountain range; the Northern Plains; and the Deccan (DEK-un) or Southern Plateau. The snow-

ANCIENT INDIA

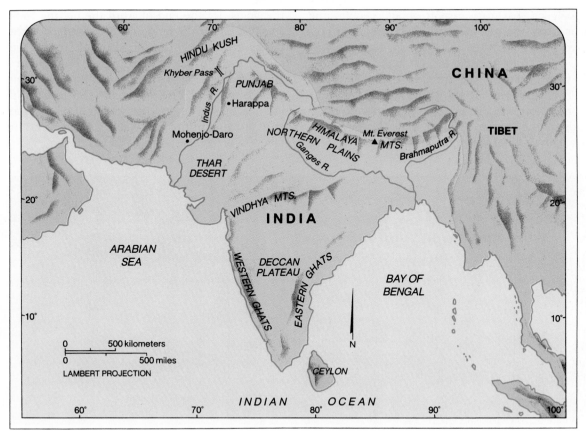

Identify the physical boundaries that isolated ancient India from other early civilizations to the east and west. What are the advantages and disadvantages of this isolation?

capped Himalayas are the world's tallest mountain range. In places as wide as 200 miles (over 320 kilometers), this range prevented travel between India and the lands of Asia to the east.

There were also mountain barriers, such as the Hindu Kush range, to the northwest in modern-day Afghanistan. However, rivers have cut passes, among them the Khyber Pass, through these mountains. Mounted invaders surged out of the mountains through such passes and into the warmer lands to the south.

These invaders entered India's second major geographical area, the Northern Plains. This plain stretches across the widest part of the country. Ancient India's four longest rivers began in the melting snows and ice of the northern mountains, then spilled down into this vast plain. The Indus to the west, and the Ganges, the Jumna, and the Brahmaputra (brah-muh-POO-truh) to the east were the four most important rivers of ancient India. Like the Nile and the Tigris-Euphrates rivers, each provided a way to transport goods, people, and ideas from one region to another. They also provided precious water for livestock and growing crops. Silt from flooding helped make this one of the world's most fertile farming regions.

The Vindhya (VIN-dyuh) Mountains separate the rich Northern Plains from the less fertile grasslands of the Deccan Plateau. The plateau is enclosed by coastal mountains called the Western Ghats and the Eastern Ghats. The major rivers of the area, the Cauvery (KAW-vuh-ree), the Godavari, and the Krishna flow eastward into the Bay of Bengal, while the Narmada flows westward into the Arabian Sea. During the rainy season from June to October, the rivers often overflow, causing great hardship and damage. Yet in the dry Deccan Plateau, flooding was a source of natural irrigation, and very important to ancient farmers.

The Monsoon Cycle

Most of ancient India's people lived in small farming villages along the river plains. The success of their crops depended in part on the waters of the rivers. The harvests also relied on the yearly arrival of great rains brought by seasonal winds called **monsoons** (mon-SOONZ). In most of India little rain fell from October until May, so fields in ancient India were irrigated by canals and ditches. These carried water from the streams and rivers to the fields. By the end of April the blazing Indian sun had baked the land dry. Crops stopped growing as irrigation ditches dried up. If farmers were lucky, torrential monsoon rains would begin in June, and for several months pounding rain would drench the land. The monsoons also restored the land each year for another season of planting and crop growing in the river valleys. If the monsoons failed to arrive, crops and animals died.

What do these ruins of Mohenjo-Daro tell you about the architectural achievements of the prehistoric people of the Indus River Valley?

Civilization in the Indus Valley

In 1921 archaeologists found the first traces of ancient Indian cities in the Indus River Valley. (See the map on page 65.) Their ruins indicate a civilization as advanced as those of Egypt and Mesopotamia. This civilization lasted from approximately 2400 B.C. to 1700 B.C. It covered an area larger than either ancient Egypt or Sumer. The economy was based on farming, trading, and shipping.

The people of the ancient Indus Valley excelled in devising an advanced system of weights and measures, town planning, and architecture. Their two largest cities, Mohenjo-Daro (moe-hen-joe-DAH-roe) and Harappa (huh-RAP-uh), were cultural centers for a region that extended for about a thousand miles along the Indus River Valley. Large and carefully planned, they had a system of brick-lined sewers, indoor bathrooms, and five-story buildings.

Streets of these two cities were laid out in perfect grids. Their design reveals a knowledge of geometry and surveying. At important intersections, remains of one-room buildings suggest that perhaps a nightwatchman stood guard. Scholars do not know who ruled the cities, although they know that such a well-organized town is indicative of a strong system of government. Moreover, cities very far apart were built in the same fashion. This indicates that the government may have had tight control over a large area.

The people were active traders, for the ruins of the cities have yielded goods from Sumer, Persia, and Egypt. They must have been skilled shipbuilders and sailors, for they built large seaports. At a port city on the Gulf of Cambay, a brick shipping dock more than 730 feet (222 meters) long had a sluice gate to control tidal water. The sluice gate swung shut to keep the water at high levels so ships could be loaded or unloaded even at low tide. Ships entered from as far away as the island of Bahrain, in the Persian Gulf.

Farming was the most important part of the economy. Farmers grew dates, melons, and other fruits, as well as the staple crops of wheat, barley, and rice. The Indians were the first to cultivate cotton. Among their domesticated animals were sheep, cattle, and pigs.

Archaeologists have unearthed many small statues of humans and animals. They have also

Bearded figures, such as this priest-king or god from Mohenjo-Daro, have also been found in Sumer. What might account for the similarities in style?

found decorated toys, jewelry, razors, pottery, mirrors, fishhooks, and woven cloth. These artifacts tell us that the artisans of the Indus Valley were skilled in many crafts.

Archaeologists can only guess the answers to many questions about life in Indus Valley cities. This is because no one has yet been able to decipher the writing of these ancient people. They used a kind of pictograph that may have been adapted from the Sumerians.

We do not know why the cities of Mohenjo-Daro and Harappa were abandoned. They might have been destroyed by the flooding of the Indus River, plague, or enemy invasion. For whatever reason, by 1500 B.C. the Indus River Valley had become a desolate place, having been overrun by invading nomads from the north.

The Aryans Invade India

You have learned how many peoples in the ancient Middle East invaded territories and, in the process, brought new ideas with them. They also acquired new ideas from the lands they conquered. The Amorites, for example, learned a new system of writing by conquering the Sumerians. In turn, the Amorites introduced new codes of law to those they ruled. Egyptians learned of ironworking and new ways to conduct military operations from Hittite and Hyksos invaders. Sometimes warlike newcomers to an area would eventually establish a more advanced civilization. The Aryans who invaded India eventually created an advanced society, but not before they destroyed the civilization they found in India.

For hundreds of years the Aryans migrated to India through the mountain passes of the northwest. (See the map on page 65.) The Aryans were a warlike people who originally came from Central Asia or Russia. Although the exact dates of the repeated migrations by Aryan tribes are not known, they probably began entering India as early as 1500 B.C. Their use of horses gave them a great advantage in warfare, for horses were not native to India. By about 1400 B.C. warrior-bowmen, led by soldiers in horse-drawn chariots, had conquered all of northern India, leaving only the people in the south independent. These people were known as the **Dravidians** (druh-VID-ee-unz).

The earliest Aryans had no interest in cities nor commerce. They destroyed the cities they entered and left the ruins to decay. These nomads scorned the settled way of life of the Indians, had no respect for Indian culture, and treated the natives as slaves. It was not until between 1000 B.C. and 500 B.C. that the Aryans became more settled and conflicts between the two cultures decreased. The people began to intermarry and adopt one another's customs.

The Aryans eventually established small kingdoms. Each was ruled by a king and a council of warriors. Within the Aryan kingdoms were many villages. Each was so independent that it resembled a small state within the kingdom. Because the kingdoms were not united under a central authority, they often warred with one another.

The settled Aryans farmed the plain between the Indus and Ganges rivers. (See the map opposite.) This is one of the most fertile areas in the world and their main crop was barley. Although land was divided among the families of a village, everyone, including women and children, worked together to keep the land irrigated. According to Aryan law, women were not permitted to inherit land nor could land be sold to strangers.

Each Indian village was governed by a council of elders, made up of the oldest inhabitants. Early Indians believed that rules for everyday actions were the most important rules of life. Religious rules were the main rules of the village. Public holidays were also religious ones.

Aryan Social Structure

As the centuries passed, Aryans settled into a social structure that drew clear lines between classes. This structure developed partly because Aryans looked down on the darker-skinned Dravidians to the south. The Aryan word *dasa* originally referred to enemies. Later it became a synonym for "dark-skinned." As the Aryan conquerers spread over more of India between 1500 B.C. and 1000 B.C., they had to find ways to live with the people they called *dasas*.

Part of their solution was to develop a class system that excluded non-Aryan people. This was done to maintain their own identity, as well as their political supremacy over the conquered people. As time progressed, this class system became progressively more rigid and structured. Eventually it was almost impossible to move from one class to another.

When the Aryans first invaded India their society was composed of three main groups. These were the nobles, priests, and ordinary tribespeople.

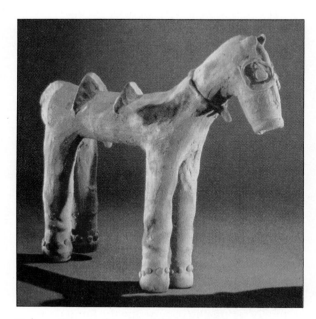

Today artisans in this region still make clay horses that are broken in a ritual based on ancient Aryan custom. What does this suggest about the transmission of culture?

EARLY INDIA

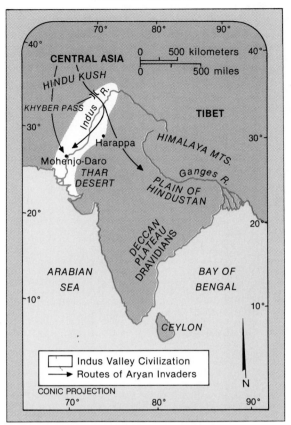

Describe the routes of the Aryan invaders. Use the distance scale to determine the approximate extent of the Indus Valley Civilization.

As the Aryans became more settled, a more formal class system developed. They reclassified themselves from three into four classes. Based on occupations, these classes were the priests, warriors, peasant farmers, and servants. The Aryans believed that the gods had assigned a role to each group. Humans, they felt, must not challenge the will of the gods. Each class had its own laws and rules of conduct for its members to follow.

The highest class was made up of the priests and scholars, called Brahmans (BRAH-munz). It was their job to study, to teach, and to perform sacrifices. Part of their task was to memorize the hymns and legends of their religion and to transmit them to the next generation. Priests also passed on behavior codes for the other classes. As centuries passed, these rules became more detailed and more complicated.

Below the Brahmans was the warrior class, or Kshatriyas (kuh-SHA-tree-uhz). Their two main duties were to protect and govern the people. The rulers of Aryan society were members of the warrior class, which also included nobles. Their job was to expand Aryan rule to other areas and to provide a just government during times of peace. During times of war, the Kshatriyas were considered to be more important than the Brahmans. During peacetime the Brahmans were considered to be of higher rank.

A third class, the Vaisyas (VYSHE-yuhz), consisted primarily of peasant farmers. They raised cattle and cultivated the land to provide food for the other classes. Lowest-ranking of the social classes were the Sudras (SOO-druhz), or laborers, whose job was to serve the other classes. This group, which included non-Aryans and prisoners of war, did the heavy manual labor for the others. As the population grew, the number of occupations increased. For instance, by about 500 B.C. trade had become so important that the artisans and merchants took over the third class, the Vaisyas. The farmers and unskilled laborers, in turn, dropped down into the Sudra class.

Non-Aryan people were virtually excluded from this complicated class structure. People who did menial or undesirable tasks did not belong to any class and were scorned by the other groups. They were very much like those who were later called pariahs (puh-RIE-uhz), or Untouchables. In the early years of Aryan rule it may have been possible, although not easy, to move between classes. This social system made it difficult for an Aryan to marry someone of a different class. However, Aryans and non-Aryans apparently did intermarry, despite the urging of the Brahmans not to do so.

Sometime between 800 B.C. and 500 B.C. the class structure developed into a **caste system.** This is more rigid than a class system. In a caste system each level of society is separated from the others not only by occupation and social rank, but by marriage and even diet. Historians believe the caste system in India was influenced by the Brahmans. To help protect their own place in society, Brahman priests insisted that only those born into their caste could become priests. They even maintained that Brahmans could not eat with members of the lower castes. As the centuries passed, the Brahmans outlined the rules of conduct for the

The Status of Women

The Laws of Manu *is a collection of social codes based on early Indian customs from about 1000 B.C. to 1 B.C. Probably written by teachers of the Vedas, they explain the duties of both the individual and the community as a whole. This selection from* The Status of Women *gives us an indication of the role played by women in early Indian society, particularly in relationship to their families.*

Women must be honoured and adorned by their fathers, brothers, husbands, and brothers-in-law, who desire [their own] welfare.

Where women are honoured, there the gods are pleased; but where they are not honoured, no sacred rite yields rewards.

The houses on which female relations, not being duly honoured, pronounce a curse, perish completely, as if destroyed by magic.

Hence men who seek [their own] welfare, should always honour women on holidays and festivals with [gifts of] ornaments, clothes, and [dainty] food.

In that family, where the husband is pleased with his wife and the wife with her husband, happiness will assuredly be lasting.

Day and night women must be kept in dependence. . . .

Her father protects [her] in childhood, her husband protects [her] in youth, and her sons protect [her] in old age; a woman is never fit for independence. . . .

She must not seek to separate herself from her father, husband, or sons; by leaving them she would make both [her own and her husband's] families contemptible.

She must always be cheerful, clever in [the management of her] household affairs, careful in cleaning her utensils, and economical in expenditure.

Him to whom her father may give her, or her brother with her father's permission, she shall obey as long as he lives, and when he is dead, she must not insult [his memory]. . . .

Source: Adapted from Sarvepalli Radhakrishnan and Charles A. Moore. *A Source Book in Indian Philosophy.* Copyright © 1957 by Princeton University Press.

1. According to *The Status of Women*, how should men treat their female relatives?
2. How can a happy household be assured?
3. How should a woman behave?
4. How does the position of women in American society today and in the past differ from early Indian society depicted in the selection above?

---

other classes. These rules became so firm and inflexible that by 500 B.C. a clear caste system existed in all of India under Aryan rule.

The Vedas

The earliest information about Aryan culture is contained in the Vedas (VAY-duhz). This is a collection of sacred compositions. The Aryans had no written language when the Vedas meaning knowledge, were composed. Therefore, these hymns and prayers were carefully memorized by the Brahman priests and handed down by word of mouth. Centuries later, the Vedas were recorded in **Sanskrit**, the Aryan written language. This language is related to most European languages, including English and Latin.

The oldest and most important of the Vedas the *Rig-Veda*, contains over a thousand hymns of praise to the gods. The *Sama-Veda* lists songs and chants, and the other two Vedas contain charms, spells, and formulas for conducting sacrifices. The

Vedas indicate that the early Aryans worshiped many gods associated with nature. Some of these writings imply, however, that these gods were considered to be different aspects of a single cosmic power.

Between 800 B.C. and 400 B.C. a three-part collection of prose and poetry was written, commenting on the meaning of the Vedas and incorporating further changes in Aryan religious beliefs. This collection is known as the **Upanishads** (oo-PAHN-ih-shads), meaning a meeting, or a lesson, with a teacher. The *Upanishads* deal with the nature of the universe and the meaning of human life. They clarify that the many Vedic gods were to be understood as aspects of one Supreme Truth. The Vedas and the *Upanishads* express the core of Aryan religious beliefs. They then became the basis of the Hindu religion.

Early Epic Literature

Between about 400 B.C. and 200 A.D., the two greatest epics of Indian literature began to take their final form. The *Mahabharata* (muh-HAH-BAH-ruh-tuh) is one of the longest epic poems in world literature. It describes an eighteen-day struggle between rival families for the throne of a kingdom in northern India. Some scholars believe that the epic may describe an actual struggle that took place near Delhi around 1400 B.C. The most famous section of this poem is called the *Bhagavad-Gita* (bug-uh-vuhd-GEE-tuh). Its message is a religious one: that unselfish good deeds and love of God are more important than ritual sacrifices. Krishna, the god Vishnu in human form, points out that life is a never-ending journey toward perfection. The goal of all life, he says, is to strive for this perfection. This leads to liberation, or immortality of the soul. This goal can only be accomplished by doing one's duty, following the codes of conduct of one's caste, and by being morally correct in one's behavior.

The second of India's two great epics is the *Ramayana* (rah-MAH-yuh-nuh), which describes the wanderings and adventures of the heroic prince Rama as he rescues his wife, Sita, from the demon-king Ravana. From both of these examples of ancient Indian literature, scholars have learned much of what we know about Aryan society and religious traditions.

SECTION REVIEW

1. Mapping: Use the map on page 61 to describe the location of Harappa and Mohenjo-Daro, and the location of India in relation to the rest of Asia.
2. In your own words, briefly define and identify: Indus Valley civilization, monsoons, Aryans, Dravidians, the Vedas, Sanskrit, the *dasas*, the *Upanishads*.
3. Explain why more facts are not known about life in Harappa or Mohenjo-Daro.
4. Describe the four classes in ancient India and how they developed into a caste system.
■ How do you think the existence of a rigid class system affected the future development of Indian society?

HINDUISM AND BUDDHISM

At about the time the *Upanishads* were completed, an Indian prince reformed ancient Aryan beliefs. He founded one of the world's major religions, Buddhism (BOO-diz-um). Though Buddhism was born in India, it became more important in other parts of Asia. In India itself, Hinduism (HIN-doo-iz-um) slowly absorbed the earlier Aryan religion.

Hinduism

In time Aryan religion evolved into **Hinduism.** This is a religion that held the *Upanishads* as the core of religious thought. Hinduism was both a religion and a way of life. Among its basic teachings was a belief that life is an evolution toward perfection. Although the body may die, the human soul is eternal. It is reborn in successive lives until the immortality of the soul is realized. This belief in the soul's cycle of rebirth is known as reincarnation.

Hinduism taught that a person's destiny is determined by his or her own **karma,** or actions in this and previous lives. The actions of the good are rewarded and the evil are punished. This is done by having their souls reborn in the body of a person of a higher or lower state. The goal of a Hindu was to live life in such a way that his or her soul would reincarnate until it reached perfection. Then it would attain *moksha*, or be liberated from the cycle of rebirth and united with Brahma, the source of all being. To accomplish this, a person might observe daily acts that were thought to benefit a believer. These acts included meditation and worship, and reading aloud from sacred writings. Other acts included avoiding forbidden foods and bathing in sacred rivers like the Ganges. Being kind to people and animals, and observing *dharma*, or caste rules, were also important.

Hindus recognized Brahma as the universal power, or supreme reality, who assumed three major forms. The first was Brahma (BRAH-muh), the source and creator of all life. Vishnu (VISH-noo) was the protector of living things, and Shiva (SHEE-vuh) was the god of destruction.

Buddhism

Around 500 B.C. another major religion appeared in India. It was called **Buddhism** and its founder was Prince Siddhartha Gautama (sih-DAHR-tuh GOW-tuh-muh).

Gautama's father ruled a small kingdom in northern India. The prince grew up surrounded by wealth and luxury, but he was troubled by the misery and poverty of the people. The prince lived at a time when Hinduism had become increasingly marked by rituals and sacrifices. Hoping to return to a simpler, more pure religion, the prince set out in search of the ultimate truth that would relieve human suffering. Years of wandering and study followed. He sought out Hindu scholars to tutor him in the *Vedas* and the *Upanishads*. One day, while meditating beneath a tree, Siddhartha felt that at last he understood the cause of human suffering and how to end it. From that time, he was known as the "Enlightened One," or the Buddha (BOOD-uh).

The Buddha spent the rest of his life instructing his followers. Legends tell that he always wore a yellow robe and relied on the goodness of others for his needs. He went from village to village, where crowds flocked to hear him preach.

Buddhism was not an entirely new religion. It shared many beliefs with Hinduism. The Buddha shared the Hindu beliefs in the sacredness of all life, and followers refused to kill an animal because they believed that all living things possessed a soul. Other common beliefs of Hindus and Buddhists include reincarnation and the soul's journey to reach perfection. This was a state of peace Buddhists call **nirvana.** Like the Hindus, the Buddha taught that human suffering was the result of desires for things such as wealth, power, and pleasures.

Buddhism, however, rejected the sacred scriptures of Hinduism. The Buddha taught that one's salvation could not be achieved by following the complex rituals performed by Hindu priests. The Buddha believed that, regardless of caste, each individual could attain perfection. Liberation could only be achieved by knowing the Four Noble Truths and following the Eightfold Path to righteous living.

Of these four truths, the first is the belief that all human life consists of some sickness, pain, and suffering. Second, human suffering is caused by desires, including those for material possessions. Third, by renouncing all desires, one can overcome suffering and achieve nirvana. Fourth, nirvana and liberation can be achieved by following the Eightfold Path. This strict moral code consisted of eight guidelines for proper living. They included renouncing all pleasures, controlling emotions, speaking the truth, acting generously, cultivating goodness, respecting all living things, acquiring knowledge, and meditating.

After the Buddha's death, many of his followers banded together under special rules he had laid down for them. They worshiped him as a god, though in his lifetime he had insisted they not do so. Living together as monks, in places known as monasteries, his disciples devoted their lives to the Buddha's teachings. Buddhist monasteries developed into important centers of learning.

The Spread of Buddhism

Buddhism spread rapidly over central and northern India for a variety of reasons. Some people turned to the new religion out of dissatisfaction with the powers of the Brahmans and the complex, elaborate rites of Hinduism. Others were unhappy with the Hindu caste system. Many Indians accepted the new religion simply because it was in many ways similar to Hinduism.

Buddhism spread from India to Burma, Thailand (TIE-land), and southeastern Asia. It entered Tibet (tih-BET) and China from India's northeast. It was carried from there to Korea and Japan. As the religion spread, it was interpreted in different ways. A variety of Buddhist sects sprang up, each having its own doctrine. Two main branches of Buddhism evolved. These were the **Theravada** (ther-uh-VAH-duh) and the **Mahayana** (mah-huh-YAH-nuh). Theravada was the school of Buddhism that spread to southeastern Asia and remained closest to the original teachings of Buddha. It taught that nirvana was achieved through proper conduct. Mahayana, however, placed more emphasis on the worship of Buddha as a god and as a savior of all humanity. Its followers became very dedicated to human service. Mahayana spread to the northern parts of central Asia, such as China, Korea, Japan, and Vietnam.

SECTION REVIEW

1. In your own words, briefly define and identify: Hinduism, reincarnation, Brahma, Buddhism, the Buddha, nirvana.
2. In what ways were the beliefs of Buddhism similar to those of Hinduism? In what ways did they differ?
3. Explain how the Four Noble Truths and the Eightfold Path would influence the behavior of a Buddhist.
■ Are any groups or individuals in your community considered better or worse than others? Why do you think this situation exists?

THE EARLY CHINESE

On the outskirts of the Chinese city of Xian, (SHEE-an), visitors can visit a stone-age village. Scientists believe that people lived here perhaps 6,000 years ago. The site is Banpo, a neolithic community of forty-five houses, two animal pens, six pottery kilns and 250 graves.

The people of Banpo made tools of stone or bone. These included chisels, knives, needles, and fishhooks. They fired pottery to use for cooking, storing, and eating. They also invented a pottery steamer, so food could be cooked with steam. This method of cooking is still in use today.

Banpo and Xian are located in the valley of the Yellow River. In this region, more than a thousand years later, a civilization emerged just as it had in the river valleys of Mesopotamia, India, and Egypt. The exact date is uncertain, but is believed to have been about 2000 B.C. The Chinese people developed one of the earliest and most durable of all early civilizations.

Early Chinese Civilization and Geography

To some extent, China's physical geography protected the country from outside forces. Today, the map of China shows a vast land that spreads from the East China Sea west across a land as wide as the United States. Ancient China was much smaller. It was a place of small kingdoms that gradually spread outward in all directions from the valleys of the Yellow and Yangtze rivers.

To the west, formidable geographical barriers separated the early Chinese from India and Europe. These included the world's driest deserts and highest mountains. To the north the grim Gobi Desert protected ancient China from northern tribes. Another desert, the Takla Makan, lies between ancient China and the Tien Shan Mountains, on the modern border of the Soviet Union. South of the Takla Makan, the bleak Plateau of Tibet borders the towering Himalayas. These landforms made a natural barrier against contact with other people.

Thus, China's geography limited the amount of foreign contact and influence it received. Overland trade to or from China was restricted. As a result, early Chinese culture developed relatively free of outside influence.

Most scholars believe civilization in China first appeared in the north along the Yellow River or Huang He. (See the map on page 70.) Despite bitter cold winters and high winds, this area of China was suitable for farming. The land was not heavily forested and the soil was fertile. Rainfall was light, but rivers and streams provided the water needed to raise crops. The Yellow River and its tributaries flood regularly, spilling water and silt over their banks. This flooding deposits a rich yellow soil, called loess, on the North China Plain. These factors created the proper environment for an agricultural civilization to develop.

Through the ages, the Yellow River has been a mixed blessing to China. The name describes the river's muddy color, which is caused by the loess it carries from the mountains and highlands to the plains. The Yellow River has also been referred to as "China's Sorrow." The very floods that replenished the soil each year also caused great suffering among the people who lived in the river valley. Sediment deposited in the riverbed slowly forced the water level higher and higher. During the monsoon season this sometimes resulted in heavy flooding that threatened the people of the river valley with death and destruction. The Chinese began building dikes to hold back the water. However, the dikes caused the water level to rise more quickly under heavy rainfall, and the threat of devastating floods increased. Living in the river valley became even more dangerous.

Early Chinese legends mention wise rulers who supposedly founded Chinese culture. For instance, Fu Xi (FOO-SEE) is said to have taught the Chinese to hunt. Another ruler, Shen Nong (SHUN-NOONG), is credited with having developed farming. According to legend, the first dynasty, or ruling family, that governed China was the **Xia** (SHYAH) **Dynasty.** Historians do not know whether or not the Xia Dynasty actually existed. Tradition claims that the Xia ruled the region from approximately 2200 B.C. to 1500 B.C.

EARLY CHINA

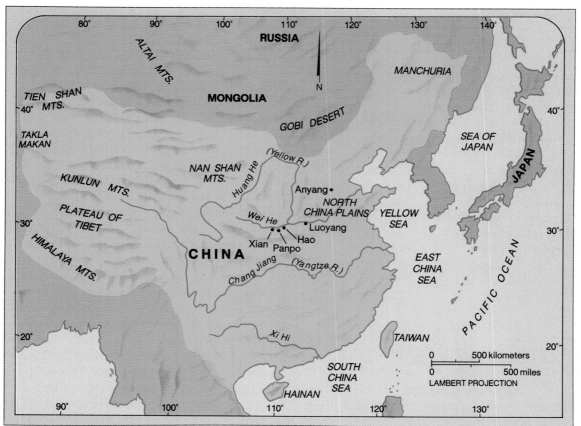

Despite formidable geographic barriers, ancient China still was frequently threatened by nomadic invaders from the north. What impact do you think the fear of invasion might have on a people and their culture?

During this period of history the family became the basic unit of Chinese life. The family included all relatives, not just parents and children. Sometimes entire villages were made up of just one family. In ancient times, a family name came from the name of a clan, or a group of families. Then, as today in China, the family name came before the name given an individual by his or her parents.

The people who lived in the river valleys of China had little or no contact with other civilized peoples. Therefore, they developed a strong sense of identity and superiority. They regarded their land as the center of civilization. They called China "the central country," or "the Middle Kingdom." Even in later periods when the Chinese traded with many other lands, they considered their own kingdoms the center of the civilized world.

The Shang Dynasty

For centuries, scholars thought that all the legends and other stories about early China were myths. In the late 1800's archaeologists began making discoveries that proved some stories were based on fact. Near the city of Anyang (AHN-YAHNG), they dug up the remains of a dynasty mentioned in the stories—the **Shang Dynasty.** The Shang is the first dynasty for which we possess real historical evidence. Chinese tradition says the Shang rule began in 1766 B.C. and lasted until 1027 B.C.

Shang Art and Architecture

The first major advances in Chinese art and architecture were probably made during this period. Evidence found at Anyang and elsewhere, such as city walls, foundations of houses and buildings, and tombs, show a high level of building skills. The upper class lived in magnificent houses of wood and stone. Nobles occupied huge palaces. Ordinary people built dwellings to cope with the fierce winds of the North China Plain. Often their houses were partially submerged in the earth.

Shang tombs were built and furnished like palaces. In them, archaeologists found the remains of many people, horses, and dogs. They have even found the wooden chariots in which Shang warriors rode to war. The furnishings included ornaments of carved stone, jade, and bone. Other items included bronze vessels and weapons. The finest

SHANG KINGDOM

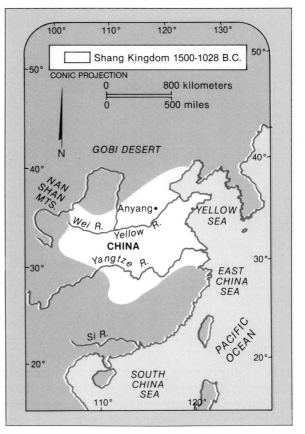

Describe the location of the Shang Kingdom in China. What influence might this location have had on the development of the economy of the Shang?

tombs were probably built for members of the royal family.

Royal tombs have yielded a wealth of information about the art of the period. An important advance in Shang times was learning how to make bronze. The tombs are filled with elaborate ceremonial vessels of this alloy. Shang artisans crafted finely made pottery and experimented with unique shapes and new glazes. Potters learned to use kaolin (KAY-uh-lun), a fine white clay, for making high quality ceramics.

In addition, the tombs have also yielded objects made of shells, ivory, and gold, and stamps for pressing designs into clay. They also found pieces of ox bone and tortoiseshell with writing cut into them. Scholars believe that these may have been the first Chinese writing.

This Shang Dynasty cup, made of bronze and richly detailed, was used to hold ceremonial foods for the gods.

Shang Oracles

Some of the writing on bones shows that the Shang consulted **oracles** (AWR-uh-kulz). An oracle is someone thought to have the power to predict the future and give wise answers to questions. For example, a person would bring a question to the oracle: "How will this year's rice crop turn out?" The oracle would then heat a bone or a tortoiseshell over a fire until it cracked. From the shape of the crack, the oracle would decide the answer to the question. The question and sometimes the answer were then written on the bone or shell, which was sometimes signed and dated. Nearly 200,000 oracle bones and shells have been found.

Shang Government

Over the centuries, Shang rulers moved their capital to several cities, among them Anyang. A king governed with the help of leading nobles. Many were the king's relatives. The king was believed to be the descendant of a god. When the king died, he was believed to join his ancestors in looking after those family members who were still alive. Ancestor worship was an important part of Chinese culture. The living considered their deceased relatives to still be members of their family.

By examining available evidence, scholars have learned many other things about Shang government. The dynasty collected its wealth from tributes, or payments from people the Shang had defeated in war. When a king died, his younger brother became ruler. If there was no younger brother, the oldest son of the king was permitted to take command. The tomb of one Shang noblewoman, Fu Hao, contains records of her leading military expeditions against hostile tribes. Scholars believe that she may have been the mother of the heir to the throne.

Each ruler was aided by an educated class of priests. These served as predictors and interpreters of the future. They also performed religious rites, and kept the lunar calendar up-to-date. Measuring time was important to this agricultural economy. Therefore astrologers, or people who predicted events by studying the positions of the stars and planets, had an important and respected place at the royal court. As early as 1400 B.C. the priests were also recording lunar eclipses and observing sunspots.

To help farmers know when to plant and harvest, Shang priests developed a lunar calendar, dividing the year into ten-day periods. Three such periods equaled a month, six such periods equaled a cycle, and six cycles made one year.

Shang Economy and Trade

Most people of Shang China were farmers who planted millet, a type of cereal, wheat, and some rice. Many fields were irrigated. Hoes and spades made of stone or shell, and a plow that was pushed with the foot were their main tools. Farmers raised cattle, horses, goats, pigs, and fowl, as well as crops. Some farmers practiced **sericulture** (SER-uh-kul-chur), or the cultivation of silkworms for the production of silk.

Shang people traded widely, importing shells from southeast Asia and tin, lead, and copper from southern China. Cowrie (KOW-ree) shells, used as money, came from islands in the Pacific Ocean, and salt was brought from the shores of the Yellow Sea. Shang merchants exported highly-valued silk to many parts of the ancient world. Because silk commanded such high prices, the techniques of sericulture were kept a closely guarded secret for almost 3,000 years.

The Chinese System of Writing

Writing in China may have begun as it did in ancient Egypt, with pictures used to represent words. By Shang times, however, the Chinese writing system had developed beyond pictures to 2,500 different symbols. Some characters or symbols, called pictographs, resembled the thing they stood for. For example, the characters for sun, moon, and tree looked like drawings of those objects. Other characters stood for sounds or ideas. The character for the number three was simply three straight lines drawn one above the other. Very often the Shang characters conveyed complex meanings, as well as simple words. For example, a joining together of the symbols for the moon and the sun meant brightness.

Writing was done with a brush and ink. Rules dictated how many brush strokes should be used to form a particular character. Some characters required twenty-five strokes to draw. As a result, **calligraphy,** or beautiful handwriting, emerged as a highly admired art form.

Writing usually began at the top of a strip of

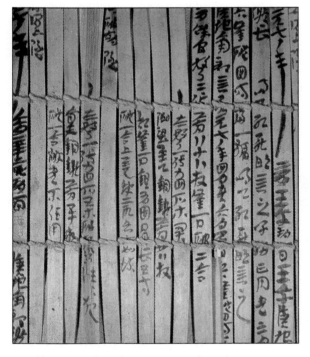

In addition to written documents, on what other sources do we rely for information about the past?

silk, bamboo, or paper, and continued vertically to the bottom. Scholars believe the first Chinese books were narrow strips of bamboo held together with a thong. These are called *Bamboo Books* or *Bamboo Annals.* One bamboo book discovered in a grave in 281 A.D. was later lost. It was then forged and, finally, reconstructed from ancient quotations. The *Bamboo Annals* contain a history of a much earlier period. Other samples of early writing can be found on oracle bones and on tortoise-shells. Shang bronzes often included written inscriptions. These, too, have helped scholars pinpoint the dates of important events.

SECTION REVIEW

1. Mapping: Use the map on page 70 to describe the location of China in relation to the rest of the ancient world of the Far East. Locate the main geographic features of China and describe how they affected early China.
2. In your own words, briefly define or identify: "China's sorrow," dynasty, oracles, sericulture, calligraphy, Xia Dynasty, Shang Dynasty.
3. What evidence about the Shang Dynasty led scholars to change their minds about the meaning of ancient Chinese legends?
4. What are "oracle bones" and how were they used by the people of the Shang Dynasty?
■ Did the culture of the Shang Dynasty have any characteristics in common with your own?

THE DEVELOPMENT OF A CHINESE EMPIRE

About 1028 B.C. the last Shang king was overthrown. Previously, the Shang had conquered the Zhou (JOE), a people from the Wei (WAY) River Valley to the northwest. As the Shang leaders became weaker, the Zhou formed an alliance with several other Chinese peoples and gradually overwhelmed the Shang, destroying the city of Anyang. Most of its inhabitants were slaughtered, but some escaped and carried Shang culture to other parts of the Far East. Some traces of Shang culture have even been found in Korea.

The Zhou Dynasty

The **Zhou Dynasty** was the longest dynasty in China's history, lasting from about 1027 B.C. to 256 B.C.—almost 800 years. The Zhou Dynasty established a new capital at Hao (HOW), near the modern city of Xian. They brought most of northern China, a vast plain, under their control. However, the lack of efficient communication and transportation made it impossible for the Zhou to unite all the lands they had conquered. Zhou rulers therefore parceled out most of their land to their descendants and allies who had helped them overthrow the Shang. Those who received land were known as **vassals.** In return for land, these nobles agreed to provide soldiers for the Zhou kings in times of war. This system of exchanging land for military aid was known as *chien-feng,* called **feudalism** in English.

Zhou Government

To keep in touch with every part of their vast territories, Zhou rulers traveled constantly. While traveling, the ruler depended on his vassals for food and shelter. Vassals also traveled to the capital city and stayed at the ruler's court.

Zhou nobles lived in walled towns and ruled the surrounding countryside. The areas under their control were known as city-states. Vassals had small courts of their own and officials to help them govern. If a vassal controlled several large areas, he appointed a governor for each one. They supervised forests and farmlands and maintained roads and bridges. Others regulated trade, acted as judges, ran prisons, or hunted criminals.

The position of vassal came to be hereditary, and vassals became powerful in their own territories. They ruled as if they were kings. Over time, the power of the Zhou vassals grew so great that they threatened the power of the Zhou ruler.

In 770 B.C. a group of Zhou vassals attacked the capital and murdered the Zhou ruler. Part of the royal family escaped to eastern China. They set up a new capital at Luoyang (LWAN-YONG), where the Zhou Dynasty continued for about another 500 years as the Eastern Zhou Dynasty.

Zhou rulers never recovered the power they had once held. As both royal power and territory lessened, city-states in eastern China grew stronger. The larger ones conquered their weaker neighbors. Between 403 B.C. and 256 B.C. there was almost constant warfare in eastern China. The Zhou ruler was no longer effective. After about 300 B.C. many vassal rulers began to call themselves kings. Until then the title had been used only by the Zhou rulers.

Despite the breakdown in royal authority and frequent wars, China prospered during the Zhou period. Trade and industry grew. People flocked to the cities to help produce silk, copper, iron, and other products. As a result, cities became centers of wealth and luxury.

Culture Under the Zhou

Education grew as rapidly as industry. People were trained in various occupations such as judges, diplomats, and doctors. Others trained to become priests, scribes, artists, poets, scientists, and historians. Some studied scientific farming and gardening. Canals were dug to improve transportation and communication.

These cultural advances under the Zhou helped to increase a sense of pride among the Chinese. They considered themselves part of a superior civilization. Their ideas produced what is known as a golden age of Chinese thought.

SECTION REVIEW

1. Mapping: Use the map on page 71 to describe the extent of the area ruled by the Shang Dynasty.
2. In your own words, briefly define or identify: Zhou Dynasty, vassals, feudalism, Hao.
3. Explain why a system of feudalism was used to govern the Zhou Dynasty.
4. Describe the advances in industry and culture made during the Zhou dynasty.
■ Cultural advances helped to increase a sense of pride among the Chinese. What examples of recent cultural advances in the United States could you cite as having increased Americans' pride in themselves and their country?

EARLY CHINESE PHILOSOPHY

The period of government weakness and endless wars from 475 B.C. to 211 B.C., called the Age of Warring States, was a time of great intellectual ferment in Zhou China. Leading thinkers and philosophers observed the chaos of their society and tried to suggest new systems to solve society's problems.

The Teachings of Confucius

Of all the wise men who pondered great ideas during Zhou times, none had more long-lasting influence on China than a scholar we call **Confucius** (kun-FYOO-shus). His name is a western variation of the name Kung Fu-tzu. Kung was his family name, and Fu-tzu meant grand master. In later times, his students quoted him by saying, "Kung, the master (tzu) says. . . ."

He traveled from place to place with his pupils, teaching his philosophy. Near the end of his life he returned to his home in northern China. There he spent his time teaching and writing. After his death in 479 B.C., Confucius' teachings were collected and written down. These are called the *Five Classics,* and the way of life they describe is called **Confucianism** (kun-FYOO-shuh-niz-um).

Confucius believed that Chinese society would be better if people followed a clear code of conduct, which especially stressed morals. He taught that three virtues—wisdom, love, and courage—were most important. Other virtues included respect for elders, generosity, sincerity, humility, self-respect, loyalty, friendliness, and eagerness to learn. Confucius believed that educated people should provide a good example for others. They should also provide moral leadership for the country. He stated that a noble man or woman was one who practiced these virtues. However, simply being a virtuous person was not enough.

Goodness, Confucius believed, should serve society. A good person was obligated to help others become virtuous. According to Confucius, society should have five things in order to be perfect. These are love between parents and children, fairness between ruler and ruled, a clear division of duties and responsibilities between husband and wife, respect between elders and the young, and good relations between friends.

According to Confucius, every person was born to play a particular role in society. If every individual was content to do whatever he or she was born to do, then society would be more stable. "Let the ruler be a ruler, and the subject a subject; let the father be a father, and the son a son," was the way Confucius put it in one of his famous proverbs.

Confucius did not challenge the authority of government, yet he did not believe a ruler had unrestricted freedom. Instead, Confucius insisted that rulers were obliged to set a proper example for all their subjects. The goal for a good ruler, if he or she wished to be a virtuous individual, was to promote virtue, not to increase his or her power.

The Mandate of Heaven

Confucius' most famous follower was Mengzi (mung-DZOO), also known as Mencius (MEN-shee-uss). This philosopher made important contributions of his own to Confucianism. Mencius taught that a moral ruler would enjoy the respect and support of subjects. This was because heaven expressed its approval of a ruler through the ruler's subjects. Thus a good ruler was thought to possess the **Mandate of Heaven,** or a divine right to govern. If a ruler governed badly or was immoral, however, the people would rise in revolt and overthrow the ruler. This meant the Mandate of Heaven had been withdrawn and the ruler no longer had the divine right to govern.

Mencius did not originate the Mandate of Heaven. It was used by the Zhou to justify overthrowing the Shang Dynasty. Throughout Chinese history, whenever there were famines, floods, or foreign invasions, rebels claimed that these disasters were signs that the Mandate of Heaven had been lost by the government in power. This thereby gave the rebels grounds for revolt.

China progressed from one dynasty to another, and Chinese scholars continued to interpret their past. A new idea about history, called the **Dynastic Cycle Theory,** began to emerge. According to this Chinese idea, cultures or civilizations repeat their history through several major developments, all of which express the use of the Mandate of

Heaven. In a simplified version, there is first an age of warring states in which a dynasty is founded. After new dynasties are established, there comes a time of unification and empire. Third, there occurs a time of disintegration and collapse of dynastic central power. Barbarians on the frontier grow more powerful and dangerous. They invade and conquer a country weakened by a corrupt or poorly ruled dynasty. These people then absorb ideas from those conquered. They, in turn, provide new vigor and ideas to the conquered people. In the fourth stage, warring states again emerge to do battle with one another. Lastly, the cycle begins again as new leaders seek to obtain the Mandate of Heaven. Floods, famine, and disease, due in part to weak government control, also come and go in this cycle. If one accepts the Chinese Dynastic Cycle Theory, the future can be predicted by studying the past.

Taoism

Next to Confucianism, the most important school of philosophy in the Zhou period was **Taoism** (DOW-iz-um). According to legend, its founder was Laozi (LOW-DZUH), who is believed to have lived from 604 B.C. to 531 B.C.

Confucianism taught a code of conduct for all society to follow. Taoism favored individualism and taught its followers to scorn the values set by society. Each individual was to see his or her own way to live in harmony with nature. The word *tao* meant a road or path to follow. The term was first used by Confucius to identify the social system he urged people to adopt. However, the Taoists gave it a different spiritual meaning, one that called followers of Taoism to a life of simplicity.

Taoists believed that the world ran smoothly on its own and in accordance to the laws of nature. Yet people were always trying to improve the world or change society. This, the Taoists taught, was often in opposition to the laws of nature. The best life, they believed, was one of spontaneity, one which "flowed like water." Even knowledge, the Taoists thought, had the power to corrupt. It created desires for things that were not essential. Taoism taught individuals to live a simpler life in order for society to return to a more pure existence.

The End of the Zhou Dynasty

Under the Zhou dynasty, Chinese economy was expanded and strengthened. Kings encouraged commerce by building, repairing roads and canals, and coining metal money. They sponsored the building of dams and other irrigation projects. Most important, the Zhou provided hundreds of years of strong and stable government. During that time, education and culture thrived.

As Zhou rulers expanded their territory, many new people were absorbed into Chinese culture. Some were from the south, near modern Thailand. Some were northerners. Once these people learned Chinese and learned to write its characters, they, too, were considered Chinese. By absorbing other people, Chinese culture was enriched with new art forms and ideas. Under the Zhou, Chinese artists continued to create great works of pottery and bronze. Pots and other writers created stories and poems that are classics of Chinese and world literature. Philosophers shaped ideas that still serve today as the spiritual foundation for the daily lives of many people.

During the years 480 B.C. to 256 B.C., the Zhou city-states had become powerful kingdoms. One of them, the kingdom of the **Qin** (CHIN), destroyed the Zhou Dynasty in 256 B.C. and then went on to conquer all its rivals. In the next fifteen years the Qin conquered all the various kingdoms and territories of China and established the first Chinese empire. Thus, the king of Qin became China's first emperor, and it was from the Qin that China derived its name.

SECTION REVIEW

1. In your own words, identify or define: Confucius, Laozi, Mandate of Heaven, Dynastic Cycle Theory, Taoism, Qin.
2. Which three virtues did Confucius deem most important?
3. What contributions to Chinese thought did Mencius make?
■ Which of the three philosophers—Confucius, Mencius, or Laozi—do you think offer the best solutions for solving the problems of our modern society? Explain.

Reviewing the Chapter

Chapter Summary

As in Egypt and Mesopotamia, the early civilizations of India and China began in river valleys where frequent flooding provided fertile soil. Because of geographical barriers impeding travel and the exchange of ideas, early Indian and Chinese civilizations were more self-contained than the civilizations of the Middle East.

The people of India's Indus Valley built large, carefully planned cities that indicate a high degree of government organization, yet little is known of this civilization. Later, Aryan invaders from the north overran northern India and introduced a class system to their society, which later developed into the more rigid caste system. Both Hinduism and Buddhism had their beginnings in India.

China's early civilization developed in even greater isolation than that of the Indus Valley. The earliest known Chinese civilization, the Shang Dynasty, developed bronze-working, advanced architecture, and a system of writing that is still in use in much of Asia today. Under the Zhou Dynasty, a strong and stable government permitted further advances in the economy, the arts, and education.

A long period of wars caused by the breakup of the Zhou Dynasty produced a period of intellectual ferment. Philosophers sought better answers to how people should behave and how governments should function. The Confucian philosophy that developed in this period has influenced China for more than 2,000 years.

1. Why were the early civilizations of India and China more self-contained than the early civilizations that developed in ancient Egypt and Mesopotamia?
2. What do the cities of early Indus Valley civilizations reveal about the government at that time?
3. What were some of the main achievements of the Shang Dynasty?
4. How did China benefit from the stability of the Zhou Dynasty?

Using Your Vocabulary

1. What is a monsoon and how does it differ from other storms?
2. In your own words, define Brahmans and describe the importance of their position in ancient Indian society.
3. What were the *Upanishads?* Explain their importance in Indian literature.
4. Define and compare the characteristics of Hinduism and Buddhism.
5. What is reincarnation?
6. Why did the people of China refer to their country as "the central country" or "the Middle Kingdom?"
7. What were oracles and how were they used during the Shang Dynasty?
8. What is sericulture? Why were the techniques of sericulture kept secret for so long a time?
9. What is calligraphy?
10. In your own words, differentiate between Confucianism and Taoism.
11. Define "Mandate of Heaven." What limits were there to this mandate?
12. In your own words, explain the Dynastic Cycle Theory.

Developing Your Geography Skills

1. Use the map on page 65 to describe what parts of India were affected by the Aryan invasions.
2. Use the map on page 71 to describe the boundaries of Shang China.
3. Use the map of page 70 to describe how the geography of China made it difficult for the rulers of China's large empires to govern their vast territories. What were some of the measures taken by China's early rulers to organize and control these large territories?

Recalling the Facts

1. What were the most important geographic features of ancient India?
2. Why are so few facts known about the people who built the ancient cities of Harappa and Mohenjo-Daro?
3. What were the main achievements of the early Indus Valley civilization?
4. What evidence indicates that the people of the Indus Valley traded with other parts of the ancient world?
5. What was the class system? How did it differ from the later caste system?
6. What are the main beliefs of Buddhism?
7. In what ways do the beliefs of Buddhism differ from those of Hinduism? In what ways are these two religions similar?
8. What conditions made the Yellow River Valley suitable for the beginnings of a civilization?
9. Describe the development of the first Chinese writing system.
10. Identify the main achievements of the Shang Dynasty.
11. Identify the main achievements of the Zhou Dynasty.
12. Why did feudalism develop under the Zhou?
13. Why did the Age of Warring States produce a golden age of philosophy in China?
14. What virtues did Confucius believe were most important? What additional virtues did he recommend?
15. What were the main differences between Taoism and Confucianism?
16. What contribution did Mencius make to the philosophy of Confucianism?
17. What were some of the results of the breakdown of royal authority near the end of the Zhou Dynasty?
18. Who were the Qin?

Essay Questions

1. Write a brief essay explaining how geographic barriers helped isolate the early civilizations of India and China.
2. Write a brief description of what a Hindu priest might suggest as the correct way for a person of the merchant class to live.
3. Explain the importance of the concept of reincarnation in Indian life, mentioning its role in Hinduism and Buddhism. Describe what a person had to achieve to escape endless rebirth.
4. Write a brief biography of Siddhartha Gautama, the founder of Buddhism.
5. Explain why the people of ancient China held scholars in great admiration.
6. Describe how Zhou rulers ran their government, explaining why this system lasted for so long. What were the strengths and weaknesses of such a system?
7. Explain why a knowledge of mathematics was helpful in an agricultural society and how the Chinese priests adjusted their calendars.
8. Describe the contributions of Mencius to Confucianism and to Chinese ideas of government.
9. In your opinion, what are the major contributions of the ancient Indians and the ancient Chinese to world civilization? Explain.

Critical Thinking

Detecting Bias

Critical thinking involves detecting **bias.** Bias is an opinion based on personal feelings that leads to distorted judgment and interferes with making fair decisions. Detecting bias requires determining if a judgment has been made on the basis of a person's or a group's feelings, or whether it is justified by supporting evidence.

1. Describe the structure of India's class system.
2. What was the basis of the division of the population into castes?
3. How did changes in the caste system reflect changes in people's feelings about which occupations were most important?
4. Do you detect any bias in the caste system? Explain your answer.
5. How might a member of each of the following groups describe the caste system: Brahmans, Kshatriya, Vaisya, Sudra, and Untouchables? Explain the role bias might play in each group's response.

Reviewing the Unit

Developing a Sense of Time

Examine the time line below and answer the questions that follow.

3000 B.C.	3000	Sumerian cities developed
	2850	Old Kingdom in Egypt
	2500	Sumer declines
	2050	Middle Kingdom in Egypt
2000 B.C.		
	1750	Code of Hammurabi
	1730	Hyksos invade Egypt
	1570	New Kingdom in Egypt
	1500	Indus Valley civilization ends; Aryan tribes enter India
	1200	Hittite Empire falls
1000 B.C.	1000	Aryans settle in India; Zhou Dynasty replaces the Shang
	926	Solomon rules
	900	Assyrians move into Mesopotamia; Phoenician trade well established
	670	Egypt invaded by Assyrians
	600	Height of Chaldean Empire
500 B.C.	500	Buddhism founded
	221	Qin Empire established

1. Which emerged first: the development of Sumerian cities or the Old Kingdom in Egypt?
2. What period of Egyptian history occurred shortly after the development of the Code of Hammurabi?
3. By what time had the trade of the Phoenicians become well established?
4. What was happening in India about the time the Zhou Dynasty was established in China?

Social Science Skills

Reading for the Main Idea

In the *Social Science Skills* in Chapter 2, you learned how to read a paragraph for the main idea. Keep this in mind as you answer the following questions.

1. In your opinion, what is the meaning of the word civilization? List as many characteristics of civilization as you can.
2. Which three things on your list do you consider to be the main ideas or points about civilization?
3. Do the ancient civilizations of the Middle East, Egypt, India, and China fit your main points about what characterizes a civilization? Why or why not?

Critical Thinking

Review the definitions of each of the following and then answer the questions that follow.

> Verifiable fact (page 35)
> Value claims (page 59)
> Bias (page 78)

1. What facts appeared with the material on the ancient Egyptians? The ancient Indians? The ancient Chinese? List three examples.
2. How can such facts be verified? Be as specific as possible in your answer.
3. What value claims did the ancient Aryans make? The ancient Chinese emperors? List two examples of each.
4. Did you detect any bias in how the ancient Egyptians viewed others? Explain.
5. How might you detect someone else's bias or values?

Linking Past and Present

The introduction and use of iron by the Hittites and Assyrians was a major innovation that provided better and stronger weapons and tools and contributed to their advanced technology. Name one recent innovation that has improved our technology. How will it improve our lives?

UNIT ·2·

CLASSICAL CIVILIZATIONS

3000 B.C.— 650 A.D.

CHAPTER ·4·

CLASSICAL CHINA and INDIA

322 B.C.–648 A.D.

Objectives

- *To describe the achievements and failures of China's first emperor*

- *To list the main contributions of Chinese civilization during the period from 221 B.C. to 648 A.D.*

- *To outline the main contributions of the Maurya, Kushan, and Gupta empires*

- *To explain how trade influenced the development of culture in ancient India*

You read in Chapter 3 how geography played a major role in isolating the early civilizations of India and China from the rest of the world. As time passed, very distinctive and lasting cultures developed in the important river valleys of each of these lands. You will read how in the period covered by this chapter, Indian and Chinese civilizations absorbed new lands, new peoples, and new ideas.

In China, strong central governments were established by the Qin and Han dynasties that expanded imperial control over many new territories. Newly-included people were considered barbaric, or uncivilized, unless they adopted Chinese culture and language. Therefore, after new territories were conquered by the Chinese, most of the conquered peoples quickly adopted Chinese ways. Even groups that conquered Chinese kingdoms usually adopted many aspects of Chinese culture.

Meanwhile, by the fourth century B.C., political unification had been brought about in India under the Mauryas. Many groups of people entered the Indian subcontinent, some as conquerers. India absorbed all of these new groups, incorporating them into the existing caste system, which was an integral part of the Hindu society.

By the third century A.D., India was once again united. The Guptas established a prosperous empire that resulted in a golden age for Indian culture. Developing in very different ways, Chinese and Indian civilizations made important advances in learning and the arts.

CHINA'S FIRST EMPIRE

As you learned in Chapter 3, the Zhou Dynasty weakened during a long period in which many city-states became powerful kingdoms. They fought among themselves to replace the Zhou Dynasty, which was destroyed by the kingdom of Qin in 256 B.C.

The Qin Dynasty

The Qin first ruled an area in western China. One by one, Qin armies defeated the other kingdoms and expanded their rule over more land.

In 221 B.C. the Qin conquered its last rival kingdom and, for the first time, all of China was

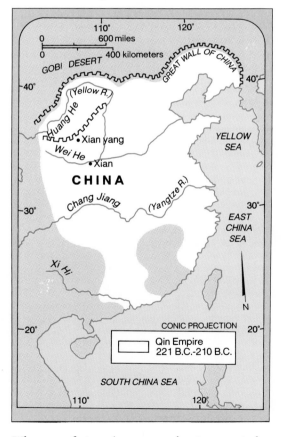

QIN EMPIRE

Why was a fast moving army and a strong central government necessary to govern the Qin Empire?

united under one rule. The area was smaller than that of modern China, but vastly larger than that controlled by previous dynasties. Although Qin rule of unified China lasted only eleven years, from 221 B.C. to 210 B.C., the precedence for a strong central government was created. This system of government would be the model that would endure for the next 2,000 years in China.

The Qin king decided to develop a new system of government to replace the Zhou feudal system. He chose not to distribute land among his family and supporters, as Zhou kings had done in the past. The Qin king knew that the wealthy nobles were often the first to rebel, and he wanted to prevent this. Instead, he destroyed the power of the nobles by giving away their land to the peasant farmers who, in turn, became taxpayers. The nobles of the former ruling class were then forced to move to new homes in the capital, Xianyang (SYEN-YONG). There the actions of these people could be watched more easily.

The country was then divided into thirty-six provinces, each governed by a governor, a military commander, and other officials who answered directly to the king. All subjects except soldiers were ordered to turn over their weapons to the government. Arms were melted down and recast into bells and statues.

Unification of the Empire

Since he now ruled not a small kingdom but a large empire, the Qin ruler took a new name and title, Shihuangdi (SHUR-HWOHNG-DEE), the First Emperor. He moved swiftly and ruthlessly to fulfill his two main goals. The emperor wanted to strengthen his rule and to unify his empire both physically and politically. He ordered roads, bridges, and canals to be built to improve communication and transportation. Five main roads fanned out from the capital. The government even dictated the width of cart and wagon axles so the wheels of all vehicles would fit the ruts in the new royal roads. Along these roads were stations where government messengers and officials could rest and change horses. The emperor did even more to unify his land. He insisted that everyone use the same system of weights and measures, form of currency, and a standard form of written Chinese. A single code of laws replaced local laws.

In carrying out his plans, Shihuangdi followed a philosophy called **Legalism.** Like Confucianism and Taoism, this system of ideas also began in the Age of Warring States when the Zhou Dynasty was breaking up. Previous governments had been based on custom and local rule. Legalists, however, believed that a more stable society could be achieved through clearly stated laws and a strong central government. The ruler was to have absolute power. The most important job of government, Legalists believed, was to ensure order and provide safety against foreign enemies. The Legalists had a very low opinion of human nature, and believed that people were basically selfish and corrupt. Rulers, therefore, enforced laws with rewards for compliance and stern punishments for disobedience. Under Legalism, the main duty of the people was to obey the laws without question.

Besides working for the government, Legalists considered only farming and warfare to be worthwhile professions. An ideal citizen, they believed, was a farmer in peacetime and a loyal soldier at times of war. They looked down on anyone who worked in trade or in the arts. They believed most scholarship and learning to be of little value.

In the name of unity, Shihuangdi tried to control people's ideas and to discourage others from expressing differing points of view. He ordered the burning of all books except those approved by the Legalists and those on medicine and farming. No historical records except those referring to Qin history were to be spared. When many scholars objected to his projects, the First Emperor ordered that 460 of them be executed and all their books destroyed. Some scholars immediately began to memorize entire books, notably the works of Confucius, so that these ideas could be preserved for future generations.

Historians view the First Emperor as China's first absolute **dictator.** A dictator is a ruler with unlimited power. However, despite his ruthless drive for power, the First Emperor left three positive, lasting achievements. First, he unified China and established a strong central government. Second, he built for himself one of the most elaborate tombs in history. In it a remarkable life-sized army of some 8,000 terra cotta soldiers stood guard. Each face on the pottery soldiers is different, and offers a vivid portrait of the people of ancient China. The bronze weapons, wooden and bronze chariots, and pottery statues found in the tomb are providing much new information on how Chinese people lived more than two thousand years ago. The emperor's third, and perhaps greatest,

An archaeologist catalogs the life-sized pottery army found in Shihuangdi's tomb. Why do you think this 1974 discovery is considered one of the greatest of all time?

Built to keep invaders out, the Great Wall also posed problems for Chinese governments. What difficulties would maintaining and patrolling the wall present?

It crosses mountains, ravines, and gullies. Built of brick over stone foundations, the wall linked hundreds of watchtowers along the northern frontier. From the towers and the road along the top of the Great Wall, soldiers watched for invaders.

The wall served other purposes in addition to defense. Chinese soldiers who were unhappy with the government were stationed at the frontier. This kept them out of the mainstream of Chinese life. The emperor also kept the army busy, because he knew that soldiers were often used to attempt the overthrow of a dynasty.

The Qin Dynasty drafted men not only for the army, but for other types of service. Tens of thousands were needed to build roads, bridges, canals, and the Great Wall. Often these projects took farmers far from their home villages. This forced labor eventually led to resentment and finally to widespread revolts. Although the empire ended with his death, the centralized government system Shihuangdi created took deep root in China.

achievement was the construction of the **Great Wall of China.**

The Great Wall of China

Shihuangdi realized that his empire could not survive unless China was protected from its northern enemies. Nomadic tribes who roamed the cold, dry plains in northern China constantly raided the rich lands of the south. Since they did not live in settled communities, the nomads could not be easily conquered. When attacked and driven off, they simply regrouped elsewhere, soon to reappear.

Earlier Chinese kings had built walls and watchtowers to keep out the mounted nomads. The First Emperor decided to connect these walls and towers in order to form an uninterrupted barrier against the nomad raiders. Work on the Great Wall of China started in 214 B.C. Thousands of peasants and prisoners were forced to work on the wall for the ten years it took to complete. So many people worked on the Great Wall that for the first time in China surnames, or family names, were used to identify people.

The wall eventually extended across some 1,400 miles (2,240 kilometers) of northern China.

SECTION REVIEW

1. Mapping: Use the map on page 83 to describe the extent of the Qin Dynasty.
2. In your own words, briefly define and identify: Qin Dynasty, the First Emperor, dictator, Legalism, the Great Wall of China.
3. Describe the steps the First Emperor took to unify the country.
4. Explain the main ideas of Legalism.
■ Explain why clothing, hairstyles, shoes, weapons, and other details of figures in the pottery army at the First Emperor's tomb might tell how civilians in early China lived.

EXPANDING CHINESE CIVILIZATION

In the centuries after the Qin Dynasty, the Chinese developed one of their most stable civilizations. Although governments changed, the basic pattern of Chinese life remained almost the same for nearly

2,000 years. Several factors helped to unite the country. Among these were an agricultural economy, an efficient, centralized government headed by the emperor, a standardized form of writing, and the Chinese sense of pride, fostered by their many achievements.

The Han Dynasty

When Shihuangdi died in 210 B.C., many generals fought for power. The victor, Liu Bang (LYOH-BONG), founded a new dynasty that was named the **Han** (HAHN), in honor of a major tributary of the Yangtze River. Unlike the aristocratic rulers of the earlier dynasties, Liu Bang was a man of humble origins. He never pretended to be a noble, and he maintained close contact with ordinary people.

He ended the harsh laws of the Qin and lowered taxes. Liu Bang kept the strong central government of the Qin Dynasty, but revived the concept of awarding land to members of his royal family. So lasting was the influence of his dynasty that even today many Asians call the Chinese the "people of Han."

The Han ruled China, with one brief interruption, from 202 B.C. until 220 A.D. During its 400-year reign the Han Dynasty expanded its rule by conquering new territories, including parts of Korea, Manchuria, and Turkestan. The Han eventually controlled an empire of about 70 million people. It was as large, as wealthy, and as powerful as any empire in the ancient world. In size, the empire was almost the equivalent of modern China.

HAN EMPIRE

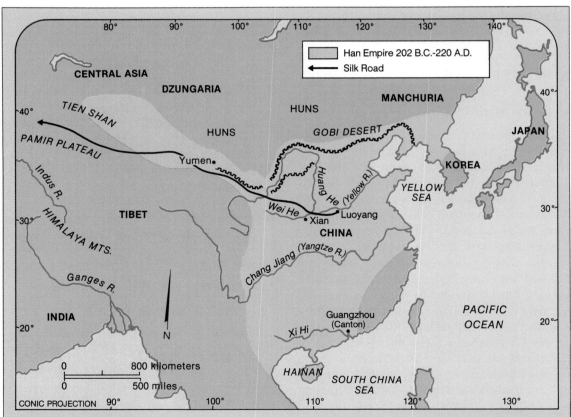

During the Han Dynasty what group of people were a threat to China's northern border? In which direction was the Great Wall extended to help meet this threat?

A great number of salaried officials were hired to help the Han emperor rule the empire. These officials made up the efficient **bureaucracy** (byooh-ROK-ruh-see), or civil service, of this centralized government. The bureaucracy became so large that there was one government official for every 500 Chinese people. These officials were given special privileges. For example, they paid no taxes and, if convicted of crimes, they received milder punishments than other citizens.

Three main classes of citizens evolved. The largest group was made up of poor, tax-paying farmers and peasants. The second largest group was composed of wealthy landowners, including feudal nobles, a large royal family, and a royal court. On the bottom of Chinese society were the slaves, often prisoners of war or criminals. This social structure was different from the class and caste systems of early India where an individual was born, lived, and died in the same class. In theory, the social position of a Chinese person during the Han period could change. For example, a rich political leader could be overthrown and enslaved. Conversely, a peasant might perhaps become a leader, as Liu Bang had done.

Han emperors were the first to make government jobs competitive, and required men who wanted these positions to take tests. To pass these civil service tests, a person had to have great knowledge of Confucian ideas and of Chinese history. Later dynasties made such tests mandatory for anyone wishing to enter government service.

In theory any male could join the bureaucracy, but most government officials were rich landowners or members of the nobility. Few others had enough leisure time to devote to studying for the local, provincial, and national examinations required of aspiring government servants.

The Economy of Han China

Farming continued to be the basis of the Chinese economy. The government built more canals to increase irrigation and to transport crops to market. Usually each farmer was required to devote at least one month's time per year to work on roads, canals, palaces, and imperial tombs. Since the majority of Chinese were farmers, this provided an enormous labor pool to work on public projects.

The greatest of the Han emperors, Wudi (WOO-DEE), imposed strict government control over the economy. During his rule from 140 B.C. to 87 B.C., he claimed many of the country's natural resources as government property. Only the government was permitted to produce salt and iron. Like many emperors before him, Wudi also wanted to reduce the power of rich merchants and to unite the country under his control. He set up a national system of transport and exchange in which government workers controlled all transportation. He also opened warehouses to store crops and goods. The emperor ordered these warehouses to buy and store goods when prices were low. When prices went up, goods were sold at a lower-than-market rate. This served two main purposes. First, it was an attempt to control the prices of goods in demand by increasing their supply. This helped to keep prices down. This concept of supply and demand is today a basic law of economics. Second, by having the government charge lower prices than the individual merchants, Wudi reduced their profits and their power.

After the government took over the iron industry and opened government warehouses, the merchant class began to decline. Wudi also reserved many luxuries for the nobles, which were not given to the merchants. For example, merchants were not permitted to wear silk or ride in carriages. Prejudice against the merchants helped keep China a predominantly agricultural society. However, some merchants and iron manufacturers in the early Han empire did manage to make fortunes or win highly-prized government jobs for their sons. Because most Han rulers were still afraid that the merchants would gain too much power, members of merchant families were not usually allowed to work for the government.

Meanwhile, Chinese artisans created goods of great value and beauty including silk, metals, and pottery. The manufacture of silk was a closely guarded secret. People in distant lands would pay enormous prices for beautiful Chinese silks, which were in great demand. Chinese pottery reached new levels of elegance. Objects of bronze, jade, and lacquered wood were highly prized in the Middle East and Europe. Maps and other drawings on silk scrolls combined calligraphy with the fine art of drawing. These new maps reflected a world much larger than the Chinese had ever imagined.

During the prosperity of the Han Dynasty, granaries like the one shown in this model were often full.

Advances Under the Han

The stability of the Han Dynasty made advances in science, education, and the arts possible. An imperial university was founded in the first century B.C. to train people for government service. During this time the Chinese invented a way to make paper, which then replaced wood and bamboo as the primary material on which to keep written records. Scholars recorded whatever they could find or recall of Confucius and other philosophers. Many scholars also wrote poetry, and others wrote books on medicine, especially on the healing powers of herbs. The first general history of China was written around this time. It contained valuable information about the economy and social conditions, as well as about kings and wars, during the Han Dynasty.

Expanding the Empire

Han armies enlarged the empire by conquering tropical lands south of China, including parts of present-day Korea and Vietnam. However, the most important wars were fought along the northern borders. Army after army was sent to fight the Turkish-speaking nomads known as the **Huns.** Mounted on fast horses, the Huns struck, raided, and vanished. Chinese armies suffered terrible losses but, encouraged by the Huns' temporary retreats, they continued their attacks.

Finally, in 119 B.C., Wudi's armies pushed the Huns to the Gobi Desert. By 52 B.C. about half the Hun tribes had submitted to Chinese rule. Some who did not accept Chinese rule moved to the Near East and Europe.

The long struggle against the Huns brought vast territories into the Chinese empire and opened new trade routes to the west. The Great Wall was extended further westward to Yumen (YOO-MEN), and thousands of Chinese colonists were sent to settle the frontiers in Manchuria and Turkestan.

It was in the wars against the Huns that the Chinese learned of other civilizations to the west. In 139 B.C. Wudi sent an official named Chang Jian to Central Asia to gain allies against the Huns. Hostile tribes imprisoned him for several years, during which time he learned their customs.

On a second trip, Chang Jian made a treaty with a nomadic tribe in Turkestan. This treaty helped create the **Silk Road,** the name given to the route caravans and traders followed between China, the Near East, and Europe. It led form the Han capital of Luoyang to the Mediterranean Sea.

Chinese silks and other luxuries reached the Roman Empire via the 4,000-mile (6,400 kilometer) long Silk Road. However, such goods must have changed hands between traders many times along the way. There is no record of any Roman having visited China, or any Chinese having been to Rome, during the time when these were the two most powerful empires. Goods were also transported to and from India by both land and sea routes.

The Chinese were introduced to new foods including sesame and caraway oil, walnuts, and cucumbers from the people they traded with or conquered. They learned to plant clover and alfalfa, and to grow grapes for wine. They paid high prices to purchase horses from Central Asia, and then began to breed herds of their own. From Persia came fine carpets for Chinese palaces.

In addition to consumer goods, the spread of

Buddhism was one of the most important results arising from the increase in trade and travel between China and other lands. Monks from India entered China from the west to teach the doctrines of Buddhism. Acceptance of this new religion was slow at first, due to the apparent contradiction between some Chinese and Buddhist philosophies. For example, Buddhist monks would leave their friends and relatives behind in order to spread their teachings. The Chinese concept of family unity taught that families should not be kept apart. Despite these and other differences, Buddhism attracted many Chinese and continued to spread eastward into other parts of Asia.

Centuries of Unrest

As the Han territories expanded, the cost of governing the empire increased. The government raised taxes to cover the higher costs, and most of the tax burden fell on the peasants. Eventually the strain became so great that some of the peasants rebelled. Imperial armies crushed the revolts, which further contributed to the rising costs of government.

In 8 A.D. the Han Dynasty was overthrown for a short time by a reformer named Wang Mang. His main contributions were to end slavery and to break up the feudal estates. However, by 25 A.D. the Han successfully regained control of the empire, and their rule continued until 220 A.D.

Later Han rulers never regained the power of the earlier emperors. Military leaders known as warlords rose to power in the provinces during periods of peasant uprisings. After the revolts had been crushed, the warlords refused to relinquish their power. Meanwhile, Han armies waged almost constant warfare against the Huns.

The end of the Han dynasty in 220 A.D. was followed by three centuries of almost continual civil war, invasion, and unrest. Between 220 A.D. and 586 A.D., six dynasties rose and fell. Invading Huns, Mongolians, Tibetans, and other groups seized parts of northern China. At this time many educated Chinese left their homes and fled to safety in southern China.

The invading Huns were finally overthrown by Yang Jian (YAHNG-JYEN), a Chinese government official. He reunited northern and southern China and founded the **Sui** (SWAY) **Dynasty** in 589

A.D. He also built the Grand Canal to connect the Yellow River of northern China to the Yangtze River of southern China. The canal provided a transportation link between the agricultural Yangtze River Valley and the highly populated northern region of China.

The success of the Sui Dynasty was short-lived. Unsuccessful attempts to conquer southern Manchuria and northern Korea weakened the government. Attacks in the northwest by Turks further weakened the Sui.

Though Chinese armies and governments were defeated, Chinese culture slowly spread to the invaders. Within a few generations, the children of most of these conquerors wanted to be considered Chinese. Although China accepted many foreigners with different cultures and traditions, Chinese civilization continued to progress.

SECTION REVIEW

1. Mapping: Use the map on page 86 to locate the Silk Road. What major land areas does the Silk Road cross?
2. In your own words, briefly define and identify: Han Dynasty, bureaucracy, the Huns, Wudi, the Silk Road, Sui Dynasty.
3. The Han Dynasty marks the height of China's power, prosperity, and culture. What role did government play in creating an environment in which the empire could flourish?
4. Discuss how wars against invaders helped expand Chinese culture.
■ If you had lived in Han China and knew you could make a great deal of money as a merchant, would you still have chosen that profession? Why or why not?

INDIA'S AGE OF EMPIRES

In India, as in ancient China, invaders often threatened the northern borders. After the Aryans, many other groups also entered India through the mountain passes of the northwest. As they conquered parts of the subcontinent, the newcomers brought new knowledge and ideas to the people of India. They also learned many things from the Indians. Repeated invasions brought a great variety of people, languages, cultures, and religions for early India to absorb. However, unlike China, much of the history of the period remains a mystery for few artifacts and records have survived.

Greek and Persian Influences

In Chapter 1 you read how Persian armies swept through Mesopotamia. In 531 B.C. Cyrus the Great of Persia led an army eastward through the Hindu Kush Mountains into northwest India. A few years later another Persian ruler, Darius, extended Persian rule into the Indus Valley. Northwest India then became a province of the Persian Empire. During the two centuries that Persia ruled this region, the people of the northwest borrowed many ideas from the well-educated Persians. Persian art and architecture had a strong influence on northwest India, the area of modern Pakistan.

Persian rule was brought to an end, not by Indians but by an invading army of Greeks. Their leader was an outstanding general, Alexander the Great, who conquered much of the Middle East. In 326 B.C. Alexander reached the Indus River, where his troops defeated both Persian and Indian forces. However, Alexander had no idea how large the Indian subcontinent was. When he tried to extend Greek rule further southeast he was defeated by India's geography. His exhausted army had difficulty crossing rivers and fighting local kings, and his soldiers wanted to return home. Finally, Alexander was forced to retreat.

More than a century later, around 200 B.C., the Greek kingdom of Bactria (BACK-tree-uh), was founded on India's northwest border. Bactrian Greeks influenced India by introducing new forms of medicine, science, drama, and art. Within the kingdom, Greek and Indian languages and cultures intermingled. However, between the time Alexander retreated and the kingdom of Bactria was founded, a major Indian empire emerged.

The Maurya Empire

Chandragupta Maurya (chun-druh-GOOHP-tuh MOW-ree-uh) was an Indian noble who studied Greek military tactics. His armies quickly replaced Alexander's in India, drove out the remaining Greeks, and defeated the small kingdoms in the north. By about 322 B.C. he controlled enough of northern India to found his own dynasty. The **Maurya Empire** lasted for almost 150 years.

The government of the Maurya Empire did much to unite, as well as control and protect, the empire it had established. A uniform tax system was created. Roads and irrigation canals were built and large areas of forest were cleared. The government took over all mines and major industries, such as shipbuilding. Chandragupta kept a huge army of infantry and cavalry, which included war elephants, to defend his empire.

The government of the Maurya Empire was a huge bureaucracy in which no one, not even the emperor himself, could be trusted. A book called the *Arthashastra,* which was probably written in part by Chandragupta's prime minister, provides a commentary on how government should be run. It not only recommends the use of spies and of lies when necessary, but also urges strong rulers to attack weak neighbors. The *Arthashastra* also recommends that government officials be watched constantly, perform only very specific tasks, and do nothing without the approval of their superiors.

The Philosopher-King

The greatest ruler of the Maurya Dynasty was Chandragupta's grandson, King Ashoka, (uh-SHOKE-uh). His reign lasted from 270 B.C. to 232 B.C., a period of almost forty years. Historians know more about Ashoka's rule than about most other early Indian rulers. Inscriptions found on stones and pillars from this period have provided detailed information about his reign.

King Ashoka provided his subjects with a just and efficient government. He sent officials throughout the empire to determine the needs of his people. Ashoka was responsible for having some of the first public hospitals and rest houses built. He also ordered wells to be dug, and trees to be planted along major roads.

In the first eight years of his rule, Ashoka launched a series of savage wars in order to further extend his empire. These victories brought all but the southern tip of India under his rule. For the first time, nearly all the huge subcontinent was ruled by a single government.

MAURYA AND KUSHAN EMPIRES

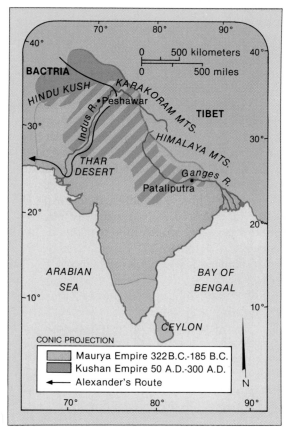

How were the invasion routes of Alexander the Great and the Kushans the same? How were they different?

Ashoka then apparently grew sick of war and became a devout Buddhist who preached nonviolence. He did all he could to help Buddhism spread throughout India. He had hundreds of monasteries built and he also sent missionaries to carry the message of Buddhism to foreign lands. Two of these missionaries were his own son and daughter. Ashoka tried to set an example for his people by governing according to Buddhist principles. He stopped hunting animals or eating meat for fear of violating his Buddhist beliefs. He also encouraged religious tolerance by declaring that all religious beliefs in his empire should be treated with equal respect.

In 250 B.C., at Ashoka's urging, important Buddhist monks met to gather the most holy writings of Buddhism. However, that collection did not appear in written form until around 80 B.C. Until then, each generation had to pass on the knowledge orally to the next generation.

The government Ashoka established did not survive long after his death. When the last Mauryan ruler was assassinated about 185 B.C., India again split into many rival kingdoms.

Invasions and Civil Wars

For nearly 500 years, kings quarreled with each other, foreigners invaded, and much of India suffered chaos and violence. Greek armies from Bactria raided far into India, and Greek influence again became strong in northwestern India. Then the Scythians from Persia raided Bactria and eventually drove out the Greeks.

Other groups of warlike nomads entered India because they had been driven out of their Asian homelands by the Huns. As you recall, the Qin and Han dynasties of China sent strong armies to defend their borders against Hun invaders. Unable to enter China, large groups of Huns had turned westward. They forced other nomadic peoples from their homelands, and some of these groups moved into India.

By 50 A.D. one group of invaders, the **Kushans** (kuh-SHANZ), had pushed into northwest India and seized most of the Greek-held territory. They destroyed Greek cities and most traces of Greek culture. The Kushans eventually controlled a vast area mostly north and west of the Indian subcontinent. In this region, people of many cultures mingled. Among them were Greeks, Persians, Indians, Romans, Arabs, and various nomadic tribal groups. In the Kushan Empire, traders from Europe and the Middle East exchanged goods with Asian merchants traveling the Silk Road from China.

The Kushans encouraged developments in Indian art and science. They adopted Buddhism, the religion of their subjects. The greatest Kushan ruler, Kanishka (kuh-NISH-kuh), came to power about 100 A.D. He established his capital at Peshawar (puh-SHAH-wuhr), in present-day Pakistan.

Kanishka called together a council of Buddhist monks for the purpose of setting forth the doctrines of Mahayana, one of the two major branches of Buddhism. Mahayana then spread eastward, following trade routes to Tibet, China, and later to Korea and Japan.

People in History

Foreign Travelers to Early India

Though India's empires never rivaled those of Rome or China in political power, Indian culture had an enormous influence over the lands of Asia and the Middle East. Accounts written by travelers from other lands offer valuable information about early India. Since the early Indians themselves did not keep written records of their economic and social history, much of what historians know comes from the accounts of foreign visitors.

One of these travelers was a Chinese Buddhist monk named Faxian (FAH-SYEN). He left his home in the Yellow River region of China, crossed deserts and mountains to present-day Afghanistan, and then reached the Indus River. He traveled along the Ganges River Valley before making his way to present-day Sri Lanka and finally returning home to China.

Faxian was in India from 399 A.D. to 405 A.D. He went there to study Buddhist writings, but he was also interested in other aspects of Indian life. He made notes describing the landscape, climate, and the way people lived. For instance, he noted that most people were vegetarians, and that laws were much less harsh in India than in China. He was amazed at the number and size of the great Indian cities, and was impressed by the free hospitals. He noted, too, the religious tolerance of Indian society.

Another Chinese Buddhist monk, Xuanzang (SEE-WAHN-DZONG) made the lengthy round trip voyage from China to India in the years 629 A.D. to 645 A.D. His observations of Indian life appear in a work called *Record of the Western Regions*.

Still another Chinese pilgrim, I-Ching, followed a southerly route to India and back. In his visit between 671 A.D. and 695 A.D., I-Ching not only recorded his own travel log but compiled the records of more than fifty other Chinese pilgrims in India.

Such journals gave the educated Chinese information about the civilization to the west. They also provide modern scholars with invaluable sources of information about India not recorded by the Indians themselves.

1. How did we learn about early Indians in a period when they themselves were not yet keeping written records?
2. To what profession did many of these early Chinese pilgrims belong? What was the purpose of their voyages?
3. What do the writings of Faxian, Xuanzang, and I-Ching reveal about life in India between the fifth and seventh centuries A.D.?
4. These three Chinese travelers made several observations about life in early India. What advantages do you see in having history recorded from the perspective of outsiders? What is the value of an impartial observation? Can you give any examples in today's society?

The Deccan

While Greeks, Kushans, and others ruled in northern India, the southern region of the Deccan was controlled by several small Indian kingdoms, each warring for power. Rugged terrain, and differences in religion, language, and culture made it extremely difficult to unite the entire southern region under one government.

Although Buddhism was popular in the north, Hinduism was the main religion of the Deccan, especially among the Dravidian peoples in the south. The Dravidians spoke a language called Tamil that was quite different from the languages of the north. However, the religious tolerance and friendly attitudes of most southern rulers toward foreigners made cultural exchanges with peoples of other lands possible.

Most of India's trade left from southern seaports, although the northern Kushans also traded with faraway lands. By the first century A.D. Indian pearls, silks, spices, muslins, and artworks were being traded in markets as far away as Egypt and Rome.

SECTION REVIEW

1. Mapping: Use the maps on pages 91 and 94 to compare the areas ruled by the Maurya, Kushan, and Gupta empires.
2. In your own words, briefly define and identify: Bactria, Maurya Empire, *Arthashastra*, Kushan Empire.
3. What were the main achievements of the Maurya Empire? The Kushan?
- Repeated invasions brought a great variety of people, languages, cultures, and religions to early India. How do you think a country benefits from this infusion of ideas and beliefs?

A GOLDEN AGE OF INDIAN CULTURE

About 320 A.D. northern India was united once again by a royal family, the **Guptas** (GOOHP-tuhz). The Gupta years, from 320 A.D. to 535 A.D., are considered the high point, or "golden age," of Indian civilization. Foreign visitors to India noted that roads were well maintained, taxes were moderate, and there was little crime. Hindus and Buddhists, who shared many beliefs, lived side by side in a spirit of religious tolerance. The separation between castes, however, had become even more rigid and the number of castes and subcastes increased into the thousands.

Gupta emperors presided over a prosperous empire in which knowledge and the arts flourished. India became a center of learning and, under the Guptas, Indian culture reached its highest level of development in ancient times. Indian merchants traded with the entire known civilized world. Therefore, ideas of other countries influenced Indian sciences and the arts. In turn, Indian culture spread throughout eastern Asia.

Trade in Ancient India

Ships from many lands docked regularly in Indian ports. There traders could exchange Asian goods for those of Europe, Africa, and the Middle East. Indian merchants traded with East Africa, the kingdoms of the Persian Gulf, China, and Southeast Asia.

India exported more than it bought from other lands. These goods included ivory, perfumes, spices, diamonds, and other precious gems. Indians may have been the first to produce cotton cloth, cashmere, and chintz, all of which were in great demand. In the first century A.D. the Roman historian Pliny complained that Romans spent too much gold in India each year for jewels, spices, and exotic animals.

Indians imported silk, wine, pottery, porcelain, copper, dates, and glassware from other lands. Many of these goods were transported overland by caravans from the ports to the rest of India, or to more distant parts of Asia. Asian merchants often bought and then resold goods to European and Middle Eastern dealers.

By the end of the Gupta Empire, Indian sailors were probably the most advanced in the world. They sailed all over the eastern and western parts of the Indian Ocean and Arabian Sea, helping to spread Indian culture to other lands. They also brought back many ideas from the lands they visited, and this influenced the development of culture within India itself.

Literature and Drama

During the Gupta Age, Indians for the first time began to write down their literature. As a result, a whole class of scribes developed. India's two great epic poems, the *Mahabharata* and the *Ramayana,* were recorded during this period. Many Indian stories, especially fables and fairy tales, were also written at this time. They then became popular in other parts of the world. The story of Sinbad the Sailor, for instance, originated in India.

Sanskrit had become the most common written language of northern India. Sacred poetry, scientific information, biographies, dramas and plays were written in Sanskrit. In dramas of the period, narratives, conversations, songs, and dances were all included as part of the performance. Romantic love was the main theme, and the dramas always had a happy ending. Kalidasa, one of fifth-century India's greatest playwrights and poets, was influenced by the past and the present. In his writings he combined ancient legends with the new theme of romantic love to produce some of the finest examples of Indian poetry and drama.

Art and Architecture

After 100 A.D. many Indians began to move into southeast Asia. As a result, Indian art influenced the rest of Asia. The temples of Cambodia, Burma, and Indonesia (in-duh-NEE-zhuh) reflect Indian architectural styles.

Particularly Indian was the **stupa** (STOO-puh), a large mound of earth, covered by brick and surrounded by a fence with elaborate stone gates. Originally, a stupa was a shrine or holy place. Some stupas marked the birthplace of a spiritual leader. As Buddhism spread to other parts of Asia, so did the building of stupas. The Chinese imitated the Indian stupa and modified it into the type of building known as the **pagoda** (puh-GOE-duh).

Some of the best Gupta art can be seen in **fresco** (FRES-koh) paintings. A fresco painting is done by pressing colors dissolved in water into fresh plaster. These paintings appear on temple walls and in Buddhist monasteries and caves not only in India, but also in China and other parts of Asia. Some of the best preserved examples of Gupta sculpture and paintings are at the cave temples of Ajanta in central India. A common subject of Indian sculptors was the Buddha, who was often portrayed as a graceful figure. Some of the statues of the Buddha show Greek influences, in that they resemble statues of the Greek god Apollo.

Science and Education

A thriving economy, plus constant contact with other civilizations, sparked major advances in knowledge. Indian scholars made lasting contributions to science and mathematics. Indians invented the concept of the zero, an idea that quickly spread

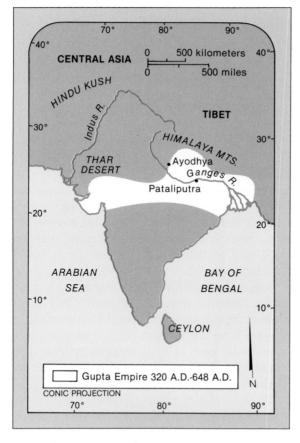

GUPTA EMPIRE

How did the extension of the Gupta Empire from coast to coast assist the Gupta's trade empire?

elsewhere. The Arabic numbers one through nine and the decimal system we use today actually began in India around the sixth century A.D. Indian mathematicians also knew how to calculate square and cube roots.

Indian scientists accurately predicted eclipses, identified the seven planets that can be seen without a telescope, and worked on developing the theory of gravity. Indian doctors made major advances in medical science. India had hospitals, something unknown in most of the world. Physicians also listed specific remedies for illnesses and performed delicate operations, including bonesetting and plastic surgery. They also kept extensive records of their research on the human body.

Behind these advances in knowledge was a strong respect for education. Only the children of the upper classes were formally educated; other young people learned crafts and trades from their parents. Ancient India had several important centers of higher learning, and their universities attracted scholars from all over Asia and the Middle East. Many students received government scholarships to study religion, philosophy, science, medicine, art, architecture, and farming.

Foremost among the scholars of the age were members of the Brahman caste and the Buddhist monks. Monks founded libraries and universities unparalleled in western Europe for almost one thousand years. The most famous early Indian University was at Nalanda (NA-land-ah) in the Ganges River Valley. Gupta rulers provided almost all funds for the school. By the late sixth century this university had more than 5,000 students, some from as far away as Korea, China, and Tibet.

The Decline of the Empire

Around 535 A.D. the Gupta Empire began to weaken. Not only were the kingdoms of central and southern India enemies of the Gupta, but invaders threatened from both the north and the south. Seemingly endless numbers of Huns attacked the northern borders of the empire. Although the Gupta armies held the invaders at bay, they were severely weakened by the struggle. By the sixth century A.D., Gupta power was broken and the Huns established their own empire in

The great stupa of Sanchi features elaborate carvings on its gate that depict events in the life of Buddha.

northern India. Indian culture was to enjoy a rebirth when a new, well-organized government reappeared in 606 A.D.

SECTION REVIEW

1. In your own words briefly define and identify: Gupta Empire, stupa, pagoda, fresco.
2. List the contributions made to science, mathematics, and the arts during the Gupta Empire.
3. How did Indian art and architecture influence the rest of Asia?
4. What role did the seaports of ancient India play in spreading culture from India to other lands?
■ Many social and economic advances are made under stable governments, like that of the Gupta. What social and economic accomplishments recently have been made under present-day governments?

Reviewing the Chapter

Chapter Summary

The civilizations of ancient China and India continued to expand and grow from the third century B.C. to the seventh century A.D. In this period, the Qin and Han dynasties for the first time united ancient China under strong central governments. At this same time India was brought together under the Mauryas and, later, the Guptas.

To keep out invaders, the First Emperor of China built a huge wall, known as the Great Wall of China, across the entire northern frontier. At times the invaders succeeded in breaking through, but within a few generations they had usually adopted Chinese language and culture. The Qin Dynasty unified China politically, by creating a strong central government; physically, by building government roads and bridges; and culturally, by standardizing writing.

Under the Han, Chinese civilization spread to southern China, Korea, and Vietnam. The Han Empire was as large and powerful as any in the ancient world. Their rulers preserved political unity, opened trade routes to the Middle East, introduced Buddhism to China, and expanded the empire.

Repeatedly invaded from the north, India absorbed many different peoples and cultures, many of whom kept their own customs. India was united under its first and largest empire, the Maurya. Industry, transportation, and communication were all improved. The Emperor Ashoka helped spread Buddhism to other lands. After 500 years of civil war and invasions, northern India was again united under the Guptas. Under the Gupta Empire trade increased and Indian culture spread to other lands. Indians made great advances in literature, the arts, the sciences, and education.

1. What was the main accomplishment of the Qin and Han dynasties?
2. How did the First Emperor of China unite his country politically, physically, and culturally?
3. How were the achievements of India's first empire similar to those of the Qin and Han dynasties?
4. What were some of the improvements made in India under the Gupta Empire?

Using Your Vocabulary

1. In your own words, describe the bureaucracy of Qin and Han China.
2. Define Legalism. How did this philosophy influence Shihuangdi?
3. In your own words, explain why the First Emperor of China was considered a dictator.
4. What was the Silk Road? Why was it important to China's economic expansion?
5. In your own words, define stupa and pagoda, then explain their relationship.
6. What is a fresco? How is it created?

Developing Your Geography Skills

1. Use the maps in the chapter to list and describe the extent of the Qin and Han dynasties in classical China and the Maurya, Kushan, and Gupta empires in India.
2. Use the map on page 86 to locate the extent of the Great Wall of China and the Silk Road.
3. Use the map on page 91 to trace the route of Alexander the Great through India.
4. Use the Atlas map of the Far East on page 755 to explain why, in ancient times, India's seagoing contacts with southeastern Asia might have been greater than with China.

Recalling the Facts

1. List at least three measures that were taken by the Qin King in developing a new system of central government.
2. Why is a dynasty as short-lived as the Qin considered so important to Chinese history?

3. What was the Great Wall of China? For what purposes was it built?
4. Who was Liu Bang? What changes did he make in the centralized government of China?
5. Describe how a person might get a government job in Han China.
6. In what ways did the Emperor Wudi control the Chinese economy? For what purpose?
7. Explain how silk helped create a trade route between India and China.
8. List some Greek and Persian influences on ancient India.
9. In what ways did Mauryan rulers control the economy of India?
10. What was the *Arthashastra*? How does it influence our opinion of the government of the Maurya Empire?
11. Why is Ashoka one of the most popular rulers of Indian history?
12. In what part of India did the Kushans establish themselves? What group of people did they overcome in this region?
13. Describe how Buddhism spread to other lands.
14. List the main imports and exports of Gupta India during the Gupta Empire.
15. Why is the Gupta period in Indian history called India's "golden age"?

Essay Questions

1. Compare and contrast life in China during the Han Dynasty with life in India under the Guptas.
2. Describe the role trade played in developing and spreading culture in classical China and India. Use specific examples to document your description.
3. Compare and contrast how early China absorbed newcomers with the way ancient India absorbed new people and ideas.
4. Imagine you are a Chinese merchant who has just arrived in India during the Kushan Empire. What might your first impressions of India be? How do these impressions compare with what you know of life in China?
5. Explain how the Huns influenced the history of both India and China. Include as many dates

and facts as you can.
6. In your own words, describe your impression of a busy Indian seaport during the Gupta Empire. Mention what foreigners you might meet and what goods are traded.

Critical Thinking

Determining Warranted and Unwarranted Claims

Another very important part of the Critical Thinking process involves **determining warranted and unwarranted claims.** A warranted claim is one that can be justified because there is evidence or proof to support its accuracy, quality, or condition. An unwarranted claim, on the other hand, cannot be substantiated by proof. Keep these definitions in mind as you answer the following questions.

1. The First Emperor, Shihuangdi, was a ruthless leader whose main goals were to unify the empire and gain power. He was therefore considered a dictator. Based on the information in the chapter, is this claim warranted or unwarranted. Why?
2. Reread the definition of Legalism on page 84. Legalists had a low opinion of human nature, and created laws to ensure that people did as required. Do you think the claims of the Legalists to be warranted or unwarranted? Why?
3. The Gupta Empire is known as India's "golden age." Would you consider this claim to be warranted? Why or why not?
4. Many people feel that in order to have an objective opinion, data has to be collected by unbiased observers. Much of what we know about early India is through the eyes of foreign observers, such as the Buddhist monks that traveled from their Chinese homeland to India. Is their claim of impartiality warranted? What evidence supports your opinion?
5. The news reporters in the media, through whose eyes we learn about the world today, also attempt to be objective observers. Is this possible? What measures should a reporter take to eliminate bias from the reports he or she presents? What methods can a reader or viewer of the reports use to detect bias?

CHAPTER 5

The WORLD of ANCIENT GREECE

3000 B.C.–133 B.C.

Objectives

- To describe the early cultures of Crete and Mycenae and explain how they affected the culture of classical Greece

- To compare and contrast the governments of Sparta and Athens and life in these two city-states

- To describe the major political, social, and economic developments that occurred during the fifth century B.C. called the Classical Age of Greece

- To explain how the spread of classical Greek culture during the Hellenistic Age influenced the future development of western civilization

*A*lthough many of the great ancient cultures originated in the Middle East and Far East, other important cultures developed further to the west. Our modern western culture is most directly descended from the great civilizations of Greece and Rome. Do you realize that you use Greek words every day? Many English words—democracy, geography, drama, and philosophy, to name a few—are derived from ancient Greek words. Many of our public buildings, particularly courthouses, libraries, and schools, are built following Greek architectural designs. Modern science, philosophy, literature, and even some sports trace their roots to ancient Greek life and thought.

This chapter is devoted to exploring the world of ancient Greece. You will learn how culture first blossomed on the island of Crete and on the Greek peninsula, and how it grew to its classical form in the fifth century B.C. You will read about the development of the Greek city-state, or polis, and the different forms of government used to manage the polis, particularly Athenian democracy. The impact of the Persian and Peloponnesian wars is discussed, as is the establishment of the empire of Alexander the Great. Then you will survey the greatest contributions of Greek culture and trace how that culture spread across much of the ancient world. Lastly, you will learn how Hellenistic culture emerged from a mixing of classical Greek and Eastern influences.

EARLY GREEK CIVILIZATION

Ancient Greece was not a unified territory but rather a group of scattered islands, rugged peninsulas, small plains, and extended shorelines. Greece was divided into many small regions, each having its own strong local traditions. Geography, therefore, played a major role in developing the independent spirit of local people and local government that characterized ancient Greece.

Unlike the early river civilizations we have studied, Greece has no great rivers. It is a peninsula of mountainous land surrounded on three sides by the sea. The Greek mainland is almost cut in two by the Gulf of Corinth. The southern area is called the Peloponnesus (pehl-uh-puh-NEE-suhs) and resembles a four-fingered hand reaching into the sea toward the island of Crete (KREET). The many islands east of Greece as well as the western coast of modern Turkey, called Ionia (i-OH-nee-a), were also part of the ancient Greek world. Greek settlers colonized Ionia and the islands nearby very early in their history, making these lands in the Aegean Sea basin almost entirely Greek.

The small fertile valleys on the Greek mainland are surrounded by mountains that isolated the towns from their neighbors. This encouraged the development of many small, independent city-states and hindered the formation of a unified nation. The limited amount of farmland forced the

ANCIENT GREECE

Greek colonies were established throughout the Aegean and Mediterranean seas. What geographical factors motivated Greek interest in trade and colonization?

Greeks, like the Phoenicians, to look to the sea for much of their livelihood. The sea, because the rugged mountains made land travel difficult, also provided the easiest means of communication. The coastline had many good harbors, and the islands made excellent landmarks—both important elements of navigation before the discovery of the compass. Yet sudden storms still made seafaring dangerous and few ships went to sea during the stormy winter months from November to March. During the summer a northwest wind kept the skies clear, the seas calm, and sea travel safe.

The majority of rain in Greece falls in the winter, so the crop cycle was to plant in the autumn and harvest in the spring.

With the exception of deposits of gold in the north, and lead and silver along the eastern seaboard, Greece had poor mineral resources and no natural supplies of iron, copper, or tin.

Minoan Crete

One of the most important early cultures was that of the Minoans (muh-NOE-unz) on the island of Crete. Historians do not know what the ancient people of Crete were actually called. According to legends, one of their great kings was Minos (MIE-nus), so archaeologists have given them the name Minoans. We have no written histories from the period of the Minoans. All we know about these interesting and highly skilled people has come from the work of archaeologists. By examining the archaeological remains that have been found, scholars have learned that people were living on the island of Crete by 6000 B.C.

The settlers on Crete prospered. They built large houses and kept oxen, sheep, pigs, and chickens. They also grew olives, grain, and grapes. The Minoans made tools and weapons of copper and bronze and founded trading colonies on several neighboring islands to help them acquire supplies of metal ore. By 2000 B.C. ships from Crete were trading with the Egyptians and the peoples of the east coast of the Mediterranean. Crete, lying between the Greek mainland and Egypt and close to the lands of the ancient Middle East, was strategically located as a trading center. A large, powerful navy protected Crete and its colonies.

The Minoans were famous for their arts and crafts, especially their paintings, carved gems, met-alwork, and pottery. Fine Minoan pottery was not only popular locally but was an important item for trade throughout the Mediterranean world.

The Minoans built several cities on the island of Crete, but the grandest was Knossos (NAHSS-us). At first this city was believed to be just part of an old Greek legend about the Minotaur, a monster part-bull and part-human, who lived in a labyrinth—a type of maze. About a century ago the English archaeologist Sir Arthur Evans uncovered ruins of a palace that resembled a labyrinth described in the legend. This palace was a vast maze of halls, storerooms, paved corridors, and great stone stairways—some centered around a large courtyard. It was not built as a fortress but as a government administration center and a place for storing items collected as taxes. Those taxes included olive oil, wine, and grain, all kept in large stone and ceramic jars. The palace complex included a theater, separate houses and work areas, baths and running water, and a sewage system that was still in working order when the archaeologists first found it.

The Minoan Trade Empire

A commercial empire on Crete developed between 2000 B.C. and 1400 B.C. Merchant ships from Crete sailed westward to trade with Italy, while to the north Minoan goods reached as far as Macedonia. Trading by Minoan merchants also extended as far east as Syria and as far south as Egypt. In addition to trade the Minoans also profited from the cultural influences of Syria, Libya, and Egypt. Largely due to Minoan enterprise and skill, Crete became the commercial and cultural crossroads of the eastern Mediterranean.

In Minoan Crete the king controlled most commercial enterprise. The king's factories were the largest and most important and produced excellent pottery, metal goods, and textiles. Small businesses were permitted to exist but their owners were forced to compete with those owned by the king.

Considering its day and age, Minoan society apparently permitted women considerable freedom and equality. They seemed to enjoy the same rights as men and to enter into many public activities and occupations. Minoan paintings show both men and women hunting game from chariots and officiating at religious and court ceremonies. Out-

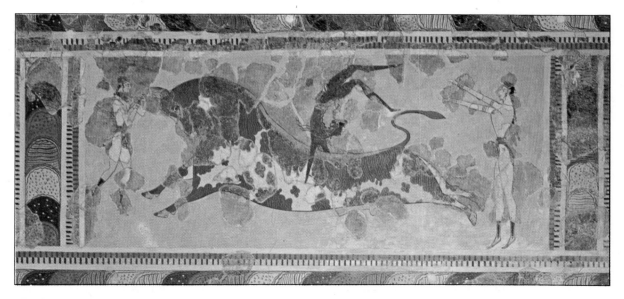

The three athletes in this Minoan wall painting from 1500 B.C are shown participating in the sport of bull vaulting. What skills were needed to perform this sport?

side the court, men and women were depicted working at crafts and trade. Women even joined in the popular ritual of bull-leaping. All this evidence suggests that in Minoan Crete women enjoyed a far higher social status than they did anywhere else in the ancient world.

The Minoans used three forms of writing: an early pictograph form and two others called Linear A and Linear B. While no one has been able to translate or decipher Linear A, Linear B—which was adapted from Linear A—was first decoded in 1952. It was found to be an early form of Greek, indicating the arrival of Greeks on Crete and their gradual takeover of Minoan society. Because of the use of Linear B, historians know that by about 1450 B.C. invaders from mainland Greece were ruling at Knossos. During the years before Knossos' final destruction around 1400 B.C., these Greek invaders, called the Mycenaeans (mie-suh-NEE-unz), adopted many aspects of Minoan culture and passed them on to mainland Greeks.

Mycenaean Greece

By about 2000 B.C.—the time that Minoan culture was flourishing in Crete—the original inhabitants of the Greek mainland had been overrun by Greek-speaking invaders from the north and east.

These invaders were part of a huge Indo-European folk migration that originated in Central Asia. It also brought the Iranians and the Hittites to the Middle East. By about 1600 B.C. a new people called the Achaeans (uh-KEE-unz) had emerged. Their language was that of the invading tribes— Greek—but their culture developed from a mixture of the native and invading peoples, with certain Cretan influences as well.

The Achaeans had the same basic form of government as the Minoans. A king, supported by a court of nobles, ruled the people. Serving the king were many government officials whose main duties included carrying out the daily bureaucratic functions of the government, maintaining and supplying armed forces, and collecting taxes.

The Achaeans, influenced by their geography, were arranged into small fortress-principalities. One, Mycenae (mie-SEE-nee), had achieved a certain preeminence, and it is from this city that the culture of the Achaeans was given its name: Mycenaean. Mycenae was also important because it helped spread Minoan culture to mainland Greece.

The center of each Achaean district, or area, was the fortification where the king resided. The farming villages and fields surrounding the citadel were also under the king's rule. Most Achaeans earned their living from the soil. There were, however, a rich variety of trades as well, including metalworking, weaving, and building. The Achaeans also grew more skilled at seafaring, trading, and warfare. By the 1400's B.C. they had taken over many of the Aegean islands and Crete.

The Dark Age

The people of the eastern Mediterranean were shaken by a wave of invasions around 1200 B.C. Dorian invaders swept down from the north and east, destroying some cultures and altering others. About 1150 B.C. the city of Mycenae was destroyed, along with the other major centers of the Achaeans. Gradually a new culture replaced the old. Since we know so little about this period and since the new culture seems to have been considerably less advanced than that of the Mycenaeans, the period from about 1200 B.C. to 800 B.C. is called the Dark Age.

The Dorians eventually settled in the Peloponnesus, the southern Aegean islands, and southern Asia Minor. Some of the Achaeans were enslaved by the Dorians while others fled to Athens, the islands of the central Aegean, and to Ionia on the central coast of Asia Minor. The latter group came to be known as Ionians.

The Dark Age in Greece was appropriately named. The Greeks withdrew from international commerce, beginning a period of isolation from the other lands of the eastern Mediterranean. The large Mycenaean kingdoms and bureaucracies were replaced by local chieftains who, with their elders, ruled small areas. An **aristocracy,** or ruling class made up of nobles, warriors, and landowners, kept all political power in their own hands. They paid little attention to the landless peasants, artisans, and tradesmen who made up the bulk of the population.

The age was not one of total darkness, however, and as new peoples settled in, changes and improvements began. Among crafts, metalworking, after a period of decline, was spurred on by the introduction of iron. Pottery improved technically and artistically. Though the diverse peoples of this period were often unfriendly to one another, eventually a common culture emerged. Each group spoke a dialect of the same language, and common political and social customs developed. Thus a tradition of independence and rivalry developed between the many small political units of Greece. At the same time, however, a growing cultural similarity caused the people to consider themselves all "Hellenes," or Greeks, and to view other people as barbarians.

The Iliad and the Odyssey

Historians know little about the period when Mycenaean power began to decline. Around 1300 B.C. food shortages for the Mycenaeans had apparently become a serious problem, and the Mycenaeans frequently raided neighboring lands.

The most famous of these raids was on the fortified city of Troy in Asia Minor around 1200 B.C. The myths surrounding the battle for Troy and its aftermath inspired two of the most famous epic poems in world literature. An epic poem tells of the adventures of great heroes, and often expresses a nation's ideals. Although the *Iliad* and the *Odyssey* were composed long after the time they describe, they offer many insights into life in Greek society. Supposedly composed by a blind poet named Homer in the eighth century B.C., the *Iliad* describes a three-day episode of the Trojan War. Ac-

The Trojan War lasted ten years, ending after Troy accepted the Trojan Horse. Soldiers hidden in the wooden horse opened Troy's gates and the Greek army took the city.

cording to the *Iliad* the war was fought between the people of Troy and the Achaeans over the kidnapping of Helen, the wife of the king of Sparta, by Paris, the son of the king of Troy. Homer's tale is concerned with the devastating effects of pride, anger, and jealousy on human society. The poem also provides a model of the aristocratic ideal in its hero, Achilles (uh-KILL-eez).

The *Odyssey* is the story of Odysseus (oe-DISS-yoos), the Achaean king of Ithaca, who spends ten years struggling to return home after the fall of Troy. After many fantastic adventures, including a fight with a one-eyed giant known as a cyclops (SIE-klops), he finally succeeds in returning home. There Odysseus rids his home of the many suitors who were trying to gain his throne by marrying his wife, Penelope.

Over the years, scholars have constantly debated whether there was any historical reality behind Homer's stories and, if so, how accurate he was. In the nineteenth century Heinrich Schliemann (HINE-rick SHLEE-mahn), a retired businessman and noted scholar of languages, admired the *Iliad* so much that he spent the last twenty years of his life trying to prove that its account of the Trojan War was true. He found the site of Troy on the northwest coast of modern-day Turkey, and later excavated, or dug up, a fabulous treasure at the site of ancient Mycenae in Greece. The tombs he discovered there dated back to about 1600 B.C. and contained gold masks, bronze weapons, and other objects similar to the ones described in the *Iliad*. Some descriptions in the stories were further confirmed when Mycenaean writing was deciphered. Clay tablets found at the sites of ancient Mycenaean cities contained lists of clothing, chariots, weapons, and other implements used at the time described in the *Iliad*.

However, Homer relied on the language and customs of his own day when describing people and events in his epic poems. While the poems often describe the everyday existence of the heroes, Homer, in order that his audience would recognize and understand the actions of his characters, actually presents us with a rich view of the Greek society that succeeded the Myceneans. From an historical point of view, Homer's work reveals more to us about Greek society in the eighth century B.C. than that of the thirteenth century B.C.

SECTION REVIEW

1. Mapping: Use the map on page 99 to locate: the Mediterranean, Aegean, and Ionian seas, Crete, Athens, Knossos, and Troy.
2. In your own words, briefly define or identify: the Minoans, the Mycenaeans, the Dorians, the *Iliad*, the *Odyssey*, aristocracy.
3. List the most important achievements of Minoan civilization.
4. Why is the period of Greek history from 1200 B.C. to 800 B.C. called the Dark Age? Did any positive developments occur during this time? Explain.
■ Before being written down, the tales of the *Iliad* and the *Odyssey* were told aloud by storytellers and poets. What kinds of stories do we have about the early heroes of the United States?

GOVERNMENT IN ANCIENT GREECE

By about 800 B.C. the culture formed during the Dark Age reached a new level of development. The population of the Greek world was increasing and the economy needed new room for expansion. These two factors influenced Greece to once again establish a major overseas trading network and to enter a period of renewed colonization, one that encompassed the entire Mediterranean region.

The Greek Polis

The political and social systems that allowed for this new wave of growth centered on the many small city-states that had emerged across Greece. The Greeks called each city-state a **polis** (POE-liss). A polis consisted of a city as well as the agricultural lands surrounding it. Each polis had its own government and all the inhabitants of the territory of the polis were expected to obey its laws and its leaders.

The city was the center of the polis. Its site was selected carefully, usually in a place that had a

Early Greek city-states were ruled by kings. This gold mask was found in a royal tomb in Mycenae. How does it compare with artwork found in Egyptian tombs?

good water supply and that could be defended easily. Some cities were built on rocky hilltops, and such a city was called an acropolis (uh-CROP-uh-liss), or "high city." A section of each polis was surrounded by strong walls behind which the people could take refuge in time of war. Each polis also had an **agora** (AHG-uh-ruh), or marketplace, which served as its economic and social center. Every polis had a patron god or goddess upon whom it relied for protection and prosperity. Places were set aside for worshiping the patron deity as well as other gods. Thus each polis was self-sufficient, having formed an economic and cultural unit quite independent of its neighbors.

By 800 B.C. a combination of landowners (who monopolized agriculture and, therefore, the economy of their times), tribal elders (who, through their knowledge, controlled government and law), and the warrior elite were able to control the polis and establish an aristocracy. Over the next century, however, several things happened to undermine the control of the aristocrats. First, the Phoenician alphabet was introduced as the basis for a new system of writing. As a result, laws could be written down and codified, thus undermining

the position of the tribal elders whose job it was to remember and interpret laws passed down through oral tradition. Second, a new type of warfare in which men fought in a large infantry group, called the **hoplite phalanx** (FAY-lanks), replaced the old heroic fighting style of a warrior elite. The political and social privileges of the warrior elite had been justified in part by their unique position as protectors of the polis. With the advent of the phalanx, the ranks of the army were opened to common citizens as long as they could afford armor. Once they assumed military responsibilities they began to demand political rights, including the right to participate in government.

Sometimes the soldiers of the hoplite phalanx chose or supported a leader who seized control of the polis. Such a leader was called a **tyrant,** and his rule was called a tyranny. The term tyrant referred only to someone who seized absolute power from the previous government. It did not have the same meaning of cruelty and misrule that it was later given. Tyranny served to break aristocratic control of the polis. In many areas of Greece, tyranny was replaced by an **oligarchy** (AHL-uh-gahr-kee), or rule by a limited group of citizens who are thought to be superior because of their wealth or family connections. In other areas there developed a system in which all male citizens could elect their leaders and cast votes on important issues. This system is called a **democracy** and, although the number of citizens could be restricted, it was not a government dominated strictly by those of aristocratic birth or wealth.

The competition for power within each city was paralleled by competition between the various city-states. Each polis wished to have the most beautiful public buildings, the best athletes, and to acquire the most honor. In economic terms, this rivalry is reflected in the great wave of expansion in international trade and colonization that characterized the period.

Trade and Colonization

Though each polis was economically self-sufficient, new prosperity led traders overseas in search of metal ores and luxury goods. A Greek trading city was established in Egypt and another in Libya. Linen, glass, papyrus, and ivory were shipped back to Greece from these areas.

Two new discoveries brought to Greece by traders were of special importance to Greece's international standing. One was the Phoenician alphabet which, as we have read, was quickly adapted by the Greeks in writing their own language. By 650 B.C. it was being used in many variations to write dozens of Greece's local dialects. Since correspondence and recordkeeping are essential to large-scale trade, the alphabet aided Greek prosperity immensely. The second discovery—that of coinage—came from Asia Minor. Until now traders had used the barter system, in which goods and services were exchanged for items of equal value. This could be awkward, because often clumsy hunks of metal were weighed and used for buying goods. About 700 B.C., however, a Lydian king from Asia Minor invented the coin, a small piece of precious metal stamped with the king's seal to ensure its quality and weight. The Greeks soon adopted the use of coinage, and trade shifted from a barter system to a monetary one, in which people used money to pay for the goods and services they needed.

Between 750 B.C. and 550 B.C. the Greeks expanded trade by establishing many new colonies. This was usually done in areas where no strong trading culture previously existed. To begin a colony, a polis would send out a group of its citizens as settlers. They would establish a new, yet independent, polis with an agora, temples, and a constitution modeled after the mother city, or metropolis (muh-TROP-uh-liss). Friendly relations were usually maintained with the new colony. In this way the older city would find room for its excess population and also establish trading contacts in a new area of the Mediterranean. Many cities on the Greek mainland, on the Aegean islands, and in Ionia followed this practice of colonization. By 550 B.C. Greek colonies were established along the Black Sea, the coasts of Sicily and southern Italy, and as far west as the southern coast of France. Although the Greeks were not a unified nation, they were now an economic power that could not be ignored.

Sparta

The two most famous Greek cities of this period, Sparta and Athens, are examples of how different Greek cities could be.

Each Greek city-state had its own coinage and used distinctive designs to celebrate the city's heritage. The above coin is Athenian from the fifth century B.C. and features the owl of Athena, patron deity of the city.

Sparta was located in a valley of the Peloponnesus, about fifteen miles (twenty-five kilometers) from the sea, and was isolated by the surrounding mountains. It was made up of three separate groups of people. The small upper class, descendants of the Dorian conquerors, were called Spartans. They made up about five or ten percent of the population and were the only ones who could be full citizens. From this group—who called themselves peers, or equals—came the rulers, landowners, and soldiers. Most of the rest of the population—the rural laborers or serfs—were called **helots** (HEL-uhts). They were the descendants of the Mycenaean settlers of the region and served as agricultural laborers. Because the Spartans constantly feared a rebellion by the helots, Sparta developed into a strong military state. The third class of people were called *perioikoi* (pair-EE-oi-koy) or "those who dwell around us." This group consisted of other non-Dorian people who lived in and around Sparta and who handled all the economic affairs of the Spartans, including their trade with foreigners. The *perioikoi* were considered citizens and fought in the army but did not have the right to vote.

Government in Sparta

Sparta was ruled by an Assembly, composed of all male Spartan citizens over the age of thirty. The Assembly elected officials and voted on proposed legislation. Voting was done orally and the Assembly was not allowed to debate the issues. A Council of Elders, chosen for life by the Assembly, proposed the laws and policies on which the Assembly voted. The Council of Elders was composed of two kings—whose positions were inherited and who served as army commanders and judges—and twenty-eight other men over the age of sixty.

A balance to the power of the kings and elders was maintained by five **ephors** (EFF-uhrs), or overseers, elected each year by the Assembly. The ephors could reprimand a king, control the helots, conduct foreign policy, accept ambassadors, and censor anyone in the city. The Spartan government was designed to discourage change since full agreement among council, kings, and ephors was necessary for any major action.

The Spartans feared that contact with outside people would weaken obedience and discipline. Therefore, Spartan citizens were not permitted to travel and foreign visitors were discouraged from coming to Sparta.

The Culture of Sparta

Militarism controlled every part of the daily lives of the Spartans. Between the ages of eighteen and sixty, Spartan men devoted their time to being citizen-soldiers of the state. Their training began much earlier, however. Spartan boys were allowed to live with their families only until they were seven years old. Then they went to live in army barracks and learned how to become strong and brave citizen-soldiers. Spartan boys were forced to undergo all kinds of physical hardships. They had to wear very light clothing in the winter. They were given little to eat and were taught to endure pain in silence. All of this training was designed to prepare future soldiers for battle.

Spartan girls also received hard physical training. The Spartans believed that women who were physically strong were more likely to produce children who would grow up to become good citizen-soldiers. Although they did not vote or take part in the government, Spartan women were granted more freedom than the women of other city-states. Women also received a better education than men because of the important role they played in educating children and managing the estates while the men trained for war. Spartan women were permitted to own property in their own name, even after marriage, and could bequeath it to whomever they wished. While the Spartan women exercised, enjoyed music, and were responsible for managing the household and its finances, the household chores were performed by helot women.

Spartans were trained to spurn all luxuries and pleasures that might divert their attention from the goals of achieving military superiority. To this day, people who live simple and self-disciplined life-styles are still referred to as "Spartan." From the Spartan point of view, poetry or philosophy was of little value unless it helped one become a well-trained, disciplined soldier.

This rigorous type of society helped Sparta's army become the main military power in Greece. Sparta became the leader of the Peloponnesian League, a military alliance of many city-states, including Corinth (KAWR-inth). Although it had only one vote at League meetings, Sparta's leadership was so strong that few dared to oppose it.

Athens

The Athenian way of life was very different from that of the Spartan. Trade, open meetings, and public discussions in the marketplace characterized daily life in ancient Athens. Athens had good areas for beaching ships, and the Athenians built harbors to carry on trade with cities around the Mediterranean. Olive oil, honey, and wine were major export items.

An important feature of Athenian society was its system of government. Though some Greek city-states practiced a form of democracy, it was usually the wealthy who governed the polis. The city of Athens, however, became famous for developing a democratic system in which all male citizens, rich and poor, participated. Women and noncitizens living in Athens, including foreigners and slaves, were not allowed to take part in Athenian democracy. The exclusion of these groups from participation in government was common to all of Greece at the time.

The movement toward a democratic form of government began in Athens about 600 B.C. Before that time an aristocracy had controlled the economic and political life of Athens and had forced many small farmers into debt.

To prevent an open rebellion in Athens, the merchant class joined with the upper class in an effort to reform the government and improve the economy. In 594 B.C. they called upon Solon (SOE-lun) to head the Athenian government. He was given full powers to bring about economic and political reforms.

One of the first things Solon did was to stop the practice of enslaving people who were unable to pay their debts. Solon also helped make agriculture more profitable by encouraging farmers to grow exportable crops, such as olives and grapes. These crops became the basis of a rich trade in oil and wine throughout the Mediterranean, and were exchanged for the staple items the Athenians needed. Solon also encouraged industry, and Athens soon had a supply of goods that could be sold in neighboring areas and overseas in exchange for grain and other items.

Before Solon, most of the political power had been controlled by a Council of Elders dominated by aristocrats. Solon began his political reforms by carefully defining this council's powers. He passed new laws that made wealth, rather than birth, the main qualification for political office. All citizens were divided into four classes based on their annual income. All four classes could participate in the Assembly, which passed legislation and approved treaties. It annually elected the city magistrates who were drawn only from the men of the two upper-income classes. One of Solon's other reforms was the introduction of a new tribal Council of 400, whose members were elected annually by the Assembly from the top three income classes. The Council of 400 conducted the daily business of state and prepared matters to be presented to the Assembly. Finally, the Council of Elders, which was composed of former magistrates, became a kind of supreme court to oversee the new constitution and hear important legal cases. Solon also rewrote the law code of Athens and put the laws on display in the agora so that all citizens would have access to them. In addition, Solon introduced a new jury system to hear criminal cases and civil disputes dealing with trade.

Though Solon's reforms were a step in the right direction, the lower classes wanted to see further reforms that would benefit them directly. As a result about 560 B.C. they supported the tyrant Pisistratus (pie-SISS-truh-tuss) who, together with his sons, would rule Athens for the next half century. Pisistratus brought about a coalition of the lower and middle classes to break the last control of the aristocrats. He also promoted overseas trade, turned Athenian pottery into a major industry and export item, and fostered a growing civic pride in Athens to celebrate its new prosperity. By 510 B.C. Athenian society, without a bloody revolution, had been unified and was ready for the next step toward full democracy.

Cleisthenes (KLYS-thuh-neez), the next reformer, divided all citizens into ten political tribes, instead of the old religious ones. Each tribe elected its own officials from among its members. All the citizens could vote in the city assembly. A special Council of 500—fifty members from each tribe—replaced the Council of 400, and performed the same function. This new council, however, was more representative. Cleisthenes also introduced a new Board of Ten Generals, elected annually by the Assembly. Unlike the annual magistrates, who could only hold office once, these generals could be reelected. Most Athenian political leaders chose to run for this office.

Pottery like this vase depicting King Theseus was a highly valued export item. How did Athenian pottery combine the interests of business, art, and state?

Cleisthenes also expanded the legal system that Solon had set up. He established popular courts to hear civil suits and cases involving trade. As many as 6,000 jurors would sit daily at various trials. Athenian juries were large—ranging between 101 to 501 jurors each—in order to make it difficult for anyone to bribe an entire jury. The right to a trial by jury and access to the law were important contributions to democracy.

Though Athenian democracy was a great step forward, it must be remembered that it was quite different from modern democracies. Although women were citizens, they were not allowed to vote. Slaves and foreigners living in Athens also were excluded from voting. Thus, even at its best, Athenian democracy, by excluding women, children, foreigners, and slaves, only involved perhaps twenty-five percent of the population.

In general, upper-class women in Athens had no part in government and did not participate in public life. They often were not given an education nor were they allowed to take part in the intellectual life of the city, own property, or represent themselves in court. Married women of good families sometimes appeared in public but only after covering their faces with a veil. They were permitted to travel only when accompanied by their husbands or a trusted slave and usually spent most of their time in the home. Some women learned to read and write, and at a later time others managed to own property, but that was unusual in ancient Athens. Women of the lower classes, however, worked side-by-side with men on farms, in shops, and in booths at the marketplaces.

One peculiarity of Athenian democracy was the practice of **ostracism** (OSS-truh-siz-uhm), or the voting of a public figure into a ten-year period of exile. Once a year in the Assembly, each citizen was asked to write on a piece of broken pottery—called an ostracon (OSS-truh-kahn)—the name of one person who should be exiled as a threat to Athens. If at least 6,000 votes were cast, the person receiving the most votes was exiled. This system was meant to be used to rid Athens of power-hungry officials or those who had misused their office. Ostracism, however, was itself sometimes misused to exile innocent but unpopular leaders.

Though Athenian democracy had its shortcomings, it has served as a model for many modern democratic institutions.

The Persian Wars

While the Greeks prospered, another empire began to emerge to the east. Cyrus (SIE-rus) the Great, who ruled from 559 B.C. to 529 B.C., amassed a vast Persian empire. He and two of his successors, Darius (DAH-rie-us) the Great and Xerxes (ZURK-seez), managed to build an empire that stretched from the borders of India in the east to the Aegean and Black seas in the west and north.

In 548 B.C. the Greeks of Ionia were conquered by Cyrus. Though the Persians did not treat them harshly, the Greeks in Asia Minor valued their independence. In 499 B.C., supported by Athens, they rebelled.

Though the Persians quickly subdued Ionia, they decided to extend their power into Greece itself. The main wars between the Greeks and the Persians lasted from 490 B.C. to 480 B.C.

In 490 B.C. the Persian fleet, under one of Darius' generals, anchored in the Bay of Marathon. This was only twenty-five miles (forty kilometers) from Athens. The Athenians sent word to Sparta asking for help, but Sparta could not send aid immediately so the Athenians were on their own. Yet when the Persians advanced they were soundly defeated at Marathon by the outnumbered Athenians, who quickly sent a runner back to Athens with the news of their victory. This run of over twenty-five miles provided the inspiration for the modern distance race that we call a marathon.

Ten years later the Persians mounted another military campaign against the Greeks, led by King Xerxes. Sparta called upon the Greeks to unite, but few came. Nevertheless, Leonidas (lee-AHN-uh-duss), the Spartan king, met the Persians at a pass between the mountains and the sea, called Thermopylae (thur-MAHP-uh-lee). There 300 Spartans, together with 700 allies, died holding the pass against thousands of Persians.

After defeating the Spartans, the army of Xerxes moved through the pass and marched unopposed all the way to Athens. The city had been evacuated, but the Persians looted it and burned its temples. The Athenian-led Greek fleet, however, under the leadership of Themistocles (thuh-MISS-tuh-kleez), lured the Persian fleet into the narrows by the island of Salamis (SAL-uh-miss). There the Greek navy won an overwhelming victory. The

ANCIENT GREECE AND THE PERSIAN WARS

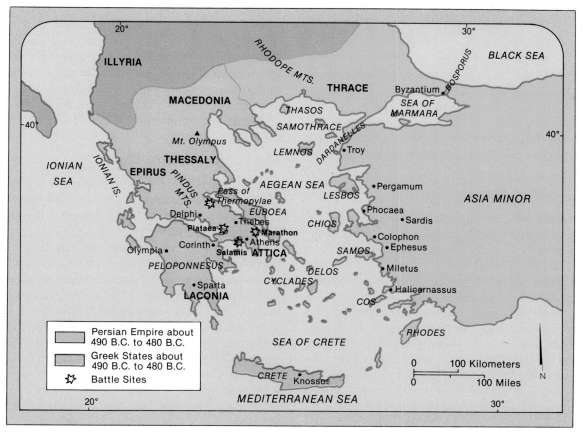

How does the location of the major battle sites of the Persian wars help to identify which side was the aggressor in these wars?

defeated Xerxes then sailed home, leaving his uncle Mardonias (mahr-DOAN-ee-uss) to continue the war in Greece. In 479 B.C. Mardonias and his army were defeated by a Spartan-led force at Plataea (pluh-TEE-uh).

Following the defeat of the Persians, Athens entered into a new era of international influence. To protect themselves against any further attack by the Persians, Athens led the formation of an alliance of city-states. The Delian (DEE-lee-uhn) League eventually numbered 300 members, and most city-states on the Aegean islands and along their shores joined the League. The League built more ships and, in 466 B.C., met and defeated a Persian fleet off the southern coast of Asia Minor. Meanwhile Athens, as the major sea power of Greece, continued to expand its trade routes, wealth, and influence.

SECTION REVIEW

1. **Mapping:** Use the scale on the map above to find the distance between Athens and Sparta, Sparta and Corinth, Athens and Corinth.
2. In your own words, briefly define or identify: polis, barter economy, monetary economy, tyrant, democracy, ostracism.
3. Compare and contrast the roles of women in Sparta and Athens.
4. How did the reforms of Solon, Pisistratus, and Cleisthenes contribute to the development of democracy in Athens?
■ How does democracy in ancient Athens compare to that of the United States? In what ways does it differ?

THE CLASSICAL AGE OF GREECE

The fifth century B.C. in Greece is known as its Classical Age. For much of the period the Greek city-states were involved in wars—first against the Persians, then in civil wars among themselves. Although the times were turbulent, there were many great advances in knowledge and the arts.

The Age of Pericles

The time from 460 B.C. to 430 B.C. is called the Age of Pericles (PAIR-uh-Kleez), in honor of the Athenian statesman in power during much of the period. One of Pericles' major contributions was in modifying the jury system. Under Pericles jurors were, for the first time, paid. Citizens who attended the Assembly meetings were also paid for their services. This reform meant that the poorer citizens, as well as the wealthy, could afford to become involved in politics. Pericles also made the courts more democratic by randomly choosing the six thousand citizens who would serve as jurors. The magistrates were also chosen at random from then on.

Pericles made other important contributions. In order to protect the growing Athenian Empire, Pericles ordered that military posts be built in strategic locations. He also had stone walls constructed from Athens to the seaport of Piraeus (pie-REE-uhs) in order to protect grain shipments arriving from Egypt, Italy, and Sicily. Pericles promoted trade by insisting that a uniform system of coinage, weights, and measures be used in all the areas of the Delian League. The stability of the economy and the free exchange of ideas sparked one of the great intellectual periods of all time. Scholars, poets, playwrights, sculptors, and philosophers were all drawn to Athens during this golden age of Greek drama, art, and philosophy.

Difficulties for Athens arose, however, when Pericles began to exercise ungranted authority over the Delian League allies. He began interfering in their internal affairs, setting up governments friendly to Athens and forcing some states to pay war taxes rather than send forces to fight the Persians. Following a military failure in 455 B.C., Pericles moved the treasury of the League from the island of Delos to Athens. He began to spend the war tax on rebuilding temples in Athens burnt by the Persians in 480 B.C. The war taxes now became tribute. Even after a peace treaty was signed with Persia, Athens collected these taxes, arguing that Athens provided security within League territory against foreign enemies, kept down piracy, and protected commerce.

The Peloponnesian War

As the influence and power of Athens continued to grow, so did the unrest over Athenian interference in the other city-states. Competition between Athens and Sparta for allies also heightened the tension on the Greek peninsula. Athens continued to pressure its allies to conform to Athenian policy and began to pressure neutral city-states to choose sides between Athens and Sparta. Pericles continued to extend the Athenian Empire on the Greek mainland, leading to war with Sparta. After some substantial skirmishes a thirty-year peace was signed in 445 B.C. According to the peace Athens would give up its land claims and Sparta would recognize Athens' sea empire. The terms of the treaty, however, were broken and Sparta and Athens again went to war. The Peloponnesian War began in 431 B.C. and lasted, on and off, for twenty-seven years. Although it involved many city-states, in essence it pitted the land power of Sparta against the sea power of Athens.

Shortly after the war broke out a plague swept through Athens killing one-quarter to one-third of the population. In 429 B.C. Pericles himself died from the plague. Without his leadership the Athenians became fearful of losing the war and their empire. Athens tried to enlist a land power on its side comparable to Sparta. Similarly, Sparta sought a strong sea power for an ally. However, unable to find allies to offset each other's strengths, the war dragged on without decisive results.

In 421 B.C. a truce was established, but in 416 B.C., after many minor violations by both sides, the peace was officially shattered when Athens attacked the neutral island of Melos. Although the Melians declared that Athens had no right to do this, Athenian representatives responded that "the strong do what they will and the weak do what they must." Athens destroyed Melos and sold the population into slavery. A year later Athens began a disastrous campaign against the city-state of Syracuse on the island of Sicily. An Athenian army 50,000 strong was destroyed.

In 411 B.C. Athenian democracy fell victim to an internal revolution. The war continued with occasional victories on both sides until Sparta asked Persia for aid. With Persian financial support, Sparta constructed and manned a fleet of warships and defeated Athens in 405 B.C. A pro-Spartan government was installed in Athens in 404 B.C., and though a new democracy was established a few years later, Athens would never again be an international power.

Early Greek Religion

Greek religious values focused on the qualities of moderation, reason, love of one's family and friends, bravery, and patriotism. The early Greeks worshiped many gods and goddesses. Most took the form of superhuman, immortal beings. These gods and goddesses had the same attributes as ordinary people. They fought with one another, required food and rest, and interacted with ordinary human beings.

The twelve most powerful gods lived on Mount Olympus. Zeus (ZOOS), the king of the gods and the father of many of the other gods and goddesses, was the most important of the Greek deities. Another important deity was Apollo, the god of art and music. Among the most popular goddesses were Aphrodite (aff-ruh-DIE-tee), the goddess of love and beauty, and Athena (uh-THEE-nuh), the goddess of wisdom and industry. In addition, each city had a special god or goddess who oversaw its affairs. Athena was said to have founded Athens, and Apollo protected Corinth. Families, too, often worshiped their own patron deities, depending on family tradition or occupation.

Many temples were built in honor of the gods. One of the most famous hilltop shrines was at Delphi (DELL-fie), where Apollo was honored. Individuals and state representatives came from far away to seek the advice of Apollo through his oracle at Delphi. Apollo's responses were given through a priestess, whose answer was then put into verse by a priest. ''Know thyself'' and ''Nothing in excess'' were two famous examples of the

Athena, partroness of Athens, is portrayed in this stone relief. How did Athenian culture reflect the qualities of the goddess Athena?

wisdom of Apollo. Usually the reply was very brief and open to several interpretations.

Funeral rituals were another important aspect of Greek religious beliefs. It was believed that without the proper burial ceremonies the dead would not be at rest. One's deceased ancestors who were properly buried—and therefore at peace—were worshiped. Thus a bond was established that kept family traditions alive through the ages.

The Greeks also held athletic games and contests in which they honored their gods. The first Olympic games took place in 776 B.C. at Olympia, and were held in honor of Zeus. Originally the games consisted only of running competitions. Gradually they came to include wrestling, chariot races, boxing, and other contests. The Olympic games, as we know them, were revived in Athens in 1896, at which time the marathon was added as an event.

Greek Theater

Early Athenian festivals honored Dionysus (die-uh-NIE-sus), the god of fertility. At these festivals Dionysus' praises were sung by Greek poets in choral performances. From these early performances of verse developed tragic drama, comedy, and other forms of Greek theater. By the fifth century B.C. there were three such annual festivals featuring plays in honor of the gods. The festivals were sponsored by the city-state and playwrights competed for prizes.

Greek tragedies and comedies were performed in huge open-air theaters that could seat audiences of as many as 30,000 people. Because many of the spectators had to sit far from the stage, special costumes, masks, and mechanical devices were used by the actors so they could be seen and heard by all. Male actors performed all roles. Costumes were designed to make it easy for the actors to be seen and their characters identified. They wore special masks that were carved or painted to show the various emotions of the characters they were portraying. When necessary, speaking tubes were used to project the voices of the actors to the audience. Some theaters were constructed in such a way that anyone in the audience could hear even a whisper at center stage.

At first, performances of Greek tragedies were given by a chorus that sang the drama. Although the chorus remained, in time individual actors were given special roles to play. Only about thirty-five of the hundreds of tragedies performed in ancient Greece have survived. Those that have been preserved include the works of the three great Athenian playwrights: Aeschylus (ESS-kuh-luss), Sophocles (SAHF-uh-kleez), and Euripides (yoo-RIP-uh-deez). Aeschylus and Sophocles wrote about fate and the interference of the gods in human lives. Euripides, however, believed that people were in control of their own destinies and were therefore responsible for their actions.

Aeschylus, who lived from 525 B.C. to 456 B.C., was the leading playwright of his generation. He had fought in the Persian Wars, and his plays emphasized courage and idealism. In the *Orestia*, a trilogy, or set of three plays, Aeschylus told of the sufferings of the family of Agamemnon after the Trojan War. Vengeance, duty, and justice are themes explored in the *Orestia*.

Sophocles grew up during the height of Periclean influence and served as a general in the

Built about 300 B.C., the theater of Epidaurus was the site of many performances of Greek drama. What helped audiences in such large theaters to follow the drama?

Athenian army. In 468 B.C. Sophocles won the first of his twenty-four first prizes at the Dionysia festivals. Sophocles wrote over a hundred and twenty plays, of which only seven have survived. All of the seven are still performed today. His most famous works include *Oedipus Rex, Antigone,* and *Oedipus at Colonus.* In *Antigone,* he used the chorus to praise the spirit of Athens, while he presented a dramatic conflict that resulted from the competing loyalties of family, state, and religion.

The third great dramatist of the Classical Age was Euripides, who wrote during the Peloponnesian War. His plays included *Electra, Medea,* and *The Trojan Women.* Through his works Euripides tried to be the conscience of Athens. As a social critic he used his plays to praise Greek ideals but condemned excess, injustice, and war.

The Greeks also enjoyed comedies that satirized, or poked fun at, public figures. Greek comedies often helped to influence public opinion by mocking contemporary customs and politicians. Aristophanes (ahr-uh-STAHF-uh-neez) wrote comedies opposing full democracy, the Peloponnesian War, and those responsible for the war. In plays like *The Wasps, The Clouds, The Birds,* and *The Frogs,* Aristophanes satirized types of people who are still recognizable in public life today.

Poets and Historians

The Greeks loved the rich, poetic sound of their language, and their literature, whether poetry or prose, is renowned for its beauty and power.

Hesiod (HEE-see-ud), who wrote soon after Homer, described ordinary lives and events. In a poem called *Works and Days,* Hesiod celebrates the life of the farmer, and provides a kind of agricultural almanac with practical advice for farmers. Another of the early poets whose works have survived into modern times was a woman named Sappho (SAFF-oh), who wrote beautiful love poems. The poet Pindar (PIN-duhr) wrote odes, or poems of praise and celebration, to glorify virtue, religion, and the winners of athletic contests.

The first great Greek historian was Herodotus (hih-RAHD-uh-tus), who lived in the middle of the fifth century B.C. In order to write a history of the Persian Wars, Herodotus traveled to Egypt, Italy, Mesopotamia, and the lands around the Black Sea to collect and record facts about Persian history

and customs. Herodotus saw the conflict between the Greeks and the Persians as an inevitable struggle between east and west—between the forces of absolute, or complete, rule and the forces of freedom. He was the first historian to conduct in-depth research, and as a result is sometimes called the "Father of History."

A short time after Herodotus, an Athenian historian named Thucydides (thoo-SID-uh-deez) wrote an account of the Peloponnesian War, in which he had fought as an Athenian general. Thucydides, who improved the methods of research and analysis introduced by Herodotus, is considered to be the first scientific historian. To write *History of the Peloponnesian Wars,* he visited the scenes of the events he described, interviewed eyewitnesses, and copied all available documents. After gathering all the available evidence, Thucydides examined it critically and recorded his conclusions. Thucydides was interested in the connection between human behavior and war itself. He hoped people would learn from the past and realize that future wars could be avoided.

The Philosophers

In ancient Greece, scholars did not specialize in just one or two particular areas of study, as they often do today. Greek scholars studied mathematics, physics, logic, music, astronomy, and the use of language. They inquired into the proper ways to govern, the workings of the universe, the relationship between mathematics and music, and the nature of reality. The Greeks coined the word philosophy, or love of wisdom, for such study of the world. Greece produced several of the world's most important philosophers. They often raised troubling questions and, therefore, were not always popular in their own time.

The earliest Greek philosopher on record was Thales of Miletus who observed nature in an attempt to understand how the world developed. Thales believed that water was the basic material of life and that all others were made from water.

At the start of the fifth century B.C., a group of philosophers appeared called **Sophists** (SAHF-ists), meaning "those who work at being wise." The most respected of the Sophists was Protagoras (proh-TAHG-uh-rus), who lived from 490 B.C. to

415 B.C. He and other Sophists formed a group of professional teachers who prepared rich, young Athenian men to be skilled debaters. They specialized in the teaching of grammar and **rhetoric,** or the use of persuasive language to influence thoughts and actions. This ability to debate one's position clearly and effectively was highly prized in Athens. Sophists believed that achieving political and social success was their first priority. This approach disturbed many Greeks who thought rhetoric was a means to an end, not the end itself. Sophists later came to be viewed negatively and were seen as people who lacked respect for tradition, law, and principle. Many Greek philosophers, including Socrates (SOCK-ruh-teez), took a different approach, using philosophy and rhetoric to discover abstract truths and moral principles.

Socrates

Socrates lived from 469 B.C. to 399 B.C. He believed the Sophists were training people to be successful rather than to develop moral character. Socrates encouraged his students to think for themselves and to search for truth through reason. His belief in the perfectibility of one's moral character made him the founder of the study of ethics.

Socrates was a well-known figure around Athens during the time of Pericles and the Peloponnesian War, and he was very popular among young people. He believed that admitting one's own ignorance was the beginning of true knowledge. Socrates taught his followers to question everything, and he said that people should never rely on traditions or on what others told them. Only by continually questioning their own beliefs, forming their own answers, and discussing these answers with others did Socrates believe people could gain knowledge. He adopted the motto "Know thyself" from Apollo and used it to characterize every facet of inquiry. This method of learning is called the **Socratic method of inquiry.**

Socrates was seen as encouraging young people to question the very foundations of the Athenian way of life. At the time, Athens was in the midst of its war with Sparta, and Socrates was considered by some to be a threat to Athens' stability. As a result, he was brought to trial in 399 B.C. for disloyalty to the state, disrespect to the gods, and for corrupting the youth of Athens. Socrates was sentenced to death and died after drinking a cup of poison hemlock.

Plato

Historians know of Socrates' teachings through the writings of another great philosopher, Plato (PLAY-toe). Plato lived from 428 B.C. to 347 B.C. and was Socrates' best-known student. He wrote about the great philosophical questions. He asked what kind of government would produce the most good, what love was, why a person should behave ethically, and many other questions that have concerned people through the ages. Plato's writings are in the form of dialogues, or conversations between two or more characters. In his works Plato, through the character of Socrates, poses questions to a group of students. The students reply and discuss the answers. When the students have answered one question, Plato poses another. In this way, his students are forced to question themselves and to justify their own responses.

In one of his most famous *Dialogues*, the *Republic*, Plato outlines his plan for an ideal society. Life in Plato's republic would be, in most respects, communal. It would consist of three classes: one of scholars; one of soldiers; and one containing merchants, artisans, and farmers. Each male citizen's membership in his group would be determined by intelligence, rather than by birth. Since the scholars had the most knowledge and intelligence, they would be the rulers. The soldiers would defend the polis. The merchants, artisans, and farmers would produce and distribute goods for the whole community.

Aristotle

Plato believed that there was an ideal behind each virtue and that people should continually try to improve themselves so that they might come nearer to these ideal virtues. Aristotle (AIR-isstot'l), another famous philosopher and a student of Plato, approached truth through the study of the natural world. He was the first to use modern scientific methods, and perfected the use of logic as one of these methods. Aristotle classified living things into groups, much as is done in biology today. He then extended this system of classification into other kinds of inquiry. He classified governments, for example, according to whether they were headed by one person, by a few people, or by many people.

Aristotle differed from Plato in his conception of the best kind of government. Aristotle believed there were three forms of good government: kingship, aristocracy, and democracy. Each had a corresponding form of bad government: tyranny was a corrupt kingship, oligarchy was a corrupt aristocracy, and mob rule a corrupt democracy. A truly ideal government would reflect the best of the three forms of government. Aristotle also believed that it was best for people to live in moderation and to avoid excess in every part of their lives. A mixed constitution would provide a moderating effect, balancing the powers within the state, and avoiding the excesses that lead to corrupt governments.

Aristotle was in a unique position to influence the course of history through his ideas of government. For three years he served as the tutor for young Prince Alexander of Macedon (MASS-uh-don), later known as Alexander the Great. Under Aristotle the young prince studied poetry, ethics, drama, and politics. When Aristotle returned to Athens he, as had Plato, established a school to carry on his philosophy.

Art and Architecture

Whatever the Greeks attempted—from philosophy to sports—they did their best to excel. They worked to perfect their skills as athletes, scholars, and poets. Nowhere was this quest for excellence more evident than in their art. Fine artwork was an important part of the life of every citizen of Athens. Even household articles like vases and jugs were created as works of art. They were painted with scenes showing the deeds of Greek gods, goddesses, and heroes. Some also showed people engaged in daily activities—weaving cloth, attending banquets, or taking part in games and athletic contests. The paintings decorating these beautiful Greek vases are almost the only ones to survive from this period. For this reason they are an important source of information on Greek life and art. Temples, gymnasiums, theaters, and other public buildings were all decorated with painted marble sculptures of the gods and military leaders.

These statues are often our only source for what many leaders of ancient Greece looked like. They are also outstanding examples of classical simplicity and elegance.

Fine examples of classical Greek architecture and sculpture can be seen in a building called the Parthenon, on the Acropolis in Athens. As you recall, the Persians sacked Athens in 480 B.C. Under Pericles an elegant new temple was built, enclosing a great statue of Athena and ringed with statues of other deities. Although the remains of the Parthenon are now unpainted, the whole building and its sculptures were once painted in bright colors. The statue of Athena was carved from wood and covered with ivory and gold. Its creator was Phidias (FID-ee-uhs), a leading sculptor of his time.

The Parthenon is perhaps the most famous example of classical Greek architecture. Built by Ictinus (ick-TIE-nuss), it shows the Greek concern

Greek art sought to personify abstract ideals of perfect beauty and natural harmony. How does this stone relief convey such ideals?

SOURCES

The Hippocratic Oath

Hippocrates ran a famous school of medicine on the island of Cos, in the Aegean Sea. His name is familiar to every modern physician as the author of the Hippocratic Oath, an ethical guide for those who practice medicine. Here are excerpts from the original version, written nearly 2,500 years ago.

I swear by Apollo Physician, by Asclepius, by Health, by Panacea and by all the gods and goddesses, by making them my witnesses, that I will carry out, according to my ability and judgment, this oath and this indenture. To hold my teacher in this art equal to my own parents; to make him partner in my livelihood; when he is in need of money to share mine with him; to consider his family as my own brothers, and to teach them this art, if they want to learn it, without fee or indenture; to impart precept, oral instruction, and all other instruction to my own sons, the sons of my teacher, and to indentured pupils who have taken the physician's oath, but to nobody else. I will use treatment to help the sick according to my ability and judgment, but never with a view to injury and wrongdoing. Neither will I administer a poison to anybody when asked to do so, nor will I suggest such a course. . . . In whatsoever houses I enter, I will enter to help the sick, and I will abstain from all intentional wrong-doing and harm, especially from abusing the bodies of man or woman, bond or free. And whatsoever I shall see as outside my profession in my . . . [dealings] with men, if it be what should not be published abroad, I will never divulge, holding such things to be holy secrets. Now if I carry out this oath, and break it not, may I gain forever reputation among all men for my life and for my art; but if I transgress it and forswear myself, may the opposite befall me.

Source: Adapted from W.H.S. Jones, *Hippocrates*, copyright © 1923 by Harvard University Press.

1. Why is Hippocrates' name still familiar to modern-day physicians?
2. According to the Oath, what is the relationship between ancient Greek physicians and their students?
3. According to the Oath, what is the goal of every physician?
4. Do the principles of the Oath differ from today's medical practices? Explain.

---

with simplicity and balance and was designed with enormous attention to detail. The pillars around the outside, for example, tilt slightly inward in order to look more solid. Each column is slightly wider in the center to adjust for the way the eye sees things at a distance.

Science, Medicine, and Mathematics

The Greeks borrowed many scientific ideas from older Middle Eastern civilizations. Reports about the scientific knowledge of Egypt and Mesopotamia were brought home to Greece by traders and travelers. Ideas also passed to the Greek mainland from the cities of Ionia, which were in contact with the civilizations of the Middle East. The great culture of ancient Greece would not have been possible without such things as the ironworking process developed by the Hittites, or the alphabet of the Phoenicians. The medical skills and geometry of Egypt and the astronomy of Babylonia greatly contributed to early Greek science.

The Greeks, however, made important changes in scientific thinking that affected modern science.

Beginning with Thales, when the Greeks wondered how things worked, they looked for answers in the natural world around them. In earlier times, people had depended solely on myths to explain events such as floods and thunderstorms.

Very early Greek medicine, for example, followed ancient Egyptian practices. Priests used charms, spells, and other kinds of "magic" to try to cure patients. A Greek named Hippocrates (hih-POCK-ruh-teez), who lived from about 460 B.C. to 377 B.C., disagreed with this approach. He argued that every disease, in addition to having a "divine" cause, also had a natural one. He used a scientific approach to the study of medicine. First, he and his students recorded the progress of a disease, noting its initial symptoms and course. Then they treated the disease based on previous studies and the results achieved. The influence of Hippocrates on modern medicine is still in evidence today. Medical students take a vow at graduation, called the Hippocratic Oath, in which they pledge to uphold the principles of their profession.

Greeks made important advances in mathematics and physics. Pythagoras (pih-THAG-uhr-us) made one of the first attempts to explain the universe in abstract mathematical language. He is probably best known for the Pythagorean theorem. This principle of geometry—studied by every high school student—states that the square of the hypotenuse of a right triangle equals the sum of the squares of the two remaining sides.

SECTION REVIEW

1. In your own words, briefly define or identify: Athena, Herodotus, Sophists, Socrates, Plato, Aristotle, Parthenon, Hippocratic Oath.
2. Name and briefly describe the works of three Greek poets.
3. Compare and contrast the philosophy of the Sophists with that of Socrates.
4. How did early Greek medicine compare with that of Egypt? How did the approach taken by Hippocrates change Greek medicine?
■ Explain why it might be impossible for someone today to try to master as many fields of knowledge as the ancient philosophers did.

THE SPREAD OF GREEK CULTURE

In 359 B.C., following a forty-year period of near anarchy on the Greek peninsula, a capable young king, Philip II, came to the throne of Macedonia. In a few short years, Philip made Macedonia, an area just to the north of Greece proper, the strongest single power on the Greek peninsula. Philip accomplished this by building a large, well-trained army, which he used to incorporate the wilder tribal areas around Macedonia into the kingdom.

A brilliant general as well as a ruthless political leader, Philip's plans to expand eastward into Thrace brought him up against a resurgent Athens, and therefore involved him in the affairs of the city-states to the south. By taking advantage of the weaknesses and quarrels among the city-states, Philip twice managed to defeat a Greek coalition set against him. In 337 B.C. he temporarily united Greece—except Sparta—in a federal league under his control. Despite his wars with the city-states, Philip admired Greek culture, particularly that of Athens, and he even brought Aristotle to Macedonia to tutor his young son, Alexander. In 336 B.C. Philip was assassinated. His son, Alexander, also had a great appreciation of Greek culture, and he wanted to emulate the exploits of the great Greek heroes he had read about.

Alexander the Great

Alexander the Great was only twenty years old when he inherited his father's kingdom. After assuming his father's position as head of the new Greek League, Alexander invaded Asia Minor and defeated the Persians. Next he advanced on Syria, Palestine, and Egypt, and easily defeated the Persian armies that held these lands. At the Nile Delta, Alexander founded the port city of Alexandria. Again turning east, Alexander took Assyria and Babylonia and pushed onward to what are now Afghanistan and Pakistan. In only twelve years Alexander created the largest empire known in the ancient world, the eastern limits of which reached as far as the Indus River in India.

Alexander brought the ideas and products of Greek culture to each region he conquered. He

EMPIRE OF ALEXANDER THE GREAT

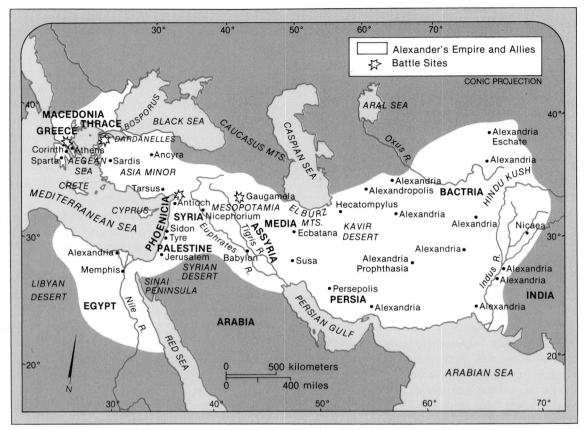

How did the military victories of Alexander contribute to the spread of Greek culture? How did Alexander's empire contribute to the creation of Hellenistic culture?

also arranged for his military leaders to marry into the important families of Persia. He created new armies and built new roads. He also founded new towns, each named Alexandria. Alexander may have founded as many as seventy Alexandrias, the farthest one more than 2,300 miles (3,680 kilometers) east of the Mediterranean. Some of these towns were only forts, but others were important centers of trade and learning.

Egypt's Alexandria, for example, became the most important trading port in the Mediterranean for the next 500 years. At its height this city had port facilities for 1,200 ships and provided the Greek world with woolen goods, glass, ivory, linen, and spices from many parts of the ancient world. It also supplied papyrus for paper, which was being used throughout the Mediterranean and Middle Eastern worlds. During this time Alexandria was also one of the world's educational centers.

Alexander ruled each area in accordance with its own traditions. He apparently adopted the eastern idea that a king was a god in human form, and he began to demand that his followers kneel before him when they were in his presence. Some of Alexander's closest friends and advisors objected to this practice and were executed as a result.

In 323 B.C., when he was only thirty-three years old, Alexander died of a fever. Almost immediately, Alexander's generals began to quarrel over the empire. Alexander's empire soon broke up, and by 275 B.C. it was divided among the descendants of three Macedonian generals: the Ptolemies (TAHL-uh-meez), who ruled Egypt, the Seleucids (suh-LOO-sids), who ruled Syria and part of Mesopotamia, and the Antigonids (an-TIG-uh-nids), who ruled Macedonia. In the second century B.C. the armies of the emerging Roman Empire began to challenge the successors of Alexander and soon absorbed Alexander's former empire.

Long after his death, Greek ideas continued to influence the areas conquered by Alexander. The cultures of these foreign lands also began to influence the Greeks themselves. New ideas brought home by Alexander's followers led to a mixing of Greek and eastern cultures. This period of cultural blending is called the **Hellenistic** (hel-uh-NISS-tik) **Age.** It lasted from Alexander's death in 323 B.C. until 30 B.C., when Rome defeated and incorporated the last major Hellenistic kingdom—Egypt. As they had in the Classical Age, the Greeks in the Hellenistic Age made enormous contributions to culture and civilization.

Hellenistic Culture

The extent and influence of the Hellenistic Age can be seen in every aspect of intellectual achievement. In the field of medicine, Herophilus (huh-ROFF-uh-luss) and Erasistratus (air-ah-SISS-trah-tuss) made important discoveries about anatomy and physiology. Both doctors used dissection to study the human body and both are credited with identifying the nervous system and distinguishing between motor and sensory nerves.

During the Hellenistic period the Greeks made many geographical discoveries. Pytheas (PITH-ee-uss) sailed northward along the coasts of Britain and Jutland and learned of the existence of the Arctic Ocean. Erastosthenes (air-uh-TAHS-thuh-neez), who worked in Alexandria, Egypt, popularized the use of longitude and latitude on maps. He computed the circumference of the earth at 24,662 miles (39,459 kilometers), very near the actual figure of 24,857 miles (39,771 kilometers). Posidonius (poe-see-DOH-nee-uss) of Rhodes learned that variations of tides in the ocean were caused by phases of the moon. He also argued that anyone sailing west from the Mediterranean Sea would eventually reach India.

Hellenistic astronomers improved upon the work done by the earlier Babylonians, Egyptians, and Greeks. Aristarchus (air-iss-TAR-kuss) discovered that the earth rotated on its axis. He also said that the earth and planets in our solar system moved in circles and may have been the first to advance the idea that the sun was the center of the universe. His ideas, however, were for the most part ignored.

Significant discoveries in mathematics and physics were also made during the Hellenistic Age. Euclid (YOO-klid) laid the foundations for modern geometry in his book *Elements*. Archimedes (ahr-kuh-MEE-deez) was both a mathematician and an inventor. He arrived at the value of pi and some of his speculations approached elementary integral calculus. He discovered the principle by which the specific gravity, or weight of a substance compared to water, can be found. Archimedes was also the inventor of the double pulley.

Many of these scientific discoveries were forgotten or discarded for hundreds of years. One reason was that such discoveries were made by men who thought of themselves as philosophers. They often felt it was not important to seek practical applications for their discoveries. A second reason was that, due to the abundance of cheap labor, any kind of machinery seemed unnecessary. The Romans, who conquered Greece in the first century B.C., borrowed greatly from all aspects of Greek culture, as you will read in the following chapter. Middle Eastern scholars would later study and adapt Greek scientific and mathematical knowledge and theory. Hundreds of years later Europe would look back to ancient Greece as a source of knowledge and inspiration for its own cultures.

SECTION REVIEW

1. Mapping: Use the map on page 118 to describe the extent of the empire of Alexander the Great.
2. In your own words, briefly define or identify: Philip of Macedon, Alexander the Great, the Hellenistic Age, Erastosthenes, Euclid, Archimedes, Herophilus and Erasistratus.
3. How did Alexander the Great contribute to Greek civilization?
■ How many examples of the spread of Greek culture can you name? In what countries do these living monuments to the ancient Greeks appear? What does this tell us about Greek influence on other cultures?

Reviewing the Chapter

Chapter Summary

More than 2,500 years ago the people of Greece created a culture that greatly influenced future civilizations. This culture developed despite a geography that made Greece difficult to unite but did foster local independence and creativity.

The Minoans built a vigorous trading empire on Crete between 2000 B.C. and 1450 B.C. Greek invaders, called the Mycenaeans, preserved and advanced Minoan culture until 1200 B.C., which marked the beginning of the Dark Age.

During the Dark Age a tradition of local self-government developed, with each polis politically independent. City-states tried various forms of government, from tyranny and oligarchy to democracy. Sparta developed a strong military oligarchy, while Athens formed a very advanced democracy and experienced a period of extraordinary cultural creativity. Women, slaves, and foreign immigrants could not participate in the governments of any of the Greek city-states.

During the Classical Age the city-states fought off Persian invasions. Later, Sparta defeated Athens in the Peloponnesian War. In the fourth century B.C. Alexander the Great made Greece part of his vast empire and helped spread Greek culture as far as India.

During both the Classical and the Hellenistic ages the Greeks made great advances in literature, science, medicine, theater, and philosophy. Homer's great epics, the Iliad and the Odyssey, are classic examples of early Greek literature. Drama was developed as an art form, and Greek sculpture, architecture, and poetry established standards of excellence that even today represent the finest ideals in classical art.

1. Who were the Minoans and what was their greatest achievement?
2. What changes occurred in government during the Dark Age?
3. What role did women, slaves, and immigrants play in the government of ancient Greece?
4. What cultural and scientific advances were made during the Dark, Classical, and Hellenistic ages?

Using Your Vocabulary

1. From what city did the culture of the Achaeans gain its name? Explain.
2. Who was Achilles? What early Greek ideal did he represent?
3. What is an epic poem? Of what value are the Iliad and the Odyssey as historical sources?
4. Define polis.
5. What was the Dark Age of Greece? How did it affect the political and cultural developments of the time?
6. How did the aristocracy influence the political development of early Greece?
7. In your own words define tyrant. Did the tyrant hinder or help the growth of democracy? Explain.
8. What is an oligarchy? A democracy? How did the two systems of government differ?
9. Define equals, helots, and perioikoi. Why did Sparta maintain a rigid class society?
10. What is the modern definition of the word Spartan? What is the origin of this meaning?
11. What is a democracy? What differences do you see between democracy in the Age of Pericles and our own? Explain briefly.
12. What was the Delian League? For what purpose was it formed?
13. What was the Age of Pericles? For what is the period most famous?
14. What was the Classical Age of Greece? How was this expressed in fifth-century Athens?
15. Define Olympic games. How is this tradition continued in the world today? Explain.
16. Define the term drama. How did this form of theater reflect Greek qualities and values? Explain briefly.

17. Who were Herodotus and Thucydides? What was the significance of their work?

Developing Your Geography Skills

1. Use the map on page 99 and the descriptions on pages 99-100 to describe the physical geography of ancient Greece.
2. How did the physical geography of ancient Greece affect the way of life that developed there?
3. Use the map on page 118 to describe the extent of the empire of Alexander the Great.

Recalling the Facts

1. List the predominant geographical features of Greece. How did these features encourage an independent spirit among the Greeks?
2. What do the Minoan forms of writing indicate about the arrival of the Greeks on Crete?
3. List the qualities and virtues important to the ancient Greeks. Which would be most valued by Athenians? By Spartans?
4. Why was the Aegean Sea as important to the ancient Greeks as the Nile River was to the Egyptians?
5. Who were the Achaeans? What was their origin? On what was their culture based?
6. What proof exists to confirm the descriptions Homer recorded of Mycenaean Greece?
7. List the reasons why Greek colonies were established. How important were they to Greece's development? Explain.
8. What two eighth-century B.C. discoveries brought to Greece by traders drastically affected international trade?
9. Why did the Spartans attempt to limit their citizens' contact with foreigners?
10. List Solon's reforms. Which do you consider the most necessary? Explain.
11. List the reforms of Cleisthenes. Why is trial by jury an important right?
12. Compare and contrast the geography of Sparta and Athens. How did it affect the culture and life in each of these two city-states?
13. Briefly describe the development of the Athenian system of government.

14. How did Pericles achieve a stable economy? How did this make Athens a more democratic city-state?

Essay Questions

1. The early Greeks have often been called the first modern westerners. Do you agree that the place of the Greeks is in the modern—rather than the ancient—world? Explain.
2. Imagine yourself a citizen of ancient Greece. Which would you consider most important: your rights or your responsibilities? Why?
3. The achievements of ancient Greece helped to lay the foundation for later western civilizations. To what cultures were the Greeks themselves indebted to for the development of their civilization?
4. Throughout history certain people have come to symbolize the times in which they lived. With which famous Greek do you most identify the culture of classical Greece?

Critical Thinking

Determining Logical Inconsistencies

Another very important part of the critical thinking process involves determining **logical inconsistencies.** A logical inconsistency develops when the evidence used to support a point actually contradicts the argument. For example, because the Athenians developed the first democracy, we assume that all citizens would have participated equally in government. This is logically inconsistent with what we know of their definitions of citizen and democracy, which are not the same as our definitions of these terms. Keep this in mind as you answer the following questions.

1. What is the logical inconsistency in the use of the Spartan term peers or equals in reference to themselves and their treatment of other classes in their society?
2. What is the logical inconsistency in the way the Athenians treated the neutral island of Melos in the Peloponnesian War, and the ideals of their own democracy?

Objectives

- To understand the main geographical and historical reasons why Rome became the ruler of Italy

- To describe the major steps by which Rome conquered the Mediterranean and to show how Rome adapted internally to its new role

- To identify the ideas the western world has inherited from the Romans

- To identify early Christianity's main ideas, its origins, and the reasons for its rapid spread throughout the Roman Empire

Rome began in the eighth century B.C. as a cluster of tiny villages. Yet by the second century A.D. it controlled an empire that stretched from the British Isles to Mesopotamia. At its greatest extent, the Roman Empire surpassed all previous empires in size, wealth, and influence. Rome left a lasting heritage in government, law, language, and architecture. The Romance languages, including French, Italian, and Spanish, the legal systems of most of Europe and Latin America, and our own federal form of government can trace their origins back to Roman civilization. Christianity, one of the world's most important and influential religions, was born and first took shape within the borders of the Roman Empire.

One of Rome's greatest contributions was the preservation and transmission of classical Greek and Hellenistic culture. The ideas and advancements of these cultures were adopted, adapted, and in many instances improved upon by the Romans. The Latin poet Horace, referring to this cultural transfusion, declared that captive Greece had actually conquered Rome. The Romans also borrowed from other cultures, quickly absorbing and using the knowledge and technical skills of the Etruscans, the Carthaginians, and other peoples.

Thus Rome not only transmitted many valuable elements of classical civilization to western Europe, but also made important contributions to our own system of law and government.

THE RISE OF ROME

The Italian peninsula occupies a central position between the eastern and western lands of the Mediterranean. The tip of the island of Sicily is only eighty miles (129 kilometers) from the coast of North Africa. Thus Italy and Sicily virtually form a bridge between Europe and Africa.

In contrast to Greece, Italy's topography, more hilly than mountainous, encouraged transportation and communication between towns. The cities of Italy were able to join politically during Roman times, whereas the Greek city-states remained independent and divided by civil wars.

The Apennines (AP-uh-nines), a large mountain range that extends down the length of the Italian peninsula, divides Italy into several large plains. The fertile valley of the Po (POE) River in the north and the coastal plain in the west were important agricultural regions. Unlike Greece, Italy has few good natural harbors in spite of its long coastline. So while the Greeks became a great seafaring people, Rome developed a strong agricultural tradition by controlling and exploiting the fertile countryside of Italy.

Peoples of Ancient Italy

People have lived on the Italian peninsula since 6000 B.C., surviving first as hunters and gatherers and later settling down as Neolithic farmers in the coastal areas and lake districts. After 2000 B.C. some significant cultural advances, such as developing the use of copper tools, were made by these early peoples. At the same time large numbers of

ANCIENT ITALY ABOUT 325 B.C.

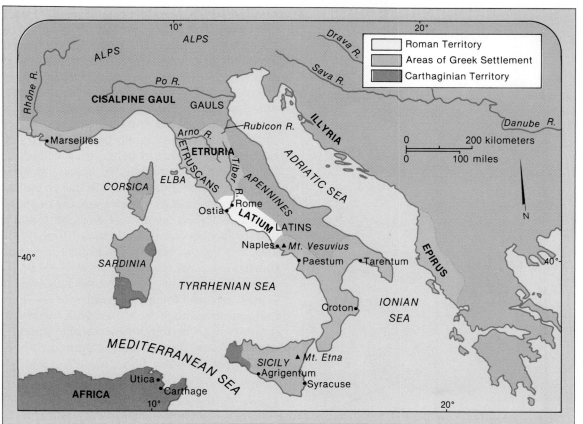

What group of people lived to the north of Latium? What group lived to the south? What groups of people shared control of Sicily?

new peoples moved into the area from the grasslands north of the Black and Caspian seas.

Later they moved inland, spreading their Bronze Age culture into central Italy. They were followed by the Villanovans, a more advanced Iron Age people. After the Villanovans a new wave of Italic speaking peoples entered the peninsula and became established in central and southern Italy.

The Italians, Etruscans, and Greeks

The Italic people lived inland. Two other groups of people occupied the coastal areas, the Etruscans along the northern part of the coast and Greek colonists on the southern part.

Of the many Italic groups of people in early Italy, the Latins, who were the smallest group,

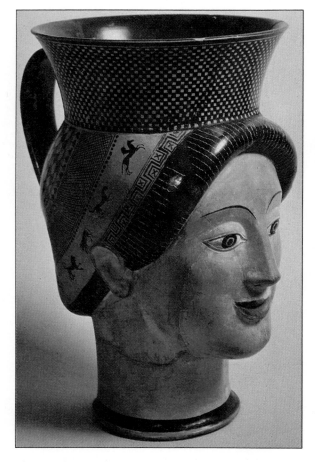

This Greek vase from about 500 B.C. was discovered in an Etruscan tomb. Women in Etruscan society had a degree of freedom that shocked both Greeks and Romans.

would prove to be the most important. The Latins, along with other early Italian peoples, settled around the Alban Hills in central Italy in a region known as Latium (LAY-shee-um). There they built a number of small farming villages.

The Etruscans arrived on the peninsula before 900 B.C., perhaps from Asia Minor. They first settled in central Italy between the Arno (AHR-noh) and Tiber rivers west of the Apennines. Later the Etruscans moved farther north into the Po Valley and south into the territory of the Latins.

The Etruscans developed a highly sophisticated civilization, borrowing and adapting the Greek alphabet for their own language. They were especially skilled in architecture and engineering, and passed both skills on to the Romans. Etruscan cities were protected by moats and walls, while the streets were laid out in a gridlike pattern. By 700 B.C. the Etruscan city-states were organized into a loose federation.

The Etruscans created a strong mixed economy based on farming, mining, and trade. Farmers grew grain and flax, as well as olives for oil and grapes for wine. Iron and copper industries were developed from natural ore deposits. Metal workers created fine weapons and jewelry of iron and bronze, which were sold to people in other Mediterranean lands. Through such trade, the Etruscans became a strong economic power.

The Etruscans eventually extended their influence over a number of neighboring villages and united them to form Rome. Etruscan kings apparently ruled Rome from about 616 B.C. to 509 B.C. The Etruscans drained the swamps and began laying out a unified city around a central forum, or marketplace, in the valley between Rome's hills. They also built an underground sewer system and constructed many temples.

A third group of people in early Italy were the Greeks, who had founded a number of colonies in southern Italy and Sicily in the eighth and seventh centuries B.C. In time, these became important city-states, and through them Rome first became familiar with Greek civilization.

Early Rome

According to legend, Rome was founded in 753 B.C. by two orphaned brothers, Romulus (RAHM-yoo-lus) and Remus (REE-muss). The abandoned brothers were then rescued and raised by a wolf. As unlikely as this legend is, archaeological evidence does show that one of Rome's seven hills was occupied for the first time around 750 B.C. Roman writers believed that from 753 B.C. to 509 B.C. Rome was ruled by seven kings.

In 509 B.C. the people of Rome cast out the last of the seven kings, an Etruscan, and founded a republic. A republic is a government in which **sovereignty,** supreme legal power, rests with all voting citizens. In republican Rome only male citizens with money and property could vote. In addition, the more wealth a citizen had, the greater was his power. Women and slaves were denied voting rights. However, as in Sparta, Roman women did have some legal rights, including the rights to inherit property and to represent themselves in court. Slaves in Rome also had some legal rights, and if manumitted, or freed, they automatically became Roman citizens.

The early history of Rome is dominated by a struggle between the two groups into which the citizens were divided, the **patricians** and **plebeians.** The patricians were a group of about 200 wealthy families who, according to legend, were descended from the earliest Roman settlers. In the early Republic, political power was completely in patrician hands. The patrician leaders met in a council of elders called the Senate and elected all other government officials from their own number. The plebeians made up the rest of the free population. Some had considerable wealth but the majority were poor.

Early Political Reform

From the founding of the Republic, the plebeians struggled to gain a greater role in government. In 494 B.C. they threatened to move away and build a new city. This threat led to the creation of **tribunes,** officials who were elected to protect plebeian interests. Ten tribunes held office and were elected annually by the plebeians. Their most powerful legal weapon was the veto, whereby any law or action of the Senate or any of the magistrates could be stopped.

In 450 B.C. a series of laws known as the Twelve Tables were codified and for the first time the power of the patricians was limited. By 287 B.C. almost all offices, and even membership in the Senate, were open to plebeians. By the late Republic the distinction between leading patrician and plebeian families had all but disappeared.

Two **consuls,** elected annually, were the chief executives of the Roman government. They were invested with **imperium,** the highest legal and political power. The consuls' duties consisted of presiding over the Assembly of Centuries, which was made up of free Roman males over the age of eighteen. In addition, the consuls convened the Senate. The consuls were not legally required to abide by the advice of the Senate, but tradition dictated that they do so.

The two consuls were the chief administrators of the Republic and commanded the Roman army. Each consul had the right to halt actions by the other. In times of crisis, such as war, consuls, with the consent of the Senate, could appoint a dictator. The dictator held absolute power for six months, the usual length of a military campaign.

Rome had several voting assemblies. The Assembly of Centuries elected the two consuls. It also elected the praetors, the magistrates responsible for criminal justice and international law, and censors, who were elected every five years to oversee public morals and count the number of citizens. The Assembly of Tribes annually elected the four aediles, or city commissioners of Rome, and the quaestors (eventually twenty in all), who served as treasury officials or as civil judges.

The Roman Army

Part of the responsibility of being a voting Roman citizen was service in the armed forces. At first Rome relied on citizen soldiers, who served only on a seasonal basis and received no set pay. These were men who owned property, and were expected to provide their own equipment, armor, and food. As compensation, these citizens were given a share of the booty at the end of the campaign. Men rich enough to own horses were members of an elite cavalry called *equites,* or knights. Men of less wealth served as infantrymen or as light-armored troops.

The Roman army was well organized. The soldiers formed mobile companies of 120 men each, with 30 such companies making up a legion. Organized as companies, they attacked their enemies in a checkerboard formation, set in three lines. In

The infantry comprised the main component of the Roman army. These bronze figures show two soldiers carrying a dead comrade. How did the risks faced by soldiers justify their claims for greater political power?

the first line were the seasoned veterans in the prime of fighting condition. The second line contained a mixture of younger and older veterans, while the third was composed of young recruits, and old veterans to steady them. Infantry fighters wore heavy body armor and were equipped with at least two kinds of weapons: spears or darts, and a sword. In close range of the enemy, the infantrymen would throw their spears and then charge with their swords. Strict training and discipline were necessary to fight in this type of formation.

Expanding the Republic

After the overthrow of the last Etruscan king, the Romans fought over the next three centuries to gain control of the Italian peninsula. In Italy, the Romans formed alliances with some Italian tribes, including the neighboring Latins, whose alliance, the Latin League, they joined. At the same time they fought with other tribes. At first, the Romans were simply trying to protect their lands. However, as each group of tribes was defeated, Rome felt itself threatened by other tribes.

In 390 B.C. a group of raiding Gauls from the Po Valley entered Italy and burned and looted most of Rome. After this defeat, Rome made a rapid recovery and by 337 B.C. had conquered all the Latins. Rome then abolished the Latin League. The Latins were given Roman citizenship but were made dependent on Rome for defense and trade. The Romans made it a practice to incorporate defeated tribes as part of the state. As a result Rome grew both in its territory and in the number of its citizens.

By 280 B.C. all of Italy, with the exception of a few Greek city-states in the south, was in Roman hands or allied to Rome. These Greek city-states in Sicily and southern Italy watched Roman expansion with concern. Some sought to remain independant through the help of the Greek League of Epirus (eh-PIE-rus). King Pyrrhus (PIHR-us), who was head of this league, twice defeated Roman forces. However, his losses were so great that he was forced to retreat. When Pyrrhus returned home to Epirus, Rome was left in complete control of Italy south of the Po River.

In its first centuries, Rome had undergone a remarkable rise—from a few obscure villages in the Alban Hills to a powerful city-state that controlled the entire Italian peninsula. In politics Rome had adopted a pragmatic philosophy that permitted the plebeians to attain full civil rights through political action without resorting to violence. This pragmatic approach also helped Rome in absorbing other city-states, in effect making the conquered city-states partners in the growing empire.

SECTION REVIEW

1. Mapping: Use the map on page 123 to locate, by means of latitude and longitude coordinates, the Greek cities in Italy and the city of Rome.
2. In your own words, define or identify: Etruscans, republic, veto, consul, praetor, aedile.
3. Who were the patricians and the plebeians? What role did each play in early Rome? How did those roles change?
■ What similarities and differences are there between the government of the Roman Republic and that of the United States?

FROM REPUBLIC TO EMPIRE

By 280 B.C. the Roman Senate had fully organized Italy under its control. Important seacoast towns were occupied by Roman army veterans and their families. These towns were regarded as colonies, and their occupants retained Roman citizenship. In a second group of towns, called *municipia* (myoo-ni-SIP-ee-ah), or municipalities, the people had most of the rights and duties of Roman citizens. They could not, however, vote or hold political office in Rome but did have to pay taxes and serve in the Roman army. A third group of towns was made up of independent allies of Rome. The people of these towns did not pay Roman taxes or serve directly in the Roman army. In theory Rome's allies were independent, but their foreign policy was in fact controlled by Rome.

As Rome emerged as the seat of a growing empire, this system of ruling through colonies and municipalities was often applied to other areas. When Rome conquered land overseas, the Romans usually let the conquered people keep their own system of local government and local customs, as long as they paid their taxes. Such flexibility allowed Rome to efficiently rule a wide variety of diverse peoples.

The Struggle with Carthage

Carthage, the former Phoenician colony, was the great naval and trading power in the western Mediterranean in the third century B.C. It controlled

ROME AND CARTHAGE, ABOUT 265 B.C.

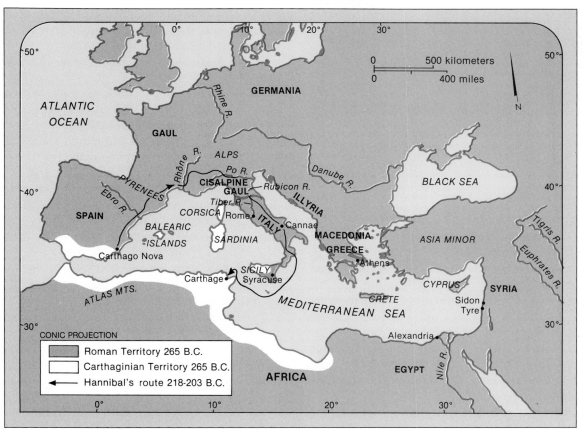

When Roman expansion confronted the Carthaginian Empire in the western Mediterranean three wars resulted. What was the main area of contention in this conflict?

The Carthaginian army featured mounted war elephants. This terra-cotta sculpture from the time of the Punic wars shows such a war elephant. What characteristics of the elephant would make them useful in warfare?

colonies on Sicily, Sardinia, and Corsica, as well as on the coast of North Africa and in Spain.

When Roman influence began to expand beyond Italy, it became inevitable that the Romans and Carthaginians would collide. In 264 B.C. Rome made the decision to invade Sicily to protect the interests of its Greek allies in southern Italy against the seapower of Carthage. Between 264 B.C. and 146 B.C., Carthage and Rome fought three wars. They are called collectively the Punic Wars—from *punicus* (PYOO-ni-kuss), the Latin word for Phoenician.

The first war between Rome and Carthage lasted for twenty-three years. At first, the Romans, who were not a maritime nation, were unsuccessful in their struggle against the strong Carthaginian navy. However, Rome built a fleet of warships and added a movable ramp to each vessel so that their soldiers could board the enemy ships. This development helped to turn the tide of the war in favor of the Romans, and the Carthaginians made peace in 241 B.C.

The peace treaty required Carthage to give Sicily to Rome. Three years later Rome also seized Sardinia and Corsica from Carthage. Rome made these territories into its first provinces. Provincials did not normally become citizens of Rome but were governed by local officials from their own upper classes. These local leaders were supervised by a Roman governor sent by the Senate and supported by contingents from the Roman army.

The Second Punic War

The Second Punic War produced two of the most brilliant military leaders in history, Hannibal and Scipio Africanus. Hannibal was a young general from Carthage determined to reassert Punic power against Rome. Scipio was the Roman general who eventually defeated Hannibal.

Since Rome now controlled the sea, Hannibal conceived a plan to use Carthage's colonies in Spain as a base for an attack on Italy. With an army of 40,000 soldiers and all their equipment, including war elephants, Hannibal marched on Italy in 218 B.C. Traveling more than 1,200 miles (1,900 kilometers), the Carthaginian army crossed the Pyrenees Mountains and the Rhône River, and passed through the treacherous mountain passes of the Alps, and across the Po River. (See map on page 127.) Hannibal's army endured many hardships, and he was required to leave many troops behind to maintain his supply lines. As a result, he reached Italy with only 26,000 solders. Yet with this army Hannibal won three major battles against the Romans. The last was at Cannae in 216 B.C. where over 70,000 Roman troops were surrounded and killed.

The Romans then appointed a dictator named Fabius Maximus to lead the army. He refused to meet Hannibal's troops in open battle, and instead tried to wear them down through hit-and-run attacks. Finally, a Roman army led by Cornelius Scipio invaded Africa, forcing Hannibal to leave Italy and to defend his homeland. In 202 B.C. Scipio and his North African allies soundly defeated Hannibal at Zama. For his African victory, Scipio was awarded the name *Africanus* (aff-ri-KAY-nuss) by the Senate. The Romans forced Carthage to give up Spain, which they organized into two Roman provinces. Carthage also had to surrender its navy and war elephants and to pay an indemnity, a huge fine, to compensate Rome for the damage it suffered from the war.

Carthage peacefully abided by the terms of the treaty of 202 B.C., but in 149 B.C. Rome declared war a third time on the now defenseless nation. In 146 B.C. the Punic capital was leveled, and the inhabitants of Carthage were sold into slavery. The city was sown with salt so that nothing would grow and no one would settle there. Its territory was made into a Roman province.

Rome's Eastern Provinces

During the Second Punic War, when the Romans seemed to be losing, Philip V of Macedonia had declared war on Rome. Although Rome eventually signed a peace treaty with Philip, the Senate still wanted to punish him. When the Greek states of Rhodes and Pergamum appealed to Rome for help against Philip, the Senate went to war with Macedonia. After a series of battles, the Romans defeated the Macedonians in 197 B.C. In 171 B.C. Rome declared war on King Philip V's son, Perseus, who was soon defeated and sent in chains to Rome. Macedonia was divided into four independent republics, and the Roman armies withdrew from Greece. However, a popular uprising to reestablish the Macedonian monarchy provoked another war. Following a victory by the Romans, Macedonia was made into a Roman province in 146 B.C. Rome had also gained a foothold in Asia Minor when King Attalus III of Pergamum died in 133 B.C., and in his will left his kingdom to Rome.

At the edges of the expanding empire, Rome still allowed local kings to rule their countries under Roman supervision. These were called **client states,** or kingdoms. The king retained complete power at home, while Romans controlled the country's foreign policy. Among the client kingdoms were Judea in Palestine, Armenia in Asia Minor, and Mauretania in North Africa. Eventually, most client kingdoms were absorbed into the empire.

Thus by the end of the second century B.C. Rome held control of Italy, the islands of Sicily, Sardinia, and Corsica, Spain, North Africa, Macedonia, Greece, and Asia Minor. In addition, most of southern France was formed into a colony in 118 B.C. Rome now had the largest empire since the time of Alexander the Great. However, Rome's relentless wars had grave economic, social, and political consequences in Italy and in the newly organized provinces.

Problems of the Expanding Empire

The rapid expansion of Rome brought a great flow of goods and money from the conquered lands into Italy. The upper classes acquired vast estates worked by thousands of slaves. Often chained together in work gangs, slaves were poorly fed and often mistreated. Prisoners of war provided the main source for slaves and the number of victims was enormous. In 176 B.C. a revolt in Sardinia ended with some 80,000 people being enslaved. In 168 B.C. over 150,000 inhabitants of Epirus on the Greek Peninsula were enslaved in a single day. Slave labor became the usual work force in Italy.

Through the accident of war, well-educated and skilled people sometimes became slaves. This was especially true of Greeks. Many Greeks served as private tutors for the children of the Roman upper classes, thus helping to spread Greek culture in Rome. Skilled slaves were sometimes allowed to earn money and, in time, buy their freedom. In general, however, most of Rome's slaves worked in the fields and were treated horribly. Old or sick slaves were sometimes abandoned because it was cheaper to buy a new slave than care for one seriously ill or no longer useful.

The large landowners who profited from cheap slave labor eventually forced the small farmers off their lands. The dispossessed peasants flocked to the cities in seach of work. There the hungry and jobless peasants began to riot in angry mobs. To keep unrest from spreading, the Roman political elite provided them with "bread and circuses," that is, free food and public entertainment. Slaves and condemned criminals were used as contestants in the public arenas, fighting wild animals or each other to the death. Some slaves were gladiators, specially trained fighters owned by wealthy Romans.

A Roman consul tries to control the factions that make up his team in the allegorical mosaic of a chariot race. What were the two main factions in Roman politics?

The increase in slavery, the forcing of small farmers into poverty, and the presence of mobs in the cities weakened the old ideals of patriotism and self-discipline. Wealth, no matter how it had been gained, replaced character and family position as the measure of a person's worth. Standards of behavior declined, and corruption began to spread. These developments would eventually contribute to the collapse of republican government in Rome.

Tiberius Gracchus and Gaius Gracchus

Tiberius Gracchus (tie-BEER-ih-us GRAK-us), a young tribune, attempted to introduce various social and economic reforms in 133 B.C. He drafted a bill that called for the enforcement of the legal limit prohibiting anyone from holding more than 300 acres (120 hectares) of public land. The land recovered from the bill's enforcement would then be redistributed to Rome's poor.

Members of the Senate, worried that such a law would endanger their estates, found another tribune to veto Gracchus' bill. Gracchus responded by having the Assembly of Tribes remove that tribune from office and pass his land bill. When, in violation of custom, Gracchus sought reelection as tribune, a violent confrontation resulted that ended with Tiberius Gracchus and 300 of his supporters being killed. This event marked the start of the Roman Revolution, a century-long period of political violence that would finally end in the collapse of the Roman Republic.

In 123 B.C. Gaius (GAY-yus) Gracchus, the younger brother of Tiberius, became a tribune, and the conflict with the Senate resumed. Gaius Gracchus wished to increase the power of the tribunate by allowing reelection to the post. He continued his brother's land reform program, helping many of the poor to acquire small farms. Gaius Gracchus also sought to grant the equites, the lower Roman classes, and the Italians who did not hold Roman citizenship more voice in the government. He also promised Roman citizenship to many non-Roman Italians.

This reform program went too far and resulted in political defeat for Gaius Gracchus. Even the Roman mobs became angry with him for granting allies rights that the Romans prized as their own. Riots broke out, and Gaius and many of his supporters were killed. In the turmoil that followed, the Senate declared martial law. Within ten years of his death, Gaius' land reform program had collapsed, and the wealthy had regained control of most of the lands that they had lost.

Marius and Sulla

The person who finally broke the power of the Senate was a young military man named Gaius Marius (MAHR-ee-us). In Africa in 105 B.C. Marius became a hero when he successfully ended a long war against an African native prince named Jugurtha. Marius was welcomed in Rome with a **triumph,** a victory procession in which captured booty and slaves were displayed for all to see. Thus, after the war with Jugurtha, Marius was the most famous and powerful man in Rome.

Marius' most important success, however, was his reorganization of the army. Eliminating all property qualifications, Marius enlisted many of Rome's poor into the army. He offered them salaries while they served on a campaign and grants of land when the campaign was over. Each man was to serve for the length of the war for which he was enlisted. Legions were now organized into self-contained units of 6,000 soldiers, including infantry, cavalry, and light armed troops. Soldiers began to feel greater loyalty to their commanders than to Rome, since it was the commanders who rewarded the troops with the spoils of war, grants of lands, and pensions. Marius made the army a means of escaping poverty and, therefore, a good career for the poor.

For a time Marius retired to the east. However, he was forced back into politics by the Social War (90 B.C.–88 B.C.) and the rise to prominence of a rival general, named Sulla.

The Social War began when soldiers from Rome's Italian allies began to demand Roman citizenship as a reward for their military service. Their demand was rejected by Rome. Outraged by this injustice, some of the Italians, who comprised roughly one-half of each army, revolted in 90 B.C. In order to maintain the loyalty of those allies who had not yet revolted, Rome granted them citizenship. The insurrection was then suppressed and Rome offered citizenship to those rebels who wished it, provided they swore loyalty to Rome. This concession was a further example of Rome's use of compromise—even in victory—to effectively govern its growing territories. The Social War also resulted in the election of Sulla, one of the war's heroes, to consul in 88 B.C.

A dispute arose between Sulla and Marius, over who would command the army that was being sent to put down a rebellion in the east. Sulla marched on the city of Rome in 88 B.C., driving Marius into exile. The following year Sulla left on the eastern campaign. In his absence Marius mustered support for a counterattack. Following Sulla's example, Marius used a private army to take Rome. He died soon after, however, and his supporters were defeated by Sulla in 82 B.C. Unopposed, Sulla had the Senate declare him dictator. His job as dictator was to reform the Roman constitution. Sulla undid those reforms of the Gracchi that were still in effect, but his attempt to restore power to the old families of the Senate was only temporary. After a reign of terror, the dictator voluntarily retired and died in 79 B.C.

Pompey, Caesar, and Crassus

For the moment Rome returned to a constitutional form of government. However, this was only a lull before a new round of conflicts began between factions of Rome's military and political leaders.

Pompey, a wealthy aristocrat, was the first of the new round of leaders to emerge, gaining extraordinary power and prestige. He made his reputation as a general in Spain and by clearing the Mediterranean of pirates. As consul, he led successful military campaigns in the east. By 63 B.C. Pompey had organized all of Asia Minor and Syria into Roman provinces and made Judea a client state. By 60 B.C. Pompey was more powerful and richer than any other Roman had ever been.

Crassus was the second richest man in Rome and a brilliant financier who had the backing of Roman business groups. Crassus also gained military fame when, in 71 B.C., he crushed a slave uprising led by the gladiator Spartacus. The revolt had lasted two years and was put down brutally.

The most controversial of the new leaders was Julius Caesar, a patrician who used his political genius to appeal to the plebeians. In 61 B.C. Caesar, Pompey, and Crassus formed an informal alliance that has become known as the First Triumvirate. A triumvirate is a ruling committee of three. In 60 B.C. Caesar was elected consul. After his consulship Caesar became governor of Gaul—part of present-day France. Between 58 B.C. and 51 B.C., he ruthlessly conquered most of what is now France and Belgium and pushed the German tribes beyond the Rhine (RINE) River. These campaigns are known as the Gallic (GAL-ik) Wars. As Caesar became more powerful because of his victories in Gaul, a struggle between the members of the triumvirate seemed likely. When Crassus died in 53 B.C. while fighting in the east, the way was opened for conflict between Pompey and Caesar.

The Collapse of the Republic

In 49 B.C. Pompey, supported by a group of senators, ordered Julius Caesar to disband his army and, despite his victories in Gaul, to return home to stand trial on trumped-up charges. Caesar refused and instead marched on Rome. Pompey and many members of the terrified Senate fled to Greece, only to be followed there by Caesar. At the Battle of Pharsalus (fahr-SAY-luss) Caesar defeated Pompey and his followers. Pompey then fled to Egypt where he was assassinated on orders from a minister of Ptolemy (TAHL-uh-mee) XII.

When he returned to Rome, Caesar declared himself dictator for life in 44 B.C. and instituted a number of reforms. He pardoned his enemies and took several steps to improve economic and social conditions. Caesar gave land to the poor and started projects that would create jobs. He extended Roman citizenship to many Spaniards and Gauls in order to win their loyalty. He reformed the law courts to make them more honest and efficient.

The aristocrats in Rome were upset that Caesar had seized so much of the power that they had once shared among themselves. A group of senators led by Brutus and Cassius, who were members of Caesar's own faction, assassinated him on the ides (fifteenth) of March, 44 B.C.

After Caesar's death, the struggle for power was renewed. Caesar had named his grandnephew Octavian to be his heir. Octavian allied himself with Caesar's aide, Mark Antony, and Lepidus (LEP-ih-dus), another of Caesar's lieutenants, to form the Second Triumvirate in 43 B.C. They defeated Caesar's murderers, Brutus and Cassius, and their forces in 42 B.C. at Philippi.

The empire then split into two zones of power. Octavian controlled the west while Antony controlled the east. Lepidus by then had been sent to North Africa and was no longer an important political rival. Antony formed an alliance with Cleopatra of Egypt and together they opposed Octavian. In a battle at Actium (AK-tee-um), off the coast of Greece, Octavian defeated Antony's forces in 31 B.C. Octavian then annexed the rich kingdom of Egypt. He was now the supreme ruler of Rome, and the Republic had come to an end.

The Roman Revolution had lasted one hundred years. Unlike the conflict that brought political equality to the plebeians, the revolution had been extremely violent. It had trampled on Rome's republican constitution and decimated the political elite of the Republic. Despite this, Rome's empire had continued to expand in wealth and territory. Sulla, Caesar, Pompey, and other Roman generals had used their successes in expanding and protecting Rome's borders to further ambitious political careers. The political conflicts, set up by military successes, destroyed republican government in Rome.

SECTION REVIEW

1. Use the map on page 127 to describe and compare the territory of Carthage at the start of the Punic Wars with that of Rome.
2. In your own words, identify or define: Hannibal, Tiberius Gracchus, Marius, Sulla, Pompey, Caesar, Octavian, client kingdom, triumvirate.
3. Explain how Marius reformed the army. How did these reforms affect the poor?
■ Many national and world leaders in this century have been the targets of assassination. What impact do you think the murder of a political or social leader has on his or her cause?

People in History

Julius Caesar

Born in 100 B.C., Julius Caesar grew up in a Rome racked with bloodshed and civil war. His aunt Julia was married to Marius, the general whose faction contested with Sulla for political power in Rome. After Marius' death Caesar quarreled with Sulla, who was now dictator, and left Rome to study philosophy and oratory at Rhodes. En route, he was captured by pirates, After being ransomed, Caesar gathered ships and men, returned to the pirates' hideout and executed them. Then he went on to Rhodes but broke off his studies there to fight in a war in Asia Minor. Back in Rome, he decided to run for office. Brilliant and charming, he was a superb speaker. With the financial backing of Crassus, Caesar was elected to various public offices.

In 61 B.C. Caesar was named governor of Spain. There he led Roman armies against the Gauls, and extended Roman rule to the Atlantic Ocean. Later he took over the provinces of northern Italy and southern Gaul (France). German tribes were pressing from the north into Gaul, and Caesar knew that if the Romans didn't take Gaul the Germans might. For nine years he maneuvered his legions across western Europe. When he was finished, Rome held western Europe east of the Rhine River. Caesar also conquered part of the British Isles.

Caesar's troops were almost always outnumbered, yet they followed him with a fierce loyalty. He had an uncanny ability to seize opportunities, and to gain victory regardless of the odds. The Roman historian Plutarch said men who were ordinary soldiers in other battles had unbeatable courage under Caesar.

Caesar commanded only one legion when Pompey ordered him to disband his army in 49 B.C. Instead, Caesar led his army across the Rubicon River, which divided the provinces from Italy. Pompey hoped Caesar's legions would desert. Instead, many of his own troops joined Caesar. Caesar soon held sole power in Rome.

He quickly showed himself a capable ruler and began much-needed reforms. He pardoned his enemies. He provided work for poor people, but reduced the number who received free food. New colonies were established, and land given to army veterans. Many Gauls received Roman citizenship. He supervised the revision of the calendar into a 365-day year with an extra day every four years. He named July for himself.

The Senate named him dictator for life in 44 B.C. To those who believed in the Republic, it was an ominous step. A group of patricians led by Brutus and Cassius murdered Caesar in 44 B.C.

1. What qualities of Caesar's are evident by his actions against the pirates? What other qualities are described in the above text?
2. What were Caesar's most important military achievements?
3. Describe the steps by which Caesar gained sole power in Rome.

IMPERIAL ROME

During almost half a century of rule, Octavian brought stability and prosperity to the now vast empire of Rome. His reign began two centuries of *Pax Romana* (PAHKS roh-MAH-nah), meaning Roman peace. It was the longest period of peace in the ancient Mediterranean world.

Augustus

Octavian acquired absolute power through a series of skillful political steps. Three years after the battle of Actium, he told the Senate that peace had been restored and offered to give up his power. Instead, the Senate, which feared a renewed civil war, voted him full powers along with the honorary title Augustus. This was the name that Octavian used after 27 B.C. Augustus had earlier been given the title Imperator (im-peh-RAH-tawr), or supreme general, by his troops. From this title, comes the modern word emperor. Because Caesar had been killed for assuming too much power, Augustus decided to maintain the facade of the Roman Republic. He allowed the nobles to become consuls and praetors, offices now without any real power. Moreover, because the idea of a monarch was hateful to the Romans, Augustus did not claim any autocratic titles. Instead he called himself *princeps* (PRIN-seps), or "First Citizen." In reality Augustus had the absolute authority of a monarch but he allowed the Roman Senate to believe it still had some powers and responsibilities.

Augustus instituted a number of reforms for the entire Roman Empire. He made the civil servants a more honest group of government workers by using professional administrators and paying them well. He also drew new boundaries for the provinces to provide them with more efficient administration. Roman roads were expanded and kept in near-perfect condition so that the armies could move quickly to keep the peace. Twenty-eight legions now guarded Rome's borders, which Augustus extended to include parts of present-day Germany, Switzerland, Austria, Hungary, Yugoslavia, and Bulgaria. The regular troops in Rome's legions were made up of Roman citizens drawn from the entire empire. Other troops, called auxiliaries, were recruited from provincials who did not yet hold Roman citizenship. However, these non-citizens would receive Roman citizenship by enlisting in the army. The army, therefore, helped to "Romanize" the provinces as well as to defend them. Rome's military force amounted to 300,000 men, half legionaires and half auxiliaries. They were stationed mostly along the frontiers of the empire and in areas of unrest.

In Italy, the only military force was the Praetorian (pre-TORE-ee-un) Guard, 9,000 elite troops stationed in a special camp near Rome and in other camps throughout Italy. The commanders of the Praetorian Guard were answerable to the emperor alone.

Augustus knew that the army was the key to imperial power. To assure that no general gained too much power, Augustus kept personal control over provinces where troops were stationed. By the end of his reign most of the legions were loyal to him alone and the memory of the Republic had faded. Gradually, imperial rule became the accepted form of government.

In Rome itself, Augustus carried on an extensive program of reform. He ordered the construction of temples and other public buildings in order to create jobs. He tried to revitalize the old state religion, and passed laws to improve morality and family life. Augustus set up the city's first fire department and police force. Finally, the emperor used Egypt to supply cheap grain for the city's poor. All of this was to insure that the city of Rome would be governed as efficiently as the empire.

The peace and stability Augustus created encouraged commerce, art, and literature. The Augustan Age is considered the high point of Roman culture. The government system he established was sturdy enough to keep the empire strong for a century, even when ruled by weak or incapable emperors.

The Julio-Claudian Dynasty

Relatives of Augustus continued his dynasty until 68 A.D. They were called the Julio-Claudian emperors because they were all related either to the Julian family through Augustus or to the Claudian family through Livia, the wife of Augustus. Throughout the Julio-Claudian period, the army backed the emperors, partly out of loyalty to the memory of Caesar and Augustus.

In 14 A.D. Tiberius, Augustus' stepson, came to the throne. He continued the policies of Augustus, ruling with a steady hand and not wasting money. The latter trait brought Tiberius into disfavor among the masses, who expected lavish gifts and entertainments from the emperor. After some years, Tiberius retired to the island of Capri, off the coast of Italy, and left Rome in the hands of an assistant. This assistant, Sejanus (seh-JAY-nus), became greedy and plotted to seize power, but was discovered and killed in 31 A.D. In 37 A.D., following Tiberius' death, Caligula (kuh-LIG-yoo-luh) was made emperor. Caligula turned out to be a cruel and incompetent ruler, who soon met death at the hands of the Praetorian Guard in 41 A.D. Then the Guard used its privileged position to choose Claudius, Caligula's uncle, as the new emperor. Claudius continued the work of Augustus in reforming the government. Under his rule, Rome conquered most of Britain, and made it a province. He also further extended grants of citizenship in Spain and Gaul. It is thought that Claudius was poisoned by his wife Agrippina so her stepson, Nero, could become emperor.

At first Nero was a shrewd and capable ruler. He appealed to the Roman masses by giving spectacular popular entertainments, including gladiatorial fights in which Christians were slaughtered. Power, however, and the fear of assassination corrupted Nero. Alarmed at Nero's excesses and irresponsibility, Rome's upper classes revolted in 68 A.D. and overthrew the emperor. He then committed suicide.

Two things had become clear since the reign of Augustus. First, imperial administration was so stable that it could survive incompetent rulers. Sec-

The Emperor Augustus is seated on the right. Livia, his wife, is seated next to him and her son Tiberius, the emperor-to-be, descends from the chariot on the left. How would the association of Tiberius with Augustus in this cameo have helped Tiberius' claim to the throne?

ond, court intrigue and the interference of the Praetorian Guard had more impact on who would rule than any other factor.

The Flavian Dynasty

With Nero's death, a civil war ensued for the first time in a hundred years. In 69 A.D. Galba, Otho, and Vitellius, who were generals and provincial governors, each proclaimed himself emperor and each lasted but a few months. Finally, Titus Flavius Vespasian (vess-PAY-zhi-an) assumed power at the end of 69 A.D. Historians have called this the Year of the Four Emperors.

Vespasian began the Flavian dynasty. The son of an Italian tax-collector in Spain, Vespasian was the first emperor who was not a member of an aristocratic family. He symbolized the potential that existed in the Roman Empire for talented individuals to achieve upward mobility. Vespasian restored dignity to the office of emperor. He also improved the empire by extending the borders in Britain, Germany, and Judea, setting up new colonies, and revitalizing the economy. In Rome, Vespasian began a giant sports arena, later called the Colosseum, and built other public works.

When Vespasian died in 79 A.D. his son Titus took over as head of state. In the same year Mount Vesuvius erupted burying the towns of Pompeii (pom-PAY) and Herculaneum (hur-kyoo-LAY-nee-um) with lava and ash. Archaeologists have excavated these cities and have gained a wealth of information from them about Roman society. The brief reign of Titus ended in 81 A.D. when he died. He was succeeded by his brother, Domitian (doh-MISH-un). Domitian was strongly disliked by the senators and upper classes for his despotic rule, and he was murdered in a palace revolt that included his wife among the conspirators.

The Five Good Emperors

At this point the Senate intervened and, for the first time, elected an emperor. They chose an elderly senator named Nerva, who protected senatorial interests. Nerva's short reign (96 A.D.–98 A.D.) ushered in a new age that historians have termed the Age of the Five Good Emperors. For over eighty years the Roman Empire enjoyed relative peace and prosperity as well as a cultural rebirth.

Nerva was afraid that if he should die without a successor anarchy would break out in the empire. Realizing that no emperor could hold power unless he had the army's support, Nerva adopted a military commander named Trajan as his heir. He also shared power with Trajan. When Nerva died Trajan's claim to the throne went uncontested. Thereafter it became standard practice for the emperor's successor not only to be associated with him but also to have an army under his command. The newly installed ruler would then offer the army bonuses and benefits for their continued support.

Trajan, who came from a Roman colony in Spain, was the first emperor from outside of Italy. He was primarily interested in warfare, and it was he who expanded the Roman Empire to its greatest limits. Trajan moved Roman frontiers further northward by conquering the Dacians (DAY-shunz) who lived north of the Danube in present-day Romania. In the east, Trajan extended the empire to the Persian Gulf, fighting battles against the inhabitants of Mesopotamia. However, a revolt broke out in these newly conquered eastern lands that soon spread throughout the Near East. As Trajan returned to Rome to raise more troops, he died of a fever.

On his death bed in 117 A.D., Trajan adopted his cousin, Hadrian, as his successor. Hadrian, unlike his predecessor, had no interest in expanding the empire further, and he did not attempt to regain Mesopotamia. Still he was concerned about the empire's defense. Hadrian spent much of his twenty-one-year reign touring the Roman provinces. He supervised the strengthening of the Roman defense system and had a protective wall built across northern Britain.

Hadrian also improved the civil service and began to systematize Roman law. At Tivoli, the imperial residence outside the capital, the emperor gathered the finest scholars and artists of his day. Hadrian himself was an accomplished architect and scholar of Greek literature and philosophy.

In 138 A.D. Antoninus Pius succeeded Hadrian, continuing his prudent policies. Imperialistic wars were avoided in favor of dealing with domestic issues. New laws were passed to help the poor and protect slaves from abusive masters.

Marcus Aurelius, the adopted son of Antoninus, came to the throne in 161 A.D. A renowned philosopher, he wrote the *Meditations,* a book giving his spiritual reflections on life. Marcus, like his two predecessors, was a man of peace; however, he spent most of his reign fighting the Germans, Britons, and Parthians along the frontier.

Roman Commerce

The saying "All roads lead to Rome" indicates that Rome during the empire was, indeed, the administrative and trade center of the Mediterranean world. To bring in products from every corner of the empire, reliable communication between Rome and the provinces was essential. Therefore, the Romans built a system of paved highways, parts of which are still being used 2,000 years later. To make their roads, the Romans first laid gravel on a solid foundation. Next, they placed a mixture of lime and stones onto that layer to form concrete. On top of the concrete they laid large paving blocks with a convex surface in order to provide proper drainage. While such roads were built primarily for military purposes, they were also used by merchants, traders, and travelers.

By the time of Augustus, Rome was a vast mercantile empire trading in all sorts of commodities. A powerful army and navy protected merchants and shippers who faced relatively few trade barriers or tariffs as they went from place to place.

Roman ships sailed along the coasts of Africa and northeast Europe as far as the Baltic Sea. Roman traders are known to have visited India and, though it is unlikely, possibly China as well. In Rome, they docked at the great port of Ostia at the mouth of the Tiber River where huge amounts of grain were imported to feed the city's population of over a million people. Rome bought more than it sold, and used taxes, tribute, and the spoils of war to pay the difference. The benefits of this economic prosperity, however, were not shared by all. Even in the best of times, great numbers of Romans did not have jobs.

With the raw materials drawn from the entire empire, Rome became a booming commercial center. Jobs ranged from wholesale shipping to selling fish, from tavernkeeping to weaving. Artisans used raw materials from the provinces to create jewelry, furniture, and other finished products.

In Roman cities, the economic center was the forum, or outdoor marketplace. In Rome several

The Appian Way was used to carry goods and people to and from ancient Rome. Like many of Rome's engineering achievements, the road has survived and is still in use today.

additional forums had to be constructed by Augustus, Vespasian, Nerva, and Trajan to handle the overflow of trade and business. Enormous aqueducts for carrying water to the cities were also constructed. Some of these aqueducts remain standing even today.

A Century of Decline

With the death of Marcus Aurelius in 180 A.D. the Age of the Five Good Emperors came to a close. Many of the ills that would destroy the empire were already at work. Pressure from foreign enemies had increased, and internal problems due to a decline in population, a slowing of the imperial economy, and inflation had set in.

Following the death of Marcus Aurelius' son and successor, Commodus, a civil war ensued much like the one that followed Nero's death in 68 A.D. The Senate tried to choose an emperor, as they had chosen Nerva. But the Senate's candidate was soon killed by the Praetorian Guard. The Guard actually put the imperial title up for sale by offering their support to the highest bidder. The Roman frontier army had meanwhile elected Septimius Severus as emperor. Severus marched on Rome, overthrew the Guard's choice, and disbanded the Guard so it would never again inter-

TRADE ROUTES AND PRODUCTS OF THE ROMAN EMPIRE

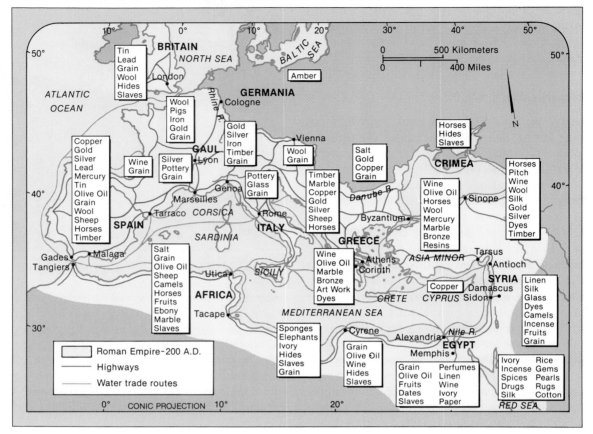

How did the efficiency of the imperial administration contribute to the economic prosperity of the Mediterranean region?

fere in the imperial succession. However, the army now assumed the emperor-making role.

Under Septimius Severus, Rome enjoyed a time of relative peace and prosperity. But this was merely a respite from the decline that had already begun. Severus, aware that his elevation to the imperial title was due solely to his troops, raised the pay of the army and allowed discipline in the ranks to slacken. He also placed soldiers who were loyal to him in top positions of government. His son Caracalla continued this policy of favoring the military, allowing it to gain more and more power. Caracalla was a brutal ruler who murdered his brother Geta to gain the throne. He did, however, introduce some beneficial reforms. The most important of these was the extension of citizenship to all free male inhabitants of the empire. Caracalla increased the number of citizens because he

needed more revenue to pay his troops; only citizens paid taxes. Now, the only groups without the full rights of citizens were women and slaves.

The dynasty that Septimius Severus founded lasted until 235 A.D. when its last member was murdered by his bodyguard. Thereafter confusion and disorder seized the empire for fifty years. The frontier provinces were again under attack by Germanic invaders. Rome also found itself at war with a new Persian Empire in the east. From now on, Roman armies would be fighting continuously either along the northern frontiers or in the east. Constant warfare drained the treasury, disrupted trade, increased taxes, and weakened the government. To make matters worse, there was a rapid succession of emperors, each proclaimed by his own army. Sometimes as many as three would-be emperors were warring with each other. The political and military confusion gave rise to rampant inflation as trade slowed and prices soared. Roman coins were cut with baser metals to save silver and gold. These precious metals were hoarded as people feared the worst for the future.

Most scholars believe the reason for the empire's fall lies in the combination of external and internal factors just mentioned. Outside pressure from foreign enemies combined with social and economic pressures within the empire. These included civil war, economic decline, rising taxes, and political instability. Moreover, the remaining power and wealth of the empire was shifting to the east.

Diocletian and Constantine

After a half century of disorder, the emperor Diocletian (die-oh-KLEE-shun) was able, at least temporarily, to restore peace and stability. Diocletian and his successors would make drastic changes in the administration of the empire in an effort to prevent its dissolution.

Diocletian, who ruled from 284 A.D. to 305 A.D., came to power with the backing of the eastern army. Although, he ruled the entire empire, Diocletian appointed one of his friends, Maximian, to supervise the western part. Both Diocletian and Maximian formally took the title of Augustus, and each appointed a second-in-command with the title of Caesar. The rule of the four together constituted what is termed the tetrarchy. This was also the beginning of the split between the eastern and western parts of the Roman Empire. Diocletian remained in the east and began the task of restoring order. To combat the threat of German tribes in the west and Persians in the east, Diocletian had special border troops stationed permanently on the frontiers. For the first time in years Rome's frontiers were stabilized.

Diocletian divided the empire into 120 provinces, each run by an administrator of his choosing. These provinces were gathered into groups of ten controlled by another official, the *vicarius* (vi-KARE-ee-us). The *vicarii* reported to the headquarters of the Augustus or Caesar ruling his area of the empire. Diocletian also sent spies to watch over the administrators. To pay for all this, new taxes were passed, the burden of which fell most heavily on small farmers and business people.

Diocletian's programs did bring order to the empire. However, on his retirement in 305 A.D., the rule of the tetrarchy broke down and the struggle to succeed Diocletian led to civil war. Constantine, the son of one of the Caesars, emerged the winner in 324 A.D. Constantine kept many of Diocletian's reforms. In 330 A.D., when Constantine made Constantinople, meaning the city of Constantine, his eastern capital, the declining fortunes of Rome and the western half of the empire were underscored. Constantinople was to eclipse Rome in splendor and importance, and would become the center of the thriving eastern empire. Though the split into western and eastern empires did not become official until 395 A.D., the start of the Eastern, or Byzantine (BIZ-uhn-teen), Empire is usually dated at 330 A.D.

The Collapse of the Western Empire

Constantine's death in 337 A.D. created a power struggle among those wishing to succeed him. Three of Constantine's sons and two of his nephews fought for the throne. Julian, one of Constantine's descendants, emerged victorious in 361 A.D., but he too ruled only a short time. Leaders of the armies selected separate rulers for the east and west, and thereafter no individual ruled the entire Roman Empire except for short times.

The collapsing western empire was under furious attack. The most immediate danger came from

The Arch of Constantine was built to honor the victories of Rome's new emperor.

the Germanic tribes on the borders. The Germanic invaders, as you read in Chapter 4, were being pressed forward by the movement of the Huns into Europe. Rome's military and economic strength collapsed under the pressure of internal unrest and frontier wars. As a result of a declining population, Rome recruited more and more of its army from the Germanic tribes within its borders. These recruits often had more in common with Rome's enemies than with Rome itself.

In the west, increasing numbers of people left the cities hoping to escape the disorder, violence, and high taxes. Twice the city of Rome was attacked and looted by invading armies. The last emperor of Rome was deposed in 476 A.D, a date that officially marks the end of the western empire. The empire in the east, however, survived, and prospered, lasting for another thousand years as the Byzantine Empire.

SECTION REVIEW

1. **Mapping:** Use the map on 138 to trace Roman trade routes. What were Rome's main imports from the Middle East? From Gaul?
2. In your own words, explain or identify: Augustus, princeps, imperator, tetrarchy.
3. List and describe seven of the most important Roman rulers between 14 A.D. and 180 A.D. Note their main accomplishments or failures.

- Lord Acton, an English historian, once said that "power tends to corrupt and absolute power corrupts absolutely." This may explain the behavior of Caligula and Nero, but does it explain Augustus? Discuss these three emperors, with Lord Acton's statement in mind.

THE BEGINNINGS OF CHRISTIANITY

As the Roman Empire slowly declined during the second, third, and fourth centuries, a powerful new force was growing. A new religion, **Christianity,** was spreading throughout the empire, re-placing traditional Roman religious beliefs and various eastern cults.

Jesus of Nazareth

Much of our knowledge of the life of Jesus, the founder of Christianity, comes from the first four books of the New Testament of the Bible. He was born in Palestine about 4 B.C. and was crucified in Jerusalem about 30 A.D. His followers believed that Jesus rose from the dead, and forty days later was taken up into Heaven. Jesus spent his adult life traveling through the towns and villages of Palestine teaching people his religious ideas. He also chose twelve of his disciples to continue his preaching. They were called the Apostles.

The teachings of Jesus were based on the religious beliefs of the Hebrews. He taught that the Ten Commandments of the Hebrews was the essential guide to proper living. Jesus also taught that all people were equal in the eyes of God, that everyone should love God above all else, and that people should treat others as they themselves wished to be treated. He further taught that God would forgive the sins of those people who asked him for forgiveness and that a happy life after death awaited such people. Jesus went to Jerusalem where he was greeted as the Messiah (meh-SIE-uh), that is, the Savior spoken of by the Old Testament prophets. These claims were opposed by some as blasphemy. The Roman government feared that Jesus' teaching might cause unrest and threaten Roman rule. For these reasons Jesus was tried as an enemy of the state and sentenced to death by crucifixion, the method of execution used for criminals who were not Roman citizens.

The Spread of Christianity

After the crucifixion of Jesus, many of his disciples became missionaries and spread the teachings of Jesus and his promise to return. Paul in particular took the lead in missionary activities, although he was not among the original Apostles. Paul was the son of a Roman citizen from the city of Tarsus in Asia Minor. His letters to Christian converts form part of the New Testament and were very influential in the development of Christian doctrine. Another great missionary, Peter, was one of the original Apostles of Jesus. He is also traditionally thought to be the first bishop of Rome. Peter and Paul are both thought to have been killed in Rome because of their Christian faith during the persecutions of the emperor Nero.

By the year 100 A.D., the new faith had spread to many of the eastern territories of the Roman Empire and was beginning to take hold in the west as well. Many early Christians were imprisoned and even put to death because they refused to honor the Roman emperor as a god. They would not make sacrifices to statues of the emperor because they believed it was sinful.

Despite their persecution, Christians continued to spread their beliefs. Christianity was appealing because it taught that everyone was equal in the sight of God. Moreover, women, who were not allowed to participate in many pagan cults, were allowed to participate, though not officiate, in Christian ceremonies. Most importantly, Christianity promised the just eternal happiness in Heaven, a hopeful message that had strong appeal in the troubled days of the late empire.

The last major attempt to crush Christianity was the severe persecution launched by Emperor Diocletian in 303 A.D. Despite its violence the persecution failed and complete reversal in Roman policy took place after Emperor Constantine came to power in 312 A.D. In 313 A.D. Constantine and Licinius, the emperor in the east, jointly issued a decree known as the Edict of Milan, which made it legal to be a Christian.

After Constantine, almost all the emperors practiced Christianity. The exception was Julian, who reigned from 360 A.D. to 363 A.D., and tried to restore paganism but had little success. Christianity became the chief religion in the empire by the late fourth century. Under Theodosius, who reigned from 379 A.D. to 395 A.D., a series of laws even prohibited other religions. In this way Christianity became the official religion of the Roman Empire replacing the former polytheistic beliefs of the state.

Early Controversies Within Christianity

The support of the Christian emperors helped Christianity grow and spread, but it also led to clashes between Church and State. While the Christian emperors aided the Church, they expected that, in return, the clergy would obey their

This early Christian era stone relief shows Jesus flanked by his disciples Peter and Paul. How is the importance of Peter and Paul underscored in this work?

commands. The emperors claimed to be all-powerful, even in Church matters. However, the bishops, or leaders of the Church, did their best to prevent the government from interfering in matters of religious concern.

The fourth and fifth centuries A.D. were a time when important Church doctrines were being clarified. Both clergy and laity were divided on many issues. One of these arose out of the teaching of Arius (uh-REE-uss), a priest at Alexandria. Arius preached that Jesus was not of the same substance as God the Father. Arius denied the doctrine of the Trinity—that God consisted of three beings of the same substance, the Father, the Son, and the Holy Spirit. Arianism spread through the eastern half of the empire and seriously split Christendom.

Eventually, Emperor Constantine decided to settle the controversy over Arianism. He summoned the bishops of the empire to a council in Asia Minor in 325 A.D. The Council of Nicaea condemned Arianism as a false teaching and outlawed it. Some years later a summary of the accepted Christian beliefs known as the Nicene Creed was written and is still used by many Christian denominations today.

The Papacy

After all the Apostles had died, a struggle for influence soon began in the Church. The bishops of the

SOCIAL SCIENCE SKILLS

USING HISTORICAL MAPS

Historical maps are useful in illustrating events, boundary changes, movements of people or goods, and other important historical data. Interpreting information on a historical map is an essential skill for all history students.

Use the title of the map below to help identify the map's purpose. Other clues to identifying and interpreting information on the map are contained in the map key. In this particular instance both lines and color are used to convey important information on the map. In other maps, symbols and boxed labels can be used for this purpose. The basic map-reading skills introduced in the Preliminary Chapter, *Building Your Geography Skills* (pages 1–7), will also help to locate direction, determine distance, and identify geographical features. Use the map below to answer the following questions.

1. Identify the purpose of this historical map.
2. In which general direction did St. Paul go after he left Tarsus?
3. St. Paul lived during the first century A.D. What evidence is there on this map to document his success as a missionary?
4. How could this map be used to describe the impact of Constantine's decision to make Christianity the state religion of the empire?

THE SPREAD OF CHRISTIANITY

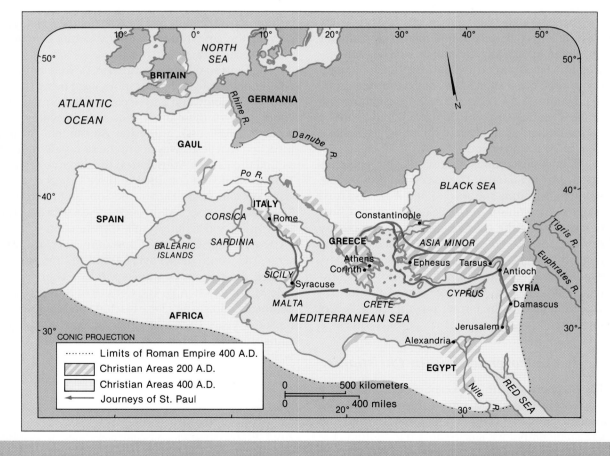

most important cities, particularly Rome, Constantinople, and Alexandria, became the most influential leaders in the Church. Each such bishop was called father, or *papa,* by his followers. Early Church councils affirmed the equality of all the bishops, but recognized five as being in direct succession from the Twelve Apostles. These were the bishops of Rome, Constantinople, Alexandria, Antioch, and Jerusalem. These bishops were called patriarchs.

As the power of the emperors in the west declined, that of the bishops, or popes, of Rome increased. One of the greatest of the early popes was Leo I, pope between 440 A.D. and 461 A.D. In 453 A.D. Leo negotiated with the invading Huns and saved the city. Leo also played a prominent role in doctrinal disputes and in establishing the Church's independence in matters of faith. Eventually most of the western empire accepted the pope in Rome as supreme, while the bishops in the east followed the patriarch of Constantinople, who was supported, and to some degree, overshadowed by the Byzantine emperor.

The sacred writings of the Christian Church consisted of the Hebrew Bible, the Old Testament as it was called by Christians, and the New Testament. The New Testament consisted of four accounts of Jesus' life, the Gospels of Matthew, Mark, Luke, and John, as well as a number of apostolic letters, or epistles. Also of great significance in shaping the doctrines and traditions of Christianity were writings of the early Christian leaders, known as the Church Fathers. Three of the most important of these were Ambrose, Jerome, and Augustine.

Ambrose gave up his position as Roman governor in northern Italy to become the bishop of Milan in 370 A.D. Ambrose was very important in the development of Church music as well as in suggesting solutions to problems such as urban poverty and the care of orphaned children. His works defended the Church's independence from imperial interference. "The emperor," he wrote, "is within the Church, not above the Church."

Jerome was a scholar fluent in many languages. He spent thirty years translating the Bible from Hebrew and Greek into Latin, the language of the Catholic Church. Jerome's translation of the Bible, called the Vulgate, was used by the Catholic Church throughout the Middle Ages.

The best known and probably the most influential of the Church Fathers was Augustine. As a teacher in Milan, he was inspired to become a Christian by the preachings of Ambrose. Later he returned to his home in North Africa and served as bishop of the city of Hippo. Augustine's autobiography, *The Confessions,* tells of his conversion to Christianity. Another of his works, *The City of God,* was a defense of Christianity, which had been blamed by pagan authors for the sack of Rome in 410 A.D. Augustine went on to expound a Christian theory of the course of history that ended with the second coming of Christ and the Final Judgment.

SECTION REVIEW

1. Mapping: Look at the map showing the spread of Christianity on page 142. What are some explanations given for the rapid spread of Christianity?
2. In your own words, define or identify: Jesus, Apostles, Paul, pope, Augustine.
3. What different responses did Diocletian and Constantine have to the growing power of the Christian Church?
■ The question of the relationship of Church to State has not yet been fully resolved. What questions does this issue raise in America today? Why are they difficult to resolve?

ROMAN CIVILIZATION

In art, science, architecture, and religion, the Romans borrowed much from the Greeks and the Etruscans, while making important adaptations. In law, government, and language, however, Rome made many original contributions.

Roman Law

Much of our legal system is based on that of the Romans, who developed the principle that justice must be fair and impartial. There are three main

The influence of Roman civilization is evident in this fifteenth-century portrait of Augustine. The monk's cell in which Augustine writes shows Roman architectural influence. Augustine himself represents Roman contributions to religion, literature, and history.

principles of Roman law. First, all law must come from one central source. Second, since all people have the same nature, laws must therefore be based on the shared characteristics of all human society. Third, laws should be flexible enough to fit special cases.

In 450 B.C. the Romans developed the Twelve Tables. These laws were similar to other ancient law codes in that specific offenses were punishable with specific penalties. Laws within the Twelve Tables provided a plaintiff with the legal right to force a defendant to appear in court. If the plaintiff won the case, the defendant had to obey the verdict. In the case of debts, if the debtor did not make the required payments, he or she became the property of the creditor.

The Twelve Tables also included rules which permitted the transfer of important kinds of property such as cattle, land, or slaves only through specific legal forms. Less valuable items, such as clothing or pottery, did not require the use of special legal forms. Other laws forbade meetings at night unless approved by the government, the cremation or burying of the dead within the city limits of Rome, or the burial of gold. There was a death penalty for anyone convicted of perjury, arson, libel, or murder.

The idea slowly developed that Roman rights belonged to a citizen anywhere within Rome's power. All Roman citizens had the right to be tried under civil law. A special Roman official, called the city praetor, interpreted the law and handled disputes involving free Roman citizens. Since most praetors were politicans or military men by profession they sought assistance from those with specialized knowledge of the law. By 242 B.C. Rome's population was becoming so cosmopolitan that a foreign praetorship was added to deal with cases where one party was not a Roman citizen. It is from this body of law that our own international law had its origins.

To handle legal matters efficiently and fairly, the praetors came to depend on the assistance of lawyers. Lawyers were unpaid and served because of the prestige and a sense of duty to the state. Eventually they also began to assist people appearing in court. Their opinions helped to establish fairness in law rather than just strict and narrow legal interpretation. Thus emerged the lasting concept that laws from a central source should be flexible enough to be applied to different circumstances.

Religion

The early Romans worshiped spirits, called *numina* (NOO-mih-nah), which they believed lived in the natural world around them—in the trees, the rivers, and on the earth. They also worshiped spirits, the *Lares* and *Penates*, who guarded their homes and granaries. Roman households included parents, unmarried children, married sons and their families, and slaves. The father, as head of the household, led the family in worship.

After contact with Greece, the Romans adopted many of the Greek gods and goddesses and gave them Roman names. Athena became Minerva, Zeus was called Jupiter, Poseidon became Neptune, and so forth. Like the Greeks, the Romans held many festivals in honor of the gods. After Augustus even the emperor was worshiped as if he were a god, and his life was celebrated on a special day of public thanksgiving, usually the emperor's birthday. The emperor also served as high priest in the religious ceremonies of the state. In addition many cults from the eastern parts of the empire became fashionable among the Romans. Mithras, a Persian deity, was worshiped in special underground sanctuaries. These symbolized the darkness from which men struggled to reach the light. Because it emphasized courage and duty, Mithraism became very popular in the Roman army. But it was a cult reserved for men only. The Egyptian goddess Isis, on the other hand, appealed primarily to women. Among the new religions was Christianity, which you read about in the previous section and which was, by far, the most enduring and significant of the new religions.

Roman Literature and Language

Rome produced many writers whose works have had a lasting impact on the literature of the western world. Rome also did much to spread the Latin language.

The Roman poets Lucretius (loo-KREE-shee-us) and Catullus (KAT-uh-lus), known for their beautiful language and the metrical balance of their poems, illustrate the great variety of Roman poetry. Lucretius wrote a long philosophical poem called *On the Nature of Things,* while Catullus wrote satire and lighthearted verses on love, desire, and fantasy.

The most famous Roman poet was Virgil, who lived from 70 B.C. to 19 B.C. His epic poem the *Aeneid* (eh-NEE-id) describes the legendary past of Rome. The chief character in Virgil's work was Aeneas. He was a hero and survivor of the Trojan war who, after many adventures, came to Italy where his descendants founded the city of Rome. In the *Aeneid,* modeled on Homer's epic poetry and written during the reign of Augustus, Virgil stressed the sacred mission of Rome and its destiny to conquer and organize the world.

One of Rome's finest writers of prose was Cicero (SISS-uh-roh), who lived from 106 B.C. to 43 B.C. Cicero held many high offices, including that of consul. Famous as a lawyer, politician, and orator, he carefully prepared speeches for the lawcourts and the Senate. A gifted stylist, he did much to perfect the use of the Latin language. Cicero also wrote essays on philosophy based on the works of Plato, Aristotle and others.

Writers of Greek ancestry also became prominent during the Roman period. One was Plutarch (PLOO-tahrk), who was born about 50 A.D. Plutarch, a writer, philosopher, and historian, produced a huge volume of work, including *Lives,* a set of historical biographies, and *Moralia* (moh-RALE-ee-ah), an influential collection of essays. The biographies in *Lives* were arranged to present a parallel history of Greece and Rome, while promoting the traditional ideals of heroism, character, and duty to the state.

Among Rome's other important historians were Livy and Tacitus. Livy wrote at the time of Augustus and his works tell the story of Rome from its beginnings through the Republic. Tacitus served in the government under several emperors, including Vespasian. In the second century A.D. Tacitus wrote a history of the early empire in which he compared what he saw as its evils to the glory of Rome's past. His *Annals* and *Histories* are the best primary sources available for the period 14 A.D. to 96 A.D.

Latin, the language of Rome, continued as the language of educated people in Europe long after the end of the Roman Empire. Today, Latin is still used to varying degrees in many fields of study, including medicine, botany, and law. Spoken Latin changed over the years and formed the basis of other European languages, including Spanish, Portuguese, Italian, and French.

Art and Architecture

The Romans were among the greatest architects of the ancient world. They learned from the Etruscans how to make rounded arches; then they devised a way to set two arches at right angles to one another to form a vault. Thus, the weight of a building was equally distributed, and walls no longer needed to be as thick in order to hold up the roof. Soon Roman builders had also perfected the use of the domed roof. Domes, vaults, and arches were used by the Romans in building palaces, outdoor theaters, and public baths.

Roman buildings were decorated with large sculptures, usually showing battle scenes or victory celebrations. Homes and public buildings also contained beautiful mosaics and wall paintings. Since the rooms in private homes were small and dark, paintings of landscapes were used to give them a feeling of space and light. In the ruins of Pompeii, archaeologists have also found paintings of the gods and Roman industries.

Roman Science

In the areas of science and medicine, the Romans made many advances in practical applications. To treat wounded soldiers, the Romans developed hospitals. They also invented several surgical instruments for special operations. Pliny (PLINN-ee)

the Elder produced a multi-volume encyclopedia, titled *Natural History,* during the first century A.D. This work includes information on the ancient sciences, including medicine and botany, which was used for centuries. Galen, a famous Greek doctor of the second century A.D., wrote treatises on medicine. They included many new and revolutionary ideas on topics such as the circulatory system, the nerves, and the brain, which served as a guide for doctors throughout the ancient world and during the Middle Ages. Another important scientist of the second century was Claudius Ptolemy, who produced works on astronomy and geography. Ptolemy's theory that the earth was the center of the solar system dominated scientific thinking for over 1,000 years.

The rich legacy of Roman civilization is still evident today. Roman contributions to world culture have had great impact in a number of areas, including administration, history, architecture, engineering, city planning, religion, literature, science, and language. It is, moreover, a living legacy, not one confined to glorious ruins and antique ornaments. It can be seen in still-working Roman aqueducts, in modern buildings and cities that follow Roman design, in the great works of literature that are still read and studied today, in the legal and governmental systems that have their foundation in Roman institutions, and in the Latin language itself.

Compare this painting to the Greek vase on page 124. What are the similarities?

SECTION REVIEW

1. Mapping: Using the map on page 138, list and locate by latitude and longitude the coordinates of Rome, Marseilles, Byzantium, Damascus, and Alexandria.
2. In your own words, identify: Lucretius, Catullus, Cicero, Livy, Tacitus, Virgil, Plutarch.
3. What were the three main principles of Roman law?
■ The historian Plutarch was concerned with the discovery of characteristics that marked individuals for greatness. Choose a modern political or social leader and describe the characteristics of that person that you feel account for his or her greatness.

Reviewing the Chapter

Chapter Summary

In 509 B.C., a republic was formed in the Italian city-state of Rome. The government of the Republic was at first in the hands of citizens of the patrician class. Later citizens of the plebeian class also took an active role in the republican government. Roman influence on the Italian peninsula grew until by the third century B.C. the entire peninsula was under Roman control.

*Between 290 B.C. and 146 B.C., Rome took over much of the eastern Mediterranean territory that had been under the rule of Alexander the Great. After the assassination of Julius Caesar in 44 B.C., Octavian won a power struggle with Mark Antony. This victory ended a period of civil war that had lasted one hundred years and resulted in the end of republican government in Rome. Octavian assumed the title of Augustus and brought stability and prosperity to the empire. Augustus' rule was followed by a period called the **Pax Romana**, which lasted for over 150 years. The emperors who followed Augustus were a mixed lot. Some were gifted rulers, others cruel and incompetent. The empire, however, continued not only to endure but to expand and prosper.*

Many of the beginnings of Roman culture can be traced to the Greeks and Etruscans. The Romans did, however, make many original contributions in law, government, and language. By the fifth century A.D., Christianity had become the official religion of the empire.

By 400 A.D., the collapse of the Roman Empire in the west had become inevitable. So great were the empire's troubles that a non-Roman ruler forced the resignation of the last emperor of Rome in 476 A.D. In the east, the Byzantine Empire continued for another thousand years.

1. What group of Roman citizens first had control of the Roman Republic?
2. What role did Octavian play in Rome's history following the assassination of Julius Caesar?
3. In what three areas did Rome make original contributions to western culture?

Using Your Vocabulary

1. Who were the Etruscans? What role did they play in the early development of Rome?
2. Define republic. In the early history of Rome what group dominated the Roman Republic?
3. Describe how the role of the plebeians changed after the founding of the Republic.
4. Who were the tribunes? How did their role affect the struggle between Rome's patricians and plebeians?
5. Who were the chief administrators of the Roman Republic?
6. Define dictator. What limitations did the Romans place on the power of the dictator?
7. Who was Scipio Africanus?
8. Identify the term client state. How did a client state differ from a province?
9. Define *Pax Romana*. What impact did the *Pax Romana* have on the prosperity of the empire? Why?
10. Define the term *princeps*. Why did Augustus choose that title over king or emperor?
11. Identify and define the phrase "The Five Good Emperors."
12. Define Christianity. How did the status of Christianity in the empire change after Diocletian's persecution ended?
13. Who were the Twelve Apostles?
14. What was the Council of Nicea? What role did it play in the controversy over Arianism?
15. Define the terms *numina*, *Lares* and *Penates*. What role did they play in Roman religion?

Developing Your Geography Skills

1. Using the map on page 756 and the descriptions on page 123, describe the physical geography of Italy.

2. Describe how the physical geography of Italy affected the way of life that developed there.
3. Using the map on page 138, describe the extent of the Roman Empire around 200 A.D.
4. How did the extent of the Roman Empire at its height compare with the empire built by Alexander the Great? Use the maps on pages 118 and 138 to make your comparison.

Recalling the Facts

1. Describe how the Etruscans developed into a strong economic power.
2. What were the Twelve Tables? What impact did they have on Roman society?
3. What were the three Punic wars? What did each accomplish for Rome?
4. Describe the reforms of Marius. How did they help the poor of Rome?
5. Who were Pompey, Julius Caesar, and Crassus? What was significant about each?
6. What role did the army play in the Roman Revolution? How did Marius and Sulla contribute to this role?
7. Who was Octavian? What did he accomplish?
8. Describe the role played by the Praetorian Guard in the Julio-Claudian Dynasty.
9. How did Diocletian seek to restore order to the Roman Empire?
10. What were some of the reasons for the decline and fall of the Roman Empire?
11. Describe the contributions of Paul and Augustine to the early Christian Church.
12. Identify the contributions of Lucretius, Virgil, and Cicero to Roman literature.
13. Identify the contributions of Pliny the Elder and Galen to Roman science.
14. What were the three main principles of Roman law as described in this chapter?
15. What was the Edict of Milan? How did it affect the growth of Christianity?
16. Identify three of the Church Fathers and name one important contribution of each.
17. Describe the role played by the emperor in the Roman state religion.
18. Who were Tacitus and Plutarch? Identify one important contribution of each.
19. What modern European languages developed from the Latin language?
20. What was Claudius Ptolemy's theory regarding the solar system?

Essay Questions

1. What do you think were the main strengths of ancient Roman culture? Why?
2. What do you consider to be the main weaknesses of ancient Roman culture? Why?
3. What were the main ideas of early Christianity? Describe how and why it spread so rapidly.
4. Describe the changes undergone by Rome as it developed from a small city-state into a large imperial power. How and why did it grow so large? What impact did these changes have on Rome's political and social institutions?

Critical Thinking

Determining Ambiguous or Equivocal Assumptions

Yet another vital aspect of the critical thinking process involves **determining ambiguous** or **equivocal assumptions.** If something is ambiguous it is doubtful, uncertain, or susceptible to multiple interpretations. Something equivocal is evasive and also of doubtful nature. Keep this in mind as you review the following.

The Roman ideal of republican government changed little over the course of its history. Yet the Roman government itself changed greatly. During the reign of Augustus, the republican formalities were maintained even though Augustus ruled with autocratic authority.

1. How does the term *princeps*, or first citizen, as applied to Augustus, represent an ambiguous or equivocal assumption?
2. Under the emperor Trajan, the Senate was freed from imperial repression by order of the new emperor. The historian Pliny viewed this as an equivocal kind of freedom, remarking that the emperor will know that "when we use the freedom we are obedient to him." Explain Pliny's remark.

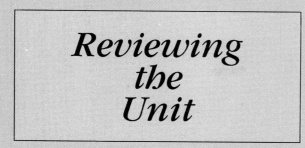

Reviewing the Unit

Developing a Sense of Time

Examine the time line below and answer the questions that follow it.

1000 B.C.	1000	Aryans begin to settle India; Zhou Dynasty replaces the Shang in China
	753	Founding of Rome
	725	The *Iliad* and the *Odyssey* are written down
	510	Democratic government established in Athens
	509	Founding of the Roman Republic
500 B.C.	500	Buddhism founded in India
	479	End of the Persian wars
	404	Sparta defeats Athens
	332	Alexander conquers Egypt
	323	Hellenistic Age in Greece begins
	322	Maurya Empire established in India
	221	Qin Empire established in China
	146	Rome defeats Carthage
	133	Roman Revolution begins
	27	Augustus rules in Rome, ending Roman Revolution
1 A.D.		
	30	Crucifixion of Jesus
	220	Fall of the Han Empire in China
	300	Christianity a major religion of the Roman Empire
	320	Gupta Empire established in India
	476	Fall of Rome
500 A.D.		

1. What was happening in India about the time the Zhou Dynasty was established in China?
2. Which empire was established first—the Maurya in India or the Qin in China?
3. How many years passed between the founding of Rome and the fall of the Roman Empire?
4. Which came first: the end of the Persian Wars or the defeat of Athens by Sparta?

Social Science Skills

Using Historical Maps

Use the map on page 123 to answer the questions below.

1. Describe the areas of Greek settlement shown on the map of ancient Italy. How do they compare with the territory of Rome?
2. Which islands west of Italy did Carthage have settlements on? Compare these holdings with those shown on the map on page 127. How had they changed?
3. Again comparing the maps on pages 123 and 127, how had Roman territories expanded? Comparing the expansion of both Rome and Carthage, why was it likely that their interests would conflict?

Critical Thinking

Review the definitions of each of the following and then answer the questions below:
Warranted and unwarranted claims (page 97)
Logical inconsistences (page 121)
Ambiguous or equivocal assumptions (page 148)

1. Would you describe the claim of pagan Roman authors that the Roman Empire collapsed because the traditional gods were abandoned as a warranted or unwarranted claim? Explain.
2. Locate the logical inconsistency in the following statement: The greatest strength of the Greeks was their fierce independence; their greatest weakness, their inability to unite.
3. How did the actual authority of Augustus render ambiguous the prescribed authority of the Senate?

Linking Past and Present

The classical civilizations that you read about in this unit enjoyed periods of great cultural achievement, featuring many significant developments that have contributed to modern culture. Name and describe five recent developments in our society that may have a lasting impact on the world of the future.

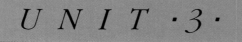

CHAPTER ·7·

BYZANTIUM and EASTERN EUROPE

330 A.D.–1605 A.D.

Objectives

- To describe the rise and development of the Byzantine Empire, and its ultimate defeat by the Turks

- To identify and describe the major political, religious, and artistic contributions of the Byzantine Empire

- To show how early Russia was greatly influenced by the Byzantine Empire

- To explain how repeated invasions brought a great cultural diversity to Eastern Europe

B y 400 A.D. the Roman Empire had been divided into the Western Roman Empire and the Eastern Roman Empire. In Western Europe this was a period of decline, not only in political stability, but in culture and trade as well. In Chapter 11 you will read more about these years of turmoil, which followed the collapse of the Western Roman Empire in the fifth century A.D.

While the West was experiencing this decline, however, the Eastern Roman Empire was flourishing, destined to survive for another thousand years. This Eastern empire is known as the Byzantine Empire, taking its name from the city of Byzantium.

Though the new empire was beset by enemies on all sides, it developed a thriving Christian culture based on trade, agriculture, and manufacturing. For several centuries the Byzantine Empire was the richest, most powerful, and most civilized of all the Christian nations. The rise of the Muslim peoples, however, eventually led to the empire's overthrow.

The legacy of Orthodoxy (AWR-thuh-dox-ee), the Byzantine religion, then passed to a new power—Russia—which rose out of Viking settlements along the Russian river system. This fledgling nation weathered a two-hundred-year Mongol invasion, and then the rulers of one of its city-states, Moscow, gained control. They took the title, ''czar,'' the Russian version of ''caesar,'' and devoted themselves to the defense of the Orthodox religion and the expansion of the Russian state.

THE BYZANTINE EMPIRE EMERGES

The fall of the Roman Empire in the fifth century A.D. plunged Western Europe into chaos. With the sacking of Rome by the Vandals in 455 A.D., the central government of the Western Empire all but vanished. In addition, trade declined, cities shrank in size and population, and much of Roman culture virtually disappeared. Recovery would come in time, but it would be a slow process. While that renewal was under way, the **Byzantine Empire,** named for the city of Byzantium in Asia Minor, discovered by Greek sailors in the seventh century B.C., served as a buffer zone for the West. It held off Asiatic invaders, fostered civilization, and preserved the learning of the past.

The Eastern Mediterranean After Rome

The Byzantines maintained the Roman system of imperial government. The emperor at Constantinople was not only an autocrat, a monarch with virtually unlimited powers, he was also the head of the Eastern Church. The Byzantines codified Roman law and preserved the learning and language of the ancient Greeks. Because of its location, the Byzantine world was profoundly influenced by Greek civilization. For example, within three centuries Greek replaced Latin as the language of the Byzantine Empire and of the Eastern Church. The linguistic difference was one of several factors that fostered a separation between the Eastern and Western churches. This was complete by the eleventh century, and from that time, the Eastern Church was known as the Greek Orthodox Church. Its missionaries brought Christianity to the Slavic (SLAHV-ik) peoples of the Balkans and Russia, and Byzantine influence played a major role in the shaping of Slavic and Russian culture. Byzantine religious art blended Greek and Asiatic influences, and Byzantine civilization developed its own unique style, which was partly Greek, highly Christian, and very colorful. During the early Middle Ages, from about 500 A.D. to 1000 A.D., it was not the West, but the Byzantine Empire that led the Christian world in learning, trade, and urban development.

Yet events were occurring in the East that would one day doom the Byzantine Empire. One was the rise of the new religion of Islam, which swept out of the Arabian peninsula in the seventh century A.D. The followers of Islam, the **Muslims** (MUHZ-lums), created a new civilization that rivaled that of the Byzantines. They conquered nearly all of the provinces of the Byzantine Empire before taking the great city of Constantinople in 1453. The Byzantine heritage, however, was carried on by yet another rising civilization in the East. This was the Slavic kingdom of Russia, which in its formative period was centered on the city of Kiev. This new power adapted much of Byzantine religion, government, and art, and consciously saw itself as the spiritual and cultural heir of the Byzantine Empire.

Thus, while Western Europe was lost in the shadows of the so-called Dark Ages, the East saw the rise of three new cultures—those of the Byzantine Empire, of the Islamic world, and of the Russian nation.

The Founding of Constantinople

In 285 A.D. Diocletian, the Roman emperor, decided to divide the empire into eastern and western halves, each with its own ruler. Diocletian himself was to take charge of the eastern provinces. This division of the empire was completed when Emperor Constantine created a new capital city for the Eastern Empire in 330 A.D. His choice of location for his city, Constantinople, was brilliant. The city sits on a narrow peninsula, protected by the Black and the Mediterranean seas on two sides. On the north is the excellent harbor known as the Golden Horn, and on the south, the Sea of Marmara. Constantinople became a thriving port and a bridge for overland trade between Europe and the Near East. Byzantine merchants were active traders in the Black, Adriatic, and Mediterranean seas, and the city prospered. Across the base of the peninsula, Constantine built a protective wall. Later, another wall would be added a mile to the west. These defenses made it possible for the city's defenders to hold off a much larger attacking force, while the superb Byzantine navy shielded the city from assault by sea. Well-protected and thriving on commerce, Constantinople quickly became one of the world's great cities. Eventually,

Constantinople even surpassed Rome as a center of wealth and civilization. After Rome fell, many looked to Constantinople as the new Rome. For many centuries the new imperial city and its empire was the richest, strongest, and most civilized Christian power. At its height in the eleventh century, Constantinople had an estimated population of one million inhabitants.

The Eastern Roman Empire Endures

The same Germanic invaders who conquered the Western Roman Empire also threatened the Byzantines. However, the Emperor Zeno, who ruled from 474 A.D. to 491 A.D., was able to rid the East of the barbarian danger. He encouraged the Germanic invaders threatening Constantinople to move westward and take Italy instead. Zeno's ability to persuade is a good indication of the talents of the Byzantine diplomats. Indeed, playing enemies against one another became a favorite Byzantine tactic. Such skillful diplomacy helps explain why the Eastern Empire was able to endure so long after Rome's fall, but there were other reasons. First, the Byzantines had much more manageable frontiers. They did not have to patrol the immense borders that were so difficult to defend for the Western emperors. Second, the Byzantines built excellent fortifications. Finally, the Byzantines had great confidence in their fleet. They had an unusual secret weapon known as Greek Fire. This was a flammable liquid that, when hurled through tubes at enemy ships, caused them to burst into flame. It was invented by a Syrian chemist named Callinicus (kuhl-li-NIK-us). Its chemical formula was so closely guarded that even today we are not sure exactly what it contained.

Government in the eastern half of the empire was more highly centralized than in the western half. In the early seventh century A.D., the Emperor Heraclius (hair-uh-KLEE-us) completely reorganized the civil service. His reforms provided loyal, well-paid, and efficient personnel that kept the Byzantine Empire running smoothly.

Even in the great days of the Roman Empire the East—with an economy based on agriculture, trade, and manufacturing—had been richer and more heavily populated than the West. With the decline of the Western Empire, the resources of the East provided the Byzantine emperors with the means to acquire even greater military and economic strength.

The Emperor Justinian

In the sixth century A.D. the Byzantine Empire underwent a brief but glorious period of territorial expansion and cultural revival. This was largely the result of one man's ambition—the Emperor Justinian (juh-STIN-ee-un), who ruled from 527 A.D. to 565 A.D. Justinian dreamed of reuniting the old Roman Empire, and though he was unable to do so, he came surprisingly close.

Surrounded by able advisers, officials, and generals, Justinian also enjoyed the support of his wife, the Empress Theodora. The orphaned daughter of a circus bear-trainer and a former actress, she proved loyal, sensible, and courageous. In 532 A.D. a rebellion broke out in Constantinople. It was known as the Nika riot, after the Greek word for victory, which was shouted by the rampaging mob. Much of the city went up in flames, and a terrified Justinian prepared to abandon his throne. In a rousing speech, Theodora inspired her husband to choose death over exile, and to make a stand in Constantinople. With the aid of Justinian's great general Belisarius (bel-uh-SAHR-ee-us), they succeeded in routing the rebels.

It was Belisarius who led the first of Justinian's campaigns to reconquer the West. After the collapse of Rome, the Roman provinces of North Africa had been conquered by a Germanic people, the Vandals (VAN-d'lz). It was toward them that Belisarius' first offensive was directed. A year after the Nika riot he sailed with an invasion fleet, landed at the North African city of Carthage, and crushed the Vandal defenders. Carthage and other parts of North Africa remained part of the Byzantine Empire until the next century when Muslim armies overran North Africa.

Justinian then turned toward Italy, a peninsula occupied by a Germanic tribe called the Ostrogoths (OSS-truh-goths), or East Goths. In 535 A.D., after the defeat of the Vandals, the Byzantine fleet sailed from North Africa and landed an army on the Italian coast. They succeeded in defeating the Ostrogoths, but it took twenty years, and the land was devastated by the conflict. Thousands died, and Rome and other cities were left in ruins.

BYZANTINE EMPIRE

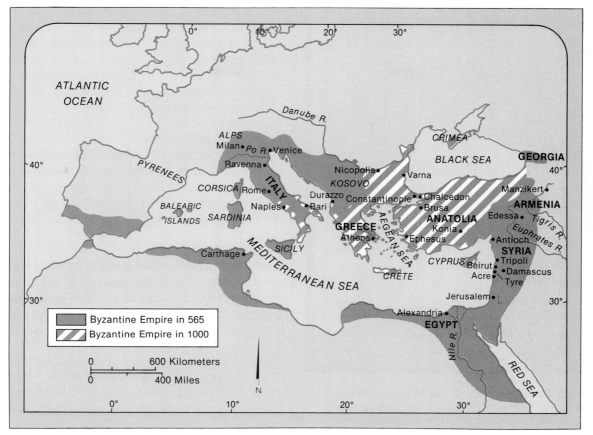

What European territories were lost by the Byzantines in the years after 565 A.D.?

In 554 A.D. Justinian's generals also tried to re-establish imperial rule in Spain, which was occupied by the Visigoths, but their success was limited. A small corner of southeastern Spain was recaptured, but the campaign's difficulty persuaded Justinian to abandon his goal of conquering France, Britain, and parts of Germany, as Roman legions had once done. As a result, Justinian's Western conquests never achieved the extent of the ancient Roman Empire. Nor did he reestablish Rome as the capital of the Western Empire, preferring instead to leave an official behind to govern in his name.

The Code of Justinian

Justinian's most lasting achievement was not military, but legal. In 528 A.D. he appointed a group of officials to sort through laws from all areas of the empire. Their goal was to simplify the laws, organize them, and produce a single legal code for the entire empire. The result of their work is called the **Code of Justinian.**

The Latin name of Justinian's great codification of Roman law is *Corpus Juris Civilis,* or Body of Civil Law. It was divided into four sections—the *Codex, Digest, Institutes,* and *Novels.* The *Codex,* which contained the empire's collected laws, and the *Digest,* which were legal opinions and scholars' interpretations, made up the main parts of the Code. The *Institutes,* which served as a text book for teachers and scholars, summarized legal principles. The *Novels,* or "new laws," were Justinian's own legal innovations. This was the only section of the code that was written in Greek, the common language, instead of Latin, the language of the highly educated. According to Justinian, this was so that the new laws "may become known to all."

Icons, such as this Madonna and Child, appear in many Orthodox churches. Look at the photo on page 166. What does the presence of an icon in this battle scene suggest about the special importance of icons?

The Code of Justinian preserved much of older Roman law and legal practice. It passed on the principle that the emperor's will was law, and that judges, serving as the emperor's representatives, interpreted the law. Justinian's code was introduced to Western Europe in the twelfth century A.D., and was very influential in the establishment of the legal system of the later Middle Ages and the growth of royal power. This principle of imperial rule would be used to justify the absolute power of European monarchies in Europe.

Invasions of the Empire

Justinian's efforts to reunite the eastern and western halves of the old Roman world cost the empire dearly. The armed forces were depleted, the treasury emptied, and the eastern borders neglected. His achievement proved transitory, as his successors could not hold the lands his generals had re-

taken. Only a few years after Justinian's death in 565 A.D., the Lombards (LAHM-burds), a new group of Germanic invaders, swept into Italy. In only seven years they overran northern Italy. By 605 A.D. nearly all of the peninsula, save for the southern tip and a few cities, had fallen to the Lombards. Meanwhile, the Visigoths quickly reestablished themselves in southeastern Spain, and by the early 700's A.D. all of North Africa had fallen to the Muslim invaders.

The rise of Islamic power in the east marked only one of several new threats to Byzantine civilization. Prior to the emergence of the Muslims, Constantinople had been regularly threatened by the Persians. In the north, migrations of peoples across the Danube menaced the empire from yet another direction. The Slavs (SLAHVS) and the Avars (AH-vahrs) pushed into the Balkans. In the seventh century A.D. another enemy, the Bulgars (BUHL-gahrs), appeared in that region. The land they settled was called Bulgaria. However, it was the Muslims who presented the gravest danger. It took them less than a century to conquer most of the southern and eastern regions of the empire. The Muslims attacked Constantinople several times without success. Surrounded by enemies, however, the Byzantine Empire was in jeopardy.

Leo III and the Iconoclastic Controversy

Between 711 A.D. and 717 A.D., no less than four emperors ascended the Byzantine throne. The last of them was Leo III. This formidable general was able to repel a huge Muslim army that attacked Constantinople just six months after he came to power. Leo reformed the government and the army and paved the way for a future restoration of Byzantine strength in the ninth century A.D. that would last for nearly two hundred years. During this revival, the emperors reconquered parts of southern Italy, defeated the Bulgars, and reclaimed those parts of Asia Minor that had been taken by the Muslims.

The popularity Leo III achieved through his military exploits was threatened by religious controversy. In 726 A.D. Leo began to speak out against the use of statues and religious paintings called icons (IE-kahnz) in the Christian churches. He believed that their use was a form of idolatry (ie-DAHL-uh-tree), or idol worship. In 730 A.D.

Leo ordered the removal of all icons—small religious panels used in daily worship—from the churches. The church walls were then painted white to cover the images. Leo's actions prompted furious protest from clergy and commoners, who often ascribed supernatural powers to icons. Troops had to be used to enforce Leo's ban. The controversy lasted for over a century and further divided the Orthodox Church from the Roman Catholic Church, which supported religious art. The dispute was finally resolved when icons, but not statues, were reinstated in the Orthodox churches.

Basil II

The military high point of the Byzantine Empire was reached during the reign of Basil (BAZ-ul) II, which lasted from 976 A.D. to 1025 A.D. A tireless soldier, Basil pushed back Constantinople's enemies and increased contacts with the emerging Russian state, whose soldiers he employed with great success. It was at this time that the Russians were converted to Christianity by Greek Orthodox missionaries. Constantinople proved a powerful model for the Russians in many ways, as they imitated Byzantine government and adopted its art and architecture. Under Basil II, the empire prospered. Trade and business thrived, and Constantinople became the richest city in all of the Mediterranean world.

Under Basil II, the Byzantines finally defeated the Bulgars, who had established a powerful empire during the ninth and tenth centuries A.D. Ambitious Bulgar leaders sought to expand their empire into Byzantine territory, but Basil in a twenty-year war brutally defeated their forces. In one campaign, he captured 15,000 Bulgarian soldiers and ordered ninety-nine out of each one hundred to be blinded. The hundredth prisoner was allowed to keep the sight of one eye so he could lead the others home. From that time on, Basil II was nicknamed Bulgaroctonus, the Bulgar slayer, and Bulgaria became part of the Byzantine Empire.

The Decline of the Empire

The borders established by the Byzantine Empire under Basil II could not be maintained by later emperors. Constantinople embarked upon a slow period of decline. Competition in commerce emerged with the growth of the Italian city-states. By the eleventh century, the rising city of Venice (VEN-us) had become an important and powerful rival to the struggling city of Constantinople.

Another powerful new threat arose in the East in the form of the Seljuk (SELL-jook) Turks. They swept out of Asia, overran Persia, and captured the Holy Land. At the battle of Manzikert in 1071, the Seljuks broke through the Byzantine defenses, and seized a large part of the eastern Byzantine Empire. The loss of Asia Minor to the Turks forced the Byzantine emperor to appeal to the Western Church for help. His request became one of the motives behind the series of crusades that were organized in Western Europe to restore Christian control over the Holy Land. However, this request for help backfired in 1204. The crusaders attacked not the Turks, but Constantinople itself. They seized and looted the city and set up their own regime, called the Latin Kingdom.

How does this decorative lamp from southern Italy reflect the influence of the Byzantine Empire and the growing wealth of Italian city-states?

The Byzantine lands not incorporated into the Latin Kingdom were divided into independent states, each with its own ruler. One of these rulers, Michael Paleologus (pay-lee-AHL-uh-guss), was able to retake Constantinople in the summer of 1261. As Michael VIII, he restored the empire, and he and his successor presided over the last days of the empire.

In the fourteenth century a new enemy appeared in the east. Another Turkish tribe, the Ottoman Turks, conquered the Seljuk Turks. Attracted by the wealth of Eastern Europe, the Ottomans bypassed Constantinople and entered the Balkans. Greece, Bulgaria, and eventually all the Balkans were gathered into the Ottoman Empire. The Byzantine Empire was reduced to the area in and around Constantinople.

The Turks closed in, surrounding Constantinople in 1453. The seige lasted seven weeks. Constantinople's walls had withstood invaders countless times before, but they could not hold up against the new Turkish guns. The Byzantines fought heroically, but the Turkish cannons destroyed the city walls, allowing the Turks to enter the city in overwhelming numbers. With the fall of Constantinople, the Byzantine Empire was officially brought to an end.

SECTION REVIEW

1. Mapping: Use the map on page 155 to explain why Constantinople was ideally situated as a trading center. Why was the Byzantine Empire considered a buffer zone for Western Europe?
2. In your own words, define or identify: the Byzantine Empire, Muslims, the Code of Justinian, Leo III, icons, Basil II, Greek Fire.
3. Describe the achievements of Emperor Justinian. What was his most lasting contribution to history?
4. Why were Justinian and Basil II considered great rulers of their times?
■ Why do nations sometimes embark on military campaigns where the possibility exists that even short-term victory might result in long-term defeat? Consider the campaigns of both Justinian and Basil II in your answer.

CONTRIBUTIONS OF THE BYZANTINE EMPIRE

The Byzantine Empire preserved much of the legacy of the Roman Empire, especially in law, government, and architecture. But it also became the world's leading Christian power and it developed a unique culture of its own, which survived long after the Turkish victory.

Government in the Byzantine Empire

Constantinople adopted Rome's imperial system of government, in which the emperor was considered the absolute ruler. Christianity was used to reinforce this belief with the idea that the ruler was God's agent on Earth. He was lawmaker, military commander, and protector of the Church, although he was not a priest. This powerful combination of roles also influenced other Eastern leaders, especially in Russia, where Byzantine autocracy was deliberately imitated.

Christianity in the Byzantine Empire

Church and State usually worked together in the Byzantine Empire. The Eastern, or Greek Orthodox, Church was supported by the government and dominated by the emperor. As in all other aspects of their subjects' lives, the emperors' decisions on religious matters were, in theory, absolute. They decided matters of belief, presided over church councils, and chose the clergy. This authority effectively prevented the clergy from achieving the power it had attained in the West. At the same time, determined opposition to the emperor's intention was sometimes successful. The iconoclastic emperors, for example, failed to bend the Church to their will.

The early Orthodox Church was divided into the four dioceses (DIE-uh-see-zuhz), or regions, of Alexandria, Antioch, Jerusalem, and Constantinople. Each was headed by a **patriarch** (PAY-tree-ahrk), or bishop. When the first three of those Middle Eastern cities fell to the Muslims in the seventh century A.D., the patriarch of Constantinople became the recognized head of the Greek Orthodox clergy. His position was not unlike that of the

People in History

Basil II

In the mid-tenth century, the Byzantine imperial throne was being sorely threatened. Usurpers and rebels sought to take advantage of a series of aloof, negligent emperors. This resulted in a dangerously powerful aristocracy and political instability. At the same time foreign enemies gathered on both the eastern and western borders of the empire.

Then, in 976 A.D., an inexperienced eighteen-year-old ruler ascended the throne. Rather than watching the empire plunge into further dissolution, Basil II turned out to be the greatest emperor since Justinian. To crush the aristocratic rebels, Basil forged an alliance with the Russians. He arranged the marriage of his sister, Anna, to Vladimir, Prince of Kiev. In turn, he accepted Christianity and sent 6,000 warriors to aid his brother-in-law, Basil. This enabled the emperor to eliminate his opponents and turn against the Bulgarian menace in the west. Again using marriage as a means of alliance, Basil joined with the Venetians and, in a war that took twenty years, ending in 1018, he annihilated the Bulgars and their leader, Samuel Cometopulos.

With further victories in the east, Basil widened the empire to the greatest extent it had known since Justinian, or would ever know again. Yet despite all the costly warfare, he lowered taxes for the poor, rebuilt the dome of Hagia Sophia (hah-jee-ah soh-FEE-ah), left the treasury full and—his most lasting achievement—permanently established Byzantine culture and religion in Russia.

Basil never married and left no heir. His reign demonstrated that all that the empire had needed in order to flourish was a vigorous, active leader. Unfortunately, one would not always be available in later periods of Byzantine history.

1. Why was the Byzantine Empire in a period of crisis when Basil came to the throne?
2. How did Basil II use diplomacy to strengthen his empire?
3. What were some of the features of Basil II's reign that illustrate his success?

pope in the West, but there were significant differences. The pope was the head of the Western Church and was elected from within that Church. The patriarch, however, was appointed by the emperor from candidates recommended by the clergy. In the West, papal power rivaled kingly power. In the East, the Church was an arm of the government and was usually a supporter of the emperors. This arrangement was referred to by the term caesaropapism (see-zuhr-oh-PAY-piz′m). In the West, the Church stood apart from government as an independent institution, although there were often close ties between Church and State.

Christianity's split into Western and Eastern churches began in the fifth century A.D. The gap widened for the next six hundred years until it became virtually unbridgeable in 1054. The primary theological dispute that divided the two Christian churches was the question of papal supremacy.

After Constantinople was taken by the Muslims, Hagia Sophia was turned into a mosque. Note the four minarets, the tall, slim towers characteristic of Islamic architecture, that were added to the church exterior and the Arabic inscriptions in the interior. Hagia Sophia is now a museum with the original Byzantine art restored.

The Orthodox Church did not recognize the Roman pope's authority over Eastern churches. An attack by the patriarch of Constantinople on Latin churches in his city led to the patriarch's excommunication in 1054. This action angered Eastern Christians and resulted in the Schism of East and West, a split that had no hope of repair after the crusaders sacked Constantinople in 1204. The two churches continued to develop separate traditions. For example, the Catholic Church requires an unmarried clergy and uses Latin as its official language; the Orthodox Church permits a married clergy and has Greek as its official language.

Like their Roman Catholic counterparts in the West, Orthodox missionaries actively spread Christian doctrine to nearby peoples. Their efforts won many converts in Eastern Europe. Between the ninth and eleventh centuries, Orthodox Christianity was accepted by the Russians, the Romanians, and the peoples of the Balkans, including the Serbs of modern Yugoslavia, and Constantinople's former enemies, the Bulgarians. In fact, the very alphabet now used in much of Eastern Europe was brought by Orthodox missionaries—the brothers Cyril and Methodius, who were sent to what is now Czechoslovakia (check-uh-sloe-VAK-ee-uh)

in the ninth century A.D. When they discovered that the Slavs had no written language, they devised a new alphabet incorporating Greek, Latin, Hebrew, plus some newly invented letters. This Slavic alphabet was named *Cyrillic* (suh-RIL-ik), after the more scholarly of the two brothers. It is still used today in Russia, Bulgaria, and Yugoslavia.

As new kingdoms were created in Eastern Europe, each nation formed its own church administration and named its own bishops. Eventually, these became independent national churches such as the Russian Orthodox, the Greek Orthodox, and the Bulgarian Orthodox churches.

Byzantine Art

Like the art of the West, Byzantine art was almost exclusively religious in nature. At first there was considerable borrowing from older Roman styles, but gradually Byzantine artists developed a style strongly influenced by oriental art. This influence can be seen in the Byzantine fondness for vivid colors and elaborate ornamentation.

Byzantine art was meant to serve religion. Its purpose was not realistic, but rather it was intended to instill religious devotion. One of the most effective forms of Byzantine religious art were the mosaics used to decorate church interiors. Mosaics are pictures created by assembling small tiles of glass, stone, wood and marble, set at angles in the mortar to catch light in even the darkest interior. The finest Byzantine mosaics represent some of the greatest artworks of the Western world. The art of painting icons also reached a highly sophisticated level. The tradition of icon painting was carried on in Slavic lands, especially Russia, long after the fall of Constantinople. This makes the Byzantine style the longest-lasting style in all of Western art.

The powerful, distinctive style of Byzantine architecture influenced all Europe. The greatest achievements, as might be expected, were churches that combined influences from Rome, Syria, and Persia. The ground plan was usually cruciform, or in the shape of a cross. However, it is clear that what really interested Byzantine architects was vertical space. They felt the need for a building that would send the viewer's thoughts to heaven. Their answer was the use of a dome. The dome had been used by the Romans, the outstanding example being Rome's Pantheon, but in Roman buildings the weight of the dome was borne by thick walls. The Byzantine builders conceived the idea of placing the dome on columns, and thus were able to place a round dome on a rectangular building—a major architectural achievement. Occasionally, Byzantine architects built five-domed churches with a large center dome and four smaller ones on each of the arms that made up the cruciform ground plan—Saint Mark's in Venice is an example. But by far the greatest example of Byzantine architecture is the great church of Hagia Sophia, which means "Holy Wisdom." This structure was begun by Justinian in Constantinople in 533 A.D. Its immense interior, lavishly decorated with murals, mosaics, and metalwork, rose at the apex of the dome to a height of 150 feet (46 meters). This church was so large that several normal-sized churches could fit comfortably inside without touching a wall. Its greatest attribute, however, was its completely novel design. Its style influenced buildings as far away as France, and set the pattern for countless Russian churches. It is no wonder that when Justinian witnessed its completion he said, "Thanks be to God who has found me worthy to complete so great a work and to surpass even thee, 0 Solomon!"

SECTION REVIEW

1. In your own words, define or identify: patriarch, the Schism of East and West, the Cyrillic alphabet, mosaics, Hagia Sophia.
2. Describe the absolute powers held by the Byzantine emperor in all matters concerning both government and religion.
■ What do you think life was like living under an absolute ruler? Do you think you would have enjoyed it? Why or why not? Is there a time when absolute rule might be justified?

THE RISE OF EARLY RUSSIA

Perhaps more than any other nation, the development of Russia was dependent on its geography. An immense nation, it stretches from the Arctic Ocean to the Black Sea and from Poland to the Pacific, a distance of 5,000 miles (8,000 kilometers). The continents of Europe and Asia, an area called Eurasia, meet at the north-south chain of the Ural Mountains. The part of Russia east of the Urals is referred to as Siberia. Lands to the west are called European Russia, the region where Russian civilization emerged.

The Geography of Russia

Russia is divided into four major geographic zones that run in long bands from east to west. Along the Arctic shores is the tundra, where the permanently frozen soil supports little vegetation. South of the tundra lies the taiga, an immense forested plain. Farther south are the treeless, grassy plains called the steppes (STEPS), known as the "Black Earth" region of Russia. Although this area is Russia's major grain producer, it suffers from insufficient rainfall. This condition subjects Russia to poor harvests, a problem that still persists to this day. Finally, there are the desert steppes of central Asia, from which have come many nomadic invaders throughout Russian history.

The Rus, like other Viking groups, were warriors and traders. How does this statue of Prince Rurik capture the Viking warrior spirit?

European Russia is criss-crossed by many rivers, including the Don, the Volga, and the Dnieper (NEE-puhr). Without these rivers, travel would have been nearly impossible in preindustrial Russia. The rivers provided transportation and trade routes for the early settlers. The rivers also linked the Baltic Sea in the north to the Black Sea and the Byzantine Empire in the south.

The Slavic Peoples of Russia

The original Slavic peoples are thought to have come from a region north of the Carpathian mountains as early as 100 B.C. They then migrated into other regions under pressure from the same barbarian invasions that destroyed Rome. Between the sixth and tenth centuries A.D., these Slavs split into three groups: the West Slavs in present-day Poland and Czechoslovakia, the South Slavs in the Balkans, and the East Slavs along the lakes and rivers of Russia.

The Slavic peoples of Russia were primarily agricultural, but in the ninth century A.D. the Vikings pushed into the region. They established a trade route linking the Baltic Sea and Constantinople, and erected fortress-cities to protect the lucrative trade.

Some historians believe that a Viking chief named Rurik (ROOH-rik) took over the city of Novgorod (NAWV-guh-raud) about 862 A.D. Other Vikings, possibly following his example, took over other Russian cities. However, none of them was able to unite all the Slavs of Russia. Instead, each Russian city-state had its own prince. Russian civilization was thus begun, not by the Slavic peoples, but by Vikings. The very name Russia comes from the name of a Norse tribe, the Rus. Eventually, the Norsemen merged into the greater Slavic population, adopting the language and taking Slavic names. The cities and the economy they established served as the basis for the Russian state.

The major assembly point for the river convoys that carried the Vikings' trade between the north and the Byzantine Empire was the city of Kiev, advantageously situated on the Dnieper river. It became, in the ninth and tenth centuries A.D., the leading Russian city-state. The area it controlled, which stretched from the Baltic Sea almost to the Black Sea, was known as Kievan (KEE-yeff-uhn) Russia. In the eleventh and twelfth centuries, Kiev was probably larger and grander than any city in Western Europe.

Kievan Russia

Kiev's princes were primarily successful merchants. They expanded their territory and collected tribute from the other cities under their rule. Unfortunately, they divided their lands equally among their sons. Since it frequently happened that a prince had more than one son, this practice often led to warfare among the heirs. This fighting fragmented Kievan Russia into many city-states, which were only loosely connected. Although Kievan Russia never achieved political unity, it did expound the idea of spiritual unity. It was believed that, as there was one Orthodox Church, there should ideally be only one Russia.

Vladimir the Great and Yaroslav the Wise

It was during the reign of Vladimir (vluh-DEE-mir) the Great, who ruled Kiev from about 972 A.D. to 1015, that Christianity was introduced to Kievan Russia. Byzantine missionaries had been active even before Vladimir took the throne. Impressed by the splendor of Byzantine ritual, Vladimir converted to Orthodoxy in 988 A.D. Two years later he married the sister of Emperor Basil II, a relationship that further strengthened Kievan-Byzantine ties. In spite of Vladimir's efforts to unite the empire, Orthodoxy had to be imposed partly by force. Pagan idols were smashed, and Vladimir ordered the people of Kiev driven to the Dnieper's banks for baptism.

Many other features of Byzantine civilization developed along with the introduction of Orthodoxy. Russian artists adopted Byzantine traditions of mural and icon painting. Architects built churches in the Byzantine style, an outstanding example of which is the Saint Sophia in Kiev, named after Justinian's great monument. Russian builders learned the Byzantine art of dome construction, but adapted it to create an onion-shaped dome. This feature became one of the most distinctive hallmarks of Russian architecture.

Byzantine theology and liturgy were more or less adopted intact. After the fall of Constantinople the Russians continued Byzantine political and legal traditions, most notably in the theory of the absolute monarch. With the Byzantine Empire's collapse, the Russian Orthodox Church was no longer a splinter of the Byzantine patriarchy. It became an independent national church, which proclaimed itself the new chief bearer of the Orthodox legacy. Vladimir, like his Byzantine counterparts, kept the Church under tight control, and the Church and State in Russia thereafter remained closely linked.

Christianity brought to Russia the first attempts at formal education, as the clergy became the bearers of literacy. Using the Cyrillic alphabet, they wrote the first examples of Russian literature. Sermons, saints' lives, and histories were translated from Greek into Slavic. The first Russian chronicle, called *The Primary Chronicle* and written in the early twelfth century, is an important source of the history of Kievan Russia. The adoption of Orthodox Christianity was of utmost significance for Russia's future. It created a religious wall between Russia and Catholic Europe, effectively cutting off Russia from many developments in the West. Though the Russians accepted Orthodoxy, they did not adopt Greek. Instead, Church Slavonic, a Bulgarian dialect favored by Cyril and Methodius, became the language of the church.

The failure to acquire Greek cut off Russia from the cultural influences of the Greek and Roman classics that the Christian church in Western Europe enjoyed. This had important political implications. Rather than follow the democratic ideas and principles of the West, early Russia was influenced by Eastern examples, which led to the development of a more autocratic system, as you will read in later chapters.

Vladimir was succeeded by his son, Yaroslav (yah-ruh-SLAHFF) the Wise, who ruled Kievan Russia from 1019 to 1054. Under his rule scholarship was encouraged, Kiev was beautified, and many churches were constructed. It was Yaroslav who ordered Kiev's Saint Sophia to be built. He also collected Russia's laws and ordered the first Russian law code to be written. To help him govern Kievan Russia, Yaroslav was assisted in his rule by the warrior noble class known as the **boyars** (boe-YAHRZ). The boyars served the ruling prince as administrators in times of peace, and provided military leadership in times of war.

Early Russian Society

At the top of Russian society were the princes of Kiev and members of their families. Below them was the boyar class, which included families related to the princes, and nobles whose ancestors had been tribal leaders of the Eastern Slavs. At first there was a great gap between princes and boyars in terms of wealth and status. The gap narrowed as time went by. By 1200 princes were considered simply the upper crust of the boyar class. The boyars often went into commerce, and shared interests with the merchant class in towns and cities.

There were no less than 300 towns and cities in early Russia, the largest being Kiev, Novgorod, and Smolensk. The development of industrial activity soon gave rise to a small middle class. Their leaders, the merchants and manufacturers, formed a group with some authority in the cities and towns.

Beneath them was a lower class of shopkeepers, hired laborers, and artisans including carpenters, blacksmiths, tailors, and masons.

In rural areas, below the boyars, were the peasants. Some peasants owned large farms and might be considered a kind of rural middle class; most, however, were small farmers. Beneath them were the wage-laborers who worked on the estates of princes or boyars. Some peasants were indentured, that is, they were bound to work the land and could not leave until their debts were paid. As the czars, as Russian rulers were called, became more powerful, peasant liberties gradually eroded until nearly the entire class of landless peasants was reduced almost to the status of slaves. These peasants tied to the estates they worked on were called serfs.

The Economy of Early Russia

The early Russian economy was based on agriculture, trade, and, to a lesser extent, industry. Surprisingly, the proportion of city dwellers to rural dwellers prior to the fourteenth century was probably higher in Russia than in Western Europe; about one-eighth of the Russian population lived in cities. Towns prospered mainly through trade in agricultural products, although the principal towns developed various industries. Metalworkers produced weapons, tools, church bells, and probably their most significant product, the axe—the fundamental tool of early Russians. Just as in America, Russian pioneers built log cabins using nothing but that one tool. As stone replaced wood in major building projects, the art of stonemasonry developed. Artisans made textiles, clothing, and felt shoes, and the early Russians were skilled boatmakers.

Wheat was the chief crop in southern Russia. In the north, where the growing season was shorter, barley, oats and, especially, rye were grown. Livestock breeding was widespread, though of poor quality. The abundance of fur-bearing animals made hunting and trapping important sidelines for peasant farmers. Furs were a major export item, and were also used by peasants to pay their taxes. Peasants obtained abundant honey and wax from bees without even having to construct hives—the bees naturally nested in hollow trees.

The Mongol Conquest of Russia

A grave threat to the new Russian state arose in the east in the form of the Mongols (MAHNG-guhls), a group of nomadic tribes from Central Asia. They united in the early thirteenth century and began a series of conquests that gave them a huge Asian empire. Within a twenty-year period Mongol domination would extend from Moscow to Korea, as you will read in Chapter 9.

The Slavic peoples of Europe were no strangers to nomadic harassment, but they were normally able to protect themselves by fleeing to the shelter of the vast forests. Invaders usually did not penetrate these areas. When, in the winter of 1236–1237, Mongol horsemen appeared deep in the forest region, a shock of terror jolted the Russian people. These riders were the advance forces of a huge Mongol army under Batu (BAH-too). His grandfather, Genghis Khan (jen-giz-KAHN) had invaded China, and later, Persia.

Batu had been promised by the Great Khan all the lands that lay in the direction of the setting sun. In 1237 Batu's army appeared before the Russian city of Ryazan (ryah-ZAHN). The prince refused to surrender. When he was unable to gather aid from other Russian city-states, the Mongols captured, looted, and burned the city. Batu's cavalry then proceeded to destroy Suzdal (SOOZ-dul), burn Moscow, and besiege the city of Vladimir. The Russian principalities were disunited and unprepared to fight alongside one another. City after city was successively captured and the inhabitants were cruelly massacred.

In 1238 the Mongols approached Novgorod. That city in the far north, however, was spared when spring rains created swamps that the Mongol cavalry could not cross. The invaders therefore rode southward toward Kiev. Destroying towns and cities as they marched, the Mongol army stormed this grandest of Russian cities, captured it, and slaughtered thousands of its people.

The Golden Horde

In their conquest of Russia, the Mongols realized that it would be almost impossible for their troops to occupy every city in order to keep the Russians under control. The Mongols therefore established Russia as a tributary state. In exchange for pay-

GROWTH OF RUSSIA FROM THE 14TH TO THE 16TH CENTURIES

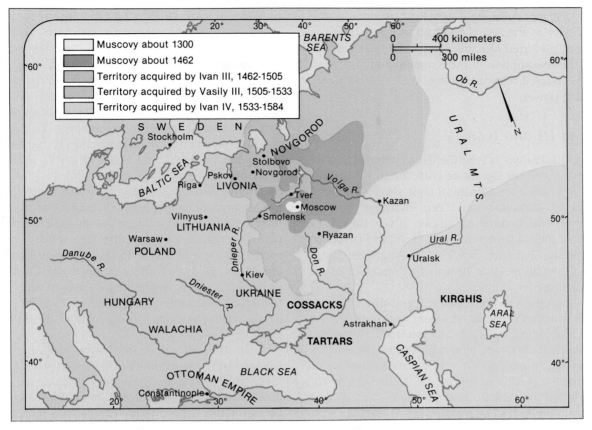

The territory of Muscovy expanded dramatically in the years after 1300. In which direction was this expansion greatest?

ments of goods and money to the Mongols, Russia was otherwise left alone to govern itself.

The Mongols set up their capital at Sarai (sah-RIE) on the Volga River, and from there administered the Russian lands. Any Russian prince that wanted to stay in power had to journey to Sarai to beg for support. The Mongols humiliated the Russian princes and sometimes even executed them. They also ruthlessly disposed of any prince who tried to escape the Mongol tax collectors. The new Mongol camp of Sarai, famous for its splendor, became the center of the Empire of the **Golden Horde.** The Mongols dominated Russia for over two hundred years, separating Russia from the West even more effectively than had the schism between the Eastern and Western churches.

It was during Mongol rule that the princes of the previously insignificant city of Moscow began their climb to the leadership of Russia. They were able to do this largely because they were the most effective collaborators with the Mongol khan.

Realizing that the princes of Moscow were their most reliable tax collectors, the Mongols gradually granted them more and more power. In the middle of the fourteenth century, three Russian cities—Tver, Novgorod, and Ryazan—decided to defy the Mongols by refusing to pay their tributes. The Mongol khan sent an army to suppress the rebellious cities, and Ivan of Moscow agreed to lead. He did this not as a supporter of the Mongols but because it gave him a splendid opportunity to weaken rival Russian cities and strengthen his own. As his reward, Ivan received the title of grand prince from the khan.

It was also during Ivan I's reign that Moscow became the religious center of Russia. In about 1300 Russia's leading clergyman, Maxim, decided to move to the city of Vladimir, but his successor, Peter, preferred Moscow. Peter built the Cathedral of the Assumption in the Kremlin, and now Moscow coupled religious prestige with its growing political power.

Ivan III and Ivan IV

Ivan III, known as Ivan the Great, married Sophia, niece of the last Byzantine emperor, in 1472, nineteen years after Constantinople's fall. The pope himself had proposed their marriage because Sophia had become a Catholic. It was hoped she could effect a union of the Catholic and Orthodox churches. For Ivan, however, the marriage meant just one thing—that he was the successor of the Byzantine royal line.

Ivan tried to preserve the Byzantine system of government. He adopted the Byzantine emblem of the double-headed eagle and referred to himself as czar. Ivan the Great, who ruled from 1462 to 1505, laid the foundation for a new Russian state called Muscovy (MUSS-kuh-vee). He refused to pay the Mongols their tribute and united the Slavic cities of Russia under his rule. Ivan also expanded the territories of Muscovy.

The first ruler actually crowned czar of all Russia, however, was Ivan the Great's grandson, Ivan IV. When Ivan was a child, he inherited the throne at the age of three, government control was assumed by the aristocratic boyars. The boyars had resented the Muscovite princes' claims to be caesars, and became powerful opponents of their regime. Ivan decided that the power of the boyars had to be destroyed. He banished many of the boyars and confiscated their estates. He was, however, unable to crush the boyars entirely, but their opposition to czarist rule was well on its way to being broken.

By this time the Mongol threat had ended, and the Muscovite czars were able to take advantage of their withdrawal to enlarge the Russian Empire. Ivan IV organized the country into military districts that were obligated to provide men for the armed forces. Ivan's forces reached the Caspian Sea. With a victory over Mongol forces in the east, he began the conquest of Siberia. It ended after his death, when the czarist armies reached the Pacific in 1639.

Ivan IV was succeeded by his son, Fyodor (FYAW-duhr). As a czar, Fyodor proved weak, and his brother-in-law, Boris Godunov, became the actual behind-the-scenes ruler of Russia. The reign of Fyodor marks the beginning of a period in Russian history known as the "Time of Troubles." Russia

What clues does the artist of this fifteenth century icon leave to identify the "good" and "bad" sides in this battle between rival Russian cities?

was subjected to bandit raids and invasions from Sweden and Poland. The "Time of Troubles" ended with the election of Michael Romanov as czar in 1613. His accession marked the emergence of the dynasty that governed Russia until the reign of the czars ended in the Russian Revolution some three hundred years later.

The People of Eastern Europe

Few formidable natural barriers separate Russia and Eastern Europe from the great land mass of the Asian continent. For thousands of years, groups of people from Central Asia have moved into or invaded the lands of Eastern Europe.

Successive waves of these nomadic peoples have pushed westward—some as temporary raiders, others as colonizers who settled down to establish farms and towns. Each group brought new customs and new languages and contributed to the cultural diversity of the region. As a result, the people of Eastern Europe can today be divided into several groups, depending on their languages and customs.

Western Europe, too, experienced nomadic invasions when the Germanic tribes flowed into the Roman Empire. By and large, however, these invasions had ended by the ninth century A.D. The Vikings raided the fringes of Europe in the tenth and eleventh centuries, but were successfully assimilated. The Mongols went as far west as Hungary and the Turks reached Vienna. Both instances, however, marked the crest of a westward wave that then receded. The east, however, suffered invasion for a much longer period. The Turks, for example, were not expelled from the Balkans until the twentieth century—a fact that accounts for this region's great ethnic diversity.

In the west, people who spoke the same language were usually able to unite politically, or at least culturally. That is, speakers of French combined to form the nation of France, and the population of England spoke English. Countries that were not united politically until much later, like Germany and Italy, were still linguistic units and felt a kind of common cultural bond. In the east, however, speakers of the same language did not always live in the same place, but were scattered from country to country. A number of different cultural groups, each speaking its own language, might be found in any one country. For example, in the early Middle Ages the kingdom of Hungary contained Germans, Hungarian-speaking Magyars (MAG-yahrz), and Croats (KROTES), who spoke Croatian (Kro-AY-shun).

Language Barriers

This linguistic confusion made the task of nation-building difficult in Eastern Europe and the drawing of national boundaries presented a problem that is still unresolved. In the west most of the nations established in the Middle Ages, whether large or small, were able to endure. In the east several medieval kingdoms either fell to foreign invaders or were absorbed by larger empires. For example, the Russians were ruled by the Mongols for two centuries, and the Serbian and Bulgarian kingdoms were incorporated into the empire of the Ottoman Turks.

Yet through the centuries the diverse peoples of Eastern Europe kept alive their desires for independence. These peoples were proud of their early history and they looked forward to the day when their territories might be reestablished. Their history became one of the chief ways by which they maintained their national identity and preserved their cultural heritage. It kept alive their pride, their sense of being different from their conquerors, and their hopes for freedom. You will read more about Eastern Europe in later chapters.

SECTION REVIEW

1. Mapping: Use the map on page 165 to explain the significance of the river system to the development of Russia. Why did the earliest Russian cities arise on rivers?
2. In your own words, define or identify: Kievan Russia, Vladimir the Great, Yaroslav the Wise, serf, the Golden Horde, Ivan IV.
3. What role did language play in the difficult task of nation-building in both Eastern and Western Europe?
■ America has often been called a "cultural melting pot." What do you think this term means? What examples of this blending of cultures do you see in your town or city? Explain.

Reviewing the Chapter

Chapter Summary

Although the Western Roman Empire collapsed in the fifth century A.D., the Eastern Roman Empire, known as the Byzantine Empire, flourished for another thousand years. The new empire prospered through trade, preserved much of Roman tradition, and established Christianity as its official religion.

The Emperor Justinian left an important legacy of legal reform and built the great church of Hagia Sophia. Under Basil II the empire flourished, and Constantinople became the richest city in the Mediterranean.

The first of several threats to Byzantine civilization came with the rise of Islam in the seventh century. Then came invasions by the Seljuk and the Ottoman Turks. By the eleventh century, commercial revival in the West, most notably in Venice, had already begun to eclipse Constantinople's economic strength.

The Byzantine heritage lived on, however, with the rise of the Slavic peoples in the East, particularly in Kievan Russia. Byzantine missionaries spread Orthodoxy throughout the Slavic lands. The split between the Eastern and Western churches created a permanent religious division in Europe.

The Golden Horde of the Mongols overran Russia in the early thirteenth century. When the Empire of the Golden Horde declined, Moscow emerged as the leading Russian city. Under Ivan the Great and Ivan IV, the territory of Muscovy was greatly extended by absorbing other city-states and taking over the former lands of the Mongols. Overall, the frequent invasions of the East brought new customs and languages to the region, leaving Eastern Europe with a diverse cultural heritage.

1. What developments were occurring in the Byzantine Empire while the Western Roman Empire was in the midst of its decline?
2. What were some of the reasons for the eventual collapse of the Byzantine Empire?
3. Where and in what ways did Byzantine heritage continue after the fall of the Eastern Roman Empire?
4. What effects can be attributed to the frequent invasions of Eastern Europe between 330 and 1605?

Using Your Vocabulary

1. Explain why the city of Constantinople was called the new Rome.
2. What was Greek Fire? Why was it such an effective weapon?
3. Identify *Corpus Juris Civilis* and name its four sections. What did it accomplish?
4. What was the Latin Kingdom? Why were the Seljuk Turks indirectly responsible for its establishment?
5. Define patriarch. How did the patriarch differ from the pope? Who was more powerful?
6. Identify Hagia Sophia. How important was its influence?
7. Who were the Rus? How did they influence Russia?
8. What was *The Primary Chronicle?* Why is it important to historians?
9. Define tributary state. How did this system influence Russia's relations with the Mongols?
10. Define czar. What does the term indicate about Roman influences on the Byzantine Empire?
11. What are icons? What role did icons play in the faith of Eastern Christians? What was the iconoclastic controversy?
12. Define the term Schism of East and West. What impact did this event have on the development of the Christian Church?
13. Define serf. How did the status of the serf evolve in early Russian society? What role did the czar play in this change?
14. Define the term "Time of Troubles." When did this period begin and end?

Developing Your Geography Skills

1. Use the map on page 155 to identify the territories lost by the Byzantine Empire between 565 A.D. and 1000.
2. Use the map on page 155 to explain how Constantinople was vulnerable to foreign invasions from several directions.
3. Use the Atlas map of Europe on page 756 to describe the practical and physical geography of Eastern Europe. Name the present-day countries, major rivers, mountain ranges, and bodies of water.

Recalling the Facts

1. List several reasons why the Byzantine Empire lasted 1,100 years after the fall of Rome. Which reason do you consider least important? Why?
2. Against which Germanic tribes did the Emperor Justinian wage war in order to restore the borders of the old Roman Empire?
3. List the events of 1453 that led to the defeat of Constantinople. Do you think that Constantinople should have surrendered? Explain briefly.
4. Identify the most important reason that led to the split in the Christian Church. What are some of the different traditions that developed in the Eastern and Western churches?
5. What were the outstanding characteristics of Byzantine art? How did it differ from the older Roman styles?
6. Why was Vladimir called "the Great"?
7. List the social classes in early Russia. What happened to peasant liberties as the power of the czar increased?
8. List the events that made Moscow the leading Russian city. Which do you consider the most important? Why?
9. What were the reasons for ethnic diversity in Eastern Europe? Why was nation-building difficult in Eastern Europe?
10. Describe the roles played by Ivan I, Ivan III, and Ivan IV in the development of Muscovy.
11. How do cultural groups within the borders of other nations maintain their own national identity?

Essay Questions

1. Explain why Western civilization owes a debt to the Byzantine Empire. If there had been no Byzantium, what do you think your world would be like today?
2. Compare the military campaigns of the Byzantines under Justinian with those under Basil II. Make sure to compare the intended goals, the success or failure, and the long term result of each of the two emperors' campaigns.
3. Explain why Russia considered itself to be the spiritual heir of the Byzantine civilization. Do you believe that the Muscovite princes had the right to call themselves czars? Explain.
4. Explain why early Russia was cut off from the West. Give historical and geographical reasons for this isolation. Do you think this isolation was beneficial or harmful? Explain.

Critical Thinking

Determining Unstated Assumptions

Another important part of the critical thinking process involves **determining unstated assumptions.** An unstated assumption is a judgment or principle taken for granted, even though the supporting evidence is not always directly presented. Keep this in mind as you answer the following questions.

1. The only section of the Code of Justinian written in Greek, the language of the common people, was the *Novels*. The other three sections were written in Latin. Why were the *Novels*, or new laws, recorded in Greek?
2. The Code of Justinian was based on the principle that the emperor's will was law. The judges, or the representatives of the emperor, interpreted the emperor's laws. On what unstated assumptions is this process of interpretation of the Code based?
3. When the Mongols established Russia as a tributary state in the thirteenth century, their administration was ruthless and cruel. On what unstated assumption was their treatment of the Russian princes and people based?
4. What do you think causes unstated assumptions to exist in any society?

CHAPTER ·8·

MUSLIM PEOPLES

600 A.D.–1500 A.D.

Objectives

- *To identify Muhammad and describe how he founded the religion of Islam*

- *To describe how Islam united the Arab nomads and sparked their political expansion*

- *To explain how divisions among Arabic Muslims led to a split in Islam and to the rise of the Seljuk Turks within the Muslim Empire*

- *To explain how the Ottoman Turks became the rulers of the Islamic world and how they extended the borders of that world*

- *To describe the Islamic achievements in art, architecture, literature, mathematics, philosophy, and science*

*I*n the seventh century one of the world's great religions, Islam (iss-LAHM), was born in the deserts of the Arabian peninsula. An Arab merchant who was about forty years of age named Muhammad announced that he had heard the voice of God and had been commanded to reveal a new and final faith to the world.

In a very short period Muhammad's new religion was accepted by all the peoples of Arabia, and their new faith inspired them to set upon an astonishingly rapid conquest that is unequalled in history. In just one hundred years they established a great empire that stretched from the borders of France in the west to the foothills of India in the east. Non-Arab Muslims, known as the Turks, became the rulers of Islam when the Balkans were added to the Muslim domain. Eventually the great Christian city of Constantinople itself became a Muslim city.

The Muslims, however, were much more than empire builders. They developed a sophisticated culture of beautiful architecture, great poetry, and brilliant mathematics and science that was far ahead of contemporary culture in the Christian West.

THE RISE OF ISLAM

Islam, meaning "submission to the will of God," was founded in the seventh century A.D. among the inhabitants of the Arabian peninsula. It is the predominant faith in North Africa, the Middle East, and parts of India and Indonesia.

The Arabs

At the time of Islam's rise in the eighth century A.D., most Arabs, the Semitic peoples of the Arabian Peninsula, were Bedouins (BED-oo-inz)—or nomads. They roamed the Arabian Desert, tending their herds of sheep, goats, horses, and camels. Other Arabs lived in small towns or villages and were known as *fellahin,* or villagers.

The Arabs were organized into tribes, and each was governed by a leader called a sheik. Loyalty to one's own tribe was intense, and the tribes were constantly at war with one another, organizing raids on their rivals' herds. Although tribal and family loyalties continued, no larger political organization was able to unite the Arab tribes until after the seventh century, A.D.

Arab Religion Before Islam

Around 610 A.D. the religious leader, Muhammad, announced his new faith to the peoples of Arabia. Pre-Islamic Arab religion was **polytheistic,** that is, the Arabs worshiped many gods. They believed that spirits, or *jinn,* dwelled in wells, trees, stones, the sun, the moon, the stars, and other natural objects. One of the many divinities they worshiped was Allah, the creator of the universe. Sometimes special significance was given to certain stones, which were thought to house spirits. There were several revered stones in Arabia, but the most famous one was in Mecca, an inland city along an important trade route near the Arabian coast. A cube-shaped temple was built to house a great black stone—which some theorize is a meteorite—and this shrine became known as the Kaaba. Many of the gods of Arabia were housed and worshiped at this site, and Mecca came to be considered a holy city. Long before Muhammad, pilgrims from all over Arabia traveled to Mecca to worship and pray.

Muslims pray and recite the Koran as they make seven circuits of the Kaaba. Then they kiss the Black Stone inside the Kaaba to complete their pilgrimage to Mecca.

Muhammad

It is generally agreed that Muhammad, the son of Abdullah, was born to a poorer branch of Mecca's leading family, the Quraish (koo-RAISH). His parents died when he was a child, and Muhammad was reared first by his grandfather and then by an uncle, Abu Talib. It is said that with his uncle, a merchant, Muhammad traveled to Syria and other places in Arabia. It appears that Muhammad became a successful businessman known for his honesty. Like other traders, caravans kept him in touch with developments in the Middle East. There is no doubt that Muhammad's commercial activities brought him into contact with both Christians and Jews and that he became familiar with their beliefs. There are no historical documents to indicate that Muhammad received any formal education, but historians do know that at age twenty-five he married a wealthy widow about fifteen years older than he. Her name was Khadija (khah-DEE-jah), and they had four daughters.

The idea of monotheism, or the belief in a single god, was not new to the Arabs. Some people, including Khadija's uncle, had even converted to Christianity. Muhammad's analysis of the differences between the ethical ideas of Judeo-Christian monotheism and Arabian polytheism may well have influenced his religious outlook.

Every year Muhammad retired to a cave to meditate in seclusion, sometimes for several nights. It was there, when he was approximately forty years old, that he heard a voice tell him that there was only one God—called Allah in Arabic—and that he, Muhammad, was his prophet. Allah's revelations to Muhammad continued for more than twenty years.

Muslim Relations with Jews and Christians

Muhammad believed that he was the last in the line of prophets that began with the biblical Abraham and continued with Moses and Jesus. Indeed, all Muslims, those believers who accept the unity of God and Muhammad as his messenger, also believe that Jesus was a great prophet and that he was born of the Virgin Mary. Each prophet before Muhammad had brought a new and more complete revelation to humanity. However, he, acting as God's messenger, was to be the last prophet and God's message was now complete.

According to Muhammad, there was no reason for Muslims to dislike Jews and Christians. He believed that Muslims were also "people of the Book," meaning the Bible, and that Muslims, Christians, and Jews alike shared common prophets and holy books. The problem with the other religions, according to Islam, was that they were incomplete and had deviated from the original message. Jews and Christians were to be tolerated and left to worship as they pleased. Although they were not persecuted in Muslim society, they could never be more than second-class citizens. However, peoples who were neither Jewish nor Christian, or those who had no "book," were good candidates for conversion to Islam.

The Spread of Islam

Much has been made of the Islamic idea of a *jihad*, or holy war, undertaken in order to spread or defend the Islamic faith. It is not at all clear that Muhammad intended to use war as a means for conversion. As Muslim armies swept across the Arabian peninsula, they spread their new religion by peaceful means as well as by violent conquest.

The Prophet's first convert to Islam, however, was his own wife, and his first group of followers numbered only about forty. Muhammad's attack on traditional beliefs offended the Meccan rulers, and they also mistrusted his growing power. It was seen as a personal threat since they feared the loss of income received from the many pilgrims who came to visit the holy Kaaba. The Meccan rulers had no way of knowing then that Muhammad would continue this tradition. As a result, the leading citizens of Mecca did not welcome Muhammad and his message, and they considered him dangerous.

In addition to Khadija, Muhammad's first converts included his cousin Ali and a merchant renamed Abu Bakr (ah-boo BAH-kur). Muhammad made few other converts in Mecca, and even members of his own family found it difficult to accept his ideas. Things worsened after Khadija's death, and people began to ridicule and even threaten the Prophet. In 622 A.D. he decided to leave Mecca for the city of Yathrib, later named Medina, where he had been invited to settle.

Medina

Muhammad's journey to Medina in 622 A.D. is known as the Hegira (hi-JIE-ruh). The event marks the beginning of the Muslim calendar: that is, the Christian year 622 A.D. is the Muslim year 1. Although Muhammad had been persecuted in his hometown of Mecca, in Medina he was treated with respect. The city had been racked with bloody disputes and, because of his honesty and religious reputation, Muhammad was accepted as an arbiter of the quarrels. He promised to restore peace by bringing in the divine law of Allah, and he became Medina's political and religious leader. Many in the city and among the Bedouin of the surrounding countryside accepted Muhammad's new message, and Islam steadily began to grow.

Muhammad's Return to Mecca

As Muhammad's community of believers grew, so did his power. Eventually he was prepared to take over Mecca itself. In 630 A.D. Muhammad assembled an army of ten thousand men. The vast force encamped outside Mecca and lit ten thousand campfires. The Meccans panicked and surrendered the city without a battle. Muhammad marched to the Kaaba, touched the sacred Black Stone and ordered that the idols of the shrine be destroyed. The temple itself was preserved and made the central place of worship for all Muslims. Mecca's status as a holy city was preserved and, from that day on, Muslims were ordered to face Mecca whenever they prayed. This custom is still observed today.

Muhammad's Death

In 632 A.D., only two years after entering Mecca in triumph, Muhammad—prophet, warrior, and lawmaker—became ill and died. Unfortunately, Muhammad had not chosen a successor and his followers were unsure of what to do. Abu Bakr, one of Muhammad's earliest converts and trusted friend, was chosen from among several candidates. He took the title **caliph** (KAY-liff), meaning successor to the prophet, and continued to pass on Muhammad's teachings.

Yet Muslim unity proved elusive after the Prophet's death. A number of tribes that had been loyal to Muhammad felt no allegiance to his successors. Each of the first four caliphs faced constant challenges to his authority—in fact, three of the four were murdered. The second caliph, Umar, had been chosen by Abu Bakr on his deathbed. He ruled from 634 A.D. until his assassination ten years later. He was succeeded by Uthman (OOTH-mahn), one of the Prophet's sons-in-law. When Uthman was murdered in 656 A.D., Ali became the fourth orthodox caliph. Even though Ali was

The Koran includes 114 suras, or chapters, and the canon, or approved text, of the Koran was established in 651-652 A.D. (the Muslim year A.H. 30).

Muhammad's cousin and the husband of the Prophet's daughter Fatima (FAT-uh-muh), many people implicated him in Uthman's assassination and, as such, refused to recognize his authority. A civil war ensued in 661 A.D. and Ali, too, fell at the hands of assassins. The split between the followers of Uthman and those of Ali created a division within Islam that persists to this day.

The Koran

God's revelations to Muhammad were first given to his followers in the form of oral recitations, and only later were they gradually written down. After his death these revelations and Muhammad's most important teachings were collected in a book known as the **Koran,** which means recitation. The Koran was written in Arabic, the language in which God had chosen to speak to Muhammad. At first its translation into other languages was not encouraged because, it was argued, the words of the Koran were not Muhammad's words, but those of God. Muhammad was merely the instrument for transmitting God's words. Later, in order to spread Islam, translation of the Koran into other languages was permitted.

Nonetheless, the Arabic language has a special importance to all Muslims, including non-Arab Muslims. As all Muslims recognize the Koran as their holy book, Arabic serves to unite Muslims everywhere. In some of the areas conquered by Islamic armies, Arabic replaced the native languages. Today the Muslim countries of North Africa and the Middle East are Arabic-speaking. Because Islam has spread over such a wide portion of the globe, today only about one-fifth of the world's Muslims speak Arabic as their native language.

Hadith

After Muhammad's death it was found among his followers that many questions arose which could not be answered solely by referring to the Koran. As a result, they collected the Prophet's other sayings and deeds and used them as a guide for correct behavior. These prophetic traditions, called Hadith (hah-DEETH), are used to supplement and to help interpret the Koran. In the first few centuries after Muhammad's death the Hadith were organized into large collections called the *Six Sound*

Books, and they assumed an importance second only to the Koran itself. Eventually a group of specially trained scholars called Ulema (oo-luh-MAH) used the Koran and other Islamic traditions to form the legal codes of Islamic countries. These Ulema still play an important role in Muslim countries because the dividing line between the purposes of religion and government are not as clear as in the West. Islam developed with no separation of Church and State: the political ruler was also the religious leader.

Muslim Duties

Islam never established an organized clergy, as did the Christian and Jewish faiths. In theory there is no clergy, and each person can approach God without an intermediary. Nevertheless, certain individuals perform religious duties. The Ulema, trained in Islamic law, served also as teachers. Those who lead the prayers in the mosque (MAHSK), the Muslim place of worship, are called Imams. Those who are chosen by the community

to call the faithful to prayer by calling out from the tops of tall towers, called minarets, are known as muezzins (myoo-EZ-ins). Prayers may be said anywhere, but it became traditional to have them said by a male congregation at the mosque. Women are normally excluded from prayer services at the mosque and usually worship at home. Friday became the Muslim holy day for worship, although it is not considered to be a day of rest like the Christian Sunday or Jewish Sabbath.

The core of the Muslim faith is known as the Five Pillars of Islam. First is the proclamation of faith, which is, "There is no God but God, and Muhammad is His messenger." Second is prayer. Besides the Friday worship, every Muslim is supposed to pray five times a day. Third is aiding the needy. Fourth is fasting during the month of Ramadan (RAM-uh-dahn), when Muslims are not permitted to eat, drink, or smoke from sunrise to sunset. Finally, all Muslims, if they can afford it, should journey to Mecca once in their lifetime to worship at the Kaaba, which they believe was built by Abraham and Ishmael.

Five hundred years separate the painting on the left from the photograph on the right. What similarities of ritual are apparent in both illustrations? What impact do you think Islam has had on the culture of its worshipers?

SPREAD OF ISLAM 632–750 A.D.

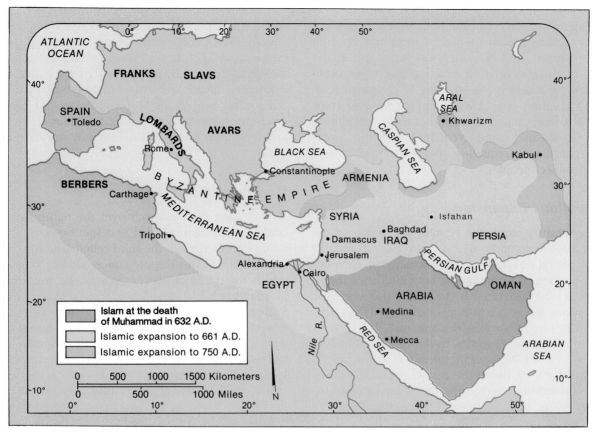

Describe the three phases of Islamic expansion.

In addition to the Five Pillars, Muslims have other beliefs and practices. They are forbidden to drink alcohol or eat certain foods, such as pork. They, as well as other religions, believe in a day of judgment and in life after death, where the blessed will be rewarded and the unjust punished. As the ultimate blessing, Muslim believers will be able to look upon the very face of God.

Islamic Political Expansion

During the reigns of the first four caliphs all of the Arabian peninsula was converted to Islam, and Muslim armies rapidly spread Islamic political rule into the bordering countries. Muslim armies quickly overran the Persian Empire, which had been weakened by its frequent wars with the Byzantine Empire, and seized much of the Middle East from Persian control.

The Arabs were courageous and fierce warriors, and were especially skilled in desert warfare. They were also quick to adopt new military techniques from the Persians and the Byzantines. Still historians have long marveled at the ease with which they were able to defeat the armies of more sophisticated cultures. An additional reason for their success may have been their belief that any Muslim killed in battle for Islam would enter Paradise. There were also economic reasons for the Arab explosion. Their harsh, barren homeland was overpopulated, and they were lured by the richer, more fertile lands around them.

The Arab conquests did not mean that the defeated peoples were forced to accept the Islamic faith. The Arabs were generally tolerant of the cultures of vanquished peoples. Although, in the eyes of Muslims, Jews and Christians were not their equals before the law, they were tolerated and allowed to continue to practice their faiths under Muslim rule. People, nevertheless, were encouraged to accept the Muslim faith. Converts to Islam were given special privileges, including freedom from most taxes. The heaviest taxes fell on the non-Islamic peoples, a practice that encouraged many to accept Islam as a way of escaping excessive taxation. The Arabs themselves never comprised more than a small part of the population of the lands they conquered. However, the Arabic language was frequently adopted by the bulk of the subject peoples.

Religious Expansion

The century immediately after the death of the Prophet, from about 632 A.D. to 750 A.D., marks the period of Islam's greatest expansion. New believers helped to spread the faith after they themselves had converted to Islam. In this way, the Muslims spread across Egypt, obliterated the Christian culture of North Africa and, in 711 A.D., took Spain from the Visigoths. In the east, the Muslims took over the Persian Empire and, at the end of the tenth century, began the conquest of India. Muslim traders brought the faith into China and southeast Asia, and caravans carried the Prophet's message into the western states of North Africa, which today include Libya, Morocco, Tunisia, and Algeria. In Asia many of the nomads, such as the Mongols and the Turks, also accepted Islam.

The Umayyid Dynasty

After Ali's murder in 661 A.D., a powerful family called the Umayyid (uh-MIE-yid) took over the caliphate and established Damascus as its capital. In order to avoid the kinds of bloody squabbles over succession that had marked the previous decades, they established the new principle that succession would pass from father to son. It was during the Umayyid period that the Berbers, a native people of North Africa, converted to Islam. It was they who carried the faith from Egypt, across North Africa and the Strait of Gibraltar, and into Spain. The Muslims even crossed the Pyrenees into France, but they were defeated by the Franks at the battle of Tours in 732 A.D.

The Umayyids also built up a formidable fleet, which was quite an accomplishment considering the Arab's desert heritage. Muslim fleets took control of the Mediterranean from the Byzantines, seized the important islands of Rhodes and Crete, and attacked Constantinople itself. Using their secret weapon, Greek Fire, the Byzantines repelled the invaders, and Byzantine armies were able to maintain control over Asia Minor. Their success temporarily held off the Muslim advance into eastern Europe, and it was not until 1453 that the Byzantine Empire was finally defeated by the Muslim Turks.

Divisions Within Islam

As you have read, quarrels over the rightful succession to Muhammad led to a split between the followers of Uthman, the third caliph, and Ali, the fourth. Part of this dispute concerned the way in which the different parties thought the successor to the Prophet should have been selected. The Sunnites (SOON-ites), the majority party and followers of Uthman, held that succession should be determined by consensus, a procedure similar to the way in which Arab shieks are chosen as tribal leaders. The followers of Ali, known as Shiites (SHEE-ites), argued that the caliphate should be hereditary. Rejecting the idea that caliphs ought to be elected, the Shiites believed that the descendants of Ali, Muhammad's cousin and son-in-law, were the rightful rulers of Islam. Thus, just as happened to Christianity, the unified religion of Islam was divided. Large numbers of non-Arab Muslims resented the heavy hand of Umayyid rule and joined the Shiites and other forces and, in the eighth century A.D., succeeded in bringing down the Umayyid Dynasty.

The gulf between the factions widened over time. The Shiites began to revise Muslim doctrine and to develop their own laws and ceremonies. Some of them developed a belief in the emergence of an infallible leader with superhuman qualities and divine inspiration, who would usher in an era of peace and justice. This messiah-like figure was called the Mahdi, but Shiites do not agree on how he is to be identified.

Today it is estimated that the Sunnites make up almost 90 percent of the world's Muslims. Although a minority in the Muslim world, the Shiites do dominate in some areas, including in present day Iran.

The Abbasid Dynasty

Opposition to the Umayyids finally united behind Abu-al-Abbas, a descendant of an uncle of Muhammad. An uprising began in Persia and in 750 A.D. the Umayyid Dynasty was overthrown. It was replaced by the Abbasid Dynasty, which moved the capital to Baghdad, now in Iraq, and ruled for five hundred years.

The first of the Abbasid caliphs was Abu-al-Abbas, who was known as "The Bloodshedder" because he tried to destroy everyone in the Umayyid family. Only one Umayyid, Abd-al-Rahman, escaped death. He fled to Spain and there started a new Umayyid Dynasty in 756 A.D. Muslim Spain now became independent of the caliphate in Baghdad. Other Muslim territories also went their own way. In 788 A.D. a descendant of Ali founded an independent dynasty in Morocco, and twelve years later the governor, or emir, of Tunisia declared that country independent.

Egypt also followed this political trend and adopted an independent course of action. To strengthen the ranks of the army, the caliphs had used slaves from the central Asian regions, including the Caucasus. These troops were called Mamelukes, and they became very powerful. In 1260 a Mameluke officer took over the throne of Egypt. For the next three centuries that land was ruled by a succession of Mameluke rulers called sultans. Theirs was a very creative and artistic society, and great mosques were built in Egypt. The Mameluke sultans were instrumental in keeping the Islamic Middle East intact when it was under pressure from crusaders and Mongols.

To complicate matters, weak Abbasid caliphs became figureheads. They delegated the governing of the empire to their viziers. Finally, the Arabs lost their dominant position in the Muslim world. Under the Abbasid Dynasty non-Arab Muslims, like the Persians and others, assumed positions of leadership in government, the military, and the arts.

The Golden Age of Islam

Despite this decline in the power of the Arab caliphs, the Abbasid Dynasty marks the Golden Age of Islam. New heights of prosperity, based on trade, were reached. The Muslim world carried on trade with Europe, Africa, and Asia. Baghdad, Cairo, and Cordoba (KAWR-thoh-bah) in Spain became centers of commerce and industry.

Baghdad even rivaled Constantinople in wealth. Baghdad, with its palaces, gardens, and mosques, was among the most splendid cities in the world. It measured two miles in diameter and was surrounded by three walls. Through the four

The great mosque of Cordoba, built between 786 A.D. and 990 A.D., is considered a masterpiece of Islamic architecture. What features does this work share with Greek and Roman architecture?

gates in these walls ran highways that extended to towns and markets throughout the globe, carrying caravans of great wealth and luxury.

Muslim industries produced textiles and metal and leather goods. The Muslims were not only skilled in industry and trade, but also in agriculture. From different regions of their empire came cotton, wheat, olives, wool, and horses. Irrigation made it possible to raise many fruits and cereals. In all, the Abbasid Dynasty's economy struck an excellent balance among commerce, industry, and agriculture.

Invasion by the Seljuk Turks

During the tenth century the warlike, nomadic Turkish tribe known as the Seljuks migrated from Central Asia into the Middle East and began to raid the Muslim frontiers of Persia. The Abbasid caliphate was already in decline, and the caliph himself was sometimes held prisoner by his own palace guards. The Seljuks had recently accepted Islam, but this did not prevent them from warring against the Muslims of Persia. The governors of Persia tried to hold off the Seljuk Turks, but in 1040 the Seljuks pushed across the frontier and won a great victory at Merv. After overrunning Persia the Seljuks aimed for Baghdad itself.

The powerless caliph at Baghdad prudently declined to war with the Seljuks and instead invited them to become his protectors. The Seljuks accepted, and in 1055 they marched into Baghdad. They left the caliph on the throne as a figurehead and a symbol of Islamic unity, but the real rulers of the empire became the Seljuk commanders, who took the title of sultan.

Seljuk armies then moved northward into Georgia and Armenia, and southward into Syria and Palestine. In 1071 the sultan, along with enormous bands of cavalry, attempted a large-scale invasion of Asia Minor. As you read in Chapter 7, he inflicted a crushing defeat on the Byzantines at the battle of Manzikert. The Seljuk sultans were thus able to add much of Asia Minor to their large, growing empire—something the Arabs had never managed to do.

Alarmed by the success of the Seljuk Turks, the eastern Christians appealed to the pope. The political fallout following the defeat of the Byzantines at Manzikert had generated a real fear in Europe that the Turks might take Constantinople and then march into Europe itself. In 1095 the Christians of western Europe formed a military crusade to defend Christianity and capture the Holy Land from the Turks.

The Fall of the Seljuk Turks

The Seljuk Empire was large but short-lived. The tendency of the Islamic territories to form independent states continued, and the sultans could not keep distant lands under their control. The empire broke up into dozens of independent states that continued to war with one another.

The final blow to the Seljuk Empire was administered by the Mongols, yet another fierce nomadic people from Asia. They swept into the Middle East, and in 1258 they sacked the city of Baghdad. They slaughtered thousands, including the caliph, and the Abbasid Dynasty came to an end. While Baghdad was being sacked, however, other Muslims continued to spread the Islamic faith peacefully into eastern Asia.

SECTION REVIEW

1. Mapping: Use the map on page 175 to find the distance between each of the following pairs of cities: Mecca and Medina, Medina and Damascus, Mecca and Baghdad. Describe the Muslim world at its greatest extent. What modern nations make up the Muslim world?
2. In your own words, identify or define: Muhammad, Allah, Mecca, Koran, Mosque, caliph, Seljuk Turks, monotheism, polytheism, Umayyid Dynasty, Abbasid Dynasty.
3. What were the main beliefs taught by Muhammad's new religion?
4. Describe the differences between the Sunnite and Shiite Muslims.
5. What motives did the Arabs have for spreading Islam?
6. Where did the Umayyid and Abbasid dynasties make their capitals?
■ A Muslim has many religious duties. Describe one of these duties and tell how it is similar to or different from religious practices in your own community.

THE OTTOMAN EMPIRE

When the Mongols poured into the Middle East, many of the inhabitants of the region fled in terror. One group, the Turkish tribe known as the Kayi, went into Asia Minor around the middle of the thirteenth century. The Seljuk sultan of Konya, in Asia Minor, welcomed the Kayi as needed military allies and gave them part of Turkey. They proved to be excellent soldiers and under their first ruler, Osman, they also became skillful government administrators. Osman, known as Ottoman to Westerners, also gave his name to the tribe and eventually, as its power grew, to the empire itself.

The Ottoman Turks in Asia Minor

As Seljuk power waned in the fourteenth century, the rapidly expanding Ottoman Turks replaced them as the dominant power in Asia Minor. The Ottoman rulers, like the Seljuks before them, took the title of sultan. They then turned westward and invaded the Byzantine Empire. Initially they were unable to capture Constantinople, however they steadily pushed back the frontiers of the Byzantine Empire. In 1345 the Ottomans invaded eastern Europe by crossing the Dardanelles (dahrd'n-ELLZ), the straits that connect the Black and Mediterranean seas. For more than a century afterward, their advance into Europe continued as they conquered the Balkan kingdoms one by one.

The Ottoman Turks in the Balkans

The Ottoman Turks had now added European land to their domains, and they made the city of Adrianople the capital of their new conquests. The city was 140 miles (224 kilometers) west of Constantinople, and it was from there that the Ottomans launched their invasion of Bulgaria. By 1376 Bulgarians were compelled to accept Ottoman rule. Next the Turks turned toward Serbia. In 1389 they defeated the Serbian army at the battle of Kossovo. The Serbian king was killed and the country became an Ottoman province, which it remained until the nineteenth century.

One corner of Serbia, the territory of Montenegro, was able to hold out against the Turks. Its rugged mountains, deep valleys, and dense forests all made it a difficult land to subdue. Many times the Ottomans assaulted Montenegro, but it stubbornly resisted Turkish control. The Serbians of Montenegro organized themselves as their own small state and selected princes to rule them. Isolated and always in danger from the Turks, the hardy people of Montenegro preserved their language, the Serbian Orthodox Church, and the use of the Cyrillic alphabet.

After defeating most of Serbia in 1389, the Ottomans once again turned their attention to Bulgaria. The Bulgarian capital, Tirnovo, fell after a brave resistance and by 1398 the entire country was under Turkish control.

The Turks spent the next seventy years conquering the rest of southeastern Europe. Besides Montenegro, only Albania and the Romanian principalities of Walachia and Moldavia were able to resist Turkish control after the fall of Constan-

Islamic elementary education was religious in nature. This miniature by Bizhad shows a class in session. What book would have been the focus of their study?

tinople. The Albanian capital was captured in 1466, however, and by 1468 the rest of the country had fallen.

The Romanians withstood repeated Turkish attacks throughout the fifteenth century. One of the most celebrated heroes in this struggle to remain independent was Stephen the Great, who ruled Moldavia from 1457 to 1504. Stephen invaded Walachia to replace a pro-Turkish ruler with one loyal to him. In 1475 he defeated the Turks at Rocova. Only after his death were the Turks able to make the Romanians their vassals.

Sultan Muhammad II, who ruled from 1451 to 1481, moved his capital to Constantinople. In just one hundred years, the Ottoman Turks had become masters of a vast empire including the Balkans and the Khanate of the Crimea.

Ottoman Government

The Ottoman Empire was divided into many provinces. Each was usually under the direct control of the central government at Constantinople, which appointed officials to act as provincial governors. In some places, however, conquered rulers were allowed to continue governing their own lands and people under Turkish supervision.

A basic Islamic belief was that the laws of the government should be based on Islamic religious teachings. As a result, the Ottomans conceded that Christians and Jews, since they did not accept Islamic beliefs, could not be expected to obey all Muslim laws. Therefore, following the pattern set by the founder of Islam, the Ottoman sultans granted Christians and Jews limited authority to

THE OTTOMAN EMPIRE
FROM THE 15TH TO THE 17TH CENTURIES

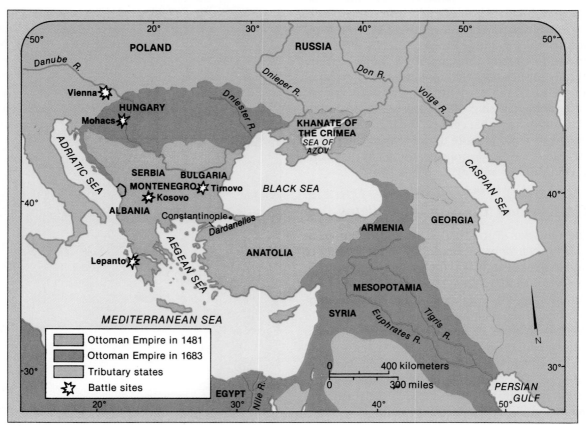

The Ottoman Empire reunited the various states of the Muslim world. What impact did this have on trade in the eastern Meditteranean?

govern themselves under their own religious leaders. Under Ottoman law, Jews and Christians were allowed to practice their religion and to carry on their business activities without Muslim interference. In fact, many Jews and Christians rose to high positions in the Ottoman government. Because of this tolerant Ottoman policy, most eastern Europeans were able to keep their original faiths. Only in Albania did a large proportion of Europeans become Muslims.

The Ottoman Army

A large army was needed to control territory as vast as the Ottoman Empire had become. Previously, male war captives had been used as soldiers, but it was illegal to enslave Muslims and the supply of non-Muslim peoples was declining. To remedy the shortage, the sultans turned to the conquered Christian populations of eastern Europe, and a percentage of the male Christian children was integrated into the Ottoman army. For a period that lasted from the late fourteenth to the early seventeenth centuries, Christian youths from ages ten to twenty were taken into the Ottoman army and raised in special schools to become Muslims. These soldiers were known as Janissaries (JAN-ih-sair-eez), from the Turkish *yeni-cheris* meaning new troops, and were among fifteenth-century Europe's finest fighting men. The most gifted of these youths were educated to serve the sultan's government. Many of these gifted slaves went on to achieve political power and some even became kings.

Weakness in the Empire

Despite the brilliant Ottoman military successes the empire had several weaknesses, which eventually created serious problems. First, little attention was paid to improving antiquated farming methods. As Europe grew stronger the Turks increased taxes and the local officials greedily pressed the already suffering farmers for more. Whole villages were abandoned as peasants fled to the cities. Crafts were a large and profitable part of Turkish industry, but most of the artisans were Christians and Jews because the dominant Turks thought commercial trading and crafts to be less worthy occupations than agriculture.

Second, the Turkish government, concentrating on military power, made little effort to absorb the peoples they conquered. Non-Muslims were allowed to make their own laws and to follow their own customs, and some groups gained special privileges. Chief among these were the Christian and Jewish trading communities, whose grants of liberty from the sultan gave them a virtual trading monopoly in the Ottoman Empire. This practice was often detrimental to the general economic interest of the Muslims.

In the beginning of the sixteenth century there emerged a powerful dynasty—the Safavid Dynasty—in Iran, then known as Persia. It not only defied the Sunnite Ottomans but also established Shiism as the state religion. Ismail, the Safavid conqueror of Persia, proclaimed himself Shah, meaning emperor. He then charted a political course that has since preserved the Iranian identity and safeguarded the territorial integrity of the Iranian state. Under him and, especially, his successor Abbas the Great, a brilliant culture developed in the capital city of Isfahan. Abbas was able to hold off the Ottomans, and he built a system of alliances with European powers.

It was at this same time that another Central Asian Turk, named Babur, was able to establish the Mogul Dynasty in India. It was not until the eighteenth century that this dynasty was replaced by British rule.

SECTION REVIEW

1. Mapping: Use the map on page 180 to describe the extent of the Ottoman Empire in the fifteenth and seventeenth centuries. Which modern European countries were once part of the Ottoman Empire?
2. In your own words, identify or define: Ottoman Turks, Montenegro, Dardanelles, Janissaries.
3. How did the Ottoman Turks treat non-Muslims who lived in their empire?
4. Why was Montenegro able to escape conquest by the Turks?
■ The Ottoman Turks adopted certain tolerant policies toward their conquered subjects. How has the United States treated enemies it has defeated in war?

CONTRIBUTIONS OF MUSLIM CIVILIZATION

The way in which art developed in the Muslim world was strongly influenced by the Islamic religion. Probably the greatest achievements were made in architecture and decoration. In such a deeply religious society it is not surprising that, as in the Christian West, the most significant architectural works were places of worship—the mosques. Their two most distinctive architectural features were the domes and the minarets. Minarets are tall, slender towers from which a muzzein called believers to their daily prayers. These two features give mosques a silhouette that is unmistakably Islamic.

Islamic Art and Architecture

Islamic law strictly forbade the use of human or animal images as decoration. Instead, the Muslim artists and sculptors devised a beautifully intricate system of geometric decoration based on flowers, plants, leaves, geometric figures, and words written in graceful Arabic script.

Handiwork and crafts from many parts of the Muslim world were highly prized. Persian rugs were already famous, as they still are. North African and Spanish leather goods were highly valued, and swords made in Toledo (tuh-LAY-thoh), in Muslim Spain, were treasured by medieval knights throughout Europe. Muslims were also noted for their trade in silks and other fabrics.

Islamic Science

The Muslims played a crucial role in the development of modern sciences such as chemistry, physics, and astronomy. Astronomy was especially important. Not only was it a navigational aid, but it was necessary for calculating the times for prayers and festivals. As a result, Muslim scientists built many observatories and invented the astrolabe, the forerunner of the sextant, a device used to measure the movements of the heavenly bodies.

The Muslims also made important contributions to the creation of modern mathematics. Although the numbers used around the world today are known as Arabic numbers, they were actually invented in early India. The ancient Indians invented the zero, too, but it was the Muslims who combined the use of the zero with the other so-called Arabic numbers. The Muslims developed the number system that we use today. They introduced it to the West in the thirteenth century, where it replaced the old system of Roman numerals.

The Arabic system of numbers was organized in the ninth century A.D. by the great Muslim scholar, Al-Khwarizmi (ahl kwah-REEZ-mee). He also helped lay the foundation for modern algebra, which is an Arabic word.

By 1000 A.D. the Muslims probably possessed the most advanced medical knowledge in the world. Their understanding of diseases was far greater than in the Christian West, and they were familiar with the contagious diseases of measles and smallpox. They translated medical books written by the ancient Greeks and built hospitals and

The astrolabe, with its decorative patterns and calligraphy, was both a work of art and a navigation tool.

People in History

Averroës

Probably no person better demonstrates the brilliance of Islamic culture than the philosopher Averroës. He was born Ibn-Rushd, in Cordoba, the center of the flourishing culture of Muslim Spain in 1126. To the Latin-speaking scholars of the Christian West, who were avid readers of his works, he was known as Averroës. His family was a distinguished one. His father was Cordoba's chief judge, a post which, as Islamic tradition mandated, Averroës eventually inherited.

Averroës was very likely the most learned man of the twelfth century. He wrote works on law, grammar, astronomy, nature, philosophy, and medicine. In fact, his medical skills were so highly prized that Averroës became court physician to the caliph of Marrakesh, a ruler who actively supported and encouraged Averroës's research.

Averroës's most fundamental and important work was undoubtedly in the area of maintaining the philosophical tradition of the Greeks. He read Plato, Aristotle, and other Greek philosophers, and he published extensive commentaries on their writings. Averroës believed that there were two kinds of truth and both were valid. Philosophical truth—that attained by the use of reason and logic—was just as worthy as religious truth which, to Averroës, meant the holy writings of the Koran. This exalted view of philosophy was criticized by more conservative religious thinkers within both the Islamic and the Christian worlds, who believed that such a high estimation of philosophy could only demean religion. Indeed, late in his life, Averroës was imprisoned briefly for his views.

Nevertheless, Averroës's reliance on the importance of reason, as found especially in the work of Aristotle, made his thought a landmark in the development of philosophy. His idea that there are two kinds of truth inspired Christian thinkers to argue the necessity of the separation of Church and State.

Averroës died in 1198. Ironically, his thought bore more fruit in the Christian West than it did in Islam. His work comes at the end of the brilliant golden age of Islamic philosophy and marks the beginning of the rise of philosophy and the rediscovery of Hellenistic thought in Europe. Orthodox Ulema in Islam prevented the spread of Averroës' ideas, but in the West, though opposition existed, his works were translated and studied by both Christian and Jewish scholars until well into the seventeenth century. The Averroist tradition, as it came to be known, stood for the separation of philosophy from theology, one of the major elements in the development of modern thought.

1. What were some of the many areas that Averroës studied?
2. Why were some thinkers opposed to Averroës's philosophy?
3. The dispute between science and religion has been a recurrent one in European history. Why do you think that is? Can you give some examples?

The central figure of this manuscript illustration represents the ideal king. What traits are emphasized?

large medical libraries where physicians could study. The famous Persian philosopher Avicenna (av-uh-SEN-uh), Ibn Sina in Arabic, compiled an encyclopedia of medical knowledge so comprehensive that it was used in European medical schools until the eighteenth century.

Muslim Philosophies

Avicenna and a Spanish philosopher and physician called Ibn Rushd, better known as Averroës (uh-VAIR-uh-weez), were probably the most renowned Muslim philosophers. They studied the writings of Plato and Aristotle and sought to reconcile Greek philosophy with Islamic teachings.

Much of the scientific knowledge that the Muslims gathered from the ancient Greek world and from India was transmitted to the West through Spain and southern Italy around 1100, the time of the Crusades. Most European scholars quickly appreciated the superiority of Islamic science and technology, and translations of Muslim writings into Latin were widely published. This preserved much of classical Greek thought at a time when it was all but forgotten in the West, and Arabic scholars spread this knowledge to other peoples. The intellectual revival of Europe in the later Middle Ages is almost unthinkable without the incentive it received from Islamic thought.

Islamic Literature

Poetry was the great vehicle of literary expression among the Arabs even in pre-Islamic times, and Muslim literature is filled with the writings of great poets. Probably the best known in the West is the twelfth-century Persian mathematician and poet, Omar Khayyam (OH-mahr kie-YAHM). His collection of poems entitled the *Rubaiyat* (ROO-bye-aht) has made him famous throughout the world.

Muslim popular literature, derived from many sources including Indian, Persian, Arabian, and Egyptian, was very imaginative and rich. The most popular collection of Islamic folktales is the *Thousand and One Nights,* sometimes known as *The Arabian Nights.* These clever and fanciful stories give us an intimate look at daily life as it was in medieval Baghdad and other cities. Islamic folktales also have given to the world such figures as Sinbad the Sailor, Ali Baba and the Forty Thieves, and Aladdin of the Magic Lamp.

SECTION REVIEW

1. How did people or products from Arabia, Persia, North Africa, Greece, and Spain contribute to Islamic cultural development?
2. In your own words, identify or define: astrolabe, Al-Khwarizmi, Avicenna, Averroës, Omar Khayyam, *The Arabian Nights.*
3. Why was astronomy especially important in the Muslim world?
4. In what way did religion affect Islamic art?
5. List three significant contributions made by the Muslims to world literature.
■ In the Muslim world religious beliefs had a great influence on art and artists. What kinds of things influence art and artists today? Why do you think this is?

SOCIAL SCIENCE SKILLS

PRIMARY AND SECONDARY SOURCES

Historians rely on many different sources to do research. These can include, for example, firsthand accounts of events, public documents of the period, works of literature, interviews, writings by early historians and, of course, critical studies by modern historians. To help sort through all this material, historians distinguish between **primary sources** and **secondary sources.**

Primary sources include information that comes from the same historical period as the events they describe. They form the essential basis for any work of history. They can include an eyewitness account of an event, a poem, a diary, a government or business record, or any item of information from the time period being studied. Primary source documents are valuable because they were written as the events occurred. They have an authenticity and a directness that comes from being part of the events they describe.

Secondary sources are works by historians or critics that try to analyze the primary sources and explain their significance. One advantage to using secondary sources is that distance in time lets us see an event's importance in ways that the original authors could not.

Here are some examples. A striking characteristic of Islamic tradition is tolerance toward other religions and races. One of the basic primary sources an historian would consult is the Koran, and this important passage might be cited:

"Let there be no constraint in religion; now is truth manifestly distinguished from error." (ii, 257)

Then, the researcher might want to quote this passage from the Hadith in which Muhammad speaks out against racial prejudice:

". . . an Arab is not superior to a foreigner or a white man to a black man except in his piety." (v, 53)

One could also search further for primary sources that support or contradict this view. Here is a passage from the Persian poet, Hallaj:

"I have reflected on the particular religions and tried to understand them, and I have come to regard them as a single principle with numerous ramifications. Therefore do not ask for a man to adopt this or that particular religion, for that would lead him away from the fundamental Principle."

These quotes clearly show that there was a real Muslim belief in religious tolerance. However, they do not tell the whole story because they do not say how the doctrine of tolerance actually worked in Muslim society. For that we can turn to authors who have studied Islam in depth and have analyzed the issue—a secondary source, in other words. The British writer D.S. Roberts, for example, explains how tolerance functioned within Islamic law.

"By tradition, under a treaty of surrender Muslims may undertake to safeguard the life and property of non-Muslims. . . . By this arrangement the non-Muslims live and work under certain disadvantages, but their freedom of religion is guaranteed and they are free to observe their own customs. . . . Non-Muslims have complete legal freedom provided they do not interfere with the religious interests of Muslims. Freedom in matters of religion is explicitly guaranteed." Source: Adapted from D.S. Roberts, *Islam: A Concise Introduction*, copyright © 1981 by D.S. Roberts. Published by Harper and Row, Publishers, Inc.

Good historical research, then, combines both primary and secondary sources. Primary sources give authenticity while secondary sources give an analysis and an important perspective.

1. Define primary and secondary sources, then give examples of each type of document.
2. What advantages are there to using each of the two types of document?
3. Why does good historical research use both primary and secondary sources?

Reviewing the Chapter

Chapter Summary

In the early seventh century A.D. Muhammad established the religion of Islam, and in a very short period virtually all of Arabia had been converted to Islam.

After Muhammad's death in 632 A.D., the Umayyids controlled the caliphate as Muhammad's successors for about one hundred years. However, they were overthrown in 750 A.D. and replaced by the Abbasid Dynasty, which ruled Islam for the next five hundred years. This period marked the Golden Age of Islamic culture. Meanwhile, a separate Umayyid Dynasty was established in Spain and became the first in a series of local movements toward independence that fragmented the once-unified Muslim world.

In 1055 the Seljuk Turks, also converts to Islam, migrated from Central Asia and added much of the Middle East to their growing empire beginning a period of Turkish domination of the Muslim world. In the fourteenth century, however, the Seljuks were replaced by yet another Turkish tribe, the Ottomans. The Ottoman Empire expanded rapidly, and by 1683 it encompassed all of the Middle East, and much of North Africa, the Balkans, and eastern Europe, once again uniting all of the Muslim territories under a single rule.

Muslim achievements in art, literature, medicine, and science rank among the world's greatest. Muslims developed the number system we use today, invented algebra, and played a crucial role in the development of modern sciences such as chemistry, physics, and astronomy.

1. What was the name of the religion founded by Muhammad? What two dynasties succeeded Muhammad?

2. Why was the Umayyid Dynasty of Spain significant?
3. What impact did the Seljuk and Ottoman Turks have on the Muslim world?
4. In which areas of culture and science have the Muslims made significant contributions to the world?

Using Your Vocabulary

1. Define Islam. Where is it the predominate faith today?
2. Who are the Bedouins? Explain their political organization before the time of Muhammad.
3. What are *jinn*? How is the history of the Kaaba connected to the *jinn*?
4. What was the Hegira? Why is Medina important to the religion of Islam?
5. Define monotheism. How does it differ from polytheism? Is Islam a monotheistic or polytheistic faith?
6. What is the Koran? What does the Koran contain? What is its relationship to the works of the Hadith?
7. What does caliph mean? How does a sultan differ from a caliph?
8. Who are the Sunnites? How do they differ from the Shiites?
9. What is a mosque? What characteristics distinguish a mosque from a church, synagogue, or temple?
10. Who were the Ulema? How did their responsibilities differ from the muezzins?
11. What was the Umayyid Dynasty? What was the Abbasid Dynasty? Describe briefly their relationship.
12. Who were the Mamelukes? What should be considered their main achievement?
13. Identify and define Janissaries.
14. Identify and define Safavid Dynasty and Shah.
15. Identify and define the word minaret.
16. Identify and define the terms primary source and secondary source.

Developing Your Geography Skills

1. Use the map on page 175 to describe the spread of Islam. What territories had become Muslim

by the year of Muhammad's death? By 661 A.D.? By 750 A.D.?

2. Use the map on page 180 to trace the growth of the Ottoman Empire. What lands and peoples had been conquered by the Ottoman Turks by 1481? By 1683? Which were considered to be tributary states?

Recalling the Facts

1. What do Islam, Christianity, and Judaism have in common? How does Islam differ?
2. Which factors brought about Islamic expansion? Which do you consider most important?
3. List the Five Pillars of Islam and Islam's other beliefs and practices. Which belief or practice would you not want to obey? Why?
4. List the accomplishments of the Umayyid Dynasty. Which do you consider the most important? Why?
5. What were the accomplishments of the Abbasid Dynasty? Which do you consider the most important? Why?
6. Explain the phrase "people of the book" and describe what impact it had on Muslim treatment of Christians and Jews.
7. What were the accomplishments of the Ottoman Turks? Which do you consider the least important? Why?
8. List the weaknesses of the Ottoman Empire. Which was the most serious? Explain briefly.
9. What is a *jihad*? What is its purpose? Were the wars of the Seljuk Turks against the Persian Muslims considered *jihads*? Why or why not?
10. Describe the significance of the Kaaba and the Black Stone to Islam.
11. Describe the contest for authority among the successors to Muhammad. How did this conflict affect Islam?
12. Explain the importance of the Arabic language to Islam. Why were Muslims reluctant to translate the Koran into other languages?
13. Who were the Kayi? Identify their leader and explain his significance to the Kayi.
14. Who was Stephen the Great? Describe the role that he played in resisting the expansion of the Ottoman Empire in the fifteenth century.

15. The Ottoman Turks did not view commercial trading or the manufacture of crafts as worthy occupations. What impact did this view have on the Ottoman Empire?
16. What contributions to modern thought were made by the Muslim philospher Averroës?

Essay Questions

1. In a brief essay describe the conflict that led to the split among the followers of Islam into the Sunnite and Shiite factions.
2. Describe the impact on the Muslim world of each of the following: the Ummayid Dynasty, the Seljuk Turks, and the Ottoman Turks. Compare the accomplishments and failures of each and determine which, in your opinion, had the greatest impact on the Muslim world.
3. Write a biographic essay describing the life of Muhammad. Include a summary that describes the significance of his life for Muslims and explains how Islam affected the history of the Mediterranean world in the centuries following Muhammad's death.
4. Based on your reading of Chapter 8, make a list of the beneficial and harmful results of Islamic expansion. Do you think Islam did more to preserve or to destroy the legacy of the classical world? Explain your answer.

Critical Thinking

Reliability of Source Data

Another important part of the critical thinking process involves determining the **reliability of source data.** The word reliability means dependability or trustworthiness. Keep this in mind as you answer the following questions.

1. What reliable sources have scholars used in order to learn about the Islamic faith? Cite at least two examples.
2. Why do you regard these sources of evidence about Islam to be reliable?
3. Identify each of the sources named in your answer to question one as either a primary source or a secondary source.

CHAPTER ·9·

INDIA, CHINA, and JAPAN

606 A.D.–1867 A.D.

Objectives

- To describe how India was affected by the invasions of the Huns, Mongols, and Turks, and by the arrival of Islam

- To describe the development of China under successive native dynasties and under the Mongols

- To identify the major cultural achievements of China from the seventh to the seventeenth centuries

- To describe how early Japanese religion and culture and the native aristocracy of Japan influenced the course of Japanese history

- To show how the Japanese adopted cultural influences from other countries, particularly China, and created a unique tradition in art and literature

*B*etween about 500 A.D. and 1500 A.D., a period of time known as the Middle Ages in Europe, three great cultures predominated in the Far East—those of India, China, and Japan. These three cultures developed in countries that were separated by formidable geographic barriers. The Himalayas, the world's highest mountains, stood between India and China. The rough waters of the Sea of Japan separated Japan from the Asian mainland. Despite these obstacles, strong cultural influences passed between these countries. Buddhism, a religion born in India, thrived in China and Japan while it nearly disappeared in the land of its origin.

The Pacific Ocean served as a shield to protect Japan from its enemies, making Japan virtually immune to invasion from outside. Japan, however, was often troubled by internal wars. India and China, on the other hand, were subjected to repeated invasions from central Asia. By the eleventh century, the Muslim Turks were beginning a series of invasions of India. As a result, Islam became rooted alongside India's native Hindu religion. From Manchuria, Mongolia, and the northwest, non-Chinese peoples pushed into China and became occupying conquerors. These invaders often replaced native emperors and set up their own dynasties.

INDIA FROM THE SIXTH TO THE EIGHTEENTH CENTURIES

As you read in Chapter 4, the Guptas established a large empire in northern India, and under their long reign Indian civilization flourished. Nevertheless, the Gupta Empire was invaded by the Huns, a warlike people from central Asia, and by 500 A.D. the Huns had overrun northwestern India. Although the Huns' brutal advance into eastern India was checked by a union of Hindu princes, the Gupta Empire had come to an end. When the Huns were finally expelled in the middle of the sixth century A.D., northern India was broken up into warring kingdoms.

The Reign of Harsha

In the early seventh century A.D. a soldier-prince named Harsha succeeded in assembling a large army. In only six years, from 606 A.D. to 612 A.D., he reunited northern India. Harsha successfully ruled the large northern empire until his death, though his attempt in 620 A.D. to conquer the Deccan Plateau was foiled by a ruler of that region. He promoted art, literature, and religion, and under his rule Hinduism began a revival that continued long after his death.

The Rajputs

Harsha died in 647 A.D., leaving no heir. India then endured several centuries of warfare and confusion as the northern empire fragmented into many small states. The northwest was ruled by a people called the Rajputs (RAHJ-poots), who were descendants of the central Asians that had settled in northwest India in the fifth and sixth centuries A.D. The Rajputs had then intermarried with the native Hindus and adopted their customs, including the caste system. The Rajputs were a military aristocracy, and they took control of the area between the Indus and the Ganges rivers—an area that came to be known as Rajputana.

Rajput literature described a warrior code similar to the ideals of chivalry in medieval western Europe. Rajput youths were taught to respect women, spare their enemies, and practice fair play. Combat was considered a form of art, courage was esteemed, and death was preferred to surrender. This military spirit was shared by women, who sometimes fought to the death alongside male warriors in defense of their cities. This tradition of the warrior code made the Rajputs splendid soldiers, but the frequency of war kept their small states divided and weak.

The Muslims Conquer India

Around the year 1000 A.D. the Turks migrated to the northwest frontier of India, overran Afghanistan, and embarked upon the conquest of India. The disunited Rajput rulers were unable to oppose them, and by the thirteenth century the Turks had overrun all of northern India. Their rulers took the title of sultan and made Delhi their capital. Their dynasty, known as the Delhi Sultanate, lasted about 300 years.

The Turks brought with them the monotheistic religion of Islam. Unlike the traditional Islamic attitude of tolerance toward "people of the book"— that is, Christians and Jews—the Turks were intolerant of Hinduism and did their best to suppress it. Nor did the Muslims have any interest in adopting Hindu customs; instead they forced many Hindus to choose between death or conversion to Islam.

Invasions are never peaceful, but the Turkish conquest of India was unusually cruel and bloody. Prisoners and innocent inhabitants of conquered cities were slaughtered. Hindu villages were destroyed and their populations either murdered or enslaved. Pre-Islamic Hindu rulers had levied a tax of one-sixth of agricultural produce; the Turks raised it to one-half. India was plundered and the Hindus impoverished.

Eventually, many Hindus adopted Muslim customs and clothing. A new language called Urdu developed, combining Persian, the language of the conquerors, with Hindi, that of the conquered. Despite their ferocity, the Delhi sultans generously supported artists, poets, and historians, some of whom were Hindus. A new architectural style emphasizing the arch was introduced. Buddhism was already in decline and Islam's advent hastened its disappearance, but Hinduism could not be eradicated. To this day Hinduism and Islam coexist in India though not always peacefully.

MOGUL EMPIRE

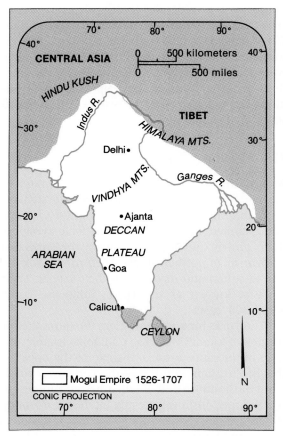

The Mogul Empire ruled India for nearly 200 years. Here it is shown at its greatest extent. How did Akbar the Great contribute to the expansion of the Mogul Empire?

The Delhi sultans restored unity to northern India for the first time since the reign of Harsha, and in the fourteenth century they even managed to subdue the Deccan Plateau. As rival sultans set up their own states, however, the inevitable fragmentation occurred. Central government broke down, the south again became independent, and then another invader appeared in the northwest.

The Mongols Invade India

In 1398 the feared Mongol leader Tamerlane entered India. Born in 1336, this fierce warrior claimed to be a descendant of the great Genghis Khan, who had conquered China and established one of history's greatest empires. From 1369 until his death in 1405, Tamerlane ruled a central Asian empire from his capital of Samarkand, in what is now the Soviet Union. He defeated the Persians and the Turks and conquered lands from the Mediterranean to China. When he struck at India, neither Hindus nor Muslims could stop him. Delhi was looted and 100,000 of its inhabitants killed. When the Mongols returned to Samarkand, they left behind political chaos. The Delhi sultans were weakened and rival sultans challenged their authority. Some of Tamerlane's followers created their own states and new Hindu and Muslim states appeared in southern India.

This political disunity endured for about a half century after Tamerlane's raids. But by 1450 the Delhi sultans were able to restore their dominance over northern India. In 1526, however, yet another Muslim invader entered India.

The Mogul Empire

This new invader was a Muslim descendant of Tamerlane named Babur, who was known as "The Tiger." With a small army of no more than 12,000 soldiers, Babur defeated the Delhi sultan at the battle of Panipat in 1526. He then took the title of sultan, defeated a Rajput rebellion, and ruled until 1530. The empire Babur created is known as the **Mogul Empire.** Mogul, the Persian word for Mongol, was a name dreaded in India for its association with Tamerlane and the terrible destruction of Delhi. The Mogul Empire, however, was blessed with a succession of extremely able and creative rulers, and it became one of history's most illustrious regimes. Europeans told many tales of its glory, and the ambitious architectural program of the Mogul emperors gave India a stunning legacy of great buildings.

Babur's grandson, Akbar, whose name means "the great," reigned from 1556 to 1605 and was among the most famous of the Mogul rulers. He came to the throne at the age of thirteen and inherited a kingdom much smaller than Babur's. Over a period of many years he was able to restore Babur's realm and gain control of all northern India. In 1590 he began the invasion of the Deccan Plateau, which proved too difficult to conquer. By the time of his death in 1605, however, much of the south had been annexed, and Akbar's successors were able to push the empire's borders even farther southward.

Akbar's achievements were more than just military. His reforms gave India an efficient, organized government. Village officials were responsible for maintaining law and order and special officials administered justice in the cities. Akbar prohibited child marriage and the practice of suttee—a custom that required widows to die on their husband's funeral pyres. He restored the agricultural tax to the pre-Islamic standard of one-sixth.

Akbar also instituted religious tolerance. He repealed the tax on non-Muslims and appointed Hindus to high positions in his government. Probably no more than one-fourth of the Indian population was Muslim, and Akbar believed that the two cultures could learn from one another. Although he was illiterate, Akbar collected a large library. He supported poets, musicians, and architects, both Muslim and Hindu, and thus the arts, especially architecture, flourished. Mogul architecture reached a high point under Akbar's grandson, Shah Jahan, who ruled from 1628 to 1658. It was he who built the Taj Mahal in Agra. This magnificent building, built between 1630 and 1648, was a tomb for Shah Jahan's wife Mumtaz Mahal, who died at age thirty-nine after giving birth to her fourteenth child.

Akbar's successors did not maintain his policy of religious tolerance. Islam was restored as the official religion and Hindu temples were destroyed. The tax on non-Muslims was reinstated and even the public playing of music was forbidden. Such intolerant measures alienated the Moguls' Hindu subjects and contributed to revolts that undermined Mogul power.

Compare this photo of the Taj Mahal to the photo of Hagia Sophia on page 160. What features characteristic of Islamic architecture do both buildings share?

Shah Jahan renewed the struggle to conquer the Deccan, but he fell ill in 1656 and a bloody rivalry erupted among his sons. The youngest son, Aurangzeb (AWR-uhng-zeb), killed one brother, blinded another, and imprisoned his father. He then took the throne for himself, which he held until his death in 1707. Much of Aurangzeb's reign was devoted to the conquest of southern India, and under him the Mogul Empire reached its greatest extent. Nevertheless, Aurangzeb's cruelty and intolerance seriously weakened his empire.

The Portuguese in India

During Roman times, Europe and India had a direct trade relationship, but it dissipated after Rome's fall. Trade did continue but it was now carried on indirectly, with other nations serving to transport goods from India to the Mediterranean. Spices, for example, were brought to India from Indonesia and then transported along several routes to either Egypt or Constantinople for shipment to Europe. With each handling the price of the goods went up. Spices were in great demand in Europe and the spice trade offered the potential for huge profits. European merchants, however, wanted to rid themselves of the many added costs connected with indirect trade.

In the fifteenth century the Portuguese set out to discover a direct trade route to India by sea. Portuguese explorers sailed south along the west coast of Africa and rounded its southern tip for the first time in 1486. In 1498, after an eleven-month voyage, Vasco da Gama arrived at the Indian port of Calicut. His return to Portugal with a shipful of spices inspired other Portuguese sailors to sail to the Far East.

The appearance of European traders in India was a threat to the Muslim traders who controlled shipping throughout the East, and the Portuguese had to fight in order to gain access to Eastern trade. However, Muslim and Hindu defenses were no match for European gunnery. Soon the Portuguese had established a network of trading posts in the East Indies and along India's southwest coast. In 1510 they seized the Indian port of Goa and made it their headquarters in India. Then they seized Ceylon, present-day Sri Lanka, as a way station for ships bound for the East Indies. The Portuguese held on to their Indian territories for about a century until other European powers took them over. Goa itself remained a Portuguese possession until well into the twentieth century.

SECTION REVIEW

1. Mapping: Use the map on page 190 to describe the extent of the Mogul Empire at its height.
2. In your own words, define or identify: Harsha, Rajputs, Delhi Sultanate, Urdu, Tamerlane, Mogul Empire, Akbar, Vasco da Gama.
3. How did the Muslim conquerors of India treat the native Hindus? How was the reign of Akbar different from those of other Mogul rulers?
4. What brought about direct contact between India and western Europe?
- The invasion of India by successive conquerors greatly affected the native Indian way of life. Can you list four ways in which foreign cultures have affected the American way of life?

CHINA UNDER NATIVE AND FOREIGN RULE

As we saw in Chapter 4, the Sui Dynasty, founded in 589 A.D., had a brief life in spite of a number of important achievements. Attempts to conquer Manchuria and Korea failed and proved costly; the northwest was assaulted by Turks, and the dynasty faced revolution at home.

The Tang Dynasty

In 617 A.D. a government official named Li Yuan (LEE YOO-AHN) formed an alliance with the Turks and succeeded in overthrowing the Sui emperor. Li Yuan took the imperial title and established his capital at Changan in northwest China. His new dynasty, the **Tang,** ruled China from 618 A.D. to 906 A.D.—a period marked by great cultural achievement.

Li Yuan ruled for only eight years and was succeeded by his son, Tai Cong (TIE TSOONG), who proved one of the outstanding Tang emperors, rul-

The women above are shown completing the silk-making process by ironing the newly made cloth. Silk-making represented a Confucian and aristocratic ideal for proper employment of women. How does the artist convey this ideal?

ing from 627 A.D. to 649 A.D. He defeated the Turks in the border region and made himself their khan. He then annexed the large Tarim Basin—an area which is still part of China. Tai Cong extended his rule into Tibet and even into the kingdoms beyond the Pamir Mountains along the Oxus River, in what is now Afghanistan. These lands were not incorporated into the Tang Empire, but their rulers became the emperor's vassals and enjoyed special trading privileges with China.

The conquest of Tibet opened a route to India, and some Chinese officials made the journey. A secure trade was never established, however, as crossing the mountains was difficult. Tai Cong was unable to conquer Korea, but during the reign of his son that peninsula was successfully joined to the Tang Empire.

In all, Tai Cong's reign saw the expansion of Chinese territory and influence far into the west. China's enemies in the north were driven back and territories that had thrown off Chinese rule after the fall of the Han dynasty were retaken.

Tai Cong and his successors were also able to restore an efficient centralized government. The bureaucracy was staffed with officials selected through a civil service examination system. Transportation was improved through the digging of new canals, the capital was beautified, and all religions were tolerated.

In 690 A.D., for the only time in Chinese history, a woman ascended the throne. During the fifteen-year reign of Wu Zhao (WOO JOW), known as Empress Wu, the government was well administered, and examinations for government posts for women were established.

Under the Zhou and other early dynasties, Chinese society had been dominated by a hereditary military aristocracy. However, the old nobility had been destroyed by the Qin and other dynasties. Under the Tang a new ruling class comprised of the gentry, or wealthy landowners, emerged and took its place. Government came to be dominated by bureaucrats who owed their success more to their talents than to birth or family ties. The gentry could afford the education necessary to pass the examinations required to become a government official, and the new gentry-scholars became the effective leaders of China.

Buddhism Spreads in China

Buddhism entered China from India during the Han Dynasty. It first was adopted by the upper classes and the rich; by the eighth or ninth century

A.D., however, Buddhism had spread to the peasantry. The religion became especially popular among the non-Chinese inhabitants of north China. Amidst the turmoil that accompanied the end of the Han Dynasty, people found solace in worshipping the Buddha as savior. Their faith helped them endure the harsh realities of their troubled times, and the new religion became as popular as Confucianism.

The school of Buddhism that took hold in China was the Mahayana form, which was more elaborate than the simple doctrines preached by the Buddha. The uneducated saw it as a new kind of magic; the educated found it a challenging set of new ideas. For many Chinese, it was their first experience with organized religion. The ceremony, art, and literature of Buddhism had great appeal, and people responded to its promises of liberation and salvation.

Yet the popularity of Buddhism in China peaked in the ninth century A.D., and Confucianism staged a comeback among the upper classes, who favored its message of civic duty and responsibility. Confucianism regained its status as China's major philosophy, a position it held until the twentieth century.

Decline of the Tang

Famine and poverty created popular discontent and led to a rebellion against the Tang government in 874 A.D. The uprisings spread and plagued the government for a decade. By the time order was restored, the provincial governors had taken control of their own regions, and some had even declared themselves kings. The persistent threat of decentralization again reared its head, the central government declined, and the Tang Dynasty lost its power.

The Song Dynasty

Tang rule finally ended in 906 A.D. and China experienced political disintegration. In the north, the age was called the period of the Five Dynasties as five dynasties came and went in only fifty-three years. In the south the situation was even more fragmented—there the post-Tang period is known as the age of the Ten Kingdoms. Overall it was a period of warfare, corruption, and hard times.

One of the generals serving the last of the Five Dynasties decided to use his army to seize the throne for himself. His name was Zhao Kuangyin (JOW KWONG-YIN) and he founded the **Song** (SOONG) **Dynasty,** which ruled China from 960 A.D. to 1279 A.D. from the capital city of Kaifeng (KIE-FUHNG) in central China.

The Song emperors, though they were unable to restore the borders that existed during the height of the Tang period, did extend their authority over south China and reunited the country. China's standard of living also reached a high level under the Song. Their cities were the most modern in the world, with wide streets, streetlights, and regular street cleaning. Each city had a fire department, restaurants, places of amusement, fairs, markets, orphanages, old-age homes, schools, and first-aid stations.

Civil Service Under the Song

The chief strength of the Song government was its civil service. It was made up of countless bureaucrats, all male, who were selected by the civil service examination system. The period of the Song Dynasty was the golden age of the scholar-official. Exams were given regularly every three years, and there were three levels of exams. First, local tests were given all across the country. Somewhere between one and ten percent of the exam-takers passed, and those men went on to an examination in the capital. Again, about ten percent passed, and they went on to a "palace examination." Those men who passed the third test were ranked, and the kind of government position that they were given was determined by their ranking. Those ranked at the top frequently rose quickly to the most important government posts. Although the examination system had originated earlier under the Sui, it was more fully developed under the Song. The process continued, relatively unchanged, until the twentieth century.

The tests consisted essentially of essay questions covering fields such as law, history, and the classics of literature and Confucianism. Emphasis was placed on the ability to write well, originality of thought, and skill in memorization and reasoning. The system brought many highly talented men into the government, but since it required an extensive education, it tended to restrict opportunity to the more prosperous social classes of Chinese society.

Sometimes unsuccessful candidates took the examinations over and over again. The government became concerned about older people who had taken the examinations many times without passing—some took the tests as many as fifteen times. Because it was thought that those who were disappointed might turn against the dynasty, some who failed repeatedly were given jobs through special examinations they were able to pass.

Under the Song foreign trade increased, especially with India and the Near East. The southern ports of Hanjzhou and Canton, or Guangzhou, grew in importance and the caravan trade brought goods like incense, ivory, coral, rock crystal, steel, and amber from central Asia and India. The Song imported horses from the Turks, Mongols, and Tibetans and paid for them with Chinese products such as tea or silk. Korea and Japan were eager for Chinese books, paintings, and other art objects. Highly prized Chinese porcelain was exported to Southeast Asia, India, and the east coast of Africa. Many foreign merchants were permitted to settle in China, and contacts with foreigners increased as a result.

Yet even though the Song emperors enjoyed great wealth, they faced difficult problems. They lacked the military strength of the Han or the Tang and were continually threatened by nomadic tribes in the north. To ward them off, the Song offered bribes.

Although the country prospered, the government found it difficult to collect sufficient revenue

TANG, SONG, AND MONGOL EMPIRES

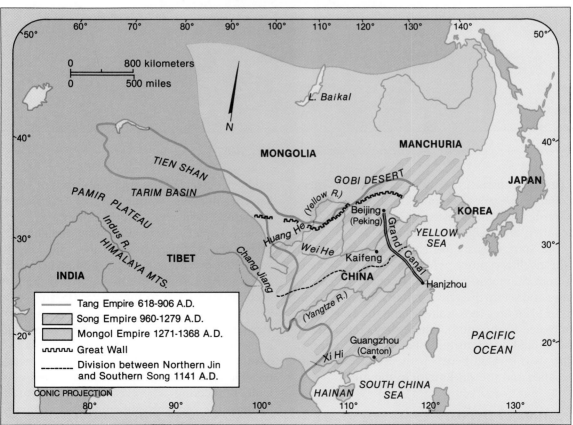

Compare the three Chinese empires shown on this map. Which extended furthest west? Which extended furthest north?

This Persian miniature shows the secret burial procession of Genghis Khan.

to pay its expenses. Many wealthy landowners were able to evade taxation. This threw a heavier tax burden onto the peasants, who responded with discontent and frequent uprisings.

The Song Dynasty lost control of north China in the twelfth century, when a non-Chinese people from the north, called the Jurchen, seized the region and set up their own dynasty, known as the Jin. In 1126 they took Kaifeng, and the Song royal family fled to the south, where they established a new capital at Hanjzhou. For over a century, China was divided between the Song Empire in the south and the Jin Empire in the north.

The Mongol Dynasty

In the thirteenth century both the Jin and the Song were conquered by the Mongols, a fierce no-madic people from the arid wastelands of Mongolia. The Mongols swarmed out of central Asia to create one of history's largest empires.

In Chapter 7 you read how Genghis Khan united the warring Mongol tribes and forged an army that overcame all opposition and created an empire that would eventually reach from the Mediterranean Sea to the Pacific Ocean. Genghis Khan was one of history's ablest and most remarkable military leaders. His warriors were skilled horsemen who could remain in the saddle for days, covering vast distances in what seemed impossible time. They carried little and lived off the land, plundering wherever they went. Ruthless fighters, the Mongols sometimes slaughtered entire town populations. News of their approach spread terror; and sometimes, hoping to be spared, cities surrendered without resistance.

In 1211 Genghis Khan turned his dreaded war machine against the Jin in northern China. The walled cities encountered by the Mongols helped to hold off the invaders and a peace was agreed to by the Mongols and the Jin. The peace was a brief one and the Mongols soon renewed their attack, capturing and destroying the Jin capital—now the modern city of Beijing. In overcoming the walled cities of the Jin, the Mongols had been assisted by Chinese advisors who taught the Mongols the siege tactics necessary to take a fortified city. The Mongols had conquered nearly all of the former Jin territory by 1227 when Genghis Khan died.

While one Mongol army was busy in China, another was conquering Turkish lands in central Asia. The Mongols then enlisted the Turks as allies and a joint Mongol-Turkish army rolled westward. Persia fell in 1231, Mesopotamia was plundered and Baghdad taken in 1258, as the Abbasid caliphate ended. Other Mongol armies overran Russia and eastern Europe.

In 1232 the Song Chinese joined with the Mongols and conquered the last of the territory controlled by the Jin. This alliance did not last long though, and in 1250 the Mongols and the Song were at war. In 1260 Kublai Khan, the grandson of Genghis Khan, assumed leadership of the Mongols and completed the final defeat of the Song in 1279. The start of the **Mongol Dynasty** in China can be dated from Kublai Khan's assumption of power as Great Khan in 1260. In 1267 Kublai Khan moved his capital from Mongolia to Beijing and four years later he gave his empire a Chinese dynastic name, Yüan. The Yüan Dynasty would last until 1368.

Beijing, the capital rebuilt by Kublai Khan, became one of the world's most magnificent cities. A description of it can be found in *The Travels of Marco Polo*, a book by an Italian merchant who visited China while Kublai Khan was on the throne. Marco Polo's accounts of what he saw in China gave Europeans their first comprehensive view of Chinese life, although many of his tales seemed incredible. He told of paper being used as money, a practice as yet unknown in Europe. He described strange black stones that burned—coal, of course—and fishermen who used birds to catch fish for them. This latter tale greatly puzzled Europeans, but today we know that cormorants, long-necked sea birds, can be used just as Marco Polo said. A cord around the cormorant's throat pre-vents it from swallowing the fish it catches and a second cord around the bird's leg prevents it from flying away.

Kublai Khan may have come from a nomadic background, but he quickly learned to appreciate the many wonders of Chinese culture. He urged his countrymen to give up their former ways and claimed that there was much to learn from Chinese civilization. The Mongols did not change the Chinese governmental structure. Although key positions were filled by Mongols, native Chinese stayed on as officials. Government business was still conducted in the Chinese language, and Mongol was used only for matters concerning the royal family. The Mongols also retained the traditional civil service system.

Decline of the Mongols

Kublai Khan died in 1294 and was followed by eight successive Mongol emperors, none of whom was strong enough to rule the empire effectively. They slowly permitted Mongol military power to decline and eventually could not even protect the coast from pirates. Banditry, famine, and floods provoked the peasantry into rebellion and by the 1350's China was once more in turmoil.

One of the many native Chinese rebellions was led by a rebel chief named Zhu Yuanzhang (JOO YOO-AHN-JAHNG). From a base in central China, he made Nanjing his capital. He led his army northward and captured Beijing in 1368. Zhu put an end to the Mongol dynasty and founded his own, the **Ming Dynasty.** By 1382, most of China had been unified under this new regime.

The Ming Dynasty

The Ming Dynasty, the last native dynasty to rule China, reigned for nearly 300 years, from 1368 to 1644. The emperors ruled from Nanjing until 1421, when the capital was moved to Beijing. The Ming emperors courted popularity by deliberately abolishing all traces of Mongol rule and reestablishing Chinese traditions. These included the practice of appointing scholars to serve the government as officials. A new law code, the Code of the Great Ming, was written. The Ming rulers also were devoted patrons, or sponsors, of the arts, and they spent lavishly on public works, constructing new buildings and bridges. Yet most of the Ming emperors were unable to restore China's military strength or recover territories that had been held by earlier dynasties. Lacking the military strength to conquer, the Ming made special arrangements to control their enemies on the border.

The Tribute System

The Ming made peace with their external enemies through an arrangement known as the **tribute system.** First established during the Han Dynasty, the tribute system was a feature of Chinese foreign policy until the late nineteenth century. Underlying this system was the assumption that China and its ruler were superior to all other countries and their rulers. According to the theory, outside peoples had much to gain from Chinese civilization.

Consequently, they should be willing to become vassals of the emperor in order to secure these invaluable assets. To become a vassal state, a foreign ruler sent a representative to the Chinese court bearing gifts. This tribute was presented to the emperor in a ceremony during which the diplomat kneeled and bowed low, touching his forehead to the ground, an act known as the kowtow. The emperor then gave gifts that were even more expensive to the representatives of the vassal states.

Chinese assumptions were not altogether imaginary—vassal states did have much to gain from becoming part of China's tribute system. They enjoyed increased trade and the promise of Chinese military protection. In the 1360's and 1370's a number of states, including Korea and Vietnam, sent tribute. Most of the other southeast Asian states also joined the system.

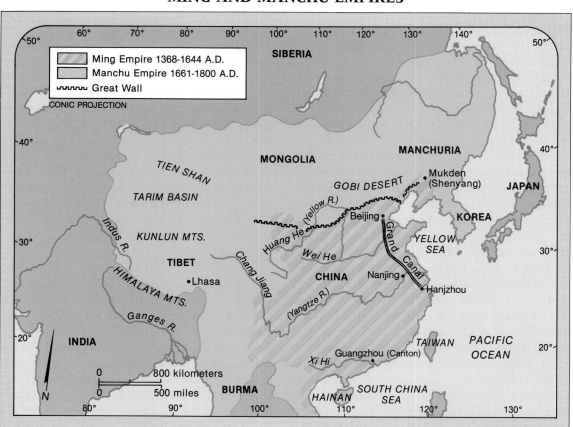

MING AND MANCHU EMPIRES

Why was the Manchu Empire more difficult to govern than previous Chinese empires?

Diplomats from vassal states were permitted to engage in private trade in special, controlled markets. This trade, however, was so lucrative that restrictions were put on the amount of goods diplomats could carry and on the frequency of their visits. Still the tribute system worked well as a method of dealing with peaceful neighbors. However, the Ming did use more aggressive measures against the Mongols, whom they frequently attacked, in order to keep them from becoming a threat to China again.

In the sixteenth and early seventeenth centuries the Ming Empire went into decline. High taxes and government corruption provoked peasant rebellions; banditry flourished and law and order broke down. In 1644 a bandit chief named Li Zizheng (LEE ZUH-JUNG) attacked Beijing with his band and the last Ming emperor, deserted by his defenders, killed himself. Li might have proclaimed himself emperor and started a new dynasty, but a Ming general opened the Great Wall and invited a foreign army, the Manchus, to enter China and destroy the bandit leader. They poured into China from Manchuria, defeated Li Zizheng, and seized the throne for themselves. Ming supporters fought back and it took the Manchus thirty years to stifle the opposition. From 1683 until 1911 their new dynasty, called the **Manchu** or Qing (CHING), controlled the entire country.

SECTION REVIEW

1. Mapping: Use the maps on pages 195 and 198 to describe and compare the empires of the Tang, Song, Mongol, Ming, and Manchu dynasties. Also give the location of central Asia and Mongolia in relation to China.
2. In your own words, define or identify: Kublai Khan, Marco Polo, Yüan Dynasty.
3. What were the main achievements of the Tang, Song, and Ming dynasties?
4. In your own words, describe the Chinese tribute system.
5. Which of the ruling Chinese dynasties came from outside China?
- China was often ruled by non-native people. Do you know of any countries in recent times whose government or rulers were foreigners?

EARLY CHINESE CULTURE

Culture under the Tang Dynasty thrived to such a degree that the period is considered a golden age of Chinese civilization. Buddhist philosophy inspired a great flowering of Chinese landscape painting, and sculptors adapted Indian ideas to create a unique Chinese sculptural style. Scholars compiled encyclopedias, and historical writings greatly increased in number.

Tang Poetry

Under the Tang, great value was placed on literary skill. Every educated person was expected to be able to read and write Chinese, and the ability to write poetry was especially treasured. As a result, no less than 48,000 poems by 2,300 Tang poets have been preserved.

The poems of the Tang period are called *shi*. These were short pieces that employed strict rules of rhyme and meter. They were able to evoke many moods and were often inspired by natural beauty describing flowers, mountains, birds, and rivers in words that carried great feeling and were sometimes colored with sadness.

The two most famous poets of the age were Li Bo, who lived from 701 A.D. to 762 A.D., and Duo Fu, who lived from 712 A.D. to 770 A.D. They were good friends and even poked fun at each other in their writings. Li Bo had been a Taoist priest, and his poems reflect the kind of love of nature often associated with Taoist ideals. Duo Fu, a Confucian official, was by nature more serious, and his poetry reflected a social concern about injustice and suffering. The works of both poets influenced Chinese writers for centuries after the end of the Tang Dynasty.

The Invention of Printing

One of the most important inventions developed during the Tang Dynasty was the art of printing. In the seventh century A.D., the Chinese became the first people to print images made from raised images or characters carved into a wood block. Then in the eleventh century they developed the art of printing from movable type.

These seventeenth-century illustrations show how the Chinese made paper. First a screen was used to pick up pulp from a large vat. The wet sheets of paper were then placed on a table to be pressed before being hung on the walls of a kiln to dry.

Before the invention of printing, texts had to be copied by hand—a tedious process that made books very expensive. Printing made it possible to produce books faster and in far greater quantity than ever before. Knowledge, therefore, could now be disseminated more quickly and to a much greater audience than ever before.

Chinese Cultural Developments

Chinese civilization advanced in other areas, too. Chinese scientists created a smallpox vaccine, developed a new and more accurate clock, and invented paper money. Cotton was introduced from India and a new, more productive kind of rice was brought from Vietnam, enabling Chinese rice growers to double their production. Algebra was developed and progress was made in zoology, botany, and chemistry. By the tenth century, the Chinese had produced gunpowder, which they first used for fireworks. Later, with the invention of hand grenades and land mines, gunpowder was used for warfare. Mapmaking developed into a high art and, by the end of the twelfth century, the Chinese were using the magnetic compass.

Painting and Pottery

Chinese landscape painting reached great heights under the Song dynasty. Unlike European artists, who concentrated on the portrayal of the human body, Chinese artists delighted in the depiction of the many aspects of nature—mountains, water, rain, and mist. Some of the finest Chinese landscape paintings were done on long horizontal scrolls, designed to be slowly unrolled and viewed about two feet at a time. The works were done with ink on silk or paper, a technique that demanded great skill from the painter. Oil paintings, as they are known in the West, can be slowly retouched or changed. When a Chinese artist uses ink and brush, however, a stroke, once made, cannot be altered—it has to be perfect the first time. For this reason, the hand of the Chinese artist was extremely well-trained through long hours of practice, and the great Chinese paintings have a unique spontaneity and freshness.

Another art that reached great heights in the Song period was the making of porcelain, a high-quality ceramic. New techniques in glazing and firing pottery made it possible for Chinese craftsmen to produce porcelain ware in an almost limitless variety. Distinctive pottery and vases from the Ming Dynasty were highly prized. Today, Ming porcelain commands a very high price.

Chinese sculpture, which had been heavily influenced by Buddhism from the sixth century A.D. on, broke away from Indian religious themes and style, to develop a character of its own. Secular, or non-religious, subjects became popular and Chinese sculpture reached a high level of achievement during the Tang Dynasty. However, Buddhist sculpture, particularly glass, jade, and ivory miniatures, remained popular until the Ming Dynasty.

Chinese Architecture

The Chinese were excellent architects and builders. As you recall, Buddhists introduced the Indian stupa to China. The Chinese modified the design and developed a structure known as the pagoda. Like the stupas, the pagodas were used originally as shrines. All pagodas follow the same basic design. The largest of many floors was the bottom level. Other floors decreased in size as they mounted upward. Furthermore, each floor of the pagoda had its own roof, with long corners curving upward.

Drama

The art of drama, which had been introduced during the Tang Dynasty, became popular under the Mongols. These dramas were love stories, such as Wang Shihfu's *Western Chamber,* or exposés of social injustice, such as *The Injustice Suffered by Widow Tou,* by Guan Hanqing. Many of these plays used satire to poke fun at the Mongol overlords. The theater had a special appeal to those who could not read, and the actors used the speech of the common people. Opera also developed during this time. Opera is a combination of singing, acting, and dancing, performed to music. China's first novel appeared in the fourteenth century and, like the drama, it avoided scholarly language and used the language of the common people.

SECTION REVIEW

1. In your own words, define or identify: *shi,* Li Bo, Wang Shihfu.
2. List some of the great Chinese inventions of this period. Which one do you think has had the greatest impact on the world? Why?
3. What are some reasons for the popularity of drama in China during the Mongol period?
- The invention of printing revolutionized the art of communication. What inventions have changed the way people communicate in the twentieth century?

EARLY JAPAN

Japan is an **archipelago** (arh-kuh-PEL-uh-goe), or group of islands, that stretches in the shape of an arc more than 1,500 miles (2,400 kilometers). It reaches from the island of Hokkaido (HAHK-KIE-DOE) in the north to the subtropical island of Kyushu (KYOO-SHOO) in the south. Of the hundreds of islands in the chain, the four largest are the most important. The largest of the four is Honshu (HAHN-SHOO), where most of Japan's major cities, including Tokyo, are located. The other three are Hokkaido, Kyushu, and the smallest of the four, Shikoku (SHEE-KOE-KOO).

Geography and Resources

The Japanese islands have a climate with four distinct seasons. Rainfall is plentiful and the growing season is long. Despite these climatic blessings, however, farming is possible on only about fifteen percent of Japan's land. Much of the country is hilly, mountainous, or heavily forested.

Mineral resources are as scarce as farmland, but the forests provide timber, and the swift flowing rivers, while inhospitable to boat traffic, are a steady source of water power. The sea has always been a major resource for the Japanese. Fishing has been a major economic activity since very early times, and for centuries the Japanese have extracted pearls from oysters for export to other areas of the world.

Japanese farmers compensate by practicing careful cultivation. Crops are planted wherever the land permits, and even steep hills and small mountains are terraced and cultivated. The main crops are barley, soybeans, wheat, fruit, vegetables, and rice. The Japanese farmers produce much the same crops today as they did in the past, with the exception of sericulture—the cultivation of silkworms—which is no longer widely practiced.

Geography has played an important role in Japanese history. The sea not only provides food and pearls, it also provides protection. Kublai Khan, the Mongol conqueror of China, twice dispatched invasion fleets to conquer Japan. In 1274 a large force of Mongols and Koreans sailed for Japan but it returned to Korea without fighting a battle. Seven years later Kublai Khan tried again, this time sending a huge force of 140,000 Mongols, Koreans, and Chinese. This was probably the greatest invasion force launched up to that time. The invaders fought the Japanese for two months, after which a violent typhoon struck the Khan's fleet and destroyed about half of the ships. This forced the remainder of the invasion force to withdraw from Japan in defeat. The Japanese claimed this storm was a wind sent from heaven. They called it the *kamikaze* and it confirmed for them the belief that Japan was a country under divine protection. In any case, the Japanese mainland was never again invaded though it was occupied by American forces after World War II.

The Japanese islands are remote from other East Asian cultural centers. Because of this, Japan's population, unlike China's, did not receive an influx of new peoples. Japan's remoteness also helps explain its long periods of cultural isolation when the Japanese deliberately shut out all foreign influences. Although at times the Japanese accepted foreign influences, especially from China, their isolation promoted a uniquely Japanese civilization and way of life.

The First Japanese Histories

The first Japanese histories are the *Kojiki*, or *Record of Ancient Things*, written in 712 A.D., and the *Nihon-shoki*, or *Chronicles of Japan*, written in 720 A.D. Scholars believe that these writings were originally legends that were transformed into historical chronicles. Yet when the information they contain is combined with evidence from archaeology, myths, and accounts of early travelers, a picture of the earliest days of Japan emerges.

The Origins of the Japanese People

The first inhabitants of the Japanese archipelago seem to have been a people called the Ainu (IE-NOO), whose features and large, round eyes suggest that they are non-Mongolian. Originally, they occupied all four of the main Japanese islands. As new settlers arrived, however, they were pushed farther and farther north until they settled on Hokkaido, where their descendants live today. The people who arrived in the islands after the Ainu are the ancestors of the modern Japanese. Some migrated east from the Asian mainland, and others came from the Philippines and the islands of the South Pacific.

Early Japanese Society

The earliest Japanese were a polytheistic people who worshipped different aspects of nature as gods. Some of their beliefs, and even their words, were likely borrowed from the Ainu. Animal sacrifices were offered to pacify the gods, and the most important deity was the sun goddess. In fact, the Japanese called their land Nippon, or Nihon, which means "source of the sun."

Early Japanese society was divided into clans, or groups of related families. Each clan had its own ruler; some were governed by kings, others by queens. Clans varied in size from 1,000 to as many

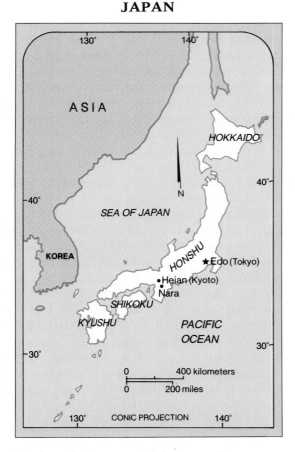

JAPAN

How have the Japanese used the surrounding seas to compensate for their lack of available farmland?

as 70,000 families. Some clans were so large that early Chinese visitors described them as countries.

Early in their history, the Japanese began to collect and preserve legends about the creation of the world, the lives of their rulers, the deeds of heroes, and other important events. These stories, combined with nature worship, became the basis of the native Japanese religion **Shinto,** or way of the gods.

No one knows when Shinto first developed, but it is clearly very ancient and its first writings date from the seventh century A.D. Followers of Shinto doctrine believe that the world is populated by gods, or *kami,* and these gods had created the nation of Japan. The *kami* could control many things in nature—a tree, a mountain, even an insect or a stone. Japanese reverence for the *kami* gave Shinto a strong feeling for nature, a characteristic trait of Japanese culture. Shinto is a bright, optimistic religion and many commentators have interpreted its love of nature as a uniquely Japanese phenomenon.

The purpose of religion, the early Japanese believed, was to seek the favor of the *kami* through simple rituals of hand clapping, bowing, and offering sacrifices. Animals were sacrificed and food was offered to show respect to the *kami.* Shrines were erected as homes for the gods and as places where worshippers could make their devotions. Gates called torii (TAWR-EE-EE) marked the locations of these shrines.

Unlike other eastern religions, Shinto did not travel beyond its birthplace but remained exclusively Japanese. Later, when Buddhist and Confucian ideas entered Japan from China, these new beliefs were blended with the native Shinto tradition. The Japanese demonstrated an impressive ability to incorporate imported faiths and still hold fast to their native Shinto ideals.

Japan Under the Yamato

Early Japanese civilization appears to have been centered in the island of Honshu, particularly near Kyoto, where the powerful Yamato (YAH-MAH-TOE) clan was established. The leaders of this clan gradually became the dominant powers in Japan, and they brought lands as far away as Tokyo under their control. The traditional Japanese histories date the beginning of the Yamato supremacy to

660 B.C. Modern historians, however, believe that the family did not achieve its leadership until the third or fourth century A.D. In any case, it was this great family that produced the first, and all the subsequent, emperors of Japan.

Each Japanese clan worshipped the particular god or goddess that was considered the clan's founder. As the clans grew in size and formed branches, the members of the branches, even though they relocated in distant territory, still paid homage to the ancestral deity. The Yamato clan worshipped the sun goddess, Amaterasu (AH-MAH-TAY-RAH-SOO), and as the clan became dominant, Amaterasu became Japan's most important deity. Hence the Yamato imperial family, and every emperor of Japan until modern times, has claimed to be descended from the sun goddess. Myths about the creation of Japan recount that Amaterasu sent her grandson Ninigi (NEE-NEE-GEE) to the island of Kyushu. Ninigi's grandson, Jimmu, conquered all the other gods on the islands and established the Yamato state. Jimmu is supposed to have been the first human emperor of Japan. To this legendary figure is traced the long line of Japanese emperors who have reigned in an unbroken succession from then until now—a record of imperial stability unequalled anywhere else in modern history.

Imperial Rule in Japan

Unlike China, Japan has had only one dynasty. The divinity of the emperor was so strongly respected that no rebellious general or ambitious official ever dared to attack the sacred figure himself. Political struggles were carried on between rival clans who hoped to gain control over the royal family, but never to replace it.

Early Japanese history is filled with clashes between powerful clans, each of which desired to be the controlling force behind the imperial facade. Though the imperial line was not to be violated, the line of succession was not always clear. When an emperor or empress died, there might be several members of the imperial family who claimed the throne, and rival clans sponsored different claimants. Many Yamato emperors and empresses reigned but did not rule; the real power was often in the hands of a close relative or a member of a related clan.

The Influence of Buddhism

The culture and civilization of Japan's great western neighbor, China, first had its impact upon Japanese civilization in the period between 600 A.D. and 900 A.D. This was the golden age of the Tang Dynasty. Japan's contact with China was not direct, but came through Korea, a land that had adopted much of Chinese thought and religion. The Koreans sent Buddhist statues and scriptures to the Yamato court in the hopes of creating a military alliance with Japan. The new faith provoked great interest and controversy. Some of the great clans supported it; others, especially those who were high officials in Shinto, thought it a dangerous foreign doctrine. It was decided to accept the new belief on a provisional basis. When a plague subsequently broke out, it was believed that the Shinto gods were displeased and the Buddhist temple was burned. This proved only a temporary delay, however. When one of the clans that admired Buddhism won a great military victory over a rival, the new religion rapidly became popular with the Japanese aristocracy.

Along with the teachings of Buddha, the Japanese also acquired the Chinese art of writing. Buddhism, much more than Shinto, was a religion that relied on the written word. In order to read the sacred texts, Japanese scholars and aristocrats schooled themselves in the Chinese language. They mastered the Chinese system of writing, in which each character stood for a specific meaning and sound. Many Chinese words were incorporated into Japanese, but many Japanese words that could not be expressed by the Chinese system of writing remained. As a result, though the two methods shared many similarities, China and Japan developed different writing systems.

China's Influences on Japan

China's cultural impact on Japan was profound in other ways. As an aid to government efficiency, Japanese bureaucrats imitated the Chinese practice of keeping written records of the past. A number of scholarly histories of Japan began to appear as early as the eighth century A.D. By learning Chinese, the Japanese were able to learn about Chinese discoveries in medicine, astronomy, and other sciences, and they also adopted the Chinese calendar. Chinese literature also provided strong models for Japanese literature, especially in its poetic descriptions of nature.

The influence of Confucianism was almost as strong as that of Buddhism. Japanese government officials admired Confucianism's promotion of civic duties, and Japanese clan members and aristocrats welcomed its emphasis on loyalty. Confucianism survived a period in which Japan was wracked by civil strife, and emerged even more popular as the Japanese looked toward its doctrines as a method for restoring responsibility and efficiency to government.

The Japanese emperors also found much to admire in Chinese architecture. For example, when a new Japanese capital was built at Nara in 710 A.D., it was done as an imitation of the grand capital of Tang China, Changan. Palaces were built in the Chinese style, and even the layout of the streets imitated the Chinese plan. When the emperor Kammu built an even newer capital in 794 A.D. at Heian (HAY-AHN), the modern city of Kyoto, it too copied the Chinese model—with one significant difference. Heian needed no walls. There were not, as there were in China, invaders against whom to defend it.

The imperial court at Heian adopted other Chinese practices. Orchestral music and society dances were introduced because they were found at the court of the Tang emperors.

Government in Early Japan

The Japanese system of government was codified in a set of laws that used Chinese codes as models. Legally, the emperor possessed all political power and was given the Chinese royal title of *Tenno*, or Heavenly Sovereign. Theoretically, the emperor's powers were unlimited. However, by the ninth century the emperors had become figureheads, and real power was exercised by the heads of aristocratic families.

The period of Japanese history between 592 A.D. and 770 A.D. records the names of several empresses, but Chinese influence also contributed to the discontinuation of the practice of having women occupy the imperial throne. With the death of Empress Koken in 700 A.D., the Japanese Council of State decided that henceforth only men could rule. This practice has been followed ever since with the exception of two female rulers in the seventeenth century.

Japan followed Chinese models of national organization, but not its system of selecting bureaucrats. The Tang system for selecting its government officials on the basis of a civil service examination system did not take hold in Japan. While a university was established to educate candidates for government service, only males from the upper class could attend the university or serve as government officials. Unlike China, Japan provided almost no opportunity for an educated commoner to rise to an important government post. Although the cost of education limited the number of Chinese who could pass the exams, one did not have to be a member of the nobility to compete. In Japan access to high positions was determined solely by birthright.

Japan's economy, like China's, was primarily based on agriculture. Japan was less successful than China in establishing a monetary system, and barter remained essential to the Japanese economy. Chinese emperors used a draft to fill the armed forces, but this was unnecessary in Japan, where there was no threat of invasion. The emperor was content with a palace guard, which was usually staffed by members of the upper class.

The Period of the Fujiwara

Shortly after the capital moved to Heian, the power of the emperors began to wane. By the ninth century authority had gradually slipped into the hands of the Fujiwara, an aristocratic family, distantly related to the imperial family. By marrying Fujiwara daughters to emperors, the family was able to gain control over the imperial line. Once a Fujiwara daughter had wed an emperor and had borne him a son, the elder Fujiwaras were usually able to persuade the emperor to abdicate in favor of his heir. The heir being only a child, it was necessary to appoint a regent to reign in his stead. It was proposed, of course, that the regent be a member of the Fujiwara family. The Fujiwara remained the power behind the imperial throne for about three centuries. To protect their power militarily, they allied themselves with other powerful families. Imperial ministers also became figureheads and the emperor's court became more a center for ceremony and ritual than for government.

How does this pagoda, part of the Horyuji Temple in Nara, represent Chinese and Korean influence?

Aristocracy in Early Japan

Theoretically, every acre of Japanese soil belonged to the emperor. In practice, the land was parceled out among the heads of the powerful clans. Also in theory, Japanese society was organized according to the Chinese model, with a well organized system of titled aristocrats serving a ruling emperor. In practice, power belonged to the man who was strong enough to keep a powerful army, control the land, and maintain a labor force to work it. By 1100 a feudal system developed, much like the one known in China during the Zhou Dynasty. Land was granted by a feudal lord who promised protection in return for military service. Bravery and loyalty were paramount virtues.

Japanese aristocrats also enjoyed freedom from taxation. This eroded the emperor's tax base, weakening the central government and contribut-

ing to the strengthening of the provincial nobility. These powerful landlords were known as **daimyo** (DIE-MYAW) and they surrounded themselves with soldiers known as **samurai** (SAH-MUH-RYE), a word meaning attendant. These soldiers were the daimyo's vassals, but he did not pay them in tracts of land. Instead they were paid in goods—usually bales of rice. This practice made the samurai much more dependent upon their lords than their counterparts in Europe. Of course, the samurai could, and did, hold lands of their own, and they generally imposed a heavy burden of taxation upon their peasants.

The number of samurai expanded so greatly that they became a separate class in Japanese society. In the sixteenth century it was decreed that no samurai could become a townsman and that no peasant could carry a sword. The sword became a samurai's symbol and prized possession. The essence of the samurai's ethic was military, but in times of peace samurai served their lords as officials and scholars.

In addition to the warrior class of the daimyo and the samurai, there were three other classes in early Japanese society. They were, in order of rank, peasant farmers, artisans, and merchants. There was also a group of people considered completely outside society, known as eta (AY-TUH), that was shunned by the other classes. As in early India, classes corresponded largely to occupation. In Japan, however, it was occasionally possible to move from one class to another.

The samurai wore a protective suit of armor and carried two swords. How did such a costume contribute to the samurai's reputation for fierceness?

SECTION REVIEW

1. Mapping: Use the map on page 202 to identify the four main islands of Japan. How did geography aid in bringing Chinese culture to Japan?
2. In your own words, define or identify: Ainu, Yamato, Kyoto, Fujiwara, samurai.
3. Summarize the main Chinese influences on early Japanese civilization.
4. Describe the relationship between the daimyo and the samurai.
■ Japanese society was clearly divided into separate classes. Do you think there are separate classes in our society? Why or why not?

THE RISE OF THE SHOGUNS

By the twelfth century it was clear that power was slipping away from the central government in Kyoto and relocating in the hands of powerful warrior clans. The Fujiwara quarreled among themselves and became increasingly threatened by ambitious rivals. Two families in particular, the Taira and the Minamoto, rose to prominence and sought to supplant the fading Fujiwara. These two great clans began an enormous military confrontation that plunged all of Japan into civil war. This period, from about 1158 to 1185, is known as the time of The Gempei War. Stories of the exploits of both sides still provide many of the popular tales and legends of modern Japan, just as accounts of medieval knights do in the West today.

The Minamoto Shogunate

In 1185 the fleets of the Minamoto and the Taira fought a great battle in which the Taira fleet was routed and many of its leaders drowned. This Minamoto victory marked the end of the civil war and the establishment of the Minamoto clan leader, Minamoto Yoritomo, as the dominant power in Japan.

Yoritomo moved quickly to establish his own government and to attain the title of **shogun,** or Supreme Military Commander, which would make him head of all Japanese military forces. This title could only be granted by the emperor and had been bestowed on certain generals in the past for limited periods of time. Yoritomo wanted the title permanently—not only for himself, but for his descendants. Finally, in 1192, the emperor gave in to Yoritomo's demands and named him shogun. The government of the shogun became known as a shogunate.

The new shogun let the imperial capital remain at Kyoto, but established his own seat of government at Kamakura. He appointed his own set of officials and installed them in place of those of the emperor. On the surface, Japan now had two governments—an imperial one in Kyoto and a military one in Kamakura. In practice, however, real power belonged to the Minamoto shogunate under Yoritomo.

Zen Buddhism

In the period of the Minamoto there was further activity in the development of Japanese Buddhism. The Mahayana form of Buddhism became popular among the common people and among philosophers at the same time other Buddhist sects arose. One sect known as Zen Buddhism was borrowed from the Chinese, and became particularly popular among Japanese warriors. Originally, Zen Buddhism was a method of attaining inner peace through meditation. Japanese warriors saw it as a method of acquiring discipline and inner strength. By submitting to the austere methods of Zen training they sought to acquire the kind of indifference to discomfort that would make them stronger, more disciplined soldiers.

Honor and the Samurai

This period was also the age of the samurai. These horsemen wore light armor, used the bow and arrow, and were especially skilled swordsmen. They developed their own code of conduct, called **Bushido** (BOO-SHEE-DOH), that stressed pride in one's family and name. Loyalty to the daimyo was prized above all else. The samurai made virtues of patience, courtesy, and indifference to suffering, but honor was the greatest virtue. Should one's honor be stained, the samurai was expected to commit sepukku (SEH-POOH-KOO), or hara-kiri (HAH-RAH-KEE-REE), a form of ritual suicide which had very specific rules. In public, the kneeling samurai plunged a special dagger into his stomach, and a fellow warrior then beheaded him. Sepukku not only wiped away disgrace, it also proved complete devotion to one's superior.

The Decline of the Minamoto

Yoritomo did not enjoy the fruits of his victory long; he died in 1199. Political power did not stay in his immediate family but went to a related branch, the Hojo. This family succeeded in giving Japan nearly a century of peace, but eventually their power declined. They were successful in repelling the Mongol invaders, but they found it expensive to maintain the defenses needed to guard against the Mongol's return. The title of shogun, which in Yoritomo's hands carried real power, slowly became, like the title of emperor, more and more a symbol. The Hojo family kept their power by remaining heads of the Council of State. The samurai, once so attached to Yoritomo, felt less loyalty to shoguns who were no more than figureheads. Once again the samurai gravitated to the service of the daimyo who would support them.

The throne again became vacant in 1318. A dispute over who should be the new emperor once more ignited a bloody struggle for power among the daimyo. By 1336, the outcome was decided in favor of the Ashikaga (AH-SHEE-KAH-GAH). They took control of the shogunate for the next two centuries and moved the capital back to Kyoto. The Ashikaga, however, were never able to centralize their rule. Japan was broken up into warring territories, each run by a powerful and independent daimyo. The ensuing civil wars did not involve the entire population of Japan but were, instead, limited to the samurai armies of the various daimyo. In fact, under the seemingly anarchic

The arrival of Portuguese merchants in Japan is captured in this Japanese painting. How does trade contribute to the exchange of culture between distant regions?

rule of the Ashikaga, Japan prospered economically and knew its greatest age of art.

The Tokugawa Dynasty

By the late sixteenth century, most of the old daimyo families had been overthrown in the civil wars, and new clans arose to replace them. The first to challenge the Ashikaga was Oda Nobunaga, who captured Kyoto. He was succeeded by one of his generals, Toyotomi Hideyoshi. One of the greatest figures in Japanese history, Hideyoshi united the country and once again brought it under the rule of a single shogun. After he died in 1598 the shogunate came into the hands of his ally Tokugawa Ieyasu (EE-YAY-AH-SOO). It was Ieyasu who founded the great Tokugawa Dynasty which gave Japan unification and peace for the next 250 years.

Ieyasu moved the capital to Edo (EH-DOE), now modern Tokyo, and set up a thorough government administration. In effect, he tried to keep Japanese society just as it was, deter change, prevent war, and perpetuate Tokugawa power. One of the ways he accomplished that was through the system known as *sankin-kotai,* or alternate attendance. Every daimyo was required to spend four months of each year at the shogun's court. When they returned to their estates for the rest of the year, they had to leave their wives and children behind as hostages. This was an effective way of preventing the daimyo from hatching plots against the rule of the shogun.

The Portuguese Discover Japan

The Tokugawa gave Japan governmental stability, but while internal order was established a new threat developed from outside Japan's borders. Japan was being discovered by Europeans. The adventurous Portuguese, having already established themselves in India, now appeared in Japan bringing trade and Christianity with them. Although the Tokugawa tried to prevent any change in Japanese life, soon some of the most powerful daimyo in the land were wearing crucifixes. Other western nations would follow the lead of the Portuguese, including the United States, and the impact of western culture on Japanese life would grow in the coming years.

EARLY JAPANESE CIVILIZATION

The introduction of Buddhism from China exercised an enormous influence on early Japan. The impact of the new religion manifested itself in many ways, including in a glorious outpouring of great art. The Tempyo period of the mid-eighth century saw exceptional developments in Buddhist sculpture in wood and metal. The most famous artistic achievement of the period was the colossal statue of Buddha in the Todaiji temple near Nara. This would be an extraordinary accomplishment in any age. In a society with as limited resources as early Japan, it is astonishing. The largest bronze statue in the world, it is fifty-three feet (16 meters) high and weighs over 500 tons (454 metric tons). The Buddhist temples erected in early Japan served as centers of art and learning. From them were disseminated Chinese techniques in sculpture and painting.

The Arts in Japan

The period of the Ashikaga shogunate in the fifteenth century marked a high point in Japanese art. Ashikaga Yoshimasa, the eighth Ashikaga shogun, was a staunch patron of the arts. His Silver Pavilion in Kyoto combines many of the most characteristic features of Japanese art. The building is restrained and tasteful. Near it is a small building that contains the first tea ceremony room in Japan. The Japanese developed a very special ceremony around the serving of tea which has become a special Japanese art form. Participants observe special rules—one comments on the beauty of the pots and bowls, on the carefully arranged flower display, and on the garments of the hostess. The effect of the tea ceremony was to instill a feeling of calm and withdrawal from the world—something precious in the often violent life of the samurai.

Outside the tea room at the Silver Pavilion is an equally subtle and tasteful garden of pine trees and mosses of different colors. Landscape architecture originated in China but became one of Japan's most distinctive art forms. Gardens were designed to bring a sense of serenity and to convey the essence of nature, and this was often accomplished with minimal means. For example, the Ryoanji Rock Garden in Kyoto consisted of nothing but a few rocks and well-raked white sand, but it suggested the beauty of a vast ocean seascape.

Japanese Painting

During the Tempyo period, Buddhist influence was felt primarily in sculpture. Later, under the Ashikaga, Buddhism, as it had in China, inspired a great flowering in the art of landscape painting. Japanese artists depicted the grandeur of nature and the subordination of humankind. Details are kept to a minimum and spaces are left deliberately unfilled. In fact, the use of empty space is one of the distinctive traits of Japanese art and one that greatly influenced western art in modern times.

Japanese Architecture

The oldest existing wooden building in the world is the Buddhist temple at Nara. This massive structure, like many early Japanese buildings, closely follows Chinese models. Sometime after 800 A.D., however, Japanese architects and builders began to develop their own styles. By the Ashikaga period Japanese buildings used natural wood finishes and avoided painted interiors. Thick rush floor mats called tatami were used instead of carpets for floor coverings.

A traditional Japanese house was surrounded by a garden. The house and garden were connected as closely as possible by a narrow platform around the outside of the house on ground level. Japanese architecture stressed harmony between buildings and their natural surroundings.

Japanese Drama

The Ashikaga period saw the development of the characteristically Japanese form of theater called **No,** which combines dance, music, and pantomime in a slow moving, dignified theatrical presentation. There are only two main actors, but they are accompanied by musicians and narrators, who together make up the chorus. Although the stage is bare, the performers wear elaborate costumes. They also wear masks to indicate their roles. *No* drama is characterized by both a religious atmosphere and a Zen influence. The plots were sometimes about the gods but they were more often about heroes from earlier periods of Japanese history. *No* drama appealed to intellectuals and aristocrats. Ordinary theater-goers tended to prefer the more popular Kabuki theater, with its more lavish display, music, and colorful stories. Bunraku, an unusual form of drama, used dolls instead of live actors. Three puppeteers were needed to control each puppet.

Japanese Literature

In addition to those written for the theater, the Japanese produced many other great literary works. The *Kojiki,* or *Record of Ancient Things,* written in 712 A.D., is not only a great work of literature but it is also an important work of history. The *Kojiki,* along with the *Nihon-shoki,* or *Chronicles of Japan,* recorded the oral traditions of ancient Shintoism. Early works of Japanese literature, such as the *Kojiki,* were written using adapted forms of Chinese ideographs. Not until the very end of the eighth century A.D. was a written form of Japanese used to record Japanese literature.

Early Japanese poetry set the tone for much of subsequent Japanese literature. It was lyrical, full of natural imagery, delicate descriptions, and concern for love. Many of these early poems were written in the tanka form, a five-line poem of thirty-one syllables with the first and third lines each being five syllables long and the other three lines containing seven syllables each.

During the Heian era, from 794 A.D. to 1185 A.D., many women became important literary figures, writing poems, diaries, and other works. Around 1000 A.D. Lady Murasaki Shikibu wrote what is considered the first Japanese novel. Called *The Tale of Genji,* this literary masterpiece describes the adventures of Prince Genji and his children as well as providing a detailed record of aristocratic life in Heian Japan.

The Tokugawa era saw two important developments in Japanese literature. One was the invention of an even shorter lyric form than the tanka. The new form, called the haiku, was three lines long and contained five syllables each in the first and third lines and seven syllables in the second line. It was a simple but very demanding form that could produce a striking effect on the reader. In the hands of a master, such as the seventeenth-century poet Matsuo Basho, it achieved a subtle blend of beauty, surprise, and simplicity. The second development of the Tokugawa era was a change from a literature that was primarily concerned with the aristocracy to one that also explored the concerns of common people.

SECTION REVIEW

1. Mapping. Use the Atlas map on page 755 to describe the geographical relationship of Japan to Korea and China. Locate the following cities by means of longitude and latitude coordinates: Kyoto, Tokyo, Nagasaki.

2. In your own words, define or identify: Todaiji temple, bunraku, Kabuki theater, *No* drama, haiku, *The Tale of Genji.*

3. How did Buddhism influence Japanese sculpture and architecture?

4. Describe a Japanese tea ceremony. What was the purpose of this ritual?

■ Much of Japanese architecture, landscaping, and painting was meant to create a feeling of peace. Do you think there are any forms of art today that try to do that? Why or why not? What do you think are some of the effects that today's art tries to achieve?

The Tale of Genji

Historians make great use of historical documents, ancient chronicles, and eyewitness accounts in their research. Works of literature, even when fictional, provide scholars with intimate glimpses of life in past ages in ways that no other primary sources can. For historians of early Japan, one of the most important sources of information is The Tale of Genji, *a long narrative of fifty-four chapters by Lady Murasaki Shikibu. This work is considered to be the first, and by many, the greatest, Japanese novel. It has even been called the first real novel in history.*

Her tale, an account of the adventures of a handsome nobleman named Genji, covers a seventy-five-year span in the history of Heian Japan, from the tenth to the early eleventh centuries. It is a work of astonishing sophistication in characterization and description, as well as a rich source of detail about life under the Heian emperors. We learn about court intrigues, methods of promotion, Korean embassies, Chinese classics, a Cherry Blossom Festival, musical instruments, Indian astrology, and child raising. When, for example, an imperial lady says, ''My son is emperor, to be sure, but no one has ever taken him seriously,'' we learn a great deal about the relative power and prestige of Heian rulers.

What was it like to attend an aristocratic banquet in tenth-century Japan? The Tale of Genji gives us details:

Though it was a quiet, unostentatious affair, the food was beautifully arranged in cypress boxes. There were numerous gifts and there were the usual diversions, Chinese poetry and the like. . . . Several of the guests presently took up instruments and began an impromptu concert. One of To no Chujo's little sons. . . . sang for them in fine voice and played on the sho pipes. . . . As the proceedings grew noisier he sang ''Takasago'' in a high, clear voice.

The novel's many descriptions of nature offer excellent examples of the traditional Japanese sensitivity to the natural world, even in its ominous aspects, as in this scene where Genji and his men are caught in a storm while performing a religious rite.

Suddenly a wind came up and even before the services were finished the sky was black: Genji's men rushed about in confusion. Rain came pouring down, completely without warning. Though the obvious course would have been to return straightway to the house, there had been no time to send for umbrellas. The wind was now a howling tempest, everything that had not been tied down was scuttling off across the beach. The surf was biting at their feet. The sea was white, as if spread over with white linen. Lightning flashed and thunder roared.

*Art, religion, politics, poetic descriptions of nature—*The Tale of Genji *is an invaluable primary source on the history of Japan. But it is more than that: It is one of history's great works of art.*
Source: Adapted from Shikibu, Murasaki *The Tale of Genji,* translated and abridged by Edward G. Seidensticker. Copyright © 1976 by Edward G. Seidensticker. Published by Random House, Inc.

1. What was one of the most notable things about the period of Japanese literature in which *The Tale of Genji* was written?
2. What period of Japanese history is covered in *The Tale of Genji?*
3. What kinds of details of early Japanese life can historians learn about from writings like *The Tale of Genji?*
■ What are some examples of present-day art and entertainment that could be studied by future historians in an effort to understand present-day life? What do you think future historians would discover about life today from studying your examples?

Reviewing the Chapter

Chapter Summary

In the early seventh century A.D. a soldier-prince named Harsha united northern India, but his empire fell apart after his death. Around 1000, the Turks began conquering India, setting up the Delhi Sultanate in 1206 and bringing the religion of Islam to India. The Turks were replaced by another Muslim invader, the Moguls, who entered India in 1526 and subsequently established a great and long lasting empire.

In China the Tang Dynasty began a period of great cultural achievement. Buddhism entered China, taking its place alongside Confucianism. The Song Dynasty rose to power in 960 A.D., beginning the age of the Chinese scholar-official. The Song Dynasty was conquered by the Mongols, who were in turn replaced by a native Chinese dynasty, established by the Ming in 1368. The Ming Dynasty ruled China until 1644.

Unlike India and China, Japan did not suffer successive invasions, though cultural influences from China were strong. The first great family to rule Japan were the Yamato, who began the imperial line. That line continued, but Japan was ruled by a succession of aristocratic families, who engaged in many civil wars. Despite the warfare, early Japanese society developed a sophisticated culture, especially in painting, drama, poetry, and landscape gardening.

1. What peoples brought Islam to India?
2. Which Chinese dynasty developed the system of government based on scholar-officials?
3. What were some of the most notable achievements of early Japanese culture?

Using Your Vocabulary

1. What was the Delhi Sultanate? How did it differ from the Mogul Empire?
2. Explain the Chinese civil service system. How did the Japanese system differ? Who were the scholar-officials?
3. Explain *kamikaze*. Do you agree that it was "a wind sent from heaven"? Explain briefly.
4. Define Shinto. How does it differ from Zen Buddhism? Explain briefly.
5. Who are the Yamato clan? Who was Jimmu? Why was he important?
6. Define *Tenno*. Who was the shogun? Which was more important? Why?
7. What was a daimyo? A samurai? Which would you have preferred to become? Explain briefly.
8. Explain Bushido. What values does Bushido stress? What social group did Bushido appeal to in particular?
9. What are the tanka and the haiku? Explain briefly how they are different.
10. What is *No* drama? How is it different from Kabuki theater?

Developing Your Geography Skills

1. Use the map on page 190 to locate by means of latitude and longitude coordinates: Ajanta, Calicut, Goa, Delhi, Ceylon (modern-day Sri Lanka).
2. Use the maps on pages 195 and 198 to list and describe the extent of the kingdoms and empires in China from the seventh to nineteenth centuries A.D.
3. Use the map of Japan on page 202 to tell how, during ancient times, Japan was more geographically secure from foreign invasion than was China.
4. Use the atlas map of the Far East on page 755 to give the distance in miles and kilometers between each of the following: the northern- and southernmost islands of Japan, the mouth of the Ganges River and the southern tip of India, Beijing and the mouth of the Chang Jiang (Yangtze) River.

Recalling the Facts

1. Describe the Rajput tradition of valor. Which trait do you admire the most? The least? Why?
2. What were the results, both positive and negative, of the Turkish invasion of India?
3. Compare the way Muslims treated Hindus to their treatment of Christians and Jews.
4. List the achievements of Akbar. Which do you consider the most important? Why?
5. How did the voyage of Vasco da Gama to Calicut in 1498 affect India?
6. Who was Li Yuan? Describe his contribution to Chinese history.
7. What accomplishments were made during the Tang Dynasty? Which do you consider the least important?
8. List the achievements of the Song Dynasty. Which do you consider the most important? Explain briefly.
9. Why did Buddhism take hold in China by the end of the Han Dynasty? Why did Confucianism regain its dominant position by the end of the Tang Dynasty?
10. What elements of Chinese culture did the Mongol conquerors appreciate?
11. Describe the tribute system as it was used during the Ming Dynasty. Upon what assumption was the tribute system based?
12. What was the importance of the invention of printing? Can you think of another invention as important? Explain briefly.
13. What were the characteristics of Chinese landscape painting? How was it different from European landscape painting?
14. Explain the influence of the sea on Japanese history. Were any other influences as important? Explain briefly.
15. What is Shinto? Who were the *Kami*? In what way did belief in Shinto and the *Kami* influence early Japanese culture?
16. What did the Tokugawa clan accomplish? Why were they not able to prevent the Japanese way of life from changing?
17. What roles did the daimyo, samurai, and shoguns play in early Japanese society?
18. How was Buddhism brought to Japan and how did it influence Japanese culture?

Essay Questions

1. India fell under the rule of two Muslim empires: the Delhi Sultanate of the Turks and the Mogul Empire of Babur and his successors. Briefly give the reasons for the decline of each empire. Which reasons do you consider the most important for the decline of each empire? Explain your answer.
2. Under the Tang and Song dynasties, China developed a civil service system. Briefly describe the system and its purpose. Is a civil service system based on merit fully democratic? Explain your answer.
3. Japan was relatively isolated from events occurring in India and China, yet was greatly influenced by them. Briefly list the influences these two countries had on Japan. What aspects of culture evolved that were typically Japanese? Explain.
4. The scholar-official of China and the samurai warrior of Japan were highly respected. Briefly define each. Which do you think did the most for his country? Explain the reasons for your choice.

Critical Thinking

1. Babur, the descendant of Tamerlane, was known as "The Tiger." Based on the facts presented in the chapter, do you believe this is a warranted or an unwarranted claim? Support your answer.
2. Are plays from the Mongol era, such as *Western Chamber* and *The Injustice Suffered by Widow Tou*, reliable sources of information about the times? Why or why not?
3. Do you think that the existence of social class systems such as the four-class system in Japan and India's caste system can result in unstated assumptions that continue to affect class relations in that society even after the system itself is abolished? Why or why not?
4. In what regard can the histories, theater, and literature of early Japan be used as reliable sources of information about Japanese history and culture? Explain.

CHAPTER 10

EARLY AFRICA and the AMERICAS

5500 B.C.–1600 A.D.

Objectives

- *To describe the geography of Africa and its effect on the life of the early peoples*
- *To discuss the early West African trading empires*
- *To identify the other African trading empires*
- *To explain early African life and society*
- *To discuss the geography of the Americas and evidence of its early peoples*
- *To describe the North American Indians and their cultures*
- *To explain the Indian civilizations of Central and South America*

*W*hile early civilizations were developing in the Middle East, India, China, Japan, and Europe, many varied and unique cultures were forming in the vast regions of Africa, the world's second largest continent. Much of what occurred there was unknown to Europeans, and this lack of knowledge led to many misconceptions about Africa. Fortunately, modern historians are now correcting these errors. Far from being a continent without a history, as was once thought, Africa is now seen as having a past as rich and as detailed as any other region of the globe. Great empires emerged, based on a thriving trade and agriculture.

In contrast, the continents of North and South America, were uninhabited until about 40,000 years ago. At that time, however, a drop in the sea level caused a land bridge to form across the Bering Strait, which separates Asia from Alaska. Peoples from Asia migrated across this strip of land and gradually populated the wilderness found on these two continents. Their descendants created the many Indian civilizations of the Western Hemisphere. The Mayas, the Aztecs, and the Incas evolved highly sophisticated cultures, which astonished Europeans when they began to explore the Americas in the early sixteenth century.

GEOGRAPHICAL INFLUENCES ON EARLY AFRICA

Africa has a varied terrain. Mountains, plateaus, deserts, lowlands, and tropical rain forests can be found in different regions of the continent. As in other areas of the world, geography influenced the development of its civilizations.

Africa's Geography and Climate

Africa can be divided into two main parts—a highland zone and a lowland zone. An imaginary line between them would extend from the mouth of the Zaire (zah-EER) River to the borders of Ethiopia and the Sudan. North of that line, the lowland zone consists of plains and basins 500–2,000 feet (150–600 meters) above sea level. To the south is a plateau ranging between 3,000–5,000 feet (900–1,500 meters) above sea level, with some higher ridges and mountains.

The lower areas of this plateau contain swamps and shallow lakes filled with a variety of fish. The sources of many rivers, such as the Nile, the Congo, and the Niger, can be found in the higher mountains. As these rivers descend the mountains they reach escarpments, or steep cliffs, and become rapids or waterfalls before moving on to the coastal plains. The numerous escarpments and waterfalls make long distance river travel impossible and prevented explorers from penetrating Africa's interior for many centuries.

The highest region in Africa lies south of the Nile and east of Zaire. There the Great Rift Valley cuts through eastern Africa, forming lakes in its lower regions. Lake Tanganyika (tan-guhn-YEE-kuh) and Lake Malawi (muh-LAH-wee) are among the deepest lakes in the world. Many extinct volcanoes mark the landscape; the highest are Mount Kilimanjaro, which is 19,340 feet (5,895 meters) high and Mount Kenya, which measures 17,058 feet (5,199 meters). Though both are practically on the equator, they are snow-capped year round. The lowlands of East Africa have a temperate Mediterranean climate.

Though there are lush tropical rain forests and arid deserts, most of the continent is a grassy wooded plateau. The northern coastal lowlands are bounded by the Atlas Mountains. South of this region is the immense Sahara Desert. Between the Sahara and the Kalahari (kah-lah-HAHR-ee) Desert in the south lies the Sudan, or the savanna region. The savannas are grasslands dotted with trees. This area is the home of Africa's famous wildlife—lions, elephants, zebras, and giraffes. At the southern tip of Africa there are coastal plains and lowlands bounded by escarpments. Farther north these escarpments form the Drakensberg Mountains.

Prehistoric Peoples

Anthropologists now consider Africa to be the cradle of the human race because the earliest human-like fossils have been found there. By about 40,000 years ago people were scattered throughout the continent. Distinct groups of peoples began to emerge about 10,000 years ago.

The early peoples of Africa can be divided into four major groups. The Bantu-speaking people originally lived in the region between the Sahara and the tropical forests to the south. Then they undertook a series of migrations, settling the entire southern portion of the continent.

North of the Sahara and east of the Nile were a people related to the inhabitants of Arabia—sometimes referred to as Hamites. The Khoi-san (KOY-sahn) were comprised of the San, also known as the Bushmen, and the Khoi, or Hottentots. These two groups were located in east Central and south Africa. The Pygmies lived in the tropical rain forests of west Central Africa. The Khoi-san and the Pygmies originally inhabited wide areas of Africa, but their populations were displaced by the migrations of the Bantu.

Though today it is the world's most forbidding desert, the Sahara was not always lifeless. Around 5500 B.C. life thrived there. Grass grew and the hills were covered with oak, cypress, and other trees. The rivers abounded with fish, and the Saharan peoples raised cattle and practiced agriculture.

By about 3000 B.C., however, the Sahara began to turn dry, and the Saharan peoples were forced to migrate. They moved north toward the Mediterranean, south toward West Africa, and east into Egypt. Some historians claim that the

How does this rock painting support the theory that the Sahara was once fertile?

cultural development of early Egypt owes much to the influx of these Saharan peoples, since there are many similarities in their religious beliefs. After the Sahara became a desert, it was populated by nomadic Berber tribes from North Africa.

The Bantu Migrations

One of the turning points in early African history was the migration of the Bantu-speaking black Africans. The languages of these peoples are derived from a common source, called original Bantu. *Ba* is a prefix meaning "many" and *ntu* means "human being." Thus Bantu means "many human beings" or "many people."

The Bantu are thought to have originated in the river valleys of eastern Nigeria or Cameroon, where they lived mainly by fishing. The men also hunted game, while the women cultivated yams, raised goats, sheep, and cattle, and grew some grains. They made fabrics of woven tree fibers.

With their families, goods, and livestock aboard canoes, the Bantu began to navigate the rivers about 2,000 years ago. Traveling over the southern half of the continent, they displaced the Pygmies and the San. The Bantu settled as far east as the Great Rift Valley, and along the Zaire and Zambezi rivers. Eventually they migrated as far north as Somalia and Lake Victoria.

One of the keys to Bantu success was their cultivation of a new type of banana, which had been brought by seafarers from southeast Asia. This crop thrived in Africa and greatly increased the food supply. In Central Africa the Bantu were unable to raise cattle because the region was infested with the tsetse fly, whose bite caused sleeping sickness, a fatal disease for both cattle and humans. Thus they moved into the east and the south. There they encountered other cattle-raising peoples, the Khoi. Today the Bantu form the largest language group in Africa, and over forty different Bantu languages are spoken. They inhabit most of Africa south of the Sahara.

SECTION REVIEW

1. Mapping: Use the map of Africa on page 222 to locate the Atlas Mountains, the Drakensberg Mountains, Lake Tanganyika, the Sahara Desert, the Zambezi and the Zaire rivers.
2. In your own words, briefly identify or define: Great Rift Valley, Mount Kilimanjaro, Sudan.
3. Name the four major groups of early Africa. Where were they located?
4. How did climatic changes in the Sahara region affect life there around 3000 B.C.?
5. Briefly describe the Bantu migrations in Africa.
■ Throughout history, people have migrated from one region to another. Give some reasons for these migrations. Why would you move to another place?

EARLY WEST AFRICAN EMPIRES

Between 300 A.D. and 1600 A.D. the African continent saw the rise and fall of several great empires. They were based primarily on long-distance trade, and their kings were renowned in distant parts of the globe. Among these mighty states were Ghana, Mali, Songhai (SONG-hie), Kanem-Bornu, and the so-called Forest Kingdoms along the Guinea coast.

Growth of Trade

As you read in Chapter 1, Carthage was established as a Phoenician trading colony on the Mediterranean coast of North Africa in 814 B.C. The colony prospered, even after gaining its independence. In 146 B.C. Carthage was defeated by the Romans during the Punic Wars, and the Romans became the masters of North Africa. They developed the region's agriculture, and about two-thirds of Rome's grain was produced there. Great cities were constructed during the Roman occupation, and impressive ruins can still be seen today on the edge of the desert.

By 400 A.D. Roman power had declined, and the Berbers, who had been pressured by the Romans to become farmers, resumed their nomadic ways. Using camels to carry their goods, the Berbers established a trading network with the inhabitants of the Sudan. Caravan routes crisscrossed the Sahara by 1000 A.D. Cities like Timbuktu, Walata (wuh-LAH-tuh), Djenné (jen-NAY), and Niani

TRADE ROUTES IN AFRICA 400–1400 A.D.

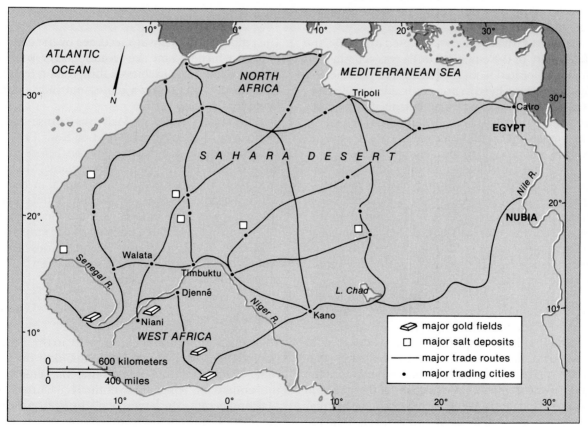

Describe the major trade routes that crossed the Sahara. Where were the major gold fields and salt deposits located?

(nee-AHN-ee) arose where trade routes intersected. West African goods carried by Berber caravans appeared in markets in the Middle East and as far away as Europe. Gold and salt were the most important items.

The Empire of Ghana

Out of this flourishing trade arose the empire of ancient Ghana, located several hundred miles north of the modern state of the same name. Ghana emerged between the fifth and sixth centuries A.D. and reached the height of its prosperity during the tenth century.

The Ghanaian kings became rich and powerful by being located at the trade crossroads between the Sudan and the southern forests. Caravans consisting of as many as 10,000 camels journeyed through the empire, and the kings charged duties on every load of salt or gold they carried. With this wealth the kings were able to support great armies, which allowed them to dominate the entire Sudan.

Ghana's royal palace was located in Kumbi, the largest city of the empire. Kumbi was actually two capitals, located about 6 miles (10 kilometers) apart. The king lived in one city inside a walled fortress. The other city contained the marketplaces and the residential areas of the merchants, teachers, craftspeople, and other workers. At its height, Kumbi had a population of about 30,000.

Like most early Africans, the people of Ghana believed that their part of Africa and the people living there had been created by a supreme being. Lesser spirits were believed to respond to the prayers of the people. These deities had different names and functions in different regions. Many were associated with nature—the sun, the moon, thunder, animals, rivers, and trees.

In some respects, the religious beliefs of the Ghanaians and other early Africans resembled those of the ancient Egyptians and Romans—deceased rulers and ancestors were believed to have influence over the affairs of the living. Ghanaian rulers were believed to be descendants of the gods. Since the health and welfare of the king and that of the country were directly related, the ruler was never allowed to die a natural death. If he became seriously ill or very old, the people feared the country would suffer the same weakness. So the sick or aged monarch was either poisoned or suffocated in an elaborate ritual. At his burial, some of his wives, servants, and other royal household members committed suicide so that they might continue to serve their lord in the next life.

About 1050 A.D. the Berbers, who had accepted the Islamic faith, began to expand south into Ghana. They conquered Kumbi in 1077 and controlled the empire for about twenty years. Though most of the Ghanaian people did not accept the invaders' new faith, a signficant number did. The Ghanaian rulers allowed Muslim scholars to establish schools in the empire's major cities, but maintained their traditional beliefs. They also employed Muslim advisers and established friendly relations with Muslim merchants to the north, which brought more wealth and power to the empire. Although the Berbers did not retain control of Ghana, the empire was weakened by their invasion and finally collapsed in 1230.

The Empire of Mali

The empire of Ghana was succeeded by the empire of Mali, which became the greatest power in West Africa by 1300. Mali achieved this position by taking control of the caravan routes and cities dominated by Ghana.

The greatest ruler of Mali was Mansa Musa (MAN-sah MOO-sah), who reigned from 1307 to 1332. Unlike the Ghanaian emperors before him, he accepted Islam. He brought many Muslim scholars from other places to his capital at Niani, which became a center of Muslim scholarship. Timbuktu was another famous educational center and home of a celebrated university. The emperors of Mali encouraged Muslim learning because their schools provided trained officials, who were necessary for the empire's stability.

The Empire of Songhai

The Saharan trade brought prosperity to the city of Gao (GOH), downstream from Timbuktu on the Niger River. From the area around Gao emerged the empire of Songhai. Eventually it surpassed Mali and became the largest of all the West African empires. During the fifteenth century Goa gained its independence from Mali.

Around 1464 the Songhai monarch Sunni Ali

People in History

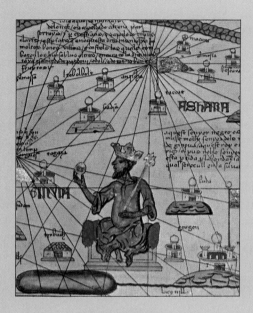

Mansa Musa

To the peoples of Europe, Africa was a mysterious, distant, and fabled land. Practically all they knew of it was its northern fringe, where Carthage and Egypt had affected their affairs since antiquity. Even the people of Europe, however, took notice of the great king Mansa Musa, emperor of Mali.

This famous monarch, who came to the throne in 1307, ruled the empire of Mali at its height—a period that would be long remembered as a golden age. His domain extended from the Atlantic eastward to present-day Nigeria, southward into the tropical rain forests, and northward into the Sahara. An Egyptian traveler who visited Mansa Musa's capital at Niani claimed that the empire was so wide that it would take a four-month journey to cross it.

Mansa Musa was a devout Muslim and an example of the Islamic penetration of Africa. Today Islam still exerts a great influence there. He supported Muslim scholars and established schools of theology and law at Timbuktu and Djenné. His representatives traveled to Egypt and present-day Morocco, and it is possible that they visited India. His pilgrimage to Mecca in 1324 was one of the most remarkable journeys in history. Great preparations were made, food and supplies were gathered, and about ninety camels were loaded with gold dust, each load weighing 300 pounds (135 kilograms). A great crowd of Mansa Musa's subjects—some claim as many as 60,000—accompanied the caravan as well as his wives and children.

Mansa Musa was a generous man. On his pilgrimage he gave gifts to the people and officials he met along the way. He also made huge donations to the cities of Mecca and Medina. His generosity was so great that he ran out of money and had to borrow from the merchants of Cairo. The repayment of these loans flooded the market with gold and, as a result, the price fell drastically. According to one source, it took more than twelve years for gold to reach its former value.

When Charles V of France had a world map prepared, the cartographers included an illustration of the great king Mansa Musa ruling his African kingdom, and on it they put these words:

> "This Negro lord is Musa Mali, lord of the Negroes of Guinea. So abundant is the gold that is found in his land that he is the richest and most noble king of all the land."

After Mansa Musa's death in 1332 the empire of Mali declined, and the empire of Songhai rose in its place.

1. When and where did Mansa Musa rule?
2. What was Mansa Musa's religion and how did it affect his rule?
3. What does Mansa Musa's pilgrimage tell you about the resources of early African empires?

came to power. He defeated Mali in a series of wars and incorporated its lands into his empire. Thus Songhai took control of the western Sudan. Sunni Ali was a Muslim, and under his rule the leading families of the major towns accepted Islam. The peoples of the countryside, however, maintained their traditional beliefs. This created religious tension and political instability within the empire and was one of its greatest weaknesses.

Sunni Ali was a ruthless conqueror and unpopular with many of his Muslim subjects. After his death the throne of Songhai was seized by one of Ali's officers, Askia Muhammad. Under his capable leadership the kingdom was divided into a group of well-administered provinces, and many reforms were instituted. The practice of civil service was established. Royal officials no longer inherited their positions, but were appointed. Since these men owed their allegiance to the king, they formed a loyal and efficient bureaucracy, which served to increase royal power.

This bronze plaque depicts a Benin ruler and his court. What evidence indicates that this city-state was wealthy?

Askia Muhammad standardized weights and measures throughout the kingdom and assigned a tax collector to each district. Timbuktu, Djenné, and Walata flourished as centers of learning, religion, and trade. One traveler wrote:

"Here in Timbuktu there is a big market for manuscript books from the Berber countries, and more profit is made from the sale of books than from any other merchandise."

A pilgrimage to Mecca in 1496 gave the monarch the authority to act as Islam's representative in West Africa. He exercised his new power with vigor, expanding the borders of his state until it more than equaled the size of Mansa Musa's earlier empire. However, Songhai lasted little more than half a century after Askia Muhammad's death. Berbers from Morocco, equipped with a new weapon, the musket, invaded the empire in 1591 and tribes within the empire revolted.

The Empire of Kanem-Bornu

East of Songhai lay another empire, that of Kanem-Bornu, which began in the eighth century. The copper mines around Lake Chad supplied its wealth. Kanem-Bornu reached its height as a trading empire under the rule of Idris Alooma, who came to power in 1570.

Kanem-Bornu was famous for its mounted cavalry that was equipped with armor, chain mail, and iron helmets by 1400. Idris Alooma brought Turkish instructors from Tripoli to train his soldiers in musketry. As a result, Kanem-Bornu's well-trained armies were able to subdue its hostile neighbors in the east central Sudan. However, war and internal strife in the other grassland empires contributed to the decline of Kanem-Bornu as a major power in the eighteenth century, and the empire ended in 1846. It was one of the last great trading empires of the Sudan.

The Forest Kingdoms

No later than the thirteenth century, the people of the Guinea coast were establishing kingdoms similar to those emerging in the Sudan. The most famous were those of the Yorubas, who founded city-states at Oyo, Ife, and Benin.

The peoples of the Forest Kingdoms were especially gifted sculptors, a tradition dating back over

2,000 years. After 1200 A.D. the bronze workers of Benin and Ife achieved a style of sensitivity and realism. Their works are among the great treasures of African art.

The Forest Kingdoms' wealth came from vast deposits of gold and an abundance of elephant tusks. These commodities were among the most valuable in the trans-Saharan trade. Rulers of the Forest Kingdoms also traded cattle, cloth, beads, and copper. Cowrie shells, which served as one form of money, came by way of Egypt from the Seychelles (say-SHELLZ), a group of islands in the Indian Ocean. A brisk trade between Africa and the Orient flourished long before Marco Polo ventured into the unknown lands of the Far East in the late thirteenth century.

SECTION REVIEW

1. Mapping: Use the map on page 222 to describe the location and extent of the empires of Ghana, Mali, Songhai, Kanem-Bornu, and the Forest Kingdoms.
2. In your own words, briefly identify or define: Berbers, Niani, Timbuktu, Gao, Sunni Ali, Idris Alooma.
3. What effect did the Berbers' expansion have on West Africa?
4. Describe the religious beliefs of the ancient Ghanaians.
5. What reforms were instituted in the Songhai Empire under Askia Muhammad?
- Gold and salt were among the most valued commodities of the early African empires. Name one of the most important commodities traded today and explain why.

OTHER AFRICAN TRADING EMPIRES

While empires and trading cities were emerging in West Africa, other empires were developing in other regions of the continent. The empires of Cush and Aksum appeared in East Africa. The Bantu established the Monomotapa, the Luba, the Lunda, and the Kongo empires in central and southern Africa.

The Empire of Cush

As early as 1000 B.C. a distinct state called Cush appeared south of Egypt. Originally colonized by the Egyptians, the rulers of Cush eventually became strong enough to conquer their northern masters. By 750 B.C. Kashta, a Cushite leader, and his sons Piankhi and Shabako, had seized an area stretching from the headwaters of the Nile to Palestine. Thus five Cushite rulers served as pharaohs of Upper Egypt. When Egypt was overrun by the Assyrians, the Cushites were forced back into the south.

The Cushites established their capital at Meroë (MEHR-oh-ee). Having learned ironworking from the Assyrians, they made Meroë one of the greatest iron-producing districts in the world by 200 B.C. Meroë had an ideal location. Lying between the Nile and the Atbara rivers, it benefited from the floods of both. The rich deposits of silt left by flooding promoted agriculture and enriched grazing lands for cattle. The city was also near a major crossroad for caravans and profited from trade. The Cushites exported iron, slaves, ivory, ebony, wood, and ostrich feathers to the Middle East.

The Cushites preserved many features of Egyptian civilization. They developed an alphabet based on hieroglyphs, constructed beautiful palaces, and built a complex irrigation system. They maintained a government similar to that of the Egyptian pharaohs. Many scholars believe that this was the source from which the empires in the Sudan received their ideas of divine kingship.

The Empire of Aksum

Cush's power was challenged by a rival empire called Aksum, or Axum, located in the northern Ethiopian highlands. Aksum's population was composed of black Africans and Arabs, who migrated there by 100 B.C. By 50 A.D. Aksum had become the center of northeastern Africa's ivory market. Trade with the Middle East and the Mediterranean brought it into contact with other peoples. The Aksumite rulers learned Greek and had excellent relations with the Roman emperors. By

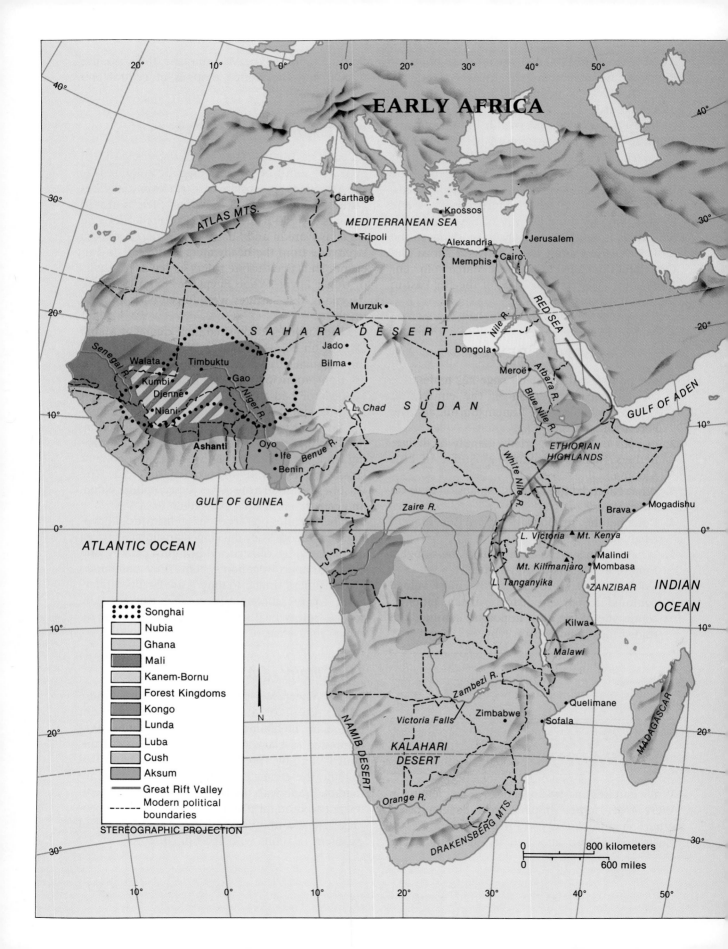

EARLY AFRICA

ATLAS MTS.

MEDITERRANEAN SEA

- Carthage
- Knossos
- Tripoli
- Alexandria
- Jerusalem
- Memphis
- Cairo

RED SEA

- Murzuk

SAHARA DESERT

- Jado
- Bilma
- Dongola

Nile R.

- Meroë

Atbara R.

Senegal R.

- Walata
- Timbuktu
- Kumbi
- Gao
- Djenne
- Niani

Niger R.

L. Chad

SUDAN

Blue Nile R.

GULF OF ADEN

Ashanti
- Oyo
- Ife
- Benin

Benue R.

ETHIOPIAN HIGHLANDS

White Nile R.

GULF OF GUINEA

Zaire R.

- Brava
- Mogadishu

ATLANTIC OCEAN

- L. Victoria
- ▲ Mt. Kenya
- ▲ Mt. Kilimanjaro
- Malindi
- Mombasa

ZANZIBAR

INDIAN OCEAN

L. Tanganyika

- Kilwa

L. Malawi

Zambezi R.

NAMIB DESERT

Victoria Falls

- Zimbabwe
- Quelimane
- Sofala

MADAGASCAR

KALAHARI DESERT

Orange R.

DRAKENSBERG MTS.

Legend

⬤⬤⬤	Songhai
	Nubia
	Ghana
	Mali
	Kanem-Bornu
	Forest Kingdoms
	Kongo
	Lunda
	Luba
	Cush
	Aksum
━━	Great Rift Valley
- - -	Modern political boundaries

STEREOGRAPHIC PROJECTION

N

0   800 kilometers
0   600 miles

How does the architecture of Kilwa compare to that of other early civilizations?

about 300 A.D. Aksum had become a Christian state, controlled and protected by the Roman Empire. This Roman link encouraged trade with Arabia, India, the Mediterranean, the East African coast, and even England.

Around 350 A.D. the Aksumites destroyed Meroë. The empire flourished until the seventh century, when the Muslims seized East African seaports. Thus Aksum's link to the outside was broken, and the empire began to decline.

The Aksumites were later absorbed by the kingdom of Ethiopia. There a unique Christian civilization evolved, almost completely cut off from that of Europe. Scholars and priests composed a sacred liturgy in the ancient language of Geez and developed a religious ritual that included music and dance. Some of the most impressive structures in Africa are the eleven churches of Lalibala (LAH-lee-bah-lah), which were carved out of solid rock in the twelfth century.

The Muslims of East Africa

The Arabs expanded their African empire, moving into the Sudan and along the East African coast. The Nubians who lived in that region agreed to a treaty with these invaders. They would supply slaves and not harm Arab traders. The Muslims, in turn, would respect Nubian independence and supply the region with items such as cloth and horses. Nevertheless, many Nubians chose to move westward into the Sudan.

The Muslims also launched invasions against Aksum and its successor, Ethiopia. This conflict lasted for centuries. Indeed, Ethiopia was not free of the Muslims until the Portuguese helped defeat them in the sixteenth century.

Although the Arabs could not subdue Ethiopia, they did establish a network of trading cities along the East African coast between 1250 and 1492. Mogadishu, now in Somalia, was the northernmost of the group, and Sofala, in present-day Mozambique, marked the southern end. Kilwa, which was located in present-day Tanzania, was one of the most impressive cities. It had wide streets and a palace with over 100 rooms and a bathing pool. Kilwa's merchants controlled the trade between the African interior and the ships that arrived from India and the Far East.

Islamic influence was especially evident in the areas that are present-day Somalia, Kenya, and Tanzania. By 1500, the people of the East African coast were a mixture of blacks and Arabs and had developed their own language, known as Swahili (swah-HEE-lee). The word Swahili is an Arab word meaning "people belonging to the coasts." Today it is a Bantu language of eastern and central Africa.

The arrival of Islamic traders in East Africa was part of Muslim expansion in the Indian Ocean region. At this time the Muslims were also moving into India, Malaya, and the Indonesian islands of Java and Sumatra. By the thirteenth century the port cities of East Africa were part of a unified Muslim trading world. This gave them political stability and access to outside markets, which enabled them to prosper. Islamic tombs and mosques still stand in these cities.

East African Trade

Trade was the main source of income for the East African coastal cities. Gold, copper, ivory, and slaves came from the interior, as did cotton, goods made from camel's hair, and iron ore. Arab ships carried cloth, carpets, jewelry, and great amounts of Chinese porcelain from the Song and the Ming dynasties to Africa.

For several centuries a vigorous trade existed between China and East Africa. In the early fifteenth century Cheng Ho, a Chinese admiral, began the first of his seven great voyages to East Africa. Between 1405 and 1453 he sailed his fleet to what are today India, Indonesia, Thailand, the Persian Gulf states, and the East African coast. In 1417 he transported the black African ambassador in Beijing home to what is now Kenya. Around 1440 the Ming dynasty began to close China to foreigners, and Chinese-African trade decreased.

The Bantu Empires

One of the most impressive remains of Bantu activity in Central Africa is the city known as Great Zimbabwe (zim-BAH-bway), which was not discovered by Europeans until 1868. The site was inhabited as early as the third century A.D. In about 1000 the people who lived there began building in stone, constructing colossal structures that now form spectacular ruins. After about 1425 a king named Mutotoa, using Great Zimbabwe as his base, embarked upon a career of conquest, creating what is known as the Monomatapa Empire. Zimbabwe also reached its height as a trading empire at this time.

At about the same time a Bantu chief, known as Kongolo, united several small states of the Luba people. He established what is called the Luba Em-

pire. Kongolo introduced the idea of *bulopwe* (boo-LOP-way), a type of sacred kingship in which all royal descendants were supposed to have a special type of blood. It was believed that anyone possessing *bulopwe* had a right to rule because it was thought that *bulopwe* could promote crop fertility and ensure the success of the hunt.

According to legend, a Luba man with *bulopwe*, named Kibinda Ilunga, visited a people to the southwest called the Lundas (LOON-dahs), who were ruled by a young queen named Rweej (ruh-WEEJ). He married Rweej and, because he had *bulopwe*, she let him rule. The Lunda state prospered and became an empire. The queen's twin brothers, however, were unhappy with this arrangement. They went to the region of Angola to establish new kingdoms for themselves.

If this story is true, the brothers were the founders of the Kongo Kingdom, located west of the Lunda and Luba empires. By 1480 the Kongo Kingdom was flourishing. Potterymaking, weaving, ironworking, and sculpture thrived. A government-regulated monetary system, using the cowrie shell as the unit of exchange, was employed throughout the kingdom. The powerful Kongo king, ruling from his capital at Mbanza (uhm-bahn-ZAH), also exacted tribute from the states that bordered his empire.

SECTION REVIEW

1. Mapping: Use the map on page 222 to describe the relative locations of the empires of Nubia, Cush, Aksum, Luba, and the Kongo Kingdom.
2. In your own words, briefly identify or define: Kashta, Meroë, Swahili, Cheng Ho, Zimbabwe, Kongolo, Rweej.
3. What attempt did the Arabs make to control East Africa? How successful were they?
4. Explain how the prosperity of the East African empires was linked to trade.
5. Describe the trade relations between China and East Africa. When did they end? Why?
6. What is *bulopwe?* How did it affect the history of the Lundas?
■ List the major types of businesses found in your community. Then use your list to analyze how they rely on trade.

AFRICAN LIFE AND SOCIETY

Though the African empires were many and great, most people lived in villages outside the bustling cities. These villages usually consisted of a family or a group of families and were seldom permanent. When the land was exhausted by crop cultivation, the people moved to new land.

The Cities

Each African empire had its important cities and towns. Some were religious centers; others served as centers for government or trade. Until recently, little was known about these towns, but Richard W. Hull, a scholar who has made a special study of African urban society, has found that these cities had three common elements: their use of walls, passageways, and urban space.

The idea of surrounding cities with concentric rings of walls can be found over much of Africa. A classic example can be seen in the towns of the Hausa (ADOH-suh), who lived in what is now Nigeria. It is theorized that walls were developed when the Hausa began to use iron and served to protect the iron-smelting industries from attack. As the towns grew, more and higher walls were built.

African city walls served many purposes. They protected against theft and controlled the number of people entering or leaving the city. During sieges, food was stored in walls. Inner walls often protected the residences of the royal family and helped preserve the mysteries of divine monarchy. They also provided privacy for the public and marked areas where businesses could operate. One of Africa's greatest city walls is at Zimbabwe. Built in the eleventh century, it had stone walls 32 feet (10 meters) high.

Many passageways ran between city walls. Some were narrow alleys, others were wide avenues. Sometimes an avenue would open onto a large plaza or marketplace, but most led to the city center where the royal palace, the main square, or the central marketplace were located.

Africans south of the Sahara believed that the land belonged to their ancestors and that the earth was the source of life. This belief led them to preserve elements of a rural setting in their cities. Trees shaded streets and plazas and, in some towns, people even raised crops along walkways or in open plots. Parks were also maintained. These features gave African towns the appearance of large villages. The urban appearance of a town varied and depended on its population, its commercial activity, and the number of people engaged in specialized occupations such as ironworking, potterymaking, or clothmaking.

Family Patterns and Village Society

The typical African village was based on the **extended family** unit, which included grandparents, uncles, aunts, and cousins under one roof. Indeed, the aunts and uncles in African families had nearly as much authority over children as the parents. Cousins were treated as brothers and sisters, and grandparents were considered the parents of the entire group. Every member of a family helped to care for the elderly, and all worked together when building houses or planting crops. In contrast the **nuclear family,** comprised of parents

This brass casting portrays an African family preparing fu-fu, a staple food made from yams.

African slaves were traded by Arab slave dealers at this market in Zanzibar. What clues indicate how slaves were treated?

and children, is the more common family structure in the United States.

A group of extended families, descended from one set of ancestors, is known as a clan. A group of clans with common ancestors is called an ethnic group. Some ethnic groups, like the Yoruba, now have populations in the millions. In Africa family patterns varied greatly. Some societies were **matrilineal;** children traced their family line through their mother, and a boy inherited wealth or property from his mother's brother rather than from his father. Other African societies were **patrilineal;** children traced their family line though their father.

Since family life was so important to the Africans, they regarded marriage as a union of two families, not just of two individuals. Certain rituals were followed, and bride wealth had to be paid by the groom or his family to the bride's family. In some societies cattle were used as payment. In other societies it might be goats, pigs, cloth, tools, or other goods. Often the bride wealth received by a bride's father was, in turn, used to finance a son's marriage.

Early African families usually lived together in a compound, or enclosed area, surrounded by fields. Farming was the village's main economic activity. Sorghum, millet, yams, okra, pumpkins, peas, watermelons, and cotton were grown in various parts of Africa. From Asia the Africans acquired rice, sugar cane, grains, dates and figs. After the discovery of the Americas, new crops like maize and the cassava were introduced.

Early African Slavery

Slavery is an ancient and widespread human institution. It existed in India, Asia, the Americas, and on Pacific islands. The Egyptians, Greeks, and Romans also practiced slavery and imported some of their slaves from Africa.

In many cultures slavery was a way in which societies disposed of prisoners of war or of criminals, and that seems to have been the form it took in Africa. Executing members of these groups wasted a valuable source of labor and income. Arab traders and African rulers enriched themselves in the slave trade, and it became a major feature of the African economy.

Early African slavery tended to be less institutionalized than slavery of more complex cultures, like that of ancient Rome. African slaves could become adopted members of a family and acquire the same social status as other family members. Children born of marriages between women slaves and free men became members of their father's clan and were automatically free. Even though slaves were expected to perform the hardest work, their owners often worked alongside them in the fields.

When the exportation of African slaves began on a large scale, the character of slavery changed. Beginning in the fifteenth century, slaves were purchased by Arab traders from black Africans. As the demand for forced labor in other parts of the world increased, slaves became a very profitable item of export and were no longer considered members of a family. African slaves were sold in Arabia, Persia, and India. The trade in slaves with Asia was known as the Indian Ocean slave trade, and the trans-Saharan slave trade provided for the Mediterranean world. When colonization of the Americas began, a new market for slaves was opened up. The increase in volume had disastrous effects on the African population. Whole areas were depopulated, and the enslaved people suffered many hardships under their new masters.

SECTION REVIEW

1. In your own words, briefly identify or define: nuclear family, extended family, clan, ethnic group, matrilineal, patrilineal.
2. What were the main features of African cities? Why did they develop?
3. Why do Africans attach so much importance to customs surrounding marriage?
4. Describe early African slavery. When did it change? Why?
■ Do you live in a nuclear family or an extended one? What are the advantages and disadvantages of each type of family?

THE ORIGINS OF EARLY AMERICANS

While Africans south of the Sahara were developing their civilizations, people in North, Central, and South America were doing the same. Indeed, by the time of Columbus' arrival in America in 1492, these native peoples had created a great variety of cultures. Europeans called the Americas the New World, but it was only new from their perspective—not from that of the Indians.

The Geography and Climate

As you know, the Western Hemisphere is comprised of two large continents, North and South America, and the Caribbean Islands. The two continents are linked by the Isthmus of Panama, a narrow strip of land about 35 miles (55 kilometers) wide. A long mountain chain runs from Alaska to the tip of South America, forming the Rockies in North America and the Andes in South America. Other mountain ranges are the Appalachians, which run along the eastern coast of North America, the Guiana highlands and the highlands of eastern Brazil.

North and South America are surrounded by great bodies of water—the Arctic Ocean to the north, the Pacific to the west, and the Atlantic to the east. The Caribbean Sea is located to the east of Central America, and the Gulf of Mexico extends along the shores of the southern United States and Mexico. The two most important rivers are the Mississippi in North America and the Amazon in South America. They serve as major arteries for transporting food, goods, and people.

Climate and vegetation vary greatly in the Americas. The northern Canadian tundra, or the arctic and subarctic plains, and the Canadian and Alaskan forests have very cold winters and cool summers. The northern United States, including the lightly forested areas of the eastern coastline, the prairies of the Great Plains, and the dense forests of the Far West generally have cold or cool winters and warm summers. The southeastern region of the United States has a humid subtropical climate with hot summers and mild winters.

There are great deserts in the southwest United States and in northern Mexico. The Atacama, one of the world's largest deserts, extends from southern Peru to northern Chile. Tropical rain forests can be found in southern Mexico, much of Central America, and in Brazil around the Amazon region. In fact, South America has the world's largest humid tropical zone. Tropical grasslands cover Brazil south of the Amazon, and northern Paraguay and parts of Argentina and Bolivia consist of tropical bush country. Farther south, the climate changes again in the cooler and drier prairie grasslands of Argentina and Uruguay. At the tip of South America is Cape Horn, a barren, frozen region whipped by Antarctic winds.

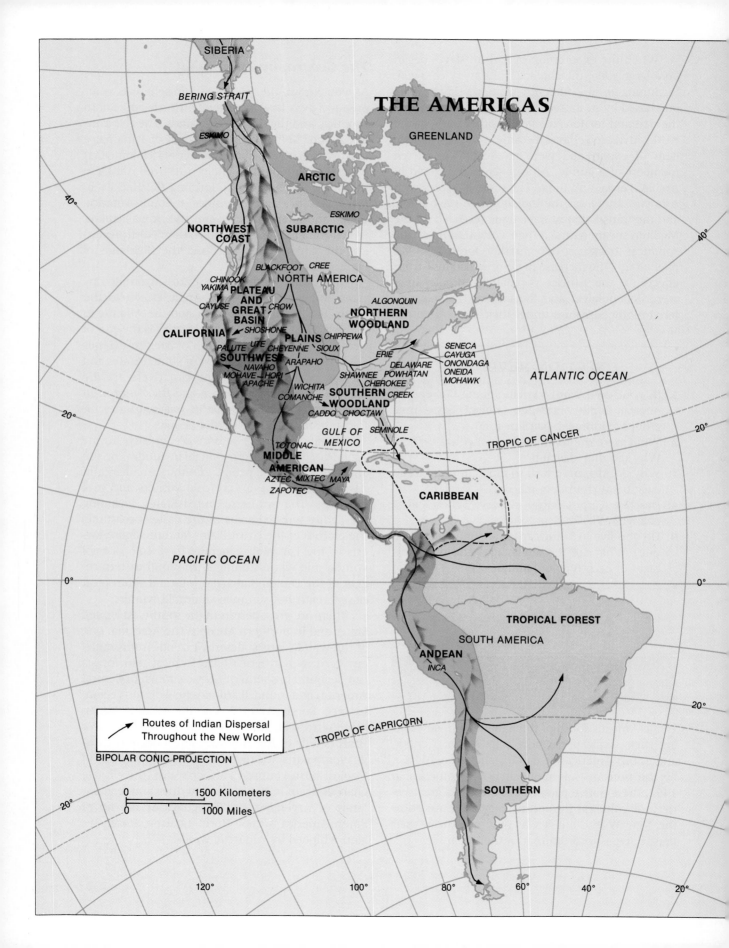

THE AMERICAS

SIBERIA

BERING STRAIT

ESKIMO

GREENLAND

ARCTIC

ESKIMO

NORTHWEST
COAST

SUBARCTIC

BLACKFOOT   CREE

CHINOOK
YAKIMA   NORTH AMERICA

CAYUSE   PLATEAU
             AND   CROW
             GREAT
             BASIN   ALGONQUIN

CALIFORNIA   SHOSHONE   NORTHERN
                              WOODLAND

              UTE   CHIPPEWA
      PAIUTE   CHEYENNE SIOUX
SOUTHWEST   ARAPAHO   ERIE   SENECA
   NAVAHO   CAYUGA
MOHAVE—HOPI   DELAWARE   ONONDAGA
   APACHE   SHAWNEE POWHATAN   ONEIDA
             WICHITA   CHEROKEE   MOHAWK   ATLANTIC OCEAN
          COMANCHE   SOUTHERN
                       WOODLAND CREEK
                  CADDO CHOCTAW

         TOTONAC   GULF OF   SEMINOLE
       MIDDLE   MEXICO   TROPIC OF CANCER
     AMERICAN
 AZTEC MIXTEC MAYA
   ZAPOTEC   CARIBBEAN

PACIFIC OCEAN

                                                TROPICAL FOREST

                                    SOUTH AMERICA

                          ANDEAN

                            INCA

                                            SOUTHERN

Routes of Indian Dispersal
Throughout the New World

BIPOLAR CONIC PROJECTION

TROPIC OF CAPRICORN

0   1500 Kilometers

0   1000 Miles

Evidence of the Earliest Americans

The best evidence indicates that the earliest inhabitants of the Americas traveled from Siberia across a land bridge in the Bering Strait. The reason for their migration is unknown. It may have been due to famine, overpopulation, or the migration of the herds that supplied their food. Perhaps they sought a milder climate. Whatever the reasons, these people eventually migrated from Alaska all the way to the southernmost part of South America.

One great pathway lay along the western slopes of the Rockies into Mexico, down Central America, and into South America. This migration may have taken as long as 40,000 years, and the first settlers probably arrived in South America about 5,000 years ago. The descendants of these first Americans were called Indians by Columbus, who mistakenly believed he had reached the East Indies.

Until 1926 few archaeologists believed that human beings had been in America for more than a few thousand years. In that year George McJunkin found some fossils of an extinct bison and a flint spearpoint in New Mexico. This discovery indicated that people lived in America more than 12,000 years ago. Since then, more sophisticated methods of dating fossils have raised the possibility that North America has been inhabited for 40,000 years.

Ample evidence exists to prove this theory. Archaeologists have found a number of ancient fire pits, or hearths, in the southwestern United States. One of them contained not only charred animal bones but also the earliest known American spearpoints. These are called Clovis points, from the place in New Mexico where they were found.

Clovis points were usually about six inches (fifteen centimeters) long and were made by chipping a piece of flint. The sharp-edged points were then placed on the end of javelins, or spears, and used by prehistoric hunters to kill large game such as the mammoth, an ancestor of the elephant, and the bison. Since Clovis points are usually found in ancient swamps or bogs, archaeologists theorize that the hunters chased their prey into the swamp, trapped it in the mud, and then hurled their javelins at it. They would then carve up the carcass, taking the meat and hide, leaving the bones.

When scientists tested the charred wood found near the Clovis points, they found that it was over 37,000 years old. Further digging in the same region yielded other spearpoints, known as Folsom points. Carbon dating of the charred bones found with the Folsom points indicates that hunters probably camped in these areas about 10,000 years ago.

The Plainview point, discovered in the Texas panhandle, is further evidence of the presence of prehistoric Americans. A Plainview point was found when archaeologists uncovered the skeletons of about 100 bison. Carbon 14 tests of the charred remains near this spearpoint revealed the site to be about 5,000 years old.

One of the most mysterious discoveries was made in gravel pits near the Trinity River in east Texas. Between 1929 and 1933, two contractors and a team of archaeologists discovered three carved stone heads. No tools or other signs of life were found, and scholars have no idea who carved the stones, nor why. They are estimated to be at least 20,000 years old.

Other Types of Evidence

In the Southwest, cave and rock paintings provide additional information about the earliest Americans. They portray subjects such as hunting scenes which are similar to those found on the rock paintings of ancient Africa, and still show traces of the vivid colors. These paintings are perhaps as old as those found in the Sahara.

One of the things about the early Americans that most puzzles scholars is why they domesticated so few crops and animals. Except for the dog and the llama in the Andes, the earliest Americans had no domestic animals and, though many plants and fruits were grown, maize was the only domesticated cereal grain.

In contrast, people on other continents domesticated many animals and plants in Neolithic times. Thus scholars theorize that the first Americans migrated from Asia before these domestications occurred, or at least before they learned about them. They believe that the sea level rose again, and washed away the land bridge across the Bering Strait, cutting North America off from Asia. As a result, there was no longer a route by which Asian cultural and agricultural developments could be transmitted to the Americas. These advances would have to wait until the arrival of the European explorers.

SECTION REVIEW

1. Mapping: Use the map on page 228 to describe the different geographical regions of North and South America.
2. In your own words, briefly define or identify: New World, Clovis points.
3. Where do historians believe the earliest Americans came from? Why and how did they arrive?
4. What evidence has been discovered to support the theory that these peoples arrived in the Americas at least 40,000 years ago?
- Imagine that you are an archeologist 5,000 years from now. So far your colleagues have uncovered only one twentieth-century site, your high school. Write a short summary of what twentieth-century life must have been like, based on that evidence.

This modern Indian tribal house and totem pole are located in Ketchikan, Alaska. What animals are represented in these totems?

THE NORTH AMERICAN INDIANS

Through careful and painstaking archeological, anthropological, and linguistic study, scholars have been fairly successful in piecing together an account of the Indian cultures of pre-Columbian America, or the period before Columbus arrived.

Indian Languages

An astounding number of languages developed among the Indians of the Americas. There were no less than 2,000. Groups who spoke the same, or similar, languages often banded together into leagues, or nations. Examples of these are the Shoshoni (shoh-SHOH-nee), the Apache, the Sioux (SOO), and the Iroquois (EER-uh-kwoy). Sharing a language did not prevent conflict, however. For example, the Iroquois massacred the Erie, Neutral, Susquehanna, and Tobacco tribes of the Great Lakes region, who spoke their language.

Native American Religious Beliefs

The Indians generally believed in many gods and spirits. They thought a supernatural force gave life to the world and believed that if a person captured this force it would enhance his or her power. The Algonquins called this power *manitou* (MAN-ih-too), the Sioux *wakan,* and the Incas *huaca* (WAH-kah). Some Indians, especially in Central and South America, formed religions based on sun worship. Others believed in a supreme being, which Europeans called the Great Spirit.

Another important part of Indian religion was their belief in a culture hero, or a mythical figure of the distant past who had taught them their arts and way of life. Certain individuals were credited with having the power to interpret the wishes of the Great Spirit. These are the familiar medicine men, or the shamans.

Indian Society

Indian society was based on the tribe or clan, not upon the individual. The tribes were groups of people who claimed a common ancestor, and in some areas tribes were named after an animal. These animals became a kind of tribal symbol, or, to use the Algonquin word, the totem. The Indian tribes of the Northwest carved figures of their totems onto poles, painted them, and placed them in front of their dwellings.

Theft among tribe members was very rare, but stealing from an enemy was an honorable act. Indeed, warfare was frequent and usually took the form of raids. Banishment from the tribe was the punishment for many crimes. These offenses included allowing another tribe member to go hungry, showing disrespect for the elderly, abandoning orphaned children, and murder.

Like other peoples, some Indian groups made slaves of their war captives. Many slaves became adopted members of their captors' clan and intermarried with clan members.

People of the North and West

Alaska was, and is, home to the northernmost Indians of the Americas. Throughout the centuries these Indian groups, the Eskimos, lived mainly by hunting seals and fishing. Their migrations took them as far east as Greenland, where some of them made contact with the Vikings as early as 1000 A.D.

In the subarctic region of Alaska and Canada Indians, such as the Cree, lived by fishing and hunting. By the time of Columbus' arrival, these Indians were thinly scattered across Canada, and probably did not number more than 200,000.

Other Indians, such as the Yakima, lived on the northwest coast and in the plateau regions of North America. These areas included parts of far-western Canada, southern Alaska, and the present states of Oregon, Washington, northern Idaho, and western Montana. They had few contacts with Europeans before the nineteenth century and lived chiefly by fishing, mainly for salmon. They were renowned for their basketweaving and wood carving.

To the south and east, in California and the Great Basin areas, were bands of Indians. They lived by trapping small game, such as rabbits and desert rodents, and by gathering foods such as acorns, berries, herbs, and roots. They supplemented their diet with fish. These Indians, which included the Yuma (YOO-muh) and the Mohave

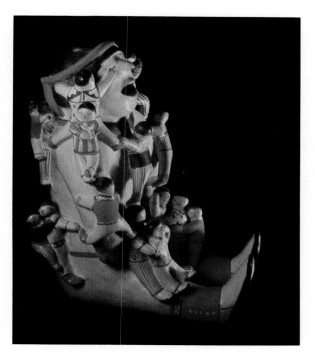

What does this modern clay figure of a storyteller reveal about the Pueblo Indians' traditions and art?

(moh-HAH-vee), inhabited the present states of California, Nevada, southern Idaho, western Wyoming and Colorado. They were also known for their baskets, which were so tightly woven that water could be stored in them.

The Great Plains Indians

The Plains Indians lived in an area extending from western Canada, east of the Rockies, to southern Texas. Most Plains tribes, such as the Sioux and Cheyenne, were nomadic hunters who roamed over large areas seeking game. Their very existence depended on the buffalo, which furnished them with food, clothing, and shelter, since the hides were used to make tepees. Dried buffalo dung was burned as fuel, bones provided tools, and sinews formed the strings for the Plains Indians' standard weapon—the bow.

Since the Plains Indians spoke different languages, they developed a system of sign language as a means of communication. This sign language consisted of commonly understood gestures, but had its limitations because it could only be used to express uncomplicated ideas.

In order to have provisions on their long journeys, the Plains Indians, among others, developed one of the first forms of concentrated food, called pemmican. It was prepared by taking dried deer or buffalo meat, pounding and mixing it with hot fat to form a paste, which was then pressed into cakes. Pemmican is very compact, keeps for a long time, and only a small amount is needed to sustain a person.

The Northern Woodlands Indians

East of the Great Plains is the northern woodland region. It includes southeastern Canada, the Great Lakes region, the northeastern United States, and part of the southern United States. Indians in these areas mastered agriculture, but their scanty harvests had to be supplemented by hunting, gathering nuts and berries, and fishing. Most of them were seminomadic, moving when food supplies declined or when threatened by powerful neighbors. The largest group of northern woodland Indians were the Iroquois, who consisted of five tribes—Mohawks, Oneidas (oh-NIE-duhz), Onondagas, Cayugas, and Senecas. To end wars among themselves, they formed a confederation known as the Iroquois League about 1570.

Women held a special position in the political organization of this league. The basic unit of society was the fireside, which consisted of a woman and her children. A group of these firesides constituted an *ohwachira* (oh-wah-CHEE-rah). The women of these *ohwachiras* appointed the men who would represent them at clan or tribal meetings. Thus women had a great deal of say in the way affairs were conducted.

Southern and Southwestern Indians

Some of the most advanced North American Indians lived in the southern woodland region, which covers the southern United States and eastern Texas. They included the Natchez, the Caddoes, the Five Nations of the Cherokees, the Chickasaws, the Creeks, the Choctaws, and the Seminoles. These tribes farmed, lived in towns, and maintained confederacies like the Iroquois.

In the southwestern United States lived a group of tribes known as the Pueblo (PWEB-loh), which means village in Spanish. Among the Pueblo tribes were the Hopi, the Acona, and later the Navaho and the Apache. They built permanent settlements and established an agricultural economy. These people were skilled potterymakers and weavers.

The Pueblo Indians constructed their apartment-style villages of adobe, or sun-dried clay brick, atop mesas, in cliff faces, and on canyon floors. One of the best examples of their architecture is Pueblo Bonito in Chaco Canyon, New Mexico. It is prehistoric America's largest apartment house. Built around 1000 A.D., the pueblo was five stories high and housed some 1,200 people in its 800 rooms. As a communal dwelling it was designed to house the members of a single clan. Pueblo Bonito was abandoned about 1300 probably because of drought.

SECTION REVIEW

1. Mapping: Use the map on page 228 to locate the following tribes: the Algonquin, the Cree, the Yakima, the Mohave, the Sioux, the Mohawk, and the Seminole.
2. In your own words, briefly identify or define: shamans, totem, Eskimos, pemmican.
3. List the various aspects of Indian society. Which do you think was the most important? Why?
4. Give three examples of how the North American Indians adapted to their environment.
5. What was unusual about the political organization of the Iroquois?
■ How does the environment affect the way you live? Give at least four examples.

CENTRAL AND SOUTH AMERICAN INDIANS

In contrast to the simple tribal societies of North American Indians, the Indians of Mexico and parts of Central and South America developed complex civilizations. Their architectural and artistic achievements rival those of ancient Egypt, India, Greece, and Rome.

The Mayas

One of the earliest civilizations to emerge was that of the Mayas. They inhabited the Yucatán Peninsula of southern Mexico, Guatemala, and Honduras. Sometime before 300 A.D. the Mayas, both men and women, became skilled farmers, cultivating beans, chilies, gourds, cacao, sweet potatoes, cotton, tobacco, and fruit. Their greatest agricultural advance, however, was the domestication of maize. The cultivation of this crop enabled them to produce food surpluses. As a result, the Mayas were able to live in cities and had time to develop crafts, arts, and sciences.

Mayan civilization flourished between 300 A.D. and 900 A.D. During this time they developed a sophisticated number system that included the idea of zero. They created an accurate calendar and learned how to predict solar and lunar eclipses. The Mayas also devised a hieroglyphic system of writing and built majestic cities and monuments, such as Palenque (puh-LEN-kay) in southern Mexico, Tikal in northern Guatemala, and Copán in western Honduras.

For some mysterious reason around 900 A.D. the Mayas abandoned many of their great urban settlements and moved north into Mexico's Yucatán Peninsula. Some scholars suggest that overpopulation prompted the move. Others theorize that epidemics and wars may have killed much of the population. However, the answer will probably not be known until scholars learn to decipher their hieroglyphs.

In Yucatán the Mayas built city-states similar to those of ancient Greece. One of these cities, Chichén Itzá (chee-CHEN eet-ZAH), was built about 1,000 years ago. Its most impressive structure is a huge pyramid called El Castillo, or The Castle. It has four stairways, each with 365 steps, or one for each day of the year. Scholars believe that the Mayas probably constructed their great pyramids because they wanted their temples to be as near as possible to their sun god.

Around 1000, the Mayas were conquered by the Itzá, who introduced Toltec customs. Between the thirteenth and fifteenth centuries the Mayas experienced oppressive rulers and constant warfare. By the time the Spanish arrived in the early sixteenth century, the Mayan Empire had greatly declined.

Indians of the Mexican Plateau

While the Mayas were creating their empire in the south, the central plateau in Mexico witnessed the development of several great Indian civilizations.

A statue of Chac Mool, the Mayan rain god, and the pyramid El Castillo can be seen at Chichén Itzá. How does it compare to the Egyptian pyramid on page 9?

The burning of the temple in this fourteenth-century codex indicates the end of a 52-year cycle. How were dates recorded by the Aztecs?

The earliest was the Olmec, which emerged along the Gulf Coast around 1000 B.C. The Olmecs were succeeded by the Totonacs, the Zapotecs, and the people of Teotihuacán (tay-oh-tee-wah-KAHN), who constructed a great religious center about 25 miles (40 kilometers) northeast of present-day Mexico City. There they built colossal pyramids, one of which is larger in bulk than the Great Pyramid of Egypt.

In the ninth century the Toltecs invaded the Valley of Mexico from the north and began to develop a culture that would later serve as the basis for the Aztec civilization. In 950 A.D. they established their capital at Tula. The Toltecs were greatly influenced by Mayan culture and were also pyramid builders. They cultivated maize and other crops. They were probably the ones who introduced the practice of human sacrifice into religious ceremonies. From their view, they were offering their god, Tezcatlipoca (tetz-kat-lee-POH-kah), the most precious gift of all—life. When the Aztecs conquered the Toltecs, they adopted the custom of human sacrifice as well as much of the Mayan culture the Toltecs had inherited.

The Aztecs

The last great Indian tribe to rule central Mexico were the Aztecs, or, as they called themselves, the Mexica (may-SHEE-kah). According to legend, they left their home in Aztlán—probably in northwestern Mexico or the southwestern United States—around 1168 and migrated southward. In 1325 they reached the shores of Lake Texcoco. There they saw a heaven-sent eagle with a snake in its beak, sitting on a cactus growing from a rock in the lake. This was considered an omen, and upon islands in the lake the Aztecs founded their capital city, Tenochtitlán (tay-notch-teet-LAHN).

Like their predecessors, the Aztecs were great builders, and magnificent temples and pyramids filled their cities. They made beautiful cloth of cotton and rabbit hair, tools of copper, and were perhaps the finest potterymakers in the New World. The Aztecs also fashioned stunning jewelry of jade, a stone they considered more precious than gold. Their work in gold and silver was judged by the Spaniards to be superior to any seen in Europe.

Aztec society was divided into four classes: nobles, commoners, serfs, and slaves. At the age of fifteen, sons of wealthy parents studied to become priests or warriors—the two most highly valued professions. One of the major subjects was Aztec history, which was told in a codex through a series of pictographs on long strips of paper. Other schools prepared boys to become soldiers, landholders, or government officials. Some Aztec women were trained to be priestesses. Others took charge of booths in the marketplaces or ran households.

The Aztecs worshipped more than sixty gods, who represented various aspects of nature, for example, the sun, the moon, and the rain. From earlier tribes, they adopted the gods Tezcatlipoca and Quetzalcóatl (ket-sahl-koh-AHT-uhl), the plumed serpent. The principal deity, however, was Huitzilopochtli (weet-zee-loh-POACH-tlee), the war god who had guided them during their migration.

The Aztec calendar, like the Mayan, had eighteen months of twenty days each, with five unlucky days left at the end of the year. The Aztecs believed that if these unlucky days came after a fifty-two-year cycle, catastrophe could occur. According to legend, four such episodes had already happened—the world had been destroyed and re-created four times. The fifth and present world was the result of Quetzalcóatl's sacrifice of his own blood. Thus the Aztecs believed that their gods needed blood to continue to survive, and the source of blood was human sacrifice in large numbers. In religious ceremonies, the victims were either war prisoners, slaves, or young men and women who were chosen from the populace.

Other tribes lived in dread of the Aztecs and their oppressive rule. This anti-Aztec sentiment proved of great benefit to the Spaniards when they arrived in the early 1500's. These tribes became their allies and helped the Spaniards overthrow the Aztec Empire.

The Incas

In the thirteenth century, about the time that the Toltec culture was at its height, another Indian civilization was emerging. This was the Inca Empire, which established itself in the Andes Mountains of Peru. Like the Aztecs, the Incas represented the culmination of many tribes that preceded them. The most notable of them was probably the Tiahuanacans, who were great builders and whose complex social system contributed greatly to Incan culture.

The Incas appeared in the Andes around 1100 A.D. and built their capital in the fertile Cuzco valley. From there they expanded in all directions, and by the sixteenth century they had established an extensive empire. Their lands were linked by a magnificent system of roads and bridges, which extended from present-day Ecuador into central Chile and eastward from the Pacific high into the mountains of Bolivia. The empire controlled twelve million people, who belonged to one hundred different tribes and spoke twenty different languages.

In the Inca Empire, political and religious power were united in one leader, who was called the Sapa Inca. He was believed to be the direct descendant of the Sun, and thus was both emperor and god, which gave him absolute authority. Incan society was strictly divided into classes, or castes, with the Inca and the royal family at the top, then nobles, warriors, religious leaders, and finally artisans and farmers. The basic unit of society was the clan, or *ayllu* (IE-yoo). A collection of clans made

up the tribe, which was presided over by a council of elders. There was no private ownership of land; all land, as well as all means of production and distribution, were owned by the state.

The land was divided into three parts—one-third for the *ayllus*, one-third for the Inca and his family, and one-third for the Sun, which, in effect, meant the priesthood. Work was done communally and the people were called to the fields by heralds who sounded shell trumpets from the tops of community towers. The Incas established a complex system of irrigation, practiced land-terracing, and developed efficient methods of food storage. Each village had silos or warehouses in which to store food in case there were bad harvests.

The Incas were also successful in domesticating the llama and the alpaca. The herds were regulated by the state, and from them the Incas obtained abundant quantities of fine wool. The llama was to the Inca what the buffalo was to the Plains Indians. Its skin provided leather, its fleece gave wool, but

The Mochicas inhabited northern Peru between about 200 to 700 A.D. What does this ear spool reveal about their culture and civilization?

unlike the buffalo, the llama also served as a beast of burden. Like the camel, it could survive for weeks without water, and its hooves were suited for traveling mountain roads.

The Incas worshipped several gods, but their primary deity was the Sun. Gold was especially prized because it was considered "the tears of the Sun." In Cuzco's great temple the walls were covered with thin sheets of gold, and a golden statue of the sun stood at the altar. When the sun's rays struck the interior of the room, it was filled with a glimmering golden light. Around the altar of the sun, the mummified bodies of Incan rulers sat upon golden thrones. An adjacent room in the temple, in honor of the moon, was covered with silver, and it contained the remains of their wives.

The Incas built majestic fortresses high in the Andes. The most impressive one remaining today is Machu Picchu, a formidable collection of walls, towers, stairways, and aqueducts 6,000 feet (1,850 meters) up in the mountains. The Incas cut stone blocks with incredible precision, using saws made from hard reeds, and brought them from quarries miles away.

The tightly-knit organization of Incan society provided the people with security, but they were subject to constant regulation and supervision. Almost every aspect of an individual's life was controlled by the state. Men were drafted into the army or into government service. Women received specialized training in religious and household activities. Even marriage was regulated. Since single men did not pay taxes, the government encouraged marriage, and if a man was not married by a certain age, a wife was assigned to him. Overall the laws were harsh, and the death penalty was carried out for even minor crimes. These strict rules had the effect of producing a remarkably crime-free society. Theft, for example, was practically unknown.

The Incas also had highly-trained doctors who used herbal medicines to treat a variety of ailments. They knew how to set broken bones, perform amputations, and even do brain surgery. Such operations could not be performed without an anesthetic, and the Incas probably used coca, the plant from which cocaine is made.

The Indians of North and South America established a great variety of cultures, but at the same

Machu Picchu remained undiscovered until 1911 when Hiram Bingham, an American explorer, saw it from an airplane. Why do you think it is considered a major engineering feat?

time retained many similarities. Geography and climate greatly influenced the shape of their societies and culture, just as it did in other parts of the world. However, the civilizations that the Indians created would all change drastically with the arrival of the Europeans in the late fifteenth and sixteenth centuries.

SECTION REVIEW

1. In your own words, briefly identify or define: El Castillo, Olmecs, codex, Sapa Inca, *ayllu*.
2. List the accomplishments of the Mayas.
3. Who were the Toltecs?
4. List the main features of Aztec society.
5. What technological advances were made by the Incas?

■ Inca society provided security for the inhabitants and was nearly crime-free, but at the price of strict regulation. Do you think that kind of strong government supervision is a price worth paying for a safe, secure society? Why or why not?

Reviewing the Chapter

Chapter Summary

The peoples of Africa can be divided into four major groups—the Bantu, the Khoi-san, the Pygmies, and the Hamites. Many great empires flourished on the African continent, beginning with the ancient empire of Egypt. Among the other African empires were those of Ghana, Mali, Songhai, Kanem-Bornu, Cush, Aksum, Lunda, and the Kongo Kingdom. Between 400 and 1400 A.D. extensive trading networks were established that crossed the Sahara to reach the markets of the Middle East and Europe. When the Muslims gained control of Africa, they established routes to India, China, and other areas of the Far East.

Asian immigrants who crossed the Bering Strait about 40,000 years ago eventually peopled the continents of North and South America. They formed a great variety of Indian cultures, such as the Eskimos in the Far North, the buffalo-hunting Plains Indians east of the Rockies, the confederated tribes of the Iroquois in the Northern Woodlands, the agricultural tribes of the South Woodlands, and the apartment-dwelling Pueblo Indians of the Southwest. The most advanced Indian civilizations, however, were found in Central and South America. There the Mayas, the Aztecs, and the Incas established sophisticated and powerful empires.

1. How far did the trading networks of early Africa extend?
2. When did the Americas become inhabited? How did this occur?
3. What Indian tribes lived in what might be called apartment buildings?
4. Where were the most advanced Indian cultures found? What were they?

Using Your Vocabulary

1. Name the four main groups to which most of the early Africans belonged.
2. Define the word Bantu.
3. What are escarpments? How did they affect exploration of Africa?
4. What is Swahili? What does the term mean?
5. What was *bulopwe?* Why was it important to the people of the Luba Empire?
6. Explain the difference between a nuclear family and an extended family.
7. How does a patrilineal society differ from a matrilineal one? To which do you belong?
8. Define the terms clan and ethnic group and explain their relationship.
9. What is bride wealth? Do we have a similar practice in our society?
10. Briefly contrast the trans-Saharan slave trade and the Indian Ocean slave trade.
11. To what time period does the term pre-Columbian refer?
12. Who were the shamans? What other term is used to describe them?
13. What is a totem? Where were they depicted?
14. What is sign language? Why was it developed?
15. Explain the term fireside as it applies to Indian society.
16. What is an *ayllu?*
17. Name the animals that were essential to Indian life and explain why.

Developing Your Geography Skills

1. Use the map on page 222 to locate the following early African cities by means of latitude and longitude coordinates: Kilwa, Mogadishu, Sofala, Timbuktu, Walata, Niani, Djenné, Benin. In which empires were these cities located? Now look at the Atlas map on page 758 and tell in what modern countries they are located.
2. Use the map on page 228 to describe the Indian migration through the Americas. Use the Atlas maps on pages 759 and 760 to explain

what geographical barriers they would have encountered.

3. Use the map on page 228 to tell which Indian tribes were located in each area of the Americas. How did the physical geography and climate of those regions affect the Indians' way of life?

Recalling the Facts

1. Describe prehistoric life in the Sahara.
2. Explain the Bantu migrations and how they affected African history.
3. How did Roman occupation of North Africa influence the region?
4. Who was Mansa Musa and why is he considered an important historical figure?
5. What changes were made in the Songhai Empire under Sunni Ali? Who succeeded him? Describe the reforms instituted by this ruler.
6. Name three important features of Kanem-Bornu.
7. What African kingdoms produced sculptures that are greatly admired?
8. What Egyptian influences can be found in the African empires?
9. Compare Aksum to the other African empires.
10. List three features of early African cities and towns and explain their purpose.
11. Briefly describe early African village society.
12. What were three features of early African slavery? How and why did it change in the 1400's?
13. List the possible explanations for the migration of Asian peoples to the Americas. Which do you think is the most likely? Explain.
14. What is one feature of American Indian languages?
15. Briefly describe early Indian religious beliefs. What other societies had similar beliefs? Give examples.
16. What was the Iroquois League? Why was it formed? Name the other Indian tribes that had similar associations.
17. List the possible reasons for the Mayas move to Yucatán. Which do you think is the most probable? Why?

18. What Indian tribes inhabited central Mexico before the Aztecs? How did their cultures influence the Aztecs?

Essay Questions

1. Compare and contrast the early African cultures and civilizations with those found in the Americas. In your opinion, which was more advanced? Explain.
2. Describe the growth of trade in early Africa and explain its role in the development of African civilization.
3. Explain how the Muslim invasions and the Islamic faith affected the early African empires. In your opinion, did the Muslims have a positive or negative effect on African civilization? Give examples to support your opinion.
4. Although there were many common elements in North American Indian life, there was great variety between tribes. How would you account for the similarities and differences?
5. Compare and contrast the Aztec and the Incan civilizations. In which would you have preferred to live? Why?

Critical Thinking

1. How have scholars been able to learn about the prehistoric Africans and the early American peoples? Give at least three examples in your answer. Would you regard this evidence as reliable sources of information? Why or why not?
2. From the information presented in this chapter, would you consider the Ghanaian kings to be biased or unbiased rulers? Explain.
3. The cartographers who prepared a world map stated that Mansa Musa was "the richest and most noble king of the land." Would you consider this a warranted or unwarranted claim?
4. What values were considered important to the early African peoples and the Indians of the Americas? Which values do they have in common? Why do you think these similarities exist? Which of these values are considered important to our society today?

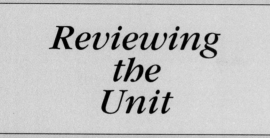

Reviewing the Unit

Developing A Sense of Time

Examine the time line below and answer the questions that follow it.

300 A.D.	300	Mayan Empire begins to flourish
	527	Justinian becomes Byzantine emperor
600 A.D.	612	Harsha unites northern India
	632	Muhammad, Islam's founder, dies
	750	Abbasid Dynasty replaces Umayyid Dynasty
900 A.D.	960	Song Dynasty begins in China
	976	Basil II becomes Byzantine emperor
	1000	Ghanaian Empire reaches its peak
	1185	Shogunate of Yoritomo begins in Japan
1200 A.D.	1211	Genghis Khan invades China
	1260	Kublai Khan starts China's Mongol Dynasty
	1300	Empire of Mali reaches its peak
	1325	Aztecs found Tenochtitlán
	1382	China unites under Ming Dynasty
	1398	Tamerlane leads Mongol invasion of India
	1453	Byzantine Empire falls to Ottoman Turks
	1462	Ivan the Great begins rule of Muscovy
1500 A.D.	1500	Inca Empire reaches its peak
	1526	Mogul Empire begins in India

1. Which came first in China: the Song or Mongol dynasties?
2. How many years passed between Justinian becoming emperor and the fall of the Byzantine Empire?
3. The Mongols conquered the Seljuk Turks in 1258. Between which two events on the time line would this event fall?

Social Science Skills

Primary and Secondary Sources

1. Is the Koran a primary or secondary source in the study of Islamic history?
2. Is Richard Hull's 1976 history, *African Cities and Towns Before the European Conquest*, a primary or secondary source?
3. Good historians work from as wide a range of primary sources as are available on their topic. What problems does an historian face who has only a few primary source documents available to work from?

Critical Thinking

1. Your biographer has a diary of someone who has known you for a long time. What must your biographer first determine before he or she accepts as accurate the descriptions of you in the diary?
2. Before battle, Spartan soldiers were presented with their long, heavy shields. The shields were very heavy to carry if running away from an enemy's charge; they were also long enough to carry a dead soldier's body. What is the unstated assumption behind the traditional command to a Spartan soldier to return with it or on it?
3. The early Japanese claimed that the wind that destroyed a Mongol invasion fleet was a *kamikaze*, or divine wind, sent from heaven to protect Japan. Why would they have thought this a warranted claim? Do you agree with this claim? Why or why not?

Linking Past and Present

Throughout this unit you have seen, and will continue to see in later units, how cultures use art—paintings, sculptures, literature, crafts, and music—to honor their religious beliefs, their rulers, their history, and their people. Describe three examples that you know of where art is used to honor aspects of our own culture. Explain how each example represents American culture.

The MEDIEVAL WORLD *of* WESTERN EUROPE

500 A.D.–1500 A.D.

CHAPTER 11

EARLY MEDIEVAL EUROPE

500 A.D.–1000 A.D.

Objectives

- *To understand the impact of the barbarian invasions in Europe during the early Middle Ages*

- *To describe medieval society and its organization*

- *To explain how growth of population, trade, and cities were interrelated*

A s you have read, the first civilizations of Europe were those of ancient Greece and Rome. This classical world, centered on the Mediterranean Sea, lost its vitality in the third and fourth centuries. By the end of the fifth century the Western Roman Empire no longer existed. Europeans, however, were already developing a new civilization. This period is known as the **Middle Ages,** *or* **medieval** *(mee-dee-EE-vul) period.*

The Middle Ages began at the time the Western Roman Empire fell, around 500 A.D., and lasted about a thousand years. Scholars gave the era its name because it was situated between the classical period and early modern times.

The first centuries of this long epoch were a time of economic and cultural decline and political turmoil. Western European civilization was less developed than the civilizations of India, China, the Byzantine Empire, and the Islamic World, where regimes were stable and important advances were being made in science, education, and the arts.

The early Middle Ages was an era of transition, during which some of the basic institutions and values of western civilization would begin to evolve. These rested on several important foundations. One was classical civilization, which never died out entirely. Another was the Christian faith and the church organization that evolved during this period. A third was the culture of the Germanic peoples.

INVASIONS OF WESTERN EUROPE

At the time the Roman Empire was crumbling, most of its territories fell into the hands of the Germanic peoples. These were warlike individuals who occupied much of northeastern Europe at least as early as the third century B.C. They were nomadic tribes, which over the years pushed west and south toward the lands ruled by the Romans. By about 200 B.C. the Germans' advance had brought them to the Danube and Rhine rivers, where they were halted by Roman armies.

Germanic Culture

The Germanic peoples had no written language, therefore most of what we know about them comes to us from Roman accounts. After the Germans conquered the Romans, they gave up their nomadic ways and settled down to practice agriculture. The actual labor, however, was left to conquered peoples and to slaves. German males were warriors and they prized the values of courage and loyalty.

Each German military leader was followed into battle by his own band of warriors who were linked to him by a personal pledge of loyalty. The Romans called this warrior band a *comitatus* (kah-muh-TAH-tuss). The leader of the *comitatus* saw that his warriors were provided with food, weapons, and shelter and that they received a share of the land and wealth gained in battle. In return, each member of the *comitatus* pledged to fight to the death alongside his leader. It was considered a disgrace to survive a battle in which the leader of the *comitatus* died.

The basic unit in German society was the family. A group of families formed a clan. Larger groups organized themselves into tribes, governed by a chieftain and tribal council. All the adult males, except slaves, belonged to the council, which discussed tribal policies. To show their agreement with the chieftain, the German warriors clashed their shields. In later years tribes united into larger units, which the Romans considered to be nations and referred to their chieftains as kings.

Germans in the Empire

The Romans looked down on the Germanic peoples, considering them to be barbarians. As you have read, Julius Caesar defended Gaul (present-day France) against the Germans. Later, Emperor Marcus Aurelius staved off determined efforts by the Germans to push across the Danube frontier.

For their part, Roman generals admired the fighting qualities of these barbarians. In the third century they permitted limited numbers of them to settle inside the empire in return for military service in the imperial armies. As the empire declined, the Romans were forced to recruit more German warriors. By the end of the fourth century the bulk of the Roman troops in western Europe were Germanic, and it was their duty to protect the frontiers against other invaders.

In the fourth century, threats to the German frontier increased because of the Huns. These skilled fighters, mounted on horseback, crossed the Volga River in 372 A.D. and quickly conquered the East Germans, or Ostrogoths (OS-truh-goths). Then they settled temporarily in what is now Hungary, raiding southward and westward. The Hun advance spread terror among other Germanic tribes. Some of them tried to escape the Hun invaders by seeking safety within the Roman Empire. The Romans did not welcome these barbarian immigrants, but the empire was powerless to keep them out. After one tribe, the West Germans, or Visigoths (VIZ-uh-goths), settled in northern Greece, disputes arose. The Roman emperor, Valens, tried to subdue the Germans. However, at the battle of Adrianople in 378 A.D., the Romans suffered a major defeat, and Valens was slain.

After Adrianople, Roman defenses became increasingly weaker. Groups of barbarians moved into the Western Empire, settling where resistance was light. The Visigoths, led by their ruler, Alaric, invaded Italy and plundered Rome in 410 A.D. Continuing westward, they settled in southern France and Spain. Another German tribe, the Vandals, swept through France and Spain, then crossed the Strait of Gibraltar to conquer Roman North Africa. The destruction they left behind was so great that the word vandal has come to mean someone who thoughtlessly destroys property. Another Germanic tribe, the Burgundians, took over eastern Gaul, while northern Gaul fell to the

Franks. From the bordering lands of modern Germany and Denmark, Jutes, Angles, and Saxons sailed to Britain. Meanwhile, Italy was overrun by the Ostrogoths.

In 451 A.D. the Huns, under the leadership of Attila, pushed into Gaul. Faced by a common danger, the Romans and Germans formed an alliance and defeated the invaders at the battle of Châlons (sha-LON). With westward movement prevented, Attila retreated to Italy where he sacked a number of Italian cities. Then he marched on Rome. As you have read, the city was saved by Pope Leo I. Attila died shortly afterward, and the Huns were driven back toward Asia. With the Hun menace ended, the Germanic tribes were free to move against the Western Roman Empire.

Germanic Control of Italy

The Vandals sailed from North Africa, raided Italy, and sacked Rome in 455 A.D. Italy was plunged into political chaos. For the next twenty years a series of weak emperors followed in rapid succession, none reigning more than a few years. These emperors were only figureheads for the real power lay with the barbarian generals and their armies. In 475 A.D. one of these generals placed his young son, Romulus, on the throne. The following year the young emperor was deposed by another general, Odoacer (oe-doe-AY-sur), and the line of Roman emperors in the West came to an end. This event, which occurred in 476 A.D., is commonly said to mark the fall of the Western Roman Empire.

In the late 400's Odoacer fought a twenty-year war with the Ostrogoths under their chieftain, Theodoric, to determine who would control Italy. In 493 A.D. Theodoric emerged the victor, but refused the title of emperor, claiming only to be king of Italy. During his reign (493 A.D. to 526 A.D.), prosperity began to return to Italy. Agriculture and commerce were revived, and cities were partially restored. Government expenses were reduced and taxes were kept low. He even preserved many Roman laws and institutions. Theodoric, who became an Arian Christian, followed a policy of religious toleration. When he died in 526 A.D., he left his kingdom to his ten-year-old grandson. Without a strong ruler, Ostrogothic domination of Italy did not survive long.

The emperor Justinian succeeded to power in Constantinople in 527 A.D. His dream was to reunite the Eastern and Western Empires, and in 535 A.D. his armies invaded Italy. After twenty years of warfare with the Byzantines, the Ostrogoths were driven out of Italy. Italy remained under Byzantine control until the invasions of a new Germanic tribe, the Lombards. Between 568 A.D. and 571 A.D. the Byzantines lost all of their Italian possessions except Rome, Ravenna, and Naples.

The Rise of the Franks

Most of the early Germanic kingdoms were short-lived. A major exception was that of the Franks, who began their rule in northern Gaul. In 481 A.D. a young warrior-chieftain named Clovis set out to expand the small kingdom he had inherited. He united all of the Franks under his authority and then defeated the other Germanic tribes until he controlled most of Gaul. After marrying a Christian, Clovis adopted his wife's religion. By this act, he gained the support of the Church in Rome,

This detail from the seventh century crown of Agiluf shows the Lombard king and two of his warriors. How does it depict the role of the king?

which in turn, made him more powerful. His people followed his example, and the Franks became one of the first barbarian groups to convert to Roman Orthodox Christianity.

Clovis ruled until 511 A.D. His dynasty was known as the Merovingians (mer-uh-VIN-jee-unz), after an ancestor named Meroveg. For 200 years after Clovis' death, some member of the Merovingian family held the Frankish throne. During the sixth and seventh centuries the Merovingians expanded their territories until they ruled most of modern-day France, the Low Countries (Belgium and the Netherlands), and western Germany. By the early eighth century the Merovingian dynasty had weakened. The real power of authority, at this time, was in the hands of royal officials, or chief stewards, known as Mayors of the Palace.

During this period, as you know, Islam was spreading across North Africa. In 711 A.D. Muslim forces attacked Spain and, by 714 A.D., they had conquered the Visigothic kingdom there. Then the Muslims, or Moors as they were called, pushed into southern France, attacking Frankish towns from 715 A.D. to 732 A.D. In this year Charles Martel, who was then Mayor of the Palace under the Merovingians, united the Franks. With the aid of the Lombards, he met and defeated the Moors at the battle of Tours in 732 A.D. As a result, the Moors retreated to Spain, and the threat of Islamic domination was averted. Martel's victory also gave him the prestige he needed to maintain control over the warring lords of his realm.

Charles Martel was king of the Franks in all but name. His son, Pepin the Short, also did not receive the title when he succeeded his father as Mayor of the Palace in 741 A.D. Pepin did become the king, however, after forcing the Merovingian ruler to abdicate ten years later.

Pepin hoped to strengthen his political position by obtaining papal approval for his rule. At that time the papacy needed an ally because the Lombards, who had invaded Italy in the sixth century, were threatening Rome. Pope Stephen II's appeals to the Byzantine emperor in Constantinople for aid were denied. So, in order to secure help, the pope journeyed to France and crowned Pepin. In return for papal recognition, Pepin sent troops into Italy against the Lombards and forced them to surrender some of the territories they had seized. The

northern part of this area, known as Lombardy, Pepin took for himself. The region to the south he gave to the pope.

This gift of land, called the Donation of Pepin, had important consequences. It strengthened the political position of both sides. The pope became a political as well as a religious leader, since he now ruled a territory that became known as the Papal States. It also initiated an alliance between the papacy and the Franks that helped to establish Frankish power in western Europe. Moreover, by crowning Pepin, Stephen II set a precedent—that the popes had the right to crown and, it would later be said, to depose monarchs.

Pepin ruled the Franks from 751 A.D. until 768 A.D. According to Germanic custom, upon his death, his lands were divided between his two sons. One of them died within three years, but the other, Charlemagne (SHAR-luh-mane), became the most outstanding ruler of the medieval period. He founded the Carolingian (kar-uh-LIN-jee-un) dynasty, which came from the Latin name for Charles, *Carolus*.

The Reign of Charlemagne

Charlemagne ruled from 768 A.D. to 814 A.D. He was an able general and devoted more than thirty years of his reign to fighting sixty military campaigns. He defeated the Saxons in northern Germany and the Lombards in Italy. He also pushed the Muslims deeper into Spain and halted the advance of Asiatic invaders in eastern Europe. As a result, he doubled the size of the Frankish kingdom and reunited large areas of the Western Roman Empire. At its height, Charlemagne's kingdom included all of modern-day France, the Low Countries, Germany, some lands to the east of Germany, northern Spain, and much of Italy.

Charlemagne governed his vast kingdom from the city of Aachen (AHK-un), the present-day Aix-la-Chapelle (eks-lah-shah-PELL). To help him, he relied on governors known as counts and margraves. Each ruled a political region in Charlemagne's name. Alongside the governors were local military commanders, the dukes. To keep an eye on his many officials, Charlemagne devised a system of supervision called the *missi dominici* (MIH-see doh-mee-NEE-kee), which is Latin for "lord's messengers." It was their duty to travel about the

This medieval miniature depicts Charlemagne's coronation at St. Peter's in Rome. How does it reflect medieval beliefs about the origin of the king's authority?

kingdom in pairs, checking on the administration of local governments. The *missi dominici* tried to learn if governors were corrupt, and even checked to see whether church services were held regularly. Any wrongdoing or neglect of duty was reported to Charlemagne.

By supporting the work of missionaries and organizing local parishes, Charlemagne helped spread Christianity. Like his father, Pepin, he had a political relationship with the papacy. In 800 A.D., when a revolt in Rome threatened to remove Leo III as pope, he took refuge with Charlemagne. The Frankish ruler then marched to Rome and subdued the rebellion. Shortly afterward, in a public ceremony on Christmas day, the pope crowned Charlemagne Emperor of the Romans. The territory of his successors came to be known as the Holy Roman Empire, to distinguish it from the earlier one. People of the time, however, regarded it as a continuation of the old Roman Empire rather than a new creation. The crowning of Charlemagne, aside from confirming the alliance between the Franks and the Western Church, indicated that Europeans still felt a strong desire for the political unity the Romans had provided.

During Charlemagne's reign there was a rebirth of culture. In Aachen, the capital, Charlemagne established a palace school to educate his children and those of the lords. He invited scholars from all over Europe to his court. He also encouraged the clergy to establish schools and libraries in their monasteries.

Charlemagne's vast empire did not last very long after his death. His son, Louis the Pious, ruled from 814 A.D. until 840 A.D. Upon Louis's death a civil war broke out as his three sons—Louis, Charles, and Lothar—fought for control of the empire. The conflict was finally resolved in 843 A.D. by the Treaty of Verdun, which arranged for the division of the empire. When invasions from all sides threatened the three brothers, they refused to unite against their common enemies. As a result, the huge empire created by their grandfather, Charlemagne, gradually disintegrated.

SOURCES

The Life of Charlemagne

The Life of Charlemagne, *the first medieval biography of a political leader, was written by Einhard, a Frankish scholar who moved to Charlemagne's capital, Aachen, around 790 A.D. During his time in Aachen, Einhard taught at the palace school, helped design the Aachen cathedral, and traveled on diplomatic missions for Charlemagne. Around 830 A.D. Einhard left the court and retired to a monastery because he did not get along well with Charlemagne's son, Louis the Pious.*

In this selection Einhard describes Charlemagne's religious observances and his coronation at Rome. It should be noted that Pope Leo III did not sustain the injuries Einhard mentions. It is possible, however, that his enemies threatened to harm him in this manner. Most modern historians also believe that the coronation was not a surprise to Charlemagne. He may have pretended that it was in order to forestall criticism from the rulers of the Byzantine empire, who claimed to be Roman emperors too.

The king practiced the Christian religion, in which he had been raised since childhood, with the greatest piety and devotion. That is why he built the beautiful basilica in Aachen and decorated it with gold and silver, candelabra, lattices, and portals of solid bronze. Since he was unable to get the columns and marble for the structure from anywhere else, he had them brought from Rome and Ravenna.

As long as his health permitted, the king attended church regularly in the morning and evening. . . . He was especially concerned that everything done in the church should be carried out with the greatest possible dignity. . . .

Charles also worked very hard at improving the quality of liturgical reading and chanting of the psalms. He himself was well versed in both, although he would never read in public or sing, except in a low voice and together with the congregation. . . .

Of all sacred and hallowed places, he loved the Cathedral of the Holy Apostle Peter in Rome most of all. He endowed its treasure room with great quantities of gold, silver, and precious stones. . . . Although he favored this church so much, he only visited it four times during his reign of forty-seven years . . . to fulfill his vows and offer his prayers.

But there were also other reasons for Charles' last visit to Rome. The Romans had forced Pope Leo, on whom they had inflicted various injuries, like tearing out his eyes and cutting out his tongue, to beg for the king's assistance. Charles therefore went to Rome to put order into the confused situation and reestablish the status of the Church. This took the whole winter. It was on this occasion that he accepted the titles of Emperor and Augustus, which at first he disliked so much that he said he would never have entered the church even on this highest of holy days [Christmas] if he had beforehand realized the intentions of the Pope. Still, he bore with astonishing patience the envy his imperial title aroused in the indignant Eastern Roman emperors. He overcame their stubborn opposition with magnanimity —of which he unquestionably had far more than they did—and sent frequent embassies to them, always calling them his brothers in his letters.

Source: Einhard, *Vita Karoli Magni: The Life of Charlemagne,* translated by Evelyn S. Firchow and Edwin H. Zeydel. Copyright © 1972 by University of Miami Press.

1. According to Einhard, what kind of person was Charlemagne?
2. According to this selection, what was the result of Charlemagne's coronation?
3. How would you account for the fact that Einhard's description of Pope Leo's injuries is not historically accurate?

CHARLEMAGNE'S EMPIRE

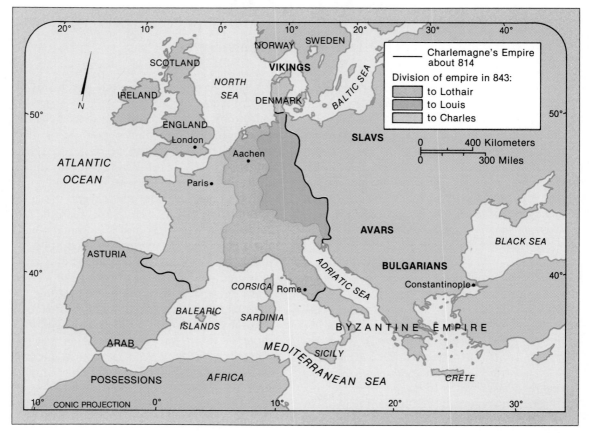

Describe the extent of Charlemagne's empire. Why do you think Charlemagne had to develop a network of supervision and communication?

Anglo-Saxon England

As you have read, the Romans invaded Britain in the first century B.C. However, they were never able to subdue the native Celts (KELTS) completely, and Roman rule was more a military occupation than a merging of cultures.

After Rome withdrew its forces from Britain, in the fifth century, German tribes began to invade the island. There are hardly any written records from this period, but it appears that Germanic invaders settled in Britain and battled the Celts for a century or more.

The three Germanic tribes that overran Britain, pushing the Celts into the western part of the island, were the Angles, the Saxons, and the Jutes. The Jutes settled in the southeast, the Saxons in

the southwest, and the Angles in the north. The territory occupied by the Angles was called Land of the Angles or simply, Angle Land. From this term developed the modern name England.

The term *Anglo-Saxon* is commonly used for the descendants of all these tribes, and the period of English history from the fifth to the eleventh centuries is known as the Anglo-Saxon period. Celtic ways, however, persisted among the Welsh, the Picts and the Scots in Scotland, and the Gaels in Ireland.

England was ruled by several Anglo-Saxon kings between the fifth and ninth centuries. The most famous was Alfred the Great, King of Wessex, from 871 A.D. to 899 A.D. During his reign the Anglo-Saxons were beset by a new wave of Germanic invaders, the Danes. After a long struggle, Alfred was able to establish peace with them. The Danes agreed to stay within the Danelaw, an area of northeastern England, and to recognize Alfred as the king of all England.

After making peace with the Danes, Alfred proceeded to unite the Anglo-Saxons and to strengthen England's government. He reorganized the army, began to build a navy, and established a common law for all Anglo-Saxons. Part of the taxes he collected were used to help the poor. Alfred also established a court school, gathered scholars about him, and tried to revive learning among the clergy. He even translated several important Latin works into the Anglo-Saxon language.

Christianity was firmly established in the British Isles by the time of Alfred the Great. Christian missionaries, like Patrick, reached Ireland in the early fifth century. Before Patrick's time, the Celts practiced a native religion called Druidism. By the mid-fifth century most of them had converted to Christianity.

The Anglo-Saxons were converted by a missionary named Augustine, sent by Pope Gregory I about 600 A.D. Augustine, who was named England's first archbishop, made the church at Canterbury his headquarters. Thereafter, the archbishops of Canterbury were considered the leaders of the Church in England.

Invasions of the Northmen

The Danes who invaded England were one group of Germanic people called Vikings, or Northmen. The Vikings were pagan seafaring warriors from Scandinavia—present-day Norway, Sweden, and Denmark. In early times they confined themselves to the role of traders. However, about the year 800 A.D., they began raiding the coasts of Europe from the North Sea to the Mediterranean. They soon gained a reputation as ruthless destroyers of towns and settlements.

Some Vikings crossed the Baltic Sea from Sweden to Russia. There they followed the rivers southward in search of loot, subduing the people who lived nearby and establishing their own kingdoms. The Vikings attacked the British Isles and later sailed to Iceland. In the tenth century they founded settlements in Greenland. It is believed that some of them reached North America about the year 1000.

This Viking rune stone shows a chieftain on a horse and a Viking ship. If you made a rune stone, what symbols would you choose to represent modern society?

Northern and western France probably suffered the most from Viking raids. In the early 900's much of western France fell into their hands. The westernmost peninsula became known as Normandy because it was the land of the Normans, or Northmen.

Muslim Piracy and Magyar Raids

Another threat to Europe at this time came from the Muslims. By the early eighth century the Muslims controlled most of North Africa. In the ninth century they seized most of the Mediterranean islands, including Crete, Sicily, Corsica, and Sardinia. From these bases in the south, Muslim pirates known as corsairs (KAWR-sairz) raided the coasts of Italy and France. Muslim domination of the Mediterranean continued throughout the Middle Ages. During this period the Mediterranean was referred to as a "Muslim lake."

Muslim control of the Mediterranean Sea had important economic impact on Europe. What trade and travel there had been between western

Europe and the Byzantine Empire was partially cut off. This led to a shortage of some goods and helped to promote the economic and cultural decline of the early medieval period.

Late in the ninth century still another group of invaders filtered into Europe. Akin to the Huns, these nomadic horsemen from the steppes of Asia were called Magyars. They established themselves along the Danube River in present-day Hungary. From there they raided northern Italy and parts of Germany and France that the Viking raids had not yet touched. In the course of their raids the Magyars, like the Vikings, destroyed many European communities. After 955 A.D. the Magyars ceased their raids, settled down permanently in Hungary, and adopted Christianity.

SECTION REVIEW

1. Mapping: Use the map on page 248 to describe how Charlemagne's empire was divided after his death.
2. In your own words, briefly define or identify: *comitatus,* Donation of Pepin, Anglo-Saxons, Danelaw, Treaty of Verdun, Northmen, corsairs, Magyars.
3. Give two reasons why Charlemagne and Alfred the Great were important figures in history.
4. Explain the significance of the battles of Tours and Châlons.
■ What qualities do you think a "great" political leader should have? Do you think a warlike ruler can be great? Why or why not?

MEDIEVAL SOCIETY

The early Middle Ages used to be described as the **Dark Ages.** The term arose from the idea that this period was a time of widespread ignorance and lack of progress. Though we now realize that this era was not as "dark" as we once thought, it is true that there was a general falling off of the cultural level of European society in comparison to the achievements of the Roman Empire.

For most Europeans, life was more difficult than it had been when the Roman Empire flourished. Charlemagne's empire temporarily restored law and order, but political turmoil returned after his death. Invasions by the Vikings, Muslims, and Magyars spread destruction and added to the political confusion.

During most of the early Middle Ages, Europe suffered from almost constant warfare. Towns and cities dwindled in size. Since rulers could no longer protect the inhabitants from raids or invasions, people moved to rural areas. There was little trade or travel because authorities could no longer keep roads and bridges in good repair, and bandits roamed the countryside. Few people were willing to venture far beyond the settlements in which they lived. To cope with all these problems, medieval society developed important new institutions.

The Development of Feudalism

For much of the early and later Middle Ages, military force was the only means of maintaining law and order. No community was safe unless guarded by soldiers. Peasants could not even work their fields without armed protection.

It was difficult for rulers like the Carolingians to have much power because their lands were too extensive to be controlled by their primitive government institutions. Authority rested instead with local lords, who carried on the tradition of the *comitatus.* By the ninth century, soldiers mounted on horseback had proved superior to foot soldiers. To manage a sword, shield, and lance while controlling a horse required skills that only developed after long training. Also, the warrior on horseback had to be rich enough to acquire weapons and to be free from farm work in order to train. Thus, there emerged a special class of mounted soldiers called knights. Frankish rulers depended on the services of a great number of knights to fight their wars and protect their lands.

Since money was scarce in this period, rulers could not pay their knights in currency. Instead, they gave each knight land as payment. This system of exchanging land in return for military service is called **feudalism** (FYOOD-ul-iz-um). The man who granted land was known as a lord. The man who received land was a vassal, and the land a vassal received from his lord was called a fief (FEEF). A fief included not only land but everything on it, even the peasants who farmed it. As time went on, vassals won the right to pass their lands on to their descendants.

Feudalism was based on a system of mutual obligations among the lords, or nobility. The public avowal of allegiance that a vassal made to his lord was called homage (HOM-uhj). As a vassal of a lord, when called upon, a man was expected to fight at his lord's side. He also advised his lord on occasion and furnished financial aid at specific times; for example, if the lord were captured in battle and a ransom were demanded for his safe return. In return for this loyalty, the lord promised to protect his vassal in case of attack and to defend him in court if he were accused of some offense. Kings were part of the feudal system, but only as lords among other lords. The title only gave him social prestige. The real authority rested in the hands of the lords who owned the largest areas of land.

As the Middle Ages progressed, feudalism developed into the accepted political system for organizing government. This system, based on personal

Medieval knights on horseback wore heavy metal armor for protection against their opponents. How did warfare then differ from that of today?

loyalties, became quite complex by the later Middle Ages. The same noble might be the vassal of several different lords. If there were a conflict among his lords, he might find it almost impossible to determine where his primary loyalty lay.

Chivalry

In the late Middle Ages European nobility followed an unwritten code of behavior called chivalry (SHIV-ul-ree), which glorified Christian virtues and the value of being a warrior. Its origins, however, can be found in the early medieval period. The term chivalry arose from the French word *chevalier*, the name for a mounted knight.

One aspect of chivalry was the preparation for knighthood. The training of a knight began at about the age of seven. First, a boy was placed as a page in the lord's house. There he served the women of the house and learned manners. As a teenager, the youth became a squire and served a knight of the household. In addition to the skills of war and hunting, he learned to play chess, to recite poetry, and to play the lute, a guitar-like instrument. He cared for his knight's weapons, equipment, and horse, and accompanied his master wherever he went, even into battle.

At about the age of twenty-one, a squire had to demonstrate his skill at fighting with the lance and sword. If he did well, he was admitted to knighthood in a solemn ceremony called dubbing. First, his sword was blessed by a member of the clergy. This was followed by prayer and the taking of an oath that defined the knight's obligations. He was to keep the Christian faith, to speak the truth at all times, and to protect the weak.

Thus, underlying chivalry were rules stressing correct behavior: politeness, courage, and respect for women and one's enemies. For example, a defeated knight was no longer to be cast into a castle dungeon while his family raised the ransom for his release. Instead, chivalry demanded that he be treated as a guest or even released on his promise to return with the ransom. Knights were also supposed to follow certain rules in battle. It was considered a disgrace to attack an unarmed knight. An opponent had to be given the opportunity to put on his armor and take up his weapons.

Another aspect of chivalry was the emphasis on courtly love. It was generally accepted that a young knight would fall in love with a lady of the court whom he admired and respected. She represented his ideal woman, and he performed acts of gallantry in her name. If necessary, he defended her name and honor. This pure devotion of a knight for his lady was celebrated in the literature and music of the time.

Law and Order

As you know, warfare was constant and fighting was the main occupation of upper-class men during the early Middle Ages. Armed force was a common way to settle disputes, and war could bring the lords material rewards. Victors often acquired new lands and gained additional wealth by taking prisoners who could be held for ransom. Some men fought simply for the joy of battle, and to die in combat was considered an honorable death.

At first, mounted soldiers were protected only by light armor called chain mail. It consisted of overlapping metal rings sewn to a coat or shirt made of cloth or leather. Mail protected a mounted knight against most sword blows that a foot soldier could deliver. Later in the Middle Ages, armor made from sheets of metal covered a knight from head to toe. Although it could protect a fighter better, it was so heavy that it made movement difficult.

Not all medieval disputes were settled on the battlefield. A lord of the manor was expected to maintain a court where the people dependent on him could have quarrels resolved or crimes punished. The lord's decisions were based on local custom or tradition rather than a written code of laws, like that of the Romans.

Sometimes, in serious cases, guilt or innocence was determined by trial by combat, whereby two men who disagreed fought a battle. Since people believed that God would not allow a guilty person to win, the accused was declared innocent if he won. Another method used by feudal courts was the trial by ordeal. In this case, the accused had to grasp a live coal or plunge an arm into boiling water. If the person recovered from his injuries, he was judged innocent because God had intervened and protected him.

Here a group of peasants is working the fields owned by the lord of the manor. What other aspects of medieval life does this painting reveal?

Manorialism

The number of lords during the early Middle Ages was quite small. Peasants who farmed the lands of the feudal lords made up perhaps 90 percent of the population of western Europe. The decline in the level of civilization that led to the development of feudalism as a political system, also led to the development of a new economic system called **manorialism** (muh-NAWR-ee-uh-liz-um). The basic unit of the manorial system was the manor, an estate belonging to a feudal lord. A large fief might have dozens of manors, while a small fief had only one.

Like feudalism, manorialism was a system of mutual obligations. The lord of a manor had to protect everyone who lived on his land. His home, the manor house, was often a castle, a combination residence and fortress that was designed to give maximum protection from raids. Usually it was surrounded by a water-filled ditch, or moat. In time of danger, all inhabitants of a manor took refuge within the manor house.

In return for the lord's protection the peasants, who lived on the manor in small villages, owed him their labor and a share of their crops. For example, they might have to work three days a week for him, tilling his fields, repairing his buildings, or operating a mill or winepress. Women frequently worked in the noble's household spinning or weaving. When peasants harvested their crops, they owed a fixed share to the lord as rent.

Some medieval peasants were free and could come and go as they pleased. Most, however, were serfs (SURFS). Although serfs were not slaves, they were bound to the land, which meant they could not leave their manor without the lord's permission. If a fief passed from one lord to another, so did its serfs. Many serfs spent their entire lives on the manor where they were born. A few lucky ones were able to accumulate enough money to buy their freedom.

Life on a Manor

A manor was a self-sufficient economic unit. Almost everything its people needed was either grown or manufactured on the estate. For example, clothing was made from the wool of sheep raised on the manor. Blacksmiths produced weapons and tools, and shoemakers made leather goods. Other skilled workers, like masons and carpenters, also lived and worked on the manor.

A manor raised almost all its own food except for such commodities as salt and spices. The chief grain crops were wheat, barley, oats, and rye. The main vegetables were cabbage, peas, beans, turnips, and carrots. Orchards yielded fruits in season. Part of every manor was set aside as pasture land for grazing cattle, sheep, and swine.

The lord of the manor had many duties connected with the administration of his estate, and his authority was unlimited. For example, he had the right to tax his people and to collect fees from everyone who used the manor's roads and bridges. As you know, he administered justice when necessary. In addition, the lord provided his peasants with access to certain facilities like a baking oven, a mill for grinding grain, and a press for making wine—all, of course, in exchange for a fee.

The chief amusements of the lord of the manor demonstrate his interest in warfare. First, there was the joust (JOWST), or tournament. In these mock battles, mounted knights with blunt weapons fought each other in groups or in single combat. Although jousts were supposed to be a form of entertainment, they often resulted in death or serious injury. For sport, the lord hunted animals, often with hawks. In the later Middle Ages, more passive games like chess and backgammon became popular with the nobility.

The lady of a manor spent her time supervising her household and servants. She also did spinning, weaving, and embroidery. She made periodic visits to the peasants on the estate and sometimes cared for the sick or injured. When her husband was away, she took over the administrative duties of the manor. She also had to be prepared to defend her home in his absence. For amusement, she played a musical instrument or, like her husband, went hunting.

In the Middle Ages marriages were arranged for economic and political reasons. They signified a union of lands and property, as well as families. Marriage was a means of acquiring territorial possessions and wealth. Women of the nobility were subordinate to men and had no property rights. A woman's entire life was spent under a man's protection—first her father's and then her husband's. A widow was placed under the protection of her eldest son or her husband's feudal lord.

The Role of the Church

Along with feudalism and manorialism, the Christian church was a powerful force in the organization of medieval life. In a time of short-lived kingdoms and decentralized government, the Church represented stability and maintained authority through its hierarchy of officials.

As you know, Christianity began in the first century and spread throughout the Roman Empire. In 395 A.D. it was proclaimed the official religion. Through the teaching of missionaries or contact with Roman civilization, conformity to Christianity was accomplished in western Europe by the ninth century.

During the early Middle Ages, a vast and complex church organization evolved that paralleled the development of feudalism. By this time, the pope in Rome was recognized as the official head of the Church in western Europe. Below him were archbishops and bishops who were chosen from the nobility. In many ways the duties and responsibilities of these high church officials were similar to those of a feudal lord. The Church owned large tracts of land that had to be administered, and taxes were collected in the form of a tithe, or a tenth of a person's income. A portion of this money was sent directly to the pope. The remainder, however, stayed in the hands of high church officials, who often lived like wealthy lords. The influence and authority of the Church permeated almost every aspect of medieval life, and there was no real separation of Church and State, or religion and government. For example, the Church maintained its own courts and made laws for members of the clergy and the nonclergy alike. It had powerful means of enforcing its laws, and no one was exempt, not even a king.

Excommunication, or the banning of a person from the sacraments, was a dreaded punishment because medieval Christians believed that salvation outside the Church was impossible. An excommunicated person, even a king or queen, was to be shunned by other Christians. If a person died while excommunicated, he or she could not receive the last rites of the faith or be buried in a church cemetery.

The interdict, or the closing of all the churches in a particular locality, was another means of controlling people. When a church was closed, Mass could not be said, marriages could not be performed, and the dead could not be buried in holy ground. Popes often used the interdict against a disobedient ruler in the hope of turning his subjects against him.

The clergy, or ordained priests of the Church, were divided into two groups, according to their way of life. The pope, archbishops, bishops, and parish priests formed the secular clergy. The term

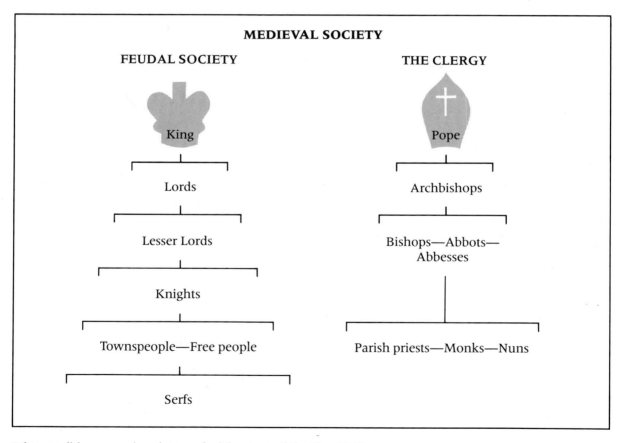

What parallels can you draw between feudal society and the Church? If you were to assign symbols to represent each of these groups, what would they be? Why?

comes from the Latin phrase *in saeculo,* meaning "in the world." The secular clergy lived and worked among the people, providing counsel, preaching, and administering the sacraments. Another group of church servants lived apart from the world, following a strictly disciplined life of poverty, chastity, and obedience. They were called regular clergy, from the Latin word *regula,* meaning "rule."

The regular clergy lived in religious communities—monasteries for men and convents for women. Monks and nuns believed that the best way to serve God was to withdraw from worldly concerns and devote themselves to prayer and good works. The most important figure in the development of this way of life was Benedict, a monk who lived in Italy in the early sixth century. He established one of the first monasteries at Monte Cassino and drew up a set of regulations to govern the daily lives of the monks. This set of rules became known as the Benedictine Rule and served as a guideline for other religious orders.

Like a manor, a monastery or convent tried to be self-sufficient. Along with the daily routine of prayer and study, monastics raised food and made the things they needed. They owed complete obedience to the abbot or abbess who directed the religious community, and were equal in rank to the bishops of the secular clergy.

The medieval Church performed many services that today are handled by other institutions. It administered charity to the poor, cared for the sick in hospitals operated by nuns, and offered shelter to travelers at monasteries or convents, because there were no inns. Some clergymen and abbesses gained significant political influence as advisors to rulers, military leaders, or as mayors of towns.

One of the greatest accomplishments of the medieval Church was the preservation of classical learning. In the Middle Ages, few people could read or write. The Church, recognizing the need for an educated clergy that could study the holy writings, maintained most of the schools. The earliest ones were opened in monasteries, and monks spent many long hours studying Latin and copying by hand the manuscripts of great classical works. The painstaking copying of these manuscripts was the only means of preserving and transmitting literature and learning from this period and earlier times. When towns began to establish themselves,

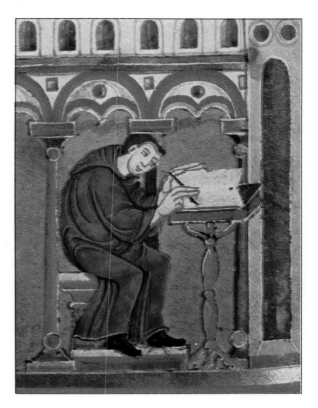

Monks copied manuscripts by hand. How do you think this method of reproducing books limited education?

cathedral schools became the most important centers of learning. The first universities were founded in the late Middle Ages.

SECTION REVIEW

1. In your own words, briefly define or identify: vassal, lord, manor, fief, monks, chivalry, excommunication, interdict.
2. Explain how and why feudalism developed.
3. Explain manorialism.
4. Explain the various stages involved in becoming a knight.
5. How did the regular clergy differ from the secular clergy?
6. What role did women play in the Church?
- You have just learned that the medieval Church performed many services that other institutions handle today. What social services do religious organizations provide in the modern world?

ECONOMIC REVIVAL AND GROWTH

The raids of Vikings, Muslims, and Magyars were for the most part ended by 950 A.D., and peace slowly brought prosperity to Europe. Trade revived, agricultural production increased, towns were established, and a middle class emerged composed of merchants and skilled artisans.

Improved Agricultural Methods

Between the sixth and tenth centuries there were several innovations in agricultural technology. In northern Europe a new kind of plow was developed that opened up more land for farming. The heavy plow, as it was called, not only dug a furrow but also turned the earth over. It was especially useful where the soil was heavy and moist. Before this invention, a simpler plow had been used but it only sufficed to turn over dry, light soil such as that found near the Mediterranean.

Another improvement was the use of horses instead of oxen as beasts of burden. This was made possible because of the invention of the horse collar. In Roman times, horses were harnessed so inefficiently that they choked if they tried to pull heavy loads. The horse collar prevented this from happening. Since horses are able to work longer hours and pull heavier loads than oxen, using them made it possible to cultivate more land and to do it more efficiently.

A new method of crop rotation, the three-field system, was also developed at this time. Under the previous two-field system, one field was left fallow, or unplanted, while the other was planted in winter wheat. With the three-field system, the land was divided into three sections. One field was left fallow, one was planted in the fall with rye or winter wheat, and the third was planted in the spring with oats, barley, or vegetables. The three-field system increased productivity and allowed a variety of crops to be planted and harvested at different times of the year.

These advances in agricultural technology increased the food supply. Invasions became less frequent as the barbarians took up farming. The combination of these factors led to an increase in population that created a demand for more farm-land. Europeans cleared forests and drained marshes to meet the need. According to one estimate, the population of western Europe almost doubled between 650 and 1000.

A Revival of Trade

A more peaceful environment and a growing population enabled more people to devote their time and energy to trade. Although commerce never died out completely, it declined significantly during the early Middle Ages due to the numerous barbarian invasions.

Trade only began to revive in the tenth century. One center of activity was the Mediterranean, where Venice, Genoa, Pisa, and Marseilles were among the principal towns. In the eastern Mediterranean, Venetian merchants negotiated agreements with the Byzantines that allowed them to travel throughout the Adriatic and Aegean seas to Constantinople and other cities in Asia Minor. In the western Mediterranean, Genoa and Pisa used armed force to win trading concessions from the Muslims. The Italians took Sardinia in 1015 and raided pirate ports in North Africa a few years later. By 1100 Sicily was free of Muslim control, and the Mediterranean was no longer a "Muslim lake." The most important commodities traded by western Europeans were grain, oil, wine, and iron, which were exchanged for silks, spices, jewels, and other luxury items from the Near and Far East.

Another center of commerical activity in the Middle Ages was in northern Europe, along the shores of the Baltic and North seas. This region dealt in such commodities as timber, furs, and fish. In the eleventh century the northern European cities began to supply manufactured goods, as Flanders (modern Belgium and northern France) became the center of a textile industry. Flemish wool was of good quality and sold for a reasonable price. Demand for this cloth grew so great that Flemish merchants began importing English wool, which was of even better quality than wool from Flanders.

Medieval commerce was conducted chiefly by shipping because there were fewer problems to overcome. When transporting goods overland, merchants had to contend with natural geographic barriers such as mountains, lakes, and rivers. The roads were usually in a state of disrepair and expensive to use because feudal lords charged tolls. Moreover, robbers roamed the countryside preying on travelers.

In the fourteenth century, German merchants in a number of cities and towns along the North and Baltic seas began to form leagues, or *Hansas,* to protect their trading and economic privileges. These associations became known as the Hanseatic League, and their fleets dominated the shipping lanes of northern Europe until the end of the fifteenth century.

The Growth of Towns and Cities

As you already know, the barbarian invasions disrupted trade and industry. As a result, manors became self-sufficient economic units and produced only a small surplus of goods for trade. Thus the need for towns and cities as centers of trade and industry declined, and their inhabitants moved to rural areas. However, with the growth of population and the increase in trade beginning in the tenth century, towns and cities started to regain their vitality.

Geography played an important role in the growth of towns and cities. They were usually established along trade routes because their location was accessible and merchants met at these places to buy and sell their goods. For example, some medieval cities, like Danzig on the Baltic Sea, had good harbors for shipping. Others, such as Antwerp and Hamburg, were on navigable rivers not far from the sea. Inland locations, where rivers could be forded or crossed by bridges, also became town sites; for instance, Oxford and Cambridge in

MEDIEVAL TRADE ROUTES

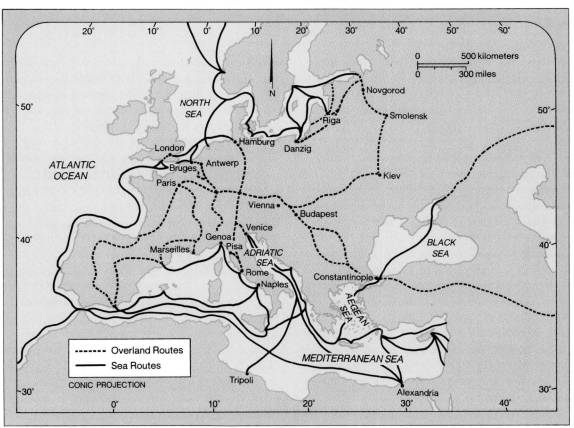

Describe the extent of medieval trading. What regions were most actively involved?

England. The German cities of Cologne and Nuremberg were favorably located at the junction of two rivers. In Italy, Milan grew up at the crossroads of two overland trade routes.

The population of towns and cities increased as peasants left their manors and moved to these new trading centers. They did this because their skills in metalworking, stonecutting, and weaving were in demand. Many serfs, who were bound to the land, ran away from their manors. According to common law, a serf who remained in a town for a year and a day was free of manorial obligations.

Economic growth was stimulated by the increase in urban population. Townspeople had to manufacture and sell goods so that they could purchase other needed goods such as food. Peasants, for their part, had to grow more food so that they would have a surplus to sell or exchange for manufactured goods they wanted or needed. Brisk trade was not only carried on locally in the town markets, but also between towns and cities.

Town Life

Medieval towns were small compared with cities of the ancient or the modern world. In northern Europe, trade centers like London or Bruges had no more than 40,000 inhabitants. Italian cities were larger; the population of Venice or Milan probably exceeded 100,000.

Most medieval towns were walled for protection. This meant that they could not expand outward, so the houses and other buildings tended to be cramped together. Streets were narrow, unpaved, and muddy, and the lack of adequate sanitation made disease a serious problem. Medieval houses were built of wood, therefore fire was a great danger. Since there were no streetlights or police, most people stayed indoors at night.

The main building in each small town was its church. Larger cities, of course, had several. By 1200 London had a total of 120 churches. If a city boasted a cathedral, it usually towered above all the other buildings and was a source of great pride to its citizens. If the town had grown up around a castle or monastery, its stone walls and towers dominated the scene.

At first, medieval towns remained under the control of feudal lords and were considered part of their fiefs. But as the population of the towns grew, there appeared a new group of people called the middle class. They were so named because, according to the social hierarchy of the feudal system, their status fell between the peasants and the lords. This new middle class was comprised of merchants, artisans, craftspeople, runaway serfs, and free peasants. Since townspeople were not serfs, they began to demand rights of their own. For example, they wanted personal freedom, an end to manorial taxes and fees, and self-government.

The political, economic, and social liberties that the townspeople won were generally set forth in town charters granted by feudal lords. Sometimes a lord made concessions in exchange for a lump sum payment. In other instances, he required an annual fee. Townspeople's demands for self-government caused difficulties and conflict. Townspeople wanted to handle their own affairs, but feudal lords did not want to give up control. Some cities and towns had to struggle for many years and even resort to armed resistance in order to gain their independence.

Guilds

With the revival of trade and towns, members of the growing middle class formed associations known as **guilds.** The chief purpose of a guild was to create a **monopoly,** that is, to gain exclusive control over a service or commodity.

Merchant guilds were the first to emerge, and they strictly regulated the buying and selling of goods and the quality of goods produced. No merchant was permitted to establish a business in a town unless he belonged to its merchant guild. If a merchant from another town or city came to do business, he had to pay a special fee to the guild of that town.

Besides regulating trade, merchant guilds provided additional services. They aided and protected their members when adverse circumstances occurred. For example, the guild would help a merchant to reestablish his business if a cargo were lost in a shipwreck or robbery. Guilds also operated schools and cared for the widows and orphans of its members.

The craft guild was another type of association that appeared at this time. Its members were people engaged in a particular craft, like weavers, shoemakers, or tanners. No one could find em-

This famous painting by Pieter Brueghel depicts city life in the Middle Ages. How many activities can you identify?

ployment in a given craft unless he belonged to the appropriate guild. Craft guilds regulated costs, set wages, and settled employer-employee disputes. In return, members guaranteed fair prices and good workmanship. Like merchant guilds, craft guilds provided charity for their members in times of need.

Craft guilds recognized three categories of members: apprentice, journeyman, and master craftsman. In the first stage of the apprentice system, a boy would go to live in a master craftsman's house in order to learn a skill. Although he was not paid for his work, he did receive food and lodging. When guilds first began, apprenticeships lasted about three years. However, in the later Middle Ages, a seven-year apprenticeship was common, and some apprentices had to serve a master craftsman for as long as twelve years.

After his initial training, the apprentice became a journeyman, or a skilled worker employed by a master craftsman for wages. In order to become a master craftsman, the journeyman had to produce an example of his craft, or a "masterpiece." If his work met the approval of the guild master, the journeyman could join their ranks and open his own shop.

SECTION REVIEW

1. Mapping: Use the map on page 257 to describe the major sea routes.
2. In your own words, briefly define or identify: three-field system, Hanseatic League, guilds, monopoly, apprentice, journeyman, master craftsman.
3. What advances were made in agriculture during the early Middle Ages?
4. What goods did Europeans trade for merchandise from the East?
5. What geographical features favored town growth? Give specific examples in your answer.

- How does a young person today go about learning a skill or trade? Compared with the craft guild apprenticeship system of the Middle Ages, do you think the modern way is better or worse? Explain.

Reviewing the Chapter

Chapter Summary

In the early Middle Ages, the time from about 500 A.D. to 1000 A.D., a new way of life began to develop in western Europe. Over a period of centuries Germanic tribes established kingdoms, the most important of which was that of the Franks. Under its ruler, Charlemagne, Europe enjoyed a brief period of stability and unification. However, invasions by the Muslims, Vikings, and Magyars soon plunged the continent into disorder again.

The early Middle Ages was a period in which western Europe experienced a general decline in culture, trade, and political stability. Three medieval institutions that helped people to survive this era were feudalism, manorialism, and the Christian church. Feudalism and manorialism, which organized political and economic life, formed the framework of medieval society.

The Christian church, however, was probably the single most important institution. Missionaries, like Patrick and Augustine, sought converts. By the ninth century most of western Europe was Christian, and the Church had developed a complex organization. The Church used its authority to influence medieval society, politics, and learning.

By the tenth century improved farming methods led to increased crop production. People were able to produce excess food. The surplus, which was exchanged for other goods, increased trade. This, in turn, helped to revive old cities and towns and create new ones.

The merchants, artisans, and craftspeople who populated the towns and cities demanded and won certain freedoms from feudal lords. Organized into guilds, they gained control over the services they provided and the products they manufactured.

1. What was the single most important force in the development of western civilization?
2. What effects did invasions have on European civilization?
3. Explain the roles of feudalism, manorialism, and the Christian church during the early Middle Ages.
4. How did agricultural improvements change European life?

Using Your Vocabulary

1. What are two other terms used to refer to the Middle Ages? Why is this time period called the Middle Ages?
2. What is a vandal? What is the origin of this word?
3. What dynasty did Clovis found? And Charlemagne? How did these dynasties receive their names?
4. Who were the Mayors of the Palace? What role did they play in politics and government?
5. Who were the *missi dominici?* What was their function?
6. Who were the Vikings? Name two characteristics of these people.
7. What is feudalism? Manorialism?
8. Name and describe two important ceremonies connected with feudalism.
9. What is a serf? What was the serf's position in medieval society?
10. Name two means by which the Church enforced its authority. Why were they considered drastic measures?
11. Briefly define Benedictine Rule. What is its significance?
12. What is a monopoly? How are monopolies related to guilds? Do monopolies exist today? Explain.

Developing Your Geography Skills

1. Use the map on page 248 to describe the location of the peoples surrounding Charlemagne's empire.

2. Use the map on page 257 to locate by means of latitude and longitude coordinates the cities of Genoa, Constantinople, Bruges, Hamburg, Danzig.
3. Use the map on page 257 to locate the cities on both overland and sea routes. Name the cities in the Middle East that were involved in trade with western Europe.

Recalling the Facts

1. What time period did the early Middle Ages encompass? List three characteristics of this period.
2. Describe two characteristics of the Germanic tribes that invaded the Western Roman Empire. How did they affect the development of Western civilization?
3. Describe German society.
4. Who was Theodoric? Describe his reign.
5. Who was Clovis? What did he accomplish? Why did he become a Christian?
6. Who was Charles Martel? What was the importance of his defeat of the Muslims?
7. What were the consequences of the Donation of Pepin?
8. Why is Charlemagne considered an important historical figure? List his accomplishments.
9. Who were the native inhabitants of the British Isles? What three Germanic tribes invaded Britain? What were the descendants of these tribes called?
10. Who was Alfred the Great? What were his achievements? With what other great medieval ruler could he be compared? Why?
11. When did Christianity reach the British Isles? Name two important Christian missionaries who reached Britain.
12. What impact did Muslim control of the Mediterranean have on the western European economy?
13. Name four ways in which disputes were settled during the Middle Ages.
14. What effects did the increase in agricultural production have on medieval society and its economy?
15. Describe two ways of transporting goods in the Middle Ages. Which one was preferable?

Essay Questions

1. Describe the relationship between feudalism and manorialism.
2. Compare and contrast the organization of feudal society and the Church.
3. During the Middle Ages, there occurred a blending of Church and State, or the combining of religion with government and politics. What examples can you give of this phenomenon? Name at least three.
4. How did the spread of Christianity affect the development of medieval society and culture? Be sure to give specific examples.
5. Describe the role of women in feudal society.
6. Explain why towns and cities dwindled in size during the early Middle Ages. When and why did they begin to revive? Why do towns and cities disappear or grow in modern times?
7. What two types of guilds were established during the Middle Ages? Why? Compare and contrast their purpose and role in society. What are organizations of workers called today? How do they compare with the guilds?

Critical Thinking

1. The Romans considered the Germanic peoples to be barbarians. Would you consider this to be a warranted or unwarranted claim? Why? Can you find any logical inconsistency in the fact that the Romans allowed these barbarians to serve in their armies and settle in their territories? Explain.
2. What traits did Germanic peoples value in their warriors? Why? Are these traits valued today?
3. At one time the medieval period was called the Dark Ages. Would you consider this an example of a warranted or unwarranted claim? Explain, giving specific reasons for your answer.
4. What evidence of bias do you detect in Einhard's biography of Charlemagne? Name two instances in which you would question the reliability of his data. Why?
5. What aspects of society did chivalry glorify? Why do you think medieval society valued these virtues?

CHAPTER ·12·

THE LATE MIDDLE AGES

1000–1500

Objectives

- *To describe the causes and effects of the Crusades*
- *To explain how the English monarchs strengthened their rule*
- *To examine the development of the French monarchy*
- *To contrast the process of centralization in Spain and Germany*
- *To discuss the major problems facing the Church in the late Middle Ages*
- *To describe the main achievements of medieval culture*

The western civilization that was developing in Europe produced lasting achievements in many fields during the late or high Middle Ages. This period lasted from about the year 1000 until 1500. It is noted for a series of overseas expeditions, the Crusades, which greatly broadened Europe's horizons. This era also witnessed the beginnings of the unified nation-state as we know it today. England, France, and Spain made important strides in achieving political unity and centralized governments under the rule of strong monarchs. The German states were united into the Holy Roman Empire, but by the end of the Middle Ages the empire had become fragmented by powerful feudal lords. The Italian states fell under the control of the German emperor and the pope.

While the Church continued to be a major force in medieval life, it faced serious difficulties and underwent a series of reforms. By the end of the Middle Ages, its power began to decline as strong monarchs challenged its authority. The vitality of the late Middle Ages was perhaps best expressed in the great accomplishments of medieval culture: the construction of great cathedrals, the establishment of universities, the writings of poets and scholars, and the development of modern languages.

· 262 ·

THE CRUSADES

To Europeans of the Middle Ages, Palestine, at the eastern end of the Mediterranean Sea, had a special significance. It had been the home of Jesus and was thus the birthplace of Christianity. Every year countless Christians, rich and poor, undertook the long and dangerous trip from western Europe to what was known as the Holy Land. Such a journey was called a pilgrimage, and those who made it pilgrims.

During the seventh century, the Holy Land fell into Muslim hands, but Muslim rulers still permitted Christian pilgrims to visit Jerusalem. Conditions changed after 1000 with the invasion of the Seljuk Turks. These Asiatic nomads, who had adopted Islam, settled in what is now eastern Turkey and rapidly created a huge empire that included the Holy Land.

Pilgrims returning to western Europe in the eleventh century told stories of Christians who had been killed or tortured by the Turks. These stories, although often exaggerated, spread throughout western Europe. It is known, however, that the Turks imposed heavy tolls and taxes on those who traveled to the Holy Land and that these tolls and the Turkish domination of the Holy Land were resented.

Calling the First Crusade

The Seljuks, an aggressive people, wanted to extend their empire westward into Byzantine territory. In 1071 the Turks and the Byzantines met at the battle of Manzikert. The Turks defeated the Byzantines and then proceeded to capture much of Asia Minor. Constantinople seemed to be in danger, and the years that followed brought no relief from the Turkish threat. In 1095 the Byzantine emperor appealed to the pope for help. At the Council of Clermont in France, Pope Urban II called for a holy war, or **Crusade,** against the Muslims. The stated purpose of the campaign was to free the Holy Land and to rescue the Byzantine Empire from Turkish domination. Privately, Urban hoped to bring Eastern and Western Christianity together and to increase papal prestige and influence. He also hoped to stop the warring between feudal lords in Europe by employing their aggressive tendencies against the Turks and in the service of Christianity.

At the Council of Clermont, Pope Urban II called for the First Crusade against the Turks. Why do you think so many people attended this meeting?

The pope's appeal brought thousands of volunteers who showed their dedication to the cause by sewing a cross on their clothes. The terms Crusade and Crusader were derived from the Spanish word *cruzada,* which means "marked with a cross." Similar terms were adopted by other languages.

Urban's call launched a series of military expeditions that continued for 200 years. Volunteers took part in them for many reasons. Some joined for purely religious motives, as it was widely believed that dying in battle for a holy cause would assure one's salvation. Others dreamed of fame, fortune, or adventure. Peasants joined Crusader armies to win freedom from serfdom, and feudal lords saw an opportunity to gain new lands. Merchants and traders hoped to gain new markets and products, besides supplying transportation for the Crusaders.

The First Crusade brought together several armies led by European noblemen. They converged on Constantinople in 1096, marched overland into Muslim lands, and defeated Muslim armies, capturing much of the eastern Mediterranean. In 1099 they stormed the city of Jerusalem, massacring most of the population, including Christians and Jews.

After their victories the Crusaders established the Kingdom of Jerusalem, which stretched from the Red Sea to Beirut, in what is now Lebanon. A French duke became the first king. Following the principles of feudalism, he distributed fiefs to vassals so that the entire eastern Mediterranean was parceled out among European nobles. The First Crusade was the only truly successful military expedition against the Muslims.

Later Crusades

Muslim power revived in the twelfth century. In 1144 the Muslims captured Edessa, a city northeast of the Kingdom of Jerusalem, and Europeans feared that the entire Holy Land might be lost. As a result a French monk, Bernard of Clairvaux (klehr-VOE), called for a Second Crusade, which was led by the French king and the German emperor. It lasted from 1147 to 1149. During this time the Crusaders tried to protect Jerusalem by capturing Damascus, but they were defeated and thousands lost their lives.

In the late 1100's a great general named Saladin restored Muslim control over much of the Holy Land. After he captured Jerusalem in 1187, Europeans organized a Third Crusade. It was called the Crusade of the Three Kings because the German, French, and English monarchs each commanded armies. The Crusaders set out for the Holy Land in 1189, but problems soon arose. The German emperor, Frederick Barbarossa, drowned in Asia Minor, and most of his army returned home. Then the French king, Philip II, quarreled with the English king, Richard I, and the French left. Thus Richard (nicknamed the Lion-Hearted) remained alone to face Saladin. His army captured the port city of Acre from the Muslims but was unable to retake Jerusalem. The Third Crusade ended in 1192, when Richard concluded a truce with Saladin that guaranteed pilgrims the right to visit Jerusalem.

The Fourth Crusade did not even reach the Holy Land. The Crusaders assembled at the Italian port of Venice in 1202, and in exchange for transport, the Venetians persuaded the Crusaders to attack Zara, a city on the coast of the Adriatic Sea. After the conquest of Zara, a claimant to the Byzantine throne in Constantinople asked the Crusaders for their help. They installed him on the throne in 1203, but received little money for their efforts. So when a rebellion broke out in 1204, they seized

This drawing shows Crusader knights in battle against the Muslims. Where do you think this battle is taking place? What techniques of warfare are employed?

THE CRUSADES

What cities were along the Crusaders' routes to the Holy Land? How do you think the Crusaders' presence affected these places?

the city. In search of loot, the Crusaders destroyed many of Constantinople's greatest art treasures and precious manuscripts. Then they established their own Latin Kingdom, which survived until 1261. As a result of this Crusade, the Byzantine Empire was seriously weakened, and Constantinople would never regain its former splendor.

The most tragic of all the Crusades was the Children's Crusade, organized in 1212 by a French peasant boy named Stephen, who persuaded thousands of children that they could accomplish what adults had been unable to do. As many as 30,000 French boys and girls may have joined Stephen. At the same time a German youth, Nicholas, gathered a force of some 20,000 children.

The young French Crusaders marched to the port of Marseilles, where most of them were car-

ried away by ship captains and sold into slavery. The German children also met a terrible fate. Many died on the long march southward across the Alps, and those who managed to board ships bound for the Holy Land were never heard from again.

Crusading continued throughout the thirteenth century but it had lost some of its appeal. Also, the population was not expanding as rapidly as before. One expedition led by the king of Hungary invaded Egypt without much success. In 1227 the German ruler, Frederick II, undertook a new Crusade, but did not lead his army against the Muslims. Instead he chose to negotiate a settlement with them. This unique Christian–Muslim truce lasted until the Muslims regained control of Jerusalem in 1244. The last Christian possession in the Holy Land, Acre, fell to the Muslims in 1291, bringing an end to the Christian Kingdom of Jerusalem. The Holy Land would remain in Muslim hands until the twentieth century.

Effects on Europe

The Crusades affected all aspects of medieval society. For example, European politics changed in several ways. There was a growth in papal authority, and this period represents the high point of Church influence in western Europe. Also, monarchs began to strengthen their governments and gain power over the feudal nobility because many nobles died or were absent from their lands for long periods of time.

Economic growth was accelerated as luxury items from the East, like spices, silk, and precious stones became more available. The demand for these products by wealthy Europeans revived trade. Italy's coastal cities became the principal ports for ships engaged in East-West trade because of their role in transporting Crusaders to the Holy Land.

New ideas and scientific knowledge were introduced to western Europeans as they learned about Arabic philosophy, medicine, and mathematics from the Moors in Spain. Thus the Crusades helped change the way in which the western Europeans lived and thought.

SECTION REVIEW

1. Mapping: Use the map on page 265 to describe the routes of the four major Crusades. Describe the location of the Holy Land.
2. In your own words, briefly identify or define: Palestine, pilgrim, Crusader, Kingdom of Jerusalem, Saladin, Children's Crusade.
3. Why did Pope Urban II call for a holy war in 1095?
4. Why did Europeans volunteer to fight in the Crusades?
5. What were the effects of the Crusades?
■ What does the word crusade mean today? Compare and contrast the modern use of the word and the Crusades of the Middle Ages.

THE GROWTH OF THE MONARCHY IN ENGLAND

From about the time of the First Crusade, European kings began to build more centralized monarchies. Their efforts brought them into conflict with the nobility and higher clergy, who did not wish to relinquish any of their wealth or privileges. By 1500, however, several monarchs had created strong national states by reducing the strength of the nobles and the power and influence of the Church. England was one of the first countries to develop in this way.

The Norman Conquest

As you know, the Danes who invaded England in the 800's eventually settled in an area of the country known as the Danelaw. Throughout most of the tenth century, Anglo-Saxons and Danes lived peacefully side by side. At the beginning of the eleventh century, new waves of Danish invaders attacked the English coast. This time the Anglo-Saxons could not ward them off, and in 1016 they accepted Canute (kuh-NYOOT) as king of England.

Canute ruled not only Denmark and England but Norway as well. He was a powerful king because the strategic location of his empire gave him control of the trade routes in the North and Baltic seas. His rule brought peace to England and encouraged a revival of trade. However, upon his death in 1035, his empire fell apart. By 1042 England was once again ruled by an Anglo-Saxon king, Edward, called the Confessor.

Edward died in 1066 without leaving an heir. So the Anglo-Saxons accepted one of their nobles, Harold the Saxon, as the new king. However, William of Normandy, whose dukedom lay across the English Channel in France, claimed that the English throne belonged to him, since he was related to the Anglo-Saxon royal family. In September he landed a Norman army on the south coast of England and met Harold at the battle of Hastings. There, the Anglo-Saxons were defeated and Harold was killed. William was crowned king of England and became the first Norman monarch to rule the country. As a result, the development of English society and culture would be altered.

This detail from an eleventh-century tapestry depicts a messenger bringing the news to William the Conqueror of Harold's defeat at the battle of Hastings. How would the President receive news of critical events today?

William the Conqueror, as he came to be called, introduced continental feudalism to England and used it to create a strong central government. Before the Norman Conquest, England maintained a political system approaching feudalism but with significant differences. For example, the lord, not the king, owned the land and provided the necessary protection for his people. Moreover, land in England was held by providing goods and services, not by military service.

When William ascended the throne, he made every vassal swear allegiance directly to him and declared himself the sole owner of all the land. He then proceeded to distribute land to his Norman followers but made certain that no large territories were under the control of any one noble. No lord was allowed to construct a fortified castle without obtaining William's permission, and he built castles of his own at strategic points, such as along the Welsh border.

William retained the old Anglo-Saxon political system, whereby the kingdom was divided into shires, each with a moot, or assembly of citizens, to administer justice as a court would. The presiding official of the moot was known as the shire reeve, or sheriff, and William made certain that the sheriffs were directly under his control. He also filled key positions in the Church with Norman clerics.

On occasion, William summoned all of his vassals to his court to advise him on matters of policy. However, he preferred to meet regularly with a smaller group of his more powerful vassals, the barons. From this smaller group, called the King's Council, William chose his permanent court officials.

In 1085 William sent clerks throughout England to make a survey of the population and its economic resources in order to determine how much tax could be assessed. Nothing seemed to escape the notice of his officials. An English monk of the time wrote that there was not "an ox, cow, or swine that was not set down in the writing." This massive report was later called the Domesday (DOOMZ-day) Book because the people felt that there was no appeal from the facts recorded in the book, any more than there was from the final judgment on doomsday.

Under the Norman rule, political and religious leaders were Normans. French became the language of the court, the law, and the government. Educated people spoke and wrote French and Latin. As a result, the Anglo-Saxon language began to absorb many French words as it developed into modern English.

William's Immediate Successors

When William the Conqueror died, his kingdom was divided between his two sons. The elder, Robert, received Normandy, and William II inherited England. William, however, managed to acquire Normandy from his brother. When William II was killed in a hunting accident, his son, Henry I, succeeded to the throne.

Henry I ruled both England and Normandy from 1100 to 1135. During his reign he strengthened royal government by creating an effective royal bureaucracy. Henry I recruited the advisers for his King's Council from the lower ranks of the nobility. These advisers were personally loyal to him because their advancement depended on their abilities, not on their wealth and power as landowners. Henry I also gave the King's Council responsibility for royal finances and revenues, creating the English Treasury and the Exchequer (eks-CHEK-ur). The Chancery was established to keep detailed records.

When Henry died, his daughter Matilda became his successor. England was thrown into a state of political chaos because some of the nobles chose to support the claim of Stephen of Blois, Henry's nephew. Stephen eventually won his claim, but England's strong central government was destroyed and the power of authority rested in the hands of the nobles.

Henry II

Henry II, Matilda's son, inherited lands in France and gained control over additional lands in France through his marriage to Eleanor of Aquitaine (AK-wih-tane), which gave him the necessary military strength to force Stephen to recognize him as the legitimate heir. In 1154 Henry and his troops marched through England, bringing the rebellious English nobles under control.

Henry II restored the administrative system of Henry I, but he is best remembered for his reform of the English legal system. He established a system of royal courts which replaced those of the feudal lords. His justices traveled regularly across the kingdom, holding court and following the same procedures, thus insuring a uniform law. As time passed, this law came to be called **common law** because it was based on custom and the decisions of other judges, rather than on a written code of laws.

In civil cases, a royal justice would call together a group of twelve men who gave evidence from personal knowledge and were sworn to tell the truth. This group became known as a jury, from the French word *jurer,* or to swear an oath, and is the ancestor of the modern jury. At first, persons were only accused of a crime by a jury, not tried. This group developed into the grand jury. Later royal courts began relying on a second jury called a petit, or trial, jury to determine guilt.

Henry's judicial innovations brought him into conflict with the Church. At this time the Archbishop of Canterbury was Thomas Becket. He had earlier served as Henry's chancellor, and Henry believed his friend would continue to support his policies. However, in 1163 when Henry demanded that clerics guilty of crimes be tried and punished in royal courts instead of church courts, Becket made his opposition clear. A series of confrontations followed until one day in 1170 the king spoke out in anger against the archbishop, and a group of his knights concluded that he wanted Becket killed. So, they traveled to Canterbury and murdered the archbishop in front of the altar of his own cathedral.

Europe was shocked, and the pope was enraged by this act of violence. Fearful of excommunication or interdict, Henry sent ambassadors to Rome to plead his innocence. The pope took advantage of the situation to obtain concessions that made the Church in England more independent of royal control.

While Henry II was in the midst of his controversy with the pope, he led a group of his barons to Ireland and established English rule there. The invaders made Dublin their capital. Although they did not win control of the entire island, they began a long campaign that eventually resulted in Ireland becoming a part of England's empire.

King John and the Magna Carta

After Henry's death in 1189, his son Richard the Lion-Hearted came to the throne. During his ten-year reign, Richard spent a total of only six months in England. He was more interested in fighting and led an army in the Third Crusade. While returning home, he was captured and held prisoner until a huge ransom was paid. The expense of the military campaign and ransom caused a severe drain on the English treasury.

Richard's brother John, who succeeded him, was a cruel and oppressive ruler. He ignored justice, threatened the privileges of the nobles, and overtaxed the people. When the French king, Philip Augustus, began his military campaign to seize English possessions in France, John's English and French vassals refused to fight for him. Between 1202 and 1204 John lost most of his French possessions, including Normandy.

In 1205 John became involved in a dispute with Pope Innocent III over the appointment of a new Archbishop of Canterbury. As a result, in 1209 the pope excommunicated John, and later declared that John was deposed. To save his kingdom, John surrendered England to the pope and received it back as a fief.

The English barons resented this situation and were angry about John's governmental policies. In 1215 they met with John at Runnymede and forced him to sign a document known as the **Magna Carta,** which is Latin for great charter.

Most of the Magna Carta's clauses dealt with feudal obligations that the king had ignored or violated, although some of its provisions benefited ordinary people. For example, it stated that no new taxes could be levied without the consent of the

Identify the people who attended the Model Parliament under Edward I.

Great Council and that any accused person was entitled to the protection of the laws and a trial by a jury of nobles. In the sixteenth and seventeenth centuries, these clauses and several others would be interpreted as guarantees of the basic rights of all English citizens.

The underlying principle of the Magna Carta was that the monarch was not above the law, but subject to it. Later generations would insist that the Magna Carta gave the English people certain rights and took matters into their own hands when a monarch failed to abide by its provisions.

The Beginnings of Parliament

After John's death in 1216 his son, Henry III, ruled until 1272. In an attempt to regain England's French possessions, Henry III became involved in fruitless and expensive wars on the Continent. His barons objected to higher taxation, believing that Henry was bound to keep the promise made by his father in the Magna Carta. In 1264 the barons revolted under the leadership of Simon de Montfort. De Montfort defeated Henry in 1264 and became England's ruler for a short time. In 1265 he summoned an assembly to discuss means of keeping the king under control. He invited representatives from the nobility, the clergy, local shires, towns, and cities to attend. However, plans for the assembly were interrupted when Henry's son led a force against de Montfort, who was killed in the fight.

De Montfort's concept of a representative assembly became an established institution during the reign of Edward I (1272–1307). In 1295 he called for a meeting of representatives of the great nobles, high-ranking clergy, rural landowners, and townspeople. This assembly was later called the Model Parliament. Like the King's Council, it discussed affairs of state, approved new taxes, and generally assisted in the business of governing.

Sometime during the next two centuries—no one knows exactly when—the **Parliament** was divided into two branches, or houses. The nobles and higher clergy formed the upper branch, or the House of Lords. The landowners and townspeople, who were considered commoners, met together as the lower branch, or the House of Commons.

Early parliaments held little power. Kings called on these legislatures to approve new taxes, establishing the tradition that no new taxes could be imposed by the monarch without the consent of Parliament. As time progressed, the Parliament enlarged the scope of its authority, minimizing that of the kings.

Rivalries for the Throne

Through most of the fourteenth and fifteenth centuries, England was governed by a succession of weak rulers and troubled by warfare on the Continent.

In the fifteenth century civil war broke out as two rival families struggled for royal power. In 1399 the House of Lancaster came to the throne. Between 1422 and 1461 the Lancastrian king, Henry VI, suffered periods of insanity, and in 1455 the House of York tried to seize power. The ensuing war was called the War of the Roses because both families had a rose as their emblem—red for the Lancastrians and white for the Yorkists.

This bloody and costly struggle lasted for thirty years. It came to an end at the battle of Bosworth Field in 1485. The Yorkist king, Richard III, was killed, and victory was claimed by Henry Tudor. According to legend, Henry discovered Richard's crown in a bush, placed it on his own head, and declared himself king.

The reign of Henry VII began the Tudor dynasty. Under the Tudors, a more efficient centralized monarchy would be established and political order restored.

SECTION REVIEW

1. In your own words, briefly identify or define: Canute, Battle of Hastings, William the Conqueror, Henry II, Becket, War of the Roses.
2. How did William the Conqueror use feudalism to strengthen England's central government?
3. What features of the English judicial system developed during the late Middle Ages?
4. What was the significance of the Magna Carta?
5. How did Parliament begin?
- The modern jury system first took shape in medieval England. What are the advantages and disadvantages of being judged by a group of your peers rather than a judge?

THE MONARCHY IN FRANCE

When the last Carolingian ruler died in the late tenth century, France was already split into numerous regions, each ruled by a powerful feudal lord. In 987 these lords revived the Frankish custom of electing their king. They chose Hugh Capet, Count of Paris, and he became the first ruler of the Capetian dynasty. Under the Capetians, a centralized monarchy would be established and France would be unified. Their rule lasted for three centuries.

The Early Capetians

The first Capetian kings were not among the great landowning nobles of France. They only ruled the Île-de-France, a small region including Paris and its surrounding lands. Under these circumstances, it was difficult for the French kings to exert any direct authority over the great feudal lords. They were kings in name only.

One of the most important achievements of the Capetians was the establishment of a continuous monarchy and the right to succession. They tried to bolster their position by allying themselves with the clergy and the towns. Church leaders in France favored a strong central government that could stop the private wars fought by the feudal lords. The towns sided with kings against the nobles because law and order, imposed by a successful central authority, favored commerce and industry.

Beginning in the 1100's, the Capetian kings had some success in extending their power and authority. Louis VI, who ruled from 1108 to 1137, was the first Capetian to have full control of his own lands. Louis the Fat, as he was called, forced feudal lords to appear in his courts and even used his armies to defend towns and monasteries against oppressive lords.

Louis' son, Louis VII, maintained the position gained by his father. His marriage to Eleanor of Aquitaine brought him sizable fiefs in France, in fact, an area far greater than what he held as king. After joining the unsuccessful Second Crusade, he returned home defeated and humiliated. He had his marriage to Eleanor annulled because she had failed to produce a male heir to the throne. She later married Henry Plantagenet, who became Henry II of England, and her fiefs were transferred to English control. Thus Henry became a more powerful landowner in France than Louis. Louis and his successors would struggle for centuries to regain control of these territories.

Philip II

One of the greatest rulers of medieval France was Louis' son, Philip II, or Philip Augustus as he was known. A shrewd and ambitious man, he spent his whole reign from 1180 to 1223 expanding the royal territories.

As you have read, Philip Augustus participated in the Third Crusade with Richard the Lion-Hearted. When Richard was taken prisoner on his way home, Philip plotted against him with John, Richard's brother. Richard never forgave Philip for this treachery, and after his release he made war against France. However, Richard was wounded in battle and died before he could defeat the French.

Although Philip had plotted with John against Richard, when John became the new king of England, Philip took advantage of the poor relationship between John and his feudal lords. By the time of John's death, the French king had regained not only Normandy but almost all the lands that had been lost when Eleanor of Aquitaine married the English king. Thus Philip more than tripled the size of his domain. When he died in 1223, the king was, for the first time, the wealthiest and most powerful landowner in France.

Developments in Government

Philip and his successors, like their counterparts in England, created new administrative systems to help them govern the lands they controlled. Under Philip, the King's Council became the chief advisory group of the king. Judicial functions were turned over to a body known as the Parlement of Paris. This was not a representative assembly like the Parliament of England, but rather a high royal court, with its own judges and court officials. Philip also established the practice of sending out royal officials, called *ballis*, to supervise and administer justice, and a financial committee, that resembled the Exchequer in England.

SOCIAL SCIENCE SKILLS

MAKING AN OUTLINE

Outlining is a method of organizing information by using a set pattern. It can be a valuable tool for studying or for preparing reports. Below is a pattern often used in outlining. The topics or main ideas are farthest to the left and are labeled with Roman numerals. Ideas supporting the topic are indented and are labeled with capital letters. The detail of the outline will vary depending on its length and use.

I. Topic or main idea

    A. Idea explaining the topic in ''I''

        1. Example or explanation of idea ''A''
        2. Another example of idea ''A''
            a. Example or explanation of ''2''
            b. Another example of ''2''

    B. Another idea explaining the topic in ''I''

II. Topic or another main idea

    A. Idea explaining the topic in ''II''
    B. Another idea explaining the topic in ''II''

Now read the following selection.

Eleanor of Aquitaine was one of the most powerful women of the late Middle Ages. She played a major role in the history of France and England during the twelfth century.

At the age of thirteen, Eleanor was married to a French prince who only a few months later became Louis VII, king of France. Upon her marriage she inherited the lands of Aquitaine, or about one-fourth of what is today France. During her reign as queen of France she exerted considerable influence over Louis. For example, Eleanor urged him to undertake the Second Crusade and even accompanied him on the journey, but it proved disastrous. When the royal pair returned to France, the marriage was annulled.

A sample outline for this selection would be:

I. Eleanor as Queen of France

    A. Inherited Aquitaine
    B. Exerted influence over Louis
    C. Accompanied Louis on the Second Crusade
    D. Returned to France where her marriage was annulled

Now read the following selection and on a separate sheet of paper develop your own outline.

Just two months after the parting with Louis, Eleanor married Henry Plantagenet who soon became Henry II of England. Eleanor spent the next sixteen years in England. In 1170 the couple separated and Eleanor moved to Poitiers. There she presided over an elegant court and encouraged the development of vernacular literature by becoming a patron of troubadours and poets. Some of the most popular courtly love poetry of the late Middle Ages was composed in her honor.

In her later years, Eleanor concerned herself with her children's welfare. In 1173 she encouraged and gave military support to two of her sons, Richard and John, when they revolted against their father in England. The rebellion failed, and Henry placed Eleanor under house arrest, where she remained until Henry died in 1189.

After Henry's death, Eleanor's son, Richard the Lion-Hearted, succeeded to the English throne. While he was absent from England fighting the Third Crusade, Eleanor administered his realm and thwarted John's conspiracy with Philip Augustus of France to take over Richard's kingdom. When Richard was captured, she led the effort to raise the huge ransom demanded. After her son John became England's king, she put down a revolt against him in France. Eleanor died in 1204—energetic, willful, and influential to the end.

One of the most revered kings of this era was Louis IX, who came to the throne in 1226. A devout Catholic, he fought in one Crusade, and was elevated to sainthood after his death. His forty-four-year reign was characterized by religious fervor and political astuteness. He tried to deal fairly with foreign rulers and provide his people with justice and peace. He urged them to use the courts, and followed the Church's example by forbidding feudal warfare and trial by ordeal and combat. Laws and customs were clarified and codified.

Preferring negotiation to battle, Louis signed a peace treaty with Henry III of England. It was said that he liked to sit under an oak tree at Vincennes and administer justice to anyone who came before him. Louis' saintliness won him the loyalty of his nobles and the devotion of the French people. According to some historians, it was during his reign that the primary loyalty of the French switched from the Church to the State.

Louis' grandson also left his mark on the late Middle Ages. Philip IV, known as Philip the Fair, ruled from 1285 to 1314. He became embroiled in a controversy with the papacy, and continued the struggle of earlier Capetians to extend the royal domains. He was at war with King Edward I of England off and on for years. His troops also fought in southern France and in Flanders.

In the Hundred Years' War, the French (left) are shown fighting with crossbows, while the English (right) use longbows. What advantages did the longbow give the English? Compare this scene to the one on page 264. How had techniques of warfare changed?

Philip's wars were expensive, and he was often in need of money. Thus the French were taxed as never before. Philip even taxed the French clergy, claiming that this was an emergency measure to help protect the kingdom from the English.

When these measures failed to bring in sufficient funds, Philip canceled debts that he owed to foreign bankers and his own nobility. He treated Jewish bankers with special severity. Many Jews had gone into the banking business during the Middle Ages because many other professions were closed to them. Philip confiscated their property and drove them from his realm.

In order to obtain public approval for his taxation of the clergy, Philip called a representative assembly in 1302. This group, the **Estates General,** consisted of three branches which met separately and represented the three orders, or classes, in France. The first estate was made up of representatives from the clergy, while the second estate was composed of delegates from the nobility. The third estate, in theory, represented all the other people of the kingdom, but in fact represented the townspeople.

Although a representative body like the Parliament of England, the Estates General differed in at least one fundamental way. Parliament was able to establish authority over taxation and could thus limit the authority of the monarch. The Estates General was never able to establish this authority and consequently never became a check on the growth of royal power.

The Hundred Years' War

After the death of Philip the Fair, three of his sons ruled in succession for brief periods. The third, Charles, had no sons. So he designated his cousin, Philip of Valois (val-WAH), as his successor and a new royal family succeeded to power. The Valois ruled France until the late sixteenth century.

England refused to recognize Philip VI as the French king. The English monarch, Edward III, was the son of Charles' sister and he argued that he should have inherited the French throne. The French, however, refused to recognize Edward's claim and the Parlement of Paris declared that succession to the French throne could not pass through the female line. This rivalry over the French throne was one cause for the Hundred Years' War which continued off and on from 1337 to 1453. Another was the matter of English fiefs in France. The immediate cause for the outbreak of fighting in 1337 was, however, control of the Flemish wool trade.

The Hundred Years' War was fought almost entirely on French soil. In the first stage of the war (1338–1360), the English success was in part due to a military innovation—the longbow. Easier to handle than the crossbow and with a greater range, it revolutionized medieval warfare. Armored knights on horseback were now vulnerable to attack by foot soldiers. First used at the battle of Crécy (kray-SEE) in 1346, the longbow tipped the scale in favor of the English at Poitiers ten years later. At Poitiers the French king, John II (1300–1364), was captured and a peace was signed. The English were awarded three counties in northern France, including Calais (KA-lay), the province of Poitou (PWA-too), and Aquitaine.

In the second phase of the war (1364–1380), the French were able to win back most of their lost territory except the coastline. During the third phase (1380–1429), France suffered from weak and incompetent rulers. In 1413 Henry V came to the English throne. A great warrior, he made an alliance with the dukes of Burgundy, invaded France, and won a major victory at Agincourt (AJ-in-kort) in 1415. The English then forced the French king, Charles VI, to sign a treaty in which he gave his daughter in marriage to Henry and agreed, upon his death, to pass the French crown to the English king. However, both Charles and Henry died in 1422. The English and Burgundians declared the infant son of Henry V to be the new king of France, and Valois supporters backed the son of Charles VI.

The war's final phase (1429–1453) began with the appearance of a teenage peasant girl named Joan of Arc who saved the French cause. Claiming to have divine inspiration, she appeared before Charles the Dauphin, heir to the throne, and demanded control of his army. Charles agreed, and in 1429 Joan led the French to victory at Orléans. Then she insisted that Charles go to Reims (REEMZ), the traditional site of French coronations, to be publicly crowned. Joan inspired a wave of patriotism and anti-English feeling among the French. She wished to continue the fight against the English, but Charles refused to give her ade-

Joan of Arc asked Charles the Dauphin for troops to continue the war against England. If Charles had refused, could Joan still have accomplished her mission?

quate support. At a later battle she fell into the hands of the Burgundians, who sold her to the English. A Church court tried her for heresy, and she was burned at the stake in 1431. Thus she became a martyr to the French cause.

After Joan of Arc's death the Hundred Years' War took a turn in favor of the French. Charles VII became determined to rid France of the English. By 1453 he had succeeded in driving the English out of all their French territories except Calais, and the war came to an end.

The Hundred Years' War effectively ended English territorial ambitions in France. Among the French people there was a growing feeling of nationalism, and they had developed a strong sense of loyalty toward their monarch. The power and authority of the French kings had increased, and later monarchs were able to retain taxes imposed during the war as permanent sources of income. The king also continued to maintain his own royal army which was not dependent on the services of

vassals. Thus the foundations were laid for the development of a strong monarchy under Louis XI, Charles' successor.

SECTION REVIEW

1. In your own words, briefly identify or define: Capetians, Philip II, Parlement, Louis IX, Philip the Fair, Estates General, longbow, Joan of Arc.
2. What new bureaucratic institutions were introduced by the medieval French kings?
3. What were the causes and effects of the Hundred Years' War?
■ The heroism of Joan of Arc aroused patriotic feelings among the French. What modern figure has stimulated similar emotions? How does this person's appeal resemble or differ from hers?

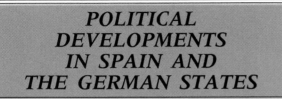

POLITICAL DEVELOPMENTS IN SPAIN AND THE GERMAN STATES

By the time the Hundred Years' War began in the fourteenth century, both England and France had established strong monarchies. In Spain this process of centralization was also occurring, although more slowly because of the long Muslim occupation. In the German states the political situation was different. Although there were many capable rulers during the late Middle Ages, none of them was able to create an effective and lasting central government. Germany would not become a unified nation until the 1800's.

Visigoths and Moors in Spain

As you know, the Visigoths conquered the whole Iberian peninsula (present-day Spain and Portugal) after the collapse of the Roman Empire. There, they created their own kingdom, with its capital at Toledo, and adopted Christianity in the early sixth century. The Visigothic rulers maintained Roman law and some elements of Roman government. Their Germanic language slowly disappeared and was replaced by a spoken form of Latin, which eventually developed into Spanish, Portuguese, and several other Romance languages.

By the early eighth century the Visigothic kings had lost most of their authority. When Muslim invaders from North Africa crossed the Strait of Gilbraltar, the Visigothic kings were unable to muster an effective army. The Muslims easily conquered the peninsula.

In Spain the Moors established a strong central government which lasted nearly eight centuries. They settled among their Christian subjects and intermarried with them. The Moors practiced a policy of religious toleration, and Muslims, Christians, and Jews lived in harmony in many places.

The Caliphate of Baghdad ruled Spain until 756 when Abd-al-Rahman proclaimed himself an independent ruler and established his capital in Cordova. The high point of Moorish rule in Spain occurred during the tenth century under the rule of Abd-al-Rahman III, the caliph of Cordova from 929 to 961. During his reign, he was able to stop the quarreling among his Muslim vassals and to defend his territories against attack. He also made Cordova one of the largest and richest cities, and

The Patio of the Lions is part of the Alhambra in Granada. It was the last palace-fortress to be occupied by the Moors. Compare Muslim architecture with the European architecture shown on page 285.

one of the leading intellectual centers of its time. His successors, however, were not so fortunate. Moorish lords battled one another, and the caliphate of Cordova was divided into small independent kingdoms, known as *taifas* (tah-EE-fas). As a result, the Christian kings were able to take advantage of this disunity and reconquer some of the Muslim territories.

The Reconquest of Spain

The Moors conquered all of Spain except for a few isolated places in the mountainous north, in the province of Asturias. In 718 the survivors of the Muslim invasion met at Covadonga to elect Pelayo, a Visigothic lord, as their king. He led an expedition against the Moors and defeated them. Thus the reconquest of Spain began. It would continue until 1492 when the Moors were expelled from their last stronghold, Granada.

Fighting between Moors and Christians was only sporadic during the ninth and tenth centuries because the Christian kings were too busy fighting each other. It was not until the mid-eleventh century that the Christian kings began a serious campaign to oust the Moors from Spain. During this time, their crusade came to be called the *Reconquista* (ray-kon-KEES-tah), which is the Spanish term for reconquest.

In 1085 Christian forces won a key victory when they captured Toledo, an important city in central Spain. By the middle of the twelfth century, about half the country was in Christian hands. In 1236 the Moorish capital of Cordova fell to the Christians. Seville, another Moorish stronghold, was taken in 1248. Only the kingdom of Granada in the southernmost part of Spain remained in Moorish hands.

During the *Reconquista* many foreign knights traveled to Spain to fight the Moors. One of them, Henry of Burgundy, so distinguished himself that in the late eleventh century the king of Castile gave him a fief in the western part of the peninsula. Henry and his son Alphonse Henry continued the *Reconquista*. In the 1140's Alphonse made Portugal a kingdom, with himself as its first ruler, and captured Lisbon from the Muslims. Lands south of Lisbon were then added to the kingdom. By the mid-thirteenth century Portugal had

reached its present extent. It was the first country in western Europe to be united under one ruler.

While the Spanish kings were fighting the Moors, they were also trying to limit the power of the nobles. This was a problem, since the monarchs usually needed the nobles' help in fighting the Muslims. Thus kings often used townspeople as soldiers, and the towns became the king's allies rather than the nobles'. By the end of the twelfth century the *Cortes* (KOR-tays), or representative assemblies, had been established. The kings also allied themselves closely with the Church. As a result Spain, unlike England and some other European countries, did not experience a power struggle between Church and State.

By the 1400's all the Spanish kingdoms, except Navarre, had been annexed by either Castile (kas-TEEL) or Aragon. In 1469 Isabella of Castile and Ferdinand of Aragon were married. The two kingdoms were officially united, forming a single nation-state in 1479 when Ferdinand succeeded to the throne of Aragon. Isabella had ascended to the throne of Castile in 1474. They then proceeded to bring religious and political unity to Spain.

Like the English and French monarchs, Ferdinand and Isabella were determined to diminish the influence of the aristocracy. They replaced the great nobles who served on the royal council with officials drawn from the lower nobility and middle class, who tended to favor a strong monarchy.

In order to impose religious uniformity on their kingdom, Ferdinand and Isabella focused their attention on the Jews. During the medieval period the Jews had developed a thriving culture and society in Spain. Since they had long been the targets of discrimination and violence, many had become outward converts to Christianity. These *Marranos*, as they were called, came under increasing suspicion. In 1480 the Spanish monarchs introduced the Inquisition to root out insincere conversions.

The Spanish Inquisition was totally controlled by the central government and used secret trials, torture, and execution to terrorize the *Marrano* population. Then, in 1492 Ferdinand and Isabella expelled all the Jews of Spain who had not converted. It is estimated that over 150,000 people, among them some of Spain's most talented doctors, government officials, and merchants were forced to leave. Most of them took refuge in Italy and the Ottoman Empire.

The Spanish rulers treated the Moors with equal harshness. When their army captured Granada in 1492, the *Reconquista* was completed, and the monarchs promised the Muslims of Spain religious freedom. A few years later, however, they reneged on their promise and ordered all Muslims either to convert or to leave the country. The thousands who converted became known as *Moriscos* (muh-RIS-koes). In the early seventeenth century, the *Moriscos* were banished from Spain.

The Early Holy Roman Empire

As you know, Charlemagne's empire was divided among his grandsons in the early ninth century. Louis inherited the eastern part of the empire, including Germany. He and his successors were unable to cope with the Magyar invasions that swept into eastern Europe at this time. As a result, several strong German lords took the title of duke, seized power, and set up duchies (DUHCH-eez) to provide protection for their peoples. By the end of the ninth century, Germany was divided into five large duchies or territories: Saxony, Lorraine, Franconia, Swabia, and Bavaria.

Nevertheless, the idea of a single monarch ruling over a unified Germany remained. When the last Carolingian king died in 911, the German dukes elected Henry of Saxony to be their new ruler. The Saxon dynasty lasted until 1024.

One of the strongest Saxon kings was Henry I, known as Henry the Fowler. He held the title from 919 to 936. During his rule he led the Germans against the Magyars and defeated them. He also pushed the Saxon borders eastward and encouraged German settlement in Slavic lands beyond the Elbe River. The Slavic peoples who had occupied this territory were forced into what is today Poland.

Henry I was succeeded by his son Otto, a warrior and an outstanding ruler. Otto the Great, as he is known, was the German king from 936 to 973. During his long reign he devoted most of his time to increasing royal power. He subdued the great dukes, taking two of the duchies for himself and giving the others to his relatives.

When the new dukes rebelled against him, Otto realized that he needed allies so he turned to the Church. He initiated the practice of **lay inves-titure,** or the installing in office of high Church officials by kings or emperors. The granting of fiefs to the clergy also seemed like a good idea. For when a clerical vassal died, the land reverted back to the crown, because there were no heirs. Thus the higher clergy became vassals of the king, and they proved to be skilled administrators, providing the German kings with educated officials and able generals.

The alliance of Church and State in Germany worked well when Otto established it, but within it lay the seed of a future problem. By eliminating the services and loyalty of the German nobility, the German monarch became dependent on the higher clergy. This meant that if the Church were to withdraw its support, the German monarch would lose his power of authority, which is what occurred under Otto's successors.

In 951 Otto and his army marched southward into Italy and he soon became king of the Lombards. However, Magyar raids soon forced him to return to Germany. He ended the Magyar threat to Germany by defeating them at the battle of Lechfeld in 955. In 961 Pope John VII appealed to

Otto III is depicted wearing the Roman imperial costume. How does this picture illustrate the relationship between Church and State in the Holy Roman Empire?

him for aid against the Lombards and Otto returned to Italy. After defeating the Lombards, the pope crowned Otto emperor.

As you know, Charlemagne had been given this same title in the year 800. Otto the Great claimed to be the heir of Charlemagne, and his lands were called the Holy Roman Empire, although they only consisted of Germany and northern Italy. For the next two and a half centuries, German involvement in Italian affairs would be deeply resented and a source of conflict.

The Investiture Controversy

Otto's successors continued the practice of lay investiture because they believed that if the popes placed their own supporters in these positions, their lands would fall under control of the pope. Thus the Church would become more powerful than the rulers. The monarchs also wanted to assure themselves of the bishops' support against the nobility if they challenged the emperor's authority. In the late eleventh century, the Church would argue that it had the right to appoint its own officials and a dispute would arise.

In 1024 a new dynasty of rulers called the Franconians, or Salians, came to the German throne. At the same time, the Western Church was in the midst of a reform movement.

Pope Gregory VII, a strong ruler, considered lay investiture a problem that plagued the Church. In 1075 he prohibited the practice and threatened excommunication for any ruler who continued appointing officials to the clergy. In response, Henry IV defied the pope by appointing a new Archbishop of Milan. Then he summoned a council of loyal German bishops to write the pope a letter informing him that they no longer owed him their obedience. At the same time, Henry ordered the pope to give up the papacy. In retaliation, Gregory excommunicated Henry and announced that the German nobles were released from their allegiance to him. A rebellion broke out among the nobles, who threatened to elect another Holy Roman Emperor. Faced with the loss of his kingdom, Henry decided to make peace with the pope and beg his forgiveness.

In 1077 Henry traveled to Canossa, in northern Italy, where the pope was staying. It is said that the emperor remained outside the gates of the pope's castle for three days, standing barefoot in the snow and dressed only in the coarse woolen garment of a penitent. As a religious leader, the pope could not refuse a man begging forgiveness. So Gregory lifted the ban of excommunication.

The emperor returned to Germany and resumed authority. However, in 1080 Pope Gregory excommunicated and deposed Henry again. A rebellion broke out among the German nobles, but Henry quickly crushed the revolt and prepared his armies to invade Italy. When Henry returned to Rome in 1084, Gregory fled the city and died soon thereafter.

Gregory's successors carried on the struggle against Henry IV and his heir, Henry V. The investiture controversy was not settled until the Concordat of Worms (VORMZ) in 1122. A concordat is an agreement between a pope and a government concerning church affairs. This compromise stated that the emperor had the right to invest the clergy with land and secular authority, the pope would invest them with spiritual authority, and the candidate had to be acceptable to both parties.

The investiture controversy had important consequences. The German emperor lost his main source of support, the Church, and the support of the nobles, who sided with the papacy. Thus the power of the German emperor had been significantly diminished.

Interference in Italy

A new line of rulers, the Hohenstaufens (HOE-uhn-shtau-fuhns), assumed the German throne in 1138 and reigned for over a century. They came into conflict with the papacy because they wanted to gain greater control of Italy, especially the northern section where the prosperous commercial centers like Milan were located. However, the Italian cities wanted to maintain their independence and were encouraged to do so by the popes, who feared the loss of their own territory, the Papal States.

Frederick I ruled from 1152 to 1190 and was known as Frederick Barbarossa, or Red Beard. He spent years trying to conquer the northern Italian cities. He was successful until the inhabitants of these cities formed the Lombard League and defeated him at the battle of Legnano in 1176. Frederick was then forced to accede to the inhabitants'

EARLY WESTERN EUROPE

Political Boundaries about 1500

CONIC PROJECTION

ATLANTIC OCEAN

SWEDEN

•Bergen
NORWAY

Stockholm•

TEUTONIC
KNIGHTS

BALTIC SEA

SCOTLAND

•Edinburgh

NORTH
SEA

DENMARK
Copenhagen•

PRUSSIA
Danzig•

IRELAND
Dublin•

ENGLAND

BRANDENBURG

Elbe R.

Oder R.

POLAND

Berlin•

Amsterdam•
London•
Thames R.
Bruges•
Calais•
Brussels•
Rheims•
Seine R.
Paris•

NETHERLANDS

•Antwerp

HOLY
ROMAN
EMPIRE

Cologne•

SAXONY
•Dresden

Trier•

•Mainz
•Worms
Rhine R.

Prague•
BOHEMIA

Danube R.

BAVARIA

Vienna•

AUSTRIA

HUNGARY

Loire R.

FRANCE

BAY OF
BISCAY

•Geneva

Milan•
•Turin

Po R.

Padua•
Venice•

V
E
N
I
C
E

Bordeaux•
Garonne R.

Rhône R.

•Avignon

•Genoa

•Bologna

OTTOMAN
EMPIRE

Marseilles•

Florence•

PAPAL
STATES

ADRIATIC SEA

CORSICA
(Genoa)

Rome•

NAPLES
(Sp.)
•Naples

PORTUGAL

Ebro R.

CASTILE
ARAGON

•Barcelona

SARDINIA (Sp.)

Tagus R.
Madrid•
•Toledo

BALEARIC ISLANDS (Sp.)

•Lisbon
SPAIN

•Cordova

•Seville
•Granada

MEDITERRANEAN SEA

SICILY (Sp.)

AFRICA

0   200   400 Kilometers

0   300 Miles

demands for control over their own towns and cities. As you read, he drowned during the Third Crusade, and his son Henry VI became emperor in 1190. Through marriage, Henry VI acquired Sicily and southern Italy.

Frederick II, Henry VI's son, became emperor of the Holy Roman Empire in 1215. Unlike the earlier emperors, he decided to ignore Germany and to make himself the undisputed ruler of Italy. To make peace with the German nobles, he gave them almost total control in their own territories.

After taking part in the Fifth Crusade, Frederick set out to unite northern and southern Italy. First he exerted his authority over the feudal lords of southern Italy and Sicily. Then his armies began the conquest of the Lombard League in northern Italy. They dealt the league a crushing defeat at the battle of Cortenuova (kor-tay-NYOOH-vah) in 1237. At this point it appeared that all northern Italy might fall into Frederick's hands. Fearing that Frederick would try to claim the Papal States, Pope Gregory IX revived the anti-imperial forces in Italy and savage fighting dragged on until Frederick died in 1250.

The Loss of Imperial Power

After the death of Frederick II, the power of the Holy Roman emperors steadily declined. The emperors had lost the support of the Church, had exhausted themselves in trying to subdue Italy, and had given away land and authority in Germany. Even Frederick's victories in Italy were short-lived. A French duke made Sicily his own kingdom and southern Italy fell to the Spanish. One by one the cities of northern Italy regained their independence. When Frederick's son, Conrad IV, died in 1254, the nobles of Germany were able to prevent the election of a new emperor for almost twenty years, causing anarchy and turmoil. Finally the pope persuaded the German nobles to meet and elect a new emperor, Rudolf of Hapsburg. For about a hundred years, assemblies of all the great nobles elected the emperors. In 1356 the Golden Bull was issued by Emperor Charles IV. This decree gave the right of naming the emperor to seven Electors, who were high-ranking nobles and clergymen. Thus real political authority rested in the hands of these Electors.

By the fifteenth century Germany had become a loose collection of over 300 political entities of varying size, each one governed by a different ruler. These lands were to remain disunited until the nineteenth century.

SECTION REVIEW

1. Mapping: Use the map on page 280, to describe the location of Spain, Portugal, and the Holy Roman Empire.
2. In your own words, briefly identify or define: Cordova, *Reconquista*, Otto I, Lombard League, Frederick Barbarossa, Golden Bull.
3. How was the kingdom of Portugal established?
4. How and when did the unification of Spain occur?
5. What was the investiture controversy?
6. How did the policies of Frederick II weaken the Holy Roman Empire?
■ The Holy Roman emperor at the end of the Middle Ages had little actual power, yet men coveted the post for its prestige. What monarchs today have ceremonial roles but no real authority? Why do you think countries retain this type of monarchy?

THE CHURCH IN THE LATE MIDDLE AGES

From the eleventh to thirteenth centuries, the Church in western Europe experienced a growth in power and influence and it was the only institution that united all Europeans. The height of papal influence was reached during the Crusades when popes were able to inspire Christians from all over Europe to join forces in the service of an ideal.

By the late Middle Ages the Church had the most organized bureaucratic system in western Europe. As you know, it had developed a hierarchy of officials, headed by the pope, to rule over its domains. A papal court, or Curia, was established to administer finances, policy, and canon or church law.

The late medieval papacy continued the practice begun by the Roman Emperor Constantine I of summoning general Church councils, attended by all the bishops of the Church. The papacy also dispatched its own personal representatives, called legates, to deal with problems throughout the Christian world. Having the power to excommunicate a person or impose an interdict on a country, the legates had to be obeyed.

Church Problems

Like other large and powerful organizations, the Church faced a number of problems. One of these was the question of Church–State relations. As you know, during the invasions of the ninth and tenth centuries, churches, monasteries, and convents were always open to attack, and many were destroyed. There was no strong emperor or king to provide protection. Therefore, the bishops and abbots appealed to feudal lords for help. By doing so, they subjected themselves to control by laymen. Great nobles took over the appointment of bishops and abbots. Feudal lords often built parish churches, appointed parish priests, and paid their wages. Not even the papacy escaped control by lay rulers. During much of the tenth and eleventh centuries, popes were chosen by either the German emperors or the nobles of Rome.

In 1059, under Pope Nicholas II, the College of Cardinals was founded and given the authority to elect popes. This action helped strengthen papal power because it took control of papal elections out of the hands of kings and nobles. When the popes tried to regain control over the selection of bishops and abbots from the feudal nobles, they ran into strong opposition. As you have read, the controversy over lay investiture was not settled until the Concordat of Worms in 1122.

Another problem facing Church leadership was the discipline of its own members. It had become common for secular rulers to sell church offices to the highest bidder, a practice known as simony. Also, some Church officials were more interested in collecting tithes and living well than in supervising the priests under their control. Even in monasteries and convents, discipline had become lax.

Reform Movements

Conscientious church leaders were aware of these problems and took steps to correct them. The first reform was undertaken by the regular clergy. A new monastery was founded at Cluny, in eastern France, early in the tenth century. Its abbots preached a return to the strict monastic principles of the Benedictine Rule. They also founded many other monasteries all over Europe. Each of these was subject to the authority of the Cluny abbot, so lay rulers could not interfere with them. At its height, Cluny directly controlled over 10,000 monks.

The Cluniac movement, as it was called, influenced the papacy. Pope Leo IX, who ruled from 1049 until 1054, assumed leadership of the reform movement. His goals were to eliminate simony, to enforce discipline among the clergy, and to free the Church from lay control. During his short reign Leo traveled to France and Germany, where he summoned councils of his bishops. Those who refused to give up their corrupt practices were either removed from their office or excommunicated.

The Schism between Rome and Constantinople also occurred at this time. The break was caused by the refusal of the Eastern Church to submit to the authority of the pope in Rome and his strict disciplinary measures. All future attempts to reunite Western and Eastern Christendom would fail.

New religious orders were established during the Church's struggle for reform. One, the Dominicans, was founded by a Spanish priest named Dominic in the early 1200's. Another, the Franciscans, evolved from the preaching of Francis of Assisi, who lived at about the same time. The members of both orders were not monks, but friars, or brothers. They preached and taught among the common people and cared for the needy. Owning no property, they lived by begging.

Not all the reform movements of the late Middle Ages were directed or approved by the Church. Some, like the Waldensians and Albigensians, gained thousands of supporters and were regarded as heresies because their doctrines conflicted with the accepted teachings of the Church. Not since the rise of Arianism in the fourth century had the problem of heresy so troubled Western Christendom. Religious belief for the people of the Middle

Otto II is shown here investing a bishop. What symbols of rank are depicted?

Ages was not a personal matter, and dissent from approved teachings was felt to endanger the very foundations of society.

In 1233 Pope Gregory IX established the Inquisition, which was a church court whose purpose was to detect and punish heretics. The inquisitors, or judges, traveled about calling on local inhabitants in order to gather information. The aim of the Inquisition was to convert suspected heretics, not to eliminate them. However, sometimes it used secret tribunals and even torture in examining the accused. Heretics who refused to renounce their beliefs were handed over to the secular governments and executed, usually by burning at the stake.

Innocent III

The peak of papal power was reached during the reign of Pope Innocent III, from 1198 to 1216. In his efforts to reinforce the papacy's position in the struggle between Church and State, Innocent used excommunication and interdict, and threatened to depose rulers who challenged him, like King John of England. He intervened in wars between kings and tried to settle disputed claims to royal thrones.

He also promoted the Fourth Crusade against the Muslims and tried to stamp out heresy.

One of Innocent's most important actions was to call the Fourth Lateran Council. It was the largest church council to be summoned and more than 1,200 church leaders, as well as rulers from all over Europe, met at Rome in 1215. The decisions made at this council had a great impact on the Church and the way religion was practiced. It passed regulations to discipline the clergy and defined the seven sacraments. It also tried to limit the sale and worship of relics or sacred objects associated with Jesus and the saints.

During Pope Innocent III's reign, papal authority came close to almost complete domination of spiritual and worldly affairs. When he died, though, his successors inherited a power struggle with secular rulers.

Troubled Times

By the fourteenth century it was no longer possible for a pope to exert the same authority as Pope Innocent III. For the next two hundred years the papacy would experience a period of decline as a world power.

In 1305 the College of Cardinals elected a French archbishop as the new pope. After his election Clement V chose to remain in France, claiming that the political situation in the Papal States was unstable. He filled the College of Cardinals with French clergy, and his six successors were also French. They governed the Church from a palace in the city of Avignon (AH-veen-yohn) from 1308 to 1377. Although this city was part of the Holy Roman Empire, it was French in language and culture.

The period of papal residence in France was called the Babylonian Captivity. This term, from the Old Testament, refers to a time when the Hebrews were captives in Babylon. The implication is that the popes were held prisoner by the French kings. Although Philip the Fair did dominate Clement V, some of Clement's successors were relatively free of royal control, and papal authority over the clergy actually increased as did papal revenues. Still, there was great dissatisfaction throughout Western Christendom with the popes' decision to remain in France, for papal prestige was closely linked to the ancient city of Rome.

In 1378 Pope Gregory IX returned to Rome, but died shortly thereafter. Roman mobs demanded that the cardinals elect a new Italian pope. Under pressure, the College of Cardinals elected Urban VI, an Italian archbishop. Urban VI remained in Rome, but when he began to institute sweeping reforms, the French cardinals declared his election invalid. Then they elected a French pope, Clement VII, who returned to Avignon.

For the next thirty-nine years there were two popes, one in Rome and one in Avignon, each with his own administration. This split, known as the Great Schism, created chaos within the Church and the European political situation because the monarchs were divided in their loyalties. Moreover, church expenses were greatly increased in order to maintain two papal courts.

In 1409 the Council of Pisa was called in order to resolve the situation. The council decided to depose both popes and to elect a third pope. However, the first two popes refused to recognize the authority of the council. So Christendom was left with three popes and the situation became even more confusing. The problem was not resolved until 1417 at the Council of Constance in Germany. The three popes were deposed or forced to

resign and a new pope, Martin V, was elected. The Council of Constance was also pledged to make reforms in the Church, but few were actually made.

SECTION REVIEW

1. Mapping: Use the map on page 265 to describe the location of Cluny.
2. In your own words, define or identify: simony, Innocent III, Babylonian Captivity, Great Schism, Council of Pisa, Council of Constance.
3. What were the three main goals of church reformers in the late Middle Ages?
4. How did the Church combat heresy in the late Middle Ages?
■ How does the role of the pope in the modern world compare with that of Innocent III?

CULTURE IN THE MIDDLE AGES

The late Middle Ages experienced a revival in artistic creativity and learning as a result of contact with other civilizations through an increase in trade and the Crusades. Almost all forms of artistic and intellectual expression were influenced by or produced for the Church.

Architecture, Art, and Music

During the Crusades there was an increase in the construction of large stone castles by feudal lords. Western Europe and the Holy Land were dotted with them. Monasteries were built, and medieval cities boasted fine guildhalls and other public buildings. The finest examples of medieval architecture, however, can be found in the churches and cathedrals.

Beginning about the year 1000, western Europeans began to construct more of their buildings from stone. Masons, or builders in stone, were in fact the architects of the Middle Ages. They developed a style that spread throughout much of the

Both of these churches were built in France during the late Middle Ages. Describe the various features of each and identify the architectural styles.

Continent called **Romanesque, (roh-mah-NESK)** meaning similar to the Roman. Like Roman buildings, Romanesque churches had vaulted or arched ceilings and domed roofs. To support the great weight of the curved stone roof, the walls of Romanesque churches had to be quite thick. It was fairly dark inside because windows tended to be small slits, with rounded tops. On the outside, these churches were decorated with stone sculptures of religious figures. Inside they sometimes had frescos, or pictures painted on wet plas-

ter on the walls or ceilings of their chapels. These paintings depicted religious figures or scenes and usually reflected a strong Byzantine influence.

About the middle of the twelfth century, a new style of architecture appeared in northern Europe. This style, very different from Romanesque, was later called **Gothic** after the Goths, the German invaders of the Roman Empire, because it was considered barbaric.

Gothic cathedrals were larger, higher, and more delicate looking than Romanesque churches.

The Cathedral of Notre Dame in Paris is considered one of the finest examples of Gothic architecture. Why? What buildings in your community have Gothic features?

The ceilings, windows, and doorways had pointed, rather than rounded, arches. These changes were made possible by the use of supporting ribs called flying buttresses, built outside the church and connected to it by arches. Since the buttresses supported the wall and ceilings, thick walls were no longer necessary and windows could be larger.

Like Romanesque churches, Gothic ones were adorned with religious sculptures, inside as well as out. Stained glass windows became a new decorative feature. Some of the windows consisted of geometrical patterns, others commemorated wealthy donors, but many depicted religious figures or biblical scenes. Like the sculptures, these windows instructed churchgoers in the Christian faith.

Gothic architecture was first introduced in northern France, where some of the most famous cathedrals were built. Notre Dame in Paris was begun about 1160. The cathedral at Chartres (SHAR-tr) was underway by 1194 and Reims by 1210. Gothic cathedrals were also constructed in England, Germany, and Spain between the thirteenth and sixteenth centuries.

The dramatic glories of Gothic architecture were accompanied by new developments in music. Before the twelfth century, church music had consisted of chants in Latin. In the 600's Pope Gregory I collected and organized the melodies used in Rome. For the next few centuries this collection of chants was considered the official music of the Church and was known as Gregorian chant.

Beginning in the 900's, parts might be added to the single melodic line of a chant. Over the next few centuries the parts became more complex, creating a multi-voiced composition. Between 500 to 1200 church musicians developed a way to notate music.

In the 1200's music began to develop outside the Church as well. As you know, wandering poet-musicians, called troubadours and *trouvères*, wrote and sang courtly love songs, often with instrumental accompaniment.

Literature and Drama

Most medieval writers used Latin in discussing serious subjects such as theology, philosophy, science, or history. These scholars wrote for other scholars, and Latin remained the language of educated people in Europe well into the early modern period.

By the late Middle Ages, however, Latin was no longer spoken by the common people. Throughout western Europe, people were developing new vernacular, or commonly spoken, languages. There were dozens of these, some based on Latin, others rooted in Germanic or Celtic languages. French, Spanish, Italian, Portuguese, and Romanian developed from Latin and are called

Romance languages because of their Roman background. The Germanic dialect of the Saxons developed into modern German, whereas other German dialects evolved into Danish, Swedish, Dutch, Flemish, and English. Celtic dialects persisted in the Welsh language of Wales and the Gaelic of Scotland and Ireland.

Between the eleventh and twelfth centuries Europeans began to use the vernacular in their writing. As you know, there were courtly love poems. A popular form of vernacular literature was the epic, a long narrative poem celebrating heroic deeds. Originally, these were recited by wandering storytellers and later written down. Almost every European people had its own epic. *Beowulf*, an Anglo-Saxon poem, describes a hero's fight with a monster and a dragon. The *Nibelungenlied* (NEE-buh-loon-guhn-leet) of the Germans contains a number of legends about a hero named Siegfried and a warrior princess, Brunhild. The *Song of Roland* tells of the death of Roland, a knight killed while defending the retreat of Charlemagne's army after fighting the Moors in Spain. *The Poem of El Cid* details the exploits of the Spanish national hero during the reconquest of Valencia, an important port on Spain's eastern coast.

Medieval vernacular literature also produced countless short stories and fables. These comic tales are usually called by their French name, *fabliaux* (FAB-lee-oe), and are designed to teach a moral. The characters of many *fabliaux* are animals who behave like humans, often quarreling, fighting, cheating, and getting into trouble.

Two of the most important vernacular writers of the Middle Ages were Dante and Chaucer. Dante Alighieri (ah-lee-GEEH-ree) was an Italian scholar and poet of the thirteenth century. He knew and admired the poems of French troubadours and, like them, wrote courtly love poetry. His greatest work, however, is the *Divine Comedy*, a long allegorical poem. The *Divine Comedy* tells of the poet's journey through Hell, Purgatory, and Paradise, accompanied by the Roman poet Virgil. On his journey Dante meets the souls of many famous individuals of his time. This device gives the poet an opportunity to criticize these people and to comment on political and social problems of his time.

Geoffrey Chaucer's *Canterbury Tales*, which shows the development of medieval English, was written in the late fourteenth century. It is a collection of twenty-four stories in verse told by a band of pilgrims on their way to Canterbury Cathedral to visit the shrine of Thomas Becket. The travelers represent almost every social class in England: a knight, a squire, a merchant, a nun, a priest, and so on. In this work Chaucer pokes fun at the English, especially the clergy, and his lively writing style presents an interesting picture of life and society in the late Middle Ages.

Medieval drama began about the twelfth century with the performances of biblical stories by priests in the churches. They were included as part of the Mass to help instruct the people, most of whom could not read the Bible. These early works developed into the mystery play and the miracle play, which was based on the life of a saint. The later morality play represented the struggle over an individual's soul by characters who represented various virtues and vices.

Medieval Universities

As you know, cathedral schools were established in towns and cities as they began to revive. In the eleventh century, students would pay wandering teachers or scholars directly for instruction. As more students and teachers congregated in cities,

This Italian miniature depicts a lecture at the University of Bologna during the late Middle Ages. How does this scene compare to a modern university?

they began to form guilds to protect their interest. Out of these guilds, called *universitates,* grew the first universities, which were for men only.

Universities were first licensed in the latter part of the eleventh century and the first part of the twelfth. The University of Salerno became famous as a medical school and the University of Bologna was noted for its law school. The University of Paris, licensed around 1200, became the model for the establishment of other universities. The universities of Oxford and Cambridge were also founded at about the same time. Between the thirteenth and fifteenth centuries there was a growth of universities throughout Europe.

University students first had to master Latin. Then they began their study of what were known as the seven liberal arts. These were divided into the trivium and the quadrivium. The trivium consisted of grammar, rhetoric, and logic, which usually improved the student's Latin. The quadrivium included the study of arithmetic, geometry, astronomy, and music.

Medieval universities were divided into faculties. The University of Paris, which was widely copied, had four: arts, law, medicine, and theology. Candidates for teaching positions took difficult examinations in order to receive degrees. A bachelor's degree indicated completion of an apprenticeship. A master's degree certified that the graduate was a master teacher. He might then advance to become a doctor of philosophy, medicine, law, or theology. The degrees granted by universities and colleges today correspond more or less to those awarded by their medieval counterparts.

Medieval Learning

The primary concern of scholars in the late Middle Ages was to link the teachings of classical thinkers, especially Aristotle, with those of the Christian Church. In particular, they searched for ways to reconcile human reason with religious faith. This search is known as **Scholasticism.** The Scholastics accepted the power of human thought to investigate and determine truth, but they also held fast to the essential teachings of Christianity. They were confident that reason and faith did not have to be in conflict.

Peter Abelard, an important Scholastic, was a brilliant teacher at the cathedral school of Notre Dame in Paris. His greatest work, *Sic et Non (Yes and No)*, was written in the early twelfth century. In it Abelard raised a series of theological questions. After each question he noted answers from various Church Fathers that contradicted each other. Furthermore, he left these contradictions unresolved so that the reader had to use logic to determine the correct answer.

Another famous Scholastic was Thomas Aquinas (uh-KWIE-nuhs), a Dominican friar of the thirteenth century. In his masterpiece, the *Summa Theologica,* Aquinas set forth basic Christian beliefs, then demonstrated how they were supported by reason and logic. Today this work is still recognized by the Roman Catholic Church as a statement of its fundamental doctrines.

In the thirteenth and fourteenth century the interest in science or experimentation was revived as a result of increased contacts with Islamic learning in mathematics, astronomy, medicine, and physical and biological science. For many years Europeans could add little to what they learned from the Muslims, but there were a few innovators.

The method of Albertus Magnus, a German Dominican and Aquinas' teacher, was to be critical of everything. He also tried to find a natural cause behind every scientific phenomenon. Roger Bacon, an English Franciscan, taught that scholars should support their hypotheses with scientific observation and experimentation and is best known for his summary criticizing this lack of method. This interest in scientific investigation and method reached its height in the seventeenth century.

SECTION REVIEW

1. In your own words, briefly define or identify: Gregorian chant, vernacular, Dante, Chaucer, *Beowulf,* Aquinas.
2. What distinguishes Romanesque from Gothic architecture?
3. Name three forms of medieval vernacular literature.
4. What was the chief goal of the Scholastics?
■ Name the subjects taught at medieval universities. How do they compare to the modern-day curriculum? Explain.

Reviewing the Chapter

Chapter Summary

The late Middle Ages was a period of varied achievement in western Europe. In response to the papacy's call to arms, thousands of people took part in the Crusades between the eleventh and thirteenth centuries. Although these expeditions to the Holy Land had little military success, they had widespread political and economic effects.

In England and France monarchs worked successfully to strengthen their authority. After the Norman Conquest of England new government institutions like the King's Council, the Treasury, the Exchequer, the Royal Courts, and Parliament helped extend royal authority into many parts of the kingdom. Similar bureaucratic institutions developed in France.

In Spain, unification meant Christian reconquest of the peninsula from the Moors—a task that was not completed until the very end of the Middle Ages. The German and Italian states, however, remained politically fragmented.

The Church, faced with many serious problems, struggled to reform and strengthen itself through the establishment of the Inquisition and new religious orders. It reached its height under Pope Innocent III in the early 1300's. However, the Babylonian Captivity and the Great Schism of the fourteenth century lessened its prestige and power, and it continued to decline through the 1400's.

The late Middle Ages produced some of the world's greatest religious art and architecture. Music began to develop and became more complex. Epic poems, short stories, fables, courtly love songs, and short plays were written for the first time in the vernacular. Latin was the language of the new universities and the conflict between faith and reason was discussed by the Scholastics.

1. What were the results of the Crusades?
2. What important institutions of English government and law began in the late Middle Ages?
3. Why did Spain not become unified until the end of the Middle Ages?
4. What western European countries failed to become united during this time?
5. Why did the power of the Church begin to decline in the fourteenth century?
6. What types of literature evolved in the late Middle Ages? In what languages were these works written?

Using Your Vocabulary

1. What were the Crusades? What is the origin of this word?
2. Define the terms moot and shire reeve. What does the word moot mean today?
3. What was the Domesday Book? How did it receive its name?
4. What is common law? How did it develop? How does it differ from a code of laws?
5. Explain the difference between a grand jury and a petit jury.
6. What was the Magna Carta? What historical importance does it have?
7. What was the Estates General? What were similar English and Spanish institutions called?
8. What term is used to describe the Spanish military campaign to oust the Moors? Why was it so named?
9. Who were the *Moriscos* and the *Marranos?* What were the political and economic effects of their expulsion from Spain?
10. Why was Otto the Great's domain called the Holy Roman Empire? Was this term accurate? Explain.
11. What is a concordat? What important concordat was reached in the late Middle Ages? What conflict did it resolve?
12. Name two new religious orders founded in the late medieval period. How did they differ from previous religious orders?
13. Name and describe two types of architecture that developed during this period.

Developing Your Geography Skills

1. Use the map on page 265 to describe the political divisions of the Iberian peninsula about 1100.
2. Use the map on page 265 and the Atlas map on page 756 to tell what present day countries were part of the Holy Roman Empire.
3. Use the map on page 280 to locate by means of latitude and longitude coordinates the cities of Rome, Venice, Genoa, Paris, and Toledo.

Recalling the Facts

1. What were the effects of the Crusades?
2. Who led the Norman Conquest of England? When was the conquest completed? What effects did Norman domination have on English politics and culture?
3. How did Henry I establish an effective bureaucracy in England?
4. Explain why a conflict developed between Thomas Becket and Henry II. What were the results?
5. What civil war occurred in England in the fifteenth century? Why was it so named? How was this conflict resolved?
6. Who founded the Capetian dynasty? What were two important accomplishments of Capetian rulers?
7. Explain the causes and effects of the Hundred Years' War.
8. Who was Joan of Arc? Why is she an important historical figure?
9. What problems did Spain have to overcome to achieve unification?
10. Describe the accomplishments of Otto the Great.
11. Why did centralization prove difficult for the rulers of the Holy Roman Empire?
12. Identify the problems of the Church in the late Middle Ages and the actions taken to correct them. What were the results?
13. Briefly define the Babylonian Captivity and the Great Schism. What were the results of these events?
14. What was Scholasticism? Name two famous Scholastics and explain their importance.

Essay Questions

1. During the Crusades, several kings left their countries unattended to lead their armies into battle. What were the advantages and disadvantages of such action? Should modern leaders follow their example?
2. Compare and contrast Parliament and the Estates General. Why was it significant to include representatives from different socio-economic groups? What input would each have contributed?
3. By the end of the Middle Ages, Italy and Germany were the only western European countries not united under the rule of a monarch. Explain how and why this occurred.
4. The struggle for power between Church and State is a continuing theme throughout history. Discuss the developments and results of this conflict in the late Middle Ages.
5. How did the Church influence the artistic and literary development of the late Middle Ages? Why did the writings of Dante and Chaucer signify a change? Why would the teachings of Abelard and Bacon be considered dangerous by the Church?

Critical Thinking

1. In the eleventh century, stories about the Muslims and their cruel treatment of pilgrims circulated throughout western Europe. Would you consider these stories a reliable source of data? Why or why not?
2. How are the explusion of the Moors and Jews from Spain an example of bias?
3. How could bias influence the judgment of officials of the medieval Inquisition?
4. How could the pope's decision to move the papal court to Avignon be an example of a value judgment? Explain.
5. Would the application of the term Gothic to the architecture of the late Middle Ages be an example of a warranted or unwarranted claim? Explain.
6. How did Peter Abelard's work *Sic Et Non* demonstrate the logical inconsistencies in Church thought?

Reviewing the Unit

Developing a Sense of Time

Examine the time line below and answer the questions that follow.

200 B.C.	200	Germanic tribes begin to invade western Europe
400 A.D.	400	Angles, Saxons, and Jutes invade England
	452	Attila the Hun invades Italy
	711	Muslims invade Spain
	732	Battle of Tours
	800	Charlemagne crowned emperor of the Romans; Viking and Magyar invasions begin
	900	Commerce and town life begin to revive in western Europe
	962	Otto the Great crowned emperor of the Holy Roman Empire
1000	1047	The Crusades begin
	1066	Norman Conquest of England
	1215	King John signs the Magna Carta
	1338	Hundred Years' War begins
	1378	The Great Schism begins
	1455	War of Roses begins
	1492	Muslims expelled from Spain

1. When did the Germanic tribes begin to invade western Europe?
2. What event took place at about the same time as the Magyars and Vikings began their invasions of western Europe?
3. What event occurred shortly after the Crusades began?
4. Which occurred first: the War of Roses or the Hundred Years' War?

Social Science Skills

Making an Outline

1. How is an outline formed? What is its purpose?
2. Use the information in the chapter summaries found in Chapters 11 and 12 to write an outline for a unit review of the Middle Ages.
3. What are the topics or main ideas of your outline? Be sure to give examples to support each idea.

Critical Thinking

1. The code of chivalry characterized women in the late Middle Ages as weak and helpless individuals who needed protection. From what you know, would you consider this a verifiable fact or an equivocal assumption?
2. Would you consider the Domesday Book a reliable source of data? Why or why not?
3. The Jews who lived in medieval Spain were government officials, merchants, and professionals, like doctors and bankers. Yet, the literature of the time always portrays them as greedy moneylenders. How would this be an example of bias?
4. The period in which the papal residence was moved from Rome to Avignon has been called the Babylonian Captivity. On what basis did the people make this claim? Do you consider this a warranted or unwarranted claim?

Linking Past and Present

Modern vernacular languages, such as English, French, Spanish, German, and Portuguese, began to develop in the late Middle Ages. Pick six words and look up their origin in the dictionary. From what language are the majority of them derived? What does this tell you about the development of modern English? How do you think new words are added to our language today? Give four words that have been added to our language in the last twenty years.

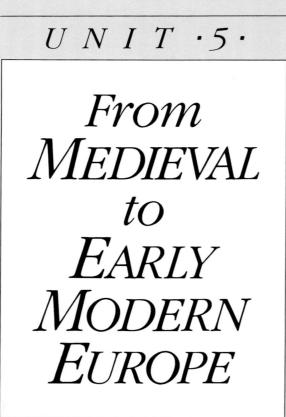

From MEDIEVAL to EARLY MODERN EUROPE

1350–1763

CHAPTER ·13·

The RENAISSANCE and the REFORMATION

1350–1600

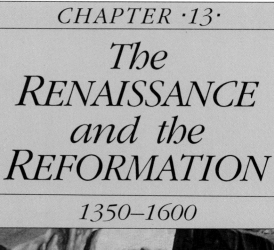

Objectives

- To describe how the Black Death affected Europe

- To discuss the meaning of the Renaissance

- To describe the New Monarchs of the late fifteenth and early sixteenth centuries

- To explain why and how the Reformation began

- To discuss the Reformation and how it was counteracted

*D*uring the long era of the Middle Ages, the people of Europe created the foundations for modern, western civilization. To protect themselves during warfare and invasions, they developed feudal institutions. Later, monarchies began to exert and strengthen their political power. The economy, after centuries of decline, revived with the growth of trade and towns.

To a great extent medieval life centered on the beliefs and practices of the Church. Its hierarchy wielded tremendous authority, not only in the spiritual realm but also in political life through its influence on lay rulers. Most of the intellectual and artistic achievements of this period developed from and reflected Christian teachings.

The final century-and-a-half of the Middle Ages is regarded by many historians as a transitional period. Europe was struck by a terrible plague that killed millions of people. At the same time, cultural and technological advances demonstrated the capacity of western civilization for revival and renewal. Attitudes toward the individual, life, and society began to change.

In some west European countries, central monarchies overcame violence and civil war to create stable regimes. The most momentous event of the sixteenth century was, however, the Protestant movement. It destroyed the religious unity of western Christendom and resulted in continuous conflict for more than a century.

SOCIAL AND TECHNOLOGICAL CHANGE

By 1300 the population of western Europe was about 54 million and seemed to be increasing steadily. Most towns and cities that exist today had been established. During the fourteenth century their rate of growth declined as the population was decimated by famine, war, and plague.

The Black Death

In 1347 a merchant ship landed in Messina, a port city of eastern Sicily. Along with its cargo it carried the plague, which proceeded to sweep northward over Europe in a vast, deadly wave.

Plague was not unknown to Europeans. For example, a mass outbreak had devastated the Byzantine Empire in the sixth century A.D. Europe, however, had been relatively free of epidemics for many centuries, and none had ever claimed as many lives as this new disease.

Europeans of the time had no idea what caused the deaths. Scholars today believe that this disease was bubonic plague, which can be transmitted to humans by fleas from infected rats. The symptoms were a high fever and black spots on the skin caused by multiple internal hemorrhages, or bleeding from blood vessels. Consequently, the disease was called the Black Death.

The plague that began in 1347 struck almost all of Europe during the next two years. It hit Paris by June 1348 and ravaged the Low Countries and England within the next year. It reached southern Norway by the end of 1349 and Russia a few months later. When it attacked a community, people refused to help the stricken, even members of their own family. Many fled to the countryside. Death came quickly, and in many cases there was no time for proper mourning and funerals. Carts moved through the streets to collect the dead, who were buried in a common grave. It is estimated that between 1347 and 1350 about one-third of the population in western Europe perished from the Black Death.

The Black Death caused immense social and economic changes. It signified the end of the eco-

nomic boom of the late Middle Ages because the demand for manufactured products, such as wool cloth, declined. Consequently, in places like Flanders and Florence, there was a high rate of unemployment. In other towns and cities the numerous deaths caused labor shortages, which allowed workers to demand higher wages and improve their standard of living.

Some landowners and townspeople became rich as they inherited property from deceased relatives. Other landowners were forced to sell their land because death and migration to the cities and towns caused labor shortages in rural areas. The lack of labor resulted in a scarcity of agricultural products, which caused a sharp rise in prices. Feudal lords were forced to make certain concessions to the peasants. They began to pay day wages and found it more productive to have peasants pay fixed rents on their land rather than requiring payment in services. Thus the feudal system was effectively ended in western Europe.

Improvements in Technology

The late Middle Ages was a period of slow but steady technological improvement. Several innovations made water travel easier and safer. By the fourteenth century Europeans were using the compass, and more detailed maps took some of the guesswork out of sea voyages. A type of sailor's chart called the *portolano*, or portolan, was especially helpful because it showed coastlines and harbors in detail. Improvements were also made in ship design. For centuries boats had been steered from the side with a long oar. During the 1300's sailors developed a new way to rig their ship's sails, enabling them to use wind power more efficiently.

In the thirteenth century western Europeans began to use paper, which they may have learned about from contact with Muslims in Spain or during the Crusades. Paper was cheaper and easier to manufacture than parchment or papyrus, the materials on which books and documents were written before this time. By the fifteenth century craftsmen had learned to mass-produce illustrations or single letters by carving images into wooden blocks that were then inked and printed on paper. However, a great deal of time and effort would have been required to print a book in this manner. Thus it was not until the invention of movable metal type around 1450 that book printing became possible.

Movable metal type enabled printers to use individual letters repeatedly and in many combinations. This led to the development of the printing press, the most far-reaching technological advance of this period. Credit for the first printed book is usually given to Johannes Gutenberg (yoh-HAHN-ness GOOT-un-burg), a German, who in 1456 published an edition of the Bible, now known as the Gutenberg Bible.

By 1500 there were printing presses in 250 European cities, and over 40,000 different books had been printed. People were encouraged to learn because books were available to a larger audience and were easier to read than manuscripts copied by hand.

SECTION REVIEW

1. In your own words, briefly define or identify: Black Death, *portolano*, Gutenberg.
2. Describe the origin and spread of the plague.
3. What were the social and economic effects of the Black Death?
4. Name the technological advances made during the late Middle Ages and explain why each was important.
- The development of printing made it possible for information to become available to a larger audience. How is information transmitted to the general public today? Which medium of communication do you consider to be the most reliable? Explain.

Early printing shops were busy places. How many job-related activities can you identify? Compare this scene with modern methods of printing.

THE RENAISSANCE

As you know, the cities of Italy were the leading centers in the revival of west European commerce in the Middle Ages. Over the years, Venice, Milan, Florence, and Genoa had developed into prosperous urban communities. Rome flourished as the center of western Christianity and the seat of the papacy.

About 1350 there began in these cities a **Renaissance** (RENN-uh-zahnts), or rebirth, which marks the period of transition between medieval and early modern times. During the Renaissance there was a revival of interest in the art, architecture, and literature of classical Rome and Greece. Also, a new attitude developed toward people and their capabilities which, in turn, inspired new ways of portraying the world in literature and art.

The Renaissance began in Italy for cultural, economic, social, and political reasons. Ties to classical traditions were strong because Italians were the direct descendants of the Romans, and the remains of Roman civilization were visible in many places. Prosperity and trade with the Byzantine Empire and Islam encouraged interest in learning and the arts. Wealthy families vied with one another to build beautiful palaces, to collect fine libraries, and to become patrons, or sponsors, of new artists and sculptors. Politically, northern Italy was divided into various independent city-states. While this situation hampered national unity, it did encourage self-government and a sense of individualism, or freedom for self-realization.

Humanism

As Italian commerce and urban population increased in the late Middle Ages, feudal law based on custom proved inadequate, and it became necessary to institute a new body of law. Thus the study of Roman civil law based on the *Corpus Juris Civilis,* or Justinian's Code, was revived in the twelfth and thirteenth centuries. Since rulers, merchants, and traders needed men possessing legal training to administer their affairs, the demand for lawyers grew. It became a profitable career, and parents urged their sons to study law.

The interest in Roman law led to a revival of the study of other Greek and Roman classical

Built of colored marble in the fourteenth century, the cathedral in Florence is one of the finest examples of early Renaissance architecture. How does it compare to Notre Dame on page 286?

works, and a new movement called **humanism** emerged. In the beginning, humanism referred mainly to educational reforms. Some fourteenth-century scholars and writers regarded scholasticism as too narrow a field of study, focused as it was on philosophy and theology. They felt that men would profit more by studying society's and people's problems and possibilities on earth. This attitude could be found in the classical writings of the Greeks and Romans.

Scholars searched throughout Europe for ancient manuscripts. When Constantinople fell to the Ottoman Turks in 1453, many Byzantine scholars took refuge in Italy, carrying Greek manuscripts with them. In 1455 the papal library at Rome had about 152 Greek manuscripts. Thirty years later its classical collection had increased to more than a thousand. The study of these manuscripts led to the establishment of a new university curriculum centered on classical studies of history, literature, and language, known as *studia humanitatis,* or the

Leonardo da Vinci labored for many years on the problem of air flight. What modern aircraft resembles this sketch?

study of humankind. From this term came humanism and the modern course of study known as the humanities.

Gradually, humanism came to mean more than just educational reform. As scholars expanded their knowledge of ancient Greece and Rome, they developed a freer, more critical way of thinking. Their interests turned to the secular and they believed that if a person lived a moral life on earth, he or she could attain salvation just as well as the person who retired from the world to a convent or monastery. Although this was a radical change from medieval thought and theology, many humanists continued to be devout Christians. Only the focus of their interest was altered.

Humanists admired the "universal" or Renaissance man, who was an educated person of wide-ranging accomplishments. Leonardo da Vinci is perhaps the best example of the universal man. His inquisitive nature led him to study painting, architecture, sculpture, literature, music, mathematics, engineering, and anatomy. While in the service of

the duke of Milan, he built a canal and designed fortifications for the city, as well as executing one of his best-known frescoes, *The Last Supper*. Later he composed music and devised cannons, a tank, and a flying machine. People never tire of studying the mysterious smile of his most famous painting, the *Mona Lisa*.

Italian Literature of the Renaissance

Humanism also influenced the literature of this period. New themes reflecting society's problems and the concept of enjoying life on earth began to emerge. References to classical writers and characters from classical myths and legends frequently appeared in Renaissance works.

One of the most important Italian humanists and lyric poets of the fourteenth century was Francesco Petrarca. Petrarch (PEH-trahrk), as he is commonly known, was a zealous collector of ancient manuscripts and wrote letters in elegant Latin. He is best known, however, for his sonnets in Italian, which were addressed to a young woman named Laura, who died of the plague in 1348.

Giovanni Boccaccio (boh-KAHCH-ee-oh) was a contemporary of Petrarch. His work, the *Decameron*, is regarded as the first prose masterpiece in Italian. It is a collection of one hundred tales told by a group of ten men and women who flee the city of Florence to escape the Black Death. In the villa where they take refuge, each is required to tell one story a day as entertainment. It is possible that Chaucer's *Canterbury Tales* was modeled on the *Decameron*.

The Book of the Courtier by Baldassare Castiglione (kahs-teel-YOH-nay), a sixteenth-century diplomat, is one of the most representative works of Renaissance thought and ideals. Through a series of lively discussions, Castiglione describes the proper behavior and qualities that a refined, educated aristocrat, or the perfect courtier, should possess. Among the participants in these discussions are some of the most famous men and women of the Italian Renaissance.

Along the same lines was the *Book of the City of Ladies*, written by Christine de Pisan, one of the few women writers of the time. Since she argued in this work for the education of women, de Pisan could be considered the first feminist.

Italian Art and Architecture

The Renaissance witnessed dramatic changes in art. Religious themes continued to dominate the scene, but figures were more realistic. Artists were inspired by classical examples, and secular themes were introduced. Renaissance artists developed new techniques that enabled them to create some of the most beautiful works of art the world has ever known. Florence was the first center of Renaissance art.

The imitation of classical models first began in sculpture. Like the great Greek and Roman masters, Renaissance sculptors were concerned with accurate representation of the human figure. They idealized the human face and figure to produce works of serene beauty in marble and in bronze.

Donatello (doh-nah-TELL-oh), a Florentine sculptor of the early 1400's, is known as the creator of the Renaissance portrait. His imposing statue of a contemporary general is the first realistic portrait in bronze of a subject on a horse. To portray people as they really looked became the norm in the Renaissance.

Giotto (jee-OHT-toh), a Florentine of the early fourteenth century, is often considered the first Renaissance painter. In his religious frescoes Giotto moved away from the portrayal of static, lifeless figures found in medieval art and developed a more natural style. His figures became more dramatic through gestures and facial expressions.

In the fifteenth century Masaccio (muh-ZAHCH-ee-oe), another great Florentine painter, created new techniques to make painting more realistic. He solved the problem of perspective, or the representation of three dimensions on a flat surface. His famous painting of the expulsion from Eden depicts Adam and Eve as real, suffering human beings.

Probably the greatest Renaissance painter and sculptor was Michelangelo. Like da Vinci, he was a man of many and varied accomplishments. The achievements of Michelangelo and da Vinci are considered among the greatest of the High Renaissance, which was centered in Rome in the late fifteenth and early sixteenth centuries.

Rafael was another outstanding painter of the High Renaissance. He is especially noted for his graceful madonnas, beautiful colors, and for the balance and harmony of his compositions. His series of religious murals in the Vatican are considered one of the greatest works of this period.

In architecture as in painting and sculpture, the Italian Renaissance turned to classical models. Domes, columns, and colonnades adorn the stately churches and palaces of the fifteenth and sixteenth century.

The architect Brunelleschi (broo-nel-LESS-kee) added a neo-classic dome to Florence's Gothic cathedral without destroying the building's design and style. Other architects, such as Palladio and Michelangelo, worked out relationships of space and volume to produce pleasing proportions.

Northern Renaissance Literature

By 1500 humanism had spread northward to France, the Low Countries, the German states, and England. The northern humanists, however, were more influenced by the medieval church and gave more attention to the study of early Christian

Michelangelo's statue portrays David as he watches his approaching foe Goliath. How is it representative of Renaissance art?

People in History

Michelangelo

Michelangelo Buonarroti (mee-kuhl-AHN-jay-loh bwoh-nahr-ROH-tee) was one of the greatest artistic geniuses of the Renaissance. He became a reknowned painter, sculptor, and architect, but his stormy temperament and moods of despair darkened his life. Nevertheless, he always remained supremely confident of his goals and his ability to carry them out.

Michelangelo expressed his creativity most dramatically through the human figure. He thought of himself primarily as a sculptor, and wrote of "liberating the figure from the marble that imprisons it." One of his most famous works is the heroic marble statue of *David*, commissioned by the city of Florence in 1501. His other well-known statues are *Moses* and the *Pietà*, which shows Mary mourning Christ. Through these works, Michelangelo provided western art with a new standard of physical beauty.

Michelangelo's paintings are noted for their sculptural quality. His masterpiece is the ceiling of the Sistine Chapel of the Vatican, done between 1508 and 1512. In the huge barrel vault, he told the story of Genesis from the Creation to the Flood. Of the hundreds of figures Michelangelo depicted, the most famous grouping shows God, surrounded by angels, reaching out to touch Adam's hand.

Some twenty years later, in the midst of the Reformation, Michelangelo was commissioned by the pope to paint a fresco of the Last Judgment, in the Sistine Chapel. Michelangelo's own self-portrait appears among the many figures.

The Sistine paintings were Michelangelo's only works to be realized as he actually conceived them. In every other case, elaborate designs for tombs, churches, and plazas were only partially executed or abandoned because of lack of funds or disagreements. For example, Michelangelo was employed by Pope Paul III to design St. Peter's in Rome, but only the dome follows his plans.

As a humanist, Michelangelo had great admiration for the classical past. He studied Greek and Roman sculpture and architecture. In some cases his work followed ancient models rather closely. For example, his tomb figure of a Medici prince shows the man in Roman military garb. In other instances the artist reworked classical models to suit himself. In a library he designed, he boldly disobeyed the rules by creating a new order of columns and leaving niches empty. According to a writer of the time, he "broke the bonds and chains of common usage."

Toward the end of his life Michelangelo expressed his feelings of disappointment and loneliness in his poetry. By the time of his death, in 1564, he seemed to have found peace in the Christian faith.

1. According to Michelangelo, what was his occupation?
2. Which of his works can be seen in the Sistine Chapel?
3. How does Michelangelo's life and work reflect Renaissance ideals?

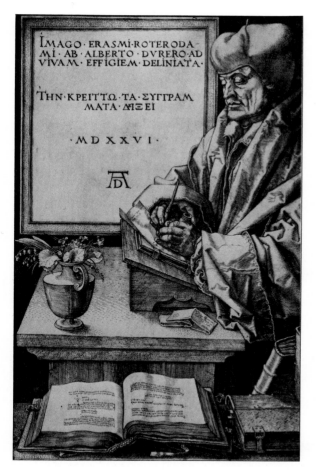

How does this engraving by Dürer characterize Erasmus?

teachings than the Italian humanists. They applied Renaissance concepts to the study of religion in an effort to modernize church doctrine and practice, and were known as Christian humanists.

The most influential humanist of northern Europe was a Dutch monk of the early sixteenth century, Erasmus (ir-RAZ-muhs). Popes and kings sought his advice, and he corresponded with the learned throughout Europe. Erasmus became the foremost biblical scholar in Europe by publishing a revised edition of the New Testament in Greek, along with a Latin translation and notes. His book, *In Praise of Folly*, made him famous as a satirist. This work ridicules the major problems of the Church and secular society, such as hypocrisy and corruption among the clergy, war, and class distinction.

The leading English humanist of the time, Sir Thomas More, was a friend of Erasmus. He spent many years as an adviser to the English king, Henry VIII, and composed religious and biographical works. He is most famous for *Utopia*, or the *Land of Nowhere*, which is an account of the perfect society in an ideal city on an imaginary island. In Utopia there is no poverty and everyone is educated and wise. The term Utopia has come to mean any place, state, or situation of ideal perfection.

François Rabelais (fran-SWA RAB-uh-lay) was a notable French humanist of the sixteenth century and a Benedictine physician. His series of books about two giants named Pantagruel (pan-tah-groo-ELL) and Gargantua (gahr-GANCH-uh-wuh), reveal a coarse sense of humor and satirical wit. By recounting the lives and adventures of these two characters, he managed to criticize most of society's problems.

In contrast were the writings of Michel de Montaigne (mahn-TAYN), another French humanist and philosopher. His collections of essays established a new literary form. As a Renaissance man, Montaigne wrote about many subjects, usually from the viewpoint of an observer. His works emphasize the individual and reliance on self-knowledge.

Art in Northern Europe

Like northern humanism, northern art differed from its Italian counterpart. Although both schools attempted to depict the world realistically, the northern artists paid more attention to small detail, especially in their landscapes. They are famous for their work in miniatures, as opposed to the great mural paintings of the Italians. This attention to detail is also reflected in their engravings.

One of the great Renaissance innovations—oil painting on canvas—originated in Flanders in the fifteenth century. A more versatile medium, oil paints soon replaced tempera, or pigment mixed with egg yolks, in most of Europe.

Among the first artists to use oils were the Flemish brothers Hubert and Jan van Eyck (IKE), who lived in the early fifteenth century. Like Giotto, they brought realism to painting. In their greatest work, the altar piece in Ghent called the *Adoration of the Lamb*, the flowers and shrubs of the landscape are shown in minute detail.

Other great northern painters were Hieronymus Bosch (heh-RON-uh-mus BOSH) and Roger van der Weyden (VIED-uhn). With respect to style and theme, Bosch broke all traditions. His paintings are like grotesque fantasies and reflect a bizarre sense of humor. Van der Weyden is best known for his religious paintings and the tragic expressions of his figures.

Albrecht Dürer (DYOOR-uhr) was one of the finest German artists of the northern Renaissance. As a naturalist, he made numerous sketches of animals, flowers, and plants. He was also a great portrait painter, but he is best remembered for his woodcuts and copper engravings of religious figures and scenes.

Hans Holbein (HOLE-bine) the Younger was another well-known German painter. As the court painter of Henry VIII of England, he painted dozens of portraits, each revealing the personality of the subject. Among his famous works are the portraits of Erasmus, Thomas More, and Henry VIII.

Renaissance Music

Just as there was an increased interest in the arts in the Renaissance, there was a corresponding interest in music. Two new developments of this period were the sacred motet and the secular madrigal. Some nobles and monarchs of the Renaissance who supported artists and sculptors were also patrons of composers and musicians.

The Renaissance motet evolved from chant and was used in church services. It is a multi-voiced composition sung in Latin and generally performed without musical accompaniment. The melodies were sung by small church choirs and usually boys or young men sang the high parts because women were not allowed to participate in the Mass.

In contrast, madrigals were sung at courtly social gatherings by small groups of men and women. Their texts were based on sentimental love poems in the vernacular.

In addition, this period witnessed the development of instrumental dance music as dancing became a popular form of entertainment among the aristocracy. Courtly dances were accompanied by music performed on a lute or harpsichord, a stringed keyboard instrument similar to a modern piano.

This detail of a fifteenth-century painting shows a wedding reception held outside a church in Florence. What aspects of Renaissance society are depicted?

1. In your own words, briefly define or identify: humanism, da Vinci, Petrarch, *Decameron, The Courtier,* Donatello, Dürer.
2. Why did the Renaissance begin in Italy?
3. How did the Renaissance attitude toward life differ from medieval ways of thinking?
4. What technical innovations in painting occurred during the Renaissance?
5. List three leading northern humanists and explain why each was important.
■ A person of varied accomplishments is still called a Renaissance man or woman. Choose a contemporary figure whom you think has these characteristics and explain why.

How does Hans Holbein depict Henry VIII's personality and position in this painting? If someone did your portrait, what would it show?

THE ERA OF NEW MONARCHIES

While the Renaissance was changing the intellectual and artistic life of Europe, strong rulers in several nation-states were seeking to restore political order. As you know, the fifteenth century was a time of turmoil in much of western Europe. It witnessed the War of the Roses in England, the end of the Hundred Years' War between France and England, and the final decades of the *Reconquista* in Spain. Rulers who came to power late in this century were determined to put an end to domestic war and violence by creating strong central monarchies. The nations where this policy was successful—England, France, and Spain—are known as New Monarchies.

Tudor England

As you have read, Henry Tudor established a new dynasty in England after defeating Richard III at the battle of Bosworth Field. Henry VII, though an unpleasant person, was a good administrator. He limited the power of the English nobles by having Parliament pass acts forbidding them to maintain private armies and allowing him to punish his ene-

mies for treason. He enriched the royal treasury through improved accounting methods and by raising fees and fines in royal courts. When he died, he was one of the richest kings in western Europe.

Henry VII also followed the example of earlier medieval rulers by strengthening his central administration. He established a new court called the Court of Star Chamber, in which there was no jury and proceedings were kept secret. Since the court was not subject to manipulation by local nobles, defendants were assured of a speedy and fair trial. Henry also increased the powers of the local officials known as justices of the peace.

By following these policies, Henry VII restored political order to England and created a well-organized state controlled by a strong central government, which was the characteristic of the New Monarchies. Henry VIII, who came to the English throne in 1509, continued the centralization process begun by his father. He is known today primarily for his many wives and for the far-reaching effects of his quarrel with the Church. One notable event of his reign was the union of England and Wales in 1536.

Valois France

The Valois dynasty came to power in France in the early fourteenth century. Many historians consider Louis XI the first New Monarch in France. As you know, his father, Charles VII, established the foundations for a strong monarchy. In order to raise an effective army to fight the Hundred Years' War, Charles gained the right to tax without the consent of the Estates General. Later he used this tax to fill the French treasury. Thus his son inherited not only one of the finest professional armies in Europe, but also a substantial treasury.

Louis XI, who ruled from 1461 to 1483, carried on his father's efforts to strengthen the monarchy. He is often called the Spider King because of the complex webs of intrigue he weaved. One of his major accomplishments was to extend the boundaries of his domain to include almost all of present-day France. Louis annexed the duchy of Burgundy after its ruler, Charles the Bold, was killed in battle in 1477. The only major region of France that remained outside the royal realm was Brittany, and it became part of the monarch's lands when Louis arranged the marriage of his son to the heiress.

Louis also curbed the power of the French nobility by dismissing many aristocratic government administrators and replacing them with civil servants from the lower nobility, or middle class, called the **bourgeoisie.** Although he imposed heavy taxes in order to raise revenues, he won the support of the bourgeoisie, on whom the heaviest tax burdens fell, by encouraging both foreign and domestic trade. From the late 1400's to the mid 1500's the power of the French monarchs increased as the government bureaucracy expanded and became more efficient.

A United Spain

Probably the two most powerful New Monarchs of the late fifteenth century were Spain's Ferdinand and Isabella. As you have read, their marriage effectively united most of Spain under a single ruling family and, after driving the Moors out of Spain, they controlled most of the Iberian peninsula except for Portugal. Under their rule, the discovery of the New World was made through the efforts of Christopher Columbus, and colonization began.

The Spanish monarchs also gained territories in Europe. They built up an effective military force and by 1504 their army had conquered Naples. At the time of Ferdinand's death in 1516, Spain had gained an enormous amount of territory and became a major power in west European politics.

Germany and Italy

The rulers of the Holy Roman Empire were also interested in establishing a New Monarchy. In 1438 the Archduke of Austria, a member of Austria's Hapsburg family, was elected emperor. With one exception, every Holy Roman Emperor from 1438 until 1806 was a Hapsburg.

Machiavelli believed that leaders should protect their states by whatever means necessary. Should modern rulers follow his advice? Why or why not?

The Hapsburgs did quite well at increasing the size of their own domains, chiefly through marriage. Although they tried to introduce the concept of centralization, they had little success in extending their control over the many German states. Under Maximilian I, who ruled from 1493 to 1519, the empire was divided into administrative circles. The leading prince in each of them was responsible for maintaining law and order in his circle. An Imperial Court was also established as overall administrator and final court of appeal. Neither move, however, accomplished much in the face of strong local interests. Later attempts at reform had little effect.

As you know, Italy was divided into many territories. In the sixteenth century the southern part of the peninsula was the home of the Kingdom of the Two Sicilies, or the kingdoms of Naples and Sicily, whereas the central portion consisted of the Papal States. Northern Italy was divided into many small city-states, the most powerful being Florence, Venice, and Milan. The Italians developed strong patriotic feelings for the state in which they lived, and war was constant as rival rulers vied to enlarge their territories. Central unification was never considered. As a result, the Italian states were constantly preyed upon by other stronger powers such as France, Spain, and the Holy Roman Empire, who wished to gain control of the Mediterranean trade.

The most noteworthy Italian of this period was not a monarch, but a statesman and writer named Niccolò Machiavelli (mack-ee-uh-VEL-ee). His masterwork, *The Prince,* was written in 1513 as a political guide for rulers and discusses the methods to be employed in the establishment of an effective central monarchy.

In *The Prince* Machiavelli decried the weakness of the Italian states and commended those New Monarchs, like Ferdinand of Aragon, who were able to build strong nation-states. He saw behind their success not the workings of divine law, but self-interest and ruthless calculation. According to Machiavelli, the end justifies the means and a ruler could lie, cheat, wage war, or do whatever was necessary to maintain his position. He also stated that it was better for a ruler to be feared than loved. In modern times the term Machiavellian has come to mean someone who is deceitful or crafty.

BEGINNINGS OF THE REFORMATION

Of all the cultural, social, and political changes about which you have been reading, none had more impact than the great division of western Christianity caused by the Protestant Reformation. It began in the early 1500's when discontent with the Church was widespread.

Background of the Reformation

As early as the tenth century, the Church had been criticized for abuses of its spiritual authority. Over the years, public awareness of these abuses increased. Humanism encouraged criticism of the Church's failure to teach, to preach, and to care for the spiritual needs of its people. Humanists, such as Erasmus, advocated a reform of the Church's practices.

The prestige of the papacy was at a low ebb in the early sixteenth century. It had been damaged by the Babylonian Captivity and by the Great Schism. Many Renaissance popes seemed to be more interested in collecting ancient manuscripts and patronizing artists than in the spiritual welfare of the people. High church offices were still bought and sold and simony was widely practiced. Politically, the New Monarchs considered the pope a competitor for national power.

Many Europeans resented the fact that the Church collected a variety of payments and that much of this money was sent to Rome. Also, people were dissatisfied with the Church's practice of selling indulgences, or remissions of punishment for sins. This custom began during the Crusades, and later popes used the sale of indulgences as a source of income for financing their projects and wars. Many devout Catholics opposed this policy because they believed the purchase of forgiveness of sins would lead to a decline in moral standards.

Some religious reformers, like Francis of Assisi and Catherine of Siena, worked within the Church. Others were denounced as heretics. The fact that would-be reformers found wide audiences indicates an eagerness among Europeans for some sort of spiritual renewal. An English scholar of the fourteenth century, John Wycliffe, preached against the wealth and worldliness of the Church and taught that the Bible was the highest source of truth. He was the first to translate the Bible into English. The Church condemned Wycliffe as a heretic, but he was allowed to live and die in peace.

John Huss, a Bohemian priest influenced by Wycliffe's teachings, was not so fortunate. After his attacks on the Church drew criticism from the papacy, he was condemned as a heretic and burned at the stake in 1415.

At the end of the fifteenth century, Girolamo Savonarola (jee-roh-LAH-moh sah-vuh-nuh-ROH-luh), a Dominican friar, gained popularity in Florence by preaching against the worldliness of the Church. His influence was so great that people threw playing cards, cosmetics, dice, and other items with a corruptive influence into bonfires. Eventually the Church declared him guilty of heresy and he was executed.

Luther's Break with the Church

The definitive split that began the Protestant Reformation occurred in Germany. Its immediate cause was the sale of indulgences to raise money for the construction of St. Peter's in Rome. One churchman who traveled around Germany collecting contributions for this purpose was a Dominican friar, Johann Tetzel (TET-suhl). When he appeared near Wittenberg, Saxony, in 1517, he aroused the anger of a monk named Martin Luther.

Why is this painting of Luther and the reformers an important document of its time?

Luther began his education by studying law. A spiritual young man, he became an Augustinian monk and later a priest. As a result of a personal religious experience, he became convinced that salvation was a free gift, given by God to all who had faith in Him. It had nothing to do with what the Church called good works, like alms-giving or receiving the sacraments. Thus when Tetzel appeared, offering, as Luther saw it, to sell salvation, the priest felt that he had to speak out.

Luther drew up a list of *Ninety-five Theses*, or statements for public debate, and posted them on the Wittenberg church door on October 31, 1517. Luther's *Theses* were copied, printed, and widely circulated. Consequently, the sale of indulgences dropped off. Various churchmen then issued counterattacks, to which Luther replied. A year later he was called before the papal legate in Germany, who ordered him to renounce his statements, but Luther refused.

During the following months Luther published pamphlets, wrote letters, and engaged in a famous debate. In this way, he stated his position in more detail. The gulf between his teachings and those of the Church became more obvious. He reasserted the importance of faith, rather than good works, in attaining salvation or the doctrine called justification by faith. He rejected the supremacy of the pope, denied the special quality of priests, and reduced the number of sacraments to achieve salvation. For him the Bible, not organized religion, was the only guide to a spiritual life. Luther also issued an appeal to German rulers asking them to reform the Church in Germany.

In 1521 the pope branded Luther a heretic, excommunicated him, and called for his arrest and punishment. He was commanded to appear before a Diet, or legislature of the Holy Roman Empire. At this Diet of Worms, Luther refused to admit that he had been in error. He ended his testimony with these defiant words: "I neither can nor will recant anything, for to go against conscience is neither right nor safe. Here I stand. I cannot do otherwise. God help me. Amen."

After the Diet of Worms, Luther was placed under the protection of Frederick III, the Elector of Saxony who favored his cause. From this time until his death in 1546, Luther continued to teach, preach, and write about his interpretation of Christianity. Aided by the new printing press, his message began to spread. Also, Luther translated the New Testament into German in about two months and headed a committee that translated the Old Testament. Luther's translation of the Bible is considered one of the great masterpieces of German literature.

Repercussions in Germany

A new sect of Christianity, Lutheranism, took shape around Luther's teachings. One of its chief tenets was justification by faith. Lutheranism emphasized preaching and teaching and the absolute authority of the Bible. The only recognized sacraments were those mentioned in the Bible, baptism and communion. Services were held in the vernacular, as opposed to Latin.

Lutheranism appealed to many partly because of its simplicity and partly because of its rejection of Rome's authority. Some of the German rulers who adopted the new religion hoped that if their domains became Lutheran, property that had belonged to the Church would now belong to them. Others saw the new religion as a means of becoming more independent from the Holy Roman Emperor, who was Catholic. The first **Protestants** were a group of Lutheran princes, lodging a protest against the decree of the Diet of Speyer in 1529 prohibiting the introduction of new religions. The term now refers to any Christian who is not a member of the Roman Catholic or Eastern Orthodox Church.

Luther welcomed the support of secular rulers, but there were other developments he bitterly denounced. For instance, he considered some religious groups that carried his ideas to extremes as

Printed in 1534, this title page is from Martin Luther's translation of the Bible. What does it reveal about the art of printing at this time?

too radical. One group, known as Anabaptists, regarded him as a kindred spirit. Their beliefs, which included adult baptism, pacifism, and free thought, offended him and he attacked them with vigor. Nor did Luther approve of armed revolt. In 1524 peasants in southern Germany rebelled against their feudal lords, demanding a number of reforms, some inspired by Luther. When Luther saw the chaos and destruction they caused, he withdrew his support and called on the German princes to put down the revolt. In the ruthless campaign that followed, about 100,000 peasants lost their lives.

This was only the beginning of decades of warfare in the name of religion. A full-fledged civil war broke out in Germany between Catholic and Lutheran princes in 1546. Although the Catholics, led by Holy Roman Emperor Charles V, won most of the battles, they could not overcome the Protestant forces entirely. The Peace of Augsburg that ended the war in 1555 provided for a compromise. Each ruler was allowed to choose the religion for his state. Whether he chose Catholicism or Lutheranism, everyone in his domain had to follow his example, or move.

SECTION REVIEW

1. In your own words, briefly define or identify: Wycliffe, Huss, Savonarola, indulgence, Tetzel, *Ninety-five Theses*, Diet of Worms.
2. Why was discontent with the church increasing in the early 1500's?
3. How did Luther's teachings differ from those of traditional western Christianity?
4. Name two reasons explaining why a German prince in the sixteenth century would convert to Lutheranism. What were the reasons for its popularity among the common people?
5. Why was Luther against the peasant's revolt?
6. When did civil war break out in Germany? What was the cause?
■ In Luther's time, churchmen and scholars often held debates to air their opinions. When are public debates held today? What topics are most often discussed?

THE REFORMATION CONTINUES

Lutheranism attracted converts not only in Germany but also in Scandinavia. By the mid-1500's it had spread to Denmark, Norway, and Sweden. In all these regions it was the established church, or the only religious organization recognized by law and supported by government funds. Protestantism also took root elsewhere but in different forms from those advocated by Luther.

The English Reformation

When the Reformation began in Germany, King Henry VIII of England upheld the pope against Luther. For this support he was awarded the title "Defender of the Faith," which English monarchs still use today. Soon, however, this alliance was broken.

As a young man, Henry had married his brother's widow, Catherine of Aragon. They had a daughter, Mary, but no sons, and the king wanted a male heir. So he asked the pope to grant him an annulment. Political considerations made this impossible, for Catherine was the aunt of the Holy Roman Emperor, a major ally of the papacy. When the pope refused, Henry had the archbishop of Canterbury annul his marriage to Catherine and he married Anne Boleyn. In 1534 he had Parliament declare him to be head of the Church in England, and the break between pope and king was complete. This act prepared the way for the spread of Protestantism in England, which led to religious conflict in the 1600's.

The Church of England, or Anglican Church, of Henry's time was essentially Catholic except for its denial of the authority of the pope. As head of the Church, Henry seized all the monasteries and convents in England and distributed their wealth and lands among his followers. This move enriched Henry and won him many new allies.

Most of the English abided by the new laws and accepted the monarch as head of the Church of England. Henry was personally popular, and resentment against the papacy and church hierarchy was strong. Those church leaders who spoke out against Henry were quickly replaced by his own

This sixteenth-century engraving shows the Calvinists vandalizing a church. Why do you think no one is trying to stop them?

supporters. A number of his subjects remained loyal to the Roman church and the king left them alone unless they were prominent people who openly defied him, like Sir Thomas More who was executed for treason.

In 1547 Henry was succeeded by Edward VI, the son of Jane Seymour, his third wife. The young king was frail, and those who ruled for him introduced more changes into the English church. When Edward died in 1553, Mary I, the daughter of Catherine of Aragon, came to the throne. Mary tried to reestablish Roman Catholicism as the state religion, but met fierce resistance. She had to use force to quell two revolts during her five-year reign and religious persecution was severe. More than 300 people were burned as heretics, and her opponents nicknamed her "Bloody Mary." She was succeeded in 1558 by Elizabeth I, the daughter of Anne Boleyn. Elizabeth was a religious moderate, and her reign brought peace and prosperity to England.

The Rise of Calvinism

In the 1530's a new religious movement founded on the teachings of John Calvin began to take shape. Attracted to Luther's doctrines, Calvin was forced to take refuge in Switzerland because of French persecution of Protestants. It was there that he published *Institutes of the Christian Religion*, outlining his basic beliefs. As a reformer, Calvin was just as influential as his predecessor, Luther.

Like Luther, Calvin believed that a person was saved by faith alone and that faith was attainable, not by the person's own efforts, but only as a free gift from God. Calvin, however, put much more emphasis than Luther on man's helplessness and God's unknowable power. He stated that God only chose to save certain people, called the elect, and only He knew who these chosen few were. This doctrine of Calvin's is known as predestination.

Calvin also differed from Luther on the relationship between Church and State. While Luther considered the State to be supreme, Calvin believed in the separation of Church and State. He argued that no government had the right to regulate religion, and in certain circumstances, it might be necessary to overthrow a ruler who acted in defiance of God's laws. Thus Calvinist beliefs contained the seeds of revolution.

A new sect, called **Calvinism,** grew out of Calvin's teachings. Preaching was the basis of Calvinist worship, and Calvinists simplified services and houses of worship. They disdained crosses, stained glass, and almost every kind of ornament.

Calvinists placed great emphasis on proper behavior they believed pleasing to God. They were convinced that God disapproved of music, dancing, and gambling. They also frowned on wearing elegant clothes or going to the theater. They set high moral standards for themselves and valued hard work.

In 1541 Calvin was invited by a group of reformers to organize the Protestant church in Geneva. There he put his teachings into effect. The Geneva church was governed by a group of ministers and laymen called the consistory. The consistory administered the church and disciplined its members. For example, it was an offense to miss church services and individuals could be fined for dancing, playing cards, or wearing inappropriate clothes.

Calvin was even less tolerant of those who differed with him than Luther had been. He disagreed strongly with the Lutherans over the nature of communion. He bitterly attacked the Spanish radical Michael Servetus (suhr-VEE-tuhs). When Servetus passed through Geneva, Calvin had him arrested, tried for heresy, and burned at the stake for arguing his position with Calvin in public.

In spite of the sternness of its beliefs, Calvinism won many followers. Unlike Anglicanism, which was imposed by the monarch, Calvinism was essentially a movement of the people. It appealed to them because it gave them a sense of purpose and a feeling of community. It spread beyond Geneva to the towns of Switzerland, and in France it won many converts, called Huguenots (HYOO-guh-nahts). It became the established religion in some German states, and in the northern Netherlands it was called the Dutch Reformed Church. The movement also attracted thousands of Poles, Hungarians, and Bohemians. Calvinism swept Scot-

land, largely through the work of John Knox, who had studied in Geneva. There it was known as the Presbyterian Church. In England the Puritans were Calvinists, and they adopted a form of church organization called Congregationalism.

The Counter Reformation

The Roman Catholic Church had been dealt several severe blows, but its leaders were determined to restore its supremacy. In the 1530's they began a movement called the **Counter Reformation.** It is also known as the **Catholic Reformation,** to emphasize the fact that it was not simply a reaction against Protestantism, but an independent movement to correct church abuses.

The reform of the Catholic Church was aided by the establishment of a new religious order, the Society of Jesus, or Jesuits. The Society of Jesus was founded in 1540 by Ignatius Loyola, a Spaniard who had been a professional soldier. His book, *Spiritual Exercises*, presents a detailed system of meditation based on the belief that one can only approach God through discipline of the will.

The Jesuits were organized, trained, and disciplined like an army and pledged to serve the pope. Influenced by humanist teachings, Loyola firmly believed in education and he encouraged the establishment of Jesuit schools and universities. Jesuit missionaries worked ceaselessly to convert and reconvert people throughout Europe. Nations that had adopted Protestantism tried to exclude Jesuit missionaries, but they worked in secret, sometimes at great peril to their lives.

Other reform measures were initiated by the papacy. Paul III, the first reforming pope of the Counter Reformation, instituted administrative and financial improvements in the Curia. He appointed a commission of cardinals to investigate church abuses and to suggest ways of correcting them. He also revived the Inquisition, which had not played a prominent role for some time, except in Spain. As before, the Inquisition's purpose was to seek out and reconvert heretics. Most rulers did not allow the Inquisition to operate in their domains. It was used mainly in parts of Italy.

Under Pope Paul IV the Index, a list of works considered dangerous to the Catholic faith, was established. Catholics were forbidden to read anything listed in the Index, nor could these works be sold in Catholic countries. In addition, existing copies of prohibited texts were destroyed, usually in large bonfires.

One of the most important aspects of the Counter Reformation was a great church council, convened by Pope Paul III in 1545 at Trent, a city in the Holy Roman Empire. The Council of Trent met three times between 1545 and 1563 to discuss theological issues. At this council, delegates reaffirmed most traditional Catholic beliefs concerning the sacraments, the Bible, and the role of priests, and strengthened the Church organization. They took care to specify exactly what the Catholic position was on such matters as indulgences, in order to avoid the kind of misinterpretation that had aroused Luther.

The Counter Reformation had a number of successes. In Spain and Italy, Protestantism failed to take hold. Areas that had substantial Protestant minorities, like southern Germany, France, Poland, Bohemia, and parts of the Netherlands, re-mained under Catholic control. But the Counter Reformation could not turn back the clock. It failed to reunify western Christendom, and Europe remained religiously divided, as it is today.

SECTION REVIEW

1. In your own words, briefly identify or define: Catherine of Aragon, Edward VI, *Institutes of the Christian Religion*, predestination, Servetus, Loyola, Council of Trent, Index.
2. Why did Henry VIII break with the Church of Rome?
3. How did Calvinism differ from Lutheranism?
4. What were the major steps taken by the Counter Reformation?
■ The Index was a form of censorship. What evidence of censorship do you see in our society today? How does it affect you?

The reforms ordered by the Council of Trent helped to restore the position of Catholicism in Europe. Identify the members of this council.

Reviewing the Chapter

1. What effects did the Black Death have on western Europe?
2. What were the most outstanding achievements of the Renaissance?
3. Who were the New Monarchs and what was their goal?
4. What event of this time had the greatest impact on western Europe? Why?
5. What were the goals of the Counter Reformation? Were they achieved?

Chapter Summary

The time between 1350 and 1600 was an era of transition in western Europe. In the mid-fourteenth century the Black Death raged over most of the continent, killing millions of Europeans. As a result, major changes occurred in west European society and economy. Technological advances of this era included navigational innovations and the printing press.

Renaissance humanism, which began in Italy and then spread northward, represented a fundamental departure from medieval attitudes toward the world. Classical learning was revived and in its wake came an outpouring of creative energy in literature, art, and architecture. Among the great works of this period are the sonnets of Petrarch, the paintings of Leonardo da Vinci and Michelangelo, and the works of Erasmus.

In the realm of politics, New Monarchs reestablished law and order after decades of turmoil. The Tudors of England, the Valois of France, and Ferdinand and Isabella of Spain strengthened the monarchy and created nation-states at the expense of the aristocracy.

The Protestant Reformation had a greater effect on west European society than any other single event of this time. Luther's message spread through Germany and Scandinavia. In England the Reformation was more a matter of politics than a reaction to church doctrine. Calvinism developed and became more widespread than Lutheranism. During the Counter Reformation the Roman Catholic Church tried to correct church abuses and took several steps to counteract the spread of Protestantism. However, it could not restore religious unity to western Europe.

Using Your Vocabulary

1. Why was the epidemic that devastated Europe called the Black Death? According to most historians, what was this disease?
2. What is *studia humanitatis?* What modern term is derived from this phrase? Why?
3. Define the term "universal" man. Name two historical figures who exemplify this concept and explain why.
4. What does the word perspective refer to in the art world? Who was the first person to develop this technique? What other connotation does this term have?
5. Explain the meaning of the term High Renaissance.
6. Who were the Christian humanists? Why were they so named?
7. What is *Utopia?* What does the term mean today?
8. Define the word bourgeoisie.
9. Who was Machiavelli? What does the term Machiavellian mean? Why?
10. Name two common Church practices that led to the call for reform in the sixteenth century.
11. What were the *Ninety-Five Theses?* Explain their historical importance.
12. What is a Diet? What was the political significance of the Diet of Worms in 1521?
13. Who were the first Protestants? How is the term used today?
14. Define the doctrine of predestination and explain why it was considered a radical concept.
15. What other term is used to describe the Catholic Reformation. Why?

Developing your Geography Skills

1. Use the map on page 280 to describe the location of the kingdoms of Sicily and Naples.
2. Use the map on page 320 to locate by means of longitude and latitude coordinates the cities of: Wittenberg, Worms, Trent, Geneva.
3. Use the map on page 320 to explain how Protestantism spread from Germany to Denmark, Sweden, and Norway.

Recalling the Facts

1. How did the Black Death change life in western Europe?
2. Name the work and the person who is given credit for the first printed book.
3. What course of study led to the development of humanism? Why?
4. Who was Petrarch? Why is he an important historical figure?
5. Name the important literary works of the Italian Renaissance. What aspects does each reveal about this period?
6. What Italian city is considered the center of the early Renaissance? Why?
7. Who is considered the first Renaissance painter? Why?
8. Explain why Erasmus is an important literary and historical figure.
9. What new technique in painting was developed in Flanders? Name the first artists to employ this technique.
10. What two new developments occurred in music during the Renaissance?
11. How did Spain's political position change during the reign of Ferdinand and Isabella?
12. Name three religious reformers of the fourteenth and fifteenth centuries.
13. Why did civil war break out in Germany in 1546? How was this conflict resolved? What other event in the sixteenth century caused political chaos in Germany?
14. How did the development of Anglicanism differ from Calvinism?
15. Who were the Jesuits? What was their role in the Counter Reformation?

Essay Questions

1. Why was the printing press such a great technological innovation? What effects did it have on society and culture?
2. Describe the characteristics of humanism and explain how it differed from medieval thought. How did humanistic concepts change society and culture?
3. Compare and contrast the Italian and Northern Renaissance with respect to art and literature.
4. Explain the characteristics of the New Monarchies and name the rulers that exemplify this type of government. Which west European countries did not develop New Monarchies? Why?
5. Describe the causes and effects of the Protestant Reformation. Why is this considered such an important historical event?
6. Explain the causes and effects of the English Reformation.
7. Compare and contrast the religious beliefs and practices of Lutheranism and Calvinism. Which had the greater impact? Explain.

Critical Thinking

1. The Renaissance has been characterized as the rebirth of culture and civilization. On what unstated assumptions is this claim based? Are these assumptions valid? Explain briefly.
2. The exact number of fatalities caused by the Black Death is unknown. What might this indicate about the reliability of source data from this period?
3. How does *The Book of the Courtier* reflect Renaissance values?
4. How might the procedures of the Court of Star Chamber have eliminated bias from judicial decisions?
5. Mary I of England was nicknamed "Bloody Mary." Based on the facts presented in this chapter, do you consider this to be a warranted or an unwarranted claim? Explain.
6. What value judgments does Machiavelli make in *The Prince?* Do you think he is correct? Why or why not?

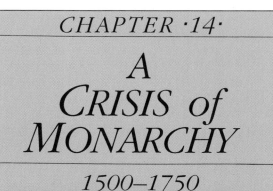

CHAPTER ·14·

A CRISIS of MONARCHY

1500–1750

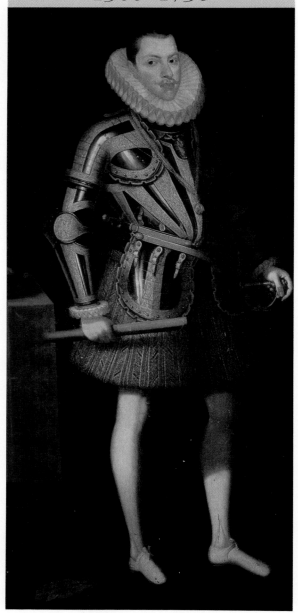

Objectives

- To describe the Spanish Empire in the sixteenth century

- To understand how religion and politics caused warfare in Europe during the sixteenth and seventeenth centuries

- To explain England's crisis in government and how it was resolved

- To describe the growth of absolutism in seventeenth-century France

*A*lthough medieval western Europe was split into many political entities, the Christian church gave a sense of unity to western civilization. By the end of the sixteenth century, or the first century of the modern period, this unity had been virtually destroyed. After the Protestant Reformation, there was no longer one universal church in western Europe. Latin was being replaced by vernacular languages, and Renaissance scholars abandoned the ideals of Scholasticism, favoring a more secular approach toward life and society's problems.

Europe in the early modern era was torn by conflict. Beginning in the mid-1500's, religion became a major justification for civil war and warfare between nations. Conflicts between nations in the sixteenth and seventeenth centuries also became dynastic wars, as various dynasties competed for power and more territory in Europe.

The techniques for warfare changed during this period. In the fourteenth century gunpowder was introduced into Europe from China and the Middle East. Guns began to replace bows and arrows. The introduction of artillery and improvements in the way the infantry fought made mounted knights obsolete. The infantry consisted mainly of mercenaries, or hired soldiers who might desert or refuse to fight if they were not paid. Troops were expected to live off the land they occupied. Innocent civilians often suffered as much as, if not more than, the actual combatants.

THE GOLDEN AGE OF SPAIN

Spain was the richest and strongest nation in sixteenth-century Europe. Under two powerful monarchs, Charles I and Philip II, it dominated much of Europe and vast overseas possessions.

One of the reasons for Spain's preeminence was its wealth, most of which came from gold and silver amassed in America. Another was its military force. Spain had the best professional army in Europe during the 1500's and developed a new way of fighting, which made its troops more effective in combat.

Charles I

In 1516 the grandson of Ferdinand and Isabella, a Hapsburg raised in Flanders, succeeded to the throne of Spain as Charles I. He had already inherited the Netherlands, and as king of Spain, Charles also ruled over Naples, Sicily, and Sardinia, as well as Spain's possessions in America. Then, in 1519, he was elected Holy Roman Emperor and received the title of Charles V. This position gave him at least nominal control of the largest European empire since Charlemagne's. The actual governing of this vast empire, however, proved to be a formidable task.

Charles was intelligent and capable, but he was not always able to shape the course of events as he wished. At first, the Spanish resented this foreigner because he filled government positions with Flemish nobles. His election as Holy Roman Emperor led to open opposition from the *Cortes*. In 1520 a popular revolt broke out but was quelled when Charles agreed to place Spanish subjects in administrative positions. In time, he became popular with his subjects, and it was said that he was "born a Fleming but grew up to be a Spaniard."

Far more serious than the Spanish revolt was the Protestant Reformation, which divided the Christian church shortly after Charles' succession to the imperial throne. As you have read, in order to bring peace to Germany, Charles had to go to war against the Lutheran princes. This conflict was ended by the Peace of Augsburg.

To protect his Hapsburg possessions, Charles had to face another formidable adversary—the Ottoman Turks. Since their capture of Constantinople in 1453, the Turks had carried on an aggressive program of expansion. In the early sixteenth century, under the strong leadership of Suleiman (SOO-lay-man) the Magnificent, the Turks pushed into Persia, Arabia, and North Africa. Most of Greece was already in Turkish hands, and other regions of eastern Europe were endangered. By 1526 the Turks occupied most of Hungary and had moved into Austria, laying siege to Vienna. Charles' forces were able to end the siege, and the Turks were pushed back into Hungary. Charles later led another successful military expedition against the Turks which resulted in the recapture of Tunis in 1535.

During most of his reign Charles was also at war with France mainly over domination of parts of the southern Netherlands and Italy. The peak of the war occurred in 1525 when Charles won a great victory at Pavia in Italy, and the French king, Francis I, was captured. Francis was released after he promised to give up his claims to the disputed territories and to cede Burgundy to Charles. Then he broke his word and the hostilities resumed. In 1527 Charles' imperial forces captured and sacked Rome. The war finally ended in 1529 with the signing of the Treaty of Cambrai (kam-BRAY). Francis agreed to renounce his claims to territories in the Netherlands and Italy, and Charles agreed to drop his claim to Burgundy. However, the peace was not permanent, and warfare would resume under Charles' successor.

In his later years Charles became increasingly devout. In 1556, tired and discouraged by his failure to eliminate Protestantism and defeat France, he disposed of his lands and titles and retired to a monastery. Spain, its overseas possessions, its Italian possessions, and the Netherlands went to Charles' son, Philip II. The remainder of the Holy Roman Empire went to Charles' brother, Ferdinand. Thus the Hapsburg dynasty was divided into two ruling families: the Spanish Hapsburgs and the Austrian Hapsburgs.

Philip II

In contrast to his father, Philip was raised as a Spaniard and his policies were generally well liked by his Spanish subjects. His other subjects, however, resented the heavy taxes he imposed and his policy of religious persecution. During Philip's reign Spain was constantly at war.

Philip's earliest wars were a continuation of his father's conflict with France over Italy. Peace was finally achieved with the signing of the Treaty of Cateau-Cambrésis (ka-TOE kam-bray-SEE) in 1559. The French agreed once more to stay out of Italy and, in return, gained territory in eastern Germany.

Philip also carried on his father's crusade by sending a Spanish fleet to take part in a naval expedition against the Ottomans. The combined European fleet won a great victory at the battle of Lepanto, off the coast of Greece, in 1571. This triumph, however, did not weaken Turkish power on land and three years later the Turks recaptured Tunis from the Spanish.

As a pious Catholic and a staunch defender of his faith, Philip used the Inquisition to keep Spain free of Protestantism, but failed elsewhere in Europe. His efforts to suppress Protestantism led to revolt in the Netherlands, and his wife, Mary Tudor, tried unsuccessfully to reinstate Catholi-

cism in England during her brief reign. After her death in 1558, Philip proposed marriage to her sister, Elizabeth, hoping in this way to gain English territories and convert Protestant England. She rejected his offer.

A major event of Philip's reign was the unification of the entire Iberian peninsula. In 1580 the Portuguese throne fell vacant and Philip inherited it through his mother, Isabella of Portugal. As a result, Spain gained control over Portugal's vast overseas empire, which remained under Spanish control for sixty years.

Philip was a diligent administrator and noted for his fondness of paper work. Distrustful of others, Philip insisted on making every decision concerning his empire. He created an immense bureaucracy to help him administer his many domains. During his reign Madrid became the capital, and Philip built a huge royal residence, the Escorial, some twenty-five miles to the northwest. There Philip set up rigidly formal rules of behavior which gave his court the reputation of being the gloomiest in Europe.

The Escorial's library contains 40,000 rare books, among them Teresa of Ávila's diary. Why would this be a valuable resource for historians?

In Las Meninas *Velásquez is painting the Princess Margarita. Her parents can be seen in the mirror. Why do experts believe he painted from a mirror image?*

By the end of Philip's reign, in 1598, Spain was facing an economic crisis. The wealth from its overseas possessions had been used to finance wars, and revenues were dwindling. Prices were constantly rising and a profitable source of income, the northern provinces of the Netherlands, had been lost. These factors would contribute to Spain's decline under Philip's successors.

Spain's Golden Age

Some of the greatest masterpieces of Spanish art and literature were created during the sixteenth and seventeenth centuries, partially as a result of the Spanish monarchs' patronage. This period is known as the *Siglo de Oro* (SEE-gloe day OR-oe), or the Golden Age.

One of the major literary figures of this period was Miguel de Cervantes (mee-GEL day sur-VAHN-tays). His masterpiece, *Don Quixote* (kee-HOE-tay), is often considered the first modern novel. In this work he describes the adventures of an idealistic but foolish knight, Don Quixote, and his squire, Sancho Panza. While ridiculing the medieval ideals of chivalry, Cervantes draws a realistic picture of sixteenth-century Spanish society and life.

Poetry also flourished during the Spanish Golden Age. In the sixteenth century Garcilaso de la Vega began to use Italian poetic forms in Spanish, and his works served as a model for Spanish poetry until about the mid-1600's. At this time a new poetic style, characterized by a sophisticated, complex sentence structure and vocabulary, emerged. The most representative poets were Luis de Góngora, Francisco de Quevedo (kay-VAY-doe), and Juana Inés de la Cruz.

Drama reached its peak during this time. The works of the two best-known playwrights, Lope de Vega and Calderón de la Barca, are still performed today. Lope was one of the most prolific writers of all time. It is believed that he wrote over 1,500 plays, although only about 400 survive. Lope broke all of the dramatic conventions of the time and developed new characters, such as the fool, in order to please his audiences.

While Lope's plays appealed to the general public, Calderón's were for a more intellectual audience. His one-act religious plays, and his longer dramas, such as *Life Is A Dream*, explore philosophical, moral, and theological questions.

As part of the Catholic reform movement a new literary theme, Christian mysticism, appeared in sixteenth-century Spain. It was based on the belief that one could attain spiritual truth and commune with God through meditation and prayer. The *Spiritual Exercises* of Ignatius of Loyola is one example of this type of writing. Another are the works of Teresa of Ávila, which describe her spiritual experiences and philosophy. A strong reformer with great organizational ability, Teresa founded a new order of Carmelite nuns and established many convents. Her work influenced John of the Cross, another great reformer of the Carmelite Order and author of some of the most beautiful religious poetry to be found in any language.

Mysticism was also reflected in the Spanish painting of the seventeenth century. Through the use of light and shadow, gestures, and facial expressions, the artists of this period managed to convey deep religious emotion. Among the best examples of this style are the works of El Greco and Zurbarán.

El Greco was also a great painter of portraits, but the undisputed master was Diego Velásquez (vay-LAHS-kayz), the court painter of Philip IV, Philip II's grandson. Velásquez's most famous painting, *Las Meninas,* is a realistic portrait of the king's young daughter with her ladies-in-waiting.

SECTION REVIEW

1. In your own words, briefly define or identify: dynastic wars, Treaty of Cateau-Cambrésis, Escorial, Cervantes, Lope de Vega, El Greco, Velásquez.
2. Summarize the military campaigns of Charles I.
3. List the accomplishments of Philip II. What were the negative effects of his reign?
4. Why are the sixteenth and seventeenth centuries in Spain considered the Golden Age?
■ In the early sixteenth century, some Europeans were afraid that Charles V would establish a universal monarchy. Do you think it would be possible for any one person or government to gain complete control over Europe today?

A CENTURY OF RELIGIOUS WARFARE

As you know, the rise of Lutheranism, Calvinism, and Anglicanism occurred in the first half of the sixteenth century. The Counter Reformation was also launched to combat these new doctrines. Hardly anyone at this time believed in religious toleration, or freedom of religion. Protestants wanted to reform their faiths, and Catholics wanted to reconvert all those who had abandoned the Church's teachings. About 1550 the conflict between Protestants and Catholics led to persecution and to a series of savage wars.

The French Religious Wars

During the reign of Francis I, in the early sixteenth century, Calvinism won many followers among France's nobility and middle class. The Huguenots, or French Calvinists, were especially strong in southern France. According to one estimate, almost one-fifth of the French population was Protestant by the 1550's.

Both Francis I and his successor, Henry II, wanted to abolish Protestantism but they were too involved in foreign wars, mainly against Spain, to devote their full attention to the matter. The oldest son of Henry II, Francis II, died after ruling only a year and a half. His two younger brothers, who reigned one after the other as Charles IX and Henry III, were dominated by their mother, Catherine de Medici (MAY-dee-chee), the chief power behind the French throne from 1560 to 1589.

Catherine was intelligent and shrewd, but her frequent resort to political intrigue had disastrous effects. Even though she was a Catholic, she did not want the major Catholic noble family, the Guises (GEEZ-uhz), to become too powerful, so she occasionally supported the Huguenot cause. By playing one side against the other, she encouraged years of civil strife that left France exhausted.

Civil war first broke out in France in 1562, and the fighting between Huguenots and Catholics continued off and on for over thirty-five years. Truces were arranged from time to time, but they brought little real peace.

This tapestry depicts Catherine de Medici entertaining the Polish ambassadors. In what ways is this scene similar to a State dinner at the White House?

In 1572 the leading Catholic and Huguenot families gathered in Paris to attend the wedding of Charles IX's sister to Henry of Navarre, the Huguenot prince of a tiny independent kingdom between France and Spain. During the celebrations, Catherine convinced Charles that the Huguenots were plotting to kill him and persuaded the king to sign an order authorizing the murder of the Protestant leaders.

Shortly after midnight on August 24—St. Bartholomew's Day—armed mobs stormed through Paris breaking into Huguenot homes, looting them, and killing their inhabitants. All the chief Protestant leaders, except Henry of Navarre, were murdered along with at least 3,000 other Huguenots. This uprising, called the St. Bartholomew's Day Massacre, led to further violence in the provinces.

In 1589 Henry III was assassinated. The next in line for the throne was Henry of Navarre. As Henry IV, he became the first monarch of a new dynasty, the Bourbons.

To restore political order to France, Henry had to defeat the Catholic nobles, who refused to accept his authority. In 1594 he became a Catholic, because the majority of his subjects were Catholic and he wished to win their loyalty. To the French a non-Catholic king was inconceivable. When Henry took up residence in the royal palace in Paris, he was said to have remarked that "Paris is well worth a Mass."

Henry brought an end to the religious wars by issuing the Edict of Nantes (NAHNT) in 1598. This proclamation gave Protestants the right to hold private services in their homes and public services in some cities and towns. It also permitted them to hold certain government offices and to retain over more than a hundred fortified towns.

Revolt in the Netherlands

As you have read, Charles V gave his possessions in the Netherlands to his son, Philip II of Spain, when he abdicated in 1556. Charles, who had been born in Flanders, was always popular in the Low Countries, but his son was almost universally hated.

The Low Countries in the sixteenth century consisted of seventeen provinces that had long been governed by a single prince, but they retained a strong sense of individual identity. People in the north spoke Dutch or Flemish, two closely related Germanic dialects, and those in the south spoke mainly French. By the middle of the sixteenth century, these provinces were also divided by their religion because Calvinism had won numerous followers in the cities and among the lesser nobility.

When Philip II took over the administration of the Low Countries he made many changes that were resented by its inhabitants. He reorganized the Church in order to gain greater control over it, causing a loss of the nobles' rights of patronage. To pay for his endless wars, Philip imposed new taxes on merchants and businessmen. Everyone objected to the quartering of Spanish troops in the Netherlands. When Philip tried to make use of the Inquisition to strengthen Catholicism and his power, a group of Protestant nobles petitioned him to stop. Philip's refusal was the culminating factor in the growing opposition to his rule.

In 1566 there was an outbreak of violence, in which Calvinists broke into Catholic churches, causing widespread destruction. As a result, Philip sent the ruthless duke of Alba along with a large Spanish army to subdue the uprising. As governor of the Netherlands the duke established a court called the Council of Troubles, better known as the

RELIGIONS IN EUROPE ABOUT 1600

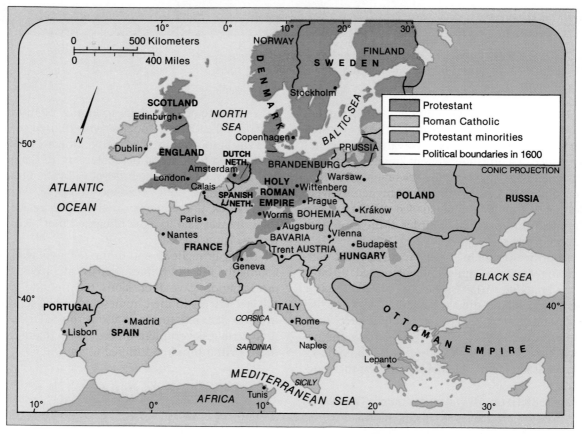

Explain why Europe by 1600 had been divided by Catholicism and Protestantism.

Queen Elizabeth rode to Tilbury, near London, to assure herself of the Spanish Armada's defeat. Why do you think so many people accompanied her?

Council of Blood, to deal with the rebels. This council ordered the arrest and execution of many Protestants and seized the property of others.

In retaliation bands of local seamen, called sea beggars, attacked Spanish ships and garrisons in port towns. In 1572 one band flying the flag of William of Orange captured Brill, a village on the North Sea. As a result of this success, many rebel leaders rallied around William of Orange.

William was determined to drive the Spanish out of the Low Countries. In 1579 he formed an alliance called the Union of Utrecht (YOO-trekt), but only the seven northern provinces joined. These provinces declared their independence in 1581 and then fought a lengthy war to win it.

The freedom of the United Provinces, or those provinces that joined the Union of Utrecht, was not officially recognized until 1648. Today this northern area is known as the Netherlands. The other ten provinces in the south, known first as the Spanish Netherlands, then as the Austrian Netherlands, now form Belgium.

The Spanish Armada

One of William's allies in his struggle against Spain was Elizabeth I of England, who distrusted the Spanish. Philip II had had designs on England ever since his marriage to Mary Tudor. When Elizabeth rejected his offer of marriage, he decided to support Mary Stuart, the queen of Scotland, who was next in line for the English throne and a Catholic. In 1568 Mary took refuge in England after she was driven out of her own country by Calvinist nobles. While Mary was in England, Elizabeth kept her under house arrest, for she was the center of many Catholic plots against the crown.

At first Elizabeth kept English financial aid to the United Provinces a secret because she feared open warfare with Spain. In 1585, however, she changed her policy and sent several thousand troops to fight alongside the Dutch. At the same time she permitted English pirates, such as Sir Francis Drake, to rob Spanish ships loaded with treasure from the New World.

As a result, Philip decided to invade England, to depose Elizabeth, and to put Mary on the throne. His plan was to send a huge fleet to attack the English coast. As the Spanish made their preparations, Elizabeth had Mary Stuart executed. Thus revenge was added to Philip's motives.

The Spanish Armada set sail from Lisbon in May 1588. With 130 ships and 22,000 men, it was the biggest naval attack force the world had ever seen. When it reached the English Channel, it was met by about 100 English ships. Since these small vessels were no match for the large ships of the Spanish fleet, the English maintained a distance and fired with long-range artillery.

After about a week of warfare, the Spanish were running out of supplies and their commander decided to dock at Calais, France. The English drove them away by barricading the harbor entrance with eight burning ship hulks. The Spanish, fleeing the fireships, were then buffeted by a fierce storm that arose in the Channel. This "Protestant wind," as the Spanish called it, drove them north into the unfamiliar waters of the North and Irish seas. The storms continued, and food and water gave out. Many of the ships went down off the coast of Ireland, and thousands of Spaniards lost their lives. When the Armada arrived home in the fall, half the fleet had been destroyed.

The failure of the Armada was a terrible blow to Philip, and he abandoned his plans for invading England. England's victory showed the world that the Spanish were not invincible and proved its superior seafaring ability.

The Thirty Years' War

The last and worst of Europe's religious conflicts, the Thirty Years' War, began in 1618. Although this war was fought mainly in German territories, most of Europe became involved in the struggle.

One of the fundamental causes of the Thirty Years' War was the religious split in the German states. Theoretically the dispute had been solved by the Peace of Augsburg, which allowed rulers to choose between Catholicism and Lutheranism. However, it had made no provision for Calvinism, which had spread to many areas of the Holy Roman Empire.

Dynastic ambitions also underlay the Thirty Years' War. The Austrian Hapsburgs wanted to strengthen their position in central Europe, and they were threatening France. The Spanish Hapsburgs were still fighting the Dutch in the Netherlands, hoping to restore this region to Spain's empire. Denmark and Sweden wished to gain German territories bordering the Baltic Sea.

The Thirty Years' War broke out in the city of Prague in Bohemia, a kingdom in the Holy Roman Empire. By the early 1600's many Bohemians were Protestants, and they had been guaranteed religious toleration by the Holy Roman Emperor Rudolf II in 1609. When Ferdinand II succeeded to the Bohemian throne in 1617, he refused to honor this pledge because he was determined to reinstate Catholicism in all his territories. As a result, the Bohemians deposed Ferdinand, placed the Calvinist Frederick V on the throne, and the struggle began. In 1619 Ferdinand became the Holy Roman Emperor and used the imperial armies to crush the Bohemian Protestants.

The defeat of the Bohemians alarmed Protestant rulers both within and outside the empire. Those in the German states, fearful that Ferdinand would impose Catholicism throughout the empire, banded together and sought foreign assistance against him. Leadership of the anti-imperial struggle was taken up by Christian IV, the Protestant king of Denmark, but he was soon defeated.

In 1629 the emperor issued the Edict of Restitution which restored all German property taken from the Catholic Church since 1552. Ferdinand's move alarmed France and Sweden. King Gustavus Adolphus II of Sweden, a devout Lutheran, superb tactician, and leader of Europe's best-trained army, entered the war in 1630 with France's support. The Swedes won brilliant victories until Gustavus Adolphus was killed in battle.

The final phase of the war became a great international struggle waged for the most part on German soil. The Spanish Hapsburgs allied themselves with the Holy Roman emperors and the French and Dutch joined the Swedish and German

Do you think the walls of a city were an effective defense in the Thirty Years' War?

Protestants. All the participants finally agreed to cease fighting in 1648.

The Peace of Westphalia (west-FAYL-yuh), ending the Thirty Years' War, is significant in European history. Not only did it end a century of religious conflict, but it also represented a new trend in international relations because all of the participants in the war attended the peace conference. One of the major provisions was the inclusion of Calvinism among the Protestant faiths a ruler could choose. Other provisions gave France some Hapsburg territories on the western border of the empire and Sweden some on the northern border along the North and Baltic seas. The Hapsburgs were also forced to recognize the independence of the Dutch Netherlands and Switzerland, and the German princes were given almost complete independence from the Holy Roman Emperor. Some German states lost or gained territory.

The Thirty Years' War had long-lasting effects on Europe. Spain's power was weakened and France now dominated Europe. In Germany the war had caused widespread destruction, the economy had been ruined, and about a third of the German population had been killed. The Peace of Westphalia left little hope of Germany establishing a strong, unified nation since it was now formally divided into hundreds of independent states.

The Peace of Westphalia ended the fear of Hapsburg domination of the Continent, or the establishment of a universal monarchy. A new political system emerged based on **the balance of power,** or a system of alliances between nations that prevented one side from gaining more power than another. This system has served as a basis for international politics up to modern times.

SECTION REVIEW

1. Mapping: Use the map on page 320 to name the major Protestant and Catholic countries. In what countries were both religions practiced?
2. In your own words, briefly identify or define: Catherine de Medici, St. Bartholomew's Day Massacre, duke of Alba, William of Orange, Mary Stuart, Spanish Armada, Christian IV, Gustavus Adolphus.
3. What was the cause for civil war in France? How was it resolved?
4. Why did the Dutch revolt during the reign of Philip II? What were the results of this conflict?
5. What were the causes and effects of the Thirty Years' War?
- Does religion sometimes play a role in modern conflicts? Explain your answer.

THE PURITAN REVOLUTION IN ENGLAND

As you know, religion played an important role in English politics during the sixteenth century. Conflict between Protestants and Catholics was constant and religious persecution severe. Only under Elizabeth was peace reestablished in England. However, after her death, the religious problems facing England reached crisis proportions.

The Elizabethan Age

Elizabeth I, the daughter of Henry VIII and Anne Boleyn, came to the throne of England in 1558 and ruled for almost fifty years. Her reign was a time of peace and prosperity, and she was one of England's most beloved and successful monarchs.

Elizabeth was a shrewd leader who put the interests of her country above her own personal desires. She pursued a skillful foreign policy and kept England out of most European wars and expensive entanglements overseas. To protect her country from invasion, she encouraged the growth of the English navy. Although she never married, she used the possibility of marriage to gain concessions in foreign negotiations from both allies and opponents.

Elizabeth maintained domestic peace by following a policy of religious moderation. Nevertheless, religious differences caused much discontent. The Catholics and the Calvinists opposed the Anglican religion instituted by her father. After the execution of Mary Stuart and the defeat of the Spanish Armada, the Catholics did not pose much of a threat. The Calvinists, on the other hand, wanted the Anglican Church to make additional

Many of Shakespeare's plays were presented in London at the Globe Theater. In his time there were few props, but elaborate costumes. Playhouses flew flags to announce performances.

reforms because they believed it followed Roman Catholicism too closely. Since these reformers aimed to purify the Church of England, they were called Puritans. Elizabeth coped with the Puritans mainly by avoiding confrontation, but religious tension was rising.

Elizabeth was a patron of the arts and the English renaissance in literature occurred in the latter part of her reign. Edmund Spenser is among the most famous writers of this period. He wrote *The Faerie Queene,* which is an allegorical poem glorifying Elizabeth.

English drama reached its peak in the works of William Shakespeare, one of the most famous playwrights of all time. His comedies and tragedies, based on timeless themes such as love, envy, and greed, still intrigue audiences to this day. Two other notable dramatists were Ben Jonson and Christopher Marlowe.

The Beginning of Stuart Rule

Since Elizabeth left no heirs, the son of Mary Stuart, the king of Scotland, was next in line for the English throne. In 1603 he became King James I, the first of the Stuart dynasty.

James did not understand the English people and his political philosophy was contrary to English tradition. He believed that monarchs had a right to rule with few limits to their power and that they were answerable only to God, who had given them their authority. This theory, known as the **divine right of kings,** is one of the foundations of **absolutism,** or rule by monarchs who regard themselves as being above the law. Thus James disregarded the tradition that Parliament and the king must share power.

James' beliefs led to a power struggle between king and legislature. Parliament was determined not to let James deprive it of its part in governing England, so the king tried to govern as if it did not exist. He instituted new measures of taxation without Parliament's consent, ignored judges whose verdicts displeased him, and imprisoned some of his political opponents who served in Parliament.

As a divine right monarch, James was determined to uphold the Church of England as the established church. This meant that all of his subjects had to attend services, pay taxes to support the Church, and conform to its beliefs and practices.

The Pilgrims emigrated to America to escape religious persecution. What hardships did they face there? How does their dress reflect their beliefs?

When the Puritans petitioned James to revise some of these practices, the monarch refused and threatened to "harry the Puritans out of the land." This anti-Puritan stand worsened his relations with Parliament, for the House of Commons contained many Puritan sympathizers.

As a result of James' persecution, many Puritans moved to Holland in search of religious freedom. Others emigrated to the New World and founded the Plymouth Colony in New England in 1620. These settlers became known as Pilgrims.

One of the greatest accomplishments of James' reign was an English translation of the Bible sponsored by the king. This Bible, known as the King James Version, appeared in 1611 and is still used by many Protestants today.

Charles I and Civil War

When James died in 1625, he was succeeded by his son, Charles I, another absolutist. Like his father, Charles tried to raise money without parliamentary consent by using forced loans and imprisoning people who failed to pay. The power struggle between monarch and Parliament reached its peak in 1628 when Parliament issued the Petition of Right. Among other things, this petition demanded an end to imprisonment without cause and taxation without the consent of Parliament. The king agreed to the petition, because he wanted Parliament to grant him money to carry on war with France and Spain, but he did not honor it.

In 1629 Charles decided to end opposition to his policies by dissolving Parliament. For eleven years he governed without Parliament, raising money by reviving old feudal dues and punishing opponents through secret proceedings of the Court of Star Chamber. His authoritarian rule turned many of his subjects against him. Religious persecution of the Puritans continued and resulted in further emigration to America and the founding of the Massachusetts Bay Colony in 1630.

When Charles tried to impose Anglicanism on the Scots, who were mainly Calvinist, they took up arms and invaded the north of England. Thus, Charles needed money to raise an army, and only a newly elected Parliament could persuade the English to pay additional taxes. So Charles summoned one in 1640. Taking advantage of the king's situation, Parliament tried to limit his powers before acceding to his demands. Charles dissolved this so-called Short Parliament in a month. Then he had to summon another one, called the Long Parliament because it was in session off and on for twenty years.

The Long Parliament was determined to exert its authority and passed a series of acts limiting the monarch's powers. It abolished the royal courts, such as the Court of Star Chamber, and passed the Triennial Act, which provided that Parliament should meet every three years, whether or not it was called into session. Parliament also dismissed the king's chief minister and the archbishop of Canterbury for abuses of their power and later had them executed.

In 1641 some members of Parliament proposed the abolition of all bishops of the Anglican Church. In response, the king invaded the House of Commons January 1642 with 400 soldiers, planning to arrest the key leaders of Parliament for treason, but they escaped. Then Parliament demanded, among other things, that it be given control over the armed forces. The king refused and both sides began to assemble armies. Civil war had begun.

The royalist cause, strongest in the north and west of the country, was supported mainly by the Anglican upper classes and gentry. The royalists were called Cavaliers because they dressed like elegant courtiers and wore their hair in long curls. Those who opposed the king, the Parliamentarians, consisted chiefly of middle-class Puritans and city workers. They cut their hair short to indicate anti-aristocratic bias and were nicknamed Roundheads.

At the beginning of the war, there were victories on both sides, but the Parliamentarians had an excellent military leader in Oliver Cromwell, a Puritan landowner and a member of Parliament. The New Model Army that he led was full of zealous, disciplined nonconformists, who marched into battle singing hymns. Charles' troops suffered a disastrous defeat at Naseby in 1645, and one year later he surrendered. Charles subsequently escaped, but was recaptured. In January 1649 the king was tried by Parliament, convicted of being "a tyrant, traitor, murderer, and public enemy," and he was beheaded.

The Interregnum

For the next eleven years there was no monarch in England. Thus this period is called the Interregnum, the Latin word for between reigns. In theory the government, called the Commonwealth, was a republic in which Cromwell and his army shared power with Parliament. In practice, however, Cromwell ruled England as a military dictator.

Under Cromwell religious toleration was decreed for everyone except atheists and Catholics, but Puritanism predominated. Alehouses and theaters were closed, and magistrates tried to enforce strict standards of morality. The majority of the English resented these policies as much as Cromwell's heavy taxes and confiscation of royalist property.

Cromwell's policies were also resented elsewhere. In 1649 his army crushed a royalist rebellion in Ireland by massacring thousands, including women and children. The ancestral estates of many Irish landowners were given to new English landlords. It is little wonder that Cromwell's name is still hated in Ireland.

As you have read, Charles I was the king of Scotland and England. After he was executed by the English, the Scots proclaimed Charles' son king and he led a revolt against Cromwell in 1650. Cromwell's army soundly defeated the Scots, and Charles II, in disguise, managed to hide from Cromwell's soldiers for forty days before escaping to France.

In hopes of increasing English trade, Cromwell had the Parliament pass the first Navigation Act banning goods from entering the country except on board English vessels. This act hurt the Dutch, many of whom made their living through commerce. In 1652 the Dutch went to war against En-

At first Cromwell and Parliament ruled England together. In 1653 Cromwell dissolved Parliament. Why? What leaders today govern without an elected legislative body?

gland, but the English won most of the battles which were fought at sea. Peace was restored in 1654.

Cromwell's rule was as arbitrary as that of an absolute monarch. When Parliament disagreed with him, he dismissed it. He then had trouble governing and so, in 1655, he divided England into military districts, appointing army officers to govern each one. Cromwell declined to be king, but he did consent to be called Lord Protector of the Commonwealth, a title he wanted passed on to his descendants. When Cromwell died in 1658, his son Richard proved unable to control the army, so Parliament asked Charles II to return from France.

The Restoration

The reign of Charles II, from 1660 to 1685, is called the Restoration because the monarchy, the House of Lords, and the authority of the Church of England were all reinstated.

Religion was still a problem, because Charles sympathized with Catholicism and his brother James was a practicing Catholic. Charles tried unsuccessfully to end religious discrimination against Catholics and to restore their civil rights. Parliament, however, responded with the Test Act, requiring that all public offices be held by members of the Anglican Church.

England's first political parties were formed during this time around the religious issue. The Tories, who favored the monarchy, drew most of their support from lesser nobles and the country gentry. In contrast, the Whigs, mainly upper class aristocrats and middle-class business people, were opposed to Catholic influence in England and favored a strong Parliament. They tried to prevent the succession of James to the throne by having Parliament pass the Exclusion Act. The Tories defeated this legislation by accepting passage of the Habeas Corpus Act in 1679.

The Habeas Corpus Act contained important guarantees of individual rights. It provided a prisoner with the right to request a judge to issue a document, called a **writ of habeas corpus,** directing authorities to bring the prisoner to court and to state the reasons for the arrest. Thus an individual was protected against arrest and imprisonment without cause. This act also provided for speedy trials and established the principle that anyone set free by a court could not be imprisoned a second time for the same offense.

James II and the Glorious Revolution

In 1685 Charles II was succeeded by his brother, James II. James tried to restore Catholicism in England by replacing high army officers with Catholics. In 1687 he ignored the Test Act and placed many Catholics in important government positions.

The situation became critical in 1688 when his second wife, a Catholic, gave birth to a son. This meant that Protestant England would have a Catholic monarchy for many years to come. To prevent further Catholic rule, English political leaders invited James' older daughter, Mary, and her Protestant husband, William of Orange, to take over the throne. The two accepted, and William landed in England with an army. James' troops refused to fight, so James fled to safety in France. This bloodless uprising of 1688 is known as the **Glorious Revolution.**

The overthrow of James II was a victory for Parliament for it had removed a king whose politics it disliked and replaced him with monarchs of its own choosing. William and Mary were not the most immediate heirs to the throne, but they owed their position to Parliament. From this time on, no English monarch could claim to rule by divine right. The Glorious Revolution proved that monarchs ruled only by consent of the governed and established a new constitutional principle.

Reforms and the Succession

William III and Mary ruled together from 1689 until her death in 1694, after which William was the sole monarch. The English felt a sense of relief at the end to the bitter religious and political controversies that had plagued their nation. Parliamentary leaders, however, wanted to guarantee that similar problems would not arise in the future. So they passed the Bill of Rights and the Act of Settlement.

The Bill of Rights prohibited certain practices such as suspension of laws, and it guaranteed English subjects some civil rights, like freedom of speech in Parliament. No provision of the Bill of

This picture shows the speaker of the House of Lords offering William and Mary the English crown. When and how is a new President officially given the power of his office? Compare the two ceremonies.

Rights has ever been repealed, and it forms a fundamental part of the English constitution. Unlike the Constitution of the United States, England's constitution is not a single document; instead it is a series of important decrees, acts of Parliament, and traditions.

Since William and Mary had no children, the Act of Settlement was passed in 1701 in order to keep the heirs of James II, who were Catholics, from succeeding to the throne. Upon the monarch's death, Mary's sister Anne received the crown.

During Anne's reign, from 1702 to 1714, the Kingdoms of England and Scotland were united. Together with Ireland and Wales, these territories became known as the United Kingdom of Great Britain. After Anne's death the crown passed to distant relatives who ruled the German Electorate of Hanover.

Constitutional Change

The first Hanoverian king, George I, who ruled from 1714 to 1727, was more interested in his continental possessions than in England. This was one of the factors that led to constitutional change in Britain during the eighteenth century.

Cabinet government was a fundamental development in this change. For centuries, English monarchs had relied on advisers. The most important of these, the ministers of the crown, headed specialized departments, such as the Exchequer, and formed the cabinet. During the reign of George I the cabinet was dominated by Sir Robert Walpole, who is now regarded by many historians as the first prime minister of England.

The cabinet, as it developed under Walpole and his successors, was responsible for drawing up and carrying out government policy. Every cabinet minister was a member of Parliament and expected to defend government measures in open debate in the legislature. The leader of the majority party in the House of Commons became prime minister and selected ministers from his party. If Parliament voted down an important measure proposed by the cabinet, declaring a no-confidence vote, Parliament was dissolved and new elections were held. This step usually resulted in the selection of a new prime minister and cabinet.

The development of cabinet government signaled the paramount position of the House of Commons, for members of the House of Lords did not serve in the cabinet.

By the nineteenth century England had become a **limited constitutional monarchy,** because the power of its rulers had been limited by the Magna Carta, the Bill of Rights, acts of Parliament, and the traditions of cabinet government. Britain was far from being democratic, however. Only property owners could vote, and several groups, like the Catholics, were still forbidden to hold public office. Also, women could not vote or hold office either.

SECTION REVIEW

1. In your own words, briefly identify or define: Shakespeare, divine right of kings, Pilgrims, Restoration, Tories, Whigs, Test Act, writ of habeas corpus, Walpole.
2. Briefly describe the domestic and foreign policies of Elizabeth I.
3. List the events that led up to the English civil war.
4. Explain why Cromwell was considered a military dictator.
5. What were the causes and effects of the Glorious Revolution?
6. List the main features of English cabinet government.
■ In England the prime minister and cabinet must resign if Parliament votes against them on an important issue. How does this system differ from the relationship between our president and Congress? What advantages and disadvantages do you see in the two systems?

ABSOLUTISM IN FRANCE

Henry IV, who came to the French throne at the end of the sixteenth century, restored peace and prosperity. As you have read, he ended the religious conflict in France by issuing the Edict of Nantes in 1598. Under the direction of his capable minister, the Duke de Sully, taxes were reduced, and industry, agriculture, and commerce were encouraged. As a result, France's financial and economic situation greatly improved. It is said that Henry wanted every family to have a "chicken in the pot on Sunday."

Richelieu and Mazarin

When Henry IV was assassinated by a religious fanatic in 1610, his successor, Louis XIII, was still a child. Henry's wife, Marie de Medici, served as Regent for several years, but had difficulty suppressing the nobility's opposition. Firm leadership,

Richelieu was a cardinal and head of the royal council. Which position gave him more power?

SOURCES

The Bill of Rights, 1689

England's Bill of Rights begins by summarizing the events of the Glorious Revolution and stating the purpose of this document. The introduction is followed by thirteen numbered provisions and a final section dealing with the succession to the throne. A portion of the introduction and all thirteen provisions are given here.

Whereas the said King James II having abdicated the government, and the throne being vacant, his Highness the prince of Orange . . . did cause letters to be written . . . for the choosing of such persons to meet and sit at Westminster upon the two-and-twentieth day of January, in this year 1689, in order . . . that their religion, laws, and liberties might not be in danger of being subverted; upon which letters elections have been accordingly made. . . . The lords spiritual and temporal [the House of Lords] and Commons . . . being now assembled in a full and free representation of this nation . . . for the vindicating and asserting their ancient rights and liberties, declare:

1. That the pretended power of suspending laws, or the execution of laws, by regal authority, without consent of parliament, is illegal.

2. That the pretended power of dispensing with laws, or the execution of laws, by regal authority, as it hath been assumed and exercised of late, is illegal.

3. That the commission for erecting the late court of commissioners for ecclesiastical causes, and all other commissions and courts of like nature, are illegal and pernicious.

4. That levying money for or to the use of the crown by pretense of prerogative, without grant of parliament, for longer time or in other manner than the same is or shall be granted, is illegal.

5. That it is the right of the subjects to petition the king, and all commitments and prosecutions for such petitioning are illegal.

6. That the raising or keeping a standing army within the kingdom in time of peace, unless it be with consent of parliament, is against law.

7. That the subjects which are Protestants may have arms for their defense suitable to their conditions, and as allowed by law.

8. That election of members of parliament ought to be free.

9. That the freedom of speech, and debates or proceedings in parliament, ought not to be impeached or questioned in any court of place out of parliament.

10. That excessive bail ought not to be required, nor excessive fines imposed, nor cruel and unusual punishments inflicted.

11. That jurors ought to be duly impaneled and returned, and jurors which pass upon men in trials for high treason ought to be freeholders.

12. That all grants and promises of fines and forfeitures of particular persons before conviction are illegal and void.

13. And that for redress of all grievances, and for the amending, strengthening, and preserving of the laws, parliament ought to be held.

Source: Edward P. Cheyney, *Readings in English History Drawn from the Original Sources.* Copyright 1908 by Ginn & Co.

1. Why was Parliment called into session in January 1689?
2. Which provisions limit the power of the English monarch?
3. What rights are guaranteed to each citizen?
4. Which provisions in the English Bill of Rights are also found in the United States Constitution?
5. Which of these provisions do you think is the most important? Why?

however, was restored when Cardinal Richelieu (REE-shul-yoo) replaced Marie as the power behind the throne.

Richelieu, as chief minister of Louis XIII, was the real ruler of France from 1624 until his death in 1642. Cold, shrewd, and ambitious, Richelieu was devoted to France and believed that a strong monarchy with unlimited authority was the best government for the nation.

To strengthen the monarchy and avoid the possibility of civil war, Richelieu decided to limit the military power the Huguenots wielded through their control of several fortified key towns. Huguenot forces protested against this policy and rose up against the monarchy. After a long siege one of their major strongholds, La Rochelle, was captured and Huguenot resistance was ended. In 1629 Richelieu issued the Edict of Grace which deprived the Huguenots of the privilege of governing towns, but allowed them to keep their religious freedom.

To undermine the nobles' power Richelieu placed royal officials, who were dependent on him, in various parts of the country to supervise local governments. These officials ruled in the king's name, and if they did not carry out his policy, they were immediately dismissed. This system helped Richelieu create an effective central administration.

In foreign affairs Richelieu tried to weaken the Hapsburgs' power, because they wanted to gain territory in France. As you have read, France played an active role in the Thirty Years' War, and the Peace of Westphalia embodied many of Richelieu's aims even though it was signed after his death.

Richelieu was better at diplomacy than finance. In order to pay the cost of his wars and the salaries of his many officials, the peasants were heavily taxed. This practice was resented and later led to revolt.

Perhaps the cardinal's most enduring legacy was his establishment of the French Academy, an organization of important literary persons. Today the academy is famous for its exhaustive dictionary of the French language and for the literary prizes it awards.

In 1643, a year after Richelieu's death, Louis XIII died. Again the French throne was occupied by a child monarch, Louis XIV, but this time Richelieu's hand-picked successor, Cardinal Mazarin (MAZ-uh-rin), had already begun to rule the country. Mazarin's continuation of Richelieu's economic and foreign policies led to a series of rebellions between 1648 and 1653, known as the Fronde.

Revolt first broke out in Paris when Mazarin refused to accede to the Parlement's demands for economic and administrative reforms. It then spread to other areas. Nobles allied themselves with the middle and lower classes in the effort to reduce Mazarin's authority but order was restored by the royal troops.

Louis XIV

When Mazarin died in 1661, Louis XIV was twenty-two, and he was determined to govern France personally. During his reign, absolutism reached its peak. Louis's concept of the monarchy is best expressed by his statement: "It is for kings to make their own decisions, for no one else either dares or is able to suggest any that are as good or as royal as those which we make ourselves."

Louis was not only a strong believer in the divine right of kings, but was quite free to govern as he saw fit because there was no representative assembly in the realm to check royal power, as in England. The Estates-General, a type of parliament, had been convened only once during the reign of Louis XIII and did not meet again until the late eighteenth century. Whether or not Louis actually said, "L'état, c'est moi." ("I am the state."), the statement is appropriate.

Louis hated Paris, mainly because when he lived there as a boy he had been frightened by popular uprisings during the Fronde. So he had a magnificent palace built at Versailles (vur-SIE), about ten miles from the capital. No expense was spared in constructing its hundreds of rooms and extensive formal gardens. Its cost will never be known, for the king himself was so appalled by the staggering bills that he burned the records.

Louis maintained a lavish court at Versailles. Hundreds of aristocrats lived in the palace or nearby and spent their days in attendance on the king. Nobles vied for the privilege of handing Louis his shirt when he dressed or of dining at his table. It was forbidden to discuss affairs of state at Versailles. Courtiers spent their time gossiping,

This painting depicts Louis XIV and his escort entering the palace at Versailles. Would you have liked to live there? Why or why not?

playing cards, and attending balls and theatrical performances. By keeping the French nobility under royal scrutiny and dependent on him for their prestige, Louis managed to control their desire for power and independence, something no other French monarch had achieved.

Domestic Policies

Although court life was frivolous, Louis worked diligently at administering his realm. He used his predecessors' system of royal officials to create an effective bureaucracy, and he appointed capable men to advise him.

Jean Baptiste Colbert (bah-TEEST kawl-BAIR), Louis' finance minister, worked to improve the French economy and to provide sufficient funds to support the king's foreign wars and extravagant life style. Like many political leaders of the time, Colbert advocated **mercantilism,** which based a nation's wealth on the amount of gold and silver in its treasury. According to this theory, the best way for a country to accumulate these precious metals was to export more than it imported, or to maintain a favorable **balance of trade.** This bal-

ance could be achieved only through strict government regulation.

As a mercantilist, Colbert encouraged manufacturing and commerce and tried to make the national economy self-sufficient. He established royal factories to make furniture, textiles, and various luxury goods for export. Other subsidized companies built ships to encourage foreign trade. To restrict imports, heavy tariffs were imposed. As a result, France became the richest country in Europe.

A believer in the divine right of kings and a devout Catholic, Louis desired religious uniformity in France and severely persecuted non-Catholics. He levied fines on the Huguenots, closed their schools, and even quartered troops in their homes. These measures had the effect of forcing many conversions. In 1685, believing that all French Protestants had been converted, he revoked the Edict of Nantes. This move led to mass emigration; some 50,000 Huguenot families left France for Germany, the Netherlands, England, and America. The Huguenot exodus damaged the French economy, for France's Protestants tended to be well-educated, prosperous business leaders.

Military Exploits

Another of Louis' goals was to create a Bourbon empire in Europe. Under François Louvois (loo-VWAH), Louis' Minister of War, France's army was reorganized and became the most powerful fighting force in Europe. To accomplish this, Louvois devised an efficient method of provisioning troops and a system of graded ranks. He also introduced the bayonet and a better musket.

During Louis' reign France was involved in four wars. The first war was fought against the Dutch and is referred to as the War of Devolution. The conflict began in 1667 because Louis claimed the Spanish Netherlands as part of his wife's inheritance. When the English and Swedes joined the Dutch in 1668, Louis was forced to withdraw his troops and the war ended. Nevertheless, Louis gained a few border towns in the Spanish Netherlands.

In 1672 Louis launched an attack on the Dutch Netherlands. This time Spain and the Holy Roman emperor joined the Dutch. At one point, French armies were at the gates of Amsterdam, but the Dutch forced their retreat by opening the dikes and flooding the land. By the end of the six-year war Louis had won additional territories to the north and west of France, but the Dutch remained free.

Louis' expansionist policies worried the rest of Europe, and Protestants were particularly alarmed by his revocation of the Edict of Nantes. As a result the Dutch, Swedes, Spanish, Austrians, and several German states formed the League of Augsburg.

The War of the League of Augsburg began in 1688 when Louis' troops invaded the Rhineland in Germany. For the next ten years the French army battled most of Europe's major powers. By the end of the war France had gained little territory and its navy had been seriously weakened.

Louis' last war, the War of the Spanish Succession, lasted from 1702 to 1713. In 1700 the king of Spain, Charles II, died leaving no heir. Louis XIV and the Holy Roman Emperor, Leopold I, claimed the throne. The other European powers, alarmed at the prospect of France and Spain under Bourbon rule, formed another alliance against Louis.

The War of the Spanish Succession was fought on many fronts. France sustained many defeats

This tapestry depicts one of Louis XIV's annual visits to the Royal Manufactory of Court Furniture. What objects do these people want to show the king?

but continued fighting. Finally, all parties agreed to a peace. According to the terms of the Treaty of Utrecht, Louis' grandson, Philip, received the Spanish throne on the condition that France and Spain would never be united under a single ruler. In addition, France lost many of its colonial possessions to the English. The Spanish Netherlands went to the Austrian Hapsburgs.

A Golden Age

The era of Louis XIV, or the Sun King as he was often called, was a golden age for French culture. Among the great playwrights of the period was Pierre Corneille (kor-NAY), whose majestic tragedies included *Le Cid*, based on the exploits of the Spanish national hero. Another tragedian, Jean Racine (zhan ra-SEEN), often presented characters from classical history and mythology, which was the style at this time. The comedies of Molière (mol-YEHR) ridiculed character types such as the miser, the hypocrite, and the hypochondriac. Jean de La Fontaine (fon-TEN) rewrote the fables of Aesop in verse, using them to make witty comments on contemporary society.

Two outstanding French painters of this period were Claude Lorraine and Nicolas Poussin (poo-SAN). Lorraine was noted for his battle scenes and landscapes. In contrast, Poussin depicted mythological scenes with Roman ruins in the background, showing a strong classical influence. In music, Jean-Baptiste Lully (loo-LEE) composed elegant operas, and François Couperin (koo-PRAN) was noted for his compositions for the organ and harpsichord.

These creative artists found an audience not only in France but elsewhere in Europe, for French culture was admired and imitated everywhere. Monarchs modeled their palaces after Versailles. Diplomats and the upper classes spoke French. French architecture, French fashion, French cooking, French court etiquette—all were copied, throughout the Continent.

SECTION REVIEW

1. In your own words, briefly identify or define: Sully, Marie de Medici, Mazarin, Fronde, mercantilism, Louvois, Molière.
2. Describe Richelieu's domestic policies.
3. What were the political effects of maintaining the French court at Versailles?
4. List the accomplishments of Louis XIV.
- During the reign of Louis XIV, French culture was imitated throughout Europe. What culture is most widely copied in the world today? Why? What do you think leads people to imitate a foreign culture?

A troop of French and Italian players performed at the Théâtre Royal in the late 1600's. What clues do you have that this was a slapstick comedy?

SOCIAL SCIENCE SKILLS

READING AND DEVELOPING AN ORGANIZATIONAL CHART

In Chapter 12 you learned that an outline can help you to organize material in a detailed manner. An organizational chart is another more general way of arranging the same material. It summarizes important events and facts in order and divides them into compact units identified by different headings. Now read the chart below and answer the questions that follow.

CONFLICTS DURING THE REIGN OF LOUIS XIV

War and Dates	Participants	Treaty and Results
War of Devolution 1667-1668	France vs. Spanish Netherlands, England, Sweden	Treaty of Aix-la-Chapelle France gains a few border towns in the Spanish Netherlands.
Dutch War 1672-1678	France vs. Dutch Netherlands, Spain, Austria, England	Treaty of Nijmegen France gains additional territories to the north and west. The Dutch Netherlands remain free.
War of the League of Augsburg 1688-1697	France vs. Dutch Netherlands, Austria, Spain, Sweden, German states	Treaty of Ryswick France gains little territory to the east.
War of Spanish Succession 1702-1713	France vs. Spain — England, Netherlands, German states, Austria, Portugal	Treaty of Utrecht A Bourbon king is placed on the Spanish throne. France loses some of its colonial possessions to England. Austria gains the Spanish Netherlands and some Spanish possessions in Italy.

1. How many wars did France fight during the reign of Louis XIV? Name them.
2. Name the treaties in which France gained territories. Where were these lands located?
3. What countries were members of the League of Augsburg?
4. Which countries fought in the Dutch War and the War of the League of Augsburg?
5. Which conflict involved most European countries? What was the cause of this war?
6. What countries benefited the most from the Treaty of Utrecht? Why?

An organizational chart can help you study. On a sheet of paper, copy the chart below. Complete it using the information in this chapter.

CONFLICTS IN EUROPE 1550 TO 1700

Conflict/Dates	Causes	Participants	Results
Dutch Revolt			
Spanish Armada			
Thirty Years' War			
Civil War in England			
Glorious Revolution			

Reviewing the Chapter

Chapter Summary

During the sixteenth century Spain was the wealthiest and most powerful country in Europe. Under Charles V and Philip II, Spain tried to prevent Turkish aggression and expand its territories in Europe. Philip II attempted to stem the spread of Protestantism. His policies led to revolt in the Netherlands, and the Armada's invasion of England failed.

Philip's crusades were not the only conflicts that troubled Europe. France suffered from a civil war that pitted Huguenots against Catholics. The nation achieved peace when Henry IV issued the Edict of Nantes.

The Thirty Years' War involved most European countries, but devastated Germany. The Peace of Westphalia established new geographical boundaries and gave the German princes almost complete control over their territories.

Conflict arose in England as Puritans and Parliament opposed the divine-right monarchs James I and Charles I. A civil war led to the establishment of the Commonwealth under Cromwell. In 1660 the monarchy was restored to Charles II. Then a bloodless revolution occurred during the reign of James II. By about 1800 the development of cabinet government and gradual constitutional changes made England a limited constitutional monarchy.

In contrast, France moved toward absolutism under Richelieu and Mazarin and reached its peak with Louis XIV. During Louis' reign, France's economy and military power were strengthened. French culture was imitated throughout the Continent. Louis' military campaigns, however, left France seriously weakened and in financial difficulties by the end of his reign.

1. When did Spanish power reach its height?
2. What were the main European conflicts between 1550 to 1650?
3. What changes were made in English government by the nineteenth century?
4. How did the reign of Louis XIV affect France?

Using Your Vocabulary

1. What is a dynastic war? Give two examples.
2. What does the term *Siglo de Oro* mean? When did it occur? Why was this period given this name?
3. Briefly define Christian mysticism and name three people who exemplify this doctrine.
4. Who were the Huguenots? What social classes did they represent? Where did they have a strong following?
5. Who were the sea beggars? What role did they play in the Dutch revolt?
6. What does the term "Protestant wind" refer to? Why do you think it was given this name?
7. Explain what is meant by a balance of power. How did this concept mark a change in international politics?
8. What is the Elizabethan Age and when did it occur?
9. Who were the Puritans? Why did they receive this name?
10. Briefly define the theory of the divine right of kings. How did it lead to absolutism?
11. What does it mean to dissolve Parliament? Under what circumstances did this occur?
12. Who were the Cavaliers and the Roundheads? Why were they given these names?
13. What does the term Interregnum mean? What time period does it refer to? Why?
14. Why was the reign of Charles II called the Restoration?
15. Briefly define limited constitutional monarchy. Under what rulers was this type of government instituted in England?
16. What was the Fronde? How did it affect Louis XIV's later life?
17. What economic theory was advocated by Colbert? On what principle was it based?

Developing Your Geography Skills

1. Use the map on page 320 to describe the location of Austria, Hungary, Bohemia, the Dutch Netherlands, and the Spanish Netherlands.
2. Use the map on page 320 to locate by means of latitude and longitude coordinates the cities of: Lepanto, Calais, Madrid. What historical importance does each place have?
3. Use the map on page 320 to locate the Ottoman Empire. From which locations could the Turks invade Europe?

Recalling the Facts

1. Why was Spain considered the greatest empire in the sixteenth century?
2. Why did Charles V lead a military expedition against the Ottoman Turks? Was he successful? Explain.
3. What happened to the empire of Charles V when he abdicated the throne?
4. List Philip II's military campaigns and their results.
5. Explain the domestic policy of Catherine de Medici and its effect on France.
6. What were the causes and effects of the St. Bartholomew's Day Massacre?
7. How did Henry IV resolve the religious conflict in France?
8. List the causes for revolt in the Netherlands. Was it successful? Explain briefly.
9. Why was Elizabeth I considered a successful monarch?
10. How did James I's belief in the divine right of kings cause problems in England?
11. Who were the Pilgrims and why did they leave England?
12. How did the Long Parliament limit the powers of Charles I?
13. Name England's first two political parties. When and why were they formed?
14. How did the Habeas Corpus Act represent an important advance for civil liberties?
15. Briefly explain the causes and effects of the Glorious Revolution.
16. Name two acts of legislation passed during the reign of William and Mary. Explain the historical significance of this legislation.
17. How is the English constitution different from that of the United States?
18. Who was Cardinal Richelieu and why is he considered an important historical figure?

Essay Questions

1. Religious differences have frequently been a cause for conflict in the world. To what extent is this true in Europe for the period from about 1560 to 1650? What other causes for conflict were there? What were the results of these conflicts? Give specific examples to support your answers.
2. Compare and contrast the rule of Charles I and Oliver Cromwell. Who do you think was the more autocratic ruler? Why?
3. In the early 1600's English monarchs spoke of divine rights, yet by the late 1600's Parliament emerged supreme. Describe the various steps taken in the development of parliamentary rule. Why do you think the growth of democracy in England has been called evolutionary rather than revolutionary?
4. Define absolutism and explain how Louis XIV's domestic and foreign policies reflected this political philosophy.

Critical Thinking

1. As a result of overwhelming opposition, Charles V was forced to sign the Treaty of Cambrai ending the war with France. How would the provisions of this treaty be an example of a logical inconsistency?
2. Henry of Navarre stated, "Paris is well worth a Mass." What value claim is implied in this statement?
3. Oliver Cromwell has often been referred to as a military dictator. From what you have read in the chapter, would you consider this a warranted or unwarranted claim? Give examples to support your opinion.
4. On what unstated assumption is the concept of balance of power based? How is this concept used in international politics today?

CHAPTER ·15·

EXPLORATION and COLONIZATION

1400–1763

Objectives

- *To explain why the Age of Exploration began in the fifteenth century*

- *To describe the major achievements of Spanish explorers*

- *To compare the overseas empires of Portugal and Spain*

- *To describe Dutch, French, and English expansion abroad*

- *To discuss the Commercial Revolution in Europe*

- *To explain how dynastic and commercial rivalries in Europe led to warfare overseas*

*T*he fourteenth and fifteenth centuries were a period of transition in western Europe. During this time, society and culture were going through a process of transformation as a result of the Renaissance and the Reformation. Another important factor to influence the changes that were occurring was European overseas expansion.

Since the time of the Crusades, Europeans had shown increasing interest in the world beyond their borders. The Italians established a commercial network, through the Mediterranean Sea, with peoples in the Near and Far East. Nevertheless, much of this world was still unknown to Europe, or known only through a few travelers' reports such as those of Marco Polo. In the fifteenth century technological advances made exploration of these and other lands possible. Thus Europeans embarked on their great voyages of discovery.

Each voyage out into the unknown seemed to inspire others, until a whole New World had been revealed. By the end of the eighteenth century only a few regions of the globe remained unknown to Europeans, and many cultures had felt the impact of western civilization. European colonists and merchants could be found in Asia, Africa, and the Americas. Major events in one part of the world began to have repercussions in other areas of the world.

THE AGE OF EXPLORATION BEGINS

The Vikings were the first Europeans to make voyages of discovery. Their sagas tell of Eric the Red, who discovered Greenland, and his son Leif Ericson, who established a settlement in Finland during the early Middle Ages. Recent discoveries of a Viking settlement in Newfoundland, dating from about 1000 A.D., prove that these sagas were probably based on fact. However, other Europeans were not acquainted with these tales, and the rediscovery of this New World would not occur until the late fifteenth century.

Motives for Exploration

The age of European exploration was influenced by many factors. A crusading spirit was probably the most important. The first voyages of discovery were undertaken by the Portuguese and the Spanish, who had been engaged for many centuries in crusades against the Muslims in Spain and North Africa. The desire to combat the infidels and to convert them to Christianity continued in their explorations. Tales of gold and other riches raised further interest.

Trade was another motive. Wealthy Europeans desired the fine fabrics, jewels, porcelain, and spices imported from the Far East. These goods passed from Asia Minor via ships or caravans to Italian merchants, who had a monopoly on their distribution in Europe. Consequently, merchants from other countries were eager to find alternate routes and gain a share of this profitable trade. Moreover, the Ottoman Turks were threatening to disrupt the established East-West trade, so it was important to find new routes.

Exploration was also encouraged by improvements in maritime technology. As you have read, Europeans began to use the compass and *portolano* during the fourteenth century. In the fifteenth century the caravel, a new type of sailing ship more suited to long voyages, was invented. Sailors also began relying on the astrolabe, which they adopted from the Muslims. For centuries, mariners had tried never to lose sight of land. These innovations gave them the confidence they needed to venture into uncharted waters.

Portuguese Voyages of Discovery

The Age of Exploration was begun by Prince Henry of Portugal. As a Crusader, Prince Henry was interested in defeating the Muslims in North Africa. He wanted to investigate the extent of Muslim power in Africa. He also hoped to form an alliance with Prester John, who supposedly ruled over a fabulous Christian kingdom somewhere in the East, and other Christian rulers for a common attack. In addition, Henry planned to convert the heathens and infidels. Moreover, he had financial motives. Since he was a younger son of the king, Henry had little money and needed African gold to live like a prince and to finance his numerous crusades. Finally, Henry was naturally curious and wished to learn about his new unexplored territory.

Thus Henry the Navigator, as he was called, established a sort of school of navigation at Sagres on Cape St. Vincent in southern Portugal. Sea captains, astronomers, and mapmakers from all over Europe gathered there, pooled their knowledge, and set off on numerous voyages to explore the western coast of Africa. Their efforts were rewarded in the 1440's when ships returned from Africa laden with gold dust, ivory, and black slaves. By the time of Henry's death in 1460, the Portuguese had established control over Madeira (muh-DEAR-uh) Island and the Azores (AY-zorz), and had traveled southward along the western coast of Africa as far as present-day Sierra Leone.

Portuguese exploration then slowed down until John II succeeded to the throne in 1481. He encouraged captains to sail their ships farther south, to chart the waters, and to explore the African coastline. In 1488 Bartholomeu Dias succeeded in rounding the Cape of Good Hope and opened the way to India.

In 1497 four ships, under the command of Vasco da Gama, left Portugal and headed for India. The expedition rounded the Cape of Good Hope and stopped at several ports along the east coast of Africa. In 1498 it reached Calicut, a port in southwest India. After establishing a trading post there, da Gama returned to Lisbon carrying a valuable cargo of spices. Thus a new water route to the

East was found, and further exploration was encouraged. Soon Portuguese ships were sailing regularly to India and the Far East. The profits from the sale of Asian goods made Portugal wealthy.

SECTION REVIEW

1. Mapping: Use the map on page 341 to locate Madeira Island, the Azores, and the Cape of Good Hope.
2. In your own words, briefly define or identify: caravel, Prester John, John II, Bartholomeu Dias, Vasco da Gama.
3. Why did Europeans become interested in exploration during the fifteenth century?
4. What role did Henry the Navigator play in Portuguese exploration?
■ People today are still interested in exploring the unknown. Why do you think this is so? What new places remain to be explored today?

SPANISH EXPLOITS IN THE NEW WORLD

Between the journeys of Dias and da Gama, another important voyage occurred. Undertaken by an Italian, Christopher Columbus, and financed by Spain, it ended in the discovery of a New World.

Christopher Columbus

Christopher Columbus spent his early years as a seaman and chart maker in the Mediterranean region. Like many educated people of his time, he believed that the world was a sphere and that it should be possible to reach the Far East by sailing west across the Atlantic. However, he had difficulty obtaining financial backing to prove his theories.

He first presented his plan for sailing to the Far East to the king of Portugal, but it was rejected. So he went to Spain. Queen Isabella finally agreed to underwrite the venture because she hoped to gain

allies in the crusade against the Muslims. She also wanted to take control of the Asian spice trade before the Portuguese could do so.

In August 1492 Columbus set sail with three caravels—the *Niña,* the *Pinta,* and the *Santa María.* After weeks at sea his crew became fearful and rebellious, and provisions were running low. On the morning of October 12, land came into sight. Columbus called the place where he and his men landed San Salvador. Actually, it was probably Watling Island in the Bahamas.

Since Columbus thought he had reached the outlying islands of Asia, or the Indies, he named the inhabitants Indians. Continuing the voyage, he sighted Cuba and founded a colony on the island of Hispaniola, now Haiti and the Dominican Republic. When he returned to Spain in the spring of 1493, he was greeted with a triumphal procession and awarded the title "Admiral of the Ocean Sea."

Columbus made three more voyages to America between 1493 and 1502. Among the places he visited were the Virgin Islands, Puerto Rico, Jamaica, and Trinidad. He also saw the mainland of South America, although he thought it was just another island. Columbus never abandoned the idea that he had reached Asia, but later exploration proved that he had actually discovered a new continent.

Exploration Continues

Technically speaking, Columbus did not discover America. The Vikings had already been there, and of course the descendants of its first settlers, the Indians, had been living in the Western Hemisphere for thousands of years. Columbus' achievement was to make this huge region known to Europe.

His initial voyage became a cause of dispute between Spain and Portugal because the Portuguese king believed that the lands Columbus had claimed were the Azores, and thus belonged to Portugal. To settle the matter, Pope Alexander VI established the Papal Line of Demarcation in 1493, which divided the unknown world between the two countries. A line was drawn around the globe from the North Pole to the South Pole, some 300 miles (483 kilometers) west of the Cape Verde Islands. All the lands west of the line not already

EUROPEAN EXPLORATIONS

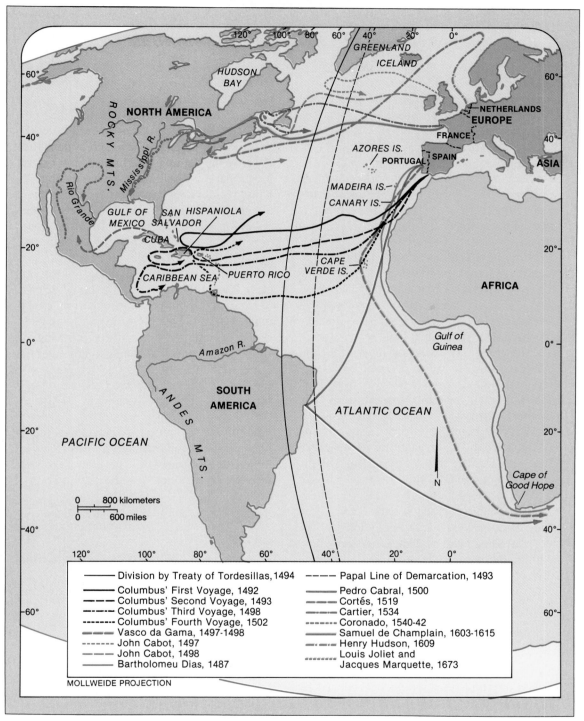

Legend	
—— Division by Treaty of Tordesillas, 1494	–––– Papal Line of Demarcation, 1493
—— Columbus' First Voyage, 1492	—— Pedro Cabral, 1500
— — Columbus' Second Voyage, 1493	– – Cortés, 1519
—·—·— Columbus' Third Voyage, 1498	—·—·— Cartier, 1534
········ Columbus' Fourth Voyage, 1502	········ Coronado, 1540-42
—— Vasco da Gama, 1497-1498	—— Samuel de Champlain, 1603-1615
– – – John Cabot, 1497	—·—·— Henry Hudson, 1609
– – John Cabot, 1498	Louis Joliet and
—— Bartholomeu Dias, 1487	········ Jacques Marquette, 1673

MOLLWEIDE PROJECTION

What areas of the world were explored by the Portuguese? The Spanish? The French? The English?

SOURCES

Writings of Christopher Columbus

Not long after he returned from his first voyage, Co-lumbus sent a long letter to Raphael Sánchez, the treasurer of Isabella and Ferdinand. The following excerpts include his descriptions of what he called Juana (Cuba) and Española (Hispaniola). Note that Columbus mentions leaving Cádiz and arriving in America thirty-three days later. He actually set sail from Palos, Spain, and his journey took seventy-three days. These errors were probably made when the letter was translated into Latin—the only version that has survived.

Knowing that it will afford you pleasure to learn that I have brought my undertaking to a successful termination, I have decided upon writing you this letter to acquaint you with all the events which have occurred in my voyage, and the discoveries which have resulted from it. Thirty-three days after my departure from Cádiz I reached the Indian sea, where I discovered many islands, thickly peopled, of which I took possession without resistance, in the name of our most illustrious Monarch. . . .

All these islands are very beautiful, and distinguished by a diversity of scenery. . . . There are . . . in the . . . island of Juana, seven or eight kinds of palm trees, which, like all the other trees, herbs and fruits, considerably surpass ours in height and beauty. The pines, also, are very handsome, and there are very extensive fields and meadows, a variety of birds, different kinds of honey, and many sorts of metals, but no iron. In that island which we named Española, there are mountains of very great size and beauty, vast plains, groves, and very fruitful fields, admirably adapted for tillage, pasture and habitation. The convenience and excellence of the harbors in this island, and the abundance of rivers, . . . surpass anything that would be believed by one who had not seen it. . . .

It has often occurred, when I have sent two or three of my men to any of the villages to speak with the natives, that they have fled in haste. . . . As soon, however, as they see that they are safe, and have laid aside all fear, they are very simple and honest, and exceedingly liberal with all they have. . . . They exhibit great love toward all others in preference to themselves; they also give objects of great value for trifles, and content themselves with very little or nothing in return. I, however, forbade that these trifles and articles of no value (such as pieces of dishes, plates and glass, keys and leather straps), should be given to them. . . . I did this in order that . . . they might be led to become Christians, and be inclined to entertain a regard for the King and Queen, our Princes and all Spaniards, and that I might induce them to take an interest in seeking out and collecting and delivering to us such things as they possessed in abundance, but which we greatly needed. They practice no kind of idolatry, but have a firm belief that all strength and power, and, indeed, all good things, are in heaven, and that I had descended from thence with these ships and sailors. . . .

Source: Paul L. Ford, ed., *Writings of Christopher Columbus,* Copyright 1892 by Charles L. Webster & Co.

1. What were Columbus' reasons for writing this letter?
2. What features of the islands does Columbus emphasize?
3. How does Columbus describe the natives?
4. Why did he forbid objects of no value to be given to the Indians?
5. If you were Sánchez, would this letter encourage you to support further explorations? Explain your answer.

ruled by some Christian prince belonged to Spain; all the lands to the east were Portugal's.

In 1494 the two countries signed the Treaty of Tordesillas (tor-day-SEE-yahs), which shifted the line about 800 miles (1,287 kilometers) farther west. In 1500 a Portuguese expedition led by Pedro Álvares Cabral was on its way south along the African coast when the ship was blown off course. It landed on the Brazilian coast, and because of the new boundary established by the treaty, the Portuguese were able to claim this land.

By the early 1500's, Europeans were becoming aware that the land Columbus had discovered was not Asia. Amerigo Vespucci (vay-SPOO-chee) explored the South American coastline between 1499 and 1502, and became convinced that he was looking at a new continent. Vespucci's reports were included with information gathered by a German mapmaker, Martin Waldseemuller. The two maps he published in 1507 not only showed the Western Hemisphere as a New World, but also labeled it *Americus* in honor of Vespucci.

From bases in the Caribbean, Spanish adventurers sailed off in many directions to explore the New World. When he was governor of Puerto Rico, Juan Ponce de León had heard tales of gold and a fountain of youth in a land to the north. In 1513 he led an expedition to Florida and explored the east and west coasts of the peninsula. In that same year, Vasco Nuñez de Balboa led an expedition of 190 Spaniards and 1,000 Indians on a difficult three-week journey across the Isthmus of Panama and discovered the Pacific Ocean, which he called the "Great South Sea."

One of the greatest expeditions of the sixteenth century was the voyage undertaken by Ferdinand Magellan, which proved Columbus' theory. Magellan sailed from Spain with five ships and about 260 men in the fall of 1519. When he reached South America, he sailed south, constantly on the lookout for a passage to the "South Sea." In October 1520 the small fleet entered the strait that now bears Magellan's name. After thirty-eight stormy days, the ships emerged into the "South Sea," which Magellan named the Pacific because it was so calm.

It took Magellan's three ships ninety-eight days to cross the Pacific. The men ran out of water and food and were reduced to eating sawdust and rats.

Many died of starvation. Finally, in March 1521, the fleet reached the Marianas Islands. A few days later it sailed to the Philippines, where Magellan was killed in a fight with some of the islanders.

By this time only one ship, the *Vittoria*, remained in the fleet. Under its captain, Sebastian del Cano, it traveled around India and Africa back to Spain, arriving with a crew of eighteen in September 1522. The *Vittoria* was the first ship to circumnavigate, or sail all the way around, the world.

In the same year Magellan set out on his voyage, a Spanish explorer named Hernando Cortés (kor-TACE) set sail from Cuba for Mexico with 508 soldiers, 16 horses, and several small cannons. At his first stop, in what is now Tabasco, Cortés subdued the Indians and gained the services of an Indian woman, Malinche (ma-LIN-chay), who learned Spanish and served as the expedition's interpreter.

Cortés then sailed northward along the coast and founded the town of Veracruz. From there the Spaniards marched overland toward the Aztec capital, Tenochtitlán. Some of the Indians Cortés encountered along the way joined forces with him because they resented Aztec rule.

The Aztecs had a large and powerful army, but their leader, Montezuma (mahn-tuh-ZOO-muh) did not employ it against the Spaniards. On the contrary, Montezuma welcomed them and invited them to enter Tenochtitlán. There he treated them like honored guests because he believed that Cortés was the Aztec god Quetzalcóatl who, according to legend, was supposed to return one day.

Cortés, however, upon seeing the great wealth of the Aztec Empire, made Montezuma a prisoner in his own palace and demanded a large ransom in gold. The ransom was paid, but resentment was growing against the Spanish. In the months that followed, warfare broke out and Montezuma was killed. Cortés was forced to abandon Tenochtitlán, but he regrouped his forces. In 1521, after a three-month siege, the Spaniards were successful in conquering the Aztec capital.

The great Inca Empire fell to the Spanish not long afterward. In 1531 Francisco Pizarro led a small expedition south from Panama along the west coast of South America and through the Andes Mountains in Peru. After almost two years

This Aztec drawing shows Cortés meeting Montezuma. What do you think is happening?

of hardship, Pizarro and his men reached the town of Cajamarca (ka-hah-MAR-kah), where they found the Inca emperor Atahualpa (ah-tah-WAHL-pah).

Pizarro invited Atahualpa to visit his encampment, then took him hostage, offering to ransom him for a huge amount of gold and silver. The Incas spent months collecting the ransom, which filled a whole room. It is estimated to have been worth at least $150 million. Pizarro, however, had no intention of releasing Atahualpa. After receiving the ransom, he charged the Inca ruler with treason and had him put to death. Without a strong leader, the Incas were easily subdued. By the end of 1533 Pizarro had taken Cuzco, the Inca capital.

Both the Aztec and Inca empires, though highly developed civilizations, fell to small Spanish invasion forces. Disunity was one factor that made this possible. The Aztecs had never succeeded in creating any feeling of loyalty among the peoples they had conquered. In fact, many were eager to rid themselves of Aztec rule, which was oppressive. The Incas were unable to present a united front because a costly civil war had been fought just before Pizarro's arrival. After the death of Atalhuapa, the Spanish prevented the new ruler from establishing control over the empire.

Another factor against the Indians was European technological superiority. The Spanish had ships, guns, and horses, none of which the Indians had ever seen. These gave the invaders not only a military, but a psychological advantage as well. They seemed able to accomplish truly superhuman feats. The character of the conquistadors, or conquerors, should also be taken into account. Men like Pizarro and Cortés were motivated to undertake these expeditions by their greed for gold and their desire to spread Christianity.

The early explorers and conquerors were followed by many others, most of them in search of riches like those found in the Aztec and Inca realms. Francisco de Orellana (oh-ray-YAH-nah) traveled the Amazon River from the interior of South America all the way to its mouth, an epic journey that took three years. In 1539 Hernando de Soto led an expedition through Florida westward and was probably the first European to see the Mississippi River. Between 1540 and 1542 Francisco Vásquez de Coronado explored what is now the southwestern United States. Members of his expedition were the first to visit Pueblo Indian villages and the Grand Canyon. By the mid-sixteenth century Spain was colonizing its new territories, which extended from northern California to southern Chile.

1. **Mapping:** Use the map on page 341 to trace the voyages of Dias and Columbus and the expeditions of Cortés and Coronado.

2. In your own words, briefly define or identify: Papal Line of Demarcation, Cabral, Vespucci, Ponce de León, Balboa, Cortés, Montezuma, Pizarro, Atahualpa, Orellana, de Soto.

3. Why did Columbus undertake his voyage? What were the results?

4. Why was Magellan's voyage a great accomplishment?

5. List the factors that made Spanish conquest of the Aztec and Inca empires possible.

■ Describe the problems faced by explorers during the fifteenth and sixteenth centuries. Would explorers today encounter similar problems? If so, which ones? What new problems might be encountered?

THE EMPIRES OF SPAIN AND PORTUGAL

After their initial discoveries in the fifteenth and early sixteenth centuries, both Portugal and Spain established extensive empires overseas. Like the early explorers, the colonists were motivated by curiosity and the spirit of adventure. Some were eager to convert nonbelievers to Christianity, while others hoped for financial gain.

Colonizing ventures were encouraged by national economic policies that aimed to benefit the mother country. Spain, for instance, claimed one-fifth of all the wealth that was brought out of the New World. Ideally, colonies provided raw materials not produced in the mother country and markets for manufactured goods.

Portugal's Trading Network

The Portuguese followed their explorations by establishing a network of trading settlements. This system was initiated by Affonso de Albuquerque in Goa, India, in the early 1500's for the purpose of exploiting the spice trade and protecting the sea links between Asia and Europe.

In Africa trading posts were established along the eastern coast in what are today Mozambique, Kenya, and Madagascar. In India they were located at Calicut, Cochin, Goa, and Diu. Outposts could be found along the Strait of Malacca and in Java, Borneo, and the Moluccas, or Spice Islands. The entire Far Eastern network was controlled by a governor who usually held the position of viceroy at Goa.

The first Portuguese ship entered Macao (muh-KOW) in 1513, and in 1557 the Ming rulers of China allowed the Portuguese to establish a colony there. Macao soon became a major center for trade with China and Japan. Japan also allowed some Portuguese missionaries to operate from a base in Kagoshima. The most well-known missionary in Portugal's Asian empire was Francis Xavier, a Jesuit who traveled extensively throughout the region. He is reported to have baptized about 30,000 people.

The major obstacle to Portuguese interests in the Far East were Arab traders, who had long dominated the spice trade. Thus Portuguese trading bases were fortified to control shipping through the Indian Ocean. When confronted on the high seas, Portuguese naval power proved superior because their ships carried mounted cannons and sailed in squadrons.

As a result of its trading interests, Portugal had created a huge commercial empire by the mid-sixteenth century. Lisbon became an important trade center. São Jorge de Mina on the Gulf of Guinea in West Africa was the center for the slave trade, which Portugal monopolized for about 150 years.

As you read in Chapter 10, there was a tradition of slavery in Africa. When the Portuguese arrived, they bought African slaves and exported them to the mother country. Then they began to use slaves to work the newly established sugar plantations on the Cape Verde Islands. They needed many workers to tend the fields and, in order to make a profit, the labor had to be cheap. This practice resulted in a new tradition, called plantation slavery, which was carried over to the New World when sugar plantations were established in the West Indies. Later, African slaves were employed to work the gold and silver mines and the new tobacco and cotton plantations. Thus the market expanded and slave trading became a profitable enterprise.

The Portuguese in Brazil

Although Cabral claimed Brazil for Portugal in 1500, colonization did not begin until the 1530's because Portugal was occupied in Africa and the Far East. The first town, São Vicente, was established in 1532.

To encourage settlement, Portugal instituted the captaincy system, which divided Brazil's territory into fifteen huge tracts of land, or captaincies. Each captaincy was given to a wealthy noble who was supposed to colonize and develop his land with his own money. However, the system proved to be a failure because many of the nobles who received land did not have enough capital or the ability to attract settlers. Thus only a few land grants were occupied and those nobles who settled their grants found it difficult to defend themselves against Indian attacks. In 1549 Brazil was brought directly under royal control and supervised by a governor general who lived at Bahia (now Salvador.) Towns were established and the population began to grow.

Portugal was not without rivals in Brazil, however. In 1555 the French founded a colony on the bay of Rio de Janeiro. In 1567 the Portuguese, fearful of French competition, drove the settlers out and founded the city of Rio de Janeiro.

In 1630 the Dutch West India Company seized Salvador and the rich sugar-growing regions along the Brazilian coast. A governor was sent out, but the Netherlands failed to support the colony because of conflict with England. The Brazilians revolted in 1654, and the colony was abandoned.

The economy of Brazil was based on its huge plantations, which grew sugar, tobacco, and cotton. These crops required much cultivation, and there were not enough Europeans to work the land. The first solution was to enslave the Indians, but it soon proved unsatisfactory. It was difficult to make the Indians work and some managed to escape. Others perished from overwork and unfamiliar diseases. Besides, they could not be replaced, for the population was limited. In Salvador, for example, some 40,000 Indians were employed as slaves in the 1560's; twenty years later only 3,000 had survived.

As a result, the Portuguese began to import African slaves. Not only did Africans find it more difficult than the Indians to escape, but they could also be replaced. According to one estimate, about

Calicut, a port on India's west coast, was one of Portugal's major trading posts in the East. What does this sixteenth-century scene tell you about Portuguese influence there? What do you think were the effects of this commerce?

one million Africans were imported into Brazil between 1530 and 1680.

The discovery of gold and diamonds in the seventeenth and early eighteenth centuries added to Brazil's appeal, and emigration increased. The different ethnic groups blended with each other, so there were peoples of mixed ancestry: white-Indian, white-black, and Indian-black. By 1800 Brazil had a total population of about 3 million—more than the mother country.

Spanish Rule in the New World

Unlike Portugal, which focused its attention primarily on the Far East, Spain concentrated most of its efforts on the Americas. During the sixteenth century the Spanish conquered and colonized a vast expanse of territory.

Spain's New World empire was governed solely for the benefit of the mother country. The chief source of wealth was mineral. Gold was mined in many regions, and rich silver deposits were found in Mexico and South America. To control this extensive empire and its wealth, Charles V established the Council of the Indies in 1524. It exercised supreme legal, administrative, and ecclesiastical authority over the colonies.

The empire was originally divided into the Viceroyalty of New Spain and the Viceroyalty of Peru. The Viceroyalty of Peru was later divided and two additional viceroyalties were created—New Granada and La Plata. These territories were governed by royal officials, called viceroys, who were responsible for executing the council's laws and instituting local legislation. Their headquarters were Mexico City, Lima, Bogota, and Buenos Aires. Like the council, the viceroys were appointed by the Spanish monarchs and ruled in their name.

To aid the viceroys in governing their territories, members were appointed to *audiencias* (ow-DAYN-see-ahs) by the king. The *audiencia* had many functions. As a court, it judged civil and criminal cases. It was also permitted to pass local legislation and performed administrative duties in the absence of the viceroy. Some *audiencias* were all but independent of viceregal control.

The Catholic Church also played an important role in extending Spanish influence and control throughout the Western Hemisphere. As you know, one of Spain's goals was to spread Christianity. Consequently, missionaries accompanied explorers and colonists to the New World.

The missionaries began their work by establishing missions, or self-sufficient religious communities, in outlying areas. Most missions included a church or chapel, workshops for teaching trades and crafts, and living quarters for missionaries and Indians. Sometimes a wall enclosed the buildings. Cultivated fields and herds of livestock surrounded the mission. Thus the Indians were not only converted to Christianity, but introduced to the European way of life.

In time, as the population of the settlement increased, control of the missions was transferred from the church to civil authority, and the missionaries would move on to found new missions. Eventually missions were established throughout Latin America and as far north as present-day Texas and California.

One of the most famous Spanish missionaries in America was Bartolomé de las Casas. He is called the "Apostle of the Indies" because he tried to improve the living conditions of Native Americans. To relieve the heavy workload placed on Indian laborers, las Casas recommended the use of African slaves. He soon regretted his decision, for these people were harshly treated too, and the death rate was high.

Life in Spanish America

The major economic system in early Spanish America, the *encomienda* (en-koe-mee-EN-dah), was first instituted in the West Indies, where land was used for agriculture and livestock raising. It was much like the captaincy in Brazil. A Spanish colonist was granted a certain amount of land, and its inhabitants were entrusted to his charge. In exchange for a fixed amount of labor and goods, the colonist was obligated to convert, to teach, and to protect the Indians under his care.

However, the system was characterized by many abuses, especially in the treatment of the Indians. Spain tried to correct these abuses and even attempted to abolish the system, but had little success. The home country was too far away to enforce its policies. As new territories were conquered, the *encomienda* was instituted in order to assure Spanish control, and the Indians were enslaved to work the fields and mines.

What job did slaves perform on this West Indies sugar plantation?

Historians' estimates differ, but all agree that the Spanish conquest had catastrophic effects on the Indians. Some areas suffered severe population losses because of harsh treatment, overwork, and contact with unfamiliar diseases, such as smallpox and measles. As a result, in the sixteenth century African slaves were imported as a substitute source of cheap labor. They were most commonly used on the sugar and tobacco plantations in the Caribbean.

A fairly rigid class system developed during colonization. At the top were the Spaniards, who held most upper-level administrative jobs. Next came American-born descendants of Spaniards, called creoles, who owned large estates or ran businesses. Below them were people of mixed heritage: mestizos were mixed white and Indian, and mulattos were mixed white and black. The lowest position was occupied by Indian and black slaves. The women in these two groups were considered even lower than the men.

Spanish colonization of the New World brought many changes. New crops like wheat, barley, oats, and sugar were introduced, as well as domesticated animals like horses, cattle, pigs, sheep, and goats. A new religion, Catholicism, and a new language, Spanish, were instituted. European culture and learning began to replace that of the Indians, and European technology changed the way the Indians lived and worked.

Spanish rule in the New World also had negative results. As you have read, millions of Indians died. Indian culture and civilization were all but destroyed. In Yucatán, for example, the Spanish bishop had hundreds of Mayan writings burned. Churches and other buildings were constructed on top of Aztec ruins in other areas. Very little of the wealth encountered in the New World was used to improve conditions there. When the supply of precious metals began to give out, no new industries were developed, and the colonies economy became mainly agricultural.

SECTION REVIEW

1. In your own words, briefly define or identify: Albuquerque, Francis Xavier, captaincy, Council of the Indies, viceroy, *audiencia,* mission, las Casas, *encomienda.*
2. Why did Portugal and Spain establish colonial empires? How did their methods of colonization differ?
3. Where and why was African slavery introduced by Europeans?
4. Briefly describe the class system that developed in Spanish America.
5. List the positive and negative effects of Spanish colonization.
- Missionaries were sent to the New World to convert the Indians, teach them new skills, and protect them. Where are missionaries active today? What other groups or agencies perform similar activities? Explain your answers.

THE EXPANSION OF NORTHERN EUROPE

The explorations and discoveries of Portugal and Spain were the envy of other European countries, especially France, England, and the Netherlands. These nations were relatively late in joining the competition for riches from abroad because of civil war and other conflicts.

The Netherlands in Asia and America

The Dutch had long been a seafaring people, but were satisfied to profit from explorations made by other countries. During the sixteenth century, Dutch merchants distributed the many foreign goods brought into Lisbon throughout Europe. However, in 1580 Portugal became a part of Spain. At the same time, the United Provinces were trying to win their independence from Spain. As a result, the port of Lisbon was closed to Dutch ships. With this source of trade cut off, the Dutch were forced to begin expansion.

The Dutch East India Company, chartered in 1602, proceeded to take over areas in the East Indies formerly controlled by the Portuguese. Dutch bases were set up first on Java, and Batavia (now Jakarta) became the company's headquarters. Later trading settlements were established on Sumatra, Ceylon (now Sri Lanka), and the Spice Islands, giving the Dutch a monopoly of the spice trade. To service its ships along the East-West trade route, the Netherlands set up posts along Africa's western coast and founded a colony at the Cape of Good Hope in 1652.

The Netherlands also began to colonize in the New World. As you have read, the Dutch maintained a colony in Brazil for a short time. In the Caribbean they laid claim to Curaçao, Saba, and St. Martin. Through the efforts of the English explorer, Henry Hudson, who sailed to America for the Dutch East India Company in 1609, the Netherlands had established a claim to lands bordering the Hudson River.

In 1624 Dutch traders founded the colony of New Netherland in order to tap the rich fur-bearing areas north and west of the Hudson River. Peter Minuit (MIN-yoo-it), the colony's first governor, bought Manhattan Island from the Indians in 1626, naming it New Amsterdam. Dutch settlements soon extended throughout the Hudson Valley. Wealthy Dutchmen, called patroons, were awarded large land grants on the condition that they transport settlers to the colony.

However, the colony soon became part of the English Empire. In 1664 the English king, Charles II, gave all the territories between the Delaware and Connecticut rivers, including New Amsterdam, to his brother, James, Duke of York. When the English fleet appeared in New Amsterdam's harbor, the Dutch governor surrendered and the colony changed hands. The names of both the colony and its principal city were changed to New York, in James' honor.

France's Overseas Empire

Like the Dutch, the French wanted a share of the riches of the Far East. America was still considered more of an obstacle than an objective. Since the southwestern passage through the Strait of Magellan was hazardous, the first French explorers and those of other northern European nations tried to find another water route through North America, or a Northwest Passage, that would lead to the Pacific and the Orient.

The first explorer to seek a Northwest Passage for the French was an Italian, Giovanni da Verrazano (ver-rah-TSAH-noe). In 1524 he sailed along the eastern coast of North America and Newfoundland. The search was continued ten years later by Jacques Cartier (kar-TYAY). Cartier explored the St. Lawrence River on this and two later voyages, claiming the land, which is now Canada, for France. The French religious conflicts, how-ever, interrupted exploration until the early seventeenth century.

In 1608 Samuel de Champlain (sham-PLAYN) led a small group of settlers up the St. Lawrence River and established a trading fort, Quebec. From Quebec Champlain traveled west and south, searching for a Northwest Passage. Among the sites he visited was the large lake that now bears his name. As a result of his extensive exploration and colonization efforts, Champlain was called "the father of New France." New France was the name given to the French territories in North America.

As the French moved outward from Quebec, they built settlements for trade and defense. The most important source of wealth in New France was the fur trade. Indian trappers exchanged the pelts of such animals as beavers and foxes with traders for tools, weapons, and other goods. Cargoes of furs were then transported by canoe to

This Dutch couple are standing on a hill overlooking the port of Batavia. Why do you think the artist portrayed them in this setting?

Quebec and to other settlements. Many of these traders lived among the Indians, adopted their way of life, and married Indian women.

New France grew rather slowly. The Huguenots, who wished to escape religious persecution in France, were forbidden to settle there. The open hostility of the Iroquois (EER-uh-kwoy) indians, who had formed an alliance with the Dutch, discouraged many colonists. Also there was a lack of financial support and interest on the part of the French monarchy because France was involved in a series of domestic and foreign wars.

Motivated by Colbert's mercantilist policies, the ministers of Louis XIV encouraged exploration and expansion. Emigration to New France was promoted by offering large grants to nobles. However, few were willing to risk the dangers. Merchants were uninterested because the French government held a monopoly on the fur trade. As a result, as late as the mid-eighteenth century New France had only about 60,000 inhabitants.

The search for a Northwest Passage was renewed during Louis XIV's reign. In the 1670's Louis Joliet (JOE-lee-et), a fur trader, and Jacques Marquette (mahr-KETT), a Jesuit priest, canoed south along the Mississippi River as far as the mouth of the Arkansas River. French clerics were active not only as explorers but also as missionaries. Several were killed by Indians, who resented European trespassers on their lands and hunting grounds.

The greatest of all French explorers in the New World was Robert Cavalier, Sieur (SYUR) de la Salle. In 1682 he traveled all the way to the mouth of the Mississippi, claiming for France the huge region through which he traveled. La Salle named this territory Louisiana in honor of Louis XIV.

Elsewhere in America, France laid claim to profitable islands in the Caribbean. Among them were Guadeloupe and Martinique, where the French grew sugar and operated a profitable rum business.

Although the French never found a Northwest Passage, they did trade with the Far East by sailing around Africa. In 1664 the French East India Company was founded. Shortly thereafter, the French set up a colony at Pondicherry, on the east coast of India, and began to extend their influence to other parts of the subcontinent as well.

English Colonies Abroad

As early as 1497, King Henry VII of England commissioned an Italian navigator, John Cabot, to explore North America. He was the first person to visit Newfoundland since the Vikings. During his two voyages Cabot sailed south along the coast, perhaps as far as Virginia. Thus England established a claim to North America, but did not begin colonization for almost a hundred years.

As you know, England supported the United Provinces in its war for independence against Spain. During this time, Queen Elizabeth I permitted English sea dogs to prey on Spanish treasure ships and seize the gold and silver they carried from the New World. The defeat of the Spanish Armada in 1588 proved English naval supremacy and gave the English enough confidence to challenge Spain in colonizing ventures. Furthermore, English merchants wanted a share of New World riches and trade.

During the sixteenth century English merchants had prospered by forming **joint-stock companies.** In these business enterprises individuals, called investors, pooled their funds by buying shares, or stock, in the companies. The investors then shared in the profits according to the number of shares they held.

In 1607 James I granted the London Company a charter, permitting it to establish a colony in Virginia. In that year the first permanent English colony in North America was founded at Jamestown. The settlement, however, did not bring its investors the returns they had hoped for. Later, more successful colonies were established to the north in the region called New England. As you have read, the Pilgrims settled on Cape Cod in 1620, and the Puritans established the Massachusetts Bay Colony in 1630.

By 1732 there were thirteen English colonies scattered along the Atlantic coast of North America. The New England colonies consisted of Rhode Island, New Hampshire, Massachusetts, and Connecticut. Strongly influenced by the Puritan ideal of a tightly knit community, the people congregated in small villages where each family had its own plot of land for cultivation. Other New Englanders were engaged in fishing, trapping, shipping, and shipbuilding.

TRIANGULAR TRADE ROUTES

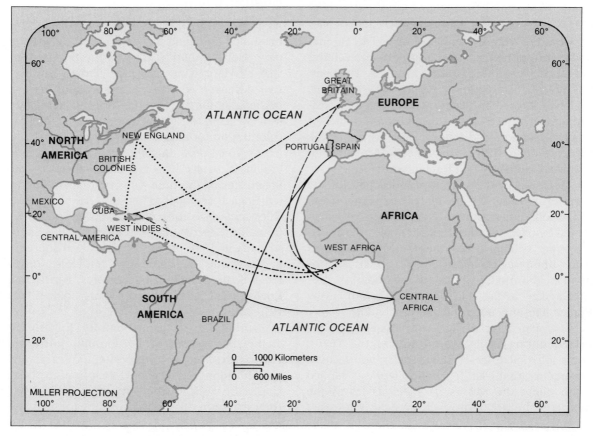

Describe the major triangular trade routes. How did they develop?

South of New England were the middle colonies: New York, New Jersey, Pennsylvania, and Delaware. Colonists in this area raised livestock and cultivated corn, wheat, and vegetables. The five southern colonies were Virginia, Maryland, North Carolina, South Carolina, and Georgia. Here, as in the West Indies and parts of Spanish America, large agricultural plantations were established for the cultivation of tobacco, rice, indigo, and later, cotton.

In England's colonies, as in those of Portugal and Spain, labor shortages made large-scale farming difficult. One solution was to employ indentured servants, or people who, in exchange for their passage to America, agreed to work for someone for four to seven years. This labor source proved inadequate, for indentured servants rarely continued to work for others after their term of service. So English colonists, like their southern counterparts, turned to black slaves.

In the eighteenth century New England ship captains began to use a triangular trade route. They would sail to Africa with colonial or European goods which they exchanged for slaves. Then they would go to the West Indies and trade their human cargoes for sugar and molasses. These products were returned to New England and used for making rum. Between the mid-1600's and the mid-1700's, colonists imported about 200,000 Africans. Slavery existed in all the colonies but was more widespread in the South.

Most of England's North American colonies were proprietary colonies, that is, they were founded by private enterprises with charters granted by the monarch. Nevertheless, by the mid-eighteenth century the crown had extended direct control over the majority of them. According to the prevailing mercantilist view, colonies were to supply raw materials England needed in exchange for manufactured goods. As a result, Parliament passed a series of Navigation Acts between 1660 and 1696 designed to restrict and control colonial trade. However, these laws were not strictly enforced and smuggling was common.

By the mid-1700's England's colonies had a population of about 1,200,000, but only about half were of English origin. Some 20 percent were blacks, most of them brought from Africa as slaves. There were also sizable numbers of Scottish, Irish, and German settlers. Colonies varied in their religious toleration, but many of Europe's persecuted minorities including the French Protestants, the English Catholics, and the Jews, found refuge in various parts of the colonies.

England had other interests in the New World as well. In 1670 it formed the Hudson's Bay Company and began to exploit the fur-trading potential of northern and western Canada. England's richest possessions, however, were in the Caribbean. The Bahamas, Barbados, and Bermuda all had profitable sugar plantations.

Like France, England began to move into the Portuguese sphere of influence in the East. In 1600 the English East India Company was founded. The company established posts at Calcutta, Surat, Madras, and Bombay. From these ports, it controlled much of the European trade with India and neighboring regions.

SECTION REVIEW

1. In your own words, briefly define or identify: New Amsterdam, patroon, Northwest Passage, New France, Louisiana, joint-stock company, indentured servant, Navigation Acts.
2. Why did England, France, and the Netherlands begin to explore and colonize overseas in the seventeenth century? Why was this process begun so late?
3. List the explorers who searched for the Northwest Passage and the results.
4. How did English colonization differ from that of other European countries?
■ France, England, and the Netherlands all established colonies in North America. In what parts of the continent can their influence be seen today? Give specific examples.

THE COMMERCIAL REVOLUTION

The Age of Exploration and expansion initiated a lengthy transformation of much of the world outside of Europe and affected European economic life. Known as the **Commercial Revolution,** this series of developments began about 1500 and lasted for some 200 years.

Social and Economic Background

One important development was an increase in population due to a drop in the death rate. Between 1500 and 1700 the number of Europeans rose from about 82 million to more than 115 million—a growth of over 40 percent. Urban population increased more than that of rural areas. London, for example, had a population of 50,000 in 1500, but over 200,000 a century later.

Population growth helped cause **inflation**, or constantly rising prices, because there was no comparable increase in production. Demand outpaced supply and the prices of basic commodities, such as food and clothing, shot upward. In general, prices tripled between 1550 and 1650, but the rate of increase was not the same for all goods or in all localities. For example, in France, hay cost fifteen times as much in 1650 as it had in 1500. In Spain during the same period, the price of wheat quadrupled. Then as now, inflation was hardest on those with fixed incomes, like the landowners.

Another factor that contributed to inflation was the tremendous influx of precious metals from America. Before the sixteenth century Europe had access to limited amounts of gold and silver, which caused a shortage of metal coins. However, with Spanish colonization of the New World, huge quantities of precious metals began flowing into Europe. According to one estimate, an average of about 5 tons of gold and 250 tons of silver were shipped to Spain every year during the sixteenth century.

Spanish bullion moved throughout Europe because Spain, with few industries of its own, bought most of its manufactured goods from other countries. The Spanish monarchs also spent great sums fighting the French, the Turks, and the Dutch. The increased money supply fueled inflation because the amount of precious metal was growing faster than the volume of goods and services produced. Thus the value of the metals declined and the prices of goods and services rose.

Growth of Business and Capitalism

The increased money supply and population growth encouraged trade and commerce. A larger market enabled merchants to establish bigger enterprises. With more money in circulation, more people were drawn into a cash economy and barter was confined to local areas.

As merchants accumulated capital, they launched more extensive ventures, which developed into a worldwide trading network. The oceans of the world were like highways, and the freight transported across them increased in volume and variety.

In the late Middle Ages only the wealthy could afford the spices and luxury products from the Far East. Now the world's goods, both exotic and common, could be obtained by the public at large. Even though prices in general were rising, prices for these former luxury goods fell drastically because of their greater availability.

Expanded trading brought additional products to Europeans. Corn and potatoes from the New World became important staples in their diet. The use of quinine and chocolate was introduced. The Middle East and, later Brazil, supplied coffee. Tea from the Far East became a popular beverage. Clothing too became more varied as lightweight cotton cloths from India supplemented the woolens and linens produced in Europe.

International shipping and shipbuilding were large-scale ventures that required sizable amounts of money. These enterprises, along with mining, printing, and the manufacturing of military weapons, attracted people who wanted to invest their funds for profit. Wealth invested to produce more wealth is called capital, and the system whereby private individuals use wealth in this manner is known as **capitalism.** The beginnings of capitalism can be traced back to the late Middle Ages, but it became more extensive during the Commercial Revolution.

Capitalism changed the method of production in the textile industry. Entrepreneurs, or those who organized and undertook the risks of a business and managed the trade, bought wool in quantity and distributed it to farm families, who spun the wool and wove it into cloth. The entrepreneur then had the cloth dyed and sold it on the national or international market. This method of manufacturing was called the **domestic system** because it was carried on in people's homes. It was also used to produce metalware, leather goods, paper, and glass.

Changes in Commercial Organization

The expansion of capitalism gave rise to other economic developments that made it easier and safer for European entrepreneurs to do business, both at home and abroad. One innovation of this period was the trading company, a capitalist association formed to facilitate overseas development. The joint-stock company was a common type of trading company.

Each joint-stock company was chartered by the government and given a monopoly to trade and settle in a given area. As you have read, England, the Netherlands, and France all established East India companies to direct their trade in Asia. Some associations, like the English East India Company and the Hudson's Bay Company, grew into what were essentially governments in themselves. Others, like the Virginia Company that founded the Jamestown colony, were absorbed by the government and ceased to exist as independent organizations.

The proliferation of trading companies resulted in the development of the stock exchange. Here would-be investors could gather to learn about speculative ventures and to buy and sell shares. One of the first European stock exchanges was established in Amsterdam in 1611.

As a result of increased trade and commerce, the institutions of banking and insurance expanded during the Commercial Revolution. In the past, banking had been carried on mainly as a private business and was limited to a small number of families with immense fortunes. With the growth of a strong and wealthy merchant class, banking became more widespread.

The development of the promissory note, or a written promise to pay a certain amount of money at a definite time, expanded the money supply and freed merchants from carrying large sums of gold

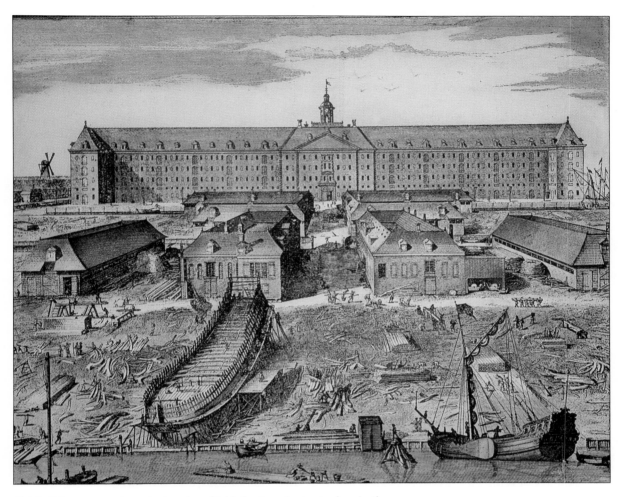

Shipbuilding was an important and profitable business in Amsterdam in the sixteenth and seventeenth centuries. Why? How were ships built at that time?

and silver. There was a tremendous rise in the number and quantity of loans. Also a great deal of money was borrowed by national governments. Two public banks, the Bank of Amsterdam, founded in 1609, and the Bank of England, established at the end of the century, regularized financial transactions and provided a secure place for deposits.

During the Middle Ages insurance had been offered to merchants and shipowners through the guilds. Now marine insurance became a thriving business. Commercial insurance was introduced in Antwerp, and fire insurance became popular after the Great London Fire in 1666. One of the most famous insurance companies, Lloyd's of London, was established in the seventeenth century.

SECTION REVIEW

1. In your own words, briefly define or identify: inflation, capitalism, trading company, promissory note.
2. List the causes for inflation during the Commercial Revolution.
3. How did the domestic system operate?
4. What developments occurred in banking and insurance during this time?
■ Today's worldwide system of trade supplies us with goods from many countries. Name some common commodities that are imported to the United States and tell where they come from.

THE STRUGGLE FOR EMPIRE

By the mid-seventeenth century it was clear that overseas expansion was immensely profitable. Few nations found the gold and silver that had made Spain wealthy, but commerce and trading brought rich returns. As trade expanded, rivalry among the commercial powers intensified. England and France struggled for control over North America. In the Far East, France and England competed in India and with the Dutch in the East Indies. All of the colonial powers, except Portugal, had rival colonies in the West Indies.

Seventeenth-Century Conflicts

As you read in Chapter 14, European nations in the latter half of the seventeenth century became embroiled in several wars. Most of these were not only dynastic struggles but also commercial wars involving overseas possessions.

War erupted between England and the Netherlands in 1665. One cause for the conflict was the seizure of the Dutch colony of New Netherland in 1664 by the Duke of York. Another was the fact that the Dutch ships were not permitted to carry goods to or from England. During this war the English suffered several setbacks. At one point Dutch ships sailed up the Thames and caused serious damage to the English fleet anchored there. England was further weakened by the Great Plague and the Great London Fire in 1666. In 1667 the two countries signed the Peace of Breda, whereby England retained control of New Netherland. In compensation the Dutch received the South American territory of Suriname and a limited amount of Dutch shipping was allowed in English ports.

The War of the League of Augsburg was the first European conflict to extend to colonial possessions in North America, where it was called King William's War. In the New World, French and Indian forces were pitted against the English. Armed conflict was sporadic and limited to the northern English colonies and eastern Canada. Both sides won some territories, but the Treaty of Ryswick in 1697 restored the boundaries that existed before the war.

Widening Rivalries

During the first half of the eighteenth century, European conflicts and New World rivalries continued. The two chief competitors in this period were Britain and France, and their rivalry culminated in the world's first global war.

In 1702 the War of the Spanish Succession broke out in Europe. In North America it was known as Queen Anne's War. This time the British won several victories. The French were forced out of Acadia and it became the British province of Nova Scotia. The Treaty of Utrecht, signed in 1713, confirmed this change, as well as Britain's possession of Newfoundland and territories in the Hudson Bay region. Thus England gained a large part of the French Empire in North America.

In 1739 the British fought a commercial war against the Spanish. Since Spain's colonial ports were closed to British shipping, smuggling was common. In a series of harsh reprisals, the Spanish captured and cut off the ear of Robert Jenkins, a British sea captain. When he appeared before Parliament brandishing his severed ear, the legislature declared war. During the War of Jenkins' Ear the British bombarded several Spanish American possessions, and the Spanish attacked Georgia, but there were no decisive results.

King George's War was the American phase of the War of the Austrian Succession. Fought between 1743 and 1748, it produced no change in the American balance of power.

Anglo-French rivalry was also intense in India because both countries wanted to control its trade. India at this time was divided into many warring states. To protect their commercial interests, Britain and France began to interfere in Indian affairs. France's interests were advanced by Joseph François Dupleix (doo-PLEX), those of Britain by Robert Clive.

Colonial rivalries between Britain and France reached a peak in the mid-eighteenth century. In 1755 warfare broke out in the Ohio Valley of North America, because the British colonists objected to French forts being constructed in this area. This conflict was called the French and Indian War because both sides relied heavily on their Native American allies. The following year fighting spread to Europe and Asia, where it was known as the Seven Years' War.

EUROPEAN EMPIRES IN THE AMERICAS, 1763

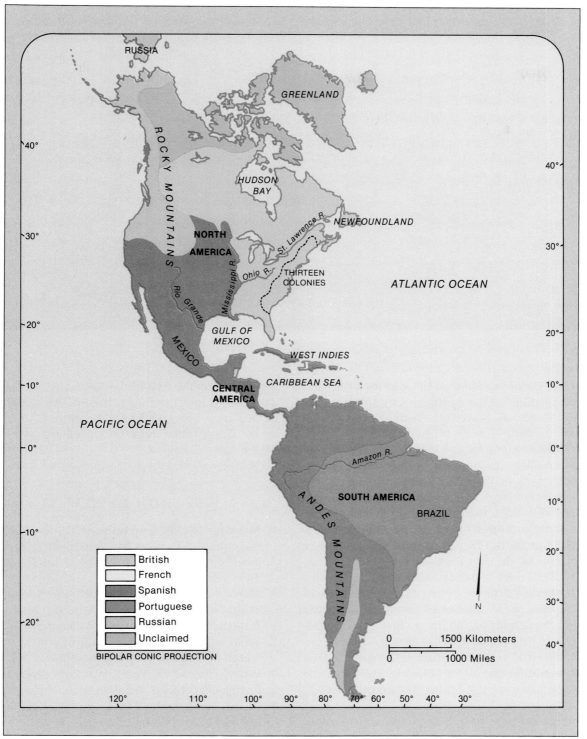

What natural geographic barrier divided the British and Spanish empires in North America? Why do you think conflict developed in this area?

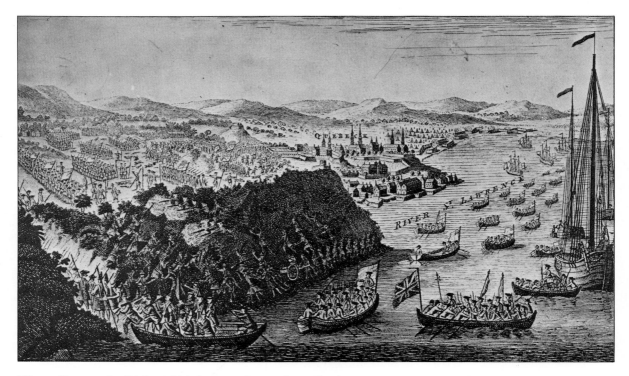

What military tactics did the British forces employ to take Quebec in 1759?

The European phase of this war involved most of the nations of the continent in a struggle over the balance of power. Its main result was to strengthen the German kingdom of Prussia.

Britain was victorious in the colonial phases of this conflict. In America British forces seized French forts in the Ohio Valley and successfully stormed Quebec. The governor-general surrendered all of New France to Britain in 1760.

In India British forces led by Clive also prevailed against the French. One of the most tragic incidents of the war took place in 1756 and involved the ruler of Bengal, who was a French ally. After Bengal's troops captured Calcutta, 146 British soldiers were imprisoned overnight in a small room. Next morning, all but 23 had died of suffocation in this "Black Hole of Calcutta." In revenge, the following year Clive attacked Bengal and won an important victory at Plassey. By 1761 the French had lost most of their Indian outposts.

The Treaty of Paris, signed in 1763, confirmed Britain's wartime gains. France lost all its territory on the North American mainland. Spain, one of France's allies, was awarded New Orleans and the French lands west of the Mississippi River. Britain received the lands east of the Mississippi, Canada, and some African outposts. Britain also acquired Florida from Spain and gained control of India's trade. Thus Britain now controlled the world's largest colonial empire.

SECTION REVIEW

1. Mapping: Use the map on page 357 to describe the extent of the Spanish, English, and Portuguese empires in the Americas in 1763. What areas remained unclaimed?
2. In your own words, briefly define or identify: Peace of Breda, Treaty of Utrecht, Jenkins, Dupleix, Clive, "Black Hole of Calcutta."
3. What were the causes for conflict in the seventeenth and eighteenth centuries?
4. Why is the Seven Years' War considered the first global conflict? What were the results?
- Do nations today still go to war over colonial possessions or trading privileges? Explain, giving examples to support your answer. For what other reasons do nations go to war?

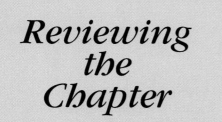

Reviewing the Chapter

Chapter Summary

The Age of Discovery began in the early fifteenth century, as a result of the efforts of Prince Henry of Portugal. Portuguese sailors first ventured south along the African coast, then to the Far East. After Columbus' voyages to the west, Spain concentrated on the exploration and conquest of the New World.

During the first half of the sixteenth century, Portugal and Spain established extensive overseas empires. That of Portugal was chiefly a trading network in Asia, although the Portuguese also colonized Brazil. Through the efforts of missionaries and settlers, Spain controlled large areas of North and South America.

Toward the end of the sixteenth century France, England, and the Netherlands began to expand. They established sizable overseas empires by claiming lands mainly in North America and by seizing Portuguese possessions in Asia.

Overseas expansion encouraged a Commercial Revolution in Europe. An increase in population and the influx of wealth from the New World led to inflation. Increased trading and commerce encouraged the growth of capitalism, the establishment of new commercial organizations, such as the joint-stock company, and innovations in banking and insurance.

During the seventeenth century rivalries developed among the colonizing nations, especially Britain and France, as they competed for territory in North America and Asia and trading rights. The numerous dynastic and commercial wars of the seventeenth and eighteenth centuries culminated in the Seven Years' War, the first global war. Britain emerged the victor in 1763.

1. When and how did the Age of Exploration begin?
2. What regions did Portugal and Spain colonize?
3. Name the northern European countries that established overseas empires and indicate when this process began.
4. How did overseas expansion change Europe?
5. What problems did overseas expansion cause?

Using Your Vocabulary

1. What was a caravel? Why was it considered an improvement?
2. Briefly define Papal Line of Demarcation and explain why it was instituted.
3. How did the term America originate?
4. How did the Pacific Ocean receive its name? By what other name was it known?
5. Identify the Spice Islands.
6. What is plantation slavery? How did this practice begin?
7. Name the economic systems employed by the Spanish and Portuguese in the New World.
8. Briefly define the terms: creoles, mestizos, and mulattos.
9. How did New York receive its name? What was it originally called?
10. Who is often considered "the father of New France"? Why?
11. How did Louisiana receive its name?
12. Name a type of trading company that emerged during this period. Describe its function and the role it played in colonization.
13. What does the term indentured servant mean? Where was this practice instituted? Was it successful? Explain briefly.
14. Briefly define the term Commercial Revolution. When did it occur?
15. What is capitalism? How does the entrepreneur reflect capitalist beliefs?
16. What innovation occurred in manufacturing during the Commercial Revolution? Why was it so named?
17. Briefly define promissory note and explain its purpose.

Developing Your Geography Skills

1. Use the Atlas map on page 758 to locate Mozambique, Madagascar, Kenya, and Sierra Leone.
2. Use the Atlas map on page 755 to locate the Strait of Malacca, Java, Borneo, and the Moluccas.
3. Use the Atlas map on page 755 to locate by means of latitude and longitude coordinates the cities of Bombay, Calcutta, Jakarta, Macao, Kyoto.
4. Use the Atlas map on page 760 to locate the Bahamas, the Dominican Republic, Puerto Rico, Guadeloupe, and Martinique. Which country claimed each island?
5. Use the map on page 357 and the Atlas map on page 760 to name the modern countries that were included in the Spanish Empire.

Recalling the Facts

1. List the factors that encouraged Europeans to begin voyages of discovery in the fifteenth century.
2. Why is Henry the Navigator considered an important historical figure? What were his accomplishments?
3. What was the significance of Columbus' discovery of America?
4. What were the consequences of the Treaty of Tordesillas?
5. Why is Magellan considered an important historical figure?
6. Name two Spanish conquistadors and the Indian civilizations they conquered. Why were these people subdued so easily?
7. Briefly explain why African slavery was introduced into the New World.
8. What problems did the Portuguese encounter in the Far East? How were they resolved?
9. Name two famous missionaries and their accomplishments.
10. What was the Northwest Passage? Why was it considered important?
11. What factors inhibited the growth of New France?

12. Describe the trade routes established by Europeans during this period.
13. List the factors that contributed to the Commercial Revolution and the ensuing results.
14. Briefly describe European expansion in India.
15. What was the War of Jenkins' Ear?
16. Name the colonial wars in which Britain made territorial gains and explain what they were for each war.

Essay Questions

1. Discuss European colonization in the Far East and the motives involved.
2. Explain the role religion played in European expansion. What were the motives and the results? Be sure to include both Protestantism and Catholicism.
3. Compare and contrast the Spanish and Portuguese empires. What factors caused the Portuguese Empire to decline in the 1600's?
4. Discuss the effects of overseas expansion on European society and economy. How did it affect colonized areas? Do you think the results were positive or negative? Explain.
5. Explain how commerce encouraged international competition and warfare in the eighteenth century. Give some examples of areas in which international competition exists today.

Critical Thinking

1. Would you consider the *Writings of Columbus* a reliable source of data? Why or why not?
2. Various tales and legends are mentioned in this chapter. Explain which ones were based on verifiable facts. Which were not?
3. What equivocal assumption was made by Columbus? When was it corrected?
4. How did the caste system that developed in Spanish America reflect bias?
5. The goals of missionaries in the New World were to convert the Indians to Christianity and to teach them European ways of life. On what unstated assumptions were these goals based?

Reviewing the Unit

Developing a Sense of Time

Examine the time line below and answer the questions that follow.

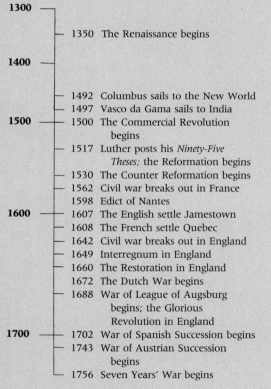

1300		
	1350	The Renaissance begins
1400		
	1492	Columbus sails to the New World
	1497	Vasco da Gama sails to India
1500	1500	The Commercial Revolution begins
	1517	Luther posts his *Ninety-Five Theses;* the Reformation begins
	1530	The Counter Reformation begins
	1562	Civil war breaks out in France
	1598	Edict of Nantes
1600	1607	The English settle Jamestown
	1608	The French settle Quebec
	1642	Civil war breaks out in England
	1649	Interregnum in England
	1660	The Restoration in England
	1672	The Dutch War begins
	1688	War of League of Augsburg begins; the Glorious Revolution in England
1700	1702	War of Spanish Succession begins
	1743	War of Austrian Succession begins
	1756	Seven Years' War begins

1. What two voyages of discovery occurred about the same time?
2. What event marks the beginning of the Reformation? What is the date?
3. Which was settled first: Quebec or Jamestown?
4. Did civil war break out first in England or France?

Reviewing Social Science Skills

Reading and Developing an Organizational Chart

1. What is the purpose of an organizational chart?
2. Using the information in Chapter 15, make an organizational chart on a separate sheet of paper listing European conflicts in North America. Your chart should include the name of the European war, the dates, the name of the North American war, and a description of the results in North America.
3. Using the information in Chapter 15, make an organizational chart on a separate sheet of paper listing the major European explorers in chronological order and their accomplishments. Your chart should include the name of the explorer, the country that financed the expedition, the date(s), and a brief description.

Critical Thinking

1. According to the divine right of kings, monarchs had the right to rule with few limits to their power, and they were accountable only to God. How was this theory proved a fallacy in England?
2. From what you have read about Louis XIV, how did his reign exemplify the values of absolutism? Give specific examples in your your answer. What other monarchs were absolutists?
3. It has been said that New World colonies were exploited, or used unfairly to gain profit, by their home countries. Would you consider this a warranted or unwarranted claim? Give examples to support your opinion.

Linking Past and Present

The ideas of Renaissance thinkers had a great impact on west European society. During this time people changed the way they lived and thought. What Renaissance concepts or ideals are still valued by our society today? Why?

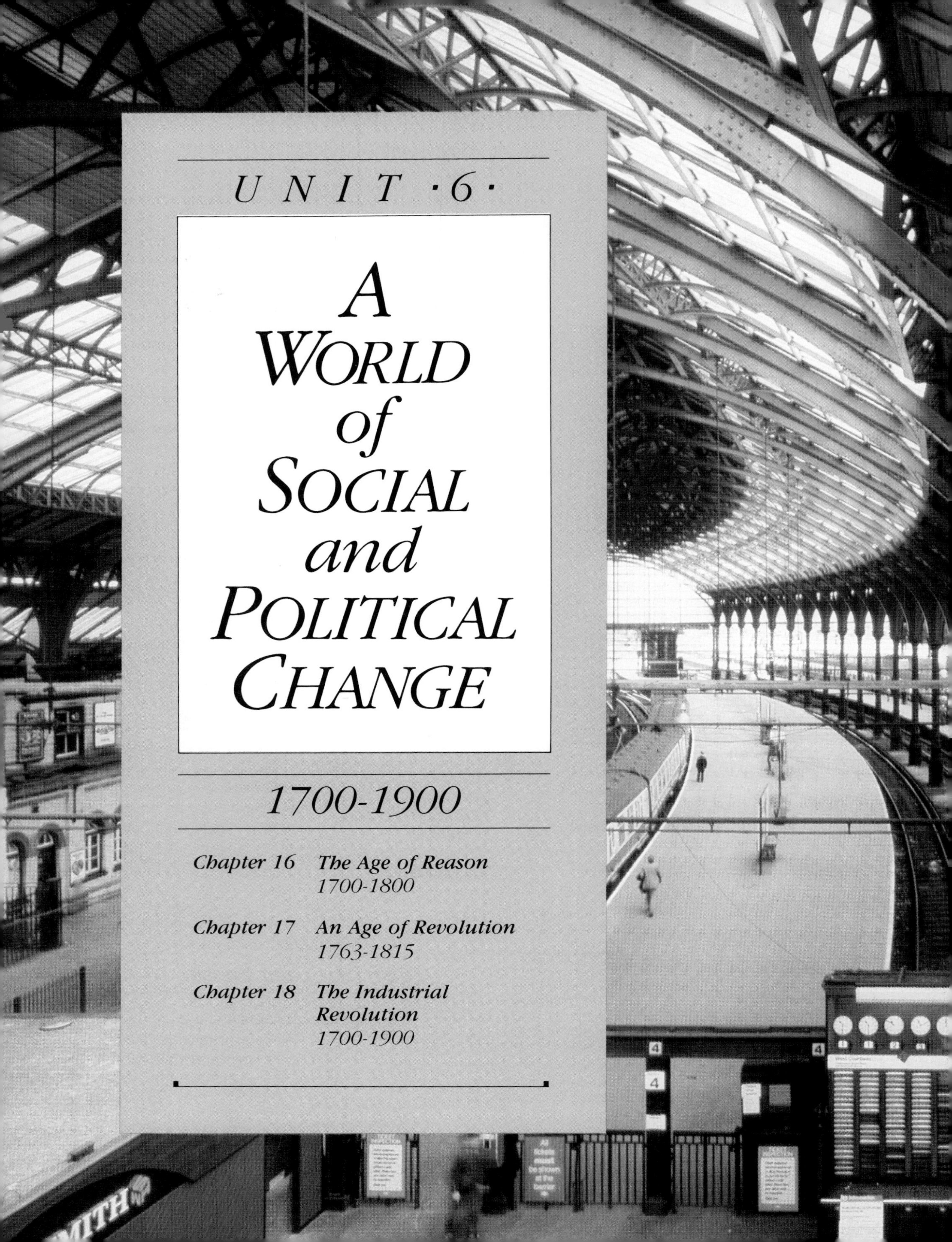

UNIT ·6·

A WORLD of SOCIAL and POLITICAL CHANGE

1700-1900

CHAPTER ·16·

THE AGE OF REASON

1700–1800

Objectives

- *To understand the major contributions of the scientific revolution to the eighteenth century*

- *To know how the Enlightenment changed European ways of thinking*

- *To explain why Prussia and Austria struggled for dominance*

- *To describe the rise of Russia as a European power*

- *To understand some of the ways eighteenth-century thought was reflected in the arts*

*T*hree concepts helped shape the development of Europe in the eighteenth century: reason, natural law, and reform. During the 1700's, a period described as the Age of Enlightenment or the Age of Reason, Europe's intellectuals believed that the use of reason would lead people to discover the natural laws, or principles basic to human nature, governing all life. Based on this discovery, people and governments then could ensure future progress.

The thinkers who held this belief and spread their ideas for change throughout Europe became known as **philosophes** (fee-luh-ZAWFS), the French word for philosophers. Not all of them, however, were French or philosophers. Many were economists, political scientists, writers, artists, and social reformers. France became the center of the Enlightenment, but the movement attracted intellectuals from all over the continent.

The intellectual advances of the seventeenth century, especially the work of English scholars and scientists such as John Locke and Sir Isaac Newton, led to the new views of the world expressed in the 1700's. Religion no longer guided every aspect of life.

Liberal reforms were proposed in education, law, and economic policy. Demands were made for freedom of speech and for limiting the privileges of kings and nobles.

The rationalist view of the world in the eighteenth century helped change the direction of culture, especially the arts. Art and music became less decorative and complex, while literature started to reflect the social problems and concerns of all classes of society.

THE SCIENTIFIC REVOLUTION

As the seventeenth century opened scientists had already begun to look at the world in new ways. The results of their research proved so far-reaching that they have been termed a scientific revolution.

Mathematics had become the language of scientists. Then in 1687 Sir Isaac Newton explained why heavenly bodies move in a certain order and why earthbound objects fall at increasing speeds. This discovery led to the Enlightenment theory that understanding the laws of nature would result in an understanding of the laws governing people and society.

Astronomy and Physics

The new era in science began taking shape in the sixteenth century in the field of astronomy. Since classical times, scholars had accepted the teachings of Ptolemy, who believed that the earth was the center of the solar system. According to this geocentric, or earth-centered, theory, the sun and all the planets revolved around the earth. Later observations made some scientists doubt this theory.

A Polish churchman and scientist, Nicholas Copernicus, was certain that the sun, not the earth, was the center of the solar system. His heliocentric, or sun-centered, theory would have been labeled heresy, however, because Christianity had embraced the Ptolemaic view. This belief placed human beings at the center of the universe. Shortly before his death in 1543, Copernicus published his startling conclusions in a book called *On the Revolutions of the Heavenly Spheres.*

The work of Copernicus was not accepted until decades later. A Danish astronomer, Tycho Brahe (TEE-koh BRAH-eh), made detailed observations of the planets that seemed to confirm the heliocentric theory.

An assistant of Brahe, Johannes Kepler, accepted the Copernican theory and was the first to offer mathematical proof of it. Although Copernicus had described planetary motion as circular, Kepler found that the planets actually moved in elliptical orbits.

Newton is said to have learned about gravity from falling apples. How do fact and fiction differ?

Galileo, the Italian scientist whose work was well-known throughout Europe by the start of the seventeenth century, offered another proof of the Copernican theory. After constructing the first complete astronomical telescope in 1609, he made lengthy observations. Among his discoveries were the moons of Jupiter. It was now clear that not all celestial bodies revolved around the earth. Like Copernicus, Galileo did not publish his theories immediately for fear of persecution by the Church and other scientists. When he did decide to publish his *Dialogue on the Two Chief Systems of the World* in 1632, he was called before the Inquisition in Rome and forced to deny his theories.

Galileo had less trouble with his experiments and discoveries in the field of physics. Kepler had developed mathematical laws to describe planetary motion, but Galileo used them to describe the motion of earthbound objects.

In the 1600's Sir Isaac Newton unified the works of Kepler and Galileo by proposing one theory that explained motion both in the heavens and on earth. Newton described this law of gravitation in his *Mathematical Principles of Natural Philosophy*, published in 1687. According to Newton's law, all the objects in the universe attract each other, and the force of their attraction is in proportion to their masses and their distance from each other. Like Kepler and Galileo, Newton used mathematics to describe his discovery. Many scholars consider Newton's work the starting point for the Enlightenment movement.

Scientific Thought

By the late seventeenth century, the general public was more receptive to revolutionary theories such as those of Newton and Francis Bacon, an English statesman and philosopher. Bacon believed that "knowledge is power." He planned a multivolume work that would reorganize the sciences, but only two books were completed. In 1620 he published the most influential of these two volumes, *Novum Organum*. In it he outlined a new approach to learning, the inductive method. This process relies on many observations in order to formulate general laws. It differs from the deductive method of reasoning favored by the medieval scholastics, which goes from the general to the specific. Bacon believed that only with the inductive method could real progress be made in science.

A French contemporary of Bacon's, René Descartes (reh-NAY day-CART), centered his scientific research on optics, especially the reflection and refraction of light, and on mathematics. He also developed the field of analytical, or coordinate, geometry. In his *Discourse on Method*, published in 1637, Descartes stressed the need for clear and or-

Christopher Wren designed this octagonal clock room for the Royal Greenwich Observatory, founded in 1675. The clocks could run without interruption for a year. What connection is there between this fact and the Scientific Revolution?

The founder of modern chemistry, Antoine Lavoisier, prepares an experiment to prove the indestructibility of matter. Marie Ann Paulze, his wife, worked with Lavoisier and recorded data. How did her role in the laboratory differ from that of the majority of women during the 1800's? During the 1900's?

derly thought. He supported Bacon's inductive method, but relied more on logic.

As the scientific revolution progressed, it became necessary to find a way to make all the new information available. New scientific associations and organizations that enabled scholars to gather together and exchange ideas were established in most European countries. One of the most famous was England's Royal Society, chartered by King Charles II in 1662. Soon afterward the Royal Observatory opened at Greenwich. By the early 1700's scientific academies for education and research had also been founded in Paris, Rome, Florence, and Berlin.

Other Discoveries

Astronomy and physics were not the only scientific areas to experience change. Almost every branch of the physical and natural sciences was af-

fected by the new trends in sixteenth- and seventeenth-century thought.

In 1543 a Flemish scientist, Andreas Vesalius, published *On the Fabric of the Human Body*. This detailed work on human anatomy was based on the dissection of cadavers, a practice that the Catholic Church opposed. Vesalius' conclusions, like those of Copernicus, contradicted traditional religious beliefs and Church authorities.

Another pioneer of this era was an English physician, William Harvey. In 1628 Harvey demonstrated the function of the heart and described the circulation of blood in his *Anatomical Treatise on the Motion of the Heart and Blood in Animals.*

Harvey had developed his theories before the invention of the microscope. However, later microscopic observations would open up a whole new world in the science of biology.

In other developments British chemists successfully isolated gases. By 1780 a French scientist,

Antoine Lavoisier (lah-vwah-ZYAY), founded modern chemistry.

A Swedish botanist of the early eighteenth century, Carolus Linnaeus (luh-NAY-us), founded the modern method of classifying plants and animals. His system, based on relationships among living things, identifies each one by family, genus, and species. By using Latin for these identifying names, Linnaeus made it the basis for a universal scientific language.

SECTION REVIEW

1. In your own words, briefly define or identify: heliocentric, Brahe, Bacon, inductive method, Descartes, Royal Society, Harvey, Linnaeus.
2. How did the work of Kepler and Galileo confirm that of Copernicus?
3. What principle did Newton formulate that initiated the Enlightenment movement?
- The discoveries of the sixteenth and seventeenth centuries were so far-reaching that they have been called a scientific revolution. Do you think that the same term can be used to describe the advances being made today?

THE ENLIGHTENMENT

The scientific revolution paved the way for the Enlightenment and a new view of the world. The rational investigations and analyses on which science depended seemed to offer hope for progress in all areas of life. If human reason could determine laws by which the universe operates, could such reason also be applied to governing society? This was the challenge of the Enlightenment.

Forerunners in Political Thought

While scientists had proved that mathematical laws governed the motion of bodies both in space and on earth, those who studied the relationships of people and nations relied on natural law. Natural law assumes that some principles are basic and fundamental to human nature everywhere. Just as physical laws govern planets, governments based on natural law were thought able to ensure the stability and order necessary for civilized society.

One of the first modern thinkers to base his work on natural law was a Dutch jurist, Hugo Grotius (GROH-shee-us). Out of his personal experiences in the Dutch revolt against the Spanish and

IMPORTANT FRENCH PHILOSOPHES DURING THE ENLIGHTENMENT		
PHILOSOPHE	DATES	CONTRIBUTIONS
Voltaire	1694–1778	Wrote *Candide* and other works using satire to attack the injustices of his time; advocated religious tolerance and freedom of speech.
Montesquieu	1689–1755	French noble and author of *The Spirit of the Laws*; proposed that the power of government should be divided among legislative, executive, and judicial branches, which would check and balance one another.
Denis Diderot	1713–1784	Edited the *Encyclopedia*, a massive work that compiled the knowledge of the 1700's including new ideas about science and government.
Jean Jacques Rousseau	1712–1778	Wrote *The Social Contract*; stressed the goodness of human nature and suggested that good government should be based on the consent of the governed.

in the Thirty Years' War, he developed principles to guide nations in their international relations.

The English political theorist, Thomas Hobbes, was less interested in international relations than in analyzing how modern states had taken shape. In his view, humans in the "state of nature," that is, before the formation of governments, suffered chaos and anarchy. Hobbes said their lives were "solitary, poor, nasty, brutish, and short." Fear of death forced people to give up some of their natural rights to a ruler. In 1651 Hobbes wrote in his *Leviathan* that to protect these natural rights required the exercise of authoritarian rule.

Another English theorist, John Locke, had a more optimistic view of the state of nature. He believed that this state was threatened by those few who would keep the majority from enjoying natural rights to life, liberty, and property. For this reason people willingly agreed to make a social contract with a ruler, who became a party to this contract, in return for protection.

Locke favored constitutional monarchy as the ideal form of government. However, if a monarch violated the people's natural rights, they were justified in revolting and installing a new ruler. Locke outlined his theories in *Two Treatises of Government*, published in 1690, the year after England's Glorious Revolution had overthrown King James II. His ideas helped shape the American colonists' Declaration of Independence.

The Philosophes

With the death of King Louis XIV of France and with the spread of scientific knowledge, France entered a new age of thought and creativity in the eighteenth century. A group of intellectuals in France known as the *philosophes* became the major figures of the Enlightenment. They represented many different points of view, but most of them glorified human reason and freedom of conscience. They examined established traditions and ridiculed those they regarded as irrational and useless. They were also quite secular in their approach and some attacked organized religion.

A major political thinker among the *philosophes* was the Baron de Montesquieu (duh-mon-tuh-SKEW), a French nobleman. In 1748 he published *The Spirit of Laws*, in which he used history as well

as Europe's growing knowledge of the peoples of Asia and Africa to try to reason out what form of government might be best or most natural. He believed that European states could form better, stronger governments by combining elements of monarchy, democracy, and aristocracy. Montesquieu proposed a separation and balance of powers among the executive, legislative, and judicial branches of government. Ideas such as these had an important impact on the men who wrote the United States Constitution.

Probably the most famous of all the *philosophes* was Voltaire (vohl-TAIR). Through his histories, poems, plays, and essays, Voltaire became the spokesperson of the Enlightenment. His writing ridiculed tradition and custom when they went against reason. He argued that oppression from any source must be opposed. Faith in reason and in the individual formed the basis of Voltaire's optimistic view of the future. Like Montesquieu, Voltaire admired the English scholars and introduced the ideas of Locke in France.

Rousseau was a strong believer in the nobility of the individual and in the natural law. How does this photo reflect his ideas?

While Voltaire recognized the strengths of European civilization, his slightly younger contemporary, Jean-Jacques Rousseau (roo-SOH), had little hope for reason or for civilization. Born in Switzerland, he first gained fame with an essay attacking civilization as corrupting.

It has been said that Rousseau urged a "return to nature." However, he recognized the need for social order. Rousseau published his most famous work, *The Social Contract,* in 1762. In it he explained how societies had come about and how they should be governed. A key concept for him was the general will, or the just law that embodies the sovereignty of the people. Rousseau challenged the rule of reason and was among the first thinkers of his time to foresee the growing nation-state movement in Europe's political system.

The ideas of the *philosophes* and other Enlightenment thinkers were gathered in the *Encyclopedia.* Denis Diderot (dee-DROH), editor of the twenty-eight volume work, obtained articles from Rousseau and Montesquieu, among many others. The first volume appeared in 1751, and the last in 1772.

Diderot's work aroused the opposition of the Church, which condemned its emphasis on material things. The *Encyclopedia* criticized religious superstition and told the public about natural law and the wonders of science. It also exposed the evils of the Old Regime and made Louis XV angry because of its criticism of his monarchy.

Describe the elements of Hobbes' political theory using this illustration from the title page of the "Leviathan." Do you agree or disagree with Hobbes' view?

The Social Contract

During the Enlightenment, one of the fundamental questions debated by the philosophes *was the essence of human nature and how it was reflected in society. Were people good or bad? What kind of government was the most rational? Jean-Jacques Rousseau explained his ideas in* The Social Contract, *published in 1762.*

The following excerpt is from Book 1. After reading this excerpt, answer the questions that follow.

Man was born free, and everywhere he is in chains. One who believes himself the master of others is nonetheless a greater slave than they. How did this change occur? I do not know. What can make it legitimate? I believe I can answer this question.

If I were to consider only force and the effect it produces, I would say that as long as a people is constrained to obey and does so, it does well; as soon as it can shake off the yoke and does so, it does even better. For in recovering its freedom by means of the same right used to steal it, either the people are justified in taking it back, or those who took it away were not justified in doing so. But the social order is a sacred right that serves as a basis for all the others. However, this right does not come from nature; it is therefore based on conventions. The problem is to know what these conventions are. . . .

Now since men cannot engender new forces, but merely unite and direct existing ones, they have no other means of self-preservation except to form, by aggregation, a sum of forces that can prevail over motivation; and make them act in concert. This sum of forces can arise only from the cooperation of many. But since each man's force and freedom are the primary instruments of his self-preservation, how is he to engage them without harming himself and without neglecting the cares he owes to himself? In the context of my subject, this difficulty can be stated in these terms:

"Find a form of association that defends and protects the person and goods of each associate with all the common force, and by means of which each one, uniting with all, nevertheless obeys only himself and remains as free as before." This is the fundamental problem which is solved by the social contract. . . .

[The social compact] can be reduced to the following terms. *Each of us puts his person and all his power in common under the supreme direction of the general will; and in a body we receive each member as an indivisible part of the whole.*

Instantly, in place of the private person of each contracting party, this act of association produces a moral and collective body, composed of as many members as there are voices in the assembly, which receives from this same act its unity, its common *self,* its life, and its will. This public person, formed thus by the union of all the others, formerly took the name *City,* and now takes that of *Republic* or *body politic,* which its members call *State* when it is passive, *Sovereign* when active, *Power* when comparing it to similar bodies. As for the associates, they collectively take the name *people;* and individually are called *Citizens* as participants in the sovereign authority, and *Subjects* as subject to the laws of the State.

Source: Adapted from Roger D. Masters, ed., *On the Social Contract, Jean-Jacques Rousseau.* Copyright © 1978 by St. Martin's Press, Inc.

1. Why is the social order necessary? On what is it based?
2. What must people do to protect themselves?
3. How does Rousseau's analysis of government compare with that of Hobbes? Of Locke?

Another way in which Enlightenment ideas were spread was through the *salons. Salons* were gatherings in the homes of intellectual women, who invited the thinkers and artists of the day to exchange ideas. Marie Thérèse Geoffrin (zhoff-RAN) was famous for her salons, as was Louise d'Epinay (deh-pee-NAY), a benefactor of Rousseau and friend of Diderot. D'Epinay was also noted for her book on the education of girls, *The Conversations of Emilie,* published in 1775. Another woman prominent during the Enlightenment, Gabrielle du Chatelet Lomont (shah-tuh-LAY loh-MAWN), was a mathematician and physicist who furthered the ideas of Newton in France.

The Enlightenment Outside France

Although centered in France, the Enlightenment was an international movement. Its most influential contributor in the British Isles was the Scottish economist, Adam Smith. In his *Wealth of Nations,* published in 1776, he applied the concept of natural law to the means of production and exchange and attacked mercantilism. Smith argued that it would be better to govern the marketplace by the natural processes of competition and of supply and demand.

Two English writers turned their attention to far different subjects. In *The Decline and Fall of the Roman Empire,* the historian Edward Gibbon shocked many of his readers by blaming Christianity for the fall of Rome. Mary Wollstonecraft, an Enlightenment figure who favored equal rights for women, could be considered a forerunner of today's women's movement. Her book, *Vindication of the Rights of Women,* was published in 1792.

In Germany, Moses Mendelssohn (MEN-duhl-sohn) urged Jews to fight political and social restrictions and to become participants in the intellectual activity of the times. In Italy Cesare Beccaria (beck-KAHR-ee-ah) became one of the first to attack capital punishment.

Enlightened Despotism

Rousseau's concept of the ideal democracy and Montesquieu's theory of separation of powers had sought to end the abuses of the Old Regime. Both

Diderot organized data on many subjects, including agriculture. How does Diderot's work fit the definition of an encyclopedia?

This painting for Josephine de Beauharnais, done in the early 1800's, imagines a typical gathering of intellectuals at one of Madame Geoffrin's famous salons. How did such meetings help to advance knowledge during the Age of Reason?

failed, so the *philosophes* looked to another movement of the Enlightenment that became known as *enlightened despotism*. As the term implies, the monarchs did not give up their belief in the principle of divine right or their prerogative of absolute rule. Instead, they based their authority to rule on the grounds of their usefulness to society.

Enlightened despotism was greatly favored by Frederick the Great in Prussia, Catherine the Great in Russia, and Joseph II in Austria—three of the period's major ruling figures. Their countries would serve as testing grounds for the Age of Reason's social, religious, and economic programs.

Enlightened despots supported a number of reforms. Most of them were designed to make administration easier and to produce more income for the royal treasuries. Some reforms sought to bring about equality before the law, religious toleration, and significant reductions of noble and clerical privileges.

SECTION REVIEW

1. In your own words, briefly define or identify: natural law, Grotius, *Leviathan,* Voltaire, Rousseau, Diderot, Wollstonecraft, Beccaria.
2. How did Locke's theory of government differ from that of Hobbes?
3. Which idea of Montesquieu was used by the men who wrote the Constitution of the United States?
4. How did Adam Smith apply the principle of natural law to economics?
■ The people of the Enlightenment had such great faith in rational thought that the eighteenth century is often called the Age of Reason. Do you live in an Age of Reason? How else would you describe the time in which you live? Give reasons for your answers.

Use the color key of this map to describe how Europe was ruled in 1715.

STATE BUILDING IN CENTRAL EUROPE

By the time of the Enlightenment, the political stage of Europe had two relatively new players, Prussia and Austria. Having greatly expanded during the 1600's, they were to perform major roles for the next two centuries.

The Growth of Prussia

Since the Middle Ages the Hohenzollerns had ruled a small north German state called Brandenburg. In the early seventeenth century the Hohenzollerns began a policy of expansion. One of their earliest acquisitions was the duchy of Prussia, toward the east.

In 1640 Frederick William became ruler of Brandenburg-Prussia. He ruled until 1688 and is known today as the Great Elector, for the Hohenzollerns were among the Electors of the Holy Roman Emperor. Through shrewd participation in the Thirty Years' War, Frederick William won some additional territories, confirmed by the Treaty of Westphalia in 1648.

Frederick William built up an army, led by Junkers (YOON-kurz), or landowners. He strongly favored the policy of **militarism,** or reliance on the army. At the same time he planned the reorganization of the state's scattered territories, encouraged manufacturing and commerce, and began to develop Berlin as a capital city.

The Great Elector's efforts abroad, however, were not as successful. He won a few territorial concessions from Poland, but made no significant impact on Sweden. His relations with Louis XIV of France gained nothing for Prussia. Yet at the time of his death, Prussia had become a state that could not be ignored.

Determined to win a royal title, the Great Elector's successor, his son Frederick III, achieved this goal by helping Emperor Leopold I against France in the War of the Spanish Succession. As a reward, the emperor gave him the title of king in Prussia, even though kingdoms could not be granted within the Holy Roman Empire. Prussia, however, was located outside its borders. The Hohenzollern ruler was crowned Frederick I in 1701. Soon the title became "king of Prussia."

In 1713 Frederick's son, Frederick William I, inherited the throne. Frederick William differed from most of his fellow absolutists by following a policy of religious toleration and by making education compulsory.

Frederick William had trouble with his heir, Frederick II, who showed no interest in the military or in administration. After several years of harsh discipline, he settled down to learn the business of kingship. Frederick II succeeded his father in 1740, and became known as Frederick the Great.

As an enlightened despot, Frederick the Great considered himself the "first servant of the state," not a divine-right ruler. He became known for his military exploits, especially those that brought him into conflict with the Hapsburgs of Austria. Under Frederick the Great's leadership Prussia became the most formidable military power in Europe, able to challenge even France and Russia.

Expanding Austria

Ever since the fifteenth century, a member of the Hapsburg family had been chosen Holy Roman Emperor. This title became less meaningful as the empire lost what little authority it had. The Hapsburgs built up a power base of their own in Austria that did not depend on imperial control. During the 1500's they added Bohemia and western Hungary to their territories.

Hapsburg expansion in the seventeenth century was mainly toward the east, at the expense of the Ottoman Turks. Although the Ottomans had been turned away at Vienna by Charles I of Spain, and defeated at Lepanto during the reign of his son

Philip II, they continued to be a strong force in the Mediterranean region.

In the early seventeenth century the Turks seized Persia and took Crete from Venice. As time went on, however, weaknesses within the Turkish state prevented its armies from keeping up with those of Europe in either administration or weaponry. When the Turks threatened Vienna again late in the 1600's, they met their match.

In 1683 Ottoman forces besieged Vienna for two months. They were defeated by a mixed army of Poles, Germans, and troops from various Austrian possessions. Under the military leadership of Eugene of Savoy, the European army drove the Turks completely out of Hungary. In 1699 the Peace of Karlowitz gave Austria not only this territory, but also Transylvania, in present-day Romania, and Croatia, now Yugoslavia.

The Austrian Hapsburgs also profited from the War of the Spanish Succession in the early eighteenth century. Eugene of Savoy, allied with the British, won several victories against the combined forces of France and Spain. The Peace of Utrecht in 1713 awarded Austria the Spanish Netherlands (now Belgium), Sardinia, Naples, and Milan.

Conflict Between Prussia and Austria

Charles VI, who ruled the Austrian domains in the early eighteenth century, was the last male Hapsburg. When it became clear that his heir would be his oldest daughter, Maria Theresa, he set about trying to protect her from future aggressions. He feared that the powers of Europe would march on Austrian territories when she came to the throne. For years Charles worked to gain approval of the Pragmatic Sanction, a document guaranteeing both the territorial integrity of the Austrian domains and his daughter's succession to the throne. By the time he died in 1740, he had the signatures of all the major European powers.

At Charles' death the Pragmatic Sanction was challenged by Frederick the Great of Prussia. Late in 1740 he invaded Silesia, a rich Austrian possession north of Bohemia. This step began the War of the Austrian Succession, which lasted until 1748. Prussia's allies included France and Spain, while Austria was joined by Britain and the Netherlands. Maria Theresa was also aided by large numbers of Hungarian troops.

As you read in Chapter 15, the War of the Austrian Succession had an impact on America, but led to no important territorial changes. In Europe, however, the war confirmed Prussia's control over Silesia. In return for agreeing to this action, Maria Theresa was successful in having her husband crowned Francis I, Holy Roman Emperor. Although Austria had failed to win back Silesia, it had kept the other powers of Europe from partitioning its territories among themselves.

During the next few years Europe underwent such drastic shifts in the balance of power that these events came to be known as the Diplomatic Revolution. Britain, formerly allied with Austria, now sided with Prussia. Austria reversed its traditional opposition to France and became its ally. This alliance was sealed with the marriage of Maria Theresa's daughter, Marie Antoinette, to the French prince who would become Louis XVI. In spite of these shifts, two situations remained constant: Britain and France were always on opposite sides, and so were Austria and Prussia.

The realignment of forces took concrete form in the Seven Years' War, which broke out in 1756. While the chief aim of the War of the Austrian Succession had been to partition Austria, now the main goal was to partition Prussia. Maria Theresa wanted to regain Silesia, and her allies, France and Russia, wanted to contain the growing power of Frederick the Great. The Prussian army, however, proved its military superiority as Frederick the Great defended his country against attack. The Peace of Hubertusburg that ended the war in 1763 left the European situation much the same, but signaled the emergence of Prussia as a first-rate European power.

In Austria, Maria Theresa now pursued a more peaceful course. When her husband died in 1765, she named her son Joseph as co-regent. However, she continued to rule until her death in 1780.

Maria Theresa of Austria and Francis I join eleven of their children for a family portrait. What role did the family play in how Europe was governed?

Maria Theresa's son, Joseph II, was less cautious than his mother. Deeply impressed by Enlightenment ideas, he was determined to make the Austrian empire more humane and efficient. Among his goals were to lessen hereditary privilege, reduce the power of the Catholic Church, abolish serfdom, and reform the judicial system. However, his achievements fell far short of his goals because he had little support in carrying out his proposed reforms. Joseph did manage to abolish serfdom and put an end to most feudal dues. He also banned the use of torture and founded hospitals, asylums, and orphanages.

SECTION REVIEW

1. Mapping: Use the map on page 374, to locate the following: Brandenburg, Prussia, Berlin, Hungary, and Transylvania. Why were these areas crucial to the Hapsburgs?
2. In your own words, briefly define or identify: Hohenzollerns, militarism, Junkers, Eugene of Savoy, Frederick the Great, Diplomatic Revolution, Pragmatic Sanction.
3. How did the Great Elector strengthen his country?
4. How did Frederick William I of Prussia differ from other European absolutists?
5. What caused the War of the Austrian Succession and what were its chief results?
6. Why did Joseph II of Austria fail to achieve most of his goals?
- Prussia and Austria expanded through the efforts of two strong families, the Hohenzollerns and the Hapsburgs. Do royal families today have this kind of power? Give reasons for your answers.

THE RISE OF RUSSIA

Like Prussia and Austria, Russia first began to exert a major influence on European affairs in the eighteenth century. Russia not only expanded geographically, but also was drawn more closely into the culture of western Europe.

An Era of Unrest

As you read in Chapter 7, the Time of Troubles in Russia ended in 1613 with the election of Michael Romanov as czar, the first of the Romanov line. Although his twenty-two-year reign was relatively peaceful, unrest would characterize the next forty years of his immediate successors' rule.

One difficulty involved the serfs and peasants who made up the vast bulk of Russia's population. During the 1640's the institution of serfdom was more firmly rooted in Russian life than ever before. Earlier, escaped serfs could gain their freedom if they avoided capture for fifteen years. This time limit was now abolished, and serfs could never change their status.

The discontented masses found a leader in Stephen Razin. He was from the Don River region and a *Cossack*, a term identifying people from several parts of eastern Europe. In 1667 he gathered a force of thousands and succeeded in capturing several towns in southern Russia. He was seized and executed in 1671, but became a hero to the peasants fighting against their oppressors.

The Russian Orthodox Church also underwent a crisis during this period. In the 1650's the Church hierarchy sought to introduce reforms in its texts and rituals. The patriarch wanted to bring Russian practices closer to those of the Church in Greece. Most of the proposed alterations involved relatively minor matters, but ritual was extremely important to the illiterate Russian peasantry.

Hundreds of thousands of Russians refused to accept the reforms, and became known as Old Believers. Many of them, convinced that the end of the world was at hand, burned themselves to death in order to avoid being called heretics. This split in the Russian Church lasted for centuries. As late as the 1880's, it was estimated that there were 13 million Old Believers.

Peter the Great

The transformation of Russia into a modern state began with Peter I, who came to the throne at the age of ten in 1682. Intelligent, energetic, and violent at times, he was known even in his own time as Peter the Great.

Because of warring factions among the royal family, Peter was named co-ruler with his men-

Peter the Great cuts off a noble's beard, symbolizing Peter's efforts to westernize Russia. How does this picture compare with modern cartoons?

tally defective half-brother Ivan. Actually Peter's mother ruled the country until her death in 1694, at which time Peter took over complete control.

One of Peter's first acts was to go abroad, something none of his predecessors had ever done. He spent fifteen months in the Netherlands and England, visiting factories, workshops, and shipyards so that he could learn as much as possible about western technology. Peter even took several hundred skilled workers back to Russia with him.

Peter's temper was displayed publicly as soon as he returned to Russia, where an uprising by the *streltsi* threatened to disrupt the country. Peter was unable to learn who of these special musketeers in the Moscow garrison had started the rebellion, so he organized a public massacre of some 1,200 of them. Then Peter began a reorganization of the Russian army to make it more efficient. He used western Europeans to train his forces, and supplied his troops with the latest weapons.

Russia was at war during most of Peter's reign. His primary enemy was Sweden, at the time one of Europe's most powerful nations. In 1700 the two countries clashed in the Great Northern War. At first Russia met with severe defeats, which inspired Peter to hasten the modernization of the armed forces. In 1708 the Swedes, under Charles XII, invaded Russia. Russian forces drew them into the interior by retreating, forcing them to spend a particularly bitter winter on the snow-swept plains. Then, in the spring of 1709, the Russians overwhelmingly defeated the Swedish army at Poltava. Further Russian victories and the death of Charles XII forced Sweden to make concessions in the Treaty of Nystadt (NIE-staht), signed in 1721. The treaty confirmed Russian control over territory along the Gulf of Finland that was important for commerce and defense.

It was in this Gulf region that Peter established a new capital city, St. Petersburg, now known as Leningrad. He hated Moscow, loved the sea, and wanted a "great window for Russia to look out at Europe." The czar built an elegant city in the style of Louis XIV's palace at Versailles, and Russian court life was revived.

An efficient army, a new navy, and a new capital were only three of Peter's achievements. Russia at this time was quite backward compared to the nations of western Europe. The country had never adopted Arabic numerals. Its women wore veils, and its men sported long beards. Peter decreed that men should shave off their beards and women should no longer wear veils. He urged people to adopt western clothing. He not only introduced the European calendar and mathematics, but also edited the country's first newspaper.

Peter the Great made important changes in order to centralize administration. When the patriarch of the Russian Church died in 1700, Peter did not replace him. Instead, he appointed a civil official to head the Church. From Peter's time on, the Russian Church was completely controlled by the czar. Another move of Peter's was to force the aristocracy to work for the state. Few nobles were exempt from serving some time in the army or civil government. To pay for all his reforms, Peter raised taxes and imposed many new ones on items from hats to coffins and on the right to marry, to grow a beard, and to be an Old Believer.

Although Peter's attempt to westernize Russia did change his country, it did not greatly affect the life of the average Russian. Aside from the upper classes, few people were exposed to western ways, and even many of the aristocrats were slow to adopt western customs. Peter's death in 1725 was followed by a period of undistinguished rulers. Russia took part in both the War of the Austrian Succession and the Seven Years' War.

Catherine the Great

In the 1740's the heir to the Russian throne, Peter III, was married to an obscure German princess, Sophia of Anhalt-Zerbst (AHN-hahlt-ZAYRBST). When she moved to Russia at the age of fifteen, she was rebaptized in the Orthodox faith and took the name of Catherine. She also learned to speak Russian and gained the good will of Russia's royal and aristocratic families.

The marriage of Peter and Catherine was not a happy one. The future czar was ignorant and immature. He loved playing with wax soldiers and irritated courtiers by wearing a Prussian military uniform. On the other hand, Catherine was intelligent and extremely ambitious. Peter III came to the throne in 1762, but within six months he died. Catherine made herself Empress.

Catherine saw herself as an enlightened despot. In practice, however, Catherine's enlightenment meant little to the people of Russia. She summoned a legal commission in 1767 to draw up a new code of laws. Although she first drafted a lengthy set of instructions, based in part on the writings of Montesquieu, few actual changes or reforms resulted.

The lot of Russia's serfs deteriorated during Catherine's reign. Landowners were allowed to transfer them to other estates, sometimes breaking up families. Many serfs were sold, and their status was comparable to that of slaves.

The miserable conditions of the Russian peasantry fueled a huge uprising in 1773, led by Emelian Pugachev (poo-gah-CHAWFF), who claimed to be Catherine's dead husband, Peter III. Declaring that he would free the serfs and eliminate taxes, Pugachev assembled an army of some 30,000 Russians. They ravaged the countryside and seized several towns in southwestern Russia. Catherine, at first reluctant to admit that her enlightened rule could lead to such an uprising, finally called out her army and defeated the rebels. Pugachev, seized and carted off to Moscow in a cage, was executed in 1775.

One of the major aims of Catherine the Great was to gain warm-water ports for Russia, outlets to the sea that would not be frozen during the winter months. The most likely region for Russian expansion was the northern territory of the Ottoman

Peter the Great's new navy routed the Swedish fleet near Cape Hango in the Baltic Sea. Why was it important for Russia to have a strong naval force?

Empire around the Black Sea. When the Turks attacked Russia in 1768, Catherine decided to overthrow Ottoman rule altogether. Russian success, however, would have seriously endangered the European balance of power, and Catherine was persuaded to stop short of complete victory.

Through the peace treaty, however, she did gain a sizable territory bordering the Sea of Azov. Russian ships were allowed to sail through Turkish waters to the Mediterranean, and Russia was recognized as the special protector of Christians in the Ottoman Empire.

Catherine also made substantial gains by taking over Polish territory. In this action she was joined by Prussia and Austria.

The Partitions of Poland

Poland was an ancient kingdom and, by the eighteenth century, was a weak one. Its rulers were elected by an assembly of nobles. For many cen-

How did Catherine the Great contribute to the growing influence of Russia in European affairs?

turies they had chosen as monarchs the legitimate heirs of the kings who had preceded them. In the sixteenth century, however, the nobles began to elect kings without regard to succession. Instead they chose whomever they could best manipulate. The resulting chaos weakened Poland internally and made it unable to ward off invasion from its surrounding neighbors.

During much of the seventeenth century the Poles were dominated by Sweden. As this northern power declined, however, Poland became the target of Russia, Austria, and Prussia. By the time of Catherine the Great, Russian influence in Poland was so strong that Frederick the Great felt it was a threat to the balance of power. He was also motivated by a desire to join the Polish lands to the rest of his kingdom. In the 1770's, therefore, Frederick persuaded Russia and Austria to join him in taking over sizable chunks of Polish territory. Catherine was reluctant because she preferred Russian influence over the entire country. Maria Theresa hesitated at first, but felt that if she did not act, Austria would lose its "fair" share.

There were three partitions of Poland. In 1772 Prussia acquired the land that had separated its eastern territory from the rest of the country. Russia gained parts of the Ukraine, and Austria took Galicia. Only Prussia and Russia participated in the second partition in 1793. Prussia took a large region south of its first acquisition, and Russia gained a huge area between the Dnieper and Dniester rivers. The Poles now realized that they were in grave danger. In 1794 a patriot named Thaddeus Kosciuszko (kahs-ee-USS-koh) gathered thousands of peasants to try and preserve Polish independence. Although at first successful, they were later defeated by a massive Russian army and Kosciuszko was taken prisoner.

The third and final partition of Poland took place in 1795. This time Russia gained the major share, although Warsaw went to Prussia and Austria gained land to the south of the Polish capital. This partition erased the Kingdom of Poland from the map of Europe. It was not to reappear for over a century.

The fall of Poland left Eastern Europe at the end of the 1700's in the hands of Austria, Prussia, Russia, and the declining Ottoman Empire. Soon these powers would be quarrelling among themselves over the control of all of Eastern Europe.

PARTITIONS OF POLAND

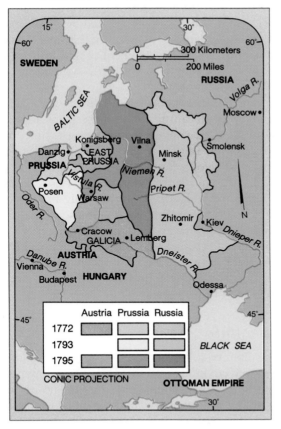

Austria Prussia Russia
1772
1793
1795

CONIC PROJECTION

Explain how partition erased the Polish nation from the map of Europe.

SECTION REVIEW

1. **Mapping:** Use the map on page 374 to locate the following: Poltava, Black Sea, Crimea, Kiev, Volga River.
2. In your own words, briefly define or identify: Razin, Old Believers, Great Northern War, Charles XII, Treaty of Nystadt, warm-water port, Kosciuszko.
3. What were some of the achievements of Peter the Great?
■ Peter the Great tried to westernize Russia in the early eighteenth century. Why do you think he faced opposition? Why do people today have a mixed reaction to western influences on their society and culture?

THE ARTS

From the late 1600's until the mid-1700's, new styles in the arts of continental Europe began to appear. The imagination of seventeenth-century Europe had been captured by the **Baroque** movement. Its style was ornate, theatrical, and boldly colorful. In the early eighteenth century the Baroque movement gave way to a lighter, more fanciful expression that came to be known as **rococo.** Finally, later in the eighteenth century, a return to simple, functional forms inspired by classical civilization would dominate the arts in the movement known as **neoclassicism.** Neoclassicism was characterized by simplicity and balance in form and function in the classic Greek and Roman style.

Architecture and Painting

In the early eighteenth century, French artists departed from the solemn dignity of earlier painters and favored a more lighthearted approach. Antoine Watteau was noted for his scenes of elegant society life. Other painters developed a rococo, or highly decorative, style. About the middle of the eighteenth century there was a reaction in France against the frivolity of rococo. The *philosophes* were among those who felt that art should serve a more serious purpose. The master of this new, neoclassical approach was Jacques-Louis David.

In England, which did not experience a rococo phase, architects had turned to a neoclassical style late in the seventeenth century. They incorporated the use of columns and symmetry, or balance, into their designs. After the Great Fire ravaged London in 1666, Christopher Wren designed fifty-two new churches to replace those that had been burned, the greatest of them being St. Paul's Cathedral. All exhibited these new design elements and a restrained elegance that had wide appeal not only in England but also in America. For instance, Jefferson's Virginia home, Monticello, employed many of the same architectural principles. The style is called Georgian, after the reigning English rulers.

Music

Music too had its baroque era, which lasted from about 1600 to the early eighteenth century. As in architecture and painting, the aim was dramatic expressiveness. Composers tried to use words or lyrics to communicate feelings. New musical instruments were introduced and others were improved including the violin, oboe, bassoon, and trumpet.

A master of early baroque was an Italian, Claudio Monteverdi (mahn-teh-VAIR-dee). In England the earliest opera came from the pen of Henry Purcell, court composer to James II and William and Mary. His *Dido and Aeneas* was first performed in 1689.

The two giants of the baroque period were both born in Germany in 1685. George Frederick Handel became a court favorite in England after his patron, the elector of Hanover, came to the throne as King George I. Handel is often regarded as primarily a composer of oratorios because of the tremendous success of his *Messiah*, first performed in 1742. Johann Sebastian Bach was famous chiefly as an organist. Almost all of his choral writings were religious, including the *Mass in B Minor*, the *Passion According to St. Matthew*, and the *Passion According to St. John*.

St. Paul's Cathedral, London's largest church, was designed in the Renaissance style. What is the relationship between Renaissance art and the Enlightenment?

In music as in art there was a reaction against the drama of the baroque in favor of greater simplicity and clarity, a trend favored by the thinkers of the Enlightenment. The era of this new classical style also saw the development of new instrumental forms such as the sonata, the symphony, and the string quartet.

The work of the Austrian Franz Joseph Haydn typifies the elegant restraint of the classical period in music. His tremendous outpouring included 104 symphonies, 14 operas, and 8 oratorios, as well as numerous works for smaller ensembles.

In the music of Mozart the classical style reached its peak. He wrote not only brilliant orchestral and chamber works but also operas that are both sparkling and profound, among them *The Marriage of Figaro* (1785) and *Don Giovanni* (1787). *The Magic Flute* (1791) embodies ideals of Freemasonry, an order that found many adherents among the men of this period.

Literature

The literary achievements of the Enlightenment period were influenced by earlier developments in France. Europe's admiration for the power and grandeur of Louis XIV's government equaled its attraction to French literature.

Classicism, which takes the writers of classical antiquity as its models of artistic and literary excellence, had become the guiding principle of the leading literary figures in France. Among those welcomed at the court of Louis XIV were Corneille and Racine, noted for their somber tragedies, and Molière, famed for his comedies. The classical literature of these seventeenth-century writers would help shape the letters and miscellaneous writings of the *philosophes* nearly a century later. They also contributed to the development of the English novel and other literary forms throughout the eighteenth century.

The English novel was one of the most important cultural achievements of the Enlightenment. Through the novel both the serious and the comical aspects of life could be revealed to large numbers of people.

The English novels, and soon those of other nations, highlighted the concerns of society in the 1800's. Daniel Defoe wrote the first volume of his adventurous tale of *Robinson Crusoe* in 1719. Then in 1727 Jonathan Swift used *Gulliver's Travels* to ridicule the follies of his time. Samuel Richardson produced a major novel in 1747, entitled *Clarissa Harlowe*. This was a sentimental tale about a young lady struggling to deal with the problems and benefits generated by love, greed, marriage, and motherhood. Richardson's novel later served as a model for Rousseau's *La nouvelle Héloïse*, which became the rage of Europe.

The characters in the English novels expressed a desire for a return to reason and traditional values. Tobias Smollett's *Roderick Random* appeared in 1748. Smollett described the cruelty and misery of life in the British navy. Henry Fielding made people laugh in his masterpiece, *Tom Jones*. Published in 1749, this novel related the adventures of a likeable, but trouble-prone, young man as he met up with all types of people.

Other literary forms were also taking shape. By the mid-1750's Denis Diderot was beginning to publish the first volumes of the *Encyclopedia*. The first *Dictionary of the English Language* was published in England by Samuel Johnson in 1755.

The literacy rate increased steadily as a result of widespread educational opportunities among the middle and lower classes of English society. This larger reading audience prompted the appearance of newspapers and other periodicals. One example of these publications, which helped influence public opinion, was *The Tatler*. The first issue of *The Tatler* was published by Richard Steele and Joseph Addison in 1709.

In Germany writers were experimenting with plays and then novels. Gotthold Lessing was a noted critic and dramatist. He wrote *Nathan the Wise* in 1779, a play that pleaded for religious toleration. Another German dramatist, Friedrich von Schiller, writing after 1770, produced plays about the spirit of freedom and liberty.

The greatest German writer of the Enlightenment, however, was Johann Goethe (GER-tuh). Among his best known works are the dramatic poem, *Faust*, and the novel, *The Sorrows of Young Werther*. Begun by Goethe in his twenties and completed some 60 years later, *Faust* is about a young man who sells his soul to the devil, symbolizing humanity's search for knowledge and power. *The Sorrows of Young Werther*, published in the 1770's, gave the novel as a literary form an important place in German letters.

Mozart began his musical career at an early age. How did his later classical compositions respond to the spirit of the Enlightenment?

SECTION REVIEW

1. In your own words, briefly define or identify: baroque, rococo, Watteau, David, Wren, Handel, Bach, neoclassicism.

2. What were the main features of the music developed during the Enlightenment? Who were some of the major musical figures of the time?

3. Name three early English novels, and their authors. How did each of these writers present the ideas of the Enlightenment in their novels?

■ Eighteenth-century novels reflected many of the social, cultural, and political ideas advanced by Enlightenment scholars and scientists. What ideas are highlighted in some of the modern novels you have read or in some of the "movie stories" you have seen? Support your answer with examples.

Reviewing the Chapter

Chapter Summary

By the mid-seventeenth century a series of developments comprised the scientific revolution. A number of advances were made in astronomy and physics, and a universal law of gravitation was proved. Reliance on the scientific method led to advances in physiology, biology, and botany.

The scientific revolution paved the way for the era of intellectual curiosity known as the Enlightenment, which began with thoughtful analyses of human nature and the need for social organization. French philosophes *such as Montesquieu, Voltaire, and Rousseau dominated the Enlightenment, and their ideas reached a wide audience through Diderot's* Encyclopedia.

Three nations in central and eastern Europe first began to play a major role during the period of the Enlightenment. After decades of expansion under the Hohenzollerns, Prussia emerged as a first-rate power under Frederick the Great. The Hapsburgs of Austria, among them Maria Theresa, ruled a large empire of diverse peoples. In Russia, Peter the Great and Catherine the Great enlarged their country and linked it more closely to western Europe. Enlightened despotism in these countries, however, was more a theory than a practice.

In the arts, the baroque style of the seventeenth and early eighteenth centuries gave way to the rococo period and then to neoclassicism. Architects like Wren introduced a new simplicity into building. The musical glories of Handel and Bach contrasted with the restrained elegance of Haydn and Mozart. Included among the literary leaders of the Enlightenment were the French philosophes, *the first English novelists, and the German poet Goethe.*

1. What revolution changed western civilization after 1600?
2. What were the most important features of the Enlightenment?
3. What major changes did Prussia and Austria experience during the eighteenth century?
4. What two achievements of Peter the Great and Catherine the Great changed Russia?
5. What styles of artistic expression emerged during the Enlightenment?

Using Your Vocabulary

1. What is the scientific revolution? Why is it considered a revolution?
2. What is the difference between a geocentric and heliocentric theory? Why did this cause trouble between Galileo and the Church?
3. In your own words, explain the difference between inductive and deductive reasoning. Why did Francis Bacon believe in the inductive method?
4. What is the Enlightenment? Why was it also called the Age of Reason?
5. In your own words, define the term natural law.
6. What is a social contract? Should people willingly agree to one?
7. Who were the *philosophes?*
8. What was the *Encyclopedia?* Why did it get Diderot in trouble?
9. What is enlightened despotism? How did it change the basis of authority?
10. What is militarism? Why is Frederick William considered a militarist?
11. What is meant by the Pragmatic Sanction? Was it successful?
12. What was the Diplomatic Revolution? Which event in this revolution linked Austria to France?
13. Who were the Old Believers? How did they protest against the new ways?
14. Who were the *streltsi?* How did their actions create the need for change?
15. Describe one difference between baroque and rococo art.

Developing Your Geography Skills

1. Use the map on page 374 to locate the major centers of Enlightenment thought and discoveries. Do you think the distance between them helped or hindered the spread of ideas during the 1700's?
2. Use the map on page 381 to describe the three partitions of Poland in terms of the territories annexed to Austria, Prussia, and Russia.
3. Use the Atlas maps on pages 756-757 and the map on page 374 to compare the size of eighteenth-century Austria, Russia, and Sweden with that of their twentieth-century land areas.

Recalling the Facts

1. List the accomplishments of Copernicus, Kepler, and Galileo.
2. What contributions did Vesalius and Harvey make to the scientific revolution?
3. Why is Hugo Grotius considered the "father of international law"?
4. Why would the ideas of John Locke, rather than those of Thomas Hobbes, be more appealing to a democratic nation?
5. Which ideas of Montesquieu and Voltaire are important to democratic thought?
6. Who was Adam Smith?
7. Who was Frederick William? What role did he play in the development of Prussia?
8. What two military actions expanded the territory of the Hapsburgs?
9. What changes occurred in Europe after the War of Austrian Succession?
10. What events marked the emergence of Prussia as a major European power?
11. Was Joseph II an enlightened despot?
12. Why were the serfs a problem for the czar?
13. Who were the Romanovs?
14. What were three changes that Peter introduced to modernize Russia?
15. What were two important territorial gains made by Catherine the Great?
16. How did Poland become erased from the map of Europe?

Essay Questions

1. The scientific revolution that began to take shape in the late sixteenth century is credited with opening the door to the Age of Enlightenment. Write a paragraph on why you agree or disagree with this statement.
2. Explain why the 1700's is also known as the Age of Reason. What contributions did scholars such as Voltaire, Rousseau, and Diderot make to the Age of Reason?
3. Both Austria and Prussia grew in power during the seventeenth and eighteenth centuries. In what ways did militarism in Prussia and Hapsburg rule in Austria shape this growth? Give examples to explain your answers.
4. Compare the reigns of Peter the Great and Catherine the Great in Russia. Were their achievements enough to merit the addition of "the Great" to their names?
5. In two or three paragraphs, explain the relationship between Enlightenment ideas and one of these areas: literature, art, or music. State how a specific idea or theory was reflected in the area of your choice.

Critical Thinking

1. What assumptions were made about the world before contributions of Copernicus, Galileo, and Kepler in the seventeenth and eighteenth centuries?
2. What trends were developing in the thought of the *philosophes* that would affect the changing values of individuals and societies in the late eighteenth century?
3. What facts can you verify regarding the accomplishments of Diderot, Madame Geoffrin, and Mary Wollstonecraft?
4. Did you detect any bias in how leaders such as Frederick the Great, Maria Theresa, Peter the Great, and Catherine the Great introduced reforms during the Enlightenment period?
5. What value claims are reflected in eighteenth-century novels? Are the same value claims made in the music and art of the eighteenth century?

CHAPTER ·17·

An AGE of REVOLUTION

1763–1815

Objectives

- To discuss the causes and results of the American Revolution

- To describe the Old Regime and the causes of the French Revolution

- To discuss the events leading up to the fall of the French monarchy

- To describe the French Revolution after the fall of Louis XVI

- To describe the rise of Napoleon Bonaparte

- To explain the effects of Napoleon on western civilization

*I*n the latter part of the eighteenth century Enlightenment ideas found practical expression through revolutions in America and France. The world that emerged out of this period is close to the one we recognize today. It is our modern political world of citizenship and representative democracy. The American and French revolutions continued the process of constitutionalism, as opposed to absolute monarchism, begun by the English in the Glorious Revolution of the seventeenth century.

Nevertheless, the two great revolutions were quite different. The American Revolution was an anticolonial independence movement. It resulted primarily in political and constitutional changes. Socially, the country carried on as it had before. It set a precedent and became a model for all the anticolonial independence movements to follow in the nineteenth and twentieth centuries.

The French Revolution, however, was a major political and social revolution, and far more radical than any comparable upheaval of the period. It was a sudden and violent overturning of the whole social order that had existed since medieval times. The monarchy and the nobility's privileges were abolished. A new government controlled by the bourgeoisie was established. The French Revolution created the political world of the nineteenth century.

THE AMERICAN REVOLUTION

To the English government, the eastern seaboard settlement that ran from Nova Scotia to Georgia was only part of a vast global empire recently enlarged by victories in the Seven Years' War. The British Empire now included Ireland, French Canada, all the land lying between the Appalachians and the Mississippi, holdings in the West Indies, and parts of India. As a result, Parliament decided to tighten control over its colonies and to bring their administration under its direct authority.

The Glorious Revolution in England had made Parliament supreme. It was this triumph that brought the growth of political stability and the English achievement of limited monarchy so admired by Montesquieu and Voltaire. England offered a unique situation: privileged people and a hereditary nobility, yet none of the worst offenses of the Old Regime, which exempted both from heavy taxes. England's powerful gentry was always willing to pay its share of taxes because it sat in Parliament; indeed, it controlled it. In Parliament it knew that if it could not change government policy, it could at least receive a fair hearing.

The End of American Tax Exemptions

The cost of the French and Indian War in North America had been expensive, and left Britain heavily in debt. Now the British government wanted the colonists to help pay the empire's debts and maintenance. After all, the colonists were only being charged for their own defense.

Before 1764 Americans paid mostly local taxes. The duties imposed by the Navigation Acts of the 1600's, which regulated colonial trade, and the Molasses Act of 1733 were often evaded by American merchants because they were not strictly enforced. In an effort to raise revenue, Britain's finance minister, George Grenville, encouraged Parliament to pass several new acts, which he was determined to enforce. Among them were the Sugar Act of 1764 and the Stamp Act of 1765. The enforcement of the Sugar Act hurt New England merchants who relied on sugar and molasses brought in from the French West Indies to make rum. Since the British West Indies were unable to supply enough of these products, some merchants had resorted to smuggling in the past. Now they had to pay the customs duties.

In contrast to earlier acts of Parliament which indirectly taxed the colonists, the Stamp Act was Parliament's first attempt at direct taxation. This

Led by Samuels Adams, a group of protestors called the Sons of Liberty dumped 342 chests of tea into the Boston Harbor. Why do you think they masqueraded as Indians?

law required all colonists to affix special stamps on newspapers, pamphlets, legal documents, playing cards, and other items. The Stamp Act sparked violent protests. Some Americans, such as Patrick Henry, claimed that, according to English law, Parliament had no right to levy such taxes on the colonists and that they were illegal.

In response to the uproar, Parliament withdrew the Stamp Act. However, Parliament mistakenly assumed that its financial problems could still be solved by a new tax. In 1767 it passed the Townshend Acts, requiring import duties to be collected at colonial ports. These new taxes also met strong resistance in America. In 1770 all were repealed, except for the tax on tea.

The Road to War

In an effort to help the British East India Company, which was experiencing financial problems, Parliament awarded it a monopoly on the tea shipped to America. It also permitted the company to lower its prices in order to undersell colonial merchants. When the first shipment arrived in Boston, the townspeople reacted. A group of men dressed as Indians dumped the tea into Boston Harbor. This act of protest was the famous Boston Tea Party of December 16, 1773.

Parliament was outraged and, in response, it passed the so-called Intolerable Acts. One of these acts closed the port of Boston, thereby threatening the city with economic ruin. Other measures forced colonists to quarter British troops in their towns, enabled the governor of Massachusetts to transfer trials of British officials to England, and restricted town meetings. Along with this legislation aimed at clamping down on Massachusetts, Parliament passed the Quebec Act.

For Canada, the Quebec Act was a masterpiece of enlightened legislation. It recognized religious toleration for French Canadian Catholics and granted Canadians the right to live under their own civil law. It also extended the boundaries of Quebec to include the whole territory north of the Ohio River, parts of which had been claimed by individual colonies. Thus the American colonists considered the Quebec Act an infringement on their westward expansion.

The Patriots, or those in favor of independence, saw the Intolerable Acts as a threat to colonial government and felt that Parliament was attempting to oppress them. On September 1, 1774, the First Continental Congress met in Philadelphia.

At this Congress, the delegates adopted a resolution asserting American rights and demanded a repeal of the Intolerable Acts. They also decided to impose a boycott on all British goods. Before adjourning, the Congress agreed to reconvene in May of the following year if Parliament did not comply with its demands. In the spring of 1775 fighting broke out between British troops, called Redcoats, and armed colonists at Lexington and Concord in Massachusetts. This event marked the beginning of the Revolutionary War.

The Declaration of Independence

The Second Continental Congress assembled a few weeks after the confrontations in Massachusetts. Though it was still reluctant to break completely with England, the Congress raised an army and made George Washington commander in chief. It also commissioned an expeditionary force to draw Canada into the war and sent diplomats to France to seek financial and military aid.

With increasing frequency the independence issue was debated in town meetings throughout the colonies. Early in 1776 Thomas Paine published a pamphlet entitled *Common Sense,* which attacked the institution of monarchy. "There is something absurd," Paine wrote, "in supposing a Continent to be perpetually governed by an island." This pamphlet was widely read, and some legislatures began to demand independence.

On June 7, 1776, Richard Henry Lee of Virginia proposed that Congress adopt a resolution that the colonies "are, and of right ought to be, free and independent states." On July 4, 1776, the delegates endorsed the Declaration of Independence, which was composed primarily by Thomas Jefferson.

The Declaration of Independence proclaimed the new American ideal.

"We hold these truths to be self evident, that all men are created equal; that they are endowed by their creator with certain unalienable rights; that among these are life, liberty and the pursuit of happiness. That, to secure these rights, governments are instituted among men, deriving their just powers from the consent of the governed. . . ."

The delegates who signed the Declaration of Independence pledged their lives, fortunes, and honor to the American cause. What does this say about these men?

Interpreting the enlightened writings of Locke and Rousseau, Jefferson raised a new standard for defining a free society and the nature of representative government. It remains the standard to which all free societies aspire today.

Victory

On a more global perspective, the American War for Independence was yet another struggle for empire between Britain and France. In the early years of the war the French provided colonists with munitions, arms, supplies, and money, but stopped short of an open commitment until the major American victory at the battle of Saratoga in 1777. After Saratoga the French felt that the Americans could win the war, so they recognized American independence and declared war on Britain. Other European powers soon followed. Some of the more well-known European military leaders to join the American forces were the Marquis de Lafayette of France, Baron Von Steuben of Prussia, and Thaddeus Kosciuszko of Poland.

The British enjoyed overwhelming financial and military superiority. The Americans, however, had the advantage of fighting on their home ground. Outstanding moral leadership, notably that of General George Washington, coupled with French participation and money, made an American victory possible.

After the defeat at Saratoga, the British abandoned the New York campaign and moved their chief theater of operation to the South, primarily the Carolinas. A combined army of American and French forces finally won a decisive victory at the battle of Yorktown in Virginia. On October 19, 1781, the British commander Cornwallis was forced to surrender. On news of the defeat Parliament voted to end the war effort and authorized peace negotiations. The Treaty of Paris in 1783 granted the United States unconditional independence and extended its boundaries north to the Great Lakes, south to Florida, and west to the Mississippi River.

The United States Constitution

From the dispute with Parliament, the colonists had learned that government should possess limited powers and function within the terms of a written constitution. Thus the states established a union of thirteen independent republics. Ratified in 1781, the Articles of Confederation embodied this idea of separatism. Congress, though it could conduct foreign policy, had neither the right to tax, nor the right to regulate trade between the states. The disadvantages of this system soon became apparent. In the spring of 1787, at a convention in Philadelphia, a new federal Constitution was drafted.

The powers of the national government were broadly defined, but the existing structure of state and local governments was retained as a check on the central government. This division of authority between federal and local governments is called the **federal system.**

To maintain an equal distribution of government power, a system of checks and balances was devised. Inspired by Montesquieu's *The Spirit of Laws,* the framers of the Constitution created three branches of government: executive, legislative, and judicial. The Constitution's chief author, James Madison, expressed the framers' intentions in the statement, "Ambition must be made to counteract ambition."

The Constitution was approved by eleven of the thirteen states by June 1788, and the new government was put into operation. The following year Washington's inauguration as president gave the Republic stability. His voluntary surrender of the presidency after two terms of office set a precedent for the peaceful transfer of power that helped assure the Republic's continuance. In 1791 the first ten amendments were added to the Constitution. Known collectively as the Bill of Rights, these amendments protect the rights of individuals. For example, they guarantee freedom of religion, freedom of speech, and freedom of the press.

Importance of the American Revolution

The American Revolution initiated an age of upheaval that lasted for over half a century. The American example inspired revolutionaries in

Why do you think crowds gathered along Washington's route to his inauguration?

France and other European countries. It also influenced patriots in Latin America. Freedom of the press, of religion, of speech, of assembly, and from arbitrary acts of government became the cries heard throughout the world. In a clean sweep the United States eliminated Europe's oldest institutions: the established church, the nobility, and the monarchy.

Nevertheless, it should be remembered that the democracy the founding fathers established was not the democracy we know today. Most blacks were slaves. Property qualifications for male voters persisted into the nineteenth century, and women were not given the vote until the twentieth century.

Still, the American experience showed that revolution was possible, indeed practical. It also demonstrated Rousseau's social contract—that the source of legal authority was derived from the people. The impact of the American Revolution and its effect on France and Latin America cannot be overestimated.

SECTION REVIEW

1. In your own words, briefly define or identify: the Boston Tea Party, *Common Sense,* the Intolerable Acts, Thomas Jefferson, the battle of Saratoga, the battle of Yorktown, the Treaty of Paris.
2. List the causes for the American Revolution.
3. Of what significance was French aid to the colonists? What other advantages did the Americans have? The British?
4. What type of government did the newly independent colonies establish? Why?
5. What were the effects of the American Revolution?
■ Not all the colonists were in favor of independence. About two-fifths were Patriots, one-fifth were Loyalists, and two-fifths remained neutral. If you had lived in 1776 would you have been in favor of American independence? Explain, giving specific reasons. What do you think life would be like in the United States today if the colonies had never won their independence?

THE OLD REGIME TO JULY 1789

The French Revolution not only transformed France, but all of Europe. At this time France was Europe's most influential country. It was the heart of the Enlightenment and, except for Russia, the Continent's most populated and powerful state. The French language was to the eighteenth century what English is today. French culture, ideas, and attitudes dominated the West. The origins of the French Revolution can be found in the problems that faced French society prior to its outbreak.

Structure of the Old Regime

In the late eighteenth century French law still recognized three Estates, or orders, as it had since medieval times. The First Estate consisted of the clergy, the Second the nobility, and the Third the commoners. Out of a population of some 24 million there were no more than 100,000 clergy and about 400,000 nobles, including children. All others, at least 96 percent of the population, were members of the Third Estate.

By law the nobility ranked second after the clergy. In fact, it was the first order and perhaps the only order to have any real sense of common identity. It corresponded to a clearly defined social and economic group, or a privileged class, which drew income from ownership of property.

At the top of the order were the great nobles, powerful, wealthy men who drew enormous incomes. At the bottom were the lesser nobility, many of whom had difficulties in making ends meet. Regardless of income however, all nobles benefited from special class privileges, the most important of which was the right to not pay taxes. Nobles also held the high government and Church posts, the exclusive right to become military officers, and most of society's other high honors.

Although in decline during the Age of Enlightenment, the Roman Catholic Church still managed to exert considerable control, especially as a landowner with income from its extensive holdings. Within the First Estate the nobility exerted great influence because its members occupied the high

Church offices, while the parish clergy were of lower-class origin.

Unlike the nobility, which was almost a closed caste, there were great social and economic differences within the Third Estate. At the top were the wealthy bourgeoisie, members of the financial and merchant classes. Many of these people drew larger incomes than the lesser nobility. Other important bourgeois members were professionals, like lawyers and judges. Of lesser prestige were the shopkeepers, artisans, craftspeople, and wealthy peasants who owned their own land. At the bottom were the wage earners in both town and country, the people without property. Most of these were servants, urban workers, or laborers on farms.

Marie Antoinette often entertained a circle of her close friends in her salon. How does this scene compare to the economic situation at this time?

Sources of Discontent

Beginning about the mid-eighteenth century, discontent in France began to increase for several reasons. The wealthy bourgeoisie resented the nobility's control of the highest offices and thus its monopoly of political power. The entire Third Estate resented the privileges that shielded the nobility from paying taxes.

Another problem was the agricultural system. Peasants, who owned about one-third of the land, were still treated as serfs. They were obliged to perform labor on public roads, and manorial lords continued to collect fees, dues, and other feudal rights. Furthermore, all peasants were burdened with the heaviest Church and state taxes.

The steady rise in prices in the 1700's pressured both nobles and peasants. To maintain their social position, manorial lords had to claim additional feudal fees. Peasants resented the privileges of a class that earned its living without managing the land. Furthermore, throughout the century the general rise in prices, most notably that of bread, was not matched by a rise in wages. This especially hurt the majority of workers.

Failure of the Monarchy

The Old Regime witnessed the strengthening of the nobility's political position at the expense of the monarchy. In the parlements, or courts, wealthy nobles who had bought their titles or inherited them from those who had bought them, exercised a great deal of power. As judges, they could block the king's laws by refusing to register them. They could even harrass or arrest the king's officials when enforcing royal edicts.

In the late 1760's Louis XV tried to correct this situation by appointing a new ministry. This ministry proceeded to abolish the courts and sent the judges into exile. A new supreme court with judges paid by salary was then established. The ministry also instituted measures aimed at reforming finances and eliminating privileges. These highly criticized reforms continued until Louis' death in 1774.

When Louis XVI ascended the throne he wanted to begin his reign with a popular decision, so he reestablished the old parlements his grandfather had abolished. By yielding to public opinion

This painting by David portrays the members of the Third Estate taking the Tennis Court Oath. What does it reveal about the political climate in 1789?

and the nobility, Louis relinquished some of his power. This process would continue throughout his reign.

The Financial Crisis

In some respects the American War for Independence was the direct cause of the French Revolution. Louis XIV's numerous expansionist wars had put France heavily into debt. By supporting the American Patriots, the debt became enormous, and France was unable to make even the interest payments. In the mid-1780's the French government faced bankruptcy.

Robert Turgot (tyoor-GOH), Louis XVI's finance minister between 1774 and 1776, tried to solve the problem by reducing government expenditures and eliminating the nobility's tax privileges. His reforms were so highly criticized that he was soon dismissed from office. His successors resorted to heavy borrowing at high rates. By 1786 the situation was so acute that bankers refused to lend money to the French government. In February 1787 Louis was forced to summon leaders of

the First and Second Estates to an Assembly of Notables.

At this assembly, Louis asked the nobility to allow themselves to be taxed. They consented, but on the condition that they would control royal revenues. Furthermore, local administrations were to be placed under assemblies that they dominated. Louis rejected this proposal and tried to tax the nobles without their consent. The provincial parlements responded by stirring up mob violence, and the king had to revoke his taxes. The aristocracy had won a victory over the monarchy.

Unable to collect taxes or borrow money, financial disaster was imminent. In the fall of 1788 the king and the parlements agreed that an assembly of the Estates General could authorize new taxes. A meeting was called for in the spring of 1789 at Versailles.

The Estates General

The Estates General had not been convened since 1614, and no one was exactly sure just what it was empowered to do. Hundreds of pamphlets were circulated. In them the authors debated how the Estates should vote and even questioned the nature of the three orders. The most famous of these pamphlets, *What is the Third Estate?* by the Abbé Sieyès (see-YEAS), advocated a prominent political role for the country's largest order.

The nobility sought to control the proceedings by insisting that each Estate be allowed only one vote. Thus the First and Second Estates would have the majority, outvoting the Third Estate two to one. Having undermined the monarchy, many of the aristocracy's leaders now sought a new political system in which they would have the authority.

However, the representatives of the Third Estate had no interest in a new aristocratic France. At the opening of the Estates General in May 1789, they insisted that members of the Estates vote individually, not collectively. They also continued their attack on the nobility as a privileged class. Moreover, the leaders claimed that it was the Third Estate's role to write a new constitution for the country.

Several weeks of confrontation and confusion followed. Louis XVI failed to display the kind of leadership to which the Third Estate might have responded. Badly advised, the king made the mistake of siding with the aristocracy against the bourgeoisie.

On June 17 the leaders of the Third Estate declared themselves a National Assembly and invited members of the other Estates to join them. On June 20, meeting at a nearby tennis court, members of the Third Estate took a pledge. In the Tennis Court Oath they swore not to separate until they had given France a constitution. On June 27 the king invited the First and Second Estates to sit with the Third in a single body to form the National Assembly. This was a revolutionary development.

The Storming of the Bastille

Tension increased throughout the country. The harvest of 1788 had been bad. Food was scarce, bread expensive, and unemployment high in

French revolutionaries stormed the Bastille on July 14, 1789. This date is now commemorated as a national holiday in France equivalent to our Fourth of July.

urban areas. Hard times were nothing new for the poor, and economic factors alone did not trigger the protests. There was real support at a popular level for the political changes the Third Estate had brought about at Versailles.

To protect himself and to pressure the National Assembly, the king summoned troops to the Paris area. The Assembly's leaders feared that the king intended to use force against them, and they demanded the army's removal. In an atmosphere charged with political tension, the people of Paris took action. On July 14, 1789, a mob in search of weapons stormed the Bastille, an old prison fortress. The following day the king announced to the Assembly the withdrawal of his troops. On July 17 he went to Paris and received from the mayor the Revolution's new emblem, a tricolored ribbon.

Although the storming of the Bastille was of no military consequence, it became a symbol of the Revolution. It demonstrated that the leaders of the Third Estate had support among the artisans and shopkeepers in Paris, and that these people had no desire to see the National Assembly dissolved until it had accomplished its purpose. Henceforth the Revolution's leadership would turn directly to the people for approval.

SECTION REVIEW

1. In your own words, briefly define or identify: the three Estates, parlement, Robert Turgot, Assembly of Notables, Tennis Court Oath, National Assembly.
2. List the reasons for discontent in France under the Old Regime.
3. How did the nobility gain power over the monarchy?
4. Why did France suffer a financial crisis in the 1780's? What measures were taken to solve the problem?
5. Of what importance was the storming of the Bastille?
■ Many historical events or political movements have been characterized by symbols, such as the tricolored ribbon. What symbols are used today to characterize such events or movements?

THE FALL OF THE MONARCHY

Violence in Paris and the countryside led to major developments in the initial stages of the Revolution. Popular support brought about several legal changes and legitimized the power of the National Assembly. Parisienne women of the working class began circulating petitions and organizing marches in order to exert pressure on legislative authorities for protection of women's trades and public education for girls.

The End of the Old Regime

In the summer of 1789 the peasantry throughout the countryside was swept up in a wave of panic known as the Great Fear. Peasants talked of troops hired by nobles coming to murder them and rumors of imaginary massacres in neighboring villages terrified the population. The initial panic gave way to violence. Groups of armed villagers descended on nobles' homes and abbeys demanding records and printed documents listing their feudal obligations to the nobility. Out of them they made bonfires, and in a few provinces they also set fire to the manor houses. The peasantry was bringing down the Old Regime by force.

These uprisings had immediate impact. In early August 1789 the National Assembly passed several decrees abolishing the feudal system, thereby ending all obligations peasants owed to nobles. Thus the Assembly earned the support of the rural masses. By destroying many nobles' tax exemptions and opening careers to persons with ability, without distinction of birth, these decrees became important to professionals and businesspeople. Insofar as the concept of privilege could be destroyed through legislation, the Assembly accomplished it.

In late August the Assembly proclaimed these reforms in the Declaration of the Rights of Man. It called for the replacement of the Old Regime by a social and political order based on the equality of free men. Louis was no longer king by the grace of God, but by the constitutional law of the state.

The Declaration's ideals of liberty, equality, and fraternity became the Revolution's rallying cry. Of

Declaration of the Rights of Man, 1789

When the French National Assembly drew up a statement declaring the rights that all citizens possessed, it included ideas shared by the English and Americans. The French declaration is a positive statement of rights. The following are excerpts from this document.

The representatives of the French people, organized as a National Assembly . . . have determined to set forth in a solemn declaration the natural, inalienable and sacred rights of man. . . .

1. Men are born and remain free and equal in rights. . . .
2. The aim of all political association is the preservation of the natural and imprescriptible rights of man. These rights are liberty, property, security and resistance to oppression.
3. The principle of all sovereignty resides in the nation. No body nor individual may exercise any authority which does not proceed directly from the nation.
4. Liberty consists in the freedom to do everything which injures no one else; hence the exercise of the natural rights of each man has no limits except those which assure to the other members of the society the enjoyment of the same rights. . . .
5. Law can only prohibit such actions as are hurtful to society. Nothing may be prevented which is not forbidden by law. . . .
6. Law is the expression of the general will. Every citizen has a right to participate personally or through his representative in its formation. . . .
7. No person shall be accused, arrested or imprisoned except in the cases and according to the forms prescribed by law. . . .
8. The laws shall provide for such punishments only as are strictly and obviously necessary, and no one shall suffer punishment except it be legally inflicted. . . .
9. . . . All persons are held innocent until they shall have been declared guilty. . . .
10. No one shall be disquieted on account of his opinions . . . provided their manifestation does not disturb the public order. . . .
11. The free communication of ideas and opinions is one of the most precious of the rights of man. Every citizen may, speak, write, and print with freedom. . . .
12. The security of the rights of man and of the citizen requires public military force. Those forces are, therefore, established for the good of all and not for the personal advantage of those to whom they shall be entrusted.
13. A common contribution is essential for the maintenance of the public forces and for the cost of administration. This should be equitably distributed among the citizens in proportion to their means.
14. All the citizens have a right to decide, either personally or by their representatives, as to the necessity of the public contribution. . . .
15. Society has the right to require of every public agent an account of his administration.

Source: Adapted from J.H. Stewart, translator and editor, *A Documentary Survey of the French Revolution.* Copyright 1951 by Macmillan Publishing Co.

1. What rights does this document guarantee?
2. How did this document establish equality for all French citizens?
3. What rights guaranteed to the French do you possess today?

Why did a crowd of Parisian women march on Versailles on October 28, 1789? What was the significance of this act?

equal importance the Declaration guaranteed the rights of free enterprise, private property, and the interests of the bourgeoisie. However, the document failed to include the rights of women. As a result, Olympe de Gouges (duh GOOZH) wrote the Declaration of the Rights of Woman, one of the first feminist documents. It was rejected by the Revolution's leaders because they did not believe women should have legal rights.

The Days of October 1789

The nobles who had supported Louis against the Assembly in early July were totally discredited after the fall of the Bastille. Pamphleteers and orators denounced them as enemies of the people, and they fled abroad. These were the first *émigrés* (ay-mee-GRAY), or emigrants, and within a couple of months another 20,000 left the country. Abroad in Italy, Prussia, and England, they plotted to end the Revolution.

Economic problems inflamed the situation, and there were rumors that troops were to be used against the people. In early October a hungry crowd, led by women, gathered in Paris and demanded bread. Out of their plea emerged a new objective: to bring the king back to Paris.

A crowd of between five and ten thousand women marched to Versailles, followed by a regiment of the National Guard. The next day some of the mob broke into the palace, murdered the bodyguards, and vandalized the queen's apartment. Order was eventually restored but at day's end, under armed escort, the king, queen, and royal children were brought back to Paris. There they were to live at the Tuileries (TWEE-ler-eez) palace under the watchful eyes of the revolutionary leadership. By the end of the week the Assembly had also moved to Paris. From this moment on, Paris became the center of the Revolution.

Reform

Between 1789 and 1791 the National Assembly enacted hundreds of laws that swept away the Old Regime and brought about new institutional changes. The majority of the French Revolution's permanent achievements date from this period.

The Assembly reformed the country's administration by abolishing the old historic provinces of France. It replaced them with districts of equal size known as departments, which still exist today. Town government was made uniform. All officials, from tax collectors to prosecuting attorneys, were now to be elected. It also adopted the metric system of weights and measures.

The Assembly seized Church lands, and with these lands it backed the issue of its new paper money. In 1790 it passed the Civil Constitution of the Clergy. This law called for priests and bishops to be elected by the voters and paid by the government. It also required the clergy to take an oath of loyalty to the state. The pope condemned the oath, and many clergy members refused to swear to it. The Civil Constitution of the Clergy led to a total break with the papacy, and caused considerable bitterness among both the clergy and lay people of France.

The Assembly also drafted a constitution, the so-called Constitution of 1791. France was transformed into a limited monarchy with a separation of executive, legislative, and judicial branches. The king could veto legislation temporarily, but in effect his power was far less than that of the President of the new United States. The key branch of this new government was a one-chamber house, known as the Legislative Assembly.

The framers of the Constitution of 1791 were members of the bourgeoisie, and by no means in favor of political democracy. All citizens, though equal under the law, were not expected to take an active role in electing a government. Only owners of property or men of sufficient financial means were allowed to vote for delegates to the Legislative Assembly.

Flight of the Royal Family

Louis XVI had absolutely no interest in being a constitutional monarch. He had seen his power steadily decrease and had watched the Paris mob humiliate his family. He had witnessed the Civil Constitution of the Clergy, and this only reinforced his conviction that the Revolution was morally wrong. Therefore, Louis decided to flee the country with his family.

Louis' wife, Marie Antoinette, was a Hapsburg and the daughter of Maria Theresa. Two of her brothers were successively the emperors of Austria, and she cultivated the support of foreign rulers and émigrés. Many people disliked Marie, and her extravagant life style led some to believe she

Louis XVI's flight to Varennes destroyed his credibility as king and emphasized the increasing gap between the monarchy and the people. What emotions do you think he experienced when he was arrested?

was responsible for the crown's bankruptcy and their economic distress.

Through secret negotiations with the Austrians, a plan was conceived. Late one night in June 1791 the royal family escaped from the Tuileries through an unguarded door. Under assumed names and in borrowed clothes they headed for the border, where it was arranged that they would be escorted to safety. However, at the village of Varennes in northern France the king was recognized and arrested. The royal family was brought back to Paris and became virtual prisoners of the Assembly.

The flight to Varennes was of great importance for the Revolution. To the people, the king's flight was a betrayal. To the members of the Assembly, it was an embarrassment. With great effort the framers of the Constitution of 1791 had worked to define the king's new role. Now they discovered their king wanted no role at all. During the months following the flight there was a great national debate.

For **conservatives,** or those who opposed changing the existing system, the monarchy was still essential because only the monarchy could maintain order. They believed the king should be forgiven, if he agreed to conduct himself according to the Constitution. For some **radicals,** or those who advocated extreme change, the king's actions only showed how useless the monarchy was. They wanted to destroy the monarchy and create a republic. **Moderates,** who wanted gradual change, wavered between the two positions because the proclamation of a republic might cause war with neighboring countries.

The Declaration of War

Not unreasonably, the people feared foreign invasion, and immediately following the king's flight there was a scramble to protect the country's borders. In August 1791 the emperor of Austria met with the king of Prussia and issued a declaration that was interpreted by some as threatening to France. The possibility of the émigrés supporting a **counterrevolution,** or a movement to reestablish the Old Regime, inflamed popular sentiments.

From the first meeting of the new Legislative Assembly in October 1791, the war issue was debated. To the Girondins (ZHEE-ron-dans), a fac-

tion within the Assembly, a war was needed to spread the Revolution's ideals. They believed that a republic could only emerge out of the conditions created by war. Also patriots in neighboring countries would aid French troops in overthrowing their monarchies and establishing new republics. The Girondins were supported by merchants who saw war as a way to revive France's economy.

Even Louis' supporters favored a war, though a limited one. If France proved victorious, the king's prestige would be restored and the republican position undermined. France would remain a constitutional monarchy and the radical element of the Revolution would be checked.

A few radical democrats, like Maximilien de Robespierre (ROHBZ-peer), tried to curb the warlike mood. In several brilliant speeches at the Jacobin Club in Paris Robespierre spoke out against a war, arguing that the émigrés were powerless. However, Robespierre's opinion was in the minority, and on April 20, 1792, the Assembly declared war against Austria.

The Second French Revolution

France was hardly prepared for war, and Austria, with Prussia's aid, quickly achieved a number of victories. At least half of France's military officers, who were nobles, had emigrated. Now soldiers mutinied on the battlefront, and French troops proved no match for the invaders. As foreign armies entered the country, the economic situation grew worse. Bread riots became widespread and peasants and grocers hoarded food. Shops were looted. The paper currency lost half of its value. The Legislative Assembly lost its popular support and proved incapable of running a successful campaign.

Bourgeois politicians from radical groups in Paris, like the Jacobin Club, took advantage of the situation and stirred up the populace. These were some of the Revolution's most famous leaders. Among them were the orator Georges Jacques Danton and the journalist Jean Paul Marat. To prevent the Revolution from being overthrown, they appealed to the radical artisans and shopkeepers of Paris who were known as the sans-culottes (sanz-kyoo-LOT).

More than ever, the king was now identified with the nation's enemies because of his Austrian

Why do you think the Mayor of Rouen accepted the tricolored ribbon of the Revolution during a bread riot? Identify the participants and their reactions.

wife. The military leaders were branded as allies of the upper classes. It was not hard to see that the advancing foreign troops had great support from a whole range of elements within the country. Once in control of the capital, thousands would flock to support the invaders: members of the clergy, aristocrats, servants of aristocrats, profiteering grain merchants, and moderates who were dissatisfied with the Legislative Assembly. In late July 1792 the commander in chief of the Prussian and Austrian forces, the Duke of Brunswick, issued the Brunswick Manifesto as he closed in on the capital. He warned that Paris risked annihilation if any harm were done to the royal family.

Meanwhile troops from Marseilles were in Paris on their way to the front. With them they brought a catchy new military tune, soon to become the French national anthem, the *Marseillaise*. The radical leadership used these troops and sympathetic members of the working class to attack the Tuileries.

On August 10, 1792, under the leadership of Danton, they stormed the king's palace, massacred many of its guards, and imprisoned Louis and his family. A revolutionary government, called the Paris Commune, was established. The monarchy had fallen and the Revolution entered its most radical phase.

1. In your own words, briefly define or identify: the Great Fear, August decrees, émigrés, Olympe de Gouges, Tuileries, sans-culottes, Paris Commune, Brunswick Manifesto.
2. List the changes instituted by the National Assembly.
3. How did the Constitution of 1791 change France's government?
4. What were the causes and effects of the royal family's flight to Varennes?
5. Why did France declare war on Austria?
■ The fall of the monarchy in August 1792 could be compared to the collapse of the presidency. What impact do you think the abolition of the presidency would have on the United States today?

THE NATIONAL CONVENTION

Not even a year old, the Legislative Assembly was forced to recognize the authority of the Paris Commune. The Assembly remained in session until a National Convention, elected by universal male suffrage, could decide the fate of the country and the king. Though all adult men were free to vote, less than 10 percent chose to exercise their right.

The Political Climate After August 10

When the Convention assembled in September 1792 the Girondins discovered that they were no longer the leaders of the most radical revolutionary groups. In the political climate that followed August 10 the radicals were dominated by the Jacobins, who were in closest touch with the Parisian sans-culottes.

The Girondin faction and their allies were generally satisfied by the establishment of the Republic. From their point of view the Revolution was now achieved. Moreover, they represented large

business interests that wanted to limit the control of the state at a local level. For the Girondins the prospect of a propertyless mob in power in Paris was something to be feared.

The Jacobins, however, saw state controls as necessary and advocated further revolutionary changes. Their role, as they saw it, was to protect the poor. They wanted to seize property from the wealthy and give to the poor so that a democratic society of small manufacturers and property owners would be formed.

The politicians on the right derived their name from their seating in the Convention hall. Those on the left sat on the opposite side, and those on the extreme left sat up in the highest section in an area nicknamed the Mountain. In the center were moderates who sat in a middle area called the Plain. Thus the right came to mean those in favor of preserving tradition, while the left signified those in favor of change.

In this way the French Revolution created the political categories of the modern age. The subsequent conflicts of the nineteenth century were essentially a struggle for or against the ideals of the Revolution. It is important to remember, however, that the terms right and left are never fixed and are always relative. What was radical in 1789 could become moderate in 1792 and conservative in 1793.

The King Must Die

On September 20, as the National Convention was first getting under way, a French victory at the battle of Valmy brought welcome news. Austrian and Prussian forces had been turned back from their march on Paris. Two days later the Convention abolished the monarchy and made France a republic.

In November the French Republic invaded the Austrian Netherlands in a new policy aimed at assisting all peoples in the struggle for liberty. The Netherlands' ports in French hands was something Britain's Prime Minister William Pitt could not accept. So Britain formed a coalition with the Dutch Netherlands, Prussia, and Austria. War was declared on February 1, 1793.

In December 1792 Louis stood trial for treason. Following one of the great debates of the Revolution, he was declared guilty by all. Yet the vote on his execution was close and by a majority of only one vote was his immediate death ordered. Half the Convention feared the consequences of his death—a dictatorship of the Mountain—and voted a stay of execution. Many people throughout the country volunteered themselves as hostages for the king rather than let him be executed. Nevertheless, on January 21, 1793, Louis was beheaded by the guillotine, and there was no turning back on the Revolution.

Defense of the Republic

In the spring of 1793 the coalition pushed the French out of the Austrian Netherlands and the Republic was threatened with invasion. Money lost its value and grain hoarding started to rise. Prices soared. In February and March the populace rioted for food. Women disrupted the Convention whenever their demands for price controls on food were not met. By June 1793 three-fourths of the departments of France were in open revolt against Paris.

In western France the counterrevolutionary movement grew in ferocity and numbers. There, in the Vendée (vahn-DAY), peasants and nobles revolted against control by Paris. In southern France foreign invasion was close at hand. A revolt led by royalists, or those in favor of a return to monarchy, surrendered the Mediterranean town of Toulon to the English.

To deal with the crisis the Convention created the Committee of Public Safety, and a tribunal was set up to deal with the Revolution's enemies. The assassination of Marat, now one of the Convention's leaders, by Charlotte Corday shocked everyone. In July 1793 the imprisonment of all traitors was declared.

To raise an army a national conscription, or draft, was proclaimed. "All Frenchmen whatever their age or sex are called by their country to defend liberty." Women were expected to help in hospitals and in the making of tents and clothes, young men served in the army. The draft created the largest patriotic fighting force ever seen up until that time. The mobilization of an entire nation at war was something new.

The Jacobins Rise to Power

During the Revolution there had been a steady rise of middle-class groups, outside the legislative body, whose influence now directed the course of politics. All over France clubs were formed by local

Dr. Guillotin introduced the guillotine in France because it was designed to make death quick and painless. Why do you think Louis XVI was guillotined in public?

revolutionaries. These clubs corresponded with the Paris Jacobins, and many gradually assumed authority at the local level. It was through the local Jacobin clubs that the extreme radicals were able to impose their rule on the rest of the country.

Under the leadership of Robespierre, the Jacobins sought to install a Republic of Virtue based on a strict civil and moral code. For the Jacobins, a temporary dictatorship of the consular type in ancient Rome was quite compatible with republican democracy. It was derived from the classical education that they knew. They had studied the teachings of the French *philosophes*, like Montesquieu and Rousseau, and those of the Roman writers. As a result, they sought to replace the decadence of the Old Regime with a government resembling the Roman Republic.

The Reign of Terror

The Reign of Terror represented the Revolution's most violent period. It lasted from the late summer of 1793 to July 1794, and it was the most gruesome display of state killings in western Europe since the wars of the sixteenth and seventeenth centuries.

People could be arrested for a remark made while standing in line waiting to buy bread, and children were used as spies on their parents and teachers. When thousands were condemned to death, even the Revolution's most enthusiastic supporters in Europe and America were shocked. Victims of the Terror ranged from Marie Antoinette and other royalists to the moderate Girondins, once the Jacobins' allies. Nevertheless, over three-fifths of those killed by the Terror were peasants or laborers. Only 8 percent were nobles.

Indeed the ruthless and fanatical executions can only be understood in the context of civil war and the threat of foreign invasion. When the Republic achieved military success and stability, the Terror ended and its leaders were arrested and executed.

Robespierre's Year

The elimination of the moderates fragmented the Mountain. Robespierre, the increasingly dominant figure on the Committee of Public Safety, started a purge of the extreme left because he accepted no deviations from his program for social change. The press and theater were tightly censored, and a system of spies and informers was instituted.

Far to the left of Robespierre were various sans-culottes leaders who indiscriminately denounced merchants and bourgeoisie. They also advocated the de-Christianization of France and attacked priests and nuns on the street, burned churches, and called for the destruction of France's great medieval cathedrals. In March Robespierre sent these radicals to the guillotine. Yet freeing the Republic of these elements did not make Robespierre secure. He accused Danton and his followers of disloyalty and corruption. In April 1794 he ordered them executed.

Many devout Catholics in the Convention were outraged by the de-Christianization of France and Danton's death. They plotted Robespierre's fall before they themselves could be accused and executed. The victory of French troops in the Austrian Netherlands at the battle of Fleurus, in June, ended the emergency situation. In late July 1794 conspirators overthrew Robespierre. The day after his fall, he and his colleagues went to the guillotine. Throughout the country a purge of Jacobins occurred. The Convention abolished the Committee of Public Safety and the Revolutionary Tribunal. The radical phase of the Revolution was over.

Accomplishments of the National Convention

The National Convention took far-reaching measures to deal with France's extraordinary circumstances. It stabilized the value of paper money by instituting price and wage controls, and it drafted the most democratic constitution of the whole revolutionary period. It abolished slavery in the colonies and developed a system of national education. By March 1794 the Convention was supporting an army of 800,000 at half the cost of March 1793.

For the first time, land confiscated from the Church and the nobility was made available to the poor peasants. The land parcels and payment terms the government offered now made it possible for even the poorer members of society to acquire land.

It was the National Convention, through two years of crisis, which enabled the Revolution to endure. By 1795 the coalition against France began to collapse. The Mountain had fallen, but the army it created would spread the Revolution throughout Europe.

SECTION REVIEW

1. In your own words, briefly define or identify: the Mountain, William Pitt, hostages for the king, the Vendée, Charlotte Corday, the Committee of Public Safety, the Reign of Terror, the battle of Fleurus.
2. List the factors that led to the establishment of the Committee of Public Safety.
3. What factors led to Robespierre's fall?
4. List the accomplishments of the National Convention.

■ The concept of a national conscription, or draft was first instituted during the French Revolution and is used by our government today. Do you think a draft is necessary during times of peace? Give reasons to support your opinion.

THE RISE OF NAPOLEON BONAPARTE

Following the Reign of Terror the Convention faced opposition from both political extremes. On the right, royalists agitated for a restoration of the Bourbon monarchy. On the left, the Paris sans-culottes rioted for bread and the values of the Constitution of 1793.

The royalists sought to install a constitutional monarchy with Louis XVI's son as Louis XVII. The young boy's death in captivity in June 1795 destroyed their hopes. Louis XVI's younger brother, the émigré count of Province, became heir to the Bourbon cause. As Louis XVIII he issued a manifesto at Verona. He proclaimed the punishment of his brother's murderers and the restoration of the Old Regime with the parlements, the nobility, and the Church fully restored to their prerevolutionary positions. The Republic dismissed his claims.

On the left, the sans-culottes attempted to use direct action because it had succeeded well in 1792 and 1793. However, many of their leaders had been executed during the Terror, and the Convention had learned from its mistakes in previous uprisings. In early October 1795 the French army was called in when about 25,000 Parisian sans-culottes tried to storm the building in which the Convention met. Henceforth the military, not the masses, would play the key political role.

The Directory

A month after the storming of the Convention a new government was created. It reflected the interests of landowners and the classes made wealthy by the Revolution—the nouveaux riches (noo-voh REESH), or the newly wealthy. The latter were the Revolution's successes: purchasers of government property, speculators, war contractors, and military men.

The democratic Constitution of 1793 was replaced by the Constitution of 1795, which called for a republic dominated by middle-class voters. Property qualifications were so high that only about 20,000 people could vote. A two-house legislature with five executives, known as Directors, was established to govern the country. The Directory lasted only four years.

In reaction to the program of austerity imposed by the Republic of Virtue, the public display of wealth again became fashionable. Dress reflected a craving for luxury. Salons resurfaced. Hosted by elegant upper-class women, they served as gathering places for politicians and important generals. One of the most famous salons was run by Madame de Staël (STAHL), a brilliant writer and the daughter of one of Louis XVI's ministers. Her salon provided a forum for intellectual society and political discussion.

Rampant inflation followed the lifting of price controls imposed by the Committee of Public Safety. Paper money fell to 15 percent of its value. Markets could not supply demand, and urban areas were only rescued from mass starvation by the distribution of free food. Corruption at all levels of government characterized the Directory's rule. Threatened by plots from both the left and the right, the Directory came to rely on the army.

General Bonaparte

The French Revolution opened up careers to many people with ability, which in the past had been reserved for the nobility. Napoleon Bonaparte's career idealized the ambitions of these professional men, and the Revolution gave him the opportunity to prove himself.

As a junior artillery officer, he was instrumental in regaining Toulon in 1793 from the enemy. The Convention rewarded him by making him a general. In 1795 he attracted attention by assisting the government in subduing a popular uprising. With the aid of his connections in Paris, the Directory gave him command of the army of Italy in 1796. He was twenty-six.

Bonaparte achieved his first major triumph in the Italian campaign of 1796–1797. He defeated the Sardinians and pushed the Austrians out of northern Italy. Had he wished, he could have marched on straight to Vienna. Living off the land, his quick-moving army was self-sufficient, and Bonaparte demonstrated his administrative skills by uniting his conquests of Italy into a new republic dependent on France. In 1797 he compelled the Austrians to accept a humiliating treaty.

Upon his return to Paris Bonaparte was greeted as a national hero. Many talked of his being the man best suited to reassert political order. Bonaparte, however, chose to continue his military conquests and devised a bold scheme. He would attack Britain indirectly by taking Egypt, the gateway to India and the Asian trade.

At first, Bonaparte's forces won a number of victories. Then the British, under the command of Admiral Horatio Nelson, dealt a crushing blow to the French fleet at the battle of the Nile in August 1798. Unable to achieve his goal, Bonaparte deserted his troops and returned to France in 1799.

Bonaparte's Coup d'État

Since 1797 the Directory had ruled the Republic as an unstable dictatorship. While Bonaparte was in Egypt, the Directory was discredited by defeats in Italy. A group of prominent people conspired to overthrow it. The most important was Sieyès, the former champion of the Third Estate, and one of the Directors. Supported by the chief of police, several bankers, and the foreign minister, Talleyrand,

Napoleon was born in 1769 on the Mediterranean island of Corsica, shortly after it was acquired by France. His family belonged to the lesser Italian nobility. Thus he was able to take advantage of the best French military training. He specialized in artillery. How was Napoleon able to rise in rank and social position?

the conspirators planned a sudden takeover.

They used the threat of a fictitious Jacobin counterrevolution to alarm the legislators. Then soldiers loyal to Bonaparte drove the legislators from the assembly at bayonet point. Thus the Directory fell in a sudden seizure of power by force, known as a *coup d'état* (koo day-TAH), literally a stroke of state. By the evening of November 9, 1799, a provisional government, the Consulate, was approved.

The Consulate was headed by three consuls, but most of the power rested in the hands of the First Consul, who was the head of state. Bonaparte was chosen for the position, and a military dictatorship was soon established.

From First Consul to Emperor

As First Consul, Bonaparte achieved unlimited power. He could issue laws, appoint and dismiss officials, conduct foreign policy, regulate finances, and make war and peace. Self-government through elected bodies was suppressed. In the weeks following his coup Bonaparte submitted his new constitution to a popular vote. The voters accepted it by a reported margin of over 99 percent. However, they had no alternative to the autocracy Bonaparte offered them. As long as the First Consul was successful militarily, he had no opposition.

Bonaparte gained loyalty and popularity at home by establishing peace abroad. He convinced the Russian czar, Alexander I, to drop out of the coalition against France by showing how England, now dominant in the Middle East, threatened Russian interests in this region more than France did. He forced Austria to sign yet another peace treaty in 1801 after he crossed the Alps and defeated its army. In the following year the English signed a treaty. For a brief time between 1802 and 1803 no European power was at war with another. Bonaparte had brought peace abroad and stability at home.

In 1804, two years after he had been made First Consul for life, a national vote approved Bonaparte's coronation as emperor. In the following years nobles of the Old Regime assumed a more active role in the administration, and many

As the pope was about to crown the emperor, Napoleon seized the crown and placed it on his head. He then crowned Josephine. What was the significance of these acts?

émigrés returned to France. Hereditary titles were brought into use again, and Napoleon maintained an extremely formal court, which had not been done since the days of Louis XIV.

Administrative Legacy

Napoleon ended the French Revolution, yet managed to preserve many of its innovations. There would be no return to the Old Regime, but neither would there be further upheaval. Although popular democracy had no place in Napoleonic France, the values of bourgeois society were retained. Within a few years France had a law code, an agreement with the Church, and a National Bank.

The law code, which jurists had been working on since the National Convention, was published in 1804. It protected private property and recognized the rights of individuals to engage freely in commerce and manufacturing. It confirmed the Revolution's ideals of freedom of worship and citizenship, and it served to abolish many feudal institutions abroad. This code, renamed the Napoleonic Code by the emperor, had a profound effect on the non-English-speaking world and was perhaps Napoleon's most lasting legacy.

In 1801, with Talleyrand's diplomatic assistance, Napoleon negotiated a treaty with the Roman Catholic Church. The Vatican recognized the seizure of Church lands, the abolition of clerical privileges, and the state's right to appoint and pay clergy. In exchange, Napoleon gave the Vatican the privilege of confirming appointments and agreed to reopen religious seminaries. In this manner Napoleon gained the support of the Catholic Church and many Catholics in France.

Official recognition of the Church, however, did not mean a restoration of the clergy's control of education. Napoleon continued the work of the National Convention in laying the foundations for modern France's secondary and higher educational system.

Thus the new French Empire rested on a contradiction. It stood for both the ideals of the Revolution of 1789 and for hereditary hierarchy as well. It advocated free competition in business and the triumph of the bourgeoisie. Yet it sanctioned monarchy and nobility, and it governed as an absolutist state.

SECTION REVIEW

1. In your own words, briefly define or identify: Louis XVIII, nouveaux riches, the Constitution of 1795, Madame de Staël, battle of the Nile, coup d'état, Napoleonic Code.
2. What opposition did the Directory face?
3. Of what importance was Bonaparte's first Italian campaign?
4. What conditions within France made Bonaparte's coup d'état possible?
5. How did Napoleon end the French Revolution yet preserve some of its achievements?

■ A coup d'état has never occurred in the United States. In your opinion, what aspects of our political tradition have prevented a coup from taking place?

NAPOLEONIC EUROPE

With political stability established in France, Napoleon began a course of military expansion in 1805 that lasted until his fall in 1814. Throughout this period he constantly faced opposition from Great Britain.

Diplomatic Overview of the Wars of 1803–1814

It is convenient to conceive of the era from 1803 to 1814 as one long military struggle, a struggle historians often refer to as the Napoleonic Wars. However, only Great Britain actually remained at war with France throughout this period. On the Continent the conflict was really a series of wars, the motives of the powers not nearly as clear as Britain's.

From Britain's view the struggle was almost exclusively economic. Britain wished to defeat its major rival in order to achieve commercial supremacy in the European and world markets. Nevertheless, Britain's small army required that it wage war on the Continent primarily through financial aid to its allies. Napoleon's far greater military superiority on land and Britain's unchallenged supremacy at sea made direct confrontation between the two powers difficult.

On the other hand, many of the European powers were capable of allying themselves with Napoleon when it was in their interest to do so. Russia was as wary of the British navy as of the French army. Prussia, in seeking mastery over north Germany, was challenged there by Austria, which in turn had its own designs on the Balkans. Spain pursued an active alliance with France until 1808. Only in 1813 did it become clear to all the powers that their primary aim was the removal of Napoleon.

The War Against Britain

Napoleon had preparations under way for a direct attack on England when Austria, Russia, and Sweden allied themselves with Great Britain to form the Third Coalition against him in 1805. The battle of Trafalgar, near the Strait of Gibraltar in the fall of 1805, destroyed his invasion plans. Under the command of Admiral Horatio Nelson, who was killed in the fighting, the English dealt a crushing blow to the combined French and Spanish fleets. Trafalgar confirmed British naval supremacy for the remainder of the war.

Unable to attack Britain directly, Napoleon resorted to economic warfare. In a series of decrees beginning in 1806, he imposed what became known as the *Continental System.* France and territories under French control were prohibited from doing business with Great Britain. British goods were not to be sold to the Continent and, if intercepted, were subject to confiscation and destruction. The Continental System was also intended to increase the wealth and production of France and its allies, and thus trigger the collapse of British industry.

The British responded with a blockade of their own on ports under French control. As a result, there was a rise in smuggling. Administrators, generals, and customs officials profited, and even Napoleon was forced to break his own laws. Europe simply could not do without British goods. Gradually the system was modified, and Napoleon sold merchants expensive licenses to do business with Britain. In the long run the system only served to alienate the commercial and industrial classes, which found it a severe economic burden.

Mastery of Europe

Napoleon displayed the full range of his military genius in the campaign of 1805–1807. Outnumbered by a combined Austrian and Russian army, he won what is considered one of his greatest victories at the battle of Austerlitz in December 1805. Challenged next by Prussia, Napoleon smashed the Prussian army and entered Berlin. He then marched straight through Poland and East Prussia, boldly confronted the Russians, and defeated them in two major engagements.

By 1807 Napoleon was the master of Europe. He forced Czar Alexander I to accept several territorial losses and reduced Prussia to little more than a buffer between the Russian Empire in the East and his own in the West. He limited the size of the Prussian army and stationed French troops in Berlin. Alexander agreed to join him in an alliance against Britain, and both Russia and Prussia accepted the Continental System. Thus the Third Coalition was effectively ended.

Between 1808 and 1811 Napoleon's power was at its height. With the exception of the Balkans, the entire European mainland was either under his control or allied to him. In addition to the empire, Napoleon dominated other states like the Confederation of the Rhine, which he created out of the ruins of the Holy Roman Empire in 1806, and the Grand Duchy of Warsaw, which he established after Prussia's defeat.

Napoleon was distressed by the lack of an heir to the throne. Though he had crowned Josephine empress in 1804, he chose to divorce her and to marry Marie Louise, the daughter of the Austrian emperor. A dynasty seemed confirmed when a son was born in 1810.

Napoleonic Europe

In many respects Napoleonic rule in Europe was beneficial. The French introduced new legal codes, improved administration, equalized tax burdens, and abolished nobles' privileges. In this sense, French occupation hastened the process of social and political reform that was to occupy Europe for the remainder of the century.

Prussia felt the impact and transformed itself into a modern state. It freed its serfs, reorganized its local governments, and reformed its educational

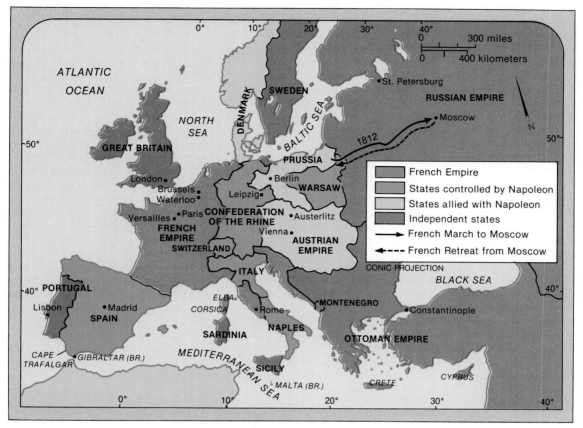

How much of Europe was under Napoleon's control by 1810? Explain how Prussia served as a buffer state for his empire.

system along Enlightenment guidelines. These reforms helped to promote the spread of nationalist sentiments among many Germans and led them to seek their political identity as a nation.

For all his innovations, however, Napoleon resorted to old-fashioned methods in the administration of his empire. He placed his family on the thrones of France's satellites and gave little thought to the fact that monarchial rule contradicted the ideals of the French Revolution. He also instituted heavy taxes and a system of spying and censorship. In general, his administrative reforms were directed at exacting as much money as possible for the continued maintenance of the French army. As a result of these policies and his endless warfare, resentment began to grow within the French Empire and its satellite states.

The Peninsular War

To ensure the success of the Continental System, Napoleon demanded that many neutral countries adhere to it. He even ordered the invasion of Portugal for the purpose of closing its ports to British trade. In a series of diplomatic moves he forced the Spanish Bourbons to abdicate and placed his elder brother Joseph on the Spanish throne. In early May 1808 a massive insurrection spread throughout Spain. It found support in all classes because the French were considered Jacobin atheists.

Seizing the chance to confront the French on land, the British sent a force to the Iberian peninsula under the command of General Arthur Wellesley, later the Duke of Wellington. Allied to Iberian armies, the British conducted a five-year campaign against France and its Spanish allies. The

After the Russian campaign, Napoleon and his shattered army returned to France. What does this painting reveal about the hardships they suffered in Russia? Why do you think Napoleon waited so long before beginning his retreat?

Peninsular War proved a drain on French reserves because Napoleon was forced to quarter many troops in Spain at the height of his continental campaigns. The French were finally driven out of Spain in 1814, and the Bourbon monarchy was restored to power.

The Russian Disaster and Abdication

Even before the empire reached its greatest extent, Napoleon's physical and mental decline began. He became irritable and his aggressions seemed increasingly illogical. Russia, the only power on the Continent that was still capable of resistance, annoyed Napoleon by its failure to observe the Continental System. Although this problem could have been settled diplomatically, for Napoleon there was no alternative except war. If successful, his empire would be greatly expanded. In the spring of 1812 Napoleon led his Grand Army of over 650,000 into Russia.

The rapid campaigns that worked so well in Germany and Italy, where French armies could live off the land and count on local support, failed in the barren wastes of Russia. Alexander's troops avoided battle and retreated into the country, burning and destroying everything in their path. This strategy forced Napoleon to lead his Grand Army deeper into Russian territory. Moreover, the one engagement Napoleon did achieve, at Borodino, was not the total victory he wanted. When he took Moscow in September 1812, he entered an empty burning city. Russia's scorched-earth policy greatly weakened Napoleon's position since his troops could not live off the land. His offers to Alexander for peace went unanswered.

Aware that he would not be able to spend the winter in Moscow, he withdrew. Famine, bitter cold, and Russian attacks exacted a heavy price. The Grand Army dwindled in size, and fearing a coup in France, Napoleon deserted his troops to return home.

The retreat from Moscow sparked revolts throughout Europe even before the Russian campaign was over. Britain, Russia, Prussia, and Austria formed a Fourth Coalition, and at the battle of Leipzig in October 1813 the French were crushed. Meanwhile Wellington's forces in Spain pushed into southern France. Napoleon could not halt the coalition's advance. In March 1814 the allied armies entered Paris. In April, Napoleon abdicated.

The emperor was given a pension and permitted to retire to the Mediterranean island of Elba, off the coast of Italy. Already in contact with Louis XVIII, Talleyrand set up a provisional government that paved the way for a restoration of the Bourbon monarchy.

The Hundred Days

The treaty that ended the war provided France with generous terms. Though stripped of most of its conquests, France still kept more territory than it had when Napoleon began his expansionist program. The country was not to be occupied. Louis XVIII, who was no longer demanding the restoration of the Old Regime, accepted the basic provisions of the Revolution's initial stages, and he ascended the throne.

For Napoleon, ten months in exile on a tiny island proved too much, and in early March 1815 he made one last desperate bid for power. He landed in southern France with a force of a thousand men and, unopposed, marched north to Paris. A few days before Napoleon's arrival in the capital, Louis XVIII fled the country.

However, the allies refused to accept Napoleon. In June 1815 a Prussian army and a British army under the command of the Duke of Wellington defeated Napoleon at the battle of Waterloo. Napoleon's final attempt to regain power had lasted little more than one hundred days.

This time the emperor abdicated again, and was exiled to the British island of St. Helena, in the South Atlantic. There he spent his declining years dictating his memoirs and arguing with the British governor. He died of stomach cancer in 1821. Ultimately, though, it was France that had to pay for Napoleon's last vain quest for glory. The peace settlement it accepted in Vienna in 1815 would not be as generous as what it had achieved in Paris the year before.

Napoleon's Impact

Through his memoirs, Napoleon helped create the legend of the superman that survived after his death. No doubt Napoleon made his achievement seem more liberal than it was. However, it cannot be denied that he cast a huge shadow over the generation that followed him.

To the nineteenth-century romantics Napoleon was the totally free individual, the one who had come out of obscurity to triumph completely over his environment. He was also the stabilizer and the rationalist, the enlightened man of the eighteenth century.

Napoleon unleashed upon Europe, and to some extent the world, the revolutionary power of 1789. He utilized the achievements of the Revolution to expose the corruption of the Old Regime. His career proved what a person of ability could accomplish if given the opportunity and means. He spread the ideals of the French Revolution, triggering nationalist movements in the nineteenth century.

There was only one thing he corrupted: the democratic ideals of the Jacobin Revolution and the Constitution of 1793. These would, ultimately, prove to be a legacy even more powerful than his own.

SECTION REVIEW

1. Mapping: Use the map on page 409 to locate the following: Gibraltar, Lisbon, Vienna, Berlin, the confederation of the Rhine, Moscow, the Baltic Sea, Leipzig, Elba, Waterloo.

2. In your own words, briefly define or identify: battle of Trafalgar, Continental System, battle of Austerlitz, Peninsular War, One Hundred Days, St. Helena.

3. Why did Napoleon institute the Continental System?

4. How did Napoleon achieve mastery of Europe? What impact did Napoleonic rule have on other countries?

5. Of what importance was the Peninsular War?

6. What were the results of the Russian campaign?

■ Napoleon's rise from junior artillery officer to emperor of Europe would not have been possible without the Revolution. What major political figures of today have achieved power through their ability and not their wealth?

Reviewing the Chapter

1. What were the results of the confrontation between the American colonies and the British Parliament?
2. How did the Revolution change French society?
3. How did the rise of Napoleon affect France and the rest of Europe?

Chapter Summary

Parliament's authority to tax its American colonies was challenged by Patriots in the 1760's and 1770's. The results of this confrontation were a war for independence and the establishment of a new political system—federalism. The American ideal of liberty, equality, and freedom of worship had great impact on France and Latin America.

In contrast, the French Revolution was a profound social and political upheaval that transformed France and affected the rest of Europe. The Revolution ended the society of orders and privileges, and eventually led to the fall of the monarchy. The Constitution of 1793 was the most democratic constitution in the world up until that time, and it made land confiscated from the nobility and the Church available to the poorer classes.

The threat of foreign invasion sparked radical extremes. Under the Reign of Terror, France suffered a year of bloodshed and fear. The fall of Robespierre brought about a return to more moderate rule under the leadership of the Directory. Six months after Robespierre's fall, the armies of the National Convention were spreading the Revolution's ideals beyond France's borders.

The Directory was seriously weakened by economic problems and corruption. After a coup d'état, a provisional government, the Consulate was established, but Napoleon Bonaparte soon emerged as dictator of France. Napoleon ended the French Revolution but managed to preserve many of its achievements. A military genius, he dominated Europe for over a decade. After a disastrous campaign in Russia, Napoleon was forced to abdicate. In 1814 France witnessed the restoration of the Bourbon monarchy, but not the Old Regime.

Using Your Vocabulary

1. What is the federal system? In what document is this system defined?
2. Name the three branches of our federal government.
3. Briefly define the three Estates in France. Which group was the largest?
4. What were the parlements? Who controlled them?
5. What was the Bastille? Why did it become a symbol of the French Revolution?
6. Who were the émigrés? How did their actions affect the Revolution?
7. What are the departments? When were they instituted?
8. Explain the difference between conservatives, moderates, and radicals.
9. Define the term counterrevolution. What group threatened to bring about a counterrevolution in France? Why?
10. Who were the Girondins? The sans-culottes? The Jacobins? What role did each play in the Revolution?
11. What do the terms left, right, and center refer to in politics? How were they derived?
12. Who were the nouveaux riches?
13. Define the term coup d'état. How does a coup d'etat differ from a revolution?
14. What was the Napoleonic Code? How did it reflect the ideals of the Revolution?
15. Define scorched-earth policy. When and why was it employed?

Developing Your Geography Skills

1. Use the map on page 357 to describe the extent of the British Empire in North America before the American War for Independence.

2. Use the map on page 409 to tell which states were controlled by Napoleon. Which states were his allies? Which were independent?
3. Use the map on page 409 to describe the Austrian Empire, the Confederation of the Rhine, the Duchy of Warsaw, and Prussia.

Recalling the Facts

1. List the causes of the American Revolution.
2. Why is the Boston Tea Party considered an important historical event? What were the causes and effects of the Boston Tea Party?
3. Why was the First Continental Congress convened? What resolutions were adopted by the delegates?
4. What event marked the beginning of the Revolutionary War?
5. Who wrote *Common Sense?* How did this pamphlet influence the colonists?
6. Why is the Declaration of Independence considered an important historical document?
7. How and when did the Revolutionary War end?
8. List the causes of the French Revolution.
9. Why was a meeting of the Estates General called in 1789? What were the results?
10. What were the accomplishments of the National Assembly? How did it change France?
11. Why did Louis XVI try to flee France? What were the results?
12. Why did France declare war on Austria in 1792? How did it affect the Revolution?
13. How did the character of the Revolution change after August 10, 1792?
14. Who was Robespierre? What role did he play in the Revolution? How did he fall from power? Why?
15. What were the positive achievements of the National Convention?
16. Why was the period after the fall of the Convention called the Directory? Describe its rule.
17. Explain the Continental System. Why was it established?
18. Describe the Hundred Days. Why do you think Napoleon was exiled to an island in the South Atlantic the second time?
19. List the effects of Napoleonic rule on France and the rest of Europe.

Essay Questions

1. Compare and contrast the American and French revolutions. Be sure to include the causes, the results, and the nature of the two movements.
2. During his reign Louis XVI went from the position of absolute monarch to being a virtual prisoner in the Tuileries. Explain the various stages in the reduction of his power. Why was it difficult to order his execution?
3. Describe the role of women in the French Revolution.
4. "Liberty, equality, and fraternity" was the slogan heard during the French Revolution. Explain its significance and how it applied or did not apply to various groups.
5. From 1803 to 1814 France was confronted with almost continual opposition from Great Britain. Describe the causes, the major events, and the effects of this conflict. Which side was ultimately victorious? Why?
6. Describe Bonaparte's rise to power. What events led to his downfall? Why do you think Bonaparte was able to crown himself emperor when the country had just undergone a revolution in order to abolish monarchy?

Critical Thinking

1. On what unstated assumptions did Parliament base its decision to tighten control over its colonies? Do you think this was a wise decision?
2. The Declaration of Independence makes certain statements with respect to the colonists' values. What were they? Why do you think the colonists valued these concepts?
3. How did life during the Old Regime reflect bias? Give specific examples.
4. What statements can you make about the values of Robespierre and the Committee of Safety? Be sure to support your opinion.
5. What logical inconsistencies existed under Napoleonic rule?

CHAPTER ·18·

The INDUSTRIAL REVOLUTION

1700–1900

Objectives

- *To understand why the Industrial Revolution began in England*

- *To explain how improvements in areas such as transportation and communications changed Western civilization*

- *To understand how industrialization changed people's lives*

A revolution is often described as any fundamental change that affects how people think, live, and govern. As you read in Chapter 16, an intellectual revolution changed the ways in which society viewed the universe and the individual's place in it. In Chapter 17 you learned that the weakening or destroying of monarchies and the appearance of republican forms of government in France and America were the results of social and political revolutions. These events altered people's understanding of human nature and society.

During the 1700's a series of changes in the manufacture of goods and in trade led to another type of revolution. The Industrial Revolution gave rise to a wave of new methods of production and reshaped the patterns of economic life. This industrial or economic revolution resulted in the introduction of labor-saving machinery in manufacturing, and of coal and steam power for hand labor. Working and living conditions were changed drastically by the new machines and the factories built to house them. The cottage, or home, industry gave way to increased factory production. The changes that stimulated **industrialization** also influenced developments in transportation, communication, and business.

Although greater wealth was produced, its unequal distribution gave rise to new economic and political theories. Huge concentrations of people in industrial areas not only led to economic and cultural growth, but also to problems such as pollution, congestion, inequality, and slums. The Industrial Revolution was not so much a historical event as a process. In fact, it is still going on in developing parts of the world.

BEGINNINGS IN ENGLAND

Several conditions favored the development of an industrial revolution in England. The country had a plentiful supply of labor. It also had large reserves of such important raw materials as coal, tin, iron ore, and wool. Any raw materials that England lacked were available from its colonies, which also provided good markets for its manufactured products.

England had a surplus of capital, the money that businesspeople spend to buy land, buildings, machinery, and other goods or services. Many wealthy merchants, bankers, and landowners in England had money to risk in new businesses and also to invest in rail and water transportation networks.

Industrialization, both in England and on the continent, was influenced to a great extent by Adam Smith. This Scottish economist advocated an end to mercantilism as an unnecessary barrier to trade and manufacture. Moreover, he and other economists of the Enlightenment opposed restraints on innovations such as merchant and craft guilds.

The geography of England also helped further its industrial development. England, Scotland, and Wales were separated geographically from the continent and, thus, from many of the wars fought during the 1700's. They were protected from invasion by geographic barriers, so the countryside was not destroyed by warfare. Water resources were more than plentiful, and the climate was suitable for growing cotton and many varieties of food products.

Changes in Agriculture

One of the most important factors in England's rise as an industrial power was a series of changes in agriculture. Farming in the early eighteenth century had not changed much since the Middle Ages. For example, the medieval three-field system was still in use. Each year one-third of a farmer's land was planted, one-third was used for pasture, and one-third was left unplanted, or fallow. Strip farming was still common. Each household received at least one strip of good soil, one of poor soil, and so on. Planting methods were not very efficient. For instance, seeds were sown in broadcast fashion, that is, a farmer planted a crop by walking across the field and just throwing seeds by hand in all directions.

Agricultural innovation began among England's large landowners in the mid-1700's. The owners of small farms had neither the funds nor the desire to alter traditional ways of working the

Members of the Royal Agricultural Society meet in Bristol, England, in 1842, to inspect the latest farm tools. What purpose did such groups serve?

land. However, the owners of large estates could afford to set aside fields or pastures for experiments. They were also able to invest money in new machines.

One of the first estate owners to improve farming was Jethro Tull. After experimenting in the early 1700's, he concluded that most crops grow best in soil that is broken up thoroughly before seeds are planted. To prepare the soil, he advocated the use of cultivators. Tull also invented a seed drill. This device dug holes in a row along the ground, placed seeds in them, and covered them up with soil. Planting with a seed drill proved much more efficient than broadcast sowing. Tilling and weeding became easier because seeds were now planted in rows.

Another pioneer in English agriculture was Charles Townshend. He proved that sections of a field need not lie fallow every third year. Soil exhaustion could be avoided by growing mineral-rich crops such as turnips and clover every third year. The turnips and clover could then be harvested and fed to livestock in winter. Traditionally, most farmers slaughtered their livestock in the fall because they lacked the feed to keep the animals alive through the winter months. More animals meant more manure for fertilizer, which also increased crop yields.

Robert Bakewell developed scientific methods of animal breeding to produce larger, heavier animals that could be raised for meat. Prior to this, most livestock was used chiefly to provide dairy products, hides, and wool.

As changes in agriculture made farming more profitable, large landowners wanted to obtain additional acreage so they bought farms from smaller owners. Another method of acquiring land was called enclosure, through which public pastureland was enclosed, or fenced in. Enclosure had been going on for many years by local agreement. However, in the eighteenth century Parliament stepped in to regulate the practice, which was being abused by large landowners. Enclosure reached its peak between 1760 and 1810, when hundreds of enclosure acts were passed. By 1850, almost all the open fields of England were gone.

Many of England's small farmers, hurt by the enclosure movement because it limited the availability of growing and planting acreage to them, gave up their farms. Some became farm laborers for large owners. Others moved to the cities to look for work. Even though many small farmers left the land, the use of more efficient methods increased agricultural productivity. Thus, although fewer people were engaged in farming, the amount of food produced rose steadily.

The Textile Industry

Textile production was one of England's largest and most prosperous industries in the 1700's. As a result, manufacturers of textiles had large sums of money available to invest in new machinery. Some of the first new inventions of England's Industrial Revolution appeared in textile factories.

This series of inventions started in the 1730's. The first was the flying shuttle, patented by John Kay in 1733. This device cut in half the time required to weave cloth from thread. A demand for more thread to keep the weavers busy led to the development of the spinning jenny by James Hargreaves in the 1760's. Richard Arkwright then improved on the spinning jenny. About 1769 he produced the water frame, a water-powered machine that produced uniformly fine- or hard-spun thread. Samuel Crompton went even further. He combined features of the spinning jenny and the water frame to produce the spinning mule. Crompton's spinning mule was able to produce the thread needed for the finest textiles, such as muslin.

At this point, the spinning process had gotten ahead of the weaving process. Hand looms could no longer keep pace with the amount of thread being produced. In 1785 Edmund Cartwright designed a power loom, which was gradually improved during the next few years.

All these advances in the textile industry increased England's need for cotton, which it had to import. At first England bought raw cotton mainly from its colonies in the West Indies and from Egypt. In 1793, however, a young American inventor, Eli Whitney, produced the cotton gin, a shortened word for engine. With this device, workers could separate cotton seeds from the fiber far more quickly than by hand. Whitney's invention stimulated the production of cotton in the United States, and America soon became the major supplier of England's cotton.

A Newcomen engine lifts ore from this eighteenth-century English mine, while men use wheelbarrows to collect coal. How can machines benefit workers?

The flying shuttle and the spinning jenny could be used by domestic workers in their own homes. However, the water frame, the spinning mule, and the power loom were too big and required water power. Therefore, a central location where workers and machinery could be brought together under one roof was needed. The first mill, or factory, was built near Manchester in 1771 by Arkwright and two of his partners. In less than twenty years England had 119 such mills.

The factory system made Britain the world's greatest producer of cotton cloth. Imports of raw cotton went from 1 million pounds in 1743 to 60 million pounds by 1800 to over 200 million pounds by 1830. Between 1790 and 1820, cotton goods rose from ninth to first place in value among British manufacturers. By 1820 cotton goods accounted for almost half of Britain's exports.

Steam, Coal, and Iron

Until the 1700's England depended on animals for farm work, water mills for power, and wood for fuel. The Industrial Revolution, however, introduced machinery that required improvements in sources of power. New uses of steam, coal, and iron changed the face of industry and commerce.

The first textile factories were powered by water mills, but these had disadvantages. Not only did a factory have to be built alongside a river, the power failed if a drought lowered the water level or cold weather froze the river. In addition, because coal miners usually dug down below the water table, a way had to be found to pump out this water. The first steam engines built in England solved these problems.

The earliest steam engines were constructed by Thomas Savery and Thomas Newcomen, but they consumed a great deal of fuel in proportion to the power they delivered. This drawback was not serious in the coal fields where fuel was available, but it limited the use of steam engines elsewhere. In 1763 a Scottish inventor, James Watt, greatly improved Newcomen's engine so that it could be used in textile factories. Watt soon formed a partnership with Matthew Boulton to produce the new steam engine in quantity. By 1800 there were almost 500 steam engines operating in Britain, and

SOCIAL SCIENCE SKILLS

GRAPHING

Social scientists have a variety of tools that they can use both to obtain and to provide information. One of the most effective visual tools is the graph. Graphs present information in such a manner that relationships or trends can be discerned quickly.

There are three common types of graphs: circle graphs, line graphs, and bar graphs. A circle graph is divided into pielike slices or wedges. The size of the slices depends on the percentage of the whole that each wedge of data is intended to represent. To indicate patterns or trends, a line or bar graph may be utilized. A line graph uses solid or dashed lines alone or in combination. A bar graph uses horizontal or vertical solid or shaded bands. To construct or interpret a graph, you must first focus on what information needs to be conveyed.

During the Industrial Revolution innovations in techniques and machinery led to significant in-

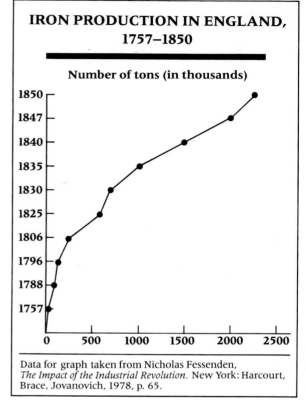

IRON PRODUCTION IN ENGLAND, 1757–1850

Number of tons (in thousands)

Data for graph taken from Nicholas Fessenden, *The Impact of the Industrial Revolution.* New York: Harcourt, Brace, Jovanovich, 1978, p. 65.

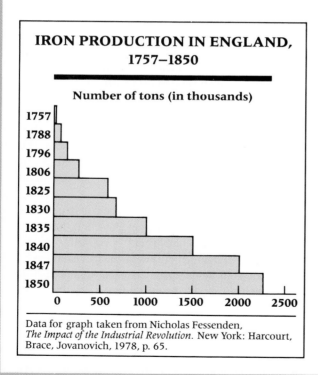

IRON PRODUCTION IN ENGLAND, 1757–1850

Number of tons (in thousands)

Data for graph taken from Nicholas Fessenden, *The Impact of the Industrial Revolution.* New York: Harcourt, Brace, Jovanovich, 1978, p. 65.

creases in the production of coal, steel, and iron. These technological developments along with England's natural resources of coal and iron ore resulted in the rapid growth of the iron industry. One way to show this growth is by using graphs, such as the bar and line graphs on this page, entitled *Iron Production in England, 1757-1850.* The same set of statistics for the number of tons produced in a given year, gathered from a written source, were used for both graphs.

1. Using either graph, what trend is most evident in the production of iron after 1800?
2. Could a circle graph have been constructed to present these data on iron ore production? Why or why not?

all were made by Watt and Boulton. Steam was soon the major source of power for a wide variety of industries and for many forms of transportation.

Meanwhile, coal had become increasingly important during the eighteenth century. Because so much of England's forests had been cut down, a new source of fuel was necessary. Coal filled this need and was one of the factors that made possible greater production of iron. Iron had long been smelted with charcoal, which is made from wood. With the disappearance of England's forests, something else had to be substituted. In the early 1700's Abraham Darby worked out a way of using coke, a by-product of coal, for smelting.

The need for large quantities of high-quality iron spurred further improvements. Steam engines were used to operate bellows for furnaces. In 1783 Henry Cort developed a process called puddling which involved reheating the iron to produce iron relatively free of impurities.

British production of both coal and iron began to rise dramatically. Between 1700 and 1800, coal output increased from 860,000 to 10 million tons a year. During the same period, iron production soared from about 6,000 tons to 250,000 tons annually. Britain was becoming known as the "workshop of the world" because of its dominance of industrial markets worldwide and leadership in metal technology.

SECTION REVIEW

1. In your own words, briefly define or identify: Tull, Townshend, Bakewell, Whitney, Watt, Darby.
2. What factors stimulated the development of the Industrial Revolution in England?
3. Summarize the importance to the English textile industry of each of the following: Kay, Hargreaves, Arkwright, Crompton, Cartwright.
■ In its early stages, the Industrial Revolution depended on new machinery, new sources of power, and new ways of organizing production. Which of these three elements do you think is the most important in today's industrial world? Why?

THE SPREAD OF INDUSTRIALIZATION

The Industrial Revolution spread from the British Isles to the continent of Europe and to North America. Its progress, however, was uneven. Political divisions in such countries as Italy and Germany prevented innovation on a large scale. Lack of capital hindered development in southern and eastern Europe. In some regions, such as Spain, entrepreneurs and business leaders were viewed unfavorably. On the other hand, the new United States had an enterprising population impatient to exploit their country's rich natural resources.

Agriculture and Industry

On the whole, agriculture did not make the rapid advances on the European continent that it did in England. In France, where a higher percentage of small owners controlled the land, there were fewer enclosures and less innovation. In southern, central, and eastern Europe, however, peasants and

Completed in 1825, the Erie Canal linked the Great Lakes with America's East Coast consumer areas. How are transportation and economic growth linked?

serfs continued to use medieval methods of planting and harvesting. A major exception to the prevailing conservatism in agriculture was the United States, where a steady movement westward opened up thousands of acres of land for settlement. American farms tended to be large, and their owners were eager to adopt such mechanical aids as the reaper, first demonstrated successfully by an American inventor, Cyrus McCormick, in 1834.

The mechanization of industry progressed more rapidly in France and the Low Countries than elsewhere on the continent of Europe. For example, the French textile industry was becoming mechanized by the late eighteenth century. Coal production expanded as well. Other zones of European industrialization included Switzerland and northern Italy. In the United States, as in England and France, the textile industry was the first to mechanize. The earliest factories in America were located along the rivers of the New England states, where water power was plentiful.

Transportation

Transportation became industrialized along with other elements of the economy. France was among the first nations to develop a better road network. Large-scale improvements, however, did not take place until the rule of Napoleon, who was concerned with efficient military transport. In the British Isles, the first men to build roads according to scientific methods were two Scots, Thomas Telford and John McAdam. McAdam's technique, which utilized layers of small stones with gravel on top, was widely adopted.

Even on improved roads, transporting goods on pack horses or in wagons was expensive, especially for bulky items such as coal. Because water travel was cheaper, miles of canals were dug to connect rivers and seaports. One of the first European canals linked the Somme and Oise rivers in northern France. England's first artificial water link was the Bridgewater Canal, which connected

Fulton's steamboat, the Clermont, *made it possible for paddle-wheelers to sail the inland waterways of the United States. Tested by the* Clermont *in 1807, Fulton's steam engine helped to revolutionize transportation. How?*

Trains of the Liverpool and Manchester Railway show great differences in classes of travel: luxury coaches (top) and open cars for people, goods, and livestock (bottom). How did the Industrial Revolution affect railway expansion? How did railway travel affect peoples's lives?

the coal fields of Worsley and the growing city of Manchester. Opened in 1761, it halved the cost of coal transport in Manchester. By 1815 England had an estimated 2,000 miles of canals.

While most of England's canals were constructed by private enterprise, those on the continent and in the United States generally relied on state aid. One of these was the Erie Canal of New York state, completed in 1825. The canal enabled goods to be shipped by water between the Great Lakes and the Atlantic Ocean, and made New York City the nation's major transportation center. In 1869 the Suez Canal joined the Mediterranean Sea and the Indian Ocean by way of the Red Sea.

Water transportation came into wider use with the application of steam. This became feasible after Watt's experiments, which made smaller engines possible. Robert Fulton, whose *Clermont* steamed up the Hudson River in 1807, is credited with the first practical steamboat. Actually, at least thirty steamers had been built before this time. Steamboats came into wide use on large inland river systems such as the Mississippi in the United States and the Rhine in Germany. The first steam-powered vessels crossed the Atlantic Ocean in the 1830's.

Although water transport was cheaper than land, it was slow and impossible in mountainous terrain. The development of the locomotive and then of railroad systems solved the problems connected to the overland movement of goods and people.

Rails had long been used in mining areas to provide tracks along which horses or mules could pull carts. An English engineer, Richard Trevithick (TREH-vih-thik), built a steam locomotive to pull loads. Credit for the first practical locomotive is usually given to George Stephenson, whose locomotive powered the Stockton and Darlington Railway. When this line opened in 1825, it signaled the beginning of the railroad industry.

A railroad network was quickly laid out over much of Great Britain. The network totaled about 6,000 miles by 1850. The German states and France were also quick to take advantage of the new method of transportation. In the 1850's, France and the United States tripled their operating mileage.

The railroad, like many other innovations of the Industrial Revolution, did not win immediate acceptance among ordinary citizens. The speed, the noise, and the sparks flying from the railway

New York City's central telephone office in 1888 had operators who manually had to connect calls by moving wires. What advances has telephone service made since?

its pioneers were an Italian, Alessandro Volta, who made the first battery about 1800, and a Dane, Hans Øersted, who discovered electromagnetism in 1819. A French scientist, André Marie Ampère (ahm-PAIR), worked out laws in the 1820's that formed the basis for the science of current electricity. Less than ten years later two inventors, Michael Faraday of England and Joseph Henry of the United States, working independently, invented the electric generator.

These discoveries made possible electric telegraphy, or sending messages by wire thousands of miles per second. Underwater telegraphy by cable was the next step. France and England were first linked in 1845, but it took many years before a successful transatlantic cable was laid. After many failures an American, Cyrus Field, accomplished this task in 1866.

Electricity also made possible the telephone, which used fluctuating currents to transmit the sound of the human voice. Alexander Graham Bell, a Scottish Canadian, patented his first instrument in 1876. Soon after, all the industrialized countries of Europe and America had telephone systems.

Another series of improvements that aided communication took place in the field of printing. In the early 1800's, a German named Friedrich Koenig (KUR-nig) had first applied steam power to printing. Another milestone was the development of the rotary press. Shortly after its introduction in the 1840's, this high-speed machine was able to print up to 10,000 sheets a minute.

Developing an individual printing machine, now known as the typewriter, challenged the ingenuity of many inventors in the early eighteenth century. Not until the 1860's, however, did an American, Christopher Sholes, succeed in developing a practical machine for commercial use.

cars and tracks were frightening to those accustomed to the slow pace of the horse and carriage. When the French opened a new line between Paris and the nearby town of St. Germain, King Louis Philippe wanted to ride on the first train. His wish was denied for fear he might be injured by harmful gases or the explosion of the locomotive.

Communications

Like transportation, European systems of communication in the early modern period were inadequate for an age that was industrializing. As late as 1700, for instance, it took three weeks for news to travel from Rome to London.

Among the first improvements was an optical telegraph, developed by Claude Chappé of France in the 1790's. It made use of poles mounted with crossbars whose position could be changed to indicate words or letters. However, stations had to be within eyesight for messages to be relayed between them.

Meanwhile, however, scientific investigations led to a new field of discovery, electricity. Among

Later Developments

Changes in technology helped foster feelings of optimism and confidence in the future. Visitors went to great international fairs to marvel at the latest wonders. One of the first of these expositions took place in London in 1851. It was held in the Crystal Palace, a revolutionary new building made entirely of iron and glass and constructed in only seven months.

Great Britain dominated the displays at the Crystal Palace Exposition, but American innovations such as the McCormick reaper and the Colt revolver also drew crowds. The reaper and the revolver were just two of the many items being turned out by **mass production,** which was utilized increasingly as the Industrial Revolution progressed. This method of making goods produced items in quantity through the use of machinery, continuous operations, interchangeable parts, and a highly structured division of labor.

Although many of the innovations of the Industrial Revolution are credited to single individuals, the final product often represented the ideas of many people. A case in point concerns interchangeable parts, or standardized components, which are essential to mass production. Eli Whitney is usually cited as the first to suggest the idea. However, in the early 1700's Christopher Polhem of Sweden used this principle to make pendulum clocks.

Among the industries that adopted mass production were those that manufactured clothing and shoes. Mass production also benefited the food processing industry. Preserving food by canning had begun during the Napoleonic era, although its principles were little understood at the time. A Frenchman, Nicholas Appert, first successfully canned meat in 1810. Gail Borden of the United States introduced condensed milk in the 1850's.

Another development of the later Industrial Revolution influenced steel production. Steel took the place of iron for many industrial uses. People had long known how to make this strong alloy, but the process of separating out the carbon impurities had made it very expensive. The problem was solved by two breakthroughs in the mid-nineteenth century. One was the Bessemer converter, developed by Henry Bessemer of England. The other was the open-hearth furnace, a joint project of William Siemens of England and Pierre Martin of France. World production of steel jumped from about one million tons in 1870 to thirty times that amount by 1900.

The applications of electricity continued to multiply. Arc lights were used to illuminate department stores in France and the United States in the 1870's. Incandescent lighting for the home fol-

London's Crystal Palace probably was the world's first prefabricated building. Its sections could be put up and taken down easily. Why was it a creation of the Industrial Revolution?

lowed the development of carbon filament lamps by Thomas Edison, among others. In 1878 New York City and London opened several central power stations.

Transportation also utilized electricity. In 1881 Berlin became the first city to operate an electric trolley car. Just a few years later London opened its subway, or underground, and powered its trains by electricity.

By the end of the nineteenth century, inventors in several different countries were working on a self-propelled vehicle that would be powered by an internal-combustion engine. Pioneers in developing the automobile included Karl Benz and Gottlieb Daimler of Germany, J.J.E. Lenoir (luh-NWAHR) and Louis Renault (reh-NO) of France, and Charles and Frank Duryea (DUHR-yay) of the United States. By 1900 many different models were being manufactured.

An early mass-produced vehicle was the Oldsmobile, first made in the United States in 1901. When Henry Ford began marketing his Model T in 1908, automobiles became truly afford-able for middle-class citizens. Ford's plants developed the assembly line, an arrangement whereby stationary workers put together a finished product as parts passed by them on a moving belt. The assembly line cut manufacturing time for a chassis from over twelve hours to ninety minutes.

Among the many far-reaching effects of the automobile was the development of the petroleum industry. Until 1900, petroleum was used mainly as a lubricant and a source of kerosene. But with automobiles and the internal-combustion engine (most of which used gasoline), the demand for petroleum soared. In the twentieth century this fuel would become as important to industry as coal had been to the Industrial Revolution.

SECTION REVIEW

1. In your own words, briefly define or identify: McCormick, McAdam, Fulton, Stephenson, Ampère, Faraday, Crystal Palace, Bessemer, assembly line.
2. Why did the Industrial Revolution spread unevenly to countries beyond England?
3. What contributions did Bell, Koenig, and Sholes make to modern communications?
4. What is mass production, and what industries utilized it during the nineteenth century?
■ The innovations introduced to agriculture in the early 1700's helped set the stage for technological advances affecting industry in the 1800's. Does this same process of development occur today? Has industry been influenced by advances in other fields?

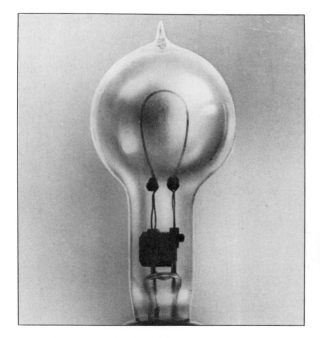

How "big" a contribution did Edison's "small" electric light bulb make to industrialization? What would you do today without electricity?

THE IMPACT OF THE INDUSTRIAL REVOLUTION

The Industrial Revolution was more than an age of new inventions and economic development. It also led to changes in cultural patterns and lifestyles. More than any other single phenomenon of the modern world, the Industrial Revolution shaped today's civilization.

Population and City Growth

Beginning about the middle of the eighteenth century, population increased rapidly. This was a worldwide phenomenon, probably due more to declining death rates than to increasing birthrates. Furthermore, fewer mothers were dying in childbirth, and infant deaths were declining.

In Europe the population rose from about 140 million in 1750 to 266 million a century later. This growth represented an increase of some 90 percent. In the United Kingdom alone, the population tripled in this period from ten million to about thirty million.

Although industrialization was not the sole cause of the population increase in Europe, it was an important factor. Improvements in agriculture provided a larger food supply, and the development of better means of transportation, especially the railroad, practically did away with local food shortages and famines. Finally, the growth of manufacturing, with a corresponding increase in overseas trade, created an expanding economy that employed growing numbers of people.

Population growth was accompanied by two great migrations. One was movement outward from Europe, especially to North America. The other population movement was a shift to the cities. Many factories were established in or near older towns, where there was a supply of labor. Others formed the basis for new cities. In either case, urban centers drew thousands of people from rural villages and farms.

In 1800 there were only twenty-two European cities with populations of over 100,000. By 1850 there were at least thirty-nine. In 1785 Scotland and England had only four cities with populations exceeding 50,000. By the mid-nineteenth century, there were thirty-two urban centers of this size. By this date, too, England's urban population exceeded that of its rural areas. This urban-rural ratio would not be reached by Germany until 1914, or by the United States until 1920.

Changes in Life-style

Along with technological and agricultural advances, the Industrial Revolution led to lasting changes in people's patterns of living and working. Industrialization, especially in the late nineteenth

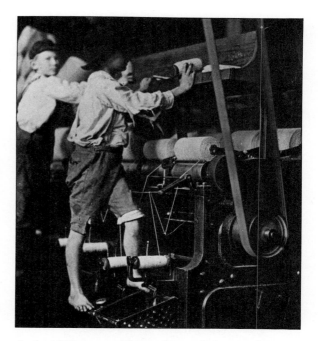

In the 1800's young children often worked at unsafe jobs. Why are the young boys shown here at risk? Must children today work as these boys did?

century, would give rise to movements for social reform and the unionization of labor. Cultural and economic progress would accompany these movements.

As the factory system expanded, working conditions became more difficult. Wages were so low that whole families often had to work in order to survive. In fact, textile manufacturers preferred women and children for some jobs because their smaller fingers were more adept at operating the complex machinery. They were also in demand in mines because they could pull carts through small tunnels. Working days were long, usually lasting from fourteen to sixteen hours.

Factories in England and other developed countries were full of safety and health hazards. Workers were often injured by machinery, especially if they were tired after long hours on the job. As did their counterparts in the coal mines, many textile workers contracted lung diseases. The factories had to maintain a hot, humid atmosphere in order to keep threads from breaking.

By 1830, as population increased and cities grew, living conditions for factory workers were

One result of industrialization was the growth of cities. Use this Doré engraving to explain how industrialization led to urban problems in the 1800's. Are today's problems the same?

often appalling. Cities were unprepared for the influx of new inhabitants who came from rural or other areas looking for jobs. Water supplies, sewage facilities, police and fire protection, and other services proved inadequate. In many cases, city water came untreated from the same river into which sewage was dumped. This condition led to widespread disease and sickness.

Housing in new industrial areas was constructed quickly and cheaply, and factories were soon surrounded by miles of slums. In some cities, entire blocks of houses were built side-by-side and back-to-back so that the only windows were in

front. Whole families crowded into one room. In Liverpool, one-third of the inhabitants lived in cellars. Coal smoke darkened the air and every surface it touched.

Life for both the working class and the rising new middle class of business and professional people changed. In the centuries when most people had made a living by farming, and artisans had worked out of their own homes, there was little division between home life and work life. Now, in working families where all the members had factory jobs except for the smallest children, family life changed. By the mid-1800's men were going out every day to the factory or office, while their wives were expected to stay at home. The home was the sphere of middle-class women. Yet single and married working-class women continued to represent a large share of the work force, particularly in the areas of clothing manufacturing, nursing services, and teaching.

Owners and Workers

As you read in Chapter 15, the Commercial Revolution that accompanied the age of exploration witnessed an expansion of capitalism. This economic system, as it existed in the sixteenth and seventeenth centuries, is often called commercial capitalism because it was based chiefly on trade. With the Industrial Revolution, capitalism entered a new phase. Now dominated by manufacturers rather than merchants, it became known as industrial capitalism.

In the early days of the Industrial Revolution, businesses were often started by single entrepreneurs or by a few partners. As industrialization progressed, however, capital needs became too great even for the wealthiest individuals. Constructing a steel mill was very different from setting up a spinning factory. Thus capitalists turned increasingly to a new form of business organization, the **corporation.** Like the joint-stock company of an earlier time, the corporation was owned by a number of investors. They were its stockholders, or shareholders. However, the stockholders of the corporation, unlike those of the joint-stock company, were not liable for the debts that the corporation might incur. In other words, they had limited liability. This provision encouraged investment, for it protected individuals from losing everything in case of bankruptcy or business failure.

Competition among businesses became intense by the late 1800's and led to ways of organizing business that continued into the twentieth century. Some businesses, instead of competing, worked out ways of cooperating with other large firms engaged in similar activities. Through arrangements called **pools,** they looked for ways to share markets and to fix prices for goods.

In another form of business organization, several firms were combined, usually when one large firm bought up a number of competitors. This new, larger firm was called a **trust.** It received this name because the stock of all the individual companies was held in trust by a single new corporation. Some trusts combined business enterprises in several countries, and these international trusts were known as **cartels** (cahr-TELLS). If all the firms in a given industry were combined, a monopoly resulted.

Pools, trusts, cartels, and monopolies played an important role in expanding the economies of Western nations in the late nineteenth century. They introduced new business techniques and more efficient production. By reducing competition, however, these practices usually resulted in higher prices for consumers.

The complex ways of doing business that developed in the nineteenth century depended more and more on bankers, who helped organize and finance trusts and similar ventures. Because of the power of financiers such as the Rothschilds in Europe and J.P. Morgan in the United States, the economy of the late nineteenth century is often referred to as finance capitalism.

Workers had little defense against organized business. If an individual laborer was dissatisfied with his or her earnings or working conditions, the only recourse was to quit and try to find a job somewhere else. Owners could fire workers without notice, and had no obligation to reimburse them or their families in case of injury or death on the job.

Workers and others interested in their welfare did make attempts to improve conditions, but little was accomplished for many decades. It was not until 1833, for example, that the British Parliament passed an effective factory act. Some of its provisions were intended to curb abuses of child labor. It prohibited child labor under the age of nine. The act set limits on children aged nine to thirteen who could be employed no more than forty-eight hours a week (or nine hours a day). Those aged thirteen to eighteen could work no more than sixty-nine hours a week (or twelve hours a day). The Factory act of 1833 applied only to the textile industry, however. Many years passed before legislation brought widespread change to British industrial workers, including children.

Another alternative would have been for workers to combine forces in labor unions, so that many people together could try to accomplish what individuals could not.

Labor unions, however, were prohibited in every country of Europe. In England the series of so-called Combination Acts that outlawed unions was repealed in 1824, but a burst of union activity immediately followed. The accompanying violence led to a new law in 1825, which allowed workers

The underwriting room of Lloyds of London is shown as it looked in 1809. By the 1900's, Lloyds was the largest insurance firm in the world. How was its growth connected to industrialization?

to join together to seek better wages and hours, but forbade them to strike. Until late in the nineteenth century the main recourse of workers was political activity such as Chartism, or socialism, about which you will read in later chapters.

Pluses and Minuses

Were people better or worse off as a result of the Industrial Revolution? Historians and other experts do not agree. Most of those who first studied the social effects of industrialization, beginning in the late nineteenth century, emphasized the negative. For example, the factory worker was almost always viewed as unhappy with the conditions under which he or she lived. Scholars are now questioning these findings.

Critics of the early Industrial Revolution tended to concentrate on conditions in this period without comparing them with those in earlier eras. In addition, they based much of their research on the findings of parliamentary committees that were deliberately searching out social ills.

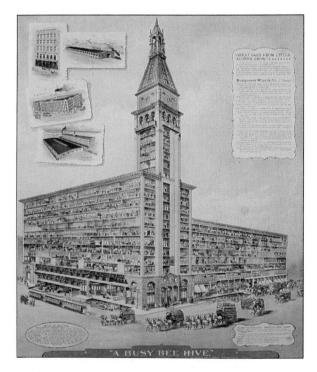

By the 1880's, large stores and mail-order firms, such as the one pictured in this historic advertisement, were popular. How did mass production and communication encourage this trend?

Certainly it is true that farmers and those engaged in domestic industry had always worked hard. For centuries before the Industrial Revolution, entire families had labored for a relatively small return. Much rural housing was crude, and people suffered from inadequate diet and poor sanitary facilities.

Overall statistics indicate that England, for example, made substantial progress during the period of industrialization. Between 1750 and 1850, per capita production increased by two-and-one-half times. Although the upper and middle classes probably benefited more from the rising standard of living than did workers, mass production did mean mass consumption.

Still, there seems little doubt that industrialization brought a good deal of misery in its wake. Farm and crafts workers labored hard, but they followed their own, and nature's, timetable. In small communities, individuals and families preserved an identity down through the generations. Factory workers were regimented according to an owner's or manager's rules, and formed part of an anonymous mass that was crowded into city housing. Independence was replaced by dependence, and the rhythms of the seasons gave way to the ebb and flow of the supply and demand of a developing market economy.

SECTION REVIEW

1. In your own words, briefly define or identify: industrial capitalism, corporation, pool, trust, cartel, monopoly.
2. How did industrialization contribute to population growth?
3. Why were women and children preferred as workers in the new industrial establishments?
4. What effect did the Industrial Revolution have on families?
5. Why did nineteenth-century workers not form labor unions?
■ The Industrial Revolution changed the lifestyles of people at all levels of society. How? Has your life-style been affected by the technological advances made in the last decade? Give reasons for your answers.

Reviewing the Chapter

Chapter Summary

The Industrial Revolution began in England, with improvements in agriculture paving the way by making farms more productive. The cotton textile industry was the first to undergo mechanization. Accompanying developments included the use of steam power, an increase in coal production, and expansion of the iron industry.

Industrialization spread from the British Isles to continental Europe and to North America. The nineteenth century witnessed vast improvements in transportation, including better roads, canal networks, steamships, and railroads. Equally important were such communication breakthroughs as the telegraph, the cable, and the telephone. Electricity was used not only to power the new communication devices, but also to light homes, businesses, and factories, and to run trolleys and subways. By 1900 the new internal-combustion engine had been adapted so that it could power automobiles. Petroleum was on its way to becoming the primary fuel of the industrialized world.

The Industrial Revolution helped stimulate population growth, which in turn led to overseas migration and increased urbanization. Industrialization, however, created difficult working and living conditions and prompted changes in family life.

As the economy grew more complex, it led to new forms of business organization, among them industrial capitalism and the corporation. In the absence of effective labor unions, most workers were at a disadvantage in dealing with their employers. Nonetheless, production rose and the standard of living improved considerably when compared with earlier times. Whether the Industrial Revolution benefited people as a whole is still being debated.

1. What industries were first affected by the Industrial Revolution?
2. What were some of the positive and negative results of the Industrial Revolution?

Using Your Vocabulary

1. In your own words, define revolution. What types of revolution have you studied?
2. Describe some of the major characteristics of the Industrial Revolution.
3. What is the difference between an event and a process?
4. Explain the role of capital in the Industrial Revolution.
5. Why was the enclosure movement important to the agricultural life of England in the 1700's?
6. What is your understanding of the terms industrialization and mechanization?
7. What are standardized components? Explain their importance to manufacturing.
8. Why was water transportation cheaper than that over land routes?
9. What was the original meaning of the word typewriter? How did its meaning change?
10. What is your understanding of the term mass production?
11. Describe some of the applications of electricity in the later 1800's.
12. What is the principal characteristic of an assembly line? How does this technique save production time?
13. How does commercial capitalism differ from industrial capitalism?
14. What are some similarities between a corporation and a joint-stock company? What are some of the differences between them?
15. In your own words, briefly explain the meaning of the following terms as they are used in business: pool, trust, monopoly, and cartel.
16. Explain the meaning of limited liability.
17. Describe the Factory act of 1833. What was its main goal?
18. What did workers have to gain if they formed labor unions?
19. Cite some of the pluses and minuses in people's lives during the Industrial Revolution.

Developing Your Geography Skills

1. Use the Atlas map on page 756 to locate England. How did the geography and location of England influence the start of the Industrial Revolution there? Can the same be said of the other countries of the British Isles? Why or why not?
2. Refer to the Atlas maps on pages 756 and 759. Identify some of the places where industrial and agricultural techniques and innovations were first introduced.

Recalling the Facts

1. How did Adam Smith's theories contribute to the rise of industrialization?
2. What medieval planting methods were still in use in the early eighteenth century?
3. Name three of the most important agricultural pioneers in the early 1700's. Briefly describe the contribution made by each.
4. What effect did the enclosure movement have on the small farmer?
5. What was the largest and most prosperous industry in England in the early 1700's? How did this industry influence the number of inventions made during the first half of the eighteenth century?
6. What was the main advantage of the cotton gin? How did it affect the relationship between America and England?
7. What was the primary advantage of the cottage industry?
8. What reasons prompted the establishment of factories?
9. Why was it necessary to find new sources of power as the Industrial Revolution progressed in the 1800's?
10. Why did agricultural innovation fail to take hold in the rest of Europe as rapidly as it had in England?
11. Describe at least two techniques or inventions that advanced each of these areas: water transport, railroads, and communications.
12. Why were exhibitions such as the one held at London's Crystal Palace important?

13. What industries were most affected by the method of mass production?
14. What two developments changed the process of steel production? How?
15. Name at least two pioneers in the development of the automobile, and what countries they represented.
16. Briefly explain the impact of industrialization on the growth of cities in the 1700's and 1800's.
17. Cite at least two ways in which the mechanization of industry affected the lives of children and their families.
18. What new techniques to organize business were prompted by competition in the late 1800's?

Essay Questions

1. Explain the factors that made England the starting place for the Industrial Revolution in the 1700's.
2. Describe the life of a working-class family in the mid-1850's. Consider such aspects as job and educational opportunities, living conditions, and roles of family members.
3. How did agricultural and mechanical innovations influence each of these events in the 1800's: migration, population growth, and the rise of cities?

Critical Thinking

1. "New uses of steam, coal, and iron changed the face of industry and commerce." What facts from Chapter 18 can you use to verify this statement?
2. It has been said that "more than any other single phenomenon of the modern world, the Industrial Revolution shaped today's civilization." Are there any unstated assumptions in this observation? Explain your answer.
3. What warranted or unwarranted claims may be made about the breakthroughs in transportation and communication that brought people and nations closer together in fact and in spirit?

Reviewing the Unit

Developing a Sense of Time

Examine the time line below and answer the questions that follow it.

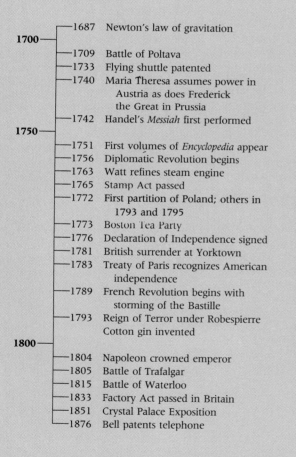

1700 —
— 1687   Newton's law of gravitation

— 1709   Battle of Poltava
— 1733   Flying shuttle patented
— 1740   Maria Theresa assumes power in
          Austria as does Frederick
          the Great in Prussia
— 1742   Handel's *Messiah* first performed

1750 —
— 1751   First volumes of *Encyclopedia* appear
— 1756   Diplomatic Revolution begins
— 1763   Watt refines steam engine
— 1765   Stamp Act passed
— 1772   First partition of Poland; others in
          1793 and 1795
— 1773   Boston Tea Party
— 1776   Declaration of Independence signed
— 1781   British surrender at Yorktown
— 1783   Treaty of Paris recognizes American
          independence
— 1789   French Revolution begins with
          storming of the Bastille
— 1793   Reign of Terror under Robespierre
          Cotton gin invented

1800 —
— 1804   Napoleon crowned emperor
— 1805   Battle of Trafalgar
— 1815   Battle of Waterloo
— 1833   Factory Act passed in Britain
— 1851   Crystal Palace Exposition
— 1876   Bell patents telephone

1. Who was crowned king of Prussia at the same time that Maria Theresa assumed power in Austria?
2. Which event marked the beginning of the French Revolution?
3. How many times was Poland partitioned? When?
4. Which occurred first: the battle of Waterloo or the battle of Trafalgar?

Social Science Skills

Graphing
1. Based on the graphs on page 418, how many tons of iron were produced in 1806 and in 1850?
2. Based on your reading of Chapter 18, what factors contributed to the steady increases in iron production?

Critical Thinking

1. What underlying connections can you identify between the progress made during the scientific revolution and the Enlightenment's emphasis on reason?
2. Based on what you have read about the conditions in factories during the 1800's, what can you deduce about the values of many factory owners who lived at that time?
3. What claims were made by the American colonists to justify revolution? Do you think they were warranted or unwarranted?
4. What facts are verifiable regarding the beginnings of the Industrial Revolution in England?

Linking Past and Present

1. The culture of the Enlightenment period reflected a world more sensitive to the needs and desires of individuals and societies for a better life. Is the same sensitivity to life evident in today's popular culture?
2. The American colonists fought for and won their independence from England during the years 1776-1783. Shortly afterward the people of France revolted against the social, economic, and political oppression of the Old Regime. In what ways do these eighteenth-century revolutions compare with the struggles of people today, both in the United States and abroad, to achieve equality or political independence?

UNIT ·7·

The
ERA
of
NATIONALISM
and
REFORM

1815–1914

CHAPTER ·19·

EUROPE after the CONGRESS of VIENNA

1815–1900

Objectives

- *To discuss the steps taken after 1815 to keep nationalism and liberalism in check*

- *To compare the changes in the political and economic systems suggested by nineteenth-century reformers*

- *To explain the changes in the electoral system achieved in Great Britain in the 1800's*

- *To describe the different governments that ruled France after 1830, 1848, 1852, and 1872*

- *To summarize the causes and the outcomes of the revolutions of 1848*

*I*n 1814 and 1815, following the defeat of Napoleon, the major European powers met in Vienna to plan the peace. After decades of turmoil, they hoped to restore lawful government and bring stability to the Continent. However, their search for order would be marked by a conflict between the ways of the past and the forces of the future. In a number of countries that had been conquered by the French, the desire to be free of foreign rule forever was taking hold. Moreover, new ideas of freedom that had arisen out of the American and the French revolutions were spreading throughout Europe.

Adding to these forces for change were the dramatic effects of the Industrial Revolution. The shift away from an agrarian society brought vast numbers of people to the cities. This migration created a middle class that wanted to be represented in government and a class of urban workers who lived and worked under harsh conditions in the crowded cities. These changes in the social system unleashed new theories about the relationship between citizens and government.

For a while reformers pressed their demands in a peaceful, nonviolent way. But in most western European countries, despite some modest changes, rulers rejected suggestions for major reform. The beliefs of those in power and the goals of the reformers were so far apart that compromise was often impossible.

The movement for reform could not be totally suppressed. The period from 1815 to 1848 was marked by uprisings and rebellions that caused serious problems for the established governments. Although most of the revolutions failed, some of the changes that came about altered forever the political and economic systems in most of the western world.

EUROPE AFTER NAPOLEON

The wars against Napoleon had not only been over territory, they had also been against revolutionary ideas. When the fighting was over, the European leaders found it easier to redraw the map than to stamp out the new ideas.

Nationalism and Liberalism

One of the most important results of the Napoleonic Wars in Europe was the revival of a spirit of **nationalism.** Nationalism is the sense of unity and common identity felt by people who share the same history, language, and culture. Spurred by recent French control, people developed feelings of national identity and a desire to overthrow foreign rule.

Besides the surge in nationalism, other forces for change were emerging in Europe. One such movement, **liberalism,** favored private property, self-government, economic freedom, and educa-

The leaders at the Congress of Vienna conferred about Europe like doctors discussing a patient. They wanted to ensure that the fever of revolution would not break out again.

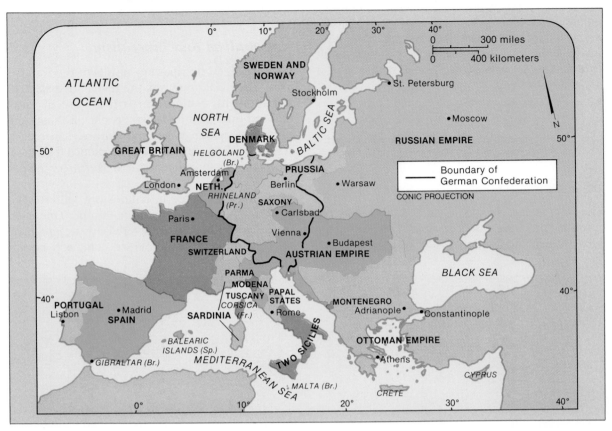

Which states bordered France and served as buffers against French expansion?

tion. Liberals—among them professionals, lawyers, and rich members of the expanding middle class—now wanted constitutions limiting the powers of government, parliaments representing the voters, and guarantees protecting their natural rights. Considered even more extreme in their demands were the radicals. These were often university students, working-class leaders, and many of the new industrialists who lacked the vote. The radicals wanted reorganization of the courts, relief for the poor, and universal manhood suffrage. Some even advocated the vote for women.

The nationalists, liberals, and radicals posed threats to the old ways. They alarmed the conservatives, people opposed to changing the existing political system. Conservatives resisted the idea that people had natural rights or that government was a contract between citizens and rulers. At first the conservatives, led by men like the British polit-

ical philosopher Edmund Burke, opposed only radical change. They felt freedom should be achieved gradually through a process of adaptation. Soon, however, conservatives in many countries were joined by reactionaries, those who not only opposed any change but also wanted to return to how things had been. During the next fifty years, all these groups would confront one another in country after country in Europe.

The Congress of Vienna

Following the overthrow of Napoleon, the leaders of Europe gathered in Vienna in 1814 and 1815. Dominating the Congress of Vienna was the aristocratic Austrian foreign minister Prince Metternich (MET-ur-nik). Other major figures included were Britain's foreign secretary Viscount Castlereagh (KASS-ul-ray) and Russia's Czar Alexander I. In addition, the French foreign minister Talleyrand (TAL-ee-rand), a master of diplomacy and negotiation, maneuvered himself into a position to protect the interests of France.

Legitimacy, the return of monarchs to their rightful thrones, was an underlying principle of the Congress. The Bourbons were restored to power in France, Spain, and Naples. But even the conservative Congress of Vienna did not wish to put the Holy Roman Empire back together. Scores of German princes were ignored as Napoleon's reorganization of Germany was maintained. A loose association of thirty-nine independent states, including Prussia and Austria, made up the German Confederation.

Establishing a balance of power was another major concern of the delegates. To this end they set up buffers around France, which was thought by many to be the major threat to European peace. Metternich and Castlereagh also worked to prevent any one power from gaining an overwhelming political or territorial advantage.

Territorial Settlements

The delegates sought to restore the balance of power in Europe through a series of trade-offs and alliances. A vital issue was the decision on Poland and Saxony. Poland had been partitioned by Russia, Prussia, and Austria in the eighteenth century and partly restored in Napoleon's duchy of Warsaw. Czar Alexander I hoped to reestablish the Kingdom of Poland under his control, thus extending Russian power into central Europe. In return for Prussia's agreement to this scheme, the czar would support Prussia's claim to Saxony, thereby increasing Prussia's influence in Germany. Great Britain and Austria would not stand by as Russia and Poland enhanced their prestige.

Through the clever arrangements of Talleyrand, the final settlements provided something for everyone, including recognition of France as a major power. Russia received most of Poland while more than half of Saxony went to Prussia. Belgium, the former Austrian Netherlands, was unwillingly united with the Dutch Netherlands. This act satisfied the British who wanted to keep the river ports of the Netherlands out of the hands of a strong country. In exchange for this loss of territory, Austria gained Italian principalities and

became the leading power in Italy. Also, the independence of Switzerland was reestablished with its neutrality guaranteed by the major powers. This system of territorial compensation often conflicted with the principle of legitimacy.

The New European Alliances

The leaders at the Congress of Vienna took more steps to ensure the success of their peace efforts. They joined together in a series of agreements to support one another against violations of the settlement. The first such pact was the Holy Alliance, a moral statement sponsored by Alexander I of Russia. The czar urged his fellow monarchs to pledge to deal with their subjects in a spirit of Christian love. Although they did not take it seriously, most of the other rulers in Europe signed the Holy Alliance. Only the Turkish sultan, the pope, and the king of England abstained. Lord Castlereagh termed the Holy Alliance "a piece of sublime mysticism and nonsense."

Of much greater potential importance was the Quadruple Alliance, a pact made in 1815 by Britain, Prussia, Russia, and Austria. Hoping to maintain peace through diplomacy, the nations agreed to meet regularly to review matters of mutual concern, particularly any threat to the balance of power. When France was admitted to the alliance in 1818, the five nations became the Quintuple Alliance. They operated in what was known as the Concert of Europe.

The Concert of Europe was not very effective because its members could not agree on what constituted a threat to peace. Britain regarded the purpose of the Quintuple Alliance as merely to protect Europe against possible new French threats. Czar Alexander, on the other hand, wanted the alliance not only to guarantee existing borders, but to safeguard "legitimate" governments as well by repressing dissent. The British representative was opposed to this added commitment and Great Britain eventually withdrew from the alliance.

By ignoring the forces of nationalism and democracy, the leaders at Vienna had sown the seeds of further trouble. Soon a series of uprisings in southern Europe brought the alliance together, without Britain. The nations promised military support for any government threatened by revolution. In time the Concert of Europe backed its words with weapons and used force to put down rebellions. No major war, however, involving the leading European powers, erupted for nearly forty years.

The Age of Metternich

Many historians call the years from 1815 to 1848 the Age of Metternich because of his impact on events. He used his influence to put down liberalism and nationalism. The centers of these movements were in the commercial and industrial cities and in the universities. Students had returned from the wars to overthrow Napoleon with hopes for national unity. They wanted constitutions that guaranteed political freedoms. Convinced by student agitation that Germany and Austria were on the verge of rebellion, Metternich masterminded the adoption of the Carlsbad Decrees by the German Confederation in 1819. These decrees limited free discussion at universities, censored publications, abolished legal reforms, and in general undid the civil gains of the French Revolution.

In response to the awakening forces of liberalism, rulers in most European countries attempted to restore the conditions that existed before the French wars. Conflict was inevitable. When a rebellion broke out in Naples, Metternich put it down. At this point Britain refused to intervene in what it considered the domestic affairs of another nation. In Spain an uprising brought about a brief return of constitutional government. However, by 1823, King Ferdinand VII was restored to absolute power by the French forces representing the Quintuple Alliance, excluding Great Britain. The break in the Concert of Europe became more apparent when Great Britain supported the independence of the Latin Americans who revolted against Spain.

Throughout Europe in the 1820's, only in Greece did revolutionaries achieve some permanent success. In 1821 Greek nationalists revolted against the oppressive rule of the Ottoman Empire. Although European rulers refused at first to come to their aid, many individuals, including the English poet Lord Byron, responded to Greek pleas for help. Finally, despite pressure from Metternich, Russia, Great Britain, and France persuaded the Ottoman ruler to meet the Greeks' demands. By 1830 Greece was declared an independent state.

1. Mapping: Use the map on page 436 to locate the Netherlands, Prussia, Switzerland, Saxony, and the Austrian Empire.
2. In your own words, identify or define: nationalism, liberalism, conservatives, reactionaries, legitimacy, Metternich, Castlereagh, Holy Alliance, Quadruple Alliance, Talleyrand.
3. What effects did nationalism and liberalism have on Europe after 1815?
■ Why did the European rulers find it almost impossible to return to the ways of the old regimes after the Congress of Vienna? What are the benefits and the difficulties of nations banding together to keep the peace?

REFORMERS OF THE POLITICAL AND ECONOMIC SYSTEMS

In the years following 1815, country after country felt the effects of industrialization. As the domestic system declined and production moved from the home to the factory, many new industrialists became wealthy. At the same time, the poverty of the lower classes became more visible as the poor were drawn from rural districts to mill towns and cities.

Adam Smith and the Classical Economists

As you have read, capitalism made great gains in the 1700's and early 1800's. Under capitalism, people invest in businesses that produce goods and services in order to make a profit. Capitalism was not a new economic system. It had existed in Europe since the end of the Middle Ages, but it had existed under mercantilist systems in which the government regulated economic activity and supported monopolies. This system made it difficult for the new breed of industrial capitalists to make profits.

In the late 1700's a new economic system, known as **free enterprise,** was first proposed. Supporters of free enterprise believed that businesses would produce the greatest amount of goods and services when capitalists were allowed to operate with the least interference from government. They wanted economic freedom as well as free trade among nations. A term describing this capitalist system is **laissez-faire** (leh-say-FAIR), from the French for "let them [businesses] do as they please" or "leave things alone."

The roots of this economic philosophy go back to French writers of the Enlightenment and the work of a Scottish economist named Adam Smith. In *The Wealth of Nations,* published in 1776, Smith argued against mercantilist restrictions. He said there are rules that govern all economic activity. Among these rules are the law of supply and demand and the law of competition. In business, according to Smith, prices and profits are determined by the relationship of supply and demand. If there is great demand for a particular good, and that item is scarce, buyers will pay a high price for it. As a result, profits from its sale will increase. When this happens, individuals with capital will invest in the manufacturing of the scarce goods in order to earn profits. Soon more of the product will be available. Then the manufacturers must compete with one another for sales. They offer customers lower prices or a higher-quality product, or both, while trying to keep their expenses low. When some producers are forced out of business, the supply will shrink once again, and prices will rise. In the end, only the better organized and more efficient manufacturers will survive and make profits. Thus, according to Adam Smith, everyone gains from free enterprise. Manufacturers produce the goods demanded by buyers, workers have jobs, investors and business owners earn profits, and buyers receive quality goods at lower prices.

Smith and other believers in laissez-faire came to be known as classical economists. Among Smith's followers were Thomas R. Malthus and David Ricardo, who held that so-called natural laws governed economic activity. In his *Essay on the Principle of Population,* published in 1798, Malthus wrote that people multiplied much faster than the supply of food they needed to stay alive. Thus, poverty and human misery were unavoidable. Even if wealth were distributed evenly, the population would expand and be reduced to poverty again. Malthus' theory promoted a laissez-faire attitude toward social reform. Later David Ricardo wrote *Principles of Political Economy and Taxation.* He applied Malthus' gloomy theory to wages. According to the law of supply and demand, when the supply of laborers was plentiful, wages went down. Therefore, as the population and consequently the labor supply increased, workers would inevitably earn less. This theory became known as the iron law of wages.

The Liberal Economists

As people became aware of the effects of industrialization on working and living conditions, a number of individuals began to urge a reform of the economic system. A key figure in this movement was Jeremy Bentham, an Englishman who founded **utilitarianism.** Bentham believed that utility, or the measure of usefulness, was the standard by which to judge a society and its government. To Bentham, a democracy was the form of government that was likely to ensure the most pleasure and the least pain to its citizens.

John Stuart Mill, a leading reformer and writer, was greatly influenced by Bentham. Mill wrote in his essay *On Liberty,* published in 1859, that the basic principle that defined the relationship between people and government was one in which power was exercised only to prevent harm to others. "That government is best that governs least," he wrote. This principle, Mill believed, was based not on natural law, as others had stated, but on utility. Mill's emphasis on the freedom of the individual had great appeal to the newly emerging middle class made up of industrialists and business people.

Unlike most nineteenth-century liberals who did not favor giving the right to vote to everyone, Mill wanted suffrage extended to all men and women. He felt that basic education should be provided at state expense to prepare people to vote.

The Utopian Socialists

Some economic reformers had more radical goals than the liberal economists. Rejecting the economic principles of Adam Smith and his followers, they believed the only way to improve the conditions of working people was to abolish capitalism. These reformers proposed an economic system called **socialism.** The socialists opposed private enterprise. They believed it was unjust for factory owners to have so much economic control. Some socialists also proposed doing away with private property. They favored government ownership of factories, mines, and railroads.

Some of the early socialists were later called Utopian socialists because they wanted to eliminate competition and create Utopian or perfect societies. Among these were Henri de Saint-Simon and Charles Fourier of France and the British capitalist Robert Owen.

Saint-Simon, a French nobleman, said government should organize society so that people would join together to exploit nature instead of exploiting one another. To help the poor and to redistribute resources, he suggested, society should operate on the premise, "From each according to his capacity, to each according to his work." He admired industrialists and managers and felt that they were of more value to society than landowners and kings.

Robert Owen was a successful industrialist whose beliefs grew out of his faith in the natural goodness of all people. According to Owen, people had been corrupted by their surroundings. If men and women could live in a society based on cooperation, in which there was no selfishness or competition, their true nature would emerge. He also believed that women should participate in government and ought to be relieved of some family responsibility so they could do so.

Owen tried to put his economic theory into practice. He bought a cotton mill in Scotland and turned the factory town nearby into a clean, safe community with good schools and a high standard of living. However, Owen's later attempts to set up similar communities in England and at New Harmony, Indiana, in the United States failed.

Owen's idea of a cooperative industrial society was adopted by Charles Fourier. He proposed another kind of Utopian community, the phalanx. Phalanxes were to be communities of fewer than two thousand people, each of which would form a self-sufficient economic unit. Work was to be assigned to people according to their interests and talents. A number of these phalanxes were tried, mostly in the United States where land was more easily available, but, like other Utopian experiments, they met with little success.

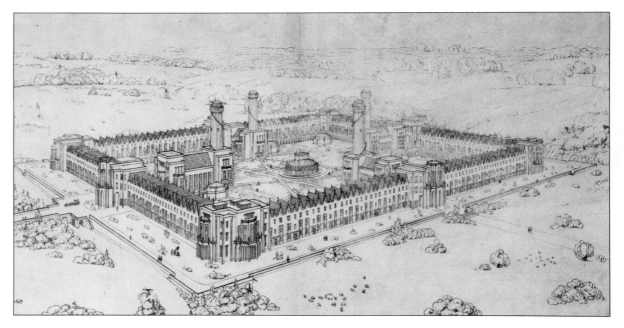

Robert Owen proposed a community in New Harmony, Indiana. The inhabitants were to work together and share the goods they produced. Why did Owen believe such Utopian communities were possible?

"Scientific Socialism"

Socialists had little influence at first. However, in the second half of the 1800's, the groundwork for socialism to become an important force was laid by a German scholar and newspaper writer named Karl Marx. Karl Marx was the most important of all the nineteenth-century socialists. Marx first published his ideas in the *Communist Manifesto,* which he wrote with the help of Friedrich Engels, the son of a wealthy German manufacturer. Later he expanded on his ideas in his major work *Das Kapital,* edited in part by Engels. Marx's ideas formed the basis for the political and economic system known as **communism.**

The socialism of Marx differed from that of the early socialists in two important ways. First, the early socialists believed that there should be a gradual and peaceful development toward ideal conditions for the workers. Marx, on the other hand, forecast a sudden and violent uprising in which the workers would seize the government and use it to secure their own welfare. Here Marx reflected the impact of the French Revolution on his theory. He felt that if a revolution could topple an economic and social system once, it could do it again. Second, Marx considered his form of socialism to be "scientific." He argued that it was based on research and observation of real world conditions. It was Marx who called other forms of socialism "utopian." To him they were based on feelings of morality and dependent upon the kindness of the rich to the poor.

Marx also developed an explanation for historical development. For him, all history was the story of class struggle. Marx believed that throughout the past there had always been two groups, or classes, of people involved in producing goods. One class controlled all the wealth and political power while the other did all the work. Marx argued that this was true during the Middle Ages, when serfs were exploited by the landowners. The struggle of serfs against nobles lasted for hundreds of years. In time capitalism developed out of this continuing struggle as the middle class replaced the landed aristrocrats. The existence of the middle-class industrialists gave rise to the working class. Under capitalism, Marx said, workers have replaced serfs, and factory owners have taken the place of the landowners.

According to Marx, the working class would grow larger as competition forced more and more small producers out of business. Economic crises would increase, causing suffering that would help motivate workers to revolt. Finally the larger worker class would overthrow the few remaining capitalists. Temporarily, the leaders would set up a **"dictatorship of the proletariat,"** that is, a rule of the workers. This dictatorship would exist as long as any form of capitalism or any differences between the classes remained. After people were educated to accept socialism, government would be unnecessary and would "wither away." All would be equally provided with what they needed. Competition would be replaced by cooperation. Marx, however, never fully explained how the future socialist system would work.

In 1864 Marx took part in a workers' meeting that became known as the First International. He used future meetings as forums for his ideas. When a bloody rebellion of workers broke out in Paris in 1871, Marx thought it was the first step of the revolution he predicted. But the middle class reacted against the violence and the First International ceased to exist. Nevertheless, socialist ideas had taken root and would continue to have an impact on social, economic, and political history with or without revolution.

Other Forms of Protest

The different methods of reform suggested by nineteenth-century economists and political philosophers appealed to many people. There were some, however, who rejected these ideas and looked for other ways to bring about change. One such group was the Christian Socialists. This group had its origins among the English clergy, many of whom felt that the evils of industrialism were bringing "ever-increasing darkness and despair" to workers in the clothing factories. The Christian Socialists suggested cooperative ventures in which people would work together in the Christian spirit of mutual self-sacrifice. Some of their ideas helped pave the way for later social reform in England.

A different form of protest arose from a group of people who, like the socialists, wanted to do away with capitalism. These were **anarchists,** individuals deeply opposed to any form of government. The anarchists were not willing to wait for the state to wither away, as Marx had predicted. Some even advocated terrorism and rebellion to overthrow it. They believed that society should be free of authority. Communities should exist in which people cooperated freely and willingly with one another.

SECTION REVIEW

1. In your own words, define or identify the following: laissez-faire, utilitarianism, socialism, Jeremy Bentham, Saint-Simon, Karl Marx, proletariat, Christian socialism, anarchist.
2. According to the classical economists, what is the law of supply and demand? The law of competition? The iron law of wages?
3. In the 1800's, what political changes did reformers think would benefit people of the middle class and working class?
■ The United States today has a mixed economy with elements of free enterprise and socialism. What examples can you give of each?

THE RISE OF DEMOCRACY IN ENGLAND

England in the 1830's

In the early nineteenth century, many Europeans who wanted political and social changes in their own countries looked to England as their model. It seemed to be rather free of the economic evils that plagued the rest of the Continent. England was a richer manufacturing and trading nation than all others. It had a representative government, the Parliament. The power of the monarch was limited, and there was considerable freedom of expression. Nevertheless, by the 1830's, a number of problems in Great Britain disrupted the apparent calm.

The population had increased greatly. With the development of urban life, tremendous growth had occurred in the industrial centers such as Manchester and Birmingham. The new cities were not equipped to handle their swelling populations. Safety and sanitary systems were lacking. Working and living conditions were poor: men, women, and children toiled long hours for low wages in the new factories.

Political rights were not evenly distributed. Common laborers and the growing middle class were closed out of the political system. Only wealthy property owners could elect members to the House of Commons in Parliament. In fact, 96 percent of the men in England and Ireland could not vote and women had no vote at all. Catholics and other non-Anglican Protestants were denied the right to hold office. Furthermore, elections were expensive and often corrupt. Candidates used bribes freely in a system that lacked the secret ballot, and rotten boroughs were widespread. A rotten borough was a district that continued to send a representative to Parliament long after its population had shrunk or disappeared entirely. One member of the House of Commons represented a district that was under the North Sea. Another device for controlling representation was the pocket borough. In these districts landlords virtually told the voters who would be the parliamentary member.

Liberals, including the new industrialists, felt the time was ripe for reform. The way their demands were handled in the next decades would strengthen British democracy and expand its power abroad.

Gradual Political Reform

Influenced by the writings of the political economists, such as Jeremy Bentham, British liberals were alert to the need for change. These reformers became convinced that the best way to end the inequalities caused by industrialization was to redistribute political power. However, their efforts were hindered by the Tory, or Conservative, party that had long controlled Parliament. The Tories had consistently blocked political or economic change. In 1830 events on the Continent shook the Tory regime as renewed revolution toppled the French government in three days. The Whigs assumed more power in Parliament and immediately presented a major bill aimed at reforming the political system and preventing violent revolution in Britain. Despite its initial failure in the House of Lords, pressure from riots and demonstrations around the country eventually brought about its passage as the Reform Bill of 1832.

There were several important provisions in this progressive legislation. It extended the vote to a portion of the merchants, businessmen, industrialists, and other members of the middle class. It eliminated many rotten boroughs and pocket boroughs and redistributed seats in Parliament. The number of seats allotted to Scotland and Ireland was increased. Provision was also made for more careful voter registration.

The Reform Bill of 1832 represented a change in that Parliament was no longer controlled only by the major landowners. It set in motion once more the liberal changes that the Congress of Vienna had tried to stop. Though factory workers, small farmers, and women still could not vote, the reform bill had lessened the chances of violence. It raised hope for a peaceful extension of suffrage in the future.

The Chartist Movement

Even with the reforms of 1832, only one out of eight adult males had the right to vote. In protest, a group of skilled workers in London drew up a

This cartoon shows Charles Grey, a strong supporter of the Reform Bill of 1832, sweeping out the rotten boroughs. How do the elements of the cartoon reflect the issue of election reform?

program in 1838 called the People's Charter. The Chartists, as they became known, demanded a number of major changes in the political system. These included voting by all adult males, a secret ballot, and annual elections. They also wanted to eliminate property requirements for Parliament, provide salaries for its members, and have districts with equal population.

The charter attracted support from a broad section of the population. There were public meetings and demonstrations. The Chartists collected more than a million signatures on a petition, which they presented to Parliament in 1839. This petition was rejected, as was another with over three million signatures that the Chartists presented in 1842. Following the rejection of yet another petition in 1848, the movement finally collapsed, defeated, in part, by lack of unity among its members.

Later British Election Reforms

In 1867 a new reform act extended voting rights to men who lived in towns and paid taxes or rent equal to at least $50. It also lowered the property requirements for voting in rural areas and provided additional representation for such industrial centers as Manchester, Birmingham, and Liverpool. By giving the vote to urban workers, the Reform Act of 1867 nearly doubled the electorate.

In the ensuing years, additional legislation extended the rights of Jews, atheists, and others to hold political office. The secret ballot was adopted in 1872, and in 1884, the vote was finally given to agricultural workers and others in the rural parts of England. This measure added another two million voters to the electorate.

Women, however, were still kept from voting, as they were elsewhere in Europe and the United States. In England, from the 1880's on, women's groups led by Emmeline Pankhurst and her daughters Christabel and Sylvia petitioned Parliament for the vote. They staged parades and took bold and sometimes violent action. But it was not until the next century, around the time the Nineteenth Amendment was passed in the United States, that women could vote in England.

The Victorian Age

In 1837 an eighteen-year-old princess, Victoria, succeeded to the throne upon the death of her uncle King William IV. Victoria would reign until 1901, in a remarkable period known as the Victorian era. Among the many great statesmen who dominated English politics during her reign two stand out—Benjamin Disraeli and William Gladstone.

Disraeli was the leader of the Conservative party from the late 1860's until his death in 1881. Queen Victoria considered him a friend, relied on his advice, and supported his decisions. A realist, Disraeli knew that having the support of Parliament was even more important to the success of his plans. In two terms as prime minister, he culti-

What methods used by suffragists to gain support for women's suffrage are revealed in this picture?

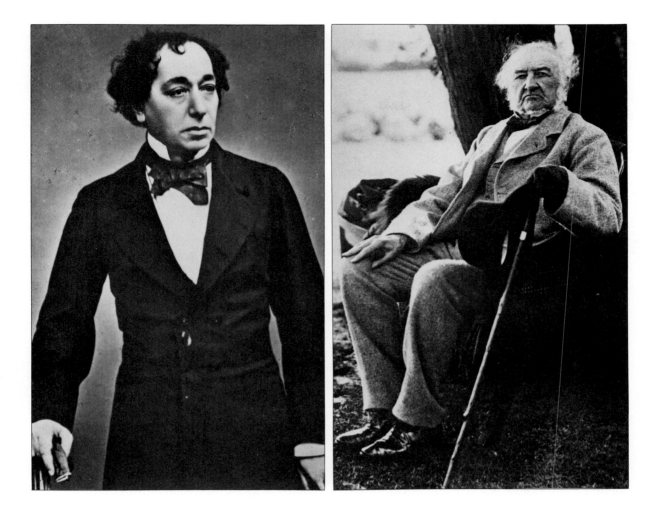

Benjamin Disraeli (left), a Conservative, devoted much of his early career to obtaining social legislation. William Gladstone (right), a Liberal, sought expansion of the vote. He did not make major gains in factory or labor reform because he opposed government intervention. What are the advantages and disadvantages of political figures having opposing views?

vated its members with wit and charm. Although Disraeli's name is associated closely with the expansion of the British Empire, he was also responsible for the passage of the Reform Bill of 1867.

William Gladstone served as prime minister four times, beginning in 1868. He was a powerful member of the Liberal party, which had succeeded the old Whig party. A man of great physical energy, Gladstone was famous for his ability to work long and hard. A contemporary said of him, "Gladstone could do in four hours what it took any other man sixteen to do, and he worked sixteen hours a day."

Gladstone was primarily interested in domestic matters, and during his years in office worked to bring about reforms. He promoted competitive exams for civil service appointments, public support for education, and reorganization of the army.

The Question of Ireland

Besides bringing about domestic reforms, Gladstone made a great effort to resolve the question of Ireland. Throughout their history, the Irish had tried to win their freedom from English rule. By the Act of Union of 1801, Ireland had been united with England into a single state known as the United Kingdom of Great Britain and Ireland. Both the English and the Irish were now to be governed by the British Parliament. The Irish bitterly resented their under-representation in Parliament, and the fact that, though Roman Catholics, they had to pay taxes to support the Anglican church. Moreover, since most Irish did not own the land they worked, they paid rent to absentee English landlords. Their rents and taxes were heavy burdens.

A number of Irish leaders, angry at their lack of political power and stirred by feelings of nationalism, wanted to free Ireland from British rule. Their protests grew stronger in the late 1840's. After a disastrous potato-crop failure, Ireland suffered from a great famine. Thousands left to start life over in the United States and elsewhere. Those who remained in Ireland supported the drive for land reform and self-government.

Gladstone, as prime minister, made numerous efforts to improve conditions in Ireland. He helped to bring about a separation of Church and State, so that the Irish no longer had to support the Anglican church. He also made several attempts at land-reform legislation, and proposed a home-rule bill. Home rule proved to be a major issue in Britain. It split the Liberal party in half in 1886 and brought about a Conservative era that was to last for sixteen years. Despite Gladstone's efforts, the problems between England and Ireland continued unresolved into the 1900's.

SECTION REVIEW

1. In your own words, define or identify: rotten boroughs, pocket boroughs, Tory, Chartists, Emmeline Pankhurst, Benjamin Disraeli, William Gladstone.
2. List the demands of the Chartists and describe the results of their movement.
3. What were the protests of the Irish and how did William Gladstone try to settle the Irish question?
- Describe the privileges and the responsibilities of universal suffrage in today's world.

CONFLICTS IN FRANCE

In France during the nineteenth century, change in the political system was accompanied by periods of rebellion. Following the policy of legitimacy adopted by the Congress of Vienna, the Bourbon dynasty was restored to the throne in the person of Louis XVIII, the brother of Louis XVI.

The Reign of Louis XVIII

Although in theory an absolute monarch, in practice Louis XVIII's power was limited. In his ten-year reign, he let the people keep many of the reforms gained between 1789 and 1815. In 1814 he had accepted a constitution. He agreed to share authority with a chamber of deputies, elected from among the wealthier citizens, and a chamber of peers, made up of nobles. Louis XVIII also retained the Bank of France, the system of laws known as the Napoleonic Code, and state-supported schools.

The king sincerely tried to unite the conflicting groups, but he met with opposition. On one side were the liberals, who urged the king to even more reform. On the other side were the royalists, who wanted to restore absolute power to the monarchy. The royalists were led by the king's reactionary brother, Charles, the count of Artois (ahr-TWAH).

Charles X

Charles succeeded Louis XVIII in 1824. Unlike his more liberal brother, Charles X wanted to turn the clock back to the time of the Old Regime. He openly announced his intention to restore the privileges of the nobles and clergy. He planned to use tax money to repay them for the land that they had lost during the revolution.

As Charles's policies became more repressive, the liberals who opposed his rule became more outspoken. When, in the spring of 1830, the Chamber of Deputies denounced his new ministry, Charles simply dismissed the Chamber and sent the deputies home. The following July, the king abolished freedom of the press, stripped the middle class of the right to vote, and reduced the power of the legislature. The people of Paris reacted to these violations of the constitution by taking to the streets in revolt. Royal troops could not, and some even would not, control the riots. Within three days Charles X was overthrown in the Revolution of 1830, or July Revolution.

During the rebellion Paris became a battleground. People overturned carts, boxes, tables, and whatever else they could find to barricade the streets. Revolutionaries, crouched behind barricades, defied the army and the police. Meanwhile from the roofs of the houses, families showered bricks, tiles, and even furniture on the troops.

Louis Philippe Becomes King

During the July Revolution, workers fought side by side with soldiers, students, and lawyers. Many of them hoped the outcome of the uprising would be a republican government for France. However, by the time the fighting was over, the leaders of the new revolution were the more moderate liberals, members of the middle class. This group favored a limited monarchy over a republic.

The aging Marquis de Lafayette, hero of both the American and French revolutions, recommended Louis Philippe, duke of Orléans, as the new king. Liberals hoped that the royalists would accept Louis Philippe because he was related to the Bourbon rulers. They hoped he would be supported by the republicans, because, as a young man, Louis Philippe had volunteered to fight with the revolutionaries in 1792.

Louis Philippe ruled from 1830 to 1848. He became known as the "citizen king," partly because of his manner and dress and partly to distinguish him from Charles X, who had claimed to rule by divine right. Under Louis Philippe, France had a liberal constitution and a free press. The right to vote was extended to the moderately wealthy class.

As time went by, the government under Louis Philippe proved to be only a little more democratic than the previous regime. High tariffs benefited manufacturers by limiting foreign goods coming into the country. But the same trade restrictions forced prices up, causing hardship for the lower classes. In addition, workers were forbidden to organize for better wages or working conditions. The common people lacked the vote and were still unable to take part in the government.

Members of the working class resented being shut out of power and disliked the favor being shown their rich employers. The Chamber of Deputies represented only a few special interests, and issues of broad public concern were rarely debated. In reaction, a strong movement developed to give the vote to a much larger part of the population.

The Revolution of 1848

By 1848 Louis Philippe faced growing opposition. Liberals wanted to maintain the constitutional monarchy but increase voting rights, and workers wanted the vote for every adult male. In February, when the king banned a protest meeting, the people of Paris once again rose against the government. As mobs seized control and proclaimed a republic, the king fled to England.

Joining forces, middle-class moderates and working-class radicals set up a temporary government. They arranged for the election of a national assembly to draw up a new constitution. One of the provisional government's first moves was to try to rebuild the economy. The year 1846 had seen economic depression throughout Europe. As a number of key industries collapsed in France, many laborers were thrown out of work. Now the republicans and socialists who dominated the new government promised that they would provide jobs. The national workshops that were set up were a watered-down version of a socialist plan for units owned and run by workers. The government never wanted them to succeed for fear they would compete with private industry.

The possibility of jobs, however, lured some 100,000 workers to Paris. Waiting for the government to fulfill its promises, the workers remained idle; the jobs that finally came amounted to almost nothing. As desperation spread among the workers, the government tried to abandon the workshops and force the workers out of Paris. Once again the distressed laborers took to the streets in bloody protest, in a new uprising called the June Days.

The Second Republic

This new wave of violence confirmed the growing conflict between the working class and the middle class. Fear of widespread revolution spread throughout France and the rest of Europe. When

Napoleon III seized power on December 2, 1851, the anniversary of one of Napoleon I's greatest victories. He tried to emulate his famous uncle by winning territory and honor for France.

order was restored, the National Assembly drew up a plan for a democratic government and wrote a new constitution. This latest constitution restored to the people many of the rights they held when Napoleon I was in power. Citizens were to elect their own president to head the Second Republic. In the 1848 election held in December, Louis Napoleon Bonaparte, a nephew of the former emperor, won a large majority and became the new president of France. He had risen to power on the fears of the people in a country nearly divided once more by revolution.

Because of his overwhelming victory, Louis Napoleon considered that he, rather than the new legislature, represented the will of the people. To that end, he encouraged the support of groups from all parts of French society. Laborers and farmers, as well as members of the middle class, viewed him as their champion. In addition, Louis Napoleon worked to gain the backing of the army and pleased French Catholics by putting down a republican rebellion in Rome. At home he strengthened the influence of the Catholic Church over French education.

His efforts at reform were mixed. He returned the vote to all adult males in 1851, but at the same time, he imposed strict censorship on public comment, and drove his critics out of the country.

Basking in public support, which he deliberately sought, Louis Napoleon next asked the people for permission to draft a new constitution for the republic. This was the opportunity he had been waiting for. The reign of Napoleon I in France was remembered by the French people as the age of glory, when an undefeated France had ruled most of Europe. Louis Napoleon, wishing to follow in his uncle's footsteps, dissolved the government on December 2, 1851, and declared himself emperor exactly one year later. Thus the Second Republic gave way to the Second Empire. In less than fifty years, the French people had lived under three different forms of government.

The Second French Empire

As emperor, Louis Napoleon worked hard to restore the glory France had known before. France was once again considered the strongest nation of the European continent.

Although the empire had the formal institutions of a republic—a constitution, an elected legislature, and universal male suffrage—it had in fact returned to absolutism. Napoleon III, as he wished to be called, ruled through his ministers, ignored the legislature, censored the press, and imposed strict limits on free speech at the universities.

To distract the French people from his dictatorial rule at home and to remind them of France's former glory, Napoleon III embarked on a series of foreign adventures. He hoped to unite the people behind him with a series of new conquests that would appeal to French nationalism.

In the early 1850's Napoleon III encouraged the Ottoman Empire to resist Russian claims in a dispute over who had the right to protect Christians in Turkey. War broke out between Russia and Turkey in 1853. By late 1854 France, Britain, and Sardinia were allied with Turkey against Russia. Most of the costly war was fought in the Crimea, a peninsula in southern Russia. Russia was defeated, and France gained little for its effort in the Crimean War except some military glory and a major role in the peace conference. But Napoleon did not give up dreams of empire.

In 1861, while the United States was involved in the Civil War, Napoleon sent troops to Mexico to seize the government and set up a new one under his control. He made Archduke Maximilian, a member of the Austrian royal family, emperor of Mexico. Almost immediately Mexican nationalists, led by their president, Benito Juárez, struggled to drive the French out of Mexico. But they were not powerful enough to retake control.

When the Civil War ended in 1865, the United States, unwilling to accept European influence in the Western Hemisphere, threatened to drive the French from Mexico. Napoleon III withdrew his troops rather than risk war with the United States. In 1867 the unfortunate Maximilian was executed by Mexican forces.

The Fall of the Second Empire

Only a few years later, Napoleon III challenged Prussia by opposing its efforts to unite the German states. But Otto von Bismarck, the Prussian prime minister, viewed war with France as an opportunity to achieve unification. By July 1870 the two powers were at war. France suffered disastrous losses in the Franco-Prussian War. Napoleon III was taken prisoner, and Paris fell to the Germans. The Second Empire had been destroyed, like the first, by a Bonaparte's ambition.

The Germans imposed harsh peace terms on France. After the fall of the empire, the type of government France would have was uncertain. Bismarck permitted the election of a national assembly by universal manhood suffrage. He wanted the peace made by a proper French government. Meanwhile, radical republicans in Paris refused the peace terms accepted by the National Assembly. The radicals established a revolutionary council or "commune." Civil war broke out and in the violent overthrow of the Paris Commune, thousands died. At this point, France probably would have remained a monarchy had it not been for disagreements over who should be the ruler. Some members of the assembly wanted to place a member of the Bourbon royal family on the throne once again. Some supported the son of Louis Philippe. Others wanted the son of Napoleon III. Partly because the three groups could not agree on who should be king, the Third Republic was proclaimed.

The Third Republic

Because of disputes among the various groups in the National Assembly, the Third Republic functioned without a constitution until 1875. The president, elected by the people, was to serve for seven years. His actions were subject to approval by a cabinet, which also set policy. There would be a senate, elected indirectly, and a chamber of deputies, to be elected by a general vote.

During the next years the new republican government struggled with a number of problems. One of the most serious began in 1894. A Jewish army officer, Alfred Dreyfus, was accused and convicted of betraying military secrets to Germany. After Dreyfus was sentenced to life imprisonment

The Dreyfus Affair revealed a sharp division in political attitudes in France. How would propaganda such as this cartoon worsen relations between opposing groups?

at Devil's Island in French Guinea, his innocence was revealed. But the army, supported by monarchists and anti-Semites, refused to reopen the case. Despite the publication of *J'Accuse,* a powerful and widely read criticism of the army written by the French novelist Émile Zola, Dreyfus was not cleared until 1906.

The Dreyfus scandal revealed the stresses among the various political groups in France. On one side were the socialists, republicans, and intellectuals. Opposing them were the army, monarchists, and conservatives. These divisions would lead to a number of **coalitions,** or temporary alliances of various groups to gain a majority in the legislature. Only in this way was the Third Republic able to survive.

SECTION REVIEW

1. Mapping: Use the map on page 436 and the information in your text to locate the states that were allied with France against Russia in the Crimean War.
2. In your own words, define or identify: Louis XVIII, Charles X, July Revolution, citizen king, national workshops, Louis Napoleon, Maximilian, Alfred Dreyfus.
3. Describe the reasons for the Revolution of 1830. Who benefited most from the reign of Louis Philippe?
4. Why did the promise of the Revolution of 1848 fail to come about for the workers and common people?
■ Louis Napoleon thought the destiny of France lay in his hands. Do you think the leader of a country is the most important factor in developing a country's destiny? Explain.

THE REVOLUTIONS OF 1830 and 1848

As you have read, the brief uprisings that followed the peace settlements of 1815 were soon put down by the great powers. But, in the decades that followed, a series of revolutionary movements brought important political changes to a number of European countries.

The Revolutions of 1830

When the people overturned the government of Charles X in 1830, the shock wave set off a series of revolutions elsewhere in Europe. The delicate balance established in Vienna in 1815 was in danger of collapse. In Belgium rioting broke out in Brussels as a wave of nationalist feeling erupted against Dutch rule. Troops sent by the Dutch king to stop the Belgians were quickly defeated. After negotiations the great powers agreed upon the terms of a treaty. Belgium was to be a permanently neutral state that could not make alliances. The five major powers would be responsible for protecting it from invasion.

In Germany and Italy, people were stirred by the example of the French, and struggled to gain reforms. The Italians hoped for support from Louis Philippe, but he feared the anger of the Austrian ruler. Therefore, Metternich was able to put down rebellion in the northern Italian states.

In Poland nationalists engaged in a struggle against the forces of Nicholas I, the Russian czar. Poles were enraged when they heard rumors that they would be sent to put down the uprisings in France and Belgium. But the Polish revolutionaries were divided into quarreling factions, and Russia was able to defeat them. As a result, Russia gained access to central Europe by absorbing Poland. In most cases throughout Europe, the wave of revolutionary change was held in check in 1830. It would not be long before other attempts would be made.

The Austrian Empire in 1848

In 1848 Europe was once more in turmoil. The fall of Louis Philippe in France touched off reactions throughout the Continent. Constitutional government and national independence were goals that had been long sought and long denied. Revolutionaries in Austria, Italy, and Germany hoped that their time had come.

It was no coincidence that Metternich had tried for thirty years to suppress liberal and national movements. There were at least twelve different

Why did the moderates become alarmed by the revolutionaries in 1848?

nationalities living within the borders of the Austrian Empire. These included Hungarians, or Magyars, Germans, Italians, and Slavs. The whole issue of the relationship of these people with their government had been avoided or ignored. Metternich envisioned the role of government as it had existed in the largely agricultural society of the eighteenth century. He did not recognize a need for a give-and-take between the governing and the governed.

When news of the events in Paris in 1848 became known, Austria tottered on the verge of collapse. Louis Kossuth, a Hungarian radical, seized the opportunity to demand independence in a speech before the Hungarian diet. Revolution spread to Vienna, and Metternich fled to England. Taken by surprise at the degree of public support for the rebels, the Austrian emperor Ferdinand promised a constitution and the abolition of censorship. Revolution then spread to non-German areas of the Austrian Empire. The Slavic people of Bohemia demanded the right to govern their own affairs, and Emperor Ferdinand granted it. In northern Italy, as you will see, Austrian troops were also under attack.

Before the end of 1848, the counterrevolutionaries were gaining strength. The leaders of the revolution were more scholars than soldiers. Emperor Ferdinand abdicated and his nephew Francis Joseph replaced him. Francis Joseph took the offensive and suppressed the rebels. The Russian czar, fearing the revolt would spread to Russian Poland, helped Austria. Nicholas I also sent his troops to put down the revolution in Hungary. Many Hungarians who surrendered were executed by the Russians. Austrian troops then restored order in other parts of the empire.

Rebellion in Italy

At the same time, in northern Italy, rebels tried to drive out Austrian forces. Under the leadership of Giuseppe Mazzini, Italians sought to unite the peninsula as a republic. Violence broke out in many parts of Italy, and republics were established in Rome and Florence.

When the rebels took over Rome they seized the pope, an act which angered Catholics throughout Europe. The French ruler, Louis Napoleon, sent troops to rescue Rome from the rebels. His forces found that many Italians had already turned against the revolution and were ready to side with the invaders. As in Austria, revolution in Italy failed partly because of foreign intervention and lack of widespread support for the revolutionaries.

Revolution in Germany

Less than two weeks after revolution broke out in Hungary, rioting began in Berlin. Stunned by the turn of events, the Prussian king Frederick William IV pledged to make government reforms. Among the reforms he promised were a parliament, a constitution, and support for a united Germany. Liberals began to plan for a national assembly to draft a constitution. Representatives from all over Germany met in the city of Frankfurt to plan a government that would unite all the German-speaking kingdoms.

Despite the revolutionary talk at the Frankfurt Assembly, very few real gains resulted. The assembly offered the Prussian king the crown of a federal union of German states, excluding Austria. He chose not to accept the role of a constitutional monarch. This weakened the assembly, and supporters of King Frederick William IV had a chance to rally their forces and undo the reformers' work. The army, which remained loyal to the king, was soon in control of Berlin. The Frankfurt Assembly was disbanded in June 1849. At that time, the king issued his own constitution, which kept nearly all of the power in the hands of the monarch and the ruling classes. By 1849 nothing but embers remained of the brief blaze of revolutionary glory in eastern Europe.

The Failure of the 1848 Rebellions

There were several reasons for the failure of the revolutions of 1848. The rebels in each country were divided over their goals, the forces of reaction were still strong, and the economic conditions that had beset Europe in the mid-1840's were lifting. But one of the strongest reasons the revolutionaries did not succeed was that they had little support outside the cities. The members of the lower classes distrusted the leadership of the well-to-do. On the other hand, the middle class, in most countries, feared the influence of the new socialist economic and political theories.

Nevertheless, there were a number of gains from the revolutions of 1848. In France, more people gained the vote. In Italy and Germany, there were some first steps toward unification. And in the Austrian Empire, the Age of Metternich came to an end. The forces for change, brought about by feelings of nationalism and liberalism, had made their mark in Europe.

SECTION REVIEW

1. Mapping: Use the map on page 436 and the information in the text to locate those countries in which rebellions occurred in 1848.
2. In your own words, define or identify: Louis Kossuth, Bohemia, Francis Joseph, Giuseppe Mazzini, Frankfurt Assembly.
3. Describe the results of the uprisings in Belgium and Poland in 1830.
4. What efforts toward unification were taken in Italy and in Germany in the mid-1800's?
■ Although there were some gains, most of the revolutions of 1848 failed. What are the techniques for bringing about change in a constitutional government?

People in History

Karl Marx

Karl Marx, the founder of modern communism, was born in Trier, Prussia, in 1818. Raised in a middle-class family, he went to universities in Bonn and in Berlin. In Berlin Marx became intensely interested in the new theories, particularly socialism. He was made editor of a newspaper in 1842, but because of its radical demands the paper was soon suppressed. The next summer Marx married, and his wife Jennie was to be his lifelong companion.

After the wedding Marx and his wife moved to Paris. There he met Friedrich Engels, a German revolutionary, with whom he would collaborate.

Forced by Prussian pressure to leave France, Marx went next to Brussels. There he came into close contact with the socialist working-class movement. With Engels he joined a secret society of German workers, the "League of the Just," which had branches in the major capitals of Europe. In early 1848 Marx and Engels issued their famous *Communist Manifesto* for the society that was then called the Communist League. In the *Manifesto* they surveyed existing socialist thought and analyzed the role of the workers in society.

Immediately after the publication of the *Communist Manifesto*, revolution erupted in France. Marx, long involved with the movement for German independence, rushed to Cologne to participate. There he attacked the middle-class democratic parties whose indecision enabled the Prussian king to stop the attempted rebellion. Marx was tried for treason; despite his acquittal he was expelled from Prussia.

With his family, Marx settled in London. He was desperately poor, and three of his young children died. In London he spent years doing research in the British Museum. He tried unsuccessfully to start a publication to express his views. Finally, he was hired as a correspondent by the *New York Tribune* and filed articles covering the Crimean War.

In 1864 the International Working Men's Association was founded, and to this organization, later known as the First International, Marx devoted his efforts over the next few years. As its leader, he lectured and wrote on education, unions, working conditions, and economic cooperation. In 1867 he published the first volume of *Das Kapital.* In it he brilliantly described his theory of the class struggle He held that forces in history would inevitably put power in the hands of the workers.

Events of the 1870's and pressure from members led to the collapse of the International, although it survived elsewhere in altered forms. Marx, now old and ill, returned to research and writing. In 1881 his wife Jennie died; he survived her by only fifteen months, dying in March 1883. His influence, however, was immense. Today Marx is considered by historians to occupy a major place in the development of economic thought.

1. What was Karl Marx's background?
2. How do you think the era in which Marx lived affected his beliefs?
3. How do workers in the United States today exercise power within a democratic and capitalistic system?

Reviewing the Chapter

Chapter Summary

After 1815, feelings of nationalism and liberalism made it difficult for European leaders to maintain peace under conditions that had existed before the French wars. At the Congress of Vienna, diplomats had restored legitimate rulers to power, traded territory, and formed the Quadruple Alliance to prevent future aggression. Led by Metternich, they were able to put down a number of small rebellions.

At the same time, life in western Europe was being greatly altered by the Industrial Revolution. Cities and populations expanded rapidly, and there was a new and prosperous middle class. However, workers lived and toiled under harsh conditions. Reformers urged changes in the political and economic systems. Some suggested that governments in which the people had the vote would be the best. More extreme reformers suggested socialism or communism, systems that would abolish capitalism, free enterprise, and private ownership and put the power in the hands of the working class.

Liberals looked to England as a model of constitutional government. There, beginning in 1832, a series of reform bills gave all adult males the vote, eliminated corrupt election practices, and established the secret ballot.

In France, uprisings in 1830, 1848, and 1871 reflected the desire for a more representative government. France endured a number of rulers and different types of government until 1873, when the Third French Republic was created. Sparked by the French Revolution of 1848, rebellions occurred elsewhere in Europe. In Austria, Slavic peoples in Bohemia sought independence, while in Italy and Germany there were early, unsuccessful attempts at unification.

1. How did the French wars and the Industrial Revolution change Europe?
2. How did the struggle for democratic reform differ in Britain and France?
3. How did the revolution in 1848 in France affect other parts of Europe?

Using Your Vocabulary

1. What is nationalism? How did the French wars contribute to the development of nationalism?
2. What was the principle of legitimacy?
3. Compare and contrast liberals, conservatives, and reactionaries. Which of them would not favor the principle of legitimacy?
4. What was the Holy Alliance? Was it effective? Explain.
5. What was the Quadruple Alliance? How did it differ from the Holy Alliance?
6. Why was the thirty-year span after the Congress of Vienna called the Age of Metternich?
7. What does laissez-faire mean in French? How was this expression applied to economic theory? With which economists is this theory associated?
8. What is meant by the law of supply and demand?
9. What is utilitarianism? How was this philosophy applied to government?
10. According to theory, what is a Utopian society? Why do you think Utopianism was generally unsuccessful when put into practice?
11. How are socialism and communism similar? How do they differ?
12. Who were the proletariat? How were they different from capitalists?
13. What is a pocket borough? A rotten borough?

Developing Your Geography Skills

1. Use the map on page 436 to locate by means of longitude and latitude coordinates: Vienna, Athens, Paris, Berlin, London, Carlsbad, and Rome.

2. In what countries or empires were these places located?

3. Use the map on page 436 to describe the extent of the German Confederation in 1815. Use the Atlas map on page 756 to identify which countries, all or in part, now occupy the territory of the former German Confederation.

Recalling the Facts

1. In general, what were the basic causes for the political uprisings in Europe between 1815 and 1848?

2. What were the two major principles guiding the Congress of Vienna?

3. What was the purpose of the Concert of Europe? Why was it ineffective?

4. Who were the major figures associated with classical economics? How did John Stuart Mill's theory of government differ from that of the classical economists?

5. Name the major political parties in nineteenth-century England. How were they different?

6. What was the importance of the Reform Bill of 1832?

7. Who were the Chartists? Why did their movement collapse?

8. What is considered the Victorian era? Who were two famous statesmen of this period?

9. When was Ireland united with England? Why did the Irish oppose British rule? Why did many Irish immigrate to other countries in the late 1840's?

10. Compare and contrast the reigns of Louis XVIII and Charles X.

11. Who was called the "citizen king"? Why?

12. What was the immediate cause of the "June Days"? How did they lead to the establishment of the Second Republic?

13. Who was the leader of the Second French Empire? How did he obtain this position? How did the Second Empire end?

14. What was the Dreyfus affair? What did it reveal about conditions in the Third French Republic?

15. What were the results of the revolutions of 1830?

Essay Questions

1. How did the French wars and the Industrial Revolution upset political and social conditions in Europe?

2. How did democracy begin to develop in Great Britain? Why did it take so long for reforms to be made in the election process? Why do you think women failed to get the vote?

3. Name the authors and works that had an impact on political, economic, and social developments in nineteenth-century Europe. Briefly explain the theory each proposed. Which one(s) do you think had the greatest impact on history? Why?

4. How were some of the basic ideas of the economic reformers in the nineteenth century similar? In what ways did they differ?

5. Compare and contrast the ways in which democracy developed in Britain and France in the nineteenth century.

6. Describe the circumstances that led to the rise and fall of the Second French Empire under Napoleon III.

7. Why can 1848 be called a year of revolution? Explain. What were the causes? What were some of the circumstances that limited their success? What gains were made?

Critical Thinking

1. How might the value claims of a capitalist and a communist differ toward private property?

2. Something that is ambiguous is subject to different interpretations. How were Karl Marx's ideas on the rise of socialism ambiguous?

3. The French people struggled for democracy and in 1848 elected Louis Napoleon as the first president of France. How were Louis Napoleon's actions inconsistent with a movement toward democracy?

4. What circumstances indicate bias in the treatment of Alfred Dreyfus?

5. What factors do you think might interfere with the reliability of information about the revolutions of 1848? What factors might interfere with the reliability of news information today?

CHAPTER ·20·

The AGE of PROGRESS

1800–1914

Objectives

- To describe advances in science during the nineteenth and early twentieth centuries

- To describe major movements in literature, art, and music in the nineteenth century

- To explain how the rise of the urban middle class led to wider education and new forms of entertainment

*T*he booming factories, speedier transportation, and swelling cities of the Industrial Revolution made more goods available to more and more people and enriched the middle class, a group that expanded in size and influence. The Industrial Revolution also brought changes in areas that may have seemed unrelated to technology and commerce. Very few areas of life remained unaffected.

Science entered an age of rapid development. The scope of knowledge expanded and became specialized. As scientific research advanced, technology capitalized on the research, and industries found ways to make practical use of new information. The methods of investigation of the natural sciences also affected the social sciences as people began to study how and why individuals and groups acted as they did. Anthropology, history, sociology, and psychology benefited from the application of the scientific method of study.

In the early nineteenth century, the Romantics, with their love of nature and glorification of emotion over reason, had gained popularity. Toward the middle of the century, emphasis shifted to Realism. Artists, writers, and musicians boldly interpreted the new world they saw, but the public did not always understand or appreciate their work.

Educational institutions expanded to meet the demands of the middle class, and the rise in literacy increased the market for books, magazines, and newspapers. Almost as a defense against the speed of change, people began to admire the past and the history of their own nations.

THE ERA OF SCIENTIFIC DISCOVERY

Until the 1800's the physical sciences, including physics, chemistry, and astronomy, were not treated separately. This body of knowledge, called the Natural Philosophies, was so limited that a person could conceivably be an expert in every branch. But during the nineteenth century, so many developments took place that the physical sciences each developed its own specialization. The nineteenth century saw not only political and industrial change, but a revolution in the way in which people thought about and examined the world. By the end of the century, science assumed its modern form.

The use of reason and logical thought has a tradition going back to antiquity. However, scientists in the seventeenth and eighteenth centuries had broken with that tradition and no longer depended on Greek and Roman works. They set the stage for radical new discoveries. People such as Galileo and Kepler had observed the natural world, but analyses of their observations were not possible until enhanced with mathematics. As you recall, Newton was the first to apply mathematics to science, using it to formulate his laws of motion. During the Enlightenment, mathematics had become so popular that it was used in parlor games. It seemed to prove the value of logical reasoning. But scientific conclusions based purely on mathematical reason came to be recognized as invalid unless they were confirmed by experiments. This realization gave birth to the modern laboratory, where data could be gathered and theories could be tested. People began to realize that logic and experimentation could unravel nature's secrets.

The Development of Chemistry

In the late eighteenth century, the flight of a hot air balloon in the sky above France thrilled spectators and motivated scientists to think about heat and fire. They wondered about the nature of fire and what happens to things when they burn. Some scientists thought that a mysterious substance was released into the air by combustion.

Antoine Lavoisier proved otherwise. By comparing changes in the weight of heated metals and the surrounding air, he proved that burning substances took oxygen from the air. Lavoisier's experiments depended on careful measurements of changes in quantities. This emphasis on quantitative analysis made modern chemistry possible.

John Dalton, a Manchester schoolmaster, went further to explain that compounds were composed of atoms linked together. He thus revived the atomic theory first conceived by ancient Greeks and then discredited by Aristotle, who claimed that all things were made of four elements—air, water, fire, and earth. Scientists now realized that if they wanted to know how substances combined or separated to form new products, they had to classify those substances by weight. They also recognized that substances always combined in the same proportion. For example, water is always two parts hydrogen and one part oxygen (H_2O).

At the beginning of the nineteenth century the work of an Italian scientist, Alessandro Volta, expanded the body of knowledge about matter. Volta gave a demonstration in France, attended by Napoleon himself, of his voltaic pile. This was the predecessor of the electric battery. The ability to produce electricity gave scientists a new tool with which to explore matter. They discovered that by passing an electric current through substances, they could be made to separate into their elements. Sir Humphry Davy used this new procedure, called electrolysis, to discover elements such as sodium, potassium, and calcium.

Scientists soon discovered that if they could separate substances into their elements, they could also combine elements to create new things. Friedrich Wöhler astonished the world by creating in his laboratory a nitrogen compound that previously occurred only in living things. The age of organic chemistry had begun. (It is no coincidence that Mary Wollstonecraft Shelley wrote *Frankenstein* at this time.) The ability to combine elements into new products brought forth a whole array of useful creations. Among them were chloroform, medicine's first painkiller, and sodium salicylate, which we know today as aspirin.

If the combination of elements was determined by weight, scientists reasoned that elements must be made up of atoms that also had specific weights. They saw that the elements fell into a pattern ranging from lightest to heaviest. They soon realized that the elements could be laid out, very logically, on a chart and that similar elements would fall into columns. This chart, known as the periodic table, was perfected by the Russian chemist Dmitri Mendeleyev. Using the table, he was able to predict the existence of elements that had not yet been discovered.

The New Physics

Although the work of Dalton revived interest in atomic theory, it was not until the late nineteenth century that scientists were able to prove the existence of atoms. Dalton's atom, like that of the Greeks, was indivisible. But toward the end of the nineteenth century, a series of discoveries led to an entirely different view of the atom. These discoveries posed questions whose answers resulted in what is termed the new physics. It differed from the classical physics of Newton, which explained the mechanical motion of bodies but could not explain atomic structure.

In 1895 Wilhelm Roentgen, a German scientist, made an exciting discovery. While working in his laboratory he noticed that when he turned on the current in a vacuum tube, a nearby substance glowed in the dark. Obviously something from the tube was making the flourescent substance glow. Since Roentgen did not know what it was, he called it the X ray—X stands for the unknown in mathematics. He observed that the ray, whatever it was, passed through lighter substances more easily than denser substances. It could also affect a photographic plate. This discovery led to many practical applications of the X ray to medicine and industry.

The following year Henri Becquerel discovered radioactivity, a phenomenon in which atoms of some elements give off particles and change into other elements. Working for years in dreadful poverty, his student Marie Curie and her husband Pierre Curie investigated this phenomenon of emitting particles. They discovered two radioactive elements—radium and polonium.

Drawing on Madame Curie's work, the English physicist Ernest Rutherford determined the basic shape of the atom—a nucleus with electrons orbiting around it. Shortly thereafter, the Danish scientist Niels Bohr realized that the classic laws of

Considering the working conditions, why were Marie Curie's accomplishments all the more outstanding?

physics could not explain how atoms hold together. Drawing on the ideas of the German physicist Max Planck, Bohr showed in 1913 that the energy emitted by atoms does not emerge in a continuous flow, but in bursts called quanta. The quantum theory, as it came to be known, was immensely important. It was further evidence that Newton's laws of physics were inadequate and would have to be revised.

In 1905, while working in a Swiss patent office, Albert Einstein published a series of papers that changed physics forever. His theory of relativity upset Newton's laws of motion by showing that time and space were interrelated. Einstein proposed that nothing can exceed the speed of light. The consequence is that time goes slower the faster one travels. He further demonstrated that matter and energy were equivalent. This led to the realization that if an atom could be split—through a process called fission—tremendous energy would be released. Einstein's research led to ever more sophisticated knowledge of subatomic physics. It revolutionized people's thinking about the physical world and ultimately gave us nuclear power and the atom bomb. For better or worse, Einstein brought the dawn of the nuclear age.

Biology and Evolution

William Smith was an English drainage engineer. As he went about his excavations at the end of the eighteenth century, he saw that the earth was divided into strata, or layers, and that each layer contained its own form of fossils. Fossils had been studied before, but Smith's observations indicated that each form belonged to a specific period and that the forms followed a certain progression.

The existence of fossils seemed to make one thing indisputable: Certain creatures that once lived on earth were now gone and new forms of life had taken their places. In an effort to explain changes in species, Jean-Baptiste Lamarck in France and James Hutton in Scotland suggested that some animal forms evolved, that is, slowly changed into newer forms. The world's leading expert on fossils, Georges Cuvier, did not agree but thought that species disappeared because of natural catastrophes.

It was in England, where the middle class had a long tradition of nature study, that the theory about the origin of species was most comprehensively developed. Principally the work of Charles Darwin, the theory was also developed independently by Alfred Wallace. Darwin's theory maintained that over vast amounts of time species did change into new forms. This came about through a process later called natural selection. Darwin suggested that an individual animal or plant is more likely to survive when it has some advantage, such as greater intelligence or strength. Its offspring will inherit the advantageous trait. In the struggle for survival, the weaker will perish. This idea certainly did not seem strange in the competitive world of the Industrial Revolution.

Darwin spent at least twenty years working on his theory before he published it in 1859. He knew it would raise a storm of protest, and it did. Many scientists embraced it, but others found weak spots that troubled them. But the real outcry came from religious groups. Many people felt it conflicted with the account of God's Creation of the universe in the Scriptures. If Darwin's theory was correct, all creatures were not formed at one time and the earth had to be much older than anyone thought. Also, evolution reduced people to the status of animals. This raised problems about human nature and the soul.

Other thinkers distorted Darwin's theory to apply it to politics. This movement was known as Social Darwinism. It is associated with the British sociologist Herbert Spencer, who coined the phrase "survival of the fittest." The idea was that if species evolved, so could human beings. On the one hand, this gave rise to a belief in progress—that science would lead us into ever higher stages. On the other hand, Social Darwinism implied that those too weak to survive the struggle for existence were best left to perish. This was a potentially dangerous political belief, because it could be extended to mean that certain groups of people were less fit to live than others. It also provided an underlying justification for imperialism, one nation subjugating another.

The Discovery of Genetics

Though scientists were impressed by Darwin's theory, they were bothered by Darwin's inability to explain how inheritance worked. Darwin had said that a certain valuable trait, like strength, would be passed on to an animal's offspring. How and why this occurred were problems for which his theory offered no solutions.

It was an obscure Austrian monk named Gregor Mendel who, working in his monastery garden raising peas, found the answer. From this ordinary task came the modern science of genetics. Observing succeeding generations of plants, Mendel realized that there had to be some unit that carried a physical trait from a parent to its offspring. This turned out to be the gene. Its discovery solved the puzzle of inheritance and opened up great new doors for science and medicine in the twentieth century. Mendel's revolutionary paper describing the outcome of his experiments with plants was published in 1869, only ten years after Darwin's book *The Origin of Species*. The theory was so far ahead of its time that its importance was not recognized until 1900, sixteen years after Mendel's death. The rediscovery of that paper gave birth to the scientific discovery of heredity. In 1903 it was shown that genes were located on parts of living cells called chromosomes.

Progress in Medicine

In the early nineteenth century only the poor went to hospitals, which were so unsanitary that a person had a much better chance of surviving illness at home. Surgery was performed only as a last resort. Not only did the patient have to endure terrible pain, but wounds became infected so quickly that only half of all people who underwent surgery recovered from it.

Several medical breakthroughs improved this situation. Chloroform was first used as an anesthetic by the Englishman James Simpson. Also, two Americans, William Morton and Horace Wells, demonstrated that ether was an effective painkiller.

Surgery without pain was now possible, but the problem of infection remained. That was solved by the great French scientist Louis Pasteur. Pasteur began his research by investigating the fermentation of alcohol, a subject of great interest to the winemakers of France. He was able to show that fermentation was caused by a tiny microorganism called a germ. He also showed that there were substances, called antiseptics, that could kill germs. This was immensely important for the treatment of disease. Pasteur also concluded that humans could be protected against germs through the process of immunization, and he used the word vaccine to describe the substance that made people immune. Finally, in his research on rabies, Pasteur demonstrated the existence of organisms too small to be seen under a microscope and opened the door to the hidden world of viruses.

Joseph Lister combined Pasteur's research with advances in chemistry to make infection-free surgery possible. His experiments convinced him that carbolic acid would destroy the organisms that caused infection. It was in Glasgow in 1865 that he carried out his first trial. He exposed himself to great ridicule when he washed everything in carbolic acid—the surgical instruments, the surgeon's hands, the bandages, the patient. He even sprayed carbolic acid into the air. But the laughter did not last. Lister's patients lived. The discoveries of Pasteur and Lister brought the laboratory methods of science to medicine. No longer were doctors limited to tradition or common sense in the treatment of disease.

How do modern hospital techniques differ from those pictured here in the 1870's?

Anthropology and History

Just as science was being applied to the natural world, it was also being used in the so-called social sciences to study people. The Industrial Revolution drew the entire globe into the net of European commerce as distant regions were reached by colonizers, merchants, and missionaries. This activity spurred greater interest in the peoples and cultures of the world. Because the scientific method was proving so fruitful, thinkers applied it to a study of the world's cultures, past and present. This gave birth to modern anthropology.

One of the first great anthropologists was an American, Lewis Henry Morgan. He methodically studied the Iroquois Indians. Morgan was influenced by the theory of evolution and believed that cultures progress, or evolve, in a series of stages that takes people from savagery to civilization.

The German-born anthropologist Franz Boas further extended his scientific study to the analysis of other human cultures. A careful and rigorous student of native peoples, he did his main work among the Kwakiutl Indians of the Pacific Northwest. Boas was the leading figure responsible for making anthropology an academic discipline.

History, too, was becoming more scientific. This movement was led by the great German historian Leopold von Ranke. He insisted that history had to explain "how it actually happened" by basing the story of the past on documentary evidence. His example inspired many countries to publish collections of historical documents; this made research much easier.

It was during the nineteenth century that understanding of prehistory developed. By chance, an amateur coin collector was given the job of organizing the overflowing collection of ancient artifacts in a Danish museum. He began to arrange the items on the basis of what they were made of and what they were used for. The resulting assortment of stone, bronze, and iron items spurred him to offer a three-age theory of prehistory. Later findings by archaeologists supported the division of ancient times into the Stone Age, the Bronze Age, and the Iron Age.

Karl Marx also claimed to have unlocked history's secrets in a scientific way. The new interest in history also drew upon the new nationalism, as people found history a source of national pride.

Another innovation was the idea of social history, the history of people, society, and economics. The idea that history should be not only about politics and great men, but also about ordinary people and about ideas as well was probably first promoted by the French philosopher Auguste Comte. Comte also promoted the objective study of social relationships. He encouraged early sociologists to apply the methods of science to their study of human society.

Psychology

The field of psychology grew out of the application of the scientific method to the study of the mind. But science demands measurement and experiment, and it was difficult to determine how these could be applied to that mysterious thing called the mind.

One of the first to try was the German scientist Wilhelm Wundt. He established the world's first psychology laboratory. Alfred Binet then developed the idea that intelligence could be measured. It was Binet who invented the IQ test. The first application of statistics to psychology was made by the Englishman Francis Galton, who was Charles Darwin's cousin.

Meanwhile, in Russia Ivan Pavlov discovered something very interesting, while doing an experiment with dogs. Whenever he fed them, he rang a bell. In time they associated the sound of the bell with the food. Then he rang the bell without feeding the dogs; they salivated, even though no food was present. The dogs had been "conditioned" to salivate when the bell rang. Psychology had discovered that through training, the body can be made by the mind to behave in a certain way. This discovery of the conditioned reflex opened up a new area of research on how the mind can affect body functions.

The most influential psychologist of all time was Sigmund Freud of Vienna, the founder of psychoanalysis. Freud was largely responsible for the theory of the unconscious mind. His studies led him to believe that long forgotten childhood experiences could cause mental illness in adulthood and that sexual feelings began in infancy. He studied the frustrations, drives, and repressions that colored a person's behavior. Freud maintained that the unconscious does not reveal its contents directly, but through the use of symbols, most significantly in dreams, which he moved from the realm of the fortune teller to that of the scientist. His idea influenced writers and artists, who began to use symbols as a way of expressing the mind's most secret feelings. Freud's theories are still controversial and have been challenged often. But dozens of his terms—such as neurosis, Oedipus complex, and repression—have entered everyday language, and he remains one of the leading figures of modern thought.

SECTION REVIEW

1. In your own words, briefly identify: voltaic pile, electrolysis, Wilhelm Roentgen, gene, antiseptic, Sigmund Freud.
2. Why was the invention of the laboratory so important to nineteenth-century science?
3. What ideas did Albert Einstein develop that changed people's understanding of the physical world?
4. What were some improvements made in health care in the nineteenth century?
5. How did nineteenth century thinkers attempt to apply the scientific method to the study of people?
■ The discovery of germs and antiseptics enabled nineteenth-century scientists to help people live longer. How are researchers using science to extend life today?

CHANGES IN LITERATURE, ART, AND MUSIC

The age of political liberty and industrialization witnessed enormous changes in literature, art, and music. Some artists felt the thrill of freedom and extended their explorations into new areas of human life. Others saw modern life sweeping

away much of what they valued and longingly turned to the past. They idealized the Middle Ages and, in the spirit of emerging nationalism, celebrated the histories of their own nations.

The artistic mood of the first half of the nineteenth century is usually labeled **Romanticism.** This term has never been clearly defined but the ideals it tends to uphold include the importance of the individual, a love of nature, a belief in the goodness of man, and a view of the artist as a liberated genius or hero. It also encompasses an interest in folk customs and the medieval past, a respect for religion, and high esteem for emotion. As the English poet William Wordsworth wrote, poetry is "the spontaneous overflow of powerful feelings." The Romantics criticized the Enlightenment as being coldly scientific and too confident in the power of reason. They were fond of the world of imagination, and they were impressed by nature and the powerful energy that it contained.

Romanticism and Realism in Literature

In England the Romantic movement expressed itself most notably in poetry. Wordsworth stressed emotion but also believed that poetry should imitate the speech of ordinary people. His friend Samuel Coleridge emphasized the use of imagination. The other three great poets of English Romanticism were John Keats, Percy Shelley, and Lord Byron. Keats' work is famous for its haunting imagery and deep emotion; Shelley was a political radical; the dashing figure of the aristocratic and witty Byron served as a model for a generation of young men. All three poets died young. Romanticism in the English novel can be found in the works of Sir Walter Scott, who wrote many stories set in the Middle Ages. One of the most famous is *Ivanhoe,* a story of Richard the Lionhearted and the Crusades.

The Middle Ages also inspired the poet and novelist Victor Hugo in France. He created the famous hunchback of Notre Dame and was criticized for dwelling on a subject too "ugly" for art. However, an interest in what was ugly or exotic or mysterious was also characteristic of Romanticism.

It was in Germany that the term Romantic was invented as a word to describe the opposite of the

People in History

George Gordon, Lord Byron

Some historical figures are so important that their names become adjectives—Marxist, Freudian, Napoleonic. From the English poet Lord Byron we get the word "Byronic." To be Byronic is to be a melancholy rebel with a mysterious sin on the conscience.

Byronic describes the heroes Byron created and it also describes Byron himself. A handsome aristocrat, he defied social convention, lived a scandalous life, took part in political intrigue, and died in the Greek war for independence. His poetry, which mixed wildness and melancholy, thrilled all of Europe. Everywhere—in Germany, Italy, Poland, and Russia—young men imitated his defiant, moody personality. "Remember certain passages of Byron if you wish for eternal inspiration," wrote Delacroix.

In 1812, Byron published an autobiographical poem *Childe Harold's Pilgrimage*. It reflected the poet's disillusionment with the world.

> "In my youth's summer I did sing of One,
> The wandering outlaw of his own dark mind;
> Again I seize the theme, then but begun,
> And bear it with me, as the rushing wind
> Bears the cloud onwards: in that Tale I find
> The furrows of long thought, and dried-up tears,
> Which, ebbing, leave a sterile track behind,
> O'er which all heavily the journeying years
> Plod the last sands of life,—where not a flower appears."

The Byronic image of the artist as a rebel set a style that influenced the entire modern age and that still persists today.

1. How did Byron reflect Romanticism?
2. Why would fighting in a war for independence appeal to a Romantic?
3. How does *Childe Harold's Pilgrimage* reflect the poet's melancholia?

---

classical spirit of the eighteenth century. Germany's greatest writer of the period, Johann Wolfgang von Goethe (GER-tuh), was a kind of bridge between the two centuries. His great work *Faust*, about a man who wagers his soul to the devil to satisfy his wish for knowledge, youth, and action, seemed to provide a symbol of the longings of the Romantic thinkers. *Faust* inspired a whole generation of Romantics.

The influence of Byron was particularly strong in Russia. It can be seen in the career of Alexander Pushkin, Russia's greatest poet. His works used themes from Russian folklore and history, but he also took Russian literature in the direction of Realism, a literary movement that closely followed Romanticism in Europe.

By 1850 most of the great names of Romanticism were dead. Also, the political mood had changed. The liberal element of the middle class that had sought greater political freedom had been disappointed, particularly by the failure of the revolutions of 1848. A conservative reaction set in.

This changed mood brought a decline in Romantic idealism and substituted a view of life as it was, rather than as it might be. In literature the movement is called **Realism,** in politics **realpolitik** (ray-AHL-po-lih-teek). Realism aims at a detailed description of society, the more scientific the better. Perhaps the leading exponent was the French novelist Gustave Flaubert (floe-BAIR), author of *Madame Bovary,* which unflatteringly depicted the dullness of life in a small French town. Works of realism were not dull, however. The writings of the great English Realists, such as Charles Dickens and George Eliot (the pen name of Mary Ann Evans), are colorful renditions of life. The same is true of the three great Russian novelists of the Realistic tradition—Leo Tolstoy (tol-STOY), Ivan Turgenev (toor-GEN-yef), and Fyodor Dostoevsky (dahs-tuh-YEF-skee). Realism is most notable for its attempt to look at the world of everyday nineteenth-century life without idealism and sometimes with disapproval. Whereas writers such as Dickens, Tolstoy, and Elizabeth Gaskell were strong critics of social injustice, other writers, such as Flaubert and Kate Chopin, were critical of the blandness of middle-class life. To some like George Sand and the Utopian socialists, the emancipation of women was a major theme.

Romanticism and Nationalism in Music

In the eighteenth century, composers such as Haydn and Mozart tended to work for the nobility or the church. The emergence of the middle class in the Industrial Revolution brought musicians a much larger audience, and the modern custom of concert-going was established. No longer tied to specific employers, composers enjoyed a freedom and frequently a poverty very much in keeping with the Romantic ideal.

The most important composer at the beginning of the nineteenth century was Ludwig van Beethoven of Vienna. His symphonies, piano sonatas, and string quartets were admired for their originality. His music was enhanced by the versatility of the piano, perfected by the early 1800's. His achievements are all the more outstanding since he accomplished them while progressively losing his hearing. Beethoven seemed to fit the new Romantic image of the artist—independent, inspired by nature, heroic, and innovative.

Hector Berlioz (BER-lee-oez) of France was closely identified with Romanticism. Audiences found his huge compositions difficult, and consequently he struggled to make a living. His career demonstrated the awkward new status of the artist in the nineteenth century. Although the audience was expanding, the public often found it hard to understand the ways in which artists were experimenting. As a result, many artists rejected middle-class standards as unappreciative and unartistic.

The growth of nationalism also inspired many composers. They looked to the histories and myths of their countries for new subject matter, and they used folk melodies in their compositions. The Polish-born pianist and composer Frederic Chopin

How does this picture of the Sultan of Morocco by Delacroix reflect the Romantic movement?

Compare George Stubbs' hunting scene in the Neoclassic style (late eighteenth century) to Impressionist Edouard Manet's horse race. How do the styles differ?

(SHOH-pan) wrote pieces based on the dances of his native land, as did the Hungarian Franz Liszt (LIST). Patriotism inspired Anton Dvorak (DVAWR-zhahk) in Czechoslovakia, Edvard Grieg (GREEG) in Norway, Jan Sibelius (suh-BAYL-yus) in Finland and a group of composers in Russia. There the most impressive achievement was probably Modest Mussorgsky's (moo-SAWRG-skee) opera, *Boris Godunov* (guh-doo-NAWF), based on Pushkin's story of a historical Russian czar.

Two great opera composers dominated the nineteenth century and inspired patriotism in their countries, both of which were struggling for unification. In Italy Giuseppe Verdi's (jyoo-SEP-pay VAIR-dee) music was adopted as the voice of the Italian drive toward liberation. In Germany, Richard Wagner drew upon ancient Germanic legends to create a poetic view of his country's past. Wagner maintained that his blending of music, singing, and theater was the "artwork of the future," and the bold new harmonies of his music had an enormous influence on later composers.

Romanticism and Realism in Art

Two greatly influential painters of Romanticism were Eugene Delacroix (del-uh-KRWAH) of France and J. M. W. Turner of England.

Delacroix's works were controversial for their brilliant colors and their subject matter. He claimed the purpose of art was "not to imitate nature but to strike the imagination." Delacroix chose subjects that related to current events, such as the Greek rebellion against the Turks. He also introduced foreign scenes, as in the paintings he did of Arab life after visiting North Africa. This taste for exotic scenes was characteristic of the Romantic school.

Turner's work demonstrates the aspect of Romanticism that idealizes nature. His art is in a long tradition of English landscape painting, but his obsession with capturing the effects of light made his later work incomprehensible to many viewers. One critic called them "pictures of nothing." In fact, the great swirls of color found in his later works anticipate twentieth-century abstract art.

Just as in the novel, the mid-century saw a shift toward Realism in painting. The painter most identified with this change is Gustave Courbet (khoohr-BAY). He rejected the brash colors and exotic subjects of Romanticism and sought to depict the world as it actually is. He flirted with political radicalism and considered his painting to be a plea for justice and a criticism of society. He took his themes from ordinary life and was denounced by many critics for his concentration on the "lowly" subject.

Later Developments in Art

The second half of the nineteenth century saw the rise of a new school of painting in France. This movement is known as **Impressionism** and its leaders were Edouard Manet (ma-NAY), Auguste Renoir (REN-wahr), Claude Monet (moe-NAY), Camille Pissaro (puh-SAHR-oe), and Edgar Degas (duh-GAH). Among the important American figures working in Europe were Mary Cassatt and James McNeil Whistler. The Impressionists developed a method of capturing light through combining small flecks of paint. In part they benefited from the developing chemical industry that was supplying pigments previously unavailable. The Impressionists tried to capture fleeting images and create the same impression of reality as that new invention, the camera. Though their works were much brighter than the paintings of Courbet, the Impressionists were in the Realistic tradition in one sense. They believed that their art was truly realistic because it relied on the scientific study of light. They discovered, for example, that shadows are not black, but colored according to the objects that cast them.

Impressionist subject matter drew upon popular activity—boating parties, railroad stations, city streets, race tracks. Their shimmering light effects and their attempts to catch spontaneous moments gave their work a sketchy quality. In that sense, Impressionism can be seen as the first modern art movement. With the exception of Turner, the Impressionists were the first to break with the traditional methods of copying nature.

Compare Cezanne's painting with the previous works. Which do you prefer? Why?

The generation that followed went even further in rejecting traditional Realism. This school is called **Postimpressionism.** Georges Seurat (suh-RAH) invented a system called **pointillism** in which scenes were built up out of thousands of tiny dots of color. He did not want the same look as the Impressionists. Seurat claimed his method was the most scientific of all. His theories demonstrate the importance science had for many artists—and writers—in the second half of the nineteenth century. The work of Paul Cézanne (say-ZAN) also was an attempt to make Impressionism "solid." His scenes revealed geometric shapes, and he advised painters to look for "the cone, the sphere, and the cylinder" in nature. Yet he boldly distorted the appearance of an object to express what he considered the essence of the subject. Cézanne is often seen as a forerunner of modern art, especially the movement known as Cubism.

Paul Gauguin (goe-GAN) shared Cézanne's interest in solidity and bold colors, but he also felt the Romantics' love of exotic locales. Gauguin rejected European civilization and sailed to the South Pacific, where he did some of his greatest works.

Other Postimpressionists used their art to reveal their emotional states. The Dutch painter Vincent van Gogh (vahn-GOE) used strong colors and nervous brushwork to create a world full of energy. The Belgian painter James Ensor was fascinated by death, skeletons, and masks. He turned his strange visions into pictures that would not be fully understood until the age of Freud. The emotional kind of painting seen in the works of van Gogh and Ensor was a forerunner of the modern movement called Expressionism.

The end of the nineteenth century also saw the development of an artistic style known as **Art Nouveau** (noo-VOE). It was not primarily a style of painting. Designers turned to things like furniture, dinnerware, and jewelry that were used every day by middle-class people. The use of Art Nouveau was one of the first uses of art in advertising, which was a growing new force for reaching a mass public; designers used the style in posters and magazine advertisements. Art Nouveau seems highly decorated today, but in contrast to the heavy ornamentation of the mid-century it was considered a bold simplification. Art Nouveau is characterized by long, sweeping curves, known as whiplash lines.

SECTION REVIEW

1. In your own words, briefly identify: Faust, Realism, Impressionism, Art Nouveau.
2. What were the reasons for the transition from Romanticism to Realism in the mid-nineteenth century?
3. Why did Romantic artists often criticize the middle class?
4. How did the progress of science affect the arts in the nineteenth century?
- Nineteenth-century writers, artists, and musicians demanded a great measure of artistic freedom. Do you think artists and performers of the present day share this attitude? Why?

CHANGES IN EDUCATION AND POPULAR CULTURE

Industrialization and political democracy enabled great numbers of people to participate in activities formerly reserved for the nobility or the wealthy. New business enterprises opened and government activity grew. The need for educated employees resulted in the expansion of educational facilities. This need for education gave rise to institutions such as libraries, museums, and zoos. As more people could read, forms of communication, like newspapers, expanded. Finally, the new middle class had more leisure time. Parks and theaters opened and team sports were organized.

Popular Entertainment

Museums had been around for centuries, but only as private collections. Now they began to admit the public. After the French Revolution the Louvre in Paris was opened and the exhibits organized. London's National Gallery followed, as well as the Hermitage in St. Petersburg and the Smithsonian Institution in Washington, D.C. Other kinds of museums also opened. An anthropological museum was founded in Paris, and an open-air museum devoted to preserving peasant life opened in Swe-

How does this scene represent the changes in society and popular entertainment?

den, a sign that urbanization was destroying traditional folkways.

Libraries developed in the same way. Private book collections were absorbed by national libraries, typifying the new nationalism. Britain and the United States led the way in establishing public circulating libraries. Books were kept on open shelves and classification schemes were invented so that users could locate books easily.

As urban congestion grew, governments saw the need for open spaces, and parks were opened. The first were the private gardens confiscated from nobles during the French Revolution. The most famous park designer was Frederick Law Olmsted, who helped design New York's Central Park. Closely related were "pleasure gardens," where city dwellers could enjoy outdoor dining, dancing, and some new attractions—slides, swings, and merry-go-rounds.

City dwellers could also keep in touch with nature in the new zoos. Nearly all the European capitals opened public zoos. In Paris, the animal collection was organized by Cuvier, the great fossil expert.

Theaters also multiplied and new technology revolutionized the stage. The Paris opera installed gas lights in the 1820's, and by the end of the century, electric lights were being used. Railroads made it possible for theater companies to tour, and soon even people living in small towns were able to see the great shows from the city.

Middle-class leisure time was also filled by the rise of organized sports—rugby and cricket in Britain, soccer in other European countries, baseball and football in the United States, and hockey in Canada. The end of the century saw the invention of basketball in Massachusetts. Almost all of today's major spectator sports began in the nineteenth century.

Education

As the countries of the West entered the modern age, it became clear that extending education to all levels of society was essential to progress. Governments began setting up nationwide educational systems. At first, Germany was most successful; this gave that country an educational edge, which was reflected in the excellence of German science. The French set up primary schools and teachers' colleges in the 1830's; England lagged slightly behind. In the last twenty years of the century, the number of public high schools in the United States went from 800 to 6,000.

By the end of the century education was seen as a civil right, and gradually women were included. The United States was a pioneer in establishing schools for women—by 1870 more than half of American high school graduates were girls. Germany and France began to organize girls' schools and admit women to universities in the 1870's. In Britain steps toward women's education began around midcentury. Following her work in military hospitals during the Crimean War, Florence Nightingale developed training programs for nurses.

Journalism

As democratic ideas spread, freedom of the press was established in Europe. This, combined with the success of education, meant a great increase in newspapers. In 1836, 39 million newspapers were printed in Britain; twenty years later, that figure had tripled. The *Times* was the best known British newspaper, but it was challenged by the *Daily Telegraph,* which sold for the unheard-of low price of one penny. By 1870 the *Daily Telegraph* was selling 180,000 copies every day. Papers flourished in France, Germany, and the United States, too; by the end of the century 1,400 newspapers were bring printed in Paris alone.

In the 1830's a process of making paper in a continuous roll was developed. Then printing presses were invented that could turn out the great volume necessary. The *Times* introduced a machine called the Walter press, which could produce 12,000 copies every hour. Also, communication was greatly speeded up by steamships, railroads, and, especially the telegraph. This gave rise to international news collecting agencies like the one founded by Julius Reuter. He was able to report the news of Lincoln's death two days earlier than anyone else in Europe.

Technology and education combined to create an era of mass communication which would later be expanded by inventions such as radio and television. The public was becoming more informed, and the world began to seem smaller.

How were schools trying to meet the needs of an industrial society? How do schools meet the needs of our society?

Reviewing the Chapter

Chapter Summary

Industrialization and the rise of democracy changed the world in many ways. Industry made practical use of scientific discoveries. Scientists used technology to develop new ways of studying the environment, and great advances were made in chemistry, physics, biology, and medicine. Thinkers also tried to apply the scientific method to the study of humanity; this led to new ways of writing history, to new forms of psychology, and to the founding of the science of anthropology.

The arts at the beginning of the nineteenth century were characterized by Romanticism, an idealistic movement that stressed love of nature and the past, valued emotion, and conceived of the artist as a hero. The latter half of the century saw the rise of Realism, an artistic movement that aimed at the depiction of ordinary life. The arts were influenced by changes in the political atmosphere in Europe. Later artistic movements broke with the traditional methods of copying nature and pointed the way to modern art.

Growing business and government demanded an educated work force, and public education expanded. As the middle class grew wealthier, new forms of entertainment developed. Greater literacy also created a boom in newspaper publishing, and the modern era of mass communication was born.

1. How did the relationship between science and industry develop in the nineteenth century?
2. What were two major schools of art during the nineteenth century?
3. How did the expansion of public education affect society?

Using Your Vocabulary

1. What is the relationship between electricity and electrolysis?
2. How did the Xray get its name?
3. What is radioactivity? What are two radioactive elements?
4. How is fission related to Einstein's theory of matter and energy?
5. How was Social Darwinism a distortion of the theory of natural selection?
6. Who coined the word vaccine? List five words that have been coined in the twentieth century.
7. What is the study of genetics?
8. How do the natural sciences differ from the social sciences? Name four social sciences.
9. How does the work of an anthropologist differ from that of an archaeologist?
10. What is social history? Write a statement about one current event that would be of interest to a social historian.
11. What is a conditioned reflex? Who is associated with its discovery?
12. What terms did Sigmund Freud introduce into everyday language?
13. What qualities are associated with Romanticism? How does Romanticism differ from Realism?
14. What characteristics are associated with the term Byronic?
15. What is Impressionism? What painters were associated with this movement?
16. What was the art technique of the pointillist Georges Seurat?

Developing Your Geography Skills

Use the Atlas maps on pages 756, 758, 759, and 760 to locate where Delacroix visited in North Africa (Morocco), where Marie Curie was born (Poland), where Darwin made observations of nature (Galapagos Islands), where Jan Sibelius composed (Finland), where Verdi's opera *Aida* was first performed (Egypt), where Ludwig van Beethoven was born (Germany), where he composed (Vienna), where Mary Cassatt was born (United States), and where she painted (Paris).

Recalling the Facts

1. What sciences composed the Natural Philosophies?
2. What scientist did experiments to determine what happened to elements when they were heated? What contribution did he make to modern science?
3. How were the discoveries of Sir Humphrey Davy dependent on the prior work of Alessandro Volta?
4. Why was Dimitri Mendeleyev's development of the periodic table important to the progress of chemistry?
5. What characteristic of the X ray made it valuable to medicine?
6. What were two revolutionary ideas proposed by Albert Einstein? What modern developments are based on Einstein's work?
7. What did Herbert Spencer mean by the expression "survival of the fittest"?
8. How did Gregor Mendel contribute to the study of genetics?
9. What were some improvements in medicine during the nineteenth century? What are some recent innovations in medicine?
10. What contribution did Leopold von Ranke make to the study of history?
11. Who were two major figures associated with the development of anthropology? Which human societies did each study?
12. What contribution did Auguste Comte make to the development of sociology?
13. Who were two major psychologists in the nineteenth century? What contributions did they make to the field of psychology?
14. Which literary movement glorified the individual and the past? Name four literary figures associated with this movement.
15. What contribution did Alexander Pushkin make to Russian literature?
16. How did the failure of the revolutions of 1848 affect art and literature?
17. How did Guiseppe Verdi and Richard Wagner each inspire nationalism?
18. How did the work of Eugene Delacroix typify Romantic art?
19. How did the work of Gustave Courbet signal a change in art in the mid-nineteenth century.

Why did critics denounce him?
20. In what sense can Impressionism be considered the first modern art movement?
21. What forms of entertainment became popular during the nineteenth century?
22. What political, social, and technological changes affected the newspaper industry?
23. How did Julius Reuter make use of the technological changes of the Industrial Revolution?

Essay Questions

1. Describe the major contributions made to the development of chemistry in the nineteenth century.
2. What theories about the atom were developed in the nineteenth and early twentieth centuries? How did they differ from earlier theories?
3. Describe how Romanticism reflected a reaction to the Enlightenment and the Industrial Revolution.
4. How did the study of history reflect the influence of science?
5. How did Realism reflect a change in the political climate of Europe? What topics were within the scope of the Realists?
6. How did art change over the course of the nineteenth century? Identify major artists and movements.
7. Describe how the uses of Art Nouveau reflected social change.
8. How did industrialization and political change affect education and popular culture?

Critical Thinking

1. How does the modern scientific method provide verifiable facts in the natural sciences? Why is the scientific method less reliable in the social sciences?
2. How did historians in the nineteenth century try to improve the reliability of their source data?
3. How did industrialization and political change affect the value placed on education, in general, and on women's education, in particular?

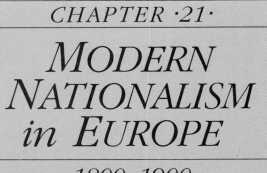

CHAPTER ·21·

MODERN NATIONALISM in EUROPE

1800–1900

Objectives

- To describe the steps that led to the unification of the Italian states

- To explain Prussia's role in the unification of Germany

- To describe the role Bismarck played in creating a strong German nation

- To discuss the impact of nationalism in the Austrian and Ottoman empires

- To discuss the situation of the Jews in Europe in the 1800's

- To summarize the nature of Russian society in the nineteenth century

*D*uring the first half of the 1800's, the Concert of Europe tried to control threats to national and international political stability. The European powers were able to avoid a major war for more than forty years. But the uprisings of 1830 and 1848 showed that rebellions spawned by liberalism and nationalism would be hard to contain. The promise of the revolutions of 1848 ended in disillusionment, but in the next fifty years strong national movements changed the politics as well as the map of Europe.

In the second half of the century, national movements absorbed some of the energy being released by political, social, and economic unrest. But the nature of nationalism was different from the idealistic nationalism of the first half of the century. Early nineteenth-century nationalism was largely a response to Napoleon. It was based on the belief that boundaries should be drawn according to national lines. People sharing a common language and heritage should be free to live together under a ruler of their choice. Mazzini and Napoleon III were among its advocates. However, with the failure of the revolutions in 1848, major players emerged who were political realists. They realized that national goals would be achieved by diplomats, armies, and strong leaders, not by popular uprisings and idealism. Nationalism displayed many different forms. It led to the unification of

Italy and Germany and the disruption of the Austro-Hungarian and Ottoman empires. In its more exaggerated form, it fostered Pan-Slavism and Russification and, when influenced by Social Darwinism, racism and imperialism.

THE UNIFICATION OF ITALY

Shortly after Napoleon's defeat, the Italian states lay in the grip of reaction. Italian nationalists never lost hope, however, and over the next fifty years they won independence, province by province, through a combination of astute leadership and courageous patriots.

Italy After the Congress of Vienna

In 1815, at the peace conference in Vienna, Italy had been divided into many states and provinces. It was not a nation in the modern sense of the term but, as Metternich called it, "a geographical expression." The states lacked the bonds of economic ties, a common language, and national government.

In the south the Kingdom of the Two Sicilies was ruled by a Bourbon despot. Central Italy was occupied by the Papal States and controlled by the pope. The north was dominated by Austria, which had been given Lombardy and Venetia by the Congress of Vienna. The rest of northern Italy was fragmented into a number of independent states. The most important was the kingdom of Sardinia, or Piedmont, which included the island of Sardinia, and the regions of Savoy, Piedmont, and Nice on the mainland. Austria also protected some of the absolute rulers in northern Italy. As a result, Italian nationalists saw Austria as the chief obstacle to unification.

Mazzini

The dream of a unified nation that would exceed the glory of ancient Rome and the Renaissance kindled nationalist spirit in Italy. The desire for a **Risorgimento** (rih-zor-jih-MEN-toe), or resurgence, began to take form during the French Revolution and crystallized when temporary unity was achieved under Napoleon. It was intensified by works such as *My Prisons,* in which Silvio Pellico described his ten years in an Austrian prison. After the Congress of Vienna, Giuseppe Mazzini, a patriot and philosopher, tried to unite the Italian states into a republic. As a young man, he had been a member of the secret Carbonari. In 1830 after a failed rebellion in Sardinia, Mazzini was exiled. He spent much of his adult life in France and England, which he used as a base for continued revolutionary activity. While in exile he founded a revolutionary society called Young Italy, to further his cause. By smuggling fiery letters and pamphlets into Italy, he spread his revolutionary zeal.

In 1848, as revolutions swept across Europe, Mazzini's followers staged uprisings throughout Italy. When a group of rebels seized Rome in early 1849, Mazzini rushed back from England and proclaimed an Italian republic.

The revolution was short-lived because it had limited appeal. The peasants would not support it, and the middle class feared the overthrow of the

Mazzini spent many years in exile or in hiding. Why is he now considered an Italian national hero?

THE UNIFICATION OF ITALY

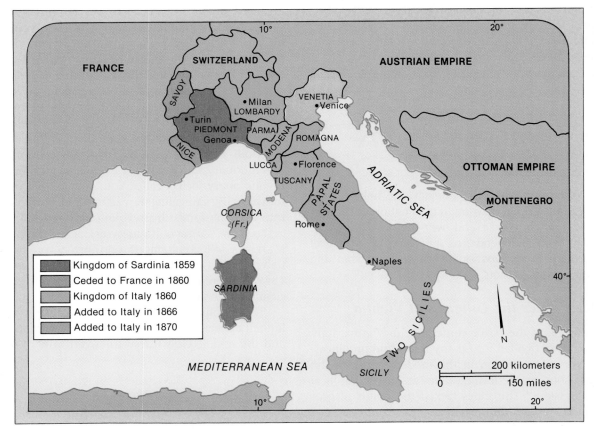

What threat did powerful neighbors pose to a disunited Italy? Why was the pope's opposition an obstacle to unity?

social as well as the political order. Those supporting the idea of unity had conflicting goals. Liberals favored a republic whereas others sought a constitutional monarchy. The clergy, in particular, feared republicanism and wanted a federation headed by the pope.

In the swift counterrevolution that followed the 1848 upheavals, Austrian troops suppressed Mazzini's followers in northern Italy. The final blow came in 1849, when an army sent by Louis Napoleon marched into Italy. The French troops advanced on Rome where they confronted an army led by Giuseppe Garibaldi. After a vigorous two-month struggle, Garibaldi gave up and fled into exile, as did Mazzini. The French took control of Rome, snuffing out the brief life of Mazzini's Roman Republic. They restored the power of the pope over the Papal States in central Italy and became the pope's defender. The French kept troops in Rome for the next twenty years, reducing Austrian influence in Italy.

Cavour

After Mazzini's defeat, leadership of the Risorgimento passed on to Count Camillo di Cavour, who had been influenced by Britain's political and economic systems. A shrewd politician, he became prime minister of the kingdom of Sardinia in 1852. As a realist, Cavour opposed the methods of the idealistic Mazzini. Cavour did not think unification could be achieved by secret societies or inflammatory pamphlets. He felt it would be accomplished under the leadership of a progressive state that

• 474 •

would serve as a model for the rest of Italy. Sardinia had been the only Italian state able to resist the Austrians effectively in 1848. Although the rebellion was crushed, Sardinia kept its independence due to British and French diplomatic intervention. Cavour wanted to capitalize on this chance to make Sardinia the leader in the unification movement.

The king of Sardinia, under Cavour's guidance, granted the people a liberal constitution and parliamentary government. Sardinia became a prosperous modern state. Railroads and docks were built, trade was expanded, and the power of the clergy was reduced. These reforms made the Sardinian king popular.

An Alliance with France

Reviewing the events of 1848, Cavour realized that Sardinia would need foreign help to oust Austria from northern Italy. His opportunity to gain an ally came in 1853, when Britain and France went to war against Russia in the Crimea, and Austria refused to join them. Cavour seized this chance to win the friendship of Louis Napoleon, now Napoleon III. Sardinia entered the Crimean War on the side of the French. By sending Italian soldiers to Russia, Cavour won a seat at the peace conference table in Paris. There he was able to raise the question of Italian unification and independence from Austria.

Then, Cavour maneuvered Austria into war with Sardinia in 1859. To obtain French help Cavour offered to give France the territories of Nice and Savoy. French and Italian troops together invaded the Austrian-held parts of Italy and had success in Lombardy. However, Prussia mobilized along the Rhine River in response to the French action. There was also an alarming increase of revolutionary fervor in Italy. These threats, combined with pressure from his Catholic citizens to support the pope, caused Napoleon III to negotiate separately with Austria for an end to the war.

The French emperor's action stunned Cavour and dashed his plan to isolate Austria. Under the peace terms arranged by Napoleon III, France gained Nice and Savoy, as promised. Sardinia acquired Lombardy, but Austria kept Venetia. France and Austria next offered a solution to the Italian question—a federation of the existing Italian governments under the control of the pope. Angered at this suggestion, nationalists rebelled throughout Italy. In Tuscany, Modena, Parma, and Romagna, they threw out their old rulers. In general elections, or **plebiscites** (PLEB-uh-sites), held in these regions, they agreed to be annexed to Sardinia. In response, the pope excommunicated the people of Romagna, which had been part of the Papal States.

The Final Steps to Unification

While this was taking place, Garibaldi, who had fought in Rome in 1848, organized an army of 1,000 nationalists called the Red Shirts. Financed by Cavour, Garibaldi invaded the island of Sicily. The corrupt government of the Two Sicilies lacked popular support. As a result, Garibaldi was able to capture Sicily within a matter of months. When

Garibaldi attracted loyal followers. What symbols depict Garibaldi's role in Italian history?

Garibaldi's army crossed to the mainland, the Bourbon king of the Two Sicilies, Francis II, fled. At this point, Cavour sent Sardinian soldiers south to seize a large area of the Papal States, avoiding Rome, which was still held by French troops. Cavour's aim was to prevent Garibaldi from attacking Rome and establishing a republic. Through skillful diplomacy, Cavour persuaded Garibaldi to support Victor Emmanuel II, the Sardinian king. Votes held in the Two Sicilies indicated a strong desire to join Sardinia.

The fighting ended and almost all the Italian peninsula was united. In 1861 Victor Emmanuel of Sardinia was proclaimed king of Italy. Venetia was added in 1866, as a prize for Italian aid to Prussia in the Seven Weeks' War. Finally, in 1870, when French troops were withdrawn from Rome as a result of the Franco-Prussian War, that city was annexed to Sardinia. This completed the formation of the modern Italian state. The capital of Italy was moved to Rome, and a section of the city set aside for the pope's use. Today the pope continues to govern the worldwide Roman Catholic Church from Vatican City, a small nation-state located within the city of Rome.

Problems Remain

The Italian states were finally united, but some problems remained. Nationalists still looked beyond Italy's borders to foreign areas where many Italians resided. In Trieste, Nice, and Savoy there were large Italian populations. Nationalists called these regions *Italia irredenta* (ee-TAHL-ee-ah ee-ree-DANE-tah), or Italy unredeemed, and began a movement called **irredentism,** to annex them to the new nation.

Within Italy, regional differences created tensions. The northern states, attempting to industrialize, looked upon the agrarian south as backward and primitive. Italy was relatively poor, with few natural resources other than agriculture. The government took on the debts of the annexed states and, despite high taxes, did little to improve education, roads, or railways. Attempts at land reform failed, since only the wealthy were able to buy confiscated church lands. The lives of laborers and peasants remained unchanged.

Tensions also existed between the Catholic Church and the government. Cavour worked hard to reduce the influence of the clergy. In addition, the church refused to recognize the state and urged the faithful not to participate in the government. With the capital of the nation in Rome–the pope's former seat of power–the rift between Church and State widened.

The most serious problem, however, was the lack of experience with constitutional government. Italy now had a parliamentary system, but it was far from democratic. At first only 600,000 out of more than 20 million Italians could vote. Agitation for more representation continued, and nationalists such as Garibaldi made unsuccessful attempts at revolution. But despite these problems, the dream of Risorgimento had been attained—Italy was a unified modern state.

SECTION REVIEW

1. Mapping: Use the map on page 474 to locate Sardinia, Nice, Savoy, Lombardy, Piedmont, Venetia, Sicily, Modena, Parma, Romagna.
2. In your own words, identify or define: Risorgimento, Giuseppe Mazzini, Young Italy, Giuseppe Garibaldi, Camillo di Cavour, Victor Emmanuel II, irredentism.
3. Describe Mazzini's association with revolution in 1830 and 1848. What were the results?
4. How did Cavour oust Austria from the Italian peninsula?
■ Italian unification was inspired by the works of writers, musicians, and artists as well as by soldiers. What examples can you describe of the work of a writer, artist, or musician today that comments on current events?

THE UNIFICATION OF GERMANY

For years, both France and Russia had encouraged rivalries among the German states to prevent the emergence of a strong nation on their borders. Before Napoleon I conquered the German states and consolidated them, there were over three hundred separate states. The Congress of Vienna reduced the number of states from about fifty to about thirty, each with its own ruler. As elsewhere, French rule had sparked feelings of nationalism. In the Revolution of 1848, liberals sought a united Germany under one ruler limited by a constitution. The rebellion failed, but the dreams did not die. Soon the example of Italy stirred nationalists in Germany. They faced problems similar to those faced by the Italians. There were numerous states with people with different heritages.

Prussia Dominates Unification Effort

At the beginning of the eighteenth century, Prussia was a small provincial kingdom. During the 1700's Prussia's rulers had expanded their power and ter-

ritory. Under Frederick II, Prussia became a major military power. In the Napoleonic Wars, however, Prussia had been defeated by the French. Napoleon seized Prussian lands, imposed restrictions on the size of the Prussian military, and forced the people to support an army of occupation. German propaganda began to promote a war for liberation and forged a sense of unity among the Prussian people. Reforms within Prussia strengthened the people's desire to be free of foreign rule.

At the Congress of Vienna, Prussia was able to enlarge its territory at the expense of some of Napoleon's former allies. As you recall, Prussia gained a large part of Saxony. Now its lands began in the west at the banks of the Rhine and stretched across the continent to Russia. Prussia also became a member of the German Confederation, a union of

THE UNIFICATION OF GERMANY

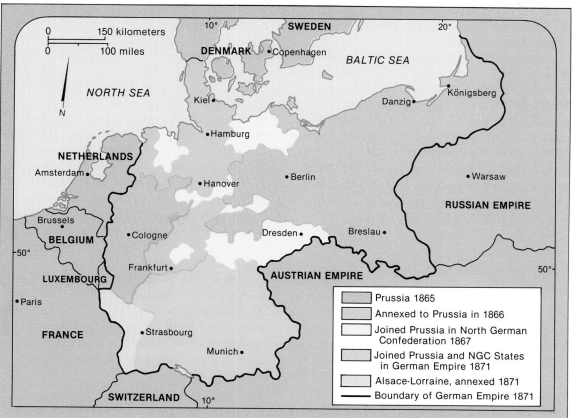

What geographic advantage did Prussia have over Austria to become the leader of German unification? What nations do you think saw German unification as a threat?

German states created by the Congress out of Napoleon's Confederation of the Rhine. The German states in the Confederation ranged from the large, powerful states of Austria, Hanover, Saxony, and Bavaria, to numerous small principalities. These were controlled by local, independent governments, with their own laws, currency, military establishment, and tariff system.

The patchwork of currency and tariffs made commerce difficult between the regions. Import taxes in each state raised the price of goods and inhibited trade. Junkers (YOON-kurz), the wealthy Prussian landowning class, persuaded their king to abolish internal tariffs so they could sell their surplus agricultural products elsewhere. The Prussians then pressed for trade treaties with the other German states. They organized a customs union, called the **Zollverein** (TSOHL-fair-ine). By 1844 most of the German states, except Austria, had joined. This economic union was a step toward unification. It was significant that it had been sponsored by Prussia. By the mid 1800's Prussia was fast becoming Austria's chief rival among the German-speaking states.

After 1862 Prussia moved with increasing speed to consolidate its power in the German Confederation. William I had become king, replacing his despotic brother, Frederick William IV. The new monarch eased restrictions on political expression and on the press, but set out to enlarge and strengthen the Prussian army. He soon met resistance from the liberal members of the Prussian parliament. To deal with this opposition, William I appointed a new prime minister, destined to become the architect of a unified Germany.

Bismarck

Otto von Bismarck, who became prime minister in 1862, was a member of the Junker class. Like Cavour in Sardinia, Bismarck's interests lay in advancing the prestige and the fortunes of his own state. He was not a nationalist, but he came to see that a German union in which Prussia played the leading role would bring his state power and glory. To this end he was willing to use any means. He was not deterred by what people would think of his actions. He showed a great toughness of mind in practicing realpolitik, the politics of reality.

Bismarck realized that for Prussia to be the leading German state it would have to prove itself more powerful than Austria. He believed he needed a war to defeat Austria and, like William I, he sought to build up the Prussian army. But his requests for taxes to increase the size of the army were turned down repeatedly by the liberal members of the Prussian parliament. Bismarck, however, was not a democrat and, when faced with opposition, he scornfully ignored it and collected the taxes anyway. In doing this, he freed himself from dependence on the regular budget that was subject to parliamentary veto. As for the liberals, whose goal was to make Prussia a model of political freedom, Bismarck said, "Not by speeches and majority votes are the great questions of the day decided—that was the great error of 1848 and 1849—but by blood and iron."

Bismarck plotted steps to isolate Austria from the other German states. The first opportunity came in 1864, when he persuaded Austria to join with Prussia in a war against Denmark. The stated purpose of the war was to prevent Denmark from annexing the border provinces of Schleswig and Holstein, where many German people lived. Bismarck's real intention, however, was to gain the provinces for Prussia. The small Danish army was quickly and easily defeated and, under the peace settlement, both Prussia and Austria were to administer the territories jointly. But as Bismarck had foreseen and desired, disagreements soon arose. Prussia complained about Austria's administration of some of the conquered territory, and in 1866 provoked Austria into a war. By skillful diplomacy, Bismarck persuaded Napoleon III to remain neutral. He also coaxed Italy into entering the war as Prussia's ally, promising to cede Venetia to the newly unified nation.

Assured of these allies, the efficient Prussian troops invaded Austrian territory. They met the Austrian army in Bohemia and stunned the Austrians at the Battle of Sadowa. Austria never recovered from its defeat and was forced to surrender soon in the so-called Seven Weeks' War.

The Dual Monarchy

Within Austria, rebellious Hungarians watched its crushing defeat at the hands of the Prussian army. The time was ripe to demand their freedom once again. The Austrian emperor, Francis Joseph I, knew that to keep his throne he must meet the Hungarians' demands. In 1867 a compromise was reached. The Hungarians were given their independence, but with the Austrian emperor as their king. This decision divided the Austrian Empire into a new state, Austria-Hungary, ruled by a Dual Monarchy. This agreement was known as the **Ausgleich** (OWS-glike), or compromise.

At the Treaty of Prague, which followed the Seven Weeks' War, Italy gained Venetia and Prussia gained the duchy of Holstein and several small states in northern Germany. The German Confederation was abandoned, curtailing Austria's chance of being included in a unified Germany. In 1867 the rest of northern Germany was united in an alliance called the North German Confederation. Prussia, as the largest state, dominated the Confederation and the Prussian monarch was its hereditary head. Only four states in southern Germany remained outside the Confederation. Bismarck soon devised a plan, to play on their fears of France and to tie them to Prussia.

The Franco-Prussian War

Prussia's sudden rise to power following the Seven Weeks' War alarmed the French. Napoleon III realized that if Bismarck could unite all of Germany, France would have an imposing power on its border. Also, as you have read in Chapter 19, the glory-hungry Napoleon believed a military victory over Prussia would unite his disillusioned country behind him. Bismarck understood that France would now do everything possible to prevent the unification of Germany. He faced the fact that France was the next obstacle to unification to be overcome. Once again he seized the opportunity to isolate his foe and then provoke a war.

Prussia and France went to war in 1870 as Napoleon III fell into Bismarck's trap. Bismarck deliberately edited a telegram he had received that described a meeting between the king of Prussia and the French ambassador at the German city of Ems. Bismarck then released the doctored text of the telegram to the press. It had been altered in such a way as to make the French believe their country

How does this picture portray the importance of Prussian militarism to the coronation of William as kaiser of Germany?

had been insulted by the Germans and to make the Germans believe they were being threatened by France. Shortly after the telegram appeared in French and German newspapers, Napoleon III declared war on Prussia.

As in the war against Austria, the Prussian army was ready for immediate action. Prussian troops quickly invaded France. As Bismarck had hoped, the small states in southern Germany—nationalistic and fearful of French domination—were quick to ally themselves with Prussia. No other power aided the French. The British felt that the French were at fault. The Austrians, who were the most likely to oppose Prussia, hated the French for the part they had played in Italian unification. The Italians saw the French preoccupation with Prussia as an opportunity to seize Rome and complete their unification. The French troops were quickly overwhelmed at the Battle of Sedan in northern France. Emperor Napoleon III surrendered on September 2, 1870. After holding out against the Germans for more than four months, Paris finally gave in and the war ended.

A New German Nation

The independent states of southern Germany joined those already annexed to Prussia to form a unified nation, which included all the German states except Austria. On January 18, 1871, while Paris was still under siege, a new Germany was proclaimed at ceremonies held at Versailles. King William of Prussia was proclaimed German emperor, and Bismarck became the Chancellor of the German Empire. It was a great humiliation for France to have this German ceremony held in the palace that was a symbol of past French power and wealth. German unification marked its emergence as the strongest nation on the Continent.

In the Treaty of Frankfurt in May 1871, Bismarck imposed peace terms so harsh that they were regarded in France and throughout Europe as immoral. The French were forced to give up their claims to Alsace and Lorraine, two important provinces rich in coal and iron. France also had to pay a huge **indemnity,** or war reparation, before German troops would withdraw from French soil. The events surrounding the end of the war and the severity of the peace terms sowed seeds of discontent that would yield a bitter harvest.

IMPERIAL GERMANY

During the period from unification until the outbreak of World War I in 1914, Germany became one of Europe's most powerful countries. To the rest of Europe, it presented a spectacle of wealth, power, and self-confidence. Many of the changes in Germany from 1871 to 1890 occurred while Bismarck was chancellor of the empire.

Governing the German Empire

With unification, Bismarck realized that he had to accept a form of democratic government for the new nation. The German Empire began with a constitution that united twenty-five German states into a loose federal system. Each state controlled its domestic affairs—education, law enforcement, public safety, health, and other matters such as the courts. But the federal government retained control over defense, international affairs, commerce, and tariffs.

At the head of the government was the kaiser, or emperor, William I of Prussia. As Bismarck wished, the kaiser had tremendous power. He could command the military forces, make foreign policy, and defend the nation against aggression.

The Krupp foundries became known for their armaments the world over. What resources did Germany need to develop industries such as this?

The chancellor was responsible to the kaiser and not to the legislature.

The kaiser's power was limited by the two-house legislature. The upper chamber, called the **Bundesrat** (BOON-dess-raht), was a council of forty-three appointed members. But since some were named to the Bundesrat by the kaiser, he could defeat any action of which he disapproved by using this block vote.

The lower house was the **Reichstag** (RIKES-tahg), an assembly of 400 representatives elected by universal manhood suffrage. Although it was chosen democratically, the power of the Reichstag was subject to the wishes of the emperor and the Bundesrat, who, acting together, could dismiss it.

Prussia dominated the new government, with the greatest representation in each house. As chancellor, Bismarck continued to strengthen Prussia's prestige and power. He also influenced the character of German government. Bismarck believed opposition to the kaiser was disloyal and morally wrong. His beliefs, backed by his power, undermined liberal sentiments in Germany. Authoritarian government cloaked by democratic practices became the norm in Germany.

The Development of Industry

The new German Empire was fortunate in its natural resources. Rich iron and coal deposits in Lorraine and in the valley of the Ruhr River provided the materials for a rapidly developing steel industry. Germany's late entry into the industrial world meant that it could acquire the latest machines and equipment for its mining and manufacturing. In the southern states, agriculture continued to flourish, and improved transportation made it easier to ship farm products. Furthermore, Germany received the indemnity it had imposed on the French after the Franco-Prussian War. Here were funds with which to consolidate its railroad system, build canals and other waterways, and fuel its industries. Bismarck also established a common monetary system, a central bank, and a unified postal system. To make it all work smoothly, he improved the efficiency of the legal and judicial systems.

Germany's industries grew rapidly and its population increased. But developments within Germany, which threatened the political system, soon forced Bismarck to a number of compromises.

Bismarck's Political Problems

With Prussian control of the Bundesrat, and strong leadership by William I and Bismarck, democracy grew very slowly in Germany. Nevertheless, problems developed that put pressure on Bismarck's authority. He was forced at times to exploit different political groups to win popular support for his projects.

Opposition came from a variety of sources. Some Germans feared the government's increasing militarism. Liberals wanted political reform to expand representation in the legislature, and social reform in education and in other institutions. Germans in the southern states, used to running their own affairs, resented federal interference in local matters.

Tensions rose sharply, particularly in southern Germany where many Catholics lived, when Bismarck began a campaign against the influence of the Catholic church. He broke diplomatic relations with the Vatican in 1873 and imposed strict laws to control the large German-Catholic population. It was the start of the **Kulturkampf** (kuhl-TOOR-kahmpf), or "struggle for culture," in which priests had to be Germans and Catholic children were forced to attend German schools. Another restrictive measure expelled Jesuits from the country. Bismarck's attack on German Catholics brought him under sharp criticism. Even non-Catholics joined the opposition, and Bismarck was forced to modify his policy. By the early 1880's, moreover, he needed Catholic and liberal support against a different threat, socialism. Therefore, he reestablished relations with the pope in 1887, and the Kulturkampf ended.

Bismarck and the Socialists

As Germany industrialized, a new class of urban workers crowded the rapidly expanding cities. These laborers, supported by the liberals in the Reichstag, wanted laws to improve their working conditions. Socialists, who had been active in Germany since the mid-1800's, wanted greater reforms, including strict regulation of industries, to prevent exploitation of the workers.

To Bismarck's alarm, socialist agitation in the cities led to the creation of the Social Democratic Party. It developed slowly at first, gaining only two

How have Bismarck and the socialists been characterized in this British cartoon? What idea is the cartoonist trying to convey?

seats in the Reichstag, but by 1877 received one half million votes and a large representation in the assembly. Although the lower house had little actual power, it provided a splendid forum to air socialist protests. Once again Bismarck enlisted liberals on his side to fight the socialists. He switched his tactics and granted many of the reforms the liberals and the socialists had asked for—insurance against sickness and accidents, shorter working hours, and improved working conditions in factories, mills, and mines. These laws gave Germany the world's most advanced social security system.

Bismarck's Foreign Policy

Following the Treaty of Frankfurt, Europe's leaders tried to reestablish the balance of power that was upset by the emergence of a strong German state. From 1871 until 1890, Bismarck was a major player in this diplomatic game. His goal was peace in Europe and German security.

A cornerstone of Bismarck's policy was German military supremacy. All German men were subject to the draft in the new German Empire, or **Second Reich** (RIKE). The German navy rivaled the great British fleet.

Conditions in Europe were tense after 1870. France had been humiliated in the Franco-Prussian War and had lost Alsace-Lorraine to Germany. Bismarck wanted the territory as a buffer against France but rightly feared French revenge. "The surrender of Alsace-Lorraine means an endless war behind the mask of peace," wrote a French official. Bismarck sought to neutralize the threat by isolating France.

The possible French ally most feared by Germany was Russia. A pact between France and Russia posed the danger of war on Germany's eastern and western borders. Bismarck devoted his efforts to preventing such an alliance.

Part of Bismarck's problem dated back to the ouster of Austria from the German Confederation in 1866. Austria then turned its attention to the Balkans to recover its prestige. Russia was also interested in the Balkans as a source for a warm-water port. As the power of the Ottoman Empire declined in the Balkans, Austrian and Russian interests clashed in that region as they vied for supremacy. But there were other forces at work as well. Germany's rise to power had alarmed Britain. In 1872 Disraeli warned the British that they must look beyond Europe to maintain their strength. As Britain's empire became more important, so did routes through the Balkans and the Middle East. Britain was willing to support the corrupt Turkish regime rather than have the Dardanelles fall under Russian control. Meanwhile Bismarck, who had no territorial ambition toward the Balkans, watched events with interest. He wanted to prevent a war between Russia and Austria because both would expect Germany's support. Once Germany was united without Austria, Bismarck had set out to repair relations between Germany and Austria.

To balance these conflicting forces, Bismarck walked a tightrope. He carefully avoided conflict with Britain. In 1879 he formed a defensive alliance with Austria-Hungary. Then the League of the Three Emperors bound Germany, Russia, and Austria together. In 1882 Bismarck organized the Triple Alliance between Germany, Austria-Hungary, and Italy, aimed at isolating France. In 1887 Bismarck negotiated the Reinsurance Treaty with Russia. By the terms of the treaty, each would remain neutral if the other went to war, unless Germany attacked France or Russia attacked Austria. In a calculated move, Bismarck made known the terms of some secret treaties as a deterrent to Russian ambitions.

For all that might be said of his methods, Bismarck did maintain peace among the major powers. In 1890, shortly after William II became kaiser, Bismarck was dismissed. As you will see, the new leader undid Bismarck's careful strategy.

SECTION REVIEW

1. In your own words, identify or define: kaiser, Bundesrat, Reichstag, Kulturkampf.
2. Describe the structure established for government of the united Germany.
3. What advantages enabled Germany to industrialize so rapidly?
4. What were the reforms in working conditions adopted during Bismarck's years of power?
■ In dealing with the threat of socialism in Germany, Bismarck worked with groups with whom he basically disagreed. Give an example from recent history of a similar action on the part of a national leader.

INDEPENDENCE MOVEMENTS IN EASTERN EUROPE

As the forces of nationalism were creating Italy and Germany, they were dividing the troubled Austro-Hungarian and Ottoman empires into smaller national states. Beginning in the early 1800's the minorities in these regions were stirred by the French Revolution and ideas of Romanticism. They developed pride in their native cultures and customs. Scholars researched and promoted national histories. Others began to collect and preserve ballads and folk tales in languages that were near extinction. As these minorities experienced a

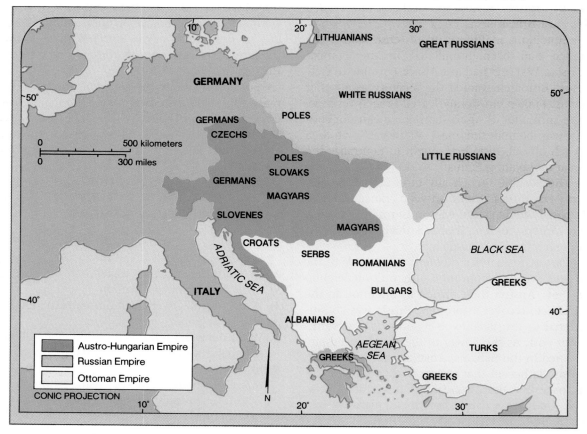

What general statement could be made about the distribution of nationalities in eastern Europe. Why do you think the rise of nationalism caused unrest?

revival of national pride, conflicts arose from their newly developed ambitions. Added to this source of unrest in eastern Europe were the complicated relationships between Austria-Hungary, Russia, the declining Ottoman Empire, and smaller states in southeastern Europe. Austria-Hungary wished to combat Slavic nationalism within its borders and in the Balkans in order to survive. Meanwhile Russia, with its Slavic population, wanted to expand into the Balkans. It also encouraged **Pan-Slavism,** the feeling that all Slavic people should help one another and be united under one ruler. This directly conflicted with Austria's aims and, in time, with those of Great Britain and Germany. Problems within the Ottoman Empire itself further threatened the fragile balance of relationships in the area.

Nationalism in Austria

Feelings of nationalism created a longing for independence. The most serious revolt against Austrian rule took place in Hungary in 1848. At that time the rebel leader, Louis Kossuth, proposed that the Hungarian kingdom of the Middle Ages be restored and ruled by the ethnic majority, the Magyars. The rebellion was brutally crushed, and it was not until Austria was weakened in the Seven Weeks' War that an opportunity for compromise developed. The result was the Dual Monarchy.

Under the Dual Monarchy the Austrian emperor, Francis Joseph I, reigned as Emperor of Austria and King of Hungary. Each country functioned independently, with its own parliament and with control over all matters except finance, foreign policy, and war. The two parts of the empire fit together well, supplying each other with needed foods and manufactured goods.

However the problems that had plagued the empire earlier soon cropped up again. Some were economic. The interests of Austria, a developing industrial nation, differed from those of Hungary, which remained primarily agricultural. Austria wanted high tariffs to protect its new manufacturers. Hungary preferred free trade and low duties.

A more serious problem for the empire was the continuing nationalist tensions that had caused the creation of the Dual Monarchy in the first place. In Austria, Germans dominated the population; in Hungary it was the Magyars. Other national minorities—the Czechs, Serbs, Croats, Romanians, and Poles—chafed under the yoke of foreign domination and sought freedom.

The Magyars Govern Hungary

After Hungary gained self-rule in 1887, it was controlled by the Magyar upper class. The Magyars ignored the poverty and other problems of the ethnic groups living in Hungary. The government insisted that there should be one national language, Magyar, or Hungarian, as it is now called. It was to be the only language used in the schools just as German was used in the Austrian portion of the empire. Since most non-Magyars could not speak Hungarian, a child belonging to another cultural group could not get an education. Speaking Hungarian and being educated were the keys to entering the bureaucracy. Furthermore, all government offices used Magyar, so that people who did not speak the language could not defend their rights. The language barrier proved to be a serious handicap for the non-Magyar population. It created resentment and helped to strengthen independence movements among the non-Magyar population of Hungary. Eventually the government did make some concessions concerning the use of native languages, but these efforts fell far short of what people wanted.

Polish Independence

Poland had been divided among Russia, Prussia, and Austria in the late 1700's, and this arrangement made it difficult for the Polish people to unite in a common independence movement. When Poles living under Russian rule revolted against the czar in 1830-1831 and again in 1863, the revolts were brutally punished. As a result, the Poles lost even more of their freedom. In both the Russian and Prussian parts of Poland, the Poles were forbidden to use their own language in official capacities. As in Hungary before the reforms, only the national language was used in schools, law courts, and government offices. All self-government was abolished. In the Russian section, many Polish rebels were sent into exile in Siberia. Many Poles fled to other countries. Because of the oppression by Russia and Prussia, there was a widespread growth of Polish nationalism and ethnic pride.

In the Austrian part of Poland, conditions were somewhat better. Poles under Austrian rule won some self-goverment by the late 1800's. In parts of the empire, the Polish and German languages were used equally. There were Polish schools, and the Polish population had privileges not enjoyed by their fellow Poles under the rule of other nations.

In the 1880's and 1890's a number of Polish political parties with different goals were organized. However, they met with little success in gaining freedom for the Poles. An independent Polish republic was not proclaimed until after World War I and the fall of the monarchies in Austria, Germany, and Russia.

Weakening of the Ottoman Empire

In the seventeenth century the empire of Ottoman Turks stretched from the north coast of Africa across southeastern Europe, westward to southern Russia, the Middle East, and western Asia. Europeans equated Turks with awesome power. But the Ottoman Empire had reached its peak. In the 1700's it was pushed back from its borders by wars and treaties. Turkish power declined as the army became corrupt and mutinous.

The Ottoman Empire included many different nationalities and religions. According to Islamic law, toleration, particularly for Christians and Jews, was encouraged. However, as state authority weakened so did protection of the rights of minorities.

At a time when modernization was taking hold in Europe, the Ottomans still operated on outdated political and economic systems. Its government was administered by officials, often corrupt, who collected such heavy taxes that whole villages were forced off the land.

In the early nineteenth century the sultan attempted major reforms. He sought advice from western Europeans and eagerly learned western ways. Though some contemporary critics felt he accomplished little, it was a start.

Following the Crimean War the Ottoman government issued an edict in 1856, calling for a wide range of reforms. Its purpose was to deal with growing nationalism. The civil authority of religious leaders was abolished. Equality before the law was guaranteed, regardless of religion. The army was opened to Muslims and Christians alike. Tax reform was begun and torture outlawed.

The spirit of this reform was encouraged by the Young Turks, a group of youthful reformers. For twenty years the empire was open to western ideas once shut out by Islamic traditions. The works of Enlightenment figures such as Montesquieu and Rousseau were translated into Turkish. Histories were written and newspapers founded.

The succession of a new sultan to power in 1876, however, signaled a reactionary era. Once his power was secure, he curtailed freedoms and brutally put down rebellions. As a result, the Ottoman Empire did not develop into a strong state that could deal with European nations on equal terms. As you will see, the result was tragic.

Early Independence Movements

Beginning in the early 1800's, dreams of independence infected the Ottoman Empire. In 1804 the first successful revolt against Turkish domination started in Serbia. During twenty years of fighting, the Turks never regained complete control over the Serbs. In 1829 the Russians joined the fight because they felt a common interest with the Serbs, who shared their Slavic nationality and Orthodox Christian religion. In the treaty settlements that followed the war, Serbia agreed to remain part of the Ottoman Empire. However, in support of their fellow Slavs, the Russians demanded that the Serbs be given the right to govern themselves. This essentially ended Ottoman control over Serbia.

This lithograph depicts a battle in the Russo-Turkish War. Why did the Russians resent the European powers who took away land the Russians had won?

The war for Greek independence in the 1820's brought renewed foreign intervention in the Balkans. Great Britain, France, and Russia came to the aid of the Greeks. The British had been drawn into the war because they feared that Russia would seize Constantinople and occupy Turkey. Russian control of the waterways would threaten Britain's vital trade routes.

The strategic importance of Turkey had long attracted Russian interests. Ships could not sail from Russian ports along the coast of the Black Sea to the Mediterranean except by passing through the Bosporus and the Dardanelles. In times of war, the Turks could close these vital waterways. As Russia came closer to achieving its long-standing ambition, the British began to support the waning Ottoman Empire to lessen Russian influence in the Balkans.

A Clash of Interests

In the second half of the nineteenth century, Pan-Slavism threatened to unsettle the fragile balance of power in Europe and trigger a widespread war. In 1875 rebellion against the Turks broke out in Bosnia and Herzegovina. It was followed in 1876 by an insurrection in Bulgaria that was viciously put down. Within a year, Russia had entered the war against Turkey. Under the mantle of Pan-Slavism, the Russian czars were renewing their drive for access to the Mediterranean.

Advancing rapidly, the Russian army reached Constantinople before the Turkish sultan made peace. By the Treaty of San Stefano, Russia acquired territory east of the Black Sea. Serbia and Rumania became independent and Bulgaria was enlarged and extended south to the Aegean Sea.

Neither Great Britain nor Austria could accept these terms. Great Britain's interest in the Balkans had paralleled its expansion in the Near East and India. The vital Suez Canal, opened in 1869, was on Ottoman territory. Austria also viewed the Balkans as important to their survival. Threat of war loomed, and Bismarck invited the great powers to Berlin for a Congress to readjust the terms of the treaty. He claimed his role was that of an "honest broker," with no ambition but peace.

At the Congress of Berlin, peace was achieved, but the cost was greater than anyone at the time realized. The dreams of the Balkan nationalists and

Russians were not satisfied. The British, who had not fired a shot, were given Cyprus. This dismayed the Greeks, who had hoped that they would fall heir to it as Turkey collapsed. Serbia was granted independence, but Bosnia, which it wanted, was given as a protectorate to Austria-Hungary. This was to balance Russian influence in the Balkans. Rumania and Montenegro won their independence. Bulgaria was divided into three regions with varying degrees of autonomy. Each was to manage its own affairs but remain nominally under the rule of the Turks.

Faced by a union of the major powers and exhausted by the war, Russia agreed to the arrangements made by the Congress of Berlin. The limits on Bulgarian independence did not last long. In 1885, in spite of Turkish opposition, the regions were combined into the new nation of Bulgaria. The Bulgarians chose a German noble to rule as their first king, and he used the title "czar" in imitation of the Russian monarchs.

SECTION REVIEW

1. Use the map on page 484 to identify the nationalities in the Austro-Hungarian, Ottoman, and Russian empires.
2. In your own words, briefly define or identify: Magyar, Francis Joseph I, Pan-Slavism, Treaty of San Stefano, Congress of Berlin.
3. After the Hungarians won their independence from Austria, how did they treat the non-Magyar people in their nation?
■ The Pan-Slavic movement united the Slavic peoples of eastern Europe in a common cause. What common movements for independence have occurred in recent years?

THE JEWS IN EUROPE

During the nineteenth century the Jews made uneven progress toward equal rights throughout Europe. The move was generally toward assimilation. The idea that legal restrictions against Jews should be abolished took hold—largely as a result of ideas of the Enlightenment, the American and French revolutions, and liberal thinkers.

Toward the end of the century two trends developed in response to Jewish assimilation in Europe. One was an increase in anti-Jewish feeling, or **anti-Semitism.** Realizing that this represented a growing threat to their existence in Europe, some Jews began to promote the establishment of a separate national Jewish state. This movement was called **Zionism.**

Napoleon and the Jews

Freedom of religion for Jews was accepted in France at the time of the French Revolution. It was based on principles of religious toleration and separation of Church and State. The Declaration of the Rights of Man stated, "No man should be molested for his beliefs, including religious beliefs, provided that their manifestation does not disturb the public order. . . ." The result of equality, or emancipation, was that the Jews looked forward to an increasing role in European society.

The price exacted by Napoleon for Jewish emancipation was high. Napoleon considered the Jews a nation, not a religion. He sought to reform the Jews and end their enforced segregation so they would blend into society. To him, Jewish community life conflicted with the aims of the state.

Napoleon's armies carried the ideas of Jewish emancipation throughout Europe. In Italy they broke down the walls of the **ghettos,** areas to which Jews were restricted. In the parts of Germany incorporated into France or under French influence, civil rights were extended to Jews.

In Poland and Prussia, Jews began to enjoy the advantages of emancipation. They were, to a greater or lesser degree, able to participate in government and become officers in the army.

After Napoleon's defeat, a reaction against the Jews set in where French laws had been imposed on conquered people. In Italy and some German cities, Jews were returned to ghettos. In other German cities, Jews were expelled entirely. A discussion of the "Jewish question" was taken up by the Germanic Federation at the Congress of Vienna. It was decided to leave the decision of how to treat the Jews up to the individual German states. Only Prussia recognized Jewish freedom.

The Jews in Western Europe

As you have read, France and England made progress toward democratic governments during the nineteenth century. This progress gradually included the rights of Jews.

After the Revolution of 1830 in France, the Jewish religion was put on equal footing with Christian religions. Rabbis, like Catholic priests and Protestant ministers, received salaries from the government. The last remnant of discriminatory law was abolished in 1846 with the removal of a special Jewish oath in law courts. From then on, there were no laws that singled out the Jews as different from others in France.

Although in theory Jews born in England were citizens, in practice they lacked equal rights. The basis of the discrimination was the requirement of an oath to get a university degree, buy certain property, engage in some businesses, and, in some cases, to vote. No Jew could swear "by the true faith of a Christian."

For years bills were introduced into Parliament to wipe out restrictions on Jews. For years they were defeated. Gradually, though, the restrictions were eliminated piecemeal. Laws were passed allowing those wishing to engage in trade in London to take the required oath in a way that would not offend their religion. In 1837, University College was opened to Jews and, by 1871, Cambridge and Oxford. But the last major obstacle was overcome in 1858 when it became possible for a Jew to sit as a member of the House of Commons.

The Jews in Eastern Europe

The Jews in eastern Europe were less successful in obtaining their rights. For centuries the largest Jewish population was in Poland. After the partition of Poland in the late eighteenth century, Jews came under the jurisdiction of Prussia, Austria, and Russia. For the Jews this was generally a change for the worse.

After the Congress of Vienna, feelings of reaction affected eastern Europe. There was an outbreak of sentiment against the Jews as aliens. The German people viewed themselves as possessing a "German spirit," based on traditions of the past. To them, the Jews did not belong. Publications denounced the Jewish demand for citizenship. It was not until 1869, under Bismarck, that a law was passed in Germany ending restrictions based on religion. In Austria Jewish emancipation was achieved by a new constitution in 1867.

The partition of Poland had given Russia the largest Jewish population in Europe. In 1791 Catherine II, the Russian monarch, forbade Jews to join merchant or artisan guilds in certain provinces. To force Jews out of ordinary life in the Russian empire, the Pale of Settlement was established. Jews were ordered by the Russian government to leave their towns and communities to be resettled and confined in the Pale. The Russians also tried to prevent Jews from practicing their religion. Beginning in the early 1800's, Jewish children were sometimes taken from their families to special schools to be reared as Christians.

Nicholas I became czar in 1825. His policies were oppressive to all the minorities living in Russian lands. To break down the solidarity of these ethnic groups, he drafted large numbers of minorities into the army. These recruits were taken far from their villages for training to weaken their ties with their people. Jews in the army were forced to serve for twenty-five years. To Nicholas the Jews, with their beliefs and customs, were a people who would never be assimilated into Russian society.

The growth of Pan-Slavism, later in the century, brought renewed trouble to the Jews in eastern Europe. In 1881, when the more liberal Czar Alexander II was assassinated, his son Alexander III ascended the throne. Alexander III's prejudices were like those of his grandfather Nicholas. Surrounded with Pan-Slavic advisers, he tried to keep the western idea of liberalism out of Russia. A series of riots against the Jews were carried out under the direction of the central government. These attacks, called **pogroms** (POE-grams), spread throughout the cities and villages of Russia, and thousands of Jews were attacked and killed. The Pale of Settlement was narrowed even further to crowd the Jews out of Russian life. Legal and economic restrictions and military obligations were intensified, bringing even more pressure on the Jewish settlements. To escape the harsh treatment, millions emigrated. Most came to the United States, more than 100,000 in 1891 alone.

This synagogue in Pinczow, Poland, was the center of community life. Why did Jews in eastern Europe form close knit communities?

Anti-Semitism and Zionism

Toward the end of the nineteenth century, when it appeared that the "Jewish question" was settled in most of Europe, a new wave of anti-Jewish feeling broke out. Anti-Semitism emerged from a narrow interpretation of nationalism. In France it was evident in the Dreyfus Affair. In Germany, as the Conservative party gained control in the 1880's, there was a marked increase in discrimination. Jews were once more banned from public office and promotions. Prejudice kept Jews from obtaining posts in universities.

At about the same time, strong anti-Semitism emerged in Austria, particularly in Vienna. The mayor of Vienna, Karl Lueger, was fiercely anti-Semitic and he promoted anti-Jewish regulations. In time the anti-Semitic political parties began to wane, but the ideas they had spread did not.

The pogroms in Russia and the renewal of anti-Semitism revived an old dream among certain Jews, the idea of a "promised land." Theodor Herzl, a Viennese Jew horrified by conditions in Europe, came to believe that assimilation of Jews into European culture was no longer possible. Herzl conceived of a return to Zion, or Palestine, where the Jewish people had originated thousands of years earlier. He gained as allies some wealthy French Jews, who had been appalled by the anti-Semitism displayed in the recent Dreyfus affair.

Many Jews already lived in the Middle East. Although Muslims allowed Jews and Christians to live among them, they restricted their religious rights. The first wave of immigrants entered Palestine in 1882. This was the beginning of the Zionist movement.

SECTION REVIEW

1. In your own words, briefly identify: anti-Semitism, ghettos, Pale of Settlement, pogroms.
2. How did the emancipation of the Jews develop in France?
3. What steps did Catherine II of Russia use to restrict Jewish life?
■ What solution to anti-Semitism did some Jews initiate in the late 1800's? What are the results today of this solution?

RUSSIA IN THE NINETEENTH CENTURY

In the nineteenth century the Industrial Revolution brought tremendous change to the societies and economies of western Europe and the United States. In western Europe the burgeoning middle class challenged the old aristocracy for power and influence. Russia, however, was still locked in its traditional and feudal agricultural society. The nobility, comprising one percent of the population, ruled over the peasants. An elite group of nobles owned about one-third of the land. The remainder was owned by the state and administered by lesser nobles. As a result, the aristocracy supported the czar's power and the czar's power was absolute. This pattern resulted in abuse of the peasants and caused deep-seated resentments.

The Need for Reform

Alexander I became czar in 1801 upon the murder of his father by political enemies. During Alexander's reign, victory over France and the defeat of Napoleon brought glory to the Russian Empire. In his early career, the czar became popular in many parts of western Europe. Within Russia, he toyed with the idea of reform but was unwilling or unable to change existing institutions. He made some mild reforms of serfdom, but hesitated to carry out measures that would disturb the status quo. As time went on, Alexander moved from liberalism to conservatism. At the Congress of Vienna he became a supporter of the Austrian statesman, Metternich. In the last ten years of his reign, Alexander instituted a hated system of military colonies. Entire farming communities were drafted into the army. When they were not training nor fighting, they continued to live and work under military discipline. These measures, and a lack of reform, spread discontent.

One source of unrest was the advent of new ideas from western Europe. Russian officers, many from the minor nobility, had contact with France during and after the Napoleonic wars. They were convinced that reforms should be made so that Russians might enjoy the freedom and rights enjoyed by western Europeans. Their goals were varied. Some wanted a constitutional monarchy and others longed for a republic. Some believed there should be full emancipation of the serfs. These officers formed secret organizations devoted to bringing about these reforms in Russia.

The Decembrist Revolt

When Alexander I died in 1825, the throne passed to his brother, Nicholas I. With the change in the monarch, the leaders of the secret organizations inside Russia saw an opportunity to revolt. Inspired by romanticism instead of realism, they were eloquent, but poorly organized. They had little support from the people, except for a few of the troops in the capital, St. Petersburg. The rebels had acted hastily and were soon put down by troops loyal to Nicholas. The leaders of the revolt were executed or exiled to Siberia. Because this attempted revolution had taken place in December, the unsuccessful rebels were called Decembrists.

Instead of reform, the Decembrist Revolt brought on the ruthless suppression of freedoms. To make sure there would be no future rebellion, Czar Nicholas instituted massive repression. The army was strengthened, and restive peasants were quickly suppressed. Nicholas established a secret police to locate the enemies of the government. Many were sent to Siberian exile, including the novelist Feodor M. Dostoevski, who wrote of his experiences in *The House of the Dead.* Controls over the press and speech were tightened since Nicholas blamed the Decembrist revolt on "harmful" ideas. A network of spies and informers reported any subversive activity to the czar.

RUSSIAN EXPANSION FROM THE 17TH TO THE 19TH CENTURY

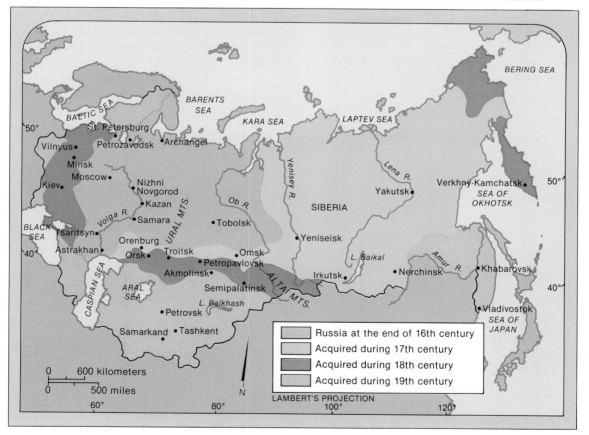

How do you think that Russian expansion affected its relationship with other countries? Why was Vladivostok important to the Russians?

Under these conditions of absolutism, there was little hope for change in Russia. Nicholas established a huge bureaucracy for keeping order and directing the lives of the people. Many who favored change decided to leave Russia rather than risk punishment for their beliefs. Others, like the writer Nicholas V. Gogol (GAW-gull), satirized the tyranny and corruption of government officials and Russian society in works such as *The Inspector General* and *Dead Souls*.

The Crimean War

Nicholas I wanted to expand the already vast territory of Russia. He wished to protect the Orthodox Christians in the Balkans and extend Russian influence over the declining Ottoman Empire. When war threatened to break out between Russia and Turkey in 1853, Great Britain and France sided with the Turks. This resulted in the Crimean War with the French, British, Piedmontese, and Turks fighting against the Russians.

Most of the war was fought in the Crimean peninsula in southern Russia on the Black Sea. The war was badly conducted on all sides. Without any allies, Russia was at a severe disadvantage. In the midst of the conflict, Nicholas died.

Nicholas I's son, Czar Alexander II, who ruled from 1855 to 1881, quickly made peace and ended the Crimean War. He recognized that the war had seriously weakened Russia.

Reforms of Alexander II

After years of repression at home and the failure of Russia's foreign policy, public support for reform began to develop. It was encouraged by writers such as Ivan Turgenev, who depicted the hardships of the serfs' lives in *A Sportsman's Sketches*. A year after becoming czar, Alexander issued a manifesto that called for important changes in education, justice, and employment. Alexander's efforts met with mixed results.

Alexander II urged his nobles to emancipate their serfs. When they were slow to do so, the czar decreed, in 1861, that the serfs were free. By this edict, forty-seven million people, out of a total population of seventy-four million, were suddenly liberated. Alexander also granted them legal rights and allowed village communes to purchase farmland. The peasants had to pay for the land over a forty-nine-year period.

The emancipation of the peasants created problems. The former serfs were seldom able to buy

The coronation of Alexander II in 1855 marked the beginning of a period of reform. Why do you think his assassination in 1881 brought a return to repression?

SOURCES

Memoirs of a Revolutionist

In the late 1860's, young people of wealthy Russian families banded together to form the populist movement. Their primary goal, represented by the slogan "Go to the people," was to establish an egalitarian peasant society in Russia. According to these revolutionaries, the peasants were Russia's only hope, since they were the only members of society not affected by the evils of the czarist regime. Prince Peter Kropotkin (kruh-PAWT-kin) was one young aristocrat who abandoned his royal title for the populist cause. In the following selection, Kropotkin describes how the populist movement developed in Russia.

All Russia read with astonishment of the indictment that was produced at the trial of Karakozov and his friends, that these young men used to live three or four in the same room. They never spent more than five dollars each a month for all their needs, and at the same time gave their fortunes to the poor. Five years later, thousands and thousands of the best of Russian youth—the best part of it— were doing the same. Their password was "V Narod!" ["Go to the people" or "Be the people."]

During the years 1860–1865, in nearly every wealthy family a bitter struggle was going on between the fathers, who wanted to maintain the old traditions, and the sons and daughters, who defended their right to do with their lives according to their own ideals. Young men left the military service, the counter, and the shop, and flocked to the university towns. Girls, bred in the most noble families, rushed penniless to St. Petersburg, Moscow, and Kiev, eager to learn a profession that would free them from their parents and, some day perhaps, also from the possible yoke of a husband. After hard and bitter struggles, many of them won that personal freedom.

Now they wanted to utilize it, not for their own personal enjoyment, but for carrying to the peasants the knowledge that had emancipated them. . . .

The aim of all reading and discussion was to solve the great question that rose before them. In what way could they be useful to the masses? Gradually, they came to the idea that the only way was to settle amongst the peasants, and to live the peasant's life. Young men went into the villages as doctors, doctor's helpers, teachers, village scribes, even as agricultural laborers, blacksmiths, woodcutters, and so on, and tried to live there in close contact with the peasants. Girls passed teachers' examinations, learned nursing, and went by the hundreds into the villages, devoting themselves entirely to the poorest part of the population. . . .

These people wanted to teach the mass of the peasants to read, to instruct them in other things, to give them medical help, and in any way to aid in raising them from their darkness and misery, and to learn at the same time what were their popular ideals of a better society.

Source: Adapted from James Allen Rogers, editor, *Memoirs of a Revolutionist*, by Peter Kropotkin. Copyright by Peter Smith, Publisher, Inc.

1. According to Kropotkin, how did the populists plan to change Russia?
2. Describe the personal and family background of the young people who became populists. Why do you think they were attracted to this revolutionary movement?
3. Do you know of any young people in your society who have left their families and changed their way of life for a particular cause? Why do you think they did so? Do you agree or disagree with their actions? Explain.

enough land to support themselves. Those who did purchase land were unable to pay for it. They were still under the control of their mir, or village commune. The edict of 1861 had given important responsibilities to the mirs. Villages had the legal right to determine how farmlands might be used, to collect taxes, and even to prevent peasants from moving away. Even if peasants left their village, they had to continue to pay taxes.

Freeing the serfs was not Alexander's only reform. During his rule, he westernized the Russian legal system and introduced trial by jury. Education became available to more people as the number of primary schools increased, and secondary schools and universities were added to the system. Alexander also modernized the army and abolished the twenty-five-year tours of duty. Elected governing bodies were created for towns, cities, and counties. Political freedom was still limited, however, because the czar refused to permit any sort of national parliament.

Demands for Change in Russia

Each reform that Alexander undertook uncovered more problems. As a result, the government became cautious, then conservative. After a brief attempt at rebellion in Poland in 1863, repression began again. A number of different groups de-manded further changes. Their ideas, aims, and ways of achieving their goals differed. Some insisted that reform must come from the czar, but without any changes in the economic or political systems of the country. This group was made up chiefly of members of the upper class. Another group, the liberals, consisted mainly of the middle class. Influenced by Pan-Slavism, they believed in Russia's special destiny and wanted citizens like themselves to have a greater share in governing the country.

The most influential of the groups was the **intelligentsia** (in-tell-uh-JENT-see-uh). The term at first referred to young, well-educated, radical reformers. Later it included anyone of any class who sought progressive reform.

Some radicals emphasized the need to destroy Russia's existing political and economic structure by any means, no matter how violent. Only by starting over completely could Russia be reformed. Many young educated Russians held this attitude, termed nihilism in Turgenev's novel *Fathers and Sons*. They joined the "To the People" movement and went to live and spread their political ideas among the peasants. But the peasants, to whom they promised so much, turned their backs on the young revolutionaries. In many cases they handed the rebels over to the secret police.

Compare this photo of Russian serfs with the picture of Alexander's coronation on page 492. What do they reveal about Russian society?

Some revolutionaries began a series of assassinations. The czar himself was a target and, after many attempts, Alexander II was murdered in 1881. The assassins were highly trained members of a band of young revolutionaries called The People's Will. The new czar had the murderers executed and destroyed their organization.

Alexander III

The murder of Alexander II convinced the new czar, Alexander III, that permitting reforms or any sort of change had been a terrible mistake. He and some of his advisers believed that western ideas such as democracy, constitutions, elections, freedom of speech, and freedom of the press were dangerous. The government tried to stamp out the revolutionaries and to silence anyone who proposed reform or political change.

The clock was turned back in Russia. During the 1880's and 1890's conditions were not very different from those in the days of Czar Nicholas I. Many of the reforms of Alexander II were abolished. In their place, Alexander III instituted harsh new measures. Political parties and labor unions were forbidden. The religious persecution of the Jewish population intensified. Newspapers and books were not permitted to criticize the government or to suggest political reform. The secret police spied on people and reported to the czar everything that was said or done. In effect, Alexander III shut the lid on liberalism, due process, civil liberties, and the free exchange or ideas.

Russian Expansion

While conditions at home worsened, Russia continued to expand its territory. The Caucasus and the desert area in central Asia beyond the Caspian Sea were both added to Russia's empire in the mid-1800's.

In the 1700's Russia had claimed Alaska as a territory. However, because Alaska was so far from Russia that control was difficult, it was sold to the United States in 1867 for just over $7 million. From the mid-1800's the Russians also were interested in exploring and settling Siberia, along the coast of the Pacific Ocean. In the 1850's they took some territory from China. Since China had recently been defeated in wars with Great Britain and France, Russia had little difficulty in forcing the weakened Chinese to give up lands north of the Amur River and along the Pacific coast. The Russians made these lands their own. At the southern end of the territory they founded the port city of Vladivostok. By the end of the 1800's, Vladivostok had become very important. To link its empire together the Russians began to build a railroad across Siberia in 1891, to connect Vladivostok with the European part of Russia.

Russia Struggles to Catch Up

By that time there was a great interest in developing Russia's trade and manufacturing. Russia had always been an agricultural country. Its failure to develop a large middle class is viewed as one reason why its political development differed so sharply from that of western countries. This lack of a middle class also affected the development of large-scale industry. Without earlier experience in small-scale entrepreneurship, Russians were not able to develop industries on a level comparable to those in western Europe. Russia turned to foreign capital and management to finance and develop industries in coal, iron, timber, oil, and cotton. The result was a surge in Russian industrialization in the late nineteenth century. Many Russians hoped that their country one day might catch up with industrial giants such as Great Britain and Germany.

SECTION REVIEW

1. Mapping: Use the map on page 491 to list the territories added to Russia in the 1700's and in the second half of the 1800's.
2. In your own words, briefly define or identify: Alexander I, Decembrist, Nicholas I, Alexander II, nihilism, Vladivostok.
3. What reforms were made by Alexander II?
4. In what ways did Russia in the 1880's and 1890's resemble Russia during the days of Nicholas I?
■ The Russian czars turned to repression and censorship to put down ideas they found threatening. What examples can you describe of similar action taken by some present-day rulers?

Reviewing the Chapter

Chapter Summary

In the second half of the 1800's, the forces of liberalism and nationalism changed existing governments and territories in much of continental Europe. Through the leadership of Mazzini, Cavour, and Garibaldi, Italy was united by 1870 under the Sardinian king, Victor Emmanuel II.

In the German states the Prussian prime minister, Otto von Bismarck, seized the opportunity, through three wars, to form a unified Germany. The first monarch of the new Germany was Kaiser William I. As his chancellor, Bismarck strengthened the army and navy, encouraged trade, and established centralized monetary and banking systems. In domestic affairs, he attacked liberals, Catholics, and socialists, then was forced to grant many liberal social reforms to gain support for his policies. Bismarck helped Germany grow strong and prosperous until 1890, when he was dismissed by the new kaiser.

In eastern Europe, nationalist feelings led subject peoples in the Austrian and Ottoman empires to try to win their independence. In 1867 the formation of the Dual Monarchy made Hungary independent. Minorities chafed under German domination, and Polish rebels were suppressed. The Ottoman Empire was slowly eroded by war and rebellion.

The Russian people, throughout the 1800's, were at the mercy of the czars, who alternated between brief periods of political reform and extended periods of repression and despotism. Jews in Russia were subject to the most harsh restrictions. They were denied certain trades and professions, and forced to crowd into the Pale of Settlement. By the end of the century millions had emigrated, seeking freedom from oppression.

1. How did Bismarck mold the new German nation?
2. What situations created tensions in eastern Europe?
3. How did Russia exemplify an autocratic state in the nineteenth century?

Using Your Vocabulary

1. How did the nationalism of political realists differ from idealistic nationalism?
2. How was the *Risorgimento* related to Italian unification?
3. What was the outcome of plebiscites held in the Italian states?
4. Why was irredentism destined to cause further unrest in Trieste, Nice, and Savoy?
5. What needs of the Junkers led to the establishment of the Zollverein?
6. In your own words define realpolitik. Contrast realpolitik with idealism.
7. How did the formation of the Dual Monarchy earn the title Ausgleich?
8. Explain the meaning of indemnity.
9. How did the Bundesrat differ from the Reichstag?
10. What is the meaning of Kulturkampf? What form did the Kulturkampf take in Germany?
11. How were Pan-Slavism and anti-Semitism both examples of extreme nationalism? How were they both related to pogroms?
12. How did the intelligentsia pose a threat to the czar?
13. Why was nihilism in Russia considered a radical theory?

Developing Your Geography Skills

1. Use the map on page 474 to explain how the shape of Italy hindered the unification of the Italian kingdoms.
2. Use the map on page 491 to explain why a warm-water port was an important goal of Russian expansion?
3. Use the Atlas maps on pages 754 and 756 to locate three key waterways in the Mediterranean Sea. Why is each important?

4. Compare the maps on pages 477 and 634. What present-day nations are located on land that was part of the German Empire in 1871?
5. Use the map on page 491 to determine how many miles would be covered by a transcontinental railroad across Russia from Vladivostok to St. Petersburg. (Do not cross Chinese territory in calculating distance.)

Recalling the Facts

1. Compare the contributions of Mazzini, Garibaldi, and Cavour to Italian unification.
2. What role did Sardinia play in the unification of Italy?
3. How did Napoleon III foster the unification of Italy?
4. What steps were taken by William I to consolidate Prussian influence in the German Confederation?
5. How did Bismarck overcome liberal opposition to the expansion of the Prussian army?
6. Why did Napoleon III fear the unification of Germany?
7. What was the cause of the Franco-Prussian War? What were the terms of the Treaty of Frankfurt ending the war?
8. Describe the economic development of Germany after its unification.
9. How had Germany attained the world's most advanced social security system by the late 1800's?
10. Describe the oppressive conditions under which Poles lived in the Russian and Prussian parts of Poland.
11. What was the outcome of the Congress of Berlin? Why was it unsatisfactory to the Russian and Balkan nationalists?
12. How did European Jews in the late 1800's respond to anti-Semitic attitudes and physical oppression?
13. What reforms were instituted in Russia by Czar Alexander II?
14. What were the goals of Russian expansion in the 1800's?
15. How and why did Russia fail to develop in the same manner as the western democracies in the 1800's?

Essay Questions

1. Explain how nationalism can be a force for both good and evil.
2. Why has Mazzini been called "the soul," Garibaldi "the sword," and Cavour "the brains" of Italian unification?
3. What factors contributed to the rise of nationalism in Europe in the 1800's?
4. Compare the role of Cavour in the unification of Italy to that of Bismarck in the unification of Germany.
5. How was Austria used as a pawn in the unification of both Italy and Germany?
6. Contrast the progress made toward equal rights in the 1800's by Jews in western and eastern Europe.
7. How did the major powers in Europe respond to the independence movements in Serbia and Greece? Why did they respond as they did?
8. How did efforts to maintain a balance of power in Europe affect the foreign policies of France and Great Britain in the 1800's?

Critical Thinking

1. As Bismarck gained power in Germany, he was often at odds with people who had different views about the nature of government in Germany. Explain which group in Germany valued universal manhood suffrage and representative government. Who valued military strength? Who valued labor reform laws? How can a society deal with groups with different values?
2. After the assassination of Czar Alexander II, Alexander III returned to the repressive measures of Nicholas I. On what basis do historians make their claim that Nicholas I and Alexander II considered liberal ideas dangerous? Do you consider this a warranted or unwarranted claim?
3. In *Memoirs of a Revolutionist,* Kropotkin describes the populist movement in Russia. Is the book a primary or secondary source? What seems to be the purpose of Kropotkin's work, to inform or to persuade? How might you test the reliability of Kropotkin's information?

CHAPTER ·22·

DEVELOPMENTS OUTSIDE EUROPE

1640–1900

Objectives

- *To compare and contrast the Latin American independence movements*

- *To discuss how China flourished in the eighteenth century but then fell victim to the West*

- *To explain how Japan ended its long isolation and learned to modernize in western fashion*

- *To discuss the United States' achievement in the nineteenth century*

*C*ontacts between the East and West were sporadic in ancient times. By the twelfth and thirteenth century European and Chinese travelers visited each others' lands. By the late Middle Ages regular trade routes reached from western Europe to Japan and the East Indies. But these contacts were not always sustained. In the seventeenth century Japan cut itself off from the rest of the world. China, a dominant force in Asia in the eighteenth century, was still a mystery to the West even though it was a major supplier of porcelain, silks, fine furniture, and tea. Only the United States and Latin America can be said to have been within the European orbit.

By the third quarter of the nineteenth century all this changed. The industrial revolution, which began in Great Britain and spread to the Continent and to the United States, unleashed a power that changed international relations. Expansion of the use of the steamship, the telegraph, and the railroad brought the whole world closer together. Modern warfare, perfected by the West, suppressed societies unable to master its techniques.

The eighteenth century proved to be the end of Chinese and Japanese late feudal civilizations. What China would learn from its contact with the West was that it had failed to industrialize fast enough. What Japan would learn was not to make China's mistake.

In the nineteenth century the world's economy became unified. The goods, money, and services a country produced were now part of a global system. Economic changes in one corner of the world triggered changes around the world. The discovery of gold in California in 1848, for example, was an event that had immediate impact on the economies of Europe and the politics of Japan. Cotton prices in the American South during the Civil War not only affected British textile workers, but also the cotton growers in India and Egypt. Indian and Egyptian growers rushed to fill the demand for a crop made scarce by war.

The globe was now intricately connected. Only in the nineteenth century can we truly begin to speak of the history of an interdependent world.

THE EMANCIPATION OF LATIN AMERICA

Soon after the American and French revolutions, South Americans began to strive for independence. Enlightenment ideas inspired the colonial patriots to seek freedom and a democratic government. The revolutionary documents—the Declaration of Independence and the Declaration of the Rights of Man—proclaimed that people should have a say in how they were governed. Fearing unrest in its colonies, Spain tried to put down the spirit of freedom.

Roots of Revolution

The Latin American independence movement was begun by upper-class creoles, people of European descent who had been born in the colonies. Many creole families were well to do. They resented the authority of the **peninsulares** (pay-neen-soo-LAH-race), the European officials born in the Iberian peninsula who held the government posts and directed colonial policy. The mestizos, those of mixed white and Indian blood, remained below the creoles on the social scale. The Indians and the African slaves were the lowest members of society. As in Europe and North America the independence movements did not end social inequality.

Three countries—the United States, Great Britain, and France—had a major impact on Latin America. The American Revolution showed that freedom could be won militarily. The French Revolution spread the ideals of democracy and served as a fountain of new ideas. Furthermore, Britain promoted Latin American independence. Engaged

as it was in its first industrial revolution, Britain wanted new markets for its manufactured goods. Britain valued dealing directly with independent countries and their businesspeople rather than with the bureaucrats of giant antique empires. The British provided the colonists with money and goods and supported national liberation movements.

Haiti

The first successful American revolution outside the United States occurred in Haiti, the western part of the sugar-rich Caribbean island of Hispaniola, then under French control. Inspired by events in France, the slaveowners demanded greater freedom. They wanted to do what they liked with their property (human or otherwise). The large black slave community also wanted freedom. In 1791 it revolted openly. Out of the rebellion rose a leader, Francois Dominique Toussaint L'Ouverture, the grandson of an African brought to the island. By 1795 he became the colony's virtual governor.

After Napoleon assumed power in France, he tried to reassert French control by sending 40,000 troops to Haiti. Toussaint tried to negotiate a settlement, but was seized and shipped to France where he died in prison. When yellow fever swept away thousands of the French troops, a group of former slaves, supported by the British, drove the French out. In 1804 Haiti declared its independence.

Haiti's slave revolt was the first and only successful slave revolt in Latin America. News of its bloody course terrified slaveowners throughout the hemisphere. For the United States it was important in another way, as well. Events in Haiti motivated Napoleon to sell the Louisiana territory.

Causes and Characteristics of Independence

The immediate trigger of Latin American independence was Napoleon's invasion of the Iberian peninsula. When the Emperor placed his elder brother Joseph on the Spanish throne in 1808, the Spanish people rebelled. It was the broadest popular uprising anywhere in Europe during that era. While Spain was divided by the chaos of warfare, its

NEW NATIONS OF LATIN AMERICA, 1825

Compare the insert map of European colonies about 1790 with the map of Latin
American nations in 1825. What changes had already begun to occur? How does the
map of Latin America in 1825 compare with a current map?

empire in America was lost by default. The Latin Americans revolted against Napoleon, not against the deposed Spanish king, Fernando VII, whom they considered the legitimate ruler of Spain.

Unlike the American Revolution, the South American struggle covered a vast continent and lasted four times as long. The Spanish colonists had no unified leadership—no Continental Congress—with a single strategy against the enemy. Rather, it was fought on a regional basis by regional interests. The rebels were separated by giant mountain chains, dense jungles, and sprawling plains.

The thirteen English colonies had united after victory to form the United States. In Latin America there was no such union. Spanish America was divided by what Simón Bolívar described in 1815 as "extremes of climate, geographical differences, opposed interests and distinct characteristics."

Mexico and Central America

The war in Spain had immediate results in Mexico. Father Miguel Hidalgo sought the distribution of land to Indians and peasants. Thousands of the poor joined his cause, which developed beyond his control. In their march to Mexico City, Hidalgo's forces resembled an unruly mob. They murdered and robbed Spaniards and creoles alike. A royalist army defeated the rebels, and Hidalgo was shot by a firing squad in 1811.

The peasant movement did not die. The fight was continued by one of Hidalgo's former pupils, the mestizo priest, José María Morelos. Morelos called for a meeting of a congress of rebels. The rebels suggested a revolutionary social and agricultural program. But in 1815 the movement was defeated and Morelos, like Hidalgo, was executed. Mexican independence would not be won by social revolution.

Again the impact of events in Spain was felt in 1814, when Ferdinand VII was restored to his throne. Like many European monarchs in the age of Metternich, Ferdinand was a reactionary. He persecuted Spanish liberals, even those who had fought for him against the Bonapartes. Mexican patriots called for independence with greater fervor. In Spain the army rose up and imposed a liberal constitution limiting the powers of the king. Mexico's wealthy conservatives allied with the liberal creoles and mestizos. They feared that Spain

might impose its liberal constitution on them.

In 1821 a creole general, Agustín de Iturbide (ee-tyoor-BEE-thay), took control of the rebel army. Under pressure, the Mexican congress made him emperor. Soon after, he was overthrown. In 1824 Mexico became a republic.

During his short reign Iturbide annexed all of Central America, stretching to what is now modern Panama. After his fall the area separated to form its own confederation. This union lasted until the 1830's when it broke up into Guatemala, Honduras, El Salvador, Nicaragua, and Costa Rica.

Spanish South America

The man most closely associated with the independence of South America is Simón Bolívar. Bolívar was born in Caracas (kah-RAH-kas) to a wealthy creole family. He was educated in French thought, notably the ideas of Jean-Jacques Rousseau. He traveled to Europe and in Rome, in 1806, made his vow to free America "from the tyrants' yoke."

After leading several unsuccessful revolts in Caracas, Bolívar planned a bold new strategy. Instead of attacking the Spanish in the north, by sea, he decided to attack from the south. Bolívar and his army crossed the Andes through icy rains and over rugged terrain. In 1819 he won a decisive victory that toppled New Granada and created the state of Great Colombia. Bolívar was made president and granted wide powers. Henceforth he would be known as The Liberator.

During Bolívar's unsuccessful campaigns in the north, a creole-led revolt broke out in Buenos Aires in May 1810. The Spanish did not attempt to take back control. The independence of the United Provinces of La Plata (later Argentina) was declared in 1816.

It was obvious, however, that permanent independence was threatened by those loyal to the Spanish king. To prevent a royalist backlash, the Argentine's José San Martín organized an army to cross the Andes into Chile. San Martín disciplined his troops in the highest standards of the European military. Dragging artillery hundreds of miles over mountain trails at an altitude of 12,000 feet (3,650 meters), San Martín's forces made a spectacular crossing. In a surprise attack they vanquished the royalists in Chile in 1818.

British and American merchants financed and

How do you think the climate and terrain of the Andes tested Simón Bolívar's determination?

supplied a navy to carry San Martín's army to Peru, where it captured the major royalist city of Lima in 1821. Bolívar then led the drive to free the rest of Peru. With this accomplished, in 1825 Upper Peru separated, to become the republic of Bolivia. It was named in Bolívar's honor.

San Martín made no attempt to challenge Bolívar's leadership. Rather than endanger the independence movement in a clash with Bolívar, he went into exile. He died in France.

Brazil

In sharp contrast to the violence in Spanish America, Brazil made its transition to independence peacefully. Again, it was Napoleon's invasion of the Iberian peninsula that started things off.

With the help of the British navy, Portugal's regent John VI and the entire Portuguese court of 15,000 were evacuated from Lisbon two days before French troops entered the city. They arrived in Brazil in the winter of 1808. The result of this unusual event was the transfer of imperial authority from the old world to the new. Overnight the colonial town of Rio de Janeiro was turned into the capital of the Portuguese Empire. In 1816 John VI granted Brazil equal status with Portugal.

In 1821, when events in Portugal demanded that John VI return home or risk losing his throne, he left his son Pedro as regent in Brazil. But when it appeared that Portugal threatened to return Brazil to its colonial status, Brazilian patriots reacted. In 1822 Pedro I became emperor of a new, independent country with its own constitution.

Recognition of Independence

In the early 1820's both Britain and the United States were quick to recognize the new republics. However, in Europe at this time reactionary policies were gaining influence. In 1823 a French army smashed the liberal movement in Spain and restored Ferdinand to his throne. British and American diplomats feared that European reactionaries might do the same in Latin America.

Secretary of State John Quincy Adams seized the moment and drafted the Monroe Doctrine. Proclaimed by President Monroe in December 1823, it proposed the following principles: The United States would not intervene in European affairs nor would it challenge the existing colonies of the European powers. At the same time, the United States would not allow any European power to recolonize any independent American country nor establish new ones in the Western Hemisphere. Furthermore, it would interpret any action in this direction as an unfriendly move against the United States. Although the Monroe Doctrine had little impact on events of the period, the European powers realized all too well what stood behind it—British naval supremacy.

Internal Problems

Only two jewels remained in the Spanish colonial empire in America—Cuba and Puerto Rico. In only a few years most of the countries of modern-day Latin America had emerged. Yet even before Bolívar's death in 1830, Great Colombia was breaking up and, years before, Paraguay had declared a separate independence from the United

Provinces of La Plata. Rivalries and political conflict seemed to be pointing to a stormy future. Freedom had not changed the makeup of Latin American society. Exhausted and discouraged near his death, Bolívar wrote: "America is ungovernable. He who serves a revolution ploughs the sea."

Simón Bolívar had ended the age of Spanish autocracy. In many ways, however, he could only replace it with a despotism of his own. The constitution of Great Colombia said that he could, when necessary, establish dictatorial powers as he saw fit. In this sense, as some historians have suggested, Bolívar was the forerunner of Latin America's nineteenth-century **caudillos** (kow-THEE-yoes), the military strongmen who ruled without parliamentary approval.

In the nineteenth century the caudillos came to govern by consent of the economic and social leaders. Certainly the wealthy landowners favored the strong rulers. In a society divided by the poverty and illiteracy of the masses and the enormous wealth of the few, repression became the norm. Unlike the United States, Latin America failed to develop a large middle class. The early nineteenth-century movements may have created independent republics, but democracy remained elusive. Similar problems continue to plague Latin America even today.

SECTION REVIEW

1. Mapping: Use the map on page 500 to locate Mexico City, Caracas, Buenos Aires, Lima, Rio de Janeiro.
2. In your own words, briefly define or identify: peninsulares, Toussaint L'Ouverture, Great Colombia, Simon Bolívar, José San Martín, Monroe Doctrine, caudillo.
3. What impact did Great Britain have on Latin American emancipation?
4. Why is Napoleon an important figure in the history of Latin American independence?
5. What factors led to Latin America's failure to unify after independence?
■ Copies of the Declaration of Independence and the Declaration of the Rights of Man had to be smuggled into South America. What are some forms of censorship in the world today?

CHINA UNDER THE QING DYNASTY

As you read in Chapter 9, the Ming dynasty was overthrown by the Manchus, northern foreigners from Manchuria. They set up a dynasty that brought generations of peace to a rich and expanding China.

The Manchu Consolidation of Power

In 1644 the Manchus entered Beijing and made it the capital of the Qing dynasty. Within fifty years they consolidated their grip on the whole country. They overran the last southern and western bases of Ming authority and seized Taiwan (Formosa) in the 1680's. They reigned until 1912.

The Manchus learned quickly that to rule China well it was necessary to rule in the Chinese style, like a Chinese dynasty. With this in mind, they kept intact the age-old institution of civil service examinations and amply paid the educated bureaucracy. They encouraged the support of the gentry, or landowning class, and the traditional ruling classes. They adapted themselves to the Chinese way of life.

Still, the Manchus kept an identity apart from that of their Chinese subjects. They did this by outlawing Manchu-Chinese marriages and restricting Chinese immigration to the Manchurian homeland. They saw to it that Manchus, not Chinese, studied the Manchu language. Thus they preserved their special status.

The powerful emperor Kangxi (KONG SEE), who ruled from 1661 to 1722, governed carefully and wisely. He and his eighteenth century successors were generally strong, capable leaders. They patronized Chinese culture and its values. They expanded the empire in an age of prosperity at home. For this reason many historians speak of the Qing eighteenth century as the final flowering of Chinese classical civilization.

An Age of Prosperity

The Chinese Empire reached its maximum size in the middle of the eighteenth century. It consisted of a vast domain, nearly four-and-a-half-million

How does this detail from a Chinese ink drawing depict the nature of the Tai Ping Rebellion? Why did it weaken China?

square miles (eleven-and-a-half-million square kilometers). Never again would China be so large. Outer Mongolia and Taiwan and territories since taken by the Soviet Union were all ruled by the Qing. Tibet was made a protectorate. In many ways, much of east Asia well beyond China's borders—Nepal, Burma, Siam, Vietnam, the Philippines, and Korea—may be said to have been under the influence of the Qing Dynasty.

The eighteenth century witnessed a period of tremendous economic growth in agriculture, manufacturing, and trade. In agriculture, for example, in addition to the old crops of wheat, barley, and rice, farmers raised new American imports. Use of the sweet potato, the peanut (for cooking oil), and maize was widespread. This made harvests possible all year round which, for China, amounted to an agricultural revolution. Now, as in Europe, even in poor climates and under conditions unsuitable for rice, peasant families enjoyed a nutritious and dependable food staple. The cultivation of mass-produced crops such as cotton, sugar cane, and tea

also expanded. The textile industry in cotton goods and rich silks supplied a growing world market. The manufacture of fine ceramics, porcelain, lacquer-ware, and furniture supplied an appreciative European market.

Political stability and the agricultural revolution sparked a population explosion. As lands were drained and crop cultivation improved, more food was produced and more people were fed. According to the **censuses,** or population counts, between 1741 and 1812 the population more than doubled, rising from 143 million to 360 million.

Culturally the age gave birth to several works of genius. Fiction reached a new peak in *The Dream of the Red Chamber,* perhaps China's greatest psychological novel. The mathematician and philosopher Dai Zhen (DIE JUN) used scientific methods to make major contributions to the study of language and literature. Some scholars worked in the fields of ethics. Others studied the methods of researching and writing history as well as the philosophy of history.

The Decline of the Qing

The first signs of the Qing decline occurred toward the end of the eighteenth century and became more obvious in the nineteenth century. Fraud spread like wildfire through all levels of the bureaucracy. Young generals, hungry for power and wealth, organized huge chains of corruption, at the expense of the people and the government they served.

In the critical area of public works, such as the regulation of rivers and dikes, local mismanagement was rampant. Rural floodings, the direct result of criminal negligence, damaged the whole economy. No less than seven major floods of the Yellow River occurred in the early nineteenth century.

In 1796 a peasant uprising broke out, the so-called White Lotus Rebellion. It was led by the secret society of the White Lotus, which had rebelled before during the Mongol and Ming eras. Its major appeal was to poor peasants who resented the higher taxes and scanty social services of corrupt administrators.

Indeed, the means of putting down the rebellion seemed to highlight the utter decay of the later Qing government. Campaigns against the rebels were unnecessarily prolonged. Generals inflated costs to line their own pockets. Cruel massacres of innocent people were pawned off as "victories" over the rebels. In 1803, when order was reestablished, the emperor simply did not have the funds to reform the bureaucracy and improve local services.

The causes of rebellion were not properly addressed. These were difficult times for the poor peasants. A growing population made land scarce and expensive. The devaluation of the currency intensified the peasants' problems. Many farmers lost their land and were driven into the ranks of the laboring poor. In sharp contrast to the prosperity of the previous era, this was an age of economic recession, rural hardship, and unrest.

Confrontation with the West

The Opium War of 1839 to 1842 was not a major affair, but it did illustrate the nature of China's problems with the West. Since the 1750's China had restricted foreign trade to the province of Canton, which angered foreign merchants. At a time when it found itself buying large quantities of Chinese tea and silk, Britain needed to establish a favorable balance of trade. To this end, it supported a profitable moneymaking opium operation.

In 1839 the Chinese government decided to stop the drug dealing. By now an alarming percentage of its population had become addicts. In an era of recession, the country was losing precious supplies of silver to pay for opium. Officials seized 20,000 cases of opium and ordered the British out. The British reacted with force.

The Chinese proved no match for the British Navy. By 1842 they sued for peace. The Treaty of Nanjing in 1842 ended the Opium War and ceded Hong Kong to Britain. It also opened Shanghai, Canton, Fuzhou (foh-JOH), and some other treaty ports to foreign trade. A year later the British were granted **extraterritoriality**, the right to try their own subjects for offenses committed in China. The Treaty of Nanjing was the first of many "unequal treaties" imposed on China by foreign powers.

Civil War

China's loss to a relatively small British naval force in the Opium War revealed the weakness of the empire. What followed was a series of devastating revolts in the 1850's and 1860's that nearly toppled the government. The ability of the industrialized nations to affect the economy and politics of China was made easier by China's civil wars.

The Tai Ping (TIE PING) Rebellion broke out in 1850 and lasted until 1864. Mixing ancient Chinese teachings with bits and pieces of Christianity, the Tai Ping, or "Great Peace," movement preached social revolution, modernization, and the ouster of the Manchus. Its chief support came from the masses. In provinces in which it gained control, the Tai Ping lowered taxes, abolished private property and prohibited opium, alcohol, and tobacco. It tried to end the practice of binding little girls' feet. Women gained land and formed all-female armies. The Tai Ping captured Nanjing, proclaimed it their Capital of Heaven, and for more than a decade controlled most of the vital Yangtze River valley. They moved north and came close to threatening Beijing.

With foreign support, the Chinese property owners and moderates who feared Tai Ping radi-

The flags over this harbor reflect the trading interests imposed on China. How do the buildings and boats reflect a contrast between China and the West?

calism put down the rebellion. There had never been such a loss of wealth and life in Chinese history. It has been estimated that between 20 and 30 million people perished during the upheaval.

Foreign Influence

Against the backdrop of civil war, a second war with Britain erupted in 1856. British soldiers attacked Canton and within two years the Qing had to deal with a British-French alliance. Under intense pressure from the European powers, the Qing government opened ten new cities to foreigners. **Consulates,** or permanent diplomatic and commercial offices, were established in the capital. Despite a treaty, however, fighting resumed. In 1860 British and French troops marched on Beijing, sacked the capital, and forced the Qing to make further concessions.

Tianjin was opened to foreigners, the British gained a peninsula opposite Hong Kong, and the Chinese were required to pay a costly penalty. Foreign ships now had the right to enter the Chinese river system. Of equal value, the British gained a hold on China's customs. As a result, foreign goods, especially textiles, could be dumped on the Chinese market free of heavy duties. The Qing government had submitted to the interests of the western powers.

By the latter part of the nineteenth century, China was under the political and economic hold of "unequal treaties." No longer could it protect its own borders, nor even its own interior. The results of these developments would become more apparent in the first half of the twentieth century. It was a legacy the Chinese would not forget.

SECTION REVIEW

1. Mapping: Use the Atlas map on page 755 to trace the increase of European influence in China in the mid-nineteenth century.
2. In your own words, briefly define or identify: Qing Dynasty, Dai Chen, Hong Kong, Tai Ping movement, "unequal treaties."
3. What impact did the civil wars have on Qing relations with the West?
■ Corruption led to the decline of the Qing. What efforts are made by governments today to lessen corruption?

TOKUGAWA JAPAN AND MEIJI RESTORATION

Throughout the 1500's Japan suffered constant civil war. Only the provincial daimyo had authority. They ruled like feudal barons at the local level. Warfare was common; the major leaders were powerless outside their own limited spheres.

In 1603 the emperor, always outside and above politics, gave to Tokugawa Ieyasu the hereditary office of shogun. The Tokugawa family maintained the title for over 250 years.

Tokugawa Seclusion under the Pax Tokugawa

The Tokugawa ruled through a system of "centralized feudalism." Though at the local level the shogunate had little direct control, its authority at the top was unchallenged.

To ensure national stability and to reinforce its own rule, the shogunate took some extreme measures. In both cases Japanese fear of foreign influences proved to be the cause.

Christianity was feared as an alien religion. It seemed responsible to an authority higher than and outside that of the imperial domain. The Spanish takeover of the Philippines in the 1500's made a sharp impression because Spanish priests held the most power in the Philippines. The Dutch and English traders of the early 1600's brought news of the religious wars that were then ravaging Europe. To discourage foreign influence, the merciless persecution of even Japanese Christians became official policy.

The Tokugawa leader feared that foreign trade would enrich daimyo lords. The nobles might then challenge the authority of the shogun himself. Rather than risk competition, the Tokugawa shogunate followed an extreme policy. In the early 1630's Japanese citizens were forbidden to travel abroad or to return to Japan once they had gone. The expulsion of the Europeans soon followed. This radical course of withdrawal from world affairs became official policy from 1640 to 1853.

There was one exception. A few Chinese and Dutch merchants, under the shogunate's direct charge, were allowed to live and do business in Nagasaki. For about two centuries this would be Japan's only direct contact with the rest of the world.

Economic and Cultural Developments

Society was ordered along the four-class system. As nobles, the shogun, daimyo, and samurai were by law separated from commoners, but Tokugawa society was by no means unchanging. Shut off as Japan was from the rest of the world, its internal trade began to thrive. National markets and a money economy developed. Wholesalers purchased goods in the countryside and sold them in the towns or cities. As a result, cities grew in size and economic importance. Kyoto and Nagasaki, and above all Osaka and Edo (modern Tokyo), became thriving commercial centers.

The rise of the merchant class produced a rich urban culture. Its ideal became known as the "floating world," the world of fashion and popular entertainment. The spread of literacy among all classes produced a wealth of popular writing and a few classic novels. In theater it was the age of the great puppet dramas and the *kabuki* with its elaborate stage performances. In the graphic arts it was the age of highly stylized woodblock prints.

How does this detail from a James McNeill Whistler painting show the influence of the East on western art?

· 507 ·

The End of Isolation

For years the question of dealing with the West had preoccupied Japanese leaders. The presence of western ships in waters off Japan was only one sign of the outside world. The study of western science and western languages, especially Dutch, was another. Upheld by a small group of samurai scholars, the study of western things steadily increased. But it was the emergence of the United States in the Pacific arena that brought Japan out of its long isolation.

With the discovery of gold in California in 1848, United States interests turned to the Far East. The United States established a shipping route between San Francisco and Shanghai. It sought to open Japan to obtain a fueling station. American whalers and merchant shippers, unhappy with the Japanese treatment of shipwrecked sailors, also wanted to negotiate a treaty.

Why do you think Admiral Perry was portrayed in this manner by a Japanese artist?

In 1852 the President of the United States ordered a fleet of seven steam warships, under the command of Matthew Perry, to sail for Japan.

Perry arrived in Edo Bay in the summer of 1853 and demanded the privilege of presenting the emperor (he meant the shogun) with a presidential letter. The Japanese knew that a limited force of British fighters had defeated China during the Opium War. If China could not resist the West, the Japanese reasoned, how could they?

In 1854 the shogun signed a commercial agreement with the United States. The treaty opened up two ports to American shipping and guaranteed fair treatment of American sailors. It also led to the appointment of a United States consul. Other nations followed with similar arrangements.

The Meiji Restoration

Confronted with the great western powers the Japanese soon learned that, in effect, their concessions amounted to a series of unequal treaties. Like the Chinese, the Japanese were being dealt with as a backward people. Behind the treaties stood the obvious threat of force. For the Japanese, this humiliation sparked a national crisis.

The country's leaders were bitterly divided. Acts of terrorism and assassination by young samurai marked the early 1860's. Many called for the end of the Tokugawa shogunate. They charged the shogunate with poor leadership and held it responsible for the nation's shame. In the name of the emperor, military forces confronted the Tokugawa shogunate. These forces were supported by the old enemies of the Tokugawa—the daimyo.

In 1868 the shogunate was abolished. After a short civil war national unity was established. The emperor, a teenager of fifteen, assumed a new name. He would be called Meiji (MAY JEE), or "Enlightened Rule." The Meiji Restoration gave its name to an era that lasted until 1912.

The Meiji Restoration proved to be more than a coup d'état. For the whole country, the Restoration effected a social, political, and economic revolution. Feudalism and the four-class system were abolished and with them the privileges of the nobility. Equality before the law was recognized, and education established. Edo, renamed Tokyo, became the nation's capital. The wave of reform unleashed a current of energy through society.

SOCIAL SCIENCE SKILLS

USING HISTORICAL PHOTOGRAPHS

The mid-nineteenth century in Japan was a time of intense change. In 1868 the Tokugawa shogunate ended and the Japanese feudal structure was abolished. In a relatively short period of time, Japan was changed by industrialization and the importation of western values.

The samurai nobility was abolished and its privileges ended. Many samurai were unable to adjust to change. Stripped of their government pensions, they took on low-paying jobs. Some even died paupers. The universal conscription, or draft laws, of 1873 had made their warrior status unimportant. Yet no society can uproot its past. The values of its age-old customs continued to affect the lives and minds of the Japanese.

The pictures above are photographic portraits of two men who lived through this period. The one on the left is a samurai noble, Kusakabe Kimbei. He is shown in traditional noble costume, the archer's dress of the Tokugawa warrior class. The picture on the right is Mutsuhito, the Emperor Meiji, or "Enlightened Rule," and symbol of Japan's modernization process. He is shown in western-style dress. It was 1872, the fifth year of his forty-five-year reign.

As portraits of an age and primary sources, photographs are invaluable. They show what words cannot describe. Study the pictures and look for valuable clues about the subjects portrayed. Pay particular attention to precise details. In the emperor's picture, for example, consider the Victorian fabric on the table and the carpet on the floor. Look at the subjects' faces, dress, and postures, and answer the questions below.

1. How would you contrast the dress, shoes, swords, and hairstyles of the two subjects portrayed here?
2. What details do these photographs offer that are valuable to the historian of late nineteenth-century Japan?
3. Why do you think it was difficult for the samurai to make the change to modern society?

Modernization and Industrialization

Unlike China, Japan had by the early nineteenth century many of the preconditions needed to industrialize. Its national economy produced surplus capital that could be used for investment. Its taxation of the peasants provided the state with constant revenue. Its strong government—which China sorely lacked—was able to organize a total modernization program.

The Japanese leadership, especially the very capable younger generation, studied the West and imported the best it had to offer. Germans helped found medical schools and historical institutes. Americans advised on the elementary school system and the postal service. The French adapted their legal code for Japanese use, and the British contributed to railway and telegraph development. The Japanese navy was revamped on the British model, the army on the Prussian. Italians were invited to teach the glories of western art.

From the start, the government carefully directed the industrialization process. Key industries that provided exports such as textiles were given top priority. Solely domestic industries were not. Thus, foreign trade that had almost no value before 1854 skyrocketed to $200 million a year by the turn of the century. In the 1890's Japan moved swiftly into steel production and shipbuilding.

The Meiji Constitution, proclaimed in 1889, placed the emperor as titular head, or ruler in name only, over a centralized bureaucracy. In the two-chamber diet, or assembly, only one chamber was elected, and that by a tiny fraction of the population. In effect, an oligarchy with few democratic sympathies came to hold political power. The Constitution freed the government from the nightmare of political unrest, enabling it to focus on the business of modernization. But it also allowed for a modern militarist state to arise, unchecked by democratic institutions.

In a relatively short number of years the country had emerged as the first Asian nation to modernize. Alone among non-western states, Japan's stunning social transformation had met the West's challenge head on. Japan soon developed an interest in a role as a world power. It began to look for alliances with European powers as recognition of its acceptance as an equal. Japan's ambition began to alter international relations in the East.

SECTION REVIEW

1. Use the Atlas map on page 755 to locate the shogun's capital of Tokyo (Edo), and the port of Nagasaki on the island of Kyushu.
2. In your own words, briefly define or identify: four-class system, "floating world," Meiji Restoration.
3. What were the motives behind Tokugawa isolation?
4. What led to the Meiji Restoration?
■ Japanese industrialization in the latter part of the nineteenth century is one of the century's great success stories. What products does Japan provide today for the world market?

THE GROWTH OF THE UNITED STATES

The nineteenth century witnessed the United States' dramatic growth from a young democracy on the Atlantic coast to a continental power. But territorial expansion was exacted at a heavy price. Sectional interests and economic differences led to civil war.

The Northwest Territory

At the Treaty of Paris in 1783 Great Britain bestowed on the United States a very generous peace settlement. Territory comprising the whole trans-Allegheny area, including the Old Northwest territory as far west as the Mississippi River, was now part of the United States.

In 1787 Congress enacted the **Northwest Ordinance** to provide for the orderly progress from a territory to a state. When a territory's population reached 60,000 free inhabitants, it could petition Congress for admission to the Union on an equal basis with the other states.

The Northwest Ordinance of 1787 was the blueprint for all future statehood in the United States. It proved to be a fair solution to the problem of westward expansion.

TERRITORIAL EXPANSION OF THE UNITED STATES

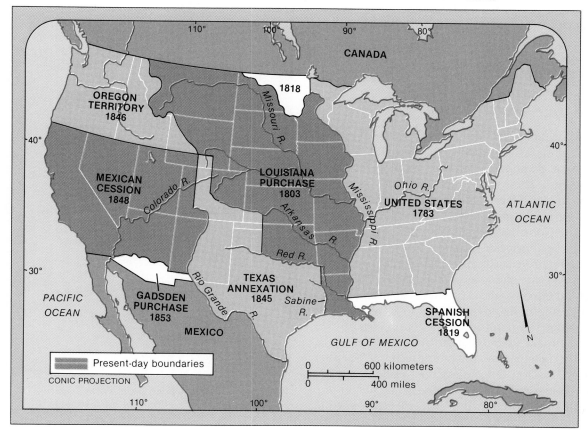

Why was the United States interested in land west of the Mississippi River?

Territorial Growth and Democratic Expansion

In 1803 the United States bought the Louisiana Territory from Napoleon for $15 million. American negotiators had gone to Paris to obtain access to the Gulf of Mexico. They returned with territory that stretched from the Mississippi River to the Rocky Mountains, as far north as modern Canada. After the War of 1812, Britain and the United States reached an agreement about part of the border between Canada and the United States. Today it is the world's longest undefended national boundary.

Under the leadership of Sam Houston, Stephen Austin, and Lorenzo de Zavala, Texas declared and won its independence from Mexico in 1836. A republic for nine years, it became part of the United States in 1845 in an action that provoked war with

Mexico. It was a war that Mexico decisively lost. Through the Mexican Cession of 1848 the United States acquired Arizona, California, Nevada, and Utah, and parts of modern New Mexico, Colorado, and Wyoming. The Oregon settlement with Great Britain in 1846 granted the United States full claim to the present states of Washington, Oregon, and Idaho, and parts of Montana and Wyoming. In 1853 the United States obtained a section of land in present-day Arizona and New Mexico by the Gadsden Purchase. By the mid-1850's America's "manifest destiny"—its goal to spread across the North American continent—had been realized.

Unlike Great Britain and France, where property qualifications restricted suffrage to the upper levels of society, the United States moved closer to genuine democracy. The "New Democracy," secured by public education, was based on white manhood suffrage. The election of Andrew Jackson to the presidency in 1828 saw the increase of elective, as opposed to appointive, offices. Modern political machines made politics a permanent profession. In comparison to Europe, it was something of a democratic revolution.

The Antislavery Impulse

As the nation grew, the issue of black slavery became progressively more explosive. It hinged on the basic economic differences between the North and South. These differences expressed themselves at the national level as **sectionalism,** the competition for power among the country's sections.

The North industrialized in the pattern of the advanced European societies. It sought generally high protective tariffs to keep out foreign manufactures and to promote its own industries. The North had no use for slavery. The agricultural South found free trade advantageous to its slave-based plantation economy. Its raw cotton exports fed Great Britain's gigantic industrial machine.

The designation of western territory as either "slave" or "free" meant essentially one thing. The territories—and future states—would be in the South's camp or in the North's. Politics was the chief weapon of the agricultural South. It simply could not challenge the North's economic might.

The South claimed protection under the Constitution. It called for states' rights, arguing that the federal government had no business telling the states whether they should be slave or free.

The moral issue of slavery was a major issue in the conflict. Britain had set an example by abolishing slavery in 1807, and in 1833 in its colonies. William Lloyd Garrison and Sarah and Angelina Grimke were among many Northerners and Southerners who made impassioned appeals to fight the spread of slavery. They and others crusaded for **abolition,** the complete end to slavery throughout the United States.

Secession and Civil War

The Republican party candidate Abraham Lincoln was elected to the presidency in 1860. It was a victory for abolition in the new territories. The South had lost the West, and with it its political future. Southerners felt sure there could be no compro-

What does this photo tell you about the military and industrial strength of the North in the Civil War?

mising with the Lincoln administration. In 1861, following South Carolina's lead in December 1860, the southern states **seceded,** or withdrew, from the Union. The secessionist states united to form their own nation, Confederate States of America. They chose Jefferson Davis as their president.

For Lincoln there could be no separation. Lincoln saw the advantages of unification and strong government in a world of industrial competition. From the South's view, this was a fight for national independence. The result was four years of bloody civil war.

With over 80 percent of the country's potential fighting force and 90 percent of its industrial production, the North had a clear-cut advantage. It had three-quarters of the nation's wealth and financial reserves, and complete naval superiority. The South's brilliant generalship and courageous army proved no match for it. By 1865, after a bitter struggle, the Union finally triumphed over the Confederacy.

American Literature Comes of Age

In retrospect, the 1850's were perhaps American literature's first golden age. Though the public was not aware of it, American writers were producing major works on a par with the European masters. Popular taste, however, craved fare like Henry Wadsworth Longfellow's *Hiawatha,* a romantic poem of a mythical native past. The public so loved Harriet Beecher Stowe's *Uncle Tom's Cabin,* as both novel and play in 1852, that Abraham Lincoln would later half-seriously attribute the Civil War to it.

The great writers of the period had a far more limited audience—or they completely failed to win an audience at all. In 1850 America's first great novel appeared. It was Nathaniel Hawthorne's tale of sin and pride and community, set in Puritan New England, *The Scarlet Letter.* The next year Herman Melville's *Moby Dick* was critically and commercially a dismal failure. It took many years for the novel to take hold. Future readers would find in it a masterpiece and one of the world's great novels. It is, on one level, an account of the American whaling industry. On another, it is an allegory on the nature of good and evil.

In 1855 Walt Whitman published his first version of *Leaves of Grass.* It was composed in a bold new style soon to be labeled free verse. Its only favorable reviews were written anonymously by the author himself. Yet Walt Whitman's achievement is considered by many critics to stand with the very finest English poetry of the century.

After the War

The pace of European emigration quickened. In the 1840's and 1850's, most immigrants had come from Ireland to escape famine and from Germany to escape political turmoil. In the latter part of the century most came from Russia, eastern Europe, Italy, and Scandinavia. The growth was so rapid that a town like Chicago with a population of 30,000 in 1850 became, by 1890, a city with more than one million inhabitants, making it the world's sixth largest urban complex.

The postwar period was an age of laissez-faire capitalism, economic expansion, and industrial growth. It was the "Gilded Age," the age of the robber barons, big business, big money, and fabulously rich self-made millionaires. The term "multi-millionaire" was coined in the late 1870's to describe Cornelius Vanderbilt's fortune. By the end of the century the United States exceeded Great Britain in industrial production.

But for the mass of workers, improvements came slowly. In the early 1900's labor legislation, though not as extensive as that in Germany and Britain, protected factory workers including women and children.

The suffrage movement also made some gains in this period. Early women's rights advocates Elizabeth Cady Stanton and Susan B. Anthony were followed by Anna Howard Shaw and Carrie Chapman Catt. By the early 1900's women had acquired the right to vote in several western states.

One of the results of the Civil War was the passage of three amendments to the Constitution. These amendments provided for the abolition of slavery, the granting of citizenship to all blacks, and suffrage for all black men. But laws did not improve the social and economic conditions of the mass of poor blacks, who remained southern sharecroppers. The minority who did become solidly middle class only fueled the racial hatred of the lower-class whites. In 1909 a coalition of black and white progressives formed the National Association for the Advancement of Colored People (NAACP). It was an organization devoted solely to ending discrimination against blacks.

SECTION REVIEW

1. Mapping: Use the map on page 511 to trace the United States' expansion.
2. In your own words, briefly define or identify: Mexican Cession, Manifest Destiny, sectionalism, Jefferson Davis, *Leaves of Grass,* Cornelius Vanderbilt, NAACP.
3. What is the importance of the Northwest Ordinance of 1787?
4. What economic factors led to the American Civil War?
■ The 1850's were a golden age of American literature. In what fields do you think our era is a golden age?

Reviewing the Chapter

Chapter Summary

South American patriots were greatly influenced by the examples of the American and French revolutions. The result of their struggle led to the establishment of many independent states. Unlike other Latin-American independence movements, Brazil's experience was remarkably peaceful. But the establishment of democracy after independence proved an elusive ideal for all of Latin America.

The economic expansion and cultural greatness of the early Qing dynasty faded in the last years of the eighteenth century. China was hit by hard economic times and rampant administrative corruption. The European powers took advantage of China's weakness. They imposed a series of "unequal treaties" on the later Qing governments.

After two centuries of total isolation, Tokugawa Japan was thrust into the modern world. Awareness of China's sad story at the hands of the West led the Japanese leadership to overthrow the shogunate and institute an era of rapid modernization. It was the social and economic marvel of the nonwestern world.

Nineteenth-century America witnessed a dramatic transformation from fledgling democracy to continental power. After bitter civil war, the United States emerged as a major industrial power on a par with the great European states.

1. What events had a major influence on the South American independence movement?
2. What did the Japanese learn from China's experience with the western powers?
3. What were two major developments in the nineteenth century in the United States?

Using Your Vocabulary

1. What was the difference between creoles and peninsulares. Why were they in conflict with each other?
2. Who was known as The Liberator? What was the meaning of the title?
3. Why did John Quincy Adams draft the Monroe Doctrine? How did the British support it?
4. What characteristics of the rule of Simón Bolívar have led some to consider him a forerunner to the caudillo?
5. What is a census? Why do you think governments undertake them?
6. Which social group in China supported the White Lotus Rebellion? Why was the Chinese emperor unable to carry out reforms?
7. Why did the British seek extraterritoriality?
8. Why do you think treaties negotiated between China and Western countries were called unequal treaties?
9. Why were consulates important to the Europeans in China?
10. What were the divisions in the four-class system in Japan?
11. What was the importance of the Meiji Restoration?
12. What is the significance of the Northwest Ordinance?
13. What territory was acquired by the United States under the terms of the Mexican Cession and the Gadsden Purchase?
14. What was sectionalism? How was it tied to the crusade for abolition?
15. Why did the states in the South secede from the Union?
16. What does the abbreviation NAACP stand for? What was the goal of this organization?

Developing Your Geography Skills

1. Using the map on page 500, describe the areas of Latin America colonized by the Spanish, the Portuguese, the French, the British, and the Dutch.
2. Use the Atlas map on page 760 to describe what areas of Latin America have the hottest climates.

What areas of Latin America have the coldest climates? How would you account for this?

3. Use the map on page 511 to name the rivers that form part of the boundaries of the Louisiana Purchase. Which river separates the Texas Annexation from Mexico? Which rivers flow into the Mississippi River?

4. Use the map on page 511 to name the territory that completed the borders of the continental United States. Use the mileage scale to estimate the distance from coast to coast and from the Canadian border to southern Texas.

Recalling the Facts

1. What was the immediate cause of the Latin American independence movements of the early nineteenth century?
2. Why was it in the economic interests of Britain for the Latin American countries to gain their independence?
3. What two leaders attempted but failed to carry out successful social revolution in Mexico?
4. What were the principles proposed by the Monroe Doctrine?
5. How were the Manchus able to rule China fairly well for over two centuries?
6. What changes took place in Chinese agriculture in the eighteenth century?
7. What were the causes and the results of the Opium War?
8. What were the goals of the Tai Ping movement?
9. Why did the Japanese persecute Christians?
10. Why did the United States want Japan open to Western contacts?
11. What marked the end of the Tokugawa shogunate? For how many years had the Tokugawa ruled Japan?
12. What were some of the provisions of the Meiji Restoration?
13. What land was acquired by the United States in the Oregon settlement of 1846?
14. Why did the Southern states secede when Abraham Lincoln was elected president?
15. What American writers were active in the mid-nineteenth century? With what works are they associated?

Essay Questions

1. Explain how Brazil obtained its independence in a relatively peaceful manner compared to the other American republics.
2. Exhausted and dying Simón Bolívar wrote "America is ungovernable. He who serves a revolution ploughs the sea." What do you think he meant?
3. Why is the eighteenth century considered an era of Chinese prosperity? Why were the Chinese unable to maintain their prosperity?
4. Compare and contrast the White Lotus and Tai Ping rebellions.
5. Why did the Japanese fear foreign influence? What measures did Japan take to cut itself off from the rest of the world?
6. Explain the "floating world" of Tokugawa society. How do you think it was fostered by the development of an urban society?
7. Describe the political and economic revolution brought about by the Meiji Restoration.
8. In the period under study in this chapter the interrelationships of the United States with Latin America, China, and Japan were beginning to expand. Describe one example of influences of each of these three on the United States and the United States' influence on them.

Critical Thinking

1. Identify the inconsistencies between Simón Bolívar as a revolutionary and as a political leader.
2. What bias is basic to the British demand for extraterritoriality from the Chinese?
3. The Southern states supported slavery as necessary to their economic well being. Do you think this was a warranted or unwarranted claim?
4. According to Amendment 9 of the United States Constitution, the rights listed in the Constitution are not necessarily the only rights that exist. Other rights shall not be denied to the people because they are not listed in the Constitution. How might either side in the American Civil War have used this Amendment to defend its position?

CHAPTER ·23·

The ERA of IMPERIALISM

1830–1914

Objectives

- *To identify the factors that caused the new imperialism*

- *To show how the European powers carved up the continent of Africa*

- *To describe how the British ruled India*

- *To discuss the outcome of imperialism in Asia and the Pacific*

- *To trace the emergence of the United States as a world power*

After an early spurt of expansion in the Age of Exploration, Europe experienced a general decline in empire building. The economic theories of Enlightenment writers made colonies seem less desirable. The French and Indian War and the American Revolution made Europeans question the value of owning colonies. The great European upheaval—the wars of the French Revolution and Napoleon—turned attention toward the struggle within Europe.

During the first half of the nineteenth century, Europe focused on its own affairs. It dealt with reaction, revolution, industrialization, and reform—not with overseas possessions. Great Britain, the victor in the Napoleonic Wars, usually supported independent nations and free trade. Only after 1870 did imperialism become widespread.

By imperialism we mean the conquest and colonization of foreign territories. Naturally this was not only a modern or western European development. Sumerians, Phoenicians, Persians, Greeks, Romans, Huns, Tartars, Ottoman Turks, and Chinese all built empires through conquest and colonization. What was different about the new imperialism of the late nineteenth century was the degree of control of markets and raw materials that the industrialized powers were able to achieve.

THE CAUSES OF MODERN IMPERIALISM

Several factors contributed to the sudden rise of imperialist activity in the last decades of the nineteenth century. Historians still debate the exact ways in which these factors interacted.

The Liberal Era

The period roughly from 1815 to 1870 may be described as the era of classical liberalism. In this period Great Britain was the unchallenged leader in world trade. As such, it generally sought open markets, free competition, and only an "informal empire." India and certain Asian and African ports were the chief exceptions. Otherwise, with its naval and industrial lead, Britain was content to keep world markets open and to profit from its superior position.

Laissez-faire theorists like Adam Smith and Jeremy Bentham believed that far more could be earned from trading with independent states than by owning and exploiting colonies. Colonies were not worth what it cost to rule and defend them. "If France took the whole of Africa," an English free trader wrote in the late 1850's, "I do not see what harm she would do us or anybody else save herself." In the spirit of laissez-faire, Britain altered its relationship with many of its existing colonies. Canada, Australia, New Zealand, and the Cape Colony in South Africa moved to a stage between colonization and independence.

After 1870 the liberal system started to erode. The unification and industrialization of Germany, the end of the American Civil War in 1865, and the emergence of modern Japan marked a shift in the relations of the major powers. A severe depression in the early 1870's dealt a blow to prices and wages. Many governments adopted protective tariffs. Free trade was under attack.

The competition for new world markets brought about the decline of classical liberalism and the rise of modern **imperialism.** People believed that an industrialized nation needed a network of colonies. In some ways this was a return to the mercantilist practices of the seventeenth and eighteenth centuries.

The New Imperialism

In the late nineteenth century imperialism's chief supporters were the great capitalists and manufacturers with specific interests at stake. They argued that colonialism made sense. Manufacturers needed fresh sources of cheap raw materials such as cotton, cocoa, rubber, and tin. They also needed new places where they could sell their excess goods and invest extra profits. Africa and Asia seemed able to provide these benefits and absorb excess population as well.

Imperialism's chief critics, mostly liberals and socialists, argued otherwise. They claimed that the only ones who really benefited from imperialism were certain well-placed capitalists: shipowners, manufacturers, and importers of tropical products. The community at large realized little profit. The capital that was being exported abroad, anti-imperialists argued, was money that could be better invested at home. It could be used to clean up slums, create jobs, and raise the standard of living.

Historical evidence indicates that the new colonialism was not especially profitable, though at the time people thought it was. In 1914, for example, Britain had more invested in the United States and Latin America than in its newly acquired empire. France had less than 10 percent of its foreign investment in its colonies, and 90 percent in independent nations. Germany had far more money invested in Great Britain, its economic rival, than in all of its colonial holdings. Japan with little, if any, excess capital for export sought colonies eagerly.

Despite these statistics, economic motives were major factors in imperialism's rise. But they were closely linked to other factors.

The Political Factor

Nationalism, which arose after the Napoleonic Wars, did not subside with the success of unification movements. For a new power, imperialism was a way of proving national worth. For an old one, like France, it was a way of reasserting itself after the disastrous defeat in the Franco-Prussian War. "There has never been great power without great colonies," wrote one French publicist in the late 1870's.

Even in Britain, the home of classical liberalism, a new call for imperialism was sounded. In the early 1870's Benjamin Disraeli, calling on Britain to ''command the respect of the world,'' advocated the revival of a formal empire. Russia's invasion of Turkestan in the mid-1860's and its pressure on Afghanistan contributed to Britain's change in policy. Chiefly out of concern for its vital interests in India, Britain reviewed its imperial position.

The rivalry of various alliance systems in Europe assumed global importance. National glory, political prestige, and strategic advantages were all elements of an imperialism that can be understood only in its relationship to European diplomacy.

Technological Factors

The technology available to industrial nations in the second half of the nineteenth century enabled them to dominate the underdeveloped world. Field artillery and disciplined fighting skills gave western-trained troops an advantage over Asian and African armies many times their size.

No less important was the technological change in ocean shipping. Europeans had been world leaders in this field since the middle of the 1500's,

Many Victorian women served as missionaries in underdeveloped regions. How do they represent one of the motives of imperialism?

but they had not been able to replace Asian ships in Asian seas. The development of steam and steel ships shifted the balance of naval power decidedly to the West.

Industrialization changed communications and medicine. In the 1820's, for example, it took a letter six months to reach Calcutta from London. An answer that was routed around the Horn of Africa could take as long as two years. By the 1870's, via submarine cable, a message to Calcutta from London could be delivered and answered in a single day. In medicine advances in the treatment of malaria and yellow fever made exploration of previously inaccessible regions possible. In many ways modern improvements contributed to imperialism.

Social Factors

The new imperialism arose out of a complex set of beliefs. Notable among these were humanitarian impulses. The developed world firmly believed it had a moral obligation to export the benefits of western civilization.

In an age influenced by Social Darwinism and ideas of racial superiority, imperialism was a powerful mission. It was a crusade. In Britain this mission was expressed as the white man's burden, in France as the civilizing mission. The Germans spoke of their unique *Kultur*, or culture. Each nation felt itself the best equipped to enlighten the undeveloped world. Colonies were a source of pride and feelings of superiority.

Missionaries from Europe and the United States devoted themselves to the service of God and humanity. Toiling for years in underdeveloped countries, they worked long and hard to advance education and to fight disease. They built churches, schools, and hospitals, and helped improve the lot of the poor. However, conflicts between the missionaries and the people sometimes were used by more powerful nations as an excuse to extend military control over an area. In this way missionaries were often the forerunners of imperialists.

Another factor promoting imperialism was its popularity. The now-educated working classes in the advanced countries delighted in reading news of overseas expansion. A novel like *King Solomon's Mines* sold 5,000 copies in its first two months of publication, and books featuring battles in exotic locales were runaway best sellers. Such books fed the popular hunger for escape and served to support the imperialist cause.

The rise of a cheap, popular press accompanied this literature. Publishers soon learned that readers wanted excitement. They wanted bold headlines of imperial conquest. The imperialist decades rode a massive wave of popular approval.

Modes of Imperialism

Imperialists of the late nineteenth century were a new breed. Centuries before, for example, the Portuguese and the Dutch were content to establish trading stations on their routes to Asia. The new imperialists sought to dominate these areas far more completely. By the end of the nineteenth century, the western powers had the technology to move into areas and take them over. Imperialists built factories, refineries, plantations, and mines. They placed the native population in wage-earning servitude. Often, where it was possible, the imperialists established total control, annexing territories as colonies. Where this was not possible, they established **protectorates.** Local rulers were kept as figureheads while a foreign country actually controlled the government.

In some cases local leadership was not challenged. The region in question fell under a **sphere of influence** in which a powerful state had economic and sometimes political influence over a weaker one. In most instances this special relationship was recognized by other nations.

SECTION REVIEW

1. In your own words, identify or define: imperialism, classical liberalism, informal empire, white man's burden.
2. How did Britain's liberal policy express itself prior to 1870?
3. What factors led to liberalism's decline?
4. What were some of the arguments offered against imperialism?
■ What nations today might fulfill the definition of a sphere of influence? What are the advantages and disadvantages to a powerful state of having a sphere of influence?

IMPERIALISM IN AFRICA

In the early nineteenth century most of tropical Africa was still isolated from the rest of the world. Europeans knew African coastal areas as stations on the route to India and Asia, or as places for trade in their own right. Interior Africa was known only to a handful of explorers, and some areas were not even known to them.

The French in Algeria

Great Britain's decisive maritime victory during the naval wars of the Napoleonic Age sparked France's entry into North Africa. After 1815 Britain became the major power in the Middle East. As a result, France focused on a region not directly under British control. It chose North Africa.

Eager to prove itself quickly, a shaky French government sent an expedition to Algeria in 1830. The alleged cause of the intervention was the recent surge in Mediterranean piracy. The naval wars between England and France had given pirates on the Barbary Coast a chance to operate boldly. They looted ships off the coasts of Morocco, Algiers, Tunis, and Tripoli.

The French met with strong resistance in Algeria. It took nearly 90,000 men and several years of heavy fighting before the Arab chief was finally captured. The war was savage. The Algerians massacred prisoners; the French burned crops and whole villages. Colonization was slow but steady, and native uprisings persisted into the 1870's.

Algeria developed into a rich agricultural colony settled by the French as well as the Spanish and the Italians. But the building of railways, schools, and hospitals only angered the native population, who were denied the best lands and access to the upper classes. Napoleon III believed that the French would one day have to face the fact that Algeria was an Arab kingdom.

The French and British in Egypt

In the mid-nineteenth century Egypt was basically an independent state. It was still officially part of the Ottoman Empire. The Ottoman ruler's viceroy,

THE
SUEZ
CANAL SHARES

A GOOD INVESTMENT.

A COMMERCIAL ADVANTAGE.

A POLITICAL NECESSITY.

EGYPT

INDIA

L-d
R-b-t M-t-u
IS COMING

No. 56.   HARD HITTING—ESPECIALLY FOR THE HITTERS.   23rd February, 1876.

Purchasing the khedive's Suez Canal shares was seen as a stroke of genius by some people. How does this cartoon portray the politicians who were opposed to it?

the khedive (kuh-DEEVZ), ruled the country as he wished. In the 1860's Egypt's wealth increased as a result of the American Civil War. The shortage of cotton sent worldwide cotton prices skyrocketing, and Egyptians rushed to fill the demand.

Egypt's economic growth attracted serious attention. Many French and English businesspeople —some respectable, others shady—swarmed into the country. They offered easy credit at very high rates to the khedive Ismail Pasha. The khedive borrowed in an attempt to modernize the country.

A major project was the construction of the Suez Canal, opened in 1869. Using the latest engineering skills, Ferdinand de Lesseps had succeeded in building a canal through the hundred miles of desert between the Mediterranean and the Red seas. Despite British opposition, the canal was financed by the French public, which bought shares

in the Suez Canal Company and by the Egyptian government. Its opening was a major event. The free-spending khedive even commissioned the opera *Aida* for the occasion.

The Suez Canal halved the length of the route from Europe to the Indian Ocean and immediately assumed military and commercial importance. Having failed to engage in its construction, the British now desperately wanted control of the canal. Their chance came in the mid-1870's, when Ismail attempted to mortgage his share of the Suez Canal Company to raise money. Without consulting Parliament, Prime Minister Disraeli quickly borrowed 4 million pounds and offered to buy the khedive's shares. In a brilliant stroke the British took outright control of the Suez Canal.

After the khedive suffered further financial setbacks, western banking interests forced him to abdicate. Britain and France placed Egypt under joint rule. In response, the Egyptians rebelled against western domination. In 1882 the British landed troops. Taking advantage of France's absence from the maneuver, the British occupied Egypt. In 1914 they declared Egypt a British protectorate.

Other Moves in North Africa

The British used Egypt as a base from which to expand into the Sudan. By the 1900's northeast Africa was in British hands with the exceptions of independent Ethiopia, French Somaliland, and Italy's two barren tracts, Italian Somaliland and Eritrea.

Closed out of northeastern Africa, France concentrated on the northwest. It already had its base of operation in Algeria and financial and cultural connections in Tunisia and Morocco. In Tunisia, France loaned the Turkish ruler money and gained an upper hand. With the approval of the Congress of Berlin, the French moved in on the bankrupt Tunisian government. In 1881 Tunisia was seized and proclaimed a French protectorate.

The French steadily expanded in the Sahara and Morocco. Morocco, however, because of strong native resistance and the rivalry of the great powers themselves, remained independent into the twentieth century. Rather than antagonize the other powers, Britain and France and—in this case—Spain preserved Morocco's neutrality.

In the early 1900's developments in Europe affected Africa. Britain and France resolved their differences, and France traded off other African territory for German recognition of a French sphere of influence in Morocco. In a series of events closely linked to the roots of the First World War, Morocco was divided up between France and Spain in the period prior to 1914.

In 1911 Italy declared war on the dying Ottoman Empire. After Ethiopians, armed by the French, defeated the invading Italians, Italy seized Tripoli, now known as Libya. The cost of administering a rebellious country of little apparent worth was hardly worthwhile.

Slave Trade

By its very nature the slave trade deterred interest in the interior of sub-Saharan Africa. Westerners had no need to go inland since the Africans themselves brought the slaves to the coasts. Many slaves were people who had been taken captive as a result of tribal warfare. It has been estimated that in the course of three centuries more than nine million slaves were acquired. Africans also offered ivory, gold, and hides in exchange for food and European manufactured goods, such as guns and cloth. Those few westerners who sought to explore or preach the faith found entry into the heartland almost impossible. Barriers included the deserts and rain forests of Africa and diseases like malaria and sleeping sickness.

Until the antislavery movement there was no motive to deal with Africa more closely. In the early 1770's crusading Christians organized pressure groups to put a stop to slavery. In the early nineteenth century Britain abolished slavery at home and then in its empire. It was assumed that only after slavery was completely ended would other kinds of African trade evolve or expand. As a result, British naval patrols policed African waters in search of slave traders.

The exploration of the African interior, romantically known as "darkest Africa," was also part of the larger humanitarian drive. The Scottish doctor and missionary David Livingstone was perhaps the best known of African explorers. In the 1850's he was presumably the first European to see Victoria Falls and to cross overland to the mouth of the Zambezi. To the Victorians "Christianity and Commerce" was the mission to rescue the peoples of Africa from ignorance, disease, and the lingering illegal slave trade.

Diplomatic Motives

As late as the 1870's only a small percentage of sub-Saharan Africa was under foreign control. The French were on the coastal fringe of Senegal and the British on the Gold Coast. The French colony of Gabon consisted basically of a small naval base and the tiny town of Libreville. Portuguese Guinea was more a sphere of influence than an active colony. As you will see, only in South Africa had significant control developed. Within thirty five years, however, all this would change. Ethiopia and American-protected Liberia would be the only African states to resist European rule.

African colonization developed within the

EUROPEAN COLONIAL POSSESSIONS IN AFRICA, 1914

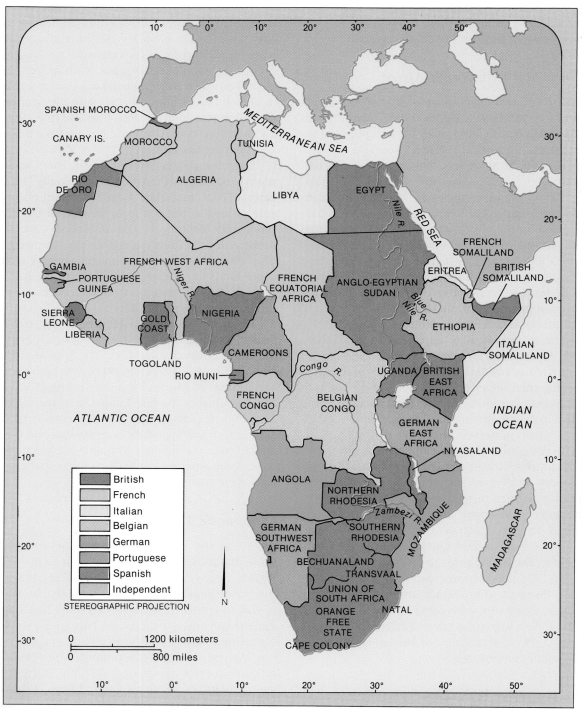

What general areas of Africa were dominated by Great Britain? In what part of Africa did France establish its colonies?

context of European political rivalry in the 1880's and 1890's. Primarily to secure Egypt, and thus the vital route to India and the Indian Ocean itself, Britain formed its African policy. France saw in the mass of Saharan North Africa a logical balance to Britain's East African empire. Germany's Bismarck personally thought African colonies useless. Yet he saw the diplomatic potential of driving a wedge between Britain and France and was prodded into colonization by German business interests. Italy, ever aware of its second-class military status, went after relatively valueless African real estate in a quest for world prestige. Even Belgium, an industrialized nation of no military importance, found itself the possessor of valuable territory in central Africa. It owed its presence there to the financial dealings of a wealthy private businessman—its king.

The Scramble for Africa

In his coast-to-coast journey across central Africa, the journalist and adventurer Henry M. Stanley came across untapped and unclaimed new territories. He offered his discoveries to King Leopold II of Belgium. Acting as a private person, Leopold set up a corporation to exploit the Congo Basin. Profit in rubber and copper were his chief motives.

The business interests that Leopold was associated with killed many of the Congo's rubber trees. People who protested the inhuman conditions they were forced to work under were repressed violently. In bold violation of basic conservation measures and human rights, Leopold and his investors made a stunning profit. Only when the Belgian government took over the administration in 1908 did the worst atrocities end.

The Belgian example encouraged German capitalists. In the space of eighteen months, from 1883 to 1885, Bismarck oversaw the annexation of Togoland, South-West Africa (now Namibia), the Cameroons, and East Africa. North and east of Leopold's Congo, French interests established the city of Brazzaville, laying claim to the French Congo.

The Berlin Conference, which lasted from late 1884 to early 1885, recognized Leopold's Congo Free State. Both the Congo and Niger river basins were declared free trade zones. All conference participants agreed to ban slavery and encourage civilization. Most important, the conference established certain ground rules for gaining "unclaimed" African lands. It now became necessary to actively occupy a territory to earn recognition by other nations. The "scramble" for Africa was under way.

In western Africa French control increased in Senegal, Guinea, the Ivory Coast, and Dahomey. The Portuguese annexed the Cape Verde Islands and huge areas in Mozambique (moe-zam-BEEK) and Angola (ang-GOE-luh). The British took the coasts of modern Nigeria, Sierra Leone (see-AIR-ruh lee-OHN), the Gold Coast, and Gambia in eastern Africa, gained influence in territories that are now Kenya and Uganda, and extended into southern Africa. Tanganyika (tan-gun-YEE-kuh) was acknowledged as German. In fifteen years the Europeans partitioned most of the continent.

The Egyptian Sudan

In the strategic Sudan, long under Egyptian rule, a major diplomatic crisis flared up in the late 1890's. Since the British occupied Egypt in 1882, the Sudan had posed a problem to them. In 1885 Britain lost its most famous general, C. G. Gordon, in the siege of Khartoum by Sudanese rebels. The British public was shocked. The government temporarily abandoned the idea of conquering the region.

In the 1890's the French dreamed of a transcontinental empire linking France's North African holdings with the Indian Ocean. They hoped to occupy the Upper Nile region and undermine the welfare of British Egypt. To achieve this end, Captain J. B. Marchand and a small band of black soldiers journeyed two years through the tropics to Fashoda on the White Nile.

Meanwhile the British dealt a brutal blow to the Sudanese in 1898 with an army under General Herbert Kitchener. At Omdurman and in other battles, at least 20,000 Sudanese lost their lives. Kitchener, learning of Marchand's arrival at Fashoda, rushed to challenge him and to demand his withdrawal. In the absence of instructions, Marchand refused to budge. The Fashoda incident placed Great Britain and France at the brink of war.

For a while in 1898 it seemed possible that the two powers would come to blows. But Britain, with a superior force, remained firm. France backed down. An agreement signed in 1899 left the Nile valley in British hands. Although the immediate French reaction was anger, France began to realize it could not afford to be on bad terms with both Germany and Britain at the same time. France began to shape its foreign policy to draw closer to Britain.

The First Europeans in Southern Africa

The first European colonists in southern Africa were the Dutch, who came in the 1650's. They were attracted by the Dutch East India Company whose way station at the Cape of Good Hope was a stop for ships en route to Asia. As their population grew, they began farming and raising cattle in the interior, away from company control. These rugged pioneers, called Boers (BOHRZ), were Calvinists. Cut off from Europe's modernizing trends,

they developed their own dialect, a variant of Dutch called Afrikaans.

When the British first seized the Cape in the Napoleonic period, it made little difference to the isolated Boers, but later developments disrupted their way of life. The abolition of slavery in the British Empire in the 1830's affected the slave-based Boer economy. The British returned lands to the Bantu that the Boers wanted. The Boers decided to push east, beyond British control.

In Natal (nuh-TAL), on the southeastern coast, they met fierce resistance from the warrior Zulus. Under their brilliant leader, Shaka, the Zulus had become well-disciplined fighters in the early 1800's. The Zulus killed the Boer leader and his followers. The Boers were forced to abandon the territory. When the British annexed Natal in 1843, the Boers decided to move.

This poster for an opera reflects the interest of the British people in their army's exploits abroad. How does the media today reflect the current political situation?

In a series of migrations known as the Great Trek, the Boers pushed north, or trekked, across the Orange River and later across the Vaal (VAHL). In the 1850's they established two republics, the Orange Free State and the Transvaal. There they built plantations and reestablished slavery.

Compared to the British Cape Colony, the Boer republics were commercially backward. The British prevented them from establishing independent access to the sea and thereby profits from direct trade. In the late 1860's, however, the discovery of diamonds forever ended Boer isolation.

The Origins of Modern South Africa

The discovery in the Orange Free State of the richest diamond deposit in the world, followed by the discovery of gold in the Transvaal, transformed the undeveloped Boer republics. Fortune hunters flooded the country. They were known to the Boers as *Uitlanders* (AIT-lan-durz), or outsiders. Soon they outnumbered the Boers.

In the 1890's British and Boer competition peaked. Cecil Rhodes, a wealthy businessman, had become Prime Minister of the Cape Colony. Rhodes pressured the Boer republics to open up Boer lands to the big diamond and gold mining interests which he headed. To Paul Kruger, the Transvaal president who had trekked as a boy and wanted to unite white South Africa under Boer leadership, Rhodes was a threat. To Rhodes, Kruger was a reactionary.

With the help of a few friends, Rhodes planned an uprising of *Uitlanders* in Johannesburg to coincide with an armed expedition into the Transvaal. Both were bungled, and Rhodes was forced to resign. But the drift toward war continued.

The Boer War, fought from 1899 to 1902, was the bloody climax to European imperialism in Africa. It took three years for the British to suppress the Boers even though the support Kruger expected from Britain's European rivals never came. The Boers finally came under British rule, but the British made some concessions.

Afrikaans continued to be used in the schools and the courts. In 1910 the Union of South Africa united Britain's South African colonies. In a gesture of conciliation to the Boers, "the native problem" was not addressed. The British expected eventually to give black Africans the vote, but the constitution did not provide for universal suffrage. The Boers, who outnumbered the British, gained control of the government of South Africa. They established a policy of **apartheid** (uh-PAHR-tide), or racial segregation.

Impact of Imperialism

There is no doubt the Europeans brought advances in housing, technology, and communications to Africa and developed untapped natural resources. But with these advances came the drawbacks of urbanization: overcrowded cities, sanitation problems, and unemployment. Also there was always the racial element. Africans became second-class citizens in their own countries.

Another major effect of foreign rule was the demand for labor. In the Congo and South Africa, workers were exploited in the worst examples of European imperialism. Elsewhere colonial officials demanded labor for the building of roads, railways, and buildings. Local chiefs were obliged to provide work details.

Colonial governments were given relatively little money to spend. They left missionaries to handle problems of medicine and education. Private interests developed the economy. The officials main concern was to keep order. This situation would last until nationalism affected North Africa after World War I and sub-Saharan Africa after World War II.

SECTION REVIEW

1. Mapping: Use the map on page 522 to locate Algeria, Cape Colony, Belgian Congo, Niger River, Natal, Transvaal, Zambezi River
2. In your own words, identify or define: David Livingstone, Leopold II, Berlin Conference, Fashoda incident, Shaka, Paul Kruger, Boer War.
3. What factors made possible Africa's isolation into the nineteenth century? What triggered the scramble for Africa?
■ The government of South Africa has had to resort to force in order to maintain apartheid. What do you think will be the final outcome of the struggle? Explain.

Cecil Rhodes (1853–1902)

The man who best personified the new capitalist imperialism in Africa during the late-Victorian Era was Cecil Rhodes. Rhodes was an impassioned empire builder. He once claimed that the British Empire was his only religion. If history had taught him anything, he wrote, it was "that expansion is everything, and that the world's surface being limited, the great object of present humanity should be to take as much of the world as it possibly could." He was personally responsible for a sizable share of the 3.5 million square miles (9 million square kilometers) of territory the British Empire annexed in the last fifteen years of the nineteenth century. His dream was a railway that would connect Egypt to South Africa through an uninterrupted stretch of British territory. Rhodes himself planned to finance and construct it.

A clergyman's son, as a boy Rhodes was physically weak and prone to illness. He went to South Africa to regain his health and made a fortune in diamonds and gold. He built monopolies by taking over small mines and overturning big businesses. He amassed a fortune but claimed that he was not interested in money, but in power. While studying at Oxford, he had become infused with the imperialist spirit.

As prime minister of the Cape Colony, Rhodes tried to topple the Boer republics. His British South Africa Company stood ready to expand Cape interests in an area soon to be known as Rhodesia. In 1895 he authorized a coup that backfired.

The raid on the Transvaal of six hundred armed men under the leadership of one of Rhodes' company associates, Dr. Jameson, was foolish and poorly organized. The raiders were captured, Rhodes' role in the plot made clear, and Rhodes' public career ruined. He resigned as prime minister and was forced to leave the board of the company. Nevertheless, he remained a major force until his death.

Rhodes' attitudes and methods were not unlike many other imperialists of the time. He was perhaps more successful than most because of his enthusiasm, vision, and ambition. He had a drive to push northward in Africa and obtain all unmapped territory for Great Britain.

After Rhodes' death in 1902, certain provisions in Rhodes' will were amended to make possible his wish for a student scholarship to Oxford University.

1. How did Cecil Rhodes personify late Victorian imperialism?
2. What aspects of his career set examples for other imperialists?
3. Mark Twain wrote of Cecil Rhodes, "When he stood on the Cape Peninsula, his shadow fell on Zambesi." How did this quote characterize the way Rhodes was seen by others?

BRITISH INDIA

After the decline of the Mogul Empire and France's defeat in the Seven Years' War, England became the chief European power in India. The Portuguese and French were restricted to a few coastal trading stations.

The British Victory in India

The end of the rivalry between Britain and France in India revealed that Europeans far outstripped Indians in firepower and military techniques. With better muskets and cannons a small number of European troops were able to subdue thousands of native soldiers. Nowhere had this been more clearly demonstrated than at Plassey in June 1757. There, with eight hundred Europeans and about two thousand Indian soldiers, John Clive defeated the nawab of Bengal's army of fifty thousand.

In the mid-1760's a key development occurred when the British East India Company insisted on its right to collect taxes in Bengal. The company was no longer simply a trading firm; it was a government in its own right.

In the decade following Clive's victory, India became a prime target for the company's corrupt and adventurous officers. They made themselves rich from unofficial trade, taxes, and bribes. In the 1770's London decided to confront the problem. It established in Bengal a governor-general and a council empowered to reform the confused administration.

The reforms meant that the government in London—not the company—was now in broad political control. India was too rich a prize to be left in the hands of private individuals.

Administrative Reform

In the 1780's a new governor-general symbolized how Britain's governing India helped compensate for the recent loss of the American colonies. The new official was Lord Cornwallis, the man defeated at the Battle of Yorktown in Virginia. Cornwallis asserted the power of government and rid the British East India Company of corruption. He separated the functions of officials into political or commercial service and demanded that officials choose between the two. A merchant was permitted to trade, but an administrator had to live solely on a salary.

Next, because he believed Indians to be corrupt beyond reform, he dismissed all the high native officials. This gave the service a distinctly European quality, but it led to lingering resentment among Indians. In the legal realm, Cornwallis assumed the task of administering criminal justice from the Indian officials and developed a code that was, for its day, truly enlightened.

Whatever their merits, however, these reforms did not alter the fabric of Indian society, because few Indians enjoyed the benefits of British rule. Those who profited were the new monied class in the towns and the new hereditary landlords created by the British reform of the tax system. In the sprawling countryside beyond British control, life continued as it had for centuries.

The Expansion of English Authority

British authority in India relied in part on Indian participation in British rule. The territory under British influence beyond the province of Bengal was Indian in nature. However, the British steadily replaced the declining Mogul political system with their own administration. In doing so they followed what some historians have described as the classic model of expansion. They established power in the central area of the Ganges River and, from there, branched out to control the rest of the subcontinent.

Most of the coastal areas and the massive valley of the Ganges River, including Delhi, fell under British control by the early 1800's. Later, with the help of Indian troops called sepoys (SEE-poyz), who were trained and commanded by the British military, other regions came under direct rule. The Marathas were defeated and most of Burma was taken by the 1820's. A war with the Afghan Empire proved disastrous, but in the 1840's the Sind was annexed. This was followed directly by the defeat of the Sikhs and the incorporation of the Punjab in the north. In the 1850's a second Burmese war brought the annexation of Rangoon. Throughout their campaigns, the British exploited the deep-rooted friction between Hindu and Muslim. They found it to their advantage to "divide and rule."

These British infantry officers and their Indian guides are heading off on a tiger shoot. Why would they choose to travel by elephant?

The Main Elements of British Policy

As the Age of Enlightenment gradually gave way to one of industry, notions of Victorian improvement gained a firmer grip on British policy. The British imposed what they believed to be the superior values of the world's most advanced society on what they deemed an old and decaying civilization.

The British suppressed those rituals of Indian religion that they found outrageous. The thugs, a secret order that robbed, kidnapped, and executed victims in honor of the goddess Kali, were outlawed. The burning of widows on the funeral pyres of their husbands was also forbidden. Though the practice of this ritual, known as *suttee,*

was greatly exaggerated, the attempt to eliminate it was considered an invasion into the sacred realm of religious worship.

The Victorians instituted the use of English rather than Persian as the exclusive language of education and government. They built railways and dug canals. They laid hundreds of miles of telegraph lines and introduced a modern postal system. They developed the country and created the framework of the modern Indian state. Nevertheless, many Indians resented what they considered interference in their traditional way of life. What they resented even worse was being treated as inferiors.

Under the direction of the Marquis of Dalhousie, who served as governor-general from 1848 to

1856, the policy of modernization accelerated. Lord Dalhousie zealously promoted western education, public works, and the expansion of the railway network. He also carried out the doctrine of lapse. Under this policy Hindu states without natural heirs were to be taken over by the British regardless of the custom of adoption. In the space of eight years, Dalhousie annexed eight states. He even informed the Mogul emperor at Delhi that his title would lapse upon his death. These developments frightened India's upper class and heightened tensions within Indian society.

The Sepoy Mutiny

The turning point of the British raj, or rule, in India came with the great uprising of 1857–1858, the so-called Sepoy Mutiny. The explosive spark was ignited in the Bengal Army.

A rumor spread that cartridges for new rifles were smeared with the grease of cows and pigs. To Hindus the eating of beef is forbidden, and to Muslims the eating of pork. Because the cartridges had to be bitten before use, both Hindu and Muslim soldiers felt dishonored. The cartridges were withdrawn and explanations were offered, but the troops mutinied. They considered the incident another crude example of the western assault on their traditions.

The rebels were savage. The British responded in kind with their share of atrocities, especially after a massacre of women and children. In the north, where fighting was heaviest, dispossessed native princes led a movement to restore the Mogul Empire. The British had to bring forces from abroad to put down the rebellion.

In 1858 the East India Company and the Mogul Empire were abolished. From that date until the British quit India in 1947 the country was administered directly by a secretary of state with cabinet status in London. In 1877, at British Prime Minister Disraeli's suggestion, Queen Victoria took the title Empress of India.

On both sides relations after the mutiny would never be the same. For the British the easy self-confidence that they had come to take for granted was profoundly upset. The future as they saw it lay in stable government. More than ever the British would pay close attention to public opinion—especially that of the conservative upper classes.

Among the Indians the results were mixed. Most of the country had not been touched by the rebellion. But the economic and social changes that accompanied British rule would encourage a young generation of Indians to westernize and learn English. From among the upper-class families in India would emerge a class of professionals, educated by the British in India and abroad.

British Imperialism in India

Throughout the nineteenth century India was the sole part of the British Empire untouched by laissez-faire theory. Economic motives were the

The Sepoy or Indian Mutiny of 1857 was not so widespread as to threaten British rule, but it was brutally put down. The penalty for mutiny in the military was death.

obvious reason. India was the key market for English cotton goods, and cotton goods were the leading export of England's first industrial revolution. In the early 1800's India's textile industry was demolished because it threatened the British mills. Afterward India was cast in the role of supplier of raw materials and consumer of manufactured goods.

India was vital to Britain's Far East trade. In 1870 nearly half of China's total imports consisted of opium. It was produced in India as a state monopoly and supplied by eager British traders. Of no less importance, India paid for the "privilege" of British government. Its interest payments on the Indian Public Debt grew steadily throughout the century. By the First World War, India was essential to Britain's balance of payments and economic well-being. Without exaggeration India was the jewel in the British imperial crown.

In terms of administration, the period saw the rise of the Indian Civil Service. This famous bureaucracy governed India with a high degree of efficiency and care. In the Civil Service historians have seen both the strengths and weaknesses of the British raj. On the one hand it provided stability and effective administration of remarkable standards. On the other hand its rigid structure did not respond to the needs of changing society.

The Indian Civil Service reinforced the racism that was so much a part of the British presence. Over 170 million Indians found themselves ruled by a small, elite corps of Britons. Indians were second-class citizens in their own country.

Emergence of Indian Nationalism

The last decades of the century witnessed a surge in British education. Liberal values challenged a new generation of Indians to look at its place in society. To many young Indians the technology, science, and values of the West were good developments. A democratic India of citizens equal under the law was worth working for, especially in a society restricted by social castes. To many educated Indians, there was no turning back to the India of the past.

When William Gladstone became British prime minister again in 1880, he embarked on a program of liberal reform. In India greater freedom of the press and a system of local self-government were met with enthusiasm. Although the liberal proposals were withdrawn as swiftly as they were offered, they raised hope in India.

It seemed natural for Indians to participate in the administration set up by the British. But British attitudes triggered Indian opposition to foreign rule. India was experiencing the birth pangs of a modern nationalist movement.

In 1885 the first meeting of the Indian National Congress was held at Bombay. It drew the support of the newly educated classes. These were the professionals, teachers, intellectuals, journalists, and university students of the Hindu majority. Though Muslims would later feel left out of the organization, the Indian National Congress developed into the chief vehicle of Indian nationalism. It dominated Indian politics into the twentieth century.

IMPERIALISM IN INDIA TO 1858

From what regions of India did the British expand their control?

1. Mapping: On the map on page 530 locate the following: Calcutta, Plassey, Delhi, the Punjab, the Sind.
2. In your own words, identify or define: Lord Cornwallis, *suttee*, Indian Civil Service, Indian National Congress.
3. Of what significance were Cornwallis' reforms in India?
4. Of what economic importance was India to Britain in the nineteenth century?

■ The British gained control of India by establishing control in one area and working out from there. Where in the world today are similar tactics being used in an effort to gain control of a region?

IMPERIALISM IN ASIA AND THE PACIFIC

As you read in Chapter 22, in the nineteenth century Japan managed a remarkable social change that brought it into the ranks of the industrialized nations. China, however, declined economically and politically and became a victim of western imperialism. Japan joined the other powers in exploiting China's weaknesses.

China and the West

Was China so very far behind the West? Some historians have suggested that because of its ancient and proud tradition China, even when it was overpowered, refused to accept the superiority of western technology. This may be partially true. But it also must be said that the first modern armsfactories and shipyards for steamship construction appeared in China in the late 1860's. Its most developed iron and steel complex, for example, was estimated to have been two years in advance of Japanese steelworks in 1896. By 1909 Chinese engineers built a railway from a northwestern prov-

ince to Beijing, through rough terrain.

China's failure to industrialize was the result of several factors. As the Qing government weakened in the nineteenth century, the West carved China up into spheres of influence. The forces that could have brought about industrialization lacked capital. The two factors that gave rise to industrial and military Japan in the Meiji era were not present in China. China had neither a strong central government nor regular sources of revenue. China was ripe for foreign domination.

Russian Advances

As early as the late 1850's Russia had occupied the territory along the Amur and east of the Ussuri River. This maritime province had been part of China since the thirteenth century. A decade later Russia took advantage of China's internal weakness to invade a region near Turkestan. Qing representatives hurried to St. Petersburg to demand withdrawal. A part of the territory was restored, but China was forced to pay indemnity.

In the Pacific region south of the Amur and east of Manchuria, the Russians constructed a new port and called it Vladivostok, meaning "Master of the East." There they built a naval base. In the early 1890's the construction of the Trans-Siberian Railway was considered throughout the world a threatening shift in Russian foreign policy. It was certain to change the whole balance of power in the region. With concern China and Japan watched Russian plans unfold.

China

Japan's first moves at China's expense were its occupation of the Ryukyu Islands and its challenge to China's claim to Formosa. In 1876 Japan opened Korea.

Korea had long been under Chinese influence, and the West wanted commercial rights to it. Sensing that a western-dominated Korea would weaken its security, Japan acted first. Japan used western tactics of gunboat diplomacy to open key Korean ports to Japanese trade. Japan obtained from China the recognition of economic privileges. Western nations followed with similar arrangements. So began a series of events that forced China to commit itself to protecting its interest in

Korea and eventually led to war with Japan.

The Sino-Japanese War marked Japan's coming of age militarily. Its relatively quick victory was a major event that showed the world that Japan had modern weaponry and was now a power in the Far East. For China the defeat was disastrous. The fleet it had attempted to build in its defense was completely destroyed. By the Treaty of Shimonoseki in 1895, China was forced to pay reparations three times the government's annual income. Japan annexed Taiwan and the Pescadores Islands, and it gained the important Liaodong (LYOW-DOONG) Peninsula.

All of this prompted the western powers to seek their share in China. Like vultures they descended on China and gained economic privileges from the Qing government. Germany seized areas in southeastern Shandong (SHAHN-DOONG). Great Britain occupied the region of Wei-hai-wei (WAY-HIE-WAY) and the far eastern part of the Shandong Peninsula. France, whose interests lay in the south, took Guangdong (GWONG-DOONG). Russia snapped up the southern tip of the Liaodong Peninsula, which western pressure had forced the Japanese to give up. There the Russians built a naval base at the strategic port of Lüshun (LOO-SHWOON), renamed Port Arthur by the westerners.

China lost more control of its economy as foreign capital poured into the country. Factories, mines, and banks multiplied. All were run by western and Japanese companies that paid low wages to the local workers and made high profits. The impact of these developments would bring about China's first twentieth-century revolution.

The Russo-Japanese War

In 1902, out of mutual concern over Russian expansion in the East, Great Britain and Japan con-

How many nations depicted in this American cartoon can you identify that had an interest in carving up China?

cluded a formal alliance treaty. This was the first alliance ever between an Asian nation and a western power. Japan had achieved its recognition of diplomatic equality.

Of particular concern were Russian business ventures in northern Korea, an area that was now a Japanese sphere of influence. Japan proposed negotiations but the czar, incited by militant factions at court, stalled. In February 1904, without any formal warning, the Japanese launched a sneak attack on the Russian navy at Port Arthur. The Russians were taken completely by surprise.

For the Russians the Russo-Japanese War was one disaster followed by another. The Russian army campaign in Manchuria ended in defeat in March 1905. It was followed in May by the greatest humiliation in Russian naval history. At the Battle of Tsushima Strait a good part of the Russian fleet, including most of the Baltic squadron, was sunk. After two years of savage warfare, the Russians sued for peace.

Japanese and Russian diplomats met at Portsmouth, New Hampshire, where they negotiated a treaty with the help of President Theodore Roosevelt. Roosevelt persuaded Japan to abandon its demands for an indemnity. The Japanese took Port Arthur and the Liaodong Peninsula, acquired half of the island of Sakhalin, and gained fishing privileges off the Siberian coast. In 1910 they annexed Korea.

The Russo-Japanese War caused a national crisis and a failed revolution in Russia. Japan's victory impressed the world by demonstrating that a nonwestern people, with discipline and direction, could deliver a stunning defeat to a major European power. For the United States, already a great power, Japan was now a rival in the Far East. Feelings of suspicion and mistrust replaced a formerly pleasant relationship.

Southeast Asia

The peoples of modern Southeast Asia are of Chinese and Tibetan origin. About 2500 years ago they began their migrations south into Indochina. From there they moved on to the Indonesian archipelago, to Polynesia and Oceania.

The cultures of Indochina, or mainland Southeast Asia, were largely influenced by India and China. Indian merchants and missionaries spread both the Hindu and Buddhist religions and the writings and mythology of classical India. Like Japan and Korea, Indochina absorbed much of China's civilization. The region saw the growth and decline of the Khmer Empire in Cambodia and the rise and fall of the Champa in what is today Vietnam.

Europe first intruded in Southeast Asia in the sixteenth century. Portuguese warships blasted their way into the Asian spice trade. They seized a number of ports that were vital to Far Eastern commerce. In the early seventeenth century the Portuguese faced the rivalry of the Dutch, who occupied Indonesia in the 1640's.

In the 1560's the Spanish colonized the Philippine Islands. What was unique here was Spain's direct rule. The Spanish united the country under a single government and converted much of the population to Catholicism.

Elsewhere in the region at this time the European presence was more commercial than colonial. Europeans shared the active East Asian seas in fierce competition with Chinese and other Asian merchants. They were not able to establish the kind of control that marked the modern period.

In the eighteenth century interest in the region shifted from spices to crops such as coffee and sugar. Europeans set up slave-based plantations similar to their West Indies operations. As industrialization made raw materials like rubber and tin valuable, the East Indies assumed new importance. In 1798 the Dutch changed their trading company in Southeast Asia into a royal colony, the Dutch East Indies. Like the British in India, the Dutch found their East Indies Company too corrupt for the proper administration of their most valuable overseas possession. Direct rule became a necessity.

The English and French in Southeast Asia

The industrial powers, Britain and France, made the biggest impact in the nineteenth century. As you have read, the British reached out to protect and extend their commercial empire in India. After a series of wars that began in the 1820's, they annexed Burma and other ports in the early 1850's. By the 1880's Burma was administered under British-Indian control.

MAJOR COLONIAL POSSESSIONS IN ASIA AND THE PACIFIC, 1914

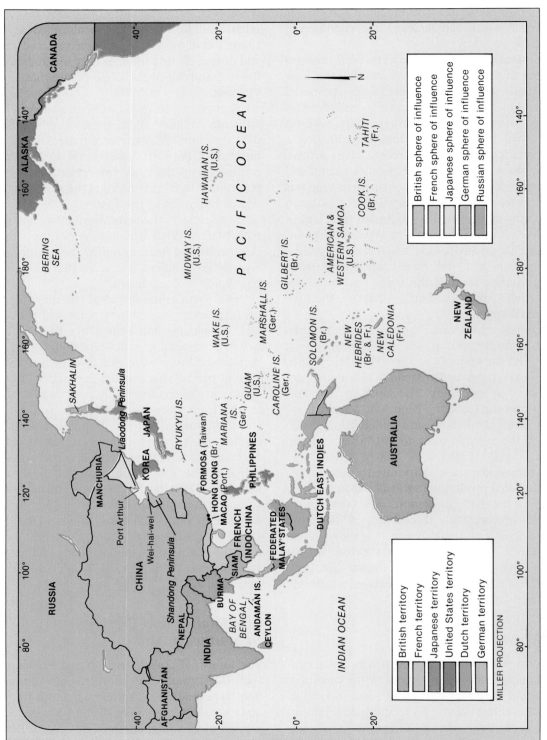

*What territories in Asia and the Pacific were under American control? What
European country had the greatest influence in the area?*

The French, under Napoleon III, spread north and west from Saigon (present-day Ho Chi Minh City), where they had established a landing in the late 1850's. Within a decade they were in control of Cochin China, or southern Vietnam, and Cambodia (present-day Kampuchea). In the early 1880's, as they pushed up the Red River valley, the French faced stiffer resistance. There the Vietnamese had the assistance of the Black Flag army, which comprised former Tai Ping soldiers who had taken refuge in northern Vietnam. To overcome the Black Flag, France resorted to direct pressure on China by carrying the war to the Chinese coast.

China was forced to sign a new treaty at Tianjin, and the French gained a free hand in Vietnam. China thus renounced its historic relations with a region long under its influence. In 1887 France formed a union of Indochina consisting of its Southeast Asian holdings. Laos was added to the union in 1893.

With the French in Indochina and the British in Burma, the kingdom of Siam found itself in the fortunate position of being caught in the middle. Out of mutual interest, Britain and France decided to preserve Siam as a **buffer state** between their territories. As a buffer Siam remained independent, serving to decrease the chance of war between the two major powers.

Island Fever

Interest in the Pacific islands was strategic as well as economic. Manufacturers and importers of tropical products pressured their governments to make gains at international bargaining tables. The governments themselves were mainly interested in these islands as fueling stations. Here steamships could stock up on coal supplies or be properly repaired or supplied.

As in Asia and Africa, the scramble peaked in the last quarter of the century. By 1900 almost all of the islands were under foreign rule. Great Britain grabbed the Fiji, Gilbert, and a few of the Solomon Islands. France, which had taken Tahiti in the 1840's, shared with Britain control of the New Hebrides. Germany bought from the crippled Spanish Empire the Carolines and, with the exception of Guam, the Mariana Islands.

The most intense Pacific rivalry involved the Samoan Islands. As early as the 1870's the United States, whose other Pacific possessions you will read about in the next section, acquired rights to a Samoan naval base at Pago Pago on the island of Tutuila. In return for using a coaling station at Pago Pago, the United States agreed to protect the native government against foreign intervention. This opened the way for problems between the United States, Great Britain and Germany.

Though Britain was the islands' chief supplier, Germany had interests here too. German firms set up large coconut plantations on one of the islands, and Germans controlled the export trade in coconut products. Tensions increased in the late 1880's, but the problem was not solved until a minor crisis in German-American relations led to treaty agreements in 1899.

Britain, it was decided, would gain compensation elsewhere. The United States took control of Tutuila and half a dozen other islands forming a territory known as American Samoa. Germany acquired the other islands in the chain in a possession called Western Samoa. "The whole of Samoa," a high-ranking German official said, "was not worth the money spent upon telegrams." For the United States the affair brought the naval base at Pago Pago. Otherwise, these islands were further evidence that the imperialist push for territories was as much symbolic as practical.

SECTION REVIEW

1. Mapping: Use the Atlas map of the Far East on page 755 to locate the following: South Korea, Vietnam, Tibet, Siam (Thailand), Taiwan, Laos, Indonesia.
2. In your own words, identify or define: Treaty of Shimonoseki, Port Arthur, French Indochina, Dutch East Indies, buffer state.
3. What impact did Russian advances into eastern Asia have on the Far East question?
4. Did the French encounter any resistance in Vietnam in the 1880's? How did they handle it?
■ The Samoan Islands were considered of such strategic importance that major powers in this period almost went to war over them. What areas of the world are considered of strategic importance today?

THE UNITED STATES EMERGES AS A WORLD POWER

Having emerged as an industrial giant in the late nineteenth century, the United States assumed a more active position in international affairs. Like many of the world's advanced nations, it too was swept up in the imperialist fever.

The New Manifest Destiny

By the 1890's most of the territory of the transcontinental United States had been explored and settled. The nation was eager to extend itself abroad. The country's population, industrial level, and sheer wealth convinced many Americans that the theories of imperialism could be applied by the United States. No doubt popular journalism played its role, too. Publishers like William Randolph Hearst and Joseph Pulitzer competed for circulation by satisfying the desire for exciting news.

In the early 1890's the new manifest destiny exhibited itself in Hawaii. American involvement there dated from the 1820's when Protestant missionaries from New England first arrived. By the end of the century, a community of American sugar planters lived on the islands. In 1893 Hawaii's Queen Liliuokalani (lee-lee-oo-oh-kah-LAH-nee) campaigned for native control of the islands. The American planters rose in open revolt. The United States helped them by landing troops. President Grover Cleveland soon discovered that Hawaii did not want to be annexed. The American public was reluctant to seize territory by force, but American plantation interests won out. In 1898 the Hawaiian Islands were annexed by a joint act of Congress.

The Venezuelans appealed to the Americans for arbitration of a border dispute with British Guiana in the 1890's. The United States invoked the Monroe Doctrine. Britain, faced with problems in South Africa, finally agreed to negotiate. As it turned out, the settlement gave the British what they had wanted in the first place. During the crisis, when open conflict seemed unavoidable, pro-war sentiment reached a fever point in the United States.

Challenge to British Interests

Until the end of the nineteenth century Great Britain was the leading economic power in Latin America. Since the independence movements, Britain had made loans, built railroads, supplied technology, and sold its manufactured goods in Latin America. The continent's other major sources of capital (the United States, France, and to a lesser extent, Germany) did not together equal that of Britain. In the early twentieth century this all changed.

United States and German products started to rival British goods in Latin American markets. Using the latest marketing skills, American and German salespeople made their pitch to Latin American buyers in the Spanish and Portuguese languages. The British, on the other hand, continued to rely on the sale of standard goods distributed by agents who knew only English. By the end of the century, Brazil and Cuba had strong economic ties to the United States that were bolstered by trade and American investments.

Cuba and the Spanish-American War

Spain's only important overseas territory was Cuba, a possession it controlled since the sixteenth century. It had a good deal of money invested in Cuba's plantation economy. As the United States replaced Spain as Cuba's natural market, many Cubans began to favor independence.

In an open rebellion in the mid-1890's, Cubans burned sugar fields and mining trains. The Spanish Army reacted with tough measures that brought cries of outrage from the American public. The American press played up the atrocities. The Cubans carried out modern guerrilla warfare against the Spanish forces.

Public opinion in the United States favored the Cuban rebels. Then, suddenly, in February 1898 the USS *Maine* mysteriously blew up. The *Maine* had been stationed in Havana to protect American citizens in case of emergency. Two hundred sixty servicemen were killed in the explosion. The American public was angered. The Spanish government tried everything it could to calm the United States short of granting Cuba its independence. In April 1898 the United States declared war on Spain.

During the Spanish-American War new warships quickly defeated the outdated Spanish fleet in the Caribbean and the Pacific. In December 1898 the Spanish sued for peace. Cuban independence was recognized and a Cuban constitution was drafted, but the Cubans had to accept the United States' Platt Amendment. The Platt Amendment gave the United States the right to intervene in Cuba's affairs should American property or citizens be threatened. It was a right the United States was to use repeatedly. The amendment also provided the United States with two naval bases on the island.

United States' Possessions

As a result of the war, the United States gained Puerto Rico in the Caribbean, and Guam and the Philippine Islands in the Pacific.

The most difficult problem was in the Philippines. The population had long been misruled by Spanish colonial officials. One consideration was to set the Philippines free. But American policymakers feared this would result in anarchy that would set the stage for intervention by some other power—Germany most likely. The result could very well lead to war.

The Filipinos assumed however that, like the Cubans, they were entitled to independence after their liberation from Spain. In early 1899 they rebelled against the United States. Quickly defeated, the Filipino armies ran a guerrilla campaign. The United States finally broke the rebellion when it captured Emilio Aguinaldo, the well-educated revolutionary leader the United States had invited back to the Philippines in 1898 for the purpose of undermining Spanish authority.

In the following years, the United States poured millions of dollars into the Philippines. It improved sanitation, roads, and communications, and it developed an important trade. It set up a first-rate school system staffed by Americans who helped establish English as a second language. But the Philippines would be satisfied with nothing less than independence.

The Panama Canal

Victorious against Spain, the United States reviewed its global needs. The United States was a

Queen Liliuokalani was the last monarch to officially rule Hawaii. Why do you think many Americans hesitated to end Hawaii's independence?

Pacific and Atlantic power with growing commercial interests and a fleet in both arenas. American policymakers were interested in a waterway that would do for the West what the Suez Canal had done for the East. Cutting a canal through Central America seemed a perfect solution. In 1903 President Theodore Roosevelt determined that the United States would build a canal, immediately. Panama and Nicaragua were the two places under consideration.

At that time Panama was part of Colombia, which refused to lease the United States the strip of territory needed for the canal. Colombia, however, was separated from Panama by dense jungle. Panamanians, who had revolted several times before, were willing to fight for a multimillion dollar project. In November 1903 a tiny revolt broke out and Panama proclaimed its independence. When Co-

Why do you think this cartoon portrays the American eagle with its wings spread from Puerto Rico to the Philippines.

lombian troops were sent to put down the rebellion, United States warships prevented them from landing.

The United States immediately recognized Panama's independence. Two weeks later Panama granted its North American neighbor rights to a coast-to-coast strip of territory. The United States purchased the territory for $10 million and an annuity of $250,000. Construction began the next year.

At great cost the United States drained swamps and brought yellow fever under control. It succeeded also in almost wiping out malaria. On August 3, 1914, the first ship passed through the Panama Canal. To critics in Latin America and elsewhere, the whole episode smacked of high-handed imperialism. To Roosevelt and his supporters, the United States had simply seized the moment.

The Roosevelt Corollary

America's new diplomatic role was also evident in the Roosevelt Corollary to the Monroe Doctrine in 1904. By this the United States redefined its role in the region. According to the Roosevelt Corollary, the United States now reserved the right to intervene in Latin America if Latin American nations defaulted on foreign loans. European gunboat diplomacy aimed at Venezuela and the Dominican Republic after these countries had so defaulted in the early 1900's prompted the corollary. The European powers had reacted to these defaults using the same tactics they employed in North Africa.

By announcing the right to exercise international police power, Roosevelt redefined the Monroe Doctrine. Critics argued that he was misusing it. The Monroe Doctrine had stated that European intervention in American affairs was not tolerable. The Roosevelt Corollary stated that the United States could intervene whenever it saw fit. The United States alone was justified in taking preventative measures in the region to secure its foreign policy objectives.

On several occasions in the next decades—in Cuba in 1906, in Nicaragua in the 1920's—the United States exercised this right. It would be interpreted by critics as yet another example of American imperialism. But there was no getting around the fact that the United States finally had emerged from its international isolation, at least for a time.

SECTION REVIEW

1. Mapping: Use the Atlas maps of the Far East and South America on pages 755 and 760 to locate the following: the United States, Cuba, the Philippines, Panama, Venezuela.

2. In your own words, identify or define: William Randolph Hearst, USS *Maine*, Platt Amendment, Emilio Aguinaldo, Panama Canal, Roosevelt Corollary.

3. What were the origins of the Spanish-American War of 1898? What problems did the United States have with the Philippines immediately following the war with Spain?

■ The United States emerged as a world power in the late nineteenth century. What countries do you think are currently world powers? Which countries seem to be decreasing in power? Which seem to be increasing?

Reviewing the Chapter

Chapter Summary

In the latter part of the nineteenth century the industrialized powers began a new competition for colonization and empire building. A great debate exists as to what caused this competition, but it is generally agreed that it was the result of various economic, diplomatic, psychological, and cultural factors.

In Africa, which for centuries had remained isolated from the West, the competition for colonies was furious. Exploitation was particularly brutal in the Congo. The bloody climax to imperialism in Africa occurred in the Boer War. In the Union of South Africa the foundations were laid for a system of apartheid.

British authority in India stemmed in part from Indian participation in British rule. The British increasingly replaced the deteriorating system of the Mogul Empire with their own rule. India proved vital to the British economy and for this reason the value of India as a colony was never seriously questioned.

Whereas Japan managed a remarkable social transformation that brought it into the ranks of the advanced nations, China did not, and was exploited by foreign powers. Japan's military status was recognized in two military victories—the first against China, the second against Russia. The United States, too, emerged as a major imperial power, above all in Latin America.

1. What was the background of nineteenth-century imperialism?
2. How did imperialism disrupt Africa?
3. How did Japan signal its membership in the ranks of advanced nations?

Using Your Vocabulary

1. What is imperialism? How does new imperialism differ from the imperialism of the seventeenth and eighteenth centuries?
2. Why did some imperialist powers establish protectorates as opposed to colonies?
3. What is meant by the term "sphere of influence"? How does it differ from a protectorate?
4. What was the position of the khedive of Egypt in the Ottoman Empire?
5. What is the meaning of humanitarian? List at least two other words built on the same base word.
6. Who are the Boers? Why did they settle in South Africa?
7. What is Afrikaans? Why did it develop in South Africa?
8. What was the Great Trek?
9. What is apartheid? What base of the word gives you a clue to its meaning?
10. Who were the Sepoys? Why did they lead a mutiny against the British?
11. Why did the British outlaw the thugs? What is the meaning of "thugs" in current usage?
12. Why did the British try to abolish suttee? Why did the Indians object?
13. Why did Lord Dalhousie's use of the Doctrine of Lapse frighten India's upper class?
14. How did the Treaty of Shimonoseki benefit Japan?
15. What is the function of a buffer state?

Developing Your Geography Skills

1. Cecil Rhodes dreamed of a Cape-to-Cairo railroad. Use the Atlas map on page 754 to locate Cairo. Use the map on page 522 to name the colonial possessions of two European nations that stood in the way of Rhodes' goal.
2. Use the map on page 530 to describe the area of India first controlled by the British. By what year had the British gained control of the Punjab? Name the last regions the British gained control of.
3. Use the map on page 534 to name Britain's major colonial possessions in Asia and the

Pacific in 1914. What European country had a major colonial possession but no spheres of influence?
4. Use the maps on pages 522 and 534 to name those European nations who had possessions in Africa but not in Asia and the Pacific.
5. The completion of the transcontinental railroad in the United States increased American interest in New Zealand and Australia. As a result the United States became interested in having a coaling station in Samoa. Using the scale of miles on the Atlas map on page 761, estimate the distance between New Zealand and Samoa.

Recalling the Facts

1. What factors limited European interest in overseas possessions during the first half of the nineteenth century?
2. Who were the chief supporters of the new imperialism?
3. Of what value was imperialism to new powers? Established powers?
4. Why did the British prime minister call for a revival of a formal empire in the 1870's?
5. How did novels such as *King Solomon's Mines* influence the public?
6. Why did Egypt's wealth increase dramatically in the 1860's?
7. Why did the Suez Canal immediately become important in both a military and commercial sense?
8. When did Britain outlaw slavery? Why did the British try to eliminate the illegal slave trade?
9. Why did the French want to extend their control to the Sudan?
10. Why did Britain become the chief European power in India?
11. What was the turning point of British rule in India?
12. Why did China fail to industrialize when Japan did?
13. What event marked Japan's coming of age militarily?
14. How did the Russian-Japanese war affect both Russia and America?
15. Why were European governments involved in acquiring islands in the Pacific in the nineteenth century?
16. What was the Roosevelt Corollary?

Essay Questions

1. Discuss several economic, political, technological, and social factors that brought about the rise of the new imperialism. How did it differ from earlier forms of imperialism?
2. Trace the rivalry between France and Britain in Africa. How did the Fashoda incident mark a change in the relationship between these two nations?
3. What were the diplomatic motives for European colonization of Africa?
4. Describe some of the differences between the British and Boers in South Africa. What was the final outcome of their rivalry?
5. Discuss some of the positive and negative effects of European imperialism in Africa.
6. Cite several examples in support of the idea that China was not so far behind the West in the late to early twentieth century.
7. What Russian advances in the Far East were looked upon by the rest of the world as a threat? Why?
8. Sometimes the imperialistic rush for territory was as much symbolic as it was a drive for valuable territory. Explain and cite examples.

Critical Thinking

1. The practice of suttee was acceptable to the Indians but not to the British. How is this an example of a clash in values? How can different values lead to problems between nations?
2. What were logical inconsistencies between the reasons imperialist nations gave for acquiring colonies and the benefits they actually received from the territories?
3. The imperialist nations claimed that their actions benefited their territories. In what ways would you consider this a warranted claim? In what ways would you consider it an unwarranted claim? How would your answer be affected by your values?

Reviewing the Unit

Developing a Sense of Time

Examine the time line below and answer the questions that follow it.

1600	1603	Tokugawa Shogunate begins in Japan
	1644	Qing Dynasty established in China
1700	1787	Northwest Ordinance
1800	1803	Louisiana Purchase
	1804	Independence of Haiti
	1814	Congress of Vienna
	1822	Independence of Brazil
	1848	Revolutions in France, Italy, Germany, and the Austrian Empire
		Karl Marx's *Communist Manifesto*
1850	1850	Tai Ping Rebellion begins
	1852	Napoleon III establishes Second French Empire
	1853	Admiral Perry visits Japan
	1857	Sepoy Mutiny in India
	1861	Russian serfs emancipated
		U.S. Civil War begins
	1868	Meiji Restoration begins in Japan
	1870	Italian unification completed
		Franco-Prussian War begins
	1871	German Empire established
	1895	Roentgen discovers X ray
	1899	Boer War begins
1900	1905	Einstein's theory of relativity

1. Which occurred first: the American Civil War or the Franco-Prussian War?
2. What dynasty ruled China during the Tai Ping Rebellion?
3. Who replaced the Tokugawa as rulers of Japan?
4. What event happened the same year as revolutions in several European countries?

Social Science Skills

Using a Historical Photograph

1. Choose a photograph from the unit and explain its relationship to the text.
2. What additional information could you learn from the photograph?
3. Choose a photograph from a current newspaper or magazine. Describe how the photograph might interest an historian.

Critical Thinking

1. The nineteenth century saw the rise of democracy in Great Britain and France. What verifiable facts could you cite to defend that statement?
2. Conflicting values can lead to problems between people, between groups, or between nations. Based on what you have read in Unit 7, give an example of such a situation. Describe the circumstances and then offer a possible solution.
3. The outcome of the Franco-Prussian War affected France, Germany, and Italy in different ways. People viewed the outcome as "good" or "bad" according to their own bias. Write a brief evaluation of the results of the war from a French, German, and Italian point of view.
4. It has been said that art reflects life. Based on what you have read in this unit, would you consider this a warranted or unwarranted claim? Explain.

Linking Past and Present

The imperialists carved up regions such as Africa without any regard for the relationships between the native populations. National borders were based on European diplomacy and not on the geographic limits of the societies. How do you think this has created problems for modern Africa?

UNIT · 8 ·

The
TWENTIETH
CENTURY
to
1945

1900–1945

CHAPTER ·24·

WORLD WAR I

1914–1918

Objectives

- To describe the system of alliances that preceded World War I

- To explain how industrial technology affected the way World War I was fought

- To discuss the importance of the entry of the United States into World War I

- To describe how the map of Europe was redrawn by treaties ending World War I, creating problems leading up to another world war

*I*n 1914 the conflicts and ambitions of Europe's largest powers touched off a war that involved most of the major nations on earth. No single event or country caused the war. Its roots could be found in the conflicts caused by nationalism, militarism, imperialism, and a system of secret treaties and alliances.

European nations dominated the globe at the start of the twentieth century. The war fought between 1914 and 1918 marked the twilight of that global power. It fulfilled the 1910 prediction of an English pacifist that the costs of a war to Europeans would be so great that there would be no winners.

The First World War hastened the collapse of old empires. It sounded the death knell for the dynasties of the Romanovs in Russia, the Hapsburgs in Austria–Hungary, and the Hohenzollerns in Germany. The Ottoman Empire was splintered.

Some historians describe World War I as the first total war. It covered a larger part of the globe, used more resources, and cost more lives than any war ever had. Governments began to plan and direct their economies to accommodate the war effort. Fearsome new weapons became part of national arsenals.

In the aftermath of the war, old boundary lines were erased and new countries were created. The war crippled economies and left unsolved problems that within a generation contributed to a second global war. Meanwhile, the United States remained almost untouched. Its economy boomed, and by the war's end the United States was a leading military and industrial power.

ORIGINS AND OUTBREAK

In the summer of 1914, an adviser to United States President Woodrow Wilson wrote to him privately, "It only needs a spark to set the whole thing off." He was referring to a heavily armed Europe that was divided into two rival camps.

Peace Efforts

By the mid-nineteenth century, European interests had become global in scope. Improved transportation and communication, as well as bonds between commerce, industry, and banking, drew nations together. People who had some common goals such as socialists, feminists, and a few remaining liberals sought out each other to share ideas. One outcome of this spirit was an international peace movement that reached its peak in the days before World War I.

Pacifists, those who oppose war, promoted their ideas in a variety of ways. In *Lay Down Your Arms!* published in 1889, the Austrian countess Bertha von Suttner tried to alert people to the effect new technology would have on modern warfare. In his will, Alfred Nobel, the Swedish scientist and developer of dynamite, provided for a prize to be awarded each year to someone who advanced the cause of world peace. The first Nobel Peace Prize was awarded in 1901. In 1911 the American industrialist Andrew Carnegie founded the Carnegie Endowment for International Peace. He also financed an international conference center built in The Hague in the Netherlands.

National leaders were also aware of the threats to peace. Two international peace conferences aimed at arms limitation were held in The Hague in 1899 and 1907. But if actions speak louder than words, nations were whispering peace and shouting war.

Militarism

Militarism, the policy of maintaining a strong fighting force in readiness for war and at the cost of other government services, had taken hold in Europe. All the major powers except Great Britain drafted men into the army. Not only were men called to active duty for a year or more, there also was a growing pool of trained civilians.

In the 1890's naval rivalry between Great Britain and Germany widened a gap already created by economic conflict. As German industries outstripped British production, German trade squeezed the British out of some of their traditional markets. Meanwhile, Germany's naval buildup alarmed Great Britain, which considered its navy its lifeline. To protect its trade and empire, Britain adopted a "two power" policy. The British would build enough ships to equal the naval strength of their two closest rivals. German activity threatened this policy and heated up the arms race.

Another unsettling influence was the blurring distinction between **mobilization** and war itself. Mobilization is the active preparation of a nation's military resources for war. In 1914 mobilization for war was almost equal to declaring war. Military leaders were so intent on being able to strike first that last-minute changes became nearly impossible. The military staffs' desire to be prepared for war conflicted with the diplomats' abilities to negotiate peace. Heads of state seemed incapable of resolving the conflict.

A Shifting Balance

During his years as German chancellor, Bismarck forged alliances to keep France isolated and Europe at peace. The Triple Alliance, first signed by Germany, Austria–Hungary, and Italy in 1882, was renewed regularly. However, no sooner had Bismarck resigned, than the fabric of his carefully woven alliance system began to fray. Emperor William II allowed the Reinsurance Treaty with Russia to lapse. Deserted by Germany, Russia welcomed an offer by France to form a defensive alliance, thus ending French isolation.

Meanwhile circumstances were altering Great Britain's tradition of freedom from alliances in peacetime. German sea power was one contributing factor. Another was British concern about Russian activity in China. To offset Russian influence, Britain made an alliance with Japan in 1902. However, when Japan defeated Russia in 1904–1905, France was left without a strong ally. In 1904 France and Britain signed an *entente cordiale* as a counterbalance to Germany. Although not a formal alliance, this friendly agreement laid the groundwork for closer ties. This agreement became the Triple Entente when Great Britain and Russia came to terms in 1907.

Setting the Stage

The scramble for colonies and influence led to dangerous rivalries that centered on North Africa and the Balkans in the decade before the war. A series of crises consolidated the alliance systems and encouraged military staffs to update war plans.

In 1905 and again in 1911 France and Germany seemed to be on a collision course in Morocco. Although both crises passed, they netted Germany little more than bad publicity and drew Britain and France closer together.

Meanwhile, the Balkans were wracked with conflict. As you read in Chapter 21, in 1878 Romania, Serbia, and Montenegro became independent. Bulgaria remained within the Ottoman Empire but was self-governing. Bosnia and Herzegovina, inhabited mainly by Slavs, were administered by Austria. Croatia and Slovenia, both Slavic regions, bordered on Bosnia but lay within Austria–Hungary.

Serbia aspired to lead a national unification movement of the South Slavs, or Yugoslavs. This desire brought Serbia into direct conflict with Austria, which annexed Bosnia and Herzegovina in 1908. Austria took this bold step because the Young Turks had carried out a successful revolution in the Ottoman Empire. Austria feared that reform would enable Turkey to become stronger and to reassert control over Bosnia.

Meanwhile, the Germans were negotiating with the Ottomans to build a railroad from Berlin to Bagdad. They also hoped to draw Turkey into the Triple Alliance. The British felt that their position in India was threatened by the railroad to Bagdad. Russia assumed that a strong Turkey would never give up the Bosporus and Dardanelles. The shared concerns of Britain and Russia drew them closer together against Germany. Meanwhile, Germany and Austria were united by a common opposition to Pan-Slavism.

In 1912, Bulgaria, Serbia, Greece, and Montenegro formed the Balkan League, defeated the Turks, and gained territory. By 1913 the winners were quarreling over the spoils. A second war aligned Serbia, Greece, and Romania against Bulgaria. Serbia gained more territory and was threatening to Austro-Hungarian ambitions.

The Archduke Francis Ferdinand and his wife Sophia are shown here shortly before their assassination. Would war have broken out if this event had not occurred?

EUROPE IN 1914

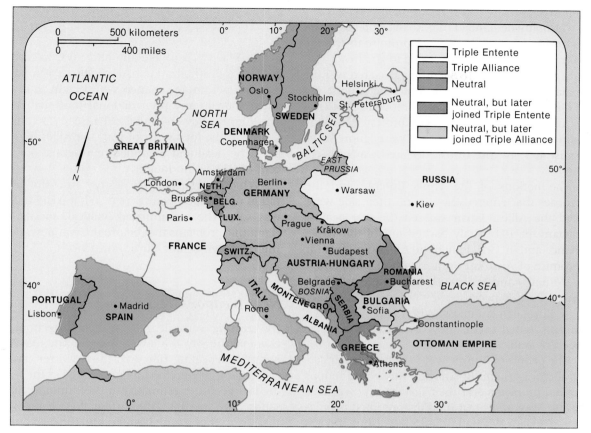

How did the alliance system contribute to the outbreak of war in 1914?

War Between Austria and Serbia

On June 28, 1914, Archduke Francis Ferdinand, heir to the throne of Austria–Hungary, was visiting the city of Sarajevo (SAHR-uh-yeh-voh) in Bosnia (part of modern Yugoslavia). His driver took a wrong turn, and slowed down to swing around in the right direction. Suddenly shots rang out—a young Serbian nationalist had assassinated the archduke and his wife. The Austrian government believed that the Serbian government had been aware of the plot. Austria was willing to risk a small-scale war involving only itself and Serbia to deal with Slavic nationalism. For assurance, the Austrian government contacted Germany, its ally. William II, believing that any war would be kept in the Balkans, offered unlimited support to Austria. With this strong backing, known as the "blank check," the Austrian government sent an ultima-

tum, or a list of demands with a time limit, to the Serbian government. Austria warned that all anti-Austrian activities in Serbia must be stopped. These demands were to be met within forty-eight hours, or Austria would declare war on Serbia.

The Serbian government was certain Russia would take its side should a war begin. Serbia, therefore, agreed to almost all of the Austrian demands. This clever move placed war-ready Austria in a difficult position. It had to back down and accept Serbia's compromise or declare war.

The Alliance System at Work

Determined to crush Serbian nationalism, Austria declared war on Serbia, on July 28, 1914. With French support Czar Nicholas II of Russia and his generals began their mobilization of the Russian army on July 30. Russia could not back down without losing its influence in the Balkans. France supported Russia for fear of losing it as an ally.

Germany demanded that Russia stop its preparations for war and that France promise to remain neutral. The czar himself decided to go ahead, and France stood by its ally. Germany declared war on Russia on August 1 and on France on August 3.

German troops immediately moved across Belgium toward France. The British protested the violation of Belgium neutrality but were ignored. On August 4, 1914, the British declared war on Germany.

The nations of the Triple Entente and the countries that entered the war on their side were called the Allies. Japan entered the war against Germany in 1914. Italy backed out of the Triple Alliance and in 1915 joined the Allies in return for a promise of Austrian territory at the war's end.

Germany and Austria–Hungary were called the Central Powers because they occupied the center of the European landmass. When Turkey and then Bulgaria joined them, they controlled a strategic sweep of land.

The people of Europe were victims of a dangerous alliance system. Austria and Russia had serious internal problems and their leaders saw war as a possible way to distract their discontented populations. Serbia felt it had little to lose. Thus the less politically stable countries pulled the rest of Europe into a whirlpool of war. The statesmen of Europe were unable to control events in 1914.

SECTION REVIEW

1. Mapping: Use the map on page 547 to locate the countries of the Triple Alliance and the Triple Entente. Identify the countries and territories occupying the Balkan peninsula in 1914.
2. In your own words, briefly identify or define: pacifists, "two power" policy, mobilization, Archduke Francis Ferdinand.
3. Explain how Germany undid Bismarck's alliance system.
4. Describe the causes of friction in the Balkans.
■ Before World War I, the Balkans were called the "powder keg of Europe." What area of the world could be considered a "powder keg" today? Explain your answer.

FIGHTING A TOTAL WAR

World War I was unlike any other war in history because industrialization had made total war possible. The percentage of men who fought in it was larger than in any prior national (not civil) war. The Central Powers mobilized nearly 23 million people in the four years of war, the Allies 42 million. The dead and wounded represented 40 percent of those who fought.

What the war did was destroy an entire generation of Europe's young men. What it did not do was solve the accumulated political, social, and economic problems that before the war beset even the most democratic European nations.

New Weapons Technology

By creating versatile new weapons, technology changed the way wars were fought. The machine gun, the repeating rifle, and the howitzer caused casualties that were no longer counted in the hundreds, but rather estimated in the hundred thousands. The internal combustion engine replaced the horse. Tanks were brought into the field by the British in 1916, but they were not used in sufficient number or with sufficient boldness to have much effect until the end of the war.

Aerial warfare also made its debut in World War I. The Germans developed a lighter-than-air craft called the zeppelin. The appearance of this cigar-shaped airship in the sky over London terrorized the populace but caused little damage below. Other aircraft were used mainly for spotting enemy movements or dropping propaganda leaflets. Later in the war, machine guns were mounted on planes. Daring fliers engaged in dogfights, and lacking parachutes, they often met an untimely end.

To many sailors, the most fearful weapon of the war was the German submarine, or U-boat. Unable to take prisoners or pick up survivors, submarines prowled the sea and threatened Britain's supply of food and materials from abroad.

As each new weapon was introduced, the other side rushed to develop a defense against it. The Allied reaction to the submarine included the use of depth charges, antisubmarine patrols, and convoys—many supply ships moving together, protected by warships. The Allies also rushed to develop a defense against poison gas, introduced by Germany in 1915 and later taken up by the Allies. Soon gas masks were part of every front-line trooper's equipment.

The War in the West, 1914–1916

Since Germany struck first, its war plan shaped the opening battles. The strategy had been worked out years before by the then German chief of staff Alfred von Schlieffen (SHLEEF-fuhn). The Schlieffen plan called for the Germans to sweep through Belgium, circle around Paris, and trap the French in a giant ring before Russian troops could reach Germany's eastern border. The German High Command expected to knock out France so quickly that Germany would not have to fight enemies on two fronts at once. It assumed that Russian forces could not reach the German borders within six weeks, so Germany would not be vulnerable while fighting France.

With the best-trained and best-equipped army in Europe, Germany advanced confidently in August of 1914. Belgium's small army faced the massed might of Germany with skill and courage. For ten days Belgium stopped the German advance at Liege, but by August 25, the Germans held most of Belgium.

The Schlieffen plan was going well, but not quite as planned. Belgian resistance had gained a few days for the French and British to prepare. On

WORLD WAR I, 1914–1918

What were the defensive advantages and disadvantages of each side in the war?

August 16, a British force of about 100,000 reached France. It joined the French forces as they were reeling back from the German assault. In these first weeks of war, the French and British suffered heavy losses.

By early September, the Germans reached the Marne River, only 37 miles (59 kilometers) from Paris. There the "miracle of the Marne" took place. With support from a small group of British troops and reinforcements that arrived by taxi from Paris, the French halted the German advance. Historians call it the crucial battle of the war. Shortly before it occurred, Russia had raced troops to Germany and invaded East Prussia. The German commander weakened the Schlieffen plan by pulling some divisions out of western Europe to defend Germany. The war could no longer be won quickly. Some military historians question if the plan would have worked anyway. The Germans had outrun their own communication and supply lines.

In the next few weeks, the armies engaged in a contest for the ports on the English Channel. The Germans hoped to cut off the short sea route used to bring British supplies and reinforcements to the Continent. British and Belgian troops stopped them in the battle of Flanders.

By the end of 1914, troop movement in the west ground to a standstill as both sides dug in along the western front, an embattled line stretching from Switzerland to the North Sea.

The Eastern Front

Meanwhile, in the east, Russia had kept its promise and attacked Austria–Hungary and Germany. Two Russian armies pushed through Poland into East Prussia in August 1914. At first the sheer numbers of Russian troops promised success. But lack of communication and cooperation undermined their efforts. The Germans were able to send new commanders and troops and turn the tide. At Tannenberg the Germans annihilated an entire Russian army. They took 90,000 Russian prisoners and captured vast quantities of supplies. Ironically, the Germans had pulled troops they did not need from the western front, weakening their forces at the Marne.

In the south, the Russian troops fared better at first. They defeated the Austrians at Lemberg in September 1914 and continued to advance. Once the Germans had wiped the Russians out of East Prussia, however, they bolstered the Austrians. By the end of 1915 they pushed the eastern front deep into Russian Poland. In 1916 a new Russian offensive against the Austrians moved the front about eighty miles until German reinforcements stemmed the tide. A failed effort in 1917 marked Russia's last offensive and led to its ultimate withdrawal from the war.

War on Other Fronts

Italy's entry into the war in 1915 did not significantly change the picture in Europe. The Italians attacked Austria, opening a new front in the Alps in 1916. There they stalled several hundred thousand Austrian troops until the Germans sent the Austrians reinforcements after Russia's defeat in 1917. The Central Powers routed the Italians at Caporetto in a battle immortalized in Ernest Hemingway's *A Farewell to Arms*. The Italians finally dug in and held their ground in northern Italy.

The Allies had even less success in their campaign to gain control of the Dardanelles. The British hoped to seize the strait in order to supply Russia through the Black Sea. The Turks resisted fiercely at Gallipoli. The neutral Balkan states, watching with interest, backed away from joining the Allies. The Allied failure also kept Russia short of equipment throughout the war since its only open route remained through Siberia.

In the long run, Allied sea power proved decisive. Britain and its allies were able to move vast quantities of troops and supplies. The Allies controlled the seas and blockaded the German coast. Not long after the war began, the British captured, sank, or drove into port most German surface ships. Only submarines escaped. Since Germany could not protect its overseas colonies, most were seized by Allied powers.

The only major naval battle of the war took place at Jutland in the North Sea. In May 1916 German ships left their ports to encounter the British fleet. Though both navies claimed victory, the British forced the German fleet back into port. There they remained for the rest of the war.

To cut British supply lines and offset the British blockade, Germany turned to submarine warfare. In 1915 Germany announced that any ship in British waters, including neutral vessels, might be

What were the obvious hardships of life in the trenches?

sunk on sight. A German U-boat sank the British passenger liner *Lusitania* (loo-suh-TANE-ee-uh) off the Irish coast in 1915. More than 1000 people died, among them many Americans. President Wilson warned the Germans about unrestricted submarine warfare. For two years Germany limited its submarine attacks for fear of drawing the United States into the war.

Stalemate

The soldiers who went to war in 1914 went with a spirit of adventure, even enthusiasm. The weather was warm, and they expected to be home before Christmas. But the nature of World War I was different from that of previous wars. Instead of the old style of flanking maneuvers, cavalry charges, and infantry advances, now there were attacks on entrenched lines defended by machine guns and the like. Only head-on frontal attacks seemed possible, and these meant the slaughter of most at-tackers. The order ''to go over the top'' and out of the trenches was often a death sentence.

The battles of Verdun and the Somme (SUM) showed the futility of an offensive on the western front. In 1916, German artillery pounded Verdun. The Germans did not expect to break the line. They hoped instead to bleed their opponent to death by inflicting five casualties for every two they suffered themselves. After ten months the Germans abandoned the attack, having received 330,000 casualties for the 350,000 they inflicted.

At the Somme River the Allies launched an of-fensive. In four months, from July to October 1916, the Allies gained about two and one-half miles of blood-soaked land at a total cost to both armies of more than one million lives.

The horrors they endured scarred a generation. This was reflected during and after the war in a large body of pacifist literature. Erich Maria Re-marque's *All Quiet on the Western Front* gave testimony to the horror of war.

The Home Front

In World War I the citizens of the belligerent, or warring nations were personally involved. It was not just the sight of a plane in the sky or a letter from the front that brought the war home. After it became clear that the war would not end quickly, governments took actions that directly affected people's lives.

With armies numbering in the millions to supply, factories and raw materials became as important as generals. Governments stepped in to direct what goods would be produced and how resources could be allotted. Laissez-faire economics was an early war casualty.

Why did many men and women do non-traditional jobs during World War I?

Germany entered the war with the world's biggest arms industry. At the Krupp works in Essen alone, 41,000 workers in sixty factories made weapons for German armies. Yet even Germany found it difficult to keep pace with the war's appetite for weapons and ammunition. On the other end of the scale, Russia found it impossible. At times when they had no ammunition, Russian soldiers were limited to night attacks with bayonets.

To keep the economy going, governments set up war production boards. Industrialists used their talents to establish priorities, secure raw materials, and direct production. Skilled people were kept home from the front. Food, clothing, and consumer goods were rationed. A radiator factory turned out guns; a piano factory, airplane wings.

The public was entreated and encouraged to support the war effort. People suffered through meatless days and wheatless bread. Daylight savings time was introduced to save coal. People planted "victory" gardens to raise food and children gathered scrap metal. Volunteers knitted socks and folded bandages. For the first time, women worked as streetcar conductors, bank tellers, and machine operators. By 1918 one-third of the workers in British arms factories were women. Women also went to the front with the Red Cross and other service organizations. Most feminist groups dropped their pacifist activities to show that they were loyal citizens.

The war was a factor in breaking down class distinctions. It marked the beginning of mass society, mainly in Russia but also elsewhere. Monarchies and the aristocracy were on the decline.

Both sides made extensive use of **propaganda**—spreading a particular set of ideas to further their cause. Posters urged people to enlist, to buy war bonds, to grow certain kinds of food. To win the support of neutral governments, stories were broadcast about atrocities committed by the other side. Allied propaganda helped build a climate of support for the United States to enter the war in 1917.

The end result was a gradual centralization of political power. Groups such as socialists and laborers temporarily stopped criticizing the government. In Germany and Austria–Hungary the military took a leading role, decreasing the power of elected officials. In Britain, France, and the United States, government authority expanded.

How is this poster an example of war propaganda?

SECTION REVIEW

1. Mapping: Use the map on page 549 to identify those areas in Europe where most of the fighting took place. Why was the British blockade effective?
2. In your own words, identify or define: total war, the "miracle of the Marne," belligerent nations, propaganda.
3. Explain why the Schlieffen plan failed.
4. Why was neither side able to advance on the western front?
■ World War I accelerated social change and altered the role of women. What circumstances today are affecting the role of women?

WAR'S END: 1917–1918

The long and deadly stalemate dissolved in 1917 when Russia quit the war and the United States entered. The enormous losses suffered by Russian troops helped trigger a long-simmering Russian revolution, which you will read about in Chapter 25. At first, Russia remained in the war, but later a Communist government made peace with Germany. The Russian withdrawal allowed Germany to shift its armies from the eastern front to the western front. However, this blow to the Allies was softened by the United States' prior entry into the war.

The American Role

From the beginning most Americans wanted to stay out of the war. Woodrow Wilson campaigned on the slogan "He kept us out of war," and won reelection in 1916. Gradually, though, American sentiment shifted toward the Allies. There were strong British–American ties of language, history, and culture. Opinion makers favored the British, and pro-British propaganda fell on willing ears. Americans sympathized with the plight of people in occupied Belgium and France. They were outraged by the German execution of Edith Cavell, a British nurse in Belgium. Though the thought of being allied with czarist Russia was troubling to some Americans, France and Britain were democratic countries at war with absolutist regimes.

By following the laws of neutrality, the United States became the banker and supplier for the Allies. By 1915 President Wilson allowed American banks to lend money to any of the belligerents; American industries were allowed to sell goods to either side. But once the blockade of Germany became effective, only the Allies could benefit.

The question of the rights of neutrals on the seas was a source of friction throughout the war. The United States insisted on the right of its citizens to travel on any nation's ship. The sinking of the *Lusitania* evoked a storm of anti-German feeling, particularly since the public was not aware that the ship was carrying munitions. Later incidents heightened the sentiment, though in the early years of the war, Germany tried not to offend the United States.

As the stalemate dragged on into 1917, German military leaders decided to risk unlimited submarine warfare. They gambled that they could starve Britain into surrendering before the United States could gear up for war. In February 1917, Germany announced that its submarines would attack any ships, military or civilian, in a war zone around Britain and western Europe.

Meanwhile, the British sent President Wilson a copy of a telegram they had intercepted and decoded. Signed by the German foreign secretary Arthur Zimmermann, it authorized the German ambassador to urge Mexico to join Germany if the United States entered the war. In return, Mexico was to regain parts of the southwestern United States it had lost in 1848. When the telegram was published, Americans became angry.

The combined effects of unlimited submarine warfare, the Zimmermann telegram, and the overthrow of the Russian czar changed Americans' attitude about entering the war. On April 2, 1917,

President Wilson asked Congress for a declaration of war.

As the Germans had predicted, the United States could give its Allies little immediate material aid. (An error in the German warplan had been overestimating what submarines could do.) It took months to enlist, equip, and train troops. But the United States entry held out hope to the battered Allies. It swung the enormous wealth, talent, and resources of the nation to their side. As the home front mobilized to make the world "safe for democracy," the first small force of Americans under General John J. Pershing reached France in June 1917.

Wilson's Fourteen Points

Deeply saddened by the need to send American troops to war, Wilson planned what would be needed for lasting peace. In January 1918, when

The Americans made a major contribution to Allied success at the Meuse-Argonne. How were troops and equipment transported to the front?

the outcome of the war was still in doubt, Wilson announced his Fourteen Points. It was a blueprint for postwar peace. Wilson's proposal called for freedom of the seas, a reduction of armaments, and an end to secret treaties. He urged reestablishment of Poland as an independent country. He called for independence and the right of self-determination for minorities in the Austro-Hungarian Empire and in the European and Arab parts of the old Ottoman Empire. The last point urged creation of an association of nations that would guarantee "political independence and territorial integrity to great and small states alike."

Leaflets explaining the Fourteen Points were dropped over enemy territory. The ideas they expressed helped sway opinion in Germany and Austria in favor of surrendering. When the Germans finally sued for peace, they approached Wilson first.

The Final Days

The entry of the United States into the war did not spell the end of problems for the Allies. During 1917 the Germans stepped up action in Europe. They held a vast region, including Poland, Romania, most of the Balkans, Belgium, and northern France. In the east, though the new Russian government pursued the war, German troops pushed the Russian Army steadily backward.

However, the strength of the Central Powers was an illusion. Turkey's armies and people were war-weary. Bulgaria, beset by poor harvests, was in a state of economic crisis. The old rivalry between the Hungarians and Austrians had broken through to the surface. In Germany itself, the British blockade had produced hunger. The failure of submarine warfare led the Reichstag to pass a resolution asking the government to consider a negotiated peace.

After a second Russian revolution in November 1917, the new Communist government asked Germany for peace terms. The Germans demanded an enormous price. By the terms of the Treaty of Brest-Litovsk, signed in March 1918, Russia lost Poland, the Ukraine, Finland, and the Baltic provinces—Estonia, Latvia, and Lithuania.

With Russia out of the war, the German military began an all-out offensive against the Allies in March 1918. Had Germany not been at the end of its strength, the results might have been different. Meanwhile, the Allies finally coordinated their efforts under the French marshal Foch. Month after month, fresh American troops poured into the field.

In June the Germans were stopped at Chateau-Thierry (sha-toh-tee-REE). In August the Allies broke through near Amiens (am-YEN). In September the American troops led the way in the battle of Meuse-Argonne (myooz-ahr-GAHN).

Meanwhile, to the east, the other Central Powers were collapsing. The Bulgarians sued for peace in September, followed quickly by Turkey. Parts of the Austro-Hungarian Empire began to break away. Hungarians, Poles, and Slavs declared their independence and planned new nations. On November 3, 1918 the Austrians agreed to an armistice.

Germany fought on alone, but in several places, German soldiers and sailors mutinied. The German High Command told the kaiser that Germany could not win, and that terms for peace should be arranged.

The German High Command urged the formation of a new government based on democratic principles. Meanwhile, Wilson demanded that the peace negotiations be made with the true representatives of the people and not the discredited leaders. The German people harbored the feeling that the Allies would grant better terms to a republican Germany. The kaiser was forced into exile on November 9, 1918. Civilian representatives of the republic, soon called the Weimar Republic, signed the armistice on November 11, 1918. By deliberately avoiding association with the surrender, the military consciously protected its image. This was to cause later difficulties for democracy in Germany.

The Costs of War

Statistics of the number of dead and wounded and of the value of property destroyed give only an incomplete picture of the cost of the war. One estimate of losses is 2 million Russians, 1.8 million Germans, 1.3 million Austro-Hungarians, and 1.25 million French. Italy lost 700,000; Serbia, which helped trigger the conflict, lost 370,000. Britain, Canada, and other parts of the British Commonwealth lost 950,000. American dead numbered

Poetry of World War I

Literature is an important source of information. It provides insight into the feelings and practices of people from the era in which it was written. The following poems reflect themes of World War I.

The Volunteer

Here lies a clerk who half his life had spent
Toiling at ledgers in a city grey,
Thinking that so his days would drift away
With no lance broken in life's tournament.
Yet ever 'twixt the books and his bright eyes
The gleaming eagles of the legion came,
And horsemen, charging under phantom
   skies,
Went thundering past beneath the oriflamme
   [banner].
And now those waiting dreams are satisfied;
From twilight to the halls of dawn he went;
His lance is broken; but he lies content
With that high hour, in which he lived and
   died.
And falling thus he wants no recompense,
Who found his battle in the last resort;
Nor need he any hearse to bear him hence,
Who goes to join the men of Agincourt.

Herbert Asquith

From *Poems 1912-1933* by Herbert Asquith, Copyright by Sedgewick and Jackson, Limited, Publishers. Used by permission.

The Dead

When you see millions of the mouthless
   dead
Across your dreams in pale battalions go,
Say not soft things as other men have said,
That you'll remember. For you need not so.
Give them not praise. For, deaf, how should
   they know
It is not curses heaped on each gashed head?
Nor tears. Their blind eyes see not your tears
   flow.
Nor honour. It is easy to be dead.
Say only this, 'They are dead.' Then add
   thereto,
'Yet many a better one has died before.
Then, scanning all the o'ercrowded mass,
   should you
Perceive one face that you loved heretofore,
It is a spook. None wears the face you knew.
Great death has made all his for evermore.

Charles Sorley

From *Marlborough and Other Poems* by Charles Sorley, Copyright by Cambridge University Press. Used by permission.

1. How do the themes of *The Volunteer* and *The Dead* differ?
2. Which of these themes do you think was felt by most of the people at home? the people on the battlefield?
3. Cite an example of a contemporary poem or song lyric that reflects people's feelings toward a current event.

115,000. The direct expense of the war was calculated at $186 billion.

Diseases and famine took many additional lives even after the fighting stopped. Epidemics of cholera, influenza, and typhus raged unchecked in Europe. After four years of war, few European farms had any livestock, or seed to replant fields. Famine threatened millions, particularly in Russia and eastern Europe.

The landscape of northern France and other places where battles had raged were scarred with trenches and craters left from heavy shelling.

European governments owed enormous amounts for loans they had taken to pay for war.

One writer spoke for many when he said the war "scorched the minds and character of a generation" of survivors. Countless poets, novelists, and artists later tried to express what they had experienced and what it had done to the human spirit.

At war's end, the troops headed home. Allied leaders headed for Paris to plan a peace.

SECTION REVIEW

1. In your own words, briefly identify: Zimmermann telegram, General John J. Pershing, Treaty of Brest-Litovsk, Fourteen Points.
2. Explain how the Russian Revolution affected the course of the war.
3. List the reasons the United States entered the war.

■ By the Fourteen Points, Woodrow Wilson hoped to eliminate the causes of war. What efforts are being made today to lessen the chance of war?

TREATIES CREATE A NEW EUROPE

Representatives of twenty-seven Allied nations met in Paris in January 1919 to discuss peace terms. They excluded the Central Powers. Russia was torn by civil war, and its former allies were backing the anti-Communist side. As a result, Russia was not represented at the conference. Japan attended, but did not play a leading role.

The key decisions at the peace conference were made by the leaders of the "Big Four" nations—the United States, Britain, France, and Italy. President Wilson, the British prime minister David Lloyd George, the French premier Georges Clemenceau (klem-uhn-SOE), and Premier Vittorio Orlando of Italy dominated the talks.

From the start, the Big Four had serious disagreements. Orlando demanded the Austrian territories that had been promised to Italy in secret treaties in 1915. One of Wilson's Fourteen Points called for an end to secret treaties, yet he yielded on the issue. Clemenceau, nicknamed the "Old Tiger," fought with fiery determination for what he thought was the good of France. His main objective was to weaken Germany forever. The British prime minister David Lloyd George hoped to prevent France from becoming powerful enough to dominate Europe. He also worked to strengthen Britain's role in the Middle East. President Wilson was the moral conscience of the peace conference but he did not fully understand the workings of European diplomacy. He argued for the major principle of the peace conference—the self-determination of nations—without realizing how difficult it would be to achieve.

Problems of Peace

Wilson's highly publicized Fourteen Points provided a basis for the talks. However, the European powers were far more concerned about protecting their own interests than about abstract principles. The Allies demanded huge reparations to pay for the costs of the war. To justify these demands Clemenceau and Lloyd George insisted that Germany accept responsibility for the war in the so-called "war guilt clause."

Ownership of former German colonies and the question of disarming Germany were other troublesome issues. After five months the Allies reached an agreement. Then they called the Germans in to tell them the terms. The draft presented to Germany did not live up to Wilson's Fourteen Points, and leaders of the new German Weimar Republic protested bitterly.

The Treaty of Versailles

The Germans protested that the settlements were a dictated peace in which they had no voice. They said they had surrendered with the belief that the Fourteen Points would be honored.

However, the new Weimar Republic of Germany had no choice but to sign the treaty. The Allies had refused to remove the blockade until the peace treaty was signed. Its continuance, which

EUROPE AFTER WORLD WAR I

Which European country lost the most territory after World War I? Why?

caused enormous food shortages, caused resentment among the German people.

The treaty signed at Versailles exacted a high price in both land and reparations from Germany. Germany lost nearly 10 percent of its prewar territory, including its richest industrial and mining regions. France regained Alsace-Lorraine, lost in the Franco-Prussian War, and Belgium claimed several small districts.

To the east, Germany had to give up Polish territory it had acquired years earlier. The treaty also gave the new state of Poland a strip of land to the Baltic sea. This "Polish Corridor" divided East Prussia from the rest of Germany.

The other major powers refused to allow France to annex the coal-rich Saar. In a compromise, the Saar was transferred for fifteen years to the newly-formed international organization, the League of Nations. After that a plebiscite was to be held to determine its status. Loss of this industrialized region made it difficult for Germany to pay the war debts set at about $33 billion in 1921.

Various countries including Japan had swept up Germany's African and Pacific colonies. In general, the treaty let those nations keep what they had gained. The British got German East Africa, and the French took the Cameroon. Japan took the Pacific islands and certain German interests in China.

Instead of weakening Germany as Clemenceau intended, the long-range effect of the treaty was to create a simmering resentment among the German people. The Weimar Republic was saddled with an agreement it had no part in making. The harsh peace terms helped create the climate in which the Nazis rose to power in the 1930's.

The New Map of Europe

The Versailles Treaty redrew the map of Europe and the Middle East. Three prewar states disappeared: Montenegro, Serbia, and Austria–Hungary. Nine new European nations were carved from lands that had been part of Germany, Russia, and Austria–Hungary.

The treaty confirmed the formation of the Baltic states of Estonia, Latvia, and Lithuania. A separate state of Poland was recreated. The Allies were trying to create a band of countries between Communist Russia and the rest of Europe.

In the Balkans, redrawing the map was even more complicated. Bulgaria lost territory to Romania and Greece, including ports on the Aegean. The new country of Yugoslavia included Serbia, and the regions of Montenegro, Macedonia, Croatia, Slovenia, Bosnia, and Herzegovina.

Boundaries of the new independent state of Hungary were drawn to include Magyars, a non-Slavic group. However, the boundaries of eastern Europe put some ethnic groups in countries dominated by people who spoke other languages. Czechoslovakia included at least three million Germans among the Slavic majority.

In a separate treaty, the Allies reduced the new republic of Austria to 6.5 million German-speaking people in territory one-tenth the size of the old Austro-Hungarian Empire. The tiny country had no seaports, and many Austrians felt that Austria should be merged with Germany. France would not agree to this out of fear of strengthening Germany. Italy took the Trieste region from Austria. The Allies divided the former Ottoman Empire into both independent countries and countries overseen by European nations. Turkey emerged as the strongest independent state.

The League of Nations

Wilson objected to the harsh reparations and to some territorial settlements. However, he went along with France and Britain to win their support for a new League of Nations. The association he had proposed came into being after the war, with headquarters in Geneva, Switzerland.

The agreement forming the League was called a covenant. The League was based on the new concept of **collective security,** or a community of power instead of a balance of power. Members promised not to go to war until three months after all other means had failed. Wilson flatly rejected Clemenceau's idea for a police force associated with the League.

The League tried to provide a way to handle the areas that were not considered ready for self-rule. By taking the territory in trust and appointing an advanced nation to administer the region, the League hoped to avoid the abuses of imperialism. France and Britain were active in the former Ottoman Empire and Africa. France received Syria as a mandate and Britain received Palestine and Iraq.

The League was weakened from the start because some major nations did not participate. The Treaty of Versailles specifically excluded Germany though it was allowed to join in 1926. The Soviet Union was also excluded until 1934. Wilson was unable to persuade the Senate to ratify the treaty forming the League, so the United States never joined.

Thus in 1920 the map of the world had been redrawn. But the "war to end all wars" had not solved the problems that caused it. The treaty ending the war created new problems that would intensify in the next two decades.

SECTION REVIEW

1. Mapping: Use the maps on pages 547 and 558 and the text to describe the location of those territories that Germany was forced to give up after World War I. Describe the locations of the lands surrendered by Austria–Hungary.
2. In your own words, briefly identify: the Paris Peace Conference, self-determination, the Treaty of Versailles, the Weimar Republic, the League of Nations.
3. Name the "Big Four" powers at the Paris Peace Conference. What did each of the powers intend to accomplish at the conference?
4. Why did Germany resent the Treaty of Versailles?
■ If you had been one of the Big Four powers, how would you have treated Germany after World War I? Why? How should any defeated nation be treated by the victors of a war?

Reviewing the Chapter

Chapter Summary

The war that engulfed Europe in 1914 changed the patterns of world power. Before World War I many of the most important countries of Europe were absolute monarchies. The war ended four empires: those of Germany, Austria–Hungary, the Ottoman Turks, and Russia.

The war pitted the Central Powers of Germany, Austria–Hungary, and Turkey against most other major nations of the world. The United States, which entered in the third year of war, tipped the balance for Allied victory.

World War I has been called the first total war because governments directed all their resources into the war effort. The costs were enormous. At least 10 million people died, and many more were wounded or left homeless.

Russia pulled out of the war early because of revolution at home and enormous losses at the front. The lands Russia lost to Germany were later divided among Romania and several nations created at the end of the war.

In drawing up a peace treaty, the victors reshaped the European balance of power and created many new countries. They increased Europe's power in the Middle East. However, peace terms left Germans embittered over what many considered unjust treatment. The problems that caused the First World War remained unsolved, and the peace treaties created disturbing new ones.

1. What empires were destroyed by World War I?
2. Why was World War I called a total war?
3. What happened to the territory lost by Russia?

Using Your Vocabulary

1. What are pacifists? How did they promote their ideas before World War I?
2. Define militarism in your own words. What actions of present governments are examples of militarism?
3. The line between mobilization for war and war itself became blurred in 1914. Explain how the belief that it was important to be able to strike first in a war contributed to this situation.
4. The *entente cordiale* was a friendly agreement. How do you think it differed from a defensive alliance?
5. How did the *entente cordiale* become the Triple Entente in 1907?
6. What was the "blank check"?
7. What is an ultimatum? How did Austria's ultimatum to Serbia increase the chance of an outbreak of war?
8. What was the the German *zeppelin*?
9. What is a convoy? How did its success affect the outcome of the war?
10. In World War I, to what did the western front refer? Why did it remain more stationary than the eastern front?
11. How does a neutral nation differ from a belligerent one? Which do you think would be favored by a pacifist?
12. Why do you think the civilian support effort during a war is called the home front? What kind of support does it provide?
13. How was propaganda a weapon of war?
14. What was the purpose of mandates from the League of Nations? In which major areas did France and Britain receive mandates?
15. What would appear to be the benefit of a system of collective security?

Developing Your Geography Skills

1. Use the map on page 549 to locate which countries bore the brunt of the fighting in their territory.
2. Use the map on page 549 and information in the text to explain the importance of control of the sea in World War I.

3. Compare the maps on pages 547 and 558. What new nations emerged after World War I? Choose one territorial settlement that was likely to cause friction in the future. Explain why.

4. Use the map on page 558 to locate land lost by Russia after World War I which formed a barrier between Russia and the rest of Europe.

Recalling the Facts

1. Out of which empire did the country of Turkey emerge after World War I?

2. What issues contributed to increasing tension between Germany and Great Britain before World War I?

3. In what two regions did conflict center in the imperialist race for colonies and influence?

4. What new technology changed the nature of warfare in World War I?

5. What was Russia's contribution to the Allied cause in World War I? Why did it withdraw from the war? What price did it pay?

6. Why did Italy join the Allies? How did Italy's entry into World War I on the side of the Allies affect the war effort?

7. Why did the Weimar Republic, rather than the Kaiser or the military, make peace with the Allies?

8. How did the failure of the Allies to gain control of the Dardanelles affect the neutral Balkan states and Russia?

9. What is the significance of the battle of Jutland?

10. Why did Germany return to unlimited submarine warfare in 1917?

11. Why were the rights of neutrals on the seas a source of friction throughout the war?

12. Why was United States' entry into World War I significant to the Allied powers?

13. Why were certain major powers not represented at the Treaty of Versailles?

Essay Questions

1. Trace the shifting balance of the network of alliances in Europe in the late nineteenth and early twentieth centuries.

2. If the Ottoman Empire had not been the "sick man of Europe," how might circumstances in the Balkans have been different?

3. How did new developments in technology affect the way World War I was fought?

4. Explain why the United States was reluctant to enter World War I. What brought about a change of attitude?

5. Describe how World War I brought about the expansion of government power in Britain, France, and the United States.

6. Discuss the significance of Woodrow Wilson's Fourteen Points. How did they reflect a reaction to the conditions that led up to World War I?

7. Describe the social and economic changes that took place as a result of World War I.

8. What were the terms of the Treaty of Versailles? Why did Germany consider it a dictated peace?

9. What was the League of Nations? What measures did it take to preserve peace and to protect underdeveloped regions?

10. Explain how World War I failed to solve the problems of imperialism, militarism, and the rights of national minorities which had been underlying causes of the war.

Critical Thinking

1. No two sources agree on the human and material costs of World War I. What factors do you think interfere with the reliability of source data?

2. By insisting on a "war guilt" clause, the Allies were blaming Germany for the outbreak of World War I. Do you consider this a warranted or unwarranted claim? Explain.

3. Write two accounts justifying some aspect of the war at sea. Write one with a pro-British bias and one with a pro-German bias, or point of view. Explain how Allied control of most means of communication between Europe and the United States could affect Americans' view of the war.

4. To make the world "safe for democracy" was a common American justification for the United States' entry into World War I. What is the unstated assumption?

CHAPTER 25

The RISE of DICTATORSHIPS in EUROPE

1905–1938

Objectives

- *To describe the underlying causes of the Russian Revolution*

- *To explain how Lenin and the Bolsheviks seized control of Russia*

- *To show how the world economy in the late 1920's and 1930's helped create a crisis for democracies*

- *To describe the rise of fascism in Italy*

- *To describe the characteristics of totalitarianism and how Stalin and Hitler put them into practice*

*T*he doors of the railroad cars were sealed as a train rolled through Germany in April 1917. Inside was a passenger who used the name Vladimir Lenin. With German aid, Lenin was hurrying home to Russia to take part in the rapidly spreading Russian Revolution. Lenin had prepared for revolution for twenty years, but when it erupted he was in exile in Switzerland. Russia's war enemy Germany controlled the route to Russia. To weaken Russia by encouraging its revolution, the Germans had agreed to slip Lenin back into the country.

Lenin helped lay the groundwork for a new kind of government called totalitarianism. It grew out of the strains of social unrest and the experiences of total war, when governments set prices and wages and determined what would be produced. Under Lenin and his successor, Joseph Stalin, Russia's new government took total control over every part of people's lives. They did not permit the full exercise of personal liberties. Suspected subversives were often imprisoned without warrant or trial.

Fears of a Communist takeover created a climate for another kind of dictatorial government, fascism. Beginning in Italy, fascism spread to many other countries. In Germany the Fascist Nazi party crushed all opposition, censored the press and radio, and stamped out personal freedoms. Like Lenin and Stalin, Hitler believed that individuals served the state.

Not until the twentieth century was total government possible. Mass communications and mass transportation made it possible for dictators to communicate quickly with all parts of their regimes. *Newspapers, magazines, radio, schools, clubs, and factories all became arms of the political party. Dissenters were not tolerated.*

Soviet communism became the model for many Communist revolutionaries around the world. The militarism of Mussolini and Hitler led to a second total war.

THE RUSSIAN REVOLUTION

The Russia that entered the twentieth century had been shaped by reforms and reaction. During the early 1900's and the final days of the last Romanov czar, Nicholas II, it looked as though this trend would continue.

In other parts of the world, nations were dealing with the changes demanded by the forces of liberalism, nationalism, and industrialization. But Nicholas II viewed these movements as "senseless dreams." In the end this view would topple the Romanovs and open the door to the revolutionary figures of Lenin, Trotsky, and Stalin—the shapers of a new Russia.

Roots of Revolution

By 1900 the masses who had been freed from serfdom were little better off than they had been in 1861. Economic and social conditions had remained the same. At least 80 percent of the Russian population were rural peasants. Most lived in mirs and were still making payments on the land. A hunger for even more land sharpened their discontent.

The serfs who had migrated to the cities to work in newly developing Russian industries soon became dissatisfied with the low wages and bad working conditions. Unions were forbidden. Since the illegal strikes of the 1890's had failed, the large groups of workers gathered in the cities became prime targets for revolutionary agitators, because they had no legal outlets for expressing their discontent. The minority nationalities and the Jews living within Russia were also victims of repression and Russification movements. These actions caused deep-rooted resentment of the government.

Political Parties

Nicholas II could not cope with the domestic problems that developed out of the working-class movement. Nor did he act to stop the decline of the peasant class. Finally, the disillusionment of liberal reformers and the influence of new revolutionary political parties in Russia proved fatal to him and his wife, the German-born Czarina Alexandra.

Underground opposition to the regime came from the Social Revolutionary party. Members favored common ownership of land and self-determination for all the national minorities. They were not above using terrorism to achieve their goals.

Followers of the doctrine of Karl Marx had formed the Social Democratic party in 1898. Most of the Social Democrats felt that before a socialist revolution could occur, Russia had to be industrialized. Then, the czar could be overthrown and a communist worker state established. In 1903 the party divided into two factions, the Bolsheviks, or majority, led by Lenin and the Mensheviks, or minority. The same year moderates and liberals banded together to form the Constitutional Democrats, or Kadets, as they were called. They favored a constitutional monarchy and a national parliament.

The activities of the political parties were closely watched by the secret police who kept the czar informed. Many of the czar's opponents were jailed, exiled, or killed.

Revolution of 1905

Events in the Far East brought about the first serious threat to the czar's rule. Pressure from Russia, France, and Germany had forced Japan to give up the Liaodong Peninsula ceded by China to Japan as a result of the Sino-Japanese War in 1894. Soon Russia obtained virtual control of the peninsula. Japan was incensed and reacted by attacking Russian warships in February 1904. Russia's embarrassing defeat in 1905 in the Russo-Japanese War revealed the empire's decay. It fanned anger over social and economic conditions.

In January 1905 striking factory workers in St. Petersburg took part in a peaceful demonstration. Together with their families, they marched to the Winter Palace of the czar to present a petition for an eight-hour day and fifty-cents minimum daily wage. In panic troops fired on the demonstrators. Hundreds of people were killed or injured on a day remembered as "Bloody Sunday." Strikes and riots became contagious. Sailors mutinied. In the countryside, peasants rose up against their landlords. Universities were in chaos. Nationalist fervor rippled through the non-Russian provinces. In Moscow and St. Petersburg, Marxist groups formed **soviets,** or councils of workers, to direct the uprising. By October a **general strike,** or widespread strike of workers in many occupations, paralyzed Russia.

The czar finally issued the so-called October Manifesto to buy time and divide his opposition. It promised a constitution, civil liberties, and an elected parliament, or **Duma** (DOO-muh). How-

ever, the revolutionaries were unable to agree on their goals. Only a few, called Octobrists, were willing to accept the concessions made by the czar. Others still sought greater change.

The end of the Russo-Japanese War marked the return of troops loyal to the czar. Meanwhile the reactionaries—the nobles, the landlords, the Orthodox Church, and the army—united behind the czar. Loans from Russia's ally, France, propped up the government. With any real threat removed, the czar weakened the power of the Duma. By changing the election laws, he packed the Duma with conservative landlords. For the time being, Russia remained what it had been—an autocracy.

Impact of World War I

One can only guess how long the czars would have ruled without the stress of war. Czar Nicholas II had taken personal control of the army in 1915. He left the government responsibility to Czarina

Members of the Russian Duma met in the woods after the Czar ordered them to disband. What do you think were the topics they discussed?

Alexandra and her court. Almost immediately the sickly and impressionable czarina fell under the spell of a bizarre Siberian adventurer named Rasputin (rahs-POO-tin). As the czarina became more dependent on Rasputin, he increased his power over the government. Jealousy, intrigue, and fear led to his murder by a group of nobles in 1916.

Continued bad management and poor leadership set the stage for the downfall of the Romanovs. On March 8, 1917, food riots broke out in Petrograd (formerly St. Petersburg). Workers poured out of the factories to join the protest. Some police and soldiers summoned to crush the revolt instead joined the protestors.

When the Duma criticized the government, it was ordered to disband. The czar once more gave notice that he would not give up his absolute authority.

Workers, joined by soldiers, formed a soviet in Petrograd and took over the city government. The Duma defied the czar's order to dissolve.

The Provisional Government

Meetings between the members of the Duma and the soviets led to the formation of a provisional government on March 14, 1917. The next day Nicholas II abdicated, or gave up, the throne held by his family for over 300 years. Both sides agreed immediately to grant political liberties and to call for a special assembly to write a constitution.

From the beginning the provisional government was weak. It was headed by Prince Georgi Lvov (LVAWFF), a liberal who inspired little confidence. The governing group also included Alexander Kerensky (Keh-REN-skee), a lawyer who had accepted membership in the provisional government though soviet members had agreed not to do so.

Neither Lvov nor Kerensky could guide the provisional government toward solving its two major concerns—land distribution and Russia's role in the last year of World War I. The government wanted to pass laws allowing the purchase of land to be distributed to the peasants, but it lacked money and took no action. The soviets favored immediate seizure. The lack of prompt action by the government left it weak and ineffective.

The provisional government felt obliged to remain in the war and avoid a separate peace with

Germany. But the people were no longer willing to fight especially after the disastrous Russian offensive of 1917. Furthermore, by calling for election of officers by the troops, the powerful Petrograd Soviet had made it impossible for the government to pursue the war. Discipline broke down and many soldiers returned to Russia in order to take advantage of the rebellion against the landowners. The stage was now set for the second revolution of 1917. While the provisional government struggled to rule with decreasing popular support, the Bolsheviks made a deal with the Germans to slip Vladimir Lenin, their most capable leader, through the war zone into Russia.

SECTION REVIEW

1. Mapping: Use the Atlas map on page 757 to locate Petrograd (now Leningrad) and Moscow. Compare their latitudes to those of other major world cities such as London, Chicago, Rome, or Paris. Explain why the fuel shortages caused by World War I would be a serious problem in Petrograd and Moscow.

2. In your own words, briefly identify or define: Nicholas II, soviet, Duma, Rasputin, Bolsheviks, provisional government, Alexander Kerensky.

3. What three major political parties arose in Russia after 1898? What was the main aim of each?

4. Briefly describe the factors that led to the Revolution of 1905.

■ Based on what you have read in this section, what differences are there between the role of political parties in prerevolutionary Russia and those in the United States?

LENIN AND THE BOLSHEVIKS

When the revolution broke out in early 1917, Lenin and his wife Krupskaya (KROOP-skuh-yuh) frantically tried to return to Petrograd from their exile in Switzerland. Because the vast majority of

Russia's people worked the land, Lenin looked for a temporary alliance with peasants and social revolutionaries. Once the provisional government had been disposed of, Lenin would shed his allies and centralize the power of the Bolsheviks.

When Lenin arrived in Petrograd in April 1917, he sided with the Petrograd Soviet against the provisional government. Driven by revolutionary zeal, he shaped the Bolshevik program to appeal to the immediate needs of the people. Lenin called for withdrawal from the war, distribution of land to the peasants, control of factories by the workers, and recognition of the soviets as the power of the people.

As the provisional government, now headed by Alexander Kerensky, was torn by plots and internal struggle, many well-placed Bolsheviks were gaining control of the soviets. The peasants and workers liked Lenin's program of "Peace, Bread, and Land." Lenin's ally, Leon Trotsky (TROT-skee), controlled the powerful Petrograd Soviet, and together they planned the swift and successful overthrow of the provisional government by force. With the help of rebellious army members, the Bolsheviks carried out this second revolution on

Lenin is seen speaking to a group of Bolsheviks. Why do you think he was so persuasive?

November 7, 1917.

At the same time several eastern European nations—Poland, Latvia, Estonia, and Finland—took advantage of the turmoil in Russia to declare their independence. Russia also lost more than one million square miles (2.5 million square kilometers) of land as a result of the 1918 Treaty of Brest-Litovsk. Huge war payments were made to Germany in the form of grain and other produce. But Lenin was not concerned. He expected that the revolution in Russia was the beginning of a socialist revolution throughout Europe.

Civil War

Within a year of returning from exile, Lenin and the Bolsheviks had seized control of the government. The Bolshevik army, now led by Leon Trotsky, fought under the red banner that identified revolutionary socialists. The Bolsheviks became known as Communists, and their followers were called "Reds." The "Whites" were the various fighting forces who opposed them.

The World War I Allies all backed the anti-Bolshevik forces because they wanted to get Russia back into the war. France and Britain sent money and troops; Japan and the United States briefly helped with troops. However, some Russians who resented this foreign interference turned against the "Whites."

The costs of the civil war were staggering. Epidemics, famine, and warfare killed an estimated twenty million people. As the regime deliberately preached class hatred, it provoked fierce battles between the poor and the not so poor. In addition, the newly formed secret police, the Cheka (CHEH-kah), executed thousands suspected of being foes of the government. Terror became a weapon. In July 1918 a group of local Communists killed Nicholas II and the rest of the royal family.

Lenin and the NEP

The period from 1918 to 1920 is referred to as the era of "war communism." Government leaders later tried to justify its excesses in the name of war. During this time the major industries were **nationalized**, or taken over to be owned and run by the government. The state also took over any businesses employing ten or more people. Banks were

Members of the bourgeoisie were reduced to poverty by the events surrounding the civil war in Russia. These women were selling their own clothes to raise money.

dissolved. Church and State were separated in an unsuccessful attempt to abolish religion. Food was in short supply and forcibly requisitioned, or taken, from farmers.

In 1921, by the end of the civil war, the Russian economy was in shambles. Industrial production was one-eighth of its prewar level. Farm production was down 30 percent. Peasants seeking universal suffrage, civil liberties, and an end to requisitioning organized a major revolt. Lenin was shocked into action and he announced a New Economic Policy (NEP).

Using free enterprise to spur the economy, Lenin temporarily turned to capitalism. Under the NEP, private ownership was permitted for small businesses and factories and peasants could sell some of their produce for profit after they paid a tax on it. Hard-line Communists were shocked by these compromises with Marxist theory.

The Union of Soviet Socialist Republics

The Russian Empire was composed of at least fifty different nationalities. The czars had tried to deal with the problem of nationalization by Russification. The result was a restless population that weakened the empire.

After the civil war ended, the Communist government had its own solution to the problem of nationalism. It set up the Union of Soviet Socialist Republics (U.S.S.R.). In theory this was a federal form of government. Individual groups would each have some self-government according to the size of their population. They would deal with issues related to education, justice, and agriculture. The national government would control trade and foreign affairs.

In the beginning there were four member republics, including the Russian Soviet Federated Republic. According to the 1924 constitution, new republics could join on an equal footing with existing members. By 1940 there were sixteen republics in the Soviet Union.

The federal system lessened some, but not all, minority grievances. The theory of self-government, however, was overshadowed by the reality of Communist party rule.

Soviet Government

The basic framework of the government established by Lenin and modified by Joseph Stalin appeared democratic. By 1936 the people elected members of the two-chamber Supreme Soviet by secret ballot. In turn, members of this parliament chose the Presidium, a few select members who assumed authority when the Supreme Soviet was not in session (which was fifty weeks out of the year). The Presidium supervised the Council of People's Commissars who were selected by the Supreme Soviet. The chairperson of this council, known since 1946 as the Council of Ministers, serves as the premier of the U.S.S.R.

What changes the democratic appearance of the system is the role of the Communist party. Lenin had never viewed the Bolsheviks as a democratic party to which anyone could belong. It was instead to be a select group of strict followers of Marxist theory as interpreted by Lenin. This dedicated band would instruct and persuade others to accept socialism. In the U.S.S.R. the only political party is the Communist party. The only candidates who can be elected to a soviet are members of the Communist party or those approved by them.

The Politburo, or political bureau, of the Communist party wields the greatest power. Often members of the Politburo are also members of the Council of Ministers of the Soviet government. Thus, while it appears that authority flows upward from the people to the government, it actually flows downward from the party to the people.

From Lenin to Stalin

Lenin suffered a stroke in 1922. The struggle to succeed him began at once. The likely heir appeared to be Trotsky. He believed that the mission of the Soviet Communist party was to lead a world revolution for socialism.

Trotsky's main rival for power was a tough and ruthless revolutionary named Joseph Stalin. The son of Georgian peasants, Stalin had been jailed often by the czar's government and just as often had escaped. In 1917 he helped Lenin and Trotsky take over Petrograd. In 1922 he served as secretary of the Communist party. At the time, few realized how powerful he was becoming. Stalin was more concerned with building socialism in the U.S.S.R. than in world revolution. Much earlier, he understood the potential power of the Communist party structure. He recognized that party functionaries, or the party and government bureaucrats, were the new ruling class. As party secretary, Stalin put people he could control into key party jobs. When

votes were taken in committee meetings, these people voted with him.

After Lenin's death in 1924, Stalin made deals with other leaders to gain their support. Then, one by one, he removed them from power until he controlled both the party and the government. In 1927 he had Trotsky expelled from the party and exiled. By 1928 Stalin had no rival for power in the U.S.S.R.

SECTION REVIEW

1. In your own words, identify or define: Lenin, "Peace, Bread, and Land," Trotsky, Reds, Whites, Cheka, Politburo, Stalin.
2. Why did the Allies choose to support the anti-Bolsheviks?
3. Explain the main differences between the aims of the provisional government and of the Bolsheviks in 1917.
4. In what ways did the New Economic Policy abandon Communist theories?
■ Compare the situation in the United States after the revolution of 1776 with that of Russia after the revolution of 1917. Why do you think that the American government was freely elected?

CRISIS OF EUROPEAN DEMOCRACY

On November 11, 1918, bells rang all over Europe as people celebrated the end of the war. After four years of fighting, a battered Europe had to rebuild.

In many ways the war had created more problems than it solved. Many of the problems stemmed from economic dislocations caused by the destruction of resources during the fighting and changing trade patterns. European nations now found it difficult to provide jobs for their veterans. The general economic problems, complicated by a worldwide depression, taxed the strength and ingenuity of democracy. In those countries where traditions of democracy were strongest, democracy survived. In others, democracy became a delayed casualty of war as people traded their freedom for what they thought would be security.

Isolationism

The League of Nations first convened in Geneva in November 1920. Perhaps more significant than who came to Geneva was who did not. Neither the United States nor Russia chose to participate. Germany was barred. This left Britain and France as the major powers, with conflicting ideas on the nature of the League.

To Britain the purpose of the League was to promote international cooperation. Britain did not want to be drawn into any direct military action.

France wanted the League to protect it against aggression. Though the United States and Britain had guaranteed France's security as part of the Treaty of Versailles, the United States Senate did not ratify the treaty.

American isolation hurt not only the prestige of the League of Nations but also other aspects of international relations. For example, because the Congress wanted to protect American industries from competing with a flood of inexpensive European goods, it passed a series of high tariffs. Economists argued that it would be impossible for other countries to repay their debts if they could not sell their goods in the world market. The United States did not recognize that, as the dominant economy in the world, its refusal to import would dangerously slow down the economic recovery of Europe.

Economic problems in Britain after World War I led to a widespread strike. How did the people and the government react?

Poor economies endangered governments.

Another spin-off of isolation was the change in United States immigration policy. In 1924 a new law limited the number of immigrants from southern and eastern Europe. As a result, a safety outlet for these economically and politically troubled areas was shut down.

Britain After the War

As British soldiers hung up their uniforms for what they hoped would be the last time, they looked forward to a normal life. But Britain and the world were no longer what they had been before the war. As did veterans everywhere, the British faced a peacetime economy that could not provide jobs.

During the war Britain had lost about 40 percent of its shipping, and other industrial nations were able to compete successfully for former British markets. Countries such as Brazil, India, and China were now manufacturing their own industrial goods instead of importing them. By 1921, 20 percent of the British labor force was still out of work. Over two million unemployed workers were on relief.

As labor unions struggled to hold on to the gains won during the war, tensions mounted. In 1922 the first of several hunger marches occurred as jobless people marched from Glasgow to London, in protest.

A strike in the hard-pressed coal mining industry in 1926 sparked a general strike in which workers in other industries walked off their jobs in support of the miners. About one-sixth of Britain's workers struck. The government declared a state of emergency and quickly provided for essential services. The strike lacked public support because people saw it as an attempt to bypass the democratic process. With the spectre of the Russian Revolution before them, many people blamed the labor unrest on Bolsheviks. Meanwhile, the government expressed support for unionism, though not the strike. The strike collapsed and serious conflict was avoided. The government passed the severe Trade Disputes Act of 1927, which outlawed general strikes intended to coerce the government. Workers channeled their energies to working within the scope of the democratic government in order to reach their goals.

The Labour party gained strength. It replaced the Liberal party as the opposition to the Conservatives. Led by Ramsay MacDonald, the Labourites promoted a gradual, democratic socialist program. They expanded unemployment insurance and public works projects. During the Depression, however, neither major party was able to launch a significant recovery program. The economy remained in a slump until the rearmament that preceded World War II.

Ireland

The problem of relations between Ireland and Britain was long-standing. When the British delayed home rule for Ireland during World War I, the Irish reacted strongly. An extremist group, the Sein Fein, launched a revolt during Easter week of 1916 with German support.

The violent revolt was put down with force. In 1918 Irish members elected to the British Parliament refused to take their seats. They formed an independent Irish Parliament in Dublin. Eamon de Valera (AY-mun deh vuh-LAIR-uh) became president. After three years of violence, Britain recognized the Irish Free State as a self-governing dominion. It was made up of the largely Catholic southern counties of Ireland. Ulster, the mainly Protestant northern county, chose to remain part of Britain.

In 1937 under a new constitution Ireland, or Eire (AIR), became an independent member of the British Commonwealth. Matters remained unsettled as the Irish agitated for reunion with Ulster. In 1949 the Irish Free State withdrew from the Commonwealth and declared themselves the Republic of Ireland. Disputes over control of Ulster have continued to disrupt relations between Ireland and Britain.

France

As mentioned, the failure of Britain and the United States to protect France from invasion caused the French to feel insecure. They reacted by using other measures to provide for their defense and weaken German forces.

With a technique that had been used against them in the past, the French sought allies to encircle Germany. The French made defense treaties, some of them secret, with Belgium, Poland, Czechoslovakia, Yugoslavia, and Romania. France also loaned these countries money to pay for armaments. The French hoped this network of armed allies would also act as a buffer against any revolution stirred up by the Soviet Union. In the hopes of preventing a German invasion, the French built a 200-mile (320-kilometer) line of fortifications—the so-called Maginot (MA-zhi-noh) Line—along the border of Germany and Luxembourg.

France, more than any other country, was determined to collect war reparations from Germany. It needed the money to repay war debts. France also wanted to use the payments to prevent Germany from rebuilding. When Germany told the Allies in July 1922 that it could not pay further reparations, France reacted immediately. With Belgian help, the French seized Germany's Ruhr Valley. France intended to occupy this rich industrial area and take the output of its factories. In retaliation the German workers walked off their jobs.

An international commission chaired by American banker Charles Dawes worked out a compromise in 1924. The Dawes Plan called for the French to leave the Ruhr. Payments on the war debt were reduced and extended over a longer period of time. In 1929 another commission further reduced the reparation debt.

French Politics

The problems of France were similar to those of Britain, but in some ways worse. Much of the war had been fought on French soil. Barbed wire, concrete bunkers, and trenches were its harvest. Factories were flattened and homes destroyed. Bridges collapsed on riverbeds, and roads and villages looked like Roman ruins. Half of the French males between the ages of twenty and thirty-two were dead.

France was heavily in debt. It owed money to its own citizens and to the United States. Though rebuilding tempered unemployment, it flamed inflation, which struck the lower classes and industrial workers the hardest.

As France struggled to recover, coalitions of different parties were necessary to carry on business. As these fragile alliances broke down, the coalition governments rose and fell rapidly.

Inflation affected the German economy. Workers were paid daily because the value of money decreased so quickly. This German woman is using her money as fuel instead of spending it. Why?

Although the economic depression of the 1930's was slower to affect France than Britain, the country was not spared. As banks and businesses failed, people blamed political leaders for the lack of jobs and loss of savings. The government looked particularly ineffective since no one party could control a majority of the National Assembly. By 1934 the conservative elements were looking for a chance to overthrow the republican government. The revelation of a huge swindle that tainted political figures provided the opportunity. The rightists cried out for a strong military leader. They stirred up anti-Semitism and denounced the government as they became more concerned with security than with democracy.

The threat to the government by the right galvanized a reaction from the left. Labor called a general strike to reinforce its demands. Liberals, democrats, trade unions, and even Communists joined in a coalition government to save the republic. The so-called Popular Front campaigned on a program of labor reform, economic revival, and the protection of democracy. A leading socialist, Leon Blum, was elected in 1936. In the year his government was in power, Blum established a forty-hour work week, paid vacations, and a system of labor arbitration. In spite of a return to antilabor measures in 1938 that split the population, democracy survived in France.

The Weimar Republic

In 1919 the constitution of the Weimar (VIE-mahr) Republic created a democratic government with a legislature elected by universal suffrage, including women. From the beginning, extremists on the left and the right threatened the republic. An early Communist revolt supported by Lenin and the Bolsheviks was put down by the government with the help of the army.

In 1920 a threat came from the army. When the government began to disband brigades to meet the terms of the Versailles Treaty, a group of army officers revolted. They staged a *putsch* (POOTSH), or armed revolt, to take over the government. The socialist workers called a general strike that ended the revolt.

Of even greater concern to the government was inflation. The German government made reparation payments on schedule until 1923. But the Weimar government depended heavily on borrowing and printing money instead of collecting taxes. The flood of paper money was worthless. The further economic crisis caused by the French invasion of the Ruhr led to a series of reforms by Gustav Stresemann (SHTRAY-zeh-mahn), the most able of Germany's postwar chancellors. He put Germany's economy back on track and prompted the Allies to establish the Dawes commission.

Stresemann then turned his attention to bringing Germany back into the circle of world nations. At a series of international conferences held in Locarno, Switzerland, in 1925, Stresemann proved to be an able and moderate spokesman. The agreements hastened the removal of Allied troops from German soil and opened the way for German membership in the League of Nations. To Europe the "spirit of Locarno" was a sign that peace could be maintained.

Stresemann died in 1929, the year the United States stock market crash signaled the start of world depression. After United States banks began to fail, Americans withdrew their funds from German banks. German prosperity collapsed as factories closed. By 1932 nearly six million Germans were jobless. Faced also with the loss of their savings, many people became bitter.

SECTION REVIEW

1. Mapping: Use the map on page 558 to locate the countries with which France made defensive agreements. Where were these countries in relation to Germany?
2. In your own words, identify or define: League of Nations, general strike, Irish Free State, Popular Front, Leon Blum, *putsch*, Gustav Stresemann, Locarno Agreements.
3. How did the British government react to the general strike by British workers?
4. Explain how France tried to protect itself from Germany.
5. List the problems facing the Weimar Republic.
■ Compare the role the United States plays in the world today with American attitudes in 1920. Could the United States withdraw into isolation today? Explain.

FASCIST ITALY

In the 1920's the idea of democracy was gaining strength in Europe. Even the newly independent nations of eastern Europe adopted liberal, democratic constitutions. Only in Russia had moderates failed to form a responsive government.

In Great Britain and France democracy survived economic unrest. But soon warning signs appeared in Italy and elsewhere. Economic problems and nationalistic ambitions threatened democracy.

Problems in Italy

Italy was the first western European country to abandon democratic institutions after the war. Disappointment over the peace settlements angered nationalists who felt that the government had allowed Italy to be cheated. Economic problems affected Italian society. Labor unrest and violence against landowners frightened the middle and upper classes as socialists in Italy embraced Bolshevik ideas.

With matters growing worse, the members of the government spent energy fighting among themselves. This apparent failure of parliamentary government undermined liberal sentiments and gave Benito Mussolini (bay-NEE-toh moo-soh-LEE-nee) the chance he was waiting for to seize power.

Benito Mussolini

Early in his political career, Benito Mussolini was an ardent socialist. While in Switzerland, he encouraged labor troubles and was expelled by the police. Upon his return to Italy, he became the editor of the leading Italian socialist paper. Mussolini opposed the church, the monarchy, militarism, and nationalism. Later he would support them.

Mussolini was guided by a desire for power. In 1915 he was ousted from the Socialist party for supporting Italy's entrance into World War I. Although previously evading military service, he joined the army and became a corporal.

After the war Mussolini began to organize a political party based on revolutionary and nationalist ideals. Its early members were discontented veterans and young nationalists who joined clubs called *fasci* (FAH-shee). The word appealed to Italy's pride in ancient Rome, where bundles of sticks called fasces were symbols of government authority. Mussolini's followers became known as Fascists (FASH-ists), and his system, **fascism.** Fascists became known by the black shirts they wore.

Fascism

After the war serious economic problems led to an outbreak of strikes and labor turmoil. Although by 1922 fear of revolution was greater than the chance of revolution, a mood of antisocialism was

How does this picture reflect the importance of the military to Mussolini's regime?

sweeping Italy. Fascism depended heavily on its anti-Communist fervor for popular support. People who otherwise found fascist ideas and tactics disturbing feared Bolshevism more.

Mussolini sensed that the time was right to seize the government. In October 1922 he announced a "March on Rome." He remained in Milan, but his Black Shirts poured into Rome. The parliament recognized too late that it had lost control and that Mussolini had succeeded in picturing parliamentary government as weak. Fearing that the army would not fight Mussolini, King Victor Emmanuel III refused to declare martial law. Instead, he bowed to the rising tide of antiliberal sentiment and asked Mussolini to form a cabinet. Within days Mussolini was prime minister.

At first Mussolini kept the outward trappings of democracy, but he appointed Fascists, responsible only to him, to all important government positions. By changing the election law, Fascists were able to capture a majority in the lower house of the Italian parliament. Mussolini was given the right to initiate all regulations and to rule the country by decree.

As with the communist regime in Russia, the party was the source of power. The state was supreme and people were subject to it. Fascism differed from communism in that it supported private property and social classes. It was a dictatorship of the right rather than the left.

Once Mussolini was securely in power, his opponents were exiled or imprisoned. The Fascists demanded absolute loyalty from anyone in a position to influence opinion. Italy became a repressive state in which the police and the army were controlled by the Fascists. Mussolini assumed the title of *Il Duce* (eel DOO-chay), or leader. King Victor Emmanuel III was only a figurehead.

The Corporate State

Mussolini formed a government that was organized according to occupation or profession. Each of the major economic interests such as commerce, banking, transportation, and agriculture made up a corporation or syndicate. Each corporation had representatives of labor organizations, employers, and the government, who together established policies and work rules for the industry. Strikes were forbidden.

The Papal Swiss Guard serves as the pope's personal guard in Vatican City. Michelangelo may have designed their Renaissance uniforms.

By 1928 the lower house of the parliament was nominated by the national councils of each syndicate. However the Fascist party could revise the list of candidates at will. Those permitted to vote could vote only "Yes" or "No" to the entire slate of nominees. By the 1930's there were twenty-two corporations firmly under the control of Mussolini. Agriculture and industry revived, but unemployment continued to be a serious problem well into the 1930's.

In 1929 Mussolini's government and Pope Pius XI settled several issues between the Roman Catholic Church and the Italian State. The **Lateran Treaty** recognized the pope as the head of the independent government of Vatican City, an area of about one hundred acres in Rome. The Italian government declared the Roman Catholic faith the official state religion and agreed to enforce church law throughout Italy.

Spread of Dictatorships

The fascist mix of nationalism, militarism, anti-communism, and state control of the economy appealed to many people of other nations. In many countries there were so many political groups that no single party or leader could gain the majority needed to govern effectively. In this climate, and suffering from the effects of the Depression, many nations longed for a strong leader who could bring order and stability. This was especially true in the new states of eastern Europe and the Balkans.

Almost all Hungarians resented the peace treaty forced on them in 1920 by the Allies. Nationalist secret societies seethed with plans to regain lost lands. The Hungarian government democratically elected in 1918 fell to Communists a year later. Then, the Communists were overthrown by a group who tried but failed to reinstate the monarchy. Hungary became a military dictatorship under Admiral Nicholas Horthy.

The new republic of Poland faced enemies on all borders. Russia hoped to reclaim lost lands in the east, while Germany wanted lost lands in the west. There were so many political parties in Poland that no one group could form an effective government. Governments rose and fell until 1926 when Marshal Josef Pilsudski (YOH-seff pil-SOOT-skee) established a military dictatorship.

By 1934 Austria, Estonia, Latvia, and Bulgaria were dictatorships. In Yugoslavia, to keep the kingdom from breaking up over disputes between Croats and Serbians, the king became a dictator. King Carol of Romania soon established his own dictatorship. Only Czechoslovakia was able to preserve a democratic government.

In Turkey, Mustapha Kemal (MOOS-tah-fah keh-MAHL) abolished the sultanate and proclaimed a republic in 1923. Kemal ruled as a dictator. However, he was a true reformer in some ways. He urged Turkish women to shed their veils, vote, and run for office.

On the Iberian peninsula, both Spain and Portugal became dictatorships. In 1923 General Miguel Primo de Rivera (mee-GAIL PREE-moh day ree-VAY-rah) dissolved the Spanish parliament and suspended the constitution. The link with Italian fascism was clear: King Alfonso XIII called Rivera "my Mussolini." Portugal's republic drifted into dictatorship under Oliveira Salazar.

SECTION REVIEW

1. Mapping: Use the map on page 558 to locate the countries discussed in this section that became dictatorships. In which areas of Europe did democratic government survive?
2. In your own words, identify or define: Mussolini, fascism, corporate state.
3. What factors led to the breakdown of democratic government in Italy?
4. What were the main similarities between communism and fascism? The main differences?
■ How can a country resist the takeover of dictators? What conditions today might lead to a takeover by a dictator? Give reasons for your answers.

TOTALITARIANISM

The systems devised by the Nazis for Germany and by the Communists for Russia gave unlimited power to the government. Both were **totalitarian** systems. In a totalitarian system a single party controls every aspect of life in the nation.

Totalitarianism is the opposite of liberal democracy, for it rejects the worth of the individual. The only valid ideas are those of the society as a whole. The only art allowed is that which expresses the ideas of society. Literature and history are used to manipulate public opinion and the entire educational system is used to reinforce the dominant values and ideas. Information available to citizens is limited and distorted. After a while it is impossible to know the truth.

In Russia Lenin had declared that the will of the Communist party was superior to that of all others. Therefore, the person who controlled the party had unlimited power. This power was always backed by force, and all totalitarian governments have been police states. No organization or institution that might become a center of protest is tolerated.

Economically, totalitarianism rejected the ideas of laissez-faire and free markets. Instead, it

Stalin thought heavy machinery could be more efficiently used on collective farms. Why do you think these tractors were made by an American company?

imposed rigid state control on production and sometimes on consumption as well.

Not all authoritarian governments went to these extremes. In the 1920's and 1930's dictators overthrew several democratic governments. Most dictatorships established during this period were of the old style. They did not extend total government control over all parts of people's lives. Some scholars do not consider Mussolini a totalitarian dictator since he lacked the technology and organization to impose complete control. By contrast, the Communist government of the Soviet Union under Stalin and the Fascist government of Germany under Adolf Hitler took total control.

Stalinist Russia

In 1928 Stalin decided it was time to end the compromises Lenin had made with pure communism in the New Economic Policy. Stalin announced a crash program to industrialize Russia and collectivize its farms. In 1928 the first of several **Five-Year Plans** set into motion Stalin's program to industri-

alize and make the U.S.S.R. entirely self-sufficient. A strong nationalist, Stalin believed that the need to buy manufactured goods abroad weakened the Soviet Union.

The Five-Year Plans stressed basic industries: building steel mills and blast furnaces, opening machine tool factories, building huge hydroelectric plants. The plans set general goals as well as production quotas for every factory.

The program to industrialize was very successful, but many goods produced were of poor quality. Steel output quadrupled, electric output increased at least tenfold in a ten-year period. By 1939 the Soviet Union, which had been a backward agricultural country in 1918, ranked third among industrial countries in the world. Only the United States and Germany produced more manufactured goods.

Stalin's plan also called for mechanizing Russia's farms and ending private ownership of land. In 1929 the party began forcing peasants off their land to work on two kinds of state-controlled farms. State farms were run like giant factories from which workers drew wages. Collective farms were run by committees under party direction. At the end of the year workers on collectives received a share of profits based on how much they had worked. Also, families were allowed to farm small plots for their own use after regular working hours.

In 1929 a decree ordered about one million kulaks, the more prosperous farmers, into collectives. The order triggered a small civil war as farmers fought to keep their property. Peasants hid their harvests from government collectors and butchered their animals rather than give them to the government.

Police arrested resisters by thousands and sent them to forced labor camps in Siberia. In a five-year period, an estimated six million members of kulak families were killed or imprisoned. In the upheaval, farm production fell sharply. Famine swept through several regions, including the Ukraine and the Volga district.

Stalin's ruthlessness also showed in a campaign of purges between 1928 and 1938. Stalin used the purges to eliminate anyone who disagreed with him, including almost all the old Bolsheviks who had worked with Lenin. Secret police arrested enormous numbers of people, then tortured them until they signed confessions.

In 1936 Stalin claimed that he had uncovered a vast treason plot. In a series of show trials, top army leaders and political figures were forced to confess to being "enemies of the people," foreign spies, or in league with the exiled Trotsky. The highly publicized trials were designed to intimidate others who might question Stalin's authority. It has been estimated that half the officers of the Red Army over the rank of colonel were killed or jailed. By 1938 an estimated twelve million people had been arrested. Of these, one million were executed and two million more died in prison.

Hitler's Early Career

Adolf Hitler was born in Austria in 1889 and orphaned at an early age. When he became a young adult, Hitler drifted to Vienna where he eked out a starvation-level existence as an artist. Although he disliked the mixture of nationalities in the city, he was sympathetic to the strong anti-Semitic atmosphere. Becoming very race conscious, Hitler

prided himself on being a "pure" German.

When World War I broke out, Hitler joined the army. Anger over Germany's defeat heightened his sense of nationalism. After the war, Hitler joined a group of extreme nationalists who formed the National Socialist German Workers' party, or Nazi (NAHT-zee) party. He quickly gained control of the party and urged a propaganda campaign to spread its doctrines. **Nazism** (NAHT-zee-ism) included elements of extreme nationalism, militarism, anticommunism, and racism, particularly anti-Semitism.

In 1923 when France seized the Ruhr, Hitler tried to spark a revolution. The Munich Putsch was easily put down, and Hitler served less than a year in jail. During this time he wrote *Mein Kampf (My Struggle)* outlining his ideas.

The Nazi Party

By the time Hitler emerged from jail the Nazi party was weak, and under Stresemann's influence the Weimar Republic was less troubled. But Hitler worked to rebuild the Nazis and bided his time.

Before the Depression the Nazis had been able to win only twelve seats in the German Reichstag, but in 1929 and 1930 as the economy collapsed, support for Nazism surged. Hitler used propaganda to inflame feelings against the Weimar government, the Treaty of Versailles, the Communists, and the Jews. In 1930 Nazi candidates won 107 seats, but no party could win a majority. Coalition governments fell often. In 1932 the Nazis won 230 seats and were the largest single party. By now the Nazis had financial support from many of Germany's landowners, army officers, and industrialists who felt they could control Hitler. In 1933 President von Hindenburg was encouraged to ask Hitler to become chancellor of Germany. Thus Hitler, like Mussolini, gained power legally.

Hitler immediately began to consolidate his power and he called for a new election. Just before the election a fire broke out in the Reichstag. Hitler blamed it on the Communists. He urged von Hindenburg to suspend civil rights. In March 1933 Hitler forced the Reichstag to pass an act giving up legislative authority. Hitler's revolution was under way. After von Hindenburg died in 1934, Hitler took the title of *führer* (FYOOR-uhr), or leader, and announced the formation of the Third Reich.

SOCIAL SCIENCE SKILLS

RECOGNIZING PROPAGANDA

Ein Volk, ein Reich, ein Führer!

Lenin's slogan, "Peace, Land, and Bread," and Hitler's "One People, One Empire, One Leader," are both **propaganda.** Both are designed to make people think and feel in certain ways. Propaganda is the one-sided presentation of information designed to persuade.

Companies use propaganda to sell products. Political parties use propaganda to win votes.

Here are some typical propaganda techniques.

- *Name-calling* is using words or labels that produce negative feelings when describing people or groups. The Soviet press refers to the United States as "war-mongering imperialists."
- *Transfer* uses admiration or loyalty to one person or thing and combines those feelings favorably with something else. The use of patriotic symbols on the stage with candidates is a transfer technique. Transfer can be negative, ·by using things about which people have bad feelings. "The candidate has accepted campaign funds from companies that pollute our rivers."
- *Testimonials* are closely related to transfer. An admired person endorses a person, product, or activity, as when a movie star says she drives a certain sportscar.
- *Glittering Generalities* are vague statements that seem to say something but actually do not. A sweeping statement like this Nazi propaganda, "We thank our German Army that it has kept spotless the shield of humanity and chivalry," is both vague and unprovable. Glittering generalities often use "virtue" words or phrases like "humanity," "honor," "one-hundred percent American."
- *Selecting Facts* or *card-stacking* is a technique by which the propagandist picks only facts that support the argument. Card-stacking leaves out damaging information and may slant the truth. Hitler admitted using the "big lie," completely false information used to sway popular opinion.
- *Plain Folks* is a technique by which a famous person tries to seem like ordinary people. A candidate photographed munching a hot dog is using the "I'm just plain folks" technique.
- *Bandwagon* methods try to convince people that everyone else is already sold on an idea or person, and that by joining in, they too will be associated with a winner. At Hitler's mass rallies a chanting chorus whipped up bandwagon feelings. "We want one leader! Heil Hitler!" With thousands cheering, people could feel they were part of a huge movement.

1. How does the poster above use the transfer technique?
2. What other techniques does it demonstrate?
3. Sum up in one or two sentences the feelings the poster tries to produce.
4. Cite examples of current propaganda from television or other sources.

The Third Reich

Hitler set out to establish a totalitarian regime and eliminate all possible opposition. He used brown-shirted "Storm Troopers" to terrorize his opponents. The secret police, or Gestapo, hunted down Hitler's enemies. Many people were shipped to concentration camps without any trial.

Racism was used to make Germans feel superior to others. Hitler hated Slavs, Hungarians, Jews, and gypsies. In 1935 the Nuremberg laws deprived Jews of the rights of citizens. They were also forbidden to marry non-Jews. A pattern of harassment and violence against Jews developed.

All political parties ceased to exist except the Nazi party. Private ownership was maintained and employers were given extensive control of their industries. Strikes were forbidden.

Nazi economic policies enjoyed wide support. Massive public works projects reduced unemployment. Women were fired in order to provide jobs for men. Nazi propaganda told women that their sphere was *Kinder, Kirche, und Küche* (KIN-der, KEER-keh, oont KUE-keh), or children, church, and cooking. Their greatest role was to be a mother of members of the Aryan master race. From 1935 on, the growth of the army and the armaments industry further reduced unemployment.

Great efforts went into creating a Nazi Youth Movement to indoctrinate the young. Textbooks were rewritten to conform to the Nazi ideals. Huge sports facilities encouraged physical strength. A program of Strength Through Joy provided entertainment and vacations for workers.

Hitler manipulated public opinion by playing on people's hopes and fears through lies and distortion. At huge public rallies the führer would work the crowds into a frenzy. He would shout out a key phrase and pause, while the mass audience roared back, *Sieg Heil! Sieg Heil!* Soon the echo of the cry would reverberate throughout Europe.

SECTION REVIEW

1. In your own words, identify or define: totalitarianism, state farms, collective farms, purges.
2. List ways in which modern totalitarianism differs from most earlier dictatorships.
3. In what ways did Stalin reshape the Soviet economy?
4. How did Hitler maintain control of Germany?
■ What governments would you describe as totalitarian in our decade? Explain your choices.

Compare this photo of Hitler to the picture on page 573. How are they similar?

Reviewing the Chapter

Chapter Summary

For a few years after the end of World War I, democracy seemed to be gaining strength in Europe. The new republics created at war's end wrote liberal constitutions and held elections. Established democracies such as France and Britain faced major economic problems, some of them caused by shifts in the world economy. Widespread unemployment created unrest throughout Europe. The withdrawal of the United States into isolation, and the issue of unpaid war debts strained relations between the former allies.

In Russia the war created a climate for revolution as people became embittered over battle losses and economic hardship. Bolsheviks, led by Vladimir Lenin, overthrew the democratically chosen provisional government and established a Communist police state. Under Joseph Stalin, the Soviet Union extended the reach of totalitarian government further into people's lives as he assumed total control of the economy and used purges to liquidate opposition.

Economic problems contributed to the collapse of democracy in Italy and Germany. Benito Mussolini created the first Fascist state in Italy. In Germany, Adolf Hitler's Nazi party created a totalitarian regime based on violence, militarism, nationalism, and anti-Semitism.

1. Compare the causes of the takeover of Russian Communists with the takeover of Germany by Hitler.
2. Who were the main figures associated with the rise of fascism and communism?
3. What conditions encouraged the spread of dictatorships in the 1920's and 1930's?

Using Your Vocabulary

1. Totalitarianism is a term coined by Mussolini. Describe what is meant by totalitarianism. Why do some historians question whether Mussolini was a totalitarian dictator in the full modern sense?
2. What were the soviets and why were they formed?
3. How did the czar weaken the power of the Duma?
4. What did the government do when it nationalized the major industries?
5. What is the origin of the term Supreme Soviet?
6. Who were the party functionaries and what was their role in the government?
7. Which counties were included in the Irish Free State? When did the Irish Free State become the Republic of Ireland?
8. What was the Maginot Line? What was its purpose?
9. What was the Dawes Plan?
10. What important issue was settled by the Lateran Treaty?
11. How does totalitarianism differ from the ideas of laissez-faire and free markets?
12. What title did Hitler take for himself? What is the meaning of that title?
13. What is propaganda? How does it achieve the goal of influencing the thoughts and feelings of its audience?

Developing Your Geography Skills

1. Use the maps on pages 436, 547, and 558 to determine what countries or regions Hitler was referring to when he talked of absorbing land that had once been German.
2. Use the map on page 558 to name the nations bordering Germany after World War I. Which countries on Germany's western border were not protected by the Maginot Line?
3. Use the Atlas map on page 756 to describe the geographic relationship between Ireland and Great Britain. How does Northern Ireland compare in size and location with the Republic of Ireland?

Recalling the Facts

1. Why was Lenin's return from exile in Switzerland to Russia important to the outcome of the Russian Revolution? Why did the Germans help Lenin return to Russia?
2. Which underground party was formed to oppose the czar's regime?
3. What two things were asked for by the striking St. Petersburg workers? What was the immediate reaction to their demonstration?
4. How was the provisional government of 1917 formed?
5. What temporary alliance did Lenin attempt to establish to bring about a socialist revolution?
6. What events weakened the provisional government? Who headed the provisional government when it was overthrown?
7. Why did Lenin temporarily turn to capitalism? Explain.
8. What role did the Presidium play in the Soviet government?
9. How did Great Britain define the purpose of the League of Nations? How did its view differ from that of France?
10. Why did the British general strike of 1926 lack public support?
11. Why was the French government unstable following World War I? What reforms were made by Leon Blum's socialist government?
12. How did the Weimar government produce the revenue to make reparation payments?
13. What was the first western European country to form a nondemocratic government after the war?
14. What group carried out Mussolini's "March on Rome" and who were they?
15. What political conditions in Italy created the desire for a strong leader?
16. Which eastern European country preserved its democratic government after the war? Name at least five countries in eastern Europe that became dictatorships in the years following World War I.
17. How did the Five-Year Plans set Stalin's program of industrialization into motion?
18. Against which groups or agreements did Hitler use his propaganda?

Essay Questions

1. Revolution broke out in Russia in 1905 and again in 1917. Describe the underlying and immediate causes that led to the outbreak of each revolution. Contrast the outcome of the revolutions.
2. Name and describe the major activities of the political parties in Russia before the revolution of 1905 through the 1940's.
3. How did Lenin bring various social and political factions together to accomplish his goal of spreading the revolution? In what ways were Lenin's actions an example of realpolitik?
4. Describe the impact American isolationism had on the economic recovery of the European nations following World War I.
5. Describe how the Depression created a crisis for democracies. How do you think a long history of parliamentary success in Great Britain and France affected the outcome of these crises?
6. Describe the underlying problems in Italy that made Mussolini's rise to power possible. How was Mussolini able to acquire leadership of Italy legally?
7. Some historians claim that Mussolini was not a totalitarian dictator because he lacked the means of total control. How did both Stalin and Hitler fill the mold of a totalitarian dictator?

Critical Thinking

1. How did Lenin, Stalin, and Hitler view the relationship between individuals and the state? What value did they assign to citizens of the state?
2. Was the idea expressed by Nicholas II of Russia that nationalism and industrialization were "useless dreams" an unwarranted claim? Explain.
3. What unstated assumption underlines the need to preserve dictatorships by force?
4. How does information used as propaganda bring into question the reliability of source data?
5. Describe the racial and political biases expressed by Hitler. How did he use bias in his propaganda against these groups?

CHAPTER ·26·

GLOBAL DEVELOPMENTS BETWEEN the WARS

1919–1939

Objectives

- To compare the manner in which Britain treated its various colonies

- To discuss developments in China in the early twentieth century

- To describe how the United States faced the Depression and increasing world tensions

- To identify political, economic, and social changes in Latin America in the early twentieth century

- To describe major social and cultural developments in the early twentieth century

A fter World War I disrupted the economic and political order of most of Europe, people wondered what kind of world would arise from the war's ashes. For centuries Europe had been the center of world power. Colonies were somewhat awed by the technology and power of the European empire builders. But the war disrupted international relationships. The idea of self-determination for nations championed by Woodrow Wilson in the Fourteen Points affected imperialist goals and raised hopes for freedom.

These sentiments encouraged change worldwide. The results were uneven. Canada, Australia, and Egypt achieved total independence, while India, African colonies, and the League of Nations mandates did not. In China, foreigners acted as a catalyst to revolution.

The economic problems which threatened European democracies left few places in the world unaffected. In Japan they gave rise to militarism. In Latin America where democracy was not firmly established, crises upset governments that were already trying to deal with peasant unrest. In the United States, where democracy was strong, the government used a variety of means to help people through hard times.

The anxieties of the world were reflected in art that broke with tradition. Artists, writers, and musicians, affected by the war and its aftermath, rebelled against the values of the past. Influenced by the psychology of Sigmund Freud and Carl Jung, they sought new ways to interpret the world they saw.

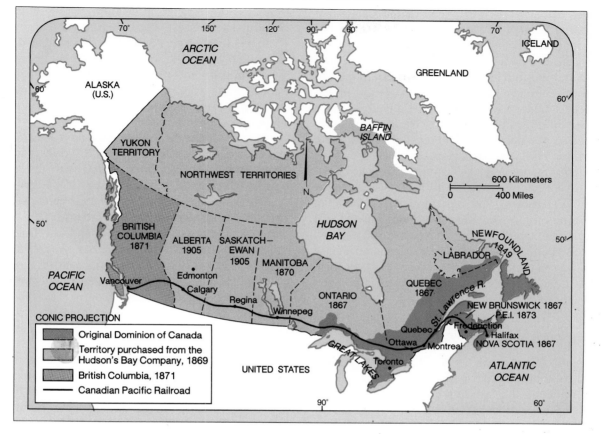

In what part of Canada did the early British and French colonists settle?

THE BRITISH EMPIRE

In the nineteenth century the liberal ideas affecting British political life led to reorganization of the British Empire. The desire to expand democracy, promote free trade, and decrease military expenses encouraged lessening control over some parts of the empire. Steps were taken that gradually led to new relationships within the empire in the twentieth century.

Canada

British North America in the nineteenth century was a patchwork of different territories with a variety of settlers. The early British settlers in Upper Canada (now Ontario) resented a new wave of immigrants from Britain. The French in Lower Can-

ada (now Quebec) feared being outnumbered by the British.

In 1837 friction between the settlers and the government led to rebellions in Upper and Lower Canada. The Earl of Durham, sent from Britain as governor, investigated the situation and wrote a series of recommendations in 1839 that came to be known as the Durham Report. Durham recommended the union of Upper and Lower Canada into one self-governing province. Consolidation would be reinforced by stressing the common citizenship of the French and British, and by building railroads and canals to link the two regions.

The following year the British army was withdrawn from British North America as Canadians took over their own defense. By the end of the decade, the governor allowed an elected assembly to make policies and appoint and remove ministers in domestic matters.

The next stage in Canadian unity occurred in 1867. The British North America Act established the Dominion of Canada with a status that lay between that of a colony and that of a fully independent nation. Parliament called for a strong central government in a federal system. The Dominion of Canada provided a way to unite other British North American territories with Canada. By once more dividing Upper and Lower Canada, it partly satisfied the desire of the French for a separate identity. The act also gave Canada greater power to govern its own affairs. Ontario, Quebec (kwi-BECK), New Brunswick, and Nova Scotia (NOH-vuh SKOH-shuh) were represented in the national government. In 1869 the country purchased a vast expanse of land from the Hudson's Bay Company. In 1885 the completion of the Canadian Pacific Railway bound Canada together. The constitutional development of Canada served as a model for other British colonies.

Australia and New Zealand

Captain James Cook explored and mapped the east coast of Australia in 1770. He took possession for Britain of the eastern portion of the continent, called New South Wales. Cook also established the British claim to New Zealand.

The colonies in Australia and New Zealand developed rapidly in the nineteenth century. New South Wales received limited self-government in the 1850's, as did other Australian colonies. Rivalry between the colonies, however, dampened enthusiasm for creating the federal system suggested by the British.

Conditions changed as the discovery of gold and the rise of the wool trade caused immigration to swell the population of Australia. In 1900 the Australian colonies were united under a federal system of government in the Commonwealth of Australia.

Britain annexed New Zealand in 1840. Its native people, the Maoris, were Polynesians who had emigrated to the islands around 600 years before. Disputes over land between the British settlers and the Maoris continued on and off for decades.

In response to unrest among the settlers, Britain granted New Zealand a constitution and an elected legislature in 1852. The country's economic development took off later in the century. The invention of refrigerated cargo ships enabled New Zealand to build an economy based on exports of cheese, meat, and butter.

In the 1890's New Zealand took a world lead in adopting progressive measures. In 1893 it became the first country to grant suffrage to women. Arbitration courts were set up to settle labor disputes; in 1898 New Zealand introduced government-supported old-age pensions.

As part of the British Empire, both Australia and New Zealand were drawn into World War I. Their troops, called Anzacs, served with distinction, notably in the Middle East and at Gallipoli.

The Statute of Westminster of 1931 created the **British Commonwealth of Nations.** This offered Canada, Australia, New Zealand, the Union of South Africa, and the Irish Free State equal partnership with Britain. The Commonwealth is made up of independent nations bound together by allegiance to the British monarchy.

The Indian Independence Movement

In British-dominated India in the late nineteenth century, educated Indians began to demand a greater role in their government. In 1885 they formed the predominantly Hindu Indian National Congress. That it had only two Muslim representatives was an ominous sign for the unity of the Indian nationalist movement. In its early years the Congress sought moderate reforms on the part of the British government. It called for greater educational opportunities for Indians and a greater role in the government.

After 1890 there was a shift to stronger demands for self-government. Many of those who advocated this more radical approach were members of the so-called Hindu Renaissance. They believed that Indians should look to their Hindu past. In their view the West was materialistic and corrupt. As Hindu nationalism spread, it became more radical in its opposition to the British and to Indian capitalists who were seen as cooperating with the British. Many Hindu nationalists began to demand home rule.

The Muslims were alarmed by Hindu activism. Since many Muslims had not taken advantage of the limited educational opportunity open to Indians, they were outnumbered by Hindus in the professions and business. Many Muslims feared for their status as a minority within a united independent India. As a result, in 1906 they formed the All-India Muslim League.

In spite of their discontent with British rule, Indians responded generously during World War I. More than one million Indians served both as soldiers and noncombatants in the war effort. As the war continued, Indians wanted to see some reward for their services. For the first time Hindus and Muslims acted together in calling for greater self-rule for India.

Although willing to increase Indian participation in government, the British were not willing to grant home rule. But Woodrow Wilson's stress on the importance of the self-determination of nations raised the hopes of colonists everywhere. After the war the movement for Indian independence gained new momentum.

Gandhi and the Independence Movement

Born to a Hindu middle-class family in 1869, Mohandas K. Gandhi (moh-HAHN-dahs GAHN-dee) trained in England to become an attorney. As a young man, he went to South Africa to practice law. He saw the treatment of the Indians there by the Europeans as part of a widespread pattern of discrimination. In response, he advocated **civil disobedience,** or peaceful refusal to cooperate, as a means of protest. It reflected his personal convictions.

Returning to India in 1915, Gandhi originally supported the British in World War I. But in the postwar years his life became entwined with the Indian independence movement. Earlier Indian nationalists came from the educated upper classes and the movement was not widespread. Perhaps Gandhi's greatest achievement was to make independence a concern of the great mass of Indians. To offer them inspiration, he lived in poverty and dressed in a garment of handwoven cloth. Gandhi adopted the spinning wheel as his symbol of protest against British economic policies that had destroyed certain handicraft industries in India.

In 1919, a British massacre of unarmed Indians intensified the Indian independence movement. Gandhi crisscrossed the country preaching nonviolence and engaging in hunger strikes. He urged the boycott of British goods. Sometimes his policy of

Crowds surrounded Gandhi when he appeared in public. Why do you think Gandhi inspired such interest and regard? Are there any public figures today who are able to sway people by the strength of their personality?

nonviolence did not work, but he would not give up. Gandhi launched a 200-mile (320-kilometer) march to the sea in 1930 to protest a British salt tax that burdened the poor. Tens of thousands followed him. Although arrested with many of his followers, he was soon released. Gandhi was now being called Mahatma, or "great soul."

By 1932 Gandhi's methods were producing results. India's import of British cloth was cut in half. By the Government of India Act of 1935, the British promised the election of a representative national parliament and a great degree of self-rule. Provincial governments were granted autonomy, or self-rule. World War II was to cause further changes that would bring full independence for India.

Palestine

In 1917 the British issued the Balfour Declaration, promising "the establishment in Palestine of a national home for the Jewish people." Under the mandate system of the League of Nations, Palestine was set up under British control in 1922. It was to be held in trust and prepared for self-government.

The terms of the Balfour Declaration were ambiguous. Although it promised a homeland for Jews in Palestine, it also said that nothing was to be done to prejudice the rights of Arabs living there. For Jews, the Balfour Declaration was a step in the Zionist dream of a Jewish state. **Zionism** was a movement that called for a state for the Jewish people in their ancient homeland. But during the war the British had also made promises to the Arabs, which seemed to conflict with the Declaration. Conflict between Jews and Arabs in Palestine became frequent. Both peoples formed their own national ruling councils to supervise their communities, but issues of land and immigration remained unresolved.

Violence escalated in the 1930's. With the rise of Nazism, Jewish immigration from Europe increased. As tensions increased, Arabs and Jews attacked each others' settlements. In 1936 Arab leaders called a general strike, and Arab rebels launched a revolt against the British. Many of the Arab leaders were deported. By 1939 the revolt was suppressed, but the problems in Palestine remained.

Africa

As you recall, on the eve of World War I, almost all of Africa was under the colonial rule of Britain, France, Italy, Belgium, Germany, Portugal, and Spain. By the terms of the Treaty of Versailles following the war, Germany was forced to give up all its colonies. Britain and France wanted the League of Nations to have a role in administering these territories.

Under the League of Nations' mandate system, colonies considered unprepared for self-rule were to be held in trust by a developed nation. As a result, Britain, France, and Belgium increased their holdings in Africa.

Throughout Africa there was a growing nationalist movement. More Africans were becoming educated and recognizing the contradiction between the idea of self-determination and their own colonial status. European powers began to feel the pressure of organized protest in their African possessions. Token reforms such as the elimination of forced labor and the encouragement of local authority could not satisfy the Africans' rising demands. For example, in Tanganyika which Great Britain administered as a League of Nations mandate, African civil servants organized and began to protest foreign rule. By the time World War II weakened the colonial powers, the seeds of opposition to imperialism had been sown.

SECTION REVIEW

1. Mapping: Use the Atlas maps in the back of the book to locate the countries that were the first members of the British Commonwealth of Nations.

2. In your own words, briefly define or identify: Durham Report, British Commonwealth of Nations, Hindu Renaissance, Zionism.

3. What were the steps in the constitutional development of Canada?

4. What was the status of Palestine after World War I? What serious problems did it face?

■ Are nonviolent methods more effective than violence in helping to change conditions? Explain your answer.

CHINA

In China many officials were resistant to change. In the late nineteenth century the reactionary Empress Dowager Ci Xi (TSUH SEE) constantly challenged her nephew, the emperor, for control of China. In 1898 he pushed her aside and initiated the Hundred Days' Reform. This series of edicts was a last-ditch effort to modernize China and ward off foreign domination. The reforms called for drastic changes in administration, foreign policy, the military, education, and commerce. The measures won support from some scholar-bureaucrats and liberals who criticized the Qing (CHING) government, but reactionary princes and nobles at court helped the Empress Dowager strike back. She imprisoned her nephew before the reforms could be carried out and resumed control of China.

How do you think the Empress Dowager Ci Xi was able to maintain her power?

Last Days of the Qing Dynasty

Among the Chinese peasants, China's weakness revived fear of foreigners, particularly missionaries. A secret society, the Society of Harmonious Fists, arose in the province of Shandong, where foreign influence was greatest. Its members practiced a traditional form of gymnastic exercise and were dubbed Boxers by the Europeans. With the apparent approval of the government, in 1900 the Boxers launched an attack on foreigners and Chinese Christians.

In what became known as the Boxer Rebellion, the foreign embassies in Beijing were beseiged for fifty-five days. The Empress Dowager, who disliked foreigners, allowed Imperial troops to help the Boxers. An international military force made up of Europeans, Americans, and Japanese saved the legations. The combined forces proceeded to take Tianjin and Beijing. The Chinese government was forced to pay reparations for damages. In addition, foreign troops were stationed in Beijing to protect the embassies. It was a revelation of the weakness of the Qing government, a sign that it had lost the Mandate of Heaven.

Meanwhile the United States was watching events in China with interest. It became apparent that foreign powers were extending their control throughout China. Spheres of influence were carving up Chinese territory. The United States government feared that China would be closed to American trade by other powers. In 1899 American Secretary of State John Hay circulated the first of a series of Open Door Notes. They called for the principle of equal trading opportunity in China for all the trading powers.

The United States government thought that the Boxer Rebellion might be used as an excuse to partition China completely. The Second Open Door Note of 1900 called for all nations to respect the territorial integrity of China.

The Qing dynasty was now on the point of collapse. Even the Empress Dowager realized that changes had to be made. Attempts were made to strengthen the military. In 1905 the examination system that had been used for almost two thousand years to fill government posts was abandoned. Reformers tried to establish western-type schools that would teach something other than the Chinese classics. But these reforms were too little, too late. The failure of China to undertake moderate and continuing reform led to a revolution that would sweep away the throne and radically change Chinese society.

The Revolution of 1911

One of the leaders of the opposition to Qing rule was Sun Yat-sen (SOON YAHT-SENN). Sun Yat-sen had lived in the United States and studied in Hawaii and Hong Kong. In 1895, after an unsuccessful attempt to overthrow the Qing government, Sun Yat-sen fled the country. He traveled to the overseas Chinese communities in Britain, Hawaii, the United States, and Japan to collect funds to back his revolutionary activities.

While Sun Yat-sen was still abroad, a revolution broke out in Hankou (HONG-JOH), now part of the city of Wuhan, and spread throughout the country. Sun Yat-sen hurried home and was named the provisional president of China by a revolutionary assembly. He resigned shortly, in favor of General Yuan Shigai (YOO-AHN SHUR-GIE), who controlled the powerful Imperial troops. In return for the presidency, Yuan Shigai negotiated the abdication of the last Qing emperor in 1912.

Yuan Shigai had little interest in the democratic reforms that Sun Yat-sen had planned for the new republic. He favored an authoritarian, centralized government. He ignored the newly established parliament and also outlawed the Kuomintang (KWOH-MIN-TANG), the political party founded by Sun Yat-sen. After Yuan Shigai's death in 1916, no single faction could control all of China. The country entered a period of civil disorder. Warlords, powerful leaders of local armies, controlled large areas of China. They fought each other and looted their provinces.

China and the First World War

The outbreak of World War I affected China because it upset the balance of power in the Pacific. Almost immediately, Japan joined the Allies and set out to expand its influence in Asia. Japan took over the German protectorate of Shandong. In 1915 Japan, taking advantage of the chaos in China, made demands to Yuan Shigai for trade concessions and special privileges throughout the country. The Japanese wanted to supervise the government and the police. Acceptance of the so-called Twenty-One Demands would have made China a virtual colony of Japan, but Japan backed down from its major political demands when the Allies objected.

In 1917, under pressure from the Allies, the Chinese government declared war on the Central Powers and sent men to serve as laborers in battalions in Europe. The Chinese hoped that the defeat of Germany would enable them to recover their territory in the Shandong peninsula. But China was unable to take active part in military operations due to its own unsettled state.

At the end of the war, the Chinese felt betrayed by the outcome of the Paris Peace Conference. In violation of Woodrow Wilson's ideal of self-determination, Japan was granted the German concession at Shandong. On May 4, 1919, demonstrations broke out in Beijing in reaction to the decision. The rebellion quickly spread throughout China as demonstrators denounced Japan and the West and called for a boycott of Japanese goods. Nearly all of China's future leaders participated in the rebellion which encouraged the rise of communist sympathies in China.

China in the 1920's

After being shunted from power by Yuan Shigai, Sun Yat-sen sought to regain influence in China. Disillusioned by lack of support from Japan and the Western powers, he turned to the Soviet Union for help in the early 1920's. Meanwhile the Chinese Communist party was formed in 1921.

With Soviet support Sun Yat-sen reorganized the Kuomintang, later called the Chinese Nationalist Party. In 1923 Sun Yat-sen agreed to cooperate with the Communists in order to defeat the warlords and unify the country. Relations between the two parties were often strained, but the fragile alliance held until the death of Sun Yat-sen in 1925.

In 1926 Chiang Kai-shek (JYANG KIE-SHECK) assumed leadership of the Kuomintang. He undertook the Northern Expedition—a military move to begin the political unification of the country. Starting from his base in Canton and supported by the Communists, Chiang moved his forces to the north. Chiang's Soviet-trained army proved effective against the warlord bands. By 1927 they were outside Shanghai. At this point Chiang, who favored the anti-Communist wing of the Kuomintang, turned against his Communist allies who, in turn, were plotting against him. With the aid of local warlords, his forces massacred Communists within the city. Communists were driven out of the Kuomintang. Advisers supplied by the Soviet Union were expelled from the country.

Chiang took Beijing in 1928. He was now recognized as the ruler of China, with his capital at Nanjing. Chiang's goal now became to wipe out the Communists entirely. Civil war erupted.

Civil War in China

In 1928 Mao Zedong (MOW DZUH-DOONG), a charter member of the Chinese Communist party, established a base with a small band of followers in a mountain stronghold in southeast China. Chiang began a series of "extermination campaigns." In 1934, after several failed efforts, he forced the Communists to leave their base.

In what was to be called the Long March, Mao Zedong and Zhu De (JOO DUH) led the Communists out of their besieged position. From southeastern China, the Communists fought their way for about 6000 miles (9600 kilometers) to northwestern China.

The Long March became the central legend of the Chinese Communist party. Having traveled through a large part of the country, the Communists got a firsthand view of conditions in China. During the trek, Mao assumed leadership of the Chinese Communist party—a position that he was never to lose. The end of the Long March in 1935 did not bring safety from Chiang's pursuit.

Now, however, Chiang met with opposition from some of his own allies. They were concerned by the Japanese inroads in China and felt the country should unite against the Japanese threat. Chiang countered, "The Japanese are a disease of

JAPANESE EXPANSION IN THE 1930'S

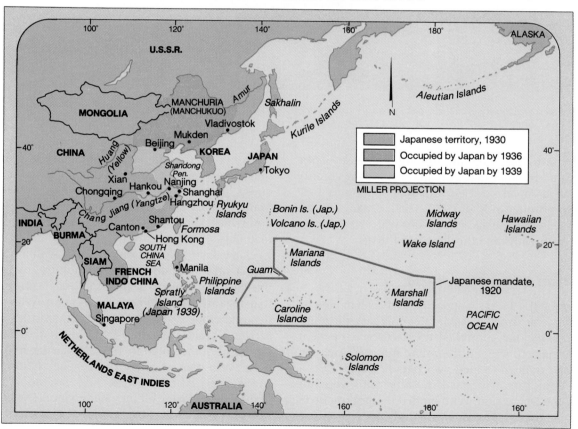

In which general directions did Japan expand?

Why was the capture of the railroad system in China vital to Japanese control?

the skin. The Communists are a disease of the heart.'' In order to get Chiang to unite the country against Japan, in 1936 Chiang's supporters took him prisoner in Xian (SHE-AHN). Chiang was released when he agreed to work with the Communists to withstand the Japanese threat.

Japan Takes Manchuria

During the 1920's it appeared that civilian government was strong in Japan. Reforms gave the political party that controlled the Diet, or parliament, the right to appoint the prime minister. The vote was extended to men over twenty-five.

Unfortunately, the democratic gains were hurt by the Depression. With limited natural resources, Japan depended strongly on trade. It exported cotton and silk and imported coal, iron, and other minerals. The slump in world trade hurt Japan's

economy. In this situation the military increased their power as people accepted the idea that conquests would solve their economic problems. Many military leaders regarded China as an area into which Japan could expand to get needed raw materials.

Japan had held a strong position within Manchuria since the late nineteenth century. In 1931 the Japanese army in Manchuria seized control of that region, citing Chinese provocation. With the deposed emperor of China as a puppet ruler, the Japanese announced the establishment of the new nation of Manchukuo in 1932. When Japan's actions were denounced by the League of Nations, the Japanese withdrew from the organization. But denunciations were all they had to face. The great powers were unwilling to take any steps to counter the Japanese. This led the Japanese to make further demands.

In 1932 the Japanese extended their control to parts of north China adjoining Manchuria. The success of their maneuvers helped the military to gain further influence within the Japanese government as well.

Japan Invades China

The seizure of Manchuria angered the Chinese, and a boycott against Japanese goods was declared. In retaliation, in 1932 Japan attacked Shanghai, the center of the boycott movement. Unexpectedly strong resistance held off the Japanese until reinforcements were called up. The Japanese took over the city but then withdrew.

In 1937 Japan began a new offensive against China. Just outside Beijing, a trumped-up incident gave the Japanese the excuse to invade China's northern provinces. Japanese forces had been stationed in this area since the Boxer Rebellion. Some historians regard this as the beginning of World War II.

The Chinese-Japanese conflict spread. Beijing and Tianjin fell to the invading Japanese troops. At the end of 1937, Nanjing, the Nationalist capital, was taken. Here the Japanese troops committed terrible acts against the civilian population. In 1938 the Japanese took Canton. They also established a blockade of China's ports.

When Nanjing fell the Chinese government moved to Hankou, but this too came under the control of the Japanese. For the duration of the war the capital was established at Chongqing (CHOONG-CHING), further west. Masses of people fled before the invading Japanese. Factories were dismantled and schoolbooks carried to the interior of the country. Teachers walked hundreds of miles to rejoin their classes.

The Japanese had conquered the major cities of eastern China, but they did not have the power to occupy the entire vast country. In battles with the Japanese, the Chinese army suffered horrendous casualties but managed to survive. Chinese guerrillas, including Communists, continued to attack isolated Japanese positions. After 1939 the war in China settled into a stalemate.

With the Japanese attack on Pearl Harbor in December 1941, the war in China became linked to a global war. China's independence now depended on the defeat of Japan by the Allies.

THE UNITED STATES BETWEEN THE WARS

The United States came out of World War I far stronger in comparison to other nations than it had been previously. While the European powers were spending their resources on the war, the United States had increased its financial power. At the end of the war the United States was a creditor nation—other nations owed it more money than it owed them. Previously it had been in debt to European nations.

American Foreign Policy

As you have read, following World War I the United States rejected the work of President Woodrow Wilson at the peace conference. The country experienced a feeling of **isolationism,** or a desire to ignore the problems of Europe and international responsibility. The Congress' refusal to approve American membership in the League of Nations hurt the League's chances for success.

The feelings of American isolationism came from disgust at the outcome of World War I and were heightened by the fear of communism. By the end of the war, the United States was in the

Not even a chilly all-day rain need upset the plans of the woman who has a Ford closed car at her disposal. Knowing it to be reliable and comfortable in all weathers, she goes out whenever inclination suggests or duty dictates.

The car is so easy to drive that it constantly suggests thoughtful services to her friends. She can call for them without effort and share pleasantly their companionship.

All remark upon the graceful outward appearance of her car, its convenient and attractive interior, and its cosy comfort. And she prides herself upon having obtained so desirable a car for so low a price.

TUDOR SEDAN, $590   FORDOR SEDAN, $685   COUPE, $525   *All prices f. o. b. Detroit

The Ford Motor Company, founded in 1903, was the first of the major automobile companies to be established. It was followed in 1908 by General Motors. How does this 1927 automobile advertisement compare to a present-day advertisement?

the navies of the United States, Britain, France, Italy, and Japan by setting quotas for different types of ships. This conference also reaffirmed the United States' commitment to the territorial integrity of China.

In 1928 Secretary of State Frank Kellogg, together with French Minister Aristide Briand, originated the Kellogg-Briand Pact that was intended to outlaw war. Although it was signed by many nations, it did not include any means of enforcement and it raised false hopes. The United States also participated in conferences on the war reparations that had been part of the Versailles Treaty.

The 1920's

In the election of 1920, Woodrow Wilson's party and most displays of international responsibility were rejected with the election of Warren G. Harding. He called for a return to "normalcy" and the American people welcomed it.

During the administrations of President Harding and his successor, Calvin Coolidge, the policy of the government was to let the country run itself. Coolidge said, "The business of America is business." Government regulation was loosened. Taxes were decreased.

The decade of the 1920's was known as the "roaring twenties." Dances like the Charleston and the foxtrot swept the nation. People thrilled to the exploits of sports figures such as Babe Ruth and Jack Dempsey. One of the great American heroes of the 1920's was Charles Lindbergh, whose solo flight across the Atlantic (the first ever) thrilled the nation. In 1928 Amelia Earhart became the first woman to fly across the Atlantic Ocean.

The 1920's were a time of great social change and economic growth in the United States. Much of the growth was fueled by the growing automobile industry. A car had formerly been a luxury only the wealthiest could afford. But in the 1920's the sales of automobiles rapidly expanded. This stimulated other industries such as oil, steel, rubber, and the electrical industry. It increased road building and brought about new occupations.

The prosperity of the 1920's was also sparked by the expansion of credit. Installment-plan buying pumped up the economy as it increased sales of new consumer products, but the prosperity was uneven. Five percent of the population received

midst of a "Red Scare" as a result of the circumstances surrounding the Russian Revolution. A few terrorist incidents, including the bombings of the homes of some public officials and some labor difficulties in the United States, were blamed on Bolsheviks. Many foreigners became suspect, and those believed to be radicals were deported with only a hearing before an immigration official. This anxiety was a factor in the failure of the United States to recognize the new government of the Soviet Union until 1933.

Isolationism and antiforeign feelings also resulted in new immigration laws in the 1920's. These limited the numbers of European immigrants and totally barred the Japanese.

Whatever efforts the United States made toward maintaining world peace had to be outside the League of Nations. Despite this trend toward isolationism, in 1921 the United States did play host to the Washington Naval Conference. The result of the conference was an agreement to limit one-third of the income. Agriculture was in its worst state in fifty years. Farmers who had increased their acreage to provide food for Europe during the war now found that they had large surpluses. Food prices dropped sharply.

Crash and Depression

Playing the stock market was the great craze of the 1920's. More than 1.5 million Americans invested in the market. This was made easier by the availability of credit. Buyers could buy stocks on margin, paying a fraction of the going price of a stock and borrowing money for the rest. When the stock price rose, buyers used their profits to pay off the loan. This led to enormous sums being invested in the market, increasing the prices of stocks far beyond their true value.

The stock market was stable as long as people had confidence in their economic future. Once people became fearful, they began to try to sell their stocks. As sellers outnumbered buyers, prices began to fall. Margin buyers had to sell their stocks in order to pay back their creditors. Selling drove the prices of stocks down further, touching off a new wave of selling.

On "Black Thursday," October 24, 1929, a record 13 million shares of stock were sold. Panic resulted with people trying to get their money out of the market as quickly as possible. Within one month stock values had plummeted by 40 percent.

The stock market crash spread from the United States to the world's financial and economic systems. The European economies depended on American dollars in exports, international loans, and trade. The sudden downturn sharply reduced buying of all kinds of products. Factories closed, and workers lost their jobs. People's life savings were wiped out. A worldwide recession, the worst in modern history, followed. It was called the Great Depression.

In the United States the Depression lasted longer and was deeper than in most other countries. Unemployment soared. The country's industrial output in 1932 was only 40 percent of what it had been in the 1920's.

President Herbert Hoover established the Reconstruction Finance Corporation to give credit to businesses, banks, insurance companies, railroads, and local public works programs. But Hoover opposed direct relief by the federal government. He believed that private agencies should provide for the needy.

The Great Depression had a profound effect on the United States. It shook many citizens' faith in the country and its economic system. Many of those who lost their jobs suffered a loss of self-respect. Without government programs to help those in need, widespread hunger arose.

The New Deal

The presidential elections of 1932 saw a landslide victory for Franklin Delano Roosevelt. He offered the American people a New Deal. In his inaugural speech in March 1933, Roosevelt told the nation, "The only thing we have to fear is fear itself." In the depth of the Depression, his words gave the nation hope.

Roosevelt declared a bank holiday, closing all banks in the country for four days. This halted the withdrawal of funds, which was creating many bank failures. The government examined the records of banks and allowed those that were solvent to reopen.

Roosevelt did not have a definite program. He promised that he would try new economic remedies, and if they did not work, he would try something else. He set up the Civilian Conservation Corps, which gave young men jobs managing natural resources. The Public Works Administration provided immediate emergency relief for the unemployed through state and local agencies.

Roosevelt tried to prop up business by the creation of the National Recovery Administration. This set up codes of competition and set prices. For agriculture, the Agricultural Adjustment Administration set quotas for farmers in an effort to solve the problems of overproduction and give farmers a fair return on their labor. The government also took measures to stop foreclosure on farm mortgages. The Tennessee Valley Authority was set up to harness the power of the Tennessee River system. It provided for cheap electrical power and spurred economic development in the surrounding seven-state area.

During the years before World War II, the Roosevelt administration revolutionized American government. For the first time the government took responsibility for the well-being of its citizens. For the elderly the Social Security System was adopted, with old age and disability insurance. Labor unions were given additional rights to collective bargaining. Banks and the stock exchange were regulated.

Roosevelt's leadership in hard times might be contrasted to Europe, where the economic crisis led to the rise of dictators. Roosevelt's programs helped the citizens but he abided by the rules of American democracy.

An Impending Crisis

Franklin Roosevelt saw the dangers of the rise of Hitler in Germany, but he was hampered by the strong isolationist sentiment within the country. Americans remembered the casualties of the First World War and wanted no part of Europe's problems. Many were resentful that European nations had not paid their war debts to the United States. Some believed that the United States had gotten involved in the war because of the actions of armaments makers and international bankers.

In response, isolationists in Congress passed neutrality acts that tied the hands of the president. Arms sales were barred to all warring nations. No distinction was made between aggressor and victim. Loans to belligerents were forbidden, and Americans were prohibited from traveling on the ships of nations at war.

As the situation in Europe worsened there was sentiment for backing the democracies, but there was a strong countermovement to keep the United States uninvolved. Roosevelt personally favored a strong response to German aggression, but he felt that he needed to have the country behind him to take any effective steps. In 1937 Roosevelt's call for a "quarantine of aggressors" met with a tepid response. He did not want to risk losing support for his domestic programs. It was difficult to get Americans interested in European problems when conditions were so grim at home.

The WPA provided jobs for construction workers such as carpenters, painters, and builders. How did the workers and communities benefit?

LATIN AMERICA

Latin America went through many changes in the early twentieth century. Its nations were affected by the First World War and the worldwide depression. Mexico experienced a revolution whose effects are still seen today.

The Mexican Revolution

Mexico was ruled in the late nineteenth and early twentieth century by Porfirio Díaz (pawr-FEER-ee-oh DEE ahs). Díaz presided over a period of economic growth in Mexico that saw the beginning of Mexico's industrialization. Much of the economic expansion, however, was fueled by foreign investments in Mexico, and Díaz gave important concessions of mineral and oil rights to British and American companies.

The mass of Mexico's Indian and mestizo population did not share in the wealth. Most were peasants who worked on large estates called haciendas (hah-see-EN-dahs). In 1911 armed uprisings, sparked by economic depression and crop failures, forced Díaz into exile. Francisco Madero (mah-DAY-roh) became president, but unrest had already spread throughout the country. Rural revolutionaries such as Pancho Villa (VEE-yah) in northern Mexico and Emiliano Zapata (zah-PAH-tah) in southern Mexico used the disturbances to press for land reform. They urged peasants in rural Mexico to seize some of the hacienda land for themselves.

In 1913, after sixteen months in office, Madero was ousted and assassinated. Victoriano Huerta (WAIR-tah), who was generally believed to have been responsible for Madero's death, took his place. Venustiano Carranza (kahr-RAHN-sah) challenged Huerta for the leadership of the government as guerrilla bands warred against landlords and against each other. The United States supplied arms to Carranza. By mid-1915, he emerged as president of Mexico, but Villa and Zapata continued their local rebellions.

Within a short time Carranza's influence was being challenged by reformers at the constitutional convention. The Constitution of 1917 provided for a degree of land reform. Some of the large estates were broken up and divided among the peasants while foreigners were limited to the location and amount of land they could hold. Mestizos and Indians were encouraged to participate fully in the government. There was to be a strict separation of Church and State. Women were given some basic rights, but were not granted suffrage.

In 1920 Carranza was ousted by a new outbreak of violence. This was the last successful revolt against the government in Mexico.

Post Revolutionary Years

In the early twenties President Obregón's education minister, José Vasconcelos (hoh-SAY vahs-cone-SAY-lohs), started a program to provide a more adequate education for a greater number of children. He was also interested in stressing the Indian roots of Mexican culture. This movement, called the Aztec Renaissance, had been one of the themes of the revolution. In encouraging it, Vasconcelos named artists to decorate public buildings. Through his efforts the great Mexican muralists Diego Rivera (ree-VAY-rah), José Clemente Orozco (oh-ROHS-koh), and David Siqueiros (see-KAIR-rohs) became known to the world.

When Lázaro Cárdenas (KAHR-day-nahs) became president in 1934, some of the waning fervor of the Revolution was revived. Cárdenas allocated more land from the large estates to the peasants than all his predecessors combined. Between 1936 and 1940, over forty million acres of land were distributed. Cárdenas also supported education and tried to encourage small business.

Cárdenas was a strong Mexican nationalist. He resented the role that the British and American oil companies played in Mexico. After the foreign-owned companies ignored his warning to raise the wages and improve working conditions of their laborers, he nationalized the oil industry. He used as justification a clause in the Mexican constitution of 1917 that gave all mineral rights to the government. In spite of the initial outrage from the British and Americans, he gave them only minor compensation for their property.

During these years Mexico was noted throughout Latin America as a leader in social and cultural developments. Its emphasis on Indian culture, called the indigenista (in-dee-hay-NEES-tah) movement, was adopted by other Latin American countries. Many people were proud of their blend of Indian and European cultures, though some chose to promote pride in only Indian culture as the basis of Latin American nationality.

The United States Latin American Policy

The United States under Theodore Roosevelt had enunciated a policy that made the Caribbean and Latin America virtually a United States protector-

How does Juan O'Gorman's painting of Father Hidalgo and his followers reflect pride in Mexico and its heritage?

ate. Woodrow Wilson had promised to be different, but the Mexican Revolution affected his policy. Wilson refused to recognize the regime of Huerta on the grounds that Huerta headed "a government of butchers." Instead, the United States adopted a policy of watchful waiting.

Wilson also faced problems caused by raids within the United States by the guerrilla bandit leader Pancho Villa. In 1916, after Villa's forces killed some people in a town in New Mexico, Wilson sent an American expeditionary force into Mexico to pursue Villa. The American force, headed by General John Pershing, never caught

Villa. But its entry into Mexico strained relations between the Mexican government and the United States. Pershing and his men withdrew from Mexico in 1917.

In the Caribbean things were not much different. Under President Wilson, American marines occupied Haiti, which was torn by revolution, and remained for more than fifteen years. The other country on the island of Hispaniola, Santo Domingo (now the Dominican Republic), was also occupied by American marines. Wilson wanted to prevent any European country from intervening and gaining a strategic hold in the Caribbean.

Nicaragua was yet another target of American military intervention. Marines occupied the country on and off from 1912 until the early 1930's. While there, they trained a National Guard led by the Somoza family. The Somozas took over the rule of the country in 1936. Armed guerrillas led opposition to the marines. One rebel leader, César Sandino (SAY-sahr sahn-DEE-noh), was regarded as a bandit by the United States and a patriot by many Nicaraguans. He was shot by Nicaraguan officers after surrendering, but his name was to be revived by later Nicaraguan rebels who succeeded in overthrowing the Somoza regime.

Relations between the United States and the Latin American countries changed during the presidency of Franklin Roosevelt. One of his first foreign policy measures was the Good Neighbor Policy. Roosevelt pledged that the United States would not interfere in the internal affairs of the nations of Latin America. Troops were removed from Haiti and Nicaragua. The Platt Amendment that had given the United States control of Cuba's foreign relations was abolished. For the first time since 1915, no American troops were on Latin American soil.

Social and Economic Change

The countries of Latin America had always had problems financing their economic development. In the nineteenth century the British helped build railroads and invested in the mines of the area. After World War I, the United States took the lead in foreign investment in Latin America.

During the First World War many Latin American countries suffered from a lack of development money. In addition they could not import products that had been available before the war. This was to have the important side effect of encouraging further development of their own domestic industries. This process continued into the 1920's, as Latin America then shared in the general world prosperity. The onset of the Depression, however, wiped out most of the gains that had been made earlier.

Some food-exporting nations of South America prospered. However, Brazil, whose major export was a nonessential—coffee—initially suffered greatly. Strikes and unrest resulted from Brazil's economic hardships.

On the eve of World War I, Argentina seemed about to take a place among the world's developed nations. It was the world's largest grain exporter and one of the largest exporters of meat. The country was becoming increasingly urbanized. In 1912 Argentina's president Roque Sáenz Peña (ROH-kay SAH-ens PAIN-yah) instituted reforms that provided for universal suffrage and the secret ballot. In 1916 the Radical Party came to power. It carried out some reforms, but labor unrest led to a general strike in 1919. In what is known as the *Semana Trágica* (say-MAH-nah TRAH-hee-kah), Argentinian government troops put down the strike with heavy loss of life. All reform ended with the onset of the Depression when a military coup brought down the government in 1930.

Chile passed some reform legislation in the 1920's, including extension of the free public school system, the granting of the vote to all men over twenty-one, improvement of the legal status of women, and an income tax. The country also instituted a welfare and public works program. But these advances were negated by the economic crisis of the 1930's.

In the 1920's Uruguay saw the beginnings of a welfare state, along with the first progressive labor legislation ever passed in Latin America. Nevertheless, the problems that had plagued the continent, such as unequal distribution of land, continued during this period.

SECTION REVIEW

1. Mapping: Use the Atlas map on page 760 to locate the countries of Latin America into which United States troops were sent during the early twentieth century.

2. In your own words, briefly define or identify: haciendas, Mexican Revolution, Aztec Renaissance, indigenista movement, Good Neighbor Policy.

3. What were the immediate reforms brought about by the Mexican Revolution?

4. What concrete actions did Roosevelt take as part of the Good Neighbor Policy?

■ Should the United States follow the Good Neighbor Policy today? Why or why not?

SOCIETY AND CULTURE

The early 1900's saw the rise of a cultural movement known as **Modernism.** Perhaps at no other period in the West were there such changes in the arts than those that occurred during the pre- and post-World War I period. Global contacts opened new horizons to artists. Developments in science changed the way people saw the world. A radical break with the past occurred in the arts. There was music without melody, there were paintings without a picture, and books without punctuation or plot. These changes are part of the Modernist movement that still influences the art world.

The Changing Role of Women

During the nineteenth century in Europe and the United States, the birthrate dropped. The decreasing number of children had a liberating effect on women. With smaller families, women of the middle class had the time to take on other interests

The flapper and the Charleston have become easily recognizable symbols of the ''roaring twenties.''

outside the home. New technology created jobs for women that did not require heavy physical labor. The development of the modern office brought many women into the job market. Growing educational opportunities slowly brought women into the ranks of doctors and lawyers and other professions formerly occupied only by men.

The changing social conditions of the post-war period, particularly in the United States, gave a new freedom to women. One of the symbols of the 1920's was the flapper. With her short ''bobbed'' hair and skirt, she exhibited a freedom in dress not known before. Bustles and other garments that were confining were thrown away. The flapper adopted an air of freedom in speech and life-style that would have shocked earlier generations.

As you have read, women in the United States, Britain, and New Zealand gained the vote. In the Soviet Union women gained the right to vote right after the Revolution. Sweden, Belgium, and other European countries followed suit. But French women had to wait until after World War II to gain suffrage.

The Revolution in Painting

Changes came about in painting in the last half of the nineteenth century. As you have read, Impressionist and Postimpressionist painters tried to take a fresh look at nature. But their work was still identifiable as a development of the traditions of western civilization.

At the beginning of the twentieth century, changes in art styles became more radical. Pablo Picasso (PAH-bloh pih-KAHS-soh) was one of the leaders of the new movements in painting. His distortions of traditional reality would become one of the hallmarks of Modernism. In the art of Henri Matisse, Modernism was expressed in the use of unusual colors. The sense that the world is not what it appears to be is a feature of modern art.

This sense was carried still further in 1910 with the completely abstract work of Wassily Kandinsky (vahs-SEEL-lee kahn-DIN-skee). The compositions of abstract artists express their message without a recognizable subject, but through the use of color and line. This was a complete break with the traditions of western art.

The styles of modern art proliferated. In the 1920's **Surrealism** was in vogue. Two of its

People in History

Picasso

The twentieth century has seen a greater variety of new forms and styles of art than any comparable period in history. The Spanish artist Pablo Picasso created or adopted many of these styles during a long and immensely productive career. He is widely regarded as the most important artist of the century.

Born in Malaga, Spain, in 1881, Picasso settled in Paris, the capital of the art world, in 1904. As a young man, Picasso had painted pictures of street people, with a heavy use of blue to create a somber mood. During his early years in Paris, the main color in his paintings shifted to pink, and his subjects were often circus performers.

Then in the winter of 1906–1907 he painted *Les Demoiselles d'Avignon*, which was to be one of the most influential paintings of the era. The painting shows five nudes, but their bodies consist of a series of angular shapes. Three of the faces are staring, cartoonlike masks; the other two are barely recognizable rearrangements of human features. Picasso had used as his models African masks and the ancient sculpture of the Iberians of Spain.

From 1909 to 1914 Picasso worked closely with his friend Georges Braque (ZHAWRZH BROCK). Together they created the technique of representing natural objects in geometric forms. This style became known as **Cubism.**

Picasso continued to work in a more naturalistic style, portraying dancers and other human forms in a heavy, rounded way that expressed both power and grace. In 1925 he painted *The Three Dancers,* which went a step beyond Cubism in breaking down human forms into shapes. More and more, he used bright colors to express a delight in life.

In 1937 the brutal German bombing of the town of Guernica during the Spanish Civil War impelled Picasso to create a huge painting that marked a break with the spirit of his past work. *Guernica* was done almost entirely in shades of gray and black. The figures are distorted in ways that suggest a scream of pain.

For the next eight years Picasso's work reflected the anguish, violence, and terror of the war. He later said, "I did not paint the war. . . . But there is no doubt that the war is there in the pictures which I painted then." He continued to live in Paris during the German occupation of World War II, defying the Germans with words and work. When the German ambassador once visited his studio, he saw a photograph of Guernica. He said, "Ah, Monsieur Picasso, so it was you who did that?" "No," Picasso retorted, "it was you."

Bright colors returned to Picasso's palette after the war, and he moved to the sunny south of France. His fame was now worldwide, and his paintings sold for high prices. Picasso continued his search for new ways of expressing himself. He continued to produce works until his death in 1973.

1. What were some of the characteristics of the styles Picasso used in his art?
2. Why would the bombing of a Spanish city cause such a change in Picasso's style?
3. What does Picasso's search for new styles of expression tell you about him?

How does this detail from Salvador Dali's Persistence of Memory *represent elements of Surrealism? How would you interpret its meaning?*

practitioners were Salvador Dali (DAH-lee) and Max Ernst, who created images from a dream world. Melting watches and misshapen human figures were strangely juxtaposed to jolt the viewer's subconscious.

Surrealism influenced other artists with its abandonment of conventional logic and attempts to portray subconscious feelings. Some artists sought to create "automatic" drawings that would be a direct extension of the artist's deepest feelings. One artist proclaimed, "We must burst the bonds of reason." The search for the power of the irrational, seen also in the psychology of Sigmund Freud and Carl Jung, reflected humanity's dismay at the horrors of World War I. These features of Modernism destroyed the traditional forms of art and reflected the restlessness of the era.

Architecture

Architecture also went through many changes in the early twentieth century. New materials and styles came into use. The most important American architect was Frank Lloyd Wright. A former pupil of Louis Sullivan, who had devised the skyscraper, Wright believed with Sullivan that "form should follow function." For example, he believed it was inappropriate for banks to look like Greek temples. He rebelled against the tradition of copying earlier styles and sought to create a new style for the modern world.

He began to develop an organic style, in which the materials were integrated with the environment. In designing a series of prairie homes, he tried to capture the spirit of the prairie. His buildings had strong horizontal lines and a simple, clean effect. The homes gained Wright international praise.

In Germany in the 1920's there arose a new architectural school, known as the Bauhaus (BOW-house). Led by Walter Gropius (GROH-pee-uhs), the Bauhaus architects carried simplicity even farther than Wright had. Clean simple lines and modern materials were the hallmarks of their style. It left the materials of a building's structure undisguised, with the intent of "civilizing technology," visually as well as functionally.

Some critics claimed that Bauhaus-designed buildings looked like glass boxes. But this architecture and the interior design of furniture and decoration that went with it became popular. After the Nazis seized power in Germany, many of the Bauhaus teachers and students left Germany, bringing the style to all parts of the world. It was one of the bases of the so-called international style that has been the dominant force in architecture up to the present day.

Music and Dance

The break with tradition was equally great in music. Igor Stravinsky's *The Rite of Spring* caused a sensation in Paris when it was first performed in 1913. A riot broke out in the theater. Most critics hated it. They found its unfamiliar sounds ugly, its rhythms strange, and its melodies lacking.

This new trend in music was carried further by Arnold Schönberg, working in Germany. He scrapped the traditional major and minor scales of western music for a new twelve-tone scale. This scale gave the listener none of the reassurance of familiarity that was offered by earlier classical music. Admired by critics, Schönberg's work had a major impact on other composers, but his music has yet to gain a widespread popular audience.

A form of music that has gained wide popular acceptance is an American cultural gift to the world—jazz. Originating in black spirituals and folk music, it began to be performed publicly as entertainment in the 1920's. In cities like St. Louis, Chicago, New Orleans, and New York, jazz greats such as Louis Armstrong and Bessie Smith popularized the new form with its strong rhythm and interesting improvisation on melodies. Jazz soon became popular in Europe and influenced the classical music of composers including Stravinsky and Darius Milhaud (meel-OH).

Dance as an art form also changed through the influence of dancers. Isadora Duncan rejected the rigid formalism of classical ballet. She shocked audiences by dressing in her own unique version of Greek costumes and performing free-form dance. Her style influenced other modern dance pioneers, among them Martha Graham.

Ballet also was transformed by new influences. The Ballet Russe under the impresario Sergei Diaghilev (sair-GAY dee-ah-GEE-leff) used modern music including Stravinsky's and sets designed by such artists as Pablo Picasso and Joan Miró. Diaghilev's troupe, which included the dancers Vaslav Nijinsky (VAHS-lahf ni-JIN-skee) and Anna Pavlova (pahv-LAWV-ah), performed works that drew on myth and folk tales as inspiration.

Literature

Changes in literature included new novels in which plot played a different role than before. Characters acted in unpredictable ways, reflecting the uncertainty of modern life. Both the French writer Marcel Proust (PROOST) and the Irish writer James Joyce sought to delve deeply into the inner feelings of their characters. Like Modernist painters, they drew on the subconscious for inspiration. In literature, the search for the subconscious led to the technique of writing down the seemingly random thoughts of a character. Joyce also drew on his wide knowledge of fantasy and

King Oliver's Creole Band included Louis Armstrong (center). What are some of the instruments used in a jazz band?

myth to produce such works as his novel *Ulysses,* which broadly retells the Homeric epic, *The Odyssey,* placing it in twentieth-century Dublin.

In many of the modern works the authors seemed to be writing for themselves and a few kindred spirits. In contrast to the great novelists of the nineteenth century such as Tolstoy and Dickens, many modern writers were read only by a small public. This division of the reading public into two groups—one of intellectuals and the other the general reading public—has continued to the present.

Among other modern masters were Virginia Woolf, who used a technique known as stream-of-consciousness to convey her own private world. Franz Kafka translated his private fantasies into images of a disturbing world. Thomas Mann wrote in a more traditional style, but he too was obsessed by discontinuities in life. In the United States, the stream-of-consciousness technique was adopted by William Faulkner to convey the drama of life in the American South. He too used elements of myth, with a particularly Southern flavor, as in his novella *The Bear.* Flannery O'Connor was known for a "Southern Gothic" style in short stories. Her characters were often disabled in some way. An-

other American, Ernest Hemingway, applied a terse, vital style to portray characters who were part of "the lost generation" that was scarred by World War I. Hemingway's style had many imitators among later American writers.

Motion Pictures

Thomas Edison's invention of motion pictures in 1889 created a new form of entertainment that won mass appeal. At first, people were content to watch brief films showing anything that moved. *The Great Train Robbery,* the first movie to use such techniques as cutting to different scenes, was made in 1903. It began a vast movie-making industry for mass entertainment. In the United States, movie-making companies set up studios in Hollywood, California, a suburb of Los Angeles. Most filming was done outdoors, and the year-round sunny climate of California was to make Hollywood the film capital of the world.

Featured actors in the movies soon became widely known and earned large sums of money for their work. Among the early movie stars, Charlie Chaplin, Douglas Fairbanks, Lillian and Dorothy Gish, and Mary Pickford had a loyal and devoted following. As movie theaters opened in cities and towns, the audience grew into the millions. Movies become the purveyors of adventure, comedy, and images of romance and glamor.

In 1927 the first motion picture with sound, *The Jazz Singer,* was released. Sound pictures attracted an even larger audience. Film became a popular entertainment form in many countries in Europe and Asia. Film directors Fritz Lang in Germany, Sergei Eisenstein in the Soviet Union, and Jean Renoir (ren-WAHR) in France created works seen around the world. But films from Hollywood had the largest worldwide audience.

In 1928 a young artist, Walt Disney, began to make animated cartoon films. His full-length feature film, *Snow White and the Seven Dwarfs,* released in 1937, became one of the most popular movies of all time. Disney's movies had a great influence on popular culture. His cartoon characters, including Mickey Mouse, became known throughout the world.

The motion picture industry continued to thrive during the Depression, as people gladly paid a dime to forget their troubles. The movies offered

Hollywood movie stars such as Mary Pickford and Johnny Mack Brown enjoyed tremendous popularity.

stories with happy endings, and elaborate musical productions. In 1930 paid admissions were running about 110 million patrons a week in the United States alone. Techniques were found to make movies in color, resulting in elaborate productions such as *Gone With the Wind* (1939).

Radio

In 1895 the Italian physicist Guglielmo Marconi discovered a way to send and receive radio waves without wires. Further discoveries by Reginald Fessenden and Lee De Forest made it possible to make inexpensive radio receiving sets. At first, radio was used for commercial and military communications. In 1915 David Sarnoff, an employee of the Marconi Wireless Telegraph Company, suggested that the company make a "radio music box" for sale to the public. Beginning in 1920 with station KDKA in Pittsburgh, radio transmitting stations broadcast the news and live music. Sarnoff became manager of the Radio Corporation of America (RCA). In 1926 he formed the National Broadcasting Company (NBC), which created programs for a chain, or network, of stations around the country.

Between 1922 and 1927 the number of home radio sets in the United States rose from 60,000 to 6.5 million. Families gathered around their large living room sets to hear symphony orchestras and jazz music bands playing in faraway cities. Soon radio dramas and comedies became a staple of radio entertainment. Stars Fred Allen, Jack Benny, Eddie Cantor, and George Burns and Gracie Allen, among others, attracted audiences larger than any entertainers had ever before reached. Singers such as Bing Crosby, and bands including Benny Goodman, Duke Ellington, and Tommy Dorsey became popular because of their radio performances. During the times when some of the most popular programs were broadcast, streets and stores all over the country were deserted.

Radio made it possible to report events as they were happening. The nation experienced a sense of unity as important news events were carried on radio. President Franklin Roosevelt was a master of the broadcast medium, using "fireside chats" to explain his various programs to the public. Roosevelt's jaunty tone made people in their living rooms feel he was speaking directly to them.

Two of the most enduring of the early radio personalities were George Burns and his wife Gracie Allen. They were among a few of the radio greats who went on to successful television careers.

Radio was also popular in European countries and in Japan. In some countries, notably Great Britain, the radio broadcasting stations were government-financed. This differed from the situation in the United States, where private businesses paid for the programming in order to advertise their products. There were no commercials on British radio (and later, television) shows.

SECTION REVIEW

1. In your own words, briefly define or identify: women's suffrage, Modernism, Surrealism, Bauhaus, network.
2. How did changing conditions in the post-war period affect women?
3. What is the main idea of Modernist painting?
■ Do you prefer abstract paintings or paintings with recognizable subjects? Give reasons for your answer.

Reviewing the Chapter

Chapter Summary

The years following World War I saw changes in the British Empire. Great Britain gave greater autonomy to Canada, Australia, and New Zealand. It organized the British Commonwealth of Nations, in which some of its former colonies were equal partners with Britain. A movement toward independence gained strength in India.

In China a revolution overthrew the Qing Dynasty. No strong government emerged to take its place, and local warlords controlled China. Nationalist party forces led by Chiang Kai-shek partially reunited the country, but the Nationalists soon were fighting a civil war with their former allies, the Communists.

Postwar prosperity brought social changes to the United States, but the economy collapsed in the stock market crash of 1929. The administration of Franklin D. Roosevelt took steps to counter the effects of the Depression that followed the crash by introducing a variety of government aid programs. The government took on a greater role than ever before in American history. The spread of the Depression strained the economies of nations around the globe.

In Mexico, revolution brought social change. Most of Latin America and the Caribbean were dominated by the United States, which sent its troops into several Latin American countries, including Mexico, Haiti and Santo Domingo. President Roosevelt established a Good Neighbor Policy that marked a change in United States relations with its southern neighbors.

Many of the arts saw new movements that were a radical departure from past styles. Both radio and motion pictures helped to create a new mass culture that was worldwide in influence.

1. How did Great Britain's policies toward its empire change?
2. What event led to the Depression of the 1930's?
3. How did President Franklin Roosevelt change relations between the United States and Latin America?

Using Your Vocabulary

1. What was the main recommendation of the Durham Report?
2. List the first member nations of the British Commonwealth of Nations. In what year was it established?
3. How did the followers of the Hindu Renaissance regard the West?
4. Describe the meaning of civil disobedience.
5. Explain the meaning of autonomy. List three words you know that begin with the prefix *auto.*
6. What was the principal aim of Zionism?
7. What was the responsibility of a nation that held a territory by mandate?
8. Describe the changes that China's Hundred Days' Reform was intended to bring about.
9. What was another name for members of the Society of Harmonious Fists?
10. Identify the Kuomintang.
11. What principle was set forth in the Open Door Notes?
12. What was the main idea of isolationism?
13. How did people buy stocks on margin?
14. What was the new idea that the New Deal brought to government?
15. Describe the principle behind the Aztec Renaissance.
16. What was the main idea of the Good Neighbor Policy?
17. Describe some changes in the arts brought about by Modernism.
18. What was the main goal of the women's suffrage movement?
19. What were two important aspects of Surrealism? Name two famous artists associated with this movement.
20. Describe the hallmarks of the Bauhaus style. In what country did this style of architecture originate?

Developing Your Geography Skills

1. Use the map on page 583 to describe the route of the Canadian Pacific Railroad. Include the names of the Canadian provinces through which it passes.
2. Use the Atlas map on page 754 to find the modern country of Israel, which was formerly the British mandate of Palestine.
3. Use the Atlas map on page 760 to locate the South American countries in which reforms were put into effect between the two world wars.
4. Use the map on page 589 to describe the areas in the Far East and the Pacific that Japan gained control of in the years between the wars. Based on its geography, why do you think Japan was reluctant to accept efforts to limit the size of its navy?

Recalling the Facts

1. What were the reasons why the British government began to reorganize its empire?
2. What four provinces were originally represented in the government of the Dominion of Canada?
3. Name the circumstances that brought new immigration to Australia in the late nineteenth century.
4. What were some of the progressive measures adopted by New Zealand in the 1890's?
5. What was Gandhi's role in the Indian independence movement?
6. Why did many Chinese people hate or fear foreigners?
7. Who was Mao Zedong? What role did he play in the development of the Communist party in China?
8. What advances did democracy make in Japan during the 1920's?
9. What were the causes of the rise of isolationist feeling in the United States?
10. What was the purpose of the Kellogg-Briand Pact? Why was it unlikely to have been successful?
11. What policies did the United States government follow during the Harding and Coolidge administrations?
12. What were the provisions of the neutrality acts passed by Congress in the 1930's?
13. Describe the provisions of the Mexican constitution of 1917.
14. Why did the United States send troops into Mexico in 1916?
15. Describe the economic effects of World War I on Latin American countries.
16. What was a popular musical form of the first part of the twentieth century?
17. Why did the motion picture industry thrive during the Depression?

Essay Questions

1. Write a brief essay explaining the effects of World War I on the Indian independence movement.
2. In your own words, explain why conflict between Jews and Arabs in Palestine developed under the British mandate.
3. Describe the means by which Japan gained control over areas of China in the 1920's and 1930's.
4. Describe, using specific examples, how the Depression was a catalyst for social and political change throughout the world.
5. How did the arts in the early 1900's reflect a change from past traditions? Give examples.

Critical Thinking

1. What bias can you see in the differences between Britain's treatment of Canada, Australia, and New Zealand and its response to the Indian independence movement?
2. What bias was there in allowing women to work in factories during World War I but forbidding them the right to vote?
3. Why did British promises to Jews and Arabs in Palestine cause problems?
4. What logical inconsistency can you see between President Wilson's call for self-determination and his policies toward Latin American nations?

CHAPTER ·27·

The WORLD in UPHEAVAL

1933–1945

UNITED

Objectives

- To describe how European tensions, heightened during the 1930's, created a climate for war

- To explain the way in which the Axis powers finally provoked war and gained early successes

- To discuss how the war became a truly global conflict

- To describe how the Allied powers were able to turn the tide and finally destroy the Axis

World War II, history's mightiest conflict, began in 1939 and lasted for six devastating years. It challenged the very existence of European society. A new war had been threatening Europe for years. As the poorer nations abandoned democratic institutions, they became enmeshed in a web of fascism that appeared to them as the only alternative to communism.

Italy, Japan, and Germany, rearmed and renewed under fascism, formed a combination of powers called the Axis. At their height, they controlled an empire in the West that reached from the Atlantic to the Ural Mountains, and an empire in the East that stretched from southeast Asia to the mid-Pacific. They had such strength that it required a combination of most of the other industrialized nations of the world to repel them. Opposing the Axis were the Allies—France, Britain, China, the Soviet Union, and the United States. This successful, though temporary, coalition combined their human and industrial resources and slowly wore down the Axis nations.

In the end the menace of international fascism and Italian, Japanese, and German territorial ambition was halted, but at a terrible price. Whole countries were devastated, great and ancient cities went up in flames, costs were extraordinary, millions died, and even more were uprooted. By the end of the war, influence in Europe was divided between two powerful nations with major ideological differences—the United States and the Soviet Union.

BUILDUP TO WAR

For all his deviousness, Adolf Hitler never kept his long-term goals a secret. In countless speeches during the 1920's, he proclaimed that once in power he would tear up the Treaty of Versailles, which had humbled and weakened Germany after World War I. He vowed to make Germany a world power once again.

Germany Rearms

When the Nazis took control of Germany in 1933, they accelerated a rearmament program that had begun in the 1920's in violation of the Treaty of Versailles. They planned to make Germany the military equal of any nation in the world within five years. Hitler made a secret speech to his staff warning them that making Germany Europe's strongest power would be risky, since he did not know if Britain and France would try to stop him. "The most dangerous period is that of rearmament," he said. "Then we shall see whether France has statesmen. If she does, she will not grant us time but will jump on us."

In 1932 a disarmament conference opened in Geneva, Switzerland. The British and French proposed an international system of supervision by which armament production could be monitored and possibly diminished in all countries. Hitler responded to this proposal not only by withdrawing from the conference in 1933 but also by leaving the League of Nations. In 1935 he instituted the military draft and began to build battleships and expand the air force.

In 1936 Hitler sent troops into the Rhineland, a German region in which military installations had been forbidden by the Versailles Treaty. It was a bold step that could have provoked a war with France that Germany could not have won. But the French, fearing that Britain would not support them, did nothing.

Some historians have suggested that if the British and the French had been willing to go to war they could have stopped Hitler in the early 1930's. With the terrors of World War I barely fifteen years in the past, peace above all else was on their minds. It was not on Hitler's mind. That is where the danger, and the tragedy, lay.

Italy Invades Ethiopia

Hitler was not the only European dictator with plans for expansion. Mussolini revived Italian ambition for an imperialist empire. In October 1935 Italian troops invaded Ethiopia, the historic kingdom where they were soundly defeated in the 1890's. This time Italy went armed with tanks, bombers, and poison gas.

Ethiopia's emperor, Haile Selassie (HIE-lee suh-LASS-see), made an impassioned plea for help to the League of Nations. The League took no military action, but imposed economic sanctions against Mussolini's regime. Credit was restricted, and no essential war materials could be shipped to Italy. The embargo caused some difficulty for Italy, but it did not stop the war. Oil, the one product Mussolini could not do without, was not limited. The British and French, faced with a dilemma, agreed not to close the Suez Canal through which the Italians shipped their African-bound war supplies. On the one hand, the British and French wanted to stay in line with other members of the League of Nations and impose sanctions. On the other hand, they hoped to use Mussolini to negotiate with Hitler. In the end, Ethiopia was overrun. The League of Nations lost whatever prestige it still had and ceased to be a force in world politics. In addition, the limited sanctions that were imposed only served to convince Mussolini that the British were his enemy. He drew closer to Germany and in October 1936 the two countries formed an alliance, which Mussolini named the Rome-Berlin Axis. Three years later, Mussolini seized Albania, which, according to the terms of the Treaty of Versailles, was already an Italian sphere of influence. In April 1939 the Italian navy bombarded the Albanian coastal towns, and the troops moved in. Albania's king fled to Turkey, and Albania became part of Mussolini's empire.

The Spanish Civil War

Soon after the problem in Ethiopia, an even larger crisis erupted in Spain. After the fall of the military dictatorship in 1930, Spain established a republican government led by socialists and liberals. They carried out a series of reforms to separate Church and State, expand suffrage to all men and women, give land to the poor, and improve conditions for

TERRITORIAL CHANGES IN EUROPE DURING THE 1930'S

British and French fear of war made it easier for Hitler to carry out territorial expansion. Control of what nations seemed to be of most strategic value to the Axis powers? Why was Poland in a very vulnerable position?

workers. Riots broke out as opposition to the government emerged. The increasingly militant communists and socialists thought the government had not done enough. The increasingly frightened conservatives, particularly monarchists, the clergy, and the army, worried that Spain was heading for a Russian-style communist regime. A more conservative government was elected in 1933 only to be replaced in 1936 by the Popular Front, a coalition of liberals, socialists, and communists.

By July 1936 some Spanish officers including Francisco Franco, decided to end Spain's leftist swing. This group and their followers, called Nationalists, led a revolt to restore the monarchy. The revolution became an international issue.

The Germans and Italians had economic interests in Spain—the Germans, for example, needed Spanish copper. But the war was also seen as a propaganda battle between fascists and communists and as a rehearsal for World War II. Hitler got a chance to test his new air force and tanks, both of which he sent to Spain to support the generals. After his success in Ethiopia, Mussolini also sent his troops to aid the revolutionaries. Stalin represented himself as the protector of the established republic, but actually he was more interested in Spain's Communist party.

Italian and German troops and weapons tilted the balance in Franco's favor. Republican appeals to France and Britain went largely unheeded, and Soviet aid was limited and sporadic. In the spring of 1939, after three years of devastating conflict, Franco and fascism triumphed. Franco became Spain's new dictator and a friend of Hitler and Mussolini—though he was shrewd enough to resist their entreaties to join them in the Second World War. Franco remained in power in Spain until his death in 1975.

The German Annexation of Austria

German-speaking peoples lived in several other European countries besides Germany—primarily Austria, Czechoslovakia, and Poland. One of Hitler's goals was to bring all of these Germans under his rule.

Hitler's first move to gather in all the Germans was made in Austria where a flourishing Nazi party already existed. Hitler made repeated demands on the Austrian chancellor, Kurt von Schuschnigg (fon SHOOSH-nig), to include more Nazis in his government, while the Nazis within Austria demanded union with Germany. Finally, Hitler lost his patience and massed his troops on the frontier. Schuschnigg resigned, and the German army moved in. Hitler rode in triumph through Vienna, and the Nazis began a crackdown on opponents of the new regime. A month later—in April 1938—Austria was officially incorporated into the German Reich, in the **Anschluss** (AHN-shloos), or union. *Anschluss* had been forbidden by the Treaty of Versailles. Britain and France protested, but their opposition went no further. Since World War I the western powers had held that peoples speaking the same language had the right to exist in their own state. As a result, Britain and France hesitated to resist Hitler.

Crisis in Czechoslovakia

Now that Austria was in the Reich, Czechoslovakia was the next target. Many Germans lived in the border area of Czechoslovakia called the Sudetenland (soo-DATE-un-land). Hitler insisted that these Germans were an oppressed minority, and he demanded the right to bring them into the German fold. The Sudetenland, like Austria, had its local Nazi party. Upon orders from Berlin, they began rioting against their "oppressors."

In May 1938 Hitler ordered his generals to prepare to invade Czechoslovakia. In contrast to Austria, Czechoslovakia was allied with the Soviet Union and had a treaty arrangement with France, Yugoslavia, and Romania in the Little Entente. Britain, France, and the Soviet Union issued warnings to Hitler that temporarily averted war. In the following months Britain and France pressured Czechoslovakia to offer concessions to the Sudetenland Germans to avoid war. But nothing that was offered satisfied Hitler. Meanwhile, Britain and France watched German rearmament with alarm and overestimated Germany's strength.

The Munich Conference

As negotiations faltered and Britain prepared for war, the British prime minister, Neville Chamberlain, prevailed upon Mussolini to communicate directly with Hitler. Mussolini succeeded in persuading Hitler to invite Britain, France, and Italy to

The Treaty Between Nazi Germany and the Soviet Union

Below is an excerpt from the treaty signed by Nazi Germany and the Soviet Union in Moscow on August 23, 1939. It bound together two countries with opposing theories of society and government. However, even though Communists around the world denounced the pact, Stalin felt that he was protecting Russia. Note that part of the treaty was kept secret and not made public until after the end of World War II.

1. Both nations promise to avoid any act of violence, any aggressive action, and any attack on each other. . . .
2. Should either Germany or the Soviet Union be attacked by a third nation, the other shall in no matter lend support to the third nation.
3. The Governments in Germany and the Soviet Union shall in the future maintain . . . contact with one another . . . to exchange information on problems affecting their common interests.
4. Neither Germany nor the Soviet Union shall become a member of any group of powers that is directly aimed against the other. . . .
5. The present treaty is concluded for a period of ten years. . . .

SECRET ADDITION TO THE TREATY

1. Should territorial changes be made in the Baltic states (Finland, Estonia, Latvia, Lithuania), the northern borders of Lithuania shall be the new boundary between the German and Soviet spheres of influence and domination.
2. Should territorial changes be made for Poland, Poland shall be divided between the German and Soviet spheres of influence and domination.
3. The question of whether Germany and the Soviet Union desire the continuation of an independent Polish state can only be determined in the course of further political developments, and both Governments shall resolve this question by means of a friendly agreement.
4. This Treaty shall be signed by both countries as strictly secret.

1. Summarize both the public and the secret sections of the treaty.
2. Why do you think the entire treaty was not revealed to the rest of the world?
3. How did the treaty give Hitler and Stalin a free hand to invade Poland?

a conference held in Munich, Germany, in September 1938. The Czech ministers, who had everything at stake, waited in an adjacent room while the four European leaders decided the fate of their nation.

Hitler demanded immediate possession of the Sudetenland with its military installations intact, and he left open the possibility of negotiating for even more territory. He insisted that all he wanted was to include Czechoslovakia's German minority in the Reich. Even Mussolini believed that Hitler did not plan to annex the entire Czech nation.

Chamberlain and the French premier, Daladier (dah-lah-DYAY), once more followed a policy of **appeasement,** yielding to Hitler's demands in the hope of preserving peace. Chamberlain stated proudly that he had achieved "peace in our time." In Paris, London, and Rome, cheering crowds, who had dreaded the prospect of war, hailed the leaders as peacemakers.

Czechoslovakia was cruelly dismembered. Hitler got an area that included not only the Sudetenland Germans, but nearly one million Czechs as well. Poland and Hungary also took pieces of the unfortunate country. Militarily, the agreement was an extraordinary achievement for Hitler. The great Czech fortifications became part of Germany. What was left of Czechoslovakia was now defenseless. In addition, Hitler acquired the powerful Czech armament factories.

In view of France's abandonment of Czechoslovakia, the other nations of the Little Entente saw that they could not rely on France for protection from Nazi ambition. They began to draw closer to Germany. France's alliance system, including the alliance with Russia, fell apart.

The Hitler-Stalin Pact

The Soviet Union had taken no clear position while Hitler was waging his diplomatic struggle with the western powers. Hitler and Stalin had opposed each other in Spain, and Hitler's political philosophy was based on anticommunism. Britain and France reluctantly sought Stalin's support. On August 1, 1939, a combined British-French diplomatic mission set sail for Russia. But this move came too late, since the Soviet Union had not been invited to Munich despite its alliances with both France and Czechoslovakia.

Hitler had no love for the Soviet Union and had even stated in *Mein Kampf* that it was there that he intended to extend his greater Nazi empire. Stalin certainly had reason to fear Hitler, but he did not trust Britain and France either. He thought that the anticommunist sentiments of their governments might lead them to abandon the Soviet Union if it was invaded by Germany.

To the astonishment of Europe, Hitler and Stalin signed a nonaggression pact on August 23, 1939. The sworn enemies who had faced each other in Spain were suddenly in accord. The agreement was explained as simply a nonaggression pact—that is, the two countries pledged not to attack each other. Its secret provisions proved, however, that it was really a plan to divide eastern Europe—especially Poland—between the powers. The Soviet action shocked and divided the international communist movement.

Crisis in Poland

Hitler hoped that his pact with Russia would deter Britain and France from offering military opposi-

tion. It had the opposite effect. In both countries people now resigned themselves to the fact that war was probably inevitable, because they realized Hitler could not be appeased.

In March 1939 Hitler took what was left of Czechoslovakia. Now Poland was the target. Hitler again proclaimed his desire to protect a German minority. In addition, he wanted the so-called Polish Corridor. This strip of land, granted to Poland after World War I as an outlet to the sea, cut off Germany from its province of East Prussia.

Anyone who believed that Hitler only wanted to restore German-speaking peoples to the Reich learned otherwise. With the incorporation of the Slavic portion of Czechoslovakia into the Reich and the seizure of the city of Memel from Lithuania, it became clear that his ambitions were far greater. Britain and France decided that if Hitler attacked Poland, they would go to war in Poland's defense. Hitler, on the other hand, had concluded that the western powers were unwilling to fight.

On August 30, 1939, Hitler issued an ultimatum to Poland demanding the return of the corridor. Actually, the orders for invasion had already been issued, and the German army crossed the frontier on September 1. Two days later, to Hitler's surprise, the British and French declared war.

SECTION REVIEW

1. Mapping: Use the map on page 608 to locate Czechoslovakia and show how Hitler was able to surround it.

2. In your own words, briefly identify or define: Rhineland, Haile Selassie, *Anschluss*, Sudetenland.

3. How did the civil war in Spain come to be a battle involving outside powers? How did this affect the way in which the civil war was fought?

4. How did Hitler justify his territorial demands in Europe?

■ Many historians have criticized Britain and France for not going to war with Germany much earlier, before Hitler had a chance to build up his army. Do you think a country today is justified in attacking a potential enemy to prevent a wider conflict later?

THE AXIS STRIKES

Many military observers rated the Polish army highly and expected it to give the Germans tough opposition. What they did not realize was that the Germans had developed a new form of warfare—the *blitzkrieg* (BLITS-kreeg), or lightning war. They used huge concentrations of tanks and air power to break through enemy lines and cut their communication. Speed and mobility were the keys.

War in Poland and Finland

The German blitzkrieg struck Poland so suddenly that the Polish troops barely had time to get into position. While the German air force hit planes still on the ground, tanks pushed into the country with dazzling speed, trapping the Polish forces in a giant pincer. Two weeks later Russians overran the eastern half of the country.

Britain and France, Poland's allies, might have tried to invade Germany from the west, but they felt their troops were unready. Because they overestimated German strength, they did nothing. The Polish campaign was over in less than a month, and the Polish nation disappeared.

The Russians took advantage of the situation to enlarge their territory. Stalin wanted a buffer zone in case Hitler eventually attacked the Soviet Union. The Russians absorbed the three Baltic nations of Lithuania, Latvia, and Estonia. They then attacked Finland, because it refused to cede its border territories. The Finns, with their white uniforms and ski troops, were well prepared for the Winter War, and the Russian tank columns were repeatedly destroyed. Western observers were enormously impressed by the staunch Finnish resistance, but in the end the sheer bulk of the Russian war machine wore down the Finns. A peace treaty signed in March 1940 gave the Russians more territory than they had originally sought.

These German soldiers were photographed in front of the Arc de Triomphe, which was built in Paris to commemorate Napoleon's victories.

Blitzkrieg in the West

Although they were officially at war with Hitler, Britain and France took no military action during the winter of 1939–1940. The situation became known as the phony war. Journalists called it the *sitzkrieg* (sit-SKREEG), or sit-down war. Hitler, however, did not stay idle. In April 1940, to assure a supply of Swedish iron ore, German forces overran Denmark and Norway. Britain offered naval resistance and landed about 45,000 troops in Norway, but the Germans repelled them easily. The fall of Norway was the final blow to Neville Chamberlain's government. He was replaced as Britain's prime minister by Winston Churchill on May 10, 1940, the same day that Germany struck Holland and Belgium. By the end of the month, Dutch and Belgian resistance had collapsed.

Now Hitler was ready to attack France. The French had been preparing for the invasion for a long time, expecting the Germans to repeat their tactics of World War I and attack by way of Belgium. They were right. That was the German plan—until a clever general convinced Hitler that the French could be caught off guard with an advance through the Ardennes Forest, an area that the French considered impenetrable. In one of history's classic military campaigns, the Germans outflanked the Maginot Line, France's fortified line of defense. They sent their tanks smashing through the Ardennes near the French-Belgian border, wheeled them with breathtaking speed toward the English Channel, and completely trapped the British and French forces who were waiting for the invasion on the Belgian border.

The Allied armies withdrew to the Channel city of Dunkirk, where most of them were rescued and evacuated to Britain by a flotilla of warships and private vessels. The Germans entered Paris on June 13. A mere six weeks after the campaign began, the French had signed a humiliating surrender. Many people thought the war was over.

The Vichy Government

As the Germans advanced into France, the French government summoned its eighty-four-year-old World War I hero, Henri Petain (PAY-tan), to save the nation. Instead of rescuing France, he presided over its surrender and formed a new government.

Under the terms of the armistice, the Germans took control of occupied France, in the northern portion of the country. The French capital was moved to the southern city of Vichy (VEE-shee). Petain's government became known as Vichy France. Though many French resisted Vichy rule, others felt that the defeat proved that democracy had made France weak, and they favored a fascist government modeled after Nazi Germany. The Vichy regime attracted many people on the far right as well as opportunists, and it cooperated with Hitler. An anti-Nazi underground movement, however, was organized in France. Partisans, as the resistance fighters were called, risked their lives to sabotage transportation and communication equipment needed by the Germans. Many of the soldiers who had escaped rallied around the French General Charles de Gaulle. Broadcasting from his exile in Britain, he exhorted the French to join him. De Gaulle formed the Free French government and promised to liberate his nation.

The Battle of Britain

Feverishly the British began preparing to meet a German invasion. Just as feverishly the Germans began preparing the cross-channel attack, which they called Operation Sea Lion. In order to invade, however, the Germans had to have control of the sea, and in order to control the sea they first had to control the air. The German air force, or *Luftwaffe* (LOOFT-vah-feh), soared into action.

The British, however, though short of equipment, had several advantages in this air war. Their new Spitfire airplane was superior to anything the Germans had. They also had radar, which enabled them to detect incoming aircraft. Finally, they had broken the German codes and were able to eavesdrop on German radio communications, learning in advance where the Germans would attack.

Nevertheless, the battle was fiercely contested and very close. An air battle of this kind had never been fought before, and both sides had great difficulty assessing the damage they were inflicting.

The Germans bombed London and terrorized the city with constant nighttime attacks known as the London Blitz. Nearly 13,000 civilians were killed in these raids, but the Londoners held fast. By the autumn of 1940 the Germans had lost thousands of planes, and it became clear that they

A stack of stretchers was a grim reminder of the toll taken by the German bombing of London.

would not be able to conquer the British skies. On September 17, Hitler postponed the invasion "until further notice." On October 12 he called off the air war. He would now turn to the east.

The United States Gets Involved

Although the Americans sympathized with France and Britain, most of them wanted to stay out of the war. In 1937 the Congress had passed neutrality acts that prohibited the exportation of arms to belligerents. The Neutrality Act of 1939 allowed the sale of armaments to belligerent nations on a "cash-and-carry" basis. As in World War I, American neutrality laws favored Britain since it controlled the seas.

Many Americans assumed that the British and French could defeat Germany without outside assistance. The fall of France changed their minds. When the British began suffering the blitz, Ameri-

can public opinion, influenced by President Roosevelt, gradually became openly pro-British.

Americans still wanted to help without actually participating in combat. In March 1941 Congress passed the Lend-Lease Act, under which massive supplies of arms could be shipped to Britain on credit. This act showed that the United States recognized and accepted that it had a stake in the outcome of the war. In August of the same year Roosevelt and Churchill met aboard ship in the North Atlantic and signed the Atlantic Charter.

The Atlantic Charter

By signing the Atlantic Charter, President Roosevelt accelerated the pace of the United States' emergence from isolationism although the debate in the nation over entry into the war was still heated. The agreement was an open declaration of the peace aims of the war. There were to be no secret agreements such as those that marred the peace efforts following World War I.

The Atlantic Charter was a brief but significant document. The principles included that neither Britain nor the United States sought any territory as a result of the war. There were to be no territorial changes without consulting the people involved. The right to choose their own government was to be guaranteed to all. There was to be freedom on the seas and access to raw materials for every nation. Social and economic progress were to be promoted by international cooperation. A basis would be established for disarmament and a wider system of national security.

The Atlantic Charter signaled that the United States would accept responsibility for the shape of the world after the war.

The Mediterranean and the Balkans

In the fall of 1940 the focus of the war shifted to the Mediterranean, where Mussolini dreamed of establishing an Italian empire in North Africa. He launched desert campaigns from Libya in September 1940. The Italians advanced into Egypt hoping to seize the Suez Canal and control the Mediterranean. Mussolini also hoped to expand outward from his base in Albania and take over Greece. The Italians in both North Africa and Greece, however, were defeated by the British. The Germans, in order to support their ally, reluctantly became involved.

Hitler's forces, meanwhile, began moving into Romania to obtain its plentiful oil fields. His army seized the country in October 1940. Yugoslavia was absorbed in April 1941, although there was strong partisan opposition under Josip Broz, later to be known as Marshal Tito. He hounded the Germans for the rest of the war. By the end of April the British were pushed out of Greece, and in May German parachute troops captured the strategic island of Crete.

The British attempt to hold Greece proved a costly diversion, for it meant pulling troops out of North Africa, an area in which the British had enjoyed considerable success against the Italians. Now the Germans entered the African campaign. In March 1941 they sent two divisions of troops and one of their ablest generals, Erwin Rommel, whom the British dubbed the Desert Fox. The forces in North Africa were now equal on both sides, and the war there would drag on until mid-May 1943.

SECTION REVIEW

1. **Mapping:** Use the map on page 608 to locate the countries that were invaded by Germany or taken over whole or in part by the Soviet Union in late 1939. How does the map help explain Mussolini's territorial ambitions and his attempts at conquest?
2. In your own words, briefly identify or define: phony war, blitzkrieg, Spitfire, Atlantic Charter.
3. What effect did the fall of France and the Battle of Britain have on people in the United States?
4. Why did the Germans decide to get involved in fighting the war in the Mediterranean?
■ Even though most of them sympathized with France and Britain, the American people were reluctant to get involved in the war. What kinds of events do you think have to happen today to persuade a country that has not been attacked to get involved in a war thousands of miles away?

THE WAR BECOMES WORLDWIDE

Even though the war so far had been devastating, it was not yet a true global war—the United States and the Soviet Union still were not in it. That all changed suddenly.

The Invasion of Russia

At 3 A.M. on June 22, 1941, the Germans overran their Russian ally with an army over three-and-a-half-million strong. Hitler was finally making his move to destroy communism and build his German empire on the eastern plains.

Elated by his success in Poland and France, Hitler expected another swift victory. The German advance in Russia was so rapid that it seemed he would get it. Only four days after the invasion started, two entire Russian armies were surrounded. Thousands of Soviet prisoners were trapped, and the German blitzkrieg rolled relentlessly onward.

The Germans crossed the Dnieper River in July and by the first week of August, Hitler's soldiers were only 200 miles (320 kilometers) from Moscow. Hitler decided not to attack the Russian capital just yet—he considered it a useless objective. Instead he sent the German forces south toward Kiev, taking 500,000 more Russian prisoners in the process.

By October 2 Hitler had changed his mind and had decided to attack Moscow after all. As the Germans neared the Russian capital, Russian resistance became more stubborn and the weather more severe. The Germans actually reached the city's outskirts, but the troops were exhausted, the supplies ran low, and the temperature dropped to 40 degrees below zero. The German offensive stalled, and both sides settled in for the winter.

When spring arrived in 1942, the German army was still in fighting shape. Held off at Moscow and lured by the Caucasus oil fields, Hitler now decided to press his efforts in the south. By the first of July German troops were masters of the Crimean peninsula. A month later they were a mere 40 miles (64 kilometers) from the city of Stalingrad, in the heart of the Soviet Union.

German intelligence officers estimated that they had already destroyed over 100 Red army divisions, but they calculated that the Russians had 300 more. The vast spaces and the deep reservoir of Russian manpower were beginning to take their toll on Hitler's army.

Russia Fights Back

Since the German drive into Russia stalled in the Moscow suburbs in the winter of 1941, Hitler's generals knew that they would not win a quick victory. They had grievously underestimated the Red army's capacity to resist. In addition, the Russians were now beginning to receive much needed supplies from the West, including tanks, airplanes, and especially trucks. With this equipment Stalin's army gained speed and maneuverability. War production was maintained by the movement of industries across the Urals, to cities out of the reach of the German army.

In early September 1942 the Red army decided to make its stand as the German Sixth Army massed to capture Stalingrad. The two armies fought fiercely. The Russians lost more soldiers in the battle for Stalingrad than the Americans lost in the entire war.

In November the Russians counterattacked to both the north and the south of the city. In two days they had Stalingrad surrounded, trapping the German Sixth Army inside. A month later, a German relief column got within 30 miles (48 kilometers) of Stalingrad, but no farther. The city became the scene of savage hand-to-hand street fighting, and the Russians tightened their grip. On February 2, 1943, the Germans surrendered, and twenty-two German divisions—or what was left of them—were captured. It was a huge defeat for Hitler's forces, one from which Germany would never recover. If there was a single turning point in the war in Europe, Stalingrad was it.

America Enters the War

Many Americans expected that, sooner or later, they would be drawn into the war, but the way in which it happened came as a surprise. At eight o'clock in the morning of December 7, 1941, a task force of Japanese aircraft attacked the United States Pacific fleet at its naval base in Pearl Harbor,

Hawaii. In less than two hours two great battleships, the *Oklahoma* and the *Arizona,* were sunk. Six more were damaged, and many smaller ships went to the bottom of the sea. Over 150 planes were destroyed; over 2000 Americans were dead. Had the aircraft carriers not been at sea, the destruction would have been even worse. As it was, America's naval strength in the Pacific was severely crippled.

Pearl Harbor was part of a long-range Japanese plan to conquer the southwest Pacific. They did not seriously believe they could conquer the United States. They did believe, however, that if they could keep America out of the Pacific for six months they could set up a defense system against which the Americans would hurl themselves in vain. The attack on Pearl Harbor reversed the isolationist sentiment of the American public.

Japan Takes the Offensive

The Japanese had been at war long before they surprised Pearl Harbor. As early as 1931, they had invaded Manchuria. In 1937 they went into China, capturing Beijing and Shanghai and then driving into the interior, where they met stubborn resistance.

When Hitler attacked the western democracies, the Japanese saw it as a great opportunity to seize the Southeast Asian colonial territories of Britain, France, and the Netherlands. The area was rich in raw materials that Japan sorely needed. In September 1940 Japan signed an alliance with the Axis powers of Germany and Italy.

The Japanese invasion of the region was carried out in two major moves—one westward into Indochina, Malaya, Burma, and the Dutch East Indies, and one to the southeast toward the Philippines and the Pacific islands. The Japanese prime minister General Hideki Tojo (HEE-DAY-KEE TOH-JOH) vowed to remove western influence from the East.

On Christmas Day, 1941, the British forces in Hong Kong surrendered. The following February the Japanese, invading through the dense Malayan jungle, seized the strategic island of Singapore. Java was taken next, and when the British were pushed out of Burma in April 1942, the Japanese were threatening India.

The Japanese attack toward the southeast was

equally successful. On December 22, 1941, the Japanese landed 43,000 troops in the Philippines, which had been a United States colony since 1898. The American commander General Douglas MacArthur tried to hold them back, but the Japanese controlled the air and sea. MacArthur's forces were pushed into the small peninsula of Bataan, where, after desperate resistance, they surrendered on April 8, 1942. The American and Filipino prisoners were marched through the jungle toward prison camps. In the Bataan Death March, thousands were executed or died. MacArthur, who had been ordered to abandon the Philippines a few weeks earlier, promised to return.

Other Pacific islands—Wake, Guam, the Gilberts, the Marshalls—were also overrun. By April 1942 the Japanese controlled an empire from the border of India to the central Pacific.

The "Final Solution"

When Hitler marched into the Soviet Union and Eastern Europe, he not only gained territory for his empire, but also extended into the conquered territory one of the most terrible tenets of the Nazi philosophy. Ever since his early days in Vienna, Hitler had borne a fanatical, irrational hatred for the Jews. Once World War II began, Hitler started shipping Jews from Germany to the areas of Poland conquered by the German army. There Jews were confined in large concentration camps. By mid-1943, the Nazis proudly announced that Berlin and most of Germany was free of all Jews.

After the start of World War II, the Nazi leaders in Germany decided to destroy all the Jews in every European country that had fallen under Germany's control. This terrible policy was re-

THE HOLOCAUST

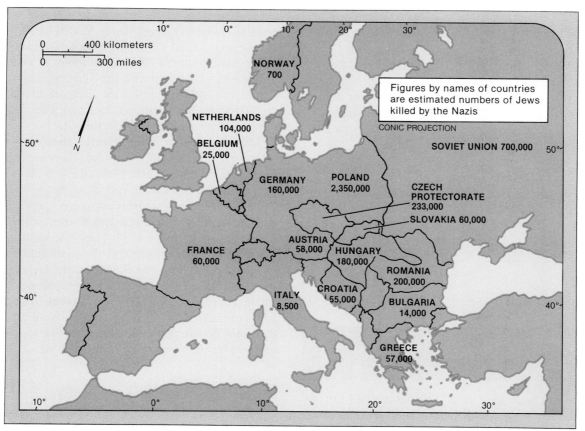

Why do you think the word genocide, meaning the organized and deliberate killing of a race or cultural group, was coined in 1944?

ferred to as the Final Solution. All over Europe, Jews were rounded up along with other peoples the Nazis considered inferior, and mass executions began. Many Jews and Slavs were sent to death camps that had been established especially to exterminate "inferior" peoples. By 1944, Nazi officials boasted that millions of Jews had been killed. They claimed that four million of these had died in the concentration camp at Auschwitz (OWSH-vits), in southern Poland. In addition to Jewish victims, it is believed the Nazis murdered at least six million non-Jews. Most of these were Slavs, who died in the death camps.

The dreadful attempt to wipe out all the Jewish people of Europe has been given the name **Holocaust** by the Jews themselves. The term holocaust means a great destruction of life. It is an appropriate word to describe the destruction of millions of innocent people by the Nazis.

SECTION REVIEW

1. Mapping: Use the map on page 622 to locate: Pearl Harbor, Japan, the Philippines, Burma, Indochina, Malaya, Dutch East Indies.
2. In your own words, briefly identify or define: Stalingrad, Singapore, Auschwitz, Holocaust.
3. What factors prevented the German army from winning a quick victory in Russia?
4. How did the attack on Pearl Harbor fit into the larger Japanese strategy in the Pacific?
■ In the Holocaust six million Jews were murdered. What kind of mentality do you think it requires to carry out a holocaust? Do you think that kind of mentality may still exist?

THE ALLIES TURN THE TIDE

The late summer and fall of 1942 marked the low point in the war for the Allies. Then while the Russians were battling the German army in Stalingrad, the Americans and British began to make headway in North Africa.

The Invasion of North Africa

General Rommel's offensives in the spring of 1942 were successful. When he routed the British at Tobruk on the Libyan coast in June, it looked as if the Germans would win in North Africa.

It was not to be. Using their ability to decode the German signals, the British under General Bernard Montgomery regrouped. By October they were able to mount an offensive. The battle at El Alamein (ell al-uh-MAYN) in Egypt resulted in a resounding British victory. Rommel found it more and more difficult to get supplies from Europe, and the British began pursuing his forces along the coast until, one by one, the North African cities were captured.

Meanwhile the Allies also fought their way across North Africa from the west. American ships and troops joined the British in the invasion called Operation Torch. In November 1942 American troops went ashore near Casablanca, and a combined Anglo-American army under the American general Dwight D. Eisenhower landed at Algiers. The Germans reinforced their troops, but this only delayed the outcome. The Allied forces in eastern North Africa linked up with the Allies coming from Casablanca and surrounded the Germans in northern Tunisia. The Germans evacuated as many troops as they could, but when the surrender came in May 1943—only three months after the German surrender at Stalingrad—the Allies took over a quarter of a million prisoners. The Axis plans for Egypt and the Suez were ended.

While the North African campaign was raging, Winston Churchill and Franklin Roosevelt met at Casablanca in January 1943. They discussed their relationship with France and their commitments to the Soviet Union. The Soviets wanted a second front opened in the West to relieve pressure on them. Fear of possible Soviet defection from the Allies motivated Churchill and Roosevelt to call for the total destruction of the Axis military power and to promise to establish another front.

The Invasion of Italy

Chances for victory looked brighter for the Allies at the opening of 1943 than they had since the outbreak of the war. The Allies could look not only to Stalingrad and North Africa but also to American

WORLD WAR II
ALLIED VICTORY IN EUROPE AND NORTH AFRICA, 1942–1945

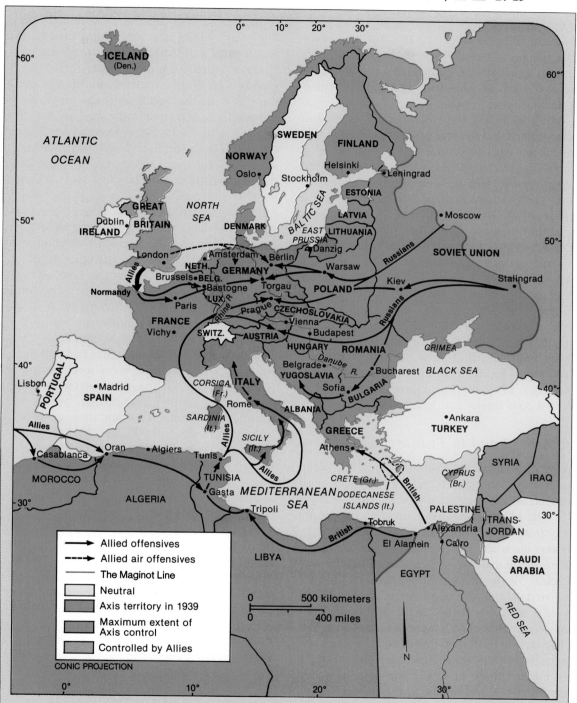

Identify the areas in Europe and the Middle East controlled by the Allied and the Axis powers. What general routes did the Allies follow once they turned the tide of the war and went on the offensive?

successes in the Pacific and the weakening of German submarine warfare in the North Atlantic.

The Allies next attempted an invasion of the strategic island of Sicily to gain control of the Mediterranean shipping lanes. On July 10, 1943, over half a million Allied troops landed on the island's southern shore. Within two weeks, they had taken control of most of the island, forcing the German and Italian forces to evacuate.

When Sicily fell, the Fascist Grand Council in Rome decided that the war was lost. Mussolini was overthrown with surprising ease. Under Marshal Pietro Badoglio (buh-DOLE-yah) Italy surrendered unconditionally and then declared war on Germany. The Germans managed to rescue Mussolini and reestablish him in an area of the Italian Alps, but his power was broken.

In September 1943 the Allies attacked the Italian peninsula as troops were put ashore at Salerno, south of Naples. As more landings followed, the Germans withdrew to strong defensive positions and resolutely determined to check the Allied advance. Their hard resistance turned the Italian campaign into a brutal, bloody stalemate. Finally in May 1944 the Allied leaders sent in enough reinforcements to break through the German lines. On June 4, 1944, the Allied forces entered Rome. The first Axis capital had fallen.

The Allies Land in France

After the Casablanca conference, at which Stalin was not present, Stalin agreed to meet with Churchill and Roosevelt at Teheran in November 1943. The Allies committed themselves to opening a new front in the west. The breakup of Germany was also discussed and Stalin proposed to enlarge Poland at the expense of Germany. Thus the way was clear for the invasion of France.

Two days after the fall of Rome, the great invasion of France—or D-Day as the Allies called it—finally came. Hitler had long been expecting it, Stalin had long been demanding it, and the Allies had long been planning it. Originally the Allies thought they might invade in 1942. The date was then moved to 1943, and finally, as the British insisted on first invading the Mediterranean, to 1944. To head this massive operation General Dwight D. Eisenhower was chosen not only for his military ability but also for his capacity to maintain harmony between the American and British generals. Having learned from their experiences in the First World War, the United States and Britain had formed a coalition called the Combined Chiefs of Staff. Early in the war they pooled their resources and formed a unified strategy for fighting.

Five beaches in the French region of Normandy were chosen for the landings. The three in the east would be assaulted by the British and the Canadians and the two in the west, by the Americans. Opposition was heavy everywhere, but especially at heavily fortified Omaha beach, where the Americans suffered 1000 casualties on the landing day. Nevertheless, the beaches were taken and secured in about a week.

The Germans were slow to send in reinforcements. The Allied deception was particularly good. Hitler thought that the Normandy landings were a diversion and that the true invasion would occur farther east, near Calais. By the time he realized that Normandy was the real target, it was too late. The Allies had landed 130,000 troops the first day and a million within a month.

The Germans fought with remarkable intensity and skill, and though the Allies had complete air superiority the invasion went more slowly than planned. In late July the Allied forces, following up a merciless bombing campaign, finally broke through the German lines and moved out of Normandy and into central France. Their armies raced across the country. Then on August 15 the invasion of southern France was launched. In Operation Anvil troops advanced over 100 miles (160 kilometers) in a week. The Germans were now being attacked at both ends of the country.

News of the invasion stirred the people of Paris, who rose up against the German occupying troops. Eisenhower had planned to bypass the city but the French troops who accompanied the invasion insisted on retaking their capital. Paris was liberated on August 25, 1944. The Germans were in orderly retreat all along the line. The only thing that slowed down the Allied armies was their inability to stretch out their supply lines and keep their racing tank columns supplied with gasoline.

The Pacific War

While the Allies were pushing back the Axis powers in Europe, they were also making gains against the Japanese in the Pacific. Using both Chinese and American troops General Joseph Stilwell struck the Japanese in northern Burma while the British, moving out of India, linked up with his forces and drove the Japanese back.

The war in the Pacific islands area was largely conducted by Americans. General Douglas MacArthur waged a successful campaign in New Guinea, constantly surprising and outmaneuvering the enemy while keeping his casualties remarkably low.

In October 1944 American troops were ready for the invasion of the Philippines. Having engineered a complex plan to destroy the United States fleet, the Japanese navy was waiting. The resulting battle of Leyte Gulf was the largest naval battle in history. When it was over, the Japanese navy was crushed. The United States troops doggedly pushed into the Philippines and took Manila, the capital, in February 1945. MacArthur had kept his promise to return. Over 14,000 Americans died in the campaign that cost the Japanese 350,000 lives.

Farther out in the Pacific, the American forces under Admiral Chester Nimitz began a process of island-hopping—capturing a series of strategic islands in succession, each one closer to Japan. The battles turned out to be unexpectedly intense and bloody. The Japanese code of honor made surrender a disgrace. The Japanese soldiers fought ferociously, preferring death to capture.

One of the most vicious battles of the war was fought on the tiny volcanic island of Iwo Jima (EE-woh JEE-mah), 750 miles (1,200 kilometers) from Tokyo. When the Marines landed on February 19, 1945, at least 21,000 Japanese defenders garrisoned Iwo Jima. When the battle was over a month later, 200 remained alive. Nearly 7000 Americans were killed.

The same kind of horrifying experience was repeated a month later, when the United States Army and Marines took Okinawa. Over 100,000 Japanese died there, many by suicide.

The price was high and the battles were savage, but the Americans were making progress. The capture of these strategic islands enabled the Americans to get their bombers within striking distance of Japan, and they rained down terrible destruction on the Japanese cities. The troops were getting closer to the day when they would be able to land on Japan itself.

Victory in Europe

By the end of 1944, the position of the Allies in western Europe looked very favorable. For over a year the Allies had been heavily bombing German cities and industries to weaken opposition. The capture of Antwerp in Belgium gave the Allies the port they needed to keep their armies supplied. They crossed the German frontier in September but were forced back. As they readied for another assault in December, the Germans mounted a completely unexpected counteroffensive in the same Ardennnes Forest through which they had attacked France three-and-a-half years earlier. The onslaught pushed a great bulge into the Allied lines, which gave the incident the name "Battle of the Bulge." Poor weather grounded the Allied air force, and the Germans had the Allies on the move for about a week. Then as reinforcements arrived,

The women in uniform and on the home front made vital contributions to the war effort.

WORLD WAR II ALLIED VICTORY IN THE PACIFIC, 1942–1945

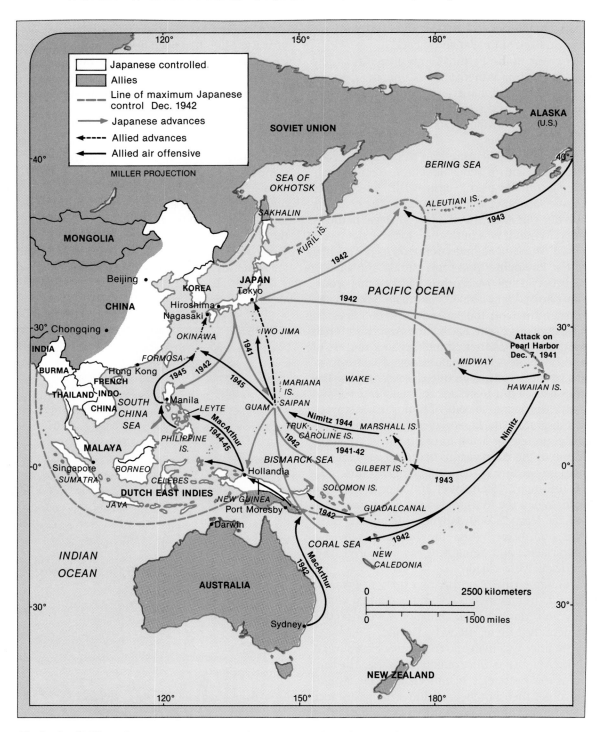

The battle of Midway (June 3–6, 1942) was an important American victory in the war in the Pacific. Why do you think the island was of strategic importance to the United States?

the skies cleared. Still, it was not until the end of January 1945 that Allies were back to their original positions. The effort so weakened the German forces that they were unable to mount an effective defense of their homeland.

In order to halt the Allied invasion of Germany, the Germans destroyed the bridges over the Rhine River. But on March 7, 1945, American troops captured a bridge at Remagen before the Germans could blow it up. They quickly poured five divisions across it. As other Rhine crossings were made, the German opposition crumbled.

In the east the Russians were also advancing. By the end of 1944 they were in Hungary, and in January of 1945 they began their drive in the north. By the end of the month they were fifty miles (eighty kilometers) from Berlin. The Germans fought hard to protect their capital, and the Russians paused to refit their forces. In April they mounted their final offensive, surrounding Berlin by the end of the month. Meanwhile German resistance in Italy collapsed. Mussolini tried to escape but was captured by Italian partisans and quickly executed. With Americans to the west and Russians to the east, Hitler finally realized that all was lost. On April 30 he committed suicide in an underground bunker to which he had retreated.

A week later—May 7, 1945—a group of the remaining members of the Nazi regime signed formal surrender papers at Eisenhower's headquarters in Rheims, France. On May 8 the end of war in Europe was declared.

Japanese Defeat

The Americans were now able to give their full attention to Japan. American bombers were already giving the enemy a pounding. The bombing of Tokyo on March 9, 1945, alone killed 83,000 people. Yet the Japanese showed no inclination to surrender and prepared a grim, unyielding defense of Japan. Having experienced the resolute zeal of the Japanese defenders of the Pacific islands, the American commanders could scarcely imagine the resistance they would have to overcome on the mainland. They fully expected that it would cost them one million casualties to invade Japan.

As it turned out, the invasion was unnecessary. On July 16, 1945, American scientists tested the atomic bomb, a new weapon so terrible it could break even the Japanese will to fight. Controversy over the decision to drop the bomb has existed ever since, but at the time there seemed to be no other choice. However horrible it was, the bomb would kill far fewer people—on both sides—than an invasion. Accordingly on August 6, 1945, the nuclear age was born, when an American B-29 dropped the atomic bomb on the Japanese city of Hiroshima (heer-uh-SHEE-muh). The gigantic explosion killed or wounded over half of the 320,000 people in the city. Two days later the Soviet Union declared war on Japan. The following day, another atomic bomb was dropped on Nagasaki (nah-guh-SAH-kee). The Russians then entered the war against Japan by invading Manchuria.

The combined effect was too much for the Japanese. The final surrender was signed on September 2, 1945, on the battleship *Missouri,* which was anchored in Tokyo Bay.

Shaping the Future of Europe

During the course of the war, the Allied leaders had to come to some agreement about the shape of the postwar world. At the meeting in November 1943 at Teheran, Churchill, Roosevelt, and Stalin formulated plans for the United Nations. In February 1945 they met again, at the Russian city of Yalta. Roosevelt, at this point, still anticipated an invasion of Japan and was eager to get the Russians to join him in the Japanese war. The Soviet Union agreed to enter the war against Japan within six months. In return it was to receive some Japanese territories.

There were difficult decisions to be made about what would happen to Germany after the war and who would take control of eastern Europe and the Balkans. It was agreed that Germany would be divided into zones of occupation among the British, French, Russians, and Americans. The Russians coveted eastern Europe, and Churchill wanted to keep them out of it. Stalin's promise that free elections would be held in the eastern European countries was quickly broken. In July 1945 another conference was held in the German city of Potsdam. By now Roosevelt was dead and Harry S Truman was president of the United States. Clement Attlee and the Labour party had replaced Winston Churchill and the Conservatives. The conference had to contend with the reality of armed strength.

Churchill, Roosevelt, and Stalin met at Yalta, Russia, in 1945 to discuss postwar plans. What were some of the issues that they had to decide?

The Red army was firmly in control of eastern Europe as far west as the Elbe River in central Germany. They had no intention of withdrawing, and eastern Europe, except Greece, came under Soviet domination, where it remains.

The Cost of War

The scale of destruction caused by World War II is so enormous that historians can only estimate it. It has been calculated that the war cost the participants well over $4 trillion. Wide areas of Europe and Asia were devastated and hundreds of famous and beautiful cities were practically wiped out. No less than 16 million soldiers lost their lives. The number of civilians who died was even greater. About 20 million died in the Soviet Union alone. One third of the population of Poland perished. When to these incredible figures are added the millions of deaths from the Holocaust, it becomes clear that World War II was probably the most destructive event in history.

SECTION REVIEW

1. Mapping: Use the map on page 622 to trace the course of the Allied advance against the Japanese. Why was Iwo Jima considered to be of such strategic importance?
2. In your own words, briefly identify or define: Omaha Beach, Chester Nimitz, Remagen, Hiroshima.
3. Who was the general in charge of the Normandy landings on D-Day? Why was he chosen for the job?
4. Why were the American attacks on islands held by the Japenese so costly in human life? How did this affect the decision to drop the atomic bomb?
■ World War II lasted six years and cost tremendous resources and numbers of lives. How does an understanding of World War II help explain the political situation in the world today?

Reviewing the Chapter

Chapter Summary

When Hitler came to power, he quickly rebuilt German military strength and then began a series of moves to create a great European empire. He formed an alliance with Italy and with Japan, forming a coalition known as the Axis.

Hitler remilitarized the Rhineland, annexed Austria, and took Czechoslovakia. Britain and France finally lost their patience and declared war when Hitler conquered Poland in September of 1939. In the spring of 1940 the Germans crushed France, but they were unable to invade Britain because they could not defeat the British air force. Hitler then turned eastward and invaded Russia, gaining enormous initial advances before his troops halted just short of Moscow. In the East, the Japanese moved into China, Indochina, the Philippines, and the Pacific islands.

When the Japanese bombed the United States naval base at Pearl Harbor, Hawaii, the United States entered the war. American industrial strength gave the Allies the arms and supplies they needed, and slowly the tide began to turn. In the west, the Allies invaded North Africa, then Italy, and finally, on June 6, 1944, France. In Russia the Red army won a great victory at Stalingrad and then began to push the Germans back.

The end in Europe came in the spring of 1945, when Berlin fell and Hitler committed suicide. With the dropping of two atomic bombs on Japan in August, the Japanese also surrendered.

1. What were the Axis powers?
2. What event caused Britain and France to declare war on Hitler's Germany?
3. How did the entrance of America into the war help turn the tide against the Axis?

Using Your Vocabulary

1. What is rearmament? Why was it important to Germany?
2. What does the term *Anschluss* mean? What country was absorbed into the Third Reich by the *Anschluss*?
3. In what country was the Sudetenland? Why did Hitler claim that it belonged to Germany?
4. Appeasement is a policy of giving in to demands in order to keep peace. What two statesmen tried to appease Hitler?
5. Which countries made up the Little Entente?
6. What is a nonaggression pact?
7. What was the blitzkrieg? What was the first country in which Hitler used this technique?
8. What was the difference between the Vichy government and the Free French government?
9. How did the provisions of the Lend-Lease Act differ from the Neutrality Act of 1939? What was the significance of the Lend-Lease Act?
10. What was the Final Solution? What name was given by the Jews themselves to this tragedy?
11. What major leader was present at the Teheran Conference who was not present at the Casablanca Conference?
12. What was D-Day?
13. At what conference was the formation of the United Nations discussed?
14. What decision about the future of Germany was made at the Yalta Conference?

Developing Your Geography Skills

1. According to the map on page 608, when did Germany move into the Saar, the Rhineland, Austria, Czechoslovakia, the Sudetenland?
2. Use the maps on pages 608, 756, and 758 to describe the location of Ethiopia and Albania in relation to Italy. What strategic value did these conquests have for Italy?
3. Use the scale of miles on the map on page 622 to give the approximate distance between Hawaii and Japan. Why was the attack on Pearl Harbor important to the Japanese?

4. Use the map on page 619 to name the countries in Europe and North Africa that were controlled by the Axis. Which countries were controlled by the Allies?
5. Use the map on page 622 to describe the area in the Pacific region and Asia controlled by the Axis. What regions or countries were members of the Allies?

Recalling the Facts

1. What sanctions were imposed on Italy for invading Ethiopia? Why were they not effective?
2. Why did France and Great Britain hesitate to interfere when Hitler incorporated Austria into the Third Reich?
3. What was the military importance of German control of the Sudetenland?
4. What was the main purpose of the secret treaty signed by Nazi Germany and the Soviet Union in 1939?
5. Which events made it clear that Hitler's intentions went beyond restoring German-speaking peoples to the Reich?
6. What was the Winter War?
7. Once Britain and France declared war on Germany, what countries did Hitler overcome?
8. Why was Hitler unable to invade Britain?
9. What factors bogged down Hitler's invasion of Russia?
10. What battle is considered by some to be the turning point of World War II in Europe?
11. What event brought the United States into the war as a belligerent?
12. Who were the major Allied and Axis powers in World War II? What was the name of the political leader of each?
13. Name four major conferences held during or immediately after World War II. What was one issue discussed at each?
14. What consideration lay behind President Truman's decision to drop the atom bomb?

Essay Questions

1. Describe the issues dividing the people in Spain at the time of the civil war. How did foreign intervention affect the outcome of the war?
2. Compare and contrast the circumstances surrounding German occupation of Austria and Czechoslovakia. Why was the failure of France to support Czechoslovakia significant politically?
4. Describe the reasons that Stalin had for allying Russia with Germany rather than with Great Britain and France.
5. Explain why Poland was wiped from the map of Europe in 1939.
6. The people of the United States did not want to participate actively in the war. Describe the gradual increase in participation of the United States from 1937 until the Japanese attack on Pearl Harbor.
7. Compare and contrast the ideas behind the Hitler-Stalin Pact and the Atlantic Charter.
8. Describe the campaign for control of North Africa. Of what strategic importance was this area?
9. Describe at least three instances in which the experience of countries in World War I affected their actions during World War II.
10. Describe the Japanese strategy in the Pacific war. How did the United States counter it?

Critical Thinking

1. What was the logical inconsistency in Stalin's decision to make a nonaggression pact and a secret treaty with Hitler? Why do you think that Communist party members throughout the world were astonished by Stalin's decision?
2. What measures were likely to be taken by the belligerents to interfere with the reliability of source data that their enemies would receive?
3. Japanese-Americans on the West Coast lost their freedom of movement and were placed in internment camps during World War II. A Japanese-American was defined as someone who had at least one grandparent who was Japanese. German-Americans did not receive similar treatment. Why do you think the Japanese-Americans considered it an unwarranted claim that they would be a danger to the country?

Reviewing the Unit

Developing a Sense of Time

Examine the time line below and answer the questions that follow it.

1900	1904	Russo-Japanese War begins
1910	1910	Mexican revolution begins
	1914	World War I begins
	1917	United States enters World War I
		Revolution begins in Russia
	1918	Civil war begins in Russia
1920	1921	Chinese Communist party founded
	1922	Mussolini gains control of Italy
	1927	Chiang Kai-shek establishes
		Nationalist government in China
	1928	Stalin emerges as Soviet leader
	1929	Great Depression begins
1930	1931	Statute of Westminster
		Japan invades Manchuria
	1933	Hitler named chancellor of
		Germany
	1934	Long March begins in China
	1936	Germany invades the Rhineland
	1938	*Anschluss* of Germany and Austria
	1939	World War II begins
1940	1941	Japan attacks Pearl Harbor
	1943	Italy surrenders
	1945	Germany surrenders
		Japan surrenders

1. How many years were there between the German occupation of the Rhineland and the outbreak of World War II?
2. Who was the leader of Germany when it invaded the Rhineland?
3. Which dictator assumed power first: Stalin, Mussolini, or Hitler?
4. What happened in Russia in 1917?

Social Science Skills

Recognizing Propaganda

1. Refer to the list of propaganda techniques on page 578. Write an example of your own for each.
2. Compare the World War I poster on page 553 to the World War II poster on page 621. What message is each trying to convey? Do you think they are effective? Why or why not?
3. Choose three current advertisements or public service announcements. Describe them and explain what propaganda technique is used in each.
4. How do you think you could best protect yourself from being swayed by propaganda?

Critical Thinking Questions

1. How do you think the reliability of source data for modern history compares with that of data for medieval or ancient history? What factors might interfere with the reliability of modern data?
2. Review the characteristics of government under a democratic system and under a totalitarian system. What was the questionable assumption in the agreement between Roosevelt and Stalin that Stalin would establish democratic governments in Eastern European countries under his control?
3. Mussolini's early political views favored socialism. Why were his earlier views inconsistent with his later ones?

Linking Past and Present

The background for World War II included a system of alliances that divided Europe into two camps, a military buildup, nationalist ambitions, and competition for territory and influence. Do similar circumstances exist today?

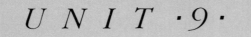

UNIT ·9·

The WORLD SINCE 1945

1945-Present

6

CHAPTER 28

EUROPE TODAY

1945–Present

Objectives

- *To describe how the Cold War began*
- *To discuss the power struggle between the two postwar superpowers*
- *To explain developments in Western European countries from the end of World War II to the present*
- *To highlight events in Eastern Europe that added to Cold War tensions*

W*orld War II was among the greatest disasters in Europe's history. The war ended Europe's dominance in international relations that had lasted for nearly 500 years. After the end of World War I there were seven major world powers— Great Britain, France, Germany, Italy, Japan, Russia, and the United States. In contrast, the postwar world saw the emergence of two dominant superpowers—the United States and the Soviet Union.*

In the early postwar period, meetings among the West's wartime leaders—Roosevelt, Churchill, and Stalin—included plans for establishing a peaceful world order. This was not to be. The Soviet Union's aim of installing Communist governments in the nations of Eastern Europe heightened Soviet–United States tensions. Western Europe looked to the United States for aid as Eastern Europe fell under Soviet influence.

The superpower conflict spread beyond Europe. Both the United States and the Soviet Union competed to exert their influence on countries around the world. With the Soviet development of an atomic bomb, the memory of Hiroshima hung over the dangerous rivalry. Both sides devoted major parts of their resources to developing more powerful weapons and better systems to launch them against the enemy.

The postwar weakness of European powers left them unable to maintain their former colonial empires. The people within these empires seized on Europe's weakness to win their independence after the war.

However, Western European nations rebuilt their societies with the help of money from the United States. Europe rose from the ashes.

EARLY POSTWAR YEARS

Europe was devastated by World War II. National economies were destroyed, and many cities were nothing but rubble. There were millions of homeless people—refugees who had fled from war areas and displaced persons who had been driven from their homes by the redrawing of national boundaries after the war. Former United States President Herbert Hoover said of the situation in Europe: "It is now 11:59 on the clock of starvation."

In 1943 the United Nations Relief and Rehabilitation Administration (UNRRA) was formed to ease the suffering from famine and disease in war-shattered Europe. The United States was by far the largest contributor.

The UNRRA, in its four years of existence, returned about seven million people to their homes. In addition, it supervised refugee camps, distributed food and medicines, and helped to restore public services in the war-ravaged countries. This aid was given to both Western and Eastern Europe as well as China.

The early postwar years were dominated by the problems of rebuilding and reestablishing political stability. These problems became complicated by the growing tension between the former wartime Allies.

In the postwar world the United States and its Allies were referred to as the West, or free world. The Soviet Union and the countries that supported it were known as the East, or Communist world. These distinctions continue to serve as a dividing line between the superpowers.

The Formation of the United Nations

On April 25, 1945, representatives from fifty Allied nations met at San Francisco to discuss the foundation of the United Nations (UN). Supporters of the United Nations hoped it would become an international organization to promote a permanent peace. The charter of the United Nations declared: "We the people of the United Nations are determined to save future generations from the scourge of war, which twice in our lifetime has brought untold sorrow to mankind. We are determined to reaffirm our faith in fundamental human rights, in the dig-

nity and worth of the human person, and in the equal rights of men and women and of nations large and small." The charter aimed to provide an organization with two main branches, the General Assembly and the Security Council. The General Assembly was made up of all the member states. The Security Council consisted of five permanent members (the United States, the USSR, China, Great Britain, and France) and six (later ten) nonpermanent members chosen by the General Assembly to represent the different regions of the world. The principal decision-making took place in the Security Council, and the five permanent members had veto power. All the members of the General Assembly pledged to comply with decisions of the Security Council. In addition, the United Nations had affiliated agencies that were to help in the fight against poverty, illiteracy, disease, and hunger. (See the chart on page 632.)

The main hope for the United Nations was that it would be a peacekeeping organization. However, the United Nations' ability to function was hampered by the political tensions between the two superpowers. The Soviet Union used its veto power to block peacekeeping efforts.

Even so, the organization scored some successes in mediating Middle East disputes (see Chapter 30) and the war between India and Pakistan in 1949 (see Chapter 29). A multinational force under the United Nations flag played a major role in defending South Korea. (See Chapter 29.)

Today, the United Nations has expanded from its original 50 members to 159. In recent years, it has shown an inability to halt conflicts between member nations, large or small. Many members have used it as a forum for defending their own national and ideological interests. Because these interests have often been in conflict with those of the United States, many of its citizens have become disillusioned with the United Nations. They resent the fact that the United States pays a large share of its budget.

The Occupation of Germany

At the Yalta and Potsdam conferences, the Allies agreed to the division of Germany into four occupation zones to be administered by the United States, the Soviet Union, Great Britain, and

France. Germany's capital, Berlin, was also divided among the four powers. At the end of the war, each administrating country had its own policy for its zone.

The Western powers soon were cooperating in their occupation and were committed to some rebuilding of Germany. In the Soviet zone, however, factories were dismantled and heavy machinery was transported to the Soviet Union as reparation, or payment, for the enormous damage that the German army had wreaked on the Soviet Union.

At Yalta it also had been decided that all traces of National Socialism were to be destroyed. This **denazification** included removing Nazi symbols from public places, changing textbooks to promote democratic principles, and removing former Nazis from positions of power and influence.

An international tribunal was set up to try major Nazi leaders for war crimes. Before the war's end, the Allies had started collecting evidence against Nazi officials. Special intelligence units accompanied the Allied army to round up suspects to be tried for atrocities. The city of Nuremberg, site of huge Nazi rallies, was chosen for the major war crimes trials.

Here, on November 20, 1945, twenty-four Nazi leaders were put on trial. Judges and prosecutors from all four Allied occupying countries participated in bringing charges that included waging aggressive war and "crimes against humanity." For almost a year, public evidence was produced to back up the charges. These included films, official and secret documents, and eyewitness accounts that documented the monstrous nature of the Nazi

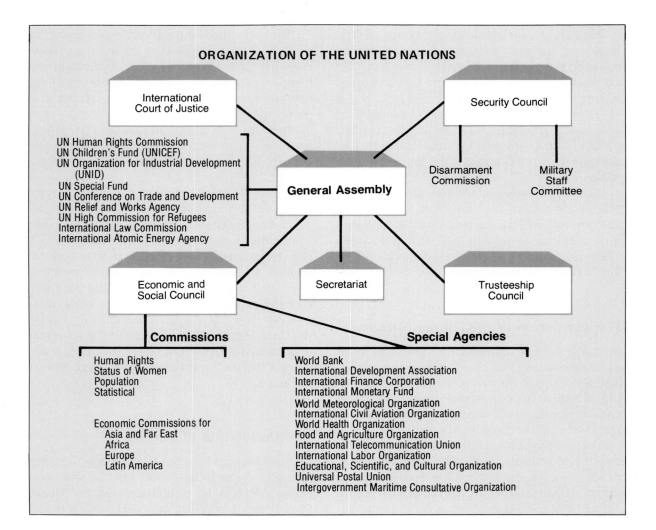

ORGANIZATION OF THE UNITED NATIONS

International Court of Justice

Security Council

UN Human Rights Commission
UN Children's Fund (UNICEF)
UN Organization for Industrial Development (UNID)
UN Special Fund
UN Conference on Trade and Development
UN Relief and Works Agency
UN High Commission for Refugees
International Law Commission
International Atomic Energy Agency

General Assembly

Disarmament Commission

Military Staff Committee

Economic and Social Council

Secretariat

Trusteeship Council

Commissions

Special Agencies

Human Rights
Status of Women
Population
Statistical

Economic Commissions for
Asia and Far East
Africa
Europe
Latin America

World Bank
International Development Association
International Finance Corporation
International Monetary Fund
World Meteorological Organization
International Civil Aviation Organization
World Health Organization
Food and Agriculture Organization
International Telecommunication Union
International Labor Organization
Educational, Scientific, and Cultural Organization
Universal Postal Union
Intergovernment Maritime Consultative Organization

Universal Declaration of Human Rights

The United Nations adopted the Universal Declaration of Human Rights in December 1948. The declaration outlines the basic civil, political, social, and economic rights and freedoms that every person on earth should have. The purpose of the declaration is to serve ''as a common standard of achievement for all peoples and all nations.'' As you read the following excerpts from the declaration, see how many are familiar to you.

All human beings are born free and equal in dignity and rights.

Everyone is entitled to all the rights and freedoms set forth in this Declaration, without distinction of any kind, such as race, color, sex, language, religion, political or other opinion, national or social origin, property, birth or other status.

No one shall be held in slavery or servitude; slavery and the slave trade shall be prohibited in all their forms.

Everyone has the right to an effective remedy by the competent national tribunals for acts violating the fundamental rights granted him by the constitution or by law.

Everyone has the right to freedom of movement and residence within the borders of each state.

Everyone has the right to seek and to enjoy . . . asylum from persecution.

No one shall be arbitrarily deprived of his nationality nor denied the right to change his nationality.

Men and women of full age, without any limitation due to race, nationality or religion, have the right to marry and to found a family.

Everyone has the right to freedom of thought, conscience and religion; this right includes freedom to change his religion or belief, and freedom, either alone or in community with others and in public or private, to manifest his religion or belief in teaching, practice, worship, and observance.

Everyone has the right to take part in the government of his country, directly or through freely chosen representatives.

Everyone has the right to rest and leisure, including reasonable limitation of working hours and periodic holidays with pay.

Everyone has the right to education. Education shall be free, at least in the elementary and fundamental stages.

1. What is the purpose of the Declaration of Human Rights?
2. What rights guaranteed in these excerpts from the declaration do we have in the United States?
3. Do you think all people have these rights? Explain using two examples.
4. What other rights do you think should be added to this list? Why?

---

regime. On October 12, 1945, twelve Nazi leaders were condemned to death. Others received prison terms, were found not guilty, or escaped trial.

Beginning of the Cold War

At the Yalta Conference, the Allies had agreed to free elections in the Eastern European countries that the Red Army was occupying on its way to Berlin. When President Harry S. Truman reminded Joseph Stalin (STAHL-un) at the Potsdam Conference of his pledge, Stalin replied: ''A freely elected government in any of these Eastern European countries would be anti-Soviet and that we could not allow.'' Stalin argued that the Soviet Union, which had been invaded by Germany twice in this century, needed friendly states to act as a buffer to a resurgent Germany.

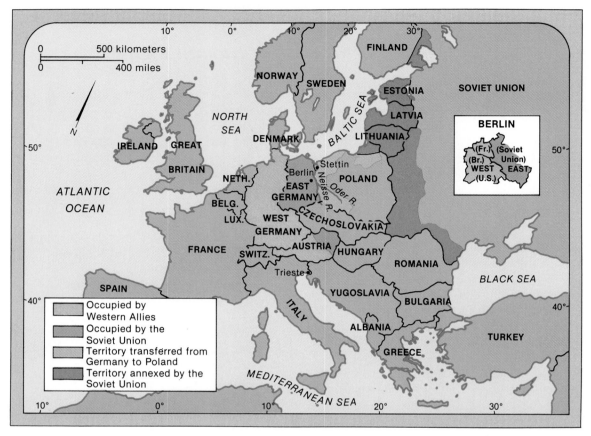

What advantages did the Soviet Union gain as a result of the territory it annexed?

In accordance with wartime Allied agreements at Yalta and Potsdam, the borders of Poland were substantially redrawn. A large part of eastern Poland was absorbed into the Soviet Union. In return, Poland was given former German territory in East Prussia and east of the Oder and Neisse rivers. A number of other adjustments in boundaries were also made.

In its march toward Germany the Soviet Army occupied Poland, Czechoslovakia, Romania, Hungary, and Bulgaria. It helped to enforce the installation of postwar Communist leaders in these countries.

At first, local Communists were part of coalition governments that included non-Communist leaders. Through force and intimidation, however, the Communists soon seized total power. In Czechoslovakia, for example, the popular foreign minister, Jan Masaryk (YAHN MAH-zuh-rik), committed suicide, thus paving the way for an election with only Communists as candidates.

By 1948 all the nations occupied by Soviet troops were under Communist control. In addition, Albania and Yugoslavia, were not occupied by the Red Army but had Communist governments and were regarded as part of the Soviet bloc. The Eastern European countries became known as satellites of the Soviet Union.

On March 5, 1946, Winston S. Churchill, now out of office, sounded the alarm in a speech in Fulton, Missouri: "From Stettin in the Baltic to Trieste in the Adriatic, an Iron Curtain has descended across the Continent. Behind that line lie all the capitals of the ancient states of Central and Eastern Europe." Churchill pointed out the control Moscow exercised over the **Iron Curtain** countries and urged Anglo-American unity to prevent further Soviet expansion.

The following year the United States diplomat George F. Kennan proposed a policy that became known as **containment.** Containment was using the resources of the United States—political, economic, and, if necessary, military forces—to prevent the further spread of Soviet influence.

The Truman Doctrine

In February 1947 the British informed the United States government that they could no longer supply aid for the Greek or Turkish governments in their fight against Communist guerrillas. It was feared that, without aid, the Greek government might fall and the country would enter the Soviet bloc. Then, Greece's neighbor Turkey, on which Moscow was applying pressure, would be threatened as well. The strategically important eastern Mediterranean then could fall into Soviet hands.

Truman went before Congress on March 12, 1947, and described the plight of war-torn Greece. He stressed: "It must be the policy of the United States to support free peoples who are resisting attempted subjugation by armed minorities or outside pressure." This policy became known as the Truman Doctrine.

Truman asked Congress for $400 million in economic and military aid for Greece and Turkey. This aid helped the Greek government to put down the Communist insurrection.

The Truman Doctrine was the first concrete response by the United States to counter aggressive pressure by the Soviet Union. It formally inaugurated the **Cold War,** a war based on propaganda, diplomacy, economic assistance, and finally military action by the United States and other free nations to aid countries threatened by communism. Despite periods of relaxed tension, the Cold War continues to the present day.

As we shall see, the Soviet Union has responded with its own aid and actions to protect its sphere of influence and enforce Communist rule in various countries. However, both the United States and the Soviet Union have attempted to avoid a direct confrontation that could lead to nuclear war. A further step in this direction may result from a meeting between the heads of the two superpowers in November 1985.

The Marshall Plan

The Truman Doctrine set the precedent for the United States to give economic assistance to other countries. But the aid to Greece and Turkey was miniscule compared to what the nations of Europe needed to rebuild their economies. Recovery was not progressing at the rate the United States had hoped. The winter of 1946–1947 had been unseasonably cold. Postwar hunger and poverty were helping to foster strong Communist parties in some Western European countries, especially in France and Italy.

In June 1947 United States Secretary of State George Marshall announced a policy of economic reconstruction for Europe. He suggested that the European nations devise a long-range plan for recovery that stressed self-help and mutual assistance. The United States would then provide them with as much assistance as practical. All European nations including the Soviet bloc were invited to participate. Marshall said that his policy was not directed "against any country or doctrine, but against hunger, poverty, desperation, and chaos."

The Soviet Union declined the offer and forced its satellites to do so also. But the Western European nations drew up the plans suggested by Marshall. The United States responded generously by pouring over $12 billion into Europe in four years. The Marshall Plan was a remarkably effective program. It provided the necessary help for Western Europe to get back on its feet and stopped the westward spread of communism. The Italian Communists were defeated in the elections of 1948.

It was also in 1948 that the Communist leader of Yugoslavia, Marshal Tito, stood firm in a dispute with Stalin. Stalin expelled Yugoslavia from the international Communist organization, the Cominform, but Yugoslavia established economic ties with Western countries. Though Yugoslavia remained Communist, it succeeded in following its own course independent from Moscow's orders.

The Berlin Airlift

The Cold War now heated up over the issue of postwar treatment of the defeated Axis countries, particularly Germany. It had been agreed at Potsdam that peace treaties would be negotiated as soon as possible. Treaties between the victors and

Italy, Bulgaria, Romania, Hungary, and Finland were signed in 1947. All provided for demilitarization, reparations, and small border rectifications.

Germany was a more difficult problem. The Soviet Union opposed the movement toward unification of the three German zones administered by the United States, Great Britain, and France. Of all the Allied nations, the Soviet Union had suffered most from the German army during the war. It wanted to prevent the reconstruction of a German nation that could again threaten its borders.

On June 24, 1948, the Soviets cut off all roads, railways, and water routes leading to Berlin. They thought that the United States, British, and French forces would not be able to supply their garrisons and the civilian population in the divided capital. Then the city would be left to the Soviets.

President Truman refused to be run out of Berlin. The United States and Great Britain immediately organized an airlift to supply not only their troops but also the civilian population in the Allied zone. At its height, the Berlin airlift was carrying 4,500 tons of food and supplies a day, including coal for heating homes.

In the first days of the airlift, the world held its breath. There were some harmless encounters between United States and Soviet aircraft. But no shots were fired. Almost a year later the Soviets lifted their blockade.

Europe Divided into Two Camps

The zones of occupation in Germany had originally been drawn as a temporary measure. It was

NEW ALLIANCES FORM

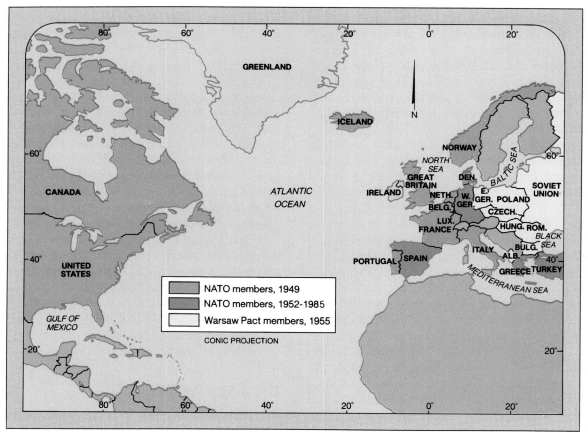

What role do national borders play in the formation of alliance systems among nations? How does the West benefit from the NATO alliance?

thought that a later conference would lead to a comprehensive peace treaty that would establish permanent German borders. But the Berlin crisis indicated that the Soviets wanted a different kind of peace with Germany.

In May 1949 the United States, Great Britain, and France combined their zones to create the German Federal Republic, or West Germany, with a new capital at Bonn. Although Allied troops remained, the new country was allowed to elect its own government. Konrad Adenauer of the Christian Democratic party became the first chancellor of West Germany in 1949. In October of the same year, the German Democratic Republic, or East Germany, was established under the control of the Soviets.

The Berlin airlift was one of several events that stimulated further cooperation between Western Europe and the United States and Canada. In April 1949 twelve nations—the United States, Canada, Great Britain, France, Italy, Belgium, the Netherlands, Luxembourg, Norway, Denmark, Iceland, and Portugal—signed the North Atlantic Treaty. It created the North Atlantic Treaty Organization (NATO), whose members pledged to defend each other in the case of armed attack. In 1952, Greece and Turkey were added. In 1955, with the final pullout of all occupying troops from West Germany, it too was admitted into NATO.

The year 1955 proved to be a turning point for many developments. After the West German entry into NATO, the Soviet Union set up the Warsaw Pact as a counter-alliance to NATO. It combined with seven other Eastern European nations to pledge mutual assistance if any of the members went to war.

Also in 1955 a treaty was reached ending the occupation of Austria. Austria received its independence on its pledge to remain neutral. It was forbidden to unite with Germany. Thus, by the end of 1955, the opposing camps were locked into rival diplomatic and military alliances.

Other world events heightened tensions between the superpowers and their allies. China's civil war ended with victory for the Communist side. Communist North Korea invaded democratic South Korea, beginning what threatened to become a wider war. You will read more about these events in Chapter 29.

SECTION REVIEW

1. Mapping: Use the map on page 634 to find how the borders of European countries were changed by the treaties after World War II.
2. In your own words, briefly define or identify: superpower, United Nations, free world, Communist world, denazification, Iron Curtain, containment, Truman Doctrine, Cold War, Marshall Plan, NATO, Warsaw Pact.
3. What was the primary purpose of the United Nations?
4. Why did the Soviet Union break its pledge to allow free elections in the countries of Eastern Europe?
5. Why did the United States give money to Europe through the Marshall Plan?
■ Is the United States still following a policy of containment today? Cite some specific examples to support your answer.

THE SOVIET BLOC AND THE COLD WAR

Relations between the Soviet Union and the United States fluctuated between confrontation and attempts at compromise. The Cold War continued at different levels of intensity. The two superpowers developed new and more powerful weapons of destruction. (See the chart on page 638.) Though they also negotiated arms control agreements, nuclear confrontation between the two powers remains a threat to the world.

The death of Stalin in early 1953 brought about changes in Eastern Europe. Relationships between the Soviet Union and the Soviet bloc countries loosened a bit, but there were limits to their freedom of action. Some movements toward independence, as in Hungary in 1956, were put down with Soviet tanks.

Within the Soviet Union itself, greater freedoms were permitted for a short time. The Soviet economy was a failure in many areas, and the Soviets had to buy grain from the West.

Year in Which Superpowers Acquired Effective Weapons

	US		USSR
Atomic (Fission) Bomb	1945	⇨	1949
Intercontinental Bomber	1948	⇨	1955
Hydrogen (Fusion) Bomb	1952	⇨	1953
Intercontinental Ballistic Missile	1958	⇦	1957
Satellite in Orbit	1958	⇦	1957
Submarine-Launched Ballistic Missile	1960	⇨	1968
Multiple Warhead	1972	⇦	1968
Anti-Ballistic Missile	1968	⇨	1972
Multiple Independently Targetable Warhead	1970	⇨	1975
Long-Range Cruise Missile	1982	⇨	?
Neutron Bomb	1983	⇨	?
Anti-Satellite Weapon	?		?
Ballistic Missile Defense	?		?

Newton showed that for every action there is an equal and opposite reaction. This law holds true for the arms race as it does in physics. Whenever one superpower devises a new weapon, the other builds the equivalent within a few years.

Source: World Military and Social Expenditures, 1983

Early Post-Stalin Years

Stalin's death in 1953 was followed by a struggle within the Communist party over who was to succeed him. By the end of 1955, Nikita Khrushchev (nih-KEE-tah kroosh-CHAWFF) emerged as the new leader of the Soviet Union.

In February 1956 Khrushchev shocked the world Communist movement in a speech denouncing Stalin and exposing some of the terrible crimes he had authorized in his lifetime. Khrushchev then began a program of **de-Stalinization.** He called for an end to the "cult of personality" that glorified the leader. He ordered statues and memorials to Stalin removed. The name of the city of Stalingrad was changed to Volgograd.

Khrushchev promised the Soviet people an improvement in their standard of living, the release of prisoners from labor camps, and greater availability of consumer goods. For a short period Soviet citizens had free speech and a free press.

Alexander Solzhenitsyn (suhl-zhuh-NEET-sin) is considered a major Soviet novelist of the con-

temporary Soviet period. He published his first work, *One Day in the Life of Ivan Denisovitch* (ee-VAHN deh-NEES-uh-vich), during this period of Soviet history, which has been called the thaw.

De-Stalinization was also carried into the Eastern European countries behind the Iron Curtain, where there was great resentment over Russian domination. Khrushchev attempted to patch the rift between the Soviet Union and Tito's independent Yugoslavia. He proclaimed that there were "differing roads to socialism."

But the cautious reforms made by the Communist governments of Eastern Europe were not adequate to satisfy the people. The policy backfired, resulting in demands for still greater freedom and revolt against Russian domination.

Revolts Against Soviet Rule in Eastern Europe

In June 1956 anti-Soviet revolts broke out among workers in Poland. Khrushchev, anxious to prevent Poland from breaking away from the Soviet orbit, rushed to Warsaw to see the new Polish Communist leader, Wladyslaw Gomulka (vwah-DISS-wahv goe-MOOHL-kuh). Khrushchev returned to the Soviet Union after getting Gomulka's assurances that Poland would remain loyal to the Soviet Union. Order was restored.

In October of the same year, Khrushchev faced another revolt. Hungarian students and workers demonstrated for human rights and the withdrawal of Soviet troops. A new Hungarian leader, Imre Nagy (IM-ree NAG-ee), promised reforms and an end to Soviet domination. He renounced the Warsaw Pact which bound Hungary to the USSR.

This was more than Khrushchev would accept. He sent Russian tanks and troops to crush the Hungarian rebellion. The Hungarians appealed to the United Nations and the West for armed assistance, but no help was offered. It was feared that direct armed conflict between Western and Soviet troops would lead to nuclear war.

Nagy was arrested, taken to the Soviet Union, and later executed. The suppression of the Hungarian Revolution cost the lives of 25,000 Hungarians and 7,000 Russians. An estimated 200,000 Hungarians fled their country.

From Peaceful Coexistence to Confrontation

The years after the Hungarian Revolution saw a relaxation of tensions between East and West. Realizing that any nuclear war between the two superpowers would mean the destruction of both, Khrushchev announced the policy of peaceful coexistence. By this he meant that although the Soviet Union and the United States would still be rivals, the rivalry would not take the form of military action. Competition would be in the areas of economic and social progress.

Khrushchev thought that the Soviet Union would overtake the United States in economic pro-duction and scientific knowledge. In 1957 the Soviet Union astonished the world by putting the first man-made satellite, *Sputnik,* into orbit around the earth. Earlier in the year the USSR test-fired the first intercontinental ballistic missile (ICBM).

The high point of this peaceful phase was the trip that Khrushchev made to the United States in 1959. The talks at Camp David between the Soviet leader and United States President Dwight D. Eisenhower helped to ease East–West tensions. Summit conferences between the leaders of the United States and the USSR were part of the administration of every United States President from Eisenhower to Ronald Reagan.

But the next year, just before a second summit conference was to be held in Paris, a United States U-2 spy plane was shot down over the Soviet Union. As a result of this incident and the refusal of the United States to restrict such activity, the summit was cancelled.

Official portraits of Communist leaders were burned during the 1956 Hungarian revolt.

The Soviets Test United States Resolve

In 1961 the Soviets wanted to stop the flow of refugees to the West and to test the newly elected United States President John F. Kennedy. In August, the Russian-dominated East German government built a wall separating East Berlin from West Berlin to keep East Germans from escaping to the West. President Kennedy responded by increasing the number of United States troops in Berlin.

The Berlin Wall became a symbol of the need of the Soviet system to keep its citizens in by force. Thousands of East Germans continued to run the gauntlet of armed guards, climbing or tunneling under the wall to reach West Berlin, the outpost of the free world.

In October 1962 the United States discovered that the Soviet Union was building missile bases in Cuba. From these bases, the Soviet Union could launch nuclear attacks against the eastern part of the United States. President Kennedy responded by setting up a naval "quarantine," or blockade, to prevent Soviet ships from reaching Cuba. The world nervously waited to see if the Soviets would challenge the blockade. In the most serious confrontation since the end of World War II, the Soviet Union backed down. Khrushchev announced the removal of Soviet missiles and the dismantling of the missile bases.

The Berlin Wall was built in 1961. It divides the city of Berlin into two parts, east and west. In what ways does the wall symbolize the difference between democracy and communism?

The Cuban missile crisis humiliated Khrushchev and led to his removal from office in 1964. But before he left, he signed the Limited Nuclear Test Ban Treaty with the United States in 1963. This treaty was the first significant arms control agreement between the two superpowers. It banned nuclear test explosions in the atmosphere, but permitted underground testing.

The Brezhnev Doctrine

The fall of Khrushchev in 1964 changed Soviet politics. The new Soviet leader, Leonid I. Brezhnev (LEE-oh-nid BREZH-nef), did not approve of Khrushchev's liberal policies. He tightened up control of the press and speech within the Soviet Union. Brezhnev enforced a tougher policy in Eastern Europe.

Later, in August 1967, the United States and the Soviet Union submitted to the United Nations a treaty to halt the spread of nuclear weapons. (By

this time Great Britain, France, and China had also tested nuclear bombs.) By the treaty nuclear nations could not supply weapons to other countries. Non-nuclear countries agreed not to manufacture such devices. The treaty became effective in 1970 when it had been ratified by forty nations. However, France, India, and China refused to sign.

In the spring of 1968 a new Communist leadership took over in Czechoslovakia. Party secretary Alexander Dubcek (DOOB-check) made promises of greater freedom to his people, calling his policy "socialism with a human face." During that "Prague spring," changes were made liberalizing freedom of expression and adopting some economic reforms.

Dubcek promised to remain friendly to the Soviet Union and to keep Czechoslovakia within the Warsaw Pact. But the Soviet Union treated Czechoslovakia just as it had Hungary. In August 1968, the Soviet Union with the aid of Warsaw Pact allies launched a sudden massive invasion of Czechoslovakia. The Czechs had no chance of resisting. Dubcek was removed from office by the Soviets and a new leader was installed. Then a purge of Dubcek's supporters began.

To justify these actions, the Soviet leader announced what became known as the Brezhnev Doctrine. This doctrine asserted the Soviet Union's right to interfere in any Eastern European satellite nation if the existing Communist system in that nation were threatened. However, in response to the invasion of Czechoslovakia, Albania formally withdrew from the Warsaw Pact.

The Years of Détente

The early years of the 1970's are known for a policy that came to be called **détente** (day-TAHNT), or relaxation of tensions. In bringing about détente, both superpowers made compromises.

With President Richard Nixon's approval, Brezhnev arranged to purchase a huge shipment of wheat from the United States. This sale offset the results of a poor wheat harvest in the Soviet Union.

The greatest benefit of détente was that it enabled the superpowers to negotiate some limitation of the arms race. The arms race was the competition for nuclear superiority that had been going on ever since the Soviets first exploded a nuclear bomb.

In May 1972 Nixon went to the Soviet Union for a summit conference with Brezhnev. Their meeting was a cordial one. Nixon was granted the unprecedented opportunity to address the Soviet people on radio and television.

At the summit, the superpower leaders signed a number of agreements that included one placing a limit on antiballistic missile systems (ABMs). Both nations had already spent billions developing ABM systems to shoot down first-strike nuclear missiles and protect their own missile sites. The treaty limited each power to two clusters of ABMs—one around the capital city and the other to protect one missile complex. It also included a cap on the number of defensive missile launchers each side could build. In effect, the treaty bound the two nations to put their population centers at the mercy of the other side, thus lessening the chances that either would start a war.

Nixon and Brezhnev also signed a strategic arms limitation treaty, known as SALT I. The result of several years of negotiation, this treaty sought to set ceilings between the two powers by limiting for five years the number of long-range offensive missiles to those already completed or in construction.

Other agreements between the superpowers during the détente period aimed to protect the environment, promote cooperation in the space programs of the two nations, and share developments in medicine, science, and technology.

An Increase in Tensions

President Jimmy Carter and Leonid Brezhnev concluded SALT II in June 1979, in Vienna. SALT II called for additional weapons arrangements between the two countries. The treaty, slated to last until the end of 1985, limited each side to 2,400 ICBM launchers and long-range bombers. To get

During his 1973 visit to Washington, Soviet leader Brezhnev chats with President Nixon.

under this level, the Soviet Union would have to destroy about 100 ICBMs. By 1981 a new ceiling of 2,250 would come into effect. The treaty also allowed each country to develop one new type of missile and to modernize existing weapons within certain limits. It also called for talks on SALT III to begin shortly afterward.

Before SALT II could be finalized, the United States Senate had to consent to ratify, or approve, it. Many senators had reservations about it. Some senators felt the treaty would, by 1985, allow the Soviets to have a greater arsenal than the United States. Some were concerned about effective ways to verify the provisions of the treaty. Many worried that it did not go far enough in limiting arms on either side.

Before the Senate could act on SALT II, the Soviet Union invaded Afghanistan in 1979, to prop up the weak Communist regime there. This action caused relations between the United States and the Soviet Union to deteriorate.

To show his disapproval of the Soviet action, President Carter had the United States' team boycott the Olympic Games in Moscow in 1980. He also placed an embargo on grain scheduled to be shipped to the Soviet Union.

Even though SALT II was never approved by the United States Senate, both countries claimed to have abided by its provisions.

Conditions Within the Soviet Union

It was an article of Communist faith that central planning would enable the economy to function efficiently. But production quotas set by a bureaucracy in Moscow for factories throughout the huge country were not always met. Factories stopped work because of lack of parts and raw materials. The morale of Soviet workers was low. The lack of incentives has made Soviet workers not as productive as those in capitalist countries.

Also, women in the Soviet Union are expected to work. Many enter fields such as medicine and engineering as well as take jobs on the farms and in the factories.

The promises of equality have not been kept, however. Soviet production of consumer goods is far behind that of the West. One reason is that a major part of the country's economy and resources is devoted to military needs. Long lines of people

waiting to buy food or scarce items such as shoes are a familiar feature of Soviet life. The more desirable items are reserved for party officials, who are the new elite of the country. The country has been plagued by an enormous black market.

Finally, Soviet agriculture traditionally has not been able to feed the entire population of the country. The situation is not improving. The 1984 grain harvest was nearly a third smaller than that of the peak year of 1978. The Soviet Union has had to rely on imports of wheat from the West.

The thaw of the Khrushchev era gradually gave way to a renewed control of expression within the country. Samizdat (sahm-eez-DAHT) pamphlets and books—typed by hand and duplicated with carbon paper—circulated as underground publications. Alexander Solzhenitsyn's later works, for which he won the Nobel Prize, first appeared as samizdat. In 1974, Solzhenitsyn was exiled from the country.

In the late 1960's and early 1970's a **dissident movement** appeared. A growing number of Soviet intellectuals began to publicly criticize the government and its policies. One of the best Soviet physicists, Andrei Sakharov (SAHK-uh-rawf), circulated public criticisms of the regime, especially about the lack of freedom of expression in the country.

In August 1975 the Soviet Union, the United States, and thirty-three other countries signed the Helsinki Accords. These pledged respect for "fundamental freedoms, including the freedom of thought, conscience, religion or belief." Fewer travel restrictions were also promised.

When the Soviet Union failed to keep the Helsinki agreement, dissidents such as Sakharov publicized the violations in interviews and letters to Western publications. The Soviet Union cracked down on dissidents by stripping them of jobs or privileges. Sakharov was subjected to "internal exile," that is, he was moved to a city where Westerners were not allowed.

Soviet Bloc Countries

The relationship of the Soviet Union with the Warsaw Pact countries has gradually changed. The USSR's closest relationships are with Bulgaria and East Germany. Hungary, after its unsuccessful rebellion, saw the growth of private enterprise and now enjoys the highest standard of living in the Soviet bloc. It traded political loyalty to the Soviet Union for a greater degree of freedom in ordering its economy.

Czechoslovakia has not yet recovered from the crushing of the Prague spring. A letter from Alexander Dubcek was published in the West protesting repression within the country. He accused the new regime of purging thousands of creative workers. Dubcek, too, was transferred to a menial job. Open protests of Czech violations of the Helsinki Accords met with police repression and jailings.

Romania has a relationship with some Western countries and maintains diplomatic relations with China. Internally, however, the Romanian regime is intolerant of its citizens' rights.

In recent years, Poland has seen the greatest unrest among the Eastern European countries. Riots in Gdansk (guh-DAHNSK) in 1970, caused by steep rises in food prices, were put down violently. Over 200 workers died. Bitterness over the event remained. The government revised its eco-

nomic goals to put more emphasis on the production of consumer goods.

In 1980 Lech Walesa (lek vuh-WEN-suh) emerged as the leader of the independent labor union Solidarity. Solidarity's activities seemed to be leading Poland toward an open break with the Soviet Union. At its height, it had a membership of nine million and seemed to have broad support.

Abruptly, in December 1981, the leader of Poland, General Jaroslav Jaruszelski (yah-roo-SHELL-skee), outlawed Solidarity and declared martial law in Poland. Walesa and other Solidarity leaders were imprisoned. Though Walesa was later released and martial law partially lifted, the regime kept its tight hold on the country.

A Look to the Future

The problem of an orderly succession of leaders is one that has never been solved by the Soviet system. Brezhnev was clearly ill and unable to carry out all his duties before he died in 1982. Meanwhile, the United States elected a new president in

Prime Minister Margaret Thatcher of Great Britain makes a point following a meeting with Soviet Premier Mikhail Gorbachev, joined here by his wife, Raisa.

1980, Ronald W. Reagan. Reagan adopted a strongly anti-Soviet foreign policy.

In 1983 President Reagan announced his approval of research on a space-based defense system against missile attack. This Strategic Defense Initiative, dubbed the "Star Wars" defense, was denounced by the Soviets as the beginning of a new round of the arms race. However, at the beginning of Reagan's second term, arms talks between the Soviets and the United States reopened in 1985 in Geneva.

Brezhnev was followed in office by two other leaders who were ill for most of their short tenures, Yuri Andropov (an-drop-OFF) and Konstantin Chernenko (chair-NYEN-koh). In 1985, immediately after the death of Chernenko, a younger and more vigorous man took control of the Soviet Union. Mikhail Gorbachev (mee-kie-EEL guhr-bah-CHAWFF), fifty-four years old, became the first Soviet leader who was not yet born at the time of the Russian Revolution. He is thought to believe that the Soviet Union needs some basic changes. His regime may mark the emergence of other young Soviet leaders with new ideas. What his effect will be on East–West relations is not yet known.

SECTION REVIEW

1. Mapping: Use the map on page 636 to list the nations that became members of NATO; then list the countries that became part of the Warsaw Pact.
2. In your own words, briefly define or identify: de-Stalinization, peaceful coexistence, Cuban missile crisis, arms control agreement, Brezhnev Doctrine, détente, SALT I, SALT II, dissident movement, and Helsinki Accords.
3. Why did the Western nations not respond to the appeal of the Hungarian leader for help during the Hungarian Revolution of 1956?
4. Why did the United States Senate not ratify SALT II?
5. How has the government of the Soviet Union failed to keep the promises of socialism?
■ From the chapter's description of Soviet life, how do you think your life would be different if you lived in the Soviet Union?

WESTERN EUROPE

The main task facing Western Europe after World War II was rebuilding from the war. By 1952, industrial production of Western Europe was about twice what it had been before World War II. This rapid recovery was also due to a willingness among European nations to cooperate for their mutual economic benefit. The new prosperity of Europe enabled its governments to extend social services. Today, despite the loss of their colonial empires in the postwar period, Western European countries enjoy one of the world's highest standards of living.

The Common Market

The Marshall Plan helped the countries of Western Europe get back on their feet. In adjusting to a new postwar world, these countries also saw the benefits of economic cooperation. The Benelux countries—Belgium, the Netherlands, and Luxembourg—organized a mutual customs union in 1949. In 1958 six countries joined together in the European Economic Community, also known as the **Common Market.** They were France, West Germany, Italy, Belgium, Luxembourg, and the Netherlands. These countries agreed to do away gradually with tariffs on the imports of one another's products and to work toward the free movement of goods and workers between countries. By 1981 Denmark, Greece, Ireland, and Great Britain had also joined. In 1985 Spain and Portugal were added.

In 1979 the Common Market countries held elections to select members to a European Parliament. Membership in this international body was determined by the population of each country represented. The Parliament has power over the administration and budget of the Common Market. A hope exists that the Parliament might some day lead to a united Europe—a dream that harks back to medieval Europe.

Postwar Britain

After World War II, Great Britain lost the vast empire it had once ruled. (See Chapters 29 and 30.) But Great Britain maintained close trade ties with its former colonies through their voluntary membership in an association called the British Commonwealth of Nations.

At home, the 1945 election brought the British Labour party to power under the leadership of Clement Attlee. The Labour government nationalized basic industries such as coal mines, steel mills, railways, and the Bank of England. The Labour program created a **welfare state** that guaranteed a minimum standard of living for its citizens. The government provided the British people with a wide variety of services, including free medical care.

However, it was difficult for the government to find tax resources to pay for the services. Great Britain did not maintain the high postwar growth levels of some other nations. Exports of British goods fell behind the amount of imported goods, creating an unfavorable trade balance. As a result, the British pound was devalued. It dropped from a value of around $4.80 to little more than $1.00 by 1985.

During the 1960's and 1970's, Great Britain suffered from inflation and unemployment. But during that time, the country produced a vigorous popular culture. British fashions and music became popular throughout the world. Four young men from Liverpool formed a rock group named the Beatles, whose records sold in the hundreds of millions.

In 1979 the Conservative party's Margaret Thatcher became Great Britain's first woman prime minister. Thatcher's platform pledged an end to socialism in Great Britain. Her cuts in government spending brought down inflation but Great Britain had an unemployment rate of more than 12 percent at the beginning of 1985. In 1982, Thatcher won the approval of many Britons when she sent ships and troops to retake the Falkland Islands, which had been seized by Argentina. (See Chapter 31.)

Tensions between the Protestant and Catholic populations in Northern Ireland led to violence. Large numbers of British troops were stationed there to try to keep order, and they then became the target of attacks. The Irish Republican Army (IRA), which seeks to unite Northern Ireland with the Republic of Ireland, has carried out a campaign of violence both in Northern Ireland and in England. Bombs planted by the IRA killed Lord Louis

Mountbatten, a member of the royal family, and blew up a hotel, narrowly missing Prime Minister Thatcher. The cycle of violence and repression has not yet ended.

Postwar France

France's government proved unstable after the war. Charles de Gaulle (duh-GOLE) headed a provisional government that was replaced by the Fourth Republic in 1945. The Fourth Republic was burdened with the cost of waging wars to retain France's former colonies in Algeria and Indochina. (See Chapter 29.) Stability was also threatened by a constitution that gave most of the governmental power to the National Assembly. Because France had many political parties, a government could be organized only through coalitions of parties. This led to frequent changes in government.

In June 1958, faced with the rebellion of the French army in Algeria, the Fourth Republic collapsed. The Assembly invited Charles de Gaulle to become premier with extraordinary powers. Under de Gaulle's direction, a new constitution was drafted that strengthened the office of the president and reduced the Assembly's power. In December de Gaulle was elected the first president of the Fifth Republic.

De Gaulle solved the Algerian problem in 1962 by negotiating Algeria's independence. De Gaulle wanted France to play an independent role in international affairs. He partially withdrew France from NATO, and demanded the withdrawal from France of all troops not under French command. By 1960 France had become an atomic power with the successful testing of a nuclear bomb.

In 1968 student revolts broke out in Paris and other French cities. The unrest spread to French workers, leading to a general strike. De Gaulle had appealed for order, promising reforms and new elections. He won an impressive victory in the elections, but the following year lost a referendum on further constitutional reforms. He resigned and retired to his country home, where he died in 1970.

Governments in the immediate post-de Gaulle years continued many of his policies. In 1981 François Mitterrand (mee-teh-RAHN), a Socialist, became president. Mitterrand proved to be a supporter of United States policies in Europe. Most of

Prior to the 1968 election, the streets of Paris were crowded with people protesting Charles de Gaulle's administration.

his Socialist reforms were mild and were soon outranked by a policy of economic and technological growth. Although Mitterrand appointed Communist ministers to his cabinet, the power of the Communist party in French politics declined under his leadership.

Postwar West Germany

Under Chancellor Konrad Adenauer's leadership from 1949 to 1953, West Germany grew to be one of Europe's major industrial powers. Helped by aid from the Marshall Plan, Germany's industrial production doubled from 1950 to 1958. Faced with the need to rebuild its industrial base, Germany modernized its factories and stimulated private investment. This boom was popularly known as the "economic miracle."

Adenauer based his foreign policy on a strong relationship with the United States. He was one of the strongest backers of NATO, which West Ger-

many entered in 1955, and also of the European community.

Although there was still talk in the 1950's of an eventual reunification of the two Germanys, any progress toward this goal was defeated by Cold War tensions. West Germany insisted that free elections be held throughout both countries, and East Germany insisted on separate elections.

When Willy Brandt (BRAHNT) became chancellor in 1969, he promised to improve relations with East Germany and the Eastern bloc. His policy became known as Ostpolitik, or eastern policy. Brandt signed a treaty with Poland accepting the borders that had been drawn after World War II. This action acknowledged a great loss of territory for Germany. Brandt also negotiated treaties with the Soviet Union and Czechoslovakia. The recognition of the boundaries between East and West Germany led to the establishment of diplomatic relations between the two countries. Though Germany now seemed permanently divided, Brandt's

Ostpolitik removed the potentially explosive issue of Germany as an active source of East–West tension. However, the goal of unification remains alive in Germany today.

Brandt's successors, Helmut Schmidt (SHMIT) and Helmut Kohl (KOLE), have had to deal with a growing antinuclear movement known as the Green Party and with a slow down in economic growth. Such growth has not been as vigorous as it was during the 1950's.

Postwar Italy

As a defeated power, Italy faced hard times in the years immediately after the war. In 1945, Italian voters replaced the monarchy with a republic. Italy's first postwar republican government, headed by Alcide de Gaspari (ahl-CHEE-day day gahs-PAH-ree), lasted until 1953. But afterward a series of weak coalition governments failed to win strong support. The Christian Democratic party remained the strongest in Italy, followed by the Communist party.

The Italian government sponsored improvements in public schools, hospitals, and transportation. Some large landed estates were broken up, and many remnants of fascism were abolished. The north of Italy had its own economic miracle in the 1950's and early 1960's, boosted by automobile manufacturing and the fashion industry.

As economic growth slowed, labor unrest increased, and there was an increase in the popularity of the Italian Communist party. The party had condemned the Soviet invasion of Czechoslovakia in 1968, showing its independence from Moscow. In 1973, the Italian Communist party leader, Enrico Berlinguer (bear-lyn-GAYHR), agreed to cooperate with other parties to improve Italian society. This compromise or cooperation with other parties and independence from the Soviet Union became known as *Eurocommunism*. Communist popularity peaked in 1975 when the party won 35 percent of the nationwide vote and control of some cities.

In recent years, Italy has faced the problem of terrorism. A terrorist organization known as the Red Brigade, formed in the 1970's, committed many violent acts including the 1978 kidnapping and murder of Aldo Moro, a former prime minister. Other acts of terrorism occurred in the 1970's and 1980's. In 1981 a Turkish terrorist made an attempt to assassinate Pope John Paul II in St. Peter's Square in Rome.

Growth of Democracy

Several European countries established democracies in the 1970's. After an interval of military rule under "the colonels," Greece regained democratic government in 1974. The current Greek Socialist government has adopted a more hostile attitude toward the United States. A substantial decrease in American financial and military aid is partly responsible for this shift in relations.

After decades of dictatorship under Antonio Salazar, a revolution in 1974 gave Portugal a military government that permitted free elections. Since popular support for maintaining Portugal's African colonies was lacking, this action also speeded up the move toward independence in Portugal's colonies.

Spain also saw the establishment of a democratic government after the death of Francisco Franco in 1975. His appointed successor, King Juan Carlos, eliminated many of the repressive institutions of the Franco dictatorship. Choosing to rule as a constitutional monarch, he permitted free elections in 1975 in which moderate and democratic Socialists formed the largest parties. Spain's democracy survived an attempted military coup in 1981 when the king made a televised appeal for support. Spain joined NATO in 1982.

SECTION REVIEW

1. Mapping: Use the map on page 636 to find the nations that belong to the Common Market.
2. In your own words, briefly define or identify: Common Market, welfare state, economic miracle, Ostpolitik.
3. What are some ways in which the members of the Common Market cooperate?
4. Why did the French Fourth Republic prove to be an unworkable form of government?
■ Some Europeans have protested the presence of United States troops in Europe as part of the NATO alliance. What do you think would happen if the NATO alliance dissolved?

Reviewing the Chapter

Chapter Summary

After World War II, Marshall Plan aid from the United States helped Western Europe to rebuild. Many Western European countries have cooperated economically through the Common Market. Today Western Europe enjoys one of the world's highest standards of living.

In Eastern Europe the presence of Soviet troops enforced the installation of Communist governments. Attempts at rebellion were put down with force. Though limited freedoms have been allowed in some countries, Eastern Europe remains under Soviet domination.

Within the Soviet Union, a repressive regime found that central economic planning could not produce a standard of living as high as that enjoyed by Western nations.

The United States and the Soviet Union emerged as the two world superpowers. The United States formed the NATO alliance with Western Europe and adopted a policy of containment to prevent the further spread of communism. The Soviet Union and its Eastern European satellites made up the Warsaw Pact alliance. Development of nuclear weapons and long-range missiles by both superpowers heightened tensions between them. During the 1970's the United States and the Soviet Union signed a series of arms control agreements. But both sides maintain huge nuclear arsenals, and the competition between West and East continues today.

1. Why did Europe break into two opposing blocs after World War II?
2. What were the advantages to both sides of the arms control agreements signed during the 1970's?

Using Your Vocabulary

1. Why is the term superpower used to refer to the United States and to the Soviet Union?
2. What is the difference between a refugee and a displaced person?
3. In your own words, explain the meaning of denazification and de-Stalinization.
4. Define the term Cold War.
5. Why do you think the term summit conference is used to describe a meeting between government leaders?
6. What is meant by détente?
7. Explain your understanding of samizdat.
8. Solidarity means fellowship. Why is this a good term for the Polish labor movement?
9. Briefly describe a welfare state. Cite some of its advantages and disadvantages.
10. What does Ostpolitik mean?
11. Describe the concept of Eurocommunism.
12. In your own words, explain the motives behind the Berlin Airlift.
13. How would you describe the arms race between the United States and the Soviet Union?
14. Why is "Star Wars" an appropriate term for the Strategic Defense Initiative proposed by the United States government?
15. What does internal exile mean?
16. What is the difference between a protest and a rebellion? Support your answer.
17. Explain the difference between a democracy and a dictatorship. Name three countries that fall into each of these categories.

Developing Your Geography Skills

1. Using the Atlas map on page 756, identify the countries of Eastern Europe that were occupied by the Soviet Union during World War II. Which are still under Soviet domination?
2. Refer to the map on page 636. Which countries joined NATO after 1949?
3. Using the Atlas map on page 756, identify the countries that today make up the Common Market. How does their nearness to each other benefit their economies?

Recalling the Facts

1. What policy was the brainchild of George F. Kennan?
2. What is the relationship between the Truman Doctrine and the Marshall Plan?
3. What countries governed Germany after World War II?
4. What was Konrad Adenauer's most significant contribution to German progress after 1945?
5. What principle of action do the NATO and the Warsaw Pact nations share?
6. What event led to the downfall of Khrushchev in the Soviet Union?
7. What was the "Prague spring"?
8. What decision did Albania make after the Soviet invasion of Czechoslovakia?
9. What was the primary objective of SALT I? SALT II?
10. What action in the late 1970's caused relations between the United States and the Soviet Union to deteriorate?
11. Name two prominent Soviet dissidents and the fields of their expertise.
12. What was the principal task facing Western Europe after World War II?
13. Why did postwar France have so many changes in its government?
14. What was the "economic miracle" of the 1950's?
15. In Spain, how did the government of King Juan Carlos differ from that of Franco?
16. Who proclaimed that there were "differing roads to socialism"?
17. What did the Soviet Union do to test the United States and its new President in the early 1960's?
18. What was Enrico Berlinguer's contribution to European politics?
19. What is one of the reasons that the production of consumer goods in the Soviet Union does not yet match that in Western nations?

Essay Questions

1. Reread the Primary Sources feature on page 633. Using at least two of the excerpts, compare how these human rights are observed in Western nations and in Soviet bloc countries?
2. Briefly state your understanding of "peaceful coexistence." Do you think people from different countries and cultures should be able to work together peacefully? Cite examples to support your views.
3. Write a short paragraph on each of the following organizations or alliances: the United Nations, NATO, Warsaw Pact, and Common Market. How did each contribute to European development after 1950?
4. Choose one of the postwar leaders you have read about in the chapter. Give the reasons for your choice, and then describe the contributions of that leader to the progress or decline of the country in the postwar period.

Critical Thinking

1. Refer to the organizational chart on page 632. Based on the information given there, identify the principal concerns of the United Nations. Are these concerns being effectively addressed by the United Nations today? Why or why not?
2. Cite one important event in either Eastern or Western Europe during the 1950's and explain its impact on the Cold War.
3. What conflicts occurred between East and West as a result of the Cold War? How do relations today between Western and Eastern bloc nations compare to those that fostered the Cold War in the 1960's? Cite examples.
4. Despite efforts such as SALT I and SALT II and détente to lessen the threat of nuclear war, what warranted claims can be made about the continued spread of nuclear weapons? Defend each claim.
5. Compare the principles of the Truman Doctrine, the Marshall Plan, and the Brezhnev Doctrine. How do these principles highlight the differences in value systems between the United States and the Soviet Union?
6. What facts can you verify about the major postwar problems facing Great Britain, France, Germany, and Italy? Describe some of the steps taken by each of these nations to solve their problems. Would you consider these steps warranted or unwarranted?

CHAPTER ·29·

MODERN ASIA

1945–Present

Objectives

- To discuss the political, social, and economic changes in China in the last forty years

- To identify the reasons for the transformation of Japan to an industrial superpower

- To explain the development of India and Pakistan from colonies to independent powers

- To describe the wars of independence in Indochina

- To describe some important developments in Southeast Asia in the last forty years

*A*sia, from Pakistan to the Pacific islands, contains more than half of the people of the world today. The first, second, and fifth most populous nations of the world—China, India, and Indonesia—are found here.

World War II quickened the movement for independence in Asia. The Japanese occupied many areas under European control, ousting the former colonial rulers. At the end of the war the Europeans often wanted to return to their former status. But they no longer had the resources to keep their colonies by force, and with varying degrees of violence the great colonial empires of Asia became a thing of the past. India, Pakistan, Burma, Malaysia, and Singapore gained their independence from Great Britain. Indonesia won its independence from the Netherlands, and after a long struggle Indochina won independence from France.

Asia became one of the battlegrounds of the Cold War. The two superpowers fought for the hearts and minds of the newly emerging nations. Some of the Asian nations became Communist, but most did not. The Cold War erupted into serious fighting in Korea in 1950 and in the long, drawn-out conflict in Indochina. Each superpower backed an opposing side, and the United States sent fighting troops to both conflicts.

Much of the energy of the new nations went into the task of modernization. Transforming agricultural economies to meet the need of the new age became a huge task that met with mixed results. Industrialization and urbanization brought social changes and new wealth.

CHINA SINCE 1945

Developments in China since World War II have been dramatic and profound. The Chinese Communists' victory in the civil war brought a new system of government that made changes greater than any others in China's long history.

Civil War

During World War II the Chinese Nationalists, led by Chiang Kai-shek (JEEAHNG kie-SHEK), and the Communists under Mao Zedong (dzu-DOONG) suspended their hostilities. They united to resist the Japanese invaders. After Japan's surrender, fighting between the Chinese Communists and the Nationalists resumed. At the end of 1945, President Harry S Truman sent General George C. Marshall to try to bring the Nationalists and the Communists together in a coalition government. Although he arranged a temporary cease-fire, his mission ended in failure.

The Chinese civil war began with some successes for the Nationalists. But in spite of superior equipment and numbers, their morale was low. In addition, the Nationalist troops were spread thinly over too large an area. Chiang Kai-shek's generals placed too great an emphasis on taking all the major cities of China. The country's poor transportation system made it difficult to supply the far-flung troops. Working from their bases in the countryside, the Communists surrounded the Nationalist-held cities. When Nationalist troops lost battles, great numbers of them defected to the Communist side.

Mao Zedong's movement was disciplined and efficient. It was more attuned to the needs of the peasants who made up the vast majority of China's population. The regime of Chiang Kai-shek, on the other hand, had become increasingly corrupt, inefficient, and authoritarian. Inflation was soaring, causing Chiang to lose support in the cities. The United States advised Chiang to begin reforms, but he resisted.

From September 1948 to January 1949, Mao Zedong's forces won a series of stunning victories. By June the Communists had virtually won the war. In October Mao stood before a cheering crowd in Beijing and proclaimed the establishment of the People's Republic of China (PRC). Chiang Kai-shek and the remnants of the Nationalist forces fled to the offshore island of Taiwan (tie-WAHN). There they established a government that they claimed represented the whole of the Chinese people.

Early Years of the People's Republic

Though victorious, the Chinese Communist government faced staggering problems. China had endured disruption and war for the last twenty years. The economy was in shambles with inflation making the money worthless.

In addition, a new system of administering the huge country had to be built almost from scratch. A coalition government was established. Most of the power went to strategically located Communists. The party organized the country from Beijing to the smallest villages.

Land redistribution gave peasants the ownership of land they had worked for centuries under the landlord system. The Marriage Law of May 1950 gave women full equality with men in marriage rights, divorce, and property ownership. The government tried to decrease the influence of the traditional Chinese extended family. It promoted the simpler nuclear family of husband, wife, and children.

The PRC's long-term economic goal was to mobilize China's resources to make it a modern industrial country. To do this required an extension of strict control of all segments of the economy. In 1953 China's first Five-Year Plan went into effect. It called for moderately rapid industrialization and growth. In the early years small private businesses were allowed to operate. Some of the former owners of industry were allowed to remain on the job as managers.

In the next two years there was a growing collectivization of agriculture. Peasant farmers were organized into cooperatives that pooled some of their resources for greater efficiency in agricultural production.

Mao Tries to Build Communism

These policies began to change in 1957. That year saw the short-lived "Hundred Flowers" campaign. With the slogan, "Let a hundred flowers bloom," the Communists encouraged the Chinese people to criticize the government. The Communists expected that the criticisms would be mild. But the unexpected freedom brought forth basic criticism of the regime, i.e., the lack of free speech and disappointment that the country had not progressed quickly enough. A short time later the "hundred flowers" were uprooted and a campaign to reeducate "rightists" was begun.

The year 1958 was a crucial one for China. Mao, dissatisfied with the progress of agriculture, shifted his policy from cooperative farms to communes. The peasants' small plots were combined into huge government-owned farms. The communes had governmental functions and military responsibilities. No private plots were allowed and the commune owned all formerly personal possessions down to pots and pans, chairs and tables. Labor was mandatory; everyone, including women and children old enough, worked twenty-eight days of the month. Children were cared for in the communes' day nurseries. Food and other necessities were provided according to need.

The establishment of agricultural communes was linked with an ambitious industrial modernization campaign called the Great Leap Forward. Peasants on the communes were encouraged to build small iron smelters to supply themselves with the materials for tools. Small factories were planned in locations all over the country to overcome the lack of good transportation. Plans were drawn up for enormous irrigation and land reclamation projects.

Mao claimed that the Great Leap Forward would enable China to surpass Great Britain in industrial production in ten years. However, the people were required to work longer hours at lower wages and make other sacrifices to industrialize their country. Mao promised that their sacrifices would bring prosperity to them and the nation, as well as help build a true Communist system. In fact the opposite resulted.

The Great Leap Forward, despite its initial support, was a failure. Lack of organized planning produced bottlenecks in production and bad weather hurt agriculture. China was forced to buy food from the Western countries to avert starvation. By the end of 1959, the Great Leap Forward program was abandoned. The Chinese people's hope for progress again proved fruitless.

The Great Proletarian Cultural Revolution

In the aftermath of the Great Leap Forward, some members of the Chinese Communist party began to question Mao's leadership. By the early 1960's anti-Maoists had gained control of important positions within the party and the government. Mao was now criticized openly or, even worse, ignored.

To recapture control in China, Mao and his supporters launched the Great Proletarian Cultural Revolution. This was an attempt to bypass the party structure and appeal to the people themselves to bring about a "true" Communist revolution.

People were advised to bombard headquarters with criticism of the party, which Mao claimed had lost its revolutionary spirit. Anti-Maoist party leaders were confronted in their offices and sometimes attacked. The movement spread throughout the country.

Mao organized students and young workers in support of his policies. These Red Guards, as they came to be known, held large rallies, demonstrations, and marches. Schools were closed and the teachings of Mao Zedong were used as a guide to all situations.

Mao's appeal to the masses for support was successful. Many of his opponents were forced out of their positions and were replaced by Maoists. But the forces Mao had unleashed did not stop there.

The Cultural Revolution produced chaos within China. Red Guard units attacked anyone suspected of anti-Maoist feelings and thoughts, dragging them from their homes and subjecting them to public trials. Intellectuals and people in managerial positions were sent to the countryside for "corrective" work on the communes. Red Guard factions began to attack each other over disputes as to who was following correctly the teachings of Mao, "the Great Helmsman." The growing number of clashes threatened China with complete anarchy. Finally, the army stepped in to restore order.

Mao's experiment with permanent revolution caused enormous damage to both the economic and the social fabric of the country. From 1966 to 1969 the country was in turmoil. Many students lost three or more years of schooling. Production was down. China's development was set back by years. The ill will between people who had been on opposing sides during the Cultural Revolution would poison the political and social system for years.

The Korean War

The early years of Communist rule in China were also disrupted by international events. Following World War II, the Soviet Union had occupied the northern half of Korea and the United States the southern half. By 1949 both superpowers had removed their troops, leaving behind two Koreas separated by the 38th parallel of latitude under different governments. The Democratic People's Republic of Korea (North Korea) was headed by Kim Il-sung. Syngman Rhee (SING-muhn REE) was president of the Republic of Korea (South Korea). The United States government favored Rhee's policies. Such support would soon be put to the ultimate test.

In June 1950 the North Koreans invaded South Korea, taking the capital, Seoul (SOHL), in the first few days of fighting. The response from the United States was prompt. President Truman sent United States forces to aid the South Koreans. The United Nations Security Council condemned North Korea as an aggressor. General Douglas MacArthur was named commander of the United Nations forces.

The North Koreans continued their swift advance, driving the opposing armies into the southeast corner of the country. On September 15, however, MacArthur launched a surprise amphibious landing at Inchon (IN-CHAHN), on the coast near Seoul behind North Korean lines. In the fighting that followed, the North Koreans were driven back to their border.

When the United Nations troops crossed the border advancing into North Korea, the Chinese watched uneasily. The Chinese warned that if the United Nations forces approached the Yalu (YAH-loo) River, the border between China and Korea,

The Chinese government used the arts, including dance groups, to instruct people about communism. What other methods are used to spread political beliefs?

China would intervene. The warning was ignored, and in late November 180,000 Chinese soldiers swept across the border. MacArthur's forces were not large enough to resist. Bitter and bloody fighting could not stem the tide and MacArthur's forces were pushed back in the longest retreat in United States military history. By December 15, 1950, the line of battle had again shifted south of the 38th parallel.

When the strength of the Communist offensive became clear, MacArthur asked for permission to attack Chinese bases in Manchuria. Truman refused, fearing that it would escalate the war and perhaps bring in the Soviet Union. A counteroffensive by United Nations forces, now headed by General Matthew B. Ridgway, pushed the Chinese back across the parallel. There the two sides stayed until an armistice was signed in July 1953.

Effects of the Korean War

The Korean War decisively affected the relations between the PRC and the United States. In the early days of the war, President Truman had sent the United States Sixth Fleet to patrol the waters between Taiwan and the People's Republic. The Communists viewed this as a hostile act since they regarded Taiwan as part of China. In addition, the United States began to arm Chiang Kai-shek and backed the Nationalist claim to the Chinese seat in the United Nations. The United States refused to recognize the PRC in any international forum. Future United States policy linked the PRC with the Soviet Union as part of a single, giant Communist foe.

The Southeast Asia Treaty Organization (SEATO) was formed in 1954 to oppose takeovers

KOREAN CONFLICT

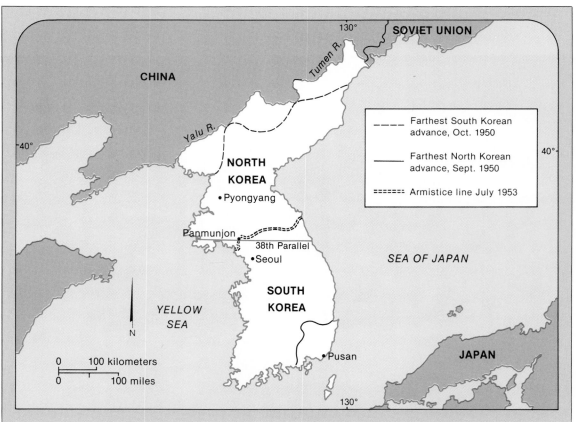

With the division of the Korean peninsula at the 38th Parallel, does South Korea gain any advantage over North Korea? Why is Korea still divided?

in that area by Communist nations or groups. Member states were the United States, Australia, France, Great Britain, New Zealand, Pakistan, the Philippines, and Thailand. The PRC regarded this action as being surrounded by enemies to prevent the final unification of their country.

The Korean War did not resolve the problem of Korean unification. Today the two countries are still not united. The intervening years have accentuated the differences between the two countries. North Korea, under communism, is much less prosperous than South Korea.

South Korea has had difficulty in achieving political stability. President Park Chung Hee, who served throughout much of the 1970's, encouraged economic growth but did not allow political opposition. He was assassinated in 1979 by a member of the Korean Intelligence Agency. After an election, Chun Doo Hwan (CHUN DOO HAWAHN) took office in 1979. He too has followed a policy of suppressing political dissent, which has sometimes strained South Korea's relationship with the United States. But 40,000 American soldiers are still there to patrol the armistice line between North and South Korea.

South Korea has become a strong economic power in the last ten years. Low wages and hard work have vastly increased the economic trade and development of the country. The area from Seoul north to the North Korean border was undeveloped in the 1960's. Today it has a network of superhighways connecting factories and apartment complexes. South Korea is a major exporter of textiles, clothing, and electronics, and is expected to be shipping cars abroad in the near future. Many observers believe South Korea is poised for an economic expansion as in Japan.

Sino-Soviet Split

In 1950 China and the Soviet Union signed a thirty-year Treaty of Friendship, Alliance, and Mutual Assistance, which provided for a military alliance between the two countries. China received a five-year $300 million loan for industrial equipment and the services of Soviet technicians. A larger loan was extended during the Korean War. While Stalin was alive, China and the Soviet Union presented a united front to the world.

Although to the outside world the Communist bloc seemed a single, united one, differences in ideology and in national interests always characterized the two countries. China had based its revolution on the peasant rather than the industrial worker, as the Soviet Union had. With the death of Stalin there was a short period of warm relations between the two countries. But when Khrushchev made fun of the Great Leap Forward to a United States senator, Mao was insulted.

With the Soviet successes in Sputnik and intercontinental ballistic missiles in 1957, Mao felt it was time to confront the United States rather than follow Khrushchev's plan for "peaceful coexistence." Mao's warlike attitude caused the Soviets to renege on their promise to supply China with an atomic bomb. By the end of the 1950's, Mao felt that Khrushchev was more interested in good relations with the United States than with China. The final straw came when the Soviet Union backed India in its border dispute with China.

The dispute became known in 1960 when Russian technicians left China. In public pronouncements China now openly laid claim to the Soviet Union's previously undisputed leadership of the Communist world. Although the Chinese Communists made diplomatic overtures to both Communist and developing nations, their successes were few.

The Chinese detonated a nuclear device in 1964, much to the dismay of the rest of the world. Relations with the Soviet Union deteriorated further as the two countries hurled abuse at each other. In late 1969 troops from the two Communist giants clashed in a border dispute.

A New Approach to the West

As China's relations with the Soviet Union worsened, it was imperative for the Chinese to seek a balance against the stronger Soviet forces. The United States involvement in the Vietnam War had awakened memories of the Korean War for the Chinese. Now, however, President Richard M. Nixon was attempting to withdraw the United States from Vietnam. He set in motion secret contacts with the PRC that helped to bring about a more peaceful relationship between the two countries. Both the PRC and the United States viewed better relations as a way to counter the Soviet Union.

A ping-pong team from the United States, playing in the Orient, was invited by the Chinese government to also play some games in the People's Republic. This so-called "ping-pong diplomacy" led to the first official visit in 1971 by United States citizens to the PRC and led to Nixon's going to China the following year.

In October 1971 the United Nations voted to accept the People's Republic as the official representative of China in the United Nations. The Taiwan government was expelled.

On February 21, 1972, President Nixon arrived in Beijing for an eight-day visit that he called "a journey for peace." The visit concluded with a joint statement known as the Shanghai Communique. The Shanghai Communique dealt with the

major issue separating the two countries. Both countries agreed that there was only one China. The two nations also agreed to work to improve relations, increase trade, and exchange scientists, artists, journalists, and athletes.

Formal diplomatic relations between China and the United States were established in 1979 during the administration of President Jimmy Carter. At that time the United States broke off diplomatic relations with Taiwan and ended its mutual defense treaty with Taiwan. Communist China agreed it would not interfere with United States investments in Taiwan and indirectly promised not to use force to unite the country.

China After Mao

The death of Mao in 1976 shocked the country. Which factions left over from the Cultural Revolution would take control? Mao's widow, Jiang Jing (JYONG JING), a leader of the extreme leftist faction, and three others (together known as the Gang of Four) were removed by the new head of state, Hua Guofeng (HWAH gwaw-FUNG).

Soon Deng Xiaoping (DUHNG syow-PING), a victim of the Cultural Revolution, emerged as the most important power in the country. His main concern was China's economic and industrial development; ideology was secondary. The theme of Deng's policy for China was "the four modernizations"—agriculture, industry, science and technology, and defense.

Deng's concern with modernization has led him to develop strong trade relations with the West. More than 33,000 students have been sent abroad to study since 1978. Between 1950 and 1978 less than half that number had left China.

Deng's aim is to quadruple China's output in farms and factories by the year 2000. In recent years China has been experimenting with greater use of incentives to increase production. After an agricultural quota set by the state has been reached, farmers can keep whatever they can produce. The peasants have enjoyed unprecedented prosperity, and farm production has risen.

Small manufacturers and craftspeople are free from the complete control of the state. In larger state-controlled factories, managers have more authority to plan, but they must compete in the marketplace with other factories.

Richard and Pat Nixon visited China and its Great Wall in 1972. This presidential visit was intended to improve relations between the United States and China. Was it successful?

Billboards are becoming commonplace in China's major cities. How does this one reflect some of the changes affecting the life of the average Chinese citizen?

China's cities have taken on a different look, with billboards that advertise televisions, cassette recorders, and cameras. People wear Western fashions and attend exercise classes. Western classical and popular music, once banned as bourgeois, is being heard again. However, the government still maintains a tight control over China's own writers and artists.

These improvements are encouraging, but with a population of one billion, China is limited in the near future to moderate increases in the living standards of its people. China has taken drastic measures in recent years to limit its population growth. The government has promoted a strict campaign to encourage one-child families. Although the rate of population growth has come down, overpopulation is still one of China's major problems.

JAPAN SINCE THE WAR

On August 15, 1945, Emperor Hirohito of Japan made a radio broadcast to his people announcing the decision to surrender. Saying that they must "endure the unendurable," he asked that the people work together for the reconstruction of their country. It was an historic moment. Most Japanese had never heard their emperor's voice. Nor had the Japanese nation ever experienced defeat. The idea of a foreign occupation of Japan filled the nation with apprehension.

An Occupied Country

Although in theory the occupation was international, in reality it was run by the United States. General Douglas MacArthur supervised the occupation. As commander of the Allied Pacific forces that had defeated Japan, MacArthur was regarded highly. His fairness and respect for Japanese traditions won the confidence of the Japanese people.

The United States felt that Japan needed a complete overhaul of its institutions in order to reform their feudal and militaristic character. First, Japanese militarism had to be eliminated. The Japanese Empire was broken up, and all Japanese soldiers and civilians abroad were returned to Japan.

Japan's military services were dissolved and military installations dismantled. Within the country, ultranationalistic organizations were disbanded, and the police force was decentralized. Political prisoners were released.

As in Germany, there were trials of war criminals. Of twenty-five military and political leaders put on trial, seven, including General Tojo, were hanged. The remainder were imprisoned for life. In the areas Japan had occupied during the war, nearly 5,000 accused war criminals were tried and more than 700 executed.

MacArthur supervised the writing of a new constitution for Japan, which went into effect in 1947. It made the country a parliamentary democracy. MacArthur understood the emperor's role as a symbol of the nation and decided not to try him for war crimes. In 1946 the emperor renounced his claim to divine right rule. His new role, described in the constitution, was as "the symbol of the state and of the unity of the people, deriving his position from the will of the people with whom resides Sovereign power."

The constitution provided for the direct election of both houses of the Diet, or Parliament. All men and women could vote. An independent judiciary was established with a Supreme Court that could rule on the constitutionality of legislation. A free press, the right of assembly, and other political and human rights were guaranteed.

The constitution attempted to put an end to Japan's former militaristic ambitions. It stated: "Aspiring sincerely to an international peace based on justice and order, the Japanese people, forever, renounce war as a sovereign right of the nation, or the threat or use of force, as a means of settling disputes with other nations."

A Changing Attitude Toward Japan

The United States started giving aid to Japan in 1947. At first the aid went toward the relief of hunger. But with the rise of Soviet power and Communist victory in China, United States attitudes toward Japan changed. Japan had now emerged as an outpost of United States influence in the Far East. To counter Communist influence in Asia, United States policy in Japan encouraged the development of a vigorous capitalist economy. This policy hoped to make Japan both prosperous and secure.

With the outbreak of the Korean War this policy took on new military significance. Japan became a staging ground for the United Nations troops. The United States encouraged the growth of Japanese Self-Defense Forces.

In September 1951 the United States and forty-seven other countries signed a peace treaty with Japan. Japan would regain its independence in April 1952. In return, Japan renounced its claims to its former colonies. China, India, and the Soviet Union were not signatories, but India and Nationalist China soon signed separate treaties with Japan. Japan was admitted to the United Nations in 1956. Japan also signed a security treaty with the United States. That treaty allowed United States troops to be based in Japan in return for a United States pledge to defend Japan in case of an attack.

Social Change in Japan

The social transformation of Japan under the occupation was comparable to that of the Meiji Restoration of the nineteenth century. The occupation authorities broke up the huge Japanese business monopolies known as **zaibatsu** (SIE-baht-SOO). In the future all Japanese companies were to sell their stock on a public market and make annual statements of their economic activities. If they created a monopoly in any field, they could be ordered by the government to sell their holdings. Workers were given the right to organize unions.

The occupation authorities also enforced land reform. All land owned by absentee landlords and other private plots over ten acres were bought by the government. This land was sold to peasants on relatively easy terms. Rent rates were strictly controlled. The amount of rented farmland decreased from 55 percent to 12 percent. Tenant farmers decreased to less than 10 percent of the total. Food prices rose rapidly after the war and increased the income of the rural population.

The greatest achievement of the occupation was directing the nation toward democracy. The hereditary nobility was abolished except for the emperor and his immediate family. Women were granted full legal equality with men. Although the father remained head of the family, his feudal authority over adult children and other relatives was abolished.

Changes were made in the educational system, shifting the emphasis from rote learning to independent thinking. Textbooks were changed to eliminate authoritarian, ultranationalist, and militarist propaganda. The number of years of required schooling went from six to nine.

Reconstruction and Growth

Japan's prospects looked bleak in 1945. Japan had a postwar population of 72 million. Its industries were destroyed and international relations severed. As a country that had to import most of its basic resources it was in dire straits. The breaking up of its huge industrial empires made economic planning difficult. Inflation soared. By 1947 Japan's production was only 37 percent of its prewar level.

The United States occupation forces started to emphasize economic recovery in 1948. Measures were enforced to control the inflation that was

Trains such as the Tokaido Super Express, dubbed "bullet trains" because of their high speed and conelike shape, are a symbol of Japan's economic success. Why?

hindering growth. The reduced prices led to a small burst of exports. But it was the Korean War that stimulated the Japanese economy. Japan received $4 billion worth of orders to meet military needs. By the mid-1950's Japan's economy had grown back to its prewar level.

Although Japan stressed exports, even more important to its economic recovery was the expansion of its domestic market. Per capita income, which had been $146 in 1951 and $395 in 1960, rose to over $2,000 in 1972. By 1981 it was $9,864. Prosperity and new patterns of living made the Japanese avid consumers. In the 1960's every household wanted "The Three Imperial Treasures"—a refrigerator, a television, and a washing machine. Giant new Japanese companies arose to meet the demands for new consumer products.

In the 1960's the economy took off as Japan reaped the benefits of economic planning and the hard work and dedication of its people. In 1968 Japan overtook West Germany to become the second largest industrial power in the free world after the United States. The Japanese economy faced a severe test in the 1970's, when the rise in oil prices caused worldwide inflation.

Japan was particularly vulnerable because it imported 90 percent of its oil from the Middle East. Though inflation increased and the rate of growth slowed, stern measures kept the economy on an upward track.

By 1980 Japan was the leading car and truck producer and the largest shipbuilder in the world. The Japanese gross national product rose from $1.3 billion in 1946 to $15.1 billion in 1962. Then it jumped to about $290 billion in 1972. Today it is over $1 trillion, the third largest gross national product in the world after the United States and the Soviet Union. These figures tell one of the most extraordinary economic success stories in history.

Reasons for the Economic Success

Many factors contributed to the Japanese success. The Japanese were, and still are, hard working, literate, and technically advanced. Japan's homogeneous society has made it easier to work toward a common goal. The Japanese people have a high rate of personal savings invested in the growth of their country.

Most of Japan's industry had been destroyed by wartime bombing. Ironically, this proved to be an advantage when Japan's industry was completely rebuilt with modern equipment. In addition, after the war Japan imported new technology, making its industries more efficient. Japanese technicians displayed a talent for improving on the imported technology.

Another factor in Japanese growth was the lack of a high military budget. The security treaty with the United States made large defense expenditures unnecessary. Thus this money could be used to invest in productive industries. Since the mid-1950's Japan's government has spent only about 1 percent of its budget on the military, a far lower figure than most other nations.

Japan, which had to trade to survive, greatly benefited from an increase in the volume of imports and exports. Japanese products were known after the war for being cheap and of low quality. Today they are highly desired all over the world.

Japan was aided by the fact that labor and management cooperated in building the country's economy. Most importantly, the government helped industry to plan for growth. The banking credit necessary for business expansion was ultimately guaranteed by the government. The term Japan, Inc., refers to the role of the Japanese government in Japan's business success.

A special government agency, the Ministry of International Trade and Industry (MITI), helped to chart Japan's economic growth. The MITI identified industries that looked favorable for development. It also set production goals through long-range planning. Much of the research necessary was done in government laboratories. Foreign markets were estimated and economic growth was rewarded with tax incentives. In recent years Japan's success at exporting huge amounts of its products has led to resentment on the part of some of Japan's trading partners.

International Relations

The guiding principle of Japan's foreign policy has been support for an open and stable world trading order. As the giant economic power of Asia, it has sought to establish conditions that maximize trade.

Japan has continued the close relationship with the United States that began in the years immediately following the occupation. Japan loyally followed the lead of the United States on most Cold War issues. But as Japan's economic power grew, some Japanese called for a more independent foreign policy. Many in Japan, remembering the devastation of Hiroshima and Nagasaki, did not want United States nuclear weapons, nor ships carrying them, in their country.

Some Japanese resented the United States retention of islands near Japan that had been Japanese-controlled. In 1972 Okinawa was returned to Japan with the understanding that the United States would be able to retain its bases.

Recently friction has occurred between the two countries because Japan's exports to the United States far outweigh United States' exports to Japan. This trade imbalance has brought calls within the United States for trade restrictions against Japan. The United States has accused Japan of closing its own country to its imports, i.e.,

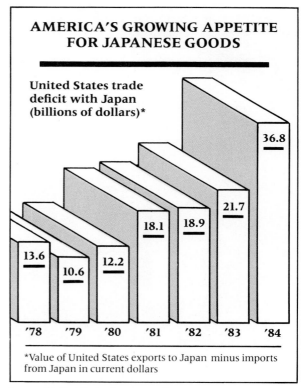

AMERICA'S GROWING APPETITE FOR JAPANESE GOODS

United States trade deficit with Japan (billions of dollars)*

'78	'79	'80	'81	'82	'83	'84
13.6	10.6	12.2	18.1	18.9	21.7	36.8

*Value of United States exports to Japan minus imports from Japan in current dollars

Source: United States Commerce Department.

high technology, lumber, and agricultural products, while the Japanese counter that their products are competitive because they have done more research to see what United States consumers want. The current Japanese prime minister, Yasuhiro Nakasone (yah-soo-HEE-roh nahk-uh-SOH-nee), has made smooth trading relationships with the United States one of his main concerns.

In the early postwar years Japan followed United States policy and withheld recognition of the People's Republic of China. But Japan established formal diplomatic relations with the PRC a year before the United States did. Today, although no longer recognizing the Nationalist Chinese government, Japan trades extensively with Taiwan.

Japan has a complex relationship with South Korea. Because of the Japanese occupation, many South Koreans feared and disliked the Japanese. In 1965 the two countries normalized relations. Japanese aid, loans, and investments helped to touch off economic growth in South Korea.

A Blend of the Old and the New

The Japanese landscape has been transformed since the war. Industrial growth has led to urbanization and overcrowding, putting a strain on transportation and service industries. Standardized housing dots the landscape. The country's limited farming areas have been threatened as well.

Industrialization has also brought the problem of pollution. This has been more severe in Japan than in most other places because of the density of the urban population and the unchecked economic growth.

One of the main aims of the Japanese has been to conserve their traditional customs in the face of the change that has engulfed the country. This they have been able to do. Shinto festivals and holidays are widely observed. Supermarkets offer courses in the traditional Japanese arts of the tea ceremony and flower arrangement. Although the Japanese admire modern and Western ways, they have conscientiously conserved their beautiful ancient arts, from pottery to garden design.

Many Japanese esthetic ideas in gardens, architecture, and furniture have had worldwide influence. A country that has made extensive use of space-age robots also has kept the traditional Ka-

The Grand Kabuki Theater Group performs in Tokyo. Kabuki drama has featured male actors in female roles for more than 300 years. What does this tell you about the traditional role of women in Japanese society?

buki (kuh-BOO-kee) and No drama. Japan has succeeded in blending the old and the new. The country's two favorite sports are baseball and traditional Japanese sumo wrestling.

SECTION REVIEW

1. Mapping: Use the map on page 654 to find Japan. Why is its closeness to China, the Soviet Union, and Korea important?
2. In your own words, briefly define or identify: zaibatsu, Japan, Inc., trade imbalance, MITI.
3. Why did the United States encourage the economic and industrial growth of Japan?
4. Summarize the reasons for Japan's economic success.
■ If the United States limited trade with Japan, what kinds of products do you think would be most affected?

THE INDIAN SUBCONTINENT

Nationalism had developed among the people of India before World War I. The British promises of self-government were not fulfilled. Instead only limited powers were granted to the Indians. The Indian movement for complete independence gained strength.

India Is Divided

Indian nationalism was complicated by internal religious differences. Although the Hindus were the majority in the country, there was a substantial Muslim minority as well as millions of people of other religions. The chief organization promoting independence, the Congress party, was dominated by Hindus although it had many Muslim members. The Muslims had ruled India for almost eight hundred years. Now they were afraid that in a united and independent India, they would be at a disadvantage. As a result, a separate Muslim movement headed by Muhammed Ali Jinnah arose. This movement adopted the goal of working for a separate independent Muslim state. The Congress party wanted a united India.

Because the Congress party launched a Quit India movement in 1942, many of its leaders, including Mohandas K. Gandhi (moh-HAHN-dahs GAHN-dee) and Jawaharlal Nehru (juh-WAH-huhr-lahl NAY-roo), were jailed by the British for most of World War II. The British, facing

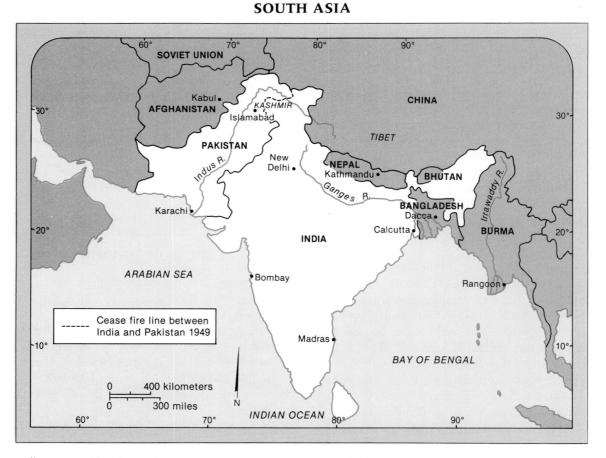

SOUTH ASIA

India's wars with Pakistan in 1949 and 1971 eventually led to the division of Pakistan into two countries. Name them, and explain how this division increased India's control of the region.

Japanese troops on the doorstep of India in World War II, felt that the Congress's demands were destructive.

In 1944 Gandhi was released from prison and negotiations for the terms of independence began between the British and the Indians. Gandhi was against any partition of the country. But Jinnah was adamant because he feared the Hindu majority. Jinnah wanted a government that would give greater freedom to various Indian provinces.

The British decided in favor of partition in 1946. Elections were to be held to determine which regions had a Muslim majority for the future state of Pakistan. The two areas of Muslim majority were found to be in the northwest and northeast of the country. Thus the new Muslim state was to have two parts, separated by over 1,000 miles of Indian territory.

In August 1947 two new countries were created—India with a Hindu majority and Pakistan with a mostly Muslim majority. Riots, which had been frequent since 1946, and religious communal killings erupted. The problem was that a geographic division did not allow for the needs nor wishes of the minorities in the respective regions. Muslims fled north, Hindus and Sikhs fled southeast and southwest. More than ten million people fled their homes in fear of religious persecution, making their way to either Hindu or Muslim territory. Hundreds of thousands were killed. Gandhi went from crisis area to crisis area trying to allay fears. He spoke out for religious tolerance and love. In 1948 he was killed by a Hindu fanatic who believed he was too soft on the Muslims.

India Under Nehru

Nehru was the first prime minister of India, and served until his death in 1964. With the horrors of partition before him, Nehru's main concern was to unify the diverse groups within India. Besides its many religions, India is splintered by language differences—hundreds of different languages and dialects are spoken by the people. Nehru pledged a secular, democratic state. The country's government was established as a parliamentary democracy.

India adopted a constitution in 1950 that divided the country into states whose borders were drawn as closely as possible along linguistic lines. Although Hindi was to be the nation's chief language, English was the common language of the educated.

To industrialize the country, Nehru guided India toward the adoption of a mixed economic system, with a combination of capitalism and socialism. In a series of five-year plans, the Indian government started vast irrigation projects and constructed new industries. The government assumed a major role in the planning of economic goals and activities but failed to lift the nation out of poverty.

Industrialization was an enormous task in a country in which more than 80 percent of the population lived in agricultural villages. Even so, India was successful in building dams to bring irrigation to farming areas and in establishing schools to educate the next generation of Indians. Steel mills were built to prepare an industrial base for the country.

In addition, Nehru faced violence over Kashmir, which stood between India and Pakistan. The United Nations sent forces to the region in a successful peacekeeping mission. But in 1965 another conflict arose between India and Pakistan.

Internationally, Nehru sought to steer a middle course between the United States and the Soviet Union. He was one of the founders of the nonaligned movement, made up of Asian and African nations that wanted to avoid allying themselves with either the Soviet Union or the United States. He was one of the leaders of the Bandung Conference of 1955, which first brought the nonaligned nations into informal agreement.

Indira Gandhi's India

In 1966 India chose Nehru's daughter, Indira Gandhi (IN-duh-ruh GAHN-dee), as prime minister. Though the country made great progress under her administration, her policies were often controversial. She instituted a sterilization program to combat India's overpopulation problem. Despite the government's continuing programs to encourage economic growth, poverty was still a major problem.

India moved forward in science and technology. Many students pursued higher education, both at home and abroad. India today is third in the number of scientists and technicians per capita after the United States and the Soviet Union. In 1974 India showed its scientific prowess by exploding a nuclear device. In 1981 India put a communications satellite into space.

In foreign relations, Indira Gandhi continued some of her father's nonalignment policies. However, she developed a strong relationship with the Soviet Union. The Soviets sent India large supplies of arms for its growing military. India's tilt toward the Soviet Union was caused by Nehru's nonalignment policy and partly because of United States' backing of Pakistan.

The war with Pakistan in 1971 was a triumph for India. The division of Pakistan into two countries made India the prime power on the Indian subcontinent. The new Pakistan was no threat, and Bangladesh was a poverty-stricken neighbor.

A Crisis for Indian Democracy

In the 1970's India suffered from political disunity, strikes, and disorder. In 1971 a massive influx of refugees from East Pakistan put strains on India's resources. In 1972 serious food shortages caused rioting. In some places provincial governments had to be taken over by the national government because of the disorder.

These conditions and a court ruling charging her with corruption in the 1971 election led Mrs. Gandhi to declare a state of emergency in 1975. This gave her the power to arrest her political opponents, restrict freedom of the press, and control prices and industrial production. Her actions led to a political crisis.

Prime Minister Gandhi was severely criticized during the time of emergency rule. Her supporters claimed her actions prevented a complete breakdown of Indian society. Others said that she had lost all respect for democratic institutions.

She lost the election of 1977 to Morarji Desai (MORE-uh-jee duh-SIE). Afterward, a government committee began to look into the question of her improper use of power during the emergency rule. Desai restored political freedom, and some of Gandhi's unpopular measures were abolished. But the next year problems of drought, food distribution, and religious conflict forced the Desai government to resign. In January 1980 Mrs. Gandhi was returned to power.

In 1984 Gandhi ordered the Indian army into the holiest shrine in the Sikh (SEEK) religion—the Golden Temple in Amritsar (ahm-RIT-sur). A band of Sikh holy men and their armed supporters were using it as a base for raids into local villages in a campaign to establish Sikh independence. As many as a thousand people were reported killed in the incident. India's fourteen million Sikhs regarded the invasion of the temple as an outrageous sacrilege. Sikh army officers mutinied. Later in the year Gandhi was murdered by a group of Sikh bodyguards. Her son Rajiv succeeded her.

Social Changes in India

Many changes have been made in Indian society since independence. The caste system, a distinctive feature of Indian society since early in its history, was legally abolished. Although the law did not end the caste system immediately, it was a start.

Rajiv Gandhi and staff campaign in New Delhi. He won the 1984 election by a large margin.

People in History

The Nehrus

No family has played a more important role in the affairs of modern India than the Nehru family. In the early years of the century Motilal Nehru, a cultivated lawyer and graduate of England's Cambridge University, was drawn to the Indian nationalist movement and became a leader of the Congress party.

His son, Jawaharlal, introduced him to Mohandas K. Gandhi. Although both Nehrus were at first skeptical of some of Gandhi's tactics, they were soon among his followers. Gandhi later declared, ''Jawaharlal is my political heir.'' After Gandhi's assassination Jawaharlal Nehru became India's first prime minister.

Nehru's only child, Indira, was born in the northern Indian city of Allahabad in 1917. Politics and the dream of independence were daily topics of discussion in her parents' home, and Gandhi was a frequent visitor.

After Indira's father became prime minister, Indira served as his hostess. Her husband died in 1960, and her father four years later. Indira became minister of Information and Broadcasting.

In January 1966 Indira became the third prime minister of independent India taking office at a critical time in India's history. The nation was in the midst of a two-year drought resulting in severe food shortages and a deepening economic crisis.

In 1975 an Indian court found Indira guilty of using illegal practices during the 1971 elections. Fearing chaos in the country; she imposed an almost dictatorial rule.

Unlike others, she chose to face elections, feeling that the people would rally as before to the family name. But she was defeated in the parliamentary elections of March 1977.

In 1978 she was again elected to Parliament but was jailed for allegedly blocking a probe of her son Sanjay's business dealings. She was soon released. Sanjay had been the favorite of her two sons and she was grooming him to succeed her. But he died in a flying accident in 1980, and Indira Gandhi became prime minister again. With the death of his brother, Indira's elder son Rajiv accepted the political tradition of the family. He ran for his brother's old seat in Parliament and won. Though he said, ''I know nothing about politics,'' his mother appointed him to a high post in the Congress party.

However, when his mother was assassinated in 1984, the members of her government turned to Rajiv as a figure who could rally the nation.

Rajiv's quiet dignity impressed the nation, and he was reelected prime minister in 1985 by a large margin. In what direction he will lead India is not yet known. He appealed for peace during the riots that resulted from his mother's death, and took the ceremonial role of lighting her funeral pyre.

1. How did childhood experiences affect Indira Gandhi's choice of her life's work?
2. How has the popularity of the Nehru family affected democratic government in India? Is the domination of one family ever good for a nation?

The caste system is woven into many aspects of Indian life but has been gradually weakened by urbanization. The growth of education has made possible professions or trades outside an individual's caste. It remains strongest in villages. The untouchables, or lowest caste, have been given equal legal rights and the government has provided a proportion of jobs and places in schools for them. However, little has changed in rural India, where the caste system remains in place.

The villages, home of the vast majority of the population, also have seen changes. The pull of tradition has been weakened by the growth of roads and railroads that link once isolated villages to the outside world. Agriculture has become more heavily mechanized, with tractors almost as common as bullock carts. As a result of education and public health facilities, the death rate has decreased significantly.

The Green Revolution, a combination of improved varieties of seeds, better irrigation, and the use of chemical fertilizer, arrived in parts of India. This technology has increased the yield from India's farms, enabling India to feed most of its enormous population.

This progress is precarious because of the problem of overpopulation. Although India was the first third-world country to have a family planning program, its population continues to grow at an alarming rate. This will be crucial for India's future development. Increasing population decreases food and water supplies, crowds classrooms, and prompts the move to the cities, which are not prepared to meet the needs of more people. Now with a population of over 700 million people, India is expected to surpass China's population by the year 2000.

Pakistan Divides

In contrast to India's secular state, Pakistan declared Islam as the state religion. It was the one unifying element of a country divided into two land areas almost a thousand miles apart. People of the two Pakistans also spoke different languages. The more populous eastern portion was poorer and had less representation in government.

Poverty was widespread and corruption was rampant. In 1958 a military coup brought Mohammed Ayub Khan (moe-HAHM-id ey-oob KAHN) to power. He was elected in 1960 and re-elected in 1965, but unrest and violent rioting in East Pakistan brought down his government in 1969. He was replaced by Mohammed Yahya Khan who declared martial law.

The Awami League, which wanted independence for East Pakistan, was growing in popularity. In the 1970 elections its supporters won a majority to an Assembly that was to write a new constitution for the country. When government troops moved in to curb rioting in East Pakistan in 1971, they committed many outrages against civilians. Millions of refugees fled into India. India entered the fighting, and full-scale war broke out between India and Pakistan. Pakistan was defeated.

The East Pakistanis established an independent nation called Bangladesh (bang-gluh-DESH). (See the map on page 662.) It has few resources and an enormous population of more than 100 million people. Like Pakistan about 70 percent of the population of Bangladesh live in villages that have no modern conveniences. In many areas electricity, telephones, and running water are unknown.

Bangladesh has suffered in recent years from a series of floods and droughts that have resulted in serious food shortages. Although one of the world's poorest nations, it has managed to survive.

Pakistan has had difficulty achieving political stability. Elections are often promised by its military governments but seldom held. The current president, Zia ul-Haq (ZEE-uh ool-HAHK), is thought to be attempting to develop nuclear weapons; there is concern as to how these would be used. To stay popular he has backed a return to a more rigorous Islam known as fundamentalism. The religious precepts of the Koran, rather than civil laws, guide public and government actions.

In foreign policy, Pakistan took a different path from India. It strongly aligned itself with the United States. After the war between India and China, it developed a friendly relation with India's foe. China and Pakistan signed agreements in trade and aid.

Since the Soviet invasion of neighboring Afghanistan, Pakistan has faced the problem of Afghan refugees. Over three million of them are now in Pakistan, which does not have the resources to absorb them and meet their needs. Their fate remains very much in doubt.

1. **Mapping:** Use the map on page 662 to locate the two parts of Pakistan that split into Pakistan and Bangladesh. How large are they in relation to India?
2. In your own words, briefly define or identify: partition, nonaligned movement, Green Revolution.
3. Why did the partition of India result in violence and a mass movement of people?
4. What factors kept Pakistan from remaining a united nation?
- Should India use its resources for building things like space satellites and nuclear weapons, or for helping build up the country's industry and agriculture to fight poverty and illiteracy? Give reasons for your answer.

CONFLICT IN INDOCHINA

The French colonized Indochina—Vietnam, Cambodia, and Laos—in the nineteenth century under Napoleon III. In Vietnam, the largest of the three countries, French settlers took over huge tracts of land for plantations. The French also exploited the country's mines and forests. French nationals administered the country; Vietnamese held only lower positions of authority. The political participation of the Vietnamese in their own country was restricted. The resentment that sprang from these conditions led to protests by many Vietnamese.

The French Phase

During World War II Vietnam fell to the Japanese. Vietnamese resistance to the Japanese occupation was organized by the League of Vietnamese Independence, also called the Viet Minh. This organization had been founded in 1941 by Ho Chi Minh (HOE-CHEE-MIN). Though himself a Communist, Ho Chi Minh believed that independence could only be achieved through the efforts of a broad coalition of Vietnamese.

By the time the Japanese surrendered, the Viet Minh represented the strongest political force in the country. On September 2, 1945, using the words of the United States Declaration of Independence, Ho Chi Minh proclaimed Vietnam a free and independent nation.

The French, however, did not want to give up their colony. They set up a rival government under their control. Negotiations failed to produce an agreement. In 1946 war broke out between the French and Vietnamese. Fighting continued until 1954, when the Vietnamese defeated the French at the crucial battle of Dien Bien Phu (DYEN-BYEN-foo).

The United States at first gave no direct support to the French. But the Soviet Union gave help to Vietnam, awakening United States fears of the spread of Communist influence. The United States gave the French forces money and supplies. By 1954 the United States was paying about 70 percent of the cost of the war.

In 1954 a conference to decide the fate of Indochina was held at Geneva. Both Laos and Cambodia were given independence. Vietnam was temporarily divided into two zones. The northern zone was to be governed by the Viet Minh. The southern zone was put temporarily under the control of the French-backed government. In 1956 elections were to be held to determine the future of the country. The United States attended the conference but did not sign the Geneva Accords.

A Growing United States Involvement

After the Geneva settlement Communist guerrillas in Laos waged a war that threatened to take over the country. The United States responded by sending aid to Laos and President Kennedy accepted a negotiated settlement in 1961, which set up a coalition government for Laos. However, internal strife continued.

In Cambodia, Prince Norodom Sihanouk (NOR-uh-dum SEE-hah-nook) was the head of government. He tried to keep Cambodia out of the strife in its two neighboring countries.

In the southern zone of Vietnam, the United States threw its support to Ngo Dinh Diem (noh-den-ZEE-ehm). In 1955 he proclaimed the southern zone of Vietnam a republic. Relying on United States backing, Diem refused to hold the national elections agreed on at Geneva. He became the first president of South Vietnam.

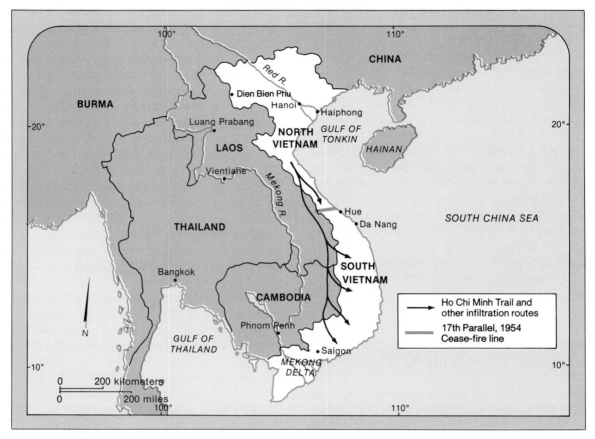

Explain why Cambodia could not have avoided being drawn into the Vietnam conflict.

A Catholic in a primarily Buddhist land, Diem ruled in an authoritarian manner. He failed to make needed reforms in the economy and government. As he lost popular support, opponents formed the National Liberation Front (NLF). Its military wing became known as the **Vietcong.** Its goal was to overthrow the Diem government and reunite North and South Vietnam.

The NLF received aid from Ho Chi Minh. The United States, which had been training the South Vietnamese army since 1956, supplied aid to Diem's forces. In 1961 President Kennedy increased military aid to South Vietnam and sent 10,000 military ''advisers'' to help.

Diem's efforts to deal with the civil war were not successful. By 1963 opposition had grown. Buddhist monks were burning themselves in public to protest his policies. On November 1, 1963, a coup by South Vietnamese generals overthrew Diem and he was assassinated.

In 1964 it was claimed that a North Vietnamese ship fired on a United States ship in the Gulf of Tonkin (TAHN-kin), off North Vietnam. At President Lyndon B. Johnson's urging, Congress passed the Tonkin Gulf Resolution. This granted the president broad powers to wage war. More importantly, it provided the legal basis for what was to become a major United States military involvement in Indochina.

The United States Sends Troops

The Vietcong drew their support from the people of South Vietnam. In hostile areas they carried out hit-and-run guerrilla warfare, often receiving food and medical supplies from friendly noncombatants. By 1965 it looked as if the NLF might defeat the government. North Vietnamese combat units arrived in the South in March of that year.

In February 1965 the United States began bombing North Vietnam in an attempt to stop the advances of the NLF. The first United States Marines in a direct combat role went ashore in March. By the end of the year 184,000 United States troops were fighting in South Vietnam.

The United States forces soon found that their superior firepower and technology were not enough to defeat the Vietcong. The Vietcong troops could not be singled out from the rest of the South Vietnamese. They knew the terrain and could attack and escape without being drawn into direct battle. The United States then resorted to tactics such as "search and destroy," in which a village suspected of harboring Vietcong could be burned and its people relocated. When this strategy failed, jungles were sprayed with chemicals to defoliate them, exposing Vietcong hiding places. "Carpet" bombing and the use of napalm were last resorts. During the war United States' planes dropped more bomb tonnage on Vietnam than during all of World War II. The enormous destruction wreaked on the country led to protests in the United States.

But the firepower was not enough. The United States government sent in more troops. At the height of its involvement, the United States had more than 550,000 troops in South Vietnam. The Soviet Union and China also sent supplies to the North Vietnamese but at much lower levels.

In January 1968 the National Liberation Front and its North Vietnamese allies launched the Tet Offensive. They attacked United States and government strongholds throughout the country, including every major city. Even the symbol of the United States presence in the country, the United States Embassy, was besieged. The United States military commander, General William Westmoreland, called for more troops. But by this time the United States was weary of the war and skeptical of predictions of victory. President Johnson called for a halt to the bombing of North Vietnam (the bombing continued in South Vietnam). He announced that he would spend the rest of his term seeking a peace. Johnson's Vice-President Hubert Humphrey ran unsuccessfully in the 1968 election against Richard Nixon.

Vietnamization

In 1969, his first year of office, President Richard Nixon announced a new policy to transfer combat operations to the South Vietnamese. The United States troops would be gradually phased out although United States air power would support the South Vietnamese troops. This policy became known as Vietnamization.

Although United States troop strength declined, the scope of the war increased. The United States and South Vietnamese forces invaded Cambodia in 1970 to attack areas where the North Vietnamese and Vietcong troops had fled, taking advantage of Cambodia's weakness. Cambodia's Prince Sihanouk was overthrown by Lon Nol, who demanded the removal of the troops. Sihanouk fled to China, where he set up a government in exile. Although no more invasions were launched, the United States continued to bomb Cambodia.

With United States air support, the South Vietnamese army invaded Laos in 1971. North Vietnam had been sending troops and supplies to the Vietcong through Laos on what became known as the Ho Chi Minh Trail.

In March 1972 North Vietnam launched a broad offensive. The United States responded with a heightened bombing campaign throughout North Vietnam and the mining of the country's major port, Haiphong (hie-FAHNG) harbor. By the autumn of 1972 a stalemate had been reached.

Negotiations had been carried on in Paris since 1968 and a breakthrough was reached near the end of 1972. But it was difficult to get the South Vietnam government, under President Nguyen Van Thieu (NWIN VAHN-TYOO), to agree. To show Thieu its commitment to South Vietnam, the United States launched the heaviest bombing of the war against North Vietnam. In early 1973 the Paris Accords were signed.

The Cost of the War

The Paris Accords allowed the North Vietnamese troops to remain in place in South Vietnam and recognized the political influence of the National Liberation Front. The agreement also permitted the United States to continue to supply Thieu's military needs. Finally, United States combat troops left South Vietnam.

Over 56,000 United States soldiers died in Vietnam and more than 300,000 had been wounded. The United States had spent $150 billion on its longest war, making it one of the costliest in the nation's history. For the Vietnamese the costs were much higher. More than one million had been killed and the fighting had destroyed parts of Vietnam.

The Paris Accords were only a temporary solution. They provided only a face-saving way of allowing the United States to remove its troops. Soon after they were signed, both sides accused the other of breaking the agreement. For a time, millions of dollars in United States aid continued to pour into South Vietnam; then aid was cut off by Congress. In 1975 the North Vietnamese conquered South Vietnam, unifying the country. The capital was at Hanoi (hah-NOY), the old North Vietnamese capital. Saigon (sie-GAHN), which had been the capital of the South, was renamed Ho Chi Minh City.

Aftermath of the War

In Cambodia at the time of the Lon Nol coup, the Communist guerrillas known as the Khmer Rouge (KMEHR ROOJ) were a small force. Their support grew with the intensive bombing that extended farther and farther into the country. By 1975 more than two million Cambodians had become refugees, and hundreds of thousands were killed. The Khmer Rouge took control of the government in April 1975 under the leadership of Pol Pot.

During the next three-and-a-half years they attempted to destroy all of Cambodia's social institutions. All places of worship were closed; many Buddhist monks were executed. The populations of the cities were driven into the countryside, where many died of starvation and exhaustion. Schools and hospitals were destroyed. Money and private trade were banned. Officials of the old regime were tortured and killed, and finally the Khmer Rouge turned on the population in a policy

In any war the land and people involved suffer destruction and bloodshed. What does this photograph tell you about the impact of the Vietnam War on that country?

The Vietnam Memorial in Washington, D.C., lists the names of 57,939 American service men and women killed in that conflict. Why are memorials important?

of national genocide. Perhaps two million out of a total population of seven million died. Many others fled to refugee camps in neighboring countries. In 1977 and 1978 the Khmer Rouge attacked villages across the border in Thailand and Vietnam.

In 1978 Vietnam invaded Cambodia, renamed Kampuchea (kam-poo-CHEE-uh), and overthrew the Pol Pot government. The Vietnamese set up a friendly government in its place and kept some troops in the country. A new civil war started in Kampuchea, with the Soviet Union supporting the North Vietnamese-backed government and China backing the remnants of Pol Pot's regime.

Relations between Vietnam and China became strained. In 1978 China ended economic aid to Vietnam. Claiming that the Vietnamese were mistreating Chinese in Vietnam, China invaded the northern border region of Vietnam in 1979. The conflict faded after the Chinese had taken and then abandoned a small part of Vietnam.

The continued fighting in Indochina produced more than 800,000 refugees between the years 1975 and 1980. Around 300,000 Vietnamese, unhappy with the Communist rule there, fled their country in very crowded boats. Known as the boat people, many of these refugees died on the open seas.

What to do with these refugees caused international problems. By 1985 the United States had taken in nearly 700,000 refugees, by far the largest

number. Many refugees remain in primitive camps in neighboring countries of the region, homeless, poverty-stricken, and without a country to aid them.

SECTION REVIEW

1. Mapping: Use the map on page 668 to locate the countries of Indochina. Where was the dividing line that separated North and South Vietnam?
2. In your own words, briefly define or identify: Vietcong, Tet Offensive, Vietnamization, Paris Accords.
3. Why was it difficult to defeat the Vietcong?
4. What were the advantages of the Vietnamization program for the United States?
5. Why did the Vietnam War spread to Laos and Cambodia?
■ What lessons do you think the United States should draw from the experience in Vietnam?

SOUTHEAST ASIA

Southeast Asia has experienced great changes since World War II. Many new independent countries have been formed. The region, so diverse in its cultures, languages, and religions, has seen great economic growth.

Southeast Asia comprises part of mainland Asia and islands scattered in the Pacific. It includes the countries of Indochina, the Philippines, Indonesia, Singapore, Malaysia, Thailand, and Burma.

The Philippines

As promised, the United States gave the Philippines its independence after World War II. On July 4, 1946, the country became a republic. It kept its close ties with the United States, which maintains military bases in the strategically located nation. The two countries signed a mutual defense treaty, and the Philippines became a member of SEATO.

During the 1950's Communist-led Huk guerrillas provoked virtual civil war in the country. They were suppressed in 1954, but political violence continued to be a problem.

High population growth aggravated poverty and unemployment. Violent protests in the 1970's caused President Ferdinand Marcos to declare martial law in 1972. Ruling by decree, he moved to stabilize prices and ordered some land reforms. Political opposition was suppressed.

In 1981 Marcos partially lifted martial law and some political prisoners were released. But the assassination of opposition leader Benigno Aquino in 1983 led to new demonstrations against the regime. Relations with the United States have been strained because of the human rights violations that have afflicted the country. The Philippine government also faces a rebellion by Muslim secessionists on the island of Mindanao.

Indonesia

The Japanese ousted the Dutch from the Dutch East Indies in 1942. The nationalist movement that supported independence from the Netherlands was strengthened. Its leader, Achmed Sukarno (AHK-med soo-KAHR-noh), declared Indonesia an independent republic in 1945. But the Netherlands wanted to retain its valuable colony and attempted to reestablish control. It took four years of bitter fighting and negotiations before the Dutch granted independence in 1949.

Sukarno became president of independent Indonesia. During his term of office the country's population rose faster than food production. (It is today the fifth most populous country in the world.) Sukarno's economic policies were not successful and resulted in unrest.

In international relations Sukarno was one of the founders of the nonaligned movement. In 1955 he hosted the Bandung Conference, which called for unity among African and Asian people and a neutral stance between the superpowers.

Various revolts in Indonesia, which Sukarno believed were encouraged by the United States, caused him to follow anti-United States policies. He involved his country in a territorial dispute with Malaysia. Soviet-trained Indonesian troops made raids into Malaysia. In 1965, when Malaysia was elected to the United Nations Security Council, Sukarno withdrew his country from the United Nations.

Indonesia's Communist party was the third largest in the world. After an attempted Communist coup in 1965, General Suharto (suh-HAHRT-oo) led the army in a campaign to eliminate the Communists. More than 300,000 people were killed. In 1967 Sukarno was stripped of his power and Suharto took his place. Suharto won reelection the following year, and has been reelected since. Indonesia's political stability has been restored under Suharto. His policies have fostered economic growth. The discovery of oil reserves within the country has increased the nation's wealth, although the state-run oil agency has been plagued by corruption.

Under Suharto, Indonesia ended its policy of hostility to the West. Suharto also reopened negotiations with Malaysia.

Malaysia and Singapore

Malaya gained its independence from Great Britain in 1957 after the suppression of a Communist uprising. In 1963 Malaya united with Singapore and other islands to form the Federation of Malaysia. However, the Federation had ethnic problems. The majority of the population were Malaysians,

A "dragon" glides across Singapore harbor. Why do people today wish to preserve their traditions?

who controlled the government. A large Chinese minority and smaller Indian minority controlled much of the business and industry. The Chinese population was heavily concentrated in Singapore. In 1965 Singapore withdrew from the Federation and declared its independence.

Singapore, one of the great ports of the world, has had extraordinary success in terms of economic development. Fueled by its position as an international banking center, Singapore has dramatically raised its standards of education and living. It has one of the highest economic growth rates in the world.

Malaysia was strongly affected by the problems of Indochina. It has been one of the stopping points for the boat people who fled Vietnam in 1978. Reluctant to admit them because they were primarily of Chinese ethnic origin, Malaysia's policy has fluctuated between prohibition and letting some of them in.

Thailand and Burma

Thailand was the only country in the region not to be colonized by a European power. During World War II it yielded to Japanese occupation and was used as a staging area for the Japanese thrust against Malaysia.

After the war Thailand fluctuated between elected governments and military coups. It had trouble with Communist uprisings in some of its outlying regions. A member of SEATO, its foreign policy was strongly pro-Western. It allowed United States troops to be based there during the Vietnam War. Thailand also sent a contingent of its own forces to fight there.

The aftereffects of the war, particularly the refugee problem, significantly affected Thailand. In 1978 and 1979 refugees flooded into the country. In spite of appeals from the United States for better treatment of the refugees, the Thai government forced them into refugee camps along the Kampuchean border. The fighting between the Vietnamese-backed Kampuchean government and the Khmer Rouge spilled over into Thailand as Vietnamese troops attacked its borders.

Burma, which was occupied by Japanese troops during World War II, was liberated by Allied forces before the end of the war. The British gave Burma its independence in 1948. Burma fluctu-

ated between civilian and military rule. Armed uprisings by both Communists and ethnic tribespeople have troubled the country. The rebels won a degree of autonomy. For some years in the late 1960's and 1970's the country was closed to the influences of the outside world. Burma has tried to remain neutral in the Cold War.

The Pacific Basin

One of the most hopeful signs in the region of Southeast Asia has been the organization known as ASEAN. The Association of Southeast Asian Nations was formed in 1967 to promote economic and political cooperation.

The original members included Thailand, Malaysia, Singapore, Indonesia, and the Philippines. The organization has annual ministerial meetings that set policy.

The ASEAN nations plus China, Japan, South Korea, Hong Kong, and Taiwan form an area known as the Pacific Basin. One of the most important world developments in recent years has been the economic transformation of this area. In the 1970's when the West suffered economic reverses, most of these countries experienced double-digit growth. They maintain a high rate of growth today. The manufacturing, trading, and economic power of this region has become as important as that of Europe and the United States. Trade between the United States and Asia is greater than American trade with Europe. This shift in economic power will have great significance for the future.

SECTION REVIEW

1. Mapping: Use the Atlas map on page 755 to find the ASEAN nations. Why is their proximity to each other important economically?
2. In your own words, briefly define or identify: ASEAN, General Suharto, Pacific Basin.
3. How did the Vietnam War affect Thailand?
4. What were some of the problems of the Philippines that led to martial law?
■ Do you think that the suppression of political opposition, as in the Philippines, is ever justified for reasons of national emergency?

Reviewing the Chapter

Chapter Summary

In China civil war resulted in the establishment of the People's Republic of China in 1949. Under the leadership of Mao Zedong, China experienced new social upheavals. After his death a new leadership set "four modernizations" as the country's goals.

In 1950 North Korea invaded South Korea, and United Nations and United States forces came to defend the South. China entered the war when the fighting neared its border. The war ended in a truce at the original border.

Japan was governed by a United States occupation force that wrote a new democratic constitution for the country. After occupation ended, Japan's economy grew at an unprecedented rate.

When India won independence in 1948 it split into Pakistan and India. India made slow progress toward modernization. Pakistan suffered a civil war dividing it into Pakistan and Bangladesh.

The countries of Vietnam, Cambodia, and Laos won independence, but the division of Vietnam led to war. The United States sent troops to help the government of South Vietnam, but the NLF won, uniting the country. The fighting sent many refugees fleeing their homes.

The democratic countries of South Asia formed the ASEAN and experienced economic growth.

1. Which Asian country experienced the greatest economic growth from World War II to the present?
2. Has the Communist government succeeded in modernizing China?
3. In what two Asian wars did the United States participate?

Using Your Vocabulary

1. How did the Chinese Communists' policy of land redistribution affect the peasants?
2. Describe the communes established by the Chinese Communists.
3. What was the major aim of China's Great Leap Forward?
4. What did Mao attempt to do in the Great Proletarian Cultural Revolution?
5. Describe the main purpose of SEATO.
6. Name the four modernizations of the leaders who followed Mao in China.
7. What is the significance of the term Japan, Inc.?
8. How did MITI contribute to Japan's postwar economic growth?
9. Explain the trade imbalance between the United States and Japan.
10. How did partition affect India?
11. What was the nonaligned movement?
12. Describe the Green Revolution.
13. What was the significance of the Vietcong?
14. Explain the Tet Offensive.
15. How did Vietnamization change United States involvement in the Vietnam War?
16. What was the purpose of ASEAN?
17. What are the countries of the Pacific Basin?
18. Explain why Singapore has been economically successful since the 1960's.
19. Describe Thailand's foreign policy. Was it primarily pro-Western or pro-Communist?
20. Identify the type of transformation that the Pacific Basin has undergone recently.

Developing Your Geography Skills

1. Use the map on page 654 to describe the major troop movements of the Korean War.
2. Use the Atlas map on page 755 to describe why China and India have trouble raising enough food to feed their people.
3. Use the map on page 668 to explain why Laos and Cambodia entered the Vietnam War.
4. Use the map on page 662 to explain why India's support for Bangladesh helped that country to become independent from Pakistan.

Recalling the Facts

1. How did the Korean War affect relations between the United States and the PRC?
2. Why did the United States and the PRC decide to seek a more peaceful relationship?
3. What has been the main concern of the Chinese leaders since the death of Mao Zedong?
4. Why did the United States want to encourage a healthy economy in Japan?
5. What economic disadvantages did Japan face in 1945?
6. What three parts of Japan's society cooperated in building economic growth?
7. Why did partition cause violence in India?
8. Why was industrialization such a difficult task for India?
9. How did the Awami League affect Pakistan?
10. Why did the United States first become involved in the Vietnam conflict?
11. What act of the United States Congress provided the legal basis for the nation's military involvement in Indochina?
12. How did the bombing of Cambodia during the Vietnam War affect that country?
13. How have conditions in Indonesia improved under General Suharto?
14. Name two countries of Southeast Asia that have been affected by the flood of refugees from war-torn countries in the area.
15. How has the economic importance of the Pacific Basin countries changed in recent years?

Essay Questions

1. In your own words, describe the reasons why the Communists defeated the Nationalists in the Chinese civil war.
2. Describe the effects of the Cultural Revolution on China's society.
3. Write a brief description of the condition of South Korea today.
4. In your own words, describe how the United States occupation changed Japanese society.
5. Write a summary of the reasons for Japanese economic success since World War II.

6. Describe how Japan's society today reflects both old traditions and new influences.
7. In your own words, explain why the Muslims opposed a united and independent India.
8. Explain how the Indian constitution attempted to reflect the country's language differences.
9. Describe how the Nehru family has influenced India.
10. Explain why the superior firepower of United States forces was not able to defeat the Vietcong. Summarize the reasons why the fighting in Southeast Asia has produced so many refugees.
11. Describe the changing relations of Indonesia and the West since World War II.
12. Explain why the Pacific Basin countries are becoming more important in the progress of the world economy.

Critical Thinking

1. What facts appeared with the material on Japan's economic progress?
2. How can such facts as you listed be verified? Be as specific as possible in your answers.
3. What were the unstated assumptions of Mao Zedong's policies toward China?
4. Indira Gandhi in India and Ferdinand Marcos in the Philippines claimed to be democratic leaders. What logical inconsistencies were there in this claim and their policies toward their countries?
5. The National Liberation Front, the government of South Vietnam, and the government of the United States all claimed to have the support of the people of South Vietnam. Which of these were warranted claims and which unwarranted claims, according to your reading of the facts?
6. Industrialization and urbanization were responsible for many social changes in Asian nations. What facts from this chapter can you use to verify this statement?
7. Although Asian nations have each introduced certain elements of Western culture to their people, what assumptions can be drawn about their efforts to preserve the past?

CHAPTER 30

AFRICA and the MIDDLE EAST TODAY

1945–Present

Objectives

· *To explain the origins of the Arab-Israeli conflict*

· *To describe recent developments in the Middle East*

· *To discuss the process of decolonization in Africa*

· *To identify the challenges facing Africa today*

Following World War II more new nations were created in the Middle East and Africa than anywhere else in the world. They varied greatly in size, wealth, and population. In some places, the march to independence was peaceful. In others, bloody fighting took place between colonial people and Europeans.

After independence, more changes meant new concerns. In the Middle East and some African countries, oil resources produced an enormous increase in wealth. Nations that were once poor now became important powers in the world. Other countries had few resources and large populations. The creation of the state of Israel resulted in a series of conflicts between Israel and its Arab neighbors.

The Middle East and Africa are at the same time ancient and new, with widely diverse peoples and cultures. In some places, attempts at modernization have met resistance by those who hold to traditional ways of life.

The task of modernization in the face of problems has been a challenge to all the new nations. Rapid urbanization and population growth have slowed progress. In Africa modernization has been made more difficult by periodic famines that threaten to be among the major tragedies of the twentieth century. By the year 2000 the population of Africa is expected to surpass the one billion mark. The ability of most African nations to meet the basic needs of this population is doubtful, particularly in the face of continuing political instability.

The strategic location of the Middle East brought the superpowers into local conflicts between nations and groups. Important mineral resources made some African countries targets of both the United States and the Soviet Union.

THE MIDDLE EAST AND NORTH AFRICA

The region of the Middle East and North Africa spreads from Morocco on the Atlantic Ocean in the west to Iran in the east. The Middle East and North Africa have been a crossroads of diverse civilizations since ancient times. Although mainly Muslim and Arab, the region has an important Jewish and Christian population. Since World War II, many nations have won their independence from former European colonial powers. Because of the Middle East's strategic location and large oil reserves, conflicts between its nations have often been important to the rivalry between the superpowers.

Modern Turkey

Spanning the continents of Europe and Asia, the modern state of Turkey came into being after World War I brought an end to the Ottoman Empire. Mustapha Kemal (MOOS-tah-fah keh-MAHL), the first leader of independent Turkey, set out on a bold course to modernize and westernize Turkey. Islam was no longer the state religion, and religious orders were suppressed. Kemal replaced the Arabic script with the Roman alphabet, adopted the western calendar, and required the use of family names. He took the name Kemal Atatürk. A western legal code was drawn up. Women were given equal rights and no longer had to wear veils. At Atatürk's death in 1938, Turkey had become the most westernized country in the Middle East.

Turkey became a charter member of the United Nations. Atatürk's attempts to make Turkey a modern European nation were continued by others. Turkey was a loyal supporter of the West, joining NATO in 1952. It plans to join the Common Market by the year 2000.

Political problems gave rise to shifts between democratic governments and military rulers. In 1983 the Motherland party won a majority in Turkish general elections, ending three years of military rule. Turkey has also been involved with Greece in a dispute over the island of Cyprus. Turkey invaded Cyprus in 1974, and continues to occupy a large portion of the island.

The Creation of Israel

In the years after the Balfour Declaration, Jewish immigration to Palestine increased. This led to friction with the Arabs who already lived there, since both peoples saw the area as their homeland. British policy fluctuated. In 1937 it proposed the creation of two states, but the Arabs rejected this proposal. Two years later a British plan to restrict new Jewish immigration was strongly opposed by the Zionist movement.

When the horrors of the Holocaust were revealed at the end of the war, the British were pressured to increase the number of Jews allowed to immigrate. In 1946 Palestine had 678,000 Jews and 1,269,000 Arabs. Fighting between the two populations was frequent. In 1947 the British asked the United Nations to find a solution to the problem.

In November 1947 the United Nations passed a resolution calling for the partition of Palestine into two states—one Arab, the other Jewish. The two states were to be joined in an economic union, and Jerusalem would be an international zone. The two proposed states were to replace Palestine no later than October 1948.

On May 14, 1948, the day the British mandate expired, David Ben-Gurion, on behalf of the Jewish National Council, proclaimed "the establishment of the Jewish State in Palestine to be called Israel." The United States recognized the new nation within hours, as did the Soviet Union a few days later.

On May 15 Lebanon, Syria, Iraq, Jordan, and Egypt attacked Israel. The Israelis, fighting for their survival, held their own and then went on the offensive. In 1949, after mediation under United Nations supervision, an armistice was signed between Israel and some of the Arab states. In the fighting, Israel had increased its territory by 50 percent over the original partition plan. Jerusalem was divided between Israel and Jordan. The territory of the Arab state that was to be created in Palestine was divided among Israel, Egypt, and Jordan.

During the fighting, hundreds of thousands of Arab Palestinians fled or were driven from their homes. Most went to refugee camps in Arab states. The problem of where these Palestinian refugees would live became a cause of continuing conflict in the Middle East.

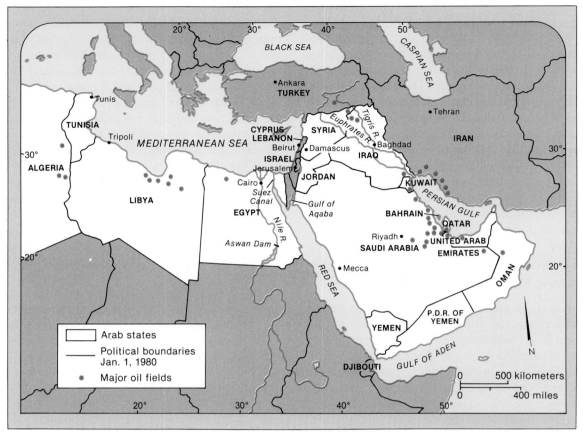

Both the Suez Canal and the major oil fields in the Persian Gulf area are of strategic importance to the Middle East. Why?

Building a Nation

The armistice did not bring peace. Israel had no road or rail connection with its neighbors and could not fly over their territory. A boycott of Israeli products was organized. The only Middle Eastern countries to recognize Israel were Turkey and Iran.

The government of Israel was a parliamentary democracy. Its first Prime Minister was David Ben-Gurion and the President was Chaim Weizmann (HIME VITES-muhn). David Ben-Gurion and his Labor party dominated Israel's politics in its early years. The country had a large number of smaller parties representing both political and religious views.

By the Law of Return, every Jew in the world had the right to citizenship in Israel. Many immigrants poured into the country, both refugees from Europe and Jews who had previously lived in Arab countries. Absorbing and educating these people put a strain on the Israeli economy. The country was helped by contributions from Jews all over the world and aid from the United States government. The West German government also paid reparations to the nation of Israel and to individual victims of the Holocaust.

The country used this aid to further its economic development. By using scientific methods and hard work, the Israelis irrigated the land. Former desert areas became citrus groves, orchards for olives and figs, and wheat fields. They experimented with different kinds of farms. One type that came to symbolize the spirit of Israel was the **kibbutz,** a farm cooperative where the people lived a communal life. Jobs were rotated among all the members of the community. From its profits, the kibbutz provided food, clothing, shelter, and medicine for its people.

New Arab States

What is today Saudi Arabia was in 1900 a patchwork of emirates, small areas with a local ruler, or emir. In the early years of the century, Ibn Saud (IH-bun sah-OOD) captured the city of Riyadh (ree-YAHD) and unified the emirates surrounding the Arabian peninsula. In 1932 the kingdom of Saudi Arabia was created. As the site of Mecca, the city to which all faithful Muslims make a pilgrimage at least once in their lives, it is the center of the Arab world.

Saud's kingdom was poor. Its only assets were pearls on the coast, date palms, and camels. He declared, "If anyone were to offer a million pounds, he would be welcome to all the concessions he wanted in my country." But the discovery of oil in 1938 transformed the country. Today it has more than one-fourth of all the world's proven oil reserves.

In 1932 Iraq (formerly Mesopotamia) became the first Arab nation to gain independence. Less affected by the 1948 war than other Arab nations, Iraq also developed its oil reserves. It was a monarchy until 1958, when a military coup ushered in a period of unstable government.

Jordan, originally part of British-controlled Palestine, gained its independence in 1946. The Arab country most affected by the 1948 war, it annexed the West Bank of the Jordan River in 1950. It had taken in the greatest number of Palestinian refugees and offered them Jordanian citizenship. The Palestinians were more westernized and highly educated than most other Jordanians. They became a majority in Jordan. In 1951 a Palestinian assassinated King Abdullah (ab-DULL-ah) for trying to make peace with Israel. Abdullah's grandson, King Hussein (hooh-SAYN), assumed the throne in 1952 and remains in power today.

French troops left Syria in 1946, and Syria became independent. Earlier the French had carved out the new nation of Lebanon from territory belonging to Syria.

Lebanon was the only Arab country in which Christians were thought to be a majority. By the National Pact of 1943 government positions were allotted by religious sect, based on a 1932 census. The president was to be a Christian and the prime minister a Muslim. Under the pact, Christians agreed not to tie the country to France, and Muslims not to reunite with Syria.

The Christian majority in Lebanon was small. The addition of 150,000 Palestinians in 1949 tipped the population balance to the Muslims. The unraveling of the pact in the 1970's brought civil war to Lebanon. Today, Lebanon is still challenged by civil war, unstable government, and terrorist-related activities.

Postwar Egypt

Since independence in 1936, Egypt had been ruled by King Farouk (fah-RUKE), a constitutional monarch. His life-style, spending millions on luxuries while 80 percent of the peasants, or *fellahin* (fel-uh-HEEN), lived in dire poverty, caused serious criticism. Many blamed the defeat of Egypt by Israel in 1948 on his corrupt government.

In early 1952 anti-British and antiroyal rioting broke out in Cairo. A coup later in the year forced King Farouk's abdication. Gamal Abdel Nasser (guh-MAHL AB-del NAH-suhr) emerged as the new leader.

Domestically, Nasser tried to deal with the economic inequalities that plagued Egypt. Many of its large business enterprises were owned by foreigners. A small native elite owned the majority of the land and buildings. In a country where almost all the people lived on the 3 percent of the land adjoining the Nile, land was particularly precious. Under Nasser, large landholdings were broken up and distributed to the poor, and attempts were made to modernize agriculture. Strong government control was exercised over major industries and utilities to divide the country's meager resources more fairly. Although Nasser worked for the welfare of his people, he did not allow any political opposition to his policies.

One of the first tests of Nasser's leadership role before becoming president in 1956 involved the Suez Canal. In 1922 pressure from Egyptian nationalists forced Great Britain to declare Egypt a partially free state. However, the British reserved the right to protect the Suez Canal and provide for Egypt's defense. In 1936 Great Britain and Egypt agreed to an alliance, cancelled later by Nasser.

In 1954 Egypt reached an agreement with Great Britain over the stationing of British troops in the Suez Canal zone. British troops would leave the canal zone over the next twenty months, but civilian technicians would remain. Egypt agreed that it would allow the Sudan, which had been ruled jointly by the Egyptians and British, to decide by plebiscite, or vote of the people, whether it would be part of Egypt or independent. In 1956 the Sudanese chose independence.

As leader of a country that lay partly in Asia and partly in Africa, Nasser wanted to play a major world role. He was one of the founders of the nonaligned movement and played a major role at the Bandung Conference in 1955. He spoke of the importance of independence from the superpowers, but in later years strongly favored support from the Soviet Union.

Nasser became a spokesperson for Arab nationalism and **Pan Arabism.** Pan Arabism was the belief that all the people who spoke Arabic were really one nation. If the Arabs unified, they could play a major role in world affairs. Egypt's location between the Asian and North African Arabs made it a natural focus for this idea. Other Arab leaders feared that Nasser's Pan Arabism was just a means to achieve Egyptian dominance.

The Arab-Israeli Conflict

In 1955 the United States agreed to give Egypt aid to build the Aswan Dam on the Nile River. However, in July 1956, when it was learned that Egypt had purchased Soviet military equipment, the United States withdrew the offer. In retaliation, Nasser nationalized the Suez Canal.

French troops arrive in Port Said for duty during the Suez Canal Crisis. How did the outcome of the Suez crisis affect United States policy in the region?

Great Britain, France, and Israel united because of their common interests in keeping the canal open. They launched an attack against Egypt in October 1956. The Israelis occupied the Sinai Peninsula. The Egyptians responded by sinking ships to block the waterway.

The United Nations demanded that the attacking nations withdraw. A United Nations peacekeeping force was sent to the end of the Sinai Peninsula, and Israel was given assurances that it could use the Gulf of Aqaba (AHK-ah-bah). The three countries withdrew.

The Suez crisis marked the end of British dominance in the Middle East. The United States, fearing the spread of communism in the area, took Great Britain's place. Then, in 1957 President Eisenhower announced that the United States would give military and economic support to any regime in the region fighting communism. Known as the Eisenhower Doctrine, it was used in 1958 when United States troops landed in Lebanon to protect its government.

In 1967, at Nasser's request, the United Nations removed its peacekeeping force from the Sinai. Egyptian soldiers took over the United Nations positions and closed the Gulf of Aqaba. Israel regarded this action as an act of war.

On June 5, 1967, Israeli bombers attacked Egyptian airfields, destroying Egypt's air force on the ground. In the Six-Day War, Israel defeated the armies of Egypt, Syria, and Jordan. A cease-fire negotiated by the United Nations halted the fighting. Israel occupied the Sinai Peninsula, Gaza Strip, Syria's Golan Heights, the Jordanian section of Jerusalem, and the West Bank of the Jordan.

Israel announced that it would not give up any territory until the Arab states agreed to recognize it. The Six-Day War was a triumph for Israel. It showed Israel's military superiority over all its neighbors.

Modern Iran

In 1921 Reza Khan (REE-zah KAHN) established a military dictatorship in Persia (later renamed Iran). In 1925 he was named hereditary shah of the Pahlavi (PAL-uh-vee) dynasty. Imitating Atatürk's westernization and modernization program, Reza Khan sent students abroad, encouraged new industry, and increased the rights of women. Reza

The Pahlavi's were Iran's ''royal family'' until the shah's overthrow and exile in 1979. His son has vowed to restore the family to power. Has the time passed for dynastic rule in modern nations?

Khan's pro-German policies resulted in the occupation of Iran by British and Soviet troops in 1941. Deposed by them, he was replaced by his son Mohammed Reza, who became the new shah. The Russians stayed on until pressure from the United States and the United Nations caused their departure in 1947.

Until 1951 foreign oil companies dominated the country. These oil companies received more profits from Iran's oil than the Iranians. In 1951 the Iranian Parliament voted to nationalize the oil industry and named Mohammed Mossadeh (MOHS-sahd-dek) as Premier. The British set up a blockade of the country. This caused the near collapse of the oil industry and serious economic problems for Iran. When the shah tried to fire Mossadeh, anti-shah riots caused him to flee the country. With the help of the United States Central Intelligence Agency, loyal troops brought an end to Mossadeh's rule and restored the shah.

The shah used his oil revenues and United States aid to build up the military forces and protect his personal power. He continued the modernization of the country.

Independence for North Africa

France had ruled Tunisia and Algeria since the nineteenth century. Many French had settled in Algeria and it was regarded as part of France.

France had gained control of Algeria in 1848. The French citizens living in Algeria, however, felt that they were not given the same rights as those living in France. For reasons similar to those the British colonists in America had put forward in 1776, many Algerians began to call for independence from France.

As in other areas, an independence movement began in Algeria after World War II. There were nine million native Algerians and one million people of French-Algerian descent living in the country. The French community owned about one-third of the land. Mines, banks, and shipping were all French-controlled. Fears that independence would lead to the expulsion of all people of French descent made the question of independence particularly sensitive.

In 1954 full-scale rebellion broke out under the leadership of the National Liberation Front (FLN). The FLN attacked French troops and settlers. The weak postwar governments in France were unable to find an acceptable settlement. Parts of the French army and many French colonists formed a Secret Army Organization (OAS) to block independence.

The OAS supported the return to power in 1958 of Charles de Gaulle in France. De Gaulle was expected to put down the rebellion. However, when he became willing to negotiate independence, the OAS turned against him. Attempts were made to assassinate de Gaulle, and a terrorism campaign spread to France. De Gaulle stood firm. In 1961 France voted to give Algeria its independence the following year.

In 1962 Ahmed Ben Bella became Algeria's first chief of state, but was overthrown by a military coup in 1965. The country then came under the leadership of Houari Beumedienne (hoo-AHR-ee boo-med-YEN). Boumedienne's followers continued to rule after his death in 1979.

Under the leadership of Chadli Bendjedid, elected president to Algeria in 1984, the nation is trying to deal with major problems being generated by the economy and by agriculture. For example, during the fifth congress of the National Liberation Front, held in December 1983, it was agreed that agriculture had the highest priority. Like other nations on the African continent, Algeria is faced with a growing population and with limited resources to meet their needs.

In Morocco, the sultan led its drive for independence. He was exiled in 1953, but an army of liberation forced the French to allow his return. In 1956 Morocco became an independent nation under King Mohammed V.

In Tunisia, Habib Bourguiba (HAH-beeb boor-GEE-buh) formed an Independence party in 1934. He continued to press his cause after the war. As in Algeria, French colonists opposed the separation of Tunisia from France. Bourguiba was arrested in 1952, and riots broke out throughout Tunisia. Because the Algerian war had strained France's resources, France wanted to avoid a similar result due to conflict in Tunisia. France granted independence to Tunisia in 1956. Bourguiba then became Tunisia's first prime minister.

Libya had been part of the African empire of Italy. The Italians were expelled during World War II and, after a transition period, Libya became independent in 1951. In 1969 Muammar el-Qaddafi (MOO-ah-mahr el-kah-DAHF-fee), leader of a military coup, came to power. The discovery of oil made Libya a rich country. It allowed Qaddafi to support a number of terrorist activities in other countries.

SECTION REVIEW

1. Mapping: Use the map on page 678 to find the boundaries of Israel in 1948. What areas did it occupy after the Six-Day War?

2. In your own words, briefly define of identify: kibbutz, emirates, *fellahin*, Pan Arabism, Suez crisis, Six-Day War, FLN, OAS.

3. How did the United Nations propose to solve the problem of Palestine in 1947?

4. Why was it difficult for France to find a peaceful solution to the problem of Algeria?

■ Do you think the United Nations should send troops to a nation fighting a war of independence? Give reasons for your answer.

THE MODERN MIDDLE EAST

Rapid changes have taken place in the Middle East in the last twenty years. Poor countries suddenly became rich from their oil reserves. Many traditional societies were disrupted by the modernization that wealth brought. These changes and ongoing area conflicts make the region one of the most explosive in the world.

The October War

Both Egypt and Israel were supplied by their superpower allies with sophisticated weapons. This action led to new conflict in the area. In 1970 Nasser died and was succeeded by Anwar al-Sadat. Sadat was less favorable toward the Soviet Union. When the Soviets would not give him all the arms he requested, he ordered Soviet technicians and advisors to leave Egypt.

Sadat's goal was to recover the Egyptian territory lost to the Israelis in the 1967 Six-Day War. To do this, he enlisted the support of Syrian President Hafez al-Assad (hah-fehz ahl-ah-SAHD), who wanted to regain the Golan Heights. The two countries attacked Israel on October 6, 1973, on Yom Kippur, the most sacred holy day in the Jewish religious calendar.

Under the protection of an artillery barrage, the Egyptians crossed the canal and overran the light Israeli defenses, to establish a position on the eastern side. The Syrians successfully attacked in the Golan Heights area. Then the Israelis counterattacked, forcing the Syrians back. They sent forces across the canal at another point and attacked the Egyptian forces from behind. When a cease-fire was arranged, the Israelis had surrounded the Egyptian army in the Sinai.

During the fighting, Arab oil-producing nations had announced an embargo on oil to countries supporting Israel. The United States Secretary of State, Henry Kissinger, worked to achieve a settlement that would lift the embargo and at the same time guarantee Israel's security. Kissinger flew back and forth between Egypt and Israel trying to persuade Sadat and Golda Meir, the Israeli prime minister, to reach an agreement. This **shuttle diplomacy** produced an agreement between Egypt

Golda Meir, both before and after she served as prime minister, helped shape the modern state of Israel. Was her leadership role any different from that of women political leaders today?

and Israel at the beginning of 1974. The Israelis agreed to withdraw from the west bank of the canal and to a partial withdrawal from the east bank. A United Nations peacekeeping force would patrol a demilitarized zone between the two sides. In May 1974 an agreement was reached between Israel and Syria. It provided for an Israeli withdrawal to the prewar lines, with a United Nations buffer zone in the area.

The October War had two major effects. It showed that the Arabs had a potent weapon in their oil wealth. It also spurred negotiations between Israel and Egypt that would eventually lead to a peace between the two former enemies.

During this period, however, continued problems with the Arabs prompted a call for a change in Israel's government. Thus Meir and other cabinet members were forced to resign. A new government was then formed under Yitzhak Rabin (YIT-zahk rah-BEEN). In 1976 he also resigned.

Egyptian-Israeli Peace

Anwar al-Sadat took the first dramatic step toward peace when he went to Jerusalem in 1977. He was welcomed by Prime Minister Menachem Begin (muh-NAHK-uhm BAY-gin), who had been elected earlier in the year. Addressing the Israeli parliament, Sadat offered Israel a peace with "security and safety" in return for its withdrawal from Arab territory and recognition of Palestinian rights. After a flurry of hope, negotiations broke down.

President Jimmy Carter, in a bold move, invited Begin and Sadat to a conference at Camp David, the United States presidential retreat. With Carter acting as a firm intermediary, an agreement was worked out after thirteen days of hard bargaining. In September 1978, Sadat and Begin signed the Camp David Accords. The accords set a framework for a peace treaty between Egypt and Israel. They also aimed for a general peace settlement through which Palestinians on the occupied West Bank and Gaza Strip would be granted "full autonomy." A final Palestinian settlement was left for later negotiations.

The other Arab countries did not support the Camp David Accords. Sadat was accused of selling out other Arab interests to get back the Sinai. Begin's policy of building more settlements on the West Bank made a settlement with the Palestinians less likely. President Carter traveled to the Middle East to ensure an agreement and in March 1979 Egypt and Israel signed a peace treaty. It provided for a three-year withdrawal from the Sinai by the Israelis, diplomatic relations between the two countries, and economic and trade relations.

For Israel, the treaty broke its diplomatic isolation. Egypt recovered the Sinai and received increased aid from the United States.

When Sadat was assassinated in 1981, his successor, Hosni Mubarak (HAHS-nee moo-BAHR-ahk), carried out the agreement. Israel withdrew its civilians and military forces as scheduled in 1982, and diplomatic relations between the two countries were established.

Egyptian President Anwar al-Sadat, President Jimmy Carter, and Israeli Prime Minister Menachem Begin signed the Camp David Accords in 1978. How did President Carter help to bring about the peace treaty settlement?

Oil Power

The Organization of Petroleum Exporting Countries (OPEC) was formed at a meeting in Baghdad in 1960. Its original members were Venezuela, Iran, Iraq, Saudi Arabia, and Kuwait. The purpose of OPEC was to advance members' interests in trade and development and to further their relations with other oil-producing states. Other countries joined later, seeing the advantage of coordinating their efforts to control the oil market.

As a result of the October War in 1973, OPEC became a household word. During the fighting, Arab oil producers agreed to reduce shipments of oil to nations that were supporting Israel. This embargo resulted in higher prices of oil in the United States, Europe, and Japan. The embargo ended the next year. Prices, however, remained high as the OPEC nations discovered their ability to control the market price.

Oil and petroleum products are part of the basic energy needs of all highly industrialized countries. The enormous increase in fuel prices affected Europe and Japan more than the United States because they were more dependent on Middle Eastern oil. For the poorer countries, the price rise was even more serious. The rising oil costs also affected the international balance of trade and financial markets.

The drastic rise in oil prices produced the biggest transfer of wealth in history, particularly for the countries of the Middle East, which held more than half of the world's oil reserves. The price of oil went from under $2 a barrel to around $34 in 1985. Billions of dollars flowed into such countries as Saudi Arabia, Iran, Iraq, Algeria, Libya, and the Gulf States—small Arabian peninsula nations including Kuwait, Bahrain, Qatar, and the United Arab Emirates.

Most of these countries had formerly been poor and weak. Now they were able to use their wealth to play an important role in world affairs. Oil became an economic weapon as powerful as military armaments.

On a per capita basis, the oil wealth is unevenly distributed. Oil-rich areas like the Gulf States, Algeria, Saudi Arabia, Iran, Iraq, and Libya are not densely populated. However, the most populous country in the region is Egypt, and it has little surplus oil.

The Iranian Revolution

As the fourth largest oil producer, Iran benefited greatly from the oil price increase. Under the shah, new industry was developed and land reform was carried out. Women were enfranchised and also given the right to divorce. The Shah was ruthless, however, in suppressing any opposition.

The shah's programs prompted opposition from the Muslim religious leaders. Leading the opposition was the Ayatollah Ruhollah Khomeini (roo-HOH-lah hoh-MAY-nee). Exiled earlier by the shah, he taped speeches that were smuggled into the country and played in mosques and bazaars. He gained a large following.

The shah countered growing opposition and mass demonstrations with force. But in early 1979 he began to lose the support of the army and was forced to leave Iran. The elderly Ayatollah arrived back in Teheran, the capital, on February 1 and announced, "I will appoint a government with the support of the Iranian people." Over time he named special Islamic Revolutionary Councils to supervise the country's affairs.

Under the new government, the rights recently won by women were revoked. A return to strict Islamic beliefs was demanded. Traditional customs that had been dropped were reinstated. This Islamic fundamentalism stressed the Koran as the basis for law.

Khomeini's policies threw the country into chaos. Industry and business almost came to a halt. Hundreds of former supporters of the shah, and others regarded as enemies of the state, were executed. The shah was condemned to death in absentia. Khomeini's rule grew stronger.

In 1979, when the Shah was admitted to the United States for medical treatment, Iranian "students," with government support, seized the United States Embassy in Iran and held fifty-two United States citizens as hostages for more than a year. Although this was a grave violation of international law, these hostages were not released until January 1981. Not obtaining the hostages' release before this time was a factor in President Carter's defeat in the 1980 elections.

In the midst of the hostage crisis, Iraq attacked Iran in an attempt to take territory that had long been in dispute. At the start Iraq scored victories due to Iran's internal disorder. However, the war

Why is PLO leader Yasir Arafat (center) always accompanied by armed bodyguards?

continues today with no settlement in sight. Cities and oil installations have been bombed. Shipping in the Gulf area has been hurt.

Civil War in Lebanon

In 1964 the Palestine Liberation Organization (PLO) was formed to regain the territory of Israel for the Palestinians. The PLO formed an army of refugees who carried out border raids against Israel. After 1971 they operated chiefly from Lebanon, under Yasir Arafat (YAH-suhr AH-rah-faht).

Bitterness between Lebanese Christians and Muslims broke into open fighting in 1975. Many religious groups in Lebanon formed their own armed militias. Soon the Palestinians joined the fighting on the side of the Muslims.

The government in Beirut was nearly powerless. The once prosperous country suffered a breakdown in law and order. The PLO attacks on Israeli settlements, from bases in south Lebanon, forced counterattacks from Israel.

In 1982 the Israelis launched a full-scale invasion of Lebanon to wipe out the PLO and establish a friendly government on their border. Earlier the Israelis had begun friendly relations with Lebanese Christians. Their troops swept up to the capital city of Beirut. During the summer Beirut was under siege, causing high numbers of civilian casualties and damage. In an agreement negotiated by the United States, the PLO was evacuated from the city and the siege ended. Soon afterward, however, Lebanese Christians entered Palestinian refugee camps and killed hundreds of people.

Government and diplomatic officials from the United States played leading roles in trying to bring these endless battles to a halt. In addition, United Nations' troops, including units from France, Italy, and the United States, were sent to Lebanon to enforce a cease fire. Members of the PLO were evacuated and sent to other Muslim nations. Talks, however, continued between the PLO and the Arab countries on establishing a homeland for the Palestinians. Nevertheless, peace in Lebanon, Israel, and the rest of the Middle East appears to be a long way off.

Although the Israelis had been successful in removing the PLO from southern Lebanon, their occupation of Lebanon proved costly. The Shiite (SHEE-ite) Muslims, many of whom were followers of Khomeini, became the largest single sect in Lebanon. They were as hostile to the other major Muslim sect, the Sunnites, as they were to Christians. Shiite suicide bombers destroyed the United States Embassy in April 1983 and then in October blew up the barracks of a United States Marine peacekeeping force, killing 237. In 1985, Israel began to withdraw from Lebanon.

Modernization and Urbanization

No region of the world has been so greatly changed in recent times as the Middle East. High-rise buildings stand where there once was nothing but sand and mud houses. Countries that were once very poor now provide housing, education, and health care for all. Superhighways cross areas that once had only dirt roads and camel tracks through the desert.

It is a growing region. Saudi Arabia's rate of population growth is the second highest in the world; Syria's is third, and Iraq's fifth. The rapid population growth results not only from a high birthrate but also from improvements in health care that have greatly increased life expectancy. Diseases such as malaria and cholera, once native to the region, are now being wiped out.

The Middle East today is a blend of the old and the new. Damascus is the oldest capital city in the world. Jerusalem, Cairo, and Baghdad are great cities with a glorious past. New cities are being built. Tel Aviv was built by Jewish pioneers. Saudi Arabia is using its oil wealth to build new cities, universities, and transportation systems. It is also investing large sums of money abroad.

The status of women in particular is changing. Traditionally women were confined to the home in their role as wives and mothers. With the exception of the very wealthy, girls were not educated. Today most girls attend at least elementary school. Most Middle Eastern governments are trying to provide high school and college programs for them as well. This education raises hope and a desire for jobs that will allow women to use their skills.

Change is spread through mass communications. The transistor radio and television have exposed the people to new cultures and ideas. Western influences are often resented by those who hold to the strict beliefs of Islam. Therefore, Khomeini's Islamic fundamentalism has a strong appeal for many who oppose modernization.

Home of the oldest civilizations and birthplace of three major religions, the Middle East faces a hard task in keeping its ancient traditions as its people adapt to their new role in the modern world. Both Arabs and Israelis have a strong sense of the importance of their past. However, Arabs take great pride in their twentieth-century wealth and prosperity and Israelis continue to build a modern state. What role the urge to preserve traditions will play in the future history of the region remains to be seen.

SECTION REVIEW

1. Mapping: Use the map on page 678 to find the Sinai Peninsula. How much area did Israel give up in the peace treaty with Egypt?
2. In your own words, briefly define or identify: shuttle diplomacy, October War, Camp David Accords, OPEC, PLO, Islamic fundamentalism.
3. Who were the three people responsible for bringing about a peace treaty between Egypt and Israel?
4. What were the policies of the Ayatollah Khomeini in Iran?
5. List some of the ways in which modernization has been introduced to the Middle East.
■ To what extent do you think the United States should have been involved in Middle Eastern affairs from 1967 to the present? Why?

AFRICAN COUNTRIES GAIN INDEPENDENCE

During the colonial period, schools for Africans were set up by missionaries and by some colonial governments. Soon a small westernized middle class arose, mainly in the urban areas of the West African countries. The steady growth of urban areas produced an African elite who served in the lower ranks of the colonial governments. Some Africans went to study in the universities of Europe and the United States.

A man whose ideas inspired many Africans was William E. B. DuBois, a United States citizen and one of the early leaders of **Pan-Africanism.** Pan-Africanism called for a united black effort to gain freedom from colonial rule in Africa. DuBois organized a series of Pan-African Congresses. They demanded justice in the colonial territories, the abolition of slavery and forced labor, and greater access to education.

During World War II tens of thousands of Africans served as troops on the Allied side. Africans believed that the victory of democracy over fascism would have benefits for Africa. African hopes rose because the war had weakened the colonial powers. Neither the United States nor the Soviet Union had colonial empires.

The Fifth Pan-African Congress took place at Manchester, England, in 1945. For the first time the majority of the delegates were Africans rather than blacks from the Caribbean or the United States. Many Africans attending the conference would lead their countries to independence, among them Kwame Nkrumah (KWAH-may NKROO-muh), Jomo Kenyatta, and Leopold Senghor (sahng-ORE).

The Fifth Pan-African Congress adopted a resolution condemning colonialism. It stated: "We are determined to be free. We want education. We want the right to earn a decent living; the right to express our thoughts and emotions, to adopt and create forms of beauty. . . . We will fight . . . for freedom, democracy, and social betterment."

The Middle East and Africa have been so affected by the impact of modernization that some camels have the chance to ride in style across the desert.

A member speaks at a meeting of the Conference of Independent African States, founded in 1958 by Nkrumah. How do such groups benefit their countries?

In 1914 Liberia and Ethiopia were the only black African countries that had escaped colonization. By 1985, there were forty-five independent black nations in Africa.

Ghana Wins Its Independence

The Gold Coast, a British colony, was rich in gold, cocoa, and timber, and the wealthiest in West Africa. An educated black middle class had some part in ruling the country.

Kwame Nkrumah, who was to lead the country to independence, studied in the United States in the 1930's and 1940's. After returning to his country, he founded the Convention People's party. The first national party in the region, it sought to attract all of the people to the cause of independence. Earlier leaders had appealed to the country's small middle class, but Nkrumah believed that a mass party would be more effective.

Starting in 1950, Nkrumah's party staged a positive action campaign, using boycotts and strikes to push independence for the country. Nkrumah was jailed. In the elections of 1951

Nkrumah and his party won easily. The British released him from prison and he took his seat in the Assembly. There he agreed to work within a new constitution to achieve his aims.

The transitional period was short. On March 6, 1957, the Gold Coast, taking the name of the ancient African empire of Ghana, became the first black colony to achieve independence. In his celebration speech, Nkrumah spoke of Ghana's freedom as being the first step in a chain of freedom that would spread over the continent.

French West Africa

While the British planned to prepare their African colonies for self-government, the French saw their mission as bringing Africans into the French cultural sphere. In their colonial schools classes were conducted in French. Educated Africans were allowed to vote in French elections. One of them, Leopold Senghor, the first leader of independent Senegal, spent much of his life in France. A brilliant poet and teacher, Senghor became a spokesman for **Negritude.** He defined this as "the affirmation of the values of African culture." He believed in unity among blacks all over the world.

He returned to Senegal after the war. At that time the French were trying to build up the French community to which their colonies would belong. In 1956 the French government offered the Outline Law, which would give internal autonomy to the territories of French West and Equatorial Africa. France would retain authority over foreign policy, defense, and strategic economic development. However, the increasing sense of African nationalism made this offer unsatisfactory.

In 1958 Charles de Gaulle came to power. Seeing that a new policy was needed, he offered the French colonies of black Africa a choice. They could have full independence with no help from the French government, or self-government within the French community with French aid. Only Guinea, under the leadership of Sekou Toure (SAY-koo toor-AY), chose full independence. President de Gaulle then canceled all aid to that country. In 1960, after negotiations with those colonies that had chosen to remain in the French community, all gained independence.

The former French colonies have kept ties with France. Receiving both economic and military aid, they have held on to many of the influences of French culture.

The Congo Crisis

Belgium had ruthlessly exploited the Congo (now known as Zaire) for its mineral wealth. There had been little preparation for self-government, and higher education had been neglected. It was only in the 1950's that local governments were allowed. More and more parties were formed, since the people of various ethnic groups felt more loyalty to their own groups than to the nation. Fighting broke out between hostile groups. In 1959 rioting in the capital resulted in the looting of European shops and schools.

Congolese leaders were invited to a conference in Belgium to discuss the future of their country. Most leaders were thinking in terms of a five-year transition to independence. Although Belgian citizens opposed this action, the government announced that independence for the Congo would be granted on June 30, 1960.

A Congolese government was formed with Patrice Lumumba (loo-MOOM-bah) as Prime Minister and his rival Joseph Kasavubu (kass-uh-VOO-boo) as president. When a mutiny of army troops resulted in the killing of Belgian officers and their families, the Belgians sought to protect European lives and property.

In July 1960 Moise Tshombe (maw-EES chome-BAY) announced that Katanga province, with its rich copper mines, was seceding from the nation. Lumumba appealed to the United Nations to save his country from division and Belgian intervention. The United Nations sent a peacekeeping mission made up primarily of African troops. When Lumumba was dissatisfied with their performance, he asked the Russians to intervene. Thus, the superpower rivalry came to the Congo.

Lumumba's turn toward the Soviets brought about his downfall. He was overthrown by a combination of the army under Colonel Joseph Mobutu (moh-BOO-too) and politicians led by Kasavubu. The Russians were expelled from the country.

Finally, United Nations troops succeeded in reuniting Katanga with the Congo. When they left in 1964, violence erupted again. In 1965 Mobutu led a military coup that restored some order, but the country remained unstable.

East African Colonies Gain Independence

In East Africa, independence was complicated by the white settlers. Because they were vastly outnumbered by blacks, they opposed governments that would be elected by popular vote. Instead, they wanted guarantees under a multiracial constitution. In this system each racial group elected a fixed number of representatives to the legislature. This usually meant that the different groups were evenly represented though their numbers might differ.

The multiracial constitution was successfully challenged by the leader of Tanganyika (tan-guhn-YEE-kuh), Julius Nyerere (nye-uh-RAY-ray). Nyerere started the most effective African national party since Nkrumah's. In 1954 he founded the Tanganyika African National Union (TANU). It soon had active branches in most districts of the country.

AFRICA TODAY

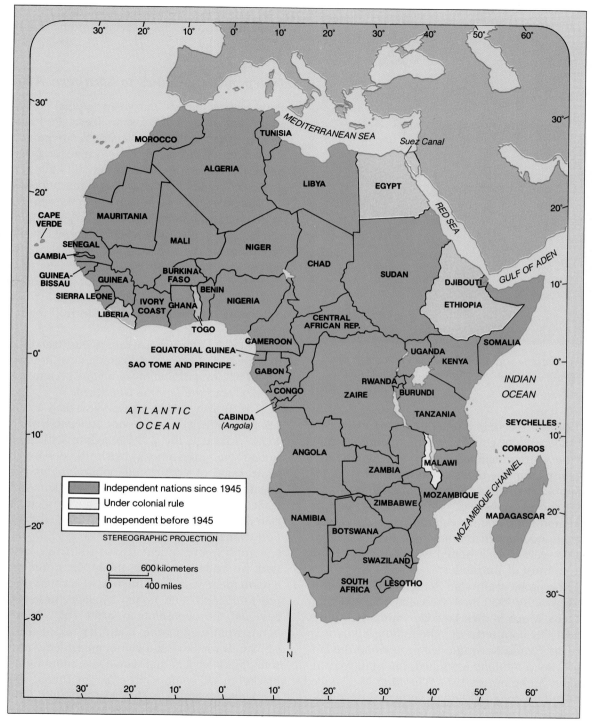

How have the movements for independence in the years since the end of World
War II changed the face of continental Africa?

Jomo Kenyatta was jailed for his role in Kenya's fight for independence. Is independence worth such risks?

During the next four years TANU worked for an independent government that would be ruled by the African majority. At the same time Nyerere promised that the rights of white people would be guaranteed under such a government. His party won the elections with white support. In a remarkably short and smooth transition, the country gained independence from Great Britain in 1961. Three years later, it united with Zanzibar to form the country of Tanzania.

The problem of white settlers was more acute in Kenya. By 1950 there were about 50,000 white citizens. Much of their land lay within the Kikuyu (ki-KOOH-yoo) territory. The leading Kikuyu nationalist, Jomo Kenyatta, led protests on the land issue. As conditions worsened, the Mau Mau rebellion broke out in 1951. The Mau Maus killed British farmers and Kikuyus suspected of collaborating with them. Kenyatta was arrested and imprisoned. The colonial government put down the rebellion by force. In four years the rebellion caused $60 million in damage. About one hundred British and several thousand Kikuyus were killed. Kenyatta's release from prison in 1961 caused great rejoicing. He became the first leader of independent Kenya in 1963, serving until his death in 1978.

Independence Comes to Southern Africa

Portugal was the first European colonial power in Africa and one of the last to leave. Portuguese were urged to settle in the "overseas provinces," as the colonies were called. The Portuguese gave no political rights to the Africans and did little to improve the colony economically or educationally.

The independence movement in the rest of Africa stimulated nationalist ideas in Angola and Mozambique. In the early 1960's guerrilla warfare broke out in the two colonies. The fighting was fierce, and Portuguese troops were sent to put down the rebellion. The struggle for independence was carried on by groups almost as hostile to each other as to the Portuguese. This fact hurt the rebel cause.

In 1974 a new government in Portugal decided that the cost of keeping the colonies was not worth it. In 1975 Angola and Mozambique became independent, but the fighting continued.

The British colony of Rhodesia had received self-government (though not independence) in 1923. Although the 250,000 white settlers controlled the government, black Rhodesians had some hope of getting full political rights while Great Britain was in charge. When Ian Smith, leader of the white Rhodesian government, declared the country independent in 1965, the situation changed.

Smith's government passed restrictive legislation; he made it clear that the blacks would be in a permanent position of inferiority. Joshua Nkomo (en-KOH-moh) and Robert Mugabe (moo-GAH-bay) led the opposition to white rule. Guerrilla bands from neighboring countries raided Rhodesia. Smith tried to put together an agreement with some black leaders that would give more rights to blacks but still retain white rule. The United States, the United Nations, and nearly all other African nations opposed this move. In 1980 elections were held for a new government. Robert Mugabe won a majority, and white Rhodesia became the black African nation of Zimbabwe (zim-BAHB-way).

SOCIAL SCIENCE SKILLS

DEVELOPING A FRAME OF REFERENCE

''. . . since the advent of British, French, Belgian, and other European nations in West Africa, there has been regression instead of progress as a result of systematic exploitation by these alien imperialist powers. The claims of 'partnership,' 'trusteeship,' 'guardianship,' and the 'mandate system' do not serve the political wishes of the people of West Africa.''

These words were part of a resolution proposed by Kwame Nkrumah at the Fifth Pan-African Congress at Manchester, England, in 1945. Nkrumah, who was to become the first leader of a black nation emerging from colonial rule, then went on to describe the colonial powers' "systematic exploitation" of the economic resources of West Africa, and their intention to make the African people "economically helpless."

Were these charges justified? To answer, you must develop a frame of reference. That is, you must examine the facts about the experience of Africa under colonization. Only then can you understand what colonialism really meant.

Forming a Frame of Reference

For example, you know that the European nations that colonized Africa took many of its people and enslaved them. Most of the African slaves were sent to European colonies in the New World. By studying the records of ships in the slave trade, it has been determined that more than 9.5 million Africans were taken from their homeland during the period 1451–1870. It is also known that there were many revolts against European rule within the African colonies during the height of the colonial period that began in the nineteenth century. How do these facts help you to understand what it meant to be colonized?

To form a frame of reference, you must try to find as much information as possible about the period you are studying. You should try to understand what conditions during that period were actually like. You should also read about some of that period's important personalities and the roles they played in their society. In this way you develop your frame of reference.

For instance, Nkrumah says there were claims made of "partnership, trusteeship, guardianship, and the mandate system." To fully understand his statement, you must understand these terms. After World War I the League of Nations set up a "mandate system" that entrusted former German colonies to other European nations. The European nations were to govern them until they were prepared for independence. At other times Europeans defended their colonial policies by saying they had to be the "guardians" of or "partners" with less-advanced peoples.

Developing Your Skills

Some Africans felt that their people could benefit from European colonization. Read the following passage, written by the Zimbabwean black nationalist leader Ndabaningi Sithole (en-dah-bah-NEEN-gee see-tole). Then answer the questions that follow.

''Colonialism has given to Africa a new, vigorous industrial pattern, a new social consciousness, new insights and visions. It has created a new environment. It has annihilated many tribal and linguistic barriers and divisions. The European colonial powers are to be praised for the work they have done in helping the emergence of African nationalism.''

1. What benefits does Sithole say have come from European colonialism?
2. How can each of these facts help you to develop a frame of reference about his assertion?

Apartheid in South Africa

The Union of South Africa was created in 1910 as a self-governing dominion within the British Empire. The British and Boer white population, existing uneasily with each other, built a prosperous society based on ruling the blacks and exploiting their labor.

In 1948 the National party came to power, representing the Afrikaner (contemporary name for Boer) population. Their policy was to establish white minority rights permanently. In a policy known as **apartheid** (apartness), they wrote into the country's laws the separation of the races. There were four classifications of race: black for the Bantu population (about 70 percent); Asians (3 percent); Coloreds, who were anyone part white, part black, or part Asian (10 percent); and whites, or Europeans (17 percent).

The apartheid system controlled the movements and political activity of blacks. All political expression was forbidden. The African Natóonal (nah-TOE-nahl) Congress, which had called for "one man, one vote," was banned. A strict system of segregation was enforced in all public places, including hospitals and schools. The Natives Act of 1952 required all blacks over sixteen to always carry a passbook that showed their residence and job. Jobs could not be changed without official permission.

Under the pretext that it was to allow the development of the unique culture of black tribes, blacks were assigned to "homelands," or Bantustans. The rest of the country, 87 percent of the land, was set aside for whites. The "homelands" contained the least desirable land in the country.

The apartheid policy roused strong opposition both within the country and in the entire world. In March 1960 South African police shot into a crowd of peaceful demonstrators at Sharpeville, killing many women and children. The action was denounced, but South Africa's response was to ignore world opinion. In 1961 South Africa declared its independence and cut its ties with the British Commonwealth.

The South Africans extended their control of apartheid to Namibia, the former German colony of Southwest Africa that had been administered by South Africa since World War I. South Africa's rule of Namibia has been opposed by the Southwest African People's Organization (SWAPO). As of 1985, Namibia is the only African region that has not been freed of colonial status.

Laws in South Africa severely restrict the movement of blacks. How is their plight similar to that of other minorities?

SECTION REVIEW

1. Mapping: Use the map on page 691 to list the names of the African countries that became independent after 1945.
2. In your own words, briefly define or identify: Pan-Africanism, Convention People's Party, Negritude, Mau Mau Rebellion, apartheid.
3. What was different about the Independence party founded by Kwame Nkrumah?
4. Why did white settlers oppose governments that would be popularly elected?
■ Is violence to attain independence ever justified? Give reasons for your answer.

To end white rule in Rhodesia, British government representatives, Rhodesian Prime Minister Ian Smith, and black leaders held meetings. How else can problems be solved?

INDEPENDENT AFRICA

With independence came new challenges. National borders often did not conform to language, ethnic, or cultural frontiers. The colonial powers had drawn boundary lines to make ruling easier. As a result, many African nations contained conflicting ethnic and tribal groups. In a continent where tribal loyalty was often stronger than national loyalty, this created explosive problems.

The new states were jealous of their newly won sovereignty, or independence. Politically, they could not afford to give up territory by drawing new borders. Thus in a continent with more than a thousand languages and dialects, the artificial frontiers between nations and groups remained.

The drive for independence had created rising hopes among Africans for a better life. New governments had to tackle the tough problems of building a system of roads and transport, modernizing agriculture, and industrializing. This had to be done in a continent where the resources were unevenly divided between countries with great mineral riches and others with few resources. To achieve modernization, a trained and educated class of administrators often had to be created. This process, however, took time.

The new nations had to build a sense of national unity and identity. Life had changed greatly during the colonial period. But many precolonial customs and traditions remained. As in other areas, conflict between old and new customs created problems.

Pan-Africanism had been the driving force behind the independence movement. To carry on this tradition, the leaders of the independent states formed the Organization of African Unity (OAU) in 1963. Its charter called for an association of sovereign states that would cooperate economically and consult about crises in the region. It was an attempt to tie the new African nations together and encourage independence movements in others.

The most important function of the organization was its specialized economic and social agencies. One of these was the Economic Community of West African States (ECOWAS). The ECOWAS wanted all the nations in that region to benefit from the oil riches of Nigeria.

Civil War in Nigeria

Nigeria's prospects looked promising in 1963. As the most populous African nation and with important oil resources, it was regarded by foreign investors as a good prospect. In addition, Nigeria's two-party system appeared to give it greater political stability.

Nigeria had been set up as a federation with a great deal of local autonomy for its four provinces. They roughly corresponded to the four main ethnic groups of the country: the Hausa and Fulani in the north, the Ibo in the southeast, and the Yoruba in the southwest. In 1966 there were disturbances within the country when attempts were made to change the government into a unified administration. Some Ibos were attacked and killed.

The violence directed against them caused leaders of the Ibos to reexamine their relation to the country. In 1967 the eastern provinces refused to transfer income from these areas to the government. Since the oil resources were in the eastern provinces, the central government was faced with a serious loss of income. After negotiations failed, the eastern province declared itself the independent country of Biafra. Fighting broke out between Nigeria and Biafra and dragged on for three years. The Nigerian government had the advantage of superior numbers and weapons. Other African states, fearing the consequences of a successful secession, supported Nigeria. Biafra surrendered in January 1970, after being subjected to a blockade that caused mass starvation.

A military government made an attempt to bind up the country's wounds. As an OPEC member, Nigeria benefited from the oil price rise. Corruption and poor use of oil revenues, however, have made Nigeria a less than prosperous country.

Sudan, the largest country in Africa, and Zaire have had problems with unity. The Muslim-controlled northern Sudan contained most of the nation's professionals and had greater political power than the Christian south. Resentment of unequal treatment led the south to try to secede. The fighting went on until the OAU arranged an uneasy settlement. The tensions still linger today. In Zaire some members of Tshombe's old organization invaded the southern province of the country in 1977. They were repelled, but secessionist feeling remains a threat.

Modernizing Efforts

In their plans for development, African nations suffered from a great disadvantage. The continent produces only a very small share of the world total of goods and services. Exports were generally minerals or farm products, and many countries had only one or two export crops. This fact made them extremely vulnerable to fluctuations in price on the world market. Most of their imports were manufactured products, which rose in price. There was clearly a need to vary their economies.

At the time of independence, Europeans owned or controlled most of Africa's major mines, manufacturing, industrial plants, and financial institutions. This situation, often called **neocolonialism,** occurred because some African nations lacked skilled managers to run large industrial concerns.

Because resources were not evenly distributed, economic progress varied greatly. In 1985 Gabon, a small country, ranked as the wealthiest black African nation, with a per capita income in excess of $6,000. Africa also has most of the poorest nations in the world.

Economic achievements have been wiped out by the increase in population. The African continent has seen a population explosion without parallel in history. Kenya has the highest growth rate in the world. An average Kenyan family has eight children. Africa's cities cannot provide the necessary services, housing, and jobs for its people, many of whom leave the rural areas for what they hope will be a better life in the city.

Most African countries have chosen a form of socialism. Ghana nationalized many businesses, but bid for aid from both the East and the West. The government built hospitals, universities, and thousands of elementary schools.

In Tanzania a form of socialism was tried that looked to the precolonial past. Ujamaa (Swahili for "family responsibility") was the term used for a program that stressed self-help and community effort. President Nyerere wanted to avoid dependence on other countries. In 1966 a two-year period of national service was required of citizens in work such as road building and irrigation projects. The banks, factories, big businesses, and plantations were nationalized. These self-help schemes have met with varying degrees of success.

One-Person Rule

Many African nations had parliamentary systems of government when granted their independence. Often these had been created in haste for the brief period before independence. As a result they had no roots in the country. Most new independent governments also had a major figure who had played a great role in the independence process. Such stature guaranteed, at least for a while, that this person would play an important role in the country's future developments. Nkrumah of Ghana is an example. Although imprisoned for opposition to the British, he allowed no opposition to his policies and only one political party when he was in power. Opponents were jailed or deported. When parliament displeased him, he overruled it. In 1962 the parliament named him president for life, but he was overthrown in a military coup in 1966.

Rising African expectations put pressure on leaders to improve the standard of living. Many felt that real political opposition would get in the way of progress. Julius Nyerere said: "Even a system based on social justice and a democratic constitution may need backing up, during the period following independence, by emergency measures of a totalitarian kind. Without discipline, freedom cannot survive." The drive toward modernization was seen as a war in which internal opposition was not acceptable.

The one-party system was the rule rather than the exception in independent Africa. The party controlled the government and trade unions. Few independent centers of power remained.

In situations where civilian governments had trouble dealing with tribal hostilities, the military came to play a major role. In Uganda, then President Milton Obote (oh-BOH-tay) was overthrown by the Ugandan army in 1971. Major General Idi Amin became the new head of government. Amin abolished the legislature and banned all political opposition. His troops killed over 100,000 Ugandans. Uganda invaded Tanzania in 1978, after border tensions. The next year Tanzania invaded Uganda and Amin was deposed. Obote returned to power in 1980, but was overthrown in 1985 during a military coup. In Africa today, military rulers are in the majority. Such rule, in most cases, continues to result in political instability.

Superpower Rivalry in Africa

Both the United States and the Soviet Union have competed for influence in Africa. They have given aid to established governments and have also backed opposition groups. Angola and the Horn of Africa are two major sites of superpower rivalry in Africa.

The Horn of Africa is the area on the east coast of the continent, south of the Sudan. It contains the nations of Ethiopia, Somalia, and Djibouti. Bordering on the Red Sea, its closeness to the Arabian Peninsula and the Persian Gulf makes it a strategic focal point for superpower bases. Ethiopia under Haile Selassie (HIE-lee suh-LASS-ee) had

HORN OF AFRICA

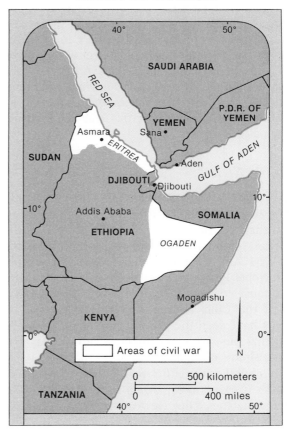

Why is Eritrea considered a valuable asset for Ethiopia and the subject of attention by the superpowers? Why are the countries that occupy the Horn of Africa important to the region's political stability?

been a close friend of the United States. The United States was its main supplier of aid and military equipment. During his reign the northern province of Eritrea had been in revolt for independence. In the south the Ogaden region was in revolt, aided by Somalia. Somalia was armed by the Soviet Union.

In 1974 Haile Selassie was overthrown by a military coup. Violence was widespread throughout the country, and more provinces revolted. In 1975 the United States stopped all aid to the country. In 1977 a coup brought a Marxist, Mengistu Haile Mariam, to power. Now the superpowers switched sides. Soviet advisors and Cuban troops arrived in Ethiopia. The next year Somali troops were cleared out of the Ogaden. The United States started aiding Somalia and set up a base on its coast.

In Angola violence did not end with independence. Fighting continued among groups trying to control the country with the military assistance of one of the two opposing superpowers. In 1976 the Soviet-backed faction gained control of the country with the help of Cuban troops. A Marxist state was established. A rival, Jonas Savimbi, with the aid of some Western countries and South Africa, has since carried on a guerrilla war and controls parts of the country.

South Africa

In spite of worldwide condemnation, the South African government was firm in carrying out its apartheid policies. Nelson Mandela, a leader of the African National Congress, was imprisoned for life in 1963. Albert Luthuli (luh-THOO-lee), who won the Nobel Peace Prize in 1960 for his nonviolent resistance to apartheid, once asked: "What have been the fruits of moderation? The past thirty years have seen the greatest number of laws restricting our rights and progress, until today we have almost no rights at all."

Conditions were the worst for the nine million blacks working in the white urban areas outside the homelands. They were under constant harassment and the threat of being repatriated, or relocated, in an unknown homeland. Blacks were not allowed to live in the cities. Their homes were in townships that surrounded the cities. To the southwest of Johannesburg was the huge town-

ship of Soweto (soh-WET-oh). In 1976 riots broke out there and were put down violently by the South African police.

The current South African government, led by President Pieter Botha (PEE-tuhr BOE-tuh), has changed a few apartheid laws. Although the law against intermarriage was repealed, the system has basically stayed in place.

The United Nations approved an arms embargo against South Africa. Since some countries have been willing to break it, it has been ineffective. South Africa has built its own arms industry, and many suspect that it has the capability to build atomic weapons.

South Africa has been able to continue its policies in the face of wide criticism because its great mineral resources are needed by other countries. Chrome and platinum are found in abundance there. The only other nation that has these minerals is the Soviet Union. Its strategic location also gives it influence and power.

Recently there has been a movement in the United States and Western Europe to pull investments out of South Africa. This **divestment** campaign is gathering force.

Famine in Africa

Agriculture in Africa suffers from severe disadvantages. There is less topsoil than elsewhere. One-third of the continent is infested with the tsetse (TSET-see) fly, which attacks livestock, humans, and some crops. The amount of arable, or crop-producing, land is decreasing due to an expansion of the Sahara Desert. Rainfall varies. Droughts that last for years have ravaged the continent.

Today Africa is threatened with a severe famine. For 150 to 200 million people in Sub-Saharan Africa, food shortages are a fact of life. Twenty-two countries are faced with severe food shortages. Of these the worst cases are found in Ethiopia, Somalia, Mozambique, Zambia, Kenya, and the Sudan.

The hunger in Africa has occurred due to a combination of human and natural factors. Besides drought, some of the factors that have contributed to this famine are civil disturbances, environmental damage, the international economic status, and in some cases the policies of the African nations.

The famine that African nations have been experiencing since the early 1980's has killed hundreds of thousands. Do other nations have an obligation to assist people such as those pictured here in Ethiopia?

The last two decades have seen a decline in per capita food production. African agriculture is still mostly unmechanized, is often women's work, and lacks status.

Government decisions have not helped the situation. To ensure the support of the populations in the cities, food prices purposely have been kept low. This takes away incentive to increase production. Some governments have also stressed the cash crop over subsistence agriculture. Cash crops can be exported, building up resources for modernization. The price trend of cash crops on the world market in recent years has been downward.

Solving the problem of hunger in Africa is an international project. While there is a desperate need for immediate food relief to save lives, there is a long-term need to create conditions that will prevent future famine.

SECTION REVIEW

1. Mapping: Use the map on page 691 to find the countries most affected by famine today. How much of Africa's land area do they occupy?
2. In your own words, briefly define or identify: Organization of African Unity, neocolonialism, ujamaa, divestment.
3. Why did the newly independent nations refuse to redraw the old colonial borders?
4. What are some of the factors that have brought about famine in Africa?
■ At some point in time many modern nations were ruled by another country. Over time they fought for and won their independence. Why is the desire to be free of outside rule as strong today as in earlier times? Cite examples.

Reviewing the Chapter

Chapter Summary

The creation of Israel in 1948 brought about an immediate war between the new nation and its Arab neighbors. Israel won this war, and the several wars that followed. A first step toward peace came when Egypt and Israel signed a peace treaty in 1979.

The northern African nations of Morocco, Libya, and Tunisia also became independent. Fighting between French settlers and Algerians finally ended in the separation of Algeria from France in 1962.

The harsh rule of the shah of Iran in attempting to modernize his country led to his loss of power. He was replaced by the Ayatollah Khomeini, who established a government based on traditional Islamic principles.

Forty-five new black-ruled nations won their independence in Africa between 1945 and 1980. They faced considerable challenges, including attempts of some groups to secede from their respective countries. In many nations, drought and other problems produced terrible famine.

The white rulers of South Africa wrote into law an apartheid system that kept power in the hands of a white minority. World condemnation failed to budge the government from its repressive course of action.

1. Describe how the movement for independence changed the map of the Middle East and Africa after World War II.
2. Explain how the conflict between old and new changed the government in Iran.
3. Discuss some of the different problems that newly independent African nations faced.

Using Your Vocabulary

1. In your own words, describe the organization of an Israeli kibbutz.
2. What type of state is an emirate?
3. What was the condition of the *fellahin* in Egypt under King Farouk?
4. What was the main idea of Pan-Arabism?
5. Explain the results of the Suez crisis.
6. Explain what roles the FLN and OAS played in the Algerian war for independence.
7. How did shuttle diplomacy bring about an agreement between Egypt and Israel in 1974?
8. What was the purpose of OPEC?
9. How did Islamic fundamentalism affect the government of Iran?
10. What was the purpose of the Palestine Liberation Organization?
11. Compare the ideas of Pan-Africanism and Negritude.
12. Explain how a multiracial constitution would treat different racial groups.
13. In your own words, explain apartheid.
14. What were the purposes of the Organization of African Unity?
15. How did neocolonialism affect new African nations?
16. What were the principles of the ujamaa program in Tanzania?
17. How does divestment seek to change the policies of the South African government?
18. Describe some of the problems faced by blacks living in South Africa.
19. In your own words, cite the reasons for the serious food shortages that have affected almost half of the nations of Africa?

Developing Your Geography Skills

1. Use the map on page 678 to locate the territory that Israel gave back to Egypt in the peace treaty. Why was this land important?
2. Use the maps on page 678 and on page 697 to tell why the Horn of Africa was important to the Middle East.
3. Use the map on page 697 to tell how Ethiopia would be affected by the loss of Eritrea.

Recalling the Facts

1. Describe the changes that Kemal Atatürk brought to Turkey.
2. What did the United Nations resolution of 1947 ask for regarding Palestine?
3. Describe the effects of the Six-Day War.
4. Explain why the OAS supported Charles de Gaulle's return to power.
5. Explain the role that the United States and the United Nations played in the Arab-Israeli agreements of 1974.
6. How did President Jimmy Carter help bring about a peace treaty between the governments of Egypt and Israel?
7. Why did Arab oil producers put an embargo on oil in 1973?
8. List some of the effects of Israel's invasion of Lebanon.
9. Describe the methods that Kwame Nkrumah used to win independence for his country.
10. What choice did Charles de Gaulle offer France's African colonies in 1958?
11. What problems did the first government of an independent Congo face?
12. Describe the methods that Julius Nyerere used to gain independence for his country.
13. List the factors that attracted foreign investment to Nigeria after independence.
14. List the disadvantages faced by African nations in their development plans.
15. List the nations of Africa in which the superpowers tried to form favorable governments.
16. Explain why South Africa has been able to withstand world pressure to change its apartheid system.

Essay Questions

1. Write a paragraph explaining how the conflict between Israel and its neighbors began.
2. Explain why Atatürk, Nasser, and Reza Khan attempted to modernize their countries. Compare the methods that each leader used.
3. Write a brief essay explaining how the problem of a homeland for the Palestinians began and how the problem has continued to foster unrest in the Middle East.

4. Select one of the countries of the Middle East, and describe the effects that modernization and change have had on it.
5. Explain how the different attitudes of the British, French, Belgians, and Portuguese toward their African colonies affected the success of their colonies after independence.
6. Explain why white governments in Rhodesia and South Africa passed laws limiting the freedom of blacks in the country. Why did Rhodesia's white government fall while South Africa's remains in power?
7. Write a paragraph about the effect that artificial boundaries between countries have had on new African nations.
8. Explain why one-person rule, rather than a democratic system, has been the pattern in many of the new African nations.
9. Write a brief essay about the problems of agriculture in Africa.

Critical Thinking

1. What logical inconsistency was there in the French regarding Algeria as a part of France?
2. What was the unstated assumption of Ibn Saud's declaration that anyone offering a million pounds "would be welcome to all the concessions he wanted in my country"? Give reasons for your answer.
3. What was the unstated assumption of the Ayatollah Khomeini's declaration, "I will appoint a government with the support of the Iranian people"?
4. Israel justified its invasion of Lebanon by claiming self-defense, in view of the fact that Palestinians in Lebanon had launched raids against Israel. Was this a warranted or unwarranted claim? Give reasons for your answer.
5. What is the bias in South Africa's policy of apartheid? Can you cite any examples of bias related to racial policy in other African nations?
6. What unstated assumptions were there in the resolution adopted by the Fifth Pan-African Congress?
7. Does the statement of Albert Luthuli about the "fruits of moderation" contain an ambiguous or equivocal assumption? Explain.

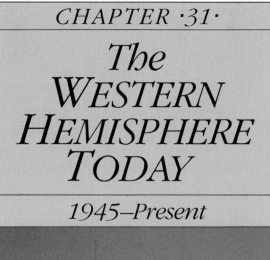

CHAPTER ·31·

The WESTERN HEMISPHERE TODAY

1945–Present

Objectives

- *To identify the challenges facing South America*
- *To describe the conflicts in the Caribbean and Central America*
- *To discuss the main issues facing Mexico and Canada since World War II*
- *To explain the changes in the society of the United States in the postwar years*

*B*y the end of World War II, all the countries of the Western Hemisphere had entered the war on the Allied side. In 1945 the United States emerged from the war as the most powerful nation in the world. It was the only one of the major combatants not to suffer damage to its industrial base. Indeed, the war helped its economy, finally ending the Depression.

The isolationist feeling that followed World War I did not recur after World War II. Instead, the United States found itself involved in the affairs of countries throughout the world. Its only rival for power was the other superpower, the Soviet Union. Both would compete for influence all over the globe, not just in the Western Hemisphere.

The power gap between the United States and the other countries in this hemisphere has often led to uneasy relations. Latin-American countries and Canada resented the dominance of their neighbor. Yet the United States has maintained good relations with most of these countries.

During the postwar years, many Latin-American nations experienced stresses in political life. Some went from dictatorships to democratic forms of government. The countries in Central America and the Caribbean, in particular, have experienced a number of revolutions. Guerrilla activity continues today. These years also saw enormous economic growth as countries modernized and industrialized. This industrialization was often uneven, leaving a great number of the people unaffected. Modernization brought about great social changes and new challenges.

SOUTH AMERICA

Foreigners controlled most of South America's plantations, public utilities, transportation, cattle ranches, meat-packing plants, and mines. Yet most South American countries remained underdeveloped. Their economies often relied on a single resource. When the markets for copper, tin, coffee, and meat decreased, South American countries suffered economic hardship. Postwar plans for diversification and industrial development brought hope for future prosperity.

Brazil Moves toward Democracy

Occupying about one-half the land mass of the continent, Brazil is the largest country in South America. Its more than 130 million Portuguese-speaking people comprise a melting pot of different nationalities. Immigrants from Germany, Italy, Lebanon, Japan, and Eastern Europe have joined Brazil's older population of Portuguese, blacks, and Indians.

During the l930's, Brazil was ruled by a dictator, Getúlio Vargas. Vargas worked to unite the country and diversify its economy. He increased government control over the economy and expanded the social welfare system. This action led to improvements in education and public health. A labor code was introduced. The government began public works programs to relieve unemployment. At the end of the war, Vargas was overthrown by a military coup. However, he returned to power in 1950, serving until 1954.

In 1955 Juscelino Kubitschek (KOO-buh-check) was elected president of Brazil. His dream was to build a new capital in the interior of the country and open that area to development. Brasilia began to take shape on a red-dust plateau where before there had been nothing but scrub trees and wild animals. It was dedicated as the nation's capital in 1960. Although it was six hundred miles from the coast, Brasilia was soon connected to the rest of the country by a network of "highways of national unity."

Discontent with Kubitschek's successors and a rise in the inflation rate to almost 100 percent surfaced in the 1960's. In 1964 the army took control. Political parties were banned, and the press was limited. Over the next eight years opponents of the regime were hunted down. In the 1970's a change to *abertura* (ah-bair-TOO-rah), or opening the door to political liberalization, was adopted. The army agreed to allow the nation's return to civilian democratic rule. In 1985 José Sarney (sahr-NAY) became the new president.

An Economic Transformation

In the last twenty years, Brazil has undergone an economic revolution. In a single generation, Brazil has become a consumer society that produces everything from automobiles to fountain pens. Older industries such as textiles, paper, chemicals, leather, cement, iron, and steel have been expanded and new industries created. Great advances have been made in agricultural technology and development. Today Brazil sells computers to China, and has the sixth largest aircraft and arms industry in the world.

Fueling this economic miracle is the industrial heart of Brazil, São Paulo. "São Paulo can never stop" is the motto for this city of an estimated ten million people, the richest in South America.

Growth was slowed by the increase in oil prices in the early 1970's. Brazil stepped up its search for oil. Meanwhile **gasahol,** a blend of gasoline and grain alcohol is being used. Today 70 percent of Brazil's cars run on gasahol. In partnership with Paraguay, Brazil constructed the largest hydroelectric complex in the world, Itaipu (ee-TIE-poo) Dam, as a new source of power.

The growing economy, however, has not benefited all of Brazil's people. Today, two societies exist within the country. One has a life-style similar to that of the United States, while the other is poor and illiterate. Brazilian Indians have been pushed off their homelands to make way for development. The slums or *favelas* in cities such as Rio de Janeiro (REE-oh dih juh-NAIR-oh) are breeding grounds of poverty and disease. Shacks, often without water and sanitary facilities, are home to almost one-fourth of Rio's population.

Much of Brazil's development has been financed by loans from foreign banks. Today, Brazil's debt of more than $100 billion is the largest in the world. With the international economic downturn in the 1980's, the debt problem became serious. When Brazil's exports fell, the country

Surrounded by a rubber plantation, a modern oil refinery in Belem, Brazil, symbolizes hope for Brazil's future development. Why?

could not meet even its interest payments. To get more foreign financing, the government had to agree to a strict budget program set up by the International Monetary Fund and subsidies of some basic products.

The building of Brasilia has increased the productivity of the undeveloped Amazon region. Homesteaders are pioneering new development there. The untapped riches of these new lands are a source of hope and optimism for Brazil's future. However, environmental groups point out that development of rain forest areas may not produce positive results.

Argentina

The second largest country in South America, Argentina is one of the great wheat- and meat-producing regions of the world. In the twentieth century, the country has shifted several times from civilian to military rule.

In 1943 Juan Perón (HWAHN pay-ROHN) was part of a military coup that overthrew the Argentine government. He was elected president in 1946. Perón's brand of authoritarianism and socialism, called *justicialismo* (hoos-tee-see-ah-LEES-moh), was originally popular with many Argentines. He shrewdly realized the power to be gained by an alliance with the growing labor movement. He formed a coalition that included the labor unions, the rural poor, and the urban middle classes. Under his administration, workers' wages were regularly increased.

Perón also fostered a strong nationalism. One of his main concerns was to remove Argentina from foreign economic domination. He bought out foreign ownership of the railroads and other large enterprises. In 1955 the army, concerned about the power of the labor unions, ousted him.

A succession of ineffective military and civilian governments followed. Perón was reelected in 1973. After his death in 1974, he was succeeded by his second wife, Isabel. She became the first woman chief-of-state in the Americas. However, her dictatorial rule led to her ouster by the military in 1976.

From 1976 to 1983 military rule was highlighted by a sharply rising debt and poor government administration. Opponents of the regime were abducted and never heard from again. Known as the "disappeareds," they numbered in the tens of thousands.

The military was weakened by the Argentine invasion of the Falkland Islands (known to the Argentines as the Malvinas) in 1982. The islands had long been claimed by both Argentina and Great Britain. The residents, however, regarded themselves as British citizens. In a ten-week war, the British regained the islands, and Argentina suffered a humiliating defeat.

Elections in 1983 restored civilian rule. President Raúl Alfonsín (rah-OOL ahl-fohn-SEEN) took office in December 1983, and shortly after began to reduce the power of the military. He repealed the law that gave amnesty to those accused of human rights violations. Civilian courts tried more than a dozen military officers involved in the disappearances of the 1970's and early 1980's. Alfonsín continues to face problems of high unemployment, a stagnating economy that was working at only 50 percent capacity in 1984, and a $46 billion debt.

Chile

Chile has the largest sources of nitrate and copper in the world. Many of these resources were owned and developed by **multinational corporations,** firms that operated in many nations. Often, their headquarters were in the United States.

Eduardo Frei (FRAY), elected president in 1964, began to nationalize the copper industry by buying 51 percent of the foreign-owned mines. He allowed foreign companies to continue management of the mines in return for their promise to increase production and pay additional taxes. In the rural areas, Frei increased farm workers' wages and distributed some land to peasants. He also proposed tax reforms to redistribute income.

However, Frei also moved to weaken the country's labor unions. As a result, workers' support for communism and socialism increased. Furthermore, inflation averaged 30 percent a year between 1967 and 1970, wiping out the economic gains Frei had promised.

In the election of 1970, the winning candidate was Salvador Allende (ah-YEN-day). He was the first Marxist to win a free election in this hemisphere. During Allende's first year in office, worker income rose by 50 percent. The government also began public financing of housing, education, sanitation, and health facilities. Inflation and the public debt rose sharply.

Allende's Marxist politics aroused opposition. His attempts to reduce the influence of the multinational companies and his recognition of the Communist government of Cuba caused the United States government to cut off credit to Chile. At home the United States also encouraged opposition to Allende. In September 1973 Allende was overthrown and died during a military coup.

The new military government in Chile has imprisoned its political opponents. Under the leadership of Augusto Pinochet (PEE-noh-shay), the socialistic measures of the Allende government were stopped.

Continuity and Change

South America is a continent of contrasts. Most of its 264 million people speak Spanish or Portuguese. Descendants of European people form the majority in such countries as Argentina, Uruguay, and Chile. But descendants of the native South Americans are in the majority in Ecuador, Peru, and Bolivia.

In most South American countries there is a great gap between the rich and the poor. The poor often are Indians and blacks, living in urban slums or leading hard lives on large farms in the interior. Attempts at mass education have increased literacy in urban areas, but it remains low in rural areas.

South American nations also vary greatly in the development of their natural resources. By 1985 the discovery of oil in Venezuela had made it the wealthiest nation on the continent. It was one of the original members of OPEC.

South America's tradition of the caudillo, or strong-man rule, has made it hard for democratic governments and political parties to establish themselves. However, what freedom of expression is allowed has often led to unrest among the poor

ECONOMIC ACTIVITY
IN LATIN AMERICA

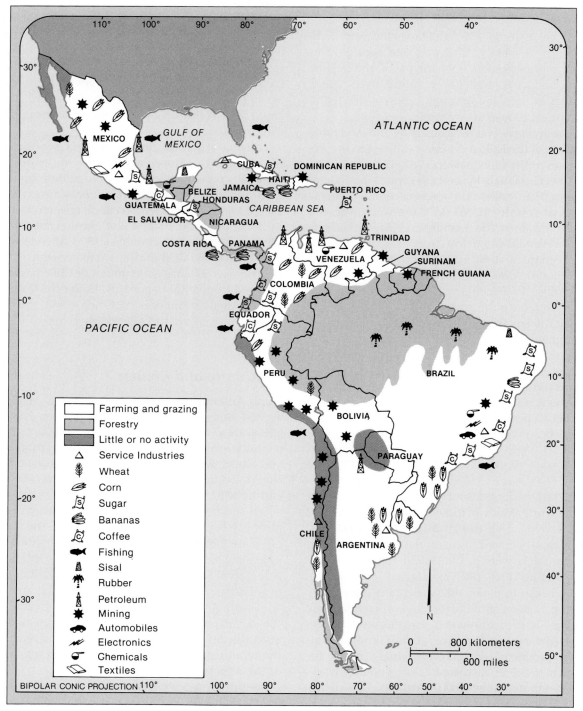

Choose three Latin American countries and name their major industries or products. Why are there fewer industries in central Brazil? Where does most economic activity occur?

and underprivileged. Military leaders have constantly been ready to overthrow elected governments to maintain order and the power of the wealthy.

There have been some encouraging signs. Venezuela has had an elected government since 1958. In 1982 Bolivia traded military rule for democracy. However, the cycle of violence is hard to break. In the 1970's, urban terrorism by the Tupamaro guerrillas resulted in military rule in Uruguay. Other countries have had similar problems. Today's democratic government in Peru faces The Shining Path, a guerrilla group that attacks both in the cities and in the countryside.

All South American countries have had a dramatic rise in population. Only Africa has a greater rate of increase. This has led to overcrowded cities, unemployment, and poverty.

Another common problem is the huge debt that many countries have incurred to develop their resources. Worldwide, most of the countries with the largest debt are in Latin America. Nations that tried to escape foreign domination by nationalizing foreign-owned resources now face a new kind of economic domination. To default, or fail to pay the debt, would mean an end to any further loans for development. To reduce the debt countries have taken funds from social programs, such as food subsidies, that are a matter of life and death for many of their people. In addition, heavy reliance on loans has placed great strains on bank resources both in the United States and in other countries that have lent money to Latin-American nations.

Inter-American Cooperation

President Franklin D. Roosevelt sought to improve relations between the United States and South America through the Good Neighbor Policy. A series of conferences between 1933 and 1947 established the principle that the United States would not interfere militarily in Latin-American affairs, as it had done in the past. In 1947 the Latin-American nations and the United States met in Rio de Janeiro. They pledged to come to the aid of any American republic that was attacked from within or without the hemisphere.

In 1948 the Organization of American States (OAS) was founded. The members included all the American nations except Canada. (Cuba was later ousted.) The members agreed that an attack on one state would be regarded as an attack on all. In 1954 the OAS, meeting in Caracas, Venezuela, agreed that members should cooperate in the defense of the hemisphere against communism.

In 1960 the Latin American Free Trade Area (LAFTA) was created. Members agreed to increase trade by lowering tariffs and breaking down other barriers. It was seen as a Latin-American counterpart of the Common Market.

President John F. Kennedy established the Alliance for Progress between the United States and Latin America in 1961. Congress set aside $10 billion for a ten-year program intended to strengthen the economies of Latin-American countries. The United States hoped that greater economic progress in the hemisphere would forestall Communist movements in the area.

Another Kennedy program, the Peace Corps, recruited Americans to help developing areas, including Latin America. Still in operation, the program sends volunteer workers to teach skills in agriculture, health care, and basic education, and to help build community projects.

President Jimmy Carter stressed the importance of human rights in his foreign policy. He threatened withdrawal of United States aid in an effort to force authoritarian countries to end abuses of human rights.

SECTION REVIEW

1. Mapping: Use the map on page 706 to find where most of Brazil's industry is located. Why does Brazil want to develop the interior of the country?
2. In your own words, briefly define or identify: *abertura*, gasohol, *favela*, *justicialismo*, multinational corporation, *caudillo*, default.
3. Why have many South American countries incurred large debts?
4. Why is it important for the United States to improve South America's economy?
■ What are some policies any nation should follow as a ''Good Neighbor''?

THE CARIBBEAN AND CENTRAL AMERICA

Most of the small countries of the Caribbean and Central America are dependent on exports of a single crop. The postwar world saw a decline in the price of such products as bananas, coffee, meat, and lumber, reducing the income of these countries. As in South America, a large gap between the rich and the poor exists in Caribbean and Central American countries. Because supporters of the two groups take extremist positions, creating a moderate reform-minded centrist party has been very difficult. Today, social and political disorders continue to affect the progress of Central American nations such as Nicaragua, El Salvador, and Honduras. In the Caribbean, Cuba remains dominated by Fidel Castro and the Soviet Union.

The Cuban Revolution

In the postwar years, Cuba was ruled by the dictator Fulgencio Batista (fool-HEN-see-oh bah-TEES-tah). Poverty was widespread because of the fluctuation of the market in sugar, Cuba's principal crop. Batista encouraged heavy foreign investment, but his regime was cruel and corrupt. In 1959 he was overthrown by a military coup.

Fidel Castro began to lead the guerrilla insurrection against the regime during the 1950's. After Batista's overthrow Castro took charge and began to transform Cuban society. He required all school-age children and illiterate adults to learn to read and write. Rural health clinics were established in areas that had never had a doctor. Agricultural land was redistributed. In the process, the government seized privately owned land and businesses, including some owned by Americans.

A lone guerrilla fighter guards a deserted village. In what way does this photograph reflect the impact of guerrilla warfare on Central American nations?

Castro permitted no opposition. He held no elections and refused to allow freedom of the press. He imprisoned or executed his political opponents. Thousands of middle-class Cubans fled the island. Most sought refuge in the United States. Castro proclaimed his Marxist beliefs and turned to the Soviet Union for aid.

In 1961 the United States broke diplomatic relations with Cuba. In April, an army of Cuban exiles landed at the Bay of Pigs on Cuba's coast. They had been trained by the United States Central Intelligence Agency. It was hoped that the Cuban people would support them in overthrowing Castro. But Castro's forces captured the invaders, who were not freed until the United States paid a large ransom for their release.

The next year saw a more dangerous confrontation involving Cuba. The Soviet Union began to place missiles with nuclear warheads on Cuban soil, only ninety miles from the United States. As part of the agreement that, much later, ended the crisis, the United States promised not to invade Cuba.

Castro's regime continued to frustrate the United States. Cuban aid and troops were sent to help Marxist insurrections both within the hemisphere and in Africa. In 1980 the Mariel boatlift operation brought many Cubans to the United States. Castro intentionally released prison inmates and mentally ill persons. He included them with other people who wanted to leave Cuba. In response to these actions, the United States has opposed all trade with the country. Castro's ability to maintain his regime in the face of opposition from the United States has earned him the admiration of some third-world nations. Cuba's ties with the Soviet Union, however, remain strong.

The Caribbean Nations

Many of the island nations of the Caribbean are small mini-states with populations around 100,000. Among these are the islands of the Lesser Antilles, such as Dominica and Grenada. The largest, Trinidad and Tobago, has a population of just over a million. In the Greater Antilles are the larger nations of Cuba, Haiti, the Dominican Republic, and Jamaica. Many of these nations depend on tourism and money sent home by people who have emigrated to the United States.

In 1952 Puerto Rico became a self-governing commonwealth territory of the United States. This allowed Puerto Ricans to come to the United States without immigration restrictions. Some Puerto Ricans wanted the island to become the fifty-first state, and others wanted independence. The status of Puerto Rico has become a major political issue on the island in recent years.

In 1965 a rebel group seized Santo Domingo, the capital of the Dominican Republic. Claiming that some of the rebels were Communists, the military government announced that it could not guarantee the safety of foreigners. The United States sent 22,000 troops to retake control of the country for the military government.

In 1983 the United States invaded the island of Grenada. This action was in response to a coup that the United States claimed endangered American students there. The United States had long wanted to rid the island of Cuban advisors. Elections were held in 1984 and a moderate pro-United States government took office.

Under President Ronald Reagan, the United States put forth a Caribbean Basin Initiative to help the economies of the countries of the region. The proposal calls for a free-trade zone for exports to the United States. It also encourages American businesses to invest in the area.

Panama and Costa Rica

Nationalistic feelings in Panama led to resentment that the United States Canal Zone divided their country. In 1964 protest over the Canal Zone led to a riot in which twenty-five persons were killed. In 1968 General Omar Torrijos (toe-REE-hohs) seized power. Torrijos demanded that the United States revoke or amend the 1903 treaty that gave it possession of the Zone. The Ford and Carter administrations negotiated two treaties, which were signed in 1977. The Canal Zone was to become Panamanian territory in 1982. Panama would gain complete control of the canal itself on the last day of 1999. However, the United States retained the right to send troops to the Zone after the year 2000 if Panama or any other country or groups closed the canal. The treaties have led to better relations between the two countries.

Costa Rica is the only Central American nation with a tradition of democratic government. Under

President José Napoléon Duarte of El Salvador joins some of his top military officers to review a parade during an anniversary celebration in 1984. Why do many Latin American leaders wish to maintain good relations with the military?

its 1949 constitution, the army was abolished. This action removed the threat of military takeovers. The people of Costa Rica enjoy the highest per capita income and the highest literacy rate in Central America. Ownership of land is widespread. Though its neighbors have experienced revolution and revolt, Costa Rica has remained at peace.

Crisis in Central America

Political instability marks the countries of Guatemala, Honduras, and El Salvador. The familiar problems of poverty, extremes between rich and poor, and military rule have produced a continuing cycle of violence.

In Guatemala, President Jacobo Arbenz's reform program threatened the monopoly on banana production held by the United Fruit Company, a company with headquarters in the United States. Arbenz also had persons suspected of being Communists in his government. In 1954 the United States helped overthrow Arbenz's elected

government. Since then, a series of regimes have put down opposition with brutal violations of human rights.

Honduras is being used as a military base and training area by United States troops. As a result, the United States has increased its economic aid to Honduras. In turn, this aid has raised the standard of living there. Even so, many people on the country's banana plantations barely make a living. In 1982 Honduras held its first national election in ten years. Internal problems, however, led to the postponement of the planned 1985 election.

El Salvador is the most densely populated country in Central America. Its economy depends on the world price of coffee. A small upper class owns most of the country's land. In 1979 a combined civilian-military leadership took power to halt recurring violence. It faced opposition by leftist rebels, who today control about 25 percent of the country. Also, right-wing death squads, made up of government officials and army officers, have killed many who advocate reforms.

The murder of four American churchwomen in 1980 resulted in a cutoff of United States aid to El Salvador. Aid resumed when the moderate José Napoleón Duarte (D'WAHR-tay) became the head of government. The Reagan administration sent American military advisors to the country. Continued violence has, however, resulted in over 40,000 deaths since 1980. Duarte has attempted to begin peace talks with the rebels to end the civil war.

Revolution in Nicaragua

When United States Marines left Nicaragua in 1933, they left the Somoza (soh-MOH-sah) family in control. The family enriched itself at the expense of their people. In 1967 Anastasio (ah-nah-STAH-s'yoe) Somoza became president, with the help of a National Guard trained by the United States. Sandinista guerrillas, named after a rebel Nicaraguan Army officer who had fought against United States Marines in the 1930's, tried to overthrow him. The movement gained support in 1978 when Somoza's forces killed the editor of an opposition newspaper. Antigovernment protests broke out. The next year Somoza resigned and fled the country.

The new Sandinista government has had some success in trying to solve the problems of illiteracy and lack of health care. But the Sandinistas' suppression of opposition and acceptance of aid and advisors from Cuba, as well as the support of the Soviet Union, brought protests from the United States government. The Reagan administration also claimed that the Sandinistas were aiding the rebels in El Salvador. The United States blocked Nicaragua's applications for loans from international organizations. Nicaragua then began to get aid from the Soviet Union.

The United States Central Intelligence Agency helped in organizing rebel opposition to the Sandinistas. These contras tried to disrupt the economy through violent actions. In 1985 the United States Congress cut off military support funds for the contras because of their human rights violations. However, non-military funds were approved totaling about $14 million.

Concern about unrest in Central America has led to the creation of the Contadora group. Composed of Panama, Mexico, Venezuela, and Colombia, this group has tried to bring a peaceful resolution to the disputes within the region. Their proposals have called for the withdrawal of all outside military advisors. The group has asked for pledges of noninterference in the internal affairs of neighboring countries.

SECTION REVIEW

1. Mapping: Use the map on page 706 to find the countries of Guatemala, Honduras, El Salvador, and Nicaragua. How do their resources compare with those found in South American countries?
2. In your own words, briefly define or identify: Bay of Pigs, Caribbean Basin Initiative, Sandinistas, contras, Contadora group.
3. Why has the United States not invaded Cuba?
4. Why did the United States oppose the Sandinistas?
■ Do you think it is important for a democratic government to permit opposition to its policies in peacetime and in wartime? Give reasons for your answers.

MEXICO AND CANADA

Mexico and Canada have always been greatly influenced by their powerful neighbor, the United States. Both, however, are important countries in their own right. Since World War II, each has increased in wealth and world influence.

Postwar Mexican Developments

With the loss of most of its foreign markets during the years of the Great Depression, Mexico began to be more independent economically. From 1934 to 1940 President Lázaro Cárdenas (LAH-sah-roh KAHR-day-nahs) encouraged Mexicans to start their own businesses. He gave more land to the peasants than all prior leaders combined had given. He also nationalized Mexico's oil industry in 1938. This action rid the country of all foreign oil interests.

Many of Cárdenas' policies were carried on by his successors, especially José López Portillo (LOE-pess pohr-TEE-yoh), who became president in 1976. He was a member of the Institutional Revolutionary party, which had ruled since 1910. (This one-party rule is credited with bringing stability to Mexico in contrast to its Central American neighbors.) He had to cope with widespread unemployment, poverty, and a population growing faster than the economy. These same problems challenge the current Mexican president Miguel de la Madrid Hurtado (oor-TAH-thoe), who took office in 1982.

However, Mexican government leaders in the postwar period seemed to be more concerned about building the nation's economy than in social reforms. Mexico began to develop its oil reserves through the state-owned oil company Pemex. Its oil resources were much more extensive than had earlier been thought. In the mid-1970's Mexico seemed to be on the edge of an economic boom. Much of the wealth, however, was misspent through corrupt and bad administration.

Today, due in part to a drop in the price of oil, President de la Madrid Hurtado rules a nation that has a foreign debt second in the world only to that of Brazil. This debt threatens to stop future development programs.

In the postwar years, Mexico has sought a foreign policy independent from the United States. Despite urgings from the United States, Mexico refused to break diplomatic relations with Cuba as many other Latin-American nations did. In recent years it has distanced itself from United States policy in Central America. It is a member of the independent Contadora group. Mexico wants to be a leader among third-world nations.

Challenges for Mexico

Since World War II, Mexico's population has risen from about 22 million to more than 75 million. Almost half its people are under 15 years of age. The high birthrate has strained the ability of Mexican agriculture to feed the nation. About 50 percent of all Mexicans are outside the "money economy." This means that they grow only enough food to support themselves. The government has begun family planning programs. As women become more educated and start to enter the work force, it is expected that average family size will diminish. Women gained the right to vote in 1955, and the country passed an equal rights law in 1974.

The depressed state of agriculture has caused many people to move to the cities in search of greater opportunities. The cities though do not have enough jobs, particularly for unskilled workers. Mexico City, for example, has seen the growth of enormous slum areas. It has a population of 16 million—twice that of New York City—and is expected to reach 30 million by the year 2000. The surrounding mountains trap the exhaust of cars and the fumes of factories to give Mexico City the world's worst air pollution. The Mexican author Carlos Fuentes (FWEN-tays) has called it "the city forever spreading like a creeping blot." Yet every day more than a thousand people leave the rural areas to live in Mexico City.

Congestion in downtown Mexico City and in other urban centers is a serious problem. Is congestion a problem in your area?

Mexico's overpopulation has affected its relations with the United States. The border of about 1,500 miles between the two countries is difficult to patrol. Many Mexicans enter the United States illegally to find better-paying jobs. The so-called undocumented aliens, some argue, put a strain on social services in the United States. These aliens are a source of concern and friction between the two countries. The influx of these aliens has led to increased border patrols and sanctions against those who employ them.

An Identity Problem for Canada

The world's second largest nation in land area, Canada is rich in resources. Petroleum, uranium, and timber are found in abundance. It is one of the great wheat-growing and exporting nations of the world. In the postwar years, Canada has tried to find its identity as a nation. To the south, the United States has long been both Canada's best trade partner and also the largest investor in Canada's economy.

Although most of Canada is English-speaking, 30 percent of its people are descendants of French colonists and speak French as their primary language. The French-speaking population lives mainly in the province of Quebec. The language division was made worse by the feeling of the French-Canadians that they were second-class citizens. They had less influence within the government and less control of the nation's economic wealth.

Led by Réné Lévesque (luh-VECK), a separatist movement arose to demand the right of Quebec to become a nation. In 1974 Quebec's provincial government voted to make French the official language of the province. Prime Minister Pierre Elliott Trudeau (troo-DOE), himself a French-Canadian, supported the move toward bilingualism, or official use of two languages. Trudeau also favored giving Quebec a degree of autonomy but opposed separation. The issue was hotly debated for several years. Later in a 1980 referendum, the people of Quebec voted against separation from Canada.

Separation was not the only divisive issue facing Canada. The western provinces, which contain valuable mineral resources, including oil, have a relatively sparse population and little political power. They began to demand a greater say in the country's affairs and in deciding how the wealth of their resources was to be used.

In 1981 Canada negotiated a new national charter. It eliminated the requirement that changes in Canada's constitution have to be ratified by the British Parliament. Although Elizabeth II of Great Britain remains queen of Canada, Britain's legal ties with Canada have been severed. The charter also provided a bill of rights.

Canada and the World

In the postwar world, Canada became a charter member of NATO and a strong partner of the West. Its important resources and strategic location have made it important to the United States. The two countries have cooperated in a common defense. They jointly erected a Distant Early Warning (DEW) radar system across northern Canada to warn of enemy missiles or aircraft. In 1958 the two nations organized the North American Aerospace Defense Command (NORAD) for the air defense of the continent. Another Canadian-American project was the St. Lawrence Seaway. This system of locks and canals, linking the Great Lakes with the Atlantic Ocean, opened in 1959.

Traditionally, Canada's relations with the United States have been positive. In foreign affairs, Canada has often supported the positions of its southern neighbor. Economic ties with the United States have helped strenghten the Canadian dollar. For example, export sales to the United States played an important role in boosting Canada's gross national product in 1984 to an estimated $387 billion.

Trudeau served as prime minister of Canada from 1968 to 1979, and again from 1980 until he retired in 1984. Under Trudeau, Canadian foreign policy stressed greater concern than ever before with the poorer countries of the world. While remaining involved in East-West issues and urging control of nuclear weapons, Trudeau frequently spoke on the north-south issue. This term refers to the relationship between rich and poor nations in this hemisphere. Efforts by Canada's government and private relief agencies to close this gap are being explored. This gap was also discussed by Pope John Paul II during a visit to Canada in 1985 during a series of meetings with Canadian officials and Church leaders.

In recent years, Canada has become involved in a dispute with the United States over the issue of acid rain. Acid rain is contaminated rainfall that is caused by industrial pollution in the Midwestern United States. It falls both on the eastern United States and within eastern Canada, causing ecological damage. President Reagan and current Canadian prime minister Brian Mulroney have agreed to study this problem.

SECTION REVIEW

1. Mapping: Use the Atlas map on page 759 to find what areas of Canada and the United States might be affected by acid rain.
2. In your own words, briefly define or identify: Pemex, undocumented aliens, separatist movement, bilingualism, north-south issue, acid rain.
3. What are the two main challenges facing Mexico today?
4. What issues threaten Canada's unity?
■ How would you view the United States if you lived in either Mexico or Canada?

POSTWAR UNITED STATES

The United States had world leadership thrust upon it after World War II. This new role caused considerable debate and division throughout the nation.

Fighting Communism at Home

The people of the United States expected that their country's postwar supremacy would lead to a period of peace. The Cold War led many to look for domestic conspiracies to explain the unexpected rise of Soviet power.

In 1950 a United States senator from Wisconsin, Joseph R. McCarthy, gave a speech in Wheeling, West Virginia. He said there were "205 card-carrying Communists" in the State Department.

Though his charge was never proven, the hunt for subversives in the government gained wide support. That same year the McCarran International Security Act required all members of the Communist party of the United States to register with the attorney general. It also barred Communists from defense plants and kept foreign Communists from coming into the United States.

McCarthy used his power to call many citizens to testify about possible Communist party connections. Simply being accused of Communist leanings caused many people to lose their jobs in government, universities, and businesses. For many years, public debate on foreign policy turned on the question of Communist influence.

In 1954 McCarthy charged that officials of the Department of the Army were involved in Communist activity. This resulted in the nationally televised Army-McCarthy hearings. When McCarthy could not back up his reckless charges, the Senate voted in December 1954 to censure him for conduct "unbecoming a member of the United States Senate." McCarthy's power faded. It was, however, one of several factors in creating an atmosphere that made stopping the spread of communism at home and abroad a major policy goal.

The Role of Government Expands

President Franklin D. Roosevelt's New Deal programs gave the government more responsibility for the economic and social life of the country, which continued after the war. President Harry S Truman's Fair Deal program extended the New Deal. It raised the minimum wage, expanded social security coverage, and improved housing for low-income citizens. President Dwight D. Eisenhower, the first Republican president elected in twenty years, continued the New Deal and Fair Deal programs. Elements of these programs are reflected in the social legislation that followed.

Elected in 1960, President John F. Kennedy proposed a New Frontier of additional social programs. Kennedy could not get Congress to pass the necessary legislation. When he was assassinated on November 22, 1963, he was succeeded by Vice-President Lyndon B. Johnson, who put through an even more ambitious program that focused on social change.

Johnson's Great Society legislation was the most sweeping social reform since the New Deal. The Great Society programs attacked poverty, discrimination, problems of the elderly, and inadequate health care. The Economic Opportunity Act of 1964 provided for job training for the poor, loans to rural farm cooperatives, aid to migrant workers, and encouragement to urban businesses. Johnson's VISTA (Volunteers in Service to America) program was intended to be a domestic version of Kennedy's Peace Corps. In 1965 Congress approved Medicare, which supported hospital care for those over 65, and Medicaid, a similar program for the needy. The Housing Act of 1965 provided federal funds for much needed low- and middle-income housing.

Johnson's Republican and Democratic successors kept and even added to his programs. Under the Nixon administration, social security benefits were tied to the cost of living. This move eventually caused financial strain on the social security program. Today, the solvency of the social security program is still a serious issue.

In 1981 President Ronald Reagan came to office with the belief that government was attempting to do too much. Under Reagan, funding for many social programs decreased, and some were eliminated. However, Reagan promised that the truly needy would not suffer from the loss of government support.

The Civil Rights Movement

The greatest social change in postwar American life was in the status of blacks. In 1945 the right of blacks to vote was effectively blocked in parts of the South by discriminatory voting requirements. In many places, **segregation,** or separation of the races, in schools and public accommodations was part of local law. Legal challenges to segregation gave rise to the civil rights movement, which sought full equality for blacks.

President Truman made a start in 1948 by desegregating the armed forces. In 1954 the United States Supreme Court in the case of *Brown* v. *Board of Education of Topeka, Kansas,* ruled that "separate

Roy Cohn, Senator Joseph McCarthy, and David Schine zeroed in on alleged Communists in the 1950's. Are public hearings in the best interests of the nation?

but equal" education for blacks was unconstitutional. School systems were ordered to desegregate "with all deliberate speed."

In 1955, Dr. Martin Luther King, Jr., led a bus boycott in Montgomery, Alabama, to protest the rule that blacks ride at the back of the bus. The boycott was a success, and the buses were desegregated. Others adopted King's lead in using nonviolent tactics such as sit-ins, occupying seats in restaurants for whites only, until they were served. Civil rights marches took place throughout the South. When some marchers were met with abusive police action, public support for the movement increased.

During the Johnson administration, Congress passed a series of Civil Rights acts. These outlawed racial discrimination in public facilities, voting registration requirements, hiring, and union membership. The acts gave the attorney general the power to bring suit in cases of racial discrimination. They also gave the government power to stop federal funding to institutions that practiced such discrimination.

To a degree, the civil rights movement helped the women's liberation movement which pressed for equal opportunity for women in jobs. Women analyzed their roles in society. Some demanded more educational opportunities, while others found they wished to have both professional careers and families. An Equal Rights Amendment (ERA) to the Constitution was passed by Congress in 1972, but was not ratified by the required number of states. Other groups, such as Native Americans and Hispanics, have also benefited from the civil rights movement.

The Vietnam Experience

The Vietnam War was the country's longest war and the first to be widely covered by television. Americans saw the brutal reality of warfare.

Martin Luther King, Jr., joined by his wife Coretta, led many civil rights marches such as this one in Selma, Alabama, in the 1960's. Did these marches make a difference?

In January 1968, the Tet Offensive, an attack by Vietcong and North Vietnamese troops against major South Vietnamese cities and towns, shocked Americans. They had been told that the United States was winning the war. Antiwar protests began on college campuses. As opposition grew, protest marches became a familiar sight.

Many political leaders questioned the involvement of the United States in Vietnam. In the presidential primaries of 1968, antiwar candidate Eugene McCarthy received a substantial vote. Johnson announced his decision not to run again. Robert Kennedy, the brother of President Kennedy, entered the race and was assassinated after a primary victory in California. Martin Luther King also fell to an assassin's bullet.

Richard Nixon was elected president in November of that year, largely on his promise to end the war. But when Nixon stepped up American involvement by invading Cambodia, campus demonstrations continued.

After Nixon finally withdrew American troops from Vietnam, his successor, President Gerald R. Ford, found it impossible to obtain support for preventing the fall of the South Vietnamese government in 1975. Within the United States, the effects of the loss were long-lasting. The inaccurate statements of the government about the nation's involvement in Vietnam led many to distrust government. Vietnam veterans came home to a country that wanted to forget their sacrifices. With the 1982 opening of the Vietnam Veteran's Memorial in the nation's capital, some of the wounds were healed. In 1985, the tenth anniversary of the fall of the South Vietnamese government and America's withdrawal, Vietnam veterans were honored in nationwide celebrations.

The Vietnam War also gave rise to the feeling that American involvement in the affairs of other nations was unwise. The holding of hostages in Iran from 1979 to 1981 caused widespread anger throughout the United States at America's unwillingness and inability to solve the crisis by force.

The Watergate Scandal

What some historians consider the worst political scandal in United States history began with a burglary of the Democratic headquarters in the Watergate apartments in Washington, D.C., during the 1972 election campaign. It soon became clear that members of President Nixon's reelection committee were involved. The Senate appointed a special committee headed by Senator Sam Ervin of North Carolina to look into the matter.

In the spring and summer of 1973, Americans watched the televised hearings of the Ervin Committee. Its most important witness, John Dean, testified that the President had approved payment of money to one of the burglars for his silence. The White House denied Dean's story, but a later witness said that the President had taped all conversations in his office. Nixon refused to release all the tapes. A special prosecutor investigated criminal activity in the Watergate affair. During this investigation, it was revealed that Vice-President Spiro Agnew had received illegal payments from a Maryland contractor. Agnew resigned, and Gerald Ford was named to succeed him.

The Judiciary Committee of the House of Representatives began hearings on the impeachment of Nixon. He was charged with obstruction of justice and various abuses of power. The committee approved three counts of impeachment, but the matter was still in doubt. The Supreme Court ordered Nixon to give up his tapes. They showed that Nixon had participated in the cover-up of the Watergate burglary. On August 9, 1974, faced with nearly certain impeachment, Nixon became the first American president to resign from office.

After Gerald Ford was sworn in as President, he gave an unconditional pardon to Nixon for any crimes he might have committed. Many of Nixon's close aides, however, went to jail. When Congress approved Nelson Rockefeller as Vice-President under Ford, for the first time neither of the nation's two highest officials had been elected.

The Economy

From 1950 to 1965 the United States produced as much as it had since the founding of Jamestown. Between 1965 and 1980 the economy again doubled, but the effects of inflation diluted the gain. Inflation occurs when the cost of goods and services increases and purchasing power declines.

Even though the number of employed workers almost doubled between 1945 and 1980, the worst inflation of the postwar period took place in the 1970's. It was spurred by two factors. One was the

People in History

Sally K. Ride

On June 18, 1983, Sally K. Ride became the first American woman to go into space. Although four men also went on the second voyage of the *Challenger* space shuttle, the shuttle trip was celebrated as "Sally's Ride" and received as much publicity as any American space feat since the first moon landing in 1969.

Sally Ride grew up in Encino, California, in the 1950's and 1960's, where she was both an outstanding student and athlete. Her parents, Dale and Joyce Ride, recalled that even before she went to school, their daughter was reading the sports pages of the daily newspaper.

When Ride went to college, she chose to study physics. That led her to astrophysics, the science that deals with the composition of heavenly or celestial objects. Ride had always been fascinated by the deeds of the early astronauts. She hardly let herself imagine she could become one herself. But she thought a career in astrophysics could help her become one of the thousands of technical workers who are part of the backup team for each space flight.

In 1977, while working for her doctoral degree in astrophysics at California's Stanford University, Sally applied to the National Aeronautics and Space Administration (NASA) for a job. Early one morning, a telephone call from NASA headquarters in Houston woke her up. She had been accepted as one of the first group of female trainees to fly in space.

Five hard years of training lay ahead before she would take her ride in space. And it was by no means sure that she would go, even if she successfully completed the training. Of the original group of six women trainees, she is the only one to go on a space mission.

She was assigned to other jobs in the space program. She helped to test the robot arm that moves satellites out of the space shuttle's hold and launches them in space. Later, she became the first woman to hold the job of chief communicator from ground control to the shuttle *Columbia's* mission in April 1982. In July of that year Ride married fellow astronaut-candidate Steven Hawley.

Sally Ride considers herself fortunate to have grown up just at the time when the women's movement was strong. It paved the way for talented women to participate in work that formerly had been reserved for men. She speaks at colleges and schools about the NASA program. "When an eight-year-old girl in the audience raises her hand to ask me what she needs to do to become an astronaut, I like that," Sally says. "It's neat! Because now there really is a way. Now it's possible!"

1. How did Sally Ride's choice of studies in college help her to become an astronaut?
2. What influences in Sally Ride's life helped her succeed in her chosen career?
3. How do her achievements help the NASA program and the women's movement today?

Vietnam War. Needing money for his domestic programs, President Johnson refused to raise taxes to support the cost of the war. This led to deficits, in which the federal government spends more than it takes in by borrowing or by printing additional money. The increased money supply decreased the value of money in circulation.

The other cause of inflation in the 1970's was the sharp rise in the price of oil. Oil or petroleum products are used in virtually every area of manufacturing. Attempts were made to find alternative sources of energy, such as coal, oil shale, atomic power, wind power, and geothermal energy. In the 1980's, however, the price of oil decreased. This has helped to stem inflation.

The nation's balance of trade is another source of concern. In the 1960's, the United States exported more goods than it imported, leaving a positive balance of trade. Today this has changed. Because of the overvaluation of the dollar, the United States imports far more than it exports. It has become a debtor nation, owing more to other countries than they owe to the United States. The results of this change will be serious if the trend continues.

In his first year in office, President Reagan cut taxes, even though there had been a large deficit in the previous year. It was claimed that the tax cut would stimulate the economy, leading to an overall gain in revenue. Increased defense spending has caused larger deficits than ever before. Many economists predict that these deficits will lead to renewed inflation in years to come.

Despite political differences and a diverse population of racial, religious, and ethnic groups, the United States remains the world's strongest nation. Enormous natural resources, farm productivity, and advanced technology have given its people the highest standard of living in history. One of the country's greatest strengths has been its ability to adapt to changing conditions.

The 1950's saw a baby boom, a sharp rise in the birthrate. New families moved into fast-growing suburban areas around major cities. Prefabricated housing, precut and ready for assembly, and government subsidies to the housing industry brought the price of a home within reach of the average American. Good roads made it possible for people to drive to workplaces many miles from their homes.

In the 1970's, population shifted toward the Sunbelt region of the South and West. One reason for this has been the decline of the "smokestack" industries of the North and East such as automobile, steel, and textile manufacturing. High-technology industries related to computers, office machines, memory chips, and communications equipment are growing in large numbers. The rise in oil prices made living in the "Snowbelt" North more expensive. People have also tended to move out of the older cities. With help from the federal government, many cities have rebuilt their central downtown areas to attract new businesses and people.

Service industries are another rising source of jobs, especially for women. The life-style of many Americans makes them wish to eat out more often, go out for entertainment, and travel. Fast-food chains and tourist attractions employ many workers.

The baby boom was followed by a marked decline in the birthrate. The country now faces the challenge of an aging population that will someday cause strains in social services. This is offset to some degree by the arrival of new immigrants. Today, these come mainly from Latin America, although many also come from the Far East. Their readiness to take advantage of opportunities in the United States makes them valued citizens.

SECTION REVIEW

1. Mapping: Use the Atlas map on page 759 to locate those states in the Sunbelt regions of the country. Give some reasons why people would want to live in these areas.
2. In your own words, briefly define or identify: Fair Deal, Great Society, segregation, women's liberation movement, deficits, debtor nation, Sunbelt, baby boom.
3. What groups benefited from the civil rights movement?
4. What were the effects of the Vietnam War on the United States?
■ How large a role do you think the federal government should play in solving social problems? Give reasons for your answer.

Reviewing the Chapter

Chapter Summary

The countries of South America struggled to expand and diversify their economies. In trying to develop untapped natural resources, they ran up large foreign debts that now exceed their ability to repay. Military groups are often ready to overthrow elected governments to prevent dissent and disorder.

The United States has moved to overthrow unfriendly governments in Central America and the Caribbean. However, only Cuba's Marxist regime has survived the active opposition of the United States government.

Mexico has succeeded in building a stronger economy. However, the nation faces the problems of a fast-growing population and large foreign debt. Canada overcame the challenge of a separatist movement. It has joined with the United States in mutual defense and development projects.

In the United States, government involvement in solving social problems continued. Both the civil rights and the women's movements led to greater freedoms for women, blacks, and other minorities. The nation was torn by dissent over the Vietnam War and disillusioned by the Watergate scandal. It saw a rise in business related to high-technology and a decline in older industry. Population shifts to the suburbs and to the Sunbelt occurred.

1. What problems hold back the development of South American countries?
2. Why has the United States often been involved in the affairs of Central America and the Caribbean nations?
3. Why is it important for the United States to maintain good relations with Mexico and Canada?

Using Your Vocabulary

1. What have been the results of *abertura* in Brazil?
2. How does the use of gasahol help Brazil deal with the rise in oil prices?
3. Describe what life is like in a *favela*.
4. What were the characteristics of *justicialismo* in Argentina?
5. What are multinational coporations?
6. How has the *caudillo* tradition affected governments in South America?
7. What are the main points of the Caribbean Basin Initiative?
8. How did the Sandinistas manage to gain power in Nicaragua?
9. What is the purpose of the Contadora group?
10. Explain how the problem of undocumented aliens has affected Mexico's relations with the United States.
11. How did the separatist movement strain the unity of Canada?
12. Explain in your own words what the north-south issue is in world affairs.
13. Why does the problem of acid rain affect relations between Canada and the United States?
14. What is segregation?
15. What was the purpose of the civil rights movement in the 1960's?
16. How are deficits in the federal budget caused?
17. What does it mean for a country to be a debtor nation?
18. How has the Sunbelt region of the United States changed in recent years?

Developing Your Geography Skills

1. Use the map on page 706 to describe which nations in South America have oil resources.
2. Use the map on page 706 to find and list the countries of Central America that have single-crop economies.
3. Use the Atlas map on page 759 to describe recent population trends in the United States.

Recalling the Facts

1. Explain the reason that Brazil built a new capital in the interior of the country.
2. List the groups that were part of the political coalition of Juan Perón.
3. Name four countries in South America that have democratic governments today.
4. Describe the purpose of the OAS.
5. Name some limitations of freedom in Cuba under Fidel Castro.
6. List three possible types of government for Puerto Rico.
7. What are the two groups causing violent political acts in El Salvador?
8. Which side is the United States helping in Nicaragua's civil war?
9. Explain why Mexico has seen a large rise in the populations of its cities.
10. List the challenges that hurt Mexico's economic growth today.
11. Explain some ways Canada and the United States have cooperated.
12. List the names for the social programs of Presidents Truman, Kennedy, and Johnson.
13. Explain President Reagan's philosophy of government regarding domestic programs.
14. List some of the tactics used by the civil rights movement.
15. Explain the two factors that caused inflation in the United States in the 1970's.
16. What relationship exists between new immigrants and America's aging population?

Essay Questions

1. Write a brief essay explaining the causes and results of the gap between rich and poor people in South American countries.
2. In your own words, explain how the problem of foreign debt affects the domestic policies of South American governments.
3. Write a brief description of the methods the United States has used to oppose the government of Fidel Castro in Cuba.
4. Explain why Costa Rica has been able to develop a tradition of democratic government.
5. Write a brief essay explaining why the United States supports the government of El Salvador against rebel opposition and supports rebels against the government of Nicaragua.
6. Explain the problems caused by Mexico's high birthrate.
7. Explain why Quebec and the western provinces of Canada want to have a greater role in the government.
8. Write a brief essay describing how the policies of the Reagan administration have differed from the policies of other postwar administrations in the United States.
9. Explain which types of industries have expanded and which have declined in recent years in the United States.
10. Compare some of the problems facing cities in the United States, Mexico, and one other Western Hemisphere country. How are they the same or different?

Critical Thinking

1. Military governments have often overthrown elected governments in South America. The military leaders claimed this was necessary to preserve order. Cite some examples given in the chapter and evaluate this claim.
2. As part of its Good Neighbor Policy, the United States agreed not to interfere militarily in South American affairs. Evaluate this claim as it applies to the events after 1945.
3. Fidel Castro claims to have the support of the people of Cuba for his government. Evaluate this claim, based on the information in the chapter.
4. Réné Lévesque claimed that the French-speaking people of Quebec wished to be independent of the rest of Canada. Evaluate this claim.
5. Senator Joseph McCarthy and his supporters claimed that Communist aggression was aided by Communist sympathizers within the United States government. Evaluate this claim.
6. President Ronald Reagan claimed that cutting taxes would produce economic growth that would increase the revenues of the United States government. Is this claim warranted or unwarranted?

CHAPTER ·32·

PERSPECTIVES on the MODERN WORLD

1945–Present

Objectives

- *To identify new developments in science and technology since the end of World War II*

- *To describe cultural trends in the postwar era*

- *To explain some of the ways in which daily life has changed since 1945*

*E*very phase of life known since World War II has experienced dramatic change. In the decades immediately following the war's end in 1945, so many revolutionary advances in science and technology had occurred that this postwar era is often referred to as the Second Industrial Revolution. As they had in other stages in the history of the world, advances in science and technology significantly influenced cultural developments.

Many of these developments were the outgrowth of research conducted during World War II. Research, first begun with military objectives in mind, would lead later to more peaceful applications.

The culture of the postwar world was influenced by the developments in science. Artists struggled to find new ways of expressing life in a technological age. Television and miniaturized electronic equipment helped to spread popular culture throughout the world.

The world became a smaller and more interconnected place as a result of innovations in transportation and communication. For the first time in history, the entire world could witness a single event simultaneously due to the wonders of satellite communications.

Concern deepened, however, about the environment, the disposal of toxic wastes, the ability to feed the world, and the threat of nuclear confrontation. Using the knowledge gained since 1945 for the betterment of society remains the world's greatest challenge.

NEW FRONTIERS IN SCIENCE AND TECHNOLOGY

World War II served as the motivating factor behind a number of the scientific and technological achievements affecting our contemporary world. The research conducted by the scientists of all countries engaged in the war led to the development of antibiotic medicines, jet-powered airplanes, synthetics, rockets, and computers.

Overshadowing all these advances was the successful harnessing of the atom. Although this development led to the first atomic bomb, the atom has since been put to peaceful purposes such as providing a new source of energy.

Technological advances made during the war years paved the way for a revolution in transportation and communications. Through the use of satellites, for example, people all over the world can observe a single event as it is happening. In 1969 hundreds of millions of people watched as American astronauts landed on the moon. Likewise, in 1985 an estimated two billion people watched concerts performed on two continents in order to raise funds for the starving people of Africa. The introduction of the computer further speeded progress in all forms of science during the postwar decades.

The Computer Revolution

Advances in computer technology have made it one of the most important elements affecting people's workplaces and life-styles. The computer can perform complicated calculations and logical processes in an incredibly short time. Work that once took years is now reduced to hours or minutes. As yet, no computer can "think," but researchers currently are studying the concept of artificial intelligence.

The first generation of computers developed during World War II used huge vacuum tubes, the size of a large room. These tubes were the principal working elements of the computer and consumed an enormous amount of power. By today's standards these large or main-frame computers were very slow.

The development of the transistor in 1948 revolutionized electronics. The transistor is an electronic device that is similar to an electron tube, but much smaller and with attached electrodes. Over time, transistors made possible the miniaturization of a variety of electronic devices. Transistorized products are also cheaper to operate and use less energy. Today, transistor radios, calculators, and even televisions are small enough to fit in the palm of your hand.

The transistor also made possible a reduction in the size of computers, which soon became common equipment in business and academic institutions. The widespread possession of computers generated new uses for them. Today they are not only a necessity in technologically advanced societies, but also in developing societies as they attempt to improve their way of living.

By 1959 the development of the silicon chip further affected the dwindling size and cost of computers. Ready-made computer programs, referred to as software, have made computers easier to use. At first, highly specialized skills were required to operate computers, but with new software they now can be operated by the average person. Today, personal or portable-type computers are in use in many homes and in a growing number of school programs at all grade levels. Likewise, computer terminals are being installed in a growing number of libraries, financial institutions, and businesses. Their future potential, however, is still being shaped.

The Exploration of Space

To many, the most wondrous achievement of science has been the exploration of space. From ancient times, people have speculated about the stars and planets. However, just since 1957, more knowledge about the universe has been gathered than in all previous times. This knowledge has enhanced many fields, especially medicine.

The space age began in 1957 with the Soviet Union's successful launch of the satellite *Sputnik*. Put into orbit around the earth, it was the first object made by humans to successfully escape earth's gravity. In 1961 the Russian cosmonaut Yuri Gagarin (YOOR-ee guh-GAH-reen) became the first person to orbit the earth.

How are America's space shuttle missions benefitting life on earth? The space shuttle program has advanced rapidly since 1980.

The Soviets' space successes spurred the United States to develop its own programs. Shortly after Gagarin's orbit of the earth, American astronaut Alan B. Shepard, Jr., rose above the earth's atmosphere in a rocket-propelled capsule. In 1962 John Glenn became the first American to orbit the earth.

The dream of landing a human being on the moon was accomplished by the American *Apollo II* expedition on July 20, 1969. As Neil Armstrong took his first step on the surface of the moon, he said, "That's one small step for a man—one giant leap for mankind."

The space programs of both the United States and the Soviet Union continued to expand. By the 1980's the United States had developed the space shuttle, which allowed a spacecraft to be reused on several missions. Shuttle flights have included researchers who performed experiments in space. One included the first American woman astronaut, Sally K. Ride. Another included participants from Saudi Arabia and France, whereas still another planned flight will include a school teacher. The Skylab program, in fact a spaceship laboratory, demonstrated the ability of people to live in space for several months without ill effects.

The space program has orbited satellites that have had immediate practical purposes. Satellites enable television and radio signals to reach all parts of the globe. They have also enhanced intelligence-gathering opportunities.

Space probes, or flights without any humans aboard, have been launched to observe the solar system. The Soviets have landed scientific laboratories on Venus, and the United States has sent space probe missions to Mars. Other American space probes have flown past Jupiter and Saturn, sending back detailed photographs of these planets and their moons. The American space probe *Voyager 2* is scheduled to pass Uranus in 1986.

Developments in Physics

The research that produced the atomic bomb eventually led to a greater understanding of the atom. Once it had been thought that the atom was made up of protons, neutrons, and electrons. In the postwar years, however, physicists discovered other particles that were among the building blocks of matter. Mesons, gluons, and quarks were added to the scientific vocabulary.

These discoveries led to further questions about the nature of matter itself. It was hoped that finding the basic building blocks of matter would lead to a greater understanding of how the universe began and developed. This work continues today, helped by the research done in the space program.

Developments in physics have been aided by new instruments. In 1985 a special telescope was lifted into space, making it possible to look deeper into the universe than ever before. Electron-scanning microscopes allowed scientists to view atoms for the first time.

Research in nuclear physics led to the ability to harness the atom for the production of usable power. The first atomic power station was built in 1951. Within twenty years, atomic power was being used in many countries. However, accidents in several nuclear plants have raised serious questions concerning their safety. Disposing of used nuclear fuel, which will remain radioactive for thousands of years, is a major environmental and health issue.

Advances in Biology

New developments in chemistry produced a breakthrough in genetic research in the 1950's. Prior to this time, scientists suspected that the nucleus of the cell contained genes, which deter-

SOME DISCOVERIES AND INVENTIONS IN THE TWENTIETH CENTURY

	Who	What	Importance
1901	Guglielmo Marconi	Invented equipment that sent first transatlantic wireless telegraphy message	Led to regular transatlantic telegraphic service in 1903.
1903	Orville and Wilbur Wright	Developed the first workable aircraft	Led to the use of aircraft for transporting people and mail in shorter time.
1904	Marie and Pierre Curie, A. H. Becquerel	Investigated radioactivity	Isolated a radioactive element for the first time; paved the way for development of X-rays.
1926	John L. Baird	Demonstrated the first successful television picture	Led to modern television, a major source of information and entertainment.
1928	Alexander Fleming	Discovered penicillin	Led to the widespread use of drugs in the fight to control disease.
1930's	Lise Meitner and Otto Hahn	Split the uranium atom	Led to experimentation with atomic chain reactions.
1930	Clarence Birdseye	First to package frozen foods	Led to the development of the frozen food industry.
1942	Enrico Fermi	Produced first controlled atomic chain reaction	Proved that nuclear energy could be harnessed.
1946	J. P. Eckert and J. W. Mauchly	Demonstrated the first electronic computer	Began era of widespread use of computers.
1948	Physicists at the Bell Telephone Laboratories	Developed the transistor	Made possible the transistor radio, portable television, pocket calculator and other portable electronic devices.
1952	Jonas E. Salk	Developed the Salk vaccine	Prevented polio.
1957	Russian scientists	Launched Sputnik	Marked the beginning of space exploration.
1960	Theodore Maiman	Perfected the laser	Made possible delicate cutting and welding procedures in industry and medicine.
1961	Yuri Gagarin	First person to orbit Earth	Made possible future space exploration.
1969	Neil Armstrong	First person to walk on Moon	Enabled scientists to study the chemical make-up of the moon.
1970	British researchers	Concorde supersonic jet	Enabled people to travel twice the speed of sound.
1970's		Microsurgery	Made possible delicate surgery for the reattachment of limbs.
1970's	Allan MacLeod Cormack, Godfrey Newbold Hounsfield	Computerized axial tomography (CAT Scan)	Combined a computer with X-rays to give a picture of sections of the body.
late 1970's		Solar energy	Research and development increased so we could decrease our dependence on fossil fuels.
1983	William C. De Vries	Artificial heart implant surgery	Replacement for diseased human heart.
1985	NASA Researchers	Special space telescope	To see deeper into the universe than ever before.

mined the traits of living things. In 1953 James Watson and Francis Crick developed a model of DNA (deoxyribonucleic acid), the genetic material that controls the characteristics of all life.

Once the model was known, it was only a matter of time before DNA could be manipulated in the laboratory. As different genes were studied, it became possible to make changes in them. Genes could be spliced together or rearranged to change the traits of living things.

This knowledge had important consequences for agriculture. It promised the possibility of developing new species of plants that might be more nutritious or resistant to drought or disease, or that might grow more rapidly. In medicine, certain diseases might be cured by rearranging the genes of persons with these illnesses.

Initially, many scientists had fears about the use of the new biological knowledge. Tampering with the genetic code was tampering with the very nature of life itself. The possibility existed that new forms of life might escape from the laboratory, with results that no one could foresee.

Yet continuing research has already created organisms that can clean up oil spills and speed up the process of growth in economically important animals. The term **bioengineering** refers to the process of applying engineering principles to construct new organisms through the manipulation of DNA. Bioengineering is becoming a science in its own right as well as a fast-growing high-tech industry.

Medicine

The number of people dying from wounds received in World War II was reduced by the discovery of penicillin and sulfa, drugs that fight bacterial infection. Since the war, millions of lives have been saved by these and other advances in medical knowledge.

Polio, a disease that once killed young and old alike, has nearly been eradicated. Dr. Jonas Salk discovered the polio vaccine in 1952, and it was approved for use in 1954. An oral polio vaccine was later developed by Dr. Albert Sabin. Other diseases, such as measles, smallpox, and tuberculosis had almost been wiped out or sharply controlled through the widespread vaccination of people in developed and underdeveloped countries. However, due to a number of nutritional, environmental, and health factors, these diseases, as well as malaria and yellow fevers are beginning to appear again in parts of Africa, Asia, and Latin America.

Many new drugs have been formulated to ease pain and tension. Sometimes these drugs have had unwanted and dangerous side effects. One drug was found to cause birth defects when given to expectant mothers. Others have led to severe nausea, loss of hair, and blindness. Government controls over the testing and use of new drugs have helped reduce these effects.

Medicine has made use of scientific discoveries in other areas. For example, computers have aided doctors in identifying the sources of epidemics. Computerized axial tomography, which is also known as the CAT scan, gives a three-dimensional view of the inside of the body. It makes possible the swift and accurate diagnosis of disease.

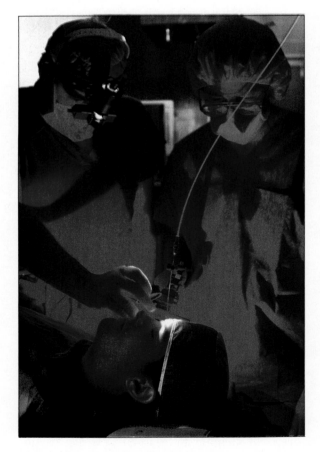

Since its discovery the laser has had many uses. Laser surgery may help to restore this person's sight.

The discovery of the laser beam in 1960 had its greatest impact on medicine. The laser beam is a concentrated form of light that does precision cutting without damaging surrounding tissue. It is now widely used in eye operations. Lasers allow many surgical procedures to be done in a doctor's office rather than in a hospital. Eventually, lasers may help to reduce the expense of medical treatment, which is among the fastest-rising of all costs today.

Other advances in surgical techniques have resulted in medical miracles. **Microsurgery,** done with the aid of microscopic lenses, enables severed limbs to be reattached to the body. Organ transplants enable a person to receive a healthy organ from a living or recently deceased donor. The first heart transplant was performed in South Africa in 1967 by Dr. Christian Barnard. Moreover, kidney and liver transplants are being performed more frequently.

Today medical researchers are beginning to develop artificial organs that can replace human ones, when necessary. The first artificial heart implant operation was performed in 1982 by Dr. William C. De Vries in California. Some patients have survived on artificial hearts for a limited amount of time. Many people use a dialysis, or blood-cleansing, machine to perform the function of their diseased kidneys. Such use of artificial organs is expected to become common in the future.

SECTION REVIEW

1. In your own words, briefly define or identify: transistor, software, *Sputnik,* space shuttle, DNA, bioengineering, CAT scan, laser beam, microsurgery, organ transplant.
2. What two inventions helped to reduce the size and cost of computers?
3. Name some practical applications of the space program.
- Generally, advances in science and technology pave the way for developments in other areas. In what ways has your life been affected by postwar scientific and technological developments? Cite examples to support your answers.

POSTWAR CULTURE

The culture of many countries in the decades following the end of World War II reflected the scale of suffering and destruction experienced by people at the time. The visual arts particularly portrayed a sense of pessimism, hopelessness, and cruelty.

As time went on, however, the war receded into memory. Artists started looking at a society being changed by technological developments. Some sought ways to use this technology to create new kinds of art.

Art became more international as advances in communications made people aware of the culture of other nations. Greater numbers of people began to enjoy works of art. Governments, especially since the 1960's, have been more willing to sponsor or to help finance the creative talent of their citizens. Furthermore, in cooperation with other groups, governments like those of Egypt, China, France, and the United States have sponsored traveling exhibits of some of their nation's greatest masterpieces.

Painting, Architecture, and Sculpture

In the postwar years the center of the art world shifted from Paris to the United States, particularly New York City. Refugees from Europe brought their talent and cultural heritage to the active New York art scene.

The first important development in the postwar world of painting was the emergence of **abstract expressionism.** Abstract painting became the sensation of the art world in the 1950's. This form of art, which had its roots in the nineteenth century, primarily uses bold forms, colors, and textures (rather than recognizable imagery) to convey attitudes and feelings. It requires the viewer to react more subjectively and immediately to what he or she sees.

Abstract art makes little effort to represent a "real" subject. The appeal of this school of art rested in the energy and bold colors that artists used in their attempt to express subconscious feelings. Artists such as Jackson Pollock (PAHL-uck), Willem de Kooning and Barnett Newman in the United States and Ben Nicholson in Great Britain were among the leaders of this art form.

In the 1960's other artistic styles began to emerge. Art took several nontraditional forms, and the definition of art was increasingly questioned. Events known as happenings became popular during this decade. People performed unusual stunts that they classified as art. Some covered their bodies with paint and rolled on a canvas. Others invited an audience to help participate in "creating" a work of art.

Pop art, which evolved from the culture highlighted by commercial advertising, movies, comic strips, and consumer products, was popularized by Andy Warhol (WAR-hall). His subjects were often canned food displays and other products immediately recognizable by the average person. Warhol and other pop artists became celebrity figures whose activities were followed by the media.

Architect Louis Kahn planned this new city in Bangladesh. Would you like living in a planned development?

The postwar years also saw the end of the careers of two of this century's great painters. Henri Matisse (muh-TEES) died in 1954 and Pablo Picasso died in 1973. Matisse was a master in the use of daring colors and bold lines. But in his later years his art became more relaxed, influenced by time spent in the Mediterranean atmosphere. Picasso contributed to the development of Cubism, an artistic style that featured subjects that were visually reassembled on the canvas in fragmented geometric shapes in order to present a number of points of view simultaneously.

Postwar sculpture was dominated by the works of Henry Moore, David Smith, and Alexander Calder. Moore's work has been influenced by ancient Egyptian, African, and Mexican art. Smith used industrial materials such as steel beams and rods to create geometric shapes. Calder, originally an engineer, invented the mobile. A mobile is a mathematically proportioned abstraction of shapes in nature, hung together and delicately balanced. Calder's work was widely imitated by commercial artists.

Most postwar architecture continued the tradition of the international style that had begun at Bauhaus in Germany in the early 1920's. This style incorporated the use of concrete, glass, and steel in architecture. Furthermore, architects began to focus on designing not just a single building but whole blocks of buildings, even entire cities. In the late 1950's and 1960's there was a reaction against the "glass boxes" of this type of architectural development.

The planned city of Brasilia represented impressive futuristic architecture, mainly the work of Brazilian architect Oscar Niemeyer. Le Corbusier (luh KOR-boo-syay), a native of Switzerland, designed an entire city, Chandigarh (CHAHN-dee-gahr), in India, to express his ideas about planning. Le Corbusier's work highlighted special-use areas for business, recreation, and residence. Like others, he utilized open spaces and light materials in construction.

Dance and Music

Two giant figures in the world of dance were George Balanchine (BAL-an-cheen) and Martha Graham. Balanchine, trained in Russia, brought the imperial tradition of ballet to the United States in the 1930's. He greatly increased the popularity

People in History

The Beatles

From 1955 until the early 1960's, rock and roll music was dominated by singers and groups from the United States. Young people in many countries listened avidly to the records of American singers like Chuck Berry, Little Richard, Elvis Presley, and Buddy Holly.

Among those who listened were some young men from Liverpool, England. John Lennon and Paul McCartney began to play American songs on their guitars in small clubs such as the Cavern in Liverpool. They soon added George Harrison to their group, and named themselves the Beatles.

On a trip to Germany in 1961, the Beatles recorded their first song. The group added a drummer, Richard Starkey, whose stage name was Ringo Starr.

The Beatles quickly became the most popular group in the lively Liverpool rock scene. Lennon and McCartney began to write their own songs. "Please Please Me" became the top hit in England in 1963.

Capitol Records released the Beatles' song "I Want to Hold Your Hand" in the United States in January 1964. It set off a national "Beatlemania" craze. In February the "Fab Four" appeared on the popular television show hosted by Ed Sullivan. By April the Beatles' songs held the top five places on the record sales charts. In August their first movie, *A Hard Day's Night,* appeared. As expected, many teenagers swarmed to see it.

Always ready to investigate new musical techniques, the Beatles influenced popular music in many ways. They introduced "psychedelic" music by recording some bars of songs backward and using various kinds of electronically produced sounds.

Before the Beatles, most rock and roll performers recorded their songs on 45 RPM disks, one song to a side. The Beatles' long-playing (LP) record *Sergeant Pepper's Lonely Hearts Club Band* contained a sequence of songs that were loosely related. Its popularity caused other performers to record similar concept LPs.

The Beatles went to India in 1968 to receive instruction in meditation from the guru, or teacher, Maharishi Mahesh Yogi. Their stay in India was cut short, as the Beatles decided they were being exploited. Later that year they released a two-record album officially titled *The Beatles,* but known as "the white album" because of its all white cover. People argued over the meaning of its mysterious lyrics.

The Beatles' music symbolized the restless, vital era of the 1960's. However, by 1970 personal conflicts had caused the group to part. After that, each Beatle recorded solo albums, but none ever reached the success of their group efforts. The 1980 death of John Lennon, who was shot outside his New York City apartment building, put an end forever to rumors that the group might reunite.

1. Name some American rock stars who influenced the Beatles.
2. What were some of the musical innovations introduced by the Beatles?
3. Compare some of today's popular singers to the Beatles.

and acceptance of this art form in this country. Earlier in this century Martha Graham pioneered modern dance. Well into her nineties, she continued to work as a teacher and choreographer, influencing many others in the field.

Classical music saw important compositions by Benjamin Britten of Great Britain and Dmitri Shostakovich (duh-MEE-tree shuh-stuh-KOE-vich) of the Soviet Union. Their music celebrated great national events and revolutionary themes. In the United States, Aaron Copland and Leonard Bernstein wrote compositions that blended theater productions with orchestral music. Edgard Varèse (vuh-REZZ) and John Cage experimented with electronically produced music.

Classical music was brought to millions through new recording methods. Long-playing records, tape recorders, hi-fidelity and stereo equipment, and laser disks brought the full richness of the concert hall into the home. Classical music today is highlighted by atonal sounds, new operatic styles, and innovative blends of old and new musical forms.

However, the music form that was to sweep the world emerged in the United States in the 1950's. Called **rock and roll,** it was a blend of rhythm-and-blues with country and gospel music. It began in the black community, but soon was being played on commercial radio stations and at concerts all over the country.

Elvis Presley, a young man from Mississippi, became the biggest star of early rock and roll. At first controversial and popular only among teenagers, he soon became the top recording artist of the time. His first name may have been the best known in the world. In the 1960's Britain made its own contribution to rock and roll. A group called The Beatles became as popular as Elvis.

The civil rights and Vietnam War protest movements often combined elements of rock and roll and folk music to rally their supporters. "We Shall Overcome" became the anthem of the civil rights movement. Folk artists such as Bob Dylan and Joan Baez were popular among the restless youth of the 1960's. The first large-scale rock and roll concert took place over a three-day period in Woodstock, New York, in 1969. Over one million people attended.

In recent years the popularity of rock and roll has been enhanced by videos, or mini-movies set to the singer's music. Recent popular stars such as Bruce Springsteen, Michael Jackson, and Cyndi Lauper became more widely known through videos. Others such as the Swedish group Abba and the Spanish singer Julio Iglesias (HOO-lee-oh ee-GLAY-see-ahs) also have attracted a large international following. Latin and Caribbean music have become very popular. By 1985 salsa and reggae had become part of the music scene both in the United States and in Europe.

Literature

No field of art was more influenced by postwar pessimism than literature. The French writers Albert Camus and Jean-Paul Sartre depicted the dilemmas of the modern age in their novels. Their novels and other works are based on existential themes. Existential thought centers on the belief that life must be faced honestly, without self-deception.

On the stage, the theater of the absurd reflected the idea that in the face of the horrors of World War II, only absurdity could express the human condition. Some plays representing this kind of theater are Sartre's *No Exit,* Eugene Ionesco's *Rhinoceros,* and Samuel Beckett's *Waiting for Godot.* Beckett's play has two characters who are waiting for a man who never appears and whose reality is in doubt. In *The Homecoming* English playwright Harold Pinter portrays the sense of menace and ambiguity in everyday life.

Latin America has produced a vital literature dealing with the realities and passions of people subjected to many social injustices. Authors of such works include Gabriel García Márquez (gahr-SEE-ah MAHR-kase), Jorge Luis Borges (BOHR-hays), Jorge Amado, Mario Vargas Llosa (YOE-sah), and Carlos Fuentes (FWEN-tays). Latin American literature also stressed the fantastic elements of life.

Through the efforts of talented translators, literature from all nations of the world has become available. The African writer Chinua Achebe (CHIN-oo-ah ah-CHAY-bay) wrote of the breakdown of traditional culture, and Wole Soyinka (VOE-lay soy-IN-kah) satirized the new bureaucratic class in Africa. Athol Fugard (AH-tole FOO-gahrd) protested against apartheid in his plays. The Japanese writers Tanazaki Junichiro (tah-nah-

ZAH-kee joo-ni-CHEE-roh) and Yasunari Kawabata (yah-soo-NAH-ree kah-wah-BAA-tah) helped create a new awareness of Japanese ideas and traditions.

The United States experienced a literary revival in the postwar years led by Jewish, black, and women writers. Jewish writers Saul Bellow and Isaac Bashevis Singer each received a Nobel Prize. Ralph Ellison and Toni Morrison wrote of the black American experience. Influential women writers in their field include anthropologist Margaret Mead and novelists Flannery O'Connor and Joyce Carol Oates.

Film

Perhaps the most popular art form of the twentieth century has been the motion picture. In the postwar years films from Europe introduced new, broader ideas of what movies could portray. Movies no longer aimed at merely entertaining audiences. Italian directors such as Vittorio De Sica (deh SEE-kah), Federico Fellini (fell-LEE-nee), and Michelangelo Antonioni (ahn-toh-nee-OH-nee) used stark realism to portray postwar life. Fellini and Antonioni went on to experiment with fantasy and ambiguity on the screen. French directors such as François Truffaut (troo-FOH) and Jean-Luc Godard (guh-DAHR) used new techniques to shoot and cut their movies. The Swedish director Ingmar Bergman showed great power in his styles and themes. His movies, such as *Wild Strawberries* and *The Seventh Seal,* are still admired.

Other countries also expanded film art as a form. The Japanese director Akira Kurosawa's (ah-KEER-uh koo-roh-SAH-wah) films *Yojimbo* and *Rashomon* influenced other filmmakers all over the world with his character development strategies. From India, Satyajit Ray's (saht-YAH-jit RAY) *Apu* trilogy moved the hearts of millions of moviegoers in other countries by focusing on the perils of life and love. Today, India has the largest film industry in the world, concentrated in Bombay. Hollywood, however, has remained the world's most influential moviemaking city attracting many of the world's best actors.

In recent years Hollywood has found a growing audience among the nation's young people. Movies such as the *Star Wars* trilogy, *E.T.*, *Ghostbusters*, and *Indiana Jones* have lured the largest audiences in history to movie theaters. Director George Lucas has been a leader in developing computerized special effects for films.

Television

In the late 1940's a new piece of furniture found a place in most American homes. This was the television set, which was first thought of only as a way of adding pictures to radio. It soon proved to be the most appealing medium ever created for spreading entertainment, information, and ideas to masses of people.

Early television programs, such as the *Texaco Star Theater, I Love Lucy,* and *The Honeymooners,* made instant celebrities of their stars—Milton Berle, Lucille Ball, and Jackie Gleason, respectively. Besides providing entertainment, television has helped unite the nation during times of stress. The assassination of President Kennedy and the Watergate crisis are two such examples.

In the 1950's 3-D movies were the rage, and required special viewing glasses. Why are fads short-lived?

Today, hardly a nation in the world does not have a television station. Television, however, has not automatically brought a higher standard of taste and knowledge to a wide audience. In the United States, most programming is created to appeal to the greatest number of people. The development of cable television has greatly increased the number of channels available, making special programming possible.

SECTION REVIEW

1. In your own words, briefly define or identify: abstract expressionism, happenings, pop art, mobile, rock and roll, videos, theater of the absurd.
2. Name three types of music and some people who made contributions to each type.
3. What are some of the effects television has had on society?
- What kind of television program would you produce if you were in charge of a television network?

CONTEMPORARY SOCIETY

Life for many people all over the world has changed radically in the postwar years as advances in technology have shrunk the distances between nations. Today people can take a jet to another continent in a matter of hours. Through mass communications, they can learn instantly what is happening on the other side of the planet.

Transportation and Communications

The jet plane was developed during World War II for military purposes. Afterward, it soon replaced propeller airplanes in civilian travel. The speed of air travel and its declining cost greatly increased pleasure travel. Attracting tourists became a prime source of income for many nations.

Some European-American flights now use SSTs, or supersonic transports, that travel faster than the speed of sound. These cut travel time across the Atlantic from six hours to about three. Many businesspeople now regularly fly transatlantic flights, and international trade has been greatly expanded due to jet travel. In addition, countries such as Japan and France have developed very fast trains that compete with airplanes for travel over short distances.

Likewise, the development of larger, speedier ocean vessels has changed international trade. Supertankers, huge ships capable of carrying enormous amounts of petroleum, were built to bring oil from the Middle East to world ports. Atomic-powered ships are now used only for military purposes, but they have the potential for increasing shipping by sea.

The telecommunications industry has drawn people closer together. Satellites in space bounce television and telephone signals from one part of the earth to another. Telephones linked to video screens make it possible to have business conferences with people thousands of miles away.

New kinds of business equipment have produced an office revolution. The development of copying machines gave office workers the ability to duplicate and distribute paperwork with ease. Electric, and then electronic, typewriters greatly increased the speed with which a document could be produced. Today, computers are linked to word processors, which make fast editing easy, and to electronic spreadsheets, which make complicated accounting work far simpler.

Transnational Problems

The postwar expansion of industry has brought new products to millions, but it has also created problems. Factories have released chemical wastes into the air and water. When left unchecked, this causes pollution, or poisoning of the environment. A link between pollution and disease may exist.

There has been a growing consciousness of the importance of **ecology**, the interdependence of all living things in nature. Problems with a pesticide commonly known as DDT, or dichloro-diphenyl-trichloroethane, focused attention on the effects of this and other chemicals. DDT was being used as a pesticide because it could increase crop yields.

Then it was discovered that DDT has a serious effect on birds that eat the insects in sprayed areas and on plant life. Most uses of the chemical were then banned.

Today a growing ecology movement is demanding comprehensive testing and study of chemicals before they are used. In some places, protests by ecologists have prevented construction projects that threatened certain types of wildlife. Yet many species of animals and plants are in danger of being eliminated because they are being killed for food or hunted for sport.

Sometimes the effects of chemicals in the workplace and in the environment do not appear for many years. Dumping of toxic wastes, harmful by-products of industry, caused serious health problems in some areas long after they had been discarded.

Atomic power has also caused unexpected problems because the long-term effects of radioactive wastes on the environment are unknown. Just as important is the immediate threat caused by **nuclear proliferation,** or the actual construction by many nations of atomic weapons. Today only the United States, the Soviet Union, Great Britain, France, China, and India are known to have exploded an atomic bomb. However, other nations such as Pakistan and Israel are thought to have nuclear weapons or to be on the way to developing them. As the number of nations with nuclear capabilities increases, so does the chance of a bomb being dropped. Fortunately, since the atomic bomb was dropped on Hiroshima and Nagasaki in 1945, no nation has used a nuclear bomb against another.

Study this photograph. How has the computer revolution affected the traditional office workplace?

Televisions, video recorders, stereos, and video games bring entertainment into millions of homes. Most people have far more leisure time than their parents or grandparents had.

With the scientific and technological advances made since 1945, the modern world has enhanced its ability to wipe out hunger and disease. For the first time in history, the technical means exist to properly feed and care for all of the planet's 4.7 billion people. Whether the people of the world have the will and determination to do so is a question the future will answer.

Better Lives Today and Tomorrow

Although the wealth of the world's nations is still unevenly divided, most people have experienced a rise in their standard of living since 1945. New machines make housework less time-consuming and far easier. Convenience foods are cheap and easy to prepare. Tomorrow's home may have robots to do many tasks.

The "cash-less" society is approaching reality. Credit cards and checks are on the way to replacing money. It may become routine for people in the near future to order products and pay their bills by using a personal computer in their home.

SECTION REVIEW

1. In your own words, briefly define or identify: supertanker, office revolution, pollution, ecology, toxic wastes, nuclear proliferation.
2. What are some of the results of fast jet plane transportation?
3. Why was DDT banned?
■ For almost every positive step taken in improving people's lives, some negative results have appeared. What are some of the benefits of modern living that have created problems for the environment?

Reviewing the Chapter

Chapter Summary

In the postwar world, science helped many people live better lives. The most important invention was the computer, which enabled scientists and businesspeople to make rapid and complex calculations. For the first time, objects and then humans were sent into space. Discoveries in biology made it possible to change the structure of life itself. In physics, the quest for the basic building blocks of matter was solved. In medicine, new techniques enabled doctors to conquer many diseases.

The arts reflected a postwar pessimism. Artists experimented with new styles to depict the stresses of the modern age. Motion pictures from many countries began to look at life more seriously. Some of the most vital new literature came from French and later from South American writers. Rock and roll appeared in the 1950's and became the most popular musical form in the world. Television quickly became a universal means of communication and entertainment.

In other developments, jet planes provided faster, cheaper transportation, and space satellites helped build a worldwide communications network. New inventions caused a revolution in office work. Pollution of the air and water created a growing consciousness about ecology. In general, most people have better lives because of the technological development that has occurred since 1945.

1. What were some of the scientific advances of the postwar years?
2. In what artistic fields did new developments appear during this period?
3. Name some of the changes in everyday life in the last forty years.

Using Your Vocabulary

1. Why did transistors make possible the miniaturization of electronic devices?
2. How did ready-made software increase computer use?
3. What significance did *Sputnik* have?
4. How did the space shuttle change the space program?
5. What did the discovery of the structure of DNA make possible?
6. What kind of scientific work involves bioengineering?
7. How do doctors use the CAT scan?
8. How is the laser used in medicine?
9. What is one use of microsurgery?
10. Where do the organs used for organ transplants come from?
11. How does abstract expressionist painting differ from painting of the past?
12. How did artists create happenings?
13. What is one of the sources of pop art?
14. Name the two principles combined in a mobile.
15. Name the musical sources of rock and roll.
16. What two artistic forms are combined in videos?
17. Describe the idea behind the theater of the absurd.
18. How did SSTs enhance international trade?
19. What is the main use of supertankers?
20. Name some of the inventions that contributed to the office revolution.
21. What is the meaning of ecology?
22. What is the chief threat of nuclear proliferation?

Developing Your Geography Skills

1. Use the Atlas map on pages 752-753 to locate the nations that are officially known to have atomic weapons.
2. Use a map of the world or a globe to find the distance across the Atlantic Ocean. Name some cities around the world between which SSTs can travel in the same time it takes to cross the Atlantic Ocean.

Recalling the Facts

1. What are the two main tasks that a computer can do?
2. What were the three effects of the transistor on electronic devices?
3. What planets have been closely observed by the successful space programs of the United States and the Soviet Union?
4. Cite one reason scientists looked for the basic building blocks of matter.
5. How did the discovery of penicillin and sulfa drugs help all people?
6. What discoveries did artists use to create new kinds of artworks?
7. How did refugees from other countries help to make New York City the capital of the art world?
8. Name two cities that were built incorporating new architectural and city-planning ideas in the postwar era.
9. What new inventions helped increase the popularity of classical music?
10. What elements did South American writers combine in their art?
11. How did jet travel increase tourism?
12. What were some causes of pollution?
13. Why was above-ground atomic testing banned?
14. What are some of the demands of the ecology movement?
15. What new inventions increased entertainment in the home?

Essay Questions

1. Write a brief essay explaining how computers developed from huge expensive machines into commonly used available items.
2. Explain why the discovery of the structure of DNA had important consequences for agriculture.
3. Describe how new scientific discoveries affected the field of medicine.
4. Explain how American musical forms changed popular music all over the world.
5. Describe the developments in world literature in the postwar period.

6. Write a brief summary of the work of some important film directors since World War II.
7. Discuss some of the ways that television has influenced people's lives.
8. Summarize the effects of the invention of the jet airplane.
9. Describe some of the harmful effects of pollution.
10. Write a brief description of the ways in which technology has improved people's lives since World War II.
11. Choose one of the following areas: transportation, communication, transnational problems. In a brief essay, describe some of the most significant advances made since the end of World War II in that area. Explain how these advances also have created problems. What do you think can be done to correct them?

Critical Thinking

1. What facts appeared in the section on the computer revolution?
2. How can the facts you listed be verified? Be as specific as possible in your answer.
3. What are some value claims that have been made relating to computer use? Cite two examples.
4. Were these warranted or unwarranted claims? Explain your answer.
5. What value claim did the playwrights of the theater of the absurd make?
6. Explain the logical inconsistency between the value claim of these playwrights and the fact that they wrote plays and sought to have them produced on stage.
7. "Most people have experienced a rise in their standard of living since 1945." What unstated assumptions exist in this assessment?
8. What facts can you use to verify that innovations in transportation and communication have drawn people closer together?
9. The scientific and technological advances made since the end of World War II have contributed in many positive ways to people's lives. They have also caused some serious problems. What logical inconsistencies are there in this relationship?

Reviewing the Unit

Developing a Sense of Time

Examine the time line below and answer the questions that follow it.

1945	1945 End of World War II
	1946 First meeting of the United Nations
	1948 State of Israel proclaimed
	1948 Berlin airlift
	1949 Formation of NATO
	1949 Establishment of People's Republic of China
1950	1950 Korean War begins
	1955 Warsaw Pact formed
	1957 Ghana becomes first black African colony to gain independence
1960	1960 French colonies in Africa receive independence
	1962 Cuban Missile Crisis
1970	1972 United States President Nixon visits China
	1972 United States and U.S.S.R. sign SALT I treaty
	1973 Yom Kippur War; OPEC oil embargo
	1978 Camp David Accords
1980	1980 Four American churchwomen murdered in El Salvador
	1980 Mariel boatlift operation
	1981 Anwar Sadat assassinated
	1982 First artificial heart implant operation performed
	1983 America's first woman astronaut on shuttle mission
	1984 Ronald Reagan reelected
1985	1985 Nuclear arms reduction talks resume between United States and U.S.S.R.
	1986 *Voyager 2* scheduled to pass Uranus

1. Which was formed first: NATO or the Warsaw Pact?
2. In what decade did the European colonies in Africa begin to gain independence?
3. In what year did the United States first take action to prevent the spread of Soviet power?
4. When was Egypt's president assassinated?
5. When did the first American woman astronaut join a space shuttle mission?

Social Science Skills

Developing a Frame of Reference

1. In your opinion, did the people of Africa benefit from colonization by the European nations?
2. Based on your readings in this unit, how did colonization and its effects influence world affairs in the postwar period?

Critical Thinking

1. What were the unstated assumptions behind giving foreign aid to help rebuild Europe?
2. What were the unstated assumptions behind the Soviet Union's establishment of control over the nations of Eastern Europe?
3. What was the logical inconsistency between the reason why the United States intervened in Vietnam and later withdrew its troops?
4. What was the logical inconsistency between the European nations' defense of colonialism and the problems that followed the independence of former colonies?

Linking Past and Present

1. The technological revolution of the twentieth century has been compared in importance to the Industrial Revolution. Compare the changes your parents have seen in their lifetimes to the changes experienced by people in the nineteenth century.
2. The greatest threat to the world community today is nuclear war. What steps would you suggest for preventing such a war?

The following abbreviations will be used: LOC, Library of Congress; MMA, Metropolitan Museum of Art, N.Y.C.; NYPL, New York Public Library; HRW, Holt, Rinehart and Winston.

COVER PHOTO: Nemrud Dagh, Turkey, formerly Anatolia. Photo by Roland and Sabrina Michaud/Woodfin Camp.

UNIT OPENER PHOTOS

UNIT 1: 8–9, aerial of the Pyramids, Egypt, Tor Eigeland. **UNIT 2:** 80–81 Acropolis, Athens, Greece, © D. J. Dianellis/The Stock Market. **UNIT 3:** 150–51, Dogubayazit Palace, Eastern Anatolia, Turkey, Roland and Sabrina Michaud/Woodfin Camp. **UNIT 4:** 240–41, Carcassonne, France, © Adam Woolfitt/Woodfin Camp. **UNIT 5:** 292–93, St. Peter's Square, Rome, Italy, Bruno del Priore/Madeline Grimoldi. **UNIT 6:** 362–63, Brighton Station, England, Manfred Hamm. **UNIT 7:** 432–33, Victoria Memorial, Calcutta, India, George Holton/Photo Researchers. **UNIT 8:** 542–43, 40th Anniversary celebration of D-Day on the beach at Normandy, France, Rene Burri/Magnum. **UNIT 9:** 628–29, Radio Astronomy Observatory, Magdalena, NM, Chuck O'Rear/Woodfin Camp.

PHOTOS WITHIN TEXT

Geography Skills: 1, NASA;

UNIT 1, Chapter 1: 10, (Bagdad Museum) Scala/Art Resource; 12,(Prehistory Museum, Rome) Alinari/Art Resource; 13, (Museum for Eastern Antiquities, Stockholm) © Wang-Go H. C. Weng; 17, Fotoarchiv Hirmer; 20, (Louvre, Paris) Scala/Art Resource; 25, MMA, lent by Norbert Schimmel, 1983; 26, (Louvre, Paris) Alinari/Art Resource; 27, (Louvre, Paris) Scala/Art Resource; 33, Scala/Art Resource. **Chapter 2:** 36, gold statuette of God Amun, ca. 900 B.C., MMA; 37, Diane Shapiro; 38–42, MMA; 43, Erich Lessing/Magnum; 46, © Hubertus Kanus, Rapho/Photo Researchers; 48, Staatliche Museen zu Berlin; 51, courtesy MMA; 52, © Thomas Hopker/Woodfin Camp; 54,55, MMA; 56, excavations of MMA; 57, mummy, ca. 1991–1786 B.C. MMA; 58, funerary mask of Tutankhamun, © Lee Boltin. **Chapter 3:** 60, Chou dynasty figure, © Lee Boltin; 62, Paolo Koch/Photo Researchers; 63, (Karachi Museum, Pakistan) Borromeo/Art Resource; 64, © Lee Boltin; 72, bronze elephant *Zun* from the loan exhibition, "The Great Bronze Age of China," courtesy of the Cultural Relics Bureau, Beijing, and MMA; 73, wooden slips, with ink writing, Han period, Academia Sinica, Taipei, © Wan-Go H. C. Weng.

UNIT 2, Chapter 4: 82, Borromeo/Art Resource; 84, An Keren/Photo Researchers; 85, Paolo Koch/Photo Researchers; 88, (The Avery Brundage Collection, San Francisco) © Bradley Smith/Gemini; 92, detail, wall painting, Tang dynasty, Dunhuang, © Wan-Go H. C. Weng; 95, Eliot Elisofan, *Life* Magazine, Time, Inc. **Chapter 5:** 98, (Staatliche Museen zu Berlin, Antikensammlung) Gjon Mili, *Life* Magazine, © 1965, Time Inc.; 101, 102, Erich Lessing/Magnum;104, (The National Museum, Athens) Scala/Art Resource; 105, Hirmer Fotoarchiv; 107, Louvre, Paris; 111, Alinari/Art Resource; 112, © Jodi Cobb/Woodfin Camp; 115, girl with pigeons, marble grave relief, 5th C. B.C., MMA. **Chapter 6:** 122, Augustus statue, portrayed as the "Pontifex Maximus," (Galleria Borghese, Rome) Scala/Art Resource; 124, (Tarquinia Museum) Scala/Art Resource; 126, (Museo di Villa Giulia, Rome) Scala/Art Resource; 128, (Museo Nazionale, Napoli) Scala/Art Resource; 130, (marble inlay from the Basilica of Junius Bassus, Rome, (Palazzo Vecchio, Florence) Scala/Art Resource; 133, (Museo Pio Clementino, Vatican) Scala/Art Resource; 135, Gemma Augustea, Rome, (Kunsthistorisches Museum, Vienna) Alinari/Art Resource; 137,

© Adam Woolfitt/Woodfin Camp; 139, Scala/Art Resource; 141, (Vatican) Scala/Art Resource; 144, detail from Botticelli, Augustine in his cell, (Uffizi, Florence) Scala/ Art Resource; 146, (Museo Archeologico, Florence) Scala/Art Resource.

UNIT 3, Chapter 7: 152, (San Vitale, Ravenna) Scala/Art Resource; 156, Scala/Art Resource; 157, (Treasury of San Marco, Venice) Scala/Art Resource; 159, (Biblioteca Marciana, Venice) Hirmer Fotoarchiv; 160, *(left)* Ara Güler, *(right)* Roland and Sabrina Michaud/ Woodfin Camp; 162, Jim Brandenburg/Woodfin Camp; 166, detail of a 15th C. Russian icon, (Museum of History, Novgorod) Granger Collection. **Chapter 8:** 170, (Kabul Library, Afghanistan) Roland and Sabrina Michaud/Woodfin Camp; 171, Robert Azzi/Woodfin Camp; 173, Roland and Sabrina Michaud/Woodfin Camp; 174, *(left)* detail from a Behzad miniature, (National Library, Cairo) Roland and Sabrina Michaud/Woodfin Camp, *(right)* Roland and Sabrina Michaud/Woodfin Camp; 177, © Bill Wassman/The Stock Market; 179, British Library; 182, MMA; 183, Tor Eigeland; 184, MMA. **Chapter 9:** 188, Museum of Fine Arts, Boston; 191, R. G. Everts/Photo Researchers; 193, Museum of Fine Arts, Boston; 196, detail from a 16th C. miniature, Ms.# OR 12988 32R 201106, British Museum; 200, Song Yingxing, *Tiangong Kaiwu*, 1637, © Wan-Go H. C. Weng; 205, Japan Information Center, New York, NY.; 206, (Stibbert Museum, Florence) Scala/Art Resource; 208, (Kobe Municipal Museum, Kobe, Japan) Bradley Smith/ Gemini. **Chapter 10:** 214, © Helen Marcus/Photo Researchers; 216, Document Mission of Henri Lhote; 219, British Museum; 220, (MMA, Michael C. Rockefeller Memorial Collection) © Lee Boltin; 223, Marc and Evelyn Bernheim/Woodfin Camp; 225, (Museum of Mankind, British Museum) Michael Holford; 226, NYPL; 230, Servizio Editoriale Fotografico/Art Resource; 231, ceramic "Storyteller" figure fashioned by Helen Cordero of New Mexico's Cochiti Pueblo, © Jerry D. Jacka; 233, © Thomas Hopker/Woodfin Camp; 234, (Museo Nacional de Antropología e Historia de México) © Bradley Smith/Gemini; 235, MMA © Lee Boltin; 236, Peter Frey/The Image Bank.

UNIT 4, Chapter 11: 242, detail from the French manuscript "Lancelot du Lac," 343, fol. 4, Bibliothèque Nationale, Paris/ Service Photographique; 244, (Museo Nazionale, Florence) Alinari/Art Resource; 246, (Musée Condé, Chantilly) Giraudon/Art Resource; 249, (National Historical Museum, Stockholm) Swedish Information Center, New York, NY; 251, © Lee Boltin; 252, Giraudon/Art Resource; 255, detail from an 11th C. German manuscript from the "Book of Pericopes," b. 21, Staatsbibliothek, Bremen; 259, Kunsthistorisches Museum, Vienna. **Chapter 12:** 262, MMA, The Cloisters Collection; 263, Bibliothèque Nationale, Paris/Service Photographique; 264, Walters Art Gallery, Baltimore; 267, with permission by the City of Bayeux; 269, Royal Library, Windsor Castle, copyright reserved, reproduced by Gracious Permission of Her Majesty the Queen; 273, 275, Bibliothèque Nationale, Paris/ Service Photographique; 276, © Gianni Tortoli/Photo Researchers; 278, Bayerische Staatsbibliothek, Munich; 283, from the bronze door of the Cathedral Gniezno, Poland, Foto Marburg/Art Resource; 285, *(left)* Rapho-Guillumette/Photo Researchers, *(right)* Fotoarchiv Hirmer; 286, © David Hundley/The Stock Market; 287, Bettmann Archive.

UNIT 5, Chapter 13: 294, (Palazzo di Schifanoia, Ferrara) Scala/Art Resource; 296, Bettmann Archive; 297, Gianni Tortoli/Photo Researchers; 298, Bibliothèque Nationale, Paris/ Service Photographique; 299, (Galleria dell'Accademia, Florence) Alinari/Art Resource; 300, (Casa Buonarroti, Florence)

THE NEW CHINESE SYSTEM OF ROMANIZATION

To standardize the spelling of Chinese in the Latin alphabet the State Council of China decided that the Chinese phonetic alphabet, Pinyin, would be the only system used in China as of January 1, 1979. Pinyin spellings are now commonly used in the media and in government. As a result, the Chinese names in this book are spelled according to the Pinyin system rather than the more familiar Wade-Giles system. Below is a list of the major people and places used in this book with their Pinyin and Wade-Giles spellings. Not all Chinese names have changed, and the State Council maintains that the traditional spellings of certain historical places and person's names need not be changed. For example, China, Tibet, Hong Kong, Shanghai, *and* Mongolia *retain their traditional spellings.*

PINYIN	WADE-GILES	PRONUNCIATION	PINYIN	WADE-GILES	PRONUNCIATION
Beijing	Peking (Peiping)	BAY-JING	Lüshun	Lü-shun	LYOOH-SHWOON
Chang Jian	Ch'ang Chien	CHONG-JYEN	Luoyang	Loyang*	LWAW-YONG
Chang Jiang	Ch'ang Chiang (Yangtze River)*	CHONG-JYONG	Mao Zedong	Mao Tse-tung	MOW DZUH-DOONG
Changan	Ch'ang-an	CHONG-ON	Mengzi	Meng-tzu (Mencius)*	MUNG-DZUH
Chongqing	Chungking*	CHOONG-CHING	Nanjing	Nanking*	NON-JING
Ci Xi	Tz'u Hsi	TSUH SEE	Qin	Ch'in	CHIN
Dai Zhen	Tai Chen	DIE JUN	Qing	Ch'ing	CHING
Deng Xiaoping	Teng Hsiao-p'ing	DUHNG SYOW-PING	Shandong	Shantung	SHON-DOONG
			Shen Nong	Shen Nung	SHUN-NOONG
Dian Ri	Tien Jih	DYEN RIH	Shihuangdi	Shih-Huang Ti	SHUR-HWONG-DEE
Duo Fu	To Fu	DWAW FOO	Song	Sung	SOONG
Faxian	Fa-hsien	FAH-SYEN	Sui	Sui	SWAY
Fu Xi	Fu Hsi	FOO-SHEE	Tai Cong	T'ai Ts'ung	TIE TSOONG
Fuzhou	Foochow*	FOO-JOH	Tai Ping	T'ai Ping	TIE PING
Guan Hanqing	Kuan Han-ch'ing	GWON HONG-CHING	Tang	T'ang	TONG
			Tianjin	Tientsin*	TYEN-JIN
Guangdong	Kuangtung*	GWONG-DOONG	Wang Shifu	Wang Shih-fu	WONG SHUR-FOO
Guangzhou	Canton	GWONG-JOH	Wei He	Wei	WAY HUH
Hankou	Hankow	HON-KOH	Wu Zhao	Wu Chao	WOO JOW
Hangzhou	Hangchow*	HONG-JOH	Wudi	Wu Ti	WOO DEE
Hao	Hao	HOW	Xia	Hsia	SYAH
Hua Guofeng	Hua Kuofeng	HWAH GWAW-FUNG	Xian	Hsien	SYEN
			Xianyang	Hsien-yang	SYEN-YONG
Huang He	Hwang Ho (Yellow River)*	HWONG-HUH	Xuanzang	Hsuan-tsang	SEE-WAHN-DZONG
			Yang Jian	Yang Chien	YAHNG JYEN
Jiang Jing	Chiang Ching	JYONG JING	Yuan Shigai	Yüan Shih-kai	YOO-AHN SHUR-GIE
Jin	Chin	JIN	Yumen	Yu-men	YOO-MEN
Kangxi	K'ang-Hsi	KONG SEE	Zhao Kuangyin	Chao K'uang-yin	JOW KWONG-YIN
Laozi	Lao-tzu	LOW-DZUH			
Li Bo	Li Po	LEE BWAW	Zhou	Chou	JOE
Li Zicheng	Li Tzu-ch'eng	LEE DZUH-CHUNG	Zhu De	Chu Teh	JOO-DUH
Liaodong	Liaotung	LYOW-DOONG	Zhu Yuanzhang	Chu Yüan-Chang	JOO YOO-AHN-JAHNG
Liu Bang	Liu Pang	LYOH BONG			

An asterisk indicates an anglicized spelling rather than Wade-Giles.

·PRONUNCIATION KEY·

When unfamiliar words or names first occur they are followed by phonetic respellings, designed wherever possible to be self-evident to the student. CAPITAL LETTERS indicate the syllable receiving major stress. The following table illustrates the pronunciation symbols generally used throughout the text.

SYMBOL	PRONOUNCED AS IN	EXAMPLE
a	map	Alaska (uh-LASS-kuh)
ay	pane	Malaya (muh-LAY-uh)
ah	father	Sangay (sahng-GIE)
e, eh	wet	Texas (TECK-suss), Hebrides (HEHB-ruh-deez)
ee	eve	Greece (GREES)
i, ih	tip	Britain (BRIT-uhn), Wisconsin (wihs-KAHN-suhn)
ie	high	Thailand (TIE-land)
ah	top	Ceylon (sih-LAHN)
oh, oe	note	Gabon (guh-BOHn), Ohio (oe-HIE-oe)
oo	moon	Rangoon (rang-GOON)
ooh	book	Cooktown (KOOHK-town)
yoo	humid	Utah (YOO-taw)
uh	sun	Kentucky (kuhn-TUHK-ee)
uh	again, audience, hypocrisy, person, curtain	Omaha (OH-muh-hah), Des Moines (duh-MOYN), Wisconsin (wihs-KAHN-suhn), Oregon (OR-uh-guhn), Duluth (duh-LOOTH)
aw	law	Balkans (BAWL-kuhnz)
ow	now	Augsburg (OWKS-boohrk)
oi, oy	boy	Detroit (dih-TROIT), Boise (BOY-zee)
s	say	Seattle (see-AT-uhl)
z	maze	Zion (ZIE-uhn)
zh	pleasure	Bruges (BROOZH)
g	go	Galilee (GAL-uh-lee)
j	jet	Nigeria (nie-JEER-ee-uh)
k	can	Grand Canyon (GRAND KAN-yuhn)

A

abolition the elimination or ending of slavery

absolutism the political theory or form of government in which a ruler has unlimited power and considers himself or herself above the law

Abstract Expressionism a style of American painting after World War II that emphasized texture and brush stroke rather than the depiction of reality

agora in ancient Greece a marketplace that served as an economic and social center

Akkadian in ancient times an inhabitant of Akkad, a city-state north of Sumer

Amarna Style in the New Kingdom of ancient Egypt a style of art characterized by expressiveness of feeling in contrast to the static quality of earlier art

Amon in ancient Egypt the ram-headed god of Thebes

Amorite in ancient times one of the invading peoples who overcame the Sumerians, gained political control of Mesopotamia, and established Babylon as capital of the region

anarchist one who believes that all forms of government are undesirable and should be destroyed, and who advocates a social and political system based on the mutual cooperation of individuals

anti-Semitism prejudice, discrimination against, or intolerance of Jews

apartheid from the Afrikaans: apartness; racial segregation and political repression of nonwhites in South Africa

appeasement granting territory or other concessions to an aggressor for the purpose of maintaining peace

aristocracy an hereditary privileged or noble class; a state governed by a privileged class

Art Nouveau a movement originating in the 1890's that applied some of the visual effects of Postimpressionism to furniture, dinnerware, jewelry, posters, and advertising

Aton the sun deity in the New Kingdom of ancient Egypt

Ausgleich from the German: compromise; the treaty of 1867 that established the dual monarchy of Austria-Hungary

B

balance of power the principle of maintaining an equilibrium of strength among nations so that one state is prevented from dominating the others

balance of trade the relationship between the value of a nation's exports and its imports

Baroque in art and architecture the seventeenth-century movement characterized by extravagance, theatrical effects, and the contortion of classical forms

bioengineering the application to medicine of engineering techniques, notably in the building of machines for diagnostic and therapeutic purposes

bourgeoisie in the Middle Ages, townspeople; in the modern era, the middle class of society

Bronze Age the period in ancient times when bronze replaced stone as the chief material in the making of implements

Buddhism a religion founded in ancient India and teaching that the ideal state of peace can be achieved through proper living and meditation

buffer state a country located between rival powers that is considered to decrease the possibility of conflict between them

Bundesrat in the German Empire of 1871–1919, the upper house of the legislature

bureaucracy a system of administration or government characterized by the specialization of departments, the adherence to fixed procedures, and a hierarchy of levels of authority

Bushido in Japanese history the code of conduct of the samurai class stressing pride in one's family and loyalty to one's *daimyo*

Byzantine Empire the eastern part of the later Roman Empire with its capital at Constantinople; 395 A.D.–1453 A.D.

C

caliph from the Arabic: successor; in the early days of Islam, a successor to the prophet Muhammad; the spiritual civil head of a Muslim state

calligraphy elegant handwriting requiring special instruments; a highly admired art form in ancient China

Calvinism the theological system based on the teachings of John Calvin and emphasizing the simplification of religious services, preaching, the doctrine of predestination, and a strict moral code

capitalism an economic system based on private or corporate ownership of the means of production in which prices and distribution are determined by a free market and open competition

carbon 14 dating a technique used by archaeologists to calculate the age of an artifact

cartel an international business syndicate with interests in a monopoly of a particular commodity or market

caste system the hereditary class structure of India and colonial Spanish America in which each level of society was rigidly separated from the others by occupation, social rank, and marriage

Catholic Reformation see *Counter Reformation*

caudillo from the Spanish: leader; a politically powerful military leader in Latin America or Spain

census an official count of a country's population with data on age, sex, marital status, and so forth

Chaldean one of the peoples of Babylon who united to defeat the Assyrian Empire

Christianity the religion that affirms the divinity of Christ; the religion based on the teachings and example of Jesus, with the Bible as its sacred text

city-state a state consisting of a city and its surrounding territory

civil disobedience a nonviolent method of opposition to an authority, or to certain civil laws; peaceful noncooperation; passive resistance

civilization a state of human society characterized by advanced levels of economic, administrative, artistic, technological, and cultural development

Classicism the aesthetic principles of balance, simplicity, and restraint as characterized by ancient Greek and Roman art and literature

client state in ancient Rome a state whose foreign policy was directed by Rome but whose internal affairs remained under the control of its own king

coalition an alliance of political factions, parties, persons, or states

Code of Hammurabi the codified laws of the most famous of the Amorite kings of Babylon

Code of Justinian the legal code of the Byzantine emperor Justinian, a code which preserved much of older Roman law and was a major influence on the legal system of medieval western Europe

codification the organization and writing down of the laws of society

Cold War after 1945 the conflict between the Communist and non-Communist blocs; a political, cultural, and economic conflict that stops short of direct military confrontation between the major powers

collective security a diplomatic system in which nations act in association to protect each other's security

Commercial Revolution the rise of commerce and economic activity, which was encouraged by overseas trade, between c. 1500 and 1700

common law the standardization of law in England based on custom and precedents set by the decisions of previous judges rather than on a written code of laws

Common Market the European Economic Community founded in 1958 whose goals are the reduction of tariffs and the free movement of goods and workers between member countries

communism a social system in which goods and services are communally shared; a Marxist theory that advocates a classless society; a political theory which, according to Lenin, promotes the violent seizure of power by a political party, the total suppression of internal opposition, and the dictatorship of the state

Confucianism the ethical and religious system of China based on the teachings attributed to Confucius and the ancient commentaries, including those of Mencius

conservative one inclined to preserve the existing social or political order

constitutional monarchy see *limited constitutional monarchy*

consul one of two chief executives, elected annually, in the Roman Republic; a governmental officer stationed in a foreign country to represent the diplomatic and commercial interests of his or her country

consulate the office of a consul, or officer, in charge of protecting his country's citizens or commercial interests in a foreign country

containment the United States foreign policy of limiting the spread of Soviet or Communist influence

Continental System Napoleon's attempt after 1806 to ruin the British economy by imposing a blockade of continental ports to British commerce; system intended to encourage production and manufacturing within the French Empire and its satellite states

corporation a modern business enterprise in which investors purchase stock, elect directors to manage policy, receive dividends based upon the number of shares owned, and are held liable only for the amount they invest in the company

Counter Reformation the sixteenth-century reform movement within the Roman Catholic Church that occurred in reaction to Protestantism and in defense of the Catholic faith

counterrevolution a movement aimed at reversing the effects of a revolution, notably by restoring the old regime

coup d'état from the French: stroke of state; a sudden seizure of the government by military force

Cro-Magnon a variety of *Homo sapiens* dominant in western Europe during the last half of the fourth Ice Age

Crusades a series of medieval military expeditions undertaken by Christians against Muslims for the purpose of gaining control of the Holy Land

Cubism a style of modern art in the early twentieth century characterized by an emphasis on abstract and geometric form

culture the integrated sum total of learning behavior patterns characteristic of the members of a society

cuneiform the wedge-shaped writing system of the ancient Sumerians

D

daimyo in Japanese history a powerful landed aristocrat

Dark Ages the Renaissance view of the medieval period in European history; the decline of culture and the level of society in comparison to the achievements of classical civilizations

democracy a system of government developed in ancient Athens in which citizens voted on key issues and elected their leaders; any system of government in which political power resides in all the people or their elected representatives

denazification the removal of anything associated with Nazism from German society after World War II

dendrochronology a method for determining the age of wood remains by comparing the growth rings on trees to those on the wood remains

de-Stalinization in the Soviet Union the policy initiated by Khrushchev in 1956 that denounced Stalin and his policies of repression

détente from the French: relaxation; the diplomatic policy of lessening tensions between the major powers

dictator a ruler with unlimited political power; during the Roman Republic an executive holding absolute power for six months with the consent of the Senate

dissident movement in the Soviet Union the open criticism by Soviet intellectuals of the government and its policies

divestment a policy advocating the withdrawal of investments in South Africa by foreign corporations as a means of effecting an end to the practice of apartheid

divine right of kings a theory of government maintaining that monarchy derives its authority directly from God

domestic system a method of production in which an entrepreneur, or businessperson, oversees the purchase of raw materials and the manufacture and distribution of finished goods by employing workers in their homes

dominion a self-governing member state of the British Commonwealth of Nations

Dravidian in ancient India inhabitants of the south who remained independent of Aryan rule

Dynastic Cycle Theory an interpretation of the whole course of Chinese history that traces the domestic political process according to a cyclical pattern of unification and disorder

dynasty a family of rulers whose power endures over generations and is passed on through inheritance

E

ecology the science that focuses on the interrelationships between organisms and their environment

émigré from the French: emigrant; one who flees to escape a revolution, especially the nobility that fled France during the French Revolution

Enlightenment a philosophical movement of the eighteenth century marked by rationalism, faith in science, and a belief in natural law

ephor in ancient Sparta one of five overseers, elected each year by the Assembly to maintain a balance of power between king and elders

Estates General the assembly in France that met irregularly in the late medieval and early modern periods and consisted of representatives of the country's three orders or estates: the clergy, the nobility, and the commoners

ethical monotheism a belief in the worship of one God that requires proper or ethical conduct on the part of its adherents

extended family a social unit consisting of parents, their children, and near relatives all living in the same household

extraterritoriality the exemption of foreign nationals from local jurisdiction or trial

F

fascism a system of government that subordinates the individual to a powerful state run by a single party supported by military force, secret police, strict censorship, and a strong leader

federal system a system of government that divides power between a federal, or central, government and local governments

Fertile Crescent an area of rich, well-watered land that extends in a great arc from the Mediterranean coast to the Persian Gulf

feudalism the system of medieval government characterized by means of the private contracts between individuals and not between a sovereign government and its subjects; the system by which vassals were granted land holdings by their lords in exchange for military service or the performance of other obligations

Five-Year Plan in Soviet history any of the programs of strictly controlled economic planning; the plan initiated in 1928 by Stalin as a crash program aimed at building up heavy industry with each branch of the national economy assigned specific production goals

fresco from the Italian: fresh; the art of painting by pressing colors dissolved in water into fresh plaster

G

general strike a strike by most workers of an industry or industries, acting together to bring a nation to a standstill and to gain concessions from its government

genocide the systematic killing of an entire national or ethnic group, first used to describe the Nazi destruction of nearly six million Jews

ghetto any area of a city inhabited by members of a minority; originally the section to which Jews were restricted

Glorious Revolution in English history the bloodless uprising of 1688 that deposed James II and placed his Protestant daughter Mary and her husband William of Orange on the throne in 1689

Golden Horde a fierce Mongol horde that conquered eastern Europe and established an empire in what is today central Russia

Gothic a style of west European architecture that originated in France and is characterized by pointed arches and flying buttresses and is best expressed in the cathedrals; c. 1200 to 1450

Great Wall of China a 1,400 mile wall extending across northern China and built to secure the country from foreign invasion

guild an association of individuals with similar interests organized for mutual aid and protection, especially, an association of merchants or artisans in medieval times

Guptas the royal family that united northern India in the fourth century A.D. and ruled during a golden age of Indian civilization

H

Han Dynasty a powerful Chinese dynasty roughly contemporaneous to the Roman Empire in the West and controlling an empire almost equivalent in size to modern China

Hellenistic Age the period—from the death of Alexander the Great to the establishment of the Roman Empire—that witnessed the spread of Greek culture and civilization over the Mediterranean world and west Asia

helot in ancient Sparta a member of the rural laboring or serf class

hieroglyphic from the Greek: sacred writing; the writing system of the ancient Egyptians in which pictures represented ideas, objects, and sounds

Hinduism the western term for the pantheistic religion of India, whose sacred writings are the *Vedas* and the *Upanishads*

Holocaust the extermination of nearly six million European Jews under the Nazis

hoplite phalanx the large infantry group of ancient Greece that replaced the earlier heroic fighting method of the warrior elite

humanism the intellectual movement of the Renaissance that emphasized the study of Greek and Roman classical works, beginning about 1350

Hun one of the nomadic Asiatic peoples who raided the western extremities of the expanding Han empire and who later invaded Europe in the fourth and fifth centuries

I

imperialism the establishment by conquest and colonization of an empire over foreign territories; the control through political or military means of the foreign trade and raw materials of underdeveloped countries

imperium the highest legal and political power; supreme command

Impressionism a style of French painting that developed out of Realism in the late nineteenth century and captures the intensity of natural light by combining small flecks of paint

indemnity payment as compensation for losses or damages caused by a war

industrialization the process of replacing old-fashioned manufacturing techniques with new developments in machinery and factory production

inflation a steady rise in prices caused by an increase in the money supply and a greater demand for goods and services

intelligentsia the well-educated and intellectual elite who held informed opinions in prerevolutionary Russia

Iron Age the period in ancient times when iron replaced bronze as the chief material in the making of weapons and implements

iron curtain a term coined by Winston Churchill to describe the Soviet sphere of influence in Eastern Europe

irredentism the political movement in Italy to acquire those European territories where Italian-speaking people lived under the rule of foreign governments

Islam the religion of the Muslims; the predominant faith in North Africa, the Middle East, Pakistan, and Indonesia; the belief in one God, Allah, whose prophet is Muhammad

J

joint-stock company in the early modern period a trading company in which investors pooled their funds, bought stock in a business enterprise, and profited according to the number of shares held

K

karma in the Hindu religion the actions in this or previous lives that determine a person's destiny

Kassite one of the foreign invaders of ancient Babylon who, with horse-drawn chariots, disrupted the relative stability of the major river valley civilizations and ruled until the invasions of the Assyrians

kibbutz from the Hebrew: gathering; a collective or cooperative settlement in Israel

Koran from the Arabic: recitation; the sacred text of Islam, which relates God's revelations to the prophet Muhammad

Kulturkampf from the German: struggle for culture; in the 1870's Bismarck's conflict with the Roman Catholic Church and his attempt to curb its social influence

Kushans invaders of India who by 50 A.D. seized Greek-held territory, destroyed most traces of Greek culture, and adopted Buddhism

L

laissez-faire from the French: let them (businesses) do as they please; the economic theory that argued that government should exercise as little influence as possible in trade and business affairs and in the regulation of industry or labor relations

lay investiture the installation of a church official by a layperson, notably a king or emperor

Legalism in Chinese history the theory that social stability could be achieved through clearly stated laws, a strong central government, and a ruler endowed with absolute power

legitimacy the policy of restoring to power after 1815 those rulers who had lost their thrones during the Napoleonic period

liberalism the political theory that, in its classical phase in the first half of the nineteenth century, promoted social reform, constitutional government, civil liberties, private enterprise, and government by taxpayers and property owners; in the twentieth century the belief in the state as the chief agent for balancing the wants of the individual against the needs of the whole society

limited constitutional monarchy a government in which the powers of the monarch are limited by constitutional laws or by a parliament

M

Magna Carta from the Latin: great charter; the political document signed in 1215 that limited the power of the English monarch and guaranteed certain rights to English citizens

Mahayana the form of Buddhism that spread to the northern parts of central Asia emphasizing the worship of Buddha as a god and a savior of humanity

Manchu the Qing Dynasty, the last Chinese dynasty (deposed in 1911); any member of the Manchu class

Mandate of Heaven in Chinese history the doctrine that a ruler's authority was based on the possession of a divine right to govern

manorialism the economic system of medieval Europe based on the social life of the manor, or estate, owned by a feudal lord and worked by peasants

mass production the methods of scientific management and standardized production first developed in the United States, which enabled industry to manufacture large quantities of standardized goods

matrilineal pertaining to tracing descent through the mother

medieval belonging to or characteristic of the Middle Ages

Meiji Restoration the end of the Tokugawa shogunate in 1868 and the establishment of a regime under the new emperor Meiji; Meiji Era (1868–1912): the first great period of industrialization and westernization in Japanese history

mercantilism an economic system of the seventeenth and eighteenth centuries aimed at increasing the wealth of a country by strict government regulation of the economy, notably through policies aimed at encouraging the increase in the amount of a country's gold and silver, a favorable balance of trade, foreign monopolies, and the development of manufacturing

Mesopotamia from the Greek: between the rivers; in ancient times the area between the lower Tigris and lower Euphrates, today located in Iraq

microsurgery the precision cutting or dissection of living structures through the use of a laser beam

Middle Ages the thousand-year period in European history between the fall of the Roman Empire and the early modern period; c. 500 to 1500

militarism the promotion of a strong national military, a large standing army, or the leadership of a strong military class

Ming Dynasty the native dynasty that ruled China from 1368 to the advent of the Manchus

mobilization the preparation of a nation's army, industry, and military resources for war

moderate characterized by political or social views that are not extreme, either to the left or the right

Modernism the course of modern art characterized by a search for new forms of expression; in twentieth-century art the shift away from the traditional methods of depicting reality toward subjectivity and abstraction

Mogul Empire the empire of northern India in the early modern period prior to British rule

Mongol Dynasty the Chinese dynasty established by Kublai Khan in 1260

monopoly the complete control of a service, commodity, or means of production with the resulting power to fix prices and eliminate competition

monotheism the belief that there is only one God

monsoon a seasonal wind that results in heavy rains of agricultural importance to India and Southeast Asia

Mosaic law the civil and religious laws of the ancient Hebrews, traditionally attributed to Moses

multinational corporation any large business enterprise with operations in several countries

Muslim a follower of Islam

N

nationalism devotion to one's nation and to its political, social, and cultural traditions

nationalize to bring an industry or resource under the control of the state

natural law the law presumed to be inherent in human nature and understandable through reason alone

Nazism the policies and ideology of the National Socialist party in Hitler's Germany as characterized by its adherence to extreme militarism, racism, fascism, and nationalism

Neanderthal a prehistoric cave-dwelling people of the Paleolithic Age

Negritude pride and awareness of one's black African origins and heritage

Neoclassicism the late eighteenth-century revival in the arts of Greek and Roman principles characterized by balance, harmony, proportion, and correctness of form; see *Romanticism*

neocolonialism the movement of industrialized powers, especially after World War II, to reassert political and economic control in any of their colonies or historic spheres of influence

neolith a stone tool or implement developed in the New Stone Age

Neolithic Age the New Stone Age, characterized by the development of polished stone tools and an agricultural society

nirvana the state of perfect peace and happiness marked by the liberation of the individual from material desires and pleasures; the ultimate goal of Buddhism and Hinduism

No the classical Japanese form of theater combining dance, music, and mime in a dignified presentation in which no single element dominates

Northwest Ordinance in the United States the 1787 law that dealt with the issue of westward expansion, territorial settlement, and statehood; new territories with 60,000 inhabitants could be admitted to the union with all the privileges of the thirteen original states

nuclear family a social unit consisting of parents and their children living in the same household

O

obelisk a tall, pointed stone column in ancient Egypt

oracle a person thought to have the power to predict the future and to give wise answers to questions

ostracism in ancient Athens the exiling of a citizen for a ten-year period, but without the loss of citizenship or property; a system used to rid the city-state of corrupt officials

P

pacifist one who opposes war and military solutions to international conflicts

pagoda a sacred tower or temple of the Far East

Pan-Africanism the political movement promoting African independence and cultural unity

Pan-Arabism the political movement promoting Arab nationalism and the unity of Arab culture

Pan-Slavism the theory and movement that called for the cultural and political unification of the Slavic peoples

papyrus a kind of paper made from plants by the ancient Egyptians

Parliament the supreme legislative body of Great Britain, consisting of the House of Lords representing the nobility and the clergy and the House of Commons representing the commoners

patriarch in the Greek Orthodox Church any of the bishops of Alexandria, Antioch, Jerusalem, or Constantinople

patrician in ancient Rome a member of the hereditary aristocracy

patrilineal pertaining to tracing descent through the father

peninsular any Iberian-born official representing Spain or Portugal in colonial Latin America

perioikoi in ancient Sparta the class that handled economic affairs, including foreign trade

pharaoh in ancient Egypt a monarch whose authority was religious as well as political

philosophe from the French: philosopher; an eighteenth-century advocate of the new faith in science; one who believed that through scientific reason one could answer the critical questions about people, society, and nature

plebeian one of the common people of ancient Rome

plebiscite a national vote by the population, usually in times of constitutional change

pogrom an officially approved local massacre, especially one against Jewish communities in czarist Russia

Pointilism the technique in painting by the Post-impressionist Georges Seurat of placing tiny dots of pure color close together so that they combine not on the surface but in the viewer's eye

polis a city-state of ancient Greece

polytheistic characterized by the belief in more than one god

pool an arrangement in which several companies fix prices for the purpose of dealing with the pressures of excessive competition

Pop Art a school of art in the United States during the 1960's characterized by wit and the use of popular commercial images such as advertisements, cartoon strips, and road signs

Postimpressionism the style of painting that followed Impressionism; the shift away from depicting things as they appear visually toward depicting their impact on the viewer's mind

prehistory history before written records, derived mostly from archaeological evidence

primary source original historical information that dates from the period it describes including eyewitness accounts, censuses, records of commercial transactions, legal documents, diplomatic correspondences, and propaganda

proletariat the working class

propaganda the organized spreading of ideas or information to support or damage a cause

prophet a religious leader or thinker; an interpreter of divine will

protectorate the relationship of control and protection assumed by a strong nation over a weaker one

Protestant a Christian who is not a member of the Roman Catholic or Eastern Orthodox Church

Protestant Reformation the sixteenth-century religious movement in Europe that broke the unity of western Christendom, denied the authority of the pope, and resulted in the establishment of numerous Christian sects

Q

Qin in Chinese history the kingdom that destroyed the Zhou Dynasty in 256 B.C., conquered the various kingdoms and territories of China, and established the first Chinese empire

R

radical one in favor of extreme social or political change

Realism the movement of the mid-1800's in literature and art that sought to convey the human condition by focusing on ordinary people in society and by emphasizing scientific, accurate, and closely observed details

realpolitik from the German: realistic politics; a political policy based on practical—as opposed to theoretical or idealistic—concerns

Reichstag in the German Empire of 1871–1919, the lower house of the legislature chosen by universal male suffrage

Renaissance the revival of interest in the art, architecture, and literature of classical Rome and Greece, which began in Italy; the period marking the transition between the medieval and modern world; c. 1350–1600

rhetoric the study of the use of persuasive and eloquent language to sway an audience; a highly prized skill in ancient Athens and Rome

Risorgimento from the Italian: resurgence; the nineteenth-century movement for the liberation and unification of Italy

rock and roll a type of popular music that emerged in the United States in the mid-1950's; a fusion of elements of several American musical styles including blues and folk, and characterized by a heavily accented beat and a simple phrase structure

Rococo an eighteenth-century movement in art and architecture of French origin characterized by curvilinear design, delicacy, and fanciful decoration

Romanesque a style in west European architecture based on classical Roman architecture and characterized by rounded arches and domed roofs; c. 1000 to 1200

Romanticism the nineteenth-century movement in music, literature, and art that encouraged subjectivity of expression, emotion, feeling, and the artist as liberated hero

S

samurai in Japanese history a military vassal of a daimyo and, until the abolition of privileged classes after the Meiji Restoration, a member of the military or bureaucratic aristocracy

Sanskrit the ancient and classical language of the Aryans in India

satrap during the ancient Persian Empire a government official in charge of a province

Scholasticism the medieval philosophy that attempted to reconcile human reason with religious faith

scribe any official writer or clerk in ancient Egypt, who was among the most important members of society

scriptures holy writings

Scythian one of the ancient peoples of the Middle East who mastered the effective handling of weapons while on horseback or camelback

secede to withdraw from a union or political organization

Second Reich from the German: empire; the German Empire from 1871 to 1919 and the Weimar Republic from 1919 to 1939; the First Reich: the Holy Roman Empire from its establishment in the ninth century to its end in 1806; the Third Reich: Hitler's regime from 1933 to 1945

secondary source a work of synthesis by an historian based on primary and secondary sources or on secondary sources alone

sectionalism allegiance to a particular section of a country rather than to the nation at large; the competition between different sections—North and South, East and West—in United States history

segregation the social practice of requiring separate facilities such as schools, transportation, and housing for whites and nonwhites

Semite in ancient times one of the nomadic peoples of Mesopotamia

sericulture the cultivation of silkworms for the production of silk

Shang Dynasty the first dynasty of ancient China, which is documented by historical evidence

Shinto the native religion of Japan characterized by the worship of nature, ancestors, and ethnic divinities

shogun from the twelfth through the nineteenth centuries, the chief military figure of Japan

shuttle diplomacy a technique of intensive diplomacy in which a negotiator travels between political capitals to reach a peace settlement; the diplomacy first used by United States Secretary of State Henry Kissinger in the 1970's to effect a peace settlement in the Middle East

socialism the public or governmental control of the basic means of production and distribution with the purpose of guaranteeing each member of society a fair share of goods, services, and benefits

Socratic method the dialectic method of inquiry and instruction used by Socrates; the pursuit of truth through the constant testing of any hypothesis and the challenging of any authority

Song Dynasty the dynasty that ruled China from 960 to 1279, a period marked by a high standard of living

Sophists a member of a school of Greek philosophy preceding that of Socrates, which specialized in the teaching of rhetoric, grammar, and logic

sovereign the supreme legal power in a state

soviet from the Russian: council; during the Russian Revolution a popular representative organization of workers, peasants, or soldiers; today, any of the legislative bodies of the Soviet Union

sphere of influence a territorial area where one power has special political or economic interests that are recognized by the other powers

sphinx in ancient Egyptian mythology a figure with the body of a lion and the head of a ram, hawk, or human being; any monumental carving of such a creature

staple crop a major crop of a country or region widely used by its inhabitants

stupa a large mound of earth, covered by brick and surrounded by a fence; originally a Buddhist shrine or holy place

Sumerian the ancient people of Sumer, among the first to leave written records

Surrealism from the French: beyond or above Realism; a style in twentieth-century art and literature that portrays the dreamlike fantasies of the subconscious mind

synagogue in ancient times a meeting place of Hebrew worship and prayer where the scriptures were read and taught; a Jewish house of worship

T

Tang Dynasty the dynasty that ruled China from 618 A.D. to 906 A.D., a period marked by great cultural achievement

Taoism from the Chinese: road or path; a Chinese philosophy founded by Laozi, which teaches that happiness can be achieved through living in harmony with the basic principles of nature

Theravada a form of Buddhism that spread to southeastern Asia and remained closest to the original teachings of Buddha

totalitarianism a system of government that denies the value of the individual and the basic principles of civil liberties in favor of the total control of the cultural, political, and economic affairs of a nation by a single party

tribune in ancient Rome an official whose responsibility was to protect plebeian interests against patrician oppression

tribute system a feature of Chinese foreign policy based on the assumption of China's superiority to other countries and marked by the payment of tribute to the emperor

triumph in ancient Rome a general's victory parade in which captured slaves and booty were displayed in a grand public procession

trust a permanent business arrangement aimed at the control of production, distribution, or price of a commodity or the management of some business

tyrant in ancient Greece a ruler who seized absolute power from the previous government without legal warrant

U

Upanishads a three-part collection of prose and poetry written as commentary on the meaning of the *Vedas* of ancient India and dealing with the nature of man and the universe

utilitarianism Jeremy Bentham's doctrine of "utility," which maintains that governments are best that secure the greatest amount of happiness for the greatest number of people

V

vassal in the feudal system one who received land from an overlord in exchange for military service

Vedas a collection of sacred compositions of ancient Aryan India

Vietcong during the Vietnam War, the military wing of the National Liberation Front whose aims were the overthrow of the government of South Vietnam and the union of North Vietnam and South Vietnam under the leadership of the Communists

vizier the most important civil official in ancient Egypt whose power increased with the decline of the pharaoh's authority during the later dynasties

W

welfare state a state in which the government guarantees a minimum standard of living for its citizens and assumes a good deal of responsibility for their social well-being, notably through unemployment and health insurance

writ of habeas corpus from the Latin: you should have the body; the legal document providing a citizen with a court order of protection from illegal imprisonment or false arrest

X Y Z

Xia Dynasty according to legend the first dynasty of ancient China

Yahweh the Hebrew name for God

zaibatsu the great commercial-industrial cartels of Japan that emerged in the 1920's

Zhou Dynasty a dynasty of ancient China, the longest in its history

ziggurat a terraced temple of ancient Sumer, built of sun-dried mud brick and several stories in height

Zionism the movement aimed at reestablishing a Jewish homeland in Palestine

Zollverein the German customs union founded in 1834

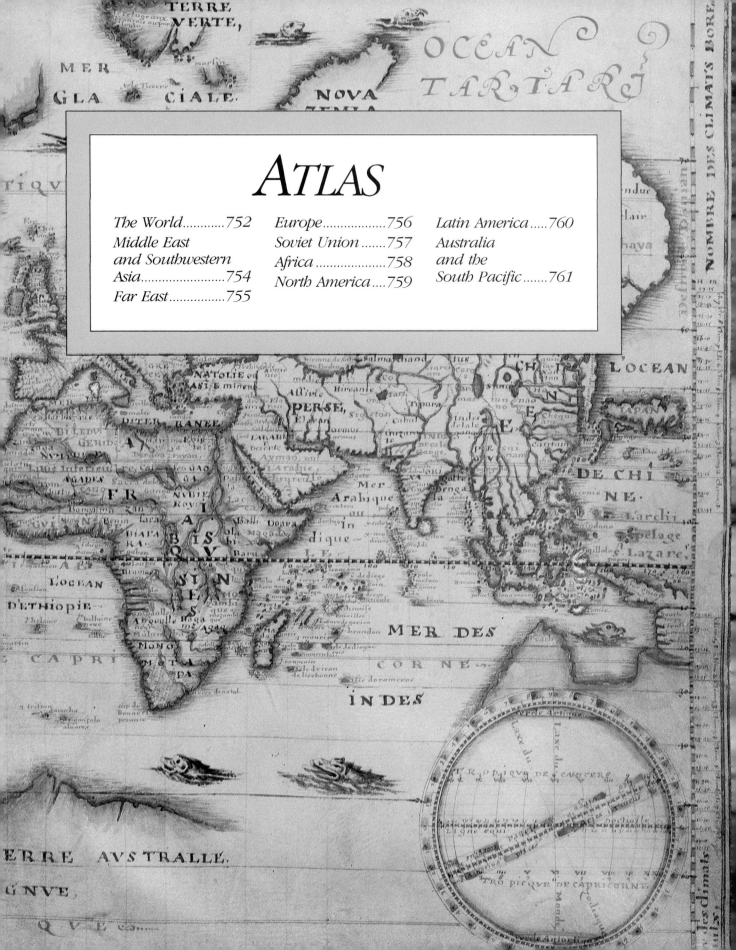

ATLAS

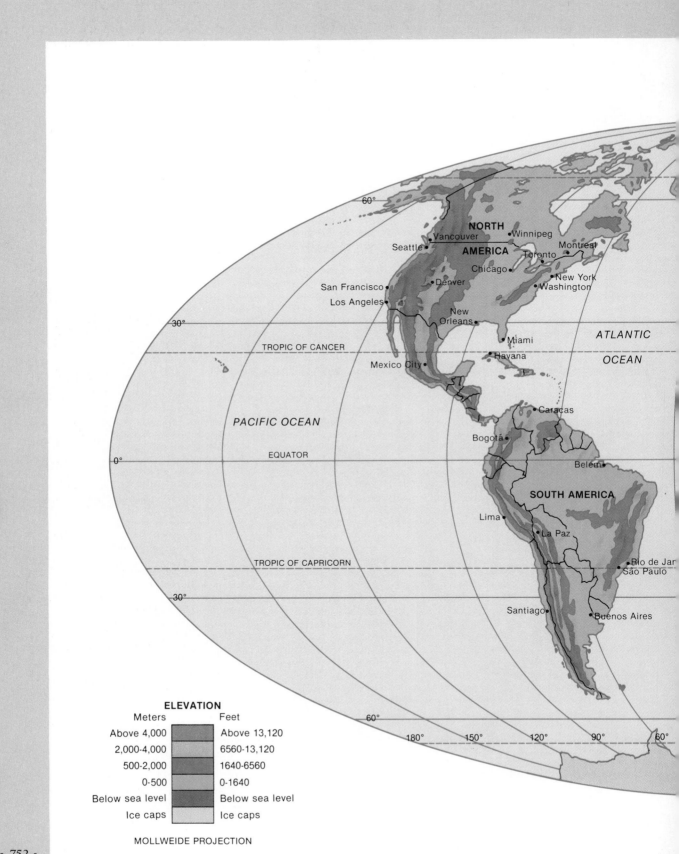

NORTH
AMERICA

Vancouver • Winnipeg
Seattle • • Montreal
Toronto •
Chicago • • New York
Denver • • Washington
San Francisco •
Los Angeles •
New
Orleans

ATLANTIC

OCEAN

Mexico City •

Miami •

Havana •

PACIFIC OCEAN

EQUATOR

Caracas •

Bogotá •

Belém •

SOUTH AMERICA

Lima •

La Paz •

Rio de Jar •
São Paulo •

Santiago •

Buenos Aires •

60°

NORTH
AMERICA

30°

TROPIC OF CANCER

0°

TROPIC OF CAPRICORN

30°

60°

180°   150°   120°   90°   60°

ELEVATION

Meters		Feet
Above 4,000		Above 13,120
2,000-4,000		6560-13,120
500-2,000		1640-6560
0-500		0-1640
Below sea level		Below sea level
Ice caps		Ice caps

MOLLWEIDE PROJECTION

ARCTIC OCEAN

NLAND

ICELAND

Oslo• •Helsinki
Stockholm •Moscow
Amsterdam •Berlin •Warsaw
London• •Prague
Paris• •Vienna •Budapest
EUROPE Belgrade• •Bucharest
Rome• •Sofia
sbon• •Madrid •Istanbul
Athens•
Rabat• •Algiers
•Tripoli Beirut• •Tehran •Kabul
ar Jerusalem• •Baghdad
Cairo•
•Riyadh

ASIA

60°

Beijing•
•Tokyo
30

Delhi•
Dacca• •Canton
Bombay• •Hanoi
Rangoon•
•Bangkok
Manila•

TROPIC OF CANCER

PACIFIC

OCEAN

AFRICA
Addis•
Ababa

•Lagos

•Nairobi
EQUATOR

INDIAN OCEAN

•Jakarta

AUSTRALIA
30

TROPIC OF CAPRICORN

•Johannesburg

•Sydney

Wellington•

60°

0° 30° 60° 90° 120° 150° 180°

ANTARCTIC CIRCLE

· 753 ·

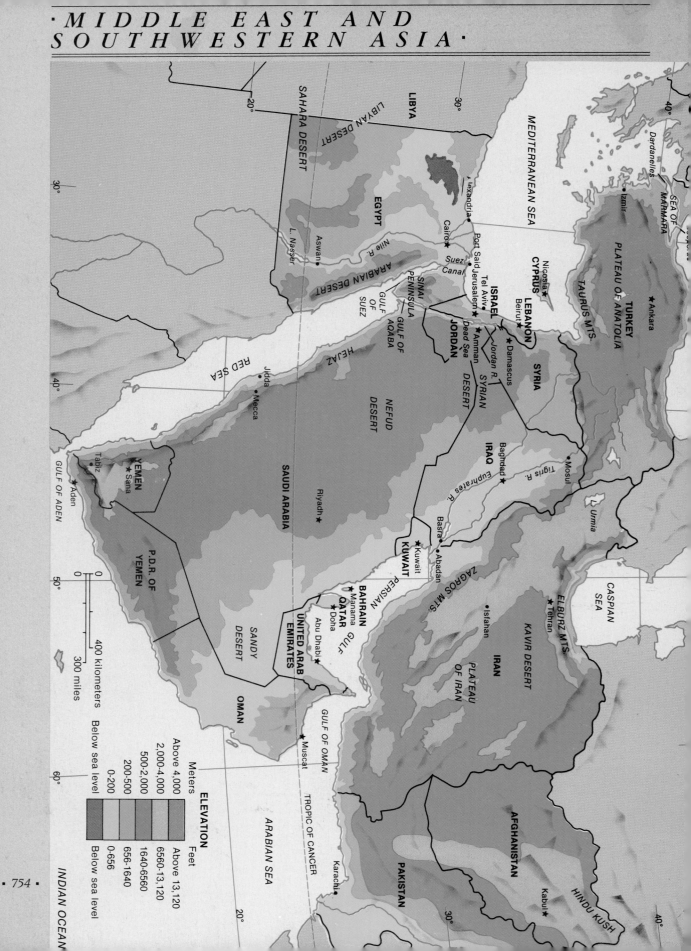

LIBYA

SAHARA DESERT

LIBYAN DESERT

20°

30°

EGYPT

ARABIAN DESERT

L. Nasser

Aswan

Nile R.

•Alexandria

•Cairo

Suez Canal

MEDITERRANEAN SEA

Port Said

Tel Aviv

Jerusalem

CYPRUS

Nicosia ★

LEBANON

Beirut ★

Damascus ★

ISRAEL

SINAI PENINSULA

GULF OF SUEZ

GULF OF AQABA

JORDAN

Amman ★

Dead Sea

Jordan R.

SYRIAN DESERT

SYRIA

IRAQ

Baghdad ★

Basra •

Abadan •

Kuwait ★

KUWAIT

HEJAZ

NEFUD DESERT

Jidda •

Mecca •

RED SEA

40°

SAUDI ARABIA

Riyadh ★

YEMEN

Sana ★

Tabiz •

Aden

GULF OF ADEN

P.D.R. OF YEMEN

50°

60°

SANDY DESERT

OMAN

UNITED ARAB EMIRATES

Abu Dhabi ★

BAHRAIN

Manama ★

QATAR

Doha •

PERSIAN GULF

ZAGROS MTS.

Isfahan •

Tehran ★

IRAN

PLATEAU OF IRAN

KAVIR DESERT

ELBURZ MTS.

CASPIAN SEA

L. Urmia

Mosul •

Tigris R.

Euphrates R.

TURKEY

PLATEAU OF ANATOLIA

Ankara ★

Izmir •

TAURUS MTS.

SEA OF MARMARA

Dardanelles

20°

30°

40°

GULF OF OMAN

Muscat •

ARABIAN SEA

TROPIC OF CANCER

AFGHANISTAN

Kabul ★

HINDU KUSH

PAKISTAN

Karachi •

30°

40°

INDIAN OCEAN

ELEVATION

Meters	Feet
Above 4,000	Above 13,120
2,000-4,000	6560-13,120
500-2,000	1640-6560
200-500	656-1640
0-200	0-656
Below sea level	Below sea level

0 400 kilometers

0 300 miles

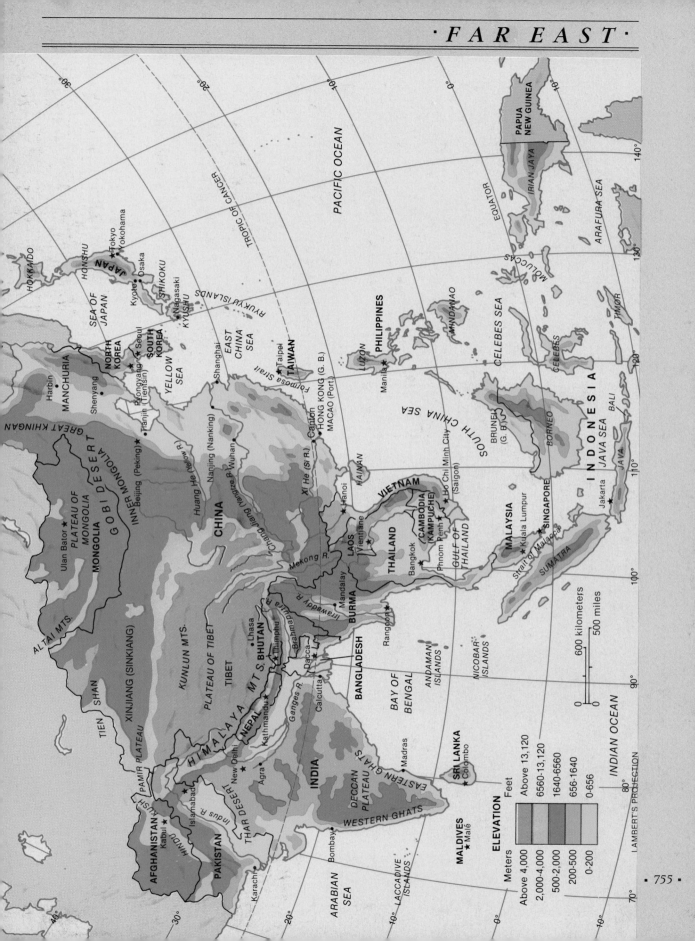

NORTH CAPE

ICELAND
★ Reykjavik

ARCTIC CIRCLE

Narvik

KJOLEN MTS.

60°

Faeroe Is.
(Den.)

GULF OF BOTHNIA

FINLAND

Shetland Is.
(G. B.)

NORWAY

SWEDEN

Helsinki ★

GULF OF FINLAND

Hebrides
(G. B.)

Orkney Is.
(G. B.)

SCOTLAND

SCOTTISH
HIGHLANDS

Bergen

Oslo ★

L. Vanern

Stockholm

BRITISH
ISLES

Firth of Forth
Glasgow ● ● Edinburgh

NORTHERN
IRELAND

Belfast ★

GREAT

L. Vattern

Göteborg

SKAGERRAK

JUTLAND
PENINSULA

BALTIC
SEA

NORTH
SEA

Dublin ●

IRISH
SEA

BRITAIN

DENMARK ★ Copenhagen

IRELAND

Liverpool ●

WALES

CAMBRIAN MTS.

ENGLAND

THE NETH.

Frisian Is.
Hamburg ●

EAST
GERMANY

Vistula R.

Berlin ★

Warsaw ★

50°

IJSSELMEER

Amsterdam ★

Cardiff ★

London ★

The Hague ● ● Rotterdam

● Cologne

POLAND

Thames R.

Antwerp ●

● Bonn

GERMANY

Elbe R.

Krakow ●

ENGLISH CHANNEL

Brussels ★

Neisse R.

Oder R.

BELGIUM

Frankfurt ●

WEST

Prague ★

CZECHOSLOVAKIA

CARPATHIAN MTS.

ATLANTIC

LUXEMBOURG

GERMANY

Brno ●

OCEAN

PLATEAU OF
BRITTANY

Seine R.

Paris ★

VOSGES MTS.

Rhine R.

BLACK FOREST

Munich ●

Vienna ★

AUSTRIA

Budapest ●

Loire R.

FRANCE

SWITZERLAND

LIECHTENSTEIN

HUNGARY

ROMANIA

BAY OF
BISCAY

L. Geneva ★ Bern

ALPS

Drava R.

Ploesti ●

Lyon ●

Geneva ●

ALPS

Trieste ●

Zagreb ●

Sava R.

Bucharest ★

CENTRAL
MASSIF

Rhone R.

● Milan

● Turin

Venice ●

Po R.

Belgrade ●

Danube R.

Bordeaux ●

Garonne R.

● Genoa

SAN
MARINO

DINARIC ALPS

YUGOSLAVIA

BULGARIA

CANTABRIAN MTS.

Florence ●

Marseilles ●

MONACO

Dubrovnik ●

Sofia ●

PYRENEES

Ebro R.

APENNINES

RHODOPE MTS.

Oporto ●

Douro R.

ANDORRA

CORSICA
(Fr.)

Tiber R.

ADRIATIC SEA

Tirana ●

Is

40°

GUADARRAMA MTS.

Barcelona ●

Rome ●

ALBANIA

Salonika ●

PORTUGAL

Madrid ★

Vatican City

ITALY

GREECE

AEGEAN SEA

Lisbon ★

Tagus R.

SPAIN

MESETA

SARDINIA
(Ital.)

TYRRHENIAN
SEA

IONIAN
SEA

Athens ★

SIERRA MORENA

BALEARIC IS.
(Sp.)

Cagliari ●

Guadalquivir R.

10°

STRAIT OF
GIBRALTAR

● Gibraltar (G. B.)

0°

Palermo ●

SICILY
(Ital.)

CRETE
(Gr.)

Valletta ★

MALTA

MEDITERRANEAN SEA

ELEVATION

Meters		Feet
Above 4,000		Above 13,120
2,000–4,000		6560–13,120
500–2,000		1640–6560
200–500		656–1640
0–200		0–656
Below sea level		Below sea level

CONIC PROJECTION

0 — 600 kilometers
0 — 500 miles

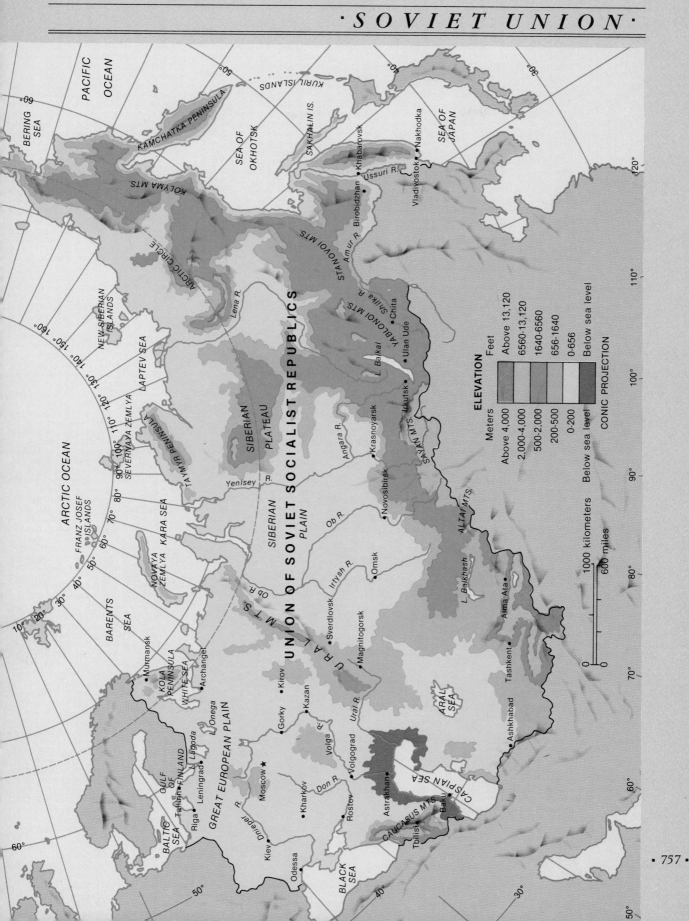

PACIFIC OCEAN

BERING SEA

KAMCHATKA PENINSULA

KOLYMA MTS.

SEA OF OKHOTSK

KURIL ISLANDS

SAKHALIN IS.

SEA OF JAPAN

Khabarovsk

Ussuri R.

Amur R. Birobidzhan

Vladivostok • Nakhodka

STANOVOI MTS.

Shilka R.

YABLONOI MTS.

Chita

L. Baikal

Ulan Ude

Irkutsk

SAYAN MTS.

Angara R.

Krasnoyarsk

Novosibirsk

ALTAI MTS.

ARCTIC CIRCLE

Lena R.

NEW SIBERIAN ISLANDS

SEVERNAYA ZEMLYA

LAPTEV SEA

TAYMYR PENINSULA

SIBERIAN PLATEAU

SIBERIAN PLAIN

Yenisey R.

Ob R.

Irtysh R.

Omsk

L. Balkhash

Alma Ata

Tashkent

UNION OF SOVIET SOCIALIST REPUBLICS

ARCTIC OCEAN

FRANZ JOSEF ISLANDS

NOVAYA ZEMLYA

KARA SEA

URAL MTS.

Ob R.

Sverdlovsk

Magnitogorsk

BARENTS SEA

Murmansk

KOLA PENINSULA

WHITE SEA

Archangel

Kirov

Kazan

Ural R.

ARAL SEA

Ashkhabad

GREAT EUROPEAN PLAIN

L. Onega

Gorky

L. Ladoga

FINLAND

GULF OF FINLAND

Tallinn

Leningrad

Riga

BALTIC SEA

Moscow ★

Volga R.

Kharkov

Don R.

Volgograd

Rostov

Astrakhan

CASPIAN SEA

Baku

CAUCASUS MTS.

Tbilisi

Dnieper R.

Kiev

Odessa

BLACK SEA

ELEVATION

Meters	Feet
Above 4,000	Above 13,120
2,000-4,000	6560-13,120
500-2,000	1640-6560
200-500	656-1640
0-200	0-656
Below sea level	Below sea level

CONIC PROJECTION

1000 kilometers

600 miles

· A F R I C A ·

MEDITERRANEAN SEA

Tangier
Rabat ★
Casablanca ★
Strait of Gibraltar
Algiers ★
Oran ●
Tunis ★
Santa Cruz de Tenerife
TUNISIA
Tripoli ★
Bengazi ●
Suez Canal
Alexandria ●
Cairo ★
MOROCCO
ATLAS MTS.
CANARY IS. (Sp.)
ALGERIA
LIBYA
EGYPT
ARABIAN DESERT
Nile R.
RED SEA
TROPIC OF CANCER

S A H A R A   D E S E R T
LIBYAN DESERT
L.Nasser
MAURITANIA
Nouakchott ★
AHAGGAR PLATEAU
NUBIAN DESERT

MALI
NIGER
CHAD
Senegal R.
Dakar ★
SENEGAL
Banjul ★
GAMBIA
Bissau ★
GUINEA BISSAU
Conakry ★
Bamako ★
BOURKINA FASO
Ouagadougou ★
Niamey ★
L.Chad
N'Djamena ★
SUDAN
Khartoum ★
Blue Nile
ERITREA
DJIBOUTI
Djibouti ★
GULF OF ADE

GUINEA
Freetown ★
SIERRA LEONE
Monrovia ★
LIBERIA
GHANA
IVORY COAST
Porto Novo ★
BENIN
NIGERIA
Niger R.
Lomé ★
Accra ★
Abijdan ★
TOGO
GULF OF GUINEA
Lagos ★
Malabo ★
CENTRAL AFRICAN REPUBLIC
Bangui ★
White Nile
Addis Ababa ★
ETHIOPIA
SOMALIA
Mogadishu ★

CAMEROON
Yaoundé ★
Oubangi R.
UGANDA
L.Turkana
São Tomé ★
SAO TOME AND PRINCIPE
EQUATORIAL GUINEA
Libreville ★
CONGO
GABON
Zaire R.
Kampala ★
L.Victoria
KENYA
Nairobi ★
Kigali ★
RWANDA
ZAIRE
Bujumbura ★
BURUNDI
INDIAN OCEAN
EQUATOR

Brazzaville ★
Kinshasa ★
Kasai R.
Dodoma ★
ZANZIBAR
Dar-es-Salaam ★
CABINDA (Angola)
L.Tanganyika
TANZANIA
ATLANTIC OCEAN
Luanda ★
KATANGA PLATEAU
COMORO ISLANDS
Moroni ★

ANGOLA
L.Nyasa
MALAWI
Lilongwe ★
ZAMBIA
Lusaka ★
Zambezi R.
Salisbury ★
ZIMBABWE (RHODESIA)
Antananarivo ★
MOZAMBIQUE
MOZAMBIQUE CHANNEL
MADAGASCAR

NAMIBIA
Windhoek ★
BOTSWANA
KALAHARI DESERT
Gaborone ★
TROPIC OF CAPRICO
Walvis Bay (South Africa)
Pretoria ★
Johannesburg ★
Maputo ★
Mbabane ★
SWAZILAND
Orange R.
LESOTHO
Maseru ★
SOUTH AFRICA
DRAKENSBERG MTS.
Capetown ★
CAPE OF GOOD HOPE

ELEVATION

Meters		Feet
Above 4,000		Above 13,120
2,000-4,000		6560-13,120
500-2,000		1640-6560
200-500		656-1640
0-200		0-656
Below sea level		Below sea level

STEREOGRAPHIC PROJECTION

0 ————— 1000 kilometers
0 ————— 600 miles

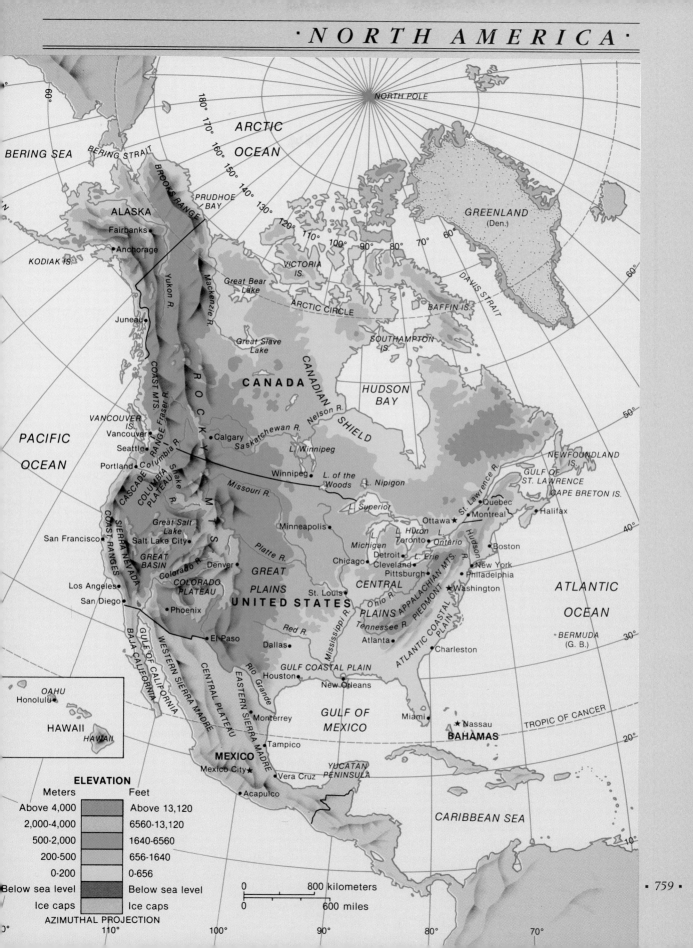

BERING SEA

BERING STRAIT

60°

ARCTIC
OCEAN

180° 170° 160° 150° 140° 130°

NORTH POLE

120°

110°

100° 90° 80° 70° 60°

ARCTIC CIRCLE

BROOKS RANGE

PRUDHOE
BAY

ALASKA

Fairbanks

Anchorage

KODIAK IS.

Juneau

Yukon R.

Mackenzie R.

VICTORIA
IS.

Great Bear
Lake

Great Slave
Lake

GREENLAND
(Den.)

DAVIS STRAIT

60°

BAFFIN IS.

SOUTHAMPTON
IS.

HUDSON
BAY

50°

CANADA

CANADIAN SHIELD

Nelson R.

COAST MTS.

VANCOUVER
IS.

Vancouver

Seattle

Portland

Calgary

Saskatchewan R.

L. Winnipeg

Winnipeg

L. of the
Woods

L. Nipigon

NEWFOUNDLAND
IS.

GULF OF
ST. LAWRENCE

CAPE BRETON IS.

PACIFIC
OCEAN

CASCADE RANGE

Fraser R.

Columbia R.

COLUMBIA
PLATEAU

Snake R.

Missouri R.

ROCKY

L. Superior

St. Lawrence R.

Quebec

Montreal

Halifax

50°

San Francisco

SIERRA NEVADA

COAST RANGES

Great Salt
Lake

Salt Lake City

GREAT
BASIN

Colorado R.

Denver

Platte R.

Minneapolis

GREAT
PLAINS

L.
Michigan

Chicago

L. Huron

Toronto

Detroit

Cleveland

L. Erie

L.
Ontario

Ottawa

Hudson R.

Boston

New York

Philadelphia

40°

Los Angeles

San Diego

COLORADO
PLATEAU

Phoenix

UNITED STATES

St. Louis

Ohio R.

CENTRAL
PLAINS

Pittsburgh

APPALACHIAN MTS.

PIEDMONT

Washington

ATLANTIC
OCEAN

El Paso

Red R.

Dallas

Mississippi R.

Tennessee R.

Atlanta

ATLANTIC COASTAL PLAIN

Charleston

BERMUDA
(G. B.)

30°

GULF COASTAL PLAIN

Houston

New Orleans

BAJA CALIFORNIA

GULF OF CALIFORNIA

WESTERN SIERRA MADRE

CENTRAL PLATEAU

EASTERN SIERRA MADRE

Rio Grande

Monterrey

GULF OF
MEXICO

Miami

Nassau

BAHAMAS

TROPIC OF CANCER

20°

OAHU

Honolulu

HAWAII

HAWAII

Tampico

MEXICO

Mexico City

Vera Cruz

Acapulco

YUCATAN
PENINSULA

CARIBBEAN SEA

10°

ELEVATION

Meters		Feet
Above 4,000		Above 13,120
2,000-4,000		6560-13,120
500-2,000		1640-6560
200-500		656-1640
0-200		0-656
Below sea level		Below sea level
Ice caps		Ice caps

AZIMUTHAL PROJECTION

0   800 kilometers

0   600 miles

110°   100°   90°   80°   70°

· 759 ·

110°   100°   90°   80°   70°   60°   50°   40°   30°

30°

BAJA CALIFORNIA
GULF OF CALIFORNIA
WESTERN SIERRA MADRE
EASTERN SIERRA MADRE
CENTRAL PLATEAU
Rio Grande
• Monterrey
GULF OF MEXICO
BAHAMAS
• Nassau
TROPIC OF CANCER

20°

• Tampico
Mexico City ★
MEXICO • Vera Cruz
Acapulco •
YUCATÁN PENINSULA
CUBA
Havana ★
GREATER
DOMINICAN REPUBLIC
HAITI
PUERTO RICO (U. S.)
VIRGIN IS. (U. S.)
San Juan •
ATLANTIC OCEA

BELIZE
• Belmopan
HONDURAS
Guatemala •
GUATEMALA
San Salvador
EL SALVADOR
Tegucigalpa ★
NICARAGUA
• Managua
San José ★
COSTA RICA
PANAMA
• Panama
PANAMA CANAL
JAMAICA ★
Kingston •
Port-au-Prince •
ANTILLES
CARIBBEAN SEA
Santo Domingo
LESSER ANTILLES
ARUBA (Neth.)
Caracas ★
GUADELOUPE (Fr.)
MARTINIQUE (Fr.)
BARBADOS
• Bridgetown
Port of Spain •
TRINIDAD AND TOBAGO

10°

Maricaibo •
Magdalena R.
Bogotá •
LLANOS
VENEZUELA
Orinoco R.
GUIANA HIGHLANDS
GUYANA
Georgetown ★
SURINAME
Paramaribo ★
FRENCH GUIANA (Fr.)
• Cayenne

0°
EQUATOR
GALÁPAGOS ISLANDS (Ec.)
COLOMBIA
Quito ★
ECUADOR
Negro R.
Amazon R.
• Manaus
• Belém

10°
A
N
D
E
S
LA MONTAÑA
PERU
Lima ★
M
T
S
.
BRAZIL
BRAZILIAN PLATEAU
Brasilia ★
São Francisco R.
Re

20°
PACIFIC OCEAN
L. Titicaca
BOLIVIA
★ La Paz
• Sucre
BRAZILIAN HIGHLANDS
• Rio de Janeir
TROPIC OF CAPRICORN
ATACAMA DESERT
GRAN CHACO
Paraguay R.
PARAGUAY
Asunción •
• São Paulo

30°
CHILE
Paraná R.
ARGENTINA
Valparaíso •
Santiago ★
Rosario •
PAMPAS
Buenos Aires ★
Uruguay R.
URUGUAY
★ Montevideo

40°

ELEVATION

Meters	Feet
Above 4,000	Above 13,120
2,000-4,000	6560-13,120
500-2,000	1640-6560
200-500	656-1640
0-200	0-656

LAMBERT'S PROJECTION

0   1000 kilomete
0   600 miles

50°

PATAGONIA
Strait of Magellan
TIERRA DEL FUEGO
FALKLAND ISLANDS
SOUTH GEORGIA (G. B.)

120°   110°   100°   90°   80°   70°   60°   50°   40°   30°   20°

·WORLD HISTORY CHRONOLOGY·

	3000 BC	2000 BC	1000 BC	1 AD
Europe	▪ 3000 Farming well established	▪ 2000 Minoan civilization prospers ▪ 1400 Mycenaeans dominate eastern Mediterranean	▪ By 900 Etruscans settle in Italy ▪ 700's Latins settle along Tiber River; Rome founded ▪ 510 Democratic government established in Athens ▪ 509 Roman Republic founded ▪ 400's Classical Age in Greece ▪ 469–322 Socrates, Plato, and Aristotle ▪ 431–404 Peloponnesian War; Sparta defeats Athens ▪ 334–323 Alexander the Great establishes Greek Empire ▪ 323 Hellenistic Age in Greece ▪ 200 Germanic tribes begin to invade western Europe ▪ 133 Roman Revolution begins ▪ 27 Augustus rules; Roman Revolution ends	
Middle East and West Asia	▪ 3000 Sumerian cities flourish ▪ 2500 Sumer declines	▪ c. 1900 Babylonian Empire established ▪ 1750 Code of Hammurabi ▪ 1600 Hittites invade Babylon ▪ 1400 Hittites develop ironworking ▪ 1200 Hittite Empire falls ▪ 1020–1004 Saul, first king of Israel	▪ 965–925 Solomon rules Israel ▪ 900 Assyrians move into Mesopotamia ▪ c. 900 Phoenician trade well established ▪ 722 Assyria destroys kingdom of Israel ▪ 600 Height of Chaldean Empire ▪ c. 600 Zoroaster ▪ 586 Nebuchadnezzar conquers Hebrews ▪ 559–529 Cyrus the Great rules Persia	▪ 30 Jesus Christ crucified
Asia and the Pacific	▪ 2400–1700 Indus Valley civilization develops and prospers; cities of Mohenjo-Daro and Harappa built ▪ 2200–1500 Legendary Xia Dynasty in Yellow River Valley	▪ c. 2000 Civilization emerges along Yellow River ▪ 1766–1027 Shang Dynasty ▪ 1500 Indus Valley civilization ends	▪ 1000 Aryans settle in India ▪ Zhou Dynasty begins in China ▪ 604–531 Lao-tzu ▪ 551–479 Confucius ▪ c. 530–330 Persian control of northwest India ▪ 500 Buddhism founded in India ▪ 403–221 Age of Warring States in China ▪ 322 Maurya Empire established in India ▪ 221 Qin Empire established in China ▪ 214 Great Wall of China begun ▪ 202 Han Dynasty begins	▪ 9–23 Interregnum of Wang Mang
Africa	▪ c. 3000 Saharan peoples migrate to Mediterranean and West Africa ▪ 2850 Old Kingdom in Egypt ▪ 2050 Middle Kingdom in Egypt	▪ 1730 Hyksos invade Egypt ▪ 1570 New Kingdom in Egypt ▪ 1468–1436 Thutmose III rules Egypt ▪ 1417–1379 Reign of Amenhotep III in Egypt ▪ 1361 Tutankhamun becomes pharoah ▪ 1279–1212 Reign of Ramses II	▪ c. 1000 Empire of Cush emerges ▪ 814 Phoenicians establish Carthage ▪ 750 Cushites control area from Nile to Palestine ▪ 670 Assyrians invade Egypt ▪ c. 500 Bantu migrations ▪ 332 Alexander the Great conquers Egypt ▪ 146 Carthage defeated by Rome in Third Punic War; Rome extends influence in North Africa	▪ c. 50 Empire of Aksum becomes a major trading center
The Americas	▪ 2500 Maize cultivated		▪ 1000 Olmec culture emerges in Mexico	

100 AD	200	300	400	500
	▪ 285–330 Roman Empire divided into East and West	▪ 313 Constantine issues Edict of Milan ▪ 372 Huns conquer Ostrogoths ▪ 379–395 Christianity becomes official religion of Roman Empire	▪ 400 Angles, Saxons, and Jutes invade England ▪ 400–500 Vandal invasions ▪ 410 Visigoths sack Rome ▪ 452 Attila the Hun invades Italy ▪ 455 Vandals sack Rome ▪ 476 Fall of Rome ▪ 481 Clovis unites the Franks	
				▪ 500–1453 Byzantine Empire ▪ c. 530 Justinian's Code
	▪ 220 Han Empire in China falls	▪ 320–535 Gupta emperors rule northern India		▪ 589 Sui Dynasty emerges; Grand Canal built
			▪ c. 400 Berbers establish trade with India	▪ c. 500–1200 Ghana Empire
		▪ 300–900 Mayan civilization flourishes		

	600	700	800	900
Europe		• 711 Muslims invade Spain • 732 Battle of Tours	• 800 Charlemagne crowned; Viking and Magyar invasions begin	• 900 Revival of commerce and town life in western Europe • 955 Magyars settle in Hungary • 962 Otto the Great crowned Holy Roman Emperor • 988 Vladimir of Kiev converts to Orthodoxy
Middle East and West Asia	• c. 610 Muhammad founds Islam	• 750 Abbasid Dynasty replaces Umayyid Dynasty		• 976 Basil II crowned Byzantine emperor
Asia and the Pacific	• 606–646 Harsha rules a reunited north India • 618–906 Tang Dynasty rules China • 690–705 Reign of Empress Wu	• 700's Age of great poetry in China		• 960–1279 Song Dynasty in China
Africa	• 632–750 Islam spreads to Egypt and North Africa			
The Americas				

1000	1100	1200	1300
- c. 1000 Vikings reach North America - 1016 Canute rules Denmark, Norway, and England - 1054 The Schism of East and West - 1066 Battle of Hastings; Norman Conquest of England - 1096 First Crusade reaches Constantinople	- 1122 Concordat of Worms - 1147–1149 Second Crusade - 1189–1192 Third Crusade - 1198–1216 Peak of papal power under Innocent III	- 1202 Fourth Crusade - 1212 Children's Crusade - 1215 Magna Carta - 1233 Pope Gregory IX establishes the Inquisition	- 1300's Renaissance begins - 1308 Babylonian Captivity begins - 1338–1453 Hundred Years' War - 1347–1350 Black Death sweeps Europe - 1378–1417 Great Schism
- 1055 Seljuk Turks move into Middle East - 1071 Seljuk Turks overcome Byzantines at Manzikert - 1096 First Crusade reaches Constantinople		- 1238 Mongols invade Russia	- 1390's Ottoman Turks invade eastern Europe
- 1000 Turks conquer India - 1000's Chinese develop movable type	- 1126 The Jin take Kaifeng from the Song, dividing China into northern and southern kingdoms - 1185 Yoritomo shogunate begins in Japan	- 1211 Mongols under Genghis Khan invade India - 1260 Kublai Khan founds Mongol Dynasty	- 1368–1644 Ming Dynasty rules China - 1398 Tamerlane invades India
- 1000 Trade routes cross Sahara; African trade centers develop - c. 1050 Muslim Berbers extend influence into West Africa		- 1250–1492 Muslims control trade in East Africa	- 1300 Empire of Mali reaches peak - 1307–1332 Mansa Musa rules empire of Mali
- c. 1000 Vikings reach North America - Mayas conquered by the Itzá	- 1100 Beginnings of Inca civilization		- 1325 Tenochtitlán founded by Aztecs

	1400	1500	1600	1700
Europe	• c. 1415 Portuguese launch the Age of Exploration • 1450's Printing press developed • 1455 War of Roses begins • 1462–1505 Reign of Ivan the Great • 1481 Spanish Inquisition begins • 1488 Bartholomeu Dias rounds Cape of Good Hope • 1492 Muslims expelled from Spain; Columbus' first voyage • 1494 Treaty of Tordesillas • 1498 Vasco da Gama reaches India	• 1500 Commercial Revolution begins • 1517 Martin Luther's *Ninety-five Theses* • 1519 Charles V crowned Holy Roman Emperor • c. 1530 The Counter Reformation • 1558–1603 Reign of Elizabeth I • 1562 Civil war breaks out in France • 1588 English defeat Spanish Armada • 1598 Edict of Nantes	• 1600's Era of scientific discoveries • 1618–1648 Thirty Years' War • 1642 Civil war in England • 1649–1660 Interregnum in England • 1660 Restoration of Charles II in England • 1682–1725 Reign of Peter the Great • 1687 Newton's law of gravitation • 1689–1697 War of League of Augsburg • 1661–1715 Reign of Louis XIV • 1688–1689 Glorious Revolution in England; Bill of Rights	• 1700's Age of Reason • 1700's Industrial Revolution begins in England • 1702 War of Spanish Succession begins • 1709 Battle of Poltava • 1713 Peace of Utrecht • 1740–1780 Reign of Maria Theresa in Austria • 1740–1748 War of the Austrian Succession
Middle East and West Asia	• 1453 Byzantine Empire falls to Ottoman Turks • 1480 Ottoman Turks control Egypt, Balkans, Middle East	• 1500's Rise of Safavid Dynasty in Persia		
Asia and the Pacific	• 1498 Vasco da Gama reaches India	• 1520's Mogul Empire begins • 1557 Portuguese establish colony in Macao • 1560's Spanish colonize Philippines	• 1600's English establish colonies in India • 1603 Tokugawa shogunate begins in Japan • 1640's Dutch occupy Indonesia • 1640–1853 Japanese isolation • 1644 Qing Dynasty established in China • 1660's French establish colony in India • 1661–1722 Kangxi rules China • 1683–1911 Manchus control China	
Africa	• 1405–1453 China-Africa trade thrives • 1460 Portuguese control Madeira and Azores • c. 1464 Sunni Ali comes to power in Songhai Empire • 1480 Kongo Kingdom flourishes • 1488 Dias sails around Cape of Good Hope	• 1500's Portuguese establish trading posts in East Africa; export of African slaves begins • 1570 Kanem-Bornu Empire reaches height	• 1650's Dutch settle in South Africa	
The Americas	• 1400–1519 Aztec Empire • 1438–1538 Inca Empire • 1492 Columbus arrives in North America • 1494 Treaty of Tordesillas • 1497 Cabot explores North America and establishes English claim • 1499–1502 Vespucci explores South American coastline	• 1500 Cabral claims Brazil for Portugal • 1513 Ponce de León explores Florida; Balboa discovers the Pacific Ocean • 1521 Cortés conquers Aztecs • 1524 Verrazano explores North American coast • 1530 Portuguese import African slaves into Brazil • 1540–1542 Coronado explores southwestern U.S. • c. 1570 Iroquois League formed	• 1607 English settle Jamestown • 1608 French settle Quebec • 1620 Plymouth Colony • 1624 New Netherland founded • 1630 Massachusetts Bay Colony founded • 1654 Brazilians revolt against the Dutch • 1660–1696 Navigation Acts • 1682 La Salle claims Louisiana territory for France • 1689 King William's War begins	• 1702 Queen Anne's War begins • 1740 King George's War begins

• 1756 Seven Years' War begins • 1762–96 Reign of Catherine II in Russia • 1769 Watt patents steam engine • 1772–1795 Poland partitioned • 1789 French Revolution begins • 1794 Fall of Robespierre • 1799 Napoleon's coup d'état	• 1800's Era of Imperialism • 1804 Napoleon crowned emperor • 1805 Battle of Trafalgar; Battle of Austerlitz • 1812 Napoleon invades Russia • 1814–1815 Congress of Vienna • 1815 Battle of Waterloo • 1815–1848 Age of Metternich • 1830 Charles X of France overthrown • 1832 Parliament passes Reform Bill • 1833 British Factory Act • 1837–1901 Reign of Victoria	• 1851 Crystal Palace Exposition in London • 1852–1870 Second French Empire • 1853–1856 Crimean War • 1861 Russian serfs emancipated • 1870 Unification of Italy completed • 1870–71 Franco-Prussian War • 1871 German Empire established • 1871–1940 Third French Republic • 1895 Roentgen discovers X Ray
		• 1869 Suez Canal opened
• 1757 Battle of Plassey; • 1763 British become leading power in India • 1795–1803 White Lotus rebellion in China • 1798 Dutch East Indies established as a royal colony	• 1839–1842 Opium War	• 1850 Tai Ping Rebellion begins • 1850's–1880's French gain control of Indochina • 1853 Admiral Perry arrives in Japan • 1857–1858 Sepoy Mutiny • 1868 Meiji Restoration in Japan • 1885 Organization of Indian National Congress • 1898 U.S. annexes Hawaii
• 1798 Battle of the Nile	• 1800's Zulu wars • 1815 Britain acquires Cape Colony • 1830 France begins colonization of Algeria • 1833 Slave trade outlawed in British Empire • 1836–1837 Great Trek in South Africa	• 1853–1856 Livingstone's transcontinental journey • 1881 Tunisia becomes French protectorate • 1882 British occupy Egypt • 1884–85 Belgium takes control of Congo • 1899–1902 Boer War
• 1754 French and Indian War begins • 1764 Sugar Act passed • 1765 Stamp Act • 1767 Townshend Acts passed • 1773 Boston Tea Party • 1775 American Revolution begins • 1776 Declaration of Independence • 1783 Treaty of Paris • 1787 U.S. Constitution drafted; Northwest Ordinance • 1793 Whitney's cotton gin	• 1803 Louisiana Purchase • 1804 Haitian independence • 1812–1815 War of 1812 • 1819 Bolívar routs Spanish from Colombia • 1821 Mexican independence declared • 1822 Brazilian independence • 1823 Monroe Doctrine • 1828 Era of Jacksonian Democracy begins • 1836 Texas declares independence from Mexico • 1846–1848 Mexican War	• 1861–1865 Civil War in U.S. • 1862 Abraham Lincoln issues Emancipation Proclamation • 1867 Canada becomes a British Dominion • 1876 Bell patents telephone • 1898 Spanish-American War

	1900	1950
Europe	■ 1905 Einstein's theory of relativity ■ 1914—1918 World War I ■ 1917 Revolution in Russia ■ 1918 Civil war in Russia ■ 1922 Mussolini assumes power in Italy ■ 1928 Stalin emerges as Soviet leader ■ 1931 Statute of Westminster ■ 1933 Hitler becomes German chancellor ■ 1936 Germany occupies Rhineland; Spanish Civil War begins ■ 1938 Anschluss of Germany and Austria ■ 1939 Germany invades Poland ■ 1939—1945 World War II ■ 1941 Atlantic Charter; U.S. enters World War II ■ 1947 Marshall Plan ■ 1948 Berlin airlift ■ 1949 NATO formed	■ 1955 Warsaw Pact ■ 1956 Revolutions in Hungary and Poland ■ 1957 Soviets launch *Sputnik* ■ 1958 Common Market in Europe formed ■ 1968 Soviets invade Czechoslovakia ■ 1975 Helsinki Accords ■ 1975 Franco of Spain dies ■ 1980 Strikes in Poland ■ 1985 New regime under Gorbachev in Soviet Union ■ 1985 Reagan-Gorbachev meet in Geneva
Middle East and West Asia	■ 1917 Balfour Declaration promises establishment of Jewish homeland ■ 1948 Israel founded; First Arab-Israeli war	■ 1956 Suez crisis ■ 1960 OPEC formed ■ 1967 Six-Day War ■ 1973 Yom Kippur War; OPEC oil embargo ■ 1975 Civil war begins in Lebanon ■ 1978 Camp David Accords between Egypt and Israel ■ 1979 Iranian Revolution ■ 1981 Anwar Sadat of Egypt assassinated ■ 1985 American hostage crisis in Lebanon
Asia and the Pacific	■ 1900 Boxer Rebellion ■ 1904—1905 Russo-Japanese War ■ 1912 Chinese republic established ■ 1920 Gandhi becomes leader of Indian National Congress ■ 1921 Chinese Communist party founded ■ 1927 Chiang Kai-shek establishes National government in China ■ 1931 Japanese invade Manchuria ■ 1934—1935 Long March in China ■ 1941 Japanese attack Pearl Harbor; World War II in Pacific begins ■ 1947 British leave India; India and Pakistan become separate independent countries ■ 1949 People's Republic of China established	■ 1950 North Korean invasion of South Korea ■ 1954 French withdraw from Indochina ■ 1956 U.S. sends military advisors to Vietnam; ■ 1966 Cultural Revolution in China ■ 1971 Bangladesh declares independence ■ 1972 U.S. President Nixon visits China ■ 1975 Saigon falls to the Communists ■ 1979 U.S.S.R. invades Afghanistan
Africa	■ 1910 British South African colonies are united ■ 1914 British declare Egypt a protectorate ■ 1923 Mustafa Kemal declares Turkish republic ■ 1948 National Party assumes power in South Africa	■ 1951 Mau Mau rebellion erupts ■ 1954 Kenyatta organizes TANU ■ 1957 Ghana becomes first black African colony to gain independence ■ 1960 French colonies in Africa receive independence ■ 1963 Organization of African Unity formed; Kenya gains independence ■ 1974 Haile Selassie overthrown in Ethiopia ■ 1980 Zimbabwe gains independence ■ 1985 Unrest in white-ruled South Africa
The Americas	■ 1900 Era of the automobile begins ■ 1910 Mexican Revolution ■ 1914 Panama Canal opens ■ 1917 U.S. enters World War I ■ 1927 First motion picture with sound ■ 1929 Great Depression begins ■ 1933 Franklin D. Roosevelt initiates the New Deal ■ 1934–1940 Lázaro Cárdenas stabilizes Mexico ■ 1941 Attack on Pearl Harbor; U.S. enters World War II ■ 1943–1955 Perón dominates Argentina ■ 1945 U.S. drops atomic bombs on Japan; Nuclear Age begins ■ 1946 United Nations founded ■ 1947 Era of the Cold War begins	■ 1950 Age of the computer begins ■ 1959 Cuban Revolution; Castro becomes premier ■ 1962 Cuban Missile Crisis ■ 1969 U.S. Astronauts land on moon ■ 1972 U.S. and U.S.S.R. sign SALT I treaty ■ 1973 Chile's Marxist government overthrown; military takes over ■ 1979 Sandinista government heads Nicaragua; junta takes control of El Salvador ■ 1983 Civilian rule restored in Argentina ■ 1985 Nuclear arms reduction talks resume between U.S. and U.S.S.R.

rule, 154–156, 161; legal system, 153, 154–155; religion, 152, 153, 156–160; Roman influence, 153, 154, 158; Russia and, 152, 153, 157, 159, 163, 166; trade, 153, 157, 250
Byzantium, 152, 153

Cabot, John, 351
Cabral, Pedro Álvares, 343
Caddoe Indians, 232
Caesar, Julius, 132, 133, 134, 243
Calderón de la Barca, 317–318
calendars, 19, 27, 52, 54, 72, 172, 233, 234
California, 231, 347, 602
Caligula, Emperor, 135
calligraphy, 73
Calvin, John, 309–310
Calvinism, 309–310, 318, 320, 323, 324
Cambodia, 94, 533, 535, 667; U.S. involvement in, 669–671, 717
Cambrai, Treaty of, 315
Cameroons, 523, 558
Camp David Accords, 684
Canaan, 30, 32, 43, 48, 50
Canaanites, 30, 32
Canada, 350, 351, 353, 358, 387, 468, 511, 517, 555, 582, 583–584, 702, 707, 713–714; geography and climate, 227; government, 584, 713; Great Britain and, 583–584; independence of, 713; Indians, 231, 232; language division in, 713; NATO, 637, 713; Quebec Act, 388; separatist movement, 713; U.S. relations with, 713–714
Canal Zone treaties, 709
Cano, Sebastian del, 343
Canterbury Tales, 287, 298
Canute, King, 266
Cape Colony, 525, 526
Cape of Good Hope, 339, 349, 524
Capetian Dynasty, 271
Cape Verde Islands, 340, 345, 523
capitalism, 354, 517; growth of, 426, 438–439; Marx on, 441
Caracalla, Emperor, 138
Cárdenas, Lázaro, 595, 711–712
Caribbean, 227, 343, 348, 349, 351, 353, 499, 537, 595, 596, 708, 709–710. *See also* names of countries
Caribbean Basin Initiative, 709
Carnarvon, Lord, 49
Caroline Islands, 535
Carolingian Dynasty, 245, 250, 271, 278
Carranza, Venustiano, 595
cartels, 426
Carter, Howard, 49
Carter, Jimmy, 641, 642, 656, 684, 707, 709
Carthage, 29–30, 154, 217; Punic Wars, 127–129
Cartier, Jacques, 350
Casablanca Conference, 618
Caspian Sea, 23, 27
Cassius, 132, 133
caste system, 65–66, 68, 93, 664, 666
Castiglione, Baldassare, 298
Castlereagh, Viscount, 436, 437
Castro, Fidel, 708–709
Cateau-Cambrésis, Treaty of, 316
Catherine of Aragon, 308, 309
Catherine II (the Great), Tsarina, 373, 379–380, 489

Catullus, 145
Cavour, Count Camillo di, 474–475
Cayuga Indians, 232
Celts, 248, 249
Central America, 227, 229, 537, 597, 708, 710–711; independence movements, 501; Indians, 214, 232–235, 343; political instability, 710, 711. *See also* Latin America; names of countries
Central Powers (World War I), 548
Cervantes, Miguel de, 317
Ceylon, 349
Cézanne, Paul, 467
Chaldeans, 27–28, 31
Chamberlain, Neville, 609, 610, 613
Chamber of Deputies (France), 446, 447
Champlain, Samuel de, 350
Chang Jian, 88
Charlemagne, 245–246, 247, 250, 278, 279
Charles IV, Holy Roman Emperor, 281
Charles V, Holy Roman Emperor, 308, 315, 319–320, 347
Charles I, King of England, 325–326
Charles II, King of England, 327, 349, 367
Charles VI, King of France, 274
Charles VII, King of France, 275, 304
Charles IX, King of France, 318, 319
Charles X, King of France, 446–447
Charles I, King of Spain, 375
Charles II, King of Spain, 333
Charles XII, King of Sweden, 378
Chartist Movement, 443–444
Chatelet Lomont, Gabrielle du, 372
Chaucer, Geoffrey, 287, 298
chemistry, 367–368, 457–458, 724
Chernenko, Konstantin, 644
Cherokee Indians, 232
Cheyenne Indians, 231
Chiang Kai-shek, 588–590, 651, 654
Chickasaw Indians, 232
child labor, 426
Children's Crusade, 265
Chile, 227, 235, 501, 597; 1960s–1980s, 705
China, 14, 91, 92, 164, 188, 192–201, 498, 503–506, 531–535, 545, 558, 587–591, 637, 640, 643, 650–657, 666, 669, 673, 733; agriculture, 69–70, 72, 86, 87, 504, 651, 652; 656; ancient times, 60, 69–89; art and architecture, 71, 76, 84, 87, 88, 94, 199–201; Boxer Rebellion, 587; Buddhism, 69, 88–89, 193–194; civil service system, 87, 193, 194–196; civil war, 89, 505–506, 589–590, 651; communism, 588–589, 651–653, 655; Confucianism, 75, 76, 84, 88, 194; Cultural Revolution, 652–653, 656; détente with U.S., 654, 655–656; Dynastic Cycle Theory, 75–76; early civilization, 69–71, 75–76, 82, 88, 89, 199–201; extraterritoriality in, 505; feudalism, 74, 83, 89; four modernizations, 656; government, 72, 74, 75, 76, 82, 83–84, 86, 87, 89, 193, 194–196, 197, 588; Great Britain and, 505–506; Great Leap Forward, 652; Great Wall, 85, 88; Han Dynasty, 86–89, 93; industrialization, 504, 531, 651, 652, 655, 656; Japanese invasion of (1937), 591,

616; Japanese invasion of Manchuria (1931), 590–591, 616; Japan influenced by, 204–205, 209; Jurchen invaders, 196; Korean War, 653–654; law codes, 83–84; literature, 199, 201, 504; Long March, 589; Manchu Dynasty, 199, 503–506, 531–532; Mandate of Heaven concept, 75–76; Ming Dynasty, 197–199, 200, 224, 345; Mongol Dynasty, 196–197, 201; Nationalist, 651, 654, 656, 658, 661; 1920s, 588–589; nuclear arms race, 655; Opium War, 505; oracle bones, 72; People's Republic of, 651–657; prehistoric, 12; Qin Dynasty, 76, 83–85, 86; Qing Dynasty, 587–588; Quing Dynasty, 503–506, 531–532; Red Guards, 652; religion, 72, 75–76, 84, 88–89, 193–194; Revolution of 1911, 588; Russia and, 495, 531, 532; science, 72, 74, 88, 200; Shang Dynasty, 71–73; Sino-Japanese War, 531–532, 563; Song Dynasty, 194–196, 197, 200; Soviet Union and, 653, 655; Sui Dynasty, 89, 192; Tai Ping Rebellion, 505–506; Tang Dynasty, 192–194, 199, 201, 204; Taoism, 76, 84; trade, 69, 72, 74, 76, 88, 89, 195, 198, 224, 345, 505; tribute system, 72, 198–199; vassals, 74; Vietnam invasion (1979), 671; warlords, 89, 588; wars against Huns, 88, 89; Western powers in, 531–532, 535, 587; White Lotus Rebellion, 505; World War I, 588; World War II, 606, 616, 621, 651; writing system, 71, 73, 86, 204; Xia Dynasty, 70–71; Zhou Dynasty, 73–76, 83, 84
chivalry, 251–252
Choctaw Indians, 232
Chopin, Frederic, 464
Christian Democratic party (Italy), 647
Christian IV, King of Denmark, 322
Christianity, 33, 263; beginnings of, 140–143; Byzantine Empire, 152, 153, 157, 158–160; early controversies, 141; in early Russia, 160, 162, 163; Middle Ages, 253–255, 281–284, 288, 294; relations with Islam, 171, 172, 180–181; in the Roman Empire, 140–141; spread of, 140–141, 246, 249, 253, 347; Western/Eastern split, 158–160, 282
Christian Socialists, 441
Churchill, Winston S., 613, 614, 618, 620, 623, 624, 630, 634
Church of England, 249, 268, 308, 324
Cicero, 145
city-states: ancient Greece, 103–110, 117; Italy, 297, 305; Mayan, 233; Phoenician, 29; Sumerian, 16, 36
Civil Constitution of the Clergy, 398
civil disobedience, 585
civil rights movement (U.S.), 715–716
civil service system, 87, 193, 194–196
Civil War (England), 325–326
Civil War (U.S.), 449, 512–513, 517
Ci Xi, Empress Dowager of China, 587
Classicism, 382
Claudius, Emperor, 135
Cleisthenes, 107–108
Clemenceau, Georges, 557, 558, 559
Clement V, Pope, 284
Clement VII, Pope, 284

Cleopatra, Queen of Egypt, 132
client states, 129
Clovis, 244–245
Clovis points, 229
Cluniac movement, 282
coal, 418, 419, 420
Code of Hammurabi, 22, 23, 32
Code of Justinian, 154–155
codification of laws, 22
Colbert, Jean Baptiste, 332
Cold War, 633, 644, 650, 714; beginning of, 633–634; Berlin Blockade, 636; division of Germany, 631–632, 635–637, 646; easing of, 641
Coleridge, Samuel, 462
collective farms, 577
Colombia, 537–538, 711
colonialism, *see* under names of countries
Colosseum (Rome), 136
Columbia (space shuttle), 718, 724
Columbus, Christopher, 340, 342, 343
Commercial Revolution, 353–355
Committee of Public Safety (France), 402, 403, 404
common law, 268
Common Market, 644
communications: nineteenth century, 421, 469, 518; twentieth century, 562–563, 602–603, 722, 732
communism, 441, 631; Marx and, 441, 453; post-World War II spread of, 634. *See also* Communist party; names of countries
Communist Manifesto, 441, 453
Communist party: China, 588, 589, 651, 652; Indonesia, 672; Italy, 635, 647; Soviet Union, 568, 575, 638; Spain, 609; United States, 714
computers, 722, 723, 732, 733
Comte, Auguste, 461
concentration camps, 618
Concert of Europe, 437–438
Concord, battle of, 388
Concordat of Worms, 279, 282
Confederate States of America, 512
Confederation of the Rhine, 408
Confucianism, 75, 76, 84, 88, 194, 203, 204
Confucius, 75, 76, 88
Congo, *see* Zaire, Republic of
Congregationalism, 310
Congress of Berlin, 487, 521
Congress of Vienna, 434, 436–437, 443, 477, 488
Congress party (India), 662
Conservative party (Great Britain), 444, 446
conservatives, 399, 436
Constantine, Emperor, 139, 141, 152, 153, 282
Constantinople, 139, 143, 152, 153–154, 156, 157, 158, 161, 162, 170, 179, 180, 263, 264–265, 282, 487; decline of, 157–158, 179; fall of (1453), 297; founding of, 153–154; Latin Kingdom of, 265; Nika riot, 154. *See also* Byzantine Empire
Constitutional Democratic party (Russia), 563
Constitution of 1791 (France), 398, 399
Constitution of 1793 (France), 404, 411

Constitution of 1795 (France), 404
Consulate (France), 406
consuls, 125
Contadora group, 711, 712
containment policy, 635
continental system, 408, 409, 410
Convention People's party (Africa), 689
convents, 282, 308
Copernicus, Nicholas, 365
Cornwallis, Lord, 389, 527
Coronado, Francisco Vásquez de, 344
corporations, 426
Corsica, 128, 129, 249
Cort, Henry, 419
Cortés, Hernando, 343, 344
Costa Rica, 501, 709–710
cotton gin, invention of, 416
Council (ancient Athens), 107
Council of Constance, 284
Council of Trent, 311
Council of Troubles, 320–321
Counter Reformation, 310–311, 318
counterrevolution, 399
coup d'état, 406, 508
craft guilds, 258–259
Crassus, 131–132, 133
Cree Indians, 231
Creek Indians, 230, 232
Crete, 98, 99, 100–101, 176, 249, 375, 615
Crimean War, 448, 469, 475, 486, 492
Croatia, 375, 546, 559
Cro-Magnon people, 12
Crompton, Samuel, 416
Cromwell, Oliver, 326, 327
Crusades, 184, 262, 263–266, 269, 271, 272, 281, 284; background of, 263; effects on Europe, 266. *See also* names of crusades
Cuba, 340, 342, 538, 597, 705, 707, 708–709, 711, 712; Bay of Pigs incident, 709; Castro revolution, 708–709; independence of, 537; Mariel boatlift operation, 709; 1950s–1980s, 708–709; Soviet missile crisis, 639–640, 709; Spanish-American War, 536–537; troops in Africa, 709
Cubism, 467, 599, 727
Cultural Revolution (China), 652–653, 656
culture, early development of, 14
cuneiform, 18–19, 26, 30, 55
Curie, Marie, 458
Cush Empire, 221
Cyprus, 487, 677
Cyril, 160, 163
Cyrillic alphabet, 160, 163, 179
Cyrus the Great, 27, 28, 90, 108
Czechoslovakia, 160, 162, 465, 559, 570, 575, 643, 646; communism, 634; Nazi seizure of, 609–611; Soviet invasion of (1968), 640–641; Warsaw Pact, 640; World War II, 609–611, 618. *See also* Bohemia

Dahomey, 523
Dalhousie, Marquis of, 528–529
Dalton, John, 457, 458
dance, twentieth century, 601, 728, 730
Danes, 248–249, 266
Dante, 287

Danton, Georges Jacques, 399, 403
Darby, Abraham, 419
Dardanelles, 179, 546, 550
Darius the Great, 90, 108
Dark Ages, 250
Darwin, Charles, 459
David, Jacques-Louis, 381
David, King, 30
Da Vinci, Leonardo, 298, 299
Dawes Plan, 571
D-Day, 620
debtor nation, 719
Decameron, The, 298
Deccan Plateau, 61, 62, 93, 189, 190
Decembrist Revolt, 491–492
Declaration of Independence, 369, 388–389
Declaration of the Rights of Man, 395–397, 488
Declaration of the Rights of Woman, 397
default, 707
deficits, 719
De Gaulle, Charles, 613, 645, 682, 690
de la Madrid Hurtado, Miguel, 712
Delhi Sultanate, 189–190
Delian League, 109, 110
democracy, 104, 106–108, 110, 111, 391, 647
Democratic People's Republic of Korea, *see* North Korea
Deng Xiaoping, 656
Denmark, 243, 249, 266, 322; Common Market, 644; NATO, 637; Reformation, 308; War of 1864, 478; World War II, 613
Depression of 1929–1930s, *see* Great Depression
Desai, Morarji, 664
Descartes, René, 366–367
De Soto, Hernando, 344
de-Stalinization, 638
détente, 641, 654, 655–656. *See also* names of countries
Dialogues, 114
Dias, Bartholomeu, 339
Diáz, Porfirio, 595
dictators, 84, 575, 576. *See also* names of countries; dictators
Diderot, Denis, 370, 383
Diem, Ngo Dinh, 667–668
Dien Bien Phu, Battle of, 667
Diocletian, Emperor, 139, 141, 153
Diplomatic Revolution, 376
Directory (France), 404, 405, 406
Disraeli, Benjamin, 444–445, 483, 518, 520, 529
Divine Comedy, The, 287
divine right of kings, 324
Djibouti, 697
domestic system, 354
Dominican Republic, 340, 538, 596, 709
Dominicans, 282, 306
Don Quixote, 317
Dorians, 102, 105
Dostoevsky, Fyodor, 464, 491
Drake, Sir Francis, 322
Dravidians, 64, 93
Dreyfus Affair, 449–450, 490
Druidism, 249
Dual Monarchy, 479, 484–485
Duarte, José Napoleón, 711
Dubcek, Alexander, 640, 641, 643

synagogues, 33; writings of the Prophets, 32–33. *See also* Hebrews; Israel; Jews
Judea, 129, 131, 136
Julio-Claudian Dynasty, 134–136
July Revolution (1830), 447
Jung, Carl, 582, 600
Jurchens, 196
Justinian, Emperor, 154–156, 161, 244
Jutes, 244, 248
Jutland, battle of, 550

Kabuki Theater, 210, 661
Kampuchea, *see* Cambodia
Kanem-Bornu Empire, 217, 220
Kangxi, Emperor, 503
Kanishka, 91
Kapital, Das, 441, 453
karma, 67–68
Kassites, 23, 43, 44
Katanga, 690
Kay, John, 416
Kellogg-Briand Pact, 592
Kemal, Mustapha, 575
Kennedy, John F., 639, 669, 707, 714, 731
Kennedy, Robert, 717
Kenya, 223, 345, 523, 696, 698; independence of, 692; Mau Mau rebellion, 692
Kenyatta, Jomo, 692
Kepler, Johannes, 365, 457
Kerensky, Alexander, 565, 566
Khadija, 171, 172
Khayyam, Omar, 184
Khmer Rouge, 670–671, 673
Khoi-san, 215, 216
Khomeini, Ayatollah Ruhollah, 685, 687
Khrushchev, Nikita, 638, 639, 640, 655
Kievan Russia, 162–163
Kilwa, 223
Kim, Il-sung, 653
King, Dr. Martin Luther, Jr., 716, 717
King George's War, 356
King William's War, 356
Kissinger, Henry, 683
Kitchener, General Herbert, 523
Knox, John, 310
Kohl, Helmut, 647
Kojiki, 210
Kongo Empire, 221, 224
Koran, 173–174, 183, 185, 666, 685
Korea, 69, 88, 89, 91, 165, 192, 195, 198, 201, 504, 650; Buddhism, 204; Chinese domination of, 531; Japanese annexation of (1910), 533. *See also* North Korea; South Korea
Korean War, 653–654, 655, 658, 659
Kosciuszko, Thaddeus, 380, 389
Kossuth, Louis, 451, 484
Kropotkin, Prince Peter, 493
Kshatriya caste, 65
Kubitschek, Juscelino, 703
Kublai Khan, 197, 201, 202
Kushan Empire, 91, 93
Kuwait, 685
Kwakiutl Indians, 461

labor unions, 426–427
Labour party (Great Britain), 570

Lafayette, Marquis de, 389, 447
Lagash, 16
laissez-faire, 439, 517
Lancaster family, 270
Laos, 535, 667; U.S. involvement in, 669
Laozi, 76
La Salle, Sieur de, 351
Las Casas, Bartolomé de, 347
Lateran Treaty, 574
Latin America, 347, 499–503, 517, 582, 594–597, 702–713, 719, 730; economic problems, 597, 707; independence movements, 499–503; 1900–1920, 594–597; Peace Corps in, 707; terrorism, 707; U.S. relations with, 502, 511, 536–538, 595–597, 705, 707, 709–713. *See also* names of countries
Latin American Free Trade Area (LAFTA), 707
Latin language, 145, 153, 184, 255, 286, 314, 368
Latins, 124, 126
Latvia, 555, 559, 566, 575, 612
Lavoisier, Antoine, 367, 457
Laws of Manu, 66
lay investiture, 278, 279, 282
League of Augsburg, War of the, 333, 356
League of Nations, 558, 559, 569, 586, 591, 607; failure of, 559, 607
League of the Three Emperors, 483
Leakey, Mary, 11
Lebanon, 29, 264, 677, 679, 681; Christian-Muslim rivalry in, 679, 686–687; civil war, 686–687
Lee, Richard Henry, 388
Legalism, 84
legal systems: Byzantine Empire, 153, 154–155; Chinese, 83–84; codification of, 22; common law, 268; Hittite, 24; Middle Ages, 252, 268, 297; Mosaic, 32; Napoleonic, 407; Roman, 136, 143–144. *See also* names of laws
Legislative Assembly (France), 398, 399, 400, 401
Leipzig, battle of, 410
Lemberg, battle of, 550
Lend-Lease Act (1941), 614
Lenin, Vladimir, 562, 563, 565–568, 575
Leo I, Pope, 143
Leo III, Pope, 246, 247
Leo IX, Pope, 282
Leo III, Emperor, 156–157
Leonidas, King, 108
Leopold I, Holy Roman Emperor, 333, 375
Leopold II, King of Belgium, 523
Lepidus, 132
Lévesque, René, 713
Lexington, battle of, 388
Leyte Gulf, battle of, 621
liberalism, 435–436, 517
Liberal party (Great Britain), 445, 446, 570
Liberia, 521, 689
Li Bo, 199
Libya, 100, 104, 176, 521, 614, 682, 685
Liliuokalani, Queen, 536
limited constitutional monarchy, 329
Limited Nuclear Test Ban Treaty (1963), 640
Lincoln, Abraham, 469, 512

Linnaeus, Carolus, 368
Lister, Joseph, 460
literature: Enlightenment period, 382–383; nineteenth century, 462–464, 469, 513, 518–519; Roman, 145; twentieth century, 601–602, 730–731. *See also* names of authors; countries; periods; titles
Lithuania, 555, 559, 611, 612
Liu Bang, Emperor, 86, 87
Livingstone, David, 521
Livy, 145
Li Yuan, Emperor, 192
Li Zizheng, 199
Lloyd George, David, 557
Locke, John, 364, 369, 389
Lombards, 156, 244, 245, 278, 279
London, 258, 353, 356, 381, 422, 443, 527, 613
Long March, 589
López Portillo, José, 712
Louis I (the Pious), Holy Roman Emperor, 246, 247
Louis VI (the Fat), King of France, 271
Louis VII, King of France, 271, 272
Louis IX, King of France, 273
Louis XI, King of France, 275, 304
Louis XIII, King of France, 329, 331
Louis XIV, King of France, 331–334, 335, 351, 369, 382, 393
Louis XV, King of France, 392
Louis XVI, King of France, 376, 392–393, 394, 395, 397, 398–399, 401–402
Louis XVIII, King of France, 404, 411, 446
Louis Philippe, King of France, 447, 449, 450
Low Countries, 419; religious wars in, 320–321. *See also* names of countries
Loyola, Ignatius, 310, 318
Luba Empire, 221, 224
Lucretius, 145
Lumumba, Patrice, 690
Lunda Empire, 221, 224
Lusitania, sinking of, 551, 553
Luther, Martin, 306–308, 309, 310
Lutheranism, 307, 308, 318, 322
Luxembourg, 637, 644

MacAdam, John, 420
Macao, 345
MacArthur, Douglas, 617, 621, 653–654, 657, 658
McCarthy, Joseph R., 714
McCormick, Cyrus, 419
Macedonia, 117, 119, 129, 559
Machiavelli, Niccolò, 305
Madagascar, 345
Madero, Francisco, 595
Magellan, Ferdinand, 343
Maginot Line, 571
Magna Carta, 269–270
Magnus, Albertus, 288
Magyars, 167, 250, 278, 484, 485, 559
Mahabharata, 67, 94
Mahayana Buddhism, 69, 91, 194, 207
Maine, USS, explosion of, 536
Malaya, 224, 616
Malaysia, 650, 671, 672–673
Mali Empire, 217, 218, 219, 220
Malthus, Thomas R., 439

Mexican venture, 449
Napoleonic Wars, 407–411, 490, 516; effects on Europe, 435; Russian campaign, 410–411. *See also* names of battles
Nasser, Gamal Abdel, 679, 680, 681, 683
Natal, Republic of, 524, 525
Natchez Indians, 232
National Aeronautics and Space Administration (NASA), 718
National Assembly (France), 394, 395, 397, 398, 448, 449, 572
National Association for the Advancement of Colored People (NAACP), 513
National Convention (France), 401–404, 405
Nationalism, 435–438, 464, 472–495; imperialism and, 517–518, 530. *See also* World War I; World War II; names of countries
Nationalist China, 651, 654, 656, 658, 661. *See also* China
National Liberation Front (NLF), 668–669, 682
National Party (China), 588
natural law, 368–373
Natural Philosophies, 457
natural selection, 459
Navaho Indians, 232
Navigation Acts (1660–1696), 353, 387
Nazi regime, 558, 575, 577–579, 586, 607–623, 632; Jews persecuted by, 579, 617–618, 624; rise to power, 577–579. *See also* Hitler, Adolf
Neanderthal people, 12
Nebuchadnezzar, King, 27, 31
Nefertiti, Queen, 47
Negritude, 689–690
Nehru, Jawaharlal, 662, 663, 664, 665
Nelson, Admiral Horatio, 405, 408
Neoclassicism, 381
Neolithic Age, 12–14, 39, 123
Nepal, 504
Nero, Emperor, 135–136, 141
Nerva, Emperor, 136
Netherlands, 311, 315, 326, 346, 375, 545; Calvinism, 310, 320; colonialism, 349, 354, 356, 524, 533, 672; Common Market, 644; Congress of Vienna, 437; French Revolution and, 401, 402, 403; NATO, 637; religious wars, 319–323; war with France (1672–1678), 333; World War II, 613
Neutral Indians, 230
Neutrality Act of 1939, 614
New Amsterdam, 349
New Brunswick, 584
Newcomen, Thomas, 417
New Deal, 593–594, 714
New Economic Policy (NEP), 567
New England Colonies (U.S.), 351
Newfoundland, 339, 350, 351, 356
New France, 350–351, 358
New Guinea, 621
New Kingdom (ancient Egypt), 40, 41, 44–49, 51, 52, 55, 56
New Netherland, 349, 356
New South Wales, 584
New Spain, 347
New Testament, 143
Newton, Isaac, 364, 365–366, 457, 458
New World, 227, 325, 338–358; European exploration and colonization of, 338–358; trade, 339, 340, 345–347, 349, 350, 352, 353, 354. *See also* United States
New York, 349, 389, 420, 468
New Zealand, 517, 584, 598, 655
Nicaragua, 501, 537, 538, 711; Sandinista government, 711; U.S. intervention in, 597
Nicholas I, Czar, 450, 452, 489, 491–492
Nicholas II, Czar, 547, 548, 563, 564, 565, 566
Nicholas II, Pope, 282
Nigeria, 216, 225, 523, 695; civil war, 696; independence of, 696
Nightingale, Florence, 469
Nile Delta, 37, 40, 43, 48, 55
Nile River, 14, 36, 37–39, 40, 60, 215; Aswan Dam project, 680; floods, 38, 41, 52, 221.
Nile Valley, 36, 37–39, 55
Ninety-five Theses, 306
Nineveh, 26
Nippur, 16
Nirvana, 68, 69
Nixon, Richard, 641, 655–656, 669, 715, 717
Nkrumah, Kwame, 688, 689, 693
No drama, 210, 661
Nol, Lon, 669
nonaligned movement, 663, 664, 672
Norman Conquest, 266–268
North Africa, 128, 129, 154, 156, 216, 243, 256, 315, 546, 676, 677; Carthage, 29–30; early history, 217; European imperialism in, 519–521, 523; independence of, 682; Muslims in, 156, 171, 173, 176, 182, 249, 339; nationalism, 525; World War II, 614–615, 618. *See also* Africa; names of countries
North America, 214, 227, 229, 350, 351, 356; geography and climate, 227; migrations from Asia, 229. *See also* Canada; United States
North Atlantic Treaty Organization (NATO), 637, 647
Northern Ireland, 645. *See also* Ireland
Northern Plains (ancient India), 61–62
North German Confederation, 479
North Korea, 637, 653–654, 655. *See also* Korea; South Korea
Northmen, 249
North Vietnam, 667–671. *See also* South Vietnam; Vietnam
Northwest Territory, 510, 584
Norway, 249, 266, 295, 465; NATO, 637; Reformation, 308; World War II, 613
Nova Scotia, 356, 584
Nubians, 223
nuclear arms race, 637, 638, 640, 641–642, 644, 655, 664, 733
nuclear power, 459, 623, 724, 733
Nuremberg trials, 632–633
Nyerere, Julius, 690, 692, 696, 697

obelisks, 52
Obote, Apollo Milton, 697
Octavian, *see* Augustus, Emperor
October Manifesto, 564
October War, 683, 685

Odyssey, 102–103
Oersted, Hans, 421
oil industry, 423; Mexico, 595, 711; Middle Eastern, 679, 681, 683, 685; 1970s energy crunch, 685, 719; Venezuelan, 705
Okinawa, 621, 660
Old Kingdom (ancient Egypt), 40–41, 42, 46, 50, 51, 52
Old Regime (France), 372, 391–392, 393, 395, 397, 404, 407, 411
Old Testament, 31, 140, 143
Olduvai Gorge, 11
oligarchy, 104
Olmec Indians, 234
Olmstead, Frederick Law, 468
Olympic Games, 111–112, 642
Oneida Indians, 232
Onondaga Indians, 232
Ontario, 583, 584
Open Door Notes, 587
opera, 201, 382, 465
Opium Wars, 505, 508
Orellana, Francisco de, 344
Orange Free State, 525
Organization of African Unity (OAU), 695
Organization of American States (OAS), 707
Organization of Petroleum Exporting Countries (OPEC), 685
Orlando, Vittorio, 557
Orthodox Christianity, 152, 153, 157, 158–160, 162, 163
Ostpolitik, 646, 647
ostracism, 108
Ostrogoths (tribe), 154, 243, 244
Otto I, Holy Roman Emperor, 278–279
Ottoman Empire, 179–181, 297, 316, 438, 448, 483, 485–487, 519–520, 521, 544, 546, 555, 559; Crimean War, 492; decline, 181, 485–487, 521; in Eastern Europe, 179–181; end of, 677; government, 180–181; independence movements, 486–487; Jews and Christians in, 180–181, 486; Russia and, 379–380
Ottoman Turks, 158, 167, 179–181, 339, 375, 485–487; Austria and, 315, 375; and Spain, 315, 316. *See also* Turks
Owen, Robert, 440

Pacific Basin, 673
Pacific Islands, European imperialism in, 535, 558. *See also* names of islands
pacifism, 545
Pago Pago, 535
Pahlavi, Shah Mohammad Reza, 681, 685
Paine, Thomas, 388
Pakistan, 91, 117, 631, 650, 663, 664, 733; division of, 664, 666; nuclear weapons, 666; SEATO, 655; war with India (1971), 664
Pale of Settlement, 489
Paleolithic Age, 11–12, 39
Palestine, 45, 117, 129, 178, 263, 490, 677; British control of, 559, 586. *See also* Holy Land; Israel
Palestine Liberation Organization (PLO), 686–687